Consolidated Ontario Education Statutes and Regulations 1999

Consulting Editor
Anthony F. Brown, LL.B., M.Ed.

CARSWELL

© 1999 Thomson Canada Limited

All rights reserved. No part of this publication may be reproduced, stored in a retrieval system, or transmitted, in any form or by any means, electronic, mechanical, photocopying, recording, or otherwise, without the prior written permission of the publisher.

This publication is designed to provide accurate and authoritative information. It is sold with the understanding that the publisher is not engaged in rendering legal, accounting or other professional advice. If legal advice or other expert assistance is required, the services of a competent professional should be sought. The analysis contained herein should in no way be construed as being either official or unofficial policy of any governmental body.

ISBN 0-459-23970-8

This work reproduces official English language versions of Ontario statutes and regulations. As the Revised Statutes of Ontario, 1990 and many Ontario Regulations also have official French versions, the reader is advised that reference to the official French language material may be warranted in appropriate circumstances.

The paper used in this publication meets the minimum requirements of the American National Standard for Information Sciences – Permanence of Paper for Printed Library Materials, ANSI Z39. 48-1984.

Canadian Cataloguing in Publication Data

The National Library of Canada has catalogued this publication as follows:

Main entry under title:

Consolidated Ontario education statutes and regulations

Annual.
Description based on: 1994.
Includes index.
ISSN 1199-6420
ISBN 0-459-23970-8 (1999)

1. Educational law and legislation — Ontario. I. Carswell Company.

KEO770.A29C7   344.713'07'0263   C94-930079-4
KF4119.A29C7

CARSWELL
Thomson Professional Publishing

One Corporate Plaza, 2075 Kennedy Road, Scarborough, Ontario M1T 3V4
Customer Service:
Toronto 1-416-609-3800
Elsewhere in Canada/U.S. 1-800-387-5164
Fax 1-416-298-5094

Introduction

This book contains a collection of the statutes and regulations that govern primary and secondary school education in the province of Ontario. It is a handy, up-to-date, comprehensive and time-saving desk-top reference for teachers, principals, administrators, trustees, school councils, parents and lawyers.

The core statute is the *Education Act*. A detailed table of contents has been included to help locate specific provisions. A table of concordance between the present Act and its predecessors allows readers to trace the history of a provision.

Other statutes and regulations, however, expand on and overlap with the *Education Act* in many areas. Readers need to refer not just to the *Education Act*, but also to the appropriate regulation and perhaps even to a different statute. The index provided in this book allows for cross-reference between the various statutes and regulations.

In addition to the regulations issued under the authority of the *Education Act*, this publication includes the General Regulation under the *Immunization of School Pupils Act* and the Regulation made under the Teaching Profession Act. The latter regulation is made by the Governing Council of the Ontario Teachers' Federation. It is not published in the Ontario Gazette because the *Regulations Act* does not apply to a regulation made under the *Teaching Profession Act*.

A number of regulations made pursuant to the *Education Act* are issued annually. Only the most recent version of each of these regulations is included. For the "grant regulations," we have omitted regulations for years prior to 1998. We have also omitted regulations that were rendered obsolete by the *Education Quality Improvement Act, 1997*. These are noted in the text.

In preparing this edition, the legislation was updated to December 17, 1998, No. 72 of Votes and Proceedings, and to April 17, 1999, volume 132:16 of the Ontario Gazette.

As noted elsewhere in this edition, the *School Boards and Teachers Collective Negotiations Act* was repealed on December 31, 1997, but has been included for the convenience of readers who wish to compare the old collective bargaining provisions to the new ones contained in Part X.1 of the *Education Act*.

This work reproduces the official English language version of the statutes and regulations. The reader is advised that the Revised Statutes of Ontario, 1990 and many Ontario Regulations also have an official French language version.

Anthony F. Brown
May, 1999

Summary Table of Contents

Introduction	iii
Education Act — Concordance	lxxvii
Education Act	1
Regulations under the Education Act [285; 291; 293-296; 298; 300; 302; 304; 306-311; 183/97; 185/97; 250/97; 460/97; 461/97; 462/97; 463/97; 464/97; 465/97; 466/97; 467/97; 468/97; 470/97; 471/97; 472/97; 494/97; 495/97; 496/97; 20/98; 21/98; 79/98; 90/98; 92/98; 118/98; 124/98; 181/98; 283/98; 284/98; 285/98; 286/98; 287/98; 288/98; 346;98; 365/98; 366/98; 392/98; 393/98; 394/98; 400/98; 444/98; 446/98; 470/98; 471/98; 472/98; 476/98; 486/98; 509/98; 712/98; 713/98; 714/98; 715/98; 213/99; 214/99; 215/99]	223
Education Quality and Accountability Office Act, 1996	789
Immunization of School Pupils Act	795
Regulation under the Immunization of School Pupils Act [645]	801
Local Government Disclosure of Interest Act, 1994	807
Municipal Conflict of Interest Act	817
Municipal Freedom of Information and Protection of Privacy Act	825
Regulation under the Municipal Freedom of Information and Protection of Privacy Act [823]	849
Ontario College of Teachers Act, 1996	855
Regulations under the Ontario College of Teachers Act [344/96; 345/96; 72/97; 184/97; 276/97; 437/97]	883
Ontario Student Record (OSR) Guideline	933
Provincial Schools Negotiations Act	951
School Boards and Teachers Collective Negotiations Act	955
Teachers' Pension Act	977
Teaching Profession Act	981
Regulation under the Teaching Profession Act	985
Index	995

Table of Contents

EDUCATION ACT

DEFINITIONS

1.	**(1)**	Definitions	1
	(1.1)	Occasional teacher	8
	(1.2.1)	Ontario Property Assessment Corporation	8
	(2)	Authority or obligation of parent vested in pupil of 18 years of age	8
	(3)	Questions re proceeding as to formation of school section	8
	(4)	Effect on separate schools	9
	(4.1)	Same	9
	(5)	Existing school arrangements continued	9
	(6)	Regulations re premanent improvements	9
	(7)	Separate school support in 1997	9
	(8)	Entitlement to vote based on residence	9
	(9)	Exception	9
	(10)	Entitlement to vote in the area of jurisdiction of a board	9
	(11)	Interpretation	9
	(12)	Trustee	10

PART I

MINISTRY OF EDUCATION AND TRAINING

2.	**(1)**	Ministry continued	10
	(2)	Minister to have charge	10
	(3)	Administration	10
	(4)	Delegation of powers and duties	10
	(5)	Limitations	10
	(6)	Application of *Executive Council Act*, s. 6	10
3.		Annual report	10
4.		Additions to enrolment in special cases	10
5.	**(1)**	Closing of school or class	10
	(2)	Pupils deemed in attendance	10
6.		[Repealed]	11
7.		[Repealed]	11
8.	**(1)**	Powers of Minister	11
	(2)	[Repealed]	15
	(3)	Identification programs and special education programs and services	15
	(4)	Application	15

vii

TABLE OF CONTENTS

9.		Accounting statement related to assistance by Ministry	15
10.		Powers of Minister	15
11.	**(1)**	Regulations	15
	(2)	[Repealed]	18
	(3)	Regulations, fees	18
	(4)	Same	18
	(5)	[Repealed]	18
	(6)	[Repealed]	18
	(7)	School year, terms, holidays, etc.	18
	(7.1)	Same	18
	(8)	Exceptions: compulsory attendance	18
	(9)	Regulations	19
		[Note: Section 11(10) to (18) inclusive repealed.]	19
12.	**(1)**	Agreements with Canada re: physical fitness	19
	(2)	Pupils at Indian schools	19
	(3)	Non-Indian pupils at Indian schools	20
	(4)	Bursaries and scholarships	20
	(5)	Learning materials	20
13.	**(1)**	Continuation of school for deaf	20
	(2)	Continuation of school for blind	20
	(3)	Administration	20
	(4)	Additional schools	20
	(4.1)	Idem	20
	(5)	Demonstration schools	20
	(6)	Idem	20
	(7)	Regulations	20
14.	**(1)**	Teacher education	21
	(2)	Practice teaching	21
	(3)	Idem	21
	(3.1)	Same	21
	(4)	Idem	22
15.		Leadership training camps	22
16.	**(1)**	Intention to operate private schools	22
	(2)	Idem	22
	(3)	Idem	22
	(4)	Offence to operate private school without filing notice of intent to operate	22
	(5)	Return	22
	(6)	Inspection of school	22
	(7)	Inspection on request	22
	(8)	Inspection of teachers	22
	(8.1)	Agreements re tests	22
	(8.2)	Same	23
	(9)	Offence for false statement	23
17.	**(1)**	Variation of scholarships and awards	23

TABLE OF CONTENTS

	(2)	Where award is repayable loan	23
17.1	(1)	Ontario Parent Council	24
	(2)	Eligibility for appointment	24
	(3)	Eligibility criteria established by Minister	24
	(4)	Non-application of *Regulations Act*	24
	(5)	Term of office	24
	(6)	Same	24
	(7)	Chair	24
	(8)	Remuneration and expenses	24
	(9)	Staff and accommodation	24
	(10)	Mandate	24
	(11)	Annual report	24
	(12)	Additional reports	24

PART II

SCHOOL ATTENDANCE

18.		Definition	24
19.	(1)	Closing of school or class by board	25
	(2)	Same	25
	(3)	Teachers' salary	25
	(4)	Definition	25
20.		Closing of schools on civic holiday	25
21.	(1)	Compulsory attendance	25
	(2)	When attendance excused	25
	(3)	Blind, deaf or mentally handicapped children	26
	(4)	Child under compulsory age	26
	(5)	Duty of parent, etc.	26
	(6)	Separate School supporters	26
22.		Where school year varied	26
23.	(1)	Suspension of pupil	26
	(1.1)	Period of suspension	26
	(1.2)	Notice	26
	(2)	Appeal against suspension	26
	(2.1)	Effect of appeal	27
	(2.2)	Review of suspensions	27
	(3)	Expulsion of pupil	27
	(4)	Parties to hearing	27
	(5)	Readmission of pupil	27
	(6)	Committee to perform board functions	27
24.	(1)	Provincial School Attendance Counsellor	27
	(2)	Inquiry by Provincial Counsellor	27
	(3)	Powers of Provincial Counsellor	28

TABLE OF CONTENTS

25.	(1)	Appointment of school attendance counsellors	28
	(2)	Idem	28
	(3)	Vacancies	28
	(4)	Notice of appointment	28
	(5)	Jurisdiction and responsibility of school attendance counsellor	28
26.	(1)	Powers of counsellors	28
	(2)	Reports	28
	(3)	To act under appropriate supervisory officer and provincial counsellor	28
	(4)	Inquiry by counsellor and notice	28
27.		Census	29
28.	(1)	Reports and information	29
	(2)	Where no school attendance counsellor	29
29.		Provincial counsellor as trustee	29
30.	(1)	Liability of parent or guardian	29
	(2)	Bond for attendance	29
	(3)	Employment during school hours	30
	(4)	Offences by corporations	30
	(5)	Habitually absent from school	30
	(6)	Proceedings under subs. (5)	30
	(7)	Reference to provincial counsellor for inquiry	30
31.	(1)	Proceedings to be taken by attendance counsellors	30
	(2)	Certificate of principal as proof in the absence of evidence to the contrary	30
	(3)	Proof of age	30
	(4)	Order re school attendance	30
32.	(1)	Resident pupil right to attend school	30
	(2)	Admission without fee	30
33.	(1)	Resident pupil qualification: elementary English-language public district school boards and elementary public school authorities	31
	(2)	Resident pupil qualification: elementary French-language public district school boards	31
	(3)	Resident pupil qualification: elementary English-language separate district school boards and elementary Roman Catholic school authorities	31
	(4)	Resident pupil qualification: elementary French-language separate district school boards	31
	(5)	Evidence as to right to attend	32
	(6)	Resident pupil, elementary	32
34.	(1)	Kindergarten	32
	(2)	Junior Kindergarten	32
	(3)	Beginners Class	32
35.	(1)	Resident pupil's right to attend more accessible elementary school	32
	(2)	Same	32
	(3)	Same	32

TABLE OF CONTENTS

36.	**(1)**	Resident pupil qualification: secondary English-language public district school boards and secondary public school authorities	33
	(2)	Resident pupil qualification: secondary French-language public district school boards	33
	(3)	Resident pupil qualification: secondary English-language separate district school boards	34
	(4)	Resident pupil qualification: secondary French-language separate district school boards	34
	(5)	Resident pupil, secondary	34
	(6)	Certain elementary-only school authorities	35
	(7)	French-speaking persons	35
	(8)	Evidence as to right to attend	35
37.	**(1)**	Admission of adult resident who is not a resident pupil	35
	(2)	Types of schools	35
38.		Limitation on right to attend without payment of fee	35
39.	**(1)**	Resident pupil's right to attend secondary school in another district or zone	36
	(2)	Types of schools	36
	(3)	Restrictions	36
	(4)	Where agreement between boards	36
40.	**(1)**	Admission to secondary school of resident pupil from other district or zone	36
	(2)	Same	36
	(3)	Notice of admission	36
	(4)	Same	37
41.	**(1)**	Admisison to secondary school	37
	(2)	Same	37
	(3)	Where admission denied	37
	(4)	Committee to perform board functions	37
	(5)	Alternative course or program	37
	(6)	Admission to continuing education class	37
42.	**(1)**	Secondary school instruction: movement from English-language public board to English-language Roman Catholic board	37
	(2)	Secondary school instruction: movement from French-language public district school board to French-language separate district school board	37
	(3)	Secondary school instruction: movement from English-language Roman Catholic board to English-language public board	37
	(4)	Secondary school instruction: movement from French-language separate district school board to French-language public district school board	38
	(5)	Secondary school instruction: movement from French-language separate district school board to English-language public board	38
	(6)	Secondary school instruction: movement from English-language public board to French-language separate district school board	38

	(7)	Secondary school instruction: movement from French-language public district school board to English-language separate district school board	38
	(8)	Secondary school instruction: movement from English-language separate district school board to French-language public district school board	38
	(9)	Fee	38
	(10)	Amount	38
	(11)	Exemption from religious studies	39
	(12)	Same	39
	(13)	Additional exemptions	39
43.	(1)	Movement from English-language public board to French-language public district school board	39
	(2)	Movement from French-language public district school board to English-language public board	39
	(3)	Movement from English-language Roman Catholic board to French-language separate district school board	39
	(4)	Movement from French-language separate district school board to English-language Roman Catholic board	39
	(5)	Fee	40
	(6)	Amount	40
43.1	(1)	Regulations: supporter non-resident attendance rights	40
	(2)	General or particular	40
	(3)	Right to continue to attend in certain circumstances	40
	(4)	Exception	40
43.2	(1)	Regulations: non-supporter resident — attendance rights based on business property	40
	(2)	General or particular	40
44.		Admission where pupil moves into residence not assessed in accordance with his or her school support	40
45.	(1)	Admission where one parent is sole support	41
	(2)	Exception: French-language rights	41
46.	(1)	Tax exempt land	41
	(2)	Resident on land exempt from taxation	41
	(3)	Fee	41
46.1	(1)	Residence on defence property	42
	(2)	Entitlement	42
	(3)	Same	42
	(4)	Regulations	42
	(5)	Retroactive	42
47.	(1)	Admission of ward, etc., of children's aid society or training school to an elementary school	42
	(2)	Admission of ward, etc., of children's aid society or training school to a secondary school	42

48.	**(1)**	Child in custody of corporation or society	42
	(2)	Fee	43
48.1	**(1)**	Right to continue attending a school: London-Middlesex Act, 1992	43
	(2)	Transportation	43
	(3)	Right to continue 1989/90 change in boundaries	43
	(4)	Exception	43
	(5)	Agreement re transportation	43
49.	**(1)**	Fee payable	43
	(2)	Same	43
	(3)	[Repealed]	44
	(4)	Admission of resident pupil to another school by reason of distance to school	44
	(5)	Admission of qualified non-resident pupil	44
	(6)	Fees for pupils	44
	(7)	Application of subs. (6)	44
49.1		Persons unlawfully in Canada	45
49.2	**(1)**	Adult persons	45
	(2)	Same	45
	(3)	Same	45
	(4)	Exception: person requires particular course	45
	(5)	Same	45
	(6)	Same	45
	(7)	Exceptional pupils	45
	(8)	Regulations	46
	(9)	Classes	46

Part II.1

MISCELLANEOUS
1997, c. 31, s. 26

Provisions Relating to Public Boards

50.	**(1)**	Visitors	46
	(2)	Same	46
	(3)	Same	46
50.1	**(1)**	Residents other than supporters entitled to vote	46
	(2)	French-language rights	46

Religious Instruction

51.	**(1)**	Religious instruction	46
	(2)	Religious exercises	46

TABLE OF CONTENTS

Provisions Relating to Roman Catholic Boards

52.		Religious education	47
53.	(1)	Visitors	47
	(2)	Same	47
	(3)	Same	47
54.	(1)	Residents other than supporters entitled to vote	47
	(2)	French-language rights	47

Representation of Pupils on Boards

55.	(1)	Regulations: pupil representatives	47
	(2)	Same	47
	(3)	Same	47
	(4)	Same	47
	(5)	Same	47

Territory Without Municipal Organization in Area of Jurisdiction of School Authority

56.	Regulations	48

Special Education Tribunals and Advisory Committees

57.	(1)	Establishment of Special Education Tribunals	48
	(2)	Regulations	48
	(3)	Right of appeal	48
	(4)	Hearing by Special Education Tribunal	48
	(5)	Decision final	48
57.1	(1)	Special education advisory committees	48
	(2)	Same	48
	(3)	Same	48
	(4)	General or particular	49

Municipal Charges

58	(1)	Municipal charges	49
	(2)	Same	49
	(3)	Exception	49

Part II.2

DISTRICT SCHOOL BOARDS

58.1	(1)	Definitions	49
	(2)	Regulations: district school boards	49
	(3)	Provisions in regulations: effect for electoral purposes	51

	(4)	Same	51
	(5)	Regulations: school outside jurisdiction of a board to be school of the board	51
	(6)	Same	52
	(7)	Purpose of clauses (2)(d), (e)	52
	(8)	Limitation re clauses (2)(d), (e)	52
	(9)	Subdelegation	52
	(10)	Number of members on a district school board	52
	(11)	Same	52
	(12)	Geographic areas	52
	(13)	Same	52
	(14)	Purpose of Clause (2)(l)	52
	(15)	Limitation	52
	(16)	Exception	52
	(17)	Transfers among district school boards and school authorities	53
	(18)	Dispute	53
	(19)	Same	53
	(20)	Clause (17)(c)	53
	(21)	Employees	53
	(22)	Tax exemption	53
	(23)	Transfer not a closing	53
	(24)	No compensation	53
	(25)	Powers of board if regulation made under subclause (2)(m)(ii)	53
	(26)	Powers of municipality if regulation made under subclause (2)(m)(ii)	54
58.2	(1)	Transfers from old boards to district school boards	54
	(2)	Clause (1)(c)	54
	(3)	Role of Education Improvement Commission	54
	(4)	Same	55
	(5)	Same	55
	(6)	Same	55
	(7)	Criteria re transfer of assets, liabilities, employees	55
	(8)	Definitions	56
	(9)	Exception	56
	(10)	Limitation	56
	(11)	Exception: ongoing disputes	56
	(12)	Employees	56
	(13)	Order, directive may be filed in court	56
	(14)	Same	56
	(15)	Order, directives final	56
	(16)	Tax exemption	56
	(17)	Transfer not a closing	57
	(18)	No compensation	57
	(19)	Effect of transfer under this Part	57
58.3	(1)	Purpose of authority under clauses 58.1(2)(p), (q), s. 58.2	57
	(2)	Same	57

	(3)	Limitation: clauses 58.1(2)(p), (q), s. 58.2	57
	(4)	Limitation: subclause 58.1(2)(q)(i)	57
	(5)	Limitation: subclause 58.1(2)(q)(ii)	57
	(6)	Same	57
	(7)	One district school board to follow directions of another	57
	(8)	Same	58
58.4	(1)	General or particular	58
	(2)	Classes	58
58.5	(1)	Corporate status	58
	(2)	Amalgamation or merger	58
	(3)	Same	58
58.6		District school boards deemed to be local boards	58
58.7		Conduct of elections	58
58.8	(1)	Electors for French-language district school boards	58
	(2)	Same	59
58.9	(1)	Election by general vote	59
	(2)	Entitlement to vote: English-language public district school boards	59
	(3)	Entitlement to vote: English-language separate district school boards	59
	(4)	Entitlement to vote: French-language public district school boards	59
	(5)	Entitlement to vote: French-language separate district school boards	59

PART III

SCHOOL AUTHORITIES — PUBLIC

1997, c. 31, s. 33

District School Areas

59.	(1)	School section to be district school area	60
	(2)	Formation and alteration of district school area	60
	(3)	Notification of assessment commissioner	60
	(4)	Arbitration	60
	(5)	Name of board	60
60.	(1)	New district school areas	60
	(2)	Alteration and formation: disposition of assets and liabilities	60
61.	(1)	Definition	61
	(2)	Composition of board	61
	(3)	Idem	61
	(4)	Increase in number of members	61
	(5)	Election year end term of office	61
	(6)	Term of office	62

Elections and Meetings of Electors

62.	(1)	Election date	62
	(2)	Notice of meeting	62

	(3)	Meeting	62
	(4)	First meeting	62
	(5)	Minutes to be sent to Ministry	62
	(6)	Special meetings	62
	(7)	Declaration where right to vote objected to	62
	(7.1)	Same	63
	(8)	Election procedures	63
63.	(1)	Conduct of elections under *Municipal Elections Act, 1996*	63
	(2)	Same	63
	(3)	Same	63
	(4)	Same	63
64.	(1)	Elections	63
	(2)	Validity of election	63
65.		[Repealed]	64
66.	(1)	District school area board to be inactive	64
	(2)	Accounts in inactive area	64
	(3)	Board dissolved	64
	(4)	Records to be forwarded to Ministry	64
	(5)	Closing of school by Minister	64

Secondary School Authorities

67.	(1)	In territorial districts	64
	(2)	Same	64
	(3)	Same	64
	(4)	[Repealed]	64
	(5)	[Repealed]	64
	(6)	[Repealed]	64
	(7)	[Repealed]	64

School Authorities on Tax Exempt Land

68.1	(1)	Public elementary school on exempt lands	65
	(2)	Public secondary school on exempt land	65
	(3)	Public secondary and elementary school on exempt land	65
	(4)	Area of jurisdiction: other boards	65
	(5)	Fee payable by non-resident	65
	(5.1)	Same	65
	(5.2)	Same	65
	(6)	Revocation of order	66
		[Note: Sections 69 through 76 inclusive repealed.]	66

PART IV

SCHOOL AUTHORITIES — ROMAN CATHOLIC

77.	[Repealed]	66

Zones

78.	(1)	Boundaries of zones	66
	(2)	Zones not in municipalities or geographic townships	66
	(3)	Zone description	66
	(4)	[Repealed]	66
79.		[Repealed]	66

Formation and Discontinuance of Zones

80.	(1)	Meeting to establish a separate school zone	66
	(2)	Procedure	67
	(3)	Certification	67
	(4)	Notification	67
	(5)	Corporate name	67
	(6)	Formation not rendered invalid	67
	(7)	Qualification of members	67
81.	(1)	Powers of board members	68
	(2)	Where school not united	68
82.		Right to vote in year of establishment of zone	68
83.		Legislative grants	68
84.	(1)	Formation of combined separate school zones	68
	(2)	[Repealed]	68
	(3)	Dissolution of boards	69
	(4)	Corporate name	69
85.	(1)	Detaching school zone from combined school zone	69
	(1.1)	Same	69
	(2)	Qualified voters detaching a separate school zone	69
	(3)	When school zone detached	69
86.	(1)	Discontinuing school authority: vote of the supporters	69
	(2)	Discontinuing school authority: other conditions	69
	(3)	Notifice to Minister, etc., of discontinuance	70
	(4)	Settling accounts	70
	(5)	Records	70
	(6)	Boundaries to be revised	70
	(7)	Sale of real property	70
	(8)	Deposit of funds from sale	70
	(9)	Re-establishing school authority	70
86.1		Regulation	70

Separate School Electors

87.	[Repealed]	70
88.	Where person residing out of urban municipality to vote	70

xviii

Rural Separate Schools

89.	(1)	Term of office of board members	71
	(2)	Same	71
	(3)	Same	71
	(4)	Organization and quorum	71
	(5)	Regularity	71
	(6)	Entitlement to vote	71
	(7)	Exception	71
90.	(1)	Duties of rural boards	71
	(2)	Appointment of auditor by the Minister	72
	(3)	Approval of new school site	72
91.		[Repealed]	72
92.	(1)	Annual meeting	72
	(2)	Election of board	72
	(3)	Idem	72
	(4)	Organization of meeting	72
	(5)	Order of business	72
	(6)	Duties of presiding officer	73
	(7)	Granting poll and proceedings in case of a poll	73
	(8)	Entries in poll book	73
	(9)	Form of ballot paper	73
	(10)	Marking of ballot paper	73
	(11)	Number of votes	73
	(12)	Manner of voting	73
	(13)	Appointment of scrutineer	73
	(14)	Declaration where right to vote objected to	73
	(15)	When poll shall close	73
	(16)	Polling at afternoon meetings	74
	(17)	Counting votes, tie vote	74
	(18)	Declaration of result	74
	(19)	Statement of result of poll	74
	(20)	Secretary to transmit minutes to Ministry	74
	(21)	Meetings called in default of first or annual meeting	74
	(22)	Validity of election	74
93.	(1)	Where municipality may conduct election	74
	(2)	Application of *Municipal Elections Act*	74

Combined Separate School Zones

94.	(1)	Secretary of board as returning officer	75
	(2)	Reporting of vote	75
	(3)	Reporting if no municipality	75
95.	(1)	Board members where combined zone is formed or altered	75
	(2)	Board members in office until organization of new board	75
	(3)	First board members	76

	(4)	Board members in combined separate school zone including urban municipality	76
	(5)	Resolution providing for board members	76
	(6)	Election and term of office	76
	(7)	Distribution of members	76
	(8)	Copy of resolution to be sent to Minister	76
	(9)	Electors' qualifications, rural combined separate school zone	76

PART IV.1

EXTENSION OF ROMAN CATHOLIC ELEMENTARY SCHOOLS

Separate School Extension Post—1997

96.	(1)	Plan re secondary school	76
	(2)	Resolution	76
	(3)	Implementation document	77
	(4)	Same	77
	(5)	Transmittal	77
	(6)	Review by Minister	77
	(7)	Notice	77
	(8)	Same	77
		[Note: sections 97 through 134 inclusive repealed.]	77

Rights Relating to Separate School Extension Pre-1998

135.	(1)	Definitions	77
		[Note: section 135(2) to (23) inclusive repealed.]	77
	(24)	Gratuity	78
	(25)	Idem	78
	(26)	Idem	78
	(26.1)	Idem	79
	(27)	[Repealed]	79
	(28)	Employment, advancement and promotion	79
	(29)	[Repealed]	79
	(30)	Deemed designated persons	79
	(31)	Interpretation	79
	(32)	Regulations: exceptions re successor board determinations	80
	(33)	Application of *Interpretation Act*	80
135.1	(1)	Interpretation: references to ten school year period	80
	(2)	Interpretation: references to Roman Catholic school board	80
136.	(1)	Hiring after ten-year period	80
	(2)	Application of *Human Rights Code* s. 5	80
	(3)	Repeal	80
137.		Enforcement	80

[Note: sections 138 through 146 inclusive repealed.] 81

Planning and Implementation Commission

[Note: sections 147 through 157 inclusive repealed.] 81

PART V

SCHOOL AUTHORITIES — PROTESTANT
1997, c. 31, s. 71

158.	**(1)**	Application to establish Protestant separate school	81
	(1.1)	Same	81
	(1.2)	Same	81
	(2)	Permission to establish	82
	(3)	Restrictions on establishment	82
	(4)	Effective date	82
159.		Protestant board: share of legislative grants	82
160.		[Repealed]	82
161.		[Repealed]	82
162.		[Repealed]	82
163.		[Repealed]	82
164.		Qualification of a voter	82
165.	(1)	Election of board members	82
	(2)	Same	82
	(3)	Number of board members	82
166.		Corporate name of board	82
167.		Powers of board	83
167.1		Attendance rights	83
168.		Discontinuing board	83
169.		Application of other sections	83

PART VI

BOARDS

Duties and Powers

170.	(1)	Duties of boards	83
	(2)	S. 67 school districts	85
	(3)	Regulations re school councils	85
170.1	(1)	Class size	85
	(2)	Same, secondary schools	85
	(3)	Exception	85

	(4)	Determination date		85
	(5)	Regulations		85
	(6)	Review of maximum amount		85
170.2	(1)	Teaching time		85
	(2)	Minimum teaching time, elementary school		85
	(3)	Minimum teaching time, secondary school		85
	(4)	Allocation to schools		85
	(5)	Allocation by principal		86
	(6)	Same		86
	(7)	Effect on collective agreements		86
	(8)	Calculation		86
	(9)	Part-time employees		86
	(10)	Definition		86
	(11)	Interpretation: provision of instruction in a secondary school		86
	(12)	Co-operative education programs: interpretation		86
	(13)	Regulations		86
170.3		Teachers' assistants, etc.		87
171.	(1)	Powers of boards		87
	(2)	Powers of board re: days of work		90
	(3)	Same		90
	(4)	Same		90
	(5)	Same		90
171.1	(1)	Definitions		90
	(2)	Agreements to co-operate		91
	(3)	Same		91
	(4)	Limitation re joint investment agreements		91
	(5)	Regulations		91
	(6)	Classes		91
	(7)	Interpretation		91
	(8)	Conflict		91
172.		[Repealed]		91
173.	(1)	Establishment of scholarships, etc.		92
	(2)	Idem		92
174.		[Repealed]		92
175.		[Repealed]		92

Benefits

176.		Powers of board		92
177.	(1)	Insurance, hospital and health services		92
	(2)	Contributions re insured services		93
	(3)	Coverage for retired persons		93
	(4)	Payment of premium		93
178.	(1)	Pensions		93
	(2)	Idem		93
	(3)	Definition		93

	(4)	Rights continued	93
	(5)	[Repealed]	93
179.	(1)	Retirement allowances	93
	(2)	Widow or widower	93
	(3)	Definition	94
	(4)	Limitation on application of section	94
180.	(1)	Sick leave credits	94
	(2)	Idem	94
	(3)	Idem	94
	(4)	Allowing of credits on transfer of employment	94
	(5)	Where transferred because of change in jurisdiction of board	94
	(6)	Idem	95
	(7)	Limitation	95
	(8)	[Repealed]	95
	(9)	[Repealed]	95
	(10)	[Repealed]	95

Agreements

181.	(1)	Agreements to provide accommodation or services for another board	95
	(2)	Where building, additions, etc., required	95
	(3)	Where cost borne by board not providing accommodation	95
	(4)	Fees, exception	95
182.	(1)	Transfer of French-language secondary school	95
	(2)	Transfer not a closing	96
183.	(1)	Definition	96
	(2)	Agreements for joint use of facilities, etc.	96
	(3)	Approval of Minister	96
	(4)	Previous agreement	96
	(5)	Facilities deemed community recreation centre	96
184.	(1)	Agreement for education at other school	97
	(2)	Calculation of fees	97
185.		Admission of pupils to Indian schools	97
186.		Closing of school by board	97
187.		Agreements re pupils in federal establishments	97
188.	(1)	Agreements re education of Indian pupils	97
	(2)	Agreements re instruction in Indian schools	97
	(3)	Agreements re accommodation for Indian pupils	98
	(4)	Cost of special services	98
	(5)	Regulations: interests of members of bands	98
	(6)	Same	98
	(7)	Same	98
	(8)	Representation on Roman Catholic boards	98
	(9)	Representation on French-language district school boards	98
	(10)	[Repealed]	98
	(11)	[Repealed]	98

	(12)	[Repealed]	98
	(13)	[Repealed]	98
189.	(1)	Definition	98
	(2)	Agreements for adult basic education	98
	(3)	Idem	98
190.	(1)	Transportation of pupils	99
	(2)	Idem	99
	(3)	Idem	99
	(4)	Idem	99
	(5)	Purchase of bus	99
	(6)	Agreements	99
	(7)	Agreements not exceeding five years	99
	(8)	Boarding of secondary school pupils	99
	(9)	Same	100
	(10)	Same	100
	(11)	Boarding of elementary school pupils	100
	(12)	Same	100
	(13)	Certification of attendance	100
	(14)	[Repealed]	101

Honoraria

191.	(1)	Honorarium for members of district school boards	101
	(2)	Maximum	101
	(3)	Chair and vice-chair: additional honorarium	101
	(4)	Maximum	101
	(5)	Different honorarium for chair, vice-chair	101
	(6)	Decrease in honorarium	101
191.1	(1)	Honorarium for members of school authorities	101
	(2)	Chair and vice-chair: additional honorarium	101
	(3)	Regulations: school authority honorariums	101
	(4)	Conflict	101
	(5)	Repeal	101
191.2	(1)	Travel expenses to attend board and committee meetings	101
	(2)	Other travel expenses	102
	(3)	Other expenses	102
	(4)	Same	102
	(5)	Deduction because of absence	102
	(6)	Committee members	102

Property

192.	(1)	School lands granted before 1850 vested in board for school purposes	102
	(1.1)	Same	102
	(2)	Property in trust vested in board	102

193.	**(1)**	Possession of property	102
	(2)	Idem	103
	(3)	Appropriation of property	103
194.	**(1)**	Disposal of realty	103
	(2)	Application for removal of restrictions on use of school lands	103
	(3)	Lease or sale of site or property	103
	(3.1)	Application of proceeds	103
	(3.2)	Conflict	103
	(3.3)	Regulations	103
	(3.4)	Same	103
	(3.5)	General or particular	104
	(3.6)	Classes	104
	(4)	Application of subs. (4.1)	104
	(4.1)	Approval of Minister re disposition, demolition	104
	(5)	Exceptions	104
195.	**(1)**	Board may purchase or expropriate within its jurisdiction	104
	(2)	Purchase or lease of site in adjoining jurisdiction	104
	(3)	School outside designated area	104
	(4)	Buildings on land owned by board	104
	(5)	Buildings on leased land	104
	(6)	Additions or alterations	105
	(7)	Regulations re land reserved for use as a school site	105
	(8)	Same	105
	(9)	Same	105
196.		Agreement for multi-use building	105

Out-of-Classroom Programs

197.	**(1)**	Acquisition of land for natural science program	105
	(2)	Application	105
	(3)	Idem	105
	(4)	Approval not required	105
	(5)	Agreement between boards	105
	(6)	Taxation	106
	(7)	Agreements with conservation authorities, etc.	106
	(8)	Idem	106
	(9)	Idem	106
	(10)	Board and lodging for courses in conservation	106

Officers

198.	**(1)**	Duties of secretary	106
	(2)	Security by officers	107
	(3)	Form of security	107
	(4)	Failure to take security	107
	(5)	Duties of treasurer	107

		(6) Business administrator	107
199.		Responsibility of officers	107

School Board Advisory Committees

200.		Definition	107
201.		Establishment of committee	107
202.	(1)	Composition	107
	(2)	English-language separate district school board	108
	(3)	French-language separate district school board	108
	(3.1)	English-language public district school board	108
	(3.2)	French-language public district school board	108
	(4)	Notice of teacher appointees	108
	(5)	Appointment and term of office	108
	(6)	Reappointment	108
	(7)	Vacancies	108
203.	(1)	First meeting	108
	(2)	Chair	108
	(3)	Quorum	108
	(4)	Sub-committees	109
204.	(1)	Recording secretary	109
	(2)	Budget	109
	(3)	Expenditures	109
205.	(1)	Powers of committee	109
	(2)	Limitation	109
	(3)	Consideration of reports	109
206.		[Repealed]	109

Access to Meetings and Records

207.	(1)	Open meetings of boards	109
	(2)	Closing of certain committee meetings	109
	(3)	Exclusion of persons	109
	(4)	Inspection of books and accounts	109

Board Meetings

208.	(1)	When board deemed constituted	110
	(2)	First meeting	110
	(3)	Supervisory officer may provide for calling first meeting	110
	(4)	Presiding officer	110
	(5)	Election of chair	110
	(5.1)	Transition: 1998	110
	(6)	Subsequent meetings	110
	(7)	Vice-chair	110
	(8)	Where equality of votes	110
	(9)	Temporary chair	110

	(10)	Temporary secretary	110
	(11)	Quorum	110
	(12)	Chair, voting; equality of votes	110
	(13)	Special meetings	111
208.1	**(1)**	Regulations: electronic meetings	111
	(2)	Same	111
	(3)	Same	111
	(4)	Same	111
	(5)	Same	111
209.	**(1)**	Declaration	111
	(2)	Idem	111
	(3)	Oath of allegiance	112
	(4)	Filing of declaration and oath	112

Arbitrators

210.	**(1)**	Arbitrators to send copy of award to board, etc.	112
	(2)	Liability of parties for costs	112
	(3)	Expenses	112
	(4)	Fees	112
	(5)	[Repealed]	112
	(6)	[Repealed]	112
	(7)	[Repealed]	112

Offences and Penalties

211.		False declaration	112
212.	**(1)**	Disturbances	113
	(2)	Idem	113
213.	**(1)**	Acting while disqualified	113
	(2)	False reports and registers	113
214.		[Repealed]	113
215.		[Repealed]	113
216.		[Repealed]	113
217.	**(1)**	Promotion or sale of books, etc., by employees of board or Ministry to board, pupil, etc., prohibited	113
	(2)	Exception for authors	113
	(3)	Employment of employee of board or Ministry to promote sale of books, etc., to board, pupil, etc., prohibited	113
	(4)	Penalty	113

Validity of Elections

218.	**(1)**	Action for declaration that seat vacant	113
	(2)	Time for bringing action	114
	(3)	Power of court	114
	(4)	Application of *Municipal Elections Act*	114

TABLE OF CONTENTS

    (5) Joining of claims 114
    (6) Validity of elections and corrupt practices 114

PART VII

BOARD MEMBERS — QUALIFICATIONS, RESIGNATIONS AND VACANCIES

219. (1) Qualifications of members 114
    (2) Same 114
    (3) Eligibility for re-election 114
    (4) Disqualifications 114
    (5) Leave of absence 114
    (6) Same 115
    (7) Disqualification: district school board by-election 115
    (8) Disqualification: school authority by-elections 115
    (9) Qualification to act as a member 116
    (10) Person not to be candidate for more than one seat 116
    (11) Vacancy where member disqualified 116
220. (1) Members to remain in office 116
    (2) Board not to cease for want of members 116
    (3) Resignation of members 116
    (4) Resignation to become candidate for some other office 116
221. (1) Vacancies 116
    (2) Optional election 116
    (3) Same 117
    (4) Notice re clause (1)(b) 117
    (5) Term of office 117
222. (1) Elections for three member boards 117
    (2) Time of meeting 117
    (3) Notice of meeting 117
    (4) Election at meeting 117
223. (1) Vacancy in rural separate school board before incorporation 117
    (2) Manner of election 117
224.   Vacancy on board 117
225. (1) Election to fill vacancy 117
    (2) Extension of time limits 118
226. (1) Appointment of trustees on failure of qualified person 118
    (2) Interim administration pending by-elections 118
227.   Tie vote 118
228. (1) Seat vacated by conviction, absence etc. 118
    (2) Exception: conviction 118
    (3) Filling of vacancies 118
229. (1) In person attendance required 118
    (2) Same 119

(3) Transition: district school boards in 1998 119

PART VIII

[Repealed 1997, c. 3, s. 5]

PART IX

FINANCE

DIVISION A

GENERAL

Estimates

231.	(1)	Estimates	119
	(2)	Balanced budget	120
	(3)	Rule for 1998	120
	(4)	Reserve fund limitation exception	120
	(5)	Same	120
	(6)	Reserve fund money	120
	(7)	Same	120
	(8)	Same	120
	(9)	Same	120
	(10)	Same	120
	(11)	Minister's powers	120
	(12)	Same	120
232.	(1)	Regulations re estimates	120
	(2)	Same	121
	(3)	Same	121
233.	(1)	Reserve following strike, lock-out	121
	(2)	Same	121
	(3)	Regulations	121

Legislative and Municipal Grants

234.	(1)	Regulations governing legislative grants	121
	(2)	Same	121
	(3)	Same	121
	(4)	Same	122
	(5)	Same	122
	(6)	Additional powers of Minister	122
	(7)	Same	122

	(8)	Payment schedule	122
	(9)	Non-application of *Regulations Act*	122
	(10)	Temporary grants	122
	(11)	Limitation	122
	(12)	Same	122
	(13)	General or particular	122
	(14)	Definition	122
235.	(1)	Definition	122
	(2)	Boards to share in municipal grants	123
	(3)	Same	123
235.1		[Repealed]	123
235.2		[Repealed]	123
235.3		[Repealed]	123

Board Support

236.	(1)	Notice re status as supporter, English-language public board	123
	(2)	Same, English-language Roman Catholic board	123
	(3)	Same, French-language public district school board	123
	(4)	Same, French-language separate district school board	124
	(5)	Same, Protestant separate school board	124
237.	(1)	School support, partnership or corporation other than designated ratepayer	124
	(2)	Non-application to designated ratepayer	124
	(3)	Right of corporation or partnership	124
	(4)	Duty of assessment commissioner	124
	(5)	Same	124
	(6)	Notice to clerk	125
	(7)	Duty of clerk	125
	(8)	Same	125
	(9)	Re corporation	125
	(10)	Same	125
	(11)	Re partnership	125
	(12)	School support if corporation, partnership is tenant	125
	(13)	Application of ss. (9), (10), (11), (14), (15) and (16)	126
	(14)	Effect of notice	126
	(15)	Same	126
	(16)	Inspection of notices	126
	(17)	Type of board	126
238.	(1)	School support, designated ratepayers	126
	(2)	Distribution of taxes	127
239.	(1)	Tenant support re distribution of amounts levied	127
	(2)	If tenant is corporation or partnership	127
	(3)	If tenant is designated ratepayer	127
	(4)	Amount to be levied if multiple tenants	127
	(5)	Agreement between owner and tenant	127

TABLE OF CONTENTS

		(6) Conflict	127

School Rate: Certain Circumstances

240.	(1)	School rate: certain circumstances	128
	(2)	Reserve account	128
	(3)	Same	128
	(4)	Use of money in account	128
	(5)	Application in area of jurisdiction of a public district school board	128
	(6)	Subclass reductions	128

Borrowing and Investment by Boards

241.	(1)	Investment powers	128
	(2)	Restrictions	129
	(3)	Same	129
	(4)	Same	129
	(5)	Report on borrowings	129
	(6)	Regulations	129
	(7)	General or particular	129
	(8)	Transition	129
	(9)	Same	129
	(10)	Definitions	129
242.	(1)	Debt, financial obligation and liability limits	130
	(2)	Approval to exceed limit	130
	(3)	Risk management activities	130
	(4)	General or particular	130
	(5)	Classes	130
243.	(1)	Current borrowing	130
	(2)	Debt charges	130
	(3)	Limit	130
	(4)	Limits for 1998	130
	(5)	Estimated revenues	131
	(6)	Exception re certain boards	131
	(7)	Approval of Minister	131
	(8)	Regulations	131
	(9)	Definition	131
244.	(1)	Provincial guarantee of debentures, etc.	131
	(2)	Form of guarantee	131
	(3)	Validity of guaranteed debentures, etc.	131
245.	(1)	Definitions	131
	(2)	Payments re debentures issued by school authorities, old boards	132
	(3)	Payments re debentures issued by municipality for school authority, old board	132
	(4)	Same	132
	(5)	Exception	132

TABLE OF CONTENTS

246.	(1)	Application of section	132
	(2)	No obligation to raise money through rates to pay debentures	133
	(3)	Deemed amendment	133
	(4)	Rights to debenture holder	133
	(5)	Same	133
	(6)	Term and conditions continued	133
247.	(1)	Borrowing for permanent improvements	133
	(2)	Same, school authorities	134
	(3)	Regulations	134
	(4)	General or particular	134
	(5)	Payments re debentures and debt instruments	134
	(6)	Exception	135
	(7)	All debentures, debt instrument rank equally	135
	(8)	Registration	135
	(9)	Certain rights and duties continued	135
	(10)	Same	135
248.	(1)	Corporation to assist with board financing	135
	(2)	Regulations	136
	(3)	Deemed reference to municipality	136
	(4)	Definition	136
	(5)	Status of securities and other financial instruments	136
	(6)	General or particular	136
	(7)	Consent of board, municipality	136
249.		Agreements	137

Miscellaneous Board Revenues

250.	(1)	Fees or charges for trailers in municipality	137
	(2)	Share to be paid to boards	137
	(3)	Same	137
	(4)	Share to be paid to two boards	137
	(5)	Same	138
	(6)	Same	138
	(7)	Fees or charges not part of annual rates	138
	(8)	Application to municipality operated trailer camps	138
	(9)	Exception	138
251.	(1)	Fee for trailers in territory without municipal organizations	138
	(2)	Same	138
	(3)	Same	138
	(4)	Same	139
	(5)	Same	139
	(6)	Notice	139
	(7)	Content of notice	139
	(8)	Notice to other boards	139
	(9)	Exception	139

	(10)	Offence	139

Financial Administration of Boards

252.	**(1)**	Financial statements	139
	(2)	Publication and notice	140
	(3)	Minister's powers	140
	(4)	Same	140
	(5)	Statements of old boards	140
	(6)	Obstruction	140
253.	**(1)**	Appointment of auditor	140
	(2)	Transition	140
	(3)	Ineligibility for appointment	140
	(4)	Duties of auditor	140
	(5)	Rights of auditor	141
	(6)	Obstruction	141
	(7)	Power to take evidence	141
	(8)	Attendance at meetings of board	141
	(9)	Rights of auditor re 1998 audit	141
	(10)	Obstruction re 1998 audit	141
	(11)	Definition	141
254.	**(1)**	Custody of books, etc.	142
	(2)	Summons for appearance	142
	(3)	Order to account	142
	(4)	Other remedy not affected	142

Miscellaneous

255.	**(1)**	Recreation committees	142
	(2)	Collection of taxes	142
	(3)	Recovery of costs	142
256.	**(1)**	Rates for certain public libraries	142
	(2)	Definition	143
257.		Court proceeding	143
257.1		When fees payable by boards	143
257.2	**(1)**	Transition: notice of support by certain partnerships, corporations	143
	(2)	Same	144
	(3)	Same	144
257.2.1	**(1)**	Tax relief, etc., in unorganized territory	144
	(2)	Exception	144
	(3)	What regulations can provide for, etc.	144
	(4)	Conflicts	144
257.3	**(1)**	Regulations re transitional matters	144
	(2)	General or particular	144
257.4		Type of board for *Assessment Act* purposes	144

DIVISION B

EDUCATION TAXES

Education Taxes

257.5		Definitions	145
257.6	(1)	Property taxable for school purposes	145
	(2)	Exemptions	145
	(3)	Same	145
	(4)	Same	145
	(5)	Regulations	145
257.7	(1)	Levying of tax rates for school purposes	146
	(2)	Exception	146
	(3)	Subclass reductions	146
257.8	(1)	Definition	146
	(2)	Business property, distribution of amounts levied	146
	(3)	Calculation by Minister	146
257.9	(1)	Residential property, distribution of amounts levied	146
	(2)	Interpretation	147
257.10	(1)	Powers of municipality, board levying rates	147
	(2)	Powers of officers	147
	(3)	Application of s. 382 of *Municipal Act*	147
	(4)	Regulations	147
	(5)	Collection of certain taxes	147
257.11	(1)	When amounts paid to boards	148
	(2)	Non-payment on due date	148
	(3)	Payment ahead of due date	148
	(4)	Rate of interest	148
	(5)	Agreement	148
	(6)	Same	148
	(7)	Limitation	148
	(8)	Termination of agreement	148
	(9)	Transition—1998	148
	(10)	Same	148
	(11)	Same	148
	(12)	Extension of instalment due dates	149
	(13)	Same	149
	(14)	Interim financing for 1998	149
	(15)	Interim financing for 1998, agreements	149
	(16)	Payments from Consolidated Revenue Fund	150
	(17)	Amounts deemed to be education funding	150
	(18)	Information relating to agreements	150
	(19)	Enforcement of requirement	150
	(20)	Additional power	150
257.12	(1)	Regulations, Minister of Finance	150

TABLE OF CONTENTS

	(1.1)	Definition	150
	(2)	Scope of regulations	150
	(3)	Tax rates may vary	151
	(4)	Uniform rate, residential/farm, multi-residential	151
	(5)	Tax rates for farmlands and managed forests	151
	(5.1)	Other rates may vary	151
	(6)	Property in subclasses	151
	(7)	Same	151
	(8)	Definition	152
	(9)	Class, etc., not to be defined in terms of board support	152
	(10)	Definition	152
257.12.1	(1)	Requisitions for amounts on business property	152
	(2)	Contents of requisition	152
	(3)	Setting of tax rates, upper-tiers	152
	(4)	When rates set	152
	(5)	Setting of tax rates, single-tiers	152
	(6)	When rates set	152
	(7)	Restrictions on tax rates	152
	(8)	Tax rates deemed to be prescribed	153
	(9)	Graduated tax rates	153
	(10)	Subclass tax reductions	153
	(11)	Definitions	153
257.12.2	(1)	School tax rates for commercial and industrial classes	153
	(2)	Application with respect to requisitions	153
	(3)	2005 and after	154
	(4)	Before 2005, municipalities at or below 3.3 per cent	154
	(5)	Before 2005, municipalities above 3.3 per cent	154
	(6)	Weighted average tax rate	154
	(7)	Rebates under section 442.2	154
	(8)	Industrial classes	155
	(9)	Definitions	155
257.13	(1)	Deferrals	155
	(2)	Same	155
257.13.1		Reductions	155
257.13.2		Regulations, unpaid taxes in territory being organized	155
257.14	(1)	Regulations, Minister of Education and Training	155
	(2)	Clause (1)(f)	156
	(3)	General or particular	157

DIVISION C

TAXES SET BY BOARDS

257.15	(1)	Definitions	157
	(2)	Types of boards	157

xxxv

TABLE OF CONTENTS

257.16	(1)	Rates set by boards	157
	(2)	Subscriptions	157
257.17		Assessment rateable under s. 257.16	157
257.18	(1)	Agreements with municipalities re collection	157
	(2)	Regulations	158
257.19	(1)	Collection powers of boards	158
	(2)	Powers of officers	158
	(3)	Application of s. 382 of *Municipal Act*	158
	(4)	Regulations	158
257.20	(1)	Designation by individuals re business property	158
	(2)	Exception	158
257.21		Limitation on s. 257.20 where residential property assessed	158
257.22		Designation by corporations sole re business assessment	159
257.23	(1)	Assessment of certain tenants	159
	(2)	Same	159
257.24	(1)	Tenant priority	159
	(2)	Same	159
257.25	(1)	Regulations re property classes and tax ratios	159
	(2)	Same	159
	(3)	Same	159
	(4)	Definition	159
257.26	(1)	Determination of rates	159
	(2)	Same	159
257.27	(1)	Regulations	160
	(2)	General or particular	160
257.28	(1)	Borrowing powers of Roman Catholic boards	160
	(2)	Terms of payment	160
	(3)	Debentures	160
	(4)	Amounts	160
	(5)	Maturity	160
	(6)	Sinking fund	160
	(7)	Investment of fund	160
	(8)	Publication of notice of by-law	161
	(9)	Non-application of s. 242	161
257.29	(1)	Notice to assessment commissioner	161
	(2)	Same	161

DIVISION D

SUPERVISION OF BOARDS' FINANCIAL AFFAIRS

257.30	(1)	Investigation of board's financial affairs	161
	(2)	Appointment of investigator	161
	(3)	Powers of investigator	161

	(4)	Same	162
	(5)	Report of investigator	162
	(6)	Same	162
257.31	(1)	Minister's powers on reviewing report: directions	162
	(2)	Vesting order; report recommendation	162
	(3)	Vesting order: board failure to comply with direction	162
	(4)	Notice to board	162
257.32	(1)	Notice to be given re board	162
	(2)	No proceedings against board without leave of Minister	162
	(3)	Suspension of limitation period	162
	(4)	Same	163
	(5)	Effect of order	163
257.33	(1)	Control exercisable by Minister	163
	(2)	Same	163
257.34	(1)	Interpretation	164
	(2)	Powers of Minister with respect to debt	164
	(3)	Limitation	164
	(4)	Publication of notice of intention to exercise powers	165
	(5)	Same	165
	(6)	Same	165
	(7)	Incidental matters	165
	(8)	Objection to be filed with Minister	165
	(9)	Approval by creditors	165
	(10)	Notice when matter to be varied	165
	(11)	Same	165
	(12)	Same	165
257.35		Certain debenture and other debt not to form part of debt after order of Minister	165
237.36		Variation or cancellation of subsisting agreements	165
257.37	(1)	Minister to approve debenture, instrument issues	166
	(2)	Approval of debenture or instrument by-laws	166
257.38	(1)	Minister to have control over money and its application	166
	(2)	Same	166
	(3)	Same	166
	(4)	Same	166
257.39		Exercise of board jurisdiction subject to order	166
257.40	(1)	Exclusive jurisdiction	166
	(2)	Review of orders, etc.	166
	(3)	Exclusive jurisdiction	167
	(4)	Review of orders, etc.	167
	(5)	Limitation	167
257.41		Powers of Minister	167
257.42		Forms of certificates, notices, etc.	167
257.43		Powers exercisable for and in name of board	167
257.44		Minister to have access to all records	167

257.45	(1)	Powers to enforce orders	167
	(2)	Liability for non-compliance	167
	(3)	Personal liability and disqualification of members of boards	167
	(4)	Dismissal of officers or employees	168
257.46		Injunction against exercise of board powers	168
257.47		Combining board offices	168
257.48	(1)	Expenses	168
	(2)	Appointment of Minister	168
	(3)	Board may be heard as to salaries	168
	(4)	Payment of salaries and expenses	168
257.49		Conflict	168
257.50	(1)	Revocation of order	168
	(2)	Same	168
257.51	(1)	Non-application of *Regulations Act*	169
	(2)	Non-application of *Statutory Powers Procedure Act*	169
	(3)	*Municipal Affairs Act*, Parts II and III	169
257.52	(1)	Denominational, linguistic and cultural issues	169
	(2)	Same	169

DIVISION E

EDUCATION DEVELOPMENT CHARGES

Definitions

257.53	(1)	Definitions	169
	(2)	Education land costs	170
	(3)	Exclusion from education land costs	170
	(4)	Education land costs, leases, etc.	170

Education Development Charge By-laws

257.54	(1)	Education development charge by-law	171
	(2)	What development can be charged for	171
	(3)	Same	171
	(4)	Application of by-law	171
	(5)	Limited exemption	171
	(6)	Conditions	171
257.55	(1)	Exemption for industrial development	171
	(2)	Enlargement 50 per cent or less	171
	(3)	Enlargement more than 50 per cent	171
257.56		When by-law effective	172
257.57		If jurisdiction divided into regions	172
257.58	(1)	Duration of education development charge by-law	172
	(2)	Board can pass new by-law	172

TABLE OF CONTENTS

257.59		Contents of by-law	172

Process Before Passing of By-Laws

257.60	(1)	Review of policies	172
	(2)	Public meeting	172
	(3)	Non-application, first by-law under new scheme	173
257.61	(1)	Education development charge background study	173
	(2)	Same	173
257.62		By-law within one year after study	173
257.63	(1)	Public meeting before by-law passed	173
	(2)	Making representations	173
	(3)	Board determination is final	173

Appeal of By-laws

257.64	(1)	Notice of by-law and time for appeal	173
	(2)	Requirements of notice	174
	(3)	Same	174
	(4)	When notice given	174
257.65		Appeal of by-law after passed	174
257.66	(1)	Secretary's duties on appeal	174
	(2)	Same	174
	(3)	Affidavit, declaration conclusive evidence	174
257.67	(1)	OMB hearing of appeal	174
	(2)	Who to get notice	174
	(3)	Powers of OMB	174
	(4)	Limitation on powers	175
	(5)	Dismissal without hearing	175
257.68		When OMB ordered repeals, amendments effective	175
257.69	(1)	Refunds, if OMB repeals by-law, etc.	175
	(2)	When refund due	175
	(3)	Interest	175
	(4)	Source of refund, interest	175
	(5)	Who refund paid to	175
	(6)	Information from municipality	175

Amendment of By-laws

257.70	(1)	Amendment of by-law	176
	(2)	Limitation	176
257.71		When amendment effective	176
257.72		Process before passing amendment	176
257.73	(1)	Notice of amendment and time for appeal	176
	(2)	Requirements of notice	176
	(3)	Same	176
	(4)	When notice given	176

257.74	(1)	Appeal of amending by-law after passed	176
	(2)	Same	177
257.75	(1)	Secretary's duties on appeal	177
	(2)	Same	177
	(3)	Affidavit, declaration conclusive evidence	177
257.76	(1)	OMB hearing of appeal	177
	(2)	Who to get notice	177
	(3)	Powers of OMB	177
	(4)	Limitations on powers	177
	(5)	Dismissal without hearing	178
257.77		When OMB ordered repeals, amendments, effective	178
257.78		Refunds, if OMB repeals by-law, etc.	178
257.79		Application to OMB amendments, etc.	178

Collection of Education Development Charges

257.80		When charge payable	178
257.81		Who charge payable to	178
257.82	(1)	Education development charge reserve funds	178
	(2)	Deposit of charges into reserve funds	178
257.83		Withholding of building permit until charge paid	179
257.84	(1)	Land given for credit	179
	(2)	Same	179

Complaints About Education Development Charges

257.85	(1)	Complaint to council of municipality	179
	(2)	Time limit	179
	(3)	Form of complaint	179
	(4)	Parties	179
	(5)	Hearing	179
	(6)	Notice of hearing	179
	(7)	Councils powers	179
257.86	(1)	Notice of decision and time for appeal	179
	(2)	Requirements of notice	180
257.87	(1)	Appeal of council's decision	180
	(2)	Additional ground	180
257.88	(1)	Clerk's duties on appeal	180
	(2)	Same	180
	(3)	Same	180
257.89	(1)	OMB hearing of appeal	180
	(2)	Notice to parties	180
	(3)	Powers of OMB	180
257.90	(1)	Refund if education development charge reduced	180
	(2)	Interest	181
	(3)	Source of refund, interest	181

257.91	**(4)**	Who refund paid to	181
		Payment if education development charge increased	181

Special Cases

257.92		Territory without municipal organization	181
257.93		Areas where province issues building permits	181

Miscellaneous

257.94		Different types of boards treated the same	181
257.95		Registration of by-law	181
257.96		Recovery of unpaid amounts, lien on land	182
257.97	**(1)**	Reports by municipalities to boards	182
	(2)	When due	182
	(3)	Contents	182
257.98	**(1)**	Statement of treasurer	182
	(2)	Requirements	182
	(3)	Copy to Minister	182
257.99		Board may borrow from reserve fund	182
257.100		No right of petition	182
257.101	**(1)**	Regulations	182
	(2)	Forms	183

Transitional Provisions

257.102	**(1)**	Definitions	184
	(2)	References to Bill 98	184
257.103	**(1)**	By-law under the old Act	184
	(2)	Continued	184
	(3)	Application of old Act, new Act	184
	(4)	Duration of continued by-law	184
	(5)	Modifications of by-law	184
	(6)	Amendment, repeal of by-law	184
	(7)	Restriction, while continued by-law in force	185
	(8)	Certain by-laws passed under old Act	185
	(9)	Same, refund of charges paid	185
257.104		Certain old requests, appeals	185
257.105	**(1)**	Regulations, transition	185
	(2)	General or particular	185

DIVISION F

Review of Education Funding

257.106	**(1)**	Operation of Division C	185
	(2)	Same	185

TABLE OF CONTENTS

	(3)	Same	185
	(4)	Same	185
	(5)	Same	186
257.107	(1)	Legislative committee review	186
	(2)	Timing	186
	(3)	Report	186
	(4)	Same	186
	(5)	Same	186
258.		[Repealed]	186
259.		[Repealed]	186

PART X

TEACHERS, PUPIL RECORDS AND EDUCATION NUMBERS

260.		[Repealed]	186
261.		Probationary teacher	186
262.	(1)	Membership in Ontario College of Teachers	186
	(2)	[Repealed]	187
	(3)	[Repealed]	187
	(4)	[Repealed]	187
263.		Termination of contract where welfare of school involved	187

Duties

264.	(1)	Duties of teacher	187
	(1.1)	Sign language	188
	(2)	Refusal to give up school property	188
	(3)	Teachers, conferences	188
265.		Duties of principal	188

Pupil Records

266.	(1)	Definition	189
	(2)	Pupil records privileged	189
	(2.1)	Information to medical officer of health	190
	(3)	Right of parent and pupil	190
	(4)	Idem	190
	(5)	Reference where disagreement	190
	(6)	Use re further education or employment	190
	(7)	Information for Minister or board	190
	(8)	No action re content	190
	(9)	Testimony re content	190
	(10)	Secrecy re contents	191
	(11)	Definition	191
	(12)	Application to former records	191

xlii

	(13)	Use of record in disciplinary cases	191

Ontario Education Numbers

266.1		Definition	191
266.2	**(1)**	Assignment of numbers	191
	(2)	Same	191
	(3)	Same	191
	(4)	Same	191
266.3	**(1)**	Privacy re education numbers	191
	(2)	Exception	191
	(3)	Same	192
	(4)	Same	192
266.4	**(1)**	Offence	192
	(2)	Penalty, individuals	192
	(3)	Penalty, corporations	192
266.5	**(1)**	Regulations	192
	(2)	General or particular	192
	(3)	Classes	192

Boards of Reference

267.		Definitions	192
268.	**(1)**	Termination of contract by board	193
	(2)	Termination of contract by teacher	193
	(3)	Application for board	193
	(4)	Service of notice	193
269.	**(1)**	Appointment in place of teacher dismissed	193
	(2)	New contract after termination of contract by teacher	193
270.	**(1)**	Application for Board of Reference	194
	(2)	Appointment	194
	(3)	Naming of representatives	194
	(4)	Failure to name representatives	194
	(5)	Idem	194
	(6)	Failure of representatives to appear	194
	(7)	Applicant deemed eligible	194
	(8)	Death or withdrawal of representative	194
	(9)	Death, etc., of chair before hearing	195
	(10)	New Board of Reference after hearing commences	195
	(11)	Procedure at new Board of Reference	195
271.		Place and time of hearing	195
272.		Duty to inquire and powers of judge	195
273.	**(1)**	Direction of Board of Reference to report	195
	(2)	Chair of Board of Reference to report	195
274.		New Board of Reference provided	196
275.	**(1)**	Direction of Board	196

xliii

	(2)	Failure to comply with direction of Board	196
	(3)	Idem	196
276.		Payment of costs	196
277.		Regulations	196

PART X.1

TEACHERS COLLECTIVE BARGAINING

Interpretation

277.1	(1)	Definitions	196
	(2)	Interpretation	196

Collective Bargaining

277.2	(1)	*Labour Relations Act, 1995*	197
	(2)	Constitutional rights	197
	(3)	Related employers	197
277.3	(1)	Teachers' bargaining units, district school boards	197
	(2)	Designated bargaining agents	197
277.4	(1)	Teachers' bargaining units, school authorities	198
	(2)	Same	198
	(3)	Designated bargaining agents	198
	(4)	Same	199
277.5	(1)	Occasional teachers	199
	(2)	Same	199
	(3)	Same	199
	(4)	Transition	199
	(5)	Outstanding grievances	199
277.6	(1)	Replacement of specified bargaining agents	199
	(2)	Same	199
	(3)	Same	199
277.7	(1)	Combined bargaining unit	199
	(2)	Discontinuation of combined bargaining unit	199
277.8	(1)	Appropriate bargaining units	200
	(2)	Certification of bargaining agents	200
	(3)	Same	200
	(4)	Same	200
277.9	(1)	Joint negotiations	200
	(2)	Same, school authorities	200
	(3)	Same, bargaining agents	200
	(4)	Agreements	200
277.10		Arbitration	200
277.11	(1)	Election by principal, vice-principal	200

	(2)	Same	200
	(3)	Same	200
	(4)	Same	200
	(5)	Effect on collective agreement	200
	(6)	Repeal	200
277.12	(1)	Education Relations Commission	200
	(2)	Certain proceedings continued	201
	(3)	Provision of information	201
	(4)	Same	201
	(5)	Testimony in proceedings	201
	(6)	Repeal	201
	(7)	Re-enactment	201
277.12	(1)	Advice re jeopardy	201
	(2)	Same	201
277.13		Conflict	201
277.13.1	(1)	Enforcement of Part X.1	201
	(2)	Same	201
	(3)	No panels	202
	(4)	Labour relation officers	202
	(5)	Interim order	202
	(6)	Timing of decisions, etc.	202
	(7)	Finality	202
	(8)	Repeal	202
277.13.2	(1)	Enforcement, *Labour Relations Act, 1995*	202
	(2)	Repeal	202

The Transition from December 31, 1997 to January 1, 1998

277.14	(1)	Terms of employment, district school boards	202
	(2)	Applicable collective agreements	202
	(3)	Same, transfer between boards	203
	(4)	Status of board	203
	(5)	Terms and conditions of employment	203
	(6)	Salary, benefits and seniority	203
	(7)	Seniority	204
	(8)	Effect	204
	(9)	Termination of agreements	204
	(10)	Definition	204
277.15	(1)	Terms of employment, school authorities	204
	(2)	Same	204
	(3)	Termination of agreements	205
277.16	(1)	Outstanding grievances	205
	(2)	Same	205
277.17	(1)	Termination of arbitrations	205
	(2)	Termination of strikes, lock-outs	205
	(3)	Right to strike	205

		(4) Right to lock-out	205
		(5) Enforcement	205

Teachers' First Collective Agreement After the Transition

277.18	(1) First collective agreements	205
	(2) Same	205
277.19	(1) Notice of desire to bargain	206
	(2) Same	206
277.20	(1) Minimum term of agreement	206
	(2) Same	206
	(3) Effective date	206
277.21	Repeal	206

PART XI

SUPERVISORY OFFICERS

278.		Qualifications of supervisory officers	206
279.		Supervisory officers and director of education: district school boards	206
280.	(1)	Appointment of director of education: school authorities	206
	(2)	Same	206
	(3)	Abolition of position	206
281.	(1)	[Repealed]	206
	(2)	[Repealed]	206
	(3)	[Repealed]	206
282.	(1)	[Repealed]	206
	(2)	[Repealed]	207
283.	(1)	Chief executive officer	207
	(1.1)	Same	207
	(2)	Idem	207
	(3)	General report of chief executive officer	207
284.	(1)	Supervisory: school authorities	207
	(2)	Agreements	207
	(3)	Same	207
	(4)	Same	207
284.1		[Repealed]	207
285.	(1)	Responsibility of supervisory officers	207
	(2)	Confirmation by Minister	207
286.	(1)	Duties of supervisory officers	207
	(2)	Responsibility to Minister	208
	(3)	Responsibility to board	208
	(4)	Full-time position	208
	(5)	Access to books and records, etc.	208
287.	(1)	Suspension or dismissal of supervisory officer by board	208

	(2)	Notice re suspension or dismissal	208
287.1	(1)	Principals, vice-principals	208
	(2)	Regulations	209
	(3)	Same	209
287.2	(1)	Employment terms, prinicpals, etc.	209
	(2)	Same	209
	(3)	Exceptions	209
	(4)	Repeal	209

PART XII

LANGUAGE OF INSTRUCTION

Provisions Relating to District School Boards

288.		French-language district school boards	209
289.		English-language district school boards	209

Provisions Relating to School Authorities

290.	(1)	Application	209
	(2)	Right to instruction in French-language instructional unit: school authorities	210
	(3)	Duty of school authority to provide French-language instructional unit	210
	(4)	Meals, lodging and transportation	210
	(5)	English-language schools or classes	210
291.	(1)	Right to instruction in French-language instructional unit: s. 67 boards	210
	(2)	Duty of s. 67 boards to provide French-language instructional unit	210
	(3)	Meals, lodging and transportation	210
	(4)	English-language classes where French-language school or classes established	211

Provisions Relating to District School Boards and School Authorities

292.	(1)	English as a subject of instruction	211
	(2)	Same, grades 5, 6, 7 and 8	211
293.	(1)	Admission of pupils other than French-speaking persons, district school boards	211
	(2)	Same, school authorities	211
	(3)	Where school authority has no French-speaking supervisory officer	212

French-Language Rights Holder Groups

294.	(1)		212
	(2)	Proposals of French-language rights holders groups	212

xlvii

TABLE OF CONTENTS

	(3)	Same	212
	(4)	Consideration of proposals by school authority	213
	(5)	Same	213
	(6)	Same	213
	(7)	Approval of proposal under clause (3)(c)	213
	(8)	Notice of refusal	213
	(9)	Referral by group to Languages of Instruction Commission	213
	(10)	Same	213

Languages of Instruction Commission of Ontario

295.	(1)	Commission continued	213
	(2)	Term, reappointment and remuneration	213
	(3)	Vacancies	213
	(4)	Commission is responsible to the Minister	213
	(5)	Quorum	214
	(6)	Recommendation	214
	(7)	Duties of commission	214
	(8)	Person to speak for group	214
	(9)	Referral to Commission by Minister	214
	(10)	Commission reponse to referral under s. 294	214
	(11)	Commission reponse to referral under subs. (9)	214
	(12)	Notice where no further action by Commission	214
	(13)	Notice where mediator appointed	214
	(14)	Parties	214
296.	(1)	Remuneration	214
	(2)	Who not eligible as mediator	215
	(3)	Duties of mediator	215
	(4)	Extension of period of mediation	215
297.	(1)	Duties of Commission	215
	(2)	Resolution by school authority	215
	(3)	Notice of resolution	215
	(4)	Where school authority resolves not to implement recommendation	215
	(5)	Time for notices and reasons	215
298.	(1)	Second resolution	215
	(2)	Conflict with by-law	215
	(3)	Time for second resolution	215
	(4)	Notice	215
299.	(1)	Reconsideration by Commission	215
	(2)	Order by Minister	215
	(3)	Report and recommendation not binding on Minister	216
	(4)	Enforcement of order	216
	(5)	Same	216
	(6)	Service of order	216
		[Note: sections 300 through 308 inclusive repealed.]	216

PART XIII

[Repealed] 216

PART XIV

MATTERS RELATED TO 1997-1998 SCHOOL SYSTEM REFORMS
1997, c. 3, s. 6; 1997, c. 31, s. 130

[Note: sections 327 through 333 inclusive repealed.] 216

Education Improvement Commission

334.	(1)	Education Improvement Commission	217
	(2)	Composition	217
	(3)	Chair and vice-chair	217
	(4)	Term of office	217
	(4.1)	Same	217
	(5)	Authority of vice-chair	217
	(6)	Authority of co-chairs	217
	(7)	Same	217
	(8)	Quorum	217
	(9)	Remuneration and expenses	217
	(10)	Staff and accommodation	217
	(11)	Expert assistance	217
	(12)	[Repealed]	217
	(13)	[Repealed]	217
	(14)	[Repealed]	217
	(15)	Court proceedings	217
	(16)	Annual report	217
	(17)	Additional reports	218
335.	(1)	[Repealed]	218
	(2)	Function of Commission	218
	(3)	Same	218
		[Note: sections 336 through 343 inclusive repealed.]	218
344.	(1)	Non-application of *Regulations Act*	219
	(2)	Non-application of *SPPA*	219
345.		[Repealed]	219
346.	(1)	Protection from liability	219
	(2)	Same	219
	(3)	Vicarious liability	219
	(4)	Protection from liability; duty, authority relating to elections	219
	(5)	Vicarious liability	219
	(6)	[Repealed]	219

	(7) Same	219
	(8) Same	220
347.	**(1)** Personal information	220
	(2) Example	220
	(3) Conflict with *FIPPA, MFIPPA*	220
	(4) Offence	220
348.	[Repealed]	220
349.	[Repealed]	220
350.	When Education Improvement Commission power may be exercised	220

Transitional Authority of District School Boards

351.	**(1)** Authority of district school boards before 1998	220
	(2) Same	220
	(3) Directions	221
	(4) Same	221
	(5) Same	221
	(6) Non-application of *Regulations Act*	221
	(7) Limitation	221
	(8) Purpose	221
	(9) Application of s. 207	221
	(10) Conflict with section 208	221
	(11) Declaration under section 209	221
351.1	Transition: membership on old board	221

REGULATIONS UNDER THE EDUCATION ACT

Regulation 283 — [Revoked]	223
Regulation 284 — *See Editor's note*	223
Regulation 285 — Continuing Education	224
Regulation 286 — *See Editor's note*	228
Regulation 287 — *See Editor's note*	228
Regulation 288 — *See Editor's note*	228
Regulation 289 — *See Editor's note*	228
Regulation 290 — *See Editor's note*	228
Regulation 291 — District School Areas	229
Regulation 293 — Fees for Transcripts and Statements of Standing and for Duplicates of Diplomas, Certificates and Letters of Standing	233
Regulation 294 — The James Bay Lowlands Secondary School Boards	234
Regulation 295 — The Northern District School Area Board	237
Regulation 296 — Ontario Schools for the Blind and the Deaf	239
Regulation 298 — Operation of Schools — General	247
Regulation 300 — Practice and Procedure — Boards of Reference	263
Regulation 302 — Purchase of Milk	267

TABLE OF CONTENTS

Regulation 304 — School Year Calendar	268
Regulation 305 — [Revoked]	271
Regulation 306 — Special Education Programs and Services	272
Regulation 307 — Special Grant	274
Regulation 308 — Supervised Alternative Learning for Excused Pupils	275
Regulation 309 — Supervisory Officers	279
Regulation 310 — Teachers' Contracts	284
Regulation 311 — Territory Without Municipal Organization Attached to a District Municipality	289
Regulation 312 — *See Editor's note*	292
Regulation 313 — *See Editor's note*	292
Regulation 7/91 — *See Editor's note*	292
Regulation 731/92 — *See Editor's note*	292
Regulation 183/97 — Letters of Permission	293
Regulation 185/97 — Establishment, Areas of Jurisdiction and Names of District School Boards	295
Regulation 250/97 — Representation on District School Boards — 1997 Regular Election	330
Regulation 460/97 — Transition From Old Boards to District School Boards	351
Regulation 461/97 — Pupil Representation on Boards	373
Regulation 462/97 — Native Representation on Boards	374
Regulation 463/97 — Electronic Meetings	376
Regulation 464/97 — Special Education Advisory Committees	378
Regulation 465/97 — Regulation under Section 46.1 of the Act (Prescribed Municipalities, Defence Property)	382
Regulation 466/97 — Borrowing for Permanent Improvements: Issuance of Debentures	383
Regulation 467/97 — Deemed District Municipalities (School Authority Jurisdiction) — Tax Rates	387
Regulation 468/97 — Deemed District Municipalities (District School Board Jurisdiction) — Tax Rates	389
Regulation 469/97 — [Revoked]	390
Regulation 470/97 — Financial Statements and Auditor's Reports for Old Boards	391
Regulation 471/97 — Eligible Investments	392
Regulation 472/97 — Principals and Vice-principals of School Authorities	395
Regulation 494/97 — Levying and Collecting by Alternative Boards	396
Regulation 495/97 — Current Borrowing Limits	397
Regulation 496/97 — Reserve for Working Funds Limit	398
Regulation 497/97 — [Revoked]	399
Regulation 498/97 — [Revoked]	400
Regulation 20/98 — Education Development Charges — General	401
Regulation 21/98 — Development Charges Act	426
Regulation 79/98 — By-elections	427
Regulation 90/98 — Principals and Vice-principals — Redundancy and Reassignment	429

TABLE OF CONTENTS

Regulation 92/98 — Interim Payments in Respect of Legislative Grants for the Period January 1, 1998 to August 31, 1998 431
Regulation 118/98 — Class Size 435
Regulation 124/98 — Transition Assistance Grants 439
Regulation 181/98 — Identification and Placement of Exceptional Pupils 440
Regulation 283/98 — Calculation of Average Daily Enrolment for the Period January 1, 1998 to August 31, 1998 455
Regulation 284/98 — Calculation of Fees for the Period January 1, 1998 to August 31, 1998 458
Regulation 285/98 — Legislative Grants for the Period January 1, 1998 to August 31, 1998 463
Regulation 286/98 — Calculation of Average Daily Enrolment for the 1998-99 Fiscal Year 524
Regulation 287/98 — Student Focused Funding — Legislative Grants for the School Board 1998-99 Fiscal Year 528
Regulation 288/98 — Calcualtion of Fees for Pupils for the 1998-99 School Board Fiscal Year 610
Regulation 346/98 — Second Instalment Payment of School Taxes in 1998 619
Regulation 365/98 — Pre-1998 School Tax Arrears 620
Regulation 366/98 — Tax Arrears in Annexed Areas 621
Regulation 392/98 — Tax Matters — Taxation of Certain Railway, Power Utility Lands 622
Regulation 393/98 — Tax Matters — Eligible Theatre Definition 649
Regulation 394/98 — Tax Matters — Definition of Business Property and Residential Property 650
Regulation 400/98 — Tax Matters — Tax Rates for School Purposes 651
Regulation 444/98 — Disposition of Surplus Real Property 662
Regulation 446/98 — Reserve Funds 672
Regulation 470/98 — School Attendance Rights — Resident Business Property Owners and Tenants 676
Regulation 471/98 — School Attendance Rights — Non-Resident Business Property Owners 677
Regulation 472/98 — Debt and Financial Obligations Limits 680
Regulation 476/98 — Transition Assistance Grants, No. 2 681
Regulation 486/98 — Calculation of Amount of Reserve Resulting from Strike or Lock-Out 683
Regulation 509/98 — Tax Matters — Relief in Unorganized Territory (Section 257.2.1 of the Act) 684
Regulation 712/98 — Tax Matters — Rates under Subsection 255(1) of the Act 693
Regulation 713/98 — Apportionment of Rates in Certain District School Areas 694
Regulation 714/98 — Levying of Certain Rates for 1998 in 1999 695
Regulation 715/98 — Deemed Attacment of Certain Territory without Municipal Organization 696
Regulation 213/99 — Calculation of Average Daily Enrolment for the 1999-2000 Fiscal Year 697

Regulation 214/99 — Student Focused Funding — Legislative Grants for the School Board 1999-2000 Fiscal Year 701
Regulation 215/99 — Calculation of Fees for Pupils for the 1999-2000 School Board Fiscal Year 778

EDUCATION QUALITY AND ACCOUNTABILITY OFFICE ACT, 1996

1.		Definitions	789
2.		Education Quality and Accountability Office established	789
3.		Objects	789
4.	(1)	Office may require co-operation of boards	789
	(2)	[Repealed]	789
	(3)	Directives: when a pupil need not take a test	789
	(4)	Non-application of *Regulations Act*	789
	(5)	Compliance of boards	790
	(6)	Compliance of pupils	790
5.	(1)	Agreements re tests	790
	(2)	Fees	790
	(3)	Capacity to enter agreements not limited	790
6.	(1)	Minister of Education and Training: directives and policies	790
	(2)	Same	790
	(3)	Non-application of *Regulations Act*	790
7.		Crown Agency	790
8.	(1)	Delegation of powers of Minister of Education and Training	790
	(2)	Delegation subject to conditions	790
9.	(1)	Capacity and powers	790
	(2)	Real property	790
	(3)	Borrowing	790
	(4)	Guarantee	791
	(5)	Same	791
	(6)	Collection of personal information	791
10.		Non-application of certain Acts	791
11.	(1)	Board of directors	791
	(2)	Term	791
	(3)	Remuneration	791
	(4)	Vacancies	791
	(5)	Temporary vacancies	791
12.	(1)	Chair	791
	(2)	Acting chair	791
13.	(1)	Meetings	791
	(2)	Quorum	791
14.		By-laws	791
15.		Conflict of interest and indemnification	791

liii

TABLE OF CONTENTS

16.	(1)	Chief Executive Officer	791
	(2)	Powers and duties	792
	(3)	Delegation	792
	(4)	Same	792
17.	(1)	Employees	792
	(2)	Same	792
	(3)	Same	792
	(4)	Professional and other assistance	792
18.	(1)	Fees	792
	(2)	Same	792
19.	(1)	Revenues and investments	792
	(2)	Payments to Consolidated Revenue Fund	792
	(3)	Reserves	792
20.		Temporary investments	792
21.		Fiscal year	793
22.	(1)	Annual budget	793
	(2)	Same	793
23.	(1)	Annual plan of operation	793
	(2)	Multi-year plan	793
	(3)	Changes required by Minister of Education and Training	793
24.	(1)	Accounting	793
	(2)	Auditors	793
	(3)	Disclosure to Provincial Auditor	793
	(4)	Audit required by Minister of Education and Training	793
	(5)	Same	793
25.	(1)	Annual report	793
	(2)	Same	793
	(3)	Tabling	793
	(4)	Other reports	794
	(5)	Same	794
26.	(1)	Regulations	794
	(2)	Consultation	794
27.	(1)	Obligation re personal information	794
	(2)	Same	794
28.	(1)	Protection from personal liability	794
	(2)	Crown not relieved of liability	794
29.		[Consequential amendments are not reproduced here]	794
30.		Commencement	794
31.		Short title	794

IMMUNIZATION OF SCHOOL PUPILS ACT

1.		Definitions	795

TABLE OF CONTENTS

2.		Purpose of Act	796
3.	(1)	Duty of parent	796
	(2)	Exception	796
	(3)	Idem	796
	(4)	Idem	796
4.		Offence	796
5.		Certificate by M.O.H. as evidence	796
6.	(1)	Order for suspension re designated diseases	796
	(2)	Grounds for order re designated diseases	796
7.		Term of suspension	796
8.	(1)	Service of copy of order upon parent	796
	(2)	Written reasons	796
	(3)	Repeated orders	797
9.		Rescission of order	797
10.		Statement by physician	797
11.	(1)	Record of immunization	797
	(2)	Review of record	797
12.	(1)	Order by M.O.H.	797
	(2)	Grounds for order	797
	(3)	Term of order	797
	(4)	Rescission of order	797
	(5)	Service of copy of order	797
	(6)	Service of copy of rescinding order	797
	(7)	Written reasons	798
13.		Hearing and submissions	798
14.	(1)	Notice of transfer of pupil	798
	(2)	Transmittal of copy of immunization record	798
15.	(1)	Notice	798
	(2)	Idem	798
	(3)	Opportunity to show compliance and to examine documents	798
	(4)	Powers of Board where hearing	798
	(5)	Time for hearing	798
	(6)	Parties	798
	(7)	Effect of order	799
	(8)	Members holding hearing not to have taken part in investigation, etc.	799
	(9)	Recording of evidence	799
	(10)	Findings of fact	799
	(11)	Only members at hearing to participate in decision	799
	(12)	Release of documentary evidence	799
16.	(1)	Appeal to court	799
	(2)	Record to be filed in court	799
	(3)	Powers of court on appeal	799
17.		Regulations	800
18.	(1)	Service	800

lv

(2) When service deemed made 800

REGULATION UNDER THE IMMUNIZATION OF SCHOOL PUPILS ACT

Regulation 645 — General 801
    1. Record of immunization 801
    2. Statement of medical exemption 801
    3. Statement of conscience or religious belief 801
    4. Notice of transfer of pupil 801
    5. Schedule 801
Form 1 802
Form 2 804
Form 3 805

LOCAL GOVERNMENT DISCLOSURE OF INTEREST ACT, 1994

  1.   Purpose 807
  2. **(1)** Definitions 807
        (2) Non-application 808
        (3) Pecuniary interest 808
        (4) Definition 808
  3.   Exceptions 808
  4. **(1)** Duty of member 809
        (2) When absent from meeting 809
        (3) Limitation 810
        (4) Interest of member 810
        (5) Filing 810
  5. **(1)** Gifts 810
        (2) Exception 810
        (3) Disclosure 810
        (4) Contents 810
  6. **(1)** Financial disclosure requirement 810
        (2) Filing form 810
        (3) Omissions 810
        (4) Changes 811
        (5) Limitation 811
        (6) Interest of member 811
  7. **(1)** Commissioner 811
        (2) Assistant commissioner 811
        (3) Restriction 811
        (4) Guidelines 811

8.	**(1)**	Applications	811
	(2)	Timing	811
	(3)	Fees	811
	(4)	Contents	811
	(5)	Investigation	811
	(6)	Same	811
	(7)	Timing	811
	(8)	Completion	811
	(9)	Court determination	812
	(10)	Application	812
	(11)	Requirement	812
	(12)	Restriction	812
	(13)	Limitation	812
9.	**(1)**	Power of court	812
	(2)	Restrictions	812
	(3)	No vacancy	813
10.	**(1)**	Appeal to Divisional Court	813
	(2)	Judgment or new trial	813
	(3)	Further appeal	813
11.		Proceedings not invalidated	813
12.		Other procedures prohibited	813
13.	**(1)**	Quorum	813
	(2)	Same	813
	(3)	Order	813
	(4)	Declaration	813
	(5)	Conditions	814
	(6)	Effect	814
14.		Minutes	814
15.	**(1)**	Register	814
	(2)	Contents	814
	(3)	Inspection	814
	(4)	Copies	814
	(5)	Retention of records	814
16.		Prohibition re information	814
17.		Offence	814
18.	**(1)**	Insurance	814
	(2)	*Insurance Act* does not apply	814
	(3)	Surplus funds	815
	(4)	Reserve funds	815
	(5)	Boards	815
	(6)	Former members	815
19.		By-laws	815
20.		Community economic development corporations	815
21.		Regulations	815
22.		Regulations	815

23.		Conflict	815
24.		Short title	815

MUNICIPAL CONFLICT OF INTEREST ACT

1.		Definitions	817
2.		Indirect pecuniary interest	818
3.		Interest of certain relatives deemed that of member	818

EXCEPTIONS

4.		Where s. 5 does not apply	819

DUTY OF MEMBER

5.	(1)	When present at meeting at which matter considered	819
	(2)	Where member to leave closed meeting	820
	(3)	When absent from meeting at which matter considered	820

RECORD OF DISCLOSURE

6.	(1)	Disclosure to be recorded in minutes	820
	(2)	Idem	820

REMEDY FOR LACK OF QUORUM

7.	(1)	Quorum deemed constituted	820
	(2)	Application to judge	820
	(3)	Power of judge to declare s. 5 not to apply	820

ACTION WHERE CONTRAVENTION ALLEGED

8.		Who may try alleged contravention of s. 5(1-3)	821
9.	(1)	Who may apply to judge	821
	(2)	Contents of notice of application	821
	(3)	Time for bringing application limited	821
10.	(1)	Power of judge to declare seat vacant, disqualify member and require restitution	821
	(2)	Saving by reason of inadvertence or error	821
	(3)	Member not to be suspended	821
	(4)	....	821
	(5)	....	821
11.	(1)	Appeal to Divisional Court	821
	(2)	Judgment or new trial	822

TABLE OF CONTENTS

	(3)	Appeal from order or new trial	822
12.		Proceedings not invalidated but voidable	822
13.		Other Procedures prohibited	822

GENERAL

14.	(1)	Insurance	822
	(2)	*Insurance Act* does not apply	822
	(3)	Surplus funds	822
	(4)	Reserve funds	822
	(5)	Local boards	823
	(6)	Former members	823
15.		Conflict with other Acts	823

MUNICIPAL FREEDOM OF INFORMATION AND PROTECTION OF PRIVACY ACT

PURPOSES

1.	(1)	Purposes	825

DEFINITIONS

2.	(1)	Definitions	825
	(2)	Personal information	826
	(3)	Bodies considered part of municipal corporation	826
3.	(1)	Designation of head	827
	(2)	Idem	827
	(3)	If no designation	827

PART I

FREEDOM OF INFORMATION

Access to Records

4.	(1)	Right of access	827
	(2)	Severability of record	827
5.	(1)	Obligation to disclose	827
	(2)	Notice	827
	(3)	Contents of notice	827
	(4)	Representation	828

Exemptions

6.	(1)	Draft by-laws, etc.	828
	(2)	Exception	828

TABLE OF CONTENTS

7.	(1)	Advice or recommendation	828
	(2)	Exception	828
	(3)	Idem	829
8.	(1)	Law enforcement	829
	(2)	Idem	829
	(3)	Refusal to confirm or deny existence of record	829
	(4)	Exception	829
	(5)	Idem	829
9.	(1)	Relations with governments	830
	(2)	Idem	830
10.	(1)	Third party information	830
	(2)	Consent to disclosure	830
11.		Economic and other interests	830
12.		Solicitor-client privilege	831
13.		Danger to safety or health	831
14.	(1)	Personal privacy	831
	(2)	Criteria re invasion of privacy	831
	(3)	Presumes invasion of privacy	832
	(4)	Limitation	832
	(5)	Refusal to confirm or deny existence of record	832
15.		Information soon to be published	832
16.		Exemptions not to apply	832

Access Procedure

17.	(1)	Request	832
	(1.1)	Frivolous request	833
	(2)	Sufficiency of detail	833
18.	(1)	Definition	833
	(2)	Request to be forwarded	833
	(3)	Transfer of request	833
	(4)	Greater interest	833
	(5)	When transferred request deemed made	833
19.		Notice by head	833
20.	(1)	Extension of time	834
	(2)	Notice of extension	834
20.1	(1)	Frivolous request	834
	(2)	Non-application	834
21.	(1)	Notice to affected persons	834
	(2)	Contents of notice	834
	(2.1)	Description	835
	(3)	Time for notice	835
	(4)	Notice of delay	835
	(5)	Representation re disclosure	835
	(6)	Representation in writing	835
	(7)	Decision re disclosure	835

TABLE OF CONTENTS

		(8) Notice of head's decision to disclose	835
		(9) Access to be given unless affected person appeals	835
22.	(1)	Contents of notice of refusal	835
	(2)	Idem	836
	(3)	Idem	836
	(3.1)	Description	836
	(4)	Deemed refusal	836
23.	(1)	Copy of record	836
	(2)	Access to original record	836
	(3)	Copy of part	836

Information to be Published or Available

24.	(1)	Publication of information re institutions	836
	(2)	Idem	837
25.	(1)	Information available for inspection	837
	(2)	Idem	837
26.	(1)	Annual report of head	837
	(2)	Contents of report	837

PART II

PROTECTION OF INDIVIDUAL PRIVACY

Collection and Retention of Personal Information

27.		Application of Part	837
28.	(1)	Definition	837
	(2)	Collection of personal information	837
29.	(1)	Manner of collection	837
	(2)	Notice to individual	838
	(3)	Exception	838
30.	(1)	Retention of personal information	838
	(2)	Standard of accuracy	838
	(3)	Exception	838
	(4)	Disposal of personal information	838

Use and Disclosure of Personal Information

31.	Use of personal information	838
32.	Where disclosure permitted	839
33.	Consistent purpose	839

Personal Information Banks

34.	(1)	Personal information bank index	839
	(2)	Ensure privacy	840

35.	(1)	Inconsistent use or disclosure	840
	(2)	Idem	840

Right of Individual to Whom Personal Information Relates to Access and Correction

36.	(1)	Right of access to personal information	840
	(2)	Right of correction	840
37.	(1)	Request	840
	(2)	Access procedures	841
	(3)	Comprehensible form	841
38.		Exemptions	841

PART III

APPEAL

39.	(1)	Right to appeal	841
	(1.1)	Fee	841
	(2)	Time for application	841
	(2.1)	Immediate dismissal	842
	(2.2)	Non-application	842
	(3)	Notice of application for appeal	842
40.		Mediator to try to effect settlement	842
41.	(1)	Inquiry	842
	(2)	Procedure	842
	(3)	Inquiry in private	842
	(4)	Powers of Commissioner	842
	(5)	Record not retained by Commissioner	842
	(6)	Examination on site	842
	(7)	Notice of entry	842
	(8)	Examination under oath	842
	(9)	Evidence privileged	842
	(10)	Protection	842
	(11)	Idem	843
	(12)	Prosecution	843
	(13)	Representations	843
	(14)	Right to counsel	843
42.		Burden of proof	843
43.	(1)	Order	843
	(2)	Idem	843
	(3)	Conditions	843
	(4)	Notice of order	843
44.		Delegation	843

TABLE OF CONTENTS

PART IV

GENERAL

45.	(1)	Fees	843
	(3)	Estimate of costs	844
	(4)	Waiver of payment	844
	(5)	Review	844
	(6)	Disposition of fees	844
46.		Powers and duties of Commissioner	844
47.	(1)	Regulations	844
	(2)	Categories of fees	845
48.	(1)	Offences	845
	(2)	Penalty	845
	(3)	Consent of Attorney General	845
49.	(1)	Delegation of head's powers	845
	(2)	Protection from civil proceeding	845
	(3)	Vicarious liability of institutions preserved	845
50.	(1)	Oral requests	846
	(2)	Pre-existing access preserved	846
51.	(1)	Information otherwise available	846
	(2)	Powers of courts and tribunals	846
52.	(1)	Application of Act	846
	(2)	Non-application of Act	846
	(3)	Same	846
	(4)	Exception	846
53.	(1)	Other Acts	846
	(2)	Idem	846
54.		Exercise of rights of deceased, etc., persons	847
55.		Review of this Act	847

REGULATION UNDER THE MUNICIPAL FREEDOM OF INFORMATION AND PROTECTION OF PRIVACY ACT

Regulation 823 — General	849
Form 1	851
Form 2	853

ONTARIO COLLEGE OF TEACHERS ACT, 1996

PART I

DEFINITIONS

1.	Definitions	855

lxiii

PART II

COLLEGE

2.	(1)	College established	855
	(2)	Body corporate	855
	(3)	Non-application of certain Acts	855
3.	(1)	Objects	855
	(2)	Duty	856
4.	(1)	Council	856
	(2)	Composition of Council	856
	(3)	Role of Registrar	856
	(4)	Expenses and remuneration	856
5.	(1)	Term of office	856
	(2)	Multiple terms	856
6.	(1)	Qualifications to vote	856
	(2)	Good standing	856
7.		Vacancies	856
8.	(1)	Council meetings	856
	(2)	Open to public	856
	(3)	Exclusion of public	856
9.	(1)	Officers	857
	(2)	Registrar	857
	(3)	Chief executive officer	857
10.	(1)	Meeting with Minister	857
	(2)	Open to public	857
11.	(1)	Annual report	857
	(2)	Tabling of report	857
12.	(1)	Powers of Minister	857
	(2)	Council to comply	857
	(3)	Regulations	857
	(4)	Authority of Lieutenant Governor in Council	857
	(5)	Copies of regulations, orders	857
	(6)	Same	858
	(7)	Expenses of College	858
13.		Annual meeting of members	858
14.	(1)	Membership	858
	(2)	Resignation of membership	858
	(3)	Same	858
	(4)	Expiry of membership	858
	(5)	Continuing jurisdiction: revocation, cancellation	858
15.	(1)	Committees	858
	(2)	Same	858
	(3)	Vacancies	858
16.		Executive Committee	858

TABLE OF CONTENTS

17. (1) Majority on committees 858
     (2) Panels 858

PART III

REGISTRATION

18. (1) Registration 859
     (2) Grounds for refusal 859
     (3) Same 859
     (4) Terms, etc., on consent 859
     (5) Same 859
19. (1) Disclosure of application file 859
     (2) Exception 859
20. (1) Notice of proposal to refuse to issue, revoke, etc. 859
     (2) Exception 859
     (3) Contents of notice 859
     (4) Request for review 859
     (5) Submissions 860
     (6) Power of Registrar where no review 860
     (7) Same 860
21. (1) Review by Registration Appeals Committee 860
     (2) Exception 860
     (3) Extension of time for requesting review 860
     (4) Same 860
     (5) Same 860
     (6) Same 860
     (7) Examination of documents, submissions 860
     (8) No hearing 860
     (9) Orders 860
    (10) Same 861
    (11) Order to return fee 861
    (12) Service of decision on parties 861
22. (1) Application for variation 861
     (2) Same 861
     (3) Limitations 861
     (4) Submissions 861
     (5) Examination of documents, submissions 861
     (6) No hearing 861
     (7) Orders 861
     (8) Limitations on application 862
     (9) Order to return fee 862
    (10) Service of decision on applicant 862
23. (1) Register 862
     (2) Contents 862

TABLE OF CONTENTS

	(3)	Inspection	862
	(4)	Copies	862
24.	(1)	Suspension: failure to pay fees, provide information	862
	(2)	Same	862
	(3)	Re-instatement	862

PART IV

INVESTIGATION COMMITTEE

25.	(1)	Composition of Investigation Committee	862
	(2)	Same	863
	(3)	Same	863
26.	(1)	Duties of Investigation Committee	863
	(2)	Same	863
	(3)	Same	863
	(4)	Same	863
	(5)	Same	863
	(6)	Decision and reasons	863
	(7)	Notice	863
	(8)	No hearing	864
	(9)	Timely disposal	864

PART V

DISCIPLINE AND FITNESS TO PRACTISE

27.	(1)	Composition of Discipline Committee	864
	(2)	Same	864
	(3)	Chair of Committee	864
28.	(1)	Composition of Fitness to Practise Committee	864
	(2)	Same	864
	(3)	Chair of Committee	864
29.	(1)	Reference by Councilor Executive Committee	864
	(2)	Same	864
	(3)	Interim suspension	864
	(4)	Restriction	864
	(5)	Same	865
	(6)	No hearing	865
	(7)	Procedure following order	865
	(8)	Duration of order	865
30.	(1)	Duties of Discipline Committee	865
	(2)	Professional misconduct	865
	(3)	Incompetence	865
	(4)	Powers of Discipline Committee	865
	(5)	Same	865

TABLE OF CONTENTS

	(6)	Same	866
	(7)	Same	866
	(8)	Publication on request	866
	(9)	Costs	866
31.	(1)	Duties of the Fitness to Practise Committee	866
	(2)	Incapacity	866
	(3)	Powers of Fitness to Practise Committee	866
	(4)	Same	866
	(5)	Same	867
	(6)	Publication on request	867
	(7)	Costs	867
32.	(1)	Procedure: s. 30 hearings	867
	(2)	Parties	867
	(3)	Examination of documentary evidence	867
	(4)	Members holding hearing not to have taken part in investigation, etc. ..	867
	(5)	Same	867
	(6)	Hearings of Discipline Committee to be public	867
	(7)	Exclusion of public	867
	(8)	Fitness to Practise Committee hearings to be closed	868
	(9)	Open on request of member in some cases	868
	(10)	Recording of evidence	868
	(11)	Only members at hearing to participate in decision	868
	(12)	Release of documentary evidence	868
	(13)	Service of decision, reasons	868
	(14)	Same	868

PART VI

REINSTATEMENT AND VARIATION

33.	(1)	Reinstatement after disciplinary proceedings	868
	(2)	Variation after disciplinary proceedings	868
	(3)	Time of application	869
	(4)	Same	869
	(5)	Referral of Discipline Committee	869
	(6)	Order	869
	(7)	Parties	869
	(8)	Examination of documentary evidence	869
	(9)	Closed hearings	869
	(10)	Recording of evidence	869
	(11)	Only members at hearing to participate in decision	869
	(12)	Release of documentary evidence	869
	(13)	Service of decision on parties	869
	(14)	Fitness to Practise Committee	869
34.		Reinstatement: no hearing	870

PART VII

APPEALS TO COURT

35.	(1)	Appeal to court	870
	(2)	Same	870
	(3)	Certified copy of record	870
	(4)	Powers of court on appeal	870

PART VIII

REGISTRAR'S POWERS OF INVESTIGATION

36.	(1)	Registrar's investigation	870
	(2)	Approval of Executive Committee	871
	(3)	Powers of investigator	871
	(4)	Same	871
	(5)	Same	871
	(6)	Obstruction of investigator	871
37.	(1)	Entries and searches	871
	(2)	Searches by day unless stated	871
	(3)	Assistance and entry by force	871
	(4)	Investigator to show identification	871
38.	(1)	Copying of documents and objects	871
	(2)	Removal for documents and objects	871
	(3)	Return of documents and objects or copies	872
	(4)	Copy as evidence	872
39.		Report of investigation	872

PART IX

REGULATIONS AND BY-LAWS

40.	(1)	Regulations subject to approval	872
	(2)	Copies of regulations	873
	(3)	Same	874
	(4)	Filling of vacancies	874
41.	(1)	By-laws	874
	(2)	Meetings by telecommunications, etc.	875
	(3)	Unanimous by-laws, etc.	875
	(4)	Copies of by-laws	875
	(5)	Same	875
42.	(1)	Regulations made by Lieutenant Governor in Council	875
	(2)	Regulations under clause (1)(c) or (d)	876
	(3)	Same	876
43.	(1)	Regulation and by-laws: general or specific	876

TABLE OF CONTENTS

| | (2) | Same | 876 |
| | (3) | Classes | 876 |

PART X

MISCELLANEOUS

44.	(1)	Right to use French	876
	(2)	Council to ensure	876
	(3)	Limitation	876
	(4)	Definition	876
45.		Official publication	876
46.	(1)	Leave of absence	876
	(2)	Employer reimbursement	876
47.	(1)	Right to obtain information	877
	(2)	Disclosure by school board: offences	877
	(3)	Disclosure by school board: conduct or actions of member	877
	(4)	Disclosure by minority language section: conduct or action of member	877
	(5)	Information provided by Minister to College	877
	(6)	Information provided by College to Minister	877
48.	(1)	Confidentiality	877
	(2)	Testimony in civil proceeding	877
	(3)	Evidence on civil proceedings	878
	(4)	Offence	878
49.		Order directing compliance	878
50.		Offence: obstruction of investigator	878
51.	(1)	Offence: false representation to obtain certificate	878
	(2)	Offence: assisting in false representation	878
52.	(1)	Service of notice or document	878
	(2)	Same	878
53.		Registrar's certificate as evidence	878
54.		*Statutory Powers Procedure Act*	878
55.		Immunity of College	878
56.	(1)	Deemed loan	879
	(2)	Same	879
	(3)	Same	879
	(4)	Same	879
	(5)	Same	879
	(6)	Same	879
	(7)	Same	879
57.	(1)	Guarantee of loans	879
	(2)	Same	879
58.	(1)	Regulations under *Teaching Profession Act*	879
	(2)	Same	879

TABLE OF CONTENTS

(3) Same 879

PART XI

TRANSITIONAL PROVISIONS

59.	(1)	Appointment of Registrar	880
	(2)	Expenses and salary of Registrar appointed by Minister	880
	(3)	Powers of Registrar appointed by Minister	880
	(4)	Same	880
	(5)	Powers of the Minister	880
	(6)	Registrar to comply	880
	(7)	Regulations	880
	(8)	By-laws	880
	(9)	Authority of Lieutenant Governor in Council	880
	(10)	Copies of regulations, by-laws made by Registrar	880
	(11)	Copies of regulations, by-laws made by Lieutenant Governor in Council	881
	(12)	Expenses	881
60.		First meeting of members	881
61.		Transition: elected Council members	881
62.	(1)	Transition: initial membership	881
	(2)	Same	881
	(3)	Same	881
	(4)	Same	881
	(5)	Same	882
	(6)	Same	882
63.	(1)	Transition: persons in programs	882
	(2)	Same	882
	(3)	Same	882

PART XII

CONSEQUENTIAL AMENDMENTS

64-67. [Consequential amendments are not reproduced here.] 882

PART XIII

COMMENCEMENT AND SHORT TITLE

68.	Commencement	882
69.	Short title	882

REGULATIONS UNDER THE ONTARIO COLLEGE TEACHERS ACT, 1996

Regulation 344/96 — First Election 883
Regulation 345/96 — Appointments to Council 891
Regulation 72/97 — General 892
Regulation 184/97 — Teachers Qualifications 900
Regulation 276/97 — Transitional Matters — Discipline 928
Regulation 437/97 — Professional Misconduct 930

ONTARIO STUDENT RECORD (OSR) GUIDELINE

	Introduction	933
1.	Establishment of the OSR	933
2.	Responsibility for the OSR	934
3.	Components of the OSR	935
3.1	The OSR Folder	935
3.1.1	Biographical data: Part A	935
3.1.2	Schools attended: Part B	935
3.1.3	Retirement from an Ontario school: Part C (Form 1A) or Parts J and K (Form 1)	936
3.1.4	Names of parents or guardians: Part D	936
3.1.5	Special health information: Part E	936
3.1.6	Photographs and information on school activities: Parts F, G, and J (Form 1A) or Parts F, G, and I (Form 1)	936
3.1.7	Additional information: Part H	936
3.2	Report Cards	936
3.2.1	Completion and use	936
3.2.2	Content	937
3.2.3	Quality of paper	938
3.3	The Ontario Student Transcript (OST)	938
3.4	The Documentation File	938
3.5	The Office Index Card	938
3.6	Student Record of Accumulated Instruction in French As a Second Language	939
3.7	Student Record of Accumulated Instruction in Native As a Second Language	940
4.	Access to the OSR	940
4.1	Students	940
4.2	Parents and Guardians	940
4.3	Educational Personnel	941
4.4	Other	941
4.4.1	Civil suits	941

4.4.2	Child and Family Services Act, 1984	941
4.4.3	Criminal Code	941
5.	Use and Maintenance of the OSR	941
6.	Transfer of the OSR	942
6.1	Transfer to Another School Board in Ontario	942
6.2	Transfer to a Private School in Ontario	942
6.3	Transfer to a DND School	943
6.4	Transfer to an Educational Institution Outside Ontario	943
7.	Retirement of a Student	943
8.	Retention, Storage, and Destruction of the OSR	943
9.	Correction or Removal of OSR Information	944
10.	Special Circumstances	945
10.1	Change of Surname	945
10.1.1	Change by repute	945
10.1.2	Change by marriage or by law	945
10.2	Adoption	946
10.2.1	Placement for adoption	946
10.2.2	Termination of adoption	946
10.3	Reports From Third Parties	946
11.	Continuing Education Records	947
	Appendix A — Definitions	948
	Appendix B — OSR Forms	949

PROVINCIAL SCHOOLS NEGOTIATIONS ACT

1.		Definitions	951
2.	(1)	Provincial Schools Authority	951
	(2)	Chair and vice-chair	951
	(3)	Secretary	951
	(4)	Remuneration	951
	(5)	Money	951
3.	(1)	Authority as employer	951
	(2)	Transition	952
	(3)	Principals, vice-principals	952
	(4)	Transition	952
	(5)	Repeal	952
4.	(1)	Employment of teachers	952
	(2)	Administration	952
	(3)	[Repealed]	952
	(4)	Pensions	952
	(5)	[Repealed]	952
	(6)	Application of Part X of *Education Act*	952
5.	(1)	Application of *Labour Relations Act, 1995*	952
	(2)	Teachers' bargaining unit	952

	(3)	Same	952
	(4)	Bargaining agent	952
	(5)	Same	952
	(6)	Same	953
	(7)	Same	953
	(8)	Closing of schools	953
	(9)	Approval for lock-out, closure	953
6.	(1)	Status of collective bargaining on January 1, 1998	953
	(2)	Collective agreement	953
	(3)	No collective agreement	953
	(4)	Same	953
7.	(1)	Regulations	953
	(2)	Same	953

SCHOOL BOARDS AND TEACHERS COLLECTIVE NEGOTIATIONS ACT

PART I

GENERAL

1.		Definitions	955
2.		Purpose of Act	956
3.	(1)	Application of Act	956
	(2)	Negotiations to be in accordance with Act	956
4.	(1)	Joint negotiations	956
	(2)	Idem	957
	(3)	Branch affiliates may negotiate as one party	957
	(4)	Agreements between individual boards and branch affiliates	957
	(5)	Continuation of agreement to act jointly	957
5.		Representation of teachers by branch affiliate	957
6.		Negotiating group	957
7.		Parties may obtain assistance	957

PART II

NEGOTIATIONS

8.		Subject-matter of negotiations	957
9.		Notice of desire to negotiate	957
10.	(1)	Notice of desire to negotiate for renewal of agreement	957
	(2)	Where notice not given of desire to negotiate renewal of agreement	958
	(3)	Working conditions may not be altered	958
11.		Obligation to negotiate	958

TABLE OF CONTENTS

12.	(1)	Parties may choose procedures to reach agreement	958
	(2)	Effect of choice of procedure	958
13.		Where Commission may assign person to assist parties	958

PART III

FACT FINDING

14.		Appointment of fact finder	959
15.		Parties may proceed to make agreement or to arbitration or selection procedure	959
16.		Persons prohibited as fact finder	959
17.		Vacancy	959
18.		Notice of appointment of fact finder	959
19.	(1)	Notice of matters agreed upon and matters in dispute	959
	(2)	Where notice not given	959
20.	(1)	Duty of fact finder	960
	(2)	What report may contain	960
21.		Matters that may be considered by fact finder	960
22.		Procedure of fact finder	960
23.		Submission of report of fact finder	960
24.		Report not binding	960
25.	(1)	Assignment of assistance	960
	(2)	Idem	960
26.	(1)	Where report confidential	960
	(2)	Release of report	961
	(3)	Deferral of release	961
27.	(1)	Parties may agree to refer matters in dispute	961
	(2)	Effect of choice of procedure	961

PART IV

VOLUNTARY BINDING ARBITRATION

28.	(1)	Parties to give notice to Commission where arbitration agreed upon	961
	(2)	Parties not to withdraw	962
	(3)	Where appointments made by Commission	962
	(4)	Appointment of chair by members	962
	(5)	Where Commission to appoint chair	962
29.		Persons prohibited as arbitrator or members of chair of board of arbitration	962
30.	(1)	Vacancy	962
	(2)	Where chair unable to act	962
	(3)	Where arbitrator unable to act	963
31.		Notice of matters agreed upon and matters in dispute	963

TABLE OF CONTENTS

32.	(1)	Procedure	963
	(2)	Idem	963
	(3)	Decision	963
33.	(1)	Powers of arbitrator or board of arbitration	963
	(2)	Stated case for contempt for failure to attend, etc.	963
34.	(1)	Duty of arbitrator or board of arbitration	964
	(2)	Matters that may be considered by arbitrator or board of arbitration	964
35.	(1)	Time for report of arbitrator or board of arbitration	964
	(1.1)	Criteria	964
	(1.2)	Transition	964
	(1.3)	Restriction	964
	(2)	Effect of decision	964
36.	(1)	Preparation and execution of document by parties	965
	(2)	Where arbitrator or board of arbitration to prepare document	965
	(3)	Failure to execute document	965

PART V

FINAL OFFER SELECTION

37.	(1)	Parties to give notice to Commission where selection agreed upon	965
	(2)	Statement by parties	965
	(3)	Parties not to withdraw	965
	(4)	Where Commission appoints selector	965
38.		Persons prohibited as selector	965
39.		Selector unable to act	966
40.		Notice of matters agreed upon and matters in dispute	966
41.		Notice of final offer	966
42.		Final offer of opposite party	966
43.		Written response	966
44.		Hearing	966
45.		Parties may dispense with hearing	966
46.	(1)	Procedure	966
	(2)	Powers of selector	966
	(3)	Stated case for contempt for failure to attend, etc.	967
47.	(1)	Selection of final offer	967
	(2)	Criteria	967
	(3)	Transition	967
	(4)	Restriction	967
48.		Effect of decision	968
49.	(1)	Preparation and execution of document by parties	968
	(2)	Where selector to prepare document	968
	(3)	Failure to execute document	968

lxxv

PART VI

AGREEMENTS

50.		Term of agreement	968
51.	(1)	Conflict	968
	(2)	Application of *Constitution Act, 1867*	968
52.	(1)	Resolution of matters arising out of agreement	968
	(2)	Enforcement of arbitration decision	969
53.		Provision against strikes and lock-outs	969
54.	(1)	Agreement to form part of contract of employment	969
	(2)	Conflict	969
55.		Notice of agreement	969
56.		Where agreement reached	969
57.		Notice to Commission of execution of agreement	969
58.		Binding effect of agreement	969

PART VII

EDUCATION RELATIONS COMMISSION

59.	(1)	Commission continued	970
	(2)	Composition	970
	(3)	Chair and vice-chair	970
	(4)	Acting chair	970
	(5)	Term of office	970
	(6)	Vacancy	970
	(7)	Reappointment	970
	(8)	Quorum	970
	(9)	Exercising powers	970
	(10)	Remuneration	970
	(11)	Employees	970
	(12)	Pension plan	970
	(13)	Professional and other assistance	970
60.	(1)	Duties of Commission	971
	(2)	Provision of information	971
	(3)	Annual report	971
61.		Testimony by member of Commission	971
62.		Money	971

PART VIII

STRIKES AND LOCK-OUTS

63.		Notice of strike	971
64.	(1)	Principals and vice-principals	972

TABLE OF CONTENTS

	(2)	Idem, membership in branch affiliate	972
65.	(1)	Unlawful strike	972
	(2)	Idem	972
66.	(1)	Unlawful lock-out	972
	(2)	Idem	972
67.	(1)	Declaration of unlawful strike	972
	(2)	Declaration of unlawful lock-out	972
	(3)	Direction by O.L.R.B.	973
	(4)	Enforcement of direction by court	973
68.	(1)	Lock-out	973
	(2)	Idem	973
	(3)	Idem	973
	(4)	Closing of school	973
	(5)	Payment of teachers	973
	(6)	Resumption of strike or new strike	973
	(7)	Application of section	973
69.		Participation in lawful strike	973
70.		Resignation, etc., by teacher	973

PART IX

MISCELLANEOUS

71.		Copies of notice to be given to Commission	974
72.		Decisions, etc., of Commission and others not subject to review	974
73.		Service of notice	974
74.	(1)	Costs	974
	(2)	Idem	974
75.		Statement as to officers of branch affiliate	974
76.	(1)	Where vote by secret ballot required	975
	(2)	Idem	975
77.	(1)	Contravention by teacher or trustee	975
	(2)	Contravention by council or Federation	975
	(3)	Contravention of decision, etc.	975
	(4)	Where officers also guilty of offence	975
	(5)	Information	975
	(6)	Consent to prosecution	975
	(7)	Practice and procedure of O.L.R.B.	975
	(8)	Decision of O.L.R.B.	975
78.		Style of prosecution	975
79.		Vicarious responsibilities	976
80.	(1)	Application	976
	(2)	Idem	976
	(3)	Idem	976
81.		Compellability of witnesses	976

TEACHERS' PENSION ACT

DEFINITIONS

1.		Definitions	977
2.	(1)	Pension plan continued	977
	(2)	Defined benefits plan	977
	(3)	Plan documents	977
	(4)	Sufficiency of assets	977
3.		Administrator	977
4.		Pension fund	977
5.	(1)	Contributions by the Crown	977
	(1.1)	Matching contributions	977
	(1.2)	Idem	978
	(2)	Payments re transitional valuation	978
	(3)	Deficiency	978
	(4)	Limitation	978
	(5)	[Repealed]	978
	(6)	[Repealed]	978
	(7)	Solvency deficiency	978
5.1	(1)	Recovery of payments	978
	(2)	Non-application of *Pension Benefits Act*, s. 78	978
6.	(1)	Board continued	978
	(2)	Application of *Corporations Act*	978
7.		Composition of the Board	978
8.	(1)	Powers, etc., of the Board	978
	(2)	Protection from liability	978
9.		[Repealed]	979
10.	(1)	Joint management	979
	(2)	Filing of amendment	979
	(3)	Conflict with *Pension Benefits Act*	979
11.	(1)	Agreement for member responsibility	979
	(2)	Filing of agreement	979
	(3)	Repeal of Schedule 1	979
12.	(1)	Investments authorized	979
	(2)	Transfer Teachers' Pensions	980
12.1	(1)	Special payments required by *Pension Benefits Act*	980
	(2)	Time for amendment	980
	(3)	Actuarial gain	980
	(4)	Interpretation	980
13.	(1)	Continued application	980
	(2)	Idem	980
14.		Payment of pensions, predecessor Acts	980

TEACHING PROFESSION ACT

1.		Definitions	981
2.		Body corporate	981
3.		Objects	981
4.	(1)	Membership in Federation	981
	(2)	Associate members	982
	(3)	Persons receiving pension	982
5.	(1)	Board of Governors	982
	(2)	Term of office	982
	(3)	Vacancies	982
6.	(1)	Executive	982
	(2)	Term of office	982
	(3)	Vacancies	982
7.		President and vice-presidents	982
8.		Secretary-treasurer	983
9.		Functions of executive	983
10.		Conferences	983
11.		[Repealed]	983
12.		Regulations	983
13.	(1)	Restriction re by-laws	984
	(2)	Changes to regulations, by-laws	984
	(3)	Same	984

REGULATION MADE UNDER THE TEACHING PROFESSION ACT

1.	Affiliated Bodies	985
2.	Voluntary Membership	985
3.	Application for Membership by a Former Member	985
4.	Fees	986
5.	Meetings of the Board of Governors	987
6.	Meetings of Executive	987
7.	Nominating Committee	988
8.	Relations and Discipline Committee	988
9.	Standing Committees	988
10.	Special Committees	988
11.	Procedure at Annual Meeting of Board of Governors	989
12.	Expenses	989
13.	General Duties of Members	989
14.	Duties of a Member to his Pupils	989
15.	Duties of a Member to Educational Authorities	989
16.	Duties of a Member to the Public	990
17.	Duties of a Member to the Federation	990

TABLE OF CONTENTS

18.	Duties of a Member to Fellow Members	990
19-28.	Relations and Discipline Procedure	991
29.	Evidencing Regulations and Resolutions	994
30.	Effective Date and Transitional Provisions	994
Index		995

EDUCATION ACT

CONCORDANCE

The following concordance shows the interrelationship between sections of the Education Act as of April 1999 and in its former versions.

R.S.O. 1990, c. E.2 (After Bill 160)	R.S.O. 1990, c. E.2	R.S.O. 1980, c. 129	R.S.O. 1974, c. 109
1(1)	1(1)	1(1)	1(1)
1(1.1)	—	—	—
1(2)	1(2)	1(2)	1(2)
1(3)	1(3)	1(3)	1(4)
1(4)	1(4)	1(4)	1(6)
1(4.1)	—	—	—
1(5)	1(5)	1(5)	—
1(6)	—	—	—
1(7)-(12)	—	—	—
2(1)-(3)	2(1)-(3)	2(1)-(3)	2(1)-(3)
2(4)-(6)	2(4)-(6)	2(4)-(6)	—
3-5	3-5	3-5	3-5
8(1)¶1-3	8(1)¶1-3	8(1)(a-c)	8(1)(a-c)
8(1)¶3.1-3.6	—	—	—
8(1)¶4	8(1)¶4	8(1)(d)	8(1)(d)
8(1)¶5	8(1)¶5	8(1)(e)	—
8(1)¶6-17	8(1)¶6-17	8(1)(f)-(q)	8(1)(e)-(p)
8(1)¶17.1	—	—	—
8(1)¶18-22	8(1)¶18-22	8(1)(r)-(v)	8(1)(q)-(u)
8(1)¶23	8(1)¶23	8(1)(w)	—
8(1)¶23.1	—	—	—
8(1)¶24-25	8(1)¶24-25	8(1)(x-y)	—
8(1)¶26	8(1)¶26	8(1)(z)	—
8(1)¶27	8(1)¶27	8(1)(za)	—
8(1)¶27.1-27.2	—	—	—
8(1)¶28-29	8(1)¶28-29	8(1)(zb)-(zc)	—
8(1)¶29.1-29.2	—	—	—
8(1)¶30	—	—	—
8(1)¶31-33	8(1)¶31-33	8(1)(ze-zg)	—
8(1)¶34-35	—	—	—
8(2)	8(2)	8(1a)	—
8(3)	8(3)	8(2)	—
8(4)	8(4)	8(3)	8(2)
9	9	8a	—
10	10	9	9

CONCORDANCE

R.S.O. 1990, c. E.2 (After Bill 160)	R.S.O. 1990, c. E.2	R.S.O. 1980, c. 129	R.S.O. 1974, c. 109
11(1)¶1-5	11(1)¶1-5	10(1)¶1-5	10(1)¶1-5
11(1)¶6	11(1)¶6	10(1)¶6	—
11(1)¶7-11	11(1)¶7-11	10(1)¶7-11	10(1)¶6-10
11(1)¶12	11(1)¶12	10(1)¶11a	—
11(1)¶13-14	11(1)¶13-14	10(1)¶12-13	10(1)¶11-13
11(1)¶15-16	11(1)¶15-16	10(1)¶14-15	10(1)¶13-14
11(1)¶17-18	11(1)¶17-18	10(1)¶15a-15b	—
10(1)¶16	10(1)¶16	10(1)¶15	—
11(1)¶19-21	11(1)¶19-21	10(1)¶17-19	10(1)¶16-18
11(1)¶22-27	11(1)¶22-27	10(1)¶20-25	10(1)¶19-24
11(1)¶28	11(1)¶28	10(1)¶26	10(1)¶25
11(1)¶29-34	11(1)¶29-34	11(1)¶27-32	10(1)¶26-31
11(1)¶35	11(1)¶35	10(1)¶33	—
11(1)¶36	11(1)¶36	10(1)¶34	—
11(2)	11(2)	10(2)	10(2)
11(3)	11(3)	10(3)	10(3)
11(4)	11(4)	10(3a)	—
11(5)-(9)	11(5)-(9)	10(4)-(8)	10(4)-(8)
—	11(10)	10(9)	—
—	11(11),(12)	10(10)-(11)	—
—	11(13-15)	10(9-11)	—
—	11(16)	10(11d)	—
—	11(17)	10(11e)	—
—	11(18)	10(12)	—
12(1),(2)	12(1),(2)	11(1),(2)	11(1),(2)
12(3)	12(3)	11(2a)	—
12(4),(5)	12(4),(5)	11(3),(4)	11(3),()
13(1)	13(1)	12(1), pt	12(1), pt
13(2)	13(2)	12(1), pt	12(1), pt
13(3)	13(3)	12(1),(2), pt	12(1),(2) pt
13(4)	13(4)	12(3)	12(3)
13(4.1)	—	—	—
13(5)	13(5)	12(4)	—
13(6)	13(6)	12(5)	—
13(7)	13(7)	12(6)	12(4)
—	—	12(7)	12(5)
14(1)-(3)	14(1)-(3)	13(1)-(3)	13(1)-13
14(3.1)	—	—	—
—	—	13(4)	13(4)
14(4)	14(4)	13(5)	13(5)
15	15	14(1)	14(1)
—	—	14(2)	14(2)

CONCORDANCE

R.S.O. 1990, c. E.2 (After Bill 160)	R.S.O. 1990, c. E.2	R.S.O. 1980, c. 129	R.S.O. 1974, c. 109
16	16	15	15
17	17	16	16
17.1	—	—	—
18	18	17	17
19(1)	19	18	18
19(2)-(4)	—	—	—
20	20	19	19
21	21	20	20
22	22	21	21
23(1)	23(1)	22(1)	22(1)
23(2)	23(2)	22(2)	22(2)
23(3)-(5)	23(3)-(5)	22(3)-(5)	22(3)-(5)
24	24	23	23
25	25	24	24
26	26	25	25
27	27	26	26
28	28	27	27
29	29	28	28
30	30	29	29
31	31	30	30
32	32	31	31
33(1)	33(1)	32(1)	32(1)
33(2)	—	—	—
33(3)	33(2)	32(2)	32(2)
33(4)	—	—	—
33(5)-(6)	33(3)-(4)	32(3)-(4)	32(3)-(4)
—	33(5)-(6)	32(5)-(6)	32(5)-(6)
34	34	33	33
35	35	34	34
35	39	38	36
36(1)-(4)	40(1)	39(1)	37(1)
36(5)	40(2)	39(2)	37(2)
36(6)-(8)	—	—	—
37	40(4)	39(5)	37(5)
38	40(5)	39(6)	37(6)
39	41	40	38
40	42	41	39
41	43	42	40
42-43.2	—	—	—
44	38	37	35
45	44	43	41
46	45	44	42

lxxxiii

R.S.O. 1990, c. E.2 (After Bill 160)	R.S.O. 1990, c. E.2	R.S.O. 1980, c. 129	R.S.O. 1974, c. 109
46.1	—	—	—
47	46	45	43
48	47	46	44
48(1)	48(1)	47(1)	—
48.1(1)-(2)	—	—	—
48.1(3)-(5)	48(2)-(3)	47(4a)-(4b)	—
49(1)-(2)	49(1)-(3)	48(1)-(3)	46(1)-(3)
49(4)-(5)	49(4)-(5)	48(4)-(5)	46(4)-(5)
49(6)-(7)	49(6)-(7)	48(6)-(7)	—
49.1	—	—	—
49.2	—	—	—
50	52	51	49
50.1	—	—	—
51	51	50	48
52	—	—	—
53	52	51	49
—	53	52	50
—	54(1),(2)	53(1),(2)	51(1),(2)
—	54(3)	53(2A)	—
—	54(4)-(6)	53(3)-(5)	51(3)-(5)
54	—	—	—
55(1)-(7)	55(1)-(7)	54(1)-(7)	52
55(8)	55(8)	54(8)	—
55	—	—	—
56(1)-(4)	56(1)-(4)	55(1)(4)	53(1)-(4)
56	—	—	—
—	—	55(5)	53(5)
57(1)-(3)	57(1)-(3)	56(1)-(3)	54(1)-(3)
—	—	56(4)-(8)	54(4)-(8)
—	—	57,58	55,56
—	—	59(1)-(9)	57(1)-(9)
—	—	59(10)	—
—	—	59(11)-(14)	57(10)-(13)
—	—	59(15)	—
—	—	59(16)-(34)	57(14)-(32)
57(1)-(2)	36	35	—
57(3)	37(1)	36(1)	—
37(2)-(4)	37(2)-(4)	36(2)-(4)	—
57(4)	37(6)	36(6)	—
57(5)	37(5)	36(5)	—
57.1	—	—	—
58	—	—	—

R.S.O. 1990, c. E.2 (After Bill 160)	R.S.O. 1990, c. E.2	R.S.O. 1980, c. 129	R.S.O. 1974, c. 109
—	58	60	58
—	—	61	59
58.1-58.9	—	—	—
59(1)-(3)	59(1)-(3)	62(1)-(3)	60(1)-(3)
—	—	—	60(4)
59(4),(5)	59(4),(5)	62(4),(5)	60(5)-(6)
60	60	63	61
61	61	64	62
62	62	65	63
63(1),(4)	63(3)	66(3)	64(3)
63(2)-(3)	63(1)-(2)	66(1)-(2)	64(1)-(2)
—	64	66A	—
—	65(1)-(6)	67(1)-(6)	65(1)-(6)
—	—	67(7)-(11)	65(7)-(11)
—	65(7)	67(12)	65(12)
66(1)-(4)	66(1)-(4)	68(1)-(4)	66(1)-(4)
—	—	—	66(5)
66(5)	66(5)	68(5)	66(6)
67(1)	67(1)	69(1)	67(1)
67(2)-(3)	—	—	—
67(2)-(7)	67(2)-(7)	69(2)-(7)	67(2)-(7)
68	68	70	68
—	69	71	69
—	70(1),(2)	72(1),(2)	70(1)-(2)
—	—	—	70(3)
—	72(3)	72(3)	—
—	—	72(4)	—
—	71	73	71
—	72(1)	74(1)	72(1)
—	74(2),(3)	74(2),(3)	—
—	74(4)-(8)	74(4),(8)	72(2)-(6)
—	73	75	73
—	74	76	74
—	—	—	75
—	—	—	76
—	75	77	77(1)
—	—	—	77(2),(3)
—	76	78	78
—	77	79	79
78(1)-(3)	78(1)-(3)	80(1)-(3)	80(1)-(3)
—	78(4)	80(4)	80(4)
—	—	80(5),(9)	80(5)-(9)

CONCORDANCE

R.S.O. 1990, c. E.2 (After Bill 160)	R.S.O. 1990, c. E.2	R.S.O. 1980, c. 129	R.S.O. 1974, c. 109
—	—	81(1),(3),(5)	81(1)-(3),(5)
—	79	81(4)	81(4)
—	—	82	82
80(1)-(5)	80(1)-(5)	83(1)-(5)	83(1)-(5)
—	—	83(6)	83(6)
80(6),(7)	80(6),(7)	83(7),(8)	83(7)-(8)
—	—	84(1),(2)	84(1)-(2)
81	81	84(3),(4)	84(3),(4)
82	82	85	85
83	83	86	86
84	84	87	87
85	85	88(1)-(3)	88(1)-(3)
—	—	88(4)	88(4)
86	86	89	89
—	—	90(1),(2)	90(1),(2)
—	—	90(2a)	—
—	—	90(3)	90(3)
—	—	91	91
—	—	92	92
—	—	93	93
—	—	94	94
86.1	—	—	—
—	87	95	95
88	88	96	96
89	89	97	97
90(1),(2)	90(1),(2)	98(1),(2)	98
93	90(3)	98(3)	—
—	91	99	99
92(1),(10)	92(1),(10)	100(1)-(10)	100(1)-(10)
92(11)	92(11)	100(10A)	—
92(12),(13)	92(12),(13)	100(11),(12)	100(11),(12)
92(14)	92(14)	100(13)	100(13)
92(15)-(22)	92(15)-(22)	100(14),(21)	100(14)-(21)
93(1)	93(1)	101(1)	100a
93(2)	93(2)	101(2)	—
94(1)	94(1)	102(1)	100b
94(2),(3)	94(2),(3)	102(2),(3)	—
95(1)-(8)	95(1)-(8)	103(1)-(8)	101(1)-(8)
—	—	103(9)	101(9)
95(9)	95(9)	103(10)	101(10)
96	—	—	—
—	96	104	102

lxxxvi

CONCORDANCE

R.S.O. 1990, c. E.2 (After Bill 160)	R.S.O. 1990, c. E.2	R.S.O. 1980, c. 129	R.S.O. 1974, c. 109
—	97(1)-(4)	105(1)-(4)	103(1)-(3)
—	97(5)-(6)	105(4a),(4b)	—
—	97(7)	105(5)	103(4)
—	98	106	103a
—	—	107	104
—	—	108	105
—	99	109	106
—	100(1)-(3)	110(1)-(3)	107(1)-(3)
—	—	110(4)-(8)	107(4)-(8)
—	100(4)	110(9)	107(9)
—	101	110a	—
—	102(1)-(4)	111(1)-(4)	108
—	102(5)	111(5)	—
—	103(1),(2)	112(1),(2)	109(1),(2)
—	103(3)	112(2a)	—
—	—	112(3)	109(3)
—	103(4)	112(4)	109(4)
—	—	113	110
—	—	114	111
—	104(1),(2)	115(1),(2)	112(1),(2)
—	—	115(3)	112(3)
—	104(3)	115(4)	112(4)
—	—	116	113
—	—	117	114
—	—	118(1)	115(1)
—	105	118(2)	115(2)
—	106(1),(2)	119(1),(2)	116(1),(2)
—	106(3)	119(2a)	—
—	106(4)-(8)	119(3),(7)	116(3)-(7)
—	107	120	117
—	—	121	118
—	108	122	119
—	108(Form 1)	122(Form 1)	—
—	109	123	120
—	110	124	121
—	111	125	122
—	112(1)	126(1)	123(1)
—	112(2)(3)	126(1a),(1b)	—
—	112(4)-(7)	126(2),(5)	123(2)-(5)
—	—	—	—
—	112(8)	126(6)	123(6)
—	112(9)	126(6a)	—

CONCORDANCE

R.S.O. 1990, c. E.2 (After Bill 160)	R.S.O. 1990, c. E.2	R.S.O. 1980, c. 129	R.S.O. 1974, c. 109
—	112(10)	126(7)	—
—	112(11)	126(8)	—
—	112(11)	126(9)	—
—	113(1)-(8)	126a(1)-(8)	—
—	113(8.1)	—	—
—	113(9)	126(9)	—
—	—	—	—
—	113(10)	126a(10)	—
—	114	127	124
—	115	128	125
—	116	129	126
—	117(1)-(5)	130(1)-(5)	127(1)-(5)
—	117(6)-(9)	130(5a)-(5d)	—
—	117(10)-(13)	130(6)-(9)	127(6-)(9)
—	117(14)	130(10)	—
—	118	131	128
—	119	132	129
—	120	133	130
—	122	135	132
—	123	136	133
—	124	136a	—
—	125	136b	—
—	126	136c	—
—	127	136d	—
—	128	136e	—
—	—	136f	—
—	129	136g	—
—	130	136h	—
—	131(1)	136i(1)	—
—	131(2),(3)	136i(1a),(1b)	—
—	—	136l(2)	—
—	131(4)	136i(3)	—
—	132	136j(1),(2)	—
—	—	136j(3)	—
—	133	136k(1),(2)	—
—	—	136k(3)	—
—	134(1)-(9)	136ka(1)-(9)	—
—	—	—	—
—	134(10)-(15)	136ka(10)-(15)	—
—	135(1)-(20)	136l(1)-(20)	136l(1)-(20)
135(1)	—	—	—
135(21)-(23)	135(21)-(23)	136l(20a)-(20c)	136¶(20a)-(26c)

CONCORDANCE

R.S.O. 1990, c. E.2 (After Bill 160)	R.S.O. 1990, c. E.2	R.S.O. 1980, c. 129	R.S.O. 1974, c. 109
135(24)-(26)	135(24)-(26)	136l(20d)-(20f)	136¶(20d)-(26f)
135(27)	135(27)	136l(20g)	—
135(28)	135(28)	136l(21)	—
135(29)	135(29)	136l(22)	—
135(30)	135(30)	136l(23)	—
135(31)-(33)	—	—	—
135.1	—	—	—
136	136	136la	—
137	—	—	—
—	137	136m	—
—	138	136ma	—
—	139	136mb	—
—	140	136mc	—
—	141	136md	—
—	142	136me	—
—	143	136n	—
—	144	136o	—
—	145	136p	—
—	146	136q	—
—	147	136r	—
—	148	136s	—
—	149	136t	—
—	150	136u	—
—	151	136v	—
—	152	136w	—
—	153	136x	—
—	154	—	—
—	155	136ra	—
—	156	136xb	—
—	157	136y	—
158	158	137	134
159	162(2)	141(2)	138(2)
—	159	138	135
—	160	139	136
—	161	140	137
—	162	141	138
—	163	142	139
164	164	143	140
165(1)	165(1)	144(1)	141(1)
165	165(2)-(3)	144(2)-(3)	141(2)-(3)
166	166	145	142
167	167	146	143

lxxxix

CONCORDANCE

R.S.O. 1990, c. E.2 (After Bill 160)	R.S.O. 1990, c. E.2	R.S.O. 1980, c. 129	R.S.O. 1974, c. 109
167.1	—	—	—
168	168	147	144
169	169	148	145
170¶1-6	170¶1-6	149¶1-6	146
170¶7-12	170¶7-12	149¶7-12	146
170¶13-17	170¶13-17	149¶13-17	146
170(1)¶17.1	—	—	—
170¶18	170¶18	149¶18	—
170.1	—	—	—
170.2	—	—	—
170.3	—	—	—
171(1)¶1	171(1)¶1	150(1)¶1	147(1)¶1
171(1)¶2	171(1)¶2	150(1)¶a	—
171(1)¶3-14	171(1)¶3-14	150(1)¶2-13	147(1)¶14
171(1)¶15	171(1)¶15	150(1)¶14	147(1)¶14
171(1)¶16-18	171(1)¶16-18	150(1)¶15-17	147(1)¶15-17
—	171(1)¶19-20	150(1)¶18-19	147(1)¶18-19
—	171(1)¶21	150(1)¶19a	—
—	171(1)¶22	150(1)¶20	147(1)¶20
171(1)¶23	171(1)¶23	150(1)¶1	—
171(1)¶24-30	171(1)¶24-30	150(1)¶22-28	—
171(1)¶31	171(1)¶31	150(1)¶29	—
171(1)¶32-39	171(1)¶32-39	150(1)¶30-37	—
171(1)¶40,pt	171(1)¶40,pt	150(1)¶38	—
171(1)¶41	171(1)¶41	150(1)¶39	—
171(1)¶40,pt	171(1)¶40,pt	150(1)¶40	—
171(1)¶42	171(1)¶42	150(1)¶41	—
171(1)¶43	171(1)¶43	150(1)¶42	—
171(1)¶44-46	171(1)¶44-46	150(1)¶43-45	—
—	171(1)¶47	150(1)¶46	—
171(1)¶48-49	—	—	—
171(2)-(5)	—	—	—
171(2)	171(2)	150(2)	147(2)
171.1	—	—	—
—	172	150a	—
173	173	151	148
—	174	152	149
—	175	153	150
176	176	154	151
177	177	155	152
178	178	156	153
179(1)-(4)	179(1)-(4)	150(1)-(4)	154(1)-(4)

xc

CONCORDANCE

R.S.O. 1990, c. E.2 (After Bill 160)	R.S.O. 1990, c. E.2	R.S.O. 1980, c. 129	R.S.O. 1974, c. 109
180(1)	180(1)	158(1)	155(1)
180(2)	180(2)	158(1a)	—
180(3)	180(3)	158(1b)	—
180(4)-(7)	180(4)-(7)	15(2)-(5)	155(2)-(5)
180(8)	180(8)	158(6)	155(6)
180(9)	180(9)	158(7)	155(7)
—	180(10)	158(8)	155(8)
181	181	159	156
182	182	159a	—
183	183	160	157
184(1)	184(1)-(2),	161(1)-(2),	158(1)-(2),
184(2)	184(4)	161(4)	158(4)
185	184(3)	161(3)	158(3)
185	185	162	159
186	185(5)	161(5)	158(5)
—	186	163	160
187	187	164	161
188(1)	188(1)	165(1)	162(1)
188(2)	188(2)	165(1a)	—
188(3)-(4)	188(3)-(4)	165(2)-(3)	163(2)-(3)
188(5)-(7)	—	—	—
188(5)-(12)	188(5)-(12)	165(4)-(10)	163(4)-(9)
188(8)	188(13)	165(11)	—
188(9)	—	—	—
189	189	165a	—
190(1)	190(1)	166(1)	163(1)
190(2)	—	166(1a)	—
190(3)-(10)	190(3)-(10)	166(2)-(9)	163(2)-(9)
190(11)	190(11)	166(10)	163(10)
190(11)-(13)	190(12)-(14)	166(11)-(13)	163(11)-(13)
191(1)-(2)	191(1)	167(1)	164(1)
191(3)-(4)	191(2)	167(2)	164(2)
191(5)	191(3)	167(2a)	—
191(4)-(5)	191(4)-(5)	167(2b)-(2c)	—
191(6)	191(6)	167(2d)	—
191(7)-(9)	191(7)-(9)	167(2e)-(2g)	—
191.1	—	—	—
191.2(1)-(2)	191(10)-(11)	167(3)-(4)	164(3)-(4)
191.2(3)-(4)	—	—	—
191.2(5)-(6)	191(12)-(13)	167(5)-(6)	164(5)-(6)
192	192	168	165
193	193	169	166

R.S.O. 1990, c. E.2 (After Bill 160)	R.S.O. 1990, c. E.2	R.S.O. 1980, c. 129	R.S.O. 1974, c. 109
194(1)-(2)	194(1)-(2)	170(1)-(2)	167(1)-(2)
194(3)-(3.6)	193(3)	170(3)	167(3)
194(4)-(4.1)	194(4)	170(4)	167(4)
195(1),(2)	195(1),(2)	171(1),(2)	168(1),(2)
—	—	171(3),(5)	168(3),(5)
195(3)	195(3)	171(4)	168(4)
195(4)-(6)	195(4)-(6)	171(6)-(8)	168(6)-(8)
195(7)-(9)	—	—	—
196	196	172	169
197(1)	197(1)	173(1)	170(1)
197(2)	197(2)	173(1a)	—
197(3)	197(3)	173(1b)	—
197(4)	197(4)	173(1c)	—
197(5)-(6)	197(5)-(6)	173(2),(3)	170(2),(3)
197(7)-(10)	197(7)-(10)	173(4)-(7)	170(4)-(7)
198	198	174	171
199	199	175	172
200	200	176	173
201	201	177	174
202(1)	202(1)	178(1)	175(1)
202(2)-(3.2)	202(2)-(3)	202(2)-(3)	175(2)-(3)
203	203	179	176
204	204	180	177
205	205	181	178
—	206(1)-(6)	182(1)-(6)	178a(1)-(6)
—	206(7)	182(7)	178a(7)
—	206(8)-(11)	182(8)-(11)	178a(8)-(11)
—	207(1)	183(1)	179(1)
207(2)	207(2)	183(1a)	—
207(3),(4)	207(3),(4)	183(2),(3)	179(2),(3)
208(1)-(5)	208(1)-(5)	184(1)-(5)	180(1)-(5)
208(5.1)	—	—	—
208(6)-(13)	208(6)-(13)	184(6)-(13)	180(6)-(13)
208.1	—	—	—
209	209	185	181
210	210	186	182
211	211	187	183
212	212	188	184
213	213	189	185
—	214	190	186
—	215	191	187
—	216	192	188

CONCORDANCE

R.S.O. 1990, c. E.2 (After Bill 160)	R.S.O. 1990, c. E.2	R.S.O. 1980, c. 129	R.S.O. 1974, c. 109
217	217	193	189
218	218	194	190
219(1)-(3)	220(1)-(3)	196(1)-(2)	192(1)-(2)
219(4)-(8)	219, 219(4)	195, 195(4)	191, 191(4)
219(9)	220(5)	196(4)	192(4)
219(10)-(11)	220(6)	196(5)	192(5)
220(1)	220(1)	196(1)	192(1)
220(2)	220(2)	196(1a)	—
220(3)-(6)	220(3)-(6)	196(2)-(5)	192(2)-(5)
220	221	197	193
221	222	198	194
222	223	199	195
223	224	200	196
224	225	202	198
225	226	203	199
226(1)	227(1)	204(1)	200
226(2)	227(2)	204(2)	—
227	228	205	201
228	229	206	202
229	—	—	—
230(1)-(4)	230(1)-(4)	206a(1)-(4)	—
230(5),(6)	230(5),(6)	206a(4a),(4b)	—
230(7)-(11)	230(7)-(11)	206a(5)-(9)	—
230(12),(13)	230(12),(13)	206a(9a),(9b)	—
230(14)	230(14)	206a(10)	—
230(15)-(28)	230(15)-(28)	206a(11)-(24)	—
231(1)-(3)	236(1)	209(1)	205(1)
—	236(2)-(3)	209(2)-(3)	205(2)-(3)
231(4)-(10)	236(4)-(6)	209(4)-(6)	205(4)-(6)
231(11)-(12)	—	—	—
—	236(7)-(13)	209(7)-(13)	205(7)-(13)
232	—	—	—
233(1)-(2)	237(2),238(2)	210(2),211(2)	205a(2),205b(2)
—	237(1),(3)-(6)	210(1),(3)-(6)	205a(1),(3)-(6)
—	238(1),(3)-(8)	211(1),(3)-(8)	205b(1),(3)-(8)
233(3)	239	212	205c
231	231	206b	—
232	232	206c	—
233	233	206d	—
235(1)-(2)	235(1)-(2)	208(1)-(2)	204(1)-(2)
235(3)-(6)	235(3)-(6)	208(3)-(6)	204(3)-(6)
234-246	—	—	—

xciii

R.S.O. 1990, c. E.2 (After Bill 160)	R.S.O. 1990, c. E.2	R.S.O. 1980, c. 129	R.S.O. 1974, c. 109
—	240(1)-(5)	214(1)-(5)	207
—	240(6)	214(6)	—
—	—	214(7)	—
—	240(7)-(16)	214(8)-(17)	—
—	241	214a	—
—	242(1)-(4)	214b(1)-(4)	—
—	243(2)-(8)	215(2)-(8)	208(2)-(8)
—	243(9)-11	215(9)-(11)	—
—	244	216	209
—	245(1)-(6)	217	210
—	246	218	211
—	247	219	212(1)-(3)
—	—	—	212(4)
—	248	220	213
—	249	221	214
—	250(1)-(3)	222(1)-(3)	215
—	250(4)	222(4)	—
—	251	223	216
—	253	225	218
—	254	226	219
—	—	—	221(8)
—	257	229	222
—	235(1)	208(1)	204(1)
247(1)-(2)	235.3	—	—
247(3)-(4)	—	—	—
247(5)-(10)	—	—	—
248	—	—	—
249	—	—	—
250	255	227	220
251	256	228(1)-(7)	221(1)-(7)
252(1)	234(9)	207(9)	203(10)
252(2)	234(7)	207(7)	203(8)
252(3)-(6)	—	—	—
253(1)	234(1)	207(1)	203(2)
253(2)	—	—	—
253(3)-(5)	234(2)-(4)	207(2)-(4)	203(3)-(5)
253(6)	—	—	—
253(7)-(8)	234(5)-(6)	207(5)-(6)	203(6)-(7)
253(9)-(11)	—	—	—
234(8)	234(8)	207(8)	203(9)
234(10)	234(10)	207(9)	203(10)
234(11)-(12)	234(11)-(12)	—	—
254	—	—	—

CONCORDANCE

R.S.O. 1990, c. E.2 (After Bill 160)	R.S.O. 1990, c. E.2	R.S.O. 1980, c. 129	R.S.O. 1974, c. 109
—	—	262(1b)	—
—	292(3)-(3)	262(1c)-(1f)	—
—	292(7),(8)	262(2),(3)	256(2),(3)
—	262(3a)	—	—
—	292(9)-(13)	262(4)-(8)	256(4)-(8)
—	292(14),(15)	262(9),(10)	—
—	293(1)	263(1)	257
—	293(2)	263(2)	—
—	294	264	258
—	295	265	259
—	296	266	260
294(1)	303	274	268
294(2)	292(1)(d)	262(1)(d)	256(1)(d)
294(3)	297(1)	267(1)	261(1)
—	297(2)-(3)	267(2)-(3)	261(2)-(3)
294(4)-(5),(8)	297(4)	267(4)	261(4)
294(6)-(7)	—	—	—
294(9)-(10)	297(5)	267(5)	261(5)
295(1)-(9)	304(1)-(9)	275(1)-(9)	269(1)-(9)
304(10)-(12)	304(10)-(12)	275(10)-(12)	269(10)-(12)
295(10)	304(13)	275(13)	269(13)
295(11)	—	—	—
295(12)	304(14)	275(14)	269(14)
295(13)-(14)	304(15)	275(15)	269(15)
296	305	276	270
297	306	277	—
298	307	277a	—
299(1)-(4)	308(1)-(4)	277b(1)-(4)	—
299(5)	—	—	—
299(6)	308(5)	277b(5)	—
—	298(1)	268(1)	262(1)
—	298(2)-(5)	268(1a)(1d)	—
—	298(6)-(8)	268(2)-(4)	262(2)-(3)
—	298(9)-(11)	268(5)-(7)	—
—	299(1)-(2)	269(1)-(2)	263(1)-(2)
—	—	—	—
—	299(3)	269(3)	263(3)
—	300	270	264
—	—	271	265
—	301(1),(2)	272(1),(2)	266(1),(2)
—	301(3),(4)	272(3),(4)	—
—	—	272(5)	—

xcvii

R.S.O. 1990, c. E.2 (After Bill 160)	R.S.O. 1990, c. E.2	R.S.O. 1980, c. 129	R.S.O. 1974, c. 109
—	302	273	267
—	309(1)	277c(1)	—
—	310	277ca	—
—	311(1)-(4)	277d(1)-(4)	—
—	—	277d(5)	—
—	311(5)	277d(6)	—
—	312	277e	—
—	—	277f	—
—	313	277g	—
—	314	277h	—
—	315(1),(2)	277i(1),(2)	—
—	—	277i(3)	—
—	315(3)-(9)	277(4)-(10)	—
—	—	277i(11)	—
—	315(10)-(12)	277i(12)-(14)	—
—	—	—	—
—	316	277j	—
—	317	277k	—
—	—	277l	—
—	318	277m	—
—	319(1)	277n(1)	—
—	—	277n(2)	—
—	319(2)-(5)	277(3)-(6)	—
—	320	277o	—
—	321(1)	277p(1)	—
—	321(2)	277p(2)	—
—	322	277q(1)-(6)	—
—	—	277q(7)-(10)	—
—	323	277r	—
—	324(1)-(3)	277s(1)-(3)	—
—	324(4)	277s(3a)	—
—	324(5)	277s(4)	—
—	325(1)(a)-(c)	277t(1)(a)-(c)	—
—	—	—	—
—	325(2)(a)-(c)	277t(2)(a)-(c)	—
—	—	—	—
—	325(3)	277t(3)	—
—	—	—	—
—	326	277u	—

CONCORDANCE

R.S.O. 1990, c. E.2 (After Bill 160)	R.S.O. 1990, c. E.2	R.S.O. 1980, c. 129	R.S.O. 1974, c. 109
—	—	277(V-2A)	—
—	—	278(1)-(2)	—
—	—	278(3),pt	—
334-351.1	—	—	—

EDUCATION ACT

R.S.O. 1990, c. E.2, as am. S.O. 1991, c. 10; 1991, c. 15; 1992, c. 15, ss. 85-89; 1992, c. 16; 1992, c. 17, ss. 1-3; 1992, c. 27, s. 59; 1992, c. 32, s. 9; 1993, c. 11, ss. 8-43; 1993, c. 23, s. 67; 1993, c. 26, ss. 44-45; 1993, c. 27, Sched.; 1993, c. 41; 1994, c. 1, s. 22; 1994, c. 17, ss. 48, 51; 1994, c. 23, s. 65 [not in force at date of publication.]; 1996, c. 11, s. 29; 1996, c. 12, s. 64; 1996, c. 13, ss. 1-12; 1996, c. 32, s. 70; 1997, c. 3, ss. 2-10; 1997, c. 16, s. 5; 1997, c. 19, s. 33; 1997, c. 22, s. 1; 1997, c. 31; 1997, c. 32, s. 10; 1997, c. 43, Sched. G, s. 20; 1998, c. 3, s. 34; 1998, c. 14, s. 1; 1998, c. 33, ss. 39-45

DEFINITIONS

1. (1) Definitions.—In this Act and the regulations, except where otherwise provided in the Act or regulations,

"assessment commissioner".—[Repealed 1997, c. 43, Sched. G, s. 20.]

"band".—"band" and "council of the band" have the same meaning as in the *Indian Act* (Canada); ("bande", "conseil de bande")

"board".—"board" means a district school board or a school authority; ("conseil")

"business property".—"business property" means business property as defined in section 257.5; ("bien d'entreprise")

"combined separate school zone".—"combined separate school zone" means a union of two or more separate school zones; ("zone unifiée d'écoles séparées")

"continuing education instructor".—"continuing education instructor" means a person employed to provide instruction in a continuing education course or class established in accordance with the regulations, other than those courses or classes for which membership in the Ontario College of Teachers is required under the regulations ("instructeur de l'éducation permanente")

"continuing education teacher".—"continuing education teacher" means a teacher employed to teach a continuing education course or class established in accordance with the regulations for which membership in the Ontario College of Teachers is required by the regulations; ("enseignant de l'éducation permanente")

"credit".—"credit" means recognition granted to a pupil by a principal as proof, in the absence of evidence to the contrary, that the pupil has successfully completed a quantity of work that,
   (a) has been specified by the principal in accordance with the requirements of the Minister, and
   (b) is acceptable to the Minister as partial fulfilment of the requirements for the Ontario secondary school diploma, the secondary school graduation diploma or the secondary school honour graduation diploma, as the case may be; ("crédit")

"current expenditure".—"current expenditure" means an expenditure, for operating purposes or for a permanent improvement, from funds other than funds,

(a) advanced under a mortgage, or
(b) arising from the sale of a debenture or an instrument prescribed under clause 247(3)(f), from a capital loan or from a loan pending the sale of a debenture or such an instrument; ("dépeses courantes")

"**current revenue**".—"current revenue" means all amounts earned by a board, together with the amounts to which it becomes entitled, other than by borrowing, that may be used to meet its expenditures; ("recettes courantes")

"**debt charge**".—"debt charge" means the amount of money necessary annually,
(a) to pay the principal due on long-term debt not payable from a sinking fund, a retirement fund or a fund prescribed under clause 247(3)(e),
(b) to provide a fund for the redemption of debentures or instruments prescribed under clause 247(3)(f) payable from a sinking fund, a retirement fund or a fund prescribed under clause 247(3)(e), and
(c) to pay the interest due on all debt referred to in clauses (a) and (b); ("service de la dette")

"**district municipality**".—"district municipality" means a municipality, except a city, in a territorial district; ("municipalité de district")

"**district school area**".—"district school area" means a school section in the territorial districts that is not a school section of a district school board or a school section designated under section 68; ("secteur scolaire de district")

"**district school board**".—"district school board" means,
(a) an English-language public district school board,
(b) an English-language separate district school board,
(c) a French-language public district school board, or
(d) a French-language separate district school board; ("conseil scolaire de district")

"**education authority**".—"education authority" means a corporation that is incorporated by one or more bands or councils of bands for the purpose of providing for the educational needs of the members of the band or bands; ("commission indienne de l'éducation")

"**elementary school**".—"elementary school" means a school in which instruction is given in some or all of the primary division, junior division and intermediate division but not in the senior division; ("école élméntaire")

"**English-language district school board**".—"English-language district school board" means an English-language public district school board or an English-language separate district school board; ("conseil scolaire de district de langue anglaise")

"**English-language public board**".—"English-language public board" means,
(a) an English-language public district school board, or
(b) a public school authority; ("conseil public de langue anglaise")

"**English-language public board supporter**".—"English-language public board supporter" means a person who is an owner or tenant of residential property in the area of jurisdiction of a board and who is not,
(a) a separate school supporter,
(b) a French-language public district school board supporter, or

(c) a Protestant separate school board supporter; ("contribuable des conseils publics de langue anglaise")

"English-language Roman Catholic board".—"English-language Roman Catholic board" means,
- (a) an English-language separate district school board, or
- (b) a Roman Catholic school authority; ("conseil catholique de langue anglaise")

"English-language Roman Catholic board supporter".—"English-language Roman Catholic board supporter" means a Roman Catholic,
- (a) who is shown as an English-language Roman Catholic board supporter on the school support list as prepared or revised by the assessment commissioner under section 16 of the *Assessment Act*, or
- (b) who is declared to be an English-language Roman Catholic board supporter as a result of a final decision rendered in proceedings commenced under the *Assessment Act*,

and includes his or her Roman Catholic spouse; ("contribuable des conseils catholiques de langue anglaise")

"exceptional pupil".—"exceptional pupil" means a pupil whose behavioural, communicational, intellectual, physical or multiple exceptionalities are such that he or she is considered to need placement in a special education program by a committee, established under subparagraph iii of paragraph 5 of subsection 11 (1), of the board,
- (a) of which the pupil is a resident pupil,
- (b) that admits or enrols the pupil other than pursuant to an agreement with another board for the provision of education, or
- (c) to which the cost of education in respect of the pupil is payable by the Minister; ("élève en difficulté")

"French-language district school board".—"French-language district school board" means a French-language public district school board or a French-language separate district school board; ("conseil scolaire de district de langue française")

"French-language district school board supporter".—"French—language district school board supporter" means a French-language public district school board supporter or a French-language separate district school board supporter; ("contribuable des conseils scolaires de district de langue française")

"French-language instructional unit".—"French-language instructional unit" means a class, group of classes or school in which the French language or Quebec sign language is the language of instruction but does not include a class, group of classes or school established under paragraph 25 of subsection 8 (1); ("module scolaire de langue française")

"French-language public district school board supporter".—"French-language public district school board supporter" means a French-language rights holder,
- (a) who is shown as a French-language public district school board supporter on the school support list as prepared or revised by the assessment commissioner under section 16 of the *Assessment Act*, or
- (b) who is declared to be a French-language public district school board supporter as a

result of a final decision rendered in proceedings commenced under the *Assessment Act*,

and includes his or her spouse if the spouse is a French-language rights holder; ("contribuable des conseils scolaires de district publics de langue française")

"French-language rights holder".—"French-language rights holder" means a person who has the right under subsection 23(1) or (2), without regard to subsection 23(3), of the *Canadian Charter of Rights and Freedoms* to have his or her children receive their primary and secondary school instruction in the French language in Ontario; ("titulaire des droits liés au français")

"French-language separate district school board supporter".—"French-language separate district school board supporter" means a Roman Catholic French-language rights holder,

(a) who is shown as a French-language separate district school board supporter on the school support list as prepared or revised by the assessment commissioner under section 16 of the *Assessment Act*, or

(b) who is declared to be a French-language separate district school board supporter as a result of a final decision rendered in proceedings commenced under the *Assessment Act*,

and includes his or her Roman Catholic spouse if the spouse is a French-language rights holder; ("contribuable des conseils scolaires de district séparés de langue française")

"French-speaking person".—"French-speaking person" means a child of a person who has the right under subsection 23(1) or (2), without regard to subsection 23(3), of the *Canadian Charter of Rights and Freedoms* to have his or her children receive their primary and secondary school instruction in the French-language in Ontario; ("francophone")

"guardian".—"guardian" means a person who has lawful custody of a child, other than the parent of the child; ("tuteur")

"head office".—"head office" of a board means the place at which the minute book, financial statements and records, and seal of the board are ordinarily kept; (siège)

"Indian".—"Indian" has the same meaning as in the *Indian Act* (Canada); ("Indien")

"intermediate division".—"intermediate division" means the division of the organization of a school comprising the first four years of the program of studies immediately following the junior division; ("cycle intermédiaire")

"judge".—"judge" means a judge of the Ontario Court (General Division); ("juge")

"junior division".—"junior division" means the division of the organization of a school comprising the first three years of the program of studies immediately following the primary division; ("cycle moyen")

"Minister".—"Minister" means the Minister of Education and Training; ("ministre")

"Ministry".—"Ministry" means the Ministry of Education and Training; ("ministère")

"municipality".—"municipality" means a city, town, village or township; ("municipalité")

"old board".—old board" has the same meaning as "board" in subsection 1 (1) of this Act, as it read immediately before the *Education Quality Improvement Act, 1997* received Royal Assent, and includes Metropolitan Toronto School Board but does not include a school authority; ("ancien conseil") "**part-time teacher**".—"part-time teacher" means a teacher employed by a board on a regular basis for other than full-time duty; ("enseignant à temps partiel")

"**permanent improvement**".—"permanent improvement" includes,
- (a) a school site and an addition or improvement to a school site,
- (b) a building used for instructional purposes and any addition, alteration or improvement to a building used for instructional purposes,
- (c) any addition, alteration or improvement to an administration building,
- (d) a teacher's residence or caretaker's residence, a storage building for equipment and supplies, and any addition, alteration or improvement to such a residence or storage building,
- (e) furniture, furnishings, library books, instructional equipment and apparatus, and equipment required for maintenance of the property described in clauses (a) to (d) or in clause (f),
- (f) a bus or other vehicle, including watercraft, for the transportation of pupils,
- (g) the obtaining of a water supply or an electrical power supply on the school property or the conveying of a water supply or an electrical power supply to the school from outside the school property,
- (h) initial payments or contributions for past service pensions to a pension plan for officers and other employees of the board,
- (i) any property, work, undertaking or matter prescribed under subsection (6); ("amélioration permanente")

"**permanent teacher**".—[Repealed 1997, c. 31, s. 1(2).]

"**population**".—"population" means the population as determined by the assessment commissioner from the last municipal enumeration as updated under the provisions of the *Assessment Act*; ("population")

"**primary division**".—"primary division" means the division of the organization of a school comprising junior kindergarten, kindergarten and the first three years of the program of studies immediately following kindergarten; ("cycle primaire")

"**principal**".—"principal" means a teacher appointed by a board to perform in respect of a school the duties of a principal under this Act and the regulations; ("directeur d'école")

"**private school**".—private school" means an institution at which instruction is provided at any time between the hours of 9 a.m. and 4 p.m. on any school day for five or more pupils who are of or over compulsory school age in any of the subjects of the elementary or secondary school courses of study and that is not a school as defined in this section; ("école privée")

"**probationary teacher**".—[Repealed 1997, c. 31, s. 1(3).]

"**provincial supervisory officer**".—"provincial supervisory officer" means a supervisory officer employed in the Ministry; ("agent provincial de supervision")

"**public board**".—"public board" means,
- (a) a public district school board, or
- (b) a public school authority; ("conseil public")

"**public district school board**".—"public district school board" means,
- (a) an English-language public district school board, or

(b) a French-language public district school board; ("conseil scolaire de district public")

"public school".—"public school" means a school under the jurisdiction of a public board; ("école publique")

"public school authority".—"public school authority" means,
- (a) a board of a district school area,
- (b) a board of a secondary school district established under section 67, or
- (c) a board established under section 68; ("administration scolaire publique")

"regulations".—"regulations" means the regulations made under this Act; ("règlements")

"reserve fund".—reserve fund" means a reserve fund established under section 163 of the *Municipal Act*; ("fonds de réserve")

"residential property".—"residential property" means residential property as defined in section 257.5; ("bien résidentiel")

"Roman Catholic".—Roman Catholic" includes a member of an Eastern Rite Catholic Church that is in union with the See of Rome; ("catholique")

"Roman Catholic board".—"Roman Catholic board" means,
- (a) a separate district school board, or
- (b) a Roman Catholic school authority; ("conseil catholique")

"Roman Catholic school authority".—"Roman Catholic school authority" means,
- (a) a board of a rural separate school zone, or
- (b) a board of a combined separate school zone; ("administration scolaire catholique")

"rural separate school".—"rural separate school" means a separate school for Roman Catholics that is not under the jurisdiction of a district school board; ("école separée rurale")

"rural separate school zone".—"rural separate school zone" means a separate school zone in respect of a rural separate school; ("zone d'école séparée rurale")

"school".—"school" means,
- (a) the body of elementary school pupils or secondary school pupils that is organized as a unit for educational purposes under the jurisdiction of the appropriate board, or
- (b) the body of pupils enrolled in any of the elementary or secondary school courses of study in an educational institution operated by the Government of Ontario,

and includes the teachers and other staff members associated with the unit or institution and the lands and premises used in connection with the unit or institution; ("école")

"school authority".—"school authority" means,
- (a) a board of a district school area,
- (b) a board of a rural separate school,
- (c) a board of a combined separate school zone,
- (d) a board of a secondary school district established under section 67,
- (e) a board established under section 68, or
- (f) a board of a Protestant separate school; ("administration scolaire")

"school day".—"school day" means a day that is within a school year and is not a school holiday; ("jour de classe")

"school section".—"school section" means the area in which a public board has jurisdiction for elementary school purposes; ("circonscription scolaire")

"school site".—"school site" means land or premises or an interest in land or premises required by a board for a school, school playground, school garden, teacher's residence, caretaker's residence, gymnasium, school offices, parking areas or for any other school purpose; ("emplacement scolaire")

"school year".—school year" means the period prescribed as such by, or approved as such under, the regulations; ("année scolaire")

"secondary school".—"secondary school" means a school in which instruction is given in some or all of the last two years of the intermediate division and the senior division; ("école secondaire")

"secondary school district".—"secondary school district" means the area in which a public board has jurisdiction for secondary school purposes; ("district d'écoles secondaires")

"secretary".—"secretary" and "treasurer" include a secretary-treasurer; ("sécretaire", "trésorier")

"senior division".—"senior division" means the division of the organization of a school comprising the years of the program of studies following the intermediate division; ("cycle supérieur")

"separate district school board".—"separate district school board" means,
   (a) an English-language separate district school board, or
   (b) a French-language separate district school board; ("conseil scolaire de district séparé")

"separate school".—"separate school" means a school under the jurisdiction of a Roman Catholic board except,
   (a) in the provisions of Part V, and
   (b) in any other provision where the context indicateds that a school under the jurisdiction of a Protestant separate school board is meant; ("école séparée")

"separate school board".—separate school board" means a board that operates a separate school for Roman Catholics; ("conseil d'écoles séparée")

"separate school supporter".—"separate school supporter" means an English-language Roman Catholic board supporter or a French-language separate district school board supporter; ("contribuable des écoles sépareés")

"separate school zone".—"separate school zone" means the area of jurisdiction of a Roman Catholic board; ("zone d'écoles séparées")

"separated town".—"separated town" means a town separated for municipal purposes from the county in which it is situated; ("ville séparée")

"special education program".—"special education program" means, in respect of an exceptional pupil, an educational program that is based on and modified by the results of continuous assessment and evaluation and that includes a plan containing specific objectives and an outline of educational services that meets the needs of the exceptional pupil; ("programme d'enseignement à l'enfance en difficulté") "**special education services**".—"special education services" means facilities and resources, including support personnel and equipment, necessary for developing and implementing a special education program; ("services à l'enfance en difficulté")

"**supervisory officer**".—"supervisory officer" means a person who is qualified in accordance with the regulations governing supervisory officers and who is employed,

(a) by a board and designated by the board, or

(b) in the Ministry and designated by the Minister

to perform such supervisory and administrative duties as are required of supervisory officers by this Act and the regulations; ("agent de supervision")

"**teacher**".—"teacher" means a member of the Ontario College of Teachers; ("enseignant")

"**temporary teacher**".—"temporary teacher" means a person employed to teach under the authority of a letter of permission; ("enseignant temporaire")

"**urban municipality**".—"urban municipality" means a city, town or village. ("municipalité urbaine")

(1.1) **Occasional teacher.**—For the purposes of this Act, a teacher is an occasional teacher if he or she is employed by a board to teach as a substitute for a teacher or temporary teacher who is or was employed by the board in a position that is part of its regular teaching staff including continuing education teachers but,

(a) if the teacher substitutes for a teacher who has died during a school year, the teacher's employment as a substitute for him or her shall not extend past the end of the school year in which the death occurred; and

(b) if the teacher substitutes for a teacher who is absent from his or her duties for a temporary period, the teacher's employment as the substitute for him or her shall not extend past the end of the second school year after his or her absence begins.

(1.2.1) **Ontario Property Assessment Corporation.**—Beginning on the day on which subsection 9(1) of the *Ontario Property Assessment Corporation Act, 1997* comes into force, a reference in this Act to the assessment commissioner or to the appropriate assessment commissioner shall be deemed to be a reference to the Ontario Property Assessment Corporation.

(2) **Authority or obligation of parent vested in pupil of 18 years of age.**—Where by or under this Act any authority or right is vested in, or any obligation is imposed upon, or any reimbursement may be made to, a parent or guardian of a pupil, such authority, right, obligation or reimbursement shall, where the pupil is an adult, be vested in or imposed upon or made to the pupil, as the case may be.

(3) **Questions re proceeding as to formation of school section.**—Where any question arises touching the validity of any proceeding with respect to the formation, alteration or dissolution of a school section or touching any by-law with respect to any of such matters, the question shall be raised, heard and determined upon a summary application to a judge, and no proceeding or by-law with respect to the formation, alteration or dissolution of a school section is invalid or shall be set aside because of failure to comply with the provisions of any Act applicable to the proceeding or by-law, unless, in the opinion of the judge before whom the

proceeding or by-law is called in question, the proceeding or by-law, if allowed to stand, would cause substantial injustice to be done to any person affected thereby.

(4) **Effect on separate schools.**—This Act does not adversely affect any right or privilege guaranteed by section 93 of the *Constitution Act*, 1867 or by section 23 of the *Canadian Charter of Rights and Freedoms*.

(4.1) **Same.**—Every authority given under this Act, including but not limited to every authority to make a regulation, decision or order and every authority to issue a directive or guideline, shall be exercised in a manner consistent with and respectful of the rights and privileges guaranteed by section 93 of the *Constitution Act*, 1867 and by section 23 of the *Canadian Charter of Rights and Freedoms*.

(5) **Existing school arrangements continued.**—Until altered under the authority of this or any other Act, all school jurisdictions and boards, including the names of the boards, as they existed on the 31st day of July, 1981, are continued subject to the provisions of this Act.

(6) **Regulations re permanent improvements.**—The Minister may make regulations prescribing any property, work, undertaking or matter for the purposes of the definition of "permanent improvement" in subsection (1).

(7) **Separate school support in 1997.**—A person who at any time in 1997 is a separate school board supporter in connection with land assessed to the support of a separate school board is also, at that time, a separate school supporter for the purpose of qualifying as a separate school elector for the English-language district school board or the French-language separate district school board, as the case may be, the area of jurisdiction of which includes that land.

(8) **Entitlement to vote based on residence.**—Despite any provision of this Act, except subsection (9), or of any other Act, including subclause 17(2)(a)(ii) of the *Municipal Elections Act*, 1996, for the purposes of regular elections and by-elections, a person is not qualified to vote for a member of a board for an area unless the person resides in the area at some time during the qualification period.

(9) **Exception.**—Subsection (8) does not apply to a person who is an owner or tenant of residential property in the area referred to in subsection (8), or who is a spouse of that person.

(10) **Entitlement to vote in the area of jurisdiction of a board.**—For the purposes of sections 50.1, 54, 58.8 and 58.9, a person is entitled to vote in the area of jurisdiction of a board if he or she,

    (a) at any time during the qualification period resides in the area or is a person to whom subsection (9) applies; and

    (b) on voting day,
- (i) is a Canadian citizen,
- (ii) is at least 18 ye%ws old, and
- (iii) is not a person referred to in subclause 17 (2) (b) (iii) of the *Municipal Elections Act*, 1996.

(11) **Interpretation.**—For the purposes of subsections (8) and (10),

    (a) "resides" and "qualification period" have the same meaning as in section 17 of the *Municipal Elections Act*, 1996; and

    (b) a person who changes residence from the area of jurisdiction of one board to the area of jurisdiction of another board during the qualification period is entitled to vote only in the area of jurisdiction where he or she resides last.

(12) **Trustee.**—A member of a board may be referred to as a trustee for any purpose related to this Act.

1992, c. 16, s. 1; 1993, c. 11, ss. 8, 9; 1993, c. 23, s. 67(1); 1996, c. 12, s. 64(1); 1996, c. 32, s. 70(1); 1997, c. 3, s. 2; 1997, c. 31, s. 1; 1997, c. 43, Sched. G, s. 20.

PART I

MINISTRY OF EDUCATION AND TRAINING

2. (1) **Ministry continued.**—The ministry of the public service known in English as the Ministry of Education and Training and in French as ministère de l'Éducation et de la Formation is continued.

(2) **Minister to have charge.**—The Minister shall preside over and have charge of the Ministry.

(3) **Administration.**—The Minister is responsible for the administration of this Act and the regulations and of such other Acts and the regulations thereunder as may be assigned to the Minister by the Lieutenant Governor in Council.

(4) **Delegation of powers and duties.**—The Minister may in writing authorize the Deputy Minister or any other officer or employee in the Ministry to exercise any power or perform any duty that is granted to or vested in the Minister under this or any other Act.

(5) **Limitations.**—The Minister may in writing limit an authorization made under subsection (4) in such manner as he or she considers advisable.

(6) **Application of *Executive Council Act*, s. 6.**—Section 6 of the *Executive Council Act* does not apply to a deed or contract that is executed under an authorization made under subsection (4).

1997, c. 31, ss. 2, 3.

3. Annual report.—The Minister shall, after the close of each fiscal year, submit to the Lieutenant Governor in Council a report upon the affairs of the Ministry for the immediately preceding fiscal year and shall then lay the report before the Assembly if it is in session or, if not, at the next session.

4. Additions to enrolment in special cases.—The Minister may, in respect of a school require to be included in the enrolment on any date the number of pupils who were absent from school because of any condition considered by the Minister to constitute a special circumstance or an emergency.

5. (1) **Closing of school or class.**—Subject to the approval of the Lieutenant Governor in Council, the Minister may order the closing of a school or any class thereof for a specified period.

(2) **Pupils deemed in attendance.**—Where a school or class is closed for a specified period under subsection (1), the pupils in such school or class shall for all purposes, including the calculation of legislative grants and fees, be deemed to be in attendance.

1997, c. 31, s. 4.

6. [Repealed 1997, c. 31, s. 5.]

PART I — MINISTRY OF EDUCATION AND TRAINING   **S. 8**

7. [Repealed 1997, c. 31, s. 5.]
8. (1) **Powers of Minister.**—The Minister may,
1. **diplomas and certificates.**—name the diplomas and certificates that are to be granted to pupils and prescribe their form and the conditions under which they are to be granted;
2. **courses of study.**—prescribe the courses of study that shall be taught and the courses of study that may be taught in the primary, junior, intermediate and senior divisions;
3. **courses and areas of study.**—in respect of schools under the jurisdiction of a board,
    (a) issue curriculum guidelines and require that courses of study be developed therefrom and establish procedures for the approval of courses of study that are not developed from such curriculum guidelines,
    (b) prescribe areas of study and require that courses of study be grouped thereunder and establish procedures for the approval of alternative areas of study under which courses of study shall be grouped, and
    (c) approve or permit boards to approve,
        (i) courses of study that are not developed from such curriculum guidelines, and
        (ii) alternative areas of study under which courses of study shall be grouped, and authorize such courses of study and areas of study to be used in lieu of or in addition to any prescribed course of study or area of study;
3.1 **reviews of effectiveness.**—conduct reviews of classroom practices and the effectiveness of educational programs and require a board or a private school inspected under subsection 16(7) to participate in the reviews and to provide information to the Minister for that purpose in such form as the Minister may prescribe;
3.2 **tests.**—assess the academic achievement of pupils attending schools under the jurisdiction of a board and, for the purpose, the Minister may,
    (a) provide for the administering and marking of tests of academic achievement,
    (b) require a board to administer tests of academic achievement to its pupils and mark the tests, within the time and in the manner and form specified by the Minister, and
    (c) require a board to report on the results of the tests to the Minister and the general public within the time and in the manner and form specified by the Minister;
3.3 **policies, guidelines; assessment of academic achievement.**—establish policies and guidelines for the assessment of the academic achievement of pupils attending schools under the jurisdiction of a board and requiring boards to comply with the policies and guidelines;
3.4 **guidelines: role and responsibilities of board members, officials.**—establish policies and guidelines respecting the roles and responsibilities of board members, directors of education, supervisory officers, principals, superintendents and other officials;
3.5 **policies and guidelines: policies re pupil representatives.**—establish policies and guidelines for the development and implementation of board policies dealing with

the representation on boards of the interests of pupils and require boards to comply with the policies and guidelines;

3.6 **policies and guidelines: policies re electronic meetings.**—establish policies and guidelines for the development and implementation of district school board policies dealing with the use of electronic means for the holding of meetings of a district school board and meetings of a committee of a district school board, including a committee of the whole board, and require district school boards to comply with the policies and guidelines;

4. **procedures.**—establish procedures by which and the conditions under which books and other learning materials are selected and approved by the Minister;

5. **textbooks and other learning materials.**—purchase and distribute textbooks and other learning materials for use in schools;

6. **textbooks, reference books, etc.**—select and approve for use in schools textbooks, library books, reference books and other learning materials;

7. **publication of book lists.**—cause to be published from time to time lists of textbooks, learning materials, reference books and library books, selected and approved by the Minister for use in elementary and secondary schools;

8. **daily register.**—prescribe the form of the register of attendance and the manner of its use in recording the daily attendance of pupils of schools, or approve the use of an alternate method of recording such daily attendance, and prescribe the form in which enrolment and attendance data shall be submitted to the Minister;

9. **application of** *Workplace Safety and Insurance Act, 1997.*—prescribe the conditions under which and the terms upon which pupils of boards shall be deemed to be workers for the purposes of the insurance plan established under the *Workplace Safety and Insurance Act, 1997*, deem pupils to be workers for those purposes and require a board to reimburse Ontario for payments made by Ontario under the insurance plan in respect of such a pupil.

10. **letter of permission.**—grant a letter of permission to a board authorizing the board to employ as a teacher a person who is not a member of the Ontario College of Teachers to teach in an elementary or secondary school if the Minister is satisfied that no member is available, but a letter of permission shall be effective only for the period, not exceeding one year, that the Minister may specify;

11. **letter of approval.**—grant a temporary letter of approval to a board authorizing the board to appoint or assign, for a period not exceeding one year, a teacher to teach a subject or hold a position where the teacher does not hold the certificate required for teaching the subject;

12. **withdraw letter.**—withdraw any letter of permission or temporary letter of approval granted under this Act;

13. **suspend or cancel.**—suspend or cancel and reinstate any certificate of qualification or letter of standing;

14. **accept equivalent qualification.**—accept in lieu of any requirement prescribed for a teacher, head of a department, principal, director, supervisor or supervisory officer, or for a candidate for a certificate or for admission to a school, such experience, academic scholarship or professional training as the Minister considers equivalent thereto, and may require such evidence thereof as the Minister considers necessary;

PART I — MINISTRY OF EDUCATION AND TRAINING S. 8

15. **medical examinations.**—require employees of school boards to submit to medical examinations;
16. **courses.**—provide or approve and review courses for teachers, principals, supervisory officers, attendance counsellors and native counsellors and grant certificates in respect of the successful completion of such courses;
17. **correspondence courses.**—provide for the development, distribution and supervision by the Ministry of correspondence courses;
17.1 **fees re correspondence courses.**—provide for fees in relation to anything referred to in paragraph 17.
18. **scholarships, bursaries.**—provide for, and prescribe the conditions of, the granting of scholarships, bursaries and awards to pupils and the granting of bursaries to teachers;
19. **teachers' colleges.**—in respect of teachers' colleges,
    (a) define courses of study and subjects to be taught,
    (b) recommend reference books and library books,
    (c) approve textbooks,
    (d) determine the number of terms and the dates upon which each term begins and ends, and
    (e) grant Bachelor of Education degrees;
20. **provincial schools.**—in respect of schools for the deaf and the blind, determine the number of terms and the dates upon which each term begins and ends;
21. **apportion federal grants.**—apportion and pay all sums received for educational purposes from the Government of Canada or any source other than an appropriation by the Legislature, in accordance with the terms of the grant, if any, and otherwise in any manner the Minister considers proper;
22. **educational advancement programs, activities and projects and accountable advances.**—make payments out of funds appropriated therefor by the Legislature to a board, an individual, a voluntary association or a corporation without share capital having objects of a charitable or educational nature,
    (a) to assist or advance programs, activities or projects for students that involve a cultural and educational exchange with other provinces and countries, provincial or interprovincial travel, school twinning and related assistance, leadership training, or summer employment, and
    (b) to foster and promote educational advancement by means of programs, activities or projects that are provided for visiting educational officials, designed to further the professional development of teachers and supervisory officers including exchange of such personnel, or considered by the Minister to be valuable in advancing a particular area of study,
    and, subject to the terms and conditions that are approved for such purpose by the Lieutenant Governor in Council, make an accountable advance to the recipient of a payment under this clause or to an individual, not being a member of the public service, who conducts or assists in conducting or participates in any such program, activity or project;
23. **agreements concerning learning materials.**—enter into an agreement with any

board, person or organization in respect of the development and production of learning materials, and pay all or part of the costs in connection therewith;

23.1 **copyright licence agreements.**—enter into a licence agreement to permit boards to copy, under the terms of the licence agreement, works protected by copyright, and to,

(a) extend the rights under the licence agreement to boards, and

(b) require boards to comply with the terms of the licence agreement;

24. **educational research and grants for promotion of advancement of education.**—initiate educational research and make grants to a board, an individual, a voluntary association or a corporation for educational research programs, activities or projects to promote the advancement of education;

25. **discretion to establish French-language programs for English-speaking pupils.**—permit a board to establish for English-speaking pupils programs involving varying degrees of the use of the French language in instruction, provided that programs in which English is the language of instruction are made available to pupils whose parents desire such programs for their children;

26. **guidelines respecting school closings.**—in respect of schools under the jurisdiction of a board, issue guidelines respecting the closing of schools and require that boards develop policies therefrom with respect to procedures to be followed prior to the closing of a school by decision of the board;

27. **guidelines respecting keeping of pupil records.**—issue guidelines respecting pupil records and require boards to comply with the guidelines;

27.1 **board reports.**—require a board,

(a) to prepare any report that the Minister may require,

(b) to submit, in the form directed by the Minister, a copy of the report to the Ministry and to such other persons as the Minister may direct, and

(c) to attach a copy of the report to the financial statements of the board referred to in section 252;

27.2 **same.**—issue guidelines respecting the form and content of a report referred to in paragraph 27.1.

28. **approve awards.**—approve awards for the purpose of subclause 49(7)(f)(iv);

29. [Repealed, 1995, c. 4, s. 2(1).]

29.1 **ethnocultural equity.**—require boards to develop and implement an ethnocultural equity and antiracism policy, to submit the policy to the Minister for approval and to implement changes to the policy as directed by the Minister;

29.2 **drug education.**—establish a drug education policy framework and require boards to develop and implement a policy on drug education in accordance with the framework.

30. **duties of auditors.**—prescribe the duties to be performed by auditors appointed under section 253.

31. [Repealed 1997, c. 31, s. 6(5).]

32. [Repealed 1997, c. 31, s. 6(5).]

33. **approval of agreements.**—approve the entering into of an agreement by boards under subsection 182(1).

34. [Repealed 1997, c. 31, s. 6(5).]

35. **education costs outside Ontario.**—make payments towards the cost of elementary or secondary education that a person receives outside Ontario, if the person is outside Ontario for the purpose of receiving insured services within the meaning of the *Health Insurance Act* and the cost of the insured services is paid for in whole or in part by the Ontario Health Insurance Plan.

(2) [Repealed, 1997, c. 31, s. 6(6).]

(3) **Identification programs and special education programs and services.**—The Minister shall ensure that all exceptional children in Ontario have available to them, in accordance with this Act and the regulations, appropriate special education programs and special education services without payment of fees by parents or guardians resident in Ontario, and shall provide for the parents or guardians to appeal the appropriateness of the special education placement, and for these purposes the Minister shall,

(a) require school boards to implement procedures for early and ongoing identification of the learning abilities and needs of pupils, and shall prescribe standards in accordance with which such procedures be implemented; and

(b) in respect of special education programs and services, define exceptionalities of pupils, and prescribe classes, groups or categories of exceptional pupils, and require boards to employ such definitions or use such prescriptions as established under this clause.

(4) **Application.**—An act of the Minister under this section is not a regulation within the meaning of the *Regulations Act*.

1991, Vol. 2, c. 10, s. 1; 1992, c. 16, s. 2; c. 27, s. 59; 1993, c. 11, s. 10; 1995, c. 4, s. 2(1); 1996, c. 11, s. 29(1); 1996, c. 12, s. 64(2); 1996, c. 13, s. 1; 1997, c. 16, s. 5; 1997, c. 31, s. 6.

9. Accounting statement related to assistance by Ministry.—The Minister may require a person or organization that has received financial assistance under this Act or the regulations to submit to the Minister a statement prepared by a person licensed under the *Public Accountancy Act* that sets out the details of the disposition of the financial assistance by the person or organization.

10. Powers of Minister.—The Minister may,

(a) **advisory body.**—appoint such advisory or consultative bodies as may be considered necessary by the Minister from time to time;

(b) **commission of inquiry.**—appoint as a commission one or more persons, as the Minister considers expedient, to inquire into and report upon any school matter, and such commission has the powers of a commission under Part II of the *Public Inquiries Act*, which Part applies to such inquiry as if it were an inquiry under that Act;

(c) **secure legal opinion.**—submit a case on any question arising under this Act to the Divisional Court for opinion and decision.

11. (1) **Regulations.**—Subject to the approval of the Lieutenant Governor in Council, the Minister may make regulations in respect of schools or classes established under this Act, or any predecessor of this Act, and with respect to all other schools supported in whole or in part by public money,

1. **general.**—for the establishment, organization, administration and government thereof;

2. **admit pupils.**—governing the admission of pupils;
3. **pupil records.**—prescribing the manner in which records in respect of pupils of elementary and secondary schools shall be established and maintained, including the forms to be used therefor and the type of information that shall be kept and recorded, and providing for the retention, transfer and disposal of such records;
4. **disposition of present pupil records.**—providing for the disposition of records established prior to the 1st day of September, 1972, in respect of pupils;
5. **special education programs.**—governing the provision, establishment, organization and administration of,
    i. special education programs,
    ii. special education services, and
    iii. committees to identify exceptional pupils and to make and review placements of exceptional pupils;
6. **identification and placement appeals.**—governing procedures with respect to parents or guardians for appeals in respect of identification and placement of exceptional pupils in special education programs;
7. **evening classes.**—defining and governing evening classes;
8. **purchase books.**—requiring boards to purchase books for the use of pupils;
9. **accommodation and equipment.**—prescribing the accommodation and equipment of buildings and the arrangement of premises;
10. **recreation programs.**—defining and governing programs of recreation, camping, physical education and adult education;
11. **certificates and letters of standing.**—governing the granting, suspending and cancelling of certificates of qualification, and letters of standing;
12. **teacher's qualifications record cards.**—providing for the issuing of teacher's qualifications record cards and governing the professional qualifications that may be recorded on such record cards;
13. **letter of permission.**—governing the granting to a board of a letter of permission and a temporary letter of approval and providing for the withdrawal of such letters;
14. **teacher's contract.**—[Repealed 1997, c. 31, s. 7(1).]
15. **schools on Crown lands.**—governing the establishment and operation of public and secondary schools on lands held by the Crown in right of Canada or Ontario or by an agency thereof, or on other lands that are exempt from taxation for school purposes;
16. **supervisory officers, examinations.**—providing for the holding of examinations for persons to become supervisory officers and governing such examinations;
17. **continuing education courses and classes.**—defining and governing continuing education courses and classes;
18. **idem.**—prescribing the continuing education courses and classes for which membership in the Ontario College of Teachers is required;
19. **fees of examiners.**—prescribing the fees to be paid to presiding officers and examiners in connection with examinations and by whom and in what manner such fees and other expenses in connection with such examinations shall be borne and paid;
20. **religious exercises and education.**—governing the provision of religious exercises and religious education in public schools and providing for the exemption of pupils

from participating in such exercises and education and of a teacher from teaching, and a public board from providing, religious education in any school or class;
21. **language of instruction.**—prescribing the language or languages in which any subject or subjects shall be taught in any year of the primary, junior, intermediate or senior division;
21.1 **sign language.**—respecting the use of American Sign Language and Quebec Sign Language as languages of instruction.
22. **exchange teachers.**—providing for and governing the exchange of teachers between Ontario and other parts of Canada and between Ontario and other jurisdictions;
23. **school libraries.**—governing school libraries;
24. **textbooks.**—listing the textbooks that are selected and approved by the Minister for use in schools;
25. [Repealed 1996, c. 12, s. 64(4)];
26. **powers and duties of teachers, etc.**—prescribing the powers, duties and qualifications, and governing the appointment of teachers, supervisors, directors, supervisory officers, heads of departments, principals, superintendents, residence counsellors, school attendance counsellors and other officials;
26.1 **effect of certificates issued under the *Ontario College of Teachers Act, 1996*.**—giving boards directions as to the effect and consequences of,
    i. a certificate issued under the *Ontario College of Teachers Act, 1996* being suspended, cancelled or revoked under that Act,
    ii. a certificate issued under the *Ontario College of Teachers Act, 1996* being subject to terms, conditions or limitations imposed under that Act,
    iii. a certificate issued under the *Ontario College of Teachers Act, 1996* being of a particular class prescribed under that Act,
    iv. a certificate of qualification that is additional to the certificate of qualification and registration being issued under the *Ontario College of Teachers Act, 1996*;
27. **pupils.**—prescribing the duties of pupils;
28. [Repealed 1993, c. 11, s. 11(2).]
29. **qualification to teach.**—prescribing the qualifications and experience required for the purpose of qualifying a person to teach;
30. **forms.**—prescribing forms and providing for their use;
31. **transportation.**—governing the transportation of pupils;
32. **practice and procedure.**—regulating the practice and procedure to be followed at any hearing provided for by or under this Act;
33. **duties of supervisory officers.**—governing the assignment by a board of duties to directors of education and other supervisory officers and prescribing the procedures in respect thereof, and defining any word or expression used in such regulation;
34. **suspension or dismissal of supervisory officers.**—prescribing the practices and procedures to be followed by a board in the case of suspension or dismissal of a director of education or other supervisory officer;
35. **competition with private sector.**—despite paragraph 28 of subsection 171(1), prohibiting or regulating and controlling any program or activity of a board that is or may be in competition with any business or occupation in the private sector and

providing that such regulations have general application or application to a particular board;

36. **language programs.**—requiring boards to offer programs that deal with languages other than English or French and governing the establishment and operation of such programs.

(2) [Repealed 1993, c. 11, s. 11(3).]

(3) **Regulations, fees.**—Subject to the approval of the Lieutenant Governor in Council, the Minister may make regulations,

(a) providing for the circumstances in which a fee is receivable by a board in respect of the provision of education by the board to elementary or secondary school pupils or any class or group of elementary or secondary school pupils; and

(b) providing for the method of determining the amount of any fee receivable under clause (a).

(4) **Same.**—A regulation made under subsection (3),

(a) may be general or particular;

(b) may prescribe the maximum amount of any fee that may be charged and may provide for the determination of fees by boards; and

(c) may be made to apply with respect to any period specified in the regulation including a period before the regulation is made.

(5) [Repealed 1997, c. 31, s. 7(3).]

(6) [Repealed 1997, c. 31, s. 7(3).]

(7) **School year, terms, holidays, etc.**—Subject to the approval of the Lieutenant Governor in Council, the Minister may make regulations,

(a) prescribing and governing the school year, school terms, school holidays, and instructional days;

(b) authorizing a board to vary one or more school terms, school holidays, or instructional days as designated by the regulations;

(c) permitting a board to designate, and to implement with the prior approval of the Minister, a school year, school terms, school holidays or instructional days for one or more schools under its jurisdiction that are different from those prescribed by the regulations; and

(d) respecting the preparation and implementation of school calendars by boards.

(7.1) **Same.**—A school calendar prepared under a regulation made under clause 7(d) shall not provide for,

(a) more than 10 examination days in any school year determined in respect of a school under the regulations made under subsection (7); or

(b) more than 4 professional activity days in any school year determined in respect of a school under the regulations made under subsection (7).

(8) **Exceptions: compulsory attendance.**—Subject to the approval of the Lieutenant Governor in Council, the Minister may make regulations prescribing the conditions under which, and establishing the procedures by which, a child who is otherwise required to attend school under Part II and who has attained the age of fourteen years may be excused from attendance at school or required to attend school only part-time.

(9) **Regulations.**—Subject to the approval of the Lieutenant Governor in Council, the Minister may make regulations,

- (a) **fee for transcripts.**—prescribing the fee to be paid to the Ministry for a transcript of standing obtained in Ontario by a pupil;
- (b) **fee for certificates and letters of standing.**—prescribing the fee to be paid to the Ministry for duplicates of Ontario Teachers' Qualifications Record Cards and duplicates of certificates issued under this Act;
- (c) [Repealed 1996, c. 12, s. 64(6).]
- (d) **fees for evaluations.**—prescribing the conditions under which fees shall be paid to the Ministry for the evaluation of academic certificates, transcripts and other documents of educational standing, and prescribing the amounts of the fees;
- (e) **fees for duplicates of certificates.**—prescribing the fees to be paid for duplicates of diplomas and certificates granted to pupils;
- (f) **fees for courses.**—prescribing the fees to be paid for courses provided by the Ministry for teachers, principals and supervisory officers or any class thereof;
- (g) **admission to teachers' college.**—prescribing the terms and conditions upon which students may be admitted to a teachers' college, remain therein and be dismissed therefrom;
- (h) **tuition fee teachers' college.**—requiring the payment of a tuition fee by students attending a teachers' college, fixing the amount and manner of payment thereof and prescribing the conditions under which a student is entitled to a refund of the fee or part thereof.

(10) [Repealed 1997, c. 31, s. 7(5).]

(11) [Repealed 1997, c. 3, s. 3.]

(12) [Repealed 1997, c. 3, s. 3.]

(13) [Repealed, 1997, c. 31, s. 7(6).]

(14) [Repealed 1997, c. 31, s. 7(7).]

(15) [Repealed 1997, c. 31 s. 7(8).]

(15.1) [Repealed 1997, c. 31, s. 7(9).]

(16) [Repealed 1997, c. 31, s. 7(10).]

(17) [Repealed 1993, c. 41, s. 1(1).]

(18) [Repealed 1997, c. 31, s. 7(10).]

1991, Vol. 2, c. 10, s. 2; 1993, c. 11, s. 11; 1994, c. 27, s. 108(1); 1996, c. 12, s. 64.

12. (1) **Agreements with Canada re: physical fitness.**—The Crown in right of Ontario, represented by the Minister, with the approval of the Lieutenant Governor in Council, may make agreements with the Crown in right of Canada, represented by the Minister of National Health and Welfare of Canada respecting physical fitness, and the Minister may authorize a board to provide training in physical fitness.

(2) **Pupils at Indian schools.**—The Crown in right of Ontario, represented by the Minister, may make agreements with the Crown in right of Canada, represented by the Minister charged with the administration of the *Indian Act* (Canada), for the admission of pupils, other than Indians, to schools for Indians operated under that Act.

(3) **Non-Indian pupils at Indian schools.**—The Crown in right of Ontario, represented by the Minister, may enter into an agreement with a band, the council of the band or an education authority where such band, council of the band or education authority is authorized by the Crown in right of Canada to provide education for Indians, for the admission of pupils who are not Indians to a school operated by the band, council of the band or education authority.

(4) **Bursaries and scholarships.**—The Crown in right of Ontario, represented by the Minister, may make agreements with the Crown in right of Canada, represented by the Minister of Manpower and Immigration, respecting the establishment, awarding and payment of bursaries and scholarships to students eligible therefor under the regulations.

(5) **Learning materials.**—The Crown in right of Ontario, represented by the Minister, may enter into an agreement with the Crown in right of Canada in respect of the development and production of learning materials and the sharing of the costs thereof.

13. (1) **Continuation of school for deaf.**—The Ontario School for the Deaf for the education and instruction of the deaf and partially deaf is continued under the name Ontario School for the Deaf in English and école provinciale pour sourds in French.

(2) **Continuation of school for blind.**—The Ontario School for the Blind for the education and instruction of the blind and partially blind is continued under the name Ontario School for the Blind in English and école provinciale pour aveugles in French.

(3) **Administration.**—Both schools are under the administration of the Minister.

(4) **Additional schools.**—Subject to the approval of the Lieutenant Governor in Council, the Minister may establish, maintain and operate one or more additional schools for the deaf or schools for the blind.

(4.1) **Idem.**—A demonstration school may provide, in a residential or non-residential setting, special education programs and special education services for exceptional pupils with learning disabilities or with hearing or visual impairments.

(5) **Demonstration schools.**—Subject to the approval of the Lieutenant Governor in Council, the Minister may,

- (a) establish, maintain and operate one or more demonstration schools; or
- (b) enter into an agreement with a university to provide for the establishment, maintenance and operation by the university, under such terms and conditions as the Minister and the university may agree upon, of a demonstration school,

for exceptional pupils whose learning disabilities are such that a residential setting is required.

(6) **Idem.**—A demonstration school referred to in subsection (5) that was established by the Minister before the 12th day of December, 1980 is deemed not to be a school operated by the Ministry of Education for the purposes of the Provincial Schools Negotiations Act, and the provincial schools authority is not responsible for any matter relating to the employment of teachers at a demonstration school.

(7) **Regulations.**—Subject to the approval of the Lieutenant Governor in Council, the Minister may, in addition to his or her powers under section 11, make regulations with respect to schools continued or established under this section,

- (a) prescribing the terms and conditions upon which pupils may,
    - (i) be admitted to, and remain in, a school,

(ii) reside in homes approved by a superintendent, and
(iii) be discharged from a school;
(b) authorizing the Minister to appoint a committee to determine any question concerning the eligibility for admission of an applicant;
(c) prescribing the fees, if any, that shall be paid in respect of pupils or any class or classes thereof;
(d) authorizing the payment of part or all of the transportation costs of pupils whose parents or guardians reside in Ontario, and fixing the maximum amount that may be paid;
(e) authorizing a superintendent to establish rules in respect of pupils admitted to the school;
(f) authorizing a superintendent to specify the type and minimum amount of clothing that a parent or guardian shall provide for a pupil;
(g) requiring a parent or guardian to deposit a sum of money with the business administrator of a school for the purpose of defraying the personal incidental expense of a pupil, and fixing the amount of the deposit;
(h) authorizing a superintendent to dismiss a pupil and prescribing procedures in respect thereof;
(i) authorizing the Minister to provide training for, and certification of, teachers of the deaf and of the blind;
(j) designating the name of each school continued or established under this section.

1991, Vol. 2, c. 10, s. 3.

14. (1) **Teacher education.**—Subject to the approval of the Lieutenant Governor in Council, the Minister may,
(a) establish, maintain and conduct a college for the professional education of teachers;
(b) enter into an agreement with a university, a college of a university or a college to provide for the professional education of teachers by the university or college, under such terms and conditions as the Minister and the university or college may agree upon.

(2) **Practice teaching.**—Where the Minister conducts a teacher education program, a board shall permit its schools to be used for observation and practice teaching purposes and shall provide for the services of any of its teachers in accordance with a schedule of payments to boards that provide accommodation for practice teaching purposes and to their principals and teachers who participate therein, and such schedule shall be approved by the Lieutenant Governor in Council.

(3) **Idem.**—Where a teacher education program is conducted pursuant to an agreement under clause (1)(b), a board shall permit its schools to be used for observation and practice teaching purposes and shall provide for the services of any of its teachers under such terms and conditions as may be agreed upon between the board and the institution conducting the program and failing agreement in accordance with the schedule of payments to boards, principals and teachers referred to in subsection (2).

(3.1) **Same.**—Where the Ontario College of Teachers has accredited a teacher education program, the Minister may require that a board shall permit its schools to be used for observation and practice teaching purposes and shall provide for the services of any of its teachers under such terms and conditions as may be agreed on between the board and the institution conducting the program and failing agreement in accordance with the schedule of payments to boards, principals and teachers referred in subsection (2).

(4) **Idem.**—The cost of providing the professional education of teachers by a university, a college of a university or a college under an agreement referred to in clause (1)(b) shall be payable out of money appropriated therefor by the Legislature.

1996, c. 12, s. 64(7); 1997, c. 31, s. 8.

15. Leadership training camps.—The Minister may establish, maintain and conduct camps for leadership training.

16. (1) **Intention to operate private schools.**—No private school shall be operated in Ontario unless notice of intention to operate the private school has been submitted in accordance with this section.

(2) **Idem.**—Every private school shall submit annually to the Ministry on or before the 1st day of September a notice of intention to operate a private school.

(3) **Idem.**—A notice of intention to operate a private school shall be in such form and shall include such particulars as the Minister may require.

(4) **Offence to operate private school without filling notice of intent to operate.**—Every person concerned in the management of a private school that is operated in contravention of subsection (1) is guilty of an offence and on conviction is liable to a fine of not more than $50 for every day such school is so operated.

(5) **Return.**—The principal, headmaster, headmistress or person in charge of a private school shall make a return to the Ministry furnishing such statistical information regarding enrolment, staff, courses of study and other information as and when required by the Minister, and any such person who fails to make such return within sixty days of the request of the Minister is guilty of an offence and on conviction is liable to a fine of not more than $200.

(6) **Inspection of school.**—The Minister may direct one or more supervisory officers to inspect a private school, in which case each such supervisory officer may enter the school at all reasonable hours and conduct an inspection of the school and any records or documents relating thereto, and every person who prevents or obstructs or attempts to prevent or obstruct any such entry or inspection is guilty of an offence and on conviction is liable to a fine of not more than $500.

(7) **Inspection on request.**—The Minister may, on the request of any person operating a private school, provide for inspection of the school in respect of the standard of instruction in the subjects leading to the Ontario secondary school diploma, the secondary school graduation diploma and to the secondary school honour graduation diploma, and may determine and charge a fee for such inspection.

(8) **Inspection of teachers.**—The Minister may, on the request of a person operating a private school or of a person in charge of a conservation authority school or field centre, provide for the inspection of a teacher in such school or centre who requires the recommendation of a supervisory officer for certification purposes.

(8.1) **Agreements re: tests.**—The Minister may enter into agreements with a person operating

(a) a private school;

(b) a school provided by the band, the council of the band or an education authority where the band, the council of the band or the education authority is authorized by the Crown in right of Canada to provide education for Indians; or

(c) a school provided by the Crown in right of Canada, about administering tests to pupils enrolled in the school, marking the tests and reporting the results of the tests.

(8.2) **Same.**—Without limiting the generality of subsection (8.1), an agreement may provide for the charging of fees by the Minister to a person operating a school described in subsection 8(1).

(9) **Offense for false statement.**—Every person who knowingly makes a false statement in a notice of intention to operate a private school or an information return under this section is guilty of an offence and on conviction is liable to a fine of not more than $500.

1996, c. 11, s. 29(2).

17. (1) **Variation of scholarships and awards.**—Where the educational object of a gift or bequest accepted by the Minister of Finance under section 6 of the Financial Administration Act is the establishment of a scholarship or an award that is available to one or more students in an elementary or a secondary school or a teacher training institution and,

(a) the selection of the recipient of the scholarship or award is based upon an examination which is no longer given;

(b) the school or teachers' college at which attendance is required for eligibility is no longer operated;

(c) reference to a county or a board in the terms and conditions of the gift or bequest is no longer appropriate by reason of the establishment of a regional municipality or a district school board; or

(d) the course or program of instruction specified in the terms and conditions is no longer available, or is no longer available at the school or teachers' college,

the Lieutenant Governor in Council on the recommendation of the Minister of Education and Training may, from time to time, vary the terms and conditions of the gift or bequest in respect of the qualifications for eligibility for the scholarship or award so as to ensure that such scholarship or award will be granted or given under such terms and conditions as in the opinion of the Minister most nearly approximate those of the original gift or bequest, and the Minister may delegate his or her powers under the original terms and conditions of such gift or bequest to a representative of the board, or the educational institution, granting the scholarship or making the award, pursuant to any variation in the terms and conditions of the gift or bequest made under this section.

(2) **Where award is repayable loan.**—In the case of an award in the form of a repayable loan for which no person has made application for seven consecutive years, the Lieutenant Governor in Council, on the recommendation of the Minister of Education and Training and with the written consent of the person making the gift or the trustee of the person making the bequest, may capitalize the fund and any interest accrued thereon held by the Minister of Finance, and may change the educational object of the gift or bequest to another object of an educational nature, in which case the provisions of subsection (1) shall apply with necessary modifications.

1997, c. 31, s. 9.

17.1 (1) **Ontario Parent Council.**—The council known in English as the Ontario Parent

Council and in French as Conseil ontarien des parents is continued and shall be composed of not more than eighteen members appointed by the Minister.

(2) **Eligibility for appointment.**—A person is eligible for appointment to the council if the person,

(a) is a parent or guardian of a child enrolled in an elementary or secondary school in Ontario; and

(b) meets the eligibility criteria established under subsection (3).

(3) **Eligibility criteria established by Minister.**—The Minister may establish such eligibility criteria for appointment to the Council as the Minister considers advisable.

(4) **Non-application of *Regulations Act*.**—The *Regulations Act* does not apply to criteria established under subsection (3).

(5) **Term of office.**—Members of the Council shall be appointed for a term of two years and may be reappointed for further terms, except that no person shall be appointed for three or more consecutive terms.

(6) **Same.**—Despite subsection (5), members appointed to the Council before the coming into force of this section are appointed for the term specified in the appointment.

(7) **Chair.**—The Minister shall designate a chair from among the members of the Council.

(8) **Remuneration and expenses.**—The members of the Council shall be paid such remuneration and expenses as are determined by the Lieutenant Governor in Council.

(9) **Staff and accommodation.**—The Ministry shall provide the Council with such staff and accommodation as the Minister considers necessary for the purposes of Council.

(10) **Mandate.**—The Council shall advise the Minister on,

(a) issues related to elementary and secondary school education; and

(b) methods of increasing parental involvement in elementary and secondary school education.

(11) **Annual report.**—The Council shall report on its activities annually to the Minister.

(12) **Additional reports.**—In addition to its annual report, the Council may report to the Minister at any time and shall comply with any requests made by the Minister for additional reports.

1993, c. 41, s. 2.

PART II

SCHOOL ATTENDANCE

18. Definition.—In sections 21, 23, 26, 28 and 30, "guardian", in addition to having the meaning ascribed in section 1, includes any person who has received into his or her home a child of compulsory school age who is not the person's child but resides with the person or is in his or her care.

19. (1) **Closing of school or class by board.**—A board may close or authorize the closing of a school or class for a temporary period where such closing appears unavoidable because of,

PART II — SCHOOL ATTENDANCE   S. 21

   (a) failure of transportation arrangements; or
   (b) inclement weather, fire, flood, the breakdown of the school heating plant, the failure of an essential utility or a similar emergency.

(2) **Same.**—In case of strike by members of a teachers' bargaining unit or a lockout of those members, the board may close one or more schools if it is of the opinion that,
   (a) the safety of pupils may be endangered during the strike or lockout;
   (b) the school building or the equipment or supplies in the building may not be adequately protected during the strike or lockout; or
   (c) the strike or lockout will substantially interfere with the operation of the school.

(3) **Teachers' salary.**—A teacher is not entitled to be paid his or her salary for the days on which the school in which he or she is employed is closed under subsection (2).

(4) **Definition.**—In this section,
"strike" and "lock-out".—"strike" and "lock-out" have the same meaning as in the *Labour Relations Act, 1995*.

                                                              1997, c. 31, s. 10.

20. Closing of schools on civic holiday.—Where the head of the council of a municipality in which a school is situate proclaims a school day as a civic holiday for the municipality, the board may, by resolution, close any of the schools under its jurisdiction on such day.

21. (1) **Compulsory attendance.**—Unless excused under this section,
   (a) every child who attains the age of six years on or before the first school day in September in any year shall attend an elementary or secondary school on every school day from the first school day in September in that year until the child attains the age of sixteen years; and
   (b) every child who attains the age of six years after the first school day in September in any year shall attend an elementary or secondary school on every school day from the first school day in September in the next succeeding year until the last school day in June in the year in which the child attains the age of sixteen years.

(2) **When attendance excused.**—A child is excused from attendance at school if,
   (a) the child is receiving satisfactory instruction at home or elsewhere;
   (b) the child is unable to attend school by reason of sickness or other unavoidable cause;
   (c) transportation is not provided by a board for the child and there is no school that the child has a right to attend situated,
      (i) within 1.6 kilometres from the child's residence measured by the nearest road if the child has not attained the age of seven years on or before the first school day in September in the year in question, or
      (ii) within 3.2 kilometres from the child's residence measured by the nearest road if the child has attained the age of seven years but not the age of ten years on or before the first school day in September in the year in question, or
      (iii) within 4.8 kilometres from the child's residence measured by the nearest road if the child has attained the age of ten years on or before the first school day in September in the year in question;
   (d) the child has obtained a secondary school graduation diploma or has completed a course that gives equivalent standing;

(e) the child is absent from school for the purpose of receiving instruction in music and the period of absence does not exceed one-half day in any week;
(f) the child is suspended, expelled or excluded from attendance at school under any Act or under the regulations;
(g) the child is absent on a day regarded as a holy day by the church or religious denomination to which the child belongs; or
(h) the child is absent or excused as authorized under this Act and the regulations.

(3) **Blind, deaf or mentally handicapped children.**—The fact that a child is blind, deaf or mentally handicapped is not of itself an unavoidable cause under clause (2)(b).

(4) **Child under compulsory age.**—Where a child under compulsory school age has been enrolled as a pupil in an elementary school, this section applies during the period for which the child is enrolled as if the child were of compulsory school age.

(5) **Duty of parent, etc.**—The parent or guardian of a child who is required to attend school under this section shall cause the child to attend school as required by this section.

(6) **Separate School Supporters.**—Nothing in this section requires the child of a Roman Catholic separate school supporter to attend a public school or a Protestant separate school, or requires the child of a public school supporter to attend a Roman Catholic separate school.

22. Where school year varied.—Where a school year approved by the Minister does not commence on the day following Labour Day, references to the first school day in September and the last school day in June in section 21 shall be read as the first school day in the school year and the last school day in the school year respectively for the purpose of compulsory attendance of pupils of the school or schools or parts thereof to which the school year applies.

23. (1) **Suspension of pupil.**—A principal may suspend a pupil because of persistent truancy, persistent opposition to authority, habitual neglect of duty, the wilful destruction of school property, the use of profane or improper language, or conduct injurious to the moral tone of the school or to the physical or mental well-being of others in the school.

(1.1) **Period of suspension.**—A suspension under subsection (1) shall be for a period fixed by the principal, not exceeding twenty school days or such shorter period as may be established by the board as the maximum period for suspensions under subsection (1).

(1.2) **Notice.**—When a pupil is suspended under subsection (1), the principal shall,
(a) notify forthwith in writing the pupil, the pupil's parent or guardian, the pupil's teachers, the board, the appropriate school attendance counselor and the appropriate supervisory officer of the suspension and the reasons for the suspension; and
(b) notify forthwith in writing the pupil and the pupil's parent or guardian of the right of appeal under subsection (2).

(2) **Appeal against suspension.**—The parent or guardian of a pupil who has been suspended or the pupil, where the pupil is an adult, may, within seven days of the commencement of the suspension, appeal to the board against the suspension and the board, after hearing the appeal or where no appeal is made, may remove, confirm or modify the suspension and, where the board considers it appropriate, may order that any record of the suspension be expunged.

(2.1) **Effect of appeal.**—An appeal under subsection (2) does not stay the suspension and, if the suspension expires before the appeal is determined, the board shall determine whether the suspension should be confirmed or whether the record of the suspension should be removed or modified.

(2.2) **Review of suspensions.**—If the pupil is suspended for the maximum period allowed under subsection (1.1) or is suspended more than once during a school year, the board shall ensure that a guidance counselor or other appropriate resource person employed by the board,
- (a) reviews the circumstances of the suspension or suspensions, as the case may be; and
- (b) where appropriate, informs the pupil and, if the pupil is not an adult, the pupil's parent or guardian, of services that are available from the board or elsewhere in the community to assist the pupil.

(3) **Expulsion of pupil.**—A board may expel a pupil from its schools on the ground that the pupil's conduct is so refractory that the pupil's presence is injurious to other pupils or persons, if,
- (a) the principal and the appropriate supervisory officer so recommend;
- (b) the pupil and the pupil's parent or guardian have been notified in writing of,
    - (i) the recommendation of the principal and the supervisory officer, and
    - (ii) the right of the pupil where the pupil is an adult and otherwise of the pupil's parent or guardian to make representations at a hearing to be conducted by the board;
- (c) the teacher or teachers of the pupil have been notified; and
- (d) such hearing has been conducted.

(4) **Parties to hearing.**—The parties to a hearing under this section shall be the parent or guardian of the pupil or the pupil, where the pupil is an adult, the principal of the school that the pupil attends and, in the case of an expulsion, the appropriate supervisory officer.

(5) **Readmission of pupil.**—A board may at its discretion readmit to school a pupil who has been expelled.

(6) **Committee to perform board functions.**—The board, by resolution, may direct that the powers and duties of the board under subsections (2) to (5) shall be exercised and performed by a committee of at least three members of the board named in the resolution or designated from time to time in accordance with the resolution.

1993, c. 11, s. 12.

24. (1) **Provincial School Attendance Counselor.**—The Lieutenant Governor in Council may appoint an officer, to be the Provincial School Attendance Counselor, who shall, under the direction of the Minister, superintend and direct the enforcement of compulsory school attendance.

(2) **Inquiry by Provincial Counselor.**—Where the parent or guardian of a child considers that the child is excused from attendance at school under subsection 21(2), and the appropriate school attendance counselor or the Provincial School Attendance Counselor is of the opinion that the child should not be excused from attendance, the Provincial School Attendance Counselor shall direct that an inquiry be made as to the validity of the reason or excuse for non-attendance and the other relevant circumstances, and for such purpose shall appoint one or more persons who are not employees of the board that operates the school that the child has the right to attend to conduct a hearing and to report to the Provincial School Attendance

Counselor the result of the inquiry and may, by order in writing signed by him or her, direct that the child,

(a) be excused from attendance at school; or
(b) attend school,

and a copy of the order shall be delivered to the board and to the parent or guardian of the child.

(3) **Powers of Provincial Counselor.**—The Provincial School Attendance Counselor has all the powers of a school attendance counselor and may exercise such powers anywhere in Ontario.

25. (1) **Appointment of school attendance counselors.**—Every board shall appoint one or more school attendance counselors.

(2) **Idem.**—Two or more boards may appoint the same school attendance counselor or counselors.

(3) **Vacancies.**—Where the office of a school attendance counselor becomes vacant, it shall be filled forthwith by the board.

(4) **Notice of appointment.**—Notice of the appointment of a school attendance counselor shall be given in writing by the board to the Provincial School Attendance Counselor and to the supervisory officers concerned.

(5) **Jurisdiction and responsibility of school attendance counselor.**—A school attendance counselor appointed by a board has jurisdiction and is responsible for the enforcement of compulsory school attendance in respect of every child who is required to attend school and who,

(a) is qualified to be a resident pupil of the board; or
(b) is or has been enrolled during the current school year in a school operated by the board, except a child who is under the jurisdiction of a person appointed under section 119 of the Indian Act (Canada).

26. (1) **Powers of counselors.**—Where a school attendance counselor has reasonable and probable grounds for believing that a child is illegally absent from school, he or she may, at the written request of the parent or guardian of the child or of the principal of the school that the child is required to attend, take the child to the child's parent or guardian or to the school from which the child is absent provided that, if exception is taken to the school attendance counselor entering a dwelling place, he or she shall not enter therein.

(2) **Reports.**—A school attendance counselor shall report to the board that appointed him or her as required by the board.

(3) **To act under appropriate supervisory officer and provincial counselor.**—A school attendance counselor is responsible to the appropriate supervisory officer, and shall carry out the instructions and directions of the Provincial School Attendance Counselor.

(4) **Inquiry by counselor and notice.**—A school attendance counselor shall inquire into every case of failure to attend school within his or her knowledge or when requested so to do by the appropriate supervisory officer or the principal of a school or a ratepayer, and shall give written warning of the consequences of such failure to the parent or guardian of a child who is not attending school as required, and shall also give written notice to the parent or guardian to

cause the child to attend school forthwith, and shall advise the parent or guardian in writing of the provisions of subsection 24 (2).

27. Census.—A board may make or obtain a complete census of all persons in the area in which the board has jurisdiction who have not attained the age of twenty-one years.

28. (1) Reports and information.—The principal of every elementary and secondary school shall,

(a) report to the appropriate school attendance counselor and supervisory officer the names, ages and residences of all pupils of compulsory school age who have not attended school as required;

(b) furnish the school attendance counselor with such other information as the counselor requires for the enforcement of compulsory school attendance; and

(c) report in writing to the school attendance counselor every case of expulsion and readmission of a pupil.

(2) **Where no school attendance counselor.**—Where a child of compulsory school age has not attended school as required and there is no school attendance counselor having jurisdiction in respect of the child, the appropriate supervisory officer shall notify the parent or guardian of the child of the requirements of section 21.

29. Provincial counselor as trustee.—Where it appears to the Minister that the board of a district school area is not providing accommodation or instruction for its resident pupils either in schools operated by the board or under an agreement with another board in schools operated by such other board, or has in other respects failed to comply with this Act and the regulations, or that the election of members of the board has been neglected and no regular board is in existence, the Minister may authorize and direct the Provincial School Attendance Counselor to do all things and exercise all powers that may be necessary for the provision and maintenance of accommodation and instruction for the resident pupils of the board including the erection of school buildings and the conduct of schools, and generally whatever may be required for the purpose of establishing, maintaining and conducting schools in accordance with this Act and the regulations, and thereupon the Provincial School Attendance Counselor has, for such period as authorized by the Minister, all the authority and powers vested in, and may, during such period, perform the duties of, the board.

1997, c. 31, s. 11.

30. (1) Liability of parent or guardian.—A parent or guardian of a child of compulsory school age who neglects or refuses to cause the child to attend school is, unless the child is legally excused from attendance, guilty of an offence and on conviction is liable to a fine of not more than $200.

(2) **Bond for attendance.**—The court may, in addition to or instead of imposing a fine, require a person convicted of an offence under subsection (1) to submit to the Minister of Finance a personal bond, in a form prescribed by the court, in the penal sum of $200 with one or more sureties as required, conditioned that the person shall cause the child to attend school as required by this Part, and upon breach of the condition the bond is forfeit to the Crown.

(3) **Employment during school hours.**—A person who employs during school hours a child who is required to attend school under section 21 is guilty of an offence and on conviction is liable to a fine of not more than $200.

(4) **Offences by corporations.**—Subsections (1) and (3) apply with necessary modifications to a corporation and, in addition, every director and officer of the corporation who authorizes, permits or acquiesces in the contravention is guilty of an offence and on conviction is liable to the same penalty as the corporation.

(5) **Habitually absent from school.**—A child who is required by law to attend school and who refuses to attend or who is habitually absent from school is guilty of an offence and on conviction is liable to the penalties under Part VI of the Provincial Offences Act and subsection 266 (2) of this Act applies in any proceeding under this section.

(6) **Proceedings under subs. (5).**—Proceedings in respect of offences under subsection (5) shall be proceeded with only in accordance with such subsection.

(7) **Reference to provincial counselor for inquiry.**—Where, in a proceeding under this section, it appears to the court that the child may have been excused from attendance at school under subsection 21(2), the court may refer the matter to the Provincial School Attendance Counselor who shall direct that an inquiry shall be made as provided in subsection 24(2) which subsection shall apply with necessary modifications except that the Provincial School Attendance Counselor shall, in lieu of making an order, submit a report to the court.

1997, c. 31, s. 12.

31. (1) **Proceedings to be taken by attendance counselors.**—Prosecutions under section 30 shall be instituted by the school attendance counselor concerned.

(2) **Certificate of principal as proof in the absence of evidence to the contrary.**—In prosecutions under section 30, a certificate as to the attendance or non-attendance at school of any child, signed or purporting to be signed by the principal of the school, is proof in the absence of evidence to the contrary of the facts stated therein without any proof of the signature or appointment of the principal.

(3) **Proof of age.**—Where a person is charged under section 30 in respect of a child who is alleged to be of compulsory school age and the child appears to the court to be of compulsory school age, the child shall, for the purposes of such prosecution, be deemed to be of compulsory school age unless the contrary is proved.

(4) **Order re school attendance.**—An order made under subsection 24(2) shall be admitted in evidence in a prosecution only where the prosecution is in respect of the school year for which the order was made.

1993, c. 27, Sch.

32. (1) **Resident pupil right to attend school.**—A person has the right, without payment of a fee, to attend a school in a school section, separate school zone or secondary school district, as the case may be, in which the person is qualified to be a resident pupil.

(2) **Admission without fee.**—Despite the other provisions of this Part, but subject to subsection 49 (6), where it appears to a board that a person who resides in the area of jurisdiction of the board is denied the right to attend school without the payment of a fee, the board, at its discretion, may admit the person from year to year without the payment of a fee.

1997, c. 31, s. 13.

33. (1) **Resident pupil qualification: elementary English-language public district school boards and elementary public school authorities.**—Subject to sections 44 and 46, a person who attains the age of six years in any year is, after September 1 in that year, qualified to be a resident pupil in respect of a school section of an English-language public district school board or of a public school authority until the last school day in June in the year in which the person attains the age of 21 years if,

(a) the person resides in the school section; and
(b) the person's parent or guardian who is not a separate school supporter or a French-language district school board supporter resides in the school section.

(2) Resident pupil qualification: elementary French-language public district school boards.—Subject to sections 44 and 46, a person who attains the age of six years in any year is, after September 1 in that year, qualified to be a resident pupil in respect of a school section of a French-language public district school board until the last school day in June in the year in which he or she attains the age of 21 years if,

(a) the person is a French-speaking person;
(b) the person resides in the school section; and
(c) the person's parent or guardian resides in the school section and,
  (i) is a supporter of the French-language public district school board, or
  (ii) is not in respect of that residence a supporter of any board.

(3) Resident pupil qualification: elementary English-language separate district school boards and elementary Roman Catholic school authorities.—Subject to sections 44 and 46, a person who attains the age of six years in any year is, after September 1 in that year, qualified to be a resident pupil in respect of a separate school zone of an English-language separate district school board or of a Roman Catholic school authority for elementary school purposes until the last school day in June in the year in which he or she attains the age of 21 years if,

(a) the person resides in the separate school zone; and
(b) the person's parent or guardian who is a separate school supporter and who is not a French-language separate district school board supporter resides in the separate school zone.

(4) Resident pupil qualification: elementary French-language separate district school boards.—Subject to sections 44 and 46, a person who attains the age of six years in any year is, after September 1 in that year, qualified to be a resident pupil in respect of a separate school zone of a French-language separate district school board for elementary school purposes until the last school day in June in the year in which he or she attains the age of 21 years if,

(a) the person is a French-speaking person;
(b) the person resides in the separate school zone; and
(c) the person's parent or guardian who is a French-language separate district school board supporter resides in the separate school zone.

(5) Evidence as to right to attend.—It is the responsibility of the parent or guardian to submit evidence that the child has a right to attend an elementary school, including proof of age.

(6) Resident pupil, elementary.—A person who is qualified to be a resident pupil in respect of a school section or a separate school zone is a resident pupil if the person enrols in an elementary school operated by the board of the school section or separate school zone, as the case may be, or in a school operated by another board,

(a) to which the board of the school section or separate school zone pays fees on the person's behalf; or

(b) with which the board of the school section or separate school zone has an agreement relating to the provision of education to the person.

1997, c. 31, s. 14.

34. (1) **Kindergarten.**—If a board operates a kindergarten in a school, a child who is otherwise qualified may become a resident pupil at an age one year lower than that referred to in section 33.

(2) **Junior kindergarten.**—If a board operates a junior kindergarten in a school, a child who is otherwise qualified may become a resident pupil at an age two years lower than that referred to in section 33.

(3) **Beginners class.**—A board may provide a class or classes for children to enter school for the first time on or after the first school day in January and, where the board so provides, a child whose birthday is on or after January 1 and before July 1, who resides in an area determined by the board and who is eligible to be admitted to an elementary school or kindergarten, as the case may be, on the first school day in the following September, may become a resident pupil in respect of such class.

1993, c. 11, s. 14; 1996, c. 13, ss. 2, 12; 1997, c. 31, s. 15.

35. (1) **Resident pupil's right to attend more accessible elementary school.**—Where a resident pupil who is an elementary school pupil of a school section or separate school zone resides,

(a) more than 3.2 kilometres by the shortest distance by road from the school that the pupil is required to attend;

(b) more than 0.8 kilometres by the shortest distance by road from any point from which transportation is provided to the school that the pupil is required to attend; and

(c) nearer by the shortest distance by road to another school of the same type that is in another section or zone than to the school that the pupil is required to attend,

the pupil shall be admitted to the nearer school of the same type, where the appropriate supervisory officer for the nearer school certifies that there is sufficient accommodation for the pupil in that school.

(2) **Same.**—Where the pupil is admitted to a nearer school, the board of the school section or separate school zone of which the pupil is a resident pupil shall pay in respect of the pupil the fee, if any, payable for the purpose under the regulations.

(3) **Same.**—For the purposes of this section, the following are types of schools:

1. English-language public schools, which are schools governed by an English-language public district school board or a public school authority.
2. French-language public schools, which are schools governed by a French-language public district school board.
3. English-language Roman Catholic schools, which are schools governed by an English-language separate district school board or a Roman Catholic school authority.

4. French-language Roman Catholic schools, which are schools governed by a French-language separate district school board.

1993, c. 11, s. 15; 1997, c. 31, s. 16.

36. (1) **Resident pupil qualification: secondary English-language public district school boards and secondary public school authorities.**—A person is qualified to be a resident pupil in respect of a secondary school district of an English-language public district school board or of a public school authority if,
- (a) the person and the person's parent or guardian who is not a separate school supporter or a French-language district school board supporter reside in the secondary school district;
- (b) the person is an English-language public board supporter and resides in the secondary school district and is an owner or tenant of residential property in the secondary school district that is separately assessed; or
- (c) the person is not a supporter of any board, is over 18 years of age and has resided in the secondary school district for the 12 months immediately before the person's admission to a secondary school in the secondary school district or to a secondary school operated by another board,
    - (i) to which the board of the secondary school district pays fees on the person's behalf, or
    - (ii) with which the board of the secondary school district has an agreement relating to the provision of education to the person.

(2) **Resident pupil qualification: secondary French-language public district school boards.**—A person is qualified to be a resident pupil in respect of a secondary school district of a French-language public district school board if,
- (a) the person is a French-speaking person, the person and the person's parent or guardian reside in the secondary school district and,
    - (i) the person's parent or guardian is a supporter of the French-language public district school board, or
    - (ii) the person's parent or guardian is not in respect of that residence a supporter of any board;
- (b) the person is a French-language public district school board supporter and resides in the secondary school district and is an owner or tenant of residential property in the secondary school district that is separately assessed; or
- (c) the person is a French-speaking person, is not a supporter of any board, is over 18 years of age and has resided in the secondary school district for the 12 months immediately before the person's admission to a secondary school in the secondary school district or to a secondary school operated by another board,
    - (i) to which the board of the secondary school district pays fees on the person's behalf, or
    - (ii) with which the board of the secondary school district has an agreement relating to the provision of education to the person.

(3) **Resident pupil qualification: secondary English-language separate district school boards.**—A person is qualified to be a resident pupil in respect of a separate school zone of an English-language separate district school board for secondary school purposes if,

(a) the person and the person's parent or guardian who is a separate school supporter and is not a French-language district school board supporter reside in the separate school zone;
(b) the person is a separate school supporter and is not a French-language district school board supporter and resides in the separate school zone and is an owner or tenant of residential property in the zone that is separately assessed; or
(c) the person is a Roman Catholic, is not a supporter of any board, is over 18 years of age and has resided in the separate school zone for the 12 months immediately before the person's admission to a secondary school in the separate school zone or to a secondary school operated by another board,
  (i) to which the board of the separate school zone pays fees on the person's behalf, or
  (ii) with which the board of the separate school zone has an agreement relating to the provision of education to the person.

(4) **Resident pupil qualification: secondary French-language separate district school boards.**—A person is qualified to be a resident pupil in respect of a separate school zone of a French-language separate district school board for secondary school purposes if,
(a) the person and the person's parent or guardian who is a French-language separate district school board supporter reside in the separate school zone;
(b) the person is a French-language separate district school board supporter and resides in the separate school zone and is an owner or tenant of residential property in the zone that is separately assessed; or
(c) the person is a French-speaking person and a Roman Catholic, is not a supporter of any board, is over 18 years of age and has resided in the separate school zone for the 12 months immediately before the person's admission to a secondary school in the separate school zone or to a secondary school operated by another board,
  (i) to which the board of the separate school zone pays fees on the person's behalf, or
  (ii) with which the board of the separate school zone has an agreement relating to the provision of education to the person.

(5) **Resident pupil, secondary.**—A person who is qualified to be a resident pupil in respect of a secondary school district or a separate school zone is a resident pupil if the person enrols in a secondary school operated by the board of the secondary school district or separate school zone, as the case may be, or in a secondary school operated by another board,
(a) to which the board of the secondary school district or separate school zone pays fees on the person's behalf; or
(b) with which the board of the secondary school district or separate school zone has an agreement relating to the provision of education to the person.

(6) **Certain elementary-only school authorities.**—Subject to subsection (7), where a person is qualified to be a resident pupil of a school authority, other than a public school authority, that provides elementary education only, and the area of jurisdiction of the school authority is the same in whole or in part as the area of jurisdiction of a public district school board, the pupil shall be admitted to a secondary school operated by the public district school board or to a secondary school operated by another board,

PART II — SCHOOL ATTENDANCE   S. 39

(a) to which the first-mentioned district school board pays fees on the person's behalf; or
(b) with which the first-mentioned district school board has an agreement relating to the provision of education to the person.

(7) **French-speaking persons.**—Only a French-speaking person may be admitted to a school of a French-language public district school board under subsection (6).

(8) **Evidence as to right to attend.**—It is the responsibility of the person or the person's parent or guardian to submit evidence that the person has a right to attend a secondary school.

1993, c. 11, s. 16; 1997, c. 31, s. 17.

37. (1) **Admission of adult resident who is not a resident pupil.**—Despite the provisions of this or any other Act, but subject to section 49.2, a person who resides in one secondary school district or separate school zone and who, except as to residence, is qualified to be a resident pupil at a secondary school in another secondary school district or in another separate school zone, as the case may be, shall be admitted, without the payment of a fee, to a secondary school of the same type that is in the other secondary school district or separate school zone operated by the board of the secondary school district or separate school zone, as the case may be, in which the person resides if,

(a) the person has attained the age of 18 years and has been promoted or transferred to a secondary school; and
(b) the appropriate supervisory officer certifies that there is adequate accommodation in the secondary school.

(2) **Types of schools.**—For the purposes of subsection (1), the following are types of schools:

1. English-language public schools, which are schools governed by an English-language public district school board or a public school authority.
2. French-language public schools, which are schools governed by a French-language public district school board.
3. English-language Roman Catholic schools, which are schools governed by an English-language separate district school board.
4. French-language Roman Catholic schools, which are schools governed by a French-language separate district school board.

1997, c. 31, s. 18.

38. Limitation on right to attend without payment of fee.—Despite section 32, where a pupil,

(a) has completed elementary school; and
(b) has attended one or more secondary schools for a total of seven or more years,

the board of the secondary school that the pupil attends may charge the fee, if any, payable for the purpose under the regulations.

1997, c. 31, s. 18.

39. (1) **Resident pupil's right to attend secondary school in another district or zone.**—Subject to subsections (2) to (4), a person who is qualified to be a resident pupil at a secondary school in a secondary school district or a separate school zone has the right to attend any secondary school of the same type,

(a) that is more accessible to the person than any secondary school in the secondary school district of which the person is qualified to be a resident pupil; or

(b) for a purpose specified in subsection 49.2 (6).

(2) **Types of schools.**—For the purposes of subsection (1), the types of schools are as set out in subsection 37(2).

(3) **Restrictions.**—Subsection (1) applies where the appropriate supervisory officer certifies that there is adequate accommodation for the person in the school.

(4) **Where agreement between boards.**—Clause (1) (b) does not apply where the board of which the person is qualified to be a resident pupil has entered into an agreement with another board to provide the relevant subjects.

1997, c. 31, s. 18.

40. (1) **Admission to secondary school of resident pupil from other district or zone.**—A person who is qualified to be a resident pupil at a secondary school in a secondary school district or separate school zone and who applies for admission to a secondary school of the same type situated in another secondary school district or separate school zone, as the case may be, shall furnish the principal of the school to which admission is sought with a statement signed by the person's parent or guardian or by the pupil where the pupil is an adult, stating,

(a) the name of the secondary school district or separate school zone in respect of which the person is qualified to be a resident pupil;

(b) whether or not the pupil or the pupil's parent or guardian is assessed in the secondary school district or separate school zone in which the school referred to in clause (a) is situated, and if so assessed the amount of the assessment; and

(c) the authority, under this Act, under which the pupil claims to have a right to attend the school to which admission is sought.

(2) **Same.**—For the purposes of subsection (1), the types of schools are as set out in subsection 37 (2).

(3) **Notice of admission.**—The principal of the school to which admission is sought shall forward the statement to the chief executive officer of the board that operates the school and, if the pupil is admitted, the chief executive officer of the board shall promptly notify the chief executive officer of the board of the secondary school district or separate school zone, as the case may be, of which the pupil is qualified to be a resident pupil of the fact of the admission and of the information included in the statement.

(4) **Same.**—Where the board that operates the school to which admission is sought has no chief executive officer, the notice required by subsection (3) shall be sent to the secretary of the board.

1993, c. 11, s. 17; 1996, c. 13, s. 3; 1997, c. 31, s. 19.

41. (1) **Admission to secondary school.**—Where a pupil has been promoted from elementary school, the pupil shall be admitted to secondary school.

(2) **Same.**—A person who has not been promoted from elementary school shall be admitted to a secondary school if the principal of the secondary school is satisfied that the applicant is competent to undertake the work of the school.

(3) **Where admission denied.**—Where an applicant for admission to a secondary school under subsection (2) is denied admission by the principal, the applicant may appeal to the board

and the board may, after a hearing, direct that the applicant be admitted or refused admission to a secondary school.

(4) **Committee to perform board functions.**—The board, by resolution, may direct that the powers and duties of the board under subsection (3) shall be exercised and performed by a committee of at least three members of the board named in the resolution or designated from time to time in accordance with the resolution.

(5) **Alternative course or program.**—Where the pupil has clearly demonstrated to the principal that the pupil is not competent to undertake a particular course or program of studies, the principal shall not permit the pupil to undertake the course or program, in which case the pupil may take a prerequisite course, or select with the approval of the principal an appropriate alternative course or program provided that, where the pupil is a minor, the consent of the pupil's parent or guardian has been obtained.

(6) **Admission to continuing education class.**—A person is entitled to enrol in a continuing education course or class that is acceptable for credit towards a secondary school diploma if the principal is satisfied that the person is competent to undertake the work of the course or class.

1997, c. 31, s. 20.

42. (1) Secondary school instruction: movement from English-language public board to English-language Roman Catholic board.—A person who is qualified to be a resident pupil of an English-language public board and to receive instruction in a secondary school grade is entitled to receive instruction provided in a secondary school operated by an English-language Roman Catholic board if the area of jurisdiction of the public board is in whole or in part the same as the area of jurisdiction of the Roman Catholic board.

(2) **Secondary school instruction: movement from French-language public district school board to French-language separate district school board.**—A person who is qualified to be a resident pupil of a French-language public district school board and to receive instruction in a secondary school grade is entitled to receive instruction provided in a secondary school operated by a French-language separate district school board if the area of jurisdiction of the public district school board is in whole or in part the same as the area of jurisdiction of the separate district school board.

(3) **Secondary school instruction: movement from English-language Roman Catholic board to English-language public board.**—A person who is qualified to be a resident pupil of an English-language Roman Catholic board and to receive instruction in a secondary school grade is entitled to receive instruction provided in a secondary school operated by an English-language public board if the area of jurisdiction of the Roman Catholic board is in whole or in part the same as the area of jurisdiction of the public board.

(4) **Secondary school instruction: movement from French-language separate district school board to French-language public district school board.**—A person who is qualified to be a resident pupil of a French-language separate district school board and to receive instruction in a secondary school grade is entitled to receive instruction provided in a secondary school operated by a French-language public district school board if the area of jurisdiction of the separate district school board is in whole or in part the same as the area of jurisdiction of the public district school board.

(5) **Secondary school instruction: movement from French-language separate district school board to English-language public board.**—A person who is qualified to be a resident pupil of a French-language separate district school board and to receive instruction in a secondary school grade is entitled to receive instruction provided in a secondary school operated by an English-language public board if the area of jurisdiction of the French-language board is in whole or in part the same as the area of jurisdiction of the English-language board.

(6) **Secondary school instruction: movement from English-language public board to French-language separate district school board.**—A French-speaking person who is qualified to be a resident pupil of an English-language public board and to receive instruction in a secondary school grade is entitled to receive instruction provided in a secondary school operated by a French-language separate district school board if the area of jurisdiction of the English-language board is in whole or in part the same as the area of jurisdiction of the French-language board.

(7) **Secondary school instruction: movement from French-language public district school board to English-language separate district school board.**—A French-speaking person who is qualified to be a resident pupil of a French-language public district school board and to receive instruction in a secondary school grade is entitled to receive instruction provided in a secondary school operated by an English-language separate district school board if the area of jurisdiction of the French-language board is in whole or in part the same as the area of jurisdiction of the English-language board.

(8) **Secondary school instruction: movement from English-language separate district school board to French-language public district school board.**—A French-speaking person who is qualified to be a resident pupil of an English-language separate district school board and to receive instruction in a secondary school grade is entitled to receive instruction provided in a secondary school operated by a French-language public district school board if the area of jurisdiction of the English-language board is in whole or in part the same as the area of jurisdiction of the French-language board.

(9) **Fee.**—The board of which the person is qualified to be a resident pupil shall pay the fee, if any, to which the other board is entitled for providing secondary school education under this section.

(10) **Amount.**—The fee to which a board is entitled under this section is the fee, if any, payable for the purpose under the regulations or such lesser amount as may be set by the board.

(11) **Exemption from religious studies.**—On written application, a Roman Catholic board shall exempt a person who is qualified to be a resident pupil in respect of a secondary school operated by a public board from programs and courses of study in religious education if,

(a) the person is enrolled in a program that is not otherwise available to the person in a secondary school operated by a public board within the area of jurisdiction of the Roman Catholic board; or

(b) it is impractical by reason of distance or terrain or by reason of physical handicap, mental handicap or multi-handicap for the person to attend a secondary school operated by a public board.

(12) **Same.**—A person who is qualified to be a resident pupil in respect of a secondary school operated by a public board who attends a secondary school operated by a Roman Catholic

board for a reason other than the one mentioned in clause (11)(a) or (b) is considered to have enrolled in all of the school's programs and courses of study in religious education.

(13) **Additional exemptions.**—In addition to the exemptions provided for in subsection (11), no person who is qualified to be a resident pupil in respect of a secondary school operated by a public board who attends a secondary school operated by a Roman Catholic board shall be required to take part in any program or course of study in religious education where a parent or guardian of the person, or the person where the person is an adult, applies in writing to the Roman Catholic board for exemption of the person from taking part.

1997, c. 31, s. 20.

43. (1) **Movement from English-language public board to French-language public district school board.**—A French-speaking person who is qualified to be a resident pupil of an English-language public board is entitled to receive instruction provided by a French-language public district school board if the area of jurisdiction of the English-language board is in whole or in part the same as the area of jurisdiction of the French-language board.

(2) **Movement from French-language public district school board to English-language public board.**—A person who is qualified to be a resident pupil of a French-language public district school board is entitled to receive instruction provided by an English-language public board if the area of jurisdiction of the French-language board is in whole or in part the same as the area of jurisdiction of the English-language board.

(3) **Movement from English-language Roman Catholic board to French-language separate district school board.**—A French-speaking person who is qualified to be a resident pupil of an English-language Roman Catholic board is entitled to receive instruction provided by a French-language separate district school board if the area of jurisdiction of the English-language board is in whole or in part the same as the area of jurisdiction of the French-language board.

(4) **Movement from French-language separate district school board to English-language Roman Catholic board.**—A person who is qualified to be a resident pupil of a French-language separate district school board is entitled to receive instruction provided by an English-language Roman Catholic board if the area of jurisdiction of the French-language board is in whole or in part the same as the area of jurisdiction of the English-language board.

(5) **Fee.**—The board of which the person is qualified to be a resident pupil shall pay the fee, if any, to which the other board is entitled for providing education under this section.

(6) **Amount.**—The fee to which a board is entitled under this section is the fee, if any, payable for the purpose under the regulations or such lesser amount as may be set by the board.

1993, c. 11, s. 18; 1997, c. 31, s. 21.

43.1 (1) **Regulations: supporter non-resident attendance rights.**—The Lieutenant Governor in Council may make regulations governing the rights of a person to attend a school operated by a board where the person does not reside in the area of jurisdiction of the board but the person or the person's parent or guardian owns property assessed for school purposes in the board's area of jurisdiction.

(2) **General or particular.**—A regulation made under subsection (1) may be general or particular.

(3) **Right to continue to attend in certain circumstances.**—A pupil who, on December 31, 1997, is enrolled in a school that he or she has the right to attend under clause 33(1)(b), 33(2)(b) or 40(1)(b) of this Act, as it read on December 31, 1997 and who on January 1, 1998, because of the repeal of those clauses, no longer has the right to attend school under any other provision of this Part, has the right to continue to attend the school so long as the pupil, or the pupil's parent or guardian, continues to be the owner of the property or the owner or the tenant of the business property in respect of which the pupil acquired the attendance right.

(4) **Exception.**—A right under subsection (1) is extinguished if,
  (a) in connection with a transfer of a school under clause 58.1(2)(p), a school that was a French-language instructional unit becomes a school of an English-language district school board;
  (b) in connection with a transfer of a school under clause 58.1(2)(p), a school that was not a French-language instructional unit becomes a school of a French-language district school board; or
  (c) the school becomes another type of school within the meaning of subsection 37(2).

1997, c. 31, s. 21.

43.2 (1) **Regulations: non-supporter resident — attendance rights based on business property.**—The Lieutenant Governor in Council may make regulations governing the rights of a person to attend a school operated by a board where,
  (a) the person and the person's parent or guardian reside in the area of jurisdiction of the board;
  (b) the person and the person's parent or guardian are not a supporter of any board the area of jurisdiction of which includes the residence of the person or of the person's parent or guardian; and
  (c) the person or the person's parent or guardian is the owner or tenant of business property in the area of jurisdiction of the board.

(2) **General or particular.**—A regulation made under this section may be general or particular.

1997, c. 31, s. 21.

44. Admission where pupil moves into residence not assessed in accordance with his or her school support.—Where a child who would otherwise have the right to attend school in a school section, separate school zone or secondary school district moves with his or her parent or guardian to a residence the assessment of which does not support that right, and the latest date on which the assessment of the residence may be changed has passed, on the filing of a notice of change of support for the following year with the appropriate assessment commissioner, the child shall be admitted, without the payment of a fee, to a school that will be supported by the taxes on the assessment of the residence on the effective date of the change of school support.

1997, c. 31, s. 22.

45. (1) **Admission where one parent is sole support.**—Subject to subsection (2), where, for any reason, one parent of a person is the sole support of the person, and that parent,
  (a) resides in a residence in Ontario that is not assessed for the purposes of any board; and

(b) boards the person in a residence that is not a children's residence as defined in Part IX (Licensing) of the *Child and Family Services Act*,

the person shall, if otherwise qualified to be a resident pupil, be deemed to be qualified to be a resident pupil in respect of,

- (c) a school section, if the residence is situate in the school section and the taxes on its assessment are directed to the support of public schools;
- (d) a separate school zone, if the person is a Roman Catholic and the residence is situate in the separate school zone and the taxes on its assessment are directed to the support of separate schools; or
- (e) a secondary school district, if the residence is situate in the secondary school district and the taxes on its assessment are directed to the support of public schools.

(2) **Exception: French-language rights.**—No person has the right under subsection (1) to attend a French-language instructional unit operated by a board unless the person is a French-speaking person.

1997, c. 31, s. 22.

46. (1) **Tax exempt land.**—A person who resides in a school section, separate school zone or secondary school district in which the person's parent or guardian resides, on land that is exempt from taxation for the purposes of any board, is not qualified to be a resident pupil of the school section, separate school zone or secondary school district, unless the person or his or her parent or guardian is assessed with respect to other property for the purposes of a board in the school section, separate school zone or secondary school district.

(2) **Resident on land exempt from taxation.**—Subject to subsection (3), a person whose education is not otherwise provided for and who is otherwise qualified to attend an elementary or secondary school and who resides on land that is exempt from taxation for the purposes of any board shall be admitted to a school that is accessible to the person where the appropriate supervisory officer has certified that there is sufficient accommodation for the person in the school for the current year.

(3) **Fee.**—The fee, if any, that is payable under the regulations in respect of a person's attendance under subsection (2) shall, except where the regulations provide otherwise in respect of such fees, be prepaid monthly by the person or by his or her parent or guardian.

1997, c. 31, s. 22.

46.1 (1) **Residence on defence property.**—In this section, "defence property" means the prescribed lands and premises of defence establishments belonging to Canada.

(2) **Entitlement.**—Despite section 46, a person who resides with his or her parent or guardian on defence property in a prescribed municipality is entitled to attend an elementary school or a secondary school, as the case requires, in accordance with this section without payment of a fee.

(3) **Same.**—A person who resides with his or her parent or guardian on defence property in a prescribed municipality,

- (a) whose parent or guardian is a Roman Catholic and a French-language rights holder, is entitled to attend a school operated by any district school board that has jurisdiction in the prescribed municipality;
- (b) whose parent or guardian is a French-language rights holder but not a Roman Cath-

olic, is entitled to attend a school operated by a public district school board that has jurisdiction in the prescribed municipality;

(c) whose parent or guardian is a Roman Catholic but not a French-language rights holder is entitled to attend a school that is operated by an English-language district school board that has jurisdiction in the prescribed municipality;

(d) in all cases other than those referred to in clauses (a), (b) and (c), is entitled to attend a school that is operated by an English-language public district school board that has jurisdiction in the prescribed municipality.

(4) **Regulations.**—The Lieutenant Governor in Council may make regulations respecting any matter that is referred to in this section as prescribed.

(5) **Retroactive.**—A regulation is, if it so provides, effective with respect to a period before it is filed.

1997, c. 31, c. 22.

47. (1) **Admission of ward, etc., of children's aid society or training school to an elementary school.**—A child who is a ward of a children's aid society, is in the care of a children's aid society or is a ward of a training school, and who is otherwise qualified to be admitted to an elementary school, shall be admitted without the payment of a fee to an elementary school operated by the board of the school section or separate school zone, as the case may be, in which the child resides.

(2) **Admission of ward, etc., of children's aid society or training school to a secondary school.**—A child who is a ward of a children's aid society, is in the care of a children's aid society or is a ward of a training school, and who is otherwise qualified to be admitted to a secondary school, shall be admitted without the payment of a fee to a secondary school operated by the board of the secondary school district or separate school zone, as the case may be, in which the child resides.

1997, c. 31, s. 22.

48. (1) **Child in custody of corporation or society.**—Subject to subsection (2), where a child who is in the custody of a corporation or society does not have the right under the other provisions of this Part to attend the school that the corporation or society elects that the child attend, and the appropriate supervisory officer certifies that there is sufficient accommodation in the school for the current school year, the board that operates the school shall, where the child is otherwise qualified to attend such school, admit the child to the school.

(2) **Fee.**—The fees, if any, that are payable under the regulations in respect of a child's attendance under subsection (1) shall, except where the regulations provide otherwise in respect of the fees, be prepaid monthly by the corporation or society.

1993, c. 11, s. 19; 1997, c. 31, s. 23.

48.1 (1) **Right to continue attending a school: London-Middlesex Act, 1992.**—If, on December 31, 1997, a pupil is enrolled in a school that the pupil has a right to attend under the London-Middlesex Act, 1992, as that Act and the regulations made under it read immediately before the Education Quality Improvement Act, 1997 received Royal Assent, the pupil has the same right to continue to attend the school after January 1, 1998 as before January 1, 1998.

(2) **Transportation.**—A pupil who attends a school by virtue of a right under subsection (1) has the same right to transportation to attend the school after January 1, 1998 as before January 1, 1998.

(3) **Right to continue 1989/90 change in boundaries.**—If, on December 31, 1989, a pupil was enrolled in a school that the pupil had a right to attend and on January 1, 1990 the pupil, because of alterations to school board boundaries, no longer had a right to attend the school under any other provision of this Part, the pupil has the same right to continue to attend the school after January 1, 1990 as before January 1, 1990.

(4) **Exception.**—A right under this section is extinguished if,

(a) in connection with a transfer of a school under clause 58.1(2)(p), a school that was a French-language instructional unit becomes school of an English-language district school board;

(b) in connection with a transfer of a school under clause 58.1(2)(p), a school that was not a French-language instructional unit becomes a school of a French-language district school board; or

(c) the school becomes another type of school within the meaning of subsection 37(2).

(5) **Agreement re transportation.**—The board of which a pupil referred to in subsection (1) or (3) is qualified to be a resident pupil may enter into an agreement with the board that operates the school, referred to in subsection (1) or (3), in respect of the transportation of the pupil to and from the school.

1997, c. 31, s. 23.

49. (1) **Fee payable.**—Where a person qualified to be a resident pupil of a secondary school district or separate school zone attends a secondary school that the person has a right to attend under subsection 39 (1), the board of which the person is qualified to be a resident pupil shall pay to the board that operates the secondary school attended by the pupil the fee, if any, payable for the purpose under the regulations.

(2) **Same.**—Where a person qualified to be a resident pupil of a board attends a public or secondary school in the area of jurisdiction of another board under section 48.1, the board of which the person is qualified to be a resident pupil shall pay to the board that operates the school attended by the pupil the fee, if any, payable for the purpose under the regulations.

(3) [Repealed, 1997, c. 31, s. 24.]

(4) **Admission of resident pupil to another school by reason of distance to school.**—A child who resides with his or her parent or guardian in a residence that is assessed to the support of public schools and who may be excused from attendance under clause 21(2)(c) may be admitted to a public school in another school section if the appropriate supervisory officer certifies that there is sufficient accommodation for the child, and the board of the section in which the child resides shall pay to the board of the other school section the fee, if any, payable for the purpose under the regulations.

(5) **Admission of qualified non-resident pupil.**—A board may admit to a school that it operates a person whose admission with or without the payment of a fee is not otherwise provided for in this Act but who, except as to residence, is qualified to attend such school, and

may, at its discretion, require the payment by or on behalf of the person of the fee, if any, payable for the purpose under the regulations.

(6) **Fees for pupils.**—Despite any other provision of this Part, if a board admits to a school that it operates a person who is a visitor within the meaning of the Immigration Act (Canada) or a person who is in possession of a student authorization issued under that Act, the board shall charge the person the maximum fee calculated in accordance with the regulations.

(7) **Application of subs. (6).**—Subsection (6) does not apply to,

(a) a person who is a participant in an educational exchange program under which a pupil of the board attends a school outside Canada without a fee;

(b) a person who enrolled in an elementary school or a secondary school prior to the 1st day of July, 1982;

(c) a person who is a dependant within the meaning of the Visiting Forces Act (Canada);

(d) a person who is in Canada under a diplomatic, consular or official acceptance issued by the Department of External Affairs;

(e) a person who claims to be or is found to be a convention refugee under the Immigration Act (Canada);

(f) a person who is in Canada while the person's parent or other person who has lawful custody of the person is in Canada,

(i) pursuant to employment authorization or ministerial permit issued by the Department of Employment and Immigration,

(ii) under a diplomatic, consular or official acceptance issued by the Department of External Affairs,

(iii) awaiting determination of a claim to be found a convention refugee under the Immigration Act (Canada),

(iv) as a graduate student who is the recipient of an award approved by the Minister for the purposes of this clause and who is in attendance at a university or institution in Ontario, including its affiliated or federated institutions, that receives operating grants from the Ministry of Colleges and Universities, or

(v) in accordance with an agreement with a university outside Canada to teach at an institution in Ontario, including its affiliated or federated institutions, that receives operating grants from the Ministry of Colleges and Universities; or

(g) a person who is in Canada while the person's parent or other person who has lawful custody of the person is in Canada as a convention refugee under the *Immigration Act* (Canada).

1993, c. 11, s. 20; 1997, c. 31, s. 24.

49.1 Persons unlawfully in Canada.—A person who is otherwise entitled to be admitted to a school and who is less than eighteen years of age shall not be refused admission because the person or the person's parent or guardian is unlawfully in Canada.

1993, c. 11, s. 21.

49.2 (1) **Adult persons.**—Despite any other provision of this Act but subject to subsection (4), a board may direct a person described in subsection (2) who is enrolled in or seeks to be admitted to a secondary school operated by the board to enrol in a continuing education course or class operated by the board in which the person may earn a credit.

(2) **Same.**—Subsection (1) applies to,
(a) a person who has attended one or more secondary schools for a total of seven or more school years;
(b) a person who did not attend secondary school for a total of four or more school years beginning after the end of the calender year in which the person attained the age of 16 years; or
(c) a person in respect of whom funding for a board is calculated in accordance with the regulations made under section 234 on the same basis as funding in respect of a person enrolled in a continuing education course or class.

(3) **Same.**—Despite any other provision of this Act but subject to subsection (4), a person who has been directed in accordance with this section to enrol in a continuing education course of class does not have a right under this Act to attend or to be admitted to any class or course provided by the board that is not a continuing education course or class.

(4) **Exception: person requires particular course.**—Where a person must take a subject for a purpose listed in subsection (6) and the board does not offer a course in the required subject as part of its continuing education courses and classes but does offer a course in the required subject in it secondary school day program, the person is entitled to enrol in the day program course in the required subject.

(5) **Same.**—Subsection (4) applies only to persons who, but for subsections (1) and (3), would be entitled to enrol in the day program course offered by the board in the required subject.

(6) **Same.**—The following are the purposes referred to in subsection (4):
1. To qualify for an Ontario secondary school diploma.
2. To qualify for admission to a university or college of applied arts and technology.
3. To enter a trade, profession or calling.

(7) **Exceptional pupils.**—This section does not apply to,
(a) a person who is identified under this Act as an exceptional pupil and in respect of whom there is a recommendation by a special Education Identification, Placement and Review Committee for placement in a day school program; or
(b) a person who is a member of a class of persons prescribed under subsection (8).

(8) **Regulations.**—The Lieutenant governor in Council may make regulation prescribing classes of persons for the purposes of clause (7)(b).

(9) **Classes.**—A class prescribed under subsection (8) may be defined with respect to any characteristic and may be defined to consist of or to include or exclude any specified member.

1996, c. 13, s. 4; 1997, c. 31, s. 25.

S. 50 EDUCATION ACT

PART II.1

MISCELLANEOUS

1997, c. 31, s. 26

Provisions Relating to Public Boards

50. (1) **Visitors.**—A parent or guardian of a child attending a public school and a member of the board that operates the school may visit the school.

(2) **Same.**—A member of the Assembly may visit a public school in the member's constituency.

(3) **Same.**—A member of the clergy may visit a public school in the area where the member has pastoral charge.

1997, c. 31, s. 27.

50.1 (1) **Residents other than supporters entitled to vote.**—Despite the provisions of this or any other Act but subject to subsection (2), a person who is not a supporter of any board who is entitled under subsection 1 (10) to vote in the area of jurisdiction of a public board and who wishes to be an elector for the public board at an election is entitled,

(a) to cause his or her name to be entered on the preliminary list for the voting subdivision in which he or she resides, as an elector for the public board; and
(b) to be enumerated as an elector for the public board.

(2) **French-language rights.**—Only a person who is a French-language rights holder has entitlements under subsection (1) in respect of a French-language public district school board.

1997, c. 31, s. 27.

Religious Instruction

51. (1) **Religious instruction.**—Subject to the regulations, a pupil shall be allowed to receive such religious instruction as the pupil's parent or guardian desires or, where the pupil is an adult, as the pupil desires.

(2) **Religious exercises.**—No pupil in a public school shall be required to read or study in or from a religious book, or to join in an exercise of devotion or religion, objected to by the pupil's parent or guardian, or by the pupil, where the pupil is an adult.

Provisions Relating to Roman Catholic Boards

52. Religious education.—A Roman Catholic board may establish and maintain programs and courses of study in religious education for pupils in all schools under its jurisdiction.

1997, c. 31, s. 28.

53. (1) **Visitors.**—A parent or guardian of a child attending a Roman Catholic school and a member of the board that operates the school may visit the school.

(2) **Same.**—A member of the Assembly may visit a Roman Catholic school in the member's constituency.

(3) **Same.**—A member of the clergy of the Roman Catholic Church may visit a Roman Catholic school in the area where the member has pastoral charge.

1997, c. 31, s. 28.

54. (1) **Residents other than supporters entitled to vote.**—Despite the provisions of this or any other Act but subject to subsection (2), a Roman Catholic who is not a supporter of any board, who is a person entitled under subsection 1 (10) to vote in the area of jurisdiction of a Roman Catholic board and who wishes to be an elector for the Roman Catholic board at an election is entitled,

(a) to cause his or her name to be entered on the preliminary list for the voting subdivision in which he or she resides, as an elector for the Roman Catholic board; and

(b) to be enumerated as an elector for the Roman Catholic board.

(2) **French-language rights.**—Only a person who is a French-language rights holder has entitlements under subsection (1) in respect of a French-language separate district school board.

1994, c. 27, s. 108(2); 1997, c. 31, s. 29.

Representation of Pupils on Boards

55. (1) **Regulations: pupil representatives.**—The Lieutenant Governor in Council may make regulations providing for representation on boards, by peer election or by appointment, of the interests of pupils in the last two years of the intermediate division and in the senior division.

(2) **Same.**—A regulation under this section may,

(a) provide for the type and extent of participation by the persons elected or appointed; and

(b) authorize boards to reimburse the persons elected or appointed for all or part of their out-of-pocket expenses reasonably incurred in connection with carrying out the responsibilities of pupil representatives, subject to such limitations or conditions as may be specified in the regulation.

(3) **Same.**—A regulation under this section shall not give voting rights to pupil representatives.

(4) **Same.**—In a regulation under this section, the Lieutenant Governor in Council may provide for any matter by authorizing a board to develop and implement a policy with respect to the matter.

(5) **Same.**—A pupil representative on a board is not a member of the board and is not entitled to be present at a meeting that is closed to the public under section 207.

1996, c. 32, s. 70(2); 1997, c. 31, s. 30.

Territory Without Municipal Organization in Area of Jurisdiction of School Authority

56. Regulations.—The Lieutenant Governor in Council may make regulations deeming, for any purpose, including but not limited to purposes related to taxation, any territory without municipal organization that is within the area of jurisdiction of a school authority,

(a) to be a district municipality, unless and until the territory becomes or is included in a municipality, or

(b) to be attached to a municipality, unless and until the territory becomes or is included in a municipality.

1997, c. 31, s. 31.

Special Education Tribunals and Advisory Committees

57. (1) **Establishment of Special Education Tribunals.**—The Lieutenant Governor in Council shall establish one or more Special Education Tribunals.

(2) **Regulations.**—The Lieutenant Governor in Council may make regulations governing,

(a) the organization and administration of a Special Education Tribunal;

(b) practices and procedures relating to a Special Education Tribunal; and

(c) the costs of persons before a Special Education Tribunal.

(3) **Right of appeal.**—Where a parent or guardian of a pupil has exhausted all rights of appeal under the regulations in respect of the identification or placement of the pupil as an exceptional pupil and is dissatisfied with the decision in respect of the identification or placement, the parent or guardian may appeal to a Special Education Tribunal for a hearing in respect of the identification or placement.

(4) **Hearing by Special Education Tribunal.**—The Special Education Tribunal shall hear the appeal and may,

(a) dismiss the appeal; or

(b) grant the appeal and make such order as it considers necessary with respect to the identification or placement.

(5) **Decision final.**—The decision of the Special Education Tribunal is final and binding on the parties to the decision.

1997, c. 31, s. 31.

57.1 (1) **Special education advisory committees.**—Every district school board shall establish a special education advisory committee.

(2) **Same.**—The Lieutenant Governor in Council may make regulations requiring school authorities to establish special education advisory committees.

(3) **Same.**—The Lieutenant Governor in Council may make regulations governing,

(a) the establishment and composition of special education advisory committees;

(b) practices and procedures relating to special education advisory committees;

(c) the powers and duties of special education advisory committees;

(d) the duties of district school boards or school authorities in relation to special education advisory committees.

(4) **General or particular.**—A regulation under subsection (3) may be general or particular and may be made to apply to any class of board and for the purpose a class may be defined with respect to any attribute and may be defined to consist of or to exclude any specified member of the class, whether or not with the same attributes.

1997, c. 31, s. 31.

Municipal Charges

58. (1) **Municipal charges.**—Despite subsection 220.1 (2) of the *Municipal Act* but subject to subsection (3), a by-law passed under that subsection does not apply to a board.

(2) **Same.**—Despite subsection 220.1 (2) of the *Municipal Act*, a by-law passed under that subsection does not apply in respect of anything provided or done by or on behalf of the municipality under sections 257.5 to 257.14 of this Act.

(3) **Exception.**—The Lieutenant Governor in Council may make regulations providing for exceptions to subsection (1).

1997, c. 31, s. 31.

PART II.2

DISTRICT SCHOOL BOARDS

58.1 (1) **Definitions.**—In this section,

"**English-language instruction**".—"English-language instruction" means instruction in the English language or in American Sign Language and includes instruction provided under a program of the type described in paragraph 25 of subsection 8(1); ("enseignement en anglais")

"**French-language instruction**".—"French-language instruction" means instruction in the French language or in Quebec Sign Language but does not include instruction provided under a program of the type described in paragraph 25 of subsection 8(1); ("enseignement en français")

"**school**".—"school" does not include a school under the jurisdiction of a school authority or an educational institution operated by the Government of Ontario. ("école")

(2) **Regulations: district school boards.**—The Lieutenant Governor in Council may make regulations providing for,

(a) the establishment of,
  (i) English-language public district school boards, to govern the provision of elementary and secondary English-language instruction in schools other than Roman Catholic separate schools,
  (ii) English-language separate district school boards, to govern the provision of elementary and secondary English-language instruction in Roman Catholic separate schools,
  (iii) French-language public district school boards, to govern the provision of elementary and secondary French-language instruction in schools other than Roman Catholic separate schools, and
  (iv) French-language separate district school boards, to govern the provision of elementary and secondary French-language instruction in Roman Catholic separate schools;
(b) the establishment of the areas of jurisdiction of district school boards;
(c) the assignment of names to district school boards;
(d) the alteration of the area of jurisdiction of a district school board;
(e) the dissolution of a district school board;

(f) the dissolution of a school authority the area of jurisdiction of which is to be included in the area of jurisdiction of a district school board;
(g) the dissolution of an old board;
(h) the amalgamation or merger of one or more old boards with a district school board to continue as a district school board;
(i) the amalgamation or merger of one or more school authorities with a district school board to continue as a district school board;
(j) the amalgamation or merger of two or more district school boards to continue as a district school board;
(k) representation on and elections to district school boards, including but not limited to regulations providing for,
 (i) the determination of the number of members of each district school board,
 (ii) the establishment, for electoral purposes, of geographic areas within the areas of jurisdiction of district school boards,
 (iii) the distribution of the members of a district school board to the geographic areas referred to in subclause (ii),
 (iv) appeals to any person or body relating to anything done under a regulation made under subclause (i), (ii) or (iii),
 (v) nomination procedures for the election of members of district school boards,
 (vi) the duties to be performed by municipal clerks, officials of old boards, officials of district school boards and others in respect of any matter relating to representation on or elections to district school boards,
 (vii) the duties to be performed by the Education Improvement Commission in respect of any matter relating to elections to district school boards in 1997 or to representation on district school boards in connection with the 1997 elections;
(l) the holding in trust, transfer and vesting of assets, including but not limited to real and personal property, the transfer of liabilities and the transfer of employees among district school boards or school authorities or both, in connection with,
 (i) the establishment, continuation or dissolution of a district school board,
 (ii) the dissolution of a school authority the area of jurisdiction of which is to be included in the area of jurisdiction of a district school board, or
 (iii) the merger or amalgamation of a school authority the area of jurisdiction of which is to be included in the area of jurisdiction of a district school board with the district school board;
(m) the deeming, for any purpose, including but not limited to purposes related to elections and taxation, of any territory without municipal organization that is within the area of jurisdiction of a district school board,
 (i) to be a district municipality, unless and until the territory becomes or is included in a municipality, or
 (ii) to be attached to a municipality, unless and until the territory becomes or is included in a municipality;
(n) the recovery of some or all of the costs incurred by a district school board in meeting any requirements under this section relating to elections in territory without municipal organization or elections to a school authority;

- (o) the conduct of elections to a school authority the area of jurisdiction of which is entirely or partly the same as the area of jurisdiction of a district school board;
- (p) the holding in trust, transfer and vesting of assets, including but not limited to real and personal property, the transfer of liabilities and the transfer of employees of old boards to and among district school boards;
- (q) such transitional matters as the Lieutenant Governor in Council considers necessary or advisable in connection with the school system reforms of 1997 and 1998, including but not limited to regulations providing for,
  - (i) such matters as the Lieutenant Governor in Council considers advisable to prevent disruption in the education of pupils,
  - (ii) the obligation of a district school board to exercise the powers and carry out the duties of another district school board for and on behalf of the other district school board,
  - (iii) the obligation of a district school board to deal with the assets, liabilities or employees or classes of assets, liabilities or employees, that are identified in the regulation, for and on behalf of another district school board,
  - (iv) the recovery of some or all of the costs incurred by a district school board in meeting any requirement under this clause;
- (r) such other matters, including transitional matters, that the Lieutenant Governor in Council considers necessary or advisable in connection with the establishment, merger, amalgamation, continuation or dissolution of one or more boards under this section, or with the alteration of the area of jurisdiction of a board under this section, including but not limited to transitional matters relating to,
  - (i) representation, by election or appointment, on a board pending the next regular elections,
  - (ii) the rights of pupils to continue to attend schools that they were enrolled in and entitled to attend immediately before the establishment, merger, amalgamation, continuation, dissolution or alteration.

(3) **Provisions in regulations: effect for electoral purposes.**—A regulation made under subsection (2) may provide that it shall be deemed to have come into force and taken effect on the day of filing or at such earlier or later time as is stated in the regulation, for any purpose related to representation on or elections to a district school board or school authority.

(4) **Same.**—Subsection (3) applies only to the extent necessary to permit the next regular election after the regulation is made, or any by-election proceeding that next regular election, to be held in a way that takes account of the provisions of the regulation.

(5) **Regulations: school outside jurisdiction of a board to be school of the board.**—The Lieutenant Governor in Council may make regulations providing that a school described in subsection (6) that is outside the area of jurisdiction of a district school board is a school of the district school board.

(6) **Same.**—Subsection (5) applies only to schools to which section 101 of this Act, as it read on December 31, 1997, applied.

(7) **Purpose of clauses (2)(d), (e).**—The purpose of clauses (2)(d) and (e) is to provide authority to the Lieutenant Governor in Council to make changes in the jurisdiction of boards on a case by case basis.

(8) **Limitation re clauses (2)(d), (e).**—A regulation shall not be made under clause (2)(d) or (e) if an area that, immediately before the regulation takes effect, was within the area of jurisdiction of a board would, immediately after the regulation takes effect, not be within the area of jurisdiction of a board.

(9) **Subdelegation.**—In a regulation under subclauses (2) (k) (i) to (iii), the Lieutenant Governor in Council may delegate to a person or body the authority to provide for anything relating to the matters mentioned in subclauses (2) (k) (i) to (iii), subject to such conditions and restrictions as are specified in the regulation.

(10) **Number of members on a district school board.**—A regulation under subclause (2)(k)(i) shall not provide for more than 22 or fewer than five members on any district school board.

(11) **Same.**—The numbers referred to in subsection (10) do not include any person elected or appointed to a district school board under section 188.

(12) **Geographic areas.**—A geographic area established under subclause (2) (k) (ii) for a district school board may,

(a) be the same as or less than the entire area of jurisdiction of the district school board;
(b) include areas within the area of jurisdiction of the district school board that do not adjoin one another; and
(c) consist of,
   (i) all or part of one or more municipalities, or
   (ii) territory without municipal organization,
or both.

(13) **Same.**—A person who establishes a geographic area under a regulation made under subclause (2)(k)(ii) shall have regard to any relevant submissions made by any person.

(14) **Purpose of Clause (2)(l).**—The purpose of clause (2)(l) is to provide authority to the Lieutenant Governor in Council to resolve questions relating to assets, liabilities and employees that arise in connection with any changes in the jurisdiction of boards that may be made on a case by case basis.

(15) **Limitation.**—The Lieutenant Governor in council has no authority under clause (2)(l) to transfer employees of a public board to a Roman Catholic board or to transfer employees of a Roman Catholic Board to a public board.

(16) **Exception.**—The limitation provided in subsection (15) does not apply in relation to the transfer of an employee between two boards if,

(a) both boards agree that the limitation should not apply in respect of the transfer;
(b) the Minister approves the agreement referred to in clause (a).

(17) **Transfers among district school boards and school authorities.**—Without limiting the generality of clause (2)(l), a regulation under that clause may provide for,

(a) processes to permit participation by classes of persons or bodies specified in the regulation in decision-making processes related to anything done under clause (2) (1);
(b) processes for the resolution of disputes among classes of persons or bodies specified in the regulation;
(c) the continuation of legal and other proceedings commenced by or against a district

school board or school authority affected by anything done under clause (2) (1) and the enforcement of court orders and other orders or determinations relating to such a district school board or school authority;

(d) deadlines for complying with any provision of the regulation; and

(e) any other matter that the Lieutenant Governor in Council considers advisable in order to achieve an efficient and fair transfer of assets, liabilities and employees among the affected district school boards and school authorities.

(18) **Dispute.**—Without limiting the generality of clause (17) (b), a regulation providing for a matter referred to in that clause may provide for disputes as to the disposition of property to be referred to an arbitrator selected by the Minister.

(19) **Same.**—Where a dispute is referred to an arbitrator as described in subsection (18), the arbitrator shall determine the matters in dispute and the decision of the arbitrator is final.

(20) **Clause (17)(c).**—Without limiting the generality of clause (17)(c), a regulation providing for a matter referred to in that clause,

(a) may substitute or add persons as parties to a proceeding continued under the clause; and

(b) may substitute or add persons against which or by which an order or determination referred to in the clause may be enforced.

(21) **Employees.**—The following rules apply where an employee is transferred under a regulation made under clause (2) (2):

1. A person who is an employee of a board on the day the regulation transferring the employee to another board is made and who would, but for that regulation, still be an employee of the transferor board on the day the regulation is to take effect is an employee of the transferee board referred to in the regulation on the day the regulation is to take effect

2. A person's employment shall be deemed not to have been terminated for any purpose by anything done under this Part.

(22) **Tax exemption.**—Taxes are not payable under the *Land Transfer Tax Act* or the *Retail Sales Tax Act* with respect to a holding in trust, transfer or vesting under clause (2)(2).

(23) **Transfer not a closing.**—A transfer of a school under clause (2)(l) is not a closing of the school.

(24) **No compensation.**—Except as provided in the regulations made under clause (2)(l), no compensation or damages are payable in connection with anything done under clause (2)(l).

(25) **Powers of board if regulation made under subclause (2)(m)(i).**—Where a board includes within its area of jurisdiction territory without municipal organization that is deemed under clause (2)(m) to be a district municipality for the purposes of elections, the officers appointed by the board have all the same powers and duties with respect to elections of members of the board in that territory as similar officers have in a municipality with respect to similar elections.

(26) **Powers of municipality if regulation made under subclause (2)(m)(ii).**—Where a board includes within its area of jurisdiction territory without municipal organization that is deemed under clause (2)(m) to be attached to a municipality for the purposes of elections, the officers of the municipality have all the same powers and duties with respect to elections of

members of the board in that territory as with respect to such elections in any part of the area of jurisdiction of the board that is within the municipality.

1997, c. 31, s. 32.

58.2 (1) **Transfers from old boards to district school boards.**—Without limiting the generality of clause 58.1(2)(p), a regulation under that clause may provide for,
- (a) processes to permit participation by classes of persons or bodies specified in the regulation in decision-making processes related to anything done under clause 58.1(2)(p);
- (b) processes for the resolution of disputes among classes of persons or bodies specified in the regulation;
- (c) the continuation of legal and other proceedings commenced by or against an old board and the enforcement of court orders and other orders or determinations affecting an old board;
- (d) deadlines for complying with any provision of the regulation; and
- (e) any other matter that the Lieutenant Governor in Council considers advisable in order to achieve an efficient and fair transfer of assets, liabilities and employees of old boards to and among district school boards.

(2) **Clause (1)(c).**—Without limiting the generality of clause (1)(c), a regulation providing for a matter referred to in that clause,
- (a) may substitute or add persons as parties to a proceeding continued under the clause; and
- (b) may substitute or add persons against which or by which an order or determination referred to in the clause may be enforced.

(3) **Role of Education Improvement Commission.**—In a regulation under clause 58.1(2)(p) or (q), the Lieutenant Governor in Council may provide for any matter referred to in clause 58.1(2)(p) or (q), in subsection (1) or (2) of this section or in subsection 58.3(7) by assigning powers and duties to the Education Improvement Commission, including but not limited to powers and duties to,
- (a) issue directives to district school boards and other persons or bodies or classes of persons or bodies specified by the Commission respecting criteria to be applied and processes to be followed in developing recommendations to the Commission on any matter referred to in clause 58.1(2) (p) or (q), in subsection (1) or (2) of this section or in subsection 58.3(7);
- (b) issue directives respecting the participation of classes of persons or bodies specified by the Commission in the development of recommendations referred to in clause (a) and respecting dispute resolution processes;
- (c) make determinations respecting the holding in trust, transfer and vesting of assets, including but not limited to real and personal property, the transfer of liabilities and the transfer of employees of old boards to and among district school boards;
- (d) issue orders that the Commission considers necessary or advisable to give effect to the determinations made under clause (c) and impose terms and conditions on its orders; and
- (e) issue directives establishing deadlines for complying with any directive or order made by the Commission under the regulations.

(4) **Same.**—In a regulation assigning powers and duties to the Education Improvement Commission, the Lieutenant Governor in Council may authorize the Commission to,

(a) make interim orders, including but not limited to interim orders respecting dealings by a district school board with any asset, liability or employee, pending final disposition of the asset or liability under this Part or final determination under this Part of which district school board will be the employer of the employee;

(b) make final orders;

(c) vary any of its orders.

(5) **Same.**—In a regulation assigning powers and duties to the Education Improvement Commission, the Lieutenant Governor in Council may,

(a) specify procedures and other rules to be followed by the Commission in carrying out its powers and duties;

(b) provide that the powers and duties of the Commission are subject to any terms and conditions specified in the regulation; and

(c) provide for the establishment of panels of the Commission and provide that a panel may exercise the powers and carry out the duties of the Commission, subject to the restrictions, if any, specified in the regulation.

(6) **Same.**—Examples of rules that may be specified under clause (5)(a) include,

(a) rules requiring the Commission to consult, in circumstances specified in the regulation, with classes of persons or bodies specified in the regulation;

(b) rules requiring the Commission to take into account, in any way that the Lieutenant Governor in Council considers appropriate, recommendations made by classes of persons or bodies specified in the regulation.

(7) **Criteria re transfer of assets, liabilities, employees.**—In making regulations under clause 58.1(2) (p) or (q) and in making determinations and issuing directives or orders under this section, the Lieutenant Governor in Council or the Education Improvement Commission, as the case may be, shall,

(a) have regard to the needs of each district school board;

(b) ensure that all assets, liabilities and employees of old boards are transferred to district school boards;

(c) ensure that all employees of old public boards are transferred to public district school boards;

(d) ensure that all employees of old Roman Catholic boards are transferred to separate district school boards.

(8) **Definitions.**—In subsection (7),

"**old public board**".—"old public board" means a board of education and the Metropolitan Toronto School Board within the meaning of this Act as it read immediately before the *Education Quality Improvement Act, 1997* received Royal Assent ("ancien conseil public"); "old Roman Catholic board" means a county combined separate school board and a district combined separate school board within the meaning of this Act as it read immediately before the *Education Quality Improvement Act, 1997* received Royal Assent ("ancien conseil catholique").

S. 58.2 EDUCATION ACT

(9) **Exception.**—Where a district school board acquires an employee as a result of merger with an old board, clauses (7)(c) and (d) do not apply in respect of the transfer of the employee to another district school board if,
- (a) both district school boards agree that clause (7)(c) or (d) as the case may be, should not apply in respect of the transfer; and
- (b) the Education Improvement Commission approves the agreement referred to in clause (a).

(10) **Limitation.**—Subject to subsection (11), clause 58.1(2)(p) does not authorize the transfer of any asset, liability or employee after August 31, 1998.

(11) **Exception: ongoing disputes.**—Where on August 31, 1998 there is an ongoing dispute between district school boards as to the appropriate disposition of an asset, liability or employee, the asset, liability or employee may be transferred, by regulation or order, as the case may be, under clause 58.1(2)(p) at any time before January 1, 1999.

(12) **Employees.**—The following rules apply where an employee is transferred from an old board to a district school board under a regulation made under clause 58.1(2)(p) or under an order issued under this section:

1. A person who is an employee of an old board on the day the order or regulation transferring the employee is issued or made and who would, but for that order or regulation, still be an employee of the old board on the day the order or regulation is to take effect is an employee of the district school board referred to in the regulation or order on the day the regulation or order is to take effect.
2. A person's employment shall be deemed not to have been terminated for any purpose by anything done under this Part.

(13) **Order, directive may be filed in court.**—An order or directive of the Education Improvement Commission under this section or a predecessor of this section may be filed in the Ontario Court (General Division).

(14) **Same.**—An order or directive that is filed under subsection (13) shall be enforceable as if it were an order of the Ontario Court (General Division).

(15) **Orders, directives final.**—Orders and directives of the Education Improvement Commission under this section or a predecessor of this section are final and shall not be reviewed or questioned in any court.

(16) **Tax exemption.**—Taxes are not payable under the *Land Transfer Tax Act* or the *Retail Sales Tax Act* with respect to a holding in trust, transfer or vesting under clause 58.1(2)(p).

(17) **Transfer not a closing.**—A transfer of a school under clause 58.1(2)(p) is not a closing of the school.

(18) **No compensation.**—Except as provided in the regulations made under clause 58.1(2)(p), no compensation or damages are payable in connection with anything done under clause 58.1(2)(p).

(19) **Effect of transfer under this Part.**—Where an asset or liability is transferred from one district school board to another district school board as a result of a regulation made under clause 58.1(2)(p) or as a result of an order made under such a regulation,
- (a) the transferee board has, immediately after the transfer, the same rights and obliga-

tions with respect to the asset or liability as the transferor board had immediately before the transfer; and

(b) the rights and obligations of a party to any agreement are not affected by reason only that the transferee board is not identical to the transferor board.

1997, c. 31, s. 32.

58.3 (1) **Purpose of authority under clauses 58.1(2)(p), (q), s. 58.2.**—The purpose of clauses 58.1(2)(p) and (q) is to provide authority to the Lieutenant Governor in Council and, where the Lieutenant Governor in Council exercises authority under section 58.2 to assign powers and duties to the Education Improvement Commission, the Education Improvement Commission, to address transitional matters that arise in connection with the school system reforms of 1997 and 1998.

(2) **Same.**—In particular, the purpose of subclauses 58.1(2)(q)(ii) and (iii) is to provide authority to the Lieutenant Governor in Council and, where the Lieutenant Governor in Council exercises authority under section 58.2 to assign powers and duties to the Education Improvement Commission, the Education Improvement Commission, to give certain district school boards time, where necessary, to prepare for the assumption of full administrative and operational responsibility for assets, liabilities and employees.

(3) **Limitation: clauses 58.1(2)(p), (q), s. 58.2.**—Neither the Lieutenant Governor in Council nor the Education Improvement Commission has any authority under clause 58.1(2)(p) or (q) or section 58.2 to address matters that, in the reasonable opinion of the Lieutenant Governor in Council or the Education Improvement Commission, as the case may be, are unrelated to the school system reforms of 1997 and 1998.

(4) **Limitation: subclause 58.1(2)(q)(i).**—Neither the Lieutenant Governor in Council nor the Education Improvement Commission has any authority under subclause 58.1.(2)(q)(i) to intervene in a strike or lock-out.

(5) **Limitation: subclause 58.1(2)(q)(ii).**—Neither the Lieutenant Governor in Council, nor the Education Improvement Commission has any authority under subclause 58.1(2)(q)(ii) or (iii) to oblige a district school board to do anything after August 1, 1998.

(6) **Same.**—Despite subsection (5), where subsections 58.2(11) applies, authority under subclauses 58.1(2)(q)(ii) and (iii) may be exercised to impose obligations on district school boards until January 1, 1999.

(7) **One district school board to follow directions of another.**—Where authority is exercised under subclause 58.1(2)(q)(ii) or (iii), the district school board acting for and on behalf of another district school board shall follow the directions of the other district school board in order to ensure that the governance role of each district school board, as described in subclause 58.1(2)(a)(i), (ii), (iii), or (iv), is respected.

(8) **Same.**—The authority to make regulations under clause 58.1(2)(q)(ii) or (iii) includes the authority to make regulations respecting how the requirements of subsection (7) are to be met.

1997, c. 31, s. 32.

58.4 (1) **General or particular.**—A regulation made under section 58.1 and a directive or order issued under section 58.2 may be general or particular.

(2) **Classes.**—A class under section 58.1 or 58.2 may be defined with respect to any

attribute and may be defined to consist of or to exclude any specified member of the class, whether or not with the same attributes.

1997, c. 31, s. 32.

58.5 (1) **Corporate status.**—Every district school board is a corporation and has all the powers and shall perform all the duties that are conferred or imposed on it under this or any other Act.

(2) **Amalgamation or merger.**—Subsection (3) applies where,

(a) one or more old boards are merged or amalgamated with a district school board to continue as a district school board;

(b) one or more school authorities are merged or amalgamated with a district school board to continue as a district school board; or

(c) two or more district school boards are merged or amalgamated to continue as a district school board.

(3) **Same.**—The district school board that is continued is a corporation and, except as otherwise provided by the regulations made under this Part, subsection 180 (7) of the *Business Corporations Act* applies with necessary modifications as if the board had been continued under that Act.

1997, c. 31, s. 32.

58.6 District school boards deemed to be local boards.—A district school board shall be deemed to be a local board and a school board for the purposes of the *Municipal Elections Act, 1996*.

1997, c. 31, s. 32.

58.7 Conduct of elections.—The election of members of a district school board shall be conducted in the same manner as the election of members of the council of a municipality.

1997, c. 31, s. 32.

58.8 (1) **Electors for French-language district school boards.**—Subject to section 58.9, a person is qualified to be an elector for a French-language district school board if the person is entitled under subsection 1 (10) to vote in the area of jurisdiction of the board and,

(a) the person is a French-language district school board supporter;

(b) the person is entered on a preliminary list under section 54 in respect of a French-language separate district school board; or

(c) the person is entered on a preliminary list under section 50.1 in respect of a French-language public district school board.

(2) **Same.**—A person qualified to be an elector for a French-language district school board may not vote for members of an English-language district school board.

1997, c. 31, s. 32.

58.9 (1) **Election by general vote.**—The members of a district school board to be elected for a geographic area established under section 58.1 shall be elected by general vote of the electors qualified to vote in the geographic area for the members of that district school board.

(2) **Entitlement to vote: English-language public district school boards.**—The members of an English-language public district school board shall be elected by persons entitled under subsection 1 (10) to vote in the area of jurisdiction of the board who,

(a) are not qualified under subsection 58.8 (1) to be electors for a French-language district school board; and

(b) are not separate school supporters or persons entered on a preliminary list under section 54.

(3) **Entitlement to vote: English-language separate district school boards.**—The members of an English-language separate district school board shall be elected by persons entitled under subsection 1 (10) to vote in the area of jurisdiction of the board who,

(a) are not qualified under subsection 58.8 (1) to be electors for a French-language district school board; and

(b) are separate school supporters or persons entered on a preliminary list under section 54.

(4) **Entitlement to vote: French-language public district school boards.**—The members of a French-language public district school board shall be elected by persons entitled under subsection 1 (10) to vote in the area of jurisdiction of the board who,

(a) are qualified under subsection 58.8 (1) to be electors for a French-language district school board; and

(b) are not separate school supporters or persons entered on a preliminary list under section 54.

(5) **Entitlement to vote: French-language separate district school boards.**—The members of a French-language separate district school board shall be elected by persons entitled under subsection 1 (10) to vote in the area of jurisdiction of the board who,

(a) are qualified under subsection 58.8 (1) to be electors for a French-language district school board; and

(b) are separate school supporters or persons entered on a preliminary list under section 54.

1997, c. 31, s. 32.

PART III

SCHOOL AUTHORITIES — PUBLIC

1997, c. 31, s. 33

District School Areas

59. (1) **School section to be district school area.**—Every school section that is in a territorial district but is not in the area of jurisdiction of a public district school board or designated as a school section under section 68 is a district school area, and the board of each such school section is a public board and shall be known as a district school area board.

(2) **Formation and alteration of district school area.**—In respect of the territorial districts, the Lieutenant Governor in Council may, by regulation,

(a) form any part thereof that is not in a school section into a district school area;

(b) combine two or more district school areas into one district school area;

(c) add a part thereof that is not in the area of jurisdiction of a public district school board to a district school area;
(d) detach a portion thereof from one district school area and attach it to another district school area or form it into a new district school area; or
(e) detach a portion thereof from a district school area.

(3) **Notification of assessment commissioner.**—Where a district school area is formed or altered under subsection (2), the Minister shall notify the assessment commissioner concerned.

(4) **Arbitration.**—Where the boundaries of a district school area are altered in accordance with clause (2)(b) or (d), the Minister shall, by order, provide for arbitration of the assets and liabilities of the boards concerned.

(5) **Name of board.**—The board of a district school area is a corporation by the name of "The .... District School Area Board" or "Conseil du secteur scolaire de district de ...." or both (inserting a name selected by the board and approved by the Minister).

1997, c. 31, s. 34.

60. (1) **New district school areas.**—Where a district school area is formed under clause 59(2)(b), upon the effective date of such formation the existing public boards in the new district school area are dissolved, and, subject to subsection 59(4),
(a) the property vested in such boards is vested in the new district school area board; and
(b) all debts, contracts, agreements and liabilities for which such boards were liable become obligations of the district school area board.

(2) **Alteration and formation: disposition of assets and liabilities.**—Where the boundaries of a district school area are altered or a new district school area is formed under clause 59(2)(d), upon the effective date of such alteration or formation, and, subject to subsection 59(4),
(a) all real and personal property of the board situate in the part of the district school area that is detached is vested in the board of the district school area to which such part is attached, or in the board of the new district school area, as the case may be; and
(b) all debts, contracts, agreements and liabilities of the board in respect of the part of the district school area that is detached become obligations of the board of the district school area to which such part is attached, or of the board of the new district school area, as the case may be.

1997, c. 31, s. 35.

61. (1) **Definition.**—In this section and in sections 62 and 63, "public school elector", in relation to a district school area board, means a person who,
(a) resides in the area of jurisdiction of the board or is the owner or tenant of residential property in the area of jurisdiction of the board,
(b) is a Canadian citizen,
(c) is at least 18 years of age,
(d) is neither a separate school supporter nor a person entered on a preliminary list under section 54, and

(e) is not qualified under subsection 58.8 (1) to be an elector for a French-language district school board.

(2) **Composition of board.**—Subject to subsections (3) and (4), a district school area board shall be composed of three members.

(3) **Idem.**—Where a school section that became a district school area on the 1st day of January, 1975, had a board of five members, the district school area board shall be composed of five members.

(4) **Increase in number of members.**—Before the 1st day of July of an election year, the board of a district school area may, by resolution approved at a meeting of the public school electors, determine that the number of members to be elected shall be increased from three to five and, at the next following election, five members shall be elected.

(5) **Election year and term of office.**—The election of members of the board of a district school area shall be held in each year in which a regular election is held under the Municipal Elections Act, 1996 and the members shall hold office until the next regular election is held under that Act and their successors are elected under this Act and the new board is organized except that,

(a) where a new district school area is formed to take effect on the 1st day of January in a year that is not a year of a regular election under the Municipal Elections Act, 1996 the first members of such board shall be elected in the year preceding such 1st day of January and shall hold office until the next regular election is held under the Municipal Elections Act, 1996 and their successors are elected under this Act and the new board is organized; or

(b) where the boundaries of a district school area are altered to take effect on the 1st day of January in a year that is not a year in which a regular election is held under the Municipal Elections Act, 1996 a new district school area board shall be elected in the year preceding such 1st day of January and the members so elected shall hold office until the next regular election is held under the Municipal Elections Act, 1996 and their successors are elected under this Act and the new board is organized.

(6) **Term of office.**—The term of office of members of the board of a district school area shall commence on the 1st day of December in the election year.

1997, c. 31, s. 36.

Elections and Meetings of Electors

62. (1) **Election date.**—Except as provided in section 63 and subject to subsection (4), a district school area board shall be elected at a meeting of the public school electors held on the second Monday in November or, where that day is Remembrance Day, on the next succeeding day in the year of an election at a time and place selected by the board.

(2) **Notice of meeting.**—At least six days before a meeting under subsection (1) or (6), the secretary of the board shall post notice of the meeting, including notice of any resolution required to be approved by the electors, in three or more of the most prominent places in the district school area and may advertise the meeting in such other manner as the board considers expedient.

S. 63   EDUCATION ACT

(3) **Meeting.**—Meetings of public school electors shall be conducted in the manner determined by the public school electors present at the meeting by a presiding officer selected by such electors, but the election of members of the board shall be by ballot, and the minutes of the meeting shall be recorded by a secretary selected by such electors.

(4) **First meeting.**—Despite subsection 61(5), the first meeting for the election of a board of a district school area formed or altered under subsection 59(2) shall be held at a time and place named by a person, designated by the Minister, who shall make the necessary arrangements for the meeting and the person so elected shall hold office until the date the next regular election is held under the Municipal Elections Act, 1996 and their successors are elected under this Act and the new board is organized.

(5) **Minutes to be sent to Ministry.**—A correct copy of the minutes of every meeting of the public school electors, signed by the presiding officer and the secretary of the meeting, shall, within ten days after the meeting, be transmitted by the presiding officer to the Ministry.

(6) **Special meetings.**—A special meeting of the public school electors shall be called by the secretary when directed by the board or upon the request in writing of five public school electors of the area, by posting notice of the meeting in three or more of the most prominent places in the district school area, and such notice shall include a clear statement of the date, time, place and objects of the meeting, and the meeting may be advertised in such other manner as is deemed necessary.

(7) **Declaration where right to vote objected to.**—If objection is made to the right of a person in territory without municipal organization to vote at a meeting under this section, or at an election under section 63, the presiding officer or the returning officer, as the case may be, shall require the person to make the following declaration in English or in French:

I, ..., declare and affirm that:

    1. I am a public school elector within the meaning of subsection 61 (1) of the *Education Act* in relation to The .... District School Area; and

    2. I have a right to vote at this election (or on the question submitted to this meeting).

(7.1) **Same.**—After making the declaration under subsection (7), the person is entitled to vote.

(8) **Election procedures.**—Subsections 92(8), (9), (10), (11), (12), (13), (15), (16), (17), (18), (19), (21) and (22) apply with necessary modifications to an election under this section.

                                                                               1997, c. 31, s. 37.

63. (1) **Conduct of elections under *Municipal Elections Act, 1996*.**—The election of the board of the district school area shall be conducted under the Municipal Elections Act, 1996 where a district school area comprises,

    (a) a municipality;

    (b) a municipality and territory without municipal organization;

    (c) all or part of two or more municipalities; or

    (d) all or parts of two or more municipalities and territory without municipal organization.

(2) **Same.**—Before July 1 in an election year, the board of a district school area may, by resolution approved at a meeting of the public school electors, determine that the board shall conduct the elections in the same manner as for the members of a district school board, except

that the members shall be elected by general vote of the public school electors of the district school area.

(3) **Same.**—The board shall give notice of the determination made under subsection (1) to the electors in the same manner as provided in subsection 62(2).

(4) **Same.**—For the purposes of an election under this section in territory without municipal organization, the secretary of the board shall be the returning officer in respect of the territory without municipal organization and shall perform all the duties that are required of a municipal clerk in relation to the election of members of a district school board.

1997, c. 31, s. 38.

64. (1) **Elections.**—Despite subsection 62(3) and (8) and section 63, where a district school area is formed under clause 59(2)(b), the Lieutenant Governor in Council may make regulations,
- (a) determining the number of members to be elected to the board of the district school area;
- (b) determining the areas each member referred to in clause (a) shall represent;
- (c) providing for the nomination of candidates to be elected; and
- (d) prescribing the manner in which the election of the members shall be conducted,

and the election of the members shall be in accordance with such regulations.

(2) **Validity of election.**—No election under this section is invalid by reason of noncompliance with the provisions of the regulations made under subsection (I) or by reason of any mistake or irregularity if it appears that the election was conducted in accordance with the principles laid down in the regulations and that the non-compliance, mistake or irregularity did not affect the result of the election.

65. [Repealed 1997, c. 31, s. 39.]

66. (1) **District school area board to be inactive.**—Where the number of public school pupils of compulsory school age residing in a district school area is fewer than ten and the board has ceased to operate a school, the Minister may declare the district school area board inactive as of the 31st day of December in any year.

(2) **Accounts in inactive area.**—When a district school area board is declared to be inactive, the board shall liquidate its assets, settle its accounts and have them audited, and forward to the Ministry the audited statement of accounts, the auditor's report and the balance of the funds for deposit in the Consolidated Revenue Fund.

(3) **Board dissolved.**—If the Minister is satisfied that the board has carried out its duties under subsection (2), the Minister shall dissolve the board and the district school area shall cease to exist as of the date that the district school area board was declared inactive under subsection (1).

(4) **Records to be forwarded to Ministry.**—The records of the dissolved board of the district school area shall be filed as the Minister may direct and, for the purposes of this Act, the pupils resident in such area shall be deemed not to reside in a school section.

(5) **Closing of school by Minister.**—Where in any district school area there are for two consecutive years fewer than eight persons between the ages of five and fourteen years residing therein, the Minister may direct that the public school of the area shall no longer remain open, and the school shall thereupon be closed until the Minister otherwise directs.

S. 67 EDUCATION ACT

Secondary School Authorities

67. (1) In territorial districts.—The Lieutenant Governor in Council may establish any area in the territorial districts that is not part of the area of jurisdiction of a public district school board as a secondary school district and may discontinue or decrease or increase the area of any such secondary school district and, if any such secondary school district is discontinued, or the area is decreased or increased, the assets and liabilities of the board shall be adjusted or disposed of as determined by the Ontario Municipal Board.

(2) **Same.**—Where a secondary school district is established under subsection (1), the Lieutenant Governor in Council may make regulations providing for,
- (a) the formation and composition of a secondary school board;
- (b) the dissolution of a secondary school board;
- (c) elections to a secondary school board, including but not limited to qualifications to vote in those elections:
- (d) disqualifications for the purposes of subsection 219(4).

(3) **Same.**—A secondary school board established under this section is a corporation by the name designated by the Lieutenant Governor in Council.

(4) [Repealed 1997, c. 31, s. 41(2).]

(5) [Repealed 1997, c. 31, s. 41(2).]

(6) [Repealed 1997, c. 31, s. 41(2).]

(7) [Repealed 1997, c. 31, s. 41(2).]

1997, c. 31, ss. 40, 41.

School Authorities on Tax Exempt Land

68. (1) Public elementary school on exempt lands.—Where, in the opinion of the Minister, it is desirable to establish and maintain a public school authority for elementary school purposes on lands held by the Crown in right of Canada or Ontario, or by an agency thereof, or on other lands that are exempt from taxation for school purposes, the Minister may by order designate any portion of such lands as a school section and may appoint as members of the board such persons as the Minister considers proper, and the board so appointed is a corporation by the name indicated in the order establishing the school section and has all the powers and duties of a public district school board for elementary school purposes.

(2) **Public secondary school on exempt land.**—Where, in the opinion of the Minister, it is desirable to establish and maintain a public school authority for secondary school purposes on lands held by the Crown in right of Canada or Ontario, or by an agency thereof, or on other lands that are exempt from taxation for school purposes, the Minister may by order designate any portion of such lands as a secondary school district, and may appoint as members of the board such persons as the Minister considers proper, and the board so appointed is a corporation by the name indicated in the order establishing the secondary school district and has all the powers and duties of a public district school board for secondary school purposes.

(3) **Public secondary and elementary school on exempt land.**—Where a secondary school district has been designated under subsection (2), the Minister may authorize the formation of a public school authority for elementary and secondary school purposes for the

district and may provide for the name of the school authority, its composition and the term or terms of office of its members, and for all other purposes the provisions in respect of public district school boards apply to the school authority.

(4) **Area of jurisdiction: other boards.**—A school section or secondary school district designated under this section shall be deemed not to be included in the area of jurisdiction of,

(a) a district school board;
(b) a board established under section 59; or
(c) a board established under section 67.

(5) **Fee payable by non-resident.**—Where a pupil attends a school that is operated by a board appointed under this section in a children's treatment centre and the pupil is not a resident pupil of the board, the board of which the pupil is a resident pupil or is qualified to be a resident pupil shall pay to the board that operates the school the fee, if any, payable for the purpose under the regulations.

(5.1) **Same.**—Where the pupil is not a resident pupil or qualified to be a resident pupil of a board and the pupil's cost of education is not payable by the Minister under the regulations, the pupil's parent or guardian shall pay to the board that operates the school a fee fixed by such board.

(5.2) **Same.**—A fee fixed under subsection (5.1) shall not be greater than the fee, if any, payable for the purpose under the regulations.

(6) **Revocation of order.**—If an order under subsection (1) or (2) is to be revoked on the 1st day of January next following a regular election under the Municipal Elections Act, 1996, the order shall, for the purpose of the election, be deemed to have been revoked.

1997, c. 31, s. 42.

69. [Repealed 1993, c. 11, s. 22.]
70. [Repealed 1993, c. 11, s. 22.]
71. [Repealed 1993, c. 11, s. 22.]
72. [Repealed 1993, c. 11, s. 22.]
73. [Repealed 1993, c. 11, s. 22.]
74. [Repealed 1993, c. 11, s. 22.]
75. [Repealed 1993, c. 11, s. 22.]
76. [Repealed 1993, c. 11, s. 22.]

PART IV

SCHOOL AUTHORITIES — ROMAN CATHOLIC

77. [Repealed 1997, c. 31, s. 44.]

Zones

78. (1) **Boundaries of zones.**—Unless otherwise determined in accordance with regulations made under subsections 58.1(2) or section 86.1, the boundaries of a separate school zone shall, in accordance with sections 80 and 84, be the boundaries of,

(a) a municipality;
(b) a geographic township;
(c) a combination of municipalities;
(d) a combination of geographic townships; or
(e) a combination of the areas referred to in clauses (a) to (d).

(2) **Zones not in municipalities or geographic townships.**—The boundaries of a separate school zone, in those parts of the territorial districts that are neither geographic townships nor townships municipalities, shall be the boundaries of a 9.6 kilometer square of land of which two sides are parallel to a line of latitude.

(3) **Zone description.**—If a separate school zone is a 9.6 kilometer square of land, the location of the zone shall be determined by the latitude and longitude of its northwest corner.

(4) [Repealed 1997, c. 31, s. 45(2).]

1997, c. 31, s. 45.

79. [Repealed 1997, c. 31, s. 46.]

Formation and Discontinuance of Zones

80. (1) **Meeting to establish a separate school zone.**—A public meeting of persons desiring to establish a separate school zone may be convened by,

(a) not fewer than five members of five families, with each member being Roman Catholic, at least 18 years of age and a householder or freeholder resident within a municipality or a geographic township that is not within the area of jurisdiction of a separate district school board, who desire to establish the area of the municipality or geographic township as a separate school zone;

(b) not fewer than 10 members of 10 families, with each member being Roman Catholic, at least 18 years of age and a householder or freeholder resident within a 9.6 kilometre square of land, that is not part of a municipality, a geographic township or a separate school zone, who desire to establish the square of land as a separate school zone; or

(c) not fewer than five members of five families, with each member being Roman Catholic, at least 18 years of age and a householder or freeholder resident within a 9.6 kilometre square of land, that is not part of a municipality, a geographic township or a separate school zone, who desire to establish the square of land as a separate school zone and unite the zone with one or more separate school zones, other than the separate school zone of a district school board.

(2) **Procedure.**—Where a meeting is held under subsection (1), the persons present shall,

(a) elect a chair and a secretary for the meeting;

(b) pass a motion to determine that the area of the municipality or geographic township or 9.6 kilometre square of land, as the case requires, be established as a separate school zone;

(c) if clause (1)(a) or (b) applies, elect the required number of board members; and

(d) require the chair of the meeting to transmit notice in writing of the holding of the meeting and of the election of board members to the clerks of the municipalities affected and to the secretary of any board that has jurisdiction in all or part of the area in which the separate school zone is to be established, designating by name and residence each of the persons elected as board members.

(3) **Certification.**—Each of the officers receiving the notice shall certify thereon the date of its receipt, and shall transmit a copy of the notice so certified to the chair of the meeting.

(4) **Notification.**—The chair of the meeting shall forthwith transmit the copy of the certified notice, a copy of the minutes of the meeting, and of the notice calling it, to,

(a) the Minister; and
(b) the appropriate assessment commissioner.

(5) **Corporate name.**—On and after transmission to the Minister of the documents referred to in subsection (4), the separate school zone is established and the board members named therein are a body corporate under the name of "The .... Roman Catholic Separate School Board" or "Conseil des écoles séparées catholiques de ...." or both (inserting the name selected by the board and approved by the Minister).

(6) **Formation not rendered invalid.**—The formation of a separate school zone is not rendered invalid by reason only of a vacancy in the office of a board member occurring before the board members become a body corporate, provided that the vacancy is filled promptly and the Minister is provided with the information required under clause (2) (d) in respect of the filling of the vacancy.

(7) **Qualifications of members.**—A person is qualified to be elected as a board member at a meeting to establish a separate school zone if he or she is,

(a) resident in the zone;
(b) a Canadian citizen;
(c) at least 18 years of age; and
(d) a Roman Catholic.

1997, c. 31, s. 47.

81. (1) **Powers of board members.**—The board members elected at a meeting convened under subsection 80(1) have all the powers of a district school area board in territory without municipal organization and are in all other respects subject to the provisions of this Act that apply to boards of rural separate schools.

(2) **Where school not united.**—Where in any year a separate school zone is established by not fewer than five members of five families under clause 80(1)(c), the public meeting for the election of board members shall be held before June 1 in that year, and the only powers and duties of the board so formed are to proceed in the same year to implement the provisions of section 84, and if the separate school zone is not united with one or more separate school zones to form a combined separate school zone before August 1 in that year under section 84, the board is dissolved on that date.

1997, c. 31, s. 48.

82. Right to vote in year of establishment of zone.—A Roman Catholic who is a householder or freeholder, who is eighteen years of age and who desires to establish the area in which the Roman Catholic is resident as a separate school zone under section 80, is entitled, in the year in which the separate school zone is established, to vote on any matter that relates to the separate school.

83. Legislative grants.—On receipt by the Minister of the documents required under section 80 that a separate school zone has been established and where the Minister is satisfied that suitable accommodation has been provided for school purposes, the Minister may pay to the board for educational purposes the sums approved for the purpose by the Lieutenant Governor in Council.

1997, c. 31, s. 49.

84. (1) Formation of combined separate school zones.—A Roman Catholic school authority or five supporters of the Roman Catholic school authority may, before July 1 in any year, hold a meeting of the supporters of the school authority to consider the question of uniting the separate school zone with one or more other separate school zones, other than the zone of a separate district school board, to form a combined separate school zone and, where the majority of the supporters present at the meeting who vote on the question, vote in favour of the union each board shall give notice of the decision, before August 1 of the same year, to the Minister, the clerks of the municipalities affected, and the appropriate assessment commissioner, and the combined separate school zone formed under this section shall be deemed to be one zone for all Roman Catholic school purposes on December 1 of the same year, except that, for the purposes of the election of board members, it shall be deemed to be one zone on the day of nomination for board members of the combined separate school board.

(2) [Repealed 1997, c. 31, s. 50]

(3) **Dissolution of boards.**—When a combined separate school zone is formed, the board of each zone forming part of the union is dissolved, and all the real and personal property vested in such board is vested in the board of the combined separate school zone.

(4) **Corporate name.**—The members of a combined separate school board are a corporation by the name of "The ....Combined Roman Catholic Separate School Board" or "Conseil unifié des écoles séparées catholiques de ...." or both *(inserting the name selected by the board and approved by the Minister)*.

1997, c. 31, s. 50.

85. (1) Detaching school zone from combined school zone.—Where, in an area that is not part of the area of jurisdiction of a separate district school board, a petition to detach a separate school zone from a combined separate school zone is submitted in any year to the combined separate school board, the board shall provide for a vote on the question within 90 days of the receipt of the petition.

(1.1) **Same.**—A petition under subsection (1) must be from at least 10 members of 10 families, with each member being at least 18 years of age, a householder or freeholder and a supporter of a combined separate school.

(2) **Qualified voters detaching a separate school zone.**—The persons who are entitled to vote on the question are the supporters of the combined separate school who reside in the portion of the combined separate school zone that it is proposed to detach.

(3) **When school zone detached.**—If, before July 1 in any year, a majority of the supporters who are entitled to vote on the question vote in favour of detaching the zone, it is detached on January 1 of the following year, except that, for the purposes of the election of board members, it shall be deemed to be detached on the day of nomination for board members,

PART IV — SCHOOL AUTHORITIES — ROMAN CATHOLIC   S. 86

and the requisite number of board members of the separate school zone so detached shall be elected as provided under section 92 or 93, as the case may be.

1997, c. 31, s. 51.

86. (1) **Discontinuing school authority: vote of supporters.**—A Roman Catholic school authority or five supporters of the school authority may, before July 1 in any year, hold a meeting of its supporters to consider the question of discontinuing the school authority and, where the majority of the supporters vote in favour of discontinuing and fewer than five supporters vote in opposition, the school authority shall within 30 days notify the Minister, the clerk of each municipality concerned and the secretary of any board that may be affected and, for assessment purposes, the zone shall be discontinued on September 30 following the meeting.

(2) **Discontinuing school authority: other conditions.**—A Roman Catholic school authority is discontinued on November 30 in any year, if,

(a) for any continuous four month period in a school year, after the year in which the school authority was established, the school authority,
   (i) fails to operate a school, or
   (ii) fails to make an agreement with another Roman Catholic board for the education of its pupils and fails to provide transportation for the pupils who would otherwise be excused from attendance under clause 21(2)(c);

(b) no one is assessed as a separate school supporter in the separate school zone in relation to property in respect of which taxes are to be levied in the following year; or

(c) the supporters fail to elect the required number of board members in two successive regular elections.

(3) **Notice to Minister, etc., of discontinuance.**—When a board is discontinued under subsection (2), the appropriate supervisory officer shall promptly notify the Minister, the clerks of the municipalities concerned and the secretaries of the affected boards.

(4) **Settling accounts.**—The board members who are in office in the year in which the school authority is discontinued under this section shall remain in office for the purpose of settling the accounts and outstanding debts of the school authority and, following an audit by a person licensed under the Public Accountancy Act, shall forward the balance of its funds to the Minister for deposit in the Consolidated Revenue Fund for safekeeping.

(5) **Records.**—The records of a school authority that has been discontinued under this section shall be filed with the Ministry.

(6) **Boundaries to be revised.**—The boundaries of the zones that are altered as a result of discontinuing a separate school zone shall be revised by the appropriate supervisory officer.

(7) **Sale of real property.**—Where a school authority that has been discontinued fails to dispose of its real property in the year in which it was discontinued and the appropriate school authority supervisory officer is notified that an offer to purchase the real property has been made, he or she shall cause notices to be posted to call a meeting of the persons who were supporters in the year in which the school authority was discontinued to elect three persons who, when elected, are a board for the purpose of selling the property.

S. 86.1

(8) **Deposit of funds from sale.**—When the school authority has sold the real property, it shall, after paying any outstanding debts, forward the balance of the money received from the sale to the Minister for deposit in the Consolidated Revenue Fund for safekeeping.

(9) **Re-establishing school authority.**—A school authority that has been discontinued in any year may, in any subsequent year, be re-established in the manner provided for in section 80, and the funds that were deposited by the school authority that was discontinued shall be returned to the school authority.

1993, c. 11, s. 23; 1997, c. 31, s. 52.

86.1 Regulation.—If the board of a separate school zone in the territorial districts applies to the Minister to extend the boundaries of the separate school zone so as to include parcels of land on which a separate school zone cannot be established because of the operation of subsection 80(1), the Lieutenant Governor in Council may by regulation extend the boundaries of the separate school zone.

1997, c. 31, s. 53.

Separate School Electors

87. [Repealed 1997, c. 31, s. 54.]

88. Where person residing out of urban municipality to vote.—When a supporter of a separate school in an urban municipality resides outside the municipality, he or she is entitled to vote in the ward or polling subdivision in which the separate school nearest to his or her residence is situate.

Rural Separate Schools

89. (1) **Term of office of board members.**—The board of a rural separate school shall consist of three members who, subject to subsection (3), shall be elected in each year in which a regular election is held under the Municipal Elections Act, 1996 and shall hold office until the date the next regular election is held under that Act and their successors are elected under this Act and the new board is organized.

(2) **Same.**—The term of office of members of a rural separate school board shall commence on December 1 in the year of a regular election.

(3) **Same.**—Where the first election of a newly established rural separate school board is held in a year in which no regular election is held under the Municipal Elections Act, 1996, the members so elected shall hold office until the date on which the next regular election is held under that Act and their successors are elected under this Act and the new board is organized.

(4) **Organization and quorum.**—A majority of the board members is a quorum, and the board shall be organized by the election of a chair and by the appointment of a secretary and a treasurer or of a secretary-treasurer.

(5) **Regularity.**—No act or proceeding is valid that is not adopted at a regular or special meeting of the board of which notice has been given as required under section 90 and at which at least two board members are present.

(6) **Entitlement to vote.**—Subject to subsection (7), the following are entitled to vote at any election of members of a board of a rural separate school and on any school question at any meeting of the supporters of the board:
1. A person who is at least 18 years of age, a Canadian citizen and a supporter of the rural separate school and who either resides in the area of jurisdiction of the board or is the owner or tenant of residential property in the area of jurisdiction of the board.
2. A Roman Catholic spouse of a person mentioned in paragraph 1.
3. A person entitled to vote under section 54 for the board.

(7) **Exception.**—Only a person described in paragraph 1 of subsection (6) is entitled to vote on a question involving the selection of a school site or an expenditure for a permanent improvement.

1997, c. 31, s. 55.

90. (1) **Duties of rural boards.**—It is the duty of every rural separate school board and it has power,
- (a) **time and place of meetings.**—to appoint the place of each annual school meeting of the supporters of the school, and the time and place of any special meeting for,
    - (i) filling any vacancy in the board,
    - (ii) the approval of a site selected by the board for a new school,
    - (iii) the appointment of a school auditor, or
    - (iv) any other school purpose,
  and to cause notices of the time and place and of the objects of such meetings to be posted in three or more public places of the neighbourhood in which the school is situate at least six days before the time of holding the meeting;
- (b) **annual report.**—to cause to be prepared and read at the annual school meeting a report for the year then ending, containing among other things a summary of the proceedings of the board during the year, together with a full and detailed account of the receipts and expenditures of all school money during such year, and signed by the chair and by one or both of the school auditors.

(2) **Appointment of auditor by the Minister.**—Where a rural separate school board the Minister neglects or the supporters at an annual or special meeting neglect to appoint an auditor, or an auditor appointed refuses or is unable to act, the Minister, upon the request in writing of any five supporters of the school, may make the appointment.

(3) **Approval of new school site.**—No site for a new school shall be acquired by a rural separate school board without approval of the site by the majority of the supporters of the rural separate school who are present at an annual or a special meeting of the board.

R.S.O. 1990, c. E.2, s. 90.

91. [Repealed 1997, c. 31, s. 56.]

92. (1) **Annual meeting.**—An annual meeting of the supporters of a rural separate school shall be held on the last Wednesday in December or, if that day is a holiday, on the next day following, commencing at the hour of 10 o'clock in the forenoon, or if the board by resolution so directs, at the hour of 1 o'clock or 8 o'clock in the afternoon, at such place as the board by resolution determines or, in the absence of such resolution, at the separate school.

S. 92   EDUCATION ACT

(2) **Election of board.**—A rural separate school board shall be elected at a meeting of the separate school supporters held on the second Monday in November or, where that day is Remembrance Day, on the next succeeding day, in the year of a municipal election at a time and place selected by the board.

(3) **Idem.**—Where the annual meeting of supporters of the school cannot conveniently be held as provided for in subsection (1), the supporters, at a regular meeting or at a special meeting called for that purpose, may pass a resolution naming another day for the holding of the annual meeting, which shall be held on that day in each year thereafter until some other day is similarly named.

(4) **Organization of meeting.**—The supporters of the school present at a meeting shall elect one of themselves to preside over its proceedings and shall also appoint a secretary who shall record the proceedings of the meeting and perform such other duties as are required of the secretary by this section.

(5) **Order of business.**—The business of the annual meeting may be conducted in the following order,

- (a) receiving and dealing with the annual report of the board members;
- (b) receiving and dealing with the annual report of the auditors;
- (c) appointing one or more auditors for the current year;
- (d) electing a board member or members to fill any vacancy or vacancies; and
- (e) miscellaneous business.

(6) **Duties of presiding officer.**—The presiding officer shall submit all motions to the meeting in the manner desired by the majority, and is entitled to vote on any motion, and,

- (a) in the case of an equality of votes with respect to the election of two or more candidates, the presiding officer shall provide for drawing lots to determine which of the candidates is elected; and
- (b) in the case of an equality of votes on a motion, the motion is lost.

(7) **Granting poll and proceedings in case of a poll.**—Where a poll is demanded by two supporters of the school at a meeting for the in case of a election of a board member, the presiding officer shall forthwith grant the poll.

(8) **Entries in poll book.**—Where a poll is granted, the secretary shall enter in a poll book the name and residence of each qualified supporter of the school offering to vote within the time prescribed and shall furnish him or her, at the time of voting, with a ballot paper on the back of which the secretary has placed his or her initials, and shall provide a pencil for the marking of the ballot paper.

(9) **Form of ballot paper.**—Ballot papers shall be pieces of plain white paper of uniform size.

(10) **Marking of ballot paper.**—A voter shall mark his or her ballot,

- (a) in the election of a board member, by marking the name of the board member on it; and
- (b) on a question, by marking thereon "for" or "pour" if in favour or "against" or "contre" if opposed.

(11) **Number of votes.**—A voter is entitled to as many votes as there are board members to be elected, but may not give more than one vote to any one candidate.

(12) **Manner of voting.**—Each voter shall mark his or her ballot paper in a compartment or other place provided for the purpose that is so arranged that the manner in which the voter marks the ballot is not visible to other persons and shall thereupon fold it so that the initials of the secretary can be seen without opening it and hand it to the secretary who shall, without unfolding it, ascertain that the secretary's initials appear upon it and shall then in full view of all present, including the voter, place the ballot in a ballot box or other suitable container that has been placed and is kept upon a table for the purpose.

(13) **Appointment of scrutineer.**—Every candidate may appoint a person to act as the candidate's scrutineer during the election.

(14) **Declaration where right to vote objected to.**—When an objection is made to the right of a person to vote at a meeting of the supporters of a rural separate school, either for a board member or on a school question, the presiding officer shall require the person whose right to vote is objected to to make the following declaration in English or in French, after which the person making the declaration is entitled to vote:

I, ..., declare and affirm that I have the right to vote at this election for .... (insert name of board) [or on the question submitted to this meeting of the ....(insert name of board)].

(15) **When poll shall close.**—The poll shall not close before noon, but shall close at any time thereafter when a full hour has elapsed without any vote being polled, and shall not be kept open later than 4 o'clock in the afternoon.

(16) **Polling at afternoon meetings.**—When a meeting for the election of meetings one or more board members is held at 8 o'clock in the afternoon the supporters present may decide by resolution that the polling shall take place forthwith or at 10 o'clock on the following morning, and if it takes place forthwith the poll shall close when ten minutes have elapsed without any vote being recorded.

(17) **Counting votes, tie vote.**—When the poll is closed, the presiding officer and secretary shall count the votes polled for the respective candidates or affirmatively and negatively upon the question submitted, and,

(a) in the case of an equality of votes with respect to the election of two or more candidates, the presiding officer shall provide for drawing lots to determine which of the candidates is elected; and

(b) in the case of an equality of votes on a motion, the motion is lost.

(18) **Declaration of result.**—In the case of an election of board members the presiding officer shall then declare the candidate elected for whom the highest number of votes has been polled, and in case of a vote on a motion the presiding officer shall declare it carried or lost as the majority of votes is in favour of or against the motion.

(19) **Statement of result of poll.**—A statement of the result of the vote shall be certified by the presiding officer and secretary and in the case of an election of board members the statement shall be signed by any scrutineer present at the counting of the ballots and a copy thereof shall be delivered to each candidate.

(20) **Secretary to transmit minutes to Ministry.**—A correct copy of the minutes of every meeting, signed by the presiding officer and secretary of the meeting, shall be transmitted forthwith by the secretary to the Ministry.

(21) **Meetings called in default of first or annual meeting.**—If from want of proper notice or other cause any meeting for the election of board members is not held at the proper time, the appropriate separate school supervisory officer or any two supporters of the school may call a meeting by giving six days notice posted in at least three of the most public places in the locality in which the school is situate.

(22) **Validity of election.**—No election under this section is invalid by reason of non-compliance with the provisions of this section as to the taking of the poll or the counting of the votes, or by reason of any mistake in the use of forms, or of any irregularity, if it appears that the election was conducted in accordance with the principles laid down in this section, and that the non-compliance or mistake or irregularity did not affect the result of the election.

1993, c. 11, s. 24; 1997, c. 31, s. 57.

93. (1) **Where municipality may conduct election.**—Despite section 92, if the rural separate school zone is a municipality or combination of municipalities, the board of the rural separate school may, by resolution passed before July 1 in the year of an election and approved at a meeting of the supporters of the rural separate school, determine that the election of members of the board shall be conducted by the municipality having the greatest population under the Municipal Elections Act, 1996 and the members of the board shall be elected by general vote of the persons entitled to vote in the election.

(2) **Application of *Municipal Elections Act*.**—Despite section 92, if the area of a rural separate school zone is not in a township or territory without municipal organization, in the year of a regular election the Municipal Elections Act, 1996 applies with necessary modifications to the election of board members of the rural separate school board, except that the voter shall take the following oath or make the following affirmation in English or French:

> You swear (or affirm) that you are the person named (or intended to be named) in the list of voters now shown to you (showing the list to the voter); That you are eighteen years of age; That you have the right to vote at this election; That you have not voted before at this election; That you have not, directly or indirectly, received any reward or gift and do not expect to receive any for the vote which you tender at this election. So help you God. (delete this sentence in an affirmation).

1997, c. 31, s. 58.

Combined Separate School Zones

94. (1) **Secretary of board as returning officer.**—If territory without municipal organization is part of a combined separate school zone and the election of members of the board for a part of the combined zone is conducted under the Municipal Elections Act, 1996, the secretary of the board shall be the returning officer and shall perform all the duties of a municipal clerk in the election for the territory without municipal organization.

(2) **Reporting of vote.**—The secretary of the board shall report forthwith the vote recorded in the territory to the returning officer for the municipality having the greatest population in the electoral area, of which the territory without municipal organization forms part.

(3) **Reporting if no municipality.**—If there is no municipality in the electoral area, the secretary of the board shall report to the returning officer of the municipality that has the

greatest population in the area of jurisdiction of the board and the returning officer shall prepare the final summary and announce the result of the vote.

1997, c. 31, ss. 59, 60.

95. (1) Board members where combined zone is formed or altered.—Where a combined separate school zone is formed or where another separate school zone is added to or detached from a combined separate school zone, the board members in office shall retire on December 1 following the election of the members of the board of the combined separate school zone and, subject to the number of board members being determined under subsection (4) or (5), five board members shall be elected by the supporters of the newly-created or altered combined separate school zone,

(a) as provided in section 92, where the combined separate school zone is formed, or where another separate school zone is added to or detached from a combined separate school zone during the two years following the year in which a regular election was held under the Municipal Elections Act, 1996, in which case the provisions of section 89 apply; or

(b) as provided in section 93, where the combined separate school zone is formed or where another separate school zone is added to or detached from a combined separate school zone in the year in which a regular election is to be held under the *Municipal Elections Act, 1996*.

(2) **Board members in office until organization of new board.**—Every board member shall continue in office until his or her successor has been elected and the new board is organized.

(3) **First board members.**—For the purpose of electing the first board members for a combined separate school zone, the boards of the separate schools forming the combined separate school zone shall, before September 1, each appoint a person to a committee, which shall arrange for the election of board members in accordance with section 92 or 93 as the case may be.

(4) **Board members in combined separate school zone including urban municipality.**—Where a combined separate school zone includes one or more urban municipalities, the board shall be composed of eight members and the zone shall be deemed to be one separate school zone.

(5) **Resolution providing for board members.**—Despite subsections (1) and (4), the board of a combined separate school zone may be composed of such number of members, not fewer than five or more than nine, representing such municipalities or parts of municipalities, or separate school zones in territory without municipal organization, within the combined separate school zone as is provided for in a resolution passed by the board, or, in the case of a newly-formed combined separate school zone, by the committee formed under subsection (3).

(6) **Election and term of office.**—Where a resolution is passed under subsection (5), the board members shall be elected at large in the areas within the combined separate school zone that they respectively represent, and sections 54 and 93 apply with necessary modifications, provided that, where a municipality is divided into wards, the resolution may provide for representation by wards.

(7) **Distribution of members.**—Where one or more board members represent two or more municipalities or parts of municipalities, or two or more municipalities or parts of

municipalities and one or more separate school zones in territory without municipal organization, and the election is conducted as provided in section 93, the provisions of the regulations made under clause 58.1(2)(k) apply with necessary modifications.

(8) **Copy of resolution to be sent to Minister.**—The board or committee that passes a resolution under subsection (5) shall promptly send a copy of it to the Minister.

(9) **Electors' qualifications, combined separate school zone.**—Every person who resides in a combined separate school zone and is entitled to vote at the election of board members under section 89 is entitled to vote at the election of board members of the combined separate school zone and, subject to subsection 89(7), on any school question.

1996, c. 32, s. 70(3); 1997, c. 31, ss. 61, 62.

PART IV.1
EXTENSION OF ROMAN CATHOLIC ELEMENTARY SCHOOLS

Separate School Extension Post—1997

96. (1) **Plan re secondary school.**—A Roman Catholic school authority may adopt a plan for the provision of secondary school education in the area of jurisdiction of the school authority.

(2) **Resolution.**—The adoption of a plan under subsection (1) shall be by resolution.

(3) **Implementation document.**—A school authority that adopts a plan under subsection (1) shall prepare an implementation document explaining how secondary school education would be provided in the area of jurisdiction of the school authority.

(4) **Same.**—The Minister may establish guidelines respecting the preparation of an implementation document.

(5) **Transmittal.**—The secretary of a school authority that adopts a plan under subsection (1) shall transmit to the Minister a copy of the resolution, certified by the secretary, together with a copy of the implementation document.

(6) **Review by Minister.**—The Minister shall review the implementation document and determine whether he or she is satisfied that the proposals set out in it would permit the provision of viable secondary school education in the area of jurisdiction of the school authority.

(7) **Notice.**—The Minister shall notify the school authority of his or her determination under subsection (6).

(8) **Same.**—If the Minister determines that the school authority's proposals would permit the provision of viable secondary school education in the area of jurisdiction of the school authority, the Minister shall advise the following persons of the determination and of the fact that implementation of the plan would require a regulation to be made under subsection 58.1(2) and provide them with a copy of the implementation document:

1. The secretary of every affected board.
2. The clerk of every municipality all or part of which is within the area of jurisdiction of the school authority.
3. The appropriate assessment commissioner.

1997, c. 31, s. 63.

PART IV.1 — EXTENSION OF ROMAN CATHOLIC ELEMENTARY SCHOOLS   S. 135

[Note: sections 97 through 132 inclusive repealed by EQIA, section 63]

133. [Repealed 1994, c. 27, s. 108(4).]

134. [Repealed 1997, c. 31, s. 64.]

Rights Relating to Separate School Extension Pre-1998

135. (1) **Definitions.**—In this section,

"**designated person**".—"designated person" means a person designated or deemed to be designated under section 135 of this Act, as it read immediately before the *Education Quality Improvement Act, 1997* received Royal Assent; ("Personne desiqnee")

"**transferred**".—"transferred" means transferred under section 135 of this Act, as it read immediately before the Education Quality Improvement Act, 1997 received Royal Assent. ("mute")

(2) [Repealed 1997, c. 31, s. 66(2).]

(3) [Repealed 1997, c. 31, s. 66(2).]

(4) [Repealed 1997, c. 31, s. 66(2).]

(5) [Repealed 1995, c. 4, s. 2(2).]

(6) [Repealed 1997, c. 31, s. 66(3).]

(7) [Repealed 1997, c. 31, s. 66(3).]

(8) [Repealed 1997, c. 31, s. 66(3).]

(9) [Repealed 1997, c. 31, s. 66(3).]

(10) [Repealed 997, c. 31, s. 66(3).]

(11) [Repealed 1997, c. 31, s. 66(3).]

(12) [Repealed 1997, c. 31, s. 66(3).]

(13) [Repealed 1997, c. 31, s. 66(3).]

(14) [Repealed 1997, c. 31, s. 66(3).]

(15) [Repealed 1997, c. 31, s. 66(3).]

(16) [Repealed 1997, c. 31, s. 66(3).]

(17) [Repealed 1997, c. 31, s. 66(3).]

(18) [Repealed 1997, c. 31, s. 66(3).]

(19) [Repealed 1997, c. 31, s. 66(3).]

(20) [Repealed 1997, c. 31, s. 66(3).]

(21) [Repealed 1997, c. 31, s. 66(3).]

(22) [Repealed 1997, c. 31, s. 66(3).]

(23) [Repealed 1997, c. 31, s. 66(3).]

(24) **Gratuity.**—On termination of employment with the board to which a designated person's teaching contract, employment contract or employment relationship is transferred, the person is entitled to payment of an amount calculated in accordance with,

    (a) the collective agreement that applied on the last date the person was employed by the public board that designated the person, as though the person had been in the continuous employ of the public board, if a collective agreement applied in respect of the person on that date; or

(b) the policy of the public board that designated the person as of the last date he or she was employed by the public board, as though the person had been in the continuous employ of the public board, if no collective agreement applied in respect of the person on that date.

(25) **Idem.**—In lieu of the payment under subsection (24), the designated person is entitled to require payment of an amount calculated in accordance with,

(a) the collective agreement that applies in respect of the person on the last date the person is employed before the termination of employment, if a collective agreement applies in respect of the person on that date; or

(b) the policy of the board with which the person is employed as of the last date he or she is employed by that board, if no collective agreement applies in respect of the person on that date.

(26) **Idem.**—The amount of the payment under subsection (24) or (25) shall be shared by the public board that designated the person and the board or boards to which the person's employment was transferred under this section in the ratio that the number of years of service of the person with each board bears to the total number of years of service of the person with such boards.

(26.1) **Idem.**—Despite subsection (26), the boards concerned may agree to share the amount of the payment under subsection (24) or (25) in any manner, including the payment of the entire amount by one of the boards.

1991, vol. 2, c. 10, s. 4(1).

(27) [Repealed 1997, c. 31, s. 66(5).]

(28) **Employment advancement and promotion.**—Section 5 of the Human Rights Code applies to designated persons employed by a Roman Catholic school board in respect of their employment, advancement and promotion by the Board, despite section 23 of the said Code.

(29) [Repealed 1997, c. 31, s. 66(6).]

(30) **Deemed designated persons.**—This section applies with necessary modifications in respect of entitlements of teachers who were employed by a public board that has jurisdiction in an area that is also the area or part of the area of jurisdiction of a Roman Catholic school board and who subsequent to a report to the Minister by the Commission under subsection 136f (1) as enacted by the Statutes of Ontario, 1986, chapter 21, section 2, but before the 24th day of June, 1986 accepted employment with the Roman Catholic school board.

1991, vol. 2, c. 10, s. 4; 1995, c. 4, s. 2(2).

(31) **Interpretation.**—For the purposes of this section, the following rules apply:

1. "Public board" in subsections (24) and (30) has the same meaning as it did immediately before the Education Quality Improvement Act, 1997 received Royal Assent.
2. A reference in subsection (26) to the public board that designated a person shall be deemed to be a reference to the successor to the old board that designated the person.
3. A reference to the board or boards to which a person's employment is transferred shall be deemed to be a reference to the successor or successors to the old board or old boards to which the person's employment was transferred.

PART IV.1 — EXTENSION OF ROMAN CATHOLIC ELEMENTARY SCHOOLS   S. 136

4. Except as otherwise provided by regulation, for the purposes of paragraph 2, the successor to an old board that designated a person,
   i. in the case of a person designated in relation to schools and classes operated under Part XII of this Act, as it read on December 31, 1997, is the French-language public district school board the area of jurisdiction of which includes all or the major part of the area of jurisdiction of the old board that designated the person, and
   ii. in the case of a designated person other than one described in subparagraph i, is the English-language public district school board the area of jurisdiction of which includes all or the major part of the area of jurisdiction of the old board that designated the person.
5. Except as otherwise provided by regulation, for the purposes of paragraph 3, the successor to an old board to which a person's employment was transferred is,
   i. in the case of a person designated in relation to schools and classes operated under Part XII of this Act, as it read on December 31, 1997, is the French-language separate district school board the area of jurisdiction of which includes all or the major part of the area of jurisdiction of the old board to which the person's employment was transferred, and
   ii. in the case of a designated person other than one described in subparagraph i, is the English-language separate district school board the area of jurisdiction of which includes all or the major part of the area of jurisdiction of the old board to which the person's employment was transferred.

(32) **Regulations: exceptions re successor board determinations.**—The Lieutenant Governor in Council may make regulations providing for exceptions to paragraphs 4 and 5 of subsection (31).

(33) **Application of *Interpretation Act*.**—The fact that section 66 of the Education Quality Improvement Act, 1997 repeals some but not all parts of section 135 of the Education Act, as that section read immediately before the coming into force of section 66 of the Education Quality Improvement Act, 1997, shall not be construed as having any effect on the application of section 14 of the Interpretation Act to the repealed parts.

1991, vol. 2, c. 10, s. 4; 1995, c. 4, s. 2; 1997, c. 31, s. 66.

135.1 (1) **Interpretation: references to ten school year period.**—A reference in this Act to hiring after the ten school year period mentioned in subsection 135(6) shall,

(a) in the case of a teacher hired by an old board after the expiration of the old board's ten-year period, as determined under subsection 135(6) of this Act as it read on December 31, 1997, be deemed to be a reference to hiring after that ten-year period; and

(b) in every other case, be deemed to be a reference to hiring on or after January 1, 1998.

(2) **Interpretation: references to Roman Catholic school board.**—A reference in this Act to a Roman Catholic school board shall be deemed to be a reference to a separate district school board.

1997, c. 31, s. 67.

136. (1) **Hiring after ten-year period.**—For the purpose of maintaining the distinctive-

S. 137 EDUCATION ACT

ness of separate schools, the Roman Catholic school board may require as a condition of employment that teachers hired by the board after the ten school year period mentioned in subsection 135(6) agree to respect the philosophy and traditions of Roman Catholic separate schools in the performance of their duties.

(2) **Application of *Human Rights Code* s. 5.**—Subject to subsection (1), and despite section 24 of the *Human Rights Code*, section 5 of the said Code applies to ensure that such teachers employed by a Roman Catholic school board will enjoy equal opportunity in respect of their employment, advancement and promotion by the board

(3) **Repeal.**—If it is finally determined by a court that subsection (1) or (2) prejudicially affects a right or privilege with respect to denominational schools guaranteed by the Constitution of Canada, subsections (1) and (2) are repealed, it being the intention of the Legislature that the remaining provisions of the Act are separate from and independent of the said subsections. R.S.O. 1990, c. E.2, s. 136.

137. Enforcement.—A right referred to in section 135 may be enforced by order of the Divisional Court on application to the court.

1997, c. 31, s. 68.

138. [Repealed 1997, c. 31, s. 68.]
139. [Repealed 1997, c. 31, s. 68.]
140. [Repealed 1997, c. 31, s. 68.]
141. [Repealed 1997, c. 31, s. 68.]
142. [Repealed 1997, c. 31, s. 68.]
143. [Repealed 1997, c. 31, s. 69.]
144. [Repealed 1997, c. 31, s. 70.]
145. [Repealed 1997, c. 31, s. 70.]
146. [Repealed 1997, c. 31, s. 70.]

Planning and Implementation Commission

147. [Repealed R.S.O. 1990, c. E.2, s. 154.]
148. [Repealed R.S.O. 1990, c. E.2, s. 154.]
149. [Repealed R.S.O. 1990, c. E.2, s. 154.]
150. [Repealed R.S.O. 1990, c. E.2, s. 154.]
151. [Repealed R.S.O. 1990, c. E.2, s. 154.]
152. [Repealed R.S.O. 1990, c. E.2, s. 154.]
153. [Repealed R.S.O. 1990, c. E.2, s. 154.]
154. [Repealed 1997, c. 31, s. 70.]
155. [Repealed 1997, c. 31, s. 70.]
156. [Repealed 1997, c. 31, s. 70.]
157. [Repealed 1997, c. 31, s. 70.]

PART V

SCHOOL AUTHORITIES — PROTESTANT

1997, c. 31, s. 71

158. (1) **Application to establish Protestant separate school.**—Subject to subsection (3), before July 1 in any year, not fewer than five members of five families, with each member being Protestant, at least 18 years of age and resident in a municipality, may apply in writing for permission to establish in the municipality one or more separate schools for Protestants.

(1.1) **Same.**—In the case of a municipality that is a township, the application shall be to the council of the township.

(1.2) **Same.**—In the case of a municipality that is an urban municipality, the application shall be to the appropriate public board.

(2) **Permission to establish.**—Subject to subsection (3), the council or the public board, as the case may be, within thirty days of the receipt of a proper application shall grant permission to the applicants to establish in the municipality one or more separate schools for Protestants.

(3) **Restrictions on establishment.**—A Protestant separate school shall not be established in a municipality except where the teacher or teachers in the public school or schools in the municipality are Roman Catholics.

(4) **Effective date.**—A Protestant separate school is established on the day following the granting of permission to establish the school by the council or public board, as the case may be.

1997, c. 31, 72.

159. Protestant board: share of legislative grants.—A Protestant separate school board shall share in the legislative grants in like manner as an English-language public board.

1997, c. 31, s. 73.

160. [Repealed 1997, c. 31, s. 73.]

161. [Repealed 1997, c. 31, s. 73.]

162. [Repealed 1997, c. 31, s. 73.]

163. [Repealed 1997, c. 31, s. 73.]

164. Qualification of a voter.—Every person who is assessed as a Protestant separate school supporter and whose name appears on the list of voters of the municipality in which the land in respect of which he or she is assessed is situate, and the wife or husband of such supporter, if she or he is a Protestant, is entitled to vote at the election of members for the Protestant separate school board and on any school question having to do with the Protestant separate school or board.

1997, c. 31, s. 74.

165. (1) **Election of board members.**—A Protestant separate school board shall have the same number of members that the board of a rural separate school would have if established in the same municipality, and the members may be elected in the same manner as the members of a board of a rural separate school may be elected, and the provisions of Part IV with respect to the election of members of a board of a rural separate school apply with necessary modifications to the election of members of Protestant separate school boards.

(2) **Same.**—Despite subsection (1), section 58.7 applies with necessary modifications to the election of members of a Protestant separate school board that is situated in an urban municipality.

(3) **Number of board members.**—Despite subsection (1), a Protestant separate school board that is situated in an urban municipality shall be composed of eight members.

1997, c. 31, s. 75.

166. Corporate name of board.—The members of every Protestant separate school board are a body corporate under the name of "The Protestant Separate School Board of the................." or "Conseil des écoles séparées protestantes de....................." or both *(inserting the name of the city, town, village or township)*.

1997, c. 31, s. 76.

167. Powers of board.—A Protestant separate school board has the same powers as a district school area board.

167.1 Attendance rights.—The provisions of Part II respecting attendance rights in ation to a Roman Catholic school authority apply with necessary modifications in relation to a Protestant separate school board.

1997, c. 31, s. 77.

168. Discontinuing board.—A Protestant separate school board is discontinued in the same manner as a Roman Catholic rural separate school board is discontinued and may be re-established in the manner provided in section 158.

1997, c. 31, s. 78.

169. Application of other sections.—Subsections 89(3) and (4), subsection 90(2), clause (1)(d) and section 239 apply in respect of Protestant separate schools and Protestant separate school boards.

1997, c. 31, s. 79.

PART VI

BOARDS

Duties and Powers

170. (1) **Duties of boards.**—Every board shall,

1. **appoint secretary-treasurer.**—appoint a secretary and a treasurer or a secretary-treasurer who, in the case of a board of not more than five elected members, may be a member of the board;
2. **security of treasurer.**—take proper security from the treasurer or secretary-treasurer;
3. **order payment of bills.**—give the necessary orders on the treasurer for payment of all money expended for school purposes and of such other expenses for promoting

the interests of the schools under the jurisdiction of the board as may be authorized by this Act or the regulations and by the board;
4. **meetings.**—fix the times and places for the meetings of the board and the mode of calling and conducting them, and ensure that a full and correct account of the proceedings thereat is kept;
5. **head office.**—establish and maintain a head office and notify the Ministry of its location and address and notify the Ministry of any change in the location or address of the head office within ten days of such change;
6. **provide instruction and accommodation.**—provide instruction and adequate accommodation during each school year for the pupils who have a right to attend a school under the jurisdiction of the board;
6.1 **kindergarten.**—operate kindergartens;
6.2 [Repealed 1996, c. 13, s. 5(1)];
7. **Special education programs and services.**—provide or enter into an agreement with another board to provide in accordance with the regulations special education programs and special education services for its exceptional pupils;
8. **repair property.**—keep the school buildings and premises in proper repair and in a proper sanitary condition, provide suitable furniture and equipment and keep it in proper repair, and protect the property of the board;
9. **insurance.**—make provision for insuring adequately the buildings and equipment of the board and for insuring the board and its employees and volunteers who are assigned duties by the principal against claims in respect of accidents incurred by pupils while under the jurisdiction or supervision of the board;
10. **conduct schools.**—ensure that every school under its charge is conducted in accordance with this Act and the regulations;
11. **school open.**—keep open its schools during the whole period of the school year determined under the regulations, except where it is otherwise provided under this Act;
12. **appoint principal and teachers.**—appoint for each school that it operates a principal and an adequate number of teachers, all of whom shall be members of the Ontario College of Teachers;
12.1 **notice of offences.**—promptly notify the Minister in writing when the board becomes aware that a teacher who is or has been employed by the board has been convicted of an offence under the Criminal Code (Canada) involving sexual conduct and minors, or of any other offence that in the opinion of the board indicates that pupils may be at risk;
13. **provide textbooks.**—subject to paragraph 31.1 of subsection 171(1) provide, without charge, for the use of the pupils attending the school or schools operated by the board, the textbooks that are required by the regulations to be purchased by the board;
14. **vehicle insurance.**—where it furnishes transportation for pupils in a vehicle that is owned by the board, provide and carry with an insurer licensed under the Insurance Act for each such vehicle at least the amount of insurance that is required to be provided in respect of such a vehicle by the licensee of a school vehicle under the Public Vehicles Act;

S. 170.1 — EDUCATION ACT

15. **report children not enrolled.**—ascertain and report to the Ministry at least once in each year in the manner required by the Minister the names and ages of all children of compulsory school age within its jurisdiction who are not enrolled in any school or private school and the reasons therefor;
16. **reports.**—transmit to the Minister all reports and returns required by this Act and the regulations;
17. **statement of sick leave credits.**—where applicable, issue to an employee, upon the termination of his or her employment with the board, a statement of the sick leave credits standing to the employee's credit with the board at the time of such termination;
17.1 **School councils.**—establish a school council for each school operated by the board, in accordance with the regulations;
18. **requirements.**—do anything that a board is required to do under any other provision of this Act or under any other Act.
19. [Repealed 1997, c. 31, s. 80.]
20. [Repealed 1997, c. 31, s. 80.]

(2) **S. 67 school districts.**—Paragraph 6.1 of subsection (1) does not apply to the board of a secondary school district established under section 67.

(3) **Regulations re school councils.**—The Lieutenant Governor in Council may make regulations respecting school councils, including regulations relating to their establishment, composition and functions.

1993, c. 11, s. 30; 1996, c. 11, s. 29; 1996, c. 12, s. 64; 1996, c. 13, ss. 5, 12; 1997, c. 31, s. 80.

170.1 (1) **Class size.**—Every board shall ensure that the average size of its elementary school classes, in the aggregate, does not exceed 25 pupils.

(2) **Same, secondary schools.**—Every board shall ensure that the average size of its secondary school classes, in the aggregate, does not exceed 22 pupils.

(3) **Exception.**—The average size of a board's classes, in the aggregate, may exceed the maximum average class size specified in subsection (1) or (2), as the case may be, to the extent that the Minister, at the request of the board, may permit.

(4) **Determination date.**—A board shall determine the average size of its classes, in the aggregate, as of October 31 each year.

(5) **Regulations.**—The Lieutenant Governor in Council may, by regulation,
(a) establish the method to be used by a board to determine the average size of its classes, in the aggregate;
(b) exclude special education classes from the determination of average class size;
(c) require boards to prepare reports (containing the information specified by the regulation) concerning the average size of its classes and to make the reports available to the public;
(d) define terms used in this section for the purposes of a regulation made under this section.

(6) **Review of maximum amount.**—Every three years, the Minister shall review the amount of the maximum average class size specified in subsections (1) and (2).

1997, c. 31, s. 81.

170.2 (1) **Teaching time.**—In this section,

"**classroom teacher**" means a teacher who is assigned in a regular timetable to provide instruction to pupils but does not include a principal or vice-principal.

(2) **Minimum teaching time, elementary school.**—Every board shall ensure that, in the aggregate, its classroom teachers in elementary schools are assigned to provide instruction to pupils for an average of at least 1300 minutes (during the instructional program) for each period of five instructional days during the school year.

(3) **Minimum teaching time, secondary school.**—Every board shall ensure that, in the aggregate, its classroom teachers in secondary schools are assigned to provide instruction to pupils for an average of at least 1250 minutes (during the instructional program) for each period of five instructional days during the school year.

(4) **Allocation to schools.**—A board may allocate to each school a share of the board's aggregate minimum time for a school year for all of its classroom teachers (during which they must be assigned to provide instruction to pupils).

(5) **Allocation by principal.**—The principal of a school, in his or her sole discretion, shall allocate among the classroom teachers in the school the school's share of the board's aggregate minimum time (as described in subsection (4)) for the school year.

(6) **Same.**—The principal shall make the allocation in accordance with such policies as the board may establish.

(7) **Effect on collective agreements.**—An allocation under subsection (4) or (5) may be made despite any applicable conditions or restrictions in a collective agreement.

(8) **Calculation.**—The calculation of the amount of time that a board's classroom teachers are assigned as required by subsection (2) or (3) shall be based upon all of the board's classroom teachers and their assignments (on a regular time-table) on every instructional day during the school year.

(9) **Part-time employees.**—For the purposes of subsection (2) or (3), the minimum time required in respect of each classroom teacher who is employed on a part-time basis by the board is correspondingly reduced.

(10) **Definition.**—In subsection (11),

"**credit**" includes a credit equivalent awarded in connection with a grade nine program in the 1998-99 school year.

(11) **Interpretation: provision of instruction in a secondary school.**—For the purposes of this section, a classroom teacher in a secondary school is assigned to provide instruction only when he or she is assigned in a regular timetable to invigilate examinations or to provide instruction in,

(a) a course or program that is eligible for credit;
(b) a special education program;
(c) a remedial class the purpose of which is to assist one or more pupils in completing a

course or program that is eligible for credit or required for an Ontario secondary school diploma;
(d) an English as a second language or actualisation linguistique en français program;
(e) an apprenticeship program;
(f) a co-operative education program; or
(g) any other class, course or program specified or described in a regulation made under clause (13)(a).

(12) **Co-operative education programs: interpretation.**—For the purposes of clause (11)(f), a teacher is assigned to provide instruction in a co-operative education program when he or she is assigned in a regular timetable to arrange placements for the program or to make site visits to monitor or evaluate the performance of pupils in such placements.

(13) **Regulations.**—The Lieutenant Governor in Council may make regulations,
(a) specifying or describing classes, courses or programs for the purposes of clause (11)(g); and
(b) clarifying the meaning of any word or expression used in subsection (11) or (12).

1997, c. 31, s. 81; 1998, c. 14, s. 1.

170.3 Teachers' assistants, etc.—The Lieutenant Governor in Council may make regulations governing duties and minimum qualifications of persons who are assigned to assist teachers or to complement instruction by teachers in elementary or secondary schools.

1997, c. 31, s. 81.

171. (1) **Powers of boards:**—A board may,
1. **committees.**—establish committees composed of members of the board to make recommendations to the board in respect of education, finance, personnel and property;
2. **idem.**—establish committees that may include persons who are not members of the board in respect of matters other than those referred to in paragraph 1;
3. **appoint employees.**—subject to Part XI, appoint and remove such officers and servants and, subject to Part X, appoint and remove such teachers, as it considers expedient, determine the terms on which such officers, servants and teachers are to be employed, prescribe their duties and fix their salaries, except that in the case of a secretary of a board who is a member of the board, the board may pay only such compensation for his or her services as is approved by the electors at a meeting of the electors;
4. **voluntary assistants.**—permit a principal to assign to a person who volunteers to serve without remuneration such duties in respect of the school as are approved by the board and to terminate such assignment;
5. **supervisors.**—appoint supervisors of the teaching staff for positions that are provided for in any Act or regulation administered by the Minister and every appointee shall hold the qualifications and perform the duties required in the Act or regulations;
6. **psychiatrist or psychologist.**—appoint one or more,
   i. psychiatrists who are on the register of specialists in psychiatry of The Royal College of Physicians and Surgeons of Canada or of the College of Physicians and Surgeons of Ontario,

PART VI — BOARDS

      ii. psychologists who are legally qualified medical practitioners are n
      the College of Psychologists of Ontario;

7. **schools and attendance areas.**—determine the number and kind of schools to be established and maintained and the attendance area for each school, and close schools in accordance with policies established by the board from guidelines issued by the Minister;
8. **courses of study.**—provide instruction in courses of study that are prescribed or approved by the Minister, developed from curriculum guidelines issued by the Minister or approved by the board where the Minister permits the board to approve courses of study;
9. **computer programming.**—in lieu of purchasing a computer or system of computer programming, enter into an agreement for the use thereof by the board;
10. **playgrounds, parks, rinks.**—operate the school ground as a park or playground and rink during the school year or in vacation or both, and provide and maintain such equipment as it considers advisable, and provide such supervision as it considers proper, provided the proper conduct of the school is not interfered with;
11. **gymnasiums.**—organize and carry on gymnasium classes in school buildings for pupils or others during the school year or in vacation or both, and provide supervision and training for such classes, provided the proper conduct of the school is not interfered with;
12. **milk.**—purchase milk to be consumed by the pupils in the schools under the jurisdiction of the board during school days in accordance with the terms and conditions prescribed by the regulations;
13. **provision of supplies, etc.**—provide school supplies, other than the textbooks that it is required to provide under paragraph 13 of section 170, for the use of pupils;
14. **libraries.**—establish and maintain school libraries and resource centres;
15. **junior kindergartens.**—operate junior kindergartens.
16. **signatures mechanically reproduced.**—provide that the signature of the treasurer and of any other person authorized to sign cheques issued by the treasurer may be written or engraved, lithographed, printed or otherwise mechanically reproduced on cheques;
17. **membership fees and traveling expenses.**—pay the traveling expenses and membership fees of any member of the board, or of any teacher or officer of the board, incurred in attending meetings of an educational association and may make grants and pay membership fees to any such organization;
18. **legal costs.**—pay the costs, or any part thereof, incurred by any member of the board or by any teacher, officer or other employee of the board in successfully defending any legal proceeding brought against him or her,
    i. for libel or slander in respect of any statements relating to the employment, suspension or dismissal of any person by the board published at a meeting of the board or of a committee thereof, or
    ii. for assault in respect of disciplinary action taken in the course of duty;
19. [Repealed 1997, c. 31, s. 82.]
20. [Repealed 1997, c. 31, s. 82.]
21. [Repealed 1997, c. 31, s. 82.]

22. [Repealed 1997, c. 31, s. 82.]
23. **student fees.**—subject to the provisions of this Act and the regulations, fix the fees to be paid by or on behalf of pupils, and the times of payment thereof, and when necessary enforce payment thereof by action in the Small Claims Court, and exclude any pupil by or on behalf of whom fees that are legally required to be paid are not paid after reasonable notice;
24. **permit use of school and school buses.**—permit the school buildings and premises and school buses owned by the board to be used for any educational or other lawful purpose;
25. **surgical treatment.**—provide for surgical treatment of children attending the school who suffer from minor physical defects, where in the opinion of the teacher and, where a school nurse and medical officer are employed, of the nurse and medical officer, the defect interferes with the proper education of the child, and includes in the estimates for the current year the funds necessary for cases where the parents are not able to pay, provided that no such treatment shall be undertaken without the consent that complies with the Health Care Consent Act, 1996;
26. **cadet corps.**—establish and maintain cadet corps;
27. **athletics.**—provide for the promotion and encouragement of athletics and for the holding of school games;
28. **activities.**—provide, during the school year or at other times, activities and programs on or off school premises, including field trips, and exercise jurisdiction over those persons participating therein;
29. **guidance.**—appoint one or more teachers qualified in guidance according to the regulations to collect and distribute information regarding available occupations and employments, and to offer such counsel to the pupils as will enable them to plan intelligently for their educational and vocational advancement;
30. **public lectures.**—conduct free lectures open to the public and include in the estimates for the current year the expenses thereof;
31. **continuing education.**—establish continuing education courses and classes.
31.1 **deposit for continuing education textbooks.**—require a pupil enrolled in a continuing education course or class that is eligible for credit towards a secondary school diploma to pay a nominal deposit for a textbook provided by the board that will be forfeited to the board in whole or in part if the textbook is not returned or is returned in a damaged condition;
32. **courses for teachers.**—establish and conduct during the school year courses for teachers;
33. **evening classes.**—establish evening classes;
34. **erect fences.**—erect and maintain any wall or fence considered necessary by the board for enclosure of the school premises;
35. **school fairs.**—contribute toward the support of school fairs;
36. **student activities.**—authorize such school activities as pertain to the welfare of the pupils and exercise jurisdiction in respect thereof;
37. **cafeteria.**—operate a cafeteria for the use of the staff and pupils;
38. **records management.**—institute a program of records management that will, subject to the regulations in respect of pupil records,

i. provide for the archival retention by the board or the Archivist of Ontario of school registers, minute books of the board and its predecessors, documents pertaining to boundaries of school sections, separate school zones and secondary school districts, original assessment and taxation records in the possession of the board and other records considered by the board to have enduring value or to be of historical interest, and

ii. establish, with the written approval of the auditor of the board, schedules for the retention, disposition and eventual destruction of records of the board and of the schools under its jurisdiction other than records retained for archival use;

39. **education of children in charitable organizations.**—employ and pay teachers, when so requested in writing by a charitable organization having the charge of children of school age, for the education of such children, whether such children are being educated in premises within or beyond the limits of the jurisdiction of the board, and pay for and furnish school supplies for their use;

40. **programs in detention homes.**—with the approval of the Minister, conduct an education program in a centre facility, home, hospital or institution that is approved, designated, established, licensed or registered under any Act and in which the Ministry does not conduct an education program, or in a demonstration school for exceptional pupils;

41. **maternity leave.**—provide for maternity leave for a teacher, not exceeding two years for each pregnancy;

42. **assumption of treatment centres, etc.**—when requested by the board of a cerebral palsy treatment centre school, a crippled children's treatment centre school, a hospital school or a sanatorium school, and with the approval of the Minister, by agreement, assume the assets and liabilities of such board and continue to operate such a school, and, upon the effective date of the agreement between the two boards, the board making the request is dissolved;

43. [Repealed 1997, c. 31, s. 82(4).]

44. **agreement for provision and use of recreational facilities.**—with the approval of the Minister, enter into an agreement with a university, college of a university, or the board of governors of a polytechnical institute or of a college of applied arts and technology, in respect of the provision, maintenance and use of educational or recreational facilities on the property of either of the parties to the agreement;

45. **election recounts.**—pass a resolution referred to in subsection 57(1) of the Municipal Elections Act 1996.

46. **insurance.**—provide for insurance against risks that may involve pecuniary loss or liability on the part of the board, and for paying premiums therefor;

47. [Repealed 1997, c. 31, s. 82(5).]

48. **Child care facilities.**—construct and renovate child care facilities in any school.

49. **day nurseries.**—establish, operate and maintain day nurseries within the meaning of the Day Nurseries Act, subject to that Act.

50. [Repealed 1996, c. 13, s. 6(2).]

(2) **Powers of boards re: days of work.**—A board may require teachers to work during some or all of the five working days preceding the start of the school year.

(3) **Same.**—A board may authorize the principal of a school to make determinations respecting the work to be done by teachers of the school during the working days referred to in subsection (2) and the principal shall exercise that discretion subject to the authority of the appropriate supervisory officer.

(4) **Same.**—For the purposes of subsections (2) and (3), a working day is a day other than Saturday, Sunday or a holiday as defined in subsection 29(1) of the Interpretation Act.

(5) **Same.**—Work that may be required under subsections (2) and (3) includes but is not limited to participation in professional development activities.

1991, vol. 2, c. 10, s. 5; 1992, c. 32, s. 9; 1993, c. 11, s. 31; 1993, c. 26, s. 44; 1994, c. 27, s. 108(5); 1996, c. 2, s. 65; 1996, c. 13, ss. 6, 12; 1996, c. 32, s. 70(4); 1997, c. 31, s. 82.

171.1 (1) **Definitions.**—In this section,

"**board**".—[Repealed 1997, c. 31, s. 83(1).]

"**college**".—"college means a board of governors of a college of applied arts and technology established in accordance with section 5 of the Ministry of Colleges and Universities Act; (collége)

"**hospital**".—"hospital" has the same meaning as "board" in section 1 of the Public Hospitals Act; (hôpital)

"**municipality**".—"municipality" includes a county, a regional municipality, The District Municipality of Muskoka and the County of Oxford; (municipalité)

"**university**".—"university" means a degree granting institution as authorized by section 3 of the *Degree Granting Act.* (université)

(2) **Agreements to co-operate.**—A board may enter into an agreement with another board or with a municipality, hospital, university or college for one or more of the following purposes:

1. The joint provision or use of transportation services.
2. The joint provision or use of administrative support services or operational support services.
3. The joint provision or use of support services for educational programs.
4. The joint provision or use of equipment or facilities of administration or operational purposes.
5. The joint investment of funds.
6. A purpose prescribed under clause (5)(a).

(3) **Same.**—A board may enter into an agreement with any class of persons or organizations prescribed under clause (5)(b) for any purpose prescribed in connection with the class of persons or organizations under clause (5)(c).

(4) **Limitation re joint investment agreements.**—No agreement entered into under this section for the joint investment of funds may,

(a) affect an education development charges account established under an education development charge by-law to which section 257.103 applies; or

(b) provide for investment by a board that is not permitted by clause 241(1)(a).

(5) **Regulations.**—The Lieutenant Governor in Council may make regulations,

(a) prescribing purposes for the purpose of paragraph 6 of subsection (2);

(b) prescribing classes of persons and organizations for the purpose of subsection (3);

(c) prescribing, in connection with any class of persons or organizations prescribed under clause (b), any of the purposes mentioned in paragraphs 1 to 5 of subsection (2) or prescribed under clause (a).

(6) **Classes.**—A class prescribed under subsection (5) may be defined with respect to any characteristic and may be defined to consist of or to include or exclude any specified member.

(7) **Interpretation.**—This section shall not be interpreted to authorize a board or any other person to acquire, provide or use any thing or service that it would not otherwise be authorized to acquire, provide or use.

(8) **Conflict.**—Where a board is permitted to do a thing by or under this section as well as by or under another provision of this or any other Act, any conditions or requirements set by or under the other provision that relate in any way to the doing of the thing must be complied with.

1993, c. 26, s. 45; 1996, c. 13, s. 7; 1997, c. 31, s. 83.

172. [Repealed 1997, c. 31, s. 84.]

173. (1) **Establishment of scholarships, etc.**—Any person may, with the approval of the board concerned, establish scholarships, bursaries or prizes.

(2) **Idem.**—A board may award bursaries or prizes to its pupils under such terms and conditions as the board may prescribe.

174. [Repealed 1997, c. 31, s. 85.]

175. [Repealed 1997, c. 31, s. 85.]

Benefits

176. Powers of board.—A board may,

1. **accident, etc., insurance.**—provide, by contract with an insurer licensed under the *Insurance Act*,
    i. group accident insurance to indemnify a member of a board or of an advisory committee appointed by a board or his or her estate against loss in case he or she is accidentally injured or killed, and
    ii. group public liability and property damage insurance to indemnify a member of a board or of an advisory committee appointed by a board or his or her estate in respect of loss or damage for which he or she has become liable by reason of injury to persons or property or in respect of loss or damage suffered by him or her by reason of injury to his or her own property,

    while traveling on the business of the board or in the performance of duties as a member of the board or of an advisory committee either within or outside the area over which the board has jurisdiction;
2. [Repealed 1997, c. 31, s. 86.]
3. **accident and public liability insurance re work-experience programs.**—where, in co-operation with business, industry or other enterprise, it provides for pupils training programs designed to supplement the courses given in its schools, provide, by contract with an insurer under the Insurance Act, accident insurance to indemnify

such pupils against loss in case they are accidentally injured while participating in such a program and public liability insurance to insure such pupils and the board against loss or damage to the person or property of others while the pupils are participating in such a program;

4. **insurance for pupils.**—provide, by contract with an insurer under the Insurance Act, accident and life insurance for pupils, the cost of which is to be paid on a voluntary basis by the parents or guardians.

1994, c. 27, s. 108(6); 1997, c. 31, s. 86.

177. (1) **Insurance, hospital and health services.**—Subject to the Health Insurance Act, a board by resolution may provide,

(a) by contract either with an insurer licensed under the Insurance Act or with an association registered under the Prepaid Hospital and Medical Services Act,

   (i) group life insurance for its employees or any class thereof and their spouses and children,

   (ii) group accident insurance or group sickness insurance for its employees or any class thereof and their spouses and children, and

   (iii) hospital, medical, surgical, nursing or dental services, or payment therefor, for employees or any class thereof and their spouses and children; and

(b) for payment by the board of the whole or part of the cost of any insurance or services provided under this subsection.

(2) **Contribution re insured services.**—A board may by resolution provide for paying the whole or part of the cost to employees of insured services under the *Health Insurance Act*.

(3) **Coverage for retired persons.**—If a person retires from employment with a board before he or she reaches 65 years of age, the board may retain the person in a group established for the purpose of a contract referred to in clause (1)(a) until the person reaches 65 years of age.

(4) **Payment of premium.**—If a person is retained in a group under subsection (3), the mium required to be paid to maintain the person's participation in the contract may be paid, in whole or in part, by the person or by the board.

1994, c. 27, s. 108(7).

178. (1) **Pensions.**—A board, by resolution, may provide pensions for employees or any class thereof under the Ontario Municipal Employees Retirement System Act.

(2) **Idem.**—Despite subsection (1), a board that makes contributions to an approved pension plan, as defined in subsection 117(1) of the Municipal Act, may continue to provide pensions under such plan, and the said section 117 applies with necessary modifications.

(3) **Definition.**—In this section, "employee" does not include a teacher or supervisory officer or an administrative officer who is a member of the Ontario College of Teachers and who is eligible to contribute to the pension fund maintained to provide benefits in respect of The Ontario Teachers' Pension Plan.

(4) **Rights continued.**—Where a person has rights under this section in relation to an old board and the old board is amalgamated or merged with a district school board under Part II.2,

the rights of the person are the same immediately after the amalgamation or merger as they e immediately before the amalgamation or merger and, for the purpose, the district school board stands in the place of the old board.

(5) [Repealed 1997, c. 31, s. 87.]

1996, c. 12, s. 64(10); 1997, c. 31, s. 87.

179. (1) **Retirement allowances.**—A board may grant an annual retirement allowance, payable weekly, monthly or otherwise for such period as the board may determine, to any employee of the board who has been in the service of the board for at least twenty years and who,

(a) is retired because of age; or
(b) while in the service has become incapable through illness or otherwise of efficiently discharging his or her duties,

provided that no retirement allowance shall be granted under this section which, together with the amount of any pension payments payable to the employee in any year under a pension plan of the board or any municipality or under the Teachers' Pension Act, will exceed three-fifths of the employee's average annual salary for the preceding three years of his or her service.

(2) **Widow or widower.**—Where an employee,

(a) has been granted an annual retirement allowance under subsection (1) and subsequently dies; or
(b) would have been eligible, except for his or her death, for such an allowance, the board may grant to the widow or widower of such employee for such period as the board may determine an annual allowance, not exceeding one-half of the maximum allowance that may be granted under subsection (1).

(3) **Definition.**—In subsection (1), ''pension payments'' means, in the case of pension payments under a board or municipal plan, only such payments that result from joint contributions of the employer and employee and does not include any such payments that result solely from contributions of the employee.

(4) **Limitation on application of section.**—Where the board has a pension plan in operation, or where a municipality has a pension plan in operation in which the employees of the board are included, this section applies only to employees who were in the employ of the board on or before the 1st day of July, 1954, and in any event does not apply to any employee who enters the service of the board after the 1st day of July, 1956.

180. (1) **Sick leave credits.**—A board, by resolution, may establish a system of sick leave credit gratuities for employees or any class thereof provided that on the termination of his or her employment no employee is entitled to more than an amount equal to the employee's salary, wages or other remuneration for one-half the number of days standing to the employee's credit and, subject to subsection (3), in any event not in excess of the amount of one-half year's earnings at the rate received by the employee immediately prior to termination of employment.

(2) **Idem.**—Where a sick leave gratuity is paid upon termination of employment, the number of days used to calculate the amount of the gratuity ceases to stand to the credit of the employee and is not available for transfer or reinstatement of credits under subsection (4).

(3) **Idem.**—Where, pursuant to a collective agreement, or a policy of the board, an employee to whom subsection (1) applies has elected to accept a reduction in employment from full-time to part-time employment in respect of one or more years or school years, as the case may be, including the year or school year immediately preceding the employee's termination of employment by reason of retirement, the limitation upon the amount of the gratuity payable under subsection (1) does not apply to the employee and, in lieu thereof, the maximum amount receivable by the employee shall not be in excess of an amount equal to one-half of the full-time annual rate of the earnings received by the employee for the last complete year or school year, as the case may be, in which the employee was employed by the board.

(4) **Allowing of credits on transfer of employment.**—Where an employee of a board that has established a sick leave credit plan under this or any other general or special Act becomes an employee of another board that has also established a sick leave credit plan under this or any other general or special Act, the latter board shall, subject to the limitation in subsection (7), place to the credit of the employee the sick leave credits standing to the credit of the employee in the plan of the first-mentioned board.

(5) **Where transferred because of change in jurisdiction of board.**—Despite subsection (4), where the contract of employment of an employee of a board has become an obligation of another board by or under any Act, the latter board shall place to the credit of the employee the sick leave credits and the termination of employment benefits standing to the employee's credit in the system of sick leave credit gratuities of the first-mentioned board.

(6) **Idem.**—Where an employee of a municipality or a local board, as defined in the Municipal Affairs Act, except a school board, that has established a sick leave credit plan under any general or special Act, becomes an employee of a board that has established a sick leave credit plan under this or any other general or special Act, the board shall, subject to the limitation in subsection (7), place to the credit of the employee the sick leave credits standing to the credit of the employee in the plan of such municipality or local board.

(7) **Limitation.**—The amount of sick leave credits placed to the credit of an employee under subsection (4) or (6) shall not exceed the amount of cumulative sick leave credits permitted under the plan to which the credits are placed.

(8) [Repealed 1993, c. 11, s. 32.]

(9) [Repealed 1993, c. 11, s. 32.]

(10) [Repealed 1997, c. 31, s. 88.]

1993, c. 11, s. 32; 1997, c. 31, s. 88.

Agreements

181. (1) **Agreements to provide accommodation or services for another board.**—A board may, subject to subsection (2), enter into an agreement with another board to provide, for the other board for such periods and under such conditions as are specified in the agreement,

(a) accommodation and equipment for administrative purposes;

(b) accommodation and equipment for instructional purposes;

(c) the services of teachers and other personnel; or

(d) the transportation of pupils,

that the board by this Act is authorized or required to provide for its own pupils.

(2) **Where building, additions, etc., required.**—Where the construction of a school building or an addition, alteration or improvement to a school building is required under an agreement made under subsection (1), the agreement shall make provision for the payment of the cost of such building, addition, alteration or improvement.

(3) **Where the cost borne by board not providing accommodation.**—Where, under an agreement, the board that does not provide the additional accommodation is required to bear and pay the cost thereof, the additional accommodation shall, for the purposes of issuing debentures, be deemed to be a permanent improvement of such board.

(4) **Fees, exception.**—An agreement under this section may, despite the regulations, provide for the calculation and payment of fees in respect of pupils covered by the agreement.

1997, c. 31, s. 89.

182. (1) **Transfer of French-language secondary school.**—A French-language public district school board that has jurisdiction in an area that is also the area or part of the area of jurisdiction of a French-language separate district school board may, with the approval of the Minister, enter into an agreement with the separate district school board to transfer a secondary school of the public district school board.

(2) **Transfer not a closing.**—A transfer of a secondary school referred to in subsection (1) is not a closing of the secondary school.

1997, c. 31, s. 90.

183. (1) **Definition.**—In this section,

"**municipality**".—"municipality" includes a county, a regional municipality, The District Municipality of Muskoka and the County of Oxford and a local board of a municipality, a county, a regional municipality, The District Municipality of Muskoka or the County of Oxford, except a board as defined in subsection 1(1).

(2) **Agreements for joint use of facilities, etc.**—One or more boards and the council of a municipality or the councils of two or more municipalities may enter into an agreement,

(a) in respect of the use of existing facilities owned by one of such parties; or
(b) for the purpose of establishing and providing for the maintenance and operation of facilities on the property of any of the parties to such agreement, for such cultural, recreational, athletic, educational, administrative or other community purposes as are set out in the agreement, and such agreement shall include provision for,
(c) the acquisition of any land that may be required for the purposes of the agreement, and the manner of approving and the method of apportioning the cost thereof;
(d) the manner of approving and the method of apportioning the cost of the construction, maintenance and operation of the facilities;
(e) the manner in which each party to the agreement shall pay its portion of the costs referred to in clauses (c) and (d) and the times when such costs shall be paid;
(f) the regulation, control and use of the facilities including the charging of fees for admission thereto; and
(g) the duration of the agreement and the manner in which and the terms upon which it may be terminated.

(3) **Approval of Minister.**—Where, pursuant to an agreement made under this section, a permanent improvement is required, it shall not be proceeded with until such plans and specifications therefor as are required by the Minister have been approved by the Minister.

(4) **Previous agreement.**—This section does not affect an agreement entered into before the 23rd day of June, 1972,
- (a) under subsection 168(2) of the *Municipality of Metropolitan Toronto Act*; or
- (b) between a board and the council of a municipality, including a regional municipality or a county, or a local board thereof, for fulfilling, executing or completing, at their joint expense or at the expense of either of the parties to the agreement, any undertaking for the joint benefit of the parties to the agreement, including the joint use of educational and municipal facilities,

but an amendment to an agreement referred to in clause (a) or (b) or an agreement to which the said subsection 168(2) applies may be made only in accordance with this section.

(5) **Facilities deemed community recreation centre.**—Where an agreement under this section or an agreement referred to in subsection (4) between one or more boards and one or more municipalities provides for the use of existing facilities or for the establishment of facilities, such facilities or any of them that come within the definition of community recreation centre under the Community Recreation Centres Act may be considered by the Minister of Community and Social Services as a community recreation centre for the purposes of making grants under section 6 of that Act.

1997, c. 31, s. 91.

184. (1) **Agreement for education at other school.**—A board may enter into an agreement with another board to provide education for pupils of the one board in a school or schools operated by the other board.

(2) **Calculation of fees.**—Where an agreement is entered into under subsection (1), the board requesting the instruction shall pay to the board providing the instruction the fees, if any, payable for the purpose under the regulations.

1997, c. 31, s. 92.

185. Admission of pupils to Indian schools.—The board of an elementary school may provide for the admission of one or more of its pupils to a school for Indian children operated by a band, council of a band or an education authority where the band, council of the band or education authority is authorized by the Crown in right of Canada to provide education for Indians, subject to the approval of the band, council of the band or education authority, and the ommodation provided under the arrangement shall be in place of the accommodation that the board is required by this Act to provide for those pupils.

1997, c. 31, s. 92.

186. Closing of school by board.—Where a board has arranged under section 184 or 185 for the admission of all its pupils to a school or schools that the board does not operate, board may close its school for the period during which the arrangement or arrangements are in effect.

1997, c. 31, s. 94.

187. Agreements re pupils in federal establishments.—A board may enter into an agreement with the Crown in right of Canada for such periods and under such conditions as are specified in the agreement whereby the board may provide for the education of pupils who reside on land held by the Crown in right of Canada in a school or schools operated by the board on land owned by the board or held by the Crown in right of Canada.

188. (1) **Agreements re education of Indian pupils.**—A board may enter into an agreement with,

- (a) the Crown in right of Canada; or
- (b) a band or the council of the band or an education authority where such band, the council of the band or education authority is authorized by the Crown in right of Canada to provide education for Indians,

to provide for Indian pupils, for the period specified in the agreement, accommodation, instruction and special services in the schools of the board, and such agreement shall provide for the payment by the Crown in right of Canada, the band, the council of the band or the education authority, as the case may be, of fees calculated in accordance with the regulation governing the fees payable by Canada.

(2) **Agreements re instruction in Indian schools.**—A board may enter into an agreement with,

- (a) the Crown in right of Canada; or
- (b) a band, the council of the band or an education authority referred to in clause (1)(b),

to provide for Indian pupils, for the period specified in the agreement, instruction and special services in schools provided by the Crown in right of Canada, the band, the council of the band or the education authority, as the case may be, and such agreement shall provide for the payment by the Crown in right of Canada, the band, the council of the band or the education authority, as the case may be, of the full cost of the provision of the instruction and special services.

(3) **Agreements re accommodation for Indian pupils.**—A board may enter into an agreement with the Crown in right of Canada for a period specified in the agreement to provide for a payment from the Crown in right of Canada to provide additional classroom accommodation and to provide tuition for a maximum of thirty-five Indian pupils for each additional classroom so provided, and the fees therefor shall be calculated in accordance with the regulations, but exclusive of expenditures for the erection of school buildings for instructional purposes and additions thereto.

(4) **Cost of special services.**—A board shall not enter into an agreement under subsection (1), (2) or (3) that requires the board to provide special services for Indian pupils that it does not provide for its resident pupils unless, in addition to the fees referred to in subsection (1) or (3), the cost of such services is payable by the Crown in right of Canada.

(5) **Regulations: interests of members of bands.**—The Lieutenant Governor in Council may make regulations providing for representation on boards, by appointment, of the interests of members of bands in respect of which there is agreement under this Act to provide instruction to pupils who are Indians within the meaning of the *Indian Act* (Canada).

(6) **Same.**—A regulation under this section may provide for the type and extent of participation by the persons appointed.

(7) **Same.**—A regulation under this section may provide that all persons, or one or more classes of persons, appointed under this section shall be deemed to be elected members of the board for all purposes or for such purposes as are specified in the regulation.

(8) **Representation on Roman Catholic boards.**—Where a person is appointed to represent the interests of Indian pupils on a Roman Catholic board, the person shall be a Roman Catholic and at least 18 years of age.

(9) **Representation on French-language district school boards.**—Where a person is appointed to represent the interests of Indian pupils on a French-language district school board, the person shall be a French-language rights holder and at least 18 years of age.

(10) [Repealed 1997, c. 31, s. 95.]

(11) [Repealed 1997, c. 31, s. 95.]

(12) [Repealed 1997, c. 31, s. 95.]

(13) [Repealed 1997, c. 31, s. 95.]

1997, c. 31, s. 95.

189. (1) **Definition.**—In this section, "adult basic education" means programs and courses that are designed to develop and improve the basic literacy and numeracy skills of adults.

(2) **Agreements for adult basic education.**—Subject to the approval of the Minister, a board may, in respect of persons who reside in the area of jurisdiction of the board, enter into an agreement in writing with a college of applied arts and technology for the area in which the board has jurisdiction under which the college of applied arts and technology provides for the board such adult basic education as is specified in the agreement.

(3) **Idem.**—A board may, in respect of persons who reside in the area of jurisdiction of the board, enter into an agreement in writing with a community group for the provision by the group of adult basic education that is approved by the Minister.

190. (1) **Transportation of pupils.**—A board may provide for,

(a) a pupil who is enrolled in a school that the board operates;

(a.1) a resident pupil of the board who is enrolled in a school operated by another board under an agreement between the boards;

(b) a pupil in respect of whom the Minister pays the cost of education under the regulations; and

(c) a child over two years of age who may, under the regulations, be admitted to a program for hearing-handicapped children,

transportation to and from the school that the pupil attends.

(2) **Idem.**—A board may provide for a pupil who is enrolled in a school that the board operates transportation to and from an activity that is part of the program of such school

(3) **Idem.**—A board may provide for a person who is qualified to be a resident pupil of the board transportation to and from the Ontario School for the Blind, an Ontario School for the Deaf, a demonstration school established by or operated under an agreement with the Minister for pupils with severe communicational exceptionalities, a centre classified as a Group K hospital under the *Public Hospitals Act*, a facility designated under the *Developmental Services Act*, a psychiatric facility designated as such under the *Mental Health Act* and a place

where an agency approved under subsection 8(1) of Part I (Flexible Services) of the *Child and Family Services Act* provides a child development service, a child treatment service or a child and family intervention service.

(4) **Idem.**—A board that operates a secondary school may assist in the provision of transportation for children who are qualified to be resident pupils of the board to and from a centre operated by a local association that is affiliated with the Ontario Association for Community Living.

(5) **Purchase of bus.**—For the purposes of this section, a board may purchase a vehicle either from current revenue or from a debenture issued for that purpose

(6) **Agreements.**—Subject to subsection (7), for the purposes of this section, a board may make an agreement or agreements for one school year or less with a corporation, commission or person for the transportation of such pupils.

(7) **Agreements not exceeding five years.**—Where a board provides transportation for more than thirty pupils, the board may, with the approval of the Ontario Municipal Board, make an agreement for a term not exceeding five years for the transportation of such pupils.

(8) **Boarding of secondary school pupils.**—Where a pupil resides in a school section of a school authority or a separate school zone of a school authority, in a territorial district, with his or her parent or guardian in a residence that is 24 kilometres or more by road or rail from a secondary school that the pupil is eligible to attend, the school authority may reimburse the parent or guardian at the end of each month for the cost of providing for the pupil, board, lodging, and transportation once a week from his or her residence to school and return, in an amount set by the authority for each day of attendance as certified by the principal of the secondary school that the pupil attends.

(9) **Same.**—Where a pupil resides in a territorial district but not in the area of jurisdiction of any board, with his or her parent or guardian in a residence that is 24 kilometres or more by road or rail from a secondary school that the pupil is eligible to attend, the board of the secondary school that the pupil attends may reimburse the parent or guardian at the end of each month for the cost of providing for the pupil, board, lodging, and transportation once a week from his or her residence to school and return, in an amount set by the board for each day of attendance as certified by the principal of the secondary school that the pupil attends.

(10) **Same.**—Where a pupil resides with his or her parent or guardian in the area of jurisdiction of a district school board or a board established under section 67, in a residence that,

(a) in a territorial district is 24 kilometres or more; or

(b) in a county or a regional municipality that is not in a territorial district is 48 kilometres or more,

by road or rail from a secondary school that the pupil attends, or where a pupil resides with his or her parent or guardian on an island in the area of jurisdiction of a district school board or a board established under section 67, the board of which the pupil is a resident pupil may reimburse the parent or guardian at the end of each month for the cost of providing for the pupil, board, lodging, and transportation once a week from his or her residence to school and return, in an amount set by the board for each day of attendance as certified by the principal of the secondary school that the pupil attends.

(11) **Boarding of elementary school pupils.**—Where a pupil resides in a territorial district but not in the area of jurisdiction of any board, with his or her parent or guardian in a residence from which daily transportation to and from an elementary school that the pupil may attend is impracticable due to distance or terrain as certified by the appropriate supervisory officer of the elementary school nearest the residence, the board of the elementary school that the pupil attends may reimburse the parent or guardian at the end of each month for the cost of providing for the pupil, board, lodging, and transportation once a week from his or her residence to school and return, in an amount set by the board for each day of attendance as certified by the principal of the elementary school that the pupil attends.

(12) **Same.**—Where a pupil resides in the area of jurisdiction of a board with his or her parent or guardian in a residence from which daily transportation to and from an elementary school that the pupil may attend is impracticable due to distance or terrain, as certified by the appropriate supervisory officer, the board of the elementary school of which the pupil is a resident pupil may reimburse the parent or guardian at the end of each month for the cost of providing for the pupil, board, lodging, and transportation once a week from his or her residence to school and return, in an amount set by the board for each day of attendance as certified by the principal of the elementary school that the pupil attends.

(13) **Certification of attendance.**—For the purpose of certifying attendance under subsections (8) to (12), the principal may add to the number of days of attendance of a pupil the number of days the pupil is excused from attendance under the regulations or is absent by reason of being ill or is absent for any other cause if the principal is of the opinion that the absence was unavoidable.

(14) [Repealed 1997, c. 31, s. 96.]

1997, c. 31, s. 96.

Honoraria

191. (1) **Honorarium for members of district school boards.**—A district school board may pay to each member of the board an honorarium in an amount determined by the board to be payable to its members.

(2) **Maximum.**—The amount determined by a district school board under subsection (1) shall not exceed $5,000 annually.

(3) **Chair and vice-chair: additional honorarium.**—A district school board may pay to its chair and vice-chair an honorarium that is additional to the honorarium payable under subsection (1), in an amount determined for the purpose by the board.

(4) **Maximum.**—The additional honorarium determined by a district school board under subsection (3) shall not exceed the amount determined by the board under subsection (1).

(5) **Different honorarium for chair, vice-chair.**—The additional honorarium payable to the chair may differ from the additional honorarium payable to the vice-chair.

(6) **Decrease in honorarium.**—A district school board may at any time decrease any honorarium payable to its members, the chair or the vice-chair.

1997, c. 31, s. 97.

191.1 (1) **Honorarium for members of school authorities.**—A school authority may pay to its members an honorarium at the same rate and on the same conditions as the allowance being paid to their members on December 1, 1996.

(2) **Chair and vice-chair: additional honorarium.**—If a school authority was paying an amount as an additional allowance to its chair or vice-chair on December 1, 1996, the school authority may pay that amount as an additional honorarium to its chair or vice-chair, at the same rate and on the same conditions as applied on December 1, 1996.

(3) **Regulations: school authority honorariums.**—The Lieutenant Governor in Council may make regulations governing the payment of honorariums to members of a school authority, including its chair and vice-chair.

(4) **Conflict.**—In the event of a conflict between subsection (1) or (2) and a regulation made under subsection (3), the regulation prevails.

(5) **Repeal.**—Subsections (1), (2) and (4) are repealed on a day to be named by proclamation of the Lieutenant Governor.

1997, c. 31, s. 97.

191.2 (1) **Travel expenses to attend board and committee meetings.**—In respect of travel of a member of a board to and from his or her residence to attend a meeting of the board, or of a committee of the board, that is held within the area of jurisdiction of the board, the board may,

(a) reimburse the member for his or her out-of-pocket expenses reasonably incurred or such lesser amount as may be determined by the board; or

(b) pay the member an allowance at a rate per kilometre determined by the board.

(2) **Other travel expenses.**—A board may by resolution authorize a member, teacher or official of the board to travel on specific business of the board and may reimburse the member, teacher or official for his or her out-of-pocket expenses reasonably incurred or such lesser amount as may be determined by the board.

(3) **Other expenses.**—A board may establish a policy under which a member of the board may be reimbursed for all or part of his or her out-of-pocket expenses reasonably incurred in connection with carrying out the responsibilities of a board member.

(4) **Same.**—A board may, in accordance with a policy established by it under subsection (3), reimburse a member for his or her out-of-pocket expenses reasonably incurred in connection with carrying out the responsibilities of a board member.

(5) **Deduction because of absence.**—A board may provide for a deduction of a reasonably amount from the allowance of a member because of absence from meetings of the board or of a committee of the board.

(6) **Committee members.**—Subsections (1) to (4) apply with necessary modifications to members of a committee established by the board who are not members of the board.

1997, c. 31, s. 97.

Property

192. (1) **School lands granted before 1850 vested in board for school purposes.**—All lands that before the 24th day of July, 1850, were granted, devised or otherwise conveyed to any person or persons in trust for common school purposes and held by such person or persons and their heirs or other successors in the trust, and have been heretofore vested in a public school board or a board of education having jurisdiction in the municipality in which the lands are situate, continue to be vested in such board, and continue to be held by it and its successors upon the like trusts and subject to the same conditions and for the estates upon or subject to or for which the lands are respectively held.

(1.1) **Same.**—In subsection (1),

"public school board" and "board of education" have the same meaning as they had immediately before the *Education Quality Improvement Act, 1997* received Royal Assent.

(2) **Property in trust vested in board.**—All property heretofore granted or devised to, acquired by or vested in any person or corporation,

(a) for the secondary school purposes of a secondary school district or any part thereof; or

(b) for the separate school purposes in a separate school zone,

is vested in the board having jurisdiction in the secondary school district or separate school zone, as the case may be.

1997, c. 31, s. 98.

193. (1) **Possession of property.**—A board may take possession of all property acquired or given for school purposes and hold and apply it according to the terms on which it was acquired or given.

(2) **Idem.**—A Roman Catholic board has power to acquire and hold as a corporation, by any title whatsoever, land, movable property, money or income given to or acquired by the board at any time for school purposes and hold or apply the same according to the terms on which it was acquired or received.

(3) **Appropriation of property.**—A public district school board may appropriate any property acquired by it or in its possession or control for any of the purposes of the board.

1994, s. 27, s. 108(8); 1997, c. 31, s. 99.

194. (1) **Disposal of realty.**—A board that is in possession of real property that was originally granted by the Crown for school purposes and that has reverted or may have reverted to the Crown may continue in possession of the real property for school purposes and when a board determines that the real property is no longer required for school purposes, the board may, with the approval of the Lieutenant Governor in Council and subject to such conditions as are prescribed by the Lieutenant Governor in Council, sell, lease or otherwise dispose of the real property.

(2) **Application for removal of restrictions on use of school lands.**—Where land, the use of which is restricted by deed in any manner to school purposes so as to appear that some other person may have an interest therein, has been vested in a board for at least fifty years, the board may apply to the Ontario Court (General Division) to remove the restriction, and the court may make such order on the application as it considers just including, where the land adjoins land being used as a farm, a requirement that the board shall, where the board intends to sell the land, first offer it at a reasonable price to the owner or owners of such adjoining land.

(3) **Lease or sale of site or property.**—Subject to subsections (3.3) and (4.1), a board has power to sell, lease or otherwise dispose of any school site or part of a school site of the board or any property of the board,

    (a) on the adoption of a resolution that the site or part or property is not required for the purposes of the board; or

    (b) on the adoption of a resolution that the sale, lease or other disposition is a reasonable step in a plan to provide accommodation for pupils on the site or part or property.

(3.1) **Application of proceeds.**—The board shall apply the proceeds of a sale, lease or other disposition under subsection (3) for the purposes of the board and shall advise the Minister of the sale or disposition or of the lease, where the term of the lease exceeds one year, of any of its schools.

(3.2) **Conflict.**—In the event of a conflict between subsection (3.1) and a regulation referred to in clause (3.4)(c), the regulation prevails.

(3.3) **Regulations.**—The Minister may make regulations governing the sale, lease or other disposition of school sites or parts of school sites or property to which resolutions referred to in clause (3)(a) apply.

(3.4) **Same.**—Regulations that may be made under subsection (3.3) include but are not limited to regulations,

    (a) respecting to whom school sites or parts of school sites or property must be offered;

    (b) respecting the price or other consideration for a disposition or class of dispositions;

    (c) respecting the use of the proceeds of a disposition or class of dispositions;

    (d) respecting the purposes for which school sites or parts of school sites or property that is disposed of to other boards must be used by the transferee board;

    (e) requiring a transferee board to return a school site or part of a school site or property to the transferor board if not longer used for the purposes referred to in clause (d);

    (f) respecting the price or other considerations for a return or class of returns required under clause (e).

(3.5) **General or particular.**—A regulation made under this section may be general or particular and may be made to apply to any class of boards.

(3.6) **Classes.**—A class may be defined with respect to any attribute and may be defined to consist of or to exclude any specified member of the class, whether or not with the same attributes.

(4) **Application of subs. (4.1).**—Subsection (4.1) does not apply in respect of a school site, part of a school site or property to which a resolution referred to in clause (3)(a) applies.

(4.1) **Approval of Minister re disposition, demolition.**—Despite any provision of this or any other Act, a board shall not sell, lease or otherwise dispose of a school site, part of a school site or property or demolish a building unless, in addition to any other approval that may be required, the board has obtained the approval of the Minister.

(5) **Exceptions.**—Subsection (4) does not apply,

    (a) to the use of a building or part thereof pursuant to an agreement under section 183; or

(b) re a building or part thereof is in use as a school, to the use of the building or part for any purpose that does not interfere with the proper conduct of the school.

1997, c. 31, s. 100.

195. (1) **Board may purchase or expropriate within its jurisdiction.**—Subject to the provisions of section 90 as to the approval of the site of a new school by a rural separate school board, every board may select and may acquire, by purchase, lease or otherwise, or may expropriate, a school site that is within its area of jurisdiction.

(2) **Purchase or lease of site in adjoining jurisdiction.**—A public board may, with the approval of the Minister, acquire by purchase, lease or otherwise a school site in an adjoining school section or secondary school district, as the case may be, for the purpose of operating a school thereon, but the board shall not expropriate any such site.

(3) **School outside designated area.**—A separate district school board may, with the approval of the Minister, acquire by purchase, lease or otherwise, a school site that is outside the area of jurisdiction established in respect of the board by regulation made under subsection 58.1(2) and may operate a separate school on the site, but a separate district school board shall not expropriate such a site.

(4) **Buildings on land owned by board.**—Subject to section 196 or subsection 197 a board may erect, add to or alter buildings for its purposes on land owned by the board.

(5) **Buildings on leased land.**—A board may erect a school building on land the leased by the board where the term of the lease, the school site and the plans of the sch building are approved by the Minister.

(6) **Additions or alterations.**—A board may, with the approval of the Minister, make ition, alteration or improvement to a school building that is acquired by the board under a lease.

1997, c. 31, s. 101(1)-(3).

(7) **Regulations re land reserved for use as a school site.**—The Minister may make regulations.

   (a) respecting the length of the extension under subsection 51(25.2) of the *Planning Act*;

   (b) prescribing conditions for the purposes of subsection 51(25.3) of the *Planning Act*;

(8) **Same.**—Without limiting the generality of clause (7)(b), regulations made under that clause may prescribe conditions that include a requirement that the board make a non-refundable deposit.

(9) **Same.**—Subsections 194(3.5) and (3.6) apply to regulations made under subsection (7).

1997, c. 31, s. 101(4) [Not in force at date of publication.]

196. Agreement for multi-use building.—Where a board plans to provide, other by way of a lease, accommodation for pupils on a school site that is not to be occupied or used exclusively by the board, the board shall obtain the prior approval of the Minister to enter negotiations with a person, other than a board or a municipality, in respect of the provision such accommodation, and an agreement for such purposes may be entered into with such person only after the proposed agreement, the plans of the school and of the building of which it may be a part and the site have been approved by the Minister.

PART VI — BOARDS — S. 197

Out-of-Classroom Programs

197. (1) **Acquisition of land for natural science program.**—Where a board acquires a school site under subsection 195(1)(2) or (3) for the purpose of conducting thereon a natural science program and other out-of-classroom programs, the board shall obtain the approval the Minister before it erects, adds to or alters buildings on or makes other improvements school site for such purpose.

(2) **Application.**—Subsection (1) does not apply with respect to a school site acquired by a Roman Catholic board under subsection 195(1) where the cost of the erection of, addition to or the alteration of the buildings on the school site or of making other improvement to the school site is provided entirely by the Roman Catholic board.

(3) **Idem.**—A board may, with the approval of the Minister, acquire by purchase or lease for the purpose of conducting a natural science program and other out-of-classroom program a school site in Ontario that it does not have the authority to acquire under section 195, and board shall obtain the approval of the Minister before it erects, adds to or alters buildings or makes other Improvements to the school site for such purpose.

(4) **Approval not required.**—An approval of the Minister is not required under section (2) or (5) for normal maintenance to a building or site.

(5) **Agreement between boards.**—Two or more boards may enter into an agreement a period specified therein for the shared use of a school site in Ontario for conducting natural science programs and other out-of-classroom programs but. where under such agreement of the boards may acquire or is to acquire by purchase or lease a school site for such purpose is to erect, add to or alter a building on or make other improvements to such site, agreement is not effective until it is approved by the Minister, and a school site situate out jurisdiction of the boards that are parties to the agreement shall not be acquired without the approval of the Minister

(6) **Taxation.**—All land acquired by a board for the purpose of conducting a natural science program and other out-of-classroom programs, so long as it is held by the board and is not situated within the jurisdiction of the board or within the jurisdiction of another board with which the board has entered into an agreement under subsection (5), is subject to taxation for municipal and school purposes in the municipality in which it is situate.

(7) **Agreements with conservation authorities, etc.**—A board may enter into an agree-with a conservation or other appropriate authority under which the board may, with the approval of the Minister, construct and maintain on lands owned by the authority the necessary facilities for the purpose of conducting a natural science program or other out-of-classroom program.

(8) **Idem.**—A board that conducts a natural science, conservation or other out-of-class program may enter into an agreement with a conservation or other appropriate authority for the use of the facilities and personnel of such authority for the purpose of conducting such a program as directed by the board

(9) **Idem.**—One or more boards may enter into an agreement with a conservation or other appropriate authority to provide for the construction, furnishing and equipping by the authority on lands owned by the authority of facilities for the purposes of conducting a natural science.

observation or other out-of-classroom program as directed by the board or one or more of the boards and, where under the agreement a board is required to pay all or part of the cost of the facilities, the construction of the facilities shall be first approved by the Minister, and the amount paid therefor by the board shall be deemed to be an expenditure made by the board for a permanent improvement.

(10) **Board and lodging for courses in conservation.**—A board may provide or pay for board and lodging for a pupil for a period not exceeding two weeks in any year while the pupil ticipates, with the consent of his or her parent or guardian and with the permission of the Board, in a natural science, conservation or other out-of classroom program.

1997, c. 31, s. 102.

Officers

198. (1) **Duties of secretary.**—The secretary of a board is responsible for,

(a) keeping a full and correct record of the proceedings of every meeting of the board in the minute book provided for that purpose by the board and ensuring that the minutes when confirmed are signed by the chair or presiding member;

(b) transmitting to the Ministry copies of reports requested by the Ministry;

(c) giving notice of all meetings of the board to each of the members by notifying the member personally or in writing or by sending a written notice to his or her residence;

(d) calling a special meeting of the board on the request in writing of the majority of the members of the board; and

(e) performing such other duties as may be required of the secretary by the regulation by this Act or by the board.

(2) **Security by officers.**—Every treasurer and collector of a board and, if required by the board, any other officer of a board shall give security for the faithful performance of his or her duties, and the security shall be deposited for safe-keeping as directed by the board.

(3) **Form of security.**—The security to be given shall be a bond of an insurer licensed under the *Insurance Act* to write surety and fidelity insurance.

(4) **Failure to take security.**—If a board refuses or neglects to take proper security the treasurer or other person to whom it entrusts money of the board and any of the mor forfeited or lost in consequence of the refusal or neglect, every member of the board is personally liable for such money, which may be recovered by the board or by any ratepayer assessed the support of the school or schools under the jurisdiction of the board suing personally on behalf of all other such ratepayers in a court of competent jurisdiction, but no member is I if the member proves that he or she made reasonable efforts to procure the taking of the security.

(5) **Duties of treasurer.**—Every treasurer of a board shall,

(a) receive and account for all money of the board;

(b) open an account or accounts in the name of the board in such place of deposit as be approved by the board;

(c) deposit all money received by the treasurer on account of the board, and no other money, to the credit of such account or accounts;

(d) disburse all money as directed by the board; and

(e) produce, when required by the board or by auditors or other competent authority papers and money in the treasurer's possession, power or control belonging to board.

(6) **Business administrator.**—Where a board determines that one or more persons shall be employed full time to carry out the duties of a secretary or treasurer or both, it may appoint one or more business administrators and one or more assistant business administrators and may ign to a person so appointed any of the duties of the secretary, treasurer and supervisor of maintenance of school buildings.

1997, c. 19, s. 33.

199. Responsibility of officers.—Every officer appointed by a board is responsible to the board through its chief executive officer for the performance of the duties assigned to him or her by the board.

School Board Advisory Committees

200. Definition.—In sections 201 to 205, "committee" means a school board advisory committee established under section 201.

201. Establishment of committee.—A district school board may establish a school board advisory committee.

1997, c. 31, s. 103.

202. (1) **Composition.**—The committee shall be composed of,

(a) three members of the board appointed by the board;
(b) the chief education officer of the board or his or her nominee;
(c) six teachers employed by the board, appointed by the teachers in the employ of the board;
(d) four persons appointed by the board who are neither teachers nor members of a board, but who are resident within the jurisdiction of the board; and
(e) the persons, if any, appointed under subsections (2) to (3.2).

(2) **English-language separate district school board.**—In the case of an English-language separate district school board where the Diocesan Council or Councils of the Federation of Catholic Parent-Teacher Associations of Ontario organized in the area of jurisdiction of the board so recommend, the board shall appoint to the committee two persons selected by the Council or Councils.

(3) **French-language separate district school board.**—In the case of a French-language separate district school board where the Fédération des associations de parents francophones de l'Ontario organized in the area of jurisdiction of the board so recommends, the board shall appoint to the committee two Roman Catholics selected by the regional section and, where there is no regional section, by the local section of the Fédération.

(3.1) **English language public district school board.**—In the case of an English-language public district school board where the Home and School Council organized in the area of jurisdiction of the board so recommends, the board shall appoint to the committee two persons selected by the Council.

(3.2) **French-language public district school board.**—In the case of a French-language public district school board where the Fédération des associations de parents francophones de l'Ontario organized in the area of jurisdiction of the board so recommends, the board shall appoint to the committee one person selected by the regional section and, where there is no regional section, by the local section of the Fédération.

(4) **Notice of teacher appointees.**—The teachers shall submit to the board, not later than the 31st day of December in each year, the names of the appointees under clause (I)(c).

(5) **Appointment and term of office.**—Members of the committee shall be appointed on or before the 31st day of December in each year and shall hold office for one year.

(6) **Reappointment.**—Except for the chief education officer. A member of the committee shall not hold office for more than three years in succession.

(7) **Vacancies.**—Every vacancy on a committee occasioned by the death or resignation of a member, or by any other cause, shall be filled by a person qualified under subsection (I) appointed by the body or person that appointed the member whose office has become vacant, and every person so appointed shall hold office for the unexpired portion of the term of such member.

1993, c. 27, Sch.; 1997, c. 31, s. 104.

203. (1) **First meeting.**—The chair of the board shall call the first meeting of the committee not later than the 31st day of January in each year, and shall preside at such meet until the chair of the committee is elected.

(2) **Chair.**—The chair of the committee shall be elected by the committee at its meeting in each year.

(3) **Quorum.**—Eight members of the committee constitute a quorum and a vote of majority of the members present is necessary to bind the committee.

(4) **Sub-committees.**—The committee may establish such sub-committees as it considers necessary.

204. (1) **Recording secretary.**—The board shall provide a recording secretary for committee.

(2) **Budget.**—The committee shall, as required by the board, submit to the board approval a budget of its estimated expenditures for the calendar year.

(3) **Expenditures.**—The board shall pay such expenditures of the committee as approved by the board.

205. (1) **Powers of committee.**—The committee may make reports and recommendations to the board in respect of any educational matter pertaining to the schools under jurisdiction of the board.

(2) **Limitation.**—Despite subsection (1), the committee shall not concern itself with salaries of employees of the board or with matters pertaining to personnel problems and policies relating to personnel.

(3) **Consideration of reports.**—The board shall consider any report or recommendation submitted to it by the committee and shall not refuse its approval without having given committee, or its representatives, an opportunity to be heard by the board.

206. [Repealed 1997, c. 31, s. 105.]

Access to Meetings and Records

207. (1) **Open meetings of boards.**—The meetings of a board and, subject to subsection (2), meetings of a committee of the board, including a committee of the whole board, shall open to the public, and no person shall be excluded from a meeting that is open to the public except for improper conduct.

(2) **Closing of certain committee meetings.**—A meeting of a committee of a board including a committee of the whole board, may be closed to the public when the subject under consideration involves,

- (a) the security of the property of the board;
- (b) the disclosure of intimate, personal or financial information in respect of a member of the board or committee, an employee or prospective employee of the board or a pupil or his or her parent or guardian;
- (c) the acquisition or disposal of a school site;
- (d) decisions in respect of negotiations with employees of the board; or
- (e) litigation affecting the board.

(3) **Exclusion of persons.**—The presiding officer may expel or exclude from any meeting, any person who has been guilty of improper conduct at the meeting.

(4) **Inspection of books and accounts.**—Any person may, at all reasonable hours, at head office of the board inspect the minute book, the audited annual financial report and current accounts of a board, and, upon the written request of any person and upon the pay to the board at the rate of 25 cents for every 100 words or at such lower rate as the board fix, the secretary shall furnish copies of them or extracts therefrom certified under the secretary's hand.

Board Meetings

208. (1) **When board deemed constituted.**—A board shall be deemed to be constituted when a majority of the members to be elected or appointed has been elected or appointed.

(2) **First meeting.**—A board that is elected at a regular election under the *Municipal Elections Act, 1996* and a board that is appointed or elected other than at a regular election under the *Municipal Elections Act, 1996* shall hold its first meeting not later than seven days after the day which the term of office of the board commences on such date and at such time and place the board determines and. failing such determination, at 8 p.m. at the head office of the on the first Wednesday following the commencement of the term of office.

(3) **Supervisory officer may provide for calling first meeting.**—Despite subsection (2), on the petition of a majority of the members of a newly elected or appointed board, private supervisory officer may provide for calling the first meeting of the board at some other time and date.

(4) **Presiding officer.**—At the first meeting in December of each year, the chief executive officer shall preside until the election of the chair or, if there is no chief executive officer or in his or her absence, the members present shall designate who shall preside at the election of the chair and if a member of the board is so designated, he or she may vote at the election of the chair.

(5) **Election of chair.**—At the first meeting in December of each year and at the first meeting after a vacancy occurs in the office of chair, the members shall elect one of themselves to be chair, and the chair shall preside at all meetings.

(5.1) **Transition: 1998.**—For the purposes of a district school board in 1998, a requirement under subsection (4) or (5) to do something at the first meeting of December in each year shall be deemed to be a requirement to do the thing at the first meeting of the board in 1998, or at an earlier meeting as directed under section 351.

(6) **Subsequent meetings.**—Subsequent meetings of the board shall be held at such time and place as the board considers expedient.

(7) **Vice-chair.**—The members of the board may also elect one of themselves to be vice-chair and he or she shall preside in the absence of the chair.

(8) **Where equality of votes.**—In the case of an equality of votes at the election of a chair or vice-chair, the candidates shall draw lots to fill the position of chair or vice-chair, as the case may be.

(9) **Temporary chair.**—If at any meeting there is no chair or vice-chair present, the members present may elect one of themselves to be chair for that meeting.

(10) **Temporary secretary.**—In the absence of the secretary from any meeting, the chair or other member presiding may appoint any member or other person to act as secretary for that meeting.

(11) **Quorum.**—The presence of a majority of all the members constituting a board is necessary to form a quorum.

(12) **Chair, voting; equality of votes.**—The presiding officer, except where he or she is the chief executive officer of the board and is not a member, may vote with the other members of the board upon all motions, and any motion on which there is an equality of votes is lost.

(13) **Special meetings.**—Special meetings of the board may be called by the chair and in such other manner as the board may determine.

1997, c. 31, s. 106.

208.1 (1) **Regulations: electronic meetings.**—The Lieutenant Governor in Council may make regulations respecting the use of electronic means for the holding of meetings of a district school board and meetings of a committee of a district school board, including a committee of the whole board.

(2) **Same.**—A regulation under subsection (1) may provide that a board member who participates in a meeting through electronic means shall be deemed to be present at the meeting for the purposes of this and every other Act, subject to such conditions or limitations as may be provided for in the regulation.

(3) **Same.**—A regulation under subsection (1) may provide for participation through electronic means by members of the board, pupil representatives and members of the public.

(4) **Same.**—In a regulation under this section, the Lieutenant Governor in Council may provide for any matter by authorizing a board to develop and implement a policy with respect to the matter.

(5) **Same.**—The minimum requirements specified in section 229 for physical presence

in the meeting room of a board shall not be interpreted to prevent a higher minimum being provided for under this section.

1997, c. 31, s. 107.

209. (1) **Declaration.**—Except as provided in subsection (2), every person elected or appointed to a board, on or before the day fixed for the first meeting of the new board, or on or before the day of the first meeting that the person attends, shall make and subscribe the following declaration in English or French before the secretary of the board or before any person authorized to administer an oath or affirmation and in default the person shall be deemed to have resigned:

DECLARATION

1. I am not disqualified under any Act from being a member of (name of board).
2. I will truly, faithfully, impartially and to the best of my ability execute the office of board member, and that I have not received and will not receive any payment or reward or promise thereof for the exercise of any partiality or malversation or other undue execution of the said office and that I will disclose any pecuniary interest, direct or indirect, as required by and in accordance with the Municipal Conflict of Interest Act.

Declared before me at ....in the

Province of Ontario ....this ....day of

.................., 19

(2) **Idem.**—Where a person is elected or appointed to fill a vacancy on a board, the person shall make such declaration on or before the day fixed for holding the first meeting of the board after his or her election or appointment or on or before the day of the first meeting that the person attends and in default the person shall be deemed to have resigned.

(3) **Oath of allegiance.**—Every person elected or appointed to a board, before entering on his or her duties as a board member, shall take and subscribe before the secretary of the board or before any person authorized to administer an oath the oath or affirmation of allegiance in the following form, in English or French:

I,............ do (swear or affirm) that I will be faithful and bear true allegiance to Her Majesty, Queen Elizabeth II (or the reigning sovereign for the time being).

(Sworn or affirmed) before me at

............in the Province of Ontario

..................this .....day

of........, 19

(4) **Filing of declaration and oath.**—The declaration and oath or affirmation of allegiance shall be filed with the secretary of the board within eight days after the making or taking thereof, as the case may be.

1994, c. 23, s. 65; 1997, c. 31, s. 108.

Arbitrators

210. (1) **Arbitrators to send copy of award to board, etc.**—Arbitrators acting under this Act shall send a copy of their award forthwith after the making thereof to the chief executive officer of the board and to the clerk of each municipality affected.

(2) **Liability of parties for costs.**—Such arbitrators shall determine the costs of the arbitration and shall direct to whom and by whom and in what manner such costs or any part thereof, and the fees under subsection (4), shall be paid, and such determination and direction is final.

(3) **Expenses.**—An arbitrator is entitled to an allowance of 10 cents for each kilometre necessarily traveled by the arbitrator to and from his or her residence to attend meetings of arbitrators together with his or her actual expenses for room and meals, incurred while attending such meetings, and such costs shall be included in the costs of the arbitration.

(4) **Fees.**—Each arbitrator shall be paid a fee,
  (a) in the case of the Ontario Municipal Board, as determined by the Board;
  (b) in the case of an arbitrator other than a supervisory officer, judge or member of the Ontario Municipal Board, at the rate of $20 for each sitting of a half-day or fraction thereof.

(5) [Repealed 1997, c. 31, s. 109.]

(6) [Repealed 1997, c. 31, s. 109.]

(7) [Repealed 1997, c. 31, s. 109.]

1993, c. 27, Sch.; 1997, c. 31, s. 109.

Offences and Penalties

211. False declaration.—Every person who wilfully makes a false statement in a declaration required to be made under this Act is guilty of an offence and on conviction is liable a fine of not more than $200.

212. (1) **Disturbances.**—Every person who wilfully interrupts or disquiets the proceedings of a school or class is guilty of an offence and on conviction is liable to a fine of not more than $200.

(2) **Idem.**—Every person who, with intent to prevent the discussion of any matter or the passing of any motion at a meeting of a board, or a committee of a board including a committee of the whole board disrupts or endeavors to disturb or interrupt the meeting after having been expelled or excluded from the meeting is guilty of an offence and on conviction is liable to a fine of not more than $200.

213. (1) **Acting while disqualified.**—Every member of a board who sits or votes at any meeting of the board after becoming disqualified from sitting is guilty of an offence and on conviction is liable to a fine of not more than $200 for every meeting at which he or she so sits or votes.

(2) **False reports and registers.**—Every member of a board who knowingly signs a false report and every teacher who keeps a false school register or makes a false return is guilty of an offence and on conviction is liable to a fine of not more than $200.

214. [Repealed 1997, c. 31, s. 110.]

215. [Repealed 1997, c. 31, s. 110.]

216. [Repealed 1997, c. 31, s. 110.]

217. (1) **Promotion or sale of books, etc., by employees of board or Ministry to board, pupil, etc., prohibited.**—No teacher, supervisory officer or other employee of a board or of the Ministry shall, for compensation of any kind other than his or her salary as such employee, promote, offer for sale or sell, directly or indirectly, any book or other teaching or learning materials, equipment, furniture, stationery or other article to any board, provincial school or teachers' college, or to any pupil enrolled therein.

(2) **Exception for authors.**—Subsection (I) does not apply to a teacher, supervisory officer or any other employee in respect of a book or other teaching or learning materials of which he or she is an author where the only compensation that he or she receives in respect thereof is a fee or royalty thereon.

(3) **Employment of employee of board or Ministry to promote sale of books, etc, to board, pupil, etc., prohibited.**—No person or organization or agent thereof shall employ a teacher, supervisory officer or other employee of a board or of the Ministry to promote, offer for sale or sell, directly or indirectly, any book or other teaching or learning materials, equipment, furniture, stationery or other article to any board, provincial school or teachers' college, or to any pupil enrolled therein, or shall, directly or indirectly, give or pay compensation to any such teacher, supervisory officer or employee for such purpose.

(4) **Penalty.**—Every person who contravenes any provision of subsection (I) or (3) is guilty of an offence and on conviction is liable to a fine of not more than $1,000.

Validity of Elections

218. (1) **Action for declaration that seat vacant.**—Any person entitled to vote at the election of members of a board may commence an application in the Ontario Court (General Division) for a declaration that the office of a member of such board has become vacant.

(2) **Time for bringing action.**—No application shall be commenced under this section more than ninety days after the facts alleged to cause the vacancy in the board came to the knowledge of the person bringing such action.

(3) **Power of court.**—Where in an application under this section the court finds that the office of a member of the board has become vacant, the court may order that the member be removed from office and declare that the office is vacant.

(4) **Application of *Municipal Elections Act*.**—Subsection 83(3) and sections 85, 86 and 87 of the *Municipal Elections Act, 1996* apply to an application made under this section, with necessary modifications.

(5) **Joining of claims.**—A claim in an application under this section may be joined with a claim in an application under section 83 of the *Municipal Elections Act, 1996*, and the claims may be heard and disposed of together.

(6) **Validity of elections and corrupt practices.**—The provisions of the *Municipal Elections Act, 1996* in respect of the validity of elections and corrupt practices apply to an election of board members that is not conducted under the Municipal Elections Act, 1996.

1996, c. 32, s. 70; 1997, c. 31, s. 111.

PART VII

BOARD MEMBERS — QUALIFICATIONS, RESIGNATIONS AND VACANCIES

219. (1) **Qualifications of members.**—A person is qualified to be elected as a member of a district school board or school authority if the person is qualified to vote for members of that district school board or that school authority and is resident in its area of jurisdiction.

(2) **Same.**—A person who is qualified under subsection (1) to be elected as a member of a district school board or school authority is qualified to be elected as a member of that district school board or school authority for any geographic area in the district school board's or school authority's area of jurisdiction, regardless of which positions on that district school board or school authority the person may be qualified to vote for.

(3) **Eligibility for re-election.**—A member of a district school board or school authority is eligible for re-election if otherwise qualified.

(4) **Disqualifications.**—Despite subsection (1), a person is not qualified to be elected or to act as a member of a district school board or school authority if the person is,

(a) an employee of a district school board or school authority;
(b) the spouse of a person mentioned in clause (a);
(c) the clerk or treasurer or deputy clerk or deputy treasurer of a county or municipality, including a regional municipality, the County of Oxford and The District Municipality of Muskoka, all or part of which is included in the area of jurisdiction of the district school board or the school authority;
(d) a member of the Assembly or of the Senate or House of Commons of Canada; or
(e) otherwise ineligible or disqualified under this or any other Act.

(5) **Leave of absence.**—Despite subsection (4), a person who is,

(a) an employee of a district school board or school authority;
(b) the spouse of a person mentioned in clause (a); or
(c) the clerk or treasurer or deputy clerk or deputy treasurer of a county or municipality, including a regional municipality, the County of Oxford and The District municipality of Muskoka, all or part of which is included in the area of jurisdiction of a district school board or school authority,

is not ineligible to be a candidate for or to be elected as a member of a district school board or school authority if he or she or, in the case of clause (b), his or her spouse, takes an unpaid leave of absence, beginning no later than nomination day and ending on voting day, in which case subsections 30(2) to (7) of the *Municipal Elections Act, 1996* apply with necessary modifications.

(6) **Same.**—In subsection (5),

"nomination day" and "voting day" have the same meaning as in the *Municipal Elections Act, 1996*.

(7) **Disqualification: district school board by-elections.**—Despite subsection (1), a person is not qualified to be elected in a by-election or to act as a member of a district school board if the person is,

(a) a member of any other district school board;
(b) a member of a school authority;
(c) a member of the council of a county or municipality, including a regional municipality, the County of Oxford and The District Municipality of Muskoka, all or part of which is included in the area of jurisdiction of the district school board; or
(d) an elected member of a local board, as defined in the *Municipal Affairs Act*, of a county or municipality, including a regional municipality, the County of Oxford and The District Municipality of Muskoka, all or part of which is included in the area of jurisdiction of the district school board,

and the person's term of office has at least two months to run after the last day for filing nominations for the by-election, unless before the closing of nominations the person has filed his or her resignation with the secretary of the other district school board, with the secretary of the school authority or with the clerk of the county or municipality, as the case may be.

(8) **Disqualification: school authority by-elections.**—Despite subsection (1), a person is not qualified to be elected in a by-election or to act as a member of a school authority if the person is,

(a) a member of any other school authority;
(b) a member of a district school board;
(c) a member of the council of a county or municipality, including a regional municipality, the County of Oxford and The District Municipality of Muskoka, all or part of which is included in the area of jurisdiction of the school authority; or
(d) an elected member of a local board, as defined in the *Municipal Affairs Act*, of a county or municipality, including a regional municipality, the County of Oxford and The District Municipality of Muskoka, all or part of which is included in the area of jurisdiction of the school authority,

and the person's term of office has at least two months to run after the last day for filing nominations for the by-election, unless before the closing of nominations the person has filed his or her resignation with the secretary of the other school authority, with the secretary of the district school board or with the clerk of the county or municipality, as the case may be.

(9) **Qualification to act as a member.**—A person is not qualified to act as a member of a district school board or school authority if the person ceases to hold the qualifications required to be elected as a member of the district school board or the school authority.

(10) **Person not to be candidate for more than one seat.**—No person shall run as a candidate for more than one seat on a district school board or school authority and any person who does so and is elected to hold one or more seats on the district school board or the school authority is not entitled to act as a member of the district school board or the school authority by reason of the election.

(11) **Vacancy where member disqualified.**—The seat of a member of a district school board or school authority who is not qualified or entitled to act as a member of that district school board or that school authority is vacated.

1996, c. 32, s. 70(10); 1997, c. 31, s. 112.

220. (1) **Members to remain in office.**—The members of a board shall remain in office until their successors are elected and the new board is organized.

S. 221 EDUCATION ACT

(2) **Board not to cease for want of members.**—A board does not cease to exist by reason only of the lack of members.

(3) **Resignation of members.**—A member of a board, with the consent of a majority of the members present at a meeting, entered on the minutes of it, may resign as a member, but he or she shall not vote on a motion as to his or her own resignation and may not resign as a member if the resignation will reduce the number of members of the board to less than a quorum.

(4) **Resignation to become candidate for some other office.**—Despite subsection (3), where it is necessary for a member of a board to resign to become a candidate for some other office, the member may resign by filing his or her resignation, including a statement that the resignation is for the purpose of becoming a candidate for some other office, with the secretary of the board and the resignation shall become effective on November 30 after it is filed or on the day preceding the day on which the term of the office commences, whichever is the earlier.

1996, c. 32, s. 70(11); 1997, c. 3, s. 4; 1997, c. 31, s. 112.

221. (1) **Vacancies.**—Subject to section 224, if the office of a member of a board becomes vacant before the end of the member's term,

(a) the remaining elected members shall appoint a qualified person to fill the vacancy within 60 days after the office becomes vacant, if a majority of the elected members remain in office; or

(b) a by-election shall be held to fill the vacancy, in the same manner as an election of the board, if a majority of the elected members do not remain in office.

(2) **Optional election.**—Despite clause (1)(a), if elections of the board are held under the *Municipal Elections Act, 1996* and the vacancy occurs in a year in which no regular election is held under that Act or before April 1 in the year of a regular election, the remaining elected members may by resolution require that an election be held in accordance with the *Municipal Elections Act, 1996* to fill the vacancy.

(3) **Same.**—The secretary of the board shall promptly send to the clerk of the appropriate municipality a certified copy of the resolution under subsection (2).

(4) **Notice re clause (1)(b).**—Where clause (1)(b) applies, the secretary of the board shall promptly send to the clerk of the appropriate municipality a notice that clause (1)(b) applies and the notice shall be deemed to be a resolution indicating a by-election is required for the purposes of section 65 of the *Municipal Election Act, 1996*.

(5) **Term of office.**—A member appointed or elected to fill a vacancy shall hold office for the remainder of the term of the member who vacated the office.

1997, c. 31, s. 112.

222. (1) **Elections for three member boards.**—If an election is required to fill a vacancy on a board that is composed of three members and there are fewer than two remaining members of the board, a meeting of the electors may be called by any two electors of the board or by the appropriate supervisory officer.

(2) **Time of meeting.**—The meeting shall take place within 60 days of the date on which the last office became vacant.

PART VII — BOARD MEMBERS — QUALIFICATIONS S. 226

(3) **Notice of meeting.**—At least six days before the meeting, the person or persons calling the meeting shall post a notice of the meeting in at least three public places within the area of jurisdiction of the board.

(4) **Election at meeting.**—The electors at the meeting shall elect the required number of board members to fill the vacancies.

1996, c. 32, s. 70(12); 1997, c. 31, s. 112.

223. (1) **Vacancy in rural separate school board before incorporation.**—If a vacancy occurs in the office of a member of the board of a rural separate school before the board members become a body corporate, the remaining board members shall promptly take steps to hold a by-election to fill the vacancy, and the person elected shall hold office for the remainder of the term of the board member who vacated the office.

(2) **Manner of election.**—The by-election shall be conducted in the same manner as an election of the whole board.

1997, c. 31, s. 112.

224. Vacancy on board.—Where a vacancy occurs on a board,
(a) within one month before the next election, it shall not be filled; or
(b) after the election, but before the new board is organized, it shall be filled immediately after the new board is organized in the same manner as for a vacancy that occurs after the board is organized.

1997, c. 31, s. 112.

225. (1) **Election to fill vacancy.**—Where an election is required to fill a vacancy on a board that is composed of more than three members and whose elections are not conducted under the *Municipal Elections Act, 1996*, the nomination shall be held on the third Monday following the day on which the office becomes vacant and the polling shall be held on the second Monday following the day of nomination, and the nomination and polling shall be held in the same manner and at the same times as for the office that became vacant.

(2) **Extension of time limits.**—The remaining members of the board may extend the time for the nomination and the polling under subsection (1), but the polling shall be held no later than 60 days after the office becomes vacant.

1997, c. 31, s. 112.

226. (1) **Appointment of board members on failure of qualified person.**—Where the appropriate supervisory officer reports that no qualified persons or an insufficient number of qualified persons are available or that the electors have failed to elect a sufficient number of members of a district school area board to form a quorum, the Minister may appoint as members of the board such persons as the Minister may consider proper, and the persons so appointed have, during the term of such appointment, all the authority of board members as though they were eligible and duly elected according to this Act.

(2) **Interim administration pending by-elections.**—Where under this Act vacancies on a board are required to be filled by an election to be conducted under the *Municipal Elections Act, 1996* and no election can be held under that Act, the Minister may by order provide for the fulfilling of the duties and obligations of the board until such time as an election is held in

accordance with the *Municipal Elections Act, 1996* and the members so elected have taken office.

1997, c. 31, s. 112.

227. Tie vote.—If two or more candidates receive an equal number of votes at a meeting held under clause 222(1)(a) to appoint a person to fill a vacancy or at a meeting to elect a person to fill a vacancy, the chair of the meeting shall provide for the drawing of lots to determine which of the candidates shall be appointed or elected.

1996, c. 32, s. 70(13); 1997, c. 31, s. 112.

228. (1) **Seat vacated by conviction, absence etc.**—A member of a board vacates his or her seat if he or she,

(a) is convicted of an indictable offence;
(b) absents himself or herself without being authorized by resolution entered in the minutes, from three consecutive regular meetings of the board;
(c) ceases to hold the qualifications required to act as a member of the board;
(d) becomes disqualified under subsection 219(4); or
(e) fails to meet the requirements of section 229.

(2) **Exception: conviction.**—Despite subsection (1), where a member of a board is convicted of an indictable offence, the vacancy shall not be filled until the time for taking any appeal that may be taken from the conviction has elapsed, or until the final determination of any appeal so taken, and in the event of the quashing of the conviction the seat shall be deemed not to have been vacated.

(3) **Filling of vacancies.**—Where a seat becomes vacant under this section, the provisions of this Act with respect to the filling of vacancies apply.

1997, c. 31, s. 112.

229. (1) **In person attendance required.**—Despite section 208.1 but subject to subsection (2), a member of a board shall be physically present in the meeting room of the board for at least three regular meetings of the board in each 12-month period beginning December 1.

(2) **Same.**—Despite section 208.1, for the period beginning when a member of a board is elected or appointed to fill a vacancy and ending on the following November 30, the member shall be physically present in the meeting room of the board for at least one regular meeting of the board for each period of four full calendar months that occurs during the period beginning with the election or appointment and ending on the following November 30.

(3) **Transition: district school boards in 1998.**—Despite section 208.1, in 1998, a member of a district school board shall be physically present in the meeting room of the board for at least three regular meetings of the board.

1993, c. 11, s. 34; 1997, c. 31, s. 112.

PART VIII

[Repealed 1997, c. 3, s. 5]

PART IX

FINANCE

DIVISION A
General

Estimates

231. (1) **Estimates.**—Every board, before the beginning of each fiscal year and in time to comply with the date set under clause (11)(c), shall prepare and adopt estimates of its revenues and expenditures for the fiscal year, and the estimates,

(a) shall set out the estimated revenues and expenditures of the board, including debt charges payable by the board or on its behalf by the council of a municipality, a county, a regional or district municipality or the County of Oxford;

(b) shall provide for a projection of any surplus or deficit arising in the fiscal year immediately preceding the fiscal year, as calculated by the treasurer of the board;

(c) shall make due allowance for a surplus of any previous fiscal year that will be available during the current fiscal year, including a surplus projected under clause (b);

(d) shall provide for any deficit of any previous fiscal year, including a deficit projected under clause (b);

(e) shall provide for allocations to reserve funds as required by the regulations made under section 232;

(f) may provide for a reserve for working funds of a sum not in excess of 5 per cent of the expenditures of the board for the preceding fiscal year, but, where the sum accumulated in the reserve is equal to or more than 20 per cent of those expenditures, no further sum shall be provided; and

(g) subject to clause (d), shall not provide for any deficit.

(2) **Balanced budget.**—In meeting the requirements of clause (1)(a), the board shall ensure that its estimated expenditures do not exceed its estimated revenues.

(3) **Rule for 1998.**—Despite clause (1)(f), in the fiscal year January 1, 1998 to August 31, 1998, a district school board may provide for a reserve for working funds of a sum not in excess of the amount prescribed by regulation under clause 232(1)(c) for the district school board.

(4) **Reserve fund limitation exception.**—The limitation on the sum that a board may allocate to a reserve fund under section 232 does not apply to revenue received by a board in any fiscal year from the sale or disposal of, or insurance proceeds in respect of, permanent improvements.

(5) **Same.**—The limitation on the sum that a board may include in its estimates for permanent improvements under section 232 does not apply to the following:

1. An expenditure from a reserve fund for the purpose for which the fund was established.

2. The portion of an expenditure for a permanent improvement receivable by way of a

grant under section 9 of the *Community Recreation Centres Act* or receivable from a municipality pursuant to an agreement under section 183.

(6) **Reserve fund money.**—Subject to section 241, the money held in a reserve fund by a board shall not be expended, pledged or applied to any purpose other than that for which the fund was established without the approval of the Minister.

(7) **Same.**—Subsections 163(2.2), (2.3) and (4) of the *Municipal Act* do not apply with respect to the money.

(8) **Same.**—The money allocated to a reserve fund shall be paid into a special account.

(9) **Same.**—Instead of keeping a separate account for each reserve fund, a board may keep a consolidated account in which there may be deposited the money allocated to all reserve funds established by the board.

(10) **Same.**—The consolidated account shall be kept in a way that permits the true state of each reserve fund to be determined.

(11) **Minister's powers.**—The Minister may,
(a) issue guidelines respecting the form and content of estimates required under this section;
(b) require boards to comply with the guidelines; and
(c) require boards to submit a copy of the estimates to the Ministry, by a date specified for the purpose by the Minister.

(12) **Same.**—The *Regulations Act* does not apply to anything done by the Minister under subsection (11).

1997, c. 3, s. 5; 1997, c. 31, s. 113(1).

232. (1) **Regulations re estimates.**—The Minister may make regulations governing estimates that a board is required to prepare and adopt, including but not limited to regulations,
(a) requiring a board, in the manner and to the extent specified in the regulations, to allocate specified amounts or types of revenues of the board to a reserve fund for permanent improvements or to a reserve fund for other purposes specified in the regulations;
(b) requiring a board, in the manner and to the extent specified in the regulations, to limit the amount of revenues of the board, or the amount of specified types of revenues of the board, that may be,
  (i) allocated by the board in a fiscal year to a reserve fund for permanent improvements or to a reserve fund for other purposes specified in the regulation, or
  (ii) expended in a fiscal year for permanent improvements or for other purposes specified in the regulation;
(c) prescribing the maximum amount that a district school board may provide for a reserve for working funds in the fiscal year January 1, 1998 to August 31, 1998 and establishing different amounts for different district school boards.

(2) **Same.**—A regulation made under this section may be general or particular and may apply in respect of any class of board or any class of permanent improvement.

(3) **Same.**—A class may be defined under this section with respect to any characteristic

and may be defined to consist of or to include or exclude any specified member of the class, whether or not with the same attributes.

1997, c. 3, s. 5; 1997, c. 31, s. 113(1).

233. (1) **Reserve following strike, lock-out.**—Where, in any fiscal year, any money that was provided in the estimates of a board for payment of salaries and wages of teachers and other employees in relation to employment in that year is not paid by reason of a strike by or lock-out of the teachers and other employees, or any of them, an amount of money calculated in accordance with the regulations shall in that fiscal year be placed in a reserve.

(2) **Same.**—The amount in the reserve at the end of the fiscal year shall be brought into the general revenues of the board for that fiscal year.

(3) **Regulations.**—The Minister, subject to the approval of the Lieutenant Governor in Council, may make regulations, which may be of general or particular application, providing for the calculation of the amounts of money to be placed in a reserve under subsection (1).

1997, c. 3, s. 5; 1997, c. 31, s. 113(1).

Legislative and Municipal Grants

234. (1) **Regulations governing legislative grants.**—Subject to subsections (2) and (3), the Lieutenant Governor in Council may make regulations governing the making of grants for educational purposes from money appropriated by the Legislature.

(2) **Same.**—Regulations made under subsection (1) shall ensure that the legislation and regulations governing education funding operate in a fair and non-discriminatory manner,
- (a) as between English-language public boards and English-language Roman Catholic boards; and
- (b) as between French-language public district school boards and French-language separate district school boards.

(3) **Same.**—Regulations made under subsection (1) shall ensure that the legislation and regulations governing education funding operate so as to respect the rights given by section 23 of the *Canadian Charter of Rights and Freedoms*.

(4) **Same.**—Without limiting the generality of subsection (1), a regulation made under subsection (1) may,
- (a) provide for the method of calculating or determining any thing for the purposes of calculating or paying all or part of a legislative grant;
- (b) prescribe the conditions governing the calculation or payment of all or part of a legislative grant;
- (c) authorize the Minister to withhold all or part of a legislative grant if a condition of the legislative grant is not satisfied or to require that all or part of a legislative grant be repaid if a condition of the grant is not satisfied.

(5) **Same.**—Without limiting the generality of clause (4)(b), the approval or confirmation of the Minister of any thing may be prescribed in a regulation made under subsection (1) as a condition governing the calculation or payment of all or part of a legislative grant.

(6) **Additional powers of Minister.**—The Minister may, for the purposes of the calculation and payment of legislative grants, prescribe the standards that shall be attained by a community group in respect of the provision of adult basic education under subsection 189 (3) and the criteria that shall be used to determine whether the standards are attainable.

(7) **Same.**—A regulation made under subsection (1),
  (a) may be general or particular in its application; and
  (b) may be made to apply with respect to any period specified in the regulation including a period before the regulation is made.

(8) **Payment schedule.**—The Minister may prescribe the number of instalments in which payments of legislative grants shall be paid to boards, the dates on which the payments shall be made and the amounts of the payments as a percentage of the total amount estimated by the Minister to be payable to the boards.

(9) **Non-application of *Regulations Act*.**—An act of the Minister under this section is not a regulation within the meaning of the *Regulations Act*.

(10) **Temporary grants.**—Despite subsection (2), the Lieutenant Governor in Council may make regulations providing for such funding to a board as the Lieutenant Governor in Council considers advisable, to assist the board in adapting to the education governance and education funding reforms of 1997 and 1998.

(11) **Limitation.**—A regulation made under subsection (10) shall not be made for the purpose of assisting a board after August 31, 2001.

(12) **Same.**—Despite subsection (11), where special circumstances exist in respect of one or more boards, a regulation may be made under subsection (10) in respect of the board or boards until August 31, 2003.

(13) **General or particular.**—A regulation made under subsection (10) may be general or particular.

(14) **Definition.**—In subsections (2) and (3) and in Division F, "education funding" means revenue available to a board,
  (a) from grants made under subsection (1),
  (b) from tax rates under Division B other than tax rates for the purposes of paying a board's share of the costs of rebates under section 442.1 or 442.2 of the *Municipal Act* or paying rebates under regulations under section 257.2.1 of this Act,
  (b.1) from taxes under Part XXII.1 of the *Municipal Act* or Division B of Part XXII.2 of the *Municipal Act* other than taxes for the purposes of paying a board's share of the costs of rebates under section 442.1 or 442.2 of the *Municipal Act* or paying rebates under regulations under section 257.2.1 of this Act, and
  (c) from education development charges under Division E.

1991, vol. 2, c. 15, s. 36; 1993, c. 27, Sch.; 1996, c. 13, s. 8; 1997, c. 31, s. 113(1).

235. (1) **Definition .**—In this section,

"Municipality".—"municipality" includes a county, a regional municipality, The District Municipality of Muskoka and the County of Oxford.

(2) **Boards to share in municipal grants.**—All grants, investments and allotments made by a municipality or by a local board of a municipality for education purposes, including but

not limited to grants referred to in section 113 of the *Municipal Act*, shall be shared in accordance with subsection (3) among the boards whose area of jurisdiction is all or partly the same as the area of jurisdiction of the municipality or the local board.

(3) **Same.**—The share of a board shall be determined by comparing the average number of pupils enrolled at the schools of the board in the area of jurisdiction of the municipality or the local board of the municipality making the grant, investment or allotment during the preceding 12 months, or during the number of months that have elapsed since the establishment of the board if it is a new board, as compared with the whole average number of pupils enrolled at the schools of all boards in the area of jurisdiction of the municipality or the local board.

1993, c. 23, s. 67; 1997, c. 31, s. 113(1); 1998, c. 33, s. 39.

235.1 [Repealed 1997, c. 31, s. 113(1).]
235.2 [Repealed 1997, c. 31, s. 113(1).]
235.3 [Repealed 1997, c. 31, s. 113(1).]

Board Support

236. (1) **Notice re status as supporter, English-language public board.**—An individual who is an owner or tenant of residential property in the area of jurisdiction of any board or outside the area of jurisdiction of all boards but within a municipality, is entitled, on application under section 16 of the *Assessment Act* to the assessment commissioner for the area in which the property is located, to have his or her name included or altered in the assessment roll as an English-language public board supporter.

(2) **Same, English-language Roman Catholic board.**—An individual who is a Roman Catholic and an owner or tenant of residential property in the area of jurisdiction of an English-language Roman Catholic board is entitled, on application under section 16 of the *Assessment Act* to the assessment commissioner for the area in which the property is located, to have his or her name included or altered in the assessment roll as an English-language Roman Catholic board supporter.

(3) **Same, French-language public district school board.**—An individual who is a French-language rights holder and an owner or tenant of residential property in the area of jurisdiction of a French-language public district school board is entitled, on application under section 16 of the *Assessment Act* to the assessment commissioner for the area in which the property is located, to have his or her name included or altered in the assessment roll as a French-language public district school board supporter.

(4) **Same, French-language separate district school board.**—An individual who is a Roman Catholic, a French-language rights-holder and an owner or tenant of residential property in the area of jurisdiction of a French-language separate district school board is entitled, on application under section 16 of the *Assessment Act* to the assessment commissioner for the area in which the property is located, to have his or her name included or altered in the assessment roll as a French-language separate district school board supporter.

(5) **Same, Protestant separate school board.**—An individual who is a Protestant and who occupies residential property as owner or tenant in a municipality in which a Protestant separate school board is established, is entitled, on application under section 16 of the *Assessment Act* to the assessment commissioner for the area in which the property is located, to have

his or her name included or altered in the assessment roll as a Protestant separate school board supporter.

1993, c. 11, s. 35; 1993, c. 23, s. 67(5); 1997, c. 31, s. 113(1).

237. (1) **School support, partnership or corporation other than designated ratepayer.**—In this section,

"**partnership**".—"partnership" means partnership within the meaning of the *Partnerships Act*.

(2) **Non-application to designated ratepayer.**—This section does not apply to a corporation that is a designated ratepayer as defined in subsection 238 (1).

(3) **Right of corporation or partnership.**—Subject to subsections (9) and (11), a corporation or partnership by notice to the assessment commissioner in a form approved by the Minister of Finance under the *Assessment Act* may,

(a) require the whole or any part of its assessment for residential property that it owns and that is within the jurisdiction of an English-language Roman Catholic board to be entered and assessed for English-language Roman Catholic board purposes;

(b) require the whole or any part of its assessment for residential property that it owns and that is within the jurisdiction of a French-language separate district school board to be entered and assessed for French-language separate district school board purposes; or

(c) require the whole or any part of its assessment for residential property that it owns and that is within the jurisdiction of a French-language public district school board to be entered and assessed for French-language public district school board purposes.

(4) **Duty of assessment commissioner.**—On receiving a notice under subsection (3) from the corporation or partnership, the assessment commissioner shall enter separately on the assessment roll to be next returned the corporation's or partnership's school support for each type of board specified in the notice.

(5) **Same.**—The assessment commissioner shall separately enter and assess for English-language public board purposes any assessment of the corporation or partnership not specified in the notice.

(6) **Notice to clerk.**—The assessment commissioner, on receipt of the notice from the corporation or partnership, shall forward a copy of the notice to the clerk of the municipality in which the residential property referred to in the notice is located.

(7) **Duty of clerk.**—On receiving the notice from the assessment commissioner, the clerk shall enter the corporation or partnership in the collector's roll and enter separately the corporation's or partnership's school support for each type of board specified in the notice.

(8) **Same.**—The clerk shall separately enter and show as assessed for English-language public board purposes any assessment of the corporation or partnership not specified in the notice.

(9) **Re corporation.**—The portions of an assessment of a corporation that are assessed other than for English-language public board purposes shall not bear a greater proportion to the whole assessment of the corporation than,

(a) in the case of assessment assessed for English-language Roman Catholic board

PART IX — FINANCE   S. 237

purposes, the number of shares held in the corporation by supporters of an English-language Roman Catholic board bears to the total number of shares of the corporation issued and outstanding;
(b) in the case of assessment assessed for French-language separate district school board purposes, the number of shares held in the corporation by supporters of a French-language separate district school board bears to the total number of shares of the corporation issued and outstanding; and
(c) in the case of assessment assessed for French-language public district school board purposes, the number of shares held in the corporation by supporters of a French-language public district school board bears to the total number of shares of the corporation issued and outstanding.

(10) **Same.**—Subsection (9) does not apply to a corporation without share capital or a corporation sole.

(11) **Re partnership.**—The portions of an assessment of a partnership that are assessed other than for English-language public board purposes shall not bear a greater proportion to the whole assessment of the partnership than,
(a) in the case of assessment assessed for English-language Roman Catholic board purposes, the interest of partners who are supporters of an English-language Roman Catholic board in the assets giving rise to the assessment bears to the whole interest of the partnership in the assets giving rise to the assessment;
(b) in the case of assessment assessed for French-language separate district school board purposes, the interest of partners who are supporters of a French-language separate district school board in the assets giving rise to the assessment bears to the whole interest of the partnership in the assets giving rise to the assessment; and
(c) in the case of assessment assessed for French-language public district school board purposes, the interest of partners who are supporters of a French-language public district school board in the assets giving rise to the assessment bears to the whole interest of the partnership in the assets giving rise to the assessment.

(12) **School support if corporation, partnership is tenant.**—A corporation or partnership that is a tenant of residential property may, subject to subsection (13), by notice to the assessment commissioner in a form approved by the Minister of Finance under the *Assessment Act* indicate the board or boards to which it wishes the amounts levied under section 257.7 in respect of such property to be distributed and the proportions of the amounts to be distributed to each board, and the amounts shall be distributed to the board or boards in the proportions indicated in the notice, and any portion of the amounts not indicated in the notice to be distributed to a specific board shall be distributed to the English-language public board that has jurisdiction in the area in which the property is located

(13) **Application of ss. (9), (10), (11), (14), (15) and (16).**—Subsections (9), (10), (11), (14), (15) and (16) apply with necessary modifications to a notice given under subsection (12).

(14) **Effect of notice.**—A notice given by a corporation under this section pursuant to a resolution of the directors or other persons having control or management over the affairs of the corporation is sufficient and shall continue in force and be acted on until it is withdrawn, varied or canceled by a notice subsequently given by the corporation pursuant to a resolution of the directors or those other persons.

(15) **Same.**—A notice given by a partnership under this section is sufficient if signed by a partner and shall continue in force and be acted on until it is withdrawn, varied or canceled by a notice subsequently given by a partner.

(16) **Inspection of notices.**—Every notice given under this section shall be kept by the assessment commissioner in his or her office, and shall at all convenient hours be open to inspection and examination.

(17) **Type of board.**—For the purposes of subsections (4) and (7), the following are types of boards:

1. English-language Roman Catholic boards.
2. French-language public district school boards.
3. French-language separate district school boards.

1997, c. 31, s. 113(1).

238. (1) **School support, designated ratepayers.**—In this section,

"**common jurisdictional area**".—"common jurisdictional area", in respect of two or more boards, means the area that is within the area of jurisdiction of both or all of those boards; ("territoire commun de compétence")

"**designated ratepayer**".—"designated ratepayer" means,

(a) the Crown in right of Canada or a province,
(b) a corporation without share capital or corporation sole that is an agency, board or commission of the Crown in right of Canada or a province,
(c) a municipal corporation,
(d) a corporation without share capital that is a local board as defined in the *Municipal Affairs Act*,
(e) a conservation authority established by or under the *Conservation Authorities Act* or a predecessor of that Act, or
(f) a public corporation; ("contribuable désigné")

"**public corporation**".—"public corporation" means,

(a) a body corporate that is, by reason of its shares, a reporting issuer within the meaning of the *Securities Act* or that has, by reason of its shares, a status comparable to a reporting issuer under the law of any other jurisdiction,
(b) a body corporate that issues shares that are traded on any market if the prices at which they are traded on that market are regularly published in a newspaper or business or financial publication of general and regular paid circulation, or
(c) a body corporate that is, within the meaning of subsections 1(1) and (2), clause 1(3)(a) and subsections 1(4), (5) and (6) of the *Securities Act*, controlled by or is a subsidiary of a body corporate or two or more bodies corporate described in clause (a) or (b) and, for the purposes of this clause, the expression "more than 50 per cent of the votes" in the second and third lines of clause 1(3)(a) of the *Securities Act* shall be deemed to read "50 per cent or more of the votes". ("société ouverte")

(2) **Distribution of taxes.**—The rates levied under Division B on the property of a designated ratepayer shall be distributed and paid in accordance with sections 257.8 and 257.9.

1997, c. 31, s. 113(1); 1997, c. 32, s. 10.

239. (1) **Tenant support re distribution of amounts levied.**—Where residential property is occupied by a tenant, the amounts levied under section 257.7 in respect of that property shall be distributed to the board of which the tenant is a supporter.

(2) **If tenant is corporation or partnership.**—If a tenant referred to in subsection (1) is a corporation or partnership referred to in section 237, for the purposes of subsection (1), the tenant shall be deemed to be a supporter of each board indicated in the notice given by the tenant under subsection 237 (12) or to be a supporter of the English-language public board as provided for by that subsection, and the amounts levied under section 257.7 in respect of the property occupied by the tenant shall be distributed to the boards of which the tenant is deemed to be a supporter in accordance with the notice and with subsection 237 (12).

(3) **If tenant is designated ratepayer.**—If a tenant referred to in subsection (1) is a designated ratepayer as defined in subsection 238 (1), for the purposes of subsection (1), the tenant shall be deemed to be a supporter of each board in whose jurisdiction the property occupied by the tenant is located and the amounts levied under section 257.7 in respect of that property shall be distributed to each of those boards in the same manner as the amounts levied on the business property of a designated ratepayer are distributed under section 257.8.

(4) **Amount to be levied if multiple tenants.**—If a parcel of residential property is occupied by more than one tenant, the amounts levied in respect of the property occupied by each tenant shall be determined as though the assessed value of the property occupied by each tenant were the assessment attributable to that tenant under subsection 14 (3) of the *Assessment Act*.

(5) **Agreement between owner and tenant.**—Where the person who occupies residential property is a tenant, no agreement between the owner and the tenant as to the application of taxes for school purposes as between themselves alters or affects subsections (1), (2), (3) or (4).

(6) **Conflict.**—Subsections (1), (2), (3) and (4) prevail in the event of a conflict between those subsections and section 237, subsection 238 (2) or section 257.9.

1997, c. 31, c. 113(1).

School Rate: Certain Circumstances

240. (1) **School rate: certain circumstances.**—Where, in a municipality,
(a) a person is entered on the collector's roll as an English-language public board supporter and there is no English-language public board to which school rates if levied in any year on the taxable property of the person in the municipality, may be paid; or
(b) a designated ratepayer as defined in subsection 238(1) is entered on the collector's roll and there is no board to which school rates levied in any year on the taxable property of the designated person in the municipality, may be paid,

there shall be levied and collected annually on the taxable property of the person referred to in clause (a) or of the designated ratepayer referred to in clause (b), as the case may be, in the municipality the same rates as are prescribed under section 257.12.

(2) **Reserve account.**—The money raised under subsection (1) shall be deposited in a reserve account for English-language public board purposes and may be invested in the securities prescribed under clause 241(6)(b), subject to the rules prescribed by the regulations for

the purposes of clause 241(1)(a), and for the purpose "invest" and "securities" have the same meaning as in section 241.

(3) **Same.**—The earnings from the investments under subsection (2) shall form part of the reserve account.

(4) **Use of money in account.**—Subject to subsection (5), where, in a municipality referred to in subsection (1), a district school area board is organized and makes provision for the education of its resident pupils, the municipal council shall pay over to the board the money that is held by the municipality under this section, and the money,

(a) shall be used for expenditures for permanent improvements for the purposes of the board that the board considers expedient; and
(b) shall be used for any other purpose approved by the Minister, in the amounts and over the periods that are approved by the Minister.

(5) **Application in area of jurisdiction of a public district school board.**—Where a municipality referred to in subsection (1) becomes part of the area of jurisdiction of an English-language public district school board, the municipal council shall pay over to the English-language public district school board the money that is held by the municipality and the money shall be used as set out in clause (4)(b).

(6) **Subclass reductions.**—Section 368.1 of the *Municipal Act* applies with necessary modifications with respect to the rates levied under this section.

1992, c. 15, s. 86; 1997, c. 31, s. 113(1).

Borrowing and Investment By Boards

241. (1) **Investment powers.**—A board may,

(a) subject to any rules prescribed under subsection (6), invest in securities prescribed under subsection (6) any money of the board that is in the board's general fund, capital fund or reserve funds and that is not immediately required by the board;
(b) advance money from the board's general fund or reserve funds that is not immediately required by the board, to the board's capital fund as interim financing of capital undertakings of the board;
(c) combine money held in the board's general fund, capital fund and reserve funds and, subject to subsection (3), deal with the money in accordance with clause (a); and
(d) despite the provisions of any other Act, borrow, for any purpose for which the board has authority to spend money, any money in any fund established by the board that is not immediately required by the board for the purposes of the fund.

(2) **Restrictions.**—Money advanced under clause (1)(b) shall be made repayable on or before the day on which the board requires the money and any interest or other earnings on the money advanced shall be credited to the fund from which it was advanced.

(3) **Same.**—Money combined under clause (1)(c) shall be made repayable on or before the day on which the board requires the money and any interest or other earnings from the combined investments shall be credited to each separate fund in proportion to the amount invested from that fund.

PART IX — FINANCE **S. 242**

(4) **Same.**—Clause (1)(d) does not apply to a sinking fund, a retirement fund, a fund prescribed under clause 247(3)(e) or to money in an education development charges account under an education development charge by-law to which section 257.103 applies.

(5) **Report on borrowings.**—At the first meeting of a board after a regular election, the treasurer shall report to the board on all borrowings under clause (1)(d) that have not been repaid.

(6) **Regulations.**—The Lieutenant Governor in Council may make regulations,
- (a) prescribing rules for the purposes of clause (1)(a);
- (b) prescribing securities or classes of securities for the purposes of clause (1)(a);
- (c) providing that a board does not have the power under this section to invest in the securities or classes of securities specified in the regulation.

(7) **General or particular.**—A regulation under subsection (6) may be general or particular in its application and may be made to apply to any class of board and for the purpose a class may be defined with respect to any attribute and may be defined to consist of or to exclude any specified member of the class, whether or not with the same attributes.

(8) **Transition.**—During the year that begins on the day that this section comes into force and ends on the first anniversary of that day, paragraphs 20 and 21 of subsection 171 (1) of the *Education Act*, as those paragraphs read immediately before the *Education Quality Improvement Act*, 1997 received Royal Assent, continue to apply to investments made before the day that this section comes into force.

(9) **Same.**—An investment to which subsection (8) applies shall not be continued past the end of the year mentioned in subsection (8) unless the investment is in a security or class of securities that is prescribed under clause (6)(b).

(10) **Definitions.**—In this section,

"invest".—"invest" includes purchase, acquire, hold and enter into; ("placer")

"securities".—"securities" includes financial agreements, investments and evidences of indebtedness. ("valeurs mobilières")

1997, c. 31, s. 113(1).

242. (1) **Debt, financial obligation and liability limits.**—The Lieutenant Governor in Council may make regulations providing for debt, financial obligation and liability limits for boards or classes of boards including,
- (a) defining the types of debt, financial obligation or liability to which the limits applies and prescribing the matters to be taken into account in calculating the limits;
- (b) prescribing the amounts to which the debts, financial obligations and liabilities under clause (a) shall be limited;
- (c) requiring a board to apply for the approval of the Minister for each specific work or class of works, the amount of debt for which, when added to the total amount of any outstanding debt, financial obligation or liability under clause (a), causes a limit under clause (b) to be exceeded;
- (d) prescribing rules, procedures and fees for the determination of the debt, financial obligation and liability limits of a board;

(e) establishing conditions that must be met by a board before undertaking any, or any class of, debt, financial obligation or liability.

(2) **Approval to exceed limit.**—A board shall not incur a debt, financial obligation or liability that would cause it to exceed a limit prescribed under clause (1)(b) unless it first obtains the approval of the Minister.

(3) **Risk management activities.**—The Lieutenant Governor in Council may make regulations allowing a board to engage in risk management activities as defined in the regulation in the circumstances specified in the regulation in order to hedge the risks specified in the regulation under or in connection with any debt instrument, financial obligation or liability of a board.

(4) **General or particular.**—A regulation made under this section can be general or particular.

(5) **Classes.**—A class may be defined with respect to any attribute and may be defined to consist of or to exclude any specified member of the class, whether or not with the same attributes.

1992, c. 15, s. 87; 1997, c. 31, s. 113(1).

243. (1) **Current borrowing.**—Despite the provisions of any Act, a board may by resolution authorize the treasurer and the chair or vice-chair to borrow from time to time the sums that the board considers necessary to meet the current expenditures of the board until the current revenue has been received.

(2) **Debt charges.**—A board may borrow the sums that the board considers necessary to meet debt charges payable in any fiscal year until the current revenue has been received.

(3) **Limit.**—The amounts that a board may borrow at any one time for the purposes mentioned in subsections (1) and (2), together with the total of any similar borrowings that have not been repaid and any accrued interest on those borrowings, shall not exceed the unreceived balance of the estimated revenues of the board, as set out in the estimates adopted for the fiscal year.

(4) **Limits for 1998.**—In the fiscal year January 1, 1998 to August 31, 1998, until the estimates for that fiscal year are adopted, the borrowing limits of a board under subsection (3) shall be calculated as prescribed by regulation under subsection (8) for the board for the purposes of this subsection.

(5) **Estimated revenues.**—For the purposes of subsection (3), estimated revenues do not include revenues derivable or derived from the sale of assets, current borrowings or issues of debentures or instruments prescribed under clause 247(3)(f) or from a surplus including arrears of taxes and proceeds from the sale of assets.

(6) **Exception re certain boards.**—A board may borrow more than the amount authorized to be borrowed under the other provisions of this section if,
(a) at the time of the borrowing, the board is subject to an order made under Division D, vesting control and charge over the administration of the affairs of the board in the Ministry under Division D; and
(b) the Minister approves the borrowing.

(7) **Approval of Minister.**—The Minister may make his or her approval under subsection (6) subject to any terms that he or she considers appropriate.

PART IX — FINANCE   S. 245

(8) **Regulations.**—The Minister may make regulations prescribing the method of calculating borrowing limits for the purposes of subsection (4).

(9) **Definition.**—In this section,

"current revenue", "estimated revenues", "revenues" do not include revenue from education development charges.

1997, c. 31, s. 113(1).

244. (1) **Provincial guarantee of debentures, etc.**—The Lieutenant Governor in Council may by order authorize the Minister of Finance to guarantee payment by the Province of the principal, interest and premium of debentures, debt instruments or other instruments prescribed under clause 247(3)(f) issued by a board or of debentures or other debt instruments issued by a corporation established under subsection 248(1) and any such authorization may relate to a single debenture or instrument or to a class of debentures or instruments as such class is defined in the authorizing order in council.

(2) **Form of guarantee.**—The form of the guarantee and the manner of its execution shall be determined by order of the Lieutenant Governor in Council, and every guarantee executed in accordance with the order is conclusive evidence of the guarantee.

(3) **Validity of guaranteed debentures, etc.**—Any debenture or debt instrument prescribed under clause 247(3)(f) or other debt instrument, payment of which is guaranteed by the Province under this section, is valid and binding on the board or corporation by which it is issued according to its terms.

1997, c. 31, s. 113(1).

245. (1) **Definitions.**—In this section, section 245 and subsection 246(5),

"**debenture**".—"debenture", in the case of a Roman Catholic board or of an old board that operated Roman Catholic schools, includes a mortgage; ("débenture")

"**general revenue**".—"general revenue" means, in respect of a board,

- (a) the amounts levied for school purposes that a board receives under Division B, and
- (b) the legislative grants received by the board that are made under subsection 234 (1); ("recettes générales")

"**municipality**".—"municipality" includes a regional or district municipality, the County of Oxford and Metro within the meaning of the *City of Toronto Act*, 1997 *(No. 2)*. ("municipalité")

(2) **Payments re debentures issued by school authorities, old boards.**—During the currency of a debenture issued by a school authority or an old board before this section comes into force, the school authority that issued the debenture or a board that assumed the obligation for a debenture issued by an old board shall,

- (a) provide in its estimates for each fiscal year for setting aside out of its general revenue in the fiscal year the amount necessary to pay the principal and interest coming due on the debenture in the fiscal year and to pay the amount required to be paid into a sinking fund or retirement fund in respect of the debenture in the fiscal year;
- (b) on or before each due date in each year, pay out of its general revenue the principal and interest coming due on the debenture in the year; and
- (c) where a sinking fund or retirement fund has been established in respect of a debenture,

on or before the anniversary in each year of the issue date of the debenture, pay out of its general revenue the amount required to be paid into the sinking fund or retirement fund in respect of the debenture in the year.

(3) **Payments re debentures issued by municipality for school authority, old board.**—During the currency of a debenture issued by a municipality before this section comes into force to raise money for a school authority or an old board, the school authority for which the debenture was issued or the board that assumed the obligation to the municipality for the debenture shall,

(a) provide in its estimates for each fiscal year for setting aside out of its general revenue in the fiscal year the amount necessary to pay to the municipality the amount of the principal and interest coming due on the debenture in the fiscal year and to pay the amount required to be paid by the municipality into a sinking fund or retirement fund in respect of the debenture in the fiscal year;

(b) on or before each due date in each year, pay out of its general revenue to the municipality the principal and interest coming due on the debenture in the year; and

(c) where a sinking fund or retirement fund has been established by the municipality in respect of a debenture, on or before each due date in each year, pay out of its general revenue to the municipality the amount required to be paid into the sinking fund or retirement fund by the municipality in respect of the debenture in the year.

(4) **Same.**—For the purposes of subsection (3), the due dates are those specified in the applicable notice given by the treasurer of the municipality to the treasurer of the board.

(5) **Exception.**—Despite clauses (2)(a) and (b) and (3)(a) and (b), the principal and interest that must be paid in a year under those clauses does not include any outstanding amount of principal specified as payable on the maturity date of a debenture to the extent that one or more refinancing debentures are issued by the school authority, board or municipality referred to in subsection (2) or (3) to repay the outstanding principal.

1992, c. 17, s. 3; 1997, c. 31, s. 113(1).

246. (1) **Application of section.**—Subsections (2) to (5) apply despite,

(a) the provisions of any other Act;
(b) any debenture;
(c) any municipal or board by-law, resolution or agreement under which a debenture is issued; or
(d) any document relating to a debenture.

(2) **No obligation to raise money through rates to pay debentures.**—A board is not obliged to raise money by way of rates,

(a) to pay the principal and interest on a debenture to which section 245 applies;
(b) to pay amounts for deposit into a sinking fund or retirement fund in respect of a debenture to which section 245 applies;
(c) to pay amounts to a municipality in respect of a debenture to which section 245 applies; or
(d) for any other purpose.

PART IX — FINANCE **S. 247**

(3) **Deemed amendment.**—A by-law, resolution, agreement or other document relating to a debenture to which section 245 applies and the debenture shall be deemed to have been amended to accord with subsections (1), (2), (4) and (5).

(4) **Rights of debenture holder.**—No holder of a debenture to which section 245 applies shall have any right to require payment, except in accordance with the payment schedule for the debenture, by reason only that the board that has assumed the obligation for the debenture may not be identical to the old board that issued the debenture or that the board that is obliged to make payments to a municipality in respect of the debenture may not be identical to the old board that was obliged to make payments to the municipality in respect of the debenture.

(5) **Same.**—None of the following shall constitute default by a district school board, a school authority, an old board or a municipality in the fulfilment of the obligations related to the debenture or a breach by a district school board, a school authority, an old board or a municipality of the terms or conditions of the debenture or of a by-law authorizing the issue of the debenture:

1. The amalgamation or merger of the old board that issued the debenture with a district school board.
2. The inability of a district school board or school authority to impose rates.
3. The elimination of a charge on the property and rates of the board that issued the debenture.
4. Anything done by a district school board or school authority in compliance with this Act or any regulation, order or directive made under this Act.

(6) **Terms and conditions continued.**—Subject to subsections (1) to (5), a debenture to which section 245 applies that is issued before this section comes into force continues to be payable on the same terms and conditions as are required by the debenture.

1997, c. 31, s. 113(1).

247. (1) **Borrowing for permanent improvements.**—Subject to any other provision of this Act and the regulations made under subsection 242(1) and subsection (3) of this section, a district school board may by by-law borrow money or incur debt for permanent improvements and may issue debentures or issue or execute any instrument prescribed under clause (3)(f) in respect of the money borrowed or the debt incurred.

(2) **Same, school authorities.**—Subject to any other provision of this Act and the regulations made under subsection 242(1) and subsection (3) of this section, and subject to the prior approval of the Minister, a school authority may by by-law borrow money or incur debt for permanent improvements and may issue debentures or issue or execute any instrument prescribed under clause (3)(f) in respect of the money borrowed or the debt incurred.

(3) **Regulations.**—The Lieutenant Governor in Council may make regulations,

(a) governing the borrowing of money and the incurring of debt by a board for permanent improvements;
(b) governing the issuance by a board of debentures and instruments prescribed under clause (f) in respect of money borrowed or debt incurred for permanent improvements;
(c) governing any dealings by a board with debentures and instruments described in

clause (b), including but not limited to regulations governing the redemption, surrender, exchange, substitution or offering as security of the debentures or instruments;

(d) governing the establishment and operation of sinking funds, retirement funds and any other type of funds that may be prescribed by the regulations and providing for the investment or other application of money held in those funds;

(e) prescribing types of funds for the purpose of clause (d);

(f) prescribing instruments other than debentures that may be issued or executed by a board in respect of money borrowed or debt incurred for permanent improvements;

(g) prescribing the duties of treasurers or other officers of boards in connection with the matters addressed in this section;

(h) providing that any provision of the *Municipal Act* relating to borrowing or debentures applies, with any modifications specified in the regulations, in relation to borrowing by a board under this section or debentures issued by a board under this section.

(4) **General or particular.**—A regulation under subsection (3) may be general or particular and may be made to apply to any class of board and for the purpose a class may be defined with respect to any attribute and may be defined to consist of or to exclude any specified member of the class, whether or not with the same attributes.

(5) **Payments re debentures and debt instruments.**—Subject to the regulations, if under subsection (1) or (2) a board issues a debenture or a debt instrument prescribed under clause (3)(f), the board shall,

(a) provide in its estimates for each fiscal year for setting aside out of its general revenue in the fiscal year the amount necessary to pay the principal and interest coming due on the debenture or debt instrument in the fiscal year and to pay the amount required to be paid into a sinking fund or retirement fund or other fund prescribed under clause (3)(e) in respect of the debenture or debt instrument in the fiscal year;

(b) on or before each due date in each year, pay out of its general revenue the principal and interest coming due on the debenture or debt instrument in the year; and

(c) where a sinking fund, retirement fund or other fund prescribed under clause (3)(e) has been established in respect of the debenture or debt instrument, on or before the anniversary in each year of the issue date of the debenture or debt instrument, pay out of its general revenue the amount required to be paid into the sinking fund, retirement fund or such prescribed fund in respect of the debenture or debt instrument in the year.

(6) **Exception.**—Despite clauses (5)(a) and (b), the principal and interest that must be paid in a year under those clauses does not include any outstanding amount of principal specified as payable on the maturity date of a debenture or debt instrument to the extent that one or more refinancing debentures or debt instruments are issued by the board to repay the outstanding principal.

(7) **All debentures, debt instruments rank equally.**—Despite any other provision of this or any other Act or any differences in date of issue or maturity, every debenture and debt instrument prescribed under clause (3)(f) issued by a board shall rank concurrently and equally in respect of payment of principal and interest with all other debentures and such debt instruments issued by the board, except as to the availability of any sinking fund, retirement fund or

other fund prescribed under clause (3)(e) applicable to any issue of debentures or such debt instruments.

(8) **Registration.**—Subsections 153(1), (2), (3), (4), (5) and (7) of the *Municipal Act* apply with necessary modifications to a by-law of a board authorizing the issue of debentures or debt instruments prescribed under clause (3)(f) that is passed under subsection (1) or (2) of this section but nothing in this subsection makes valid a by-law if it appears on the face of the by-law that it does not substantially comply with a provision of a regulation under subsection (3) that specifies the maximum term within which a debenture or debt instrument prescribed under clause (3)(f) may be made payable.

(9) **Certain rights and duties continued.**—Subject to subsection (10), the rights and duties of,

(a) a treasurer or a clerk-treasurer of a county or municipality;
(b) a treasurer of an old board;
(c) the council of a municipality;
(d) a school authority; or
(e) an old board,

under subsections 234 (3) to (6) of this Act, as those provisions read immediately before subsection 113 (1) of the *Education Quality Improvement Act*, 1997 came into force, continue with respect to debentures to which those subsections applied.

(10) **Same.**—The rights and duties described in subsection (9) of an old board or the treasurer of an old board are, respectively, the rights and duties of the district school board or treasurer of the district school board that is obliged to make payments in respect of the debenture as a result of a regulation made under clause 58.1(2)(p) or as a result of an order made under such a regulation.

1997, c. 31, s. 113(1).

248. (1) **Corporation to assist with board financing.**—The Lieutenant Governor in Council may, by regulation, establish a corporation under the name specified in the regulation,

(a) to provide financial services to boards in accordance with the regulations;
(b) to borrow money as principal or agent on behalf of boards in accordance with the regulations; and
(c) to lend money to boards on the terms and conditions that the corporation may impose.

(2) **Regulations.**—The Lieutenant Governor in Council may make regulations,

(a) providing for the composition, management, administration and control of the corporation and prescribing the powers and duties of the corporation;
(b) authorizing the corporation to provide financial services as specified in the regulations to boards in connection with their borrowing, investing, risk management and cash management activities;
(c) authorizing the corporation to borrow money in the capital markets in its own name or in the name of one or more boards on behalf of which the corporation is authorized to act;
(d) establishing terms, conditions and restrictions attaching to securities or other financial

instruments issued by the corporation in connection with borrowing described in clause (c) including,
- (i) the maximum aggregate principal amount of the securities or other financial instruments authorized for issue at any one time or from time to time,
- (ii) any restrictions on the rate or rates of interest payable, the term to maturity, redemption rights, a bonus or discount payable, the currency of issue and selling restrictions,
- (iii) any collateral that may be pledged or charged as security, and
- (iv) the terms of any guarantee by the Province of repayment by the corporation;

(e) respecting lending by the corporation to boards;

(f) governing the application or non-application to the corporation of any provision of the *Business Corporations Act*, the *Corporations Act* and the *Corporations Information Act*;

(g) authorizing the corporation to provide financial services to municipalities, to borrow money as principal or agent on behalf of municipalities and to lend money to municipalities;

(h) governing matters necessary or advisable to enable the corporation to carry out its duties.

(3) **Deemed reference to municipality.**—If a regulation is made under clause (2)(g) respecting a matter referred to in this section or in section 249, a reference to a board in this section or in section 249 in respect of that matter shall be deemed to include a municipality.

(4) **Definition.**—In clause (2)(g) and subsection (3),

"**municipality**".—"municipality" includes a county, a regional or district municipality and the County of Oxford.

(5) **Status of securities and other financial instruments.**—Securities and other financial instruments issued by the corporation shall be deemed to be investments authorized for registered corporations under subsection 162(1) of the *Loan and Trust Corporations Act* and authorized for insurers under subsection 433(1) of the *Insurance Act*.

(6) **General or particular.**—A regulation made under this section may be general or particular.

(7) **Consent of board, municipality.**— The corporation shall not provide financial services to a board or a municipality except at the request of the board or municipality and shall not borrow money in the name of a board or a municipality except with the prior approval of the board or municipality.

249. Agreements.—A board may enter into an agreement with the corporation established under subsection 248(1),

(a) for the provision to the board of financial services that the corporation is authorized to provide to a board section 248;

(b) for the borrowing of money as principal or agent on behalf of the board as authorized under section 248; and

(c) for the lending of money to the board as authorized under section 248.

1997, c. 31, s. 113(1).

PART IX — FINANCE   S. 250

Miscellaneous Board Revenues

250. (1) **Fees or charges for trailers in municipality.**—In this section and in section 251, "trailer".—"trailer" means any vehicle, whether self-propelled or so constructed that it is suitable for being attached to a motor vehicle for the purpose of being drawn or propelled by the motor vehicle, that is capable of being used for the living, sleeping or eating accommodation of persons, although the vehicle is jacked-up or its running gear is removed; ("roulotte")

"trailer camp".—"trailer camp" or "trailer park" means land in or on which any trailer is located but not including any such vehicle unless it is used for the living, sleeping or eating accommodation of persons. ("parc à roulottes")

(2) **Share to be paid to boards.**—Where a trailer is located in a trailer camp or elsewhere in a municipality and fees or charges are collected by the municipality for the trailer or for the land occupied by the trailer in a trailer camp in any year, the council of the municipality shall pay to the English-language public district school board, the district school area board or the secondary school board established under section 67 having jurisdiction in the area in which the trailer is located, 25 per cent of the fees or charges.

(3) **Same.**—Despite subsection (2), where the occupant of a trailer located in a municipality is a Roman Catholic and has given to the clerk of the municipality a notice in writing stating that the occupant is a Roman Catholic and wishes to be a supporter of the English-language Roman Catholic board that has jurisdiction in the area in which the trailer is located, the council of the municipality shall pay 25 per cent of the fees or charges to the English-language Roman Catholic board.

(4) **Share to be paid to two boards.**—Despite subsections (2) and (3), if a trailer is located in the area of jurisdiction of the two boards mentioned in paragraphs 1, 2 or 3, the municipality shall pay 12.5 per cent of the fees or charges to each of the boards:

1. A district school area board and a secondary school board established under section 67.
2. A Roman Catholic school authority and a secondary school board established under section 67.
3. A Roman Catholic school authority and an English-language public district school board.

(5) **Same.**—Despite subsection (2), where the occupant of a trailer located in a municipality is a Roman Catholic and a French-language rights holder and has given to the clerk of the municipality a notice in writing stating that the occupant is a Roman Catholic and wishes to be a supporter of the French-language separate district school board that has jurisdiction in the area in which the trailer is located, the council of the municipality shall pay 25 per cent of the fees or charges to the French-language separate district school board.

(6) **Same.**—Despite subsection (2), where the occupant of a trailer located in a municipality is a French-language rights holder and has given to the clerk of the municipality a notice in writing stating that the occupant wishes to be a supporter of the French-language public district school board that has jurisdiction in the area in which the trailer is located, the council of the municipality shall pay 25 per cent of the fees or charges to the French-language public district school board.

(7) **Fees or charges not part of annual rates.**—The share of the fees or charges payable to a board by the council of a municipality under this section shall be in addition to any other amount that is payable to the board by the municipality, and shall be paid to the board on or before December 15 in the year for which the fees or charges are collected.

(8) **Application to municipality operated trailer camps.**—This section does not apply to trailer camps and trailer parks operated by a municipality.

(9) **Exception.**—No fees shall be charged under this section in respect of a trailer assessed under the *Assessment Act*.

1992, c. 15, .88; 1997, c. 31, s. 113(1).

251. (1) **Fee for trailers in territory without municipal organization.**—Except as provided in subsections (2) to (5), the owner, lessee or person having possession of a trailer that is located in territory without municipal organization in the area of jurisdiction of a district school area board, a secondary school board established under section 67 or an English-language public district school board, shall pay to the board, on or before the first day of each month, a fee of $5.00 in respect of the trailer for each month or part of a month, except July and August, that the trailer is so located.

(2) **Same.**—Where the occupant of a trailer that is located in territory without municipal organization within the area of jurisdiction of an English-language Roman Catholic board is a Roman Catholic and signifies in writing to the board that he or she is Roman Catholic and wishes to be a supporter of the English-language Roman Catholic board, the owner or lessee of the trailer shall pay to the board, on or before the first day of each month a fee of $5.00 in respect of the trailer for each month or part of a month, except July and August, that the trailer is so located.

(3) **Same.**—If a trailer is located in the area of jurisdiction of the two boards mentioned in paragraphs 1, 2 or 3, the municipality shall pay $2.50 to each of the boards:

1. A district school area board and a secondary school board established under section 67.
2. A Roman Catholic school authority and a secondary school board established under section 67.
3. A Roman Catholic school authority and an English-language public district school board.

(4) **Same.**—Where the occupant of a trailer that is located in territory without municipal organization within the area of jurisdiction of a French-language separate district school board is a Roman Catholic and a French-language rights holder and signifies in writing to the board that he or she is a Roman Catholic and wishes to be a supporter of the French-language separate district school board, the owner or lessee of the trailer shall pay to the board, on or before the first day of each month, a fee of $5.00 in respect of the trailer for each month or part of a month, except July and August, that the trailer is so located.

(5) **Same.**—Where the occupant of a trailer that is located in territory without municipal organization within the area of jurisdiction of a French-language public district school board is a French-language rights holder and signifies in writing to the board that he or she wishes to be a supporter of the board, the owner or lessee of the trailer shall pay to the board, on or before

the first day of each month, a fee of $5.00 in respect of the trailer for each month or part of a month, except July and August, that the trailer is so located.

(6) **Notice.**—No person is required to pay a fee under this section until the person has been notified in writing by the secretary of the board concerned or the tax collector that the person is liable to pay the fee, and on receipt of the notice the person shall promptly pay all fees for which the person has been made liable under this section before receipt of the notice and shall, after that, pay fees in accordance with subsections (1) to (5).

(7) **Content of notice.**—Every notice under this section shall make reference to this section and shall specify,
- (a) the amount of fees for which the person is liable on receipt of the notice;
- (b) the amount of the monthly fee to be paid after receipt of the notice;
- (c) the date by which payment is required to be made;
- (d) the place at which payment may be made; and
- (e) the fine provided under this section.

(8) **Notice to other boards.**—A board that receives a notice under this section from an owner, occupant, lessee or person having possession of a trailer shall transmit a copy of the notice to every other board the jurisdiction of which includes the trailer camp or trailer park in which the trailer is located.

(9) **Exception.**—No fees shall be charged under this section in respect of a trailer assessed under the *Assessment Act*.

(10) **Offence.**—Every owner or lessee or person having possession of a trailer who permits the trailer to be located in any part of territory without municipal organization in which the owner, lessee or person is liable for any fee under this section without paying the fee as required under this section is guilty of an offence and on conviction is liable to a fine of not less than $20 and not more than $100 and each day that this subsection is contravened shall be deemed to constitute a separate offence.

1997, c. 31, s. 113(1).

Financial Administration of Boards

252. (1) **Financial statements.**—Every year, the treasurer of every board shall prepare the financial statements for the board by the date prescribed under subsection (3) and, on receiving the auditor's report on the financial statements, shall promptly give the Ministry two copies of the financial statements and the auditor's report.

(2) **Publication and notice.**—Within one month after receiving the auditor's report on the board's financial statements, the treasurer shall,
- (a) publish the financial statements and the auditor's report, in the form the Minister may prescribe, in a daily or weekly newspaper that, in the opinion of the treasurer, has sufficient circulation within the area of jurisdiction of the board to provide reasonable notice to those affected by them;
- (b) mail or deliver a copy of the financial statements and auditor's report, in the form the Minister may prescribe, to each of the board's supporters; or

(c) otherwise make the information in the financial statements and auditor's report available to the public, to the extent and in the manner directed by the Minister.

(3) **Minister's powers.**—The Minister may prescribe the date in each year by which the treasurer of a board shall prepare the financial statements of the board and forward them to the auditor.

(4) **Same.**—The *Regulations Act* does not apply to anything done by the Minister under subsection (3).

(5) **Statements of old boards.**—The Lieutenant Governor in Council may make regulations respecting the preparation, audit, publication and reporting of statements relating to the financial affairs of old boards, including but not limited to regulations assigning duties and powers to classes of persons in connection with those statements.

(6) **Obstruction.**—A person who refuses or neglects to comply with the request of an auditor made under the authority of a regulation under subsection (5) is guilty of an offence and on conviction is liable to a fine of not more than $200, but no person is liable if the person proves that he or she has made reasonable efforts to comply.

1997, c. 31, s. 113(1).

253. (1) **Appointment of auditor.**—Every board shall appoint one or more auditors for a term not exceeding five years who shall be a person licensed under the *Public Accountancy Act*.

(2) **Transition.**—Except as provided in a regulation made under subsection 252(5), the rights and obligations of an auditor appointed under subsection 234(1) of this Act, as it read immediately before the coming into force of subsection 113(1) of the *Education Quality Improvement Act*, 1997, terminate immediately before the coming into force of subsection 113(1) of the Education *Quality Improvement Act*, 1997.

(3) **Ineligibility for appointment.**—No person shall be appointed as an auditor of a board who is or during the preceding year was a member of the board or who has or during the preceding year had any direct or indirect interest in any contract or any employment with the board other than for services within the person's professional capacity, and every auditor, on appointment, shall make and subscribe a declaration to that effect.

(4) **Duties of auditor.**—An auditor of a board shall perform the duties that are prescribed by the Minister under paragraph 30 of subsection 8(1) and the duties that may be required by the board that do not conflict with the duties prescribed by the Minister.

(5) **Rights of auditor.**—An auditor of a board has the right of access at all reasonable hours to all records of the board and is entitled to require from the members and officers of the board any information and explanation that in the auditor's opinion may be necessary to enable the auditor to carry out his or her duties.

(6) **Obstruction.**—Every member and every officer of a board who,
 (a) refuses or neglects to provide the access to the records of the board to which the auditor is entitled under subsection (5); or
 (b) refuses or neglects to provide information or an explanation required by the auditor under subsection (5), is guilty of an offence and on conviction is liable to a fine of not more than $200, but no person is liable if the person proves that he or she has made reasonable efforts to provide the access or the information or explanation.

(7) **Power to take evidence.**—An auditor of a board may require any person to give evidence on oath or affirmation for the purposes of the audit and, for the purposes of the testimony, the auditor has the powers of a commission under Part II of the *Public Inquiries Act* and that Part applies as if the auditor were conducting an inquiry under that Act.

(8) **Attendance at meetings of board.**—An auditor of a board is entitled to attend any meeting of the board or of a committee of the board and to receive all notices relating to that meeting that a member is entitled to receive and to be heard at the meeting that the auditor attends on any part of the business of the meeting that concerns him or her as auditor.

(9) **Rights of auditor re 1998 audit.**—In addition to his or her rights under subsection (5), an auditor of a district school board has, for the purposes of carrying out his or her duties in respect of the fiscal year January 1, 1998 to August 31, 1998, the right of access at all reasonable hours to all records of the predecessor boards of the district school board that are in the possession of another district school board and is entitled to require from persons who were members or officers of those predecessor boards or who are members or officers of the other district school board any information and explanation that in the auditor's opinion may be necessary to enable the auditor to carry out his or her duties.

(10) **Obstruction re 1998 audit.**—Every person who was a member or officer of a predecessor board or who is a member or officer of the other board referred to in subsection (9), who,

(a) refuses or neglects to provide the access to records to which the auditor is entitled under subsections (5) and (9); or

(b) refuses or neglects to provide information or an explanation required by the auditor under subsection (9),

is guilty of an offence and on conviction is liable to a fine of not more than $200, but no person is liable if the person proves that he or she has made reasonable efforts to provide the access or the information or explanation.

(11) **Definition.**—In subsections (9) and (10),

"**predecessor board**".—"predecessor board", in relation to a district school board, means an old board an asset, liability or employee of which has become an asset, liability or employee of the district school board as a result of a regulation made under clause 58.1(2)(p) or as a result of an order made under such a regulation.

1992, c. 15, s. 89; 1997, c. 31, s. 113(1).

254. (1) **Custody of books, etc.**—A person who has in his or her possession a book, paper, chattel or money of a board shall not wrongfully,

(a) withhold it from a person specified by the board or the Minister;
(b) neglect or refuse to give it to the specified person in the manner specified by the board or the Minister;
(c) neglect or refuse to account for it to the specified person in the manner specified by the board or the Minister.

(2) **Summons for appearance.**—On application to a judge by the board or the Minister, supported by affidavit, showing that a person failed to comply with subsection (1), the judge may summon the person to appear before the judge at a time and place appointed by the judge.

(3) **Order to account.**—The judge shall, in a summary manner, and whether the person complained against does or does not appear, hear the application and may order the person complained against to deliver up, account for and pay over the book, paper, chattel or money by a day to be named by the judge in the order, together with any reasonable costs incurred in making the application that the judge may allow.

(4) **Other remedy not affected.**—A proceeding before a judge under this section does not impair or affect any other remedy that the board or the Minister may have against the person complained against or against any other person.

1997, c. 31, s. 113(1).

Miscellaneous

255. (1) **Recreation committees.**—If a recreation committee or a joint recreation committee is appointed under a regulation made under the *Ministry of Tourism and Recreation Act* for territory without municipal organization within the jurisdiction of a board, the board,

(a) may exercise the powers and shall perform the duties of a municipal council with respect to preparing estimates of the sums required during the year for the purposes of the committee or joint committee, and levying rates and collecting taxes for those purposes on all rateable property in that territory; and

(b) if there is a joint recreation committee, shall apportion the costs of the joint committee by agreement with the other board or boards concerned.

(2) **Collection of taxes.**—The officers of the board have the same powers and duties as similar officers in a municipality, including the powers and duties with respect to the sale of land for tax arrears.

(3) **Recovery of costs.**—The costs incurred by a board in exercising its powers under this section are recoverable by the board and shall be included in determining the rates to be levied under subsection (1).

1997. c. 31, s. 113(1).

256. (1) **Rates for certain public libraries.**—Where a public library has been established for a school section in territory without municipal organization that is deemed to be a district municipality within the area of jurisdiction of an English-language public district school board under subsection 58.1 (2), the English-language public district school board shall be deemed to be an appointing council for the district municipality under section 15 of the *Local Control of Public Libraries Act, 1997* and the amount of the estimates of the board of the public library appropriated for the board of the public library by the English-language public district school board shall be raised by a levy imposed by the English-language public district school board on all the rateable property in the district municipality and the estimated expenses to be incurred by the English-language public board in connection with raising the levy shall be recoverable by the board and shall be included in the levy imposed under this section.

(2) **Definition.**—In this section,

"**rateable property**".—"rateable property" means real property, other than property that is exempt from taxation under the *Assessment Act*.

1997, c. 31, s. 113(1).

257. Court proceeding.—In addition to any other remedy possessed by a board in territory without municipal organization for the recovery of taxes to be collected by the board under the authority of this Act, the board, with the approval of the Minister, may bring an action in a court of competent jurisdiction for the recovery of any taxes in arrears against the person assessed for those taxes.

1997, c. 31, s. 113(1).

257.1 When fees payable by boards.—The fees, if any, payable by a board for the education of pupils shall be paid, when requested by the treasurer of the board that provides the education, on an estimated basis at least quarterly during the year in which the education is provided, with any adjustment that may be required when the actual financial data and enrolment for the year have been finally determined.

1994, c. 27, s. 108(9); 1997, c. 31, s. 113(1).

257.2 (1) Transition: notice of support by certain partnerships, corporations.—A notice that was given under a provision included in the list set out in subsection (2) and that was not withdrawn or cancelled continues in effect or, if varied under one of those provisions, continues in effect as varied, until a new notice is given under section 237, except that,

(a) a notice requiring assessment to be entered, rated and assessed for separate school purposes shall be deemed to be a notice requiring assessment to be entered and assessed for English-language Roman Catholic board purposes;

(b) a notice requiring assessment to be entered, rated and assessed for the purposes of The Prescott and Russell County Roman Catholic English-Language Separate School Board shall be deemed to be a notice requiring assessment to be entered and assessed for English-language Roman Catholic board purposes;

(c) a notice requiring assessment to be entered, rated and assessed for the purposes of the Roman Catholic sector of The Ottawa-Carleton French-language School Board or of the Conseil des écoles catholiques de langue française de la région d'Ottawa-Carleton or of the Conseil des écoles séparées catholiques de langue française de Prescott School Board or of the Conseil des écoles publiques d'Ottawa-Carleton shall be deemed to be a notice requiring assessment to be entered and assessed for French-language public district school board purposes.

(2) **Same.**—The following is the list of provisions referred to in subsection (1):

1. Subsection 112 (3) of this Act, as that subsection read immediately before the coming into force of this section.
2. Subsection 17 (4) of the *Ottawa-Carleton French-language School Board Act*, as that subsection read immediately before the coming into force of this section.
3. A predecessor of the subsection referred to in paragraph 1 or 2.
4. Section 48 of Ontario Regulation 425/94, as amended by Ontario Regulations 453/94 and 689/94.
5. Section 16.4 of Ontario Regulation 479/91, as amended by Ontario Regulations 144/94 and 93/95.

(3) **Same.**—A notice mentioned in clause (1)(a), (b), (c) or (d) that was given by a partnership or corporation in respect of property of which the partnership or corporation is a tenant shall be deemed to be a notice given under subsection 237(12).

1996, c. 13, s. 9; 1997, c. 31, s. 113(1).

257.2.1 (1) **Tax relief, etc., in unorganized territory.**—The Minister of Finance may make regulations to limit the changes in taxes for school purposes from the taxes for school purposes in 1997 or to give relief from taxes for school purposes in territory without municipal organization.

(2) **Exception.**—This section does not apply with respect to territory without municipal organization that is deemed to be attached to a municipality for the purposes of taxation.

(3) **What regulations can provide for, etc.**—The following apply with respect to regulations under subsection (1);

1. Without limiting what a regulation may provide for, the regulations may provide for any matter provided for under sections 372, 372.1, 373, 442.1, 442.2 and 444.1 of the *Municipal Act* or Part XXII.2 of the *Municipal Act*.
2. A regulation may require rebates to be paid by boards.
3. A regulation made in 1998 or a later year may relate to the entire year in which it is made.
4. A regulation may delegate anything to boards or other persons or bodies and may attach conditions to such delegations.
5. A regulation may be general or specific in its application.

(4) **Conflicts.** In this case of a conflict between a regulation and this Act or the *Provincial Land Tax Act*, the regulation prevails.

1998, c. 3, s. 34; 1998, c. 33, s. 40.

257.3 (1) **Regulations re transitional matters.**—The Lieutenant Governor in Council may make regulations providing for such transitional matters as the Lieutenant Governor in Council considers necessary or advisable in connection with the education funding reforms of 1997 and 1998.

(2) **General or particular.**—A regulation made under subsection (1) may be general or particular.

1997, c. 31, s. 113(1).

257.4 Type of board for *Assessment Act* **purposes.**—For the purposes of the *Assessment Act*, the following are the types of board that a person may support:

1. English-language public board.
2. English-language Roman Catholic board.
3. French-language public district school board.
4. French-language separate district school board
5. Protestant separate school board.

1997, c. 31, s. 113(1).

DIVISION B

EDUCATION TAXES

Education Taxes

257.5 Definitions.—In sections 257.6 to 257.14,

"business property".—"business property" means,
- (a) property in the commercial property class, the industrial property class or the pipeline property class, all as prescribed under the *Assessment Act*,
- (b) property in a class of real property, not listed in subsection 7 (2) of the *Assessment Act*, that is prescribed under 257.12(1)(a) for the purposes of this clause, or
- (c) property described in paragraphs 1 and 2 of subsection 368.3(1) of the *Municipal Act*. ("bien d'entreprise")

"residential property".—"residential property" means,
- (a) property in the residential/farm property class, the farmlands property class, the managed forests property class or the multi-residential property class, all as prescribed under the *Assessment Act*, or
- (b) property in a class of real property, not listed in subsection 7(2) of the *Assessment Act*, that is prescribed under clause 257.12(1)(a) for the purposes of this clause. ("bien résidentiel")

1997, c. 31, s. 113(2); 1998, c. 3, s. 34(2).

257.6 (1) Property taxable for school purposes.—Except as otherwise provided under this or any other Act, real property that is liable to assessment and taxation under the *Assessment Act* is taxable for school purposes.

(2) **Exemptions.**—Subject to subsection (3), an exemption under this or any other Act that applied in relation to taxes for school purposes immediately before this Division came into force applies in relation to taxes for school purposes under this Division.

(3) **Same.**—Where a private Act gives a board or an old board a power of decision or approval in relation to an exemption from taxes for school purposes, the power shall be exercised by the Minister of Finance instead of the board.

(4) **Same.**— An eligible theatre in the City of Toronto incorporated by the *City of Toronto Act, 1997* is exempt from taxes for school purposes.

(5) **Regulations.**—The Minister of Finance may make regulations defining eligible theatre for the purposes of subsection (4).

1997, c. 31, s. 113(2).

257.7 (1) Levying of tax rates for school purposes.—Subject to the regulations, the following shall in each year levy and collect the tax rates prescribed under section 257.12 for school purposes on the property indicated:

1. Every municipality, on residential property and business property in the municipality, including territory without municipal organization that is deemed under section 56 or subsection 58.1(2) to be attached to the municipality, taxable for school purposes, according to the last returned assessment roll.

2. Every English-language public district school board the area of jurisdiction of which includes territory without municipal organization that is not deemed under section 56 or subsection 58.1 (2) to be attached to a municipality, on the residential property and business property in that territory taxable for school purposes, according to the last returned assessment roll.
3. Every district school area board the area of jurisdiction of which includes territory without municipal organization that is not deemed under section 56 or subsection 58.1 (2) to be attached to a municipality, on the residential property and business property in that territory taxable for school purposes, according to the last returned assessment roll.

(2) **Exception.**—This section does not apply in respect of property taxed under section 240.

(3) **Subclass reductions.**—Section 368.1 of the *Municipal Act* applies with necessary modifications with respect to the rates levied under this section on land in a municipality.

1997, c. 31, s. 113(2).

257.8 (1) **Definition.**—In this section,

"**common jurisdictional area**".—"common jurisdictional area", in respect of two or more boards, means the area that is within the area of jurisdiction of both or all of those boards.

(2) **Business property, distribution of amounts levied.**—A municipality or board that is required to levy tax rates for school purposes on business property shall distribute the amounts levied in accordance with the following:

1. Where the property is located in the area of jurisdiction of only one board, the amount levied on the property shall be distributed to that board.
2. Where the property is located in the area of jurisdiction of more than one board, the amount shall be distributed among the boards in proportion to enrolment as determined and calculated by the Minister under subsection (3) in the common jurisdictional area of the boards.

(3) **Calculation by Minister.**—The Minister shall determine enrolment and shall calculate the proportions for each year for each common jurisdictional area and shall publish the proportions in *The Ontario Gazette*, for each municipality and for territory without municipal organization in each common jurisdictional area.

257.9 (1) **Residential property, distribution of amounts levied.**—A municipality or board that is required to levy tax rates for school purposes on residential property shall distribute the amounts levied in accordance with the following:

1. An amount levied on property taxable for English-language public board purposes shall be distributed to the English-language public district school board or public school authority in the area of jurisdiction of which the property is located.
2. An amount levied on property taxable for English-language Roman Catholic board purposes shall be distributed to the English-language separate district school board or Roman Catholic school authority in the area of jurisdiction of which the property is located.
3. An amount levied on property taxable for French-language public district school

board purposes shall be distributed to the French-language public district school board in the area of jurisdiction of which the property is located.
4. An amount levied on property taxable for French-language separate district school board purposes shall be distributed to the French-language separate district school board in the area of jurisdiction of which the property is located.
5. An amount levied on property taxable for Protestant separate school board purposes shall be distributed to the Protestant separate school board in the area of jurisdiction of which the property is located.
6. An amount levied on property of a partnership within the meaning of section 237 or of a corporation to which section 237 applies, that is taxable for the purposes of one or more boards shall be distributed in accordance with the proportions of its assessment that result from the application of that section.
7. An amount levied on property of a designated ratepayer within the meaning of section 238 shall be distributed in the same manner as is provided in section 257.8 for rates levied on business property of the designated ratepayer.

(2) **Interpretation.**—Property is taxable for a board's purposes if it is assessed to the support of a board.

1997, c. 31, s. 113(2).

257.10 (1) Powers of municipality, board levying rates.—A municipality or board that is required to levy rates for school purposes under this Division has, for purposes of the collection, chargeback, cancellation, refund or rebate of the rates, the same powers and duties as a municipality has in respect of the collection, chargeback, cancellation, refund or rebate of rates levied for municipal purposes, including powers and duties relating to the sale of land for tax arrears.

(2) **Powers of officers.**—The officers of a municipality or of a board required to levy a rate for school purposes under this Division have the same powers and duties in respect of the collection, chargeback, cancellation, refund or rebate of rates levied under this Division, including powers and duties relating to the sale of land for tax arrears, as officers of a municipality have in respect of rates levied for municipal purposes.

(3) **Application of s. 382 of *Municipal Act*.**—Section 382 of the *Municipal Act* applies to taxes levied under this Division.

(4) **Regulations.**—The Minister of Finance may make regulations, which may be general or particular in their application, varying, limiting or excluding the powers and duties under this section of municipalities and boards and of the officers of municipalities and boards.

(5) **Collection of certain taxes.**—This section applies with necessary modifications in respect of the collection of a tax under section 21.1 of the *Provincial Land Tax Act*.

1997, c. 31, s. 113(2); 1998, c. 3, s. 34(3).

257.11 (1) When amounts paid to boards.—In each calendar year, a municipality or board shall pay amounts levied for school purposes in the following instalments:
1. Twenty-five per cent of the amount levied for the previous calendar year, on or before March 31.
2. Fifty per cent of the amount levied for the current calendar year less the amount of the instalment under paragraph 1, on or before June 30.

3. Twenty-five per cent of the amount levied for the current calendar year, on or before September 30.
4. The balance of the amount levied for the current calendar year, on or before December 15.

(2) **Non-payment on due date.**—Where an instalment or a part of an instalment is not paid on the due date, the municipality or board in default shall pay interest to the recipient board from the date of default to the date that the payment is made, at the rate specified in subsection (4).

(3) **Payment ahead of due date.**—Where, with the consent of the recipient board, an instalment or a part of an instalment is paid in advance of the due date, the recipient board shall allow the municipality or payor board a discount from the date of payment to the date on which the payment is due, at the rate specified in subsection (4).

(4) **Rate of interest.**—For the purposes of subsections (2) and (3), the rate of interest payable or the rate of discount allowable, as the case may be, is the lowest prime rate reported to the Bank of Canada by any of the banks listed in Schedule I to the *Bank Act* (Canada) at the date of default, in the case of subsection (2), or at the date of payment, in the case of subsection (3).

(5) **Agreement.**—Despite subsection (1), a board may, by agreement with a majority of the municipalities in its area of jurisdiction where the municipalities represent at least two-thirds of the assessment taxable for the purposes of the board, according to the last returned assessment roll, vary the number of instalments and their amounts and due dates.

(6) **Same.**—Where an agreement is entered into under subsection (5), it applies to all municipalities in the area of jurisdiction of the board.

(7) **Limitation.**—Subsection (5) applies only if the agreement requires at least one instalment to be paid in each quarter of the year.

(8) **Termination of agreement.**—Where an agreement under subsection (5) does not provide for its termination, it shall continue in force from year to year until it is terminated on December 31 in any year by notice given before October 31 in the year,

(a) by the secretary of the board as authorized by a resolution of the board, or
(b) by the clerks of a majority of the municipalities in the board's area of jurisdiction where the municipalities represent at least two-thirds of the assessment taxable for the purposes of the board, according to the last returned assessment roll,

and where no agreement is in effect under subsection (5), the payments shall be made as provided in subsection (1).

(9) **Transition – 1998.**—For 1998, the total payment to be made under paragraph 1 of subsection (1) by a municipality or board shall be the sum of,

(a) 12.5 per cent of the amount levied for school purposes for 1997 on residential and farm assessment, within the meaning of section 248 of this Act as it read on December 31, 1997, in the area in respect of which the municipality or board levies taxes under section 257.7; and
(b) 25 per cent of the amount levied for school purposes for 1997 on commercial assessment, within the meaning of section 248 of this Act as it read on December

31, 1997, in the area in respect of which the municipality or board levies taxes under 257.7.

(10) **Same.**—Where there is more than one board with jurisdiction in the area in respect of which the municipality or board levies taxes under section 257.7, the total payment determined under section 257.7, the total payment determined under subsection (9) shall be distributed in accordance with the following:
1. Apportion the total amount among public boards, Roman Catholic boards and Protestant boards in accordance with the proportions of that amount that were levied for public schools, Roman Catholic schools and Protestant schools.
2. Apportion each of the portions determined under paragraph 1 among English-language and French-language boards in proportion to enrolment.

(11) **Same.**—The Minister shall determine enrolment and calculate proportions for the purposes of paragraph 2 of subsection (10) and shall publish the proportions in *The Ontario Gazette*.

(12) **Extension of instalment due dates.**—The Minister may make regulations relating to instalments under subsection (1),
(a) extending the time for paying the instalments even if the time for paying the instalments has passed,
(b) in conjunction with the provision of interim financing to boards under subsection (14), directing the instalments to be paid to the Province.

(13) **Same.**—A regulation under subsection (12) may be general or particular.

(14) **Interim financing for 1998.**—The Minister may provide interim financing to boards in respect of instalments to be paid to the Province as directed under a regulation under clause (12)(b) and the following apply with respect to such financing:
1. The Minister may pay amounts, on behalf of the municipality or board required to pay an instalment, to the boards to which the instalment would have been distributed in the absence of the direction to pay the instalment to the Province.
2. The amount of the instalment to be paid to the Province by the municipality or the board shall be equal to the total of the amounts paid by the Minister, on behalf of the municipality or board, under paragraph 1.
3. Subsections (2), (3) and (4) apply with respect to the Minister as though the Minister were the recipient board.

(15) **Interim financing for 1998, agreements.**—The Minister may provide interim financing to a board that is a party to an agreement under subsection (5) and the following apply with respect to such financing:
1. The Minister may pay to the board, on behalf of a municipality to which the agreement applies, an amount the municipality is required to pay under the agreement and the amount shall be deemed to be an amount paid by the municipality under the agreement.
2. A municipality on whose behalf the Minister pays an amount under paragraph 1 shall repay the Province for that amount. The municipality shall repay the amount on the dates and in the amounts specified by the Minister and the municipality shall pay

interest, at the rate specified in subsection (4), on any of those amounts that are paid late.

(16) **Payments from Consolidated Revenue Fund.**—Amounts paid by the Minister under subsection (14) or (15) shall be paid out of the Consolidated Revenue Fund.

(17) **Amounts deemed to be education funding.**—Amounts paid by the Minister under subsection (14) or (15), other than amounts for the purposes of paying a board's share of the costs of rebates under section 442.1 or 442.2 of the *Municipal Act* or paying rebates under regulations under section 257.2.1 of this Act, shall be deemed to be education funding within the meaning of subsection 234(14).

(18) **Information relating to agreements.**—For the purposes of interim financing under subsection (15), the Minister may require a municipality or board to provide,

(a) a copy of any agreement under subsection (5);
(b) information about amounts paid under the agreement; and
(c) information about amounts levied under section 370 of the *Municipal Act*.

(19) **Enforcement of requirement.**—The Minister may apply to the Ontario Court (General Division) for an order requiring a municipality or board to comply with a requirement of the Minister under subsection (18).

(20) **Additional power.**—Subsection (19) is additional to and not intended to replace any other available means of enforcement.

1997, c. 31, s. 113; 1998, c. 3, s. 34(4); 1998, c. 33, s. 41.

257.12 (1) **Regulations, Minister of Finance.**—The Minister of Finance may make regulations,

(a) prescribing classes of real property prescribed under the *Assessment Act*, other than classes listed in subsection 7 (2) of the *Assessment Act*, for the purposes of clause (b) of the definition of "business property" in section 257.5 or clause (b) of the definition of "residential property" in that section;
(b) prescribing the tax rates for school purposes for the purposes of section 257.7; and
(c) prescribing rates for the purposes of calculating payments in lieu of taxes, within the meaning of section 361.1 of the *Municipal Act*, for real property that is exempt from taxation for school purposes.

(1.1) **Definition.**—In clause (1)(b),
"tax rates for school purposes" includes tax rates for the purposes of paying a board's share of the costs of rebates under section 442.1 or 442.2 of the *Municipal Act* or paying rebates under regulations under section 257.2.1 of this Act.

(2) **Scope of regulations.**—The use of "business" or "residential" in the defined terms "business property" or "residential property" does not limit the discretion of the Minister of Finance in making regulations under clause (1)(a).

(3) **Tax rates may vary.**—Subject to subsections (4) and (5), regulations under clause (1)(b) may prescribe different tax rates for,

(a) different municipalities;
(b) different parts of a municipality as specified in an Act, regulation or order implementing municipal restructuring within the meaning of subsection 25.2 (1) of the *Municipal Act*;

(c) different parts of territory without municipal organization that are deemed under section 56 or subsection 58.1 (2) to be attached to a municipality for purposes related to taxation or that are deemed under the *Moosonee Development Area Board Act* to be a locality;
(d) different classes of property prescribed by the regulations under this Act or the *Assessment Act*;
(e) different subclasses of real property prescribed by the regulations made under the *Assessment Act*;
(f) real property on any basis on which a municipality or Ontario is permitted to set different tax rates for real property for municipal purposes;
(g) different portions of a property's assessment;
(h) different geographic areas established for purposes of paragraph 1 of subsection 368.3 (1) of the *Municipal Act*;
(i) different geographic areas established for purposes of paragraph 2 of subsection 368.3 (1) of the *Municipal Act*; and
(j) different parts of a municipality based on whether or not the parts are in the area of jurisdiction of an English-language public board.

(4) **Uniform rate, residential/farm, multi-residential.**—Subject to subsections (6) and (7), the regulations under clause (1)(b) shall prescribe a single tax rate for the residential/farm property class and the multi-residential property class.

(5) **Tax rates for farmlands and managed forests.**—The tax rate for the farmlands property class and the managed forests property class shall be 25 per cent of the tax rate prescribed for the residential/farm property class.

(5.1) **Other rates may vary.**—Subsection (3) applies, with necessary modifications, with respect to regulations under clause (1)(c).

(6) **Property in subclasses.**—Except where subsection (7) applies, for property in the residential/farm property class or the multi-residential property class that is also in a subclass of real property prescribed by the regulations made under the *Assessment Act*, the tax rate set in accordance with subsection (4) shall be reduced by the rate of reduction in taxes for municipal purposes that results from the application of paragraph 1 of subsection 368.1(1) and subsection 368.1(2) and (2.1) of the *Municipal Act* to property in that subclass.

(7) **Same.**—For property described in subsection (6) that is not located in a municipality, the tax rate set in accordance with subsection (4) shall be reduced by the rate of reduction in taxes for municipal purposes that results from the application of paragraph 1 of subsection 368.1(1) and subsections 368.1(2) and (2.1) of the *Municipal Act* to property in that subclass, as though that paragraph and those subsections did not provide for tax reductions by the council of a municipality.

(8) **Definition.**—In subsection (7),
"municipality" does not include any part of territory without municipal organization that is deemed to be a district municipality.

(9) **Class, etc., not to be defined in terms of board support.**—Despite subsections 7(2) and (3) of the *Assessment Act*, regulations made by the Minister of Finance under subsection 7(1) of that Act shall not use the school support of persons assessed to define a class of real property.

S. 257.12.1   EDUCATION ACT

(10) **Definition.**—Except as provided by subsection (8), in this section, **"municipality"**.—"municipality" means,
- (a) a municipality within the meaning of subsection 1(1), and
- (b) a county, a regional municipality, The District Municipality of Muskoka and the County of Oxford.

1997, c. 31, s. 113(2); 1998, c. 3, s. 34, 1998, c. 33, s. 42.

257.12.1 (1) **Requisitions for amounts on business property.**—The Minister of Finance may requisition amounts for a year from an upper-tier municipality or a single-tier municipality to be raised by levying tax rates on business property, other than property taxed under section 368.3 of the *Municipal Act*.

(2) **Contents of requisition.**—The requisition shall specify an amount to be raised on each of the following:
1. The commercial classes.
2. The industrial classes.
3. The pipeline property class prescribed under the *Assessment Act*.

(3) **Setting of tax rates, upper-tiers.**—The council of an upper-tier municipality that is requisitioned shall, for the purposes of raising the amounts requisitioned, pass a by-law directing the council of each lower-tier municipality to levy tax rates, as specified in the by-law, on the assessment in the lower-tier municipality rateable for school purposes.

(4) **When rates set.**—A by-law required under subsection (3) shall be passed on or before the date by which the council of the upper-tier municipality must pass the upper-tier rating by-law for the year.

(5) **Setting of tax rates, single-tiers.**—The council of a single-tier municipality that is requisitioned shall, for the purposes of raising the amounts requisitioned, pass a by-law levying tax rates, as specified in the by-law, on the assessment in the municipality rateable for school purposes.

(6) **When rates set.**—A by-law required under subsection (5) shall be passed on or before the day the council passes the by-law for the year under subsection 368(2) of the *Municipal Act*.

(7) **Restrictions on tax rates.**—The following apply with respect to the tax rates specified in a by-law under subsection (3) or (5):
1. The rates shall be set so that, when levied on the applicable assessment,
    - i. the amount that the requisition requires to be raised on the commercial classes is raised from the commercial classes,
    - ii. the amount that the requisition requires to be raised on the industrial classes is raised from the industrial classes, and
    - iii. the amount that the requisition requires to be raised on the pipeline property class is raised from the pipeline property class.
2. There shall be a single rate for each class of real property prescribed under the *Assessment Act*.
3. If there are two or more commercial classes, the rates for the commercial classes must be in the same proportion to each other as the tax ratios established under section 363 of the *Municipal Act* for the classes are to each other.

4. If there are two or more industrial classes, the rates for the industrial classes must be in the same proportion to each other as the tax ratios established under section 363 of the *Municipal Act* for the classes are to each other.

(8) **Tax rates deemed to be prescribed.**—The tax rates specified in a by-law under subsection (3) or (5) shall be deemed to be tax rates prescribed by the Minister of Finance under clause 257.12(1)(b).

(9) **Graduated tax rates.**—Subsections 368.2(2.1) and (4) of the *Municipal Act* and the regulations under clause 368.2(3)(b) and (c) of that Act apply, with necessary modifications, with respect to the tax rates specified in a by-law under subsection (3) or (5).

(10) **Subclass tax reductions.**—Section 368.1 of the *Municipal Act* applies, with necessary modifications, with respect to the tax rates specified in a by-law under subsection (3) or (5).

(11) **Definitions.**—In this section,

"commercial classes" has the same meaning as in subsection 363(20) of the *Municipal Act*; ("catégories commerciales")

"industrial classes" has the same meaning as in subsection 363(20) of the *Municipal Act*; ("catégories industrielles")

"lower-tier municipality" means a municipality within the meaning of subsection 1(1) that forms part of an upper-tier municipality for municipal purposes; ("municipalité de palier inférieur")

"single-tier municipality" means a municipality within the meaning of subsection 1(1) that is not a lower-tier municipality; ("municipalité à palier unique")

"upper-tier municipality" means a county, a regional municipality, The District Municipality of Muskoka and the County of Oxford. ("municipalité de palier supérieur")

1998, c. 3, s. 34; 1998, c. 33, s. 43.

257.12.2 (1) **School tax rates for commercial and industrial classes.**—The authority of the Minister of Finance to prescribe tax rates for school purposes under section 257.12 shall be used so that the requirements in this section are satisfied.

(2) **Application with respect to requisitions.**—The authority of the Minister of Finance to requisition amounts under section 257.12.1 shall be used so that the tax rates set by the council of the municipality pursuant to the requisition result in the requirements in this section being satisfied.

(3) **2005 and after.**—The weighted average tax rate for school purposes for the commercial classes for a municipality for 2005 and later years must not exceed 3.3 per cent.

(4) **Before 2005, municipalities at or below 3.3 per cent.**—For a year after 1998 but before 2005, if the weighted average tax rate for school purposes for the commercial classes for the municipality for the previous year was 3.3 per cent or less, the weighted average tax rate for school purposes for the commercial classes for the municipality for the current year must not exceed 3.3 per cent.

(5) **Before 2005, municipalities above 3.3 per cent.**—For a year after 1998 but before 2005, if the weighted average tax rate for school purposes for the commercial classes for the municipality for the previous year was greater than 3.3 per cent, the weighted average tax rate

for school purposes for the commercial classes for the municipality for the current year must not exceed a maximum determined in accordance with the following.

1. Determine the amount by which the weighted average tax rate for school purposes for the commercial classes for the municipality for the previous year exceeds 3.3 per cent.
2. Determine the number of years until 2005, including the current year and the year 2005.
3. Divide the amount determined under paragraph 1 by the number of years under paragraph 2.
4. The maximum is the weighted average tax rate for school purposes for the commercial classes for the municipality for the previous year minus the amount determined under paragraph 3.

(6) **Weighted average tax rate.**—For the purposes of this section, the weighted average tax rate for school purposes for the commercial classes for a municipality is a percentage determined in accordance with the following:

1. The weighted average tax rate for school purposes for the commercial classes for a municipality for a year shall be determined by adding the taxes for school purposes for the year on all property in the commercial classes in the municipality for the year, dividing that sum by the total assessment of such property, as set out in the assessment roll returned for the year, and multiplying by 100.
2. The weighted average tax rate for school purposes for the commercial classes for a municipality for a previous year shall be determined by adding the taxes for school purposes for the previous year on all property that is in the municipality in the current year and was in the commercial classes for the previous year, dividing that sum by the total assessment of such property, as set out in the assessment roll returned for the previous year, and multiplying by 100.
3. For the purposes of paragraph 2, the taxes for school purposes for a property with respect to which Part XXII.1 of the *Municipal Act* or Division B of Part XXII.2 of the *Municipal Act* applied shall be deemed to be equal to the taxes that would have been raised by the tax rate prescribed by the Minister of Finance under section 257.12 or, if the Minister of Finance requisitioned an amount under section 257.12.1, by the tax rate set by the council of a municipality pursuant to the requisition.

(7) **Rebates under section 442.2.**—The following apply with respect to rebates under section 442.2 of the *Municipal Act*:

1. The weighted average tax rate for school purposes for the commercial classes may be greater than would be allowed under subsections (3), (4) and (5) to the extent necessary to raise additional taxes to fund the costs of the rebates with respect to property in the commercial classes that are shared by boards.
2. In determining the weighted average tax rate for school purposes for the commercial classes for a previous year for the purposes of this section, the taxes for school purposes shall be reduced by any additional taxes raised, as authorized under paragraph 1, to fund the costs of the rebates with respect to property in the commercial classes that are shared by boards.

(8) **Industrial classes.**—Subsections (3) to (7) also apply, with necessary modifications, with respect to the industrial classes.

(9) **Definitions.**—In this section,

"commercial classes" has the same meaning as in subsection 363(20) of the *Municipal Act*; ("catégories commerciales")

"industrial classes" has the same meaning as in subsection 363(20) of the *Municipal Act*; ("catégories industrielles")

"municipality" means a single-tier municipality or upper-tier municipality both as defined in subsection 257.12.1(11). ("municipalité")

1998, c. 33, s. 44.

257.13 (1) **Deferrals.**—Where a by-law under subsection 373(1) of the *Municipal Act* is in effect in a municipality, the amount of payments that shall be made by the municipality to a board under section 257.11 shall be reduced by the total of all taxes levied by the municipality for the board under this Division that were deferred under the by-law.

(2) **Same.**—Deferred taxes described in subsection (1), and interest on those taxes as provided under the by-law, shall be paid by the municipality to the board when the amounts are paid to the municipality.

1997, c. 31, s. 113(2).

257.13.1 Reductions.—A tax levied under this Division shall be deemed to be a municipal property tax for the purposes of section 136 of the *Tenant Protection Act, 1997*.

1997, c. 31, s. 113(2).

257.13.2 Regulations, unpaid taxes in territory being organized.—The Lieutenant Governor in Council may make regulations governing the collection of unpaid taxes for school purposes, including unpaid taxes under section 21.1 of the *Provincial Land Tax Act*, on property in unorganized territory that is annexed to a municipality or that is incorporated as a municipality including, without limiting the generality of the foregoing,

(a) requiring the municipality to make payments in respect of unpaid taxes to boards;

(b) for the purposes prescribed in the regulations, deeming the taxes to be taxes for municipal purposes levied by the municipality.

1998, c. 3, s. 34.

257.14 (1) **Regulations, Minister of Education and Training.**—The Minister of Education and Training may make regulations,

(a) providing that a board specified in the regulation in the area of jurisdiction of an English-language public district school board or a district school area board mentioned in paragraph 2 or 3 of subsection 257.7(1) perform the duties imposed by those paragraphs instead of the English-language public district school board or the district school area board in that board's area of jurisdiction;

(b) providing that a board specified in the regulation that is not mentioned in paragraphs 2 or 3 of subsection 257.7(1), the area of jurisdiction of which includes territory without municipal organization that is not deemed under section 56 or subsection 58.1(2) to be attached to a municipality, perform the duties imposed by those paragraphs in its area of jurisdiction even if the area of jurisdiction of that board is in whole or in part the area of jurisdiction of a board mentioned in paragraphs 2 and 3 of subsection 257.7 (1);

(c) providing that a board specified in the regulation perform the duties of a board mentioned in section 256 or subsection 255(1) of this Act or subsection 21.1 (1) of the *Provincial Land Tax Act*, or any of them, respecting the levying and collecting of rates, taxes or tax rates, as the case may be, in the area of jurisdiction of the board it is replacing;

(c.1) providing for boards that are required to levy tax rates under section 257.7 of this Act or section 21.1 of the *Provincial Land Tax Act* to levy tax rates, in accordance with the regulations, for the purposes of raising interim levies including, without limiting the generality of the foregoing, providing for anything provided for under section 370 of the *Municipal Act*.

(d) providing for the apportionment and distribution of amounts levied under subsection 257.7(1) on residential property taxable for English-language public board purposes between a district school area board and a board established under section 67, where the property is in the area of jurisdiction of both boards.

(e) respecting the form and contents of the collector's roll in connection with taxes for school purposes.

(f) providing, despite any provision of this Act or the *Provincial Land Tax Act*, that parts of territory described in subsection (2) shall be deemed, until the territory becomes or is included in a municipality, to be attached to a municipality under section 56 or clause 58.1(2)(m), for the purposes of this Division and of section 21.1 of the *Provincial Land Tax Act*;

(g) providing for such transitional matters as the Minister considers necessary or advisable in connection with a change as to which board or municipality is required to do a thing under this Division or under section 21.1 of the *Provincial Land Tax Act* in relation to territory without municipal organization;

(h) governing the levying of rates under subsection 255(1) or 256(1);

(i) providing, despite any provision of this Act, the *Municipal Act* or the *Provincial Land Tax Act*, for boards and municipalities to levy, in 1999, rates for 1998 under this Part on property in territory without municipal organization, subject to conditions set out in the regulation.

(2) **Clause (1)(f).**—The territory referred to in clause (1)(f) is territory without municipal organization that, on December 31, 1997, was attached to a municipality for school purposes and that, on January 1, 1998, was not so attached.

(3) **General or particular.**—A regulation under subsection (1) may be general or particular.

1997, c. 31, s. 113(2); 1998, c. 3, s. 34; 1998, c. 33, s. 45.

DIVISION C

TAXES SET BY BOARDS

257.15 (1) **Definitions.**— In this Division,

"**common jurisdictional area**".—"common jurisdictional area", in respect of two or more boards, means the area that is within the area of jurisdiction of both or all of those boards; ("territoire commun de compétence")

"**municipality**".—"municipality" includes a county, a regional municipality, the District Municipality of Muskoka and the County of Oxford. ("municipalité")

(2) **Types of boards.**—For the purposes of this Division, the following are types of boards:

1. English-language public board.
2. English-language Roman Catholic board.
3. French-language public district school board.
4. French-language separate district school board.
5. Protestant separate school board.

1997, c. 31, s. 113(3).

257.16 (1) **Rates set by boards.**—For the purpose of raising money for its purposes, a board may determine, levy and collect rates on assessment for real property that is rateable for the board's purposes as provided in section 257.17.

(2) **Subscriptions.**—For the purpose of raising money for its purposes, a Roman Catholic board may collect subscriptions on and from persons sending children to or subscribing towards the support of the board.

257.17 Assessment rateable under s. 257.16.—For the purposes of section 257.16, the following assessment for real property is rateable for a board's purposes:

1. The assessment of residential property that is entered against an individual who is in respect of that property a supporter of that type of board.
2. The assessment of residential property that is entered against a partnership or corporation to which section 237 applies, to the extent that the assessment is entered and assessed for the purposes of that type of board.
3. The assessment of business property that is entered against an individual who is in respect of that property a supporter of that type of board.
4. The assessment of business property that is entered against a corporation sole and assessed for the purposes of that type of board.

1997, c. 31, s. 113(3).

257.18 (1) **Agreements with municipalities re collection.**—Subject to the regulations, a board and a municipality may enter into an agreement providing for the municipality to levy and collect rates determined by a board under section 257.16.

(2) **Regulations.**—The Lieutenant Governor in Council may make regulations, which may be general or particular, respecting the terms of agreements referred to in subsection (1).

1997, c. 31, s. 113(3).

257.19 (1) **Collection powers of boards.**—A municipality or board that levies or collects rates for school purposes under this Division has, for purposes of the collection, chargeback, cancellation, refund or rebate of the rates, the same powers and duties as a municipality has in respect of the collection, chargeback, cancellation, refund or rebate of rates levied for municipal purposes, including powers and duties relating to the sale of land for tax arrears.

(2) **Powers of officers.**—The officers of a municipality or of a board that levies or collects rates for school purposes under this Division have the same powers and duties in respect of the collection, chargeback, cancellation, refund or rebate of rates levied under this Division, including powers and duties relating to the sale of land for tax arrears, as officers of a municipality have in respect of rates levied for municipal purposes.

(3) **Application of s. 382 of *Municipal Act*.**—Section 382 of the *Municipal Act* applies to rates levied under this Division.

(4) **Regulations.**—The Minister of Finance may make regulations, which may be general or particular in their application,

(a) varying, limiting or excluding the powers and duties under this section of municipalities and boards and of the officers of municipalities and boards; and

(b) providing for anything that the Minister considers necessary or advisable to ensure that tax collection by municipalities and boards under the provisions of this Division is co-ordinated with tax collection under any other provisions of this Act or under the provisions of any other Act and, for the purpose, varying, limiting or excluding the application of any provision of this or any other Act.

1997, c. 31, s. 113(3).

257.20 (1) **Designation by individuals re business property.**—For the purposes of rates levied under this Division, section 236 applies with necessary modifications to permit an individual to give notice in respect of assessment for business property and, for the purpose, a reference to "residential property" shall be deemed to be a reference to "business property".

(2) **Exception.**—Despite subsection (1), a person who is an owner or tenant of business property outside the area of jurisdiction of all boards is not entitled to apply under this section.

257.21 Limitation on s. 257.20 where residential property assessed.—If an individual is an owner or tenant of residential property in the area of jurisdiction of a board and is also the owner or tenant of business property in the area of jurisdiction of that board,

(a) the person shall be deemed to have applied in respect of the business property under section 16 of the *Assessment Act* to the assessment commissioner for the area in which the business property is located, to have his or her name included or altered in the assessment roll as a supporter of that board in respect of the business property; and

(b) despite section 257.20, the person is not entitled to apply under section 16 of the *Assessment Act* to have his or her name included or altered in the assessment roll as upporter of a different board in respect of business property within the area of jurisdiction of that board.

1997, c. 31, s. 113(3).

257.22 Designation by corporations sole re business assessment.—For the purpose of rates levied under this Division, section 237 applies with necessary modifications to permit a corporation sole to give notice in respect of its assessment for business property and, for the purpose, a reference to "residential property" shall be deemed to be a reference to "business property".

1997, c. 31, s. 113(3).

257.23 (1) **Assessment of certain tenants.**—For the purposes of rates levied under this

Division, subsections 237(1) to (11) and (14) to (17) apply with necessary modifications to the assessment of residential property entered against a partnership or corporation, other than a designated ratepayer as defined in subsection 238(1), that is a tenant of the property.

(2) **Same.**—For the purposes of rates levied under this Division, a notice in respect of residential property given under subsection 237(12) indicating the proportions of amounts to be distributed to each board shall be deemed to be a notice given under subsection 237 (3) requiring the same proportions of the assessment of the property to be entered and assessed for the purposes of the same boards.

257.24 (1) **Tenant priority.**—The tenant of land shall be deemed to be the person primarily liable for the payment of school rates imposed under this Division and for determining the type of board to which those rates shall be applied.

(2) **Same.**—No agreement between the owner and tenant as to the payment of rates as between themselves alters or affects the operation of this section.

1997, c. 31, s. 113(3).

257.25 (1) **Regulations re property classes and tax ratios.**—The Lieutenant Governor in Council may make regulations for the purposes of this Division prescribing property classes and establishing school purpose tax ratios for municipalities and territory without municipal organization that are situated within the area of jurisdiction of a board.

(2) **Same.**—A regulation made under subsection (1) may establish different school purpose tax ratios for the areas of jurisdiction of different boards.

(3) **Same.**—A regulation made under subsection (1) prescribing property classes shall prescribe the residential/farm property class as prescribed under the *Assessment Act*.

(4) **Definition.**—In subsection (1),

"**school purpose tax ratio**".—"school purpose tax ratio" means the ratio that the rate levied for a board's purposes for each property class prescribed under subsection (1) must be to the rate levied for the board's purposes for the residential/farm property class.

1997, c. 31, s. 113(3).

257.26 (1) **Determination of rates.**—Where a board determines rates under this Division, the board shall determine the rates in such a way that the rates on the different classes of property are in the same proportion to each other as the tax ratios established under section 257.25 for the property classes are to each other.

(2) **Same.**—A board may determine different rates under subsection (1) for a municipality, a part of a municipality, territory without municipal organization or part of territory without municipal organization.

1997, c. 31, s. 113(3).

257.27 (1) **Regulations.**—The Minister may make regulations,

(a) governing the form and content of tax notices and the giving of tax notices in connection with rates imposed under this Division;
(b) requiring boards that determine rates under this Division to prepare documents respecting,
   (i) the budgeting process and financial planning relied on in determining the rates, and

(ii) the revenues raised or expected to be raised by the rates;
(c) respecting the form and contents of the documents referred to in clause (b);
(d) requiring boards to report to the Minister and to the ratepayers of the board on any matter referred to in subclause (b)(i) or (ii), in the form and manner specified in the regulations.

(2) **General or particular.**—A regulation made under this section may be general or particular.

1997, c. 31, s. 113(3).

257.28 (1) **Borrowing powers of Roman Catholic boards.**—A Roman Catholic board may pass by-laws for borrowing money, by mortgages or other instruments, on the security of the schoolhouse property and premises and any other real or personal property vested in the board and on the security of the board's rates imposed under this Division, for the purpose of paying the cost of school sites, school buildings or additions or repairs to them, or for any other board purposes.

(2) **Terms of payment.**—The principal money may be made payable in annual or other instalments, with or without interest, and the board, in addition to all other rates or money that it may levy in any one year, may levy and collect in each year such further sum as may be required for paying all principal and interest falling due in that year, and the same shall be levied and collected in each year in the same manner and from the like persons and property by, from, on or out of which other separate school rates may be levied and collected.

(3) **Debentures.**—The mortgages and other instruments may in the discretion of the board be made in the form of debentures, and the debentures are a charge on the same property and the same rates as in the case of mortgages thereof made by the board.

(4) **Amounts.**—The debentures issued under the by-law may be for the amounts that the board considers expedient.

(5) **Maturity.**—The debt to be so incurred and the debentures to be issued for it may be made payable in 30 years at the furthest, and in equal annual instalments of principal and interest, or in any other manner authorized by the regulations made under subsection 247 (3).

(6) **Sinking fund.**—Where the debt is not payable by instalments, the board shall levy in each year during the currency of the debt in addition to the amount required to pay the interest falling due in that year a sum such that the aggregate amount so levied during the currency of the debt, with the estimated interest on the investments of the aggregate amount, will be sufficient to discharge the debt when it becomes payable.

(7) **Investment of fund.**—The sum referred to in subsection (6) shall be deposited into a fund established under clause 247(3)(d) and, subject to the other provisions of this section, a regulation made under clause 247(3)(d), (g) or (h) applies with necessary modifications to the application of the money in the fund.

(8) **Publication of notice of by-law.**—Before a by-law for borrowing money for a permanent improvement is acted on, notice of the passing of the by-law shall be published for three consecutive weeks in a newspaper having general circulation within the separate school zone stating,
(a) the purpose for which the money is to be borrowed;
(b) the amount to be borrowed and the security for the amount; and

(c) the terms of repayment including the rate of interest,

and, if no application to quash the by-law is made for three months after publication of notice of the passing of the by-law, the by-law is valid despite any want of substance or form in the by-law or in the time or manner of passing the by-law.

(9) **Non-application of s. 242.**—Section 242 does not apply in relation to borrowing under this section.

1997, c. 31, s. 113(3).

257.29 (1) **Notice to assessment commissioner.**—A board shall give written notice to the assessment commissioner of its intention to levy rates under this Division at least 12 months before January 1 of the first year in respect of which a board levies rates under this Division.

(2) **Same.**—A board is not entitled to determine, levy or collect rates under this Division unless it has given the notice referred to in subsection (1).

1997, c. 31, s. 113(3).

DIVISION D

SUPERVISION OF BOARDS' FINANCIAL AFFAIRS

257.30 (1) **Investigation of board's financial affairs.**—The Minister may direct an investigation of the financial affairs of a board if,

- (a) the financial statements of the board for a fiscal year, or the auditor's report on the statements, required to be submitted to the Ministry under section 252, indicate that the board had a deficit for that year;
- (b) the board has failed to pay any of its debentures or instruments prescribed under clause 247(3)(f) or interest on them, after payment of the debenture, instrument or interest is due and has been demanded;
- (c) the board has failed to pay any of its other debts or liabilities when due and default in payment is occasioned from financial difficulties affecting the board; or
- (d) the Minister has concerns about the board's ability to meet its financial obligations.

(2) **Appointment of investigator.**—The Minister may appoint as an investigator a person licensed under the *Public Accountancy Act* or an employee in the Ministry.

(3) **Powers of investigator.**—An investigator may,

- (a) require the production of any records that may in any way relate to the financial affairs of the board;
- (b) examine and copy any records required under clause (a); and
- (c) require any officer of the board or any other person to appear before him or her and give evidence, on oath or affirmation, relating to the financial affairs of the board.

(4) **Same.**—For the purposes of carrying out an investigation, an investigator has the powers of a commission under Part II of the *Public Inquiries Act* and that Part applies to an investigation as if it were an inquiry under that Act.

(5) **Report of investigator.**—On completion of an investigation, an investigator shall report in writing to the Minister, who shall promptly transmit a copy of the report to the secretary of the board.

(6) **Same.**—The investigator may not recommend that control and charge over the administration of the affairs of the board be vested in the Ministry unless the investigation discloses evidence of financial default or probable financial default, of a deficit or a probable deficit or of serious financial mismanagement.

1997, c. 31, s. 113(4).

257.31 (1) **Minister's powers on reviewing report: directions.**—After reviewing the report made under subsection 257.30(5), the Minister may give any directions to the board that he or she considers advisable to address the financial affairs of the board.

(2) **Vesting order: report recommendation.**—If the report recommends that control and charge over the administration of the affairs of the board should be vested in the Ministry, the Lieutenant Governor in Council may make any order that the Lieutenant Governor in Council considers necessary or advisable to vest in the Ministry control and charge over the administration of the affairs of the board.

(3) **Vesting order: board failure to comply with direction.**—If the Minister advises the Lieutenant Governor in Council that he or she is of the opinion that the board has failed to comply with a direction given under subsection (1), the Lieutenant Governor in Council may make any order that the Lieutenant Governor in Council considers necessary or advisable to vest in the Ministry control and charge over the administration of the affairs of the board.

(4) **Notice to board.**—The order shall be promptly transmitted to the secretary of the board.

1997, c. 31, s. 113(4).

257.32 (1) **Notice to be given re board.**—Where a board is subject to an order under subsection 257.31(2) or (3),

(a) the Minister shall publish notice of the order in *The Ontario Gazette*; and
(b) the persons directed by the Minister to do so shall give notice of the order to the persons specified by the Minister, in the form specified by the Minister.

(2) **No proceedings against board without leave of Minister.**—After notice has been published in *The Ontario Gazette* under clause (1)(a),

(a) no proceeding against the board shall be commenced or continued in any court without leave of the Minister; and
(b) no order of any court shall be enforced against the board without leave of the Minister.

(3) **Suspension of limitation period.**—Subject to subsection (4), where the commencement or continuance of any proceeding or the enforcement of a court order is prevented under this section,

(a) the running of any limitation period relating to the proceeding or enforcement is suspended until the Minister gives leave to commence or continue the proceeding or to enforce the court order, as the case may be; and
(b) the person having the right to commence or continue the proceeding or to enforce the court order shall, immediately after the leave is given, have the same length of time within which to commence or continue the proceeding or enforce the court order, as the case may be, as the person had when the notice was published in *The Ontario Gazette* under clause (1)(a).

PART IX — FINANCE   S. 257.34

(4) **Same.**—Subsection (3) does not apply unless application is made to the Minister for leave to commence or continue the proceeding or to enforce the order within the relevant limitation period and the Minister refuses to give the leave.

(5) **Effect of order.**—Subsection (2) does not apply in relation to a board that is subject to an order under subsection 257.31(2) or (3) after the Minister makes an order under clause 257.34(2)(b) or (i) with respect to the board.

1997, c. 31, s. 113(4).

257.33 (1) **Control exercisable by Minister.**—Where the Lieutenant Governor in Council has made an order under subsection 257.31(2) or (3) in respect of a board, the Minister has control and charge over the board generally with respect to any matter in any way affecting the board's affairs.

(2) **Same.**—Without limiting the generality of subsection (1), where the Lieutenant Governor in Council has made an order under subsection 257.31(2) or (3) in respect of a board, the Minister has control and charge over the exercise and performance by the board of its powers, duties and obligations with respect to,

(a) the appointment and dismissal of the board's officers and employees and their powers, duties, salaries and remuneration;
(b) the board's revenues and expenditures;
(c) the boards sinking funds, retirement funds and the funds prescribed under clause 247(3)(e) and the money belonging to those funds;
(d) the boards accounting and audit systems and dealings with the board's assets, liabilities, revenues and expenditures;
(e) the yearly or other estimates of the board, financial statements of the board and other reports of the board required by the Minister as well as the form, preparation and completion of them, and the times when they shall be made;
(f) the amounts to be provided for in the yearly or other estimates;
(g) the borrowing of money for the current expenditures of the board until the current revenue has been received;
(h) the imposition, charging and collection of all fees, charges and expenses;
(i) the sale or other disposition of any of the board's assets.

1997, c. 31, s. 113(4).

257.34 (1) **Interpretation.**—In this section,

"indebtedness".—"indebtedness" includes,

(a) any debenture, instrument prescribed under clause 247(3)(f) or other debt of the board,
(b) any interest on any indebtedness of the board.

(2) **Powers of Minister with respect to debt.**—Where a board is subject to an order under subsection 257.31(2) or (3), the Minister, with respect to the board's indebtedness, has the power by order to authorize or direct,

(a) the consolidation of all or any part of the board's indebtedness;
(b) the issue, on the terms and conditions, in the manner and at the times that the Minister may approve, of debentures, instruments prescribed under clause 247(3)(f) or other

evidences of indebtedness, in substitution and exchange for any debentures or such debt instruments that are outstanding or in payment and satisfaction of all or any part of any other indebtedness, and compulsory acceptance of these debentures, instruments or other evidences of indebtedness in payment and satisfaction of the debentures or other such instruments that are outstanding or other indebtedness;

(c) the issue of new debentures or instruments prescribed under clause 247(3)(f) to cover any consolidation under clause (a) or (b);

(d) the retirement and cancellation of all or any part of the existing debenture debt and debt incurred by any instrument prescribed under clause 247(3)(f) and debentures or debt instruments prescribed under clause 247(3)(f) that are outstanding, on the issue of new debentures or such debt instruments to cover them or in exchange for them;

(e) the terms, conditions, places and times for exchange of new debentures or instruments prescribed under clause 247(3)(f) for debentures or such debt instruments that are outstanding;

(f) the variation of the basis, terms, times and places of payment of all or any part of the board's indebtedness;

(g) the creation and setting aside of sinking funds, retirement funds, funds prescribed under clause 247(3)(e) and special reserves out of any portion of the revenues of the board for meeting obligations relating to all or any part of the board's indebtedness;

(h) the custody, management, investment and application of sinking funds, retirement funds, funds prescribed under clause 247(3)(e) reserves and surpluses;

(i) the ratification and confirmation of any agreement, arrangement or compromise entered into with any of the board's creditors respecting all or any part of the board's indebtedness;

(j) any amendment or cancellation of any order made by the Minister under this section or of the terms of any agreement, arrangement or compromise ratified and confirmed by the Minister under clause (i);

(k) the implementation of an interim plan, pending a final plan, or of a final plan, which may cancel all or any portion of interest in arrears and may alter, modify or compromise the rights of debenture holders, holders of instruments prescribed under clause 247(3)(f) or other creditors during any period of time between the relevant date of default and the end of the fifth year following the date on which the final plan was ordered implemented by the Minister.

(3) **Limitation.**—The Minister shall not make any order under clause (2)(k) unless creditors, representing not less than two-thirds in amount of the aggregate of the indebtedness of the board, excluding indebtedness in respect of which the board is not directly but only contingently or collaterally liable, have filed in writing with the Minister their approval of the making of the order.

(4) **Publication of notice of intention to exercise powers.**—Where the Minister intends to exercise a power under subsection (2), he or she shall first give notice of the intention in *The Ontario Gazette* and by any other publication and to the persons and in the manner that the Minister considers proper.

(5) **Same.**—The notice shall state the date after which the matter is to be dealt with by the Minister.

(6) **Same.**—The time stated under subsection (5) shall be at least two months after the notice is published in *The Ontario Gazette*.

(7) **Incidental matters.**—Subsection (4) does not apply with respect to any matter that, in the opinion of the Minister, is merely incidental to the exercise of a power under subsection (2).

(8) **Objection to be filed with Minister.**—The Minister shall not make any order under subsection (2) if an objection in writing to the making of the order is filed with the Minister by creditors representing not less than one-third in amount of the aggregate of the indebtedness of the board, excluding indebtedness in respect of which the board is not directly but only contingently or collaterally liable.

(9) **Approval by creditors.**—If creditors, representing not less than two-thirds in amount of the aggregate of the indebtedness of the board, excluding indebtedness in respect of which the board is not directly but only contingently or collaterally liable, have filed in writing with the Minister their approval of the making of any order of the Minister under subsection (1), it is not necessary that two months referred to in subsection (6) elapse.

(10) **Notice when matter to be varied.**—When a matter is being dealt with by the Minister under this section and the Minister intends to vary the terms of any indebtedness, he or she shall first give notice of the intention to the persons and in the manner that the Minister considers proper.

(11) **Same.**—The notice shall state the date after which the variation is to be dealt with by the Minister.

(12) **Same.**—The time stated under subsection (11) shall be at least two weeks after the notice.

1997, c. 31, s. 113(4).

257.35 Certain debenture and other debt not to form part of debt after order of Minister.—After an order of the Minister has been made under section 257.34, no portion of the debenture debt of the board represented by debentures or debt incurred by any instrument prescribed under clause 247(3)(f) ordered to be canceled, retired or exchanged forms part of its debt within the meaning of a provision of this or any other Act limiting the board's borrowing powers.

1997, c. 31, s. 113(4).

257.36 Variation or cancellation of subsisting agreements.—The board may, with the approval of the Minister, enter into an agreement with any person with whom the board has previously entered into an agreement or obligation that, or some term or obligation of which, remains in whole or in part or in any manner to be carried out by the board, for the amendment or cancellation of the subsisting agreement or obligation.

1997, c. 31, s. 113(4).

257.37 (1) **Minister to approve debenture, instrument issues.**—Without the approval of the Minister first being obtained, the board shall not, under this or any other Act, exercise or be required to exercise any of its powers if that exercise will or may require money to be provided by the issue of debentures or instruments prescribed under clause 247(3)(f) of the board.

(2) **Approval of debenture or instrument by-laws.**—The board may, with the approval of the Minister, pass by-laws providing for the issue of debentures or instruments prescribed under clause 247(3)(f) or authorizing the sale of debentures or such instruments or the offering of debentures or such instruments as security, but no such by-law has any force and effect until approved by the Minister.

1997, c. 31, s. 113(4).

257.38 (1) **Minister to have control over money and its application.**—The Minister has full charge and control over all money belonging to the board and received by any person for or on its behalf and the money shall be deposited in one of the following institutions, to be designated by the board or, in the absence of designation by the board, by the Minister:

1. A bank listed in Schedule I or II to the *Bank Act* (Canada).
2. The Province of Ontario Savings Office.
3. A loan or trust corporation registered under the *Loan and Trust Corporations Act*.
4. A credit union as defined in section 1 of the *Credit Unions and Caisses Populaires Act, 1994*.

(2) **Same.**—When money is deposited as required by subsection (1), it shall only be applied for the purposes, in the manner and at the times that the Minister may approve.

(3) **Same.**—All cheques drawn and issued by the board shall be signed and countersigned by the persons and in the manner that the Minister may authorize.

(4) **Same.**—No money belonging to or revenues of the board may be applied by any person except with the approval of or otherwise than as directed by the Minister.

1997, c. 31, s. 113(4).

257.39 Exercise of board jurisdiction subject to order.—The powers and duties under this or any other Act of a board that is subject to an order under subsection 257.31(2) or (3) shall only be exercised or performed in accordance with and subject to this Division and any order made or agreement entered into under it.

1997, c. 31, s. 113(4).

257.40 (1) **Exclusive jurisdiction.**—Subject to subsection (4), the Minister has exclusive jurisdiction as to all matters arising under this Division or out of the exercise by the board or any person of any of the powers conferred by this Division, and that jurisdiction is not open to question or review in any proceeding or by any court.

(2) **Review of orders, etc.**—The Minister may at any time review any order, direction or decision made by him or her under this Division and confirm, amend or revoke it.

(3) **Exclusive jurisdiction.**—The Lieutenant Governor in Council has exclusive jurisdiction as to the making of an order under subsection 257.31(2) or (3), and that jurisdiction is not open to question or review in any proceeding or by any court.

(4) **Review of orders, etc.**—The Lieutenant Governor in Council may at any time review any order made by the Lieutenant Governor in Council under subsection 257.31(2) or (3) and confirm, amend or revoke it.

(5) **Limitation.**—This section is subject to section 257.52.

1997, c. 31, s. 113(4).

257.41 Powers of Minister.—The Minister may make any orders from time to time that he or she considers advisable to carry out the provisions of this Division or any agreement made under it and may make rules in respect of any thing done under this Division.

1997, c. 31, s. 113(4).

257.42 Forms of certificates, notices, etc.—Every certificate, notice or other form that is in substantial conformity with the form required for it under this Division is not open to objection on the ground that it is not in the form required by this Division.

1997, c. 31, s. 113(4).

257.43 Powers exercisable for and in name of board.—Where a board has become subject to an order made under subsection 257.31(2) or (3), all things done by or for the Minister under this Division in relation to the affairs of the board shall for all purposes be deemed to have been done by and for the board and in its name.

1997, c. 31, s. 113(4).

257.44 Minister to have access to all records.—The Minister shall have access at all times to all records of the board, including but not limited to all by-laws, assessment rolls, collectors' rolls, minute books, books of account, vouchers and other records relating to the board's financial transactions, and may inspect and copy them.

1997, c. 31, s. 113(4).

257.45 (1) **Powers to enforce orders.**—Where a board fails to comply with any order, direction or decision of the Minister under this Division, the Minister may, on the notice, if any, that he or she considers appropriate, do or order done all things necessary for compliance with the order, direction or decision, and may exercise all the powers of the board for the purpose, under its name.

(2) **Liability for non-compliance.**—The board and each of its members, officers and employees shall comply with the orders, directions and decisions of the Minister in any matter relating to the administration of the affairs of the board, and any such person who knowingly fails to comply with any such order, direction or decision, or who, as a member of the board, votes contrary to such order, direction or decision, is guilty of an offence.

(3) **Personal liability and disqualification of members of boards.**—If a board that is subject to an order made under subsection 257.31(2) or (3) applies any of its funds otherwise than as ordered or authorized by the Minister, the members of the board who voted for the application are,

(a) jointly and severally liable for the amount so applied, which amount may be recovered in a court of competent jurisdiction; and
(b) disqualified for five years from holding any office for which elections are held under the *Municipal Elections Act*, 1996 or under this Act.

(4) **Dismissal of officers or employees.**—The Minister may dismiss from office any officer or employee of a board who fails to carry out any order, direction or decision of the Minister.

1997, c. 31, s. 113(4).

257.46 Injunction against exercise of board powers.—The Minister may by injunction proceedings prevent the exercise by or for a board of any of its powers that has not been approved by the Minister, if that approval is required under this Division.

1997, c. 31, s. 113(4).

257.47 Combining board offices.—The Minister may direct that two or more of the offices of the board shall be combined and held by the same officer, and may subsequently separate any of the offices so combined.

1997, c. 31, s. 113(4).

257.48 (1) Expenses.—The Minister may direct payment of the fees or remuneration and expenses reasonably incurred by the Ministry under this Division that he or she may determine.

(2) **Appointment of Minister.**—The Minister may appoint a person, who may be an officer of the board, to exercise the powers and perform the duties that the Minister may provide, and the person so appointed shall be paid the salary and allowed the expenses that the Minister may determine.

(3) **Board may be heard as to salaries.**—The Minister, in determining the salaries to be paid to any person appointed under subsection (2), shall give consideration to any representations that the board may at any time make.

(4) **Payment of salaries and expenses.**—All salaries, fees, remuneration and expenses payable under this section and all other expenses incurred by the Minister in carrying out the provisions of this Division or in the exercise of his or her powers under it shall be paid by the board and be chargeable to such of its accounts as the Minister may direct.

1997, c. 31, s. 113(4).

257.49 Conflict.—The powers contained in this Division shall be deemed to be in addition to and not in derogation of any power of the Minister under this or any other Act but, where the provisions of any Act or any other provision of this Act conflict with the provisions of this Division, the provisions of this Division prevail.

1997, c. 31, s. 113(4).

257.50 (1) Revocation of order.—The Lieutenant Governor in Council shall revoke an order made under subsection 257.31(2) or (3) if the Lieutenant Governor in Council is of the opinion that the affairs of a board no longer need to be administered under this Division.

(2) **Same.**—The Lieutenant Governor in Council shall revoke an order made under subsection 257.31(2) or (3) if the financial statements of a board for a fiscal year and the auditor's report on the statements submitted to the Ministry under section 252 indicate that the board did not have a deficit for the fiscal year.

1997, c. 31, s. 113(4).

257.51 (1) Non-application of *Regulations Act*.—The *Regulations Act* does not apply to anything done under any provision of this Division.

(2) **Non-application of *Statutory Powers Procedure Act*.**—The *Statutory Powers Procedure Act* does not apply to anything done under this Division.

(3) **Municipal Affairs Act, Parts II and III.**—Parts II and III of the *Municipal Affairs Act* do not apply in relation to boards.

1997, c. 31, s. 113(4).

257.52 (1) **Denominational, linguistic and cultural issues.**— Nthing in this Division authorizes the Minister to interfere with or control,

(a) the denominational aspects of a Roman Catholic board;

(b) the denominational aspects of a Protestant separate school board; or

(c) the linguistic or cultural aspects of a French-language district school board.

(2) **Same.**—The powers under this Division shall be exercised in a manner that is consistent with,

(a) the denominational aspects of a Roman Catholic board;

(b) the denominational aspects of a Protestant separate school board; or

(c) the linguistic or cultural aspects of a French-language district school board.

1997, c. 31, s. 113(4).

DIVISION E

EDUCATION DEVELOPMENT CHARGES

Definitions

257.53 (1) **Definitions.**—In this Division,

"board".—"board" means a board other than a board established under section 68; ("conseil")

"building permit".—"building permit" means a permit under the *Building Code Act, 1992* in relation to a building or structure; ("permis de construire")

"development".—"development" includes redevelopment; ("aménagement")

"education development charge".—"education development charge" means a development charge imposed under a by-law passed under subsection 257.54 (1) respecting growth-related net education land costs incurred or proposed to be incurred by a board; ("redevance d'aménagement scolaire")

"education development charge by-law".—"education development charge by-law" means a by-law passed under subsection 257.54 (1); ("règlement de redevances d'aménagement scolaires")

"education development charge reserve fund".—"education development charge reserve fund" means a reserve fund established under subsection 257.82 (1); ("fonds de réserve de redeances d'aménagement scolaire")

"education land cost".—"education land cost" means education land cost within the meaning of subsections (2), (3) and (4); ("dépense immobilière a fin scolaire")

"growth-related net education land cost".—"growth-related net education land cost" means the portion of the net education land cost reasonably attributable to the need for such net education land cost that is attributed to or will result from development in all or part of the area of jurisdiction of a board; ("dépense immobilière nette à fin scolaire liée à la croissance")

"**municipality**".—"municipality" includes a county, a regional or district municipality or the County of Oxford; ("municipalité")

"**net education land cost**".—"net education land cost" means the education land cost reduced by any capital grants and subsidies paid or that may be paid to the board in respect of such education land cost; ("dépense immobilière nette à fin scolaire")

"**non-residential development**".—"non-residential development" means development other than residential development; ("aménagement non résidentiel")

"**owner**".—"owner" means the owner of the land or a person who has made application for an approval for the development of the land on which an education development charge is imposed; ("propriétaire")

"**pupil accommodation**".—"pupil accommodation" means a building to accommodate pupils or an addition or alteration to a building that enables the building to accommodate an increased number of pupils. ("installations d'accueil pour les élèves")

(2) **Education land costs.**—Subject to subsections (3) and (4), the following are education land costs for the purposes of this Division if they are incurred or proposed to be incurred by a board:

1. Costs to acquire land or an interest in land, including a leasehold interest, to be used by the board to provide pupil accommodation.
2. Costs to provide services to the land or otherwise prepare the site so that a building or buildings may be built on the land to provide pupil accommodation.
3. Costs to prepare and distribute education development charge background studies as required under this Division.
4. Interest on money borrowed to pay for costs described in paragraphs 1 and 2.

Costs to undertake studies in connection with an acquisition referred to in paragraph 1.

(3) **Exclusions from education land costs.**—The following are not education land costs:

1. Costs of any building to be used to provide pupil accommodation.
2. Costs that are prescribed in the regulations as costs that are not education land costs.

(4) **Education land costs, leases, etc.**—Only the capital component of costs to lease land or to acquire a leasehold interest is an education land cost.

1997, c. 31, s. 113(5).

Education Development Charge By-laws

257.54 (1) **Education development charge by-law.**—If there is residential development in the area of jurisdiction of a board that would increase education land costs, the board may pass by-laws for the imposition of education development charges against land in its area of jurisdiction undergoing residential or non-residential development.

(2) **What development can be charged for.**—An education development charge may be imposed only for development that requires,

(a) the passing of a zoning by-law or of an amendment to a zoning by-law under section 34 of the *Planning Act*;
(b) the approval of a minor variance under section 45 of the Planning Act;
(c) a conveyance of land to which a by-law passed under subsection 50 (7) of the *Planning Act* applies;
(d) the approval of a plan of subdivision under section 51 of the *Planning Act*;
(e) a consent under section 53 of the *Planning Act*;
(f) the approval of a description under section 50 of the *Condominium Act*; or
(g) the issuing of a permit under the *Building Code Act*, 1992 in relation to a building or structure.

(3) **Same.**—An action mentioned in clauses (2)(a) to (g) does not satisfy the requirements of subsection (2) if the only effect of the action is to,
(a) permit the enlargement of an existing dwelling unit; or
(b) permit the creation of one or two additional dwelling units as prescribed, subject to the prescribed restrictions, in prescribed classes of existing residential buildings.

(4) **Application of by-law.**—An education development charge by-law may apply to the entire area of jurisdiction of a board or only part of it.

(5) **Limited exemption.**—No land, except land owned by and used for the purposes of a board or a municipality, is exempt from an education development charge under a by-law passed under subsection (1) by reason only that it is exempt from taxation under section 3 of the *Assessment Act*.

(6) **Conditions.**—The imposition of an education development charge by a board is subject to the prescribed conditions.

1997, c. 31, s. 113(5).

257.55 (1) Exemption for industrial development.—If a development includes the enlargement of the gross floor area of an existing industrial building, the amount of the education development charge that is payable in respect of the enlargement is determined in accordance with this section.

(2) **Enlargement 50 per cent or less.**— If the gross floor area is enlarged by 50 per cent or less, the amount of the education development charge in respect of the enlargement is zero.

(3) **Enlargement more than 50 per cent.**—If the gross floor area is enlarged by more than 50 per cent the amount of the education development charge in respect of the enlargement is the amount of the education development charge that would otherwise be payable multiplied by the fraction determined as follows:
1. Determine the amount by which the enlargement exceeds 50 per cent of the gross floor area before the enlargement.
2. Divide the amount determined under paragraph 1 by the amount of the enlargement.

1997, c. 31, s. 113(5).

257.56 When by-law effective.—An education development charge by-law comes into force on the fifth day after the day on which it is passed or the day specified in the by-law, whichever is later.

1997, c. 31, s. 113(5).

257.57 If jurisdiction divided into regions.—If the regulations divide the area of the jurisdiction of a board into prescribed regions for the purposes of this section the following apply:

1. Despite subsection 257.54 (4), an education development charge by-law of the board shall not apply with respect to land in more than one region.
2. The education development charges collected under an education development charge by-law that applies to land in a region shall not, except with the prior written approval of the Minister, be used in relation to land that is outside that region.

1997, c. 31, s. 113(5).

257.58 (1) **Duration of education development charge by-law.**—Unless it expires or is repealed earlier, an education development charge by-law expires five years after the day it comes into force.

(2) **Board can pass new by-law.**—Subsection (1) does not prevent a board from passing a new education development charge by-law.

1997, c. 31, s. 113(5).

257.59 Contents of by-law.—An education development charge by-law shall,

(a) designate the categories of residential development and non-residential development on which an education development charge shall be imposed;
(b) designate those uses of land, buildings or structures on which an education development charge shall be imposed;
(c) designate the areas in which an education development charge shall be imposed; and
(d) subject to the regulations, establish the education development charges to be imposed in respect of the designated categories of residential and non-residential development and the designated uses of land, buildings or structures.

1997, c. 31, s. 113(5).

Process Before Passing of By-Laws

257.60 (1) **Review of policies.**—Before passing an education development charge by-law, the board shall conduct a review of the education development charge policies of the board.

(2) **Public meeting.**—In conducting a review under subsection (1), the board shall ensure that adequate information is made available to the public, and for this purpose shall hold at least one public meeting, notice of which shall be given in at least one newspaper having general circulation in the area of jurisdiction of the board.

(3) **Non-application, first by-law under new scheme.**—A board is not required to conduct a review under this section before passing the first education development charge by-law it passes after December 31, 1997.

1997, c. 31, s. 113(5).

257.61 (1) **Education development charge background study.**—Before passing an education development charge by-law, the board shall complete an education development charge background study.

(2) **Same.**—The education development charge background study shall include,

(a) estimates of the anticipated amount, type and location of residential and non-residential development;
(b) the number of projected new pupil places and the number of new schools required to provide those new pupil places;
(c) estimates of the education land cost, the net education land cost and the growth-related net education land cost of the new schools required to provide the projected new pupil places; and
(d) such other information as may be prescribed.

1997, c. 31, s. 113(5).

257.62 By-law within one year after study.—An education development charge by-law may only be passed within the one-year period following the completion of the education development charge education development charge background study.

1997, c. 31, s. 113(5).

257.63 (1) Public meeting before by-law passed.—Before passing an education development charge by-law, the board shall,
(a) hold at least one public meeting;
(b) give at least 20-days notice of the meeting or meetings in accordance with the regulations; and
(c) ensure that the proposed by-law and the education development charge background study are made available to the public at least two weeks prior to the meeting or, if there is more than one meeting, prior to the first meeting.

(2) **Making representations.**—Any person who attends a meeting under this section may make representations relating to the proposed by-law.

(3) **Board determination is final.**—If a proposed by-law is changed following a meeting under this section, the board shall determine whether a further meeting under this section is necessary and such a determination is final and not subject to review by a court or the Ontario Municipal Board.

1997, c. 31, s. 113(5).

Appeal of By-laws

257.64 (1) Notice of by-law and time for appeal.—The secretary of a board that has passed an education development charge by-law shall give written notice of the passing of the by-law, and of the last day for appealing the by-law, which shall be the day that is 40 days after the day the by-law is passed.

(2) **Requirements of notice.**—Notices required under this section must meet the requirements prescribed in the regulations and shall be given in accordance with the regulations.

(3) **Same.**—Every notice required under this section must be given not later than 20 days after the day the by-law is passed.

(4) **When notice given.**—A notice required under this section shall be deemed to have been given,
(a) if the notice is by publication in a newspaper, on the day that the publication occurs;

(b) if the notice is given by mail, on the day that the notice is mailed.

1997, c. 31, s. 113(5).

257.65 Appeal of by-law after passed.—Any person or organization may appeal an education development charge by-law to the Ontario Municipal Board by filing with the secretary of the board that passed the by-law, on or before the last day for appealing the by-law, a notice of appeal setting out the objection to the by-law and the reasons supporting the objection.

1997, c. 31, s. 113(5).

257.66 (1) Secretary's duties on appeal.—If the secretary of the board receives a notice of appeal on or before the last day for appealing an education development charge by-law, the secretary shall compile a record that includes,

(a) a copy of the by-law certified by the secretary;
(b) a copy of the education development charge background study;
(c) an affidavit or declaration certifying that notice of the passing of the by-law and of the last day for appealing it was given in accordance with this Division; and
(d) the original or a true copy of all written submissions and material received in respect of the by-law before it was passed.

(2) **Same.**—The secretary shall forward a copy of the notice of appeal and the record to the secretary of the Ontario Municipal Board within 30 days after the last day of appeal and shall provide such other information or material as the Ontario Municipal Board may require in respect of the appeal.

(3) **Affidavit, declaration conclusive evidence.**—An affidavit or declaration of the secretary of a board that notice of the passing of the by-law and of the last day for appealing it was given in accordance with this Division is conclusive evidence of the facts stated in the affidavit or declaration.

1997, c. 31, s. 113(5).

257.67 (1) OMB hearing of appeal.—The Ontario Municipal Board shall hold a hearing to deal with any notice of appeal of an education development charge by-law forwarded by the secretary of a board.

(2) **Who to get notice.**—The Ontario Municipal Board shall determine who shall be given notice of the hearing and in what manner.

(3) **Powers of OMB.**—After the hearing, the Ontario Municipal Board may,

(a) dismiss the appeal in whole or in part;
(b) order the board to repeal or amend the by-law in accordance with the Ontario Municipal Board's order;
(c) repeal or amend the by-law in such manner as the Ontario Municipal Board may determine.

(4) **Limitation on powers.**—The Ontario Municipal Board may not amend or order the amendment of a by-law so as to,

(a) increase the amount of an education development charge that will be payable in any particular case;

(b) remove, or reduce the scope of, an exemption;
(c) change the date the by-law will expire.

(5) **Dismissal without hearing.**—Despite subsection (1), the Ontario Municipal Board may, where it is of the opinion that the objection to the by-law set out in the notice of appeal is insufficient, dismiss the appeal without holding a full hearing after notifying the appellant and giving the appellant an opportunity to make representations as to the merits of the appeal.

1997, c. 31, s. 113(5).

257.68 When OMB ordered repeals, amendments effective.—The repeal or amendment of an education development charge by-law by the Ontario Municipal Board, or by a board pursuant to an order of the Ontario Municipal Board, shall be deemed to have come into force on the day the by-law came into force.

1997, c. 31, s. 113(5).

257.69 (1) **Refunds, if OMB repeals by-law, etc.**—If the Ontario Municipal Board repeals or amends an education development charge by-law or orders a board to repeal or amend an education development charge by-law,

(a) in the case of a repeal, any education development charge paid under the by-law shall be refunded;

(b) in the case of an amendment, the difference between any education development charge paid under the by-law and the education development charge that would have been payable under the by-law as amended shall be refunded.

(2) **When refund due.**—A refund required under subsection (1) shall be made,

(a) if the Ontario Municipal Board repeals or amends the by-law, within 30 days after the Board's order;

(b) if the Ontario Municipal Board orders the board to repeal or amend the by-law, within 30 days after the repeal or amendment by the board.

(3) **Interest.**—Interest shall be paid on an amount refunded under subsection (1) at the prescribed interest rate from the time the amount was paid to the time it is refuded.

(4) **Source of refund, interest.**—An amount refunded under subsection (1) and interest paid under subsection (3) shall be paid out of the appropriate education development charge reserve fund.

(5) **Who refund paid to.**—An amount refunded under subsection (1) and any interest on it shall be paid to the person who paid the education development charge.

(6) **Information from municipality.**—If a refund is required under subsection (1), the municipality to which the education development charge was paid shall provide the board with the information necessary to determine the amount to be refunded, the interest payable on that amount and the person to whom the refund and interest should be paid.

1997, c. 31, s. 113(5).

Amendment of By-laws

257.70 (1) **Amendment of by-law.**—Subject to subsection (2), a board may pass a by-law amending an education development charge by-law.

(2) **Limitation.**—A board may not amend an education development charge by-law so as to do any one of the following more than once in the one-year period immediately following the coming into force of the by-law or in any succeeding one-year period:
1. Increase the amount of an education development charge that will be payable in any particular case.
2. Remove, or reduce the scope of, an exemption.
3. Extend the term of the by-law.

1997, c. 31, s. 113(5).

257.71 When amendment effective.—A by-law amending an education development charge by-law comes into force on the fifth day after it is passed.

1997, c. 31, s. 113(5).

257.72 Process before passing amendment.—Before passing a by-law amending an education development charge by-law, the board shall,
(a) give notice of the proposed amendment in accordance with the regulations; and
(b) ensure that the following are made available to the public,
  (i) the education development charge background study for the by-law being amended, and
  (ii) sufficient information to allow the public to understand the proposed amendment.

1997, c. 31, s. 113(5).

257.73 (1) Notice of amendment and time for appeal.—The secretary of a board that has passed a by-law amending an education development charge by-law shall give written notice of the passing of the amending by-law, and of the last day for appealing the amending by-law, which shall be the day that is 40 days after the day the amending by-law is passed.

(2) **Requirements of notice.**—Notices required under this section must meet the requirements prescribed in the regulations and shall be given in accordance with the regulations.

(3) **Same.**—Every notice required under this section must be given not later than 20 days after the day the amending by-law is passed.

(4) **When notice given.**—A notice required under this section shall be deemed to have been given,
(a) if the notice is by publication in a newspaper, on the day that the publication occurs:
(b) if the notice is given by mail, on the day that the notice is mailed.

1997, c. 31, s. 113(5).

257.74 (1) Appeal of amending by-law after passed.—Any person or organization may appeal a by-law amending an education development charge by-law to the Ontario Municipal Board by filing with the secretary of the board that passed the amended by-law, on or before the last day for appealing the amending by-law, a notice of appeal setting out the objection to the amending by-law and the reasons supporting the objection.

(2) **Same.**—An appeal under subsection (1) may not raise an issue that could have been raised in an appeal under section 257.65.

1997, c. 31, s. 113(5).

257.75 (1) Secretary's duties on appeal.—If the secretary of the board receives a notice of appeal on or before the last day for appealing a by-law amending an education development charge by-law, the secretary shall compile a record that includes,

(a) a copy of the education development charge by-law, as amended to the day the amending by-law was passed, certified by the secretary;
(b) a copy of the amending by-law certified by the secretary;
(c) a copy of the education development charge background study for the education development charge by-law;
(d) a copy of the information made available to the public under subclause 257.72(b)(ii) for the amending by-law and all previous amending by-laws amending the education development charge by-law; and
(e) an affidavit or declaration certifying that notice of the passing of the amending by-law and of the last day for appealing it was given in accordance with this Division.

(2) **Same.**—The secretary shall forward a copy of the notice of appeal and the record to the secretary of the Ontario Municipal Board within 30 days after the last day of appeal and shall provide such other information or material as the Ontario Municipal Board may require in respect of the appeal.

(3) **Affidavit, declaration conclusive evidence.**—An affidavit or declaration of the secretary of a board that notice of the passing of the amending by-law and of the last day for appealing it was given in accordance with this Division is conclusive evidence of the facts stated in the affidavit or declaration.

1997, c. 31, s. 113(5).

257.76 (1) **OMB hearing of appeal.**—The Ontario Municipal Board shall hold a hearing to deal with any notice of appeal of a by-law amending an education development charge by-law forwarded by the secretary of a board.

(2) **Who to get notice.**—The Ontario Municipal Board shall determine who shall be given notice of the hearing and in what manner.

(3) **Powers of OMB.**—After the hearing, the Ontario Municipal Board may,

(a) dismiss the appeal in whole or in part;
(b) order the board to repeal or amend the amending by-law in accordance with the Ontario Municipal Board's order;
(c) repeal or amend the amending by-law in such manner as the Ontario Municipal Board may determine.

(4) **Limitation on powers.**—The Ontario Municipal Board may not amend or order the amendment of an amending by-law so as to,

(a) increase the amount of an education development charge that will be payable in any particular case under the education development charge by-law as amended by the amending by-law;
(b) remove, or reduce the scope of, an exemption under the education development charge by-law as amended by the amending by-law;
(c) change the date the education development charge by-law will expire as provided in that by-law as amended by the amending by-law.

(5) **Dismissal without hearing.**—Despite subsection (1), the Ontario Municipal Board may, where it is of the opinion that the objection to the amending by-law set out in the notice

of appeal is insufficient, dismiss the appeal without holding a full hearing after notifying the appellant and giving the appellant an opportunity to make representations as to the merits of the appeal.

1997, c. 31, s. 113(5).

257.77 When OMB ordered repeals, amendments effective.—The repeal or amendment of a by-law amending an education development charge by-law by the Ontario Municipal Board, or by a board pursuant to an order of the Ontario Municipal Board, shall be deemed to have come into force on the day the amending by-law came into force.

1997, c. 31, s. 113(5).

257.78 Refunds, if OMB repeals by-law, etc.—Section 257.69 applies, with necessary modifications, with respect to the repeal or amendment of a by-law amending an education development charge by-law by the Ontario Municipal Board or pursuant to an order of the Ontario Municipal Board.

1997, c. 31, s. 113(5).

257.79 Application to OMB amendments, etc.—Subsection 257.70 (2) and sections 257.71 to 257.77 do not apply with respect to the amendment, by the Ontario Municipal Board or pursuant to an order of the Ontario Municipal Board, of an education development charge by-law or a by-law amending an education development charge by-law.

1997, c. 31, s. 113(5).

Collection of Education Development Charges

257.80 When charge payable.—An education development charge is payable upon a building permit being issued.

1997, c. 31, s. 113(5).

257.81 Who charge payable to.—An education development charge is payable to the municipality issuing the building permit.

1997, c. 31, s. 113(5).

257.82 (1) Education development charge reserve funds.—A board that has passed an education development charge by-law shall establish reserve funds in accordance with the regulations.

(2) **Deposit of charges into reserve funds.**—A municipality that receives an education development charge shall deposit the charge in the appropriate education development charge reserve fund not later than the 25th day of the month after the month in which the charge was received.

1997, c. 31, s. 113(5).

257.83 Withholding of building permit until charge paid.—Despite any other Act, a municipality shall not issue a building permit for development to which an education development charge applies unless the charge has been paid.

1997, c. 31, s. 113(5).

257.84 (1) Land given for credit.—A board that has passed a by-law imposing education development charges on land of an owner may, with the consent of the Minister, accept land for pupil accommodation in place of the payment of all or a part of the education development charges.

(2) **Same.**—A board that accepts land under subsection (1) shall, in accordance with the regulations made under section 257.101, give the owner credits toward the education development charges imposed on the owner by the board.

1997, c. 31, s. 113(5).

Complaints About Education Development Charges

257.85 (1) **Complaint to council of municipality.**—An owner, the owner's agent or a board, may complain to the council of the municipality to which an education development charge is payable that,

 (a) the amount of the education development charge was incorrectly determined;
 (b) a credit is or is not available to be used against the education development charge, or that the amount of the credit was incorrectly determined; or
 (c) there was an error in the application of the education development charge by-law.

(2) **Time limit.**—A complaint may not be made under subsection (1) later than 90 days after the day the education development charge, or any part of it, is payable.

(3) **Form of complaint.**—The complaint must be in writing, must state the complainant's name, the address where notice can be given to the complainant and the reasons for the complaint.

(4) **Parties.**—The parties to the complaint are the complainant and,

 (a) the board if the complainant is the owner or the owner's agent; or
 (b) the owner if the complainant is the board.

(5) **Hearing.**—The council shall hold a hearing into the complaint and shall give the parties an opportunity to make representations at the hearing.

(6) **Notice of hearing.**—The clerk of the municipality shall mail a notice of the hearing to the parties at least 14 days before the hearing.

(7) **Councils powers.**—After hearing the evidence and submissions of the parties, the council may dismiss the complaint or rectify any incorrect determination or error that was the subject of the complaint.

1997, c. 31, s. 113(5).

257.86 (1) **Notice of decision and time for appeal.**—The clerk of the municipality shall mail to the parties a notice of the council's decision, and of the last day for appealing the decision, which shall be the day that is 40 days after the day the decision is made.

(2) **Requirements of notice.**—The notice required under this section must be mailed not later than 20 days after the day the council's decision is made.

1997, c. 31, s. 113(5).

257.87 (1) **Appeal of council's decision.**—A party may appeal the decision of the council of the municipality to the Ontario Municipal Board by filing with the clerk of the municipality, on or before the last day for appealing the decision, a notice of appeal setting out the reasons for the appeal.

(2) **Additional ground.**—A party may also appeal to the Ontario Municipal Board if the council of the municipality does not deal with the complaint within 60 days after the complaint is made by filing with the clerk of the municipality a notice of appeal.

1997, c. 31, s. 113(5).

257.88 (1) **Clerk's duties on appeal.**—If a notice of appeal under subsection 257.87 (1) is filed with the clerk of the municipality on or before the last day for appealing a decision, the clerk shall compile a record that includes,

(a) a copy of the education development charge by-law certified by the clerk;
(b) the original or a true copy of the complaint and all written submissions and material received from the parties;
(c) a copy of the council's decision certified by the clerk; and
(d) an affidavit or declaration certifying that notice of the council's decision and of the last day for appealing it was given in accordance with this Division.

(2) **Same.**—If a notice of appeal under subsection 257.87 (2) is filed with the clerk of the municipality, the clerk shall compile a record that includes,

(a) a copy of the education development charge by-law certified by the clerk; and
(b) the original or a true copy of the complaint and all written submissions and material received from the parties.

(3) **Same.**—The clerk shall forward a copy of the notice of appeal and the record to the secretary of the Ontario Municipal Board within 30 days after the notice is received and shall provide such other information and material that the Board may require in respect of the appeal. 1997, c. 31, s. 113(5).

257.89 (1) **OMB hearing of appeal.**—The Ontario Municipal Board shall hold a hearing to deal with any notice of appeal relating to a complaint forwarded by the clerk of a municipality.

(2) **Notice to parties.**—The Ontario Municipal Board shall give notice of the hearing to the parties.

(3) **Powers of OMB.**—After the hearing, the Ontario Municipal Board may do anything that could have been done by the council of the municipality under subsection 257.85 (7).

1997, c. 31, s. 113(5).

257.90 (1) **Refund if education development charge reduced.**—If an education development charge that has already been paid is reduced by the council of a municipality under section 257.85 or by the Ontario Municipal Board under section 257.89, the overpayment shall immediately be refunded.

(2) **Interest.**—Interest shall be paid on an amount refunded under subsection (1) at the prescribed interest rate from the time the amount was paid to the time it is refunded.

(3) **Source of refund, interest.**—An amount refunded under subsection (1) and interest paid under subsection (2) shall be paid out of the appropriate education development charge reserve fund.

(4) **Who refund paid to.**—An amount refunded under subsection (1) and any interest on it shall be paid to the person who paid the education development charge.

1997, c. 31, s. 113(5).

257.91 Payment if education development charge increased.—If an education development charge that has already been paid is increased by the council of a municipality under section 257.85 or by the Ontario Municipal Board under section 257.89, the increase shall immediately be paid by the person who paid the education development charge.

1997, c. 31, s. 113(5).

Special Cases

257.92 Territory without municipal organization.—If there is an education development charge on land that is in territory without municipal organization, sections 257.81 to 257.91 apply with the following modifications:

1. Under section 257.81, the charge is payable to the board under whose by-law the charge is imposed and subsection 257.82 (2) applies to the board.
2. Section 257.83 applies to the official responsible for issuing building permits for the area the land is in.
3. Complaints under section 257.85 may be made to the board by the owner or the owner's agent. The complainant is the only party to the complaint. In sections 257.85 to 257.90, all references to the municipality or the council of the municipality shall be deemed to be references to the board and all references to the clerk of the municipality shall be deemed to be references to the secretary of the board.
4. If the decision of the board is appealed to the Ontario Municipal Board under section 257.87, the parties to the appeal are the complainant and the board.

1997, c. 31, s. 113(5).

257.93 Areas where province issues building permits.—If the council of a municipality has entered into an agreement providing for the enforcement of the *Building Code Act*, 1992 by Ontario, sections 257.81 to 257.91 apply with the modifications set out in the regulations.

1997, c. 31, s. 113(5).

Miscellaneous

257.94 Different types of boards treated the same.—In doing anything under this Division the Ontario Municipal Board shall treat English-language public boards, English-language Roman Catholic boards, French-language public district school boards and French-language separate district school boards in the same manner.

1997, c. 31, s. 113(5).

257.95 Registration of by-law.—A board that has passed an education development charge by-law may register the by-law or a certified copy of it against the land to which it applies.

1997, c. 31, s. 113(5).

257.96 Recovery of unpaid amounts, lien on land.—Section 382 of the *Municipal Act* applies with necessary modifications with respect to an education development charge or any part of it that remains unpaid after it is payable.

1997, c. 31, s. 113(5).

257.97 (1) Reports by municipalities to boards.—Each month a municipality shall make a report to a board if, in the period that the report would cover, any education development charges payable under an education development charge by-law of the board would be payable to the municipality.

(2) **When due.**—The monthly reports shall be made on or before the 5th day of each month.

(3) **Contents.**—The monthly reports shall contain the prescribed information.

1997, c. 31, s. 113(5).

257.98 (1) **Statement of treasurer.**—The treasurer of a board shall each year on or before such date as the board may direct, give the board a financial statement relating to education development charge by-laws and education development charge reserve funds.

(2) **Requirements.**—A statement must include, for the preceding year, statements of the opening and closing balances of the education development charge reserve funds and of the transactions relating to the reserve funds and such other information as is prescribed in the regulations.

(3) **Copy to Minister.**—The treasurer shall give a copy of a statement to the Minister within 60 days after giving the statement to the board.

1997, c. 31, s. 113(5).

257.99 Board may borrow from reserve fund.—A board may borrow money from an education development charge reserve fund but if it does so, the board shall repay the amount used plus interest at a rate not less than the prescribed minimum interest rate.

1997, c. 31, s. 113(5).

257.100 No right of petition.—Despite section 95 of the *Ontario Municipal Board Act*, there is no right to file a petition under that section in respect of any order or decision of the Ontario Municipal Board under this Division.

1997, c. 31, s. 113(5).

257.101 (1) **Regulations.**—The Lieutenant Governor in Council may make regulations that may have general or particular application in respect of a board,

   (a) prescribing any matter that is referred to as prescribed in this Division;
   (b) for the purposes of clause 257.54(3)(b), prescribing classes of residential buildings, prescribing the maximum number of additional dwelling units, not exceeding two, for buildings in such classes, prescribing restrictions and governing what constitutes a separate building;
   (c) defining or clarifying gross floor arrear and existing industrial building for the purposes of this Division;
   (d) dividing the area of the jurisdiction of a board into two or more prescribed regions for the purposes of section 257.57;
   (e) governing the expiry of education development charge by-laws that are passed by different boards but that apply to the same area;
   (f) for the purposes of clause 257.63(1)(b), subsection 257.64(2), clause 257.72(a) and subsection 257.73(2), governing notices referred to in those provisions;
   (g) prescribing modifications to the application of sections 257.81 to 257.91 in the circumstances set out in section 27.93;

(h) prescribing information to be included in monthly reports under section 257.97 and prescribing the period that each report must cover;
(i) prescribing the interest rate or a method for determining the interest rate that shall be paid under subsections 257.69(3) and 257.90(2);
(j) prescribing the minimum interest rate or a method for determining the minimum interest rate that boards shall pay under section 257.99;
(k) governing education development charge reserve funds including,
  (i) governing the establishment and administration of such reserve funds,
  (ii) the use of money from such reserve funds,
  (iii) varying the application of section 163 of the *Municipal Act* with respect to such reserve funds,
  (iv) requiring the approval of the Minister in respect of the manner in which or the rate at which the money is withdrawn from such reserve funds;
(l) requiring the approval of the Minister to any factor, criterion, rate, amount, portion, estimate or project used in determining an education development charge;
(m) prescribing the manner of calculating or determining education development charges and prescribing classes of persons that may make determinations necessary for the calculation of education development charges;
(n) providing for the sharing of proceeds where more than one board establishes education development charges in respect of the same area;
(o) prescribing information that boards must provide to other boards and to the Minister for the purposes of developing education development charges under this Division;
(p) prescribing the terms of agreements for credit in lieu of payment of education development charges, determining the amount of the credit and governing the allocation of the credit between or among boards;
(q) requiring a board to exempt an owner from an educational development charge if the owner meets the prescribed conditions;
(r) requiring boards to give notice of the particulars of education development charge by-laws that are in force, in the manner, and to the persons, prescribed in the regulations;
(s) requiring boards to prepare and distribute pamphlets to explain their education development charge by-laws and governing the preparation of such pamphlets and their distribution by boards and others.

(2) **Forms.**—Regulations under subsection (1) may require the use of forms approved by the Minister.

1997, c. 31, s. 113(5).

Transitional Provisions

257.102 (1) **Definitions.**—In sections 257.103 and 257.105,

"**old Act**".—"old Act" means,

(a) if section 71 of Bill 98 of the 1st Session, 36th Legislature (*Development Charges Act, 1997*) comes into force on or before the day this section comes into force, the *Education Development Charges Act* (formerly the Development Charges Act, entitled by Bill 98) as it reads immediately before this section comes into force,

(b) if section 71 of Bill 98 comes into force after the day this section comes into force, the *Development Charges Act* as it reads immediately before this section comes into force; ("ancienne loi")

"**successor board**".—"successor board" means a board that, for the purposes of this Division, is prescribed in the regulations as a successor board to an old board. ("conseil qui succède")

(2) **References to Bill 98.**—In this section the references to section 71 of Bill 98 are references to the section with that number in the version of Bill 98 reprinted as amended by the Resources Development Committee.

1997, c. 31, s. 113(5).

257.103 (1) **By-law under the old Act.**—This section applies with respect to an education development charge by-law under the old Act.

(2) **Continued.**—An education development charge by-law of an old board continues as an education development charge by-law of each successor board of the old board whose area of jurisdiction includes part of the area to which the by-law applies.

(3) **Application of old Act, new Act.**—The old Act continues to apply to a by-law continued under subsection (2) except that sections 257.80 to 257.91 and 257.94 to 257.100 apply instead of the corresponding provisions of the old Act.

(4) **Duration of continued by-law.**—Unless it expires or is repealed earlier, a by-law continued under subsection (2) expires at the end of August 31, 1999.

(5) **Modifications of by-law.**—The following apply to a by-law of a board continued under subsection (2):

1. The area to which the by-law applies is restricted to the area that the by-law applied to immediately before this section comes into force that is within the area of jurisdiction of the board.
2. If the education development charge by-law of the old board was continued as a by-law of more than one successor board and any of the areas to which the continued by-laws apply overlap, the education development charges payable in respect of land in the areas of overlap shall be determined, in accordance with the regulations, so that the education development charges payable under the continued by-laws do not exceed the amount that would have been payable had the by-law continued as the by-law of a single board.

(6) **Amendment, repeal of by-law.**—A board may, under the old Act, amend or repeal an education development charge by-law continued under subsection (2) but the board may not pass a new education development charge by-law under that Act.

(7) **Restriction, while continued by-law in force.**—A board shall not pass an education development charge by-law under this Division that applies to an area to which a by-law of the board continued under subsection (2) applies.

(8) **Certain by-laws passed under old Act.**—Despite subsection (2), an education development charge by-law of an old board passed on or after September 22, 1997 but before the day this section comes into force expires upon the coming into force of this section.

(9) **Same, refund of charges paid.**—An education development charge paid under a bylaw of an old board described under subsection (8) shall be refunded to the person who paid

it and the obligation to refund the charge shall be deemed to be a liability of the old board that shall be transferred to one or more boards.

1997, c. 31, s. 113(5); 1998, c. 33, s. 46.

257.104 Certain old requests, appeals.—Despite the repeal of section 46 of the *Education Development Changes Act* (formerly the *Development Charges Act*), that section continues to apply with respect to the requests and appeals described in that section made before November 23, 1989.

1997, c. 31, s. 113(5).

257.105 (1) **Regulations, transition.**—Without limiting the generality of section 257.3, the Lieutenant Governor in Council may make regulations,

(a) prescribing boards as successor boards for the purposes of this Division;

(b) governing the determination of education development charges in the circumstances referred to in paragraph 2 of subsection 257.103(5);

(c) varying, limiting or excluding the application of any provision of the old Act and the regulations under the old Act to by-laws continued under subsection 257.103(2);

(d) setting out transitional rules dealing with matters not specifically dealt with in sections 257.102 to 257.104;

(e) clarifying the transitional rules set out in sections 257.102 to 257.104.

(2) **General or particular.**—A regulation made under subsection (1) may be general or particular.

1997, c. 31, s. 113(5).

DIVISION F

Review of Education Funding

257.106 (1) **Operation of Division C.**—Division C is inoperative with respect to English-language public boards.

(2) **Same.**—Division C is inoperative with respect to French-language public district school boards.

(3) **Same.**—Division C is inoperative with respect to English-language Roman Catholic boards.

(4) **Same.**—Division C is inoperative with respect to French-language separate district school boards.

(5) **Same.**—Division C is inoperative with respect to a board of a Protestant separate school.

1997, c. 31, s. 113(6).

257.107 (1) **Legislative committee review.**—The Lieutenant Governor in Council shall by order appoint a committee to consider whether the legislation and regulations governing education funding meet the standard set out in subsection 234 (2) of the *Education Act*.

(2) **Timing.**—The order shall specify when the committee shall commence its work and the date specified shall not be before June 30, 2003.

(3) **Report.**—On or before December 31, 2003, the committee shall prepare a written report on its deliberations.

(4) **Same.**—The chair of the committee shall promptly sign the report and submit it to the Minister.

(5) **Same.**—The Minister shall submit the report to the Lieutenant Governor in Council and shall then table the report in the Legislative Assembly.

1997, c. 31, s. 113(6).

258. [Repealed 1997, c. 31, s. 114.]

259. [Repealed 1997, c. 31, s. 114.]

[Note subsection 114(2) of the *Education Quality Improvement Act, 1997*, which states:

(2) On the day that subsection (1) comes into force [repeal of s. 258 and s. 259, *Education Act*] every permanent teacher's contract, probationary teacher's contract and continuing education teacher's contract between a board and a teacher that is made in accordance with the regulations ceases to be in force.]

PART X

TEACHERS, PUPIL RECORDS AND EDUCATION NUMBERS

260. (1) [Repealed 1997, c. 31, s. 116(1).]

(1.1) [Repealed 1997, c. 31, s. 116(3).]

(2) [Repealed 1997, c. 31, s. 116(4).]

(3) [Repealed 1996, c. 13, s. 10(3).]

(4) [Repealed 1996, c. 13, s. 10(3).]

(4.1) [Repealed 1996, c. 13, s. 10(5).]

(5) [Repealed 1997, c. 31, s. 116(6).]

(6) [Repealed 1997, c. 31, s. 116(6).]

(6.1) [Repealed 1997, c. 31, s. 116(8).]

(7) [Repealed 1997, c. 31, s. 116(9).]

(8) [Repealed 1997, c. 31, s. 116(9).]

1996, c. 13, s. 10; 1997, c. 31, ss. 115, 116.

261. Probationary period.—The probationary period, if any, for teachers when they first become employed by a board shall not exceed two years.

1997, c. 31, s. 117.

262. (1) **Membership in Ontario College of Teachers.**—Except as otherwise provided in or under this Act, no person shall be employed in an elementary or secondary school to teach or to perform any duty for which membership in the College is required under this Act unless the person is a member of the Ontario College of Teachers.

(2) [Repealed 1996, c. 12, s. 64(11).]

(3) [Repealed 1996, c. 12, s. 64(11).]

(4) [Repealed 1996, c. 12, s. 64(11).]

1996, c. 12, s. 64(11).

263. Termination of contract where welfare of school involved.—Despite the other provisions of this Part and despite any provision in a collective agreement, if any, when a teacher is employed by a board and a matter arises that in the opinion of the Minister adversely affects the welfare of the school in which the teacher is employed,

(a) the board or the teacher may, with the consent of the Minister, give the other party thirty days written notice of termination, and the teacher's employment is terminated at the expiration of thirty days from the date the notice is given; or

(b) the board may, with the consent of the Minister, give the teacher written notice of immediate termination together with one-tenth of the teacher's yearly salary in addition to the amount to which the teacher would otherwise be entitled, and, on doing so, the teacher's employment is terminated.

1997, c. 31, s. 118, 119.

Duties

264. (1) Duties of teacher.—It is the duty of a teacher and a temporary teacher,

(a) **teach.**—to teach diligently and faithfully the classes or subjects assigned to the teacher by the principal;

(b) **learning.**—to encourage the pupils in the pursuit of learning;

(c) **religion and morals.**—to inculcate by precept and example respect for religion and the principles of Judaeo-Christian morality and the highest regard for truth, justice, loyalty, love of country, humanity, benevolence, sobriety, industry, frugality, purity, temperance and all other virtues;

(d) **co-operation.**—to assist in developing co-operation and co-ordination of effort among the members of the staff of the school;

(e) **discipline.**—to maintain, under the direction of the principal, proper order and discipline in the teacher's classroom and while on duty in the school and on the school ground;

(f) **language of instruction.**—in instruction and in all communications with the pupils in regard to discipline and the management of the school,

(i) to use the English language, except where it is impractical to do so by reason of the pupil not understanding English, and except in respect of instruction in a language other than English when such other language is being taught as one of the subjects in the course of study, or

(ii) to use the French language in schools or classes in which French is the language of instruction except where it is impractical to do so by reason of the pupil not understanding French, and except in respect of instruction in a language other than French when such other language is being taught as one of the subjects in the course of study;

(g) **timetable.**—to conduct the teacher's class in accordance with a timetable which shall be accessible to pupils and to the principal and supervisory officers;

(h) **professional activity days.**—to participate in professional activity days as designated by the board under the regulations;
(i) **absence from school.**—to notify such person as is designated by the board if the teacher is to be absent from school and the reason therefor;
(j) **school property.**—to deliver the register, the school key and other school property in the teacher's possession to the board on demand, or when the teacher's agreement with the board has expired, or when for any reason the teacher's employment has ceased; and
(k) **textbooks.**—to use and permit to be used as a textbook in a class that he or she teachers in an elementary or a secondary school,
  (i) in a subject area for which textbooks are approved by the Minister, only textbooks that are approved by the Minister, and
  (ii) in all subject areas, only textbooks that are approved by the board.

(1.1) **Sign language.**—Despite clause (1)(f), a teacher or temporary teacher may use American Sign Language or Quebec Sign Language in accordance with the regulations.

(2) **Refusal to give up school property.**—A teacher who refuses, on demand or order of the board that operates the school concerned, to deliver to the board any school property in the teacher's possession forfeits any claim that the teacher may have against the board.

(3) **Teachers, conferences.**—Teachers may organize themselves for the purpose of conducting professional development conferences and seminars.

1993, c. 11, s. 36.

265. Duties of principal.—It is the duty of a principal of a school, in addition to the principal's duties as a teacher,
(a) **discipline.**—to maintain proper order and discipline in the school;
(b) **co-operation.**—to develop co-operation and co-ordination of effort among the members of the staff of the school;
(c) **register pupils and record attendance.**—to register the pupils and to ensure that the attendance of pupils for every school day is recorded either in the register supplied by the Minister in accordance with the instructions contained therein or in such other manner as is approved by the Minister;
(d) **pupil records.**—in accordance with this Act, the regulations and the guidelines issued by the Minister, to collect information for inclusion in a record in respect of each pupil enrolled in the school and to establish, maintain, retain, transfer and dispose of the record;
(e) **timetable.**—to prepare a timetable. to conduct the school according to such timetable and the school year calendar or calendars applicable thereto, to make the calendar or calendars and the timetable accessible to the pupils, teachers and supervisory officers and to assign classes and subjects to the teachers;
(f) **examinations and reports.**—to hold, subject to the approval of the appropriate supervisory officer, such examinations as the principal considers necessary for the promotion of pupils or for any other purpose and report as required by the board the progress of the pupil to his or her parent or guardian where the pupil is a minor and otherwise to the pupil;

(g) **promote pupils.**—subject to revision by the appropriate supervisory officer, to promote such pupils as the principal considers proper and to issue to each such pupil a statement thereof;

(h) **textbooks.**—to ensure that all textbooks used by pupils are those approved by the board and, in the case of subject areas for which the Minister approves textbooks, those approved by the Minister;

(i) **reports.**—to furnish to the Ministry and to the appropriate supervisory officer any information that it may be in the principal's power to give respecting the condition of the school premises, the discipline of the school, the progress of the pupils and any other matter affecting the interests of the school, and to prepare such reports for the board as are required by the board;

(j) **care of pupils and property.**—to give assiduous attention to the health and comfort of the pupils, to the cleanliness, temperature and ventilation of the school, to the care of all teaching materials and other school property, and to the condition and appearance of the school buildings and grounds;

(k) **report to M.O.H.**—to report promptly to the board and to the medical officer of health when the principal has reason to suspect the existence of any communicable disease in the school, and of the unsanitary condition of any part of the school building or the school grounds;

(l) **persons with communicable diseases.**—to refuse admission to the school of any person who the principal believes is infected with or exposed to communicable diseases requiring an order under section 22 of the *Health Protection and Promotion Act* until furnished with a certificate of a medical officer of health or of a legally qualified medical practitioner approved by the medical officer of health that all danger from exposure to contact with such person has passed;

(m) **access to school or class.**—subject to an appeal to the board, to refuse to admit to the school or classroom a person whose presence in the school or classroom would in the principal's judgment be detrimental to the physical or mental well-being of the pupils; and

(n) **visitor's book.**—to maintain a visitor's book in the school when so determined by the board.

1991, vol. 2, c. 10, s. 6.

Pupil Records

266. (1) **Definition.**—In this section, except in subsection (12), "record", in respect of a pupil, means a record under clause 265(d).

(2) **Pupil records privileged.**—A record is privileged for the information and use of supervisory officers and the principal and teachers of the school for the improvement of instruction of the pupil, and such record,

(a) subject to subsections (2.1), (3) and (5), is not available to any other person; and

(b) except for the purposes of subsection (5), is not admissible in evidence for any purpose in any trial, inquest, inquiry, examination, hearing or other proceeding, except to prove the establishment, maintenance, retention or transfer of the record, without the written permission of the parent or guardian of the pupil or, where the pupil is an adult, the written permission of the pupil.

(2.1) **Information to medical officer of health.**—The principal of a school shall, upon request by the medical officer of health serving the area in which the school is located, give that medical officer of health the following information in respect of pupils enrolled in the school;

1. The pupil's name, address and telephone number.
2. The pupil's birth date.
3. The name, address and telephone number of the pupil's parent or guardian.

(3) **Right of parent and pupil.**—A pupil, and his or her parent or guardian where the pupil is a minor, is entitled to examine the record of such pupil.

(4) **Idem.**—Where, in the opinion of a pupil who is an adult, or of the parent or guardian of a pupil who is a minor, information recorded upon the record of the pupil is,

(a) inaccurately recorded; or
(b) not conducive to the improvement of instruction of the pupil,

such pupil, parent or guardian, as the case may be, may, in writing, request the principal to correct the alleged inaccuracy in, or to remove the impugned information from, such record.

(5) **Reference where disagreement.**—Where the principal refuses to comply with a request under subsection (4), the pupil, parent or guardian who made the request may, in writing, require the principal to refer the request to the appropriate supervisory officer who shall either require the principal to comply with the request or submit the record and the request to a person designated by the Minister, and such person shall hold a hearing at which the principal and the person who made the request are the parties to the proceeding, and the person so designated shall, after the hearing, decide the matter, and his or her decision is final and binding upon the parties to the proceeding.

(6) **Use re further education or employment.**—Nothing in subsection (2) prohibits the use by the principal of the record in respect of a pupil to assist in the preparation of,

(a) a report required by this Act or the regulations; or
(b) a report,
    (i) for an educational institution or for the pupil or former pupil, in respect of an application for further education, or
    (ii) for the pupil or former pupil in respect of an application for employment,
where a written request is made by the former pupil, the pupil where he or she is an adult, or the parent or guardian of the pupil where the pupil is a minor.

(7) **Information for Minister or board.**—Nothing in this section prevents the compilation and delivery of such information as may be required by the Minister or by the board.

(8) **No action re content.**—No action shall be brought against any person in respect of content of a record.

(9) **Testimony re content.**—Except where the record has been introduced in evidence as provided in this section, no person shall be required in any trial or other proceeding to give evidence in respect of the content of a record.

(10) **Secrecy re contents.**—Except as permitted under this section, every person shall preserve secrecy in respect of the content of a record that comes to the person's knowledge in the course of his or her duties or employment, and no such person shall communicate any such knowledge to any other person except,

(a) as may be required in the performance of his or her duties; or
(b) with the written consent of the parent or guardian of the pupil where the pupil is a minor; or
(c) with the written consent of the pupil where the pupil is an adult.

(11) **Definition.**—For the purposes of this section, "guardian" includes a person, society or corporation who or that has custody of a pupil.

(12) **Application to former records.**—This section, except subsections (3), (4) and (5), applies with necessary modifications to a record established and maintained in respect of a pupil or retained in respect of a former pupil prior to the 1st day of September, 1972.

(13) **Use of record in disciplinary cases.**—Nothing in this section prevents the use of a record in respect of a pupil by the principal of the school attended by the pupil or the board that operates the school for the purposes of a disciplinary proceeding instituted by the principal in respect of conduct for which the pupil is responsible to the principal.

1991, Vol. 2, c. 10, s. 7.

Ontario Education Numbers

266.1 Definition.—In sections 266.2 to 266.5,

"personal information" means personal information within the meaning of section 38 of the *Freedom of Information and Protection of Privacy Act* and section 28 of the *Municipal Freedom of Information and Protection of Privacy Act*.

266.2 (1) **Assignment of numbers.**—The Minister may assign an Ontario education number to a person who is enrolled or who seeks admission to be enrolled in a prescribed educational or training institution.

(2) **Same.**—For the purpose of assigning an Ontario education number, the Minister and prescribed educational and training institutions are authorized to collect, directly or indirectly, personal information.

(3) **Same.**—Subsection 39 (2) of the *Freedom of Information and Protection of Privacy Act* and subsection 29 (2) of the *Municipal Freedom of Information and Protection of Privacy Act* do not apply to a collection under subsection (2).

(4) **Same.**—For the purpose of assigning an Ontario education number, the Minister and prescribed educational and training institutions may use or disclose personal information and the disclosure shall be deemed to be for the purposes of complying with this Act.

266.3 (1) **Privacy re education numbers.**—Except as permitted by this section or otherwise by law, no person shall collect, use, disclose or require the production of another person's Ontario education number.

(2) **Exception.**—A prescribed educational or training institution may collect, use, disclose or require the production of a person's Ontario education number for purposes related to the provision of educational services to that person.

(3) **Same.**—The Minister and a person prescribed under clause 266.5 (1) (b) may collect, use or disclose or require the production of Ontario education numbers for purposes related to education administration, funding, planning or research.

(4) **Same.**—The Minister and a prescribed educational or training institution may collect, use, disclose or require the production of a person's Ontario education number for purposes related to the provision of financial assistance associated with the person's education.

266.4 (1) **Offence.**—Every person who contravenes subsection 266.3 (1) is guilty of an offence.

(2) **Penalty, individuals.**—An individual who is convicted of an offence under this section is liable to a fine of not more than $5,000 or to imprisonment for a term of not more than six months, or to both.

(3) **Penalty, corporations.**—A corporation that is convicted of an offence under this section is liable to a fine of not more than $25,000.

266.5 (1) **Regulations.**—The Lieutenant Governor in Council may make regulations,

   (a) prescribing educational institutions, training institutions or classes of such institutions for the purposes of this section and sections 266.2 to 266.4;
   (b) prescribing persons or classes of persons for the purposes of subsection 266.3 (3);
   (c) for purposes associated with Ontario education numbers, authorizing personal information to be collected by the Ministry or by prescribed educational or training institutions, other than directly from the individual to whom the information relates, and regulating the manner in which the information is collected;
   (d) requiring the use of Ontario education numbers by prescribed educational or training institutions for the purposes specified in the regulations;
   (e) respecting any matter that the Lieutenant Governor in Council considers necessary or advisable to carry out effectively the intent and purpose of sections 266.2 to 266.4.

(2) **General or particular.**—A regulation under this section may be general or particular.

(3) **Classes.**—A class may be defined with respect to any attribute and may be defined to consist of or to exclude any specified member of the class, whether or not with the same attributes.

Boards of Reference

Note: Under section 121(1) of Bill 160, sections 267 to 277 of the Act are repealed by Bill 160, section 121(2) but continue to apply with respect to applications for a Board of Reference that are made before September 1, 1998 and that have not been finally determined by that date. Regulation 300 (Practice and Procedure—Boards of Reference) of the Revised Regulations of Ontario, 1990, as it reads on August 31, 1998, also continues to apply with respect to those applications.
As such, the text of the repealed provisions is maintained for reference purposes.

267. Definitions.—In sections 268 to 277,

"**contract**".—"contract" means a contract of employment between a teacher and a board; ("contract") "employed" means employed as a permanent teacher by a board; ("employé")

PART X — TEACHERS, PUPIL RECORDS AND EDUCATION NUMBERS   S. 269

"judge".—"judge" means a judge of the Ontario Court (General Division) or a former judge of the court; ("juge")

"teacher".—"teacher" means a person qualified to teach in an elementary or secondary school and employed by a board on the terms and conditions contained in the form of contract prescribed for a permanent teacher. ("enseignant")

[Repealed 1997, c. 31, s. 121(1)].

268. (1) **Termination of contract by board.**—The dismissal of a teacher, or the termination of the contract of a teacher, by a board shall be by notice in writing, which shall state the reasons therefor, in accordance with the terms of the contract. [Repealed, EQIA, 1997, s. 121(1).]

(2) **Termination of contract by teacher.**—Where a teacher is employed by a board, the termination of the contract by the teacher shall be by notice in writing in accordance with the terms of the contract.

(3) **Application for board.**—Where a teacher is dismissed or the contract of a teacher is terminated by the board or the teacher, the teacher or board if not in agreement with the dismissal or termination may at any time within twenty-one days after receiving the notice referred to in subsection (1) or (2), as the case may be, apply in writing by registered letter to the Minister for a Board of Reference, stating the disagreement.

(4) **Service of notice.**—The applicant shall send a copy of the application by registered mail to the other party to the disagreement on the same day as the application is sent to the Minister.

[Repealed 1997, c. 31, s. 121(1).]

269. (1) **Appointment in place of teacher dismissed.**—A board shall not make a permanent appointment to take the place of a teacher who is dismissed or whose contract has been terminated in a manner not agreeable to the teacher until,

(a) the time prescribed for applying for a Board of Reference has elapsed and the teacher has not applied for a Board of Reference and sent a copy of the application to the board, as provided in section 268;

(b) the board has received from the teacher notice in writing that no application will be made under section 268;

(c) the board has received from the Minister notice in writing that an application made by the teacher under section 268 has been withdrawn;

(d) the board has received from the Minister notice in writing that the Minister has refused an application made by the teacher under section 268;

(e) the board has received from the Minister notice in writing that the teacher, being the applicant, has failed to comply with the requirements of subsection 270(3); or

(f) the board has received from the Minister a copy of the direction of the Board of Reference under section 273 directing the discontinuance of the contract, whichever first occurs.

[Repealed, EQIA, 1997, s. 121(1).]

(2) **New contract after termination of contract by teacher.**—A teacher who terminates a contract in a manner not agreeable to the board shall not enter into a contract with another

board after the teacher has received notice of the application of the board for a Board of Reference until,

(a) the teacher has received from the Minister notice in writing that an application made by the board under section 268 has been withdrawn;
(b) the teacher has received from the Minister notice in writing that the Minister has refused an application made by the board under section 268;
(c) the teacher has received from the Minister notice in writing that the board, being the applicant, has failed to comply with the requirements of subsection 270(3); or
(d) the teacher has received from the Board of Reference a copy of the direction of the Board of Reference under section 273 directing the discontinuance of the contract, whichever first occurs.

[Repealed, EQIA, 1997, s. 121(1).]

270. (1) **Application for Board of Reference.**—Upon receipt of an application for a Board of Reference, the Minister shall cause notice of the application to be sent by registered mail to the other party to the disagreement and shall within thirty days of sending the notice inquire into the disagreement and shall, within the same time,

(a) refuse to grant the Board of Reference; or
(b) grant the Board of Reference and appoint a judge to act as chair thereof.

(2) **Appointment.**—Where, under subsection (1), a judge is appointed after the expiry of thirty days referred to therein to act as chair of a Board of Reference, the failure to make the appointment within the thirty-day period does not invalidate the Board of Reference or the appointment of the judge as chair thereof, provided the Board of Reference is granted in accordance with subsection (1).

(3) **Naming of representatives.**—Upon appointing a judge to act as chair of a Board of Reference, the Minister shall cause notice thereof to be sent by registered mail to the board and teacher involved in the disagreement and the notice shall require each of them to name to the Board of Reference a representative who is not the teacher involved or a member of the board and to send or cause to be sent by hand or by registered mail to the Minister a notice of such nomination within twelve days of the sending of the notice by the Minister.

(4) **Failure to name representatives.**—If the applicant fails to comply with the requirements of subsection (3), the application shall be deemed to be abandoned and the Minister shall cause notice thereof to be sent by registered mail to the other party to the disagreement.

(5) **Idem.**—If the respondent fails to comply with the requirements of subsection (3), the Minister shall direct the continuance of the contract.

(6) **Failure of representatives to appear.**—If the representative of the board or the teacher, having been named, fails to appear at the hearing, the chair of the Board of Reference shall name a representative for the board or teacher, as the case may be.

(7) **Applicant deemed eligible.**—Where the Minister grants a Board of Reference, the applicant shall be deemed to have met the conditions precedent to the granting of a Board of Reference.

(8) **Death or withdrawal of representative.**—Where, after the hearing has commenced, the representative of the board or of the teacher dies, for any reason is unable to continue to

PART X — TEACHERS, PUPIL RECORDS AND EDUCATION NUMBERS   S. 273

act or withdraws from the Board of Reference, the other representative shall withdraw and the decision of the Board of Reference shall be made by the chair.

(9) **Death, etc., of chair before hearing.**—Where, before the hearing has commenced, the chair of a Board of Reference dies, disqualifies himself or herself, for any reason is unable to act or is prohibited from acting, the Minister shall appoint another judge to act as chair and the Board of Reference shall proceed in accordance with this Part except that for the purposes of section 271 the date of appointment of the chair is the date of appointment of the chair appointed to act under this section.

(10) **New Board of Reference after hearing commences.**—Where, after the hearing has commenced and before the chair of a Board of Reference reports to the Minister and to the parties,

(a) the chair dies, disqualifies himself or herself, for any reason is unable to continue as chair, or is prohibited from acting; or

(b) the Board of Reference is prohibited from acting or proceeding,

the Board of Reference is terminated and, where, within ninety days after the death, disqualification, inability to continue or prohibition referred to in clause (a) or (b), the person who applied for the Board of Reference requests the Minister in writing to grant another Board of Reference, the Minister may grant a new Board of Reference, in which case the provisions of this Part apply with necessary modifications except that the representatives named to the new Board of Reference shall not be the representatives named to the Board of Reference terminated under this subsection and the determination and direction of the costs under section 276 may include the costs, if any, incurred in respect of the Board of Reference terminated under subsection.

(11) **Procedure at new Board of Reference.**—Where a new Board of Reference is granted under subsection (10), the hearing shall proceed as if the hearing by the Board of Reference terminated under subsection (10) had not commenced.

[Repealed EQIA, 1997, s. 121(1).]

271. Place and time of hearing.—The chair of the Board of Reference shall, within thirty days of his or her appointment, and upon reasonable notice thereof to the parties, convene the Board of Reference in any appropriate and convenient court house or municipal or school building and at such time as the chair may appoint.

[Repealed 1997, c. 31, s. 121(1)]

272. Duty to inquire and powers of judge.—The Board of Reference shall inquire into the matter in dispute and for such purposes the chair has the powers of a commission under Part II of the *Public Inquiries Act*, which Part applies to such inquiry as if it were an inquiry under that Act.

[Repealed 1997, c. 31, s. 121(1)].

273. (1) **Direction of Board of Reference to report.**—A Board of Reference shall direct the continuance of the contract or the discontinuance of the contract.

(2) **Chair of Board of Reference to report.**—The chair of a Board of Reference shall, within seven days after,

(a) the application for the Board of Reference is withdrawn; or

(b) the matter in dispute has been settled by the parties to the Board of Reference; or

(c) the completion of the hearing and the receipt of any written submissions required by the chair,

report to the Minister and the parties the disposition of the application.

[Repealed 1997, c. 31, s. 121(1).]

274. New Board of Reference provided.—Where, pursuant to an application for judicial review under the *Judicial Review Procedure Act*, the report or the direction of a Board of Reference is set aside, the Minister may grant a new Board of Reference if the board or teacher applies therefor to the Minister by registered mail within fifteen days after the date of the order of the court setting aside the report or direction, and sections 267 to 277 apply with necessary modifications in respect of the new Board of Reference.

[Repealed 1997, c. 31, s. 121(1).]

275. (1) **Direction of Board.**—The direction of the Board of Reference under section 273 is binding upon the board and the teacher.

(2) **Failure to comply with direction of Board.**—If a board fails to comply with the direction of the Board of Reference under section 273, the Minister may direct that any portion of the amounts then or thereafter payable to the board under the authority of any Act of the Legislature shall not be paid to the board until it has complied with the direction.

(3) **Idem.**—If a teacher fails to comply with the direction of the Board of Reference under section 273, the Executive Committee of the Ontario College of Teachers may suspend the teacher's certificate of qualification and registration for such period as the Executive Committee considers advisable.

[Repealed 1997, c. 31, s. 121(1).]

276. Payment of costs.—Subject to the regulations made under section 277, the chair of the Board of Reference shall determine and direct the costs to be paid by either or both parties in the disagreement, and every such order may be enforced in the same manner as an order as to costs made in an action in the Ontario Court (General Division).

[Repealed 1997, c. 31, s. 121(1).]

277. Regulations.—The Lieutenant Governor in Council may make regulations,

(a) fixing the remuneration of members of Boards of Reference and defining, prescribing and limiting other items of expense, including traveling and living expenses, which shall be included in the costs of a Board of Reference;

(b) regulating the practice and procedure to be followed upon any reference; and

(c) respecting any matter necessary or advisable to carry out effectively the intent and purpose of sections 268 to 276.

[Repealed 1997, c. 31, s. 121(1).]

PART X.1

TEACHERS COLLECTIVE BARGAINING

Interpretation

277.1 (1) **Definitions.**—In this Part,

"designated bargaining agent" for a teachers' bargaining unit means the bargaining agent described in subsection 277.3 (2), 277.4 (3) or (4) as the bargaining agent for the unit; ("agent négociateur désigné")

"Part X.1 teacher" means a teacher employed by a board to teach but does not include a supervisory officer, a principal, a vice-principal or an instructor in a teacher-training institution; ("enseignant visé par la partie X.1")

"person" includes a designated bargaining agent and a trade union; ("personne")

"teachers' bargaining unit" means a bargaining unit described in subsection 277.3 (1), 277.4 (1) or (2) or 277.7 (1). ("unité de négociation denseignants")

(2) **Interpretation.**—Unless a contrary intention appears, expressions used in this Act relating to collective bargaining have the same meaning as in the *Labour Relations Act, 1995*.

Collective Bargaining

277.2 (1) *Labour Relations Act, 1995.*—The *Labour Relations Act, 1995* applies with necessary modifications with respect to boards, designated bargaining agents and Part X.1 teachers, except where otherwise provided or required by this Part.

(2) **Constitutional rights.**—The *Labour Relations Act, 1995* shall not be interpreted so as to adversely affect any right or privilege guaranteed by section 93 of the *Constitution Act, 1867* or by section 23 of the *Canadian Charter of Rights and Freedoms*.

(3) **Related employers.**—No person is entitled to make an application to the Ontario Labour Relations Board under subsection 1 (4) of the *Labour Relations Act, 1995* with respect to a board.

277.3 (1) **Teachers' bargaining units, district school boards.**—Each district school board has the following bargaining units:

1. One bargaining unit composed of every Part X.1 teacher, other than occasional teachers, who is assigned to one or more elementary schools or to perform duties in respect of such schools all or most of the time.
2. One bargaining unit composed of every Part X.1 teacher, who is an occasional teacher and who is on the board's roster of occasional teachers who may be assigned to an elementary school.
3. One bargaining unit composed of every Part X.1 teacher, other than occasional teachers, who is assigned to one or more secondary schools or to perform duties in respect of such schools all or most of the time.
4. One bargaining unit composed of every Part X.1 teacher who is an occasional teacher and who is one the board's roster of occasional teachers who may be assigned to a secondary school.

(2) **Designated bargaining agents.**—The following bargaining agents represent the corresponding bargaining units:

1. For each of the elementary school teachers' units at an English-language public district school board, The Federation of Women Teachers' Associations of Ontario and The Ontario Public School Teachers' Federation, acting jointly, are the bargaining agent.

2. For each of the secondary school teachers' units at an English-language public district school board, The Ontario Secondary School Teachers' Federation is the bargaining agent.
3. For every teachers' bargaining unit at an English-language separate district school board, The Ontario English Catholic Teachers' Association is the bargaining agent.
4. For every teachers' bargaining unit at a French-language district school board, l'Association des enseignantes et des enseignants franco-ontariens is the bargaining agent.

277.4 (1) **Teachers' bargaining units, school authorities.**—Every school authority (other than a board established under section 68) has the following bargaining units:
1. One bargaining unit composed of every Part X.1 teacher, other than occasional teachers, who is assigned to teach pupils enrolled in a French-language instructional unit or to perform duties in respect of such instructional units all or most of the time.
2. One bargaining unit composed of every Part X.1 teacher who is an occasional teacher and who is on the school authority's roster of occasional teachers who may be assigned to teach pupils enrolled in a French-language instructional unit.
3. One bargaining unit composed of every Part X.1 teacher, other than occasional teachers, who is not assigned to teach pupils enrolled in a French-language instructional unit or to perform duties in respect of such instructional units all or most of the time.
4. One bargaining unit composed of every Part X.1 teacher who is an occasional teacher and who is on the school authority's roster of occasional teachers who may be assigned to teach pupils other than those enrolled in a French-language instructional unit.

(2) **Same.**—Every board established under section 68 has the following bargaining units:
1. One bargaining unit composed of every Part X.1 teacher, other than occasional teachers, who is assigned to one or more elementary schools or to perform duties in respect of such schools all or most of the time.
2. One bargaining unit composed of every Part X.1 teacher who is an occasional teacher and who is on the board's roster of occasional teachers who may be assigned to an elementary school.
3. One bargaining unit composed of every Part X.1 teacher, other than occasional teachers, who is assigned to one or more secondary schools or to perform duties in respect of such schools all or most of the time.
4. One bargaining unit composed of every Part X.1 teacher who is an occasional teacher and who is on the board's roster of occasional teachers who may be assigned to a secondary school.

(3) **Designated bargaining agents.**—The bargaining agent for a bargaining unit is each of the following organizations, acting jointly, that, on December 31, 1997, had a branch affiliate representing a member of the bargaining unit for collective bargaining purposes under the *School Boards and Teachers Collective Negotiations Act*:
1. L'Association des enseignantes et des enseignants franco-ontariens.
2. The Federation of Women Teachers' Associations of Ontario.
3. The Ontario English Catholic Teachers' Association.

PART X.1 — TEACHERS COLLECTIVE BARGAINING   **S. 277.7**

    4.   The Ontario Public School Teachers' Federation
    5.   The Ontario Secondary School Teachers' Federation.

(4) **Same.**—Despite subsection (3), the bargaining agent for a bargaining unit described in paragraph 1 or 2 of subsection (1) is L'Association des enseignantes et des enseignants franco-ontariens.

277.5 (1) **Occasional teachers.**—An occasional teacher may be a member of more than one teachers' bargaining unit.

(2) **Same.**—An occasional teacher is on a board's roster of occasional teachers if he or she is on a list of occasional teachers maintained by a school operated by the board.

(3) **Same.**—Upon request, a board shall give a designated bargaining agent a copy of the roster and a principal of a school operated by the board shall give a designated bargaining agent a copy of the list of occasional teachers maintained by the school.

(4) **Transition.**—On January 1, 1998, occasional teachers who are members of a bargaining unit composed primarily of occasional teachers (other than a teachers' bargaining unit established under this Part) cease to be members of that unit.

(5) **Outstanding grievances.**—A grievance with respect to an occasional teacher that is not finally determined on January 1, 1998 is continued and the designated bargaining agent for the teachers' bargaining unit in which the teacher is a member represents the teacher for the purposes of the grievance, instead of the bargaining agent that represented the teacher on December 31, 1997.

277.6 (1) **Replacement of specified bargaining agents.**—On a day to be named by proclamation of the Lieutenant Governor, paragraph 1 of subsection 277.3 (2) is repealed and the following substituted:

    1.   For the elementary school teachers' unit at an English-language public district school board, the Elementary Teachers' Federation of Ontario is the bargaining agent.

(2) **Same.**—On the day named by proclamation under subsection (1), paragraphs 2 and 4 of subsection 277.4 (3) are repealed and the following substituted:

    1.   The Elementary Teachers' Federation of Ontario.

(3) **Same.**—On the day named by proclamation under subsection (1), the Elementary Teachers' Federation of Ontario replaces The Federation of Women Teachers' Associations of Ontario and the Ontario Public School Teachers' Federation as a party to all proceedings, negotiations and collective agreements under this Part.

[Editor's note: The day named by proclamation is July 1, 1998.]

277.7 (1) **Combined bargaining unit.**—One or more teachers' bargaining units (the ''predecessor bargaining units'') may be combined to establish one teachers' bargaining unit,

    (a) if the designated bargaining agent for each of the predecessor bargaining units is the same; and

    (b) if the employer and the designated bargaining agent agree.

(2) **Discontinuation of combined bargaining unit.**—If the employer and the designated bargaining agent agree, the combined bargaining unit may be discontinued and, in that case, the predecessor bargaining units are re-established.

277.8 (1) **Appropriate bargaining units.**—The teachers' bargaining units shall be deemed to be appropriate bargaining units.

(2) **Certification of bargaining agents.**—Each designated bargaining agent shall be deemed to be certified as the bargaining agent for the corresponding bargaining unit as specified in subsection 277.3 (2), 277.4 (3) or (4) or 277.7 (1).

(3) **Same.**—No trade union is entitled to apply for certification as the bargaining agent for a teachers' bargaining unit.

(4) **Same.**—No person is entitled to apply for a declaration that a designated bargaining agent no longer represents the members of a teachers' bargaining unit.

277.9 (1) **Joint negotiations.**—In negotiations for a collective agreement, two or more district school boards may act jointly as a party and two or more bargaining agents may act jointly as a party if the boards and the agents all agree to do so.

(2) **Same, school authorities.**—Subsection (1) applies with respect to school authorities, with necessary modifications.

(3) **Same, bargaining agents.**—In negotiations with one district school board or school authority, two or more bargaining agents may act jointly as a party.

(4) **Agreements.**—The joint parties may negotiate one agreement or may negotiate separate agreements for each board and bargaining unit.

277.10 Arbitration.—When resolving matters in dispute, an arbitrator or board of arbitration appointed under section 40 or 43 of the *Labour Relations Act, 1995* shall consider the factors and criteria set out in subsection 35 (1.1) of the *School Boards and Teachers Collective Negotiations Act* as it reads immediately before its repeal.

277.11 (1) **Election by principal, vice-principal.**—This section applies with respect to principals and vice-principals who are employed by an old board or a school authority on December 31, 1997 and become employed by a board after that date as a result of an order made by the Commission under section 58.2 or otherwise under a regulation authorized by clause 58.1 (2) (p).

(2) **Same.**—Before April 1, 1998, a principal or a vice-principal may elect in writing to resign his or her position as principal or vice-principal and to continue his or her employment with the board as a teacher.

(3) **Same.**—The election takes effect on August 31, 1998 or on such earlier date as the board and the principal or vice-principal may agree upon.

(4) **Same.**—When the principal or vice-principal becomes a member of a teachers' bargaining unit, his or seniority is determined as if he or she had been employed as a teacher when he or she was a principal or vice-principal.

(5) **Effect on collective agreement.**—The collective agreements that apply with respect to teachers in the bargaining unit in which the principal or vice-principal becomes a member are inoperative to the extent necessary to permit his or her assumption of a position within the bargaining unit.

(6) **Repeal.**—This section is repealed on January 1, 2001.

277.12 (1) **Education Relations Commission.**—Despite the repeal of section 59 of the *School Boards and Teachers Collective Negotiations Act*, the Education Relations Commission is continued for the purposes of,

PART X.1 — TEACHERS COLLECTIVE BARGAINING S. 277.13.1

(a) advising the Lieutenant Governor in Council when, in the opinion of the Commission, the continuation of a strike, lock-out or closing of a school or schools will place in jeopardy the successful completion of courses of study by the affected pupils;

(b) making determinations under clause 60(1)(f) of the *School Boards and Teachers Collective Negotiations Act* in respect of applications made but not finally determined before January 1, 1998; and

(c) compiling statistical information on the supply, distribution, professional activities and salaries of teachers.

(2) **Certain proceedings continued.**—A proceeding seeking a determination under clause 60 (1) (f) of the *School Boards and Teachers Collective Negotiations Act* that is commenced but not finally determined before January 1, 1998 is continued and, for that purpose, the *School Boards and Teachers Collective Negotiations Act*, as it read immediately before its repeal, continues to apply.

(3) **Provision of information.**—The Commission may request a board to provide information for the purpose described in clause (1) (c) and the board shall comply with the request within a reasonable period of time.

(4) **Same.**—The Commission may request a board to provide a copy of collective agreements to which the board is a party and the board shall comply with the request within a reasonable period of time.

(5) **Testimony in proceedings.**—Section 61 of the *School Boards and Teachers Collective Negotiations Act*, as it reads immediately before its repeal, continues to apply with respect to the members of the Commission acting under the authority of this section.

(6) **Repeal.**—Clause (1) (c) and subsections (3) and (4) are repealed on a day to be named by proclamation of the Lieutenant Governor.

(7) **Re-enactment.**—On a day to be named by proclamation of the Lieutenant Governor, this section is repealed and the following substituted:

277.12 (1) **Advice re jeopardy.**—The Lieutenant Governor in Council may, by order, appoint a person or entity to advise the Lieutenant Governor in Council when, in the opinion of the person or entity, the continuation of a strike, lockout or closing of a school or schools will place in jeopardy the successful completion of courses of study by the affected pupils.

(2) **Same.**—The Lieutenant Governor in Council may give the persons or entity such directions as the Lieutenant Governor in Council considers appropriate with respect to the discharge of his, her or its duties under the order.

277.13 Conflict.—In case of conflict, this Act and regulations made under it prevail over the provisions of a collective agreement.

277.13.1 (1) **Enforcement of Part X.1.**—This part may be enforced as if it formed part of the *Labour Relations Act, 1995* and, for that purpose, that Act shall be read as if it included this Part.

(2) **Same.**—Without limiting the generality of subsection (1),

(a) a designated bargaining agent shall be deemed to be a trade union for the purposes of the *Labour Relations Act, 1995*;

(b) sections 110 to 118 of the *Labour Relations Act, 1995* apply with necessary modifications with respect to anything the Ontario Labour Relations Board does under this Part;

(c) subsections 96 (4), (6) and (7) and sections 122 and 123 of the *Labour Relations Act, 1995* apply with necessary modifications with respect to proceedings before the Ontario Labour Relations Board and its decisions, determinations and orders;

(d) the Ontario Labour Relations Board has, in relation to any proceedings under this Part, the same powers to make rules to expedite proceedings as the Board has under subsection 110 (18) of the *Labour Relations Act, 1995*, and the rules apply despite anything in the *Statutory Powers Procedure Act* and they are not regulations within the meaning of the Regulations Act.

(3) **No panels.**—Where the Ontario Labour Relations Board is given authority to make a decision, determination or order under this Part, it shall be made,

(a) by the chair or, if the chair is absent or unable to act, by the alternate chair; or

(b) by a vice-chair selected by the chair in his or her sole discretion or, if the chair is absent or unable to act, selected by the alternate chair in his or her sole discretion.

(4) **Labour relations officers.**—The Ontario Labour Relations Board may authorize a labour relations officers to inquire into any matter that comes before it under this Part and to endeavour to settle any such matter.

(5) **Interim order.**—The Ontario Labour Relations Board may make interim orders with respect to a matter that is or will be the subject of a pending or intended proceeding.

(6) **Timing of decisions, etc.**—The Ontario Labour Relations Board shall make decisions, determinations and orders under this Part in an expeditious fashion.

(7) **Finality.**—A decision, determination or order made by the Ontario Labour Relations Board is final and binding for all purposes.

(8) **Repeal.**—Clause (2) (d) and subsection (3) are repealed on January 1, 2001.

277.13.2 (1) **Enforcement,** *Labour Relations Act, 1995.*—Clause 277.13.1 (2) (d) and subsections 277.13.1 (3) to (7) apply with necessary modifications with respect to the enforcement of the *Labour Relations Act, 1995* by the Ontario Labour Relations Board.

(2) **Repeal.**—This section is repealed on January 1, 2001.

The Transition from December 31, 1997 to January 1, 1998

277.14 (1) **Terms of employment, district school boards.**—This section applies with respect to teachers who,

(a) on December 31, 1997, are employed by an old board and are represented for collective bargaining purposes by a branch affiliate within the meaning of the *School Boards and Teachers Collective Negotiations Act*; and

(b) on January 1, 1998 are employed by a district school board as a result of an order made by the Commission under section 58.2 or otherwise under a regulation authorized by clause 58.1(2)(p).

(2) **Applicable collective agreements.**—On January 1, 1998, the district school board is bound by the following collective agreements as if it had been a party to them:

1. A collective agreement that applies with respect to a teacher on December 31, 1997.

PART X.1 — TEACHERS COLLECTIVE BARGAINING   S. 277.14

2. If no collective agreement applies with respect to a teacher on December 31, 1997, the most recent collective agreement that applied with respect to the teacher. The most recent agreement shall be deemed to have been amended to reflect alterations to terms and conditions that were made under the *School Boards and Teachers Collective Negotiations Act* after the agreement expired and before September 22, 1997.

3. Every collective agreement that applies with respect to teachers employed on December 31, 1997 at a particular school or school site that, on January 1, 1998, is within the board's jurisdiction.

4. If, on December 31, 1997, no collective agreement applies with respect to teachers described in paragraph 3, the most recent collective agreement that applied with respect to the teachers. The most recent agreement shall be deemed to have been amended to reflect alterations to terms and conditions that were made under the *School Boards and Teachers Collective Negotiations Act* after the agreement expired and before September 22, 1997.

(3) **Same, transfer between boards.**—If a teacher is transferred (by an order made by the Commission under section 58.2 or otherwise under a regulation authorized by clause 58.1 (2) (p)) from one district school board to another on or after January 1, 1998 and before September 1, 1998,

(a) the board from which the teacher is transferred ceases to be bound by the collective agreement described in paragraph 1 or 2 of subsection (2) with respect to the teacher when the transfer occurs: and

(b) the board to which the teacher is transferred is bound by the collective agreement described in paragraph 1 or 2 of subsection (2) with respect to the teacher when the transfer occurs as if it had been a party to the agreement.

(4) **Status of board.**—The district school board shall be deemed to be the employer under each collective agreement described in subsection (2) with respect to the teachers employed by the board.

(5) **Terms and conditions of employment.**—Subject to subsection (6), the terms and conditions of employment that apply on and after January 1, 1998 with respect to a teacher employed at a particular school or school site within the district school board's jurisdiction are determined,

(a) by the collective agreement that applies with respect to teachers employed in a similar position at that school or school site on December 31, 1997; or

(b) if no such agreement applies, by the most recent collective agreement that applied before December 31, 1997 (including the deemed amendments described in paragraph 2 of subsection (2)) with respect to teachers employed in a similar position at that school or school site.

(6) **Salary, benefits and seniority.**—The salary, benefits and seniority of a teacher on and after January 1, 1998 are determined,

(a) by the collective agreement that applies to him or her on December 31, 1997; or

(b) if no such agreement applies, by the most recent collective agreement (including the deemed amendments described in paragraph 4 subsection (2)) that applied to him or her before December 31, 1997.

S. 277.15   EDUCATION ACT

(7) **Seniority.**—Despite subsection (6), the following rules apply for the purpose of determination the seniority of teachers in a bargaining unit if two or more collective agreements apply with respect to teachers in the unit:

1. The board shall give the bargaining agent a proposed definition of seniority on or before March 31, 1998 to be used to determine the seniority of all teachers in the bargaining unit.
2. The bargaining agent shall respond to the proposal within five days after receiving it.
3. The parties may negotiate with a view to agreeing upon a definition of seniority.
4. If the parties do not wish to negotiate or if they do not agree upon a definition of seniority, either party may apply to the Ontario Labour Relations Board for an order specifying the definition of seniority to be used.
5. If, before May 1, 1998, the parties do not reach an agreement or the Ontario Labour Relations Board does not make an order, the definition of seniority first proposed by the board is the definition to be used to determine the seniority of all teachers in the bargaining unit before the first collective agreement for the bargaining unit commences.

(8) **Effect.**—The provisions of any applicable collective agreement are inoperative to the extent that they are inconsistent with the determination of seniority under subsection (7).

(9) **Termination of agreements.**—Every collective agreement continued in force by his section terminates on the earliest of,

(a) the day on which the first collective agreement for the applicable teachers' bargaining unit is entered into after December 31, 1997; or

(b) seven days after the day the Minister of Labour has released (or is deemed pursuant to subsection 122 (2) of the *Labour Relations Act, 1995* to have released) to the parties the report of a conciliation board or mediator; or

(c) fourteen days after the day the Minister of Labour has released (or is deemed pursuant to subsection 122 (2) of the *Labour Relations Act, 1995* to have released) to the parties a notice that he or she does not consider it advisable to appoint a conciliation board.

(10) **Definition.**—In subsections (2) and (5),

"collective agreement" means an agreement within the meaning of the *School Boards and Teachers Collective Negotiations Act* as the Act reads on December 31, 1997.

277.15 (1) **Terms of employment, school authorities.**—An agreement within the meaning of the *School Boards and Teachers Collective Negotiations Act* between a school authority and one or more branch affiliates that is in force on January 1, 1998 constitutes a collective agreement for the purposes of the *Labour Relations Act, 1995*.

(2) **Same.**—If there is no agreement described in subsection (1) in force on January 1, 1998, the terms and conditions of employment of the teachers shall be those determined by the most recent agreement that applied to them before that date, including any alterations to the terms and conditions made under the *School Boards and Teachers Collective Negotiations Act* after the agreement expired and before September 22, 1997.

(3) **Termination of agreements.**—Every collective agreement described in subsection (1) terminates on the earliest of,
  (a) the date specified in the agreement;
  (b) the day on which the first collective agreement for the applicable teachers' bargaining unit is entered into after December 31, 1997;
  (c) seven days after the day the Minister of Labour has released (or is deemed pursuant to subsection 122 (2) of the *Labour Relations Act, 1995* to have released) to the parties the report of a conciliation board or mediator; or
  (d) 14 days after the day the Minister of Labour has released (or is deemed pursuant to subsection 122 (2) of the *Labour Relations Act, 1995* to have released) to the parties a notice that he or she does not consider it advisable to appoint a conciliation board.

277.16 (1) **Outstanding grievances.**—This section applies with respect to a grievance under an agreement or an expired agreement made under the *School Boards and Teachers' Collective Negotiations Act* that arises before January 1, 1998 and is not finally determined by that date.

(2) **Same.**—If the grievance relates to a Part X.1 teacher, the grievance is continued and the designated bargaining agent for the teacher is the bargaining agent representing the teacher for the purposes of the grievance, instead of the branch affiliate that represented him or her before January 1, 1998.

277.17 (1) **Termination of arbitrations.**—Proceedings before an arbitrator or arbitration board that are commenced under Part IV of the *School Boards and Teachers Collective Negotiations Act* before January 1, 1998 and in which a final decision has not been issued and served before that date are terminated on January 1, 1998.

(2) **Termination of strikes, lock-outs.**—Every strike and lock-out commenced before January 1, 1998 under the *School Board and Teachers Collective Negotiations Act* is terminated on January 1, 1998.

(3) **Right to strike.**—Beginning on January 1, 1998, no Part X.1 teacher shall strike against a board unless the strike is authorized by the *Labour Relations Act, 1995*.

(4) **Right to lock-out.**—Beginning on January 1, 1998, no board shall lock out a Part X.1 teacher unless the lock-out is authorized by the *Labour Relations Act, 1995*.

(5) **Enforcement.**—Sections 81 to 85 and 100 to 108 of the *Labour Relations Act, 1995* apply with necessary modifications with respect to the enforcement of this section.

Teachers' First Collective Agreement After the Transition

277.18 (1) **First collective agreements.**—Sections 277.18 to 277.20 apply only with respect to negotiations for the first collective agreement entered into after December 31, 1997 for each teachers' bargaining unit and with respect to the agreement.

(2) **Same.**—Sections 68 (successor rights) and 69 (sale of a business) of the *Labour Relations Act, 1995* do not apply upon the occurrence of any of the following things before the first collective agreement for a bargaining unit commences:
  1. A transfer of teachers from an old board to a district school board.

2. A transfer of teachers between district school boards.

3. A transfer of assets or liabilities from an old board to a district school board.

4. A transfer of assets or liabilities between district school boards.

277.19 (1) **Notice of desire to bargain.**—On January 1, 1998, each designated bargaining agent shall be deemed to have given the appropriate board written notice under section 16 of the *Labour Relations Act, 1995* of its desire to bargain with a view to making a first collective agreement.

(2) **Same.**—On January 1, 1998, each designated bargaining agent shall be deemed to be entitled under the *Labour Relations Act, 1995* to give notice under section 16 of that Act.

277.20 (1) **Minimum term of agreement.**—Every first collective agreement must provide for a term of operation of at least two years.

(2) **Same.**—An agreement that does not provide for a term of operation of two years or longer shall be deemed to provide for a two-year term.

(3) **Effective date.**—Every first collective agreement must take effect no later than September 1, 1998.

277.21 Repeal.—Section 277.14 to 277.21 are repealed on January 1, 2001.

PART XI

SUPERVISORY OFFICERS

278. Qualifications of supervisory officers.—Every supervisory officer appointed under this Part shall hold the qualifications required by the regulations for a supervisory officer.

279. Supervisory officers and director of education: district school boards.—Every district school board shall, subject to the regulations, employ a supervisory officer as director of education and such other supervisory officers as it considers necessary to supervise all aspects of the programs under its jurisdiction.

1997, c. 31, s. 123.

280. (1) **Appointment of director of education: school authorities.**—Two or more public school authorities may with the approval of the Minister agree to appoint a supervisory officer as director of education to supervise all aspects of the programs under their jurisdictions.

(2) **Same.**—Two or more Roman Catholic school authorities may with the approval of the Minister agree to appoint a supervisory officer as director of education to supervise all aspects of the programs under their jurisdictions.

(3) **Abolition of position.**—A school authority that appoints a director of education with the approval of the Minister shall not abolish the position of director of education without the approval of the Minister.

1997, c. 31, s. 123.

281. (1) [Repealed 1993, c. 31, s. 123.]

(2) [Repealed 1997, c. 31, s. 123.]

(3) [Repealed 1997, c. 31, s. 123.]

282. (1) [Repealed 1997, c. 31, s. 123.]

(2) [Repealed 1997, c. 31, s. 123.]

283. (1) **Chief executive officer.**—A board shall not appoint or employ a person as a director of education unless the person is a supervisory officer who qualified as such as a teacher.

(1.1) **Same.**—A director of education is the chief education officer and the chief executive officer of the board by which he or she is employed.

(2) **Idem.**—The chief executive officer of a board shall, within policies established by the board, develop and maintain an effective organization and the programs required to implement such policies.

(3) **General report of chief executive officer.**—At the first meeting in December of each year, the chief executive officer of a board shall submit to the board a report in a format approved by the Minister on the action he or she has taken during the preceding 12 months under subsection (2) and a copy of such report shall be submitted to the Minister on or before the 31st day of January next following.

1997, c. 31, s. 124.

284. (1) **Supervisory officers: school authorities.**—Subject to subsection (2), every school authority shall appoint one or more English-speaking supervisory officers for schools and classes where English is the language of instruction and one or more French-speaking supervisory officers for schools and classes where French is the language of instruction.

(2) **Agreements.**—Subsection (1) does not apply where a school authority has entered into an agreement under subsection (3) or (4).

(3) **Same.**—With the approval of the Minister, a school authority may enter into an agreement with another board to obtain the services of an English-speaking or French-speaking supervisory officer appointed by the other board.

(4) **Same.**—A school authority may enter into an agreement with the Minister to obtain the services of an English-speaking or French-speaking supervisory officer appointed by the Minister.

1993, c. 11, s. 38; 1997, c. 31, s. 125.

284.1 [Repealed 1997, c. 31, s. 125.]

285. (1) **Responsibility of supervisory officer.**—A board with a supervisory officer,

(a) shall, subject to the regulations, designate the title and area of responsibility of the supervisory officer; and

(b) may assign to the supervisory officer such administrative duties, in addition to those prescribed in section 286 and the regulations, as the board considers expedient.

(2) **Confirmation by Minister.**—No person shall be appointed as a supervisory officer by a board until notice in writing of the proposed appointment and the area of responsibility to be assigned has been given to the Minister and the Minister has confirmed that the person to be appointed is eligible for the position.

1993, c. 11, s. 40.

286. (1) **Duties of supervisory officers.**—Subject to the policies and guidelines established under paragraph 3.4 of subsection 8(1) and subject to the regulations, a board or the Minister shall assign the following duties to its or the Minister's supervisory officer or officers,

(a) **assist teachers.**—to bring about improvement in the quality of education by assisting teachers in their practice;
(b) **co-operate with boards.**—to assist and co-operate with boards to the end that the schools may best serve the needs of the pupils;
(c) **visit schools.**—to visit schools and classrooms as the Minister may direct and, where the supervisory officer has been appointed by a board, as the board may direct;
(d) **prepare reports.**—to prepare a report of a visit to a school or classroom when required by the Minister and, where the supervisory officer has been appointed by a board, when required by the board and to give to a teacher referred to in any such report a copy of the portion of the report that refers to the teacher;
(e) **Acts and regulations.**—to ensure that the schools under his or her jurisdiction are conducted in accordance with this Act and the regulations;
(f) **annual report to Minister.**—to make a general annual report as to the performance of his or her duties and the condition of the schools in his or her area of jurisdiction when required by the Minister and, where the supervisory officer has been appointed by a board, when required by the board;
(g) **report to M.O.H.**—to report to the appropriate medical officer of health any case in which the school buildings or premises are found to be in an unsanitary condition;
(h) **report to the Minister.**—to furnish the Minister with information respecting any school in his or her area of jurisdiction whenever required to do so;
(i) **supervise business.**—to supervise the business functions of the board; and
(j) **supervise buildings and property.**—to supervise the use and maintenance of the buildings and property of the board.

(2) **Responsibility to Minister.**—Every supervisory officer appointed by the Minister is responsible to the Minister for the performance of his or her duties.

(3) **Responsibility to board.**—Every supervisory officer appointed by a board is responsible to the board through the chief executive officer for the performance of the duties assigned to the supervisory officer by the board.

(4) **Full-time position.**—Except as otherwise provided by this Act or the regulations, a supervisory officer shall not, without the approval of the Minister, hold any other office, have any other employment or follow any other profession or calling, during his or her tenure as a supervisory officer.

(5) **Access to books and records, etc.**—A provincial supervisory officer or a person designated by the Minister shall have access, as required by the Minister, to any school and to the books and records of a board or a school.

1997, c. 31, s. 126.

287. (1) **Suspension or dismissal of supervisory officer by board.**—A supervisory officer appointed by a board may be suspended or dismissed by the board, in accordance with the regulations, for neglect of duty, misconduct or inefficiency.

(2) **Notice re suspension or dismissal.**—Where a board suspends or dismisses a supervisory officer, the board shall forthwith notify in writing the supervisory officer and the Minister of the suspension or dismissal and the reasons therefor.

287.1 (1) **Principals, vice-principals.**—A principal or a vice-principal may perform the duties of a teacher despite any provision in a collective agreement.

(2) **Regulations.**—The Lieutenant Governor in Council may make regulations governing terms and conditions of employment for principals and for vice-principals.

(3) **Same.**—A regulation may establish different requirements for different classes of principal or vice-principal.

1997, c. 31, s.1 27.

287.2 (1) **Employment terms, principals, etc.**—This section applies with respect to principals and vice-principals who are employed by an old board or a school authority on December 31, 1997 and become employed by a board after that date as a result of an order made by the Commission under section 58.2 or otherwise under a regulation authorized by clause 58.1(2)(p).

(2) **Same.**—The terms and conditions of employment for a principal or vice-principal that are in effect on December 31, 1997 continue in effect from January 1, 1998 until August 31, 1998 or until such earlier date as may be agreed upon in writing by him or her and the board that becomes his or her employer.

(3) **Exceptions.**—Terms and conditions of employment relating to the following matters do not apply with respect to the principal or vice-principal beginning on January 1, 1998:

1. Membership in The Ontario Teachers' Federation or in an affiliate or a branch affiliate.
2. Seniority.
3. Grievances under a collective agreement or an expired collective agreement.
4. Recall and redundancy rights.

(4) **Repeal.**—This section is repealed on September 1, 2000.

1997, c. 31, s. 127.

PART XII

LANGUAGE OF INSTRUCTION

Provisions Relating to District School Boards

288. French-language district school boards.—A French-language district school board shall only operate classes, groups of classes and schools that are French-language instructional units.

1993, c. 27, Sch.; 1997, c. 31, s. 128.

289. English-language district school boards.—An English-language district school board shall not operate classes, groups of classes or schools that are French-language instructional units.

1997, c. 31, s. 128.

Provisions Relating to School Authorities

290. (1) **Application.**—This section does not apply to a board established under section 67.

(2) **Right to instruction in French-language instructional unit: school authorities.**—Every French-speaking person who is qualified under this Act to be a resident pupil of a school authority has the right to receive elementary school instruction in a French-language instructional unit operated or provided by the school authority.

(3) **Duty of school authority to provide French-language instructional unit.**—Every school authority that has one or more resident pupils who notify the school authority that they wish to exercise their right to receive elementary school instruction in a French-language instructional unit shall establish and operate one or more French-language instructional units for those pupils or shall enter into an agreement with another board to enable those pupils to receive instruction in a French-language instructional unit operated by the other board.

(4) **Meals, lodging and transportation.**—A school authority that provides a French-language instructional unit for elementary school instruction by means of an agreement with another board shall provide to each French-speaking person who is a resident pupil of the school authority for whom French-language instruction is provided under the agreement and who resides with the parent or other person who has lawful custody of the pupil more than 24 kilometres from the French-language instructional unit,

(a) an allowance payable monthly in an amount set by the school authority for meals and lodging for each day of attendance as certified by the principal for the French-language instructional unit and for transportation once a week from the pupil's residence to the lodging and return; or

(b) daily transportation in a manner determined by the school authority from the pupil's residence to the French-language instructional unit and return, where the parent or other person who has lawful custody of the pupil elects to have daily transportation.

(5) **English-language schools or classes.**—Where a school authority operates or provides one or more elementary French-language instructional units, a resident pupil of the school authority has the right to receive elementary school instruction in the English language and subsections (2), (3) and (4) apply with necessary modifications in respect of the resident pupil and the school authority.

1997, c. 31, s. 128.

291. (1) **Right to instruction in French-language instructional unit: s. 67 boards.**—Every French-speaking person who is qualified under this Act to be a resident pupil of a school authority established under section 67 has the right to receive secondary school instruction in a French-language instructional unit operated or provided by the school authority.

(2) **Duty of s. 67 boards to provide French-language instructional unit.**—Every school authority established under section 67 that has one or more resident pupils who notify the school authority that they wish to exercise their right to receive secondary school instruction in a French-language instructional unit shall establish and operate one or more French-language instructional units for those pupils or shall enter into an agreement with another board to enable those pupils to receive instruction in a French-language instructional unit operated by the other board.

(3) **Meals, lodging and transportation.**—A school authority established under section 67 that provides a French-language instructional unit for secondary school instruction by means of an agreement with another board shall provide to each French-speaking person who is

qualified to be a resident pupil of the school authority for whom French-language instruction is provided under the agreement and who resides with the parent or other person who has lawful custody of the pupil more than 24 kilometres from the French-language instructional unit,

(a) an allowance payable monthly in an amount set by the school authority for meals and lodging for each day of attendance as certified by the principal for the French-language instructional unit and for transportation once a week from the pupil's residence to the lodging and return; or

(b) daily transportation in a manner determined by the school authority from the pupil's residence to the French-language instructional unit and return, where the parent or other person who has lawful custody of the pupil elects to have daily transportation.

(4) **English-language classes where French-language school or classes established.**—Where a school authority established under section 67 operates or provides one or more secondary French-language instructional units, a resident pupil of the school authority has the right to receive secondary school instruction in the English language and subsections (1) to (3) apply with necessary modifications in respect of the resident pupil and the school authority.

1997, c. 31, s. 128.

Provisions Relating to District School Boards and School Authorities

292. (1) **English as a subject of instruction.**—English may be a subject of instruction in any grade in a French-language instructional unit.

(2) **Same, grades 5, 6, 7 and 8.**—English shall be a subject of instruction in grades 5, 6, 7 and 8 in every French-language instructional unit.

1997, c. 31, s. 128.

293. (1) **Admission of pupils other than French-speaking persons, district school boards.**—A French-language district school board, on the request of the parent of a pupil who is not a French-speaking person, or of a person who has lawful custody of a pupil who is not a French-speaking person, or of a pupil who is an adult and is not a French-speaking person, may admit the pupil to a school of the board if the admission is approved by majority vote of an admissions committee appointed by the board and composed of,

(a) the principal of the school to which admission is requested;

(b) a teacher of the board; and

(c) a supervisory officer employed by the board.

(2) **Same, school authorities.**—A school authority that operates a French-language instructional unit, on the request of the parent of a pupil who is not a French-speaking person, or of a person who has lawful custody of a pupil who is not a French-speaking person, or of a pupil who is an adult and is not a French-speaking person, may admit the pupil to the French-language instructional unit if the admission is approved by majority vote of an admissions committee appointed by the school authority and composed of,

(a) the principal of the school to which admission is requested;

(b) a teacher who uses the French-language in instruction in the school; and

(c) a French-speaking supervisory officer employed by the school authority or arranged for in accordance with subsection (3).

(3) **Where school authority has no French-speaking supervisory officer.**— Where a school authority does not employ a French-speaking supervisory officer, it shall arrange for a French-speaking supervisory officer employed by another board or by the Minister to serve as a member of the admissions committee.

1997, c. 31, s. 128.

French-Language Rights Holder Groups

294. (1) In this section and in sections 295 to 299,

"commission" means the Languages of Instruction Commission of Ontario continued under section 295; ("Commission")

"French-language rights holder", in relation to a school authority, means a person who is entitled to vote at an election of members of the school authority and who has the right under subsection 23(1) or (2), without regard to subsection 23(3), of the *Canadian Charter of Rights and Freedoms* to have his or her children receive their primary and secondary school instruction in the French-language in Ontario. ("titulaire des droits liés au français")

(2) **Proposals of French-language rights holders groups.**—A group of 10 French-language rights holders of a school authority may develop a proposal designed to meet the educational and cultural needs of the French-speaking persons who are resident pupils of the school authority and of the French-speaking community served by the school authority.

(3) **Same.**—A proposal under this section may relate to,

(a) the provision of suitable sites, accommodation and equipment;
(b) the establishment, operation and management of French-language instructional units;
(c) the establishment of or alteration of the area of jurisdiction of a French-language district school board;
(d) the use of the French-language and of the English language in French-language instructional units;
(e) the use of Quebec Sign Language as a language of instruction;
(f) the recruitment and appointment of the required teaching, supervisory and administrative personnel;
(g) the establishment of the course of study and the use of textbooks;
(h) the development and establishment of special education programs;
(i) the establishment of attendance areas for French-language instructional units;
(j) the provision of transportation for pupils;
(k) the entering into agreements with other boards in respect of the provision of instruction in the French-language and supervisory and consultative services;
(l) the provision of board, lodging, and transportation for pupils;
(m) the development and establishment of adult education programs;
(n) the use of any facility and means necessary to meet the educational and cultural needs of the French-speaking community;
(o) the provision of summer school programs; and
(p) any other matter pertaining to French-language education for French-speaking persons.

(4) **Consideration of proposals by school authority.**—The school authority shall consider any proposal that is developed by a French-language rights holder group under this section and submitted to the school authority in writing.

(5) **Same.**—The school authority shall not refuse to approve the proposal without having given the French-language rights holder group an opportunity to be heard by the school authority.

(6) **Same.**—For the purposes of subsection (5), a group shall name one of its members to speak for the group.

(7) **Approval of proposal under clause (3)(c).**—Where a school authority approves a proposal made under clause (3)(c), it shall give notice of the approval to the Minister, together with a recommendation that a regulation be made under subsection 58.1(2) implementing the proposal.

(8) **Notice of refusal.**—A school authority that refuses to approve a proposal shall, within 30 days after receiving the proposal of the French-language rights holder group, forward to the group written reasons for the refusal.

(9) **Referral by group to Languages of Instruction Commission.**—On receipt of a refusal and the reasons for it under subsection (8), the French-language rights holder group may refer the matter to the Commission by sending to the Commission,

(a) a written request for consideration of the matter:
(b) the written proposal of the group; and
(c) the written reasons of the school authority for its refusal.

(10) **Same.**—A French-language rights holder group that refers a matter to the Commission shall send to the school authority a copy of the written request for consideration referred to in clause (9)(a).

1997, c. 31, s. 128.

Languages of Instruction Commission of Ontario

295. (1) **Commission continued.**—The Languages of Instruction Commission of Ontario is continued under the name Languages of Instruction Commission of Ontario in English and Commission des langues d'enseignement de l'Ontario in French and shall be composed of five members appointed by the Lieutenant Governor in Council, at least two of whom shall be French-speaking and at least two of whom shall be English-speaking, and one of the members shall be appointed as chair.

(2) **Term, reappointment and remuneration.**—Members of the Comission shall hold office for a term of one, two or three years as may be determined from time to time by the Lieutenant Governor in Council, may be reappointed and shall be paid such remuneration as is determined by the Lieutenant Governor in Council.

(3) **Vacancies.**—Where a vacancy occurs in the membership of the Commission, the vacancy may be filled for the unexpired portion of the term of the person whose office has become vacant.

(4) **Commission is responsible to the Minister.**—The Commission is responsible to the Minister for its operation and shall be assisted by such employees in the public service of

Ontario as the Minister may assign for the purpose and may, as required from time to time, obtain the services of a lawyer.

(5) **Quorum.**—A quorum consists of three members of whom at least one shall be French-speaking and one English-speaking.

(6) **Recommendation.**—A recommendation of the Commission under section 297 or 298 requires the approval of at least a majority of the members of the Commission.

(7) **Duties of Commission.**—The Commission shall consider matters referred to it by a French-language rights holders group under section 294 or by the Minister under subsection (9).

(8) **Person to speak for group.**—The group shall name one of its members to speak for it.

(9) **Referral to Commission by Minister.**—The Minister may refer to the Commission any matter relating to instruction in the French-language or, where the pupils of a school authority who receive instruction in the English language are a minority of the pupils of the school authority, any matter relating to instruction in the English language.

(10) **Commission response to referral under s. 294.**—When a matter is referred to the Commission by a French-language rights holders group, the Commission shall,

(a) promptly appoint one or more mediators where it considers that the furtherance of the matter may be conducive to meeting the educational and cultural needs of the French-speaking or the English-speaking community; or

(b) take no further action where it considers that the furtherance of the matter is not conducive to meeting the educational and cultural needs of the French-speaking or the English-speaking community.

(11) **Commission response to referral under subs. (9).**—When a matter is referred to the Commission by the Minister, the Commission shall promptly appoint one or more mediators.

(12) **Notice where no further action by Commission.**—Where the Commission takes no further action on a referral from a French-language rights holder group, it shall promptly send notice in writing of its decision, with written reasons, to the school authority, the Minister and the person named under subsection (8).

(13) **Notice where mediator appointed.**—Where the Commission makes an appointment under subsection (10) or (11), it shall give to each party the name and address of each mediator and of each party.

(14) **Parties.**—The following are the parties to the mediation:

1. The Minister.
2. The school authority.
3. Where the referral was from a French-language rights holder group, the person named under subsection (8).
4. Any other person specified by the Commission.

1997, c. 31, s. 128.

296. (1) **Remuneration.**—Mediators shall be paid such remuneration as the Lieutenant Governor in Council may determine.

(2) **Who not eligible as mediator.**—A mediator shall not be a member of the Commission.

(3) **Duties of mediator.**—The mediator or mediators shall, after inquiring into the matter referred for mediation and conferring with the parties, endeavour to bring about an agreement and shall, within 21 days of being appointed, report to the Commission the agreement that has been reached, or the failure to bring about an agreement.

(4) **Extension of period of mediation.**—The period referred to in subsection (3) may be extended by the Commission or by agreement of the parties to the mediation.

1997, c. 31, s. 128.

297. (1) **Duties of Commission.**—Where the report of the mediator or mediators to the Commission indicates failure to bring about an agreement, the Commission shall consider and inquire into all pertinent aspects of the matter referred to mediation and shall, within 21 days of its receipt of the report, recommend in writing a course of action that it considers appropriate to settle the matter and send copies of its recommendation to each party to the mediation.

(2) **Resolution by school authority.**—Except where implementation of the recommendation would require a regulation under subsection 58.1 (2), within 30 days of the receipt by the school authority of the recommendation of the Commission, the school authority shall resolve either to implement the recommendation or not to implement the recommendation.

(3) **Notice of resolution.**—The school authority shall give written notice of the resolution to each party.

(4) **Where school authority resolves not to implement recommendation.**—A school authority that resolves not to implement the recommendation shall also give written reasons for the resolution to each party.

(5) **Time for notices and reasons.**—The school authority shall give the notices and reasons within the 30-day period mentioned in subsection (2).

1993, c. 41, s. 4; 1997, c. 31, s. 128.

298. (1) **Second resolution.**—A school authority that resolves not to implement the recommendation of the Commission may rescind the resolution and resolve to implement the recommendation.

(2) **Conflict with by-law.**—In the event of a conflict between subsection (1) and a by-law of the school authority, subsection (1) prevails.

(3) **Time for second resolution.**—A school authority must act under subsection (1) within 60 days after receiving the recommendation of the Commission.

(4) **Notice.**—A school authority that acts under subsection (1) shall give written notice of its action to each party.

1997, c. 31, s. 128.

299. (1) **Reconsideration by Commission.**—Where a school authority does not resolve to implement the recommendation of the Commission within the period of time mentioned in section 297 or 298, as the case requires, the Commission shall reconsider the matter and shall make a written report and recommendation to the Minister in respect of the matter.

(2) **Order by Minister.**—The Minister shall consider the report and recommendation of the Commission under subsection (1) and shall make such order to the school authority or the

Commission, or both, or take such other action, to deal with the matter as the Minister considers appropriate in the circumstances.

(3) **Report and recommendation not binding on Minister.**—The report and recommendation of the Commission are not binding on the Minister, and the Minister is not required to give to any person an opportunity to make submissions or to be heard before making an order under subsection (2).

(4) **Enforcement of order.**—An order by the Minister under subsection (2), exclusive of the reasons, if any, therefor may be filed in the Ontario Court (General Division).

(5) **Same.**—An order filed under subsection (4) shall be entered in the same way as a judgment or order of the Ontario Court (General Division) and is enforceable as an order of that court.

(6) **Service of order.**—An order by the Minister under subsection (2),
- (a) to a school authority is effective according to its terms when a copy is served on the secretary of the school authority; and
- (b) to the Commission is effective according to its terms when a copy is served on the chair of the Commission.

1993, c. 41, s. 4; 1997, c. 31, s. 128.

300. [Repealed 1997, c. 31, s. 128.]
301. [Repealed 1997, c. 31, s. 128.]
302. [Repealed 1997, c. 31, s. 128.]
303. [Repealed 1997, c. 31, s. 128.]
304. [Repealed 1997, c. 31, s. 128.]
305. [Repealed 1997, c. 31, s. 128.]
306. [Repealed 1997, c. 31, s. 128.]
307. [Repealed 1997, c. 31, s. 128.]
308. [Repealed 1997, c. 31, s. 128.]

PART XIII

[Repealed 1997, c. 31, s. 129.]

PART XIV

MATTERS RELATED TO 1997–1998 SCHOOL SYSTEM REFORMS

1997, c. 3, s. 6; 1997, c. 31, s. 130

327. [Repealed 1997, c. 31, s. 131.]
328. [Repealed 1997, c. 31, s. 131.]
329. [Repealed 1997, c. 31, s. 131.]
330. [Repealed 1997, c. 31, s. 131.]

331. [Repealed 1997, c. 31, s. 131.]

332. [Repealed 1997, c. 31, s. 131.]

333. [Repealed 1997, c. 31, s. 131.]

Education Improvement Commission

334. (1) **Education Improvement Commission.**—A commission to be known in English as the Education Improvement Commission and in French as Commission d'amelioration de l'education is established.

(2) **Composition.**—The Commission shall consist of not fewer than five and not more than seven members, appointed by the Lieutenant Governor in Council.

(3) **Chair and vice-chair.**—The Lieutenant Governor in Council shall designate a chair and a vice-chair or, in the alternative, two chairs from among the members of the Commission.

(4) **Term of office.**—The members of the Commission shall hold office during the pleasure of the Lieutenant Governor in Council.

(4.1) **Same.**—The term of office of a member of the Commission shall end on or before December 31, 2000.

(5) **Authority of vice-chair.**—If a vice-chair is designated under subsection (3) and the chair is absent or unable to act or there is a vacancy in the office of chair, the vice-chair shall act as and have all the powers of the chair.

(6) **Authority of co-chairs.**—Subject to Subsection (7), if two chairs are designated under subsection (3), the chairs may agree on how the powers and duties of the chair shall be shared.

(7) **Same.**—The Minister may give directions regarding how the powers and duties of the chair shall be shared and the chairs shall comply with the directions.

(8) **Quorum.**—A majority of the members of the Commission constitutes a quorum.

(9) **Remuneration and expenses.**—The members of the Commission shall be paid the remuneration fixed by the Lieutenant Governor in Council and the reasonable expenses incurred in the course of their duties under this Part.

(10) **Staff and accommodation.**—The Ministry shall provide the Commission with such staff and accommodation as the Minister considers necessary for the purposes of the Commission.

(11) **Expert assistance.**—Within its budget, the Commission may retain expert services to assist it in its work.

(12) [Repealed 1997, c. 31, s. 133(2).]

(13) [Repealed 1997, c. 31, s. 133(2).]

(14) [Repealed 1997, c. 31, s. 133(2).]

(15) **Court proceedings.**—The Commission, in its name, may be a party to any court proceeding.

(16) **Annual report.**—The Commission shall make an annual report to the Minister and the Minister shall submit the report to the Lieutenant Governor in Council and shall then lay the report before the Assembly if it is in session or, if not, at the next session.

(17) **Additional reports.**—In addition to its annual report, the Commission may report to the Minister at any time and shall report to the Minister in such form and manner, with such information and at such times as the Minister requires.

1997, c. 3, s. 8; 1997, c. 31, ss. 132, 133.

335. (1) [Repealed 1997, c. 31, s. 134(1).]

(2) **Function of Commission.**—The Education Improvement Commission shall oversee the transition to the new system of education governance in Ontario.

(3) **Same.**—Without limiting the generality of subsection (2), for the purpose of overseeing the transition to the new system of education governance in Ontario, the Commission shall,

(a) [Repealed 1997, c. 31, s. 134(2).]
(b) [Repealed 1997, c. 31, s. 134(2).]
(c) identify issues relating to the establishment of French-language district school boards that should, in the opinion of the Commission, be addressed and consider and make recommendations to the Minister on those issues;
(d) identify issues that should, in the opinion of the Commission, be addressed, relating to representation on district school boards and school authorities of the interests of members of bands in respect of which there is agreement under this Act to provide instruction to pupils who are Indians within the meaning of the *Indian Act (Canada)*, and consider and make recommendations to the Minister on those issues;
(e) identify other key issues that should, in the opinion of the Commission, be addressed and consider and make recommendations to the Minister on those issues;
(f) consider, conduct research, facilitate discussion and make recommendations to the Minister on how to facilitate, where appropriate, the out-sourcing of non-instructional services by district school boards;
(g) consider, conduct research, facilitate discussion and make recommendations to the Minister on the feasibility of strengthening the role of school councils over time;
(h) consider, conduct research, facilitate discussion and make recommendations to the Minister on the feasibility of increasing parental involvement in education governance;
(i) [Repealed 1997, c. 31, s. 134(3).]
(j) [Repealed 1997, c. 31, s. 134(4).]
(k) [Repealed 1997, c. 31, s. 134(5).]
(l) [Repealed 1997, c. 31, s. 134(5).]
(m) [Repealed 1997, c. 31, s. 134(6).]
(n) consider and make recommendations to the Minister on any issue referred to the Commission by the Minister;
(o) perform any other duties assigned or delegated to the Commission by the regulations.

1997, c. 3, s. 8; 1997, c. 31, s. 134.

336. [Repealed 1997, c. 31, s. 135.]

337. [Repealed 1997, c. 31, s. 135.]

338. [Repealed 1997, c. 31, s. 135.]

339. [Repealed 1997, c. 31, s. 135.]

340. [Repealed 1997, c. 31, s. 135.]

341. [Repealed 1997, c. 31, s. 135.]

342. [Repealed 1997, c. 31, s. 135.]

343. [Repealed 1997, c. 31, s. 135.]

344. (1) **Non-application of *Regulations Act*.**—The *Regulations Act* does not apply to anything done by the Education Improvement Commission under this Act.

(2) **Non-application of *SPPA*.**—The *Statutory Powers Procedure Act* does not apply to the Education Improvement Commission.

1997, c. 3, s. 8; 1997, c. 31, s. 136.

345. [Repealed 1997, c. 31, s. 137.]

346. (1) **Protection from liability.**—No proceeding for damages shall be brought against,

(a) the Education Improvement Commission or a member or delegate of it;

(b) a member of a committee established by the Education Improvement Commission under this Act;

(c) a person retained by or acting under the direction of the Education Improvement Commission or a committee referred to in clause (b),

for an act done in good faith in the execution or intended execution of any duty or authority related directly or indirectly, to the carrying out of the mandate of the Education Improvement Commission under this Act or for any alleged neglect or default in the execution in good faith of such duty or authority.

(2) **Same.**—Subsection (1) also applies in respect of an employee or agent of an old board or a district school board acting under the direction of,

(a) a member of the Education Improvement Commission or of a committee referred to in clause (1) (b): or

(b) the old board or district school board.

(3) **Vicarious liability.**—Despite subsections 5 (2) and (4) of the *Proceedings Against the Crown Act,* subsections (1) and (2) do not relieve any person, other than one mentioned in those subsections, of any liability to which the person would otherwise be subject.

(4) **Protection from liability: duty, authority relating to elections.**—No proceeding for damages shall be brought against any person or against the Education Improvement Commission for an act done in good faith in the execution or intended execution of any duty or authority under the *Municipal Elections Act, 1996,* the *Assessment Act* or this Part relating to elections to a district school board, to an old board or to a school authority, or for any alleged neglect or default in the execution in good faith of such duty or authority.

(5) **Vicarious liability.**—Despite subsections 5(2) and (4) of the Proceedings Against the Crown Act, subsection (4) does not relieve the Crown of any liability to which it would otherwise be subject.

(6) **[Repealed 1997, c. 31, s. 138(3).]**

(7) **Same.**—A proceeding for damages against any person for an act or alleged neglect or default to which subsection (1) or (4) applies that is brought before the *Fewer School Boards*

Act, 1997 receives Royal Assent shall be deemed to have been dismissed without costs on the day that Act receives Royal Assent.

(8) **Same.**—A decision in a proceeding described in subsection (7) is unenforceable.

1997, c. 3, s. 8; 1997, c .31, s. 138.

347. (1) **Personal information.**—A person who obtains under sections 335 to 343 of this Act, a those sections read immediately before the *Education Quality Improvement Act, 1997* received Royal Assent information that is personal information as defined in the *Freedom of Information and Protection of Privacy Act* shall use and disclose it only for the purposes of Part II.2 or this Part.

(2) **Example.**—Without limiting the generality of subsection (1), the information that may be used or disclosed under that subsection includes information relating to,

(a) a financial transaction or proposed financial transaction of an old board or a district school board;

(b) anything done or proposed to be done in connection with the finances of an old board or a district school board by a member, employee or agent of the old board or district school board.

(3) **Conflict with *FIPPA, MFIPPA*.**—Section 335 applies despite anything in the *Freedom of Information and Protection of Privacy Act* or the *Municipal Freedom of Information and Protection of Privacy Act*.

(4) **Offence.**—A person who wilfully uses or discloses, except for the purposes of Part II.2 or this Part, information that the person obtained under sections 335 to 343 of this Act, as those sections read immediately before the *Education Quality Improvement Act, 1997* received Royal Assent and that is personal information as defined in the *Freedom of Information and Protection of Privacy Act* is guilty of an offence and on conviction is liable to a fine of not more than $2,000.

1997, c. 3, ss. 8, 9; 1997, c. 31, s. 139.

348. [Repealed 1997, c. 31, s. 140.]

349. [Repealed 1997, c. 31, s. 140.]

350. When Education Improvement Commission power may be exercised.— Where a regulation made under section 58.2 confers a power on the Education Improvement Commission to do a thing, that power may be exercised at any time after the making of the regulation but an instrument made under the power does not come into operation until subsection 58.2 (1) and the regulation come into operation.

1997, c. 31, s. 141.

Transitional Authority of District School Boards

351. (1) **Authority of district school boards before 1998.**—For the purposes of this section, a district school board shall be deemed to be constituted as a body corporate when a majority of its members have been elected or appointed.

(2) **Same.**—A district school board has the power and duty to comply with the directions of the Education Improvement Commission under this section.

(3) **Directions.**—The Education Improvement Commission may issue the directions that it considers appropriate respecting organizational meetings of district school boards before January 1, 1998, including but not limited to directions respecting the business to be conducted at the meetings and the procedures to be followed at the meetings.

(4) **Same.**—A direction under subsection (3) may be general or particular.

(5) **Same.**—The following are examples of business in respect of which the Education Improvement Commission may give directions under subsection (3):
1. The adoption of by-laws.
2. The appointment of temporary and permanent staff and officers.
3. The appointment of committees.
4. Developing, together with other district school boards, recommendations and agreements to be proposed to the Education Improvement Commission, respecting the holding in trust, transfer and vesting of assets, including but not limited to real and personal property, the transfer of liabilities and the transfer of employees of old boards to and among district school boards.

(6) **Non-application of *Regulations Act*.**—A direction of the Education Improvement Commission under subsection (3) is not a regulation within the meaning of the *Regulations Act*.

(7) **Limitation.**—The authority of the Education Improvement Commission to give directions under this section respecting the business to be conducted and the procedures to be followed at organizational meetings does not include authority to give directions respecting the substance of any decision about any business to be conducted at the meetings.

(8) **Purpose.**—The purpose of this section is to facilitate the organization of the affairs of district school boards in order to permit an orderly assumption of powers and duties by them.

(9) **Application of s. 207.**—Section 207 applies, with necessary modifications, to a meeting under this section.

(10) **Conflict with section 208.**—In the event of a conflict between section 208 and a direction under this section, the direction under this section prevails.

(11) **Declaration under section 209.**—A meeting held in accordance with a direction under this section is a meeting for the purposes of determining when the requirements of section 209 must be met.

1997, c. 31, s. 141.

351.1 Transition: membership on old board.—Section 40 of the *Municipal Act* does not prevent a person who holds office on an old board from being a candidate for, being elected to and holding an office election to which is governed by the *Municipal Elections Act, 1996*.

1997, c. 31, s. 142.

REGULATION 283
CALCULATION OF AMOUNT OF RESERVE OR REDUCTION IN REQUIREMENT RESULTING FROM STRIKE OR LOCK-OUT
R.R.O. 1990, Reg. 283

[Revoked O. Reg. 486/98.]

REGULATION 284
CONDITIONS FOR EXTENDED FUNDING
R.R.O. 1990, Reg. 284

[*Editor's note: Although not revoked at the time of publication, this regulation was not included because it refers to sections of the Education Act that have been repealed.*]

REGULATION 285
CONTINUING EDUCATION
R.R.O. 1990, Reg. 285; Fr. version O. Reg. 441/92, as am. O. Reg. 96/95; 97/96

PART I

1. (1) The following classes or courses provided by a board other than as part of the day school program on an instructional day as defined in Regulation 304 of Revised Regulations of Ontario, 1990 (School Year and School Holidays) are continuing education courses or classes for the purpose of paragraph 31 of subsection 171(1) of the Act and the regulations:

1. A class or course that is designed to develop or to improve the basic literacy and numeracy skills of adults to a level that does not exceed the grade 8 level of competency.
2. A class or course in English or French for adults whose first language learned and still understood is neither English nor French and that is not a class in which a pupil may earn a credit in English or French as a second language.
3. A class or course in citizenship and, where necessary, in language instruction in the English or the French language for persons admitted to Canada as permanent residents under the *Immigration Act* (Canada).
4. A class or course in driver education in which a pupil may not earn a credit.
5. A class or course in the primary or junior division or in the first two years of the intermediate division in which a language other than English or French is the subject of instruction.
6. A class or course in which a pupil may earn a credit.
7. A class for the purpose of extending the knowledge of adults, for the purpose of improving the skills of adults, for the specific interest of adults or for the enhancement of the knowledge or skills of elementary or secondary school pupils beyond that expected or required of the pupils as part of the regular program in an elementary or secondary school,
    i. for which the board charges registration fees to persons taking the class and the fees are not calculated in accordance with the regulations, or
    ii. in which the work required for its successful completion is not acceptable to the Minister as partial fulfilment of the requirements for a diploma granted by the Minister.

(1.1) A continuing education course or class referred to in subsection (1) may be provided by a board at any time of the day or evening.

(2) The following classes or courses provided by a board between the hours of 8.00 a.m. and 5.00 p.m. that start after the completion of one school year and that end before the next following school year are continuing education classes or courses for the purposes of paragraph 31 of subsection 171(1) of the Act and the regulations:

1. A class or course for remedial purposes for pupils who are enrolled in an elementary school operated by the board and that is,
    i. a class or course that the board is required or authorized to provide during the

school day to pupils enrolled in elementary schools and, in the school year immediately preceding commencement of the class or course, was a class or course that was provided to its elementary school pupils, and
   ii. approved by the Minister.
2. A class or course that is for trainable retarded pupils who are enrolled in an elementary school or school or class for trainable retarded pupils operated by the board.
3. A class or course in which a pupil may earn a credit. O. Reg. 97/96

2. (1) Subject to subsection (2) and Part II, a board that establishes continuing education courses or classes shall determine the courses to be given in each of its continuing education classes, the number of times that each continuing education course or class is held per week, the length of time per session of each continuing education course or class and the dates and the time of the day or evening upon which each continuing education course or class is given.

(2) An elementary school board may offer continuing education courses and classes only in courses of study that the board is authorized or required to provide in its day school program in the primary and junior divisions and the intermediate division.

(3) An elementary school board may, subject to Part II, offer as a subject a language other than English or French in the primary and junior divisions and in the first two years of the intermediate division in its continuing education courses and classes.

(4) The principal of a school shall be the principal of the continuing education courses and classes in the school unless the board appoints as principal thereof another person who holds the appropriate principal's qualifications set out in section 9 of Regulation 298 of Revised Regulations of Ontario, 1990 (Operation of Schools — General).

(5) A school site that was used for school purposes and a school site that is used as a school during the school year may be used for a continuing education course or class.

(6) Two or more boards may jointly establish continuing education courses and classes in a school or schools operated by one or more of the boards concerned and determine where such courses and classes shall be conducted.

3. (1) A valid certificate of qualification or a letter of standing is required to be held by a person,
   (a) who provides the classroom teaching in a continuing education course or class referred to in paragraph 6 of subsection 1(1) or in subsection 1(2); or
   (b) who is employed in respect of the development or co-ordination of the program of which a continuing education course or class referred to in clause (a) is a part.

(2) A board may employ a person who is not a teacher to provide instruction in a continuing education course or class, other than a continuing education course or class referred to in paragraph 6 of subsection 1(1) or in subsection 1(2), if the person holds qualifications acceptable to the board for such employment.

PART II

4. In this Part,

"board", other than in section 6, means a board of education, public school board, Roman Catholic separate school board or Protestant separate school board, The Metropolitan

Toronto French-Language School Council and the public sector and the Roman Catholic sector of The Ottawa-Carleton French-language School Board;

"commencement date" means the last school day of the month of January or September, as the case requires;

"parent" includes guardian;

"program" means a program of instruction in a continuing education course or class referred to in paragraph 5 of subsection 1(1);

"qualified person", in respect of a board, means a person who is enrolled or is eligible to be enrolled in an elementary school, a kindergarten or a junior kindergarten operated by the board, and who is not enrolled or is not eligible to be enrolled in a secondary school operated by the board, but if the board does not operate a secondary school, does not include a person who is enrolled or is eligible to be enrolled in the last two years of the intermediate division.

5. (1) If a board is not providing a program and receives from parents written requests on behalf of twenty-five or more qualified persons of the board for the establishment of a program, the board shall establish the program requested.

(2) If a board is providing one or more programs and the board receives from parents written requests on behalf of twenty-five or more qualified persons of the board for the establishment of a program that the board is not providing, the board shall establish the program requested.

(3) Despite subsections (1) and (2), a board may enter into an agreement with another board for the other board to provide the program requested.

(4) A program established under this section shall start not later than the commencement date that first occurs ninety days or more after the date of the request.

(5) A board that establishes a program under this section shall provide a class or course in the program for all qualified persons of the board who wish to attend if at least ten qualified persons of the board attend the first scheduled class or course of the program.

(6) A program provided by a board shall be provided throughout the school year in which the program was established so long as a person attends the class or course in the program.

(7) If a board, other than a Roman Catholic separate school board or the Roman Catholic sector of The Ottawa-Carleton French-language School Board, establishes a program under this section, it shall admit to a class or course in the program a qualified person in respect of another board that is not a Roman Catholic separate school board or the Roman Catholic sector of The Ottawa-Carleton French-language School Board.

(8) If a Roman Catholic separate school board establishes a program under this section, it shall admit to a class or course in the program a qualified person in respect of another Roman Catholic separate school board or the Roman Catholic sector of The Ottawa-Carleton French-language School Board.

(9) If the Roman Catholic sector of The Ottawa-Carleton French-language School Board establishes a program under this section, it shall admit to a class or course in the program a qualified person in respect of a Roman Catholic separate school board.

(10) A board may admit to a class or course in a program a person who is enrolled or eligible to be enrolled in an elementary school, a kindergarten or a junior kindergarten operated

by a board and the person is not enrolled or eligible to be enrolled in a secondary school operated by a board, despite the fact that the board is not required to admit the person under this section.

6. (1) In this section,

"board" means the Conseil des écoles publiques d'Ottawa-Carleton, the Conseil des écoles catholiques de langue française de la région d'Ottawa-Carleton, the Conseil des écoles séparées catholiques de langue française de Prescott-Russell and The Metropolitan Toronto French-Language School Council; ("conseil")

"French-speaking person" means a child of a person who has the right under subsection 23(1) or (2), without regard to subsection 23(3), of the *Canadian Charter of Rights and Freedoms* to have his or her children receive their primary and secondary school instruction in the French language in Ontario.

(2) Despite section 5, a board shall not admit to a program that it operates or provides for another board a person who is not a French-speaking person.

(3) Subsection (2) does not apply to a person who is enrolled in an elementary school, a kindergarten or a junior kindergarten operated by the board or another board. O. Reg. 96/95

7. (1) Subject to subsections (2) and (3), a qualified person of a board may attend one or more programs provided in one or more languages by one or more boards.

(2) The maximum period in each week during the school year that a qualified person of a board may attend a program in any one language is two and one-half hours.

(3) The maximum period during a day that falls after the completion of one school year and before the commencement of the next following school year that a qualified person of a board may attend a program in any one language is two and one-half hours.

8. A board that provides a program before the end of the instructional program of a school day may do so only in a school site that is used for school purposes by the board during the school day.

9. (1) A board that provides a program following the end of the instructional program of a school day or on a day that is not a school day may provide a class or course in the program in a place that is not a school site.

(2) If a board conducts a class or course in a program in a place that is not used as a school site during the school day, the time that the class begins shall be not earlier than the time at which the instructional program of the board ends.

(3) A board that conducts a class or course in a program in a place that is not used as a school site during the school day shall allow an interval of time between the end of the instructional program and the beginning of the class sufficient to permit pupils enrolled in the instructional program to travel to the place in which the class is being conducted.

10. (1) A board may discontinue a program at the end of the school year if the number of qualified persons of the board enrolled in courses or classes provided under the program is fewer than twenty-five at the conclusion of the school year in which the program is provided.

(2) A board that proposes to discontinue a program shall advise any person who participated in the program to the end of the school year that the program will be discontinued and that the program may be re-established in accordance with this Part.

REGULATION 286
COUNTY COMBINED SEPARATE SCHOOL ZONES
R.R.O. 1990, Reg. 286; Fr. version O. Reg. 377/92

[Editor's note: Although not revoked at the time of publication, this regulation refers to matters that are no longer relevant after the Education Quality Improvement Act, 1997.]

REGULATION 287
DESIGNATION OF SCHOOL DIVISIONS
R.R.O. 1990, Reg. 287, as am. O. Reg. 527/92; 413/93; 94/95

[Editor's note: Although not revoked at the time of publication, this regulation refers to matters that are no longer relevant after the Education Quality Improvement Act, 1997.]

REGULATION 288
DESIGNATION OF SUPPORT STAFF
R.R.O. 1990, Reg. 288

[Editor's note: Although not revoked at the time of publication, this regulation deals with matters that can no longer arise.]

REGULATION 289
DESIGNATION OF TEACHERS
R.R.O. 1990, Reg. 289

[Editor's note: Although not revoked at the time of publication, this regulation deals with matters that can longer arise.]

REGULATION 290
DISTRICT COMBINED SEPARATE SCHOOL ZONES
R.R.O. 1990, Reg. 290, as am. O. Reg. 526/92; 730/92; 412/93

[Editor's note: Although not revoked at the time of publication, this regulation refers to matters that are no longer relevant after the Education Quality Improvement Act, 1997.]

REGULATION 291
DISTRICT SCHOOL AREAS
R.R.O. 1990, Reg. 291

The Airy and Sabine District School Area

1. The Airy District School Area and The Sabine District School Area are combined into one district school area to be known as The Airy and Sabine District School Area.

The Caramat District School Area

2. The lands described in the following Schedule are formed into a district school area to be known as The Caramat District School Area:

Schedule

All and singular that tract of land in the Compact Rural Community of Caramat and surrounding area in the Territorial District of Thunder Bay more particularly described as follows:

Beginning at a point distant 2 miles measured north astronomically from the intersection of the northeasterly limit of the Canadian National Railway with the northerly limit of Location JK 320;

Thence west astronomically 2 miles;

Thence south astronomically 4 miles;

Thence east astronomically 4 miles;

Thence north astronomically 4 miles;

Thence west astronomically 2 miles, more or less, to the place of beginning.

The Collins District School Area

3. The lands described in the following Schedule are formed into a district school area to be known as The Collins District School Area:

Schedule

All and singular that tract of land situate in the Territorial District of Thunder Bay, having an area of one square mile and bounded as follows:

On the north by a line drawn due east and west astronomically through a point distant one half-mile measured due north astronomically from mile board 21 on the main line of the Canadian National Railway at the hamlet of Collins; on the east by a line drawn due north and south astronomically through a point distant one half-mile due east astronomically from the said mile board; on the south by a line drawn due east and west astronomically through a point distant one half-mile due south astronomically from the said mile board; and on the west by a line drawn due north and south astronomically through a point distant one half-mile due west astronomically from the said mile board.

The Connell and Ponsford District School Area

4. The part of the Improvement District of Pickle Lake in the Patricia Portion of the Territorial District of Kenora that is not within The Connell and Ponsford District School Area is added to such district school area.

The Kilkenny District School Area

5. The lands in the geographic Township of Kilkenny in the Territorial District of Thunder Bay described in the following Schedule that comprise The Kilkenny District School Area are altered by excluding therefrom the lands comprising the Rocky Bay Indian Reserve Number 1 and by adding thereto the portion of the geographic Township of Kilkenny not included in the Schedule:

Schedule

In the geographic Township of Kilkenny in the Territorial District of Thunder Bay, being that area originally comprising school section No. 1 MacDiarmid and being an area five miles square whose boundaries begin at a point one mile south from north latitude 49 degrees, 30 minutes and one mile west from 88 degrees west longitude and that extends five miles due west, then five miles due south, then five miles due east and then five miles due north to the point of beginning.

The McCullagh District School Area

6. The portion of The Connell and Ponsford District School Area that is in the geographic Township of McCullagh in the Patricia Portion of the Territorial District of Kenora, being all that portion of such district school area that is not in the Improvement District of Pickle Lake, is detached from The Connell and Ponsford District School Area and formed into The McCullagh District School Area.

The Moose Factory Island District School Area

7. The lands described in the following Schedule are formed into a district school area to be known as The Moose Factory Island District School Area:

Schedule

The area in the Territorial District of Cochrane consisting of the islands in the Moose River that are situate in their entirety north of the line formed by the projection easterly of the southerly boundary of the geographic Township of Horden to the westerly limit of Indian Reserve No. 68, except Indian Reserve No. 1 on Moose Factory Island.

The Moosonee District School Area

8. The following parts of the Territorial District of Cochrane are added to The Moosonee District School Area:
1. The geographic Township of Caron.
2. The parts of the geographic townships of Horden and Moose that are not in The Moosonee District School Area, except the parts of such geographic townships that are composed of islands and parts of islands in the Moose River.

The Northern District School Area

9. The Allanwater District School Area, The Armstrong District School Area, The Auden District School Area, The Ferland District School Area and The Savant Lake District School Area are combined into one district school area to be known as The Northern District School Area.

The Slate Falls District School Area

10. The lands described in the following Schedule are formed into a district school area to be known as The Slate Falls District School Area:

Schedule

All and singular that tract of land situate in the Patricia Portion of the Territorial District of Kenora, more particularly described as follows:

Beginning at the place of intersection of the Ninth Base Line and the Fourth Meridian; thence easterly along the Ninth Base Line a distance of six miles to a point; thence northerly and parallel to the Fourth Meridian a distance of six miles to a point; thence westerly and parallel to the Ninth Base Line to a point in the Fourth Meridian; thence southerly along the Fourth Meridian to the place of beginning.

The Sturgeon Lake District School Area

11. The lands described in the following Schedule are formed into a district school area to be known as The Sturgeon Lake District School Area:

Schedule

All and singular that tract of land situate in the Territorial District of Kenora being within an area four miles in width lying on both sides of the centre line of secondary highway No. 599 and within two miles of and measured at right angles to that portion of the said centre line extending from the easterly boundary of the Township of Ignace northeasterly a distance of forty-five miles.

The Summer Beaver District School Area

12. The lands described in the following Schedule are formed into a district school area to be known as The Summer Beaver District School Area:

Schedule

All and singular that tract of land situate in the Patricia Portion of the Territorial District of Kenora being within a radius of two miles from a point having a latitude of 52° 45' North and a longitude of 88° 30' West.

REGULATION 293
FEES FOR TRANSCRIPTS AND STATEMENTS OF STANDING AND FOR DUPLICATES OF DIPLOMAS, CERTIFICATES AND LETTERS OF STANDING

R.R.O. 1990, Reg. 293; as am. O. Reg. 341/92; 522/93

1. (1) The fee for a transcript of standing, or for a duplicate of a diploma or certificate, obtained in Ontario by a pupil is $20.

(2) The fee set out in subsection (1) shall be adjusted as follows:

1. As of October 1, 1993, to $21.
2. As of July 1, 1994, to $22.
3. As of July 1, 1995, to $23.
4. As of July 1, 1996, to $24. O. Reg. 341/92, s. 1; O. Reg. 522/93, s. 1.

2. (1) The fee for a duplicate of an Ontario Teacher's Certificate is $37.

(2) The fee set out in subsection (1) shall be adjusted as follows:

1. As of October 1, 1993, to $39.
2. As of July 1, 1994, to $41
3. As of July 1, 1995, to $43.
4. As of July 1, 1996, to $45. O. Reg. 341/92, s. 2; O. Reg. 522/93, s. 2.

3. (1) The fee for a duplicate of a letter of standing, or of a certificate of qualification as a teacher other than an Ontario Teacher's Certificate, is $20.

(2) The fee set out in subsection (1) shall be adjusted as follows:

1. As of October 1, 1993, to $21.
2. As of July 1, 1994, to $22.
3. As of July 1, 1995, to $23.
4. As of July 1, 1996, to $24. O. Reg. 341/92, s. 3; O. Reg. 522/93, s. 3.

4. (1) The fee for the preparation by the Ministry, on the request of a teacher, of a statement of standing obtained, and a description of courses completed, at a teacher's education institution in Ontario is $20.

(2) The fee set out in subsection (1) shall be adjusted as follows:

1. As of October 1, 1993, to $21.
2. As of July 1, 1994, to $22.
3. As of July 1, 1995, to $23.
4. As of July 1, 1996, to $24. O. Reg. 341/92, s. 4; O. Reg. 522/93, s. 4.

REGULATION 294
THE JAMES BAY LOWLANDS SECONDARY SCHOOL BOARD
R.R.O. 1990, Reg. 294, as am. O. Reg. 394/97; 474/97

1. In this Regulation,

"board" means The James Bay Lowlands Secondary School Board;

"elector", in respect of an area for which one or more members of the board are to be elected, means a Canadian citizen of the full age of 18 years who is,

(a) resident in the area,

(b) an owner or tenant or residential property in the area, or

(c) the spouse of an owner or tenant of residential property in the area;

"equalized assessment" [Revoked O. Reg. 474/97, s. 1.]

"residential property" [Revoked O. Reg. 474/97, s. 1.] O. Reg. 394/97, s. 1; O. Reg. 474/97, s. 1.

2. The James Bay Lowlands Secondary School Board is continued and has jurisdiction in The James Bay Lowlands Secondary School District described in the Schedule.

3. (1) On and after December 1, 1997, the board shall be composed of three members of whom,

(a) two shall be elected by and from among the electors in respect of the mainland portion of the geographic townships of Caron, Horden and Moose; and

(b) one shall be elected by and from among the electors in respect of the islands in the Moose River that form part of the secondary school district, not including the portion of Moose Factory Island that is an Indian Reserve.

(2) Subsection (1) applies for the purposes of elections to the board in November, 1997. O. Reg. 394/97, s. 2.

4. (1) In addition to the disqualifications set out in the Act, a person is not qualified to be elected or to act as a member of the board who is a member of, or the secretary-treasurer of, The Moosonee Development Area Board.

(2) A member of the board who ceases to be an elector in respect of the area for which he or she was elected is thereupon disqualified to act as a member of the board.

5. (1) Meetings shall be held in the year 1982 and in every third year thereafter on such date in the month of November and at such places and times as the board may determine for the purpose of electing the members of the board referred to in section 3.

(2) The term of office of a member of the board shall be three years commencing on the 1st day of December next following his or her election to the board.

(3) Where a vacancy occurs from any cause in the office of an elected member of the board, the remaining members shall, subject to section 225 of the Act, forthwith hold a new election to fill the vacancy in the manner provided by this Regulation for holding an election of the board, except that the election shall be held only in respect of the area for which the vacancy occurs.

(4) At least six days before a meeting under this section, the secretary of the board shall post notice of the meeting in two or more of the most prominent places in the area from which one or more members are to be elected at the meeting and shall advertise the meeting in such other manner as the board considers expedient.

(5) A meeting under this section shall be conducted in the manner determined by the electors in respect of the area for which the meeting is held who are present at the meeting, by a presiding officer selected by such electors, but the election of the member or members of the board shall be by ballot, and the minutes of the meeting shall be recorded by a secretary who shall,

    (a) in the case of the meeting to elect the members provided for in clause 3(1)(a), be the secretary of The Moosonee Development Area Board;

    (b) in the case of the meeting to elect the member provided for in clause 3(1)(b), be the secretary of The Moose Factory Island District School Area Board.

    (c) [Revoked O. Reg. 394/97, s. 3]

(6) If objection is made to the right of a person to vote at a meeting under this section or section 8, the presiding officer shall require the person to make the following declaration:

I .... declare and affirm that,

1. I am of the full age of eighteen years.
2. I am a Canadian citizen.
3. I have a right to vote at this election (*or* on the question submitted to this meeting).

and after making such declaration, the person making it may vote.

(7) Subsections 92(9), (10), (12), (13), (17), (18), (19), (20) and (22) of the Act apply with necessary modifications to a meeting under this Regulation. O. Reg. 394/97, s. 3.

6. (1) The sum required by the board for secondary school purposes in each year shall be apportioned between the Moosonee Development Area and the remainder of the James Bay Lowlands Secondary School District in the ratio of the equalized assessment of the property rateable for secondary school purposes in the Moosonee Development Area to the equalized assessment of such property in the remainder of such secondary school district.

(2) For the purpose of subsection (1), the Moosonee Development Area is deemed to be a municipality and the portion of The James Bay Lowlands Secondary School District that is not in the Moosonee Development Area is deemed to be a locality.

7. [Revoked O. Reg. 474/97.]

8. (1) A special meeting of the electors of the secondary school district shall be called by the secretary of the board when directed by the board or upon the request in writing of five such electors, by posting, at least six days before the meeting, notice of the meeting in three or more of the most prominent places in the secondary school district and such notice shall include the date, time, place and objects of the meeting, and the meeting shall be advertised in such other manner as the board considers expedient.

(2) A special meeting under this section shall be conducted in the manner determined by the electors of the secondary school district who are present at the meeting, by a presiding officer selected by such electors and the minutes of the meeting shall be recorded by the secretary of the board.

Sched. REGULATIONS UNDER THE EDUCATION ACT

Schedule
The James Bay Lowlands Secondary School District

That part of the Territorial District of Cochrane comprised of the geographic townships of Caron, Horden and Moose and the unsurveyed territory consisting of the islands in the Moose River that are situate in their entirety north of a line formed by the projection easterly of the southerly boundary of the geographic Township of Horden to the westerly limit of Indian Reserve No. 68.

REGULATION 295
THE NORTHERN DISTRICT SCHOOL AREA BOARD
R.R.O. 1990, Reg. 295, as am. O. Reg. 14/96; 186/97; 395/97; 473/97

1. In this Regulation,

"Board" means The Northern District School Area Board;

"elector", in respect of an area for which one or more members of the board are to be elected, means a Canadian citizen of the full age of 18 years who is,

(a) resident in the area,

(b) the owner or tenant of residential property in the area, or

(c) the spouse of an owner or tenant of residential property in the area;

"residential property" [Revoked O. Reg. 473/97, s. 1] O. Reg. 186/97, s. 1; O. Reg. 395/97, s. 1; O. Reg. 473/97, s. 1.

2. The Board is continued with jurisdiction in The Northern District School Area set out in section 9 of Regulation 291 of Revised Regulations of Ontario, 1990.

3. (1) The Board shall be composed of eight members,

(a) one of whom shall be elected by and from the electors of the school section formerly known as The Allanwater District School Area;

(b) three of whom shall be elected by and from the electors of the school section formerly known as The Armstrong District School Area;

(c) one of whom shall be elected by and from the electors of the school section formerly known as The Auden District School Area;

(d) one of whom shall be elected by and from the electors of the school section formerly known as The Ferland District School Area; and

(e) two of whom shall be elected by and from the electors of the school section formerly known as The Savant Lake District School Area.

(2) Where a member of the Board ceases to be an elector in respect of the area for which he or she was elected he or she ceases to be qualified to act as a member of the Board.

4. (1) Meetings of the Board shall be held in the year 1982 and in every third year thereafter on such date in the month of November and, subject to subsection (2), at such places and times as the Board may determine for the purpose of electing the members of the Board referred to in subsection 3(1).

(2) The members of the Board shall be elected at a general meeting of the electors of each former district school area held separately within each former district school area.

(3) The term of office of a member of the Board shall be three years commencing on the 1st day of December next following the member's election to the Board.

(4) Where a vacancy occurs from any cause in the office of a member of the Board, the remaining members shall, subject to section 225 of the Act, forthwith hold an election to fill the vacancy in the manner provided by this Regulation for holding an election of the Board, except that the election shall be held only in respect of the area for which the vacancy occurs.

(4.1) If the electors at an election under subsection (4) fail to elect a member to fill the vacancy, and if a majority of elected members of the Board remain in office, the remaining members shall forthwith elect a person who is an elector for any area within the jurisdiction of the Board to fill the vacancy.

(4.2) Subsections 38(3), (4), and (5) of the *Municipal Elections Act, 1996* apply to an election under subsection (4.1). O. Reg. 186/97, s. 2.

(5) At least six days before holding a meeting under this section, the secretary of the Board shall post a notice of the meeting in two or more prominent places in the area from which a member or members is or are to be elected and shall, where instructed by the Board, advertise the meeting in such other manner as the Board considers expedient.

(6) A meeting under this section shall be conducted by a presiding officer selected by the electors in respect of the area for which the meeting is held and who are present at the meeting, in such manner as the electors determine, provided that the election of the member or members of the Board shall be by ballot and the minutes of the meeting shall be recorded by a secretary selected by such electors.

(7) An elector is entitled to vote for as many candidates for the Board in his or her area as there are Board members to be elected in such area, but only once for each candidate.

(8) If objection is made to the right of a person to vote at a meeting under this section, the presiding officer shall require the person to make the declaration set out in subsection 62(7) of the Act and after making such declaration, the person making it is entitled to vote.

(9) Subsections 92(9), (10), (12), (13), (17), (18), (19), (20) and (22) of the Act apply with necessary modifications to a meeting under this Regulation. O. Reg. 14/96

REGULATION 296
ONTARIO SCHOOLS FOR THE BLIND AND THE DEAF
R.R.O. 1990, Reg. 296

Interpretation

1. In this Regulation,

"applicant" means an applicant for admission to a School;

"bursar" means the business administrator of a School;

"Director" means the Executive Director of the Regional Services Division of the Ministry;

"Indian" means,
  (a) an Indian as defined in the *Indian Act* (Canada), or
  (b) an Eskimo,

who is not qualified to be a resident pupil of a board;

"parent" includes a guardian;

"residence counsellor" means a person employed as a residence counsellor in a School;

"School" means a school referred to in section 2;

"Superintendent" means the Superintendent of a School.

Designations

2. (1) The Ontario School for the Blind, Brantford is designated as The W. Ross Macdonald School.

(2) The Ontario School for the Deaf, Belleville is designated as The Sir James Whitney School.

(3) The Ontario School for the Deaf, Milton is designated as The Ernest C. Drury School.

(4) The Ontario School for the Deaf, London is designated as The Robarts School.

Admissions

3. (1) Where an applicant who is not an Indian, or the parent of such applicant, submits to the Superintendent evidence satisfactory to the Superintendent that,
  (a) the applicant will be under the age of twenty-one years on the first day of the school year for which he or she seeks admission;
  (b) because of a visual or an auditory handicap, or both, as certified by a legally qualified medical practitioner, the applicant is in need of a special educational program in the School;
  (c) if the applicant is under eighteen years of age, the applicant's parent is a resident of Ontario; and
  (d) if the applicant is eighteen years of age or over, the applicant is a resident of Ontario,

the Superintendent shall, subject to subsection (2) and subsection 8(1), admit the applicant to the School.

(2) An applicant who is qualified to be a resident pupil of a board that operates a day class for the hearing impaired that would be appropriate to the applicant shall not be admitted to an Ontario School for the Deaf except where in the opinion of the Minister the admission is in the best interests of the applicant.

(3) Where an applicant who is not an Indian and who will be twenty-one years of age or over on the first day of the school year for which he or she seeks admission submits to the Superintendent evidence satisfactory to the Superintendent under clauses (1)(b) and (d), and the Minister approves the admission of the applicant, the Superintendent shall admit the applicant to the School.

4. Where the minister of education for a province of Canada other than Ontario,
- (a) requests admission for an applicant,
    - (i) whose parent resides in that province or who, being eighteen years of age or over, himself or herself resides in that province,
    - (ii) to whom clause 3(1)(b) applies, and
    - (iii) who is not inadmissible under subsection 8(1); and
- (b) agrees to pay such fees as are payable for the instruction and maintenance of the applicant, and the Minister approves the admission of the applicant, the Superintendent shall admit the applicant.

5. Where the Minister of Indian Affairs and Northern Development for Canada,
- (a) requests admission for an applicant who,
    - (i) is an Indian to whom clause 3(1)(b) applies; and
    - (ii) is not inadmissible under subsection 8(1); and
- (b) agrees to pay such fees as are payable for the instruction and maintenance of the applicant,

and the Minister approves the admission of the applicant, the Superintendent shall admit the applicant.

6. Where an applicant who is not an Indian and who,
- (a) has not attained the age of eighteen years and whose parent is not a resident of any province of Canada; or
- (b) has attained the age of eighteen years and is not a resident of any province of Canada,

submits to the Superintendent evidence satisfactory to the Superintendent under clause 3(1)(b), the Superintendent shall, where the Minister approves the admission of the applicant, admit the applicant to the School upon payment of a fee, determined by the Minister, that shall be not greater than the fee payable under section 10 or 11, as the case may be.

7. Where an applicant is eligible for admission under section 3, 4, 5 or 6, the Superintendent may admit him or her at any time during the school year provided that accommodation and a program are available.

8. (1) An applicant shall not be admitted to a School if he or she is unable to profit from instruction in a program at the School.

(2) Where, in respect of an applicant, doubt exists as to whether,

(a) evidence submitted under clause 3(1)(b) establishes that the applicant is in need of a special educational program; or
(b) the applicant is able to profit from instruction in a program,

at the School, the admission of the applicant may be for a trial period.

(3) Upon the request of the Superintendent, or of the parent of an applicant, or of an applicant who is eighteen years of age or over, the Minister may appoint a committee to hear and determine any question concerning the eligibility for admission of the applicant.

Fees

9. No fee is payable in respect of a pupil admitted to a School under section 3.

10. (1) The fee payable in a fiscal year on behalf of a pupil who is admitted under section 4 or 5 to a School referred to in subsection 2(2), (3) or (4) and is in residence at such School shall be equal to the average of the quotients obtained by dividing, for each School,

(a) the estimated operating costs of the School for such fiscal year, excluding where applicable the estimated costs of extension and resource services, teacher education, daily transportation of pupils, food services for the staff and for pupils who are not in residence, the summer course for parents, the media centre, the program for emotionally disturbed pupils and special projects,

by,

(b) 425 in the case of The Sir James Whitney School and The Ernest C. Drury School, and 250 in the case of The Robarts School.

(2) The fee payable in a fiscal year on behalf of a pupil who is admitted under section 4 or 5 to a School referred to in subsection 2(2), (3) or (4) and is not in residence at such School shall be equal to the average of the quotients obtained by dividing, for each School,

(a) the estimated operating costs of the School for such fiscal year, excluding where applicable the estimated costs of extension and resource services, teacher education, the laundry, residence counsellors and residence operating expenses, food services for the staff and for pupils who are in residence, the summer course for parents, the media centre, the program for emotionally disturbed pupils and special projects,

by,

(b) 425 in the case of The Sir James Whitney School and The Ernest C. Drury School, and 250 in the case of The Robarts School.

11. (1) Subject to subsection (2), the fee payable in a fiscal year on behalf of a pupil who is admitted under section 4 or 5 to The W. Ross Macdonald School shall be equal to the quotient obtained by dividing by 275 the estimated operating costs of the School for such fiscal year, excluding the estimated costs of the deaf-blind program, the large-print library and the total stimulation program.

(2) The fee payable in a fiscal year on behalf of a deaf-blind pupil who is admitted under section 4 or 5 to The W. Ross Macdonald School shall be equal to the quotient obtained by dividing,

(a) the sum of the amounts allocated in the estimates of such School for such fiscal year to salaries of teachers, counsellors and aides in the deaf-blind program and to transportation and communication services and supplies for pupils in such program,

by,

(b) the number of pupils enrolled in such program on the last school day in June of such fiscal year.

12. Where in any month a pupil for whom a fee is payable attends a School for only a part of the month, his or her fee for such month shall be reduced proportionately.

Transportation

13. (1) The Superintendent may provide daily transportation to and from a School for pupils of the school who are not in residence at the School.

(2) The Minister may pay all or part of the transportation costs for a pupil admitted to a School under section 3 where the board of which such pupil is qualified to be a resident pupil does not provide transportation to and from the School.

Duties of Pupils

14. A pupil at a School shall,

(a) except with the permission of the Superintendent, be in attendance on the first day in the school year and attend classes punctually and regularly during the school year;
(b) take such tests and examinations as may be required by the Superintendent;
(c) exercise self-discipline and accept such discipline as would be exercised by a kind, firm and judicious parent;
(d) be clean in his or her person and habits, diligent in his or her studies and courteous to other pupils and to the teaching and non-teaching staff of the School;
(e) be responsible to the Superintendent for his or her conduct on the school premises, on out-of-school activities and programs sponsored by the School and while travelling on a bus under contract to or owned by the Ministry;
(f) leave the school premises only under conditions specified by the Superintendent; and
(g) if the pupil is in residence at the School, participate in the programs provided by the residence counsellor for his or her residence area.

Duties of Teachers

15. A person employed to teach at a School shall, in addition to the duties of a teacher under the Act,

(a) be responsible for effective instruction in the subjects assigned to him or her by the Superintendent, the management of his or her classes and the discipline in his or her classroom;
(b) co-operate with officials of the Ministry and the Superintendent for the purposes of planning and evaluating the program of instruction;

(c) make adequate provision in his or her daily program for the individual differences of the pupils in his or her classes so that each pupil may experience a reasonable amount of success;
(d) prepare for use in his or her class or classes such teaching plans and outlines as are required by the Superintendent and submit the plans and outlines to the Superintendent on request;
(e) assist in maintaining discipline in the School and in fostering school spirit and morale; and
(f) carry out such supervisory duties as may be assigned by the Superintendent.

Duties of Residence Counsellors

16. A residence counsellor shall,
(a) be responsible for the residence area assigned to him or her by the Superintendent and provide for the safety, health, comfort and well-being of pupils in such area;
(b) plan and provide programs to encourage and promote the growth and development of each pupil in the residence area and evaluate such programs;
(c) make adequate provision for individual differences of the pupils in the programs that he or she provides;
(d) record the growth and development of each pupil in the residence area;
(e) assist in maintaining school spirit, morale and discipline;
(f) carry out such supervisory duties as may be assigned to him or her by the Superintendent; and
(g) co-operate with the Superintendent in all matters affecting the School.

Parents

17. (1) There shall be deposited with the bursar a sum of at least $20.00 to defray the personal incidental expenses of a pupil enrolled in a School.

(2) As a condition of admission of a pupil to a School, the parent of the pupil or the pupil, where he or she is over eighteen years of age, shall agree,
(a) to supply on request of the Superintendent personal items necessary to enable the pupil to participate in school programs;
(b) to provide transportation and escort for the pupil where necessary to ensure regular attendance if such transportation and escort is not otherwise provided;
(c) to authorize the Superintendent, upon recommendation of the school physician, to arrange in case of emergency for the admission of the pupil to a hospital for treatment or surgery;
(d) to permit such medical treatment of the pupil as may be recommended by the school physician, subject to any other consent that may be required;
(e) to guarantee payment for medical and dental services required by the pupil during the school year, except such services that are provided by the School; and
(f) to notify the Superintendent promptly of the reason for the absence of the pupil.

(3) The parent of a pupil may visit with the pupil at the School in which the pupil is enrolled as authorized by the Superintendent.

Duties of Superintendent

18. There shall be for each School a Superintendent who shall,
(a) admit pupils in accordance with this Regulation;
(b) determine the pupils who shall be in residence at the School and the pupils who shall reside in homes approved by him or her;
(c) determine the mode of transportation to and from School to be used by a pupil for whom such transportation is provided by the School;
(d) assign pupils to classes and programs;
(e) transfer and promote such pupils as he or she considers proper;
(f) establish and maintain, and retain, transfer and dispose of, a pupil record in respect of each pupil enrolled in the School, in the manner prescribed by the regulations;
(g) at least once in every calendar year provide for a review of the placement of each pupil to ensure that the program is appropriate for the capabilities and needs of the pupil;
(h) recommend for a Secondary School Graduation Diploma or a Secondary School Honour Graduation Diploma a pupil of the School who has completed the requirements for such diploma;
(i) be in charge of the organization, management and discipline of the School and ensure that proper supervision is maintained at all times;
(j) furnish to the Director, on his or her request, information on any matter affecting the interests of the School;
(k) arrange for regular inspection of the school premises and report promptly to the Ministry of Government Services any repairs required to be made by that Ministry;
(l) determine the times at which pupils may leave the school premises and the times at which they may be visited at the School;
(m) notify the parent immediately if a pupil becomes seriously ill or requires hospital treatment off the school property;
(n) notify the parent if a pupil damages or destroys school property and request suitable compensation;
(o) hold emergency drills at the School and the residences at least six times during the school year and require that every pupil and staff member take part therein;
(p) report promptly to the local medical officer of health and the Director any cases of infectious or contagious disease in the School; and
(q) report at least once each term the progress of each pupil to his or her parent, or to the pupil where the pupil is eighteen years of age or over.

19. (1) The Superintendent may dismiss a pupil from a School or from a program in the School for a period not exceeding thirty days because of misconduct, persistent opposition to authority, habitual neglect of duty, the wilful destruction of school property, the use of profane or wilfully insulting language, or conduct injurious to the moral tone of the School or to the physical or mental well-being of others in the School and, where a pupil has been so dismissed, the Superintendent shall notify forthwith in writing the pupil, his or her teachers, the parent of the pupil and the Director of the dismissal, the reasons therefor and the right of appeal under subsection 2.

(2) The parent of a pupil who has been dismissed under subsection (1), or the dismissed pupil where the pupil is eighteen years of age or over, may, within seven days of the commencement of the dismissal, appeal to the Director against the dismissal, and the Director, after hearing the appeal or where no appeal is made, may remove, confirm or modify the dismissal and, where he or she considers it appropriate, may order that any record of the dismissal be expunged.

(3) The Director may dismiss a pupil permanently from a School on the ground that the pupil's conduct is so refractory that his or her presence is injurious to other pupils where,
- (a) the Superintendent so recommends;
- (b) the pupil and his or her parent have been notified in writing of,
    - (i) the recommendation of the Superintendent, and
    - (ii) the right of the pupil where the pupil is eighteen years of age or over, and otherwise of his or her parent, to make representations at a hearing to be conducted by the Director; and
- (c) such hearing has been conducted.

(4) The parties to a hearing under this section shall be the parent of the pupil, or the pupil where he or she is eighteen years of age or over, and the Superintendent.

20. (1) The Superintendent may discharge a pupil,
- (a) for failure to make progress satisfactory to the Superintendent; or
- (b) where the pupil is no longer in need of a special educational program in the School and another program placement would be more appropriate for the pupil.

(2) Where a pupil has been discharged under subsection (1), the Superintendent shall,
- (a) notify in writing the pupil and the parent of the pupil, of the discharge, the reason therefor and the right of appeal to the Director;
- (b) counsel the parent of the pupil, or the pupil where he or she is eighteen years of age or over, in respect of the opportunities available to the pupil; and
- (c) give supportive guidance to the parent and to the pupil where, in the opinion of the Superintendent, such guidance is necessary.

(3) The parent of a pupil who has been discharged under subsection (1), or the discharged pupil where he or she is eighteen years of age or over, may, within seven days of the discharge, appeal to the Director against the discharge, and the Director, after hearing the appeal or where no appeal is made, may confirm the discharge or order that the pupil be readmitted to the School.

(4) The parties to a hearing under this section shall be the parent of the pupil, or the pupil where he or she is eighteen years of age or over, and the Superintendent.

21. A Superintendent may cause a pupil to be sent home because of,
- (a) serious or continued ill-health of the pupil; or
- (b) the need of the pupil for medical treatment, certified by the school physician.

Superintendent's Advisory Council

22. (1) A Superintendent may establish a Superintendent's Advisory Council for his or her School to make recommendations to the Superintendent in respect of the organization, administration and government of the School.

(2) A Superintendent's Advisory Council established under subsection (1) shall be composed of at least six persons appointed by the Superintendent, and such Council shall meet at the call of the Superintendent at least twice during each school year.

(3) A member of a Superintendent's Advisory Council is entitled to be reimbursed for his or her expenses necessarily incurred to attend a meeting of the Superintendent's Advisory Council.

Qualifications of Teachers

23. (1) A teacher employed to teach the deaf at a School shall hold,
 (a) a certificate of qualification to teach in an elementary school or a secondary school in Ontario or a letter of standing; and
 (b) the Diploma in Deaf Education granted by the Minister or qualifications in education of the deaf that the Minister considers equivalent thereto.

(2) A deaf adult may be employed to teach the deaf at a School if he or she holds a Permanent Letter of Standing valid for the teaching of the deaf.

(3) A teacher employed to teach the blind at a School shall,
 (a) hold a certificate of qualification to teach in an elementary school or a secondary school in Ontario or a letter of standing; and
 (b) have completed, or be actively engaged in completing, the requirements for the specialist qualification for teaching the blind, or hold qualifications in education of the blind that the Minister considers equivalent thereto.

(4) A teacher employed to teach the deaf-blind at a School shall,
 (a) hold a certificate of qualification to teach in an elementary school or a secondary school in Ontario or a letter of standing; and
 (b) have completed, or be actively engaged in completing, the requirements for the specialist qualification for teaching the deaf-blind, or hold qualifications in education of the deaf-blind that the Minister considers equivalent thereto.

REGULATION 298
OPERATION OF SCHOOLS — GENERAL

R.R.O. 1990, Reg. 298, as am. O. Reg. 339/91 (Fr. version); 242/92; 95/96; 425/98

1. In this Regulation,

"business studies" means the courses in general studies that are developed from curriculum guidelines listed under the heading "Business Studies" in Appendix B to OSIS;

"division" means the primary division, the junior division, the intermediate division or the senior division;

"French as a second language" includes programs for English speaking pupils in which French is the language of instruction;

"general studies" means the courses developed from curriculum guidelines that are issued by the Minister for the intermediate division and senior division and listed under a heading other than "Technological Studies" in Appendix B to OSIS;

"OSIS" means the circular entitled "Ontario Schools Intermediate and Senior Divisions Program and Diploma Requirements" issued by the Minister including any document issued by the Minister in accordance with paragraphs 1, 2, 3, 4 and 25 of subsection 8(1) of the Act;

"parent" includes guardian;

"technological studies" means the courses developed from curriculum guidelines that are issued by the Minister for the intermediate division and senior division and listed under the heading "Technological Studies" in Appendix B to OSIS.

Accommodation

2. (1) A board shall file with the Ministry plans for the erection of, addition to, or alteration of a school building together with details of the site thereof.

(2) It is a condition of the payment of a legislative grant in respect of capital cost that the plans and details referred to in subsection (1) be approved by the Minister.

Daily Sessions

3. (1) The length of the instructional program of each school day for pupils of compulsory school age shall be not less than five hours a day excluding recesses or scheduled intervals between classes.

(2) The instructional program on a school day shall begin not earlier than 8 a.m. and end not later than 5 p.m. except with the approval of the Minister.

(3) Despite subsection (1), a board may reduce the length of the instructional program on each school day to less than five hours a day for an exceptional pupil in a special education program.

(4) Every board may establish the length of the instructional program on each school day for pupils in junior kindergarten and kindergarten.

(5) A scheduled interval between classes for the lunch break for pupils and teachers shall be not less than forty consecutive minutes.

(6) In the intermediate division and the senior division, a principal may, subject to the approval of the board, provide for recesses or intervals for pupils between periods.

(7) Every board shall determine the period of time during each school day when its school buildings and playgrounds shall be open to its pupils, but in every case the buildings and the playgrounds shall be open to pupils during the period beginning fifteen minutes before classes begin for the day and ending fifteen minutes after classes end for the day.

(8) There shall be a morning recess and an afternoon recess, each of which shall be not less than ten minutes and not more than fifteen minutes in length, for pupils in the primary and junior divisions.

Opening or Closing Exercises

4. (1) Every public elementary and secondary school shall hold opening or closing exercises.

(2) Opening or closing exercises shall include *O Canada* and may include *God Save The Queen*.

(3) Opening or closing exercises may include the following types of readings that impart social, moral or spiritual values and that are representative of Ontario's multicultural society:
1. Scriptural writings including prayers.
2. Secular writings.

(4) Opening or closing exercises may include a period of silence.

(5) No pupil enrolled in a public elementary or secondary school shall be required to take part in any opening or closing exercises where a parent or guardian of the pupil or the pupil, where the pupil is an adult, applies to the principal of the school that the pupil attends for exemption therefrom.

Flag

5. (1) Every school shall fly both the National Flag of Canada and the Provincial Flag of Ontario on such occasions as the board directs.

(2) Every school shall display in the school the National Flag of Canada and the Provincial Flag of Ontario.

Emergency Procedures

6. (1) In addition to the drills established under the fire safety plan required under Regulation 454 of Revised Regulations of Ontario, 1990 (Fire Code), every board may provide for the holding of drills in respect of emergencies other than those occasioned by fire.

(2) Every principal, including the principal of an evening class or classes or of a class or classes conducted outside the school year, shall hold at least on emergency drill in the period during which the instruction is given.

(3) When a fire or emergency drill is held in a school building, every person in the building shall take part in the fire or emergency drill.

Textbooks

7. (1) The principal of a school, in consultation with the teachers concerned, shall select from the list of the textbooks approved by the Minister the textbooks for the use of pupils of the school, and the selection shall be subject to the approval of the board.

(2) Where no textbook for a course of study is included in the list of the textbooks approved by the Minister the principal of a school, in consultation with the teachers concerned, shall, where they consider a textbook to be required, select a suitable textbook and, subject to the approval of the board, such textbook may be introduced for use in the school.

(3) In the selection of textbooks under subsection (2), preference shall be given to books that have been written by Canadian authors and edited, printed and bound in Canada.

(4) Every board shall provide without charge for the use of each pupil enrolled in a day school operated by the board such textbooks selected under subsections (1) and (2) as relate to the courses in which the pupil is enrolled.

Elementary School Boards

8. (1) Where the area of jurisdiction of a district school area board, a Roman Catholic separate school board, other than a Roman Catholic school board, or a Protestant separate school board is not within a secondary school district, the board shall provide instruction that would enable its resident pupils to obtain sixteen credits towards a secondary school graduation diploma or an Ontario secondary school diploma.

(2) A board referred to in subsection (1) that offers courses of instruction during July or August or both in any year may provide instruction that would enable its resident pupils to obtain two credits in addition to the sixteen credits referred to in subsection (1).

(3) Where a board referred to in subsection (1) provides,
(a) daily transportation for its resident pupils; or
(b) reimbursement for board and lodging and for transportation once a week to and from the places of residence of its resident pupils,

that it considers necessary to enable its resident pupils to attend a school operated by another board, the other board may provide such instruction as would enable such resident pupils to obtain the number of credits referred to in subsections (1) and (2).

(4) A Roman Catholic separate school board, other than a Roman Catholic school board, or a Protestant separate school board that has jurisdiction in a secondary school district may provide instruction for its resident pupils that would enable the pupils to obtain up to eighteen credits towards a secondary school graduation diploma or an Ontario secondary school diploma.

Qualifications for Principals and Vice-Principals

9. (1) The principal and vice-principal of a school having an enrolment greater than 125 shall each be a teacher who,

(a) holds or is deemed to hold, under Regulation 297 of Revised Regulations of Ontario, 1990, principal's qualifications; or
(b) holds a principal's certificate that is a qualification to be principal or vice-principal, as the case may be, in the type of school identified on the certificate, or is deemed under section 47 of Regulation 297 of Revised Regulations of Ontario, 1990 to hold such a certificate,

and, in the case of a school,

(c) in which English is the language of instruction; or
(d) that is established under Part XII of the Act and in which French is the language of instruction,

shall each be a person who is eligible to teach in such school under subsection 19(11), (12) or (13), as the case may be.

(2) Despite subsection (1), where a teacher who does not hold the degree of Bachelor of Arts or Bachelor of Science from an Ontario university or a degree that the Minister considers equivalent thereto was, prior to the 1st day of September, 1961, employed by a board as principal or vice-principal of an elementary school that had an enrolment of 300 or more pupils, the teacher shall be deemed to be qualified as principal or vice-principal, as the case may be, of any elementary school operated by that board or its successor board.

(3) Despite subsection (1), where a teacher who does not hold the qualifications referred to in subsection (1),

(a) was employed by a board prior to the 1st day of September, 1972 as principal of an elementary school that had an enrolment of 300 or more pupils and is employed by such board as principal of an elementary school on the 8th day of September, 1978;
(b) was employed by a board on the 1st day of September, 1978 as vice-principal of an elementary school that had an enrolment on the last school day in April, 1978 of 300 or more pupils; or
(c) was employed by a board on the 1st day of September, 1978 as principal or vice-principal of an elementary school that had an enrolment on the last school day in April, 1978 that was greater than 125 and less than 300,

such teacher shall be deemed to be qualified as principal or vice-principal, as the case may be, of any elementary school operated by that board or its successor board.

(4) A board may appoint a person who holds the qualifications required by subsection (1) as a supervising principal to supervise the administration of two or more elementary schools operated by the board and such person shall be subject to the authority of the appropriate supervisory officer.

(5) A supervising principal may be principal of only one school.

(6) Despite subsection (1), a teacher who, before the 1st day of September, 1970, held the necessary qualifications as principal of a secondary school continues to be qualified as principal or vice-principal of a secondary school.

10. (1) The principal and vice-principal of a school for trainable retarded pupils having an enrolment greater than 100 or of a school in which there are classes for trainable retarded pupils and the enrolment in such classes is greater than 100 shall each be a teacher who,

(a) holds or is deemed to hold, under Regulation 297 of Revised Regulations of Ontario,

1990, principal's qualifications, or holds a certificate referred to in section 46 of such Regulation or is deemed to hold such certificate under section 47 thereof; and

(b) holds an additional qualification in special education as recorded on the teacher's Ontario Teacher's Qualifications Record Card.

(2) The principal of an elementary or secondary school that includes one or more classes for trainable retarded pupils shall be the principal of such classes, and the vice-principal of such a school shall be the vice-principal of such classes except where a vice-principal is appointed to be in charge of such classes exclusively.

(3) Despite subsection (1), where a teacher who does not hold the qualifications referred to in subsection (1) was, on the 1st day of September, 1978 employed by a board as principal or vice-principal of a school for trainable retarded pupils that had an enrolment greater than 100 or of a school in which there were classes for trainable retarded pupils and the enrolment in such classes was greater than 100, the teacher shall be deemed to be qualified as principal or vice-principal, as the case may be, of a school for trainable retarded pupils or of a school in which there are classes for trainable retarded pupils the enrolment in which is greater than 100 that is operated by that board or its successor board.

Duties of Principals

11. (1) The principal of a school, subject to the authority of the appropriate supervisory officer, is in charge of,

(a) the instruction and the discipline of pupils in the school; and

(b) the organization and management of the school.

(2) Where two or more schools operated by a board jointly occupy or use in common a school building or school grounds, the board shall designate which principal has authority over those parts of the building or grounds that the schools occupy or use in common.

(3) In addition to the duties under the Act and those assigned by the board, the principal of a school shall, except where the principal has arranged otherwise under subsection 26(3),

(a) supervise the instruction in the school and advise and assist any teacher in co-operation with the teacher in charge of an organizational unit or program;

(b) assign duties to vice-principals and to teachers in charge of organizational units or programs;

(c) retain on file up-to-date copies of outlines of all courses of study that are taught in the school;

(d) upon request, make outlines of courses of study available for examination to a resident pupil of the board and to the parent of the pupil, where the pupil is a minor;

(e) provide for the supervision of pupils during the period of time during each school day when the school buildings and playgrounds are open to pupils;

(f) provide for the supervision of and the conducting of any school activity authorized by the board;

(g) where performance appraisals of members of the teaching staff are required under a collective agreement or a policy of the board, despite anything to the contrary in such collective agreement or board policy, conduct performance appraisals of members of the teaching staff;

(h) subject to the provisions of the policy of the board or the provisions of a collective agreement, as the case may be, in respect of reporting requirements for performance appraisals, report thereon in writing to the board or to the supervisory officer on request and give to each teacher so appraised a copy of the performance appraisal of the teacher;

(i) where the performance appraisals of members of the teaching staff are not required by board policy or under a collective agreement, report to the board or to the supervisory officer in writing on request on the effectiveness of members of the teaching staff and give to a teacher referred to in any such report a copy of the portion of the report that refers to the teacher;

(j) make recommendations to the board with respect to,
   (i) the appointment and promotion of teachers, and
   (ii) the demotion or dismissal of teachers whose work or attitude is unsatisfactory;

(k) provide for instruction of pupils in the care of the school premises;

(l) inspect the school premises at least weekly and report forthwith to the board,
   (i) any repairs to the school that are required, in the opinion of the principal,
   (ii) any lack of attention on the part of the building maintenance staff of the school, and
   (iii) where a parent of a pupil has been requested to compensate the board for damage to or destruction, loss or misappropriation of school property by the pupil and the parent has not done so, that the parent of the pupil has not compensated the board;

(m) where it is proposed to administer a test of intelligence or personality to a pupil, inform the pupil and the parent of the pupil of the test and obtain the prior written permission for the test from the pupil or from the parent of the pupil, where the pupil is a minor;

(n) report promptly any neglect of duty or infraction of the school rules by a pupil to the parent or guardian of the pupil;

(o) promote and maintain close co-operation with residents, industry, business and other groups and agencies of the community;

(p) provide to the Minister or to a person designated by the Minister any information that may be required concerning the instructional program, operation or administration of the school and inform the appropriate supervisory officer of the request;

(q) assign suitable quarters for pupils to eat lunch.

(4) A principal shall only make a recommendation to the board under subclause (3)(j)(ii) after warning the teacher in writing, giving the teacher assistance and allowing the teacher a reasonable time to improve.

(5) A principal of a school,

(a) in which there is a French-language instructional unit as defined in section 309 of the Act, who does not hold qualifications to teach in the French-language as required by subsection 19(12) or is qualified to teach in such unit only under subsection 19(13); or

(b) in which there is an English-language instructional unit as mentioned in subsection 325(1) of the Act, who does not hold qualifications to teach in the English language as required by subsection 19(11) or is qualified to teach in each unit only under subsection 19(13),

shall notify the appropriate supervisory officer in writing of the impracticability of the duty placed on the principal, having regard to the qualifications of the principal, to supervise the instruction, to conduct performance appraisals and to assist and advise the teachers referred to in the notice.

(6) Where arrangements are made under subsection 26(3), the principal is relieved from compliance with clauses (3)(a), (g), (h) and (i) to the extent that such duties are performed by another qualified person or persons.

(7) The other qualified person or persons who perform the duties shall be responsible to the board for the performance of such duties.

(8) The outlines of the courses of study mentioned in clause (3)(c) shall be written and provided,
- (a) in the French language in the case of courses of study provided in a French-language instructional unit operated under Part XII of the Act; and
- (b) in both the English and French languages in the case of a course of study in a program established in the school under paragraph 25 of subsection 8(1) of the Act.

(9) Where, after reasonable notice by the principal, a pupil who is an adult, or the parent of a pupil who is a minor, fails to provide the supplies required by the pupil for a course of study, the principal shall promptly notify the board.

(10) A principal shall transmit reports and recommendations to the board through the appropriate supervisory officer.

(11) A principal, subject to the approval of the appropriate supervisory officer, may arrange for home instruction to be provided for a pupil where,
- (a) medical evidence that the pupil cannot attend school is provided to the principal; and
- (b) the principal is satisfied that home instruction is required.

(12) The principal of a school shall provide for the prompt distribution to each member of the school council any materials received by the principal from the Ministry that are identified by the Ministry as being,
- (a) relevant to the functions of the school council; and
- (b) for distribution to the members of school councils.

(13) In each school year, the principal of a school shall make the names of the members of the school council known to the parents of the pupils enrolled in the school, by publishing those names in a school newsletter or by such other means as is likely to bring the names to the attention of the parents.

(14) The principal shall meet the requirements of subsection (13) in each school year by the later of,
- (a) the end of September; and
- (b) 30 days following the day on which the membership of the school council for the school year is determined.

(15) The principal of a school shall promptly provide the names of the members of the school council to a supporter of the board that governs the school or to a parent of a pupil enrolled in the school, on the request of the supporter or the parent. O. Reg. 425/98.

Vice-Principals

12. (1) A board may appoint one or more vice-principals for a school.

(2) A vice-principal shall perform such duties as are assigned to the vice-principal by the principal.

(3) In the absence of the principal of a school, a vice-principal, where a vice-principal has been appointed for the school, shall be in charge of the school and shall perform the duties of the principal.

Principals, Vice-Principals and Teachers in Charge of Schools and Classes Established Under Part XII of the Act

13. (1) Where, under section 289 of the Act, more than two classes where French is the language of instruction are established in an elementary school that is not a French-language elementary school, the board that operates the school shall appoint one of the teachers of such classes or a teacher who holds the qualifications required to teach such classes to be responsible to the principal for the program of education in such classes.

(2) Where the enrolment in classes established under section 291 of the Act in a secondary school that is not a French-language secondary school is more than seventy-five but not more than 200 pupils, the board that operates the school shall appoint one of the teachers of such classes or a teacher who holds the qualifications required to teach such classes to be responsible to the principal for the program of education in such classes.

(3) Where, in a secondary school, the enrolment in the classes referred to in subsection (2) is more than 200 pupils, the board shall appoint for such school a vice-principal who is qualified to teach in such classes and who shall be responsible to the principal for the program of education in such classes.

(4) Despite subsections (1), (2) and (3), where a teacher who does not hold the qualifications referred to in such subsections was, on the 8th day of September, 1978, employed by the board as a teacher or vice-principal, as the case may be, to carry out the responsibility referred to in such subsections, the teacher shall be deemed to be qualified for such position in any elementary or secondary school, as the case may be, operated by that board or its successor board.

(5) Subsections (1) to (4) apply with necessary modifications to schools or classes for English-speaking pupils established under sections 289 and 301 of the Act.

Teachers in Charge of Organizational Units

14. (1) The organization of a secondary school may be by departments or other organizational units.

(2) The organization of an elementary school may be by divisions or other organizational units.

(3) A board may appoint for each organizational unit of an elementary or secondary school a teacher to direct and supervise, subject to the authority of the principal of the school, such organizational unit.

(4) A teacher appointed under subsection (3) may be appointed to direct and supervise more than one organizational unit. O. Reg. 95/96.

15. [Revoked O. Reg. 95/96]

16. [Revoked O. Reg. 95/96]

Subject and Program Supervision and Co-Ordination

17. (1) A board may, in respect of one or more subjects or programs in the schools under its jurisdiction, appoint a teacher to supervise or co-ordinate the subjects or programs or to act as a consultant for the teachers of the subjects or programs.

(2) A teacher appointed under subsection (1) shall hold specialist or honour specialist qualifications, if such are available, in one or more of the subjects or programs in respect of which the teacher is appointed.

(3) Despite subsection (1), a teacher who, on the 8th day of September, 1978, was employed by a board to supervise or co-ordinate a subject or program in its schools or to act as a consultant shall be deemed to be qualified for such position in the schools operated by that board or its successor board.

18. (1) Subject to the authority of the appropriate supervisory officer, a teacher appointed in a subject or program under section 17 shall assist teachers in that subject or program in maintaining proper standards and improving methods of instruction.

(2) A teacher appointed under section 17 in performing duties in a school is subject to the authority of the principal of that school.

Qualifications of Teachers

19. (1) A teacher in a school shall, subject to subsection (2), be a person who holds or is deemed under Regulation 297 of Revised Regulations of Ontario, 1990 to hold an Ontario Teacher's Certificate and shall, subject to subsections (4), (5), (11) and (12), be assigned or appointed to teach according to a qualification recorded on the teacher's Ontario Teacher's Qualifications Record Card or the record of qualification in respect of such teacher held by the Ministry.

(2) A teacher who does not hold and is not deemed under Regulation 297 of Revised Regulations of Ontario, 1990 to hold an Ontario Teacher's Certificate but who,

(a) holds a Temporary Letter of Standing or a Provisional Letter of Standing or a Permanent Letter of Standing; or

(b) holds a certificate or Letter of Standing referred to in subsection 26(3) or 27(1) of Regulation 297 of Revised Regulations of Ontario, 1990,

may teach in a school in a subject or program for which the Letter of Standing or certificate is valid or in which the teacher has received professional education as indicated on the Temporary Letter of Standing or Provisional Letter of Standing.

(3) A person who does not hold any of the qualifications referred to in subsection (2) but who holds a Letter of Eligibility issued under section 12 or 13 of Regulation 297 of Revised Regulations of Ontario, 1990 may be employed by a board as an occasional teacher only,

(a) in classes where English is the language of instruction if the Letter of Eligibility is in Form 5 to Regulation 297 of Revised Regulations of Ontario, 1990; or

(b) in classes where French is the language of instruction if the Letter of Eligibility is in Form 5a to Regulation 297 of Revised Regulations of Ontario, 1990.

(4) Subject to subsections (6), (11), (12), (14) and (15), and with due regard for the safety and welfare of the pupils and the provision of the best possible program, a teacher whose Ontario Teacher's Qualifications Record Card, or the record of qualification in respect of such teacher held by the Ministry, indicates qualification in the primary division, the junior division, the intermediate division in general studies or the senior division in general studies may, by mutual agreement of the teacher and the principal of a school and with the approval of the appropriate supervisory officer, be assigned or appointed to teach in a division or a subject in general studies for which no qualification is recorded on the teacher's Ontario Teacher's Qualifications Record Card or the record of qualification in respect of such teacher held by the Ministry.

(5) Subject to subsections (11), (12) and (15), and with due regard for the safety and welfare of the pupils and the provision of the best possible program, a teacher whose Ontario Teacher's Qualifications Record Card, or the record of qualification in respect of such teacher held by the Ministry, has entries indicating qualifications in technological studies may by mutual agreement of the teacher and the principal of a school, with the approval of the appropriate supervisory officer, be assigned or appointed to teach a subject in technological studies for which no qualification is recorded on the Ontario Teacher's Qualification Record Card or the record of qualification in respect of such teacher held by the Ministry.

(6) Subject to subsections (7), (8), (9) and (10), a teacher who does not hold an acceptable university degree as defined in the definition of "acceptable university degree" in section 1 of Regulation 297 of Revised Regulations of Ontario, 1990 shall not be assigned or appointed to teach general studies in a secondary school, except that where the teacher is qualified to teach in the primary division, the junior division and the intermediate division of an elementary school and,

(a) on the 30th day of June, 1981 was teaching in a secondary school; or

(b) on or before the 2nd day of October, 1981 was assigned or appointed to teach general studies in a secondary school, and on the 30th day of June, 1982 was teaching in a secondary school,

the teacher may be assigned or appointed to teach general studies to pupils enrolled in a modified or basic level course by that board or its successor board.

(7) Despite subsection (1), a teacher who holds,

(a) a commercial-vocational qualification; or

(b) technological studies qualifications in any one or more of clerical practice, merchandising or warehousing,

may be assigned or appointed to teach the courses in business studies equivalent to the courses in business studies shown on the teacher's Ontario Teacher's Qualifications Record Card or the record of qualification in respect of the teacher held by the Ministry.

(8) A teacher who holds qualifications in technological studies in sewing and dressmaking, or textiles and clothing, or home economics may be assigned or appointed to teach in a secondary school the clothing portion of the family studies course.

(9) A teacher who holds qualifications in technological studies in food and nutrition or home economics may be assigned or appointed to teach in a secondary school the food and nutrition portion of the family studies course.

(10) A teacher who holds qualifications in technological studies in vocational art, instrumental music or vocal music may be assigned or appointed to teach art, instrumental music or vocal music, as the case may be, in general studies in a secondary school.

(11) A teacher who has not received basic teacher education in the English language or who is not otherwise qualified under the regulations for such assignment or appointment shall not be assigned or appointed to teach in classes where English is the language of instruction.

(12) A teacher who has not received basic teacher education in the French language or who is not otherwise qualified under the regulations for such assignment or appointment shall not be assigned or appointed to teach in schools or classes established under Part XII of the Act where French is the language of instruction.

(13) Despite subsections (11) and (12), a teacher who holds qualifications to teach in the intermediate division and the senior division may be assigned or appointed to teach in either or both of such divisions in classes where English or French is the language of instruction.

(14) No teacher shall,

(a) be assigned, or appointed to teach, in any of grades 9, 10, 11, 12 and 13 in any one school year for more than the time required for two courses that are recognized for credit in art, business studies, guidance including counselling, family studies, instrumental music, vocal music or physical education; or

(b) be placed in charge of,
   (i) a school library program,
   (ii) a guidance program, or
   (iii) special education; or

(c) be assigned or appointed to teach,
   (i) French as a second language,
   (ii) English as a second language,
   (iii) design and technology,
   (iv) subject to subsections (5) and (15), technological studies,
   (v) in a special education class,
   (vi) in a class for deaf, hard of hearing, blind or limited vision pupils, or
   (vii) as a resource or withdrawal teacher in special education programs,

unless,

(d) the teacher's Ontario Teacher's Qualifications Record Card or the record of qualification in respect of such teacher held by the Ministry indicates qualifications in the subject or program to which the teacher is to be assigned or appointed or placed in charge; or

(e) the teacher is qualified for such assignment, appointment or placement under subsection (2) or (16) or deemed to be qualified therefor under subsection (17).

(15) On or after the 1st of September, 1982, no teacher shall be assigned or appointed to teach courses in the senior division in technological studies at the General or Advanced levels unless the teacher's Ontario Teacher's Qualifications Record Card or the record of qualification in respect of such teacher held by the Ministry indicates advanced level qualifications in the area of technological studies to which the teacher is to be assigned or appointed.

(16) A teacher in a school or class for trainable retarded pupils shall,

(a) have an entry on the teacher's Ontario Teacher's Qualifications Record Card or on the record of qualification in respect of such teacher held by the Ministry, indicating qualifications in the area of teaching the trainable retarded; or

(b) hold one of the following:
 1. Elementary Certificate in Teaching Trainable Retarded Children.
 2. Intermediate Certificate in Teaching Trainable Retarded Children.
 3. Certificate as Teacher of the Trainable Retarded.
 4. Provisional or Permanent Letter of Standing valid for the teaching of the trainable retarded.

(17) A teacher who, on the 8th day of September, 1978, was employed by a board to teach,

(a) French as a second language or English as a second language in an elementary school or a secondary school; or

(b) industrial arts in an elementary school,

and is not qualified for such position under subsection (14), shall be deemed to be qualified for such position in the elementary schools or the secondary schools, as the case may be, that are operated by that board or its successor board.

(18) Where a teacher's Ontario Teacher's Qualifications Record Card or record of qualification has entries indicating qualifications both in technological studies and in guidance, the teacher may be assigned or appointed to teach guidance and counselling in general studies in a secondary school.

(19) The provision of subsection (14) that no teacher shall be assigned or appointed to teach in a special education class or program unless the teacher holds qualifications in special education does not apply to the teaching of classes in general studies or technological studies in what was formerly designated a special vocational or occupational program until the 1st day of September, 1985.

(20) A teacher may be assigned or appointed to teach those courses that are equivalent to those courses that appear on the teacher's Ontario Teacher's Qualifications Record Card or the record of qualification in respect of the teacher held by the Ministry. O. Reg. 243/92, s. 1.

Duties of Teachers

20. In addition to the duties assigned to the teacher under the Act and by the board, a teacher shall,

(a) be responsible for effective instruction, training and evaluation of the progress of pupils in the subjects assigned to the teacher and for the management of the class or classes, and report to the principal on the progress of pupils on request;

(b) carry out the supervisory duties and instructional program assigned to the teacher by the principal and supply such information related thereto as the principal may require;
(c) where the board has appointed teachers under section 14 or 17, co-operate fully with such teachers and with the principal in all matters related to the instruction of pupils;
(d) unless otherwise assigned by the principal, be present in the classroom or teaching area and ensure that the classroom or teaching area is ready for the reception of pupils at least fifteen minutes before the commencement of classes in the school in the morning and, where applicable, five minutes before the commencement of classes in the school in the afternoon;
(e) assist the principal in maintaining close co-operation with the community;
(f) prepare for use in the teacher's class or classes such teaching plans and outlines as are required by the principal and the appropriate supervisory officer and submit the plans and outlines to the principal or the appropriate supervisory officer, as the case may be, on request;
(g) ensure that all reasonable safety procedures are carried out in courses and activities for which the teacher is responsible; and
(h) co-operate with the principal and other teachers to establish and maintain consistent disciplinary practices in the school. O. Reg. 95/96.

Appointment to Teach in the Case of an Emergency

21. (1) Where no teacher is available, a board may appoint, subject to section 22, a person who is not a teacher or a temporary teacher.

(2) A person appointed under subsection (1) shall be eighteen years of age or older and the holder of an Ontario secondary school diploma, a secondary school graduation diploma or a secondary school honour graduation diploma.

(3) An appointment under this section is valid for ten school days commencing with the day on which the person is appointed.

Cancelled and Suspended Certificates

22. (1) A board shall not appoint a person whose teaching certificate is cancelled or under suspension to teach under section 21 or in accordance with a Letter of Permission.

(2) A person whose teaching certificate is cancelled or under suspension ceases to hold teacher's qualifications during the period of cancellation or suspension and shall not be appointed as a teacher.

Requirements For Pupils

23. (1) A pupil shall,
(a) be diligent in attempting to master such studies as are part of the program in which the pupil is enrolled;
(b) exercise self-discipline;

(c) accept such discipline as would be exercised by a kind, firm and judicious parent;
(d) attend classes punctually and regularly;
(e) be courteous to fellow pupils and obedient and courteous to teachers;
(f) be clean in person and habits;
(g) take such tests and examinations as are required by or under the Act or as may be directed by the Minister; and
(h) show respect for school property.

(2) When a pupil returns to school after an absence, a parent of the pupil, or the pupil where the pupil is an adult, shall give the reason for the absence orally or in writing as the principal requires.

(3) A pupil may be excused by the principal from attendance at school temporarily at any time at the written request of a parent of the pupil or the pupil where the pupil is an adult.

(4) Every pupil is responsible for his or her conduct to the principal of the school that the pupil attends,
(a) on the school premises;
(b) on out-of-school activities that are part of the school program; and
(c) while travelling on a school bus that is owned by a board or on a bus or school bus that is under contract to a board.

Advertisements and Announcements

24. No advertisement or announcement shall be placed in a school or on school property or distributed or announced to the pupils on school property without the consent of the board that operates the school except announcements of school activities.

Canvassing and Fund-Raising

25. (1) It is the duty of a pupil to ensure that any canvassing or fund-raising activity on school property by the pupil is carried on only with the consent of the board that operates the school.

(2) No principal, vice-principal or teacher, without the prior approval of the board that operates the school at which they are employed, shall authorize any canvassing or fund-raising activity that involves the participation of one or more pupils attending the school.

Supervision

26. (1) The appropriate supervisory officer, in addition to the duties under the Act, may, during a visit to a school, assume any of the authority and responsibility of the principal of the school.

(2) Psychiatrists, psychologists, social workers and other professional support staff employed by a board shall perform, under the administrative supervision of the appropriate supervisory officer, such duties as are determined by the board and, where such persons are

performing their duties in a school, they shall be subject to the administrative authority of the principal of that school.

(3) A supervisory officer who is notified under subsection 11(5) shall forthwith notify the French-language education council or section, English-language education council or section or majority language section of the board, as the case requires, and arrange for,

(a) the provision of supervision of instruction;
(b) assistance and advice to the teachers in respect of whom the supervisory officer was given notice under subsection 11(5); and
(c) the conducting of performance appraisals, where appropriate, of the teachers in respect of whom the supervisory officer was given notice under subsection 11(5),

in the language in which the instruction is provided.

Religion in Schools

27. Sections 28 and 29 do not apply to a separate school board or to the Roman Catholic sector of The Ottawa-Carleton French-Language School Board.

28. (1) A board may provide in grades one to eight and in its secondary schools an optional program of education about religion.

(2) A program of education about religion shall,

(a) promote respect for the freedom of conscience and religion guaranteed by the *Canadian Charter of Rights and Freedoms*; and
(b) provide for the study of different religions and religious beliefs in Canada and the world, without giving primacy to, and without indoctrination in, any particular religion or religious belief.

(3) A program of education about religion shall not exceed sixty minutes of instruction per week in an elementary school.

29. (1) Subject to subsections (2) and (3), a board shall not permit any person to conduct religious exercises or to provide instruction that includes indoctrination in a particular religion or religious belief in a school.

(2) A board may enter into an agreement with a separate school board or the Roman Catholic sector of The Ottawa-Carleton French-Language School Board that permits the separate school board or the Roman Catholic sector to use space and facilities to conduct religious exercises or provide religious instruction for the purposes of the separate school board or the Roman Catholic sector.

(3) A board may permit a person to conduct religious exercises or to provide instruction that includes indoctrination in a particular religion or religious belief in a school if,

(a) the exercises are not conducted or the instruction is not provided by or under the auspices of the board;
(b) the exercises are conducted or the instruction is provided on a school day at a time that is before or after the school's instructional program, or on a day that is not a school day;
(c) no person is required by the board to attend the exercises or instruction; and

(d) the board provides space for the exercises or instruction on the same basis as it provides space for other community activities.

(4) A board that permits religious exercises or instruction under subsection (3) shall consider on an equitable basis all requests to conduct religious exercises or to provide instruction under subsection (3).

Special Education Programs and Services

30. A hearing-handicapped child who has attained the age of two years may be admitted to a special education program for the hearing-handicapped.

31. The maximum enrolment in a special education class shall depend upon the extent of the exceptionalities of the pupils in the class and the special education services that are available to the teacher, but in no case shall the enrolment in a self-contained class exceed,

(a) in a class for pupils who are emotionally disturbed or socially maladjusted, for pupils who have severe learning disabilities, or for pupils who are younger than compulsory school age and have impaired hearing, eight pupils;

(b) in a class for pupils who are blind, for pupils who are deaf, for pupils who are trainable retarded, or for pupils with speech and language disorders, ten pupils;

(c) in a class for pupils who are hard of hearing, for pupils with limited vision, or for pupils with orthopaedic or other physical handicaps, twelve pupils;

(d) in a class for pupils who are educable retarded children, twelve pupils in the primary division and sixteen pupils in the junior and intermediate divisions;

(e) in an elementary school class for pupils who are gifted, twenty-five pupils;

(f) in a class for aphasic or autistic pupils, or for pupils with multiple handicaps for whom no one handicap is dominant, six pupils; and

(g) on and after the 1st day of September, 1982, in a class for exceptional pupils consisting of pupils with different exceptionalities, sixteen pupils.

REGULATION 300
PRACTICE AND PROCEDURE — BOARDS OF REFERENCE
R.R.O. 1990, Reg. 300, as am. O. Reg. 122/95

1. In this Regulation,

"applicant" means a person in respect of whose application the Minister has granted a Board;

"Board" means a Board of Reference that is granted by the Minister under section 270 of the Act;

"reference" means proceedings before a Board; and

"respondent" means a party to a reference other than the applicant.

2. the parties to a reference shall be,
- (a) where a board is the applicant, the board and the teacher who terminated his or her contract; and
- (b) where a teacher is the applicant, the teacher and the board that dismissed the teacher or terminated his or her contract.

3. Except as provided by section 7, the minimum rules for proceedings provided in Part I of the *Statutory Powers Procedure Act*, apply to a reference.

4. The chair of the Board shall cause three reference books to be prepared from the documents filed with him or her under section 5.

5. (1) Where a teacher is the applicant, the teacher shall file with the chair of the Board three copies of each of,
- (a) the contract of the teacher with the board where the teacher holds a copy of the contract, or an affidavit that the teacher does not hold a copy of the contract;
- (b) the notice of dismissal or termination of contract;
- (c) the statement of the disagreement with the dismissal or termination of contract as sent to the Minister;
- (d) the notice from the Minister that he or she has directed a judge to act as chair of the Board; and
- (e) the notice of the nomination by the teacher of a representative to the Board.

(2) Where a teacher is the applicant, the board shall file with the chair of the Board three copies of each of,
- (a) the contract of the teacher with the board;
- (b) the resolution, if any, of the board dismissing the teacher or terminating his or her contract;
- (c) the copy of the application for a Board provided by the applicant;
- (d) the notice of the application for a Board provided by the Minister;
- (e) the notice from the Minister that he or she has directed a judge to act as chair of the Board; and
- (f) the notice of the nomination by the board of a representative to the Board.

(3) The Minister shall cause to be filed with the chair of the Board three copies of each of,
- (a) the application for a Board;

(b) the notice of the application for a Board sent to the respondent; and
(c) [Revoked O. Reg. 122/95]

(4) Where a board is the applicant, the teacher shall file with the chair of the Board three copies of each of,

(a) the contract of the teacher with the board where the teacher holds a copy of the contract, or an affidavit that the teacher does not hold a copy of the contract;
(b) the copy of the application for a Board provided by the applicant;
(c) the notice of the application for a Board provided by the Minister;
(d) the notice from the Minister that he or she has directed a judge to act as chair of the Board; and
(e) the notice of the nomination by the teacher of a representative to the Board.

(5) Where a board is the applicant, the board shall file with the chair of the Board three copies of each of,

(a) the contract of the teacher with the board;
(b) the notice of termination of contract;
(c) the statement of the disagreement with the termination of the contract as sent to the Minister;
(d) the notice from the Minister that he or she has directed a judge to act as chair of the Board; and
(e) the notice of the nomination by the board of a representative to the Board.

(6) The documents to be filed with the chair under this section shall be filed with him or her not less than three days before the day upon which the hearing is to begin.

(7) A copy of the documents filed with the chair by an applicant shall be served by the applicant upon the respondent and a copy of the documents filed with the chair by a respondent shall be served by the respondent upon the applicant, and such service shall be made by personal service or by registered mail upon the party or upon the solicitor of the party to be served and shall be made not less than three days before the day upon which the hearing is to begin.

(8) A reference shall not be defeated by any error or omission in the supply of the documents referred to in this section, but the chair may require any such error or omission to be corrected upon such terms as to adjournment, costs and otherwise as he or she may determine. O. Reg. 122/95

6. (1) At a reference, the respondent shall begin and at the conclusion of the case for the respondent,

(a) where the applicant states an intention not to adduce evidence and the applicant has not adduced evidence, the respondent has the right to sum up the evidence and the applicant has the right to reply; and
(b) where the applicant wishes to adduce evidence, the applicant has the right to open the applicant's case and after the conclusion of such opening to adduce evidence and, when all the evidence is concluded, to sum up the evidence, and the respondent has the right to reply.

(2) Where a party to a reference is represented by counsel or an agent, a right conferred upon the party by subsection (1) may be exercised by the party's counsel or agent at the option of the party.

(3) Where, for any reason, a party to a reference omits or fails to adduce evidence that is material, the Board, at the request of such party made prior to the giving of the direction of the Board, may permit the party to adduce such evidence upon such conditions in respect of cross-examination, introduction of rebuttal evidence, reply, costs and any other matters as the chair may direct.

7. Despite section 15 of the *Statutory Powers Procedure Act*, the findings of fact of the Board shall be based exclusively on evidence admissible under the law of evidence and on matters of which notice may be taken under section 16 of that Act.

8. (1) The evidence before a Board shall be recorded by a person approved and appointed by the chair of the Board and who, before acting, shall make an oath or affirmation that he or she will truly and faithfully record the evidence to the best of his or her abilities.

(2) It is not necessary to transcribe the evidence recorded at a reference unless,

(a) the chair orders that it be done, in which case the costs thereof shall be included in the costs of the reference; or

(b) a party to the reference requests that it be done and pays the costs of the preparation of the transcript.

(3) Where evidence at a reference is transcribed, the transcript shall be accompanied by an affidavit or affirmation of the person recording the evidence that it is a true report of the evidence.

9. A reference shall be conducted, and the report and direction of the Board shall be, in the English language, except where the Board and the parties to the reference agree that the reference be conducted in the French language, in which case the report and direction of the Board may, at the option of the Board, be in the French language.

10. (1) The chair may, and if required by a party to the reference shall, appoint a person to act as an interpreter at the reference, and such person before acting shall make an oath or affirmation that he or she will truly and faithfully translate the evidence to the best of his or her abilities.

(2) The costs of an interpreter shall be included in the costs of the reference.

11. (1) An application for judicial review of a decision of the Board operates as a stay in the reference.

(2) Where an application for judicial review of a decision of the Board is made where the reference was conducted in the French language, the decision of the Board and the reasons therefor, where reasons have been given, and the transcript, if any, of the oral evidence given at the hearing, shall be translated into the English language, and the costs thereof shall be included in the costs of the reference.

12. A member of a Board who participates in a decision of the Board shall have been present throughout the reference.

13. (1) The remuneration of members of a Board other than the chair shall not be less than $85 per day or greater than $150 per day.

(2) In addition to the remuneration under subsection (1), a member of a Board is entitled to his or her actual travelling and living expenses incurred while engaged in his or her duties as a member of the Board.

(3) Counsel fees, interpreter fees, fees in respect of the recording and transcribing of the evidence, allowances to court attendants and other costs incurred in respect of a reference shall be at the rate for such fees, allowances and costs in matters before a county or district court.

14. A party to a reference who desires to call as a witness an opposite party may either request the Board to summons the party or give the party or the party's solicitor at least five days notice of the intention to examine the party as a witness, paying at the same time the amount proper for attendance money, and, if such opposite party does not attend on such summons or notice, the reference may be postponed at the direction of the chair of the Board.

15. The chair of the Board may, where it appears necessary for the purposes of the reference, make an order for the examination on oath or affirmation before any person and at any place of a person who has knowledge respecting the matters before the Board and who, because of illness or other reasonable cause, is unable to attend the reference and may permit such deposition to be placed in evidence.

16. The chair of the Board at a reference may,
- (a) order a witness who is not a party to the reference to be excluded from the reference until called to give evidence; and
- (b) exclude the testimony of any person who does not comply with an order made under clause (a).

17. A record of a reference, compiled by a Board shall be forwarded as soon as practicable by the chair of the Board to the Minister, and such record shall be retained by the Minister for a period of at least two years after which time it may be destroyed without the necessity of notice thereof being given to either party to the reference.

REGULATION 302
PURCHASE OF MILK
R.R.O. 1990, Reg. 302

1. A board is authorized to purchase milk for free distribution to pupils in schools under its jurisdiction.

2. The authority of a board may be exercised on condition that,

(a) the distribution is effected only on school days between 8.45 a.m. and 4.00 p.m. and under the supervision and direction of the principal; and

(b) the milk is consumed on the school premises.

REGULATION 304
SCHOOL YEAR CALENDAR
R.R.O. 1990, Reg. 304; Fr. version 664/91, as am. O. Reg. 91/98

1. (1) In this Regulation,

"instructional day" means a school day that is designated as an instructional day on a school calendar and upon which day an instructional program that may include examinations is provided for each pupil whose program is governed by such calendar;

"professional activity" includes evaluation of the progress of pupils, consultation with parents, the counselling of pupils, curriculum and program evaluation and development, professional development of teachers and attendance at educational conferences;

"professional activity day" means a school day that is designated as a day for professional activities on a school calendar;

"school day" means a day that is within a school year and is not a school holiday;

"school year" means the period prescribed as such by or approved as such under this Regulation.

(2) A board may designate half a school day an instructional program and the remainder of the day for professional activities, but such a day constitutes a half-day in determining the number of instructional days in the school year.

2. (1) Subject to section 5, the school year shall commence on or after the 1st day of September and end on or before the 30th day of June.

(2) [Revoked O. Reg. 91/98.]

(3) [Revoked O. Reg. 91/98, s. 2(4).]

(3.1) Subject to section 5, every school year after the 1997-1998 school year shall include a minimum of 194 school days of which up to 4 days may be designated by the board as professional activity days and the remaining school days shall be instructional days.

(4) Subject to section 5, the following are school holidays:

1. Every Saturday and Sunday.
2. When the school is open during July, Canada Day.
3. Labour Day.
4. A day appointed by the Governor General or the Lieutenant Governor as a public holiday or for Thanksgiving.
5. A Christmas vacation consisting of fourteen consecutive days commencing on the Monday next following the Friday preceding the 21st day of December, but when the 21st day of December is a Thursday or a Friday, commencing on the Monday next following.
6. Five consecutive days commencing on the Monday next following the Friday preceding the 14th day of March.
7. Good Friday.
8. Easter Monday.
9. Victoria Day. O. Reg. 91/98, s. 2.

3. (1) [Revoked, O. Reg. 91/98, s. 3(2).]

(2) [Revoked O. Reg. 91/98, s. 3(4).]

(3) Where a school has a policy of granting exemptions to pupils from the writing of examinations, such exemptions may be granted only from the final examinations in a course and only where at least one other set of examinations has been held.

(3.1) With respect to every school year after the 1997-1998 school year, a board may designate up to 10 instructional days as examination days.

(4) The teaching staff shall be in school during regular school hours on examination days and accessible to pupils, unless the board directs otherwise. O. Reg. 91/98, s. 3.

4. (1) In each year every board shall, except in respect of a school or class for which the board has submitted a proposed school calendar under section 5, prepare, adopt and submit to the Minister on or before the 1st day of May in respect of the school year next following, the school calendar or school calendars to be followed in the schools under its jurisdiction, and each such school calendar shall,

(a) state the school or schools in which the calendar is to be followed;
(b) conform to section 2; and
(c) identify each day of the school year as an instructional day, a professional activity day or a school holiday.

(2) In preparing a school calendar under subsection (1), the board shall ensure that some of the professional activity days are designated for the purposes of curriculum development, implementation and review.

(3) A school calendar submitted under subsection (1) shall be accompanied by a general outline of the activities to be conducted on the professional activity days identified on the calendar.

5. (1) For one or more schools under its jurisdiction a board may designate a school year and school holidays that are different from those prescribed in section 2 and, where a board does so, the board shall submit to the Minister on or before the first day of March a proposed school calendar for the school year next following in respect of such school or schools, identifying thereon each day of the school year as an instructional day, a professional activity day or a school holiday, and the board may, upon approval thereof by the Minister, implement such school calendar.

(2) Where the Minister informs a board that he or she does not approve the school calendar submitted under subsection (1), the board may amend its proposed school calendar and submit to the Minister a revised school calendar and, upon approval thereof by the Minister, the board may implement the revised school calendar.

(3) Where a board has submitted a proposed school calendar under subsection (1) and the Minister has not approved on or before the 15th day of April such calendar or a revision thereof submitted under subsection (2), the board shall, on or before the 1st day of May, prepare, adopt and submit to the Minister a school calendar in accordance with section 4.

6. (1) Where in the opinion of the board it is desirable to alter the date of a professional activity day or an examination day on a school calendar that has been submitted under section

4 or subsection 5(3) or approved and implemented under subsection 5(1) or (2), the board may alter the school calendar.

(2) Where, the board alters a school calendar under subsection (1), the board shall notify the parents concerned and the Minister of the altered date as far in advance as possible.

(3) The prior approval of the Minister is required for changes other than to the date of a professional activity day or an examination day.

(4) Where,

(a) a school or class is closed for a temporary period because of failure of transportation arrangements, inclement weather, fire, flood, a breakdown of the school heating plant or a similar emergency, or a school is closed under the *Health Protection and Promotion Act* or the *Education Act*; and

(b) the school calendar is not altered under subsection (1),

the day on which the school or class is closed remains an instructional day or a professional activity day, as the case may be, as designated on the school calendar applicable to such school or class.

7. (1) Every board shall publish annually its school calendar or school calendars and ensure that copies thereof are available at the beginning of the school year for the information of parents and pupils.

(2) A school calendar or school calendars published under subsection (1) shall, in addition to the information required to be listed under subsection 4(1), indicate in a general manner the activities to be conducted on professional activity days.

8. In each year, every board shall undertake an annual evaluation of the activities of the professional activity days of the previous year and retain such evaluations on file.

9. (1) A Remembrance Day service shall be held in every school on the 11th day of November or, when the 11th day of November is a Saturday or a Sunday, on the Friday preceding the 11th day of November.

(2) Subsection (1) does not apply where the school participates in a service of remembrance at a cenotaph or other location in the community.

REGULATION 305
SPECIAL EDUCATION IDENTIFICATION PLACEMENT AND REVIEW COMMITTEES AND APPEALS
R.R.O. 1990, Reg. 305; Fr. version O. Reg. 663/91

[Revoked O. Reg. 181/98.]

REGULATION 306
SPECIAL EDUCATION PROGRAMS AND SERVICES
R.R.O. 1990, Reg. 306

1. A Special Education Program Placement and Review Committee heretofore established by a board under the regulations shall be deemed to be a committee referred to in subparagraph iii of paragraph 5 of subsection 11(1) of the *Education Act* for the purposes of identifying exceptional pupils and making and reviewing placements of exceptional pupils.

2. (1) In this Regulation, "special education plan" means,
- (a) in respect of the school year 1985-86, a plan in effect during the school year prepared by a board that discloses the methods by which and the time within which the board will be in compliance with paragraph 7 of section 170 of the Act; and
- (b) in respect of a school year that commences in September in the year 1986 or any year thereafter, a plan in effect during the school year 1985-86 that is reviewed from year to year in accordance with subsection (3).

(2) Every board shall maintain the special education plan in respect of the board and ensure that the special education plan is amended from time to time to meet the current needs of the exceptional pupils of the board.

(3) Every board shall ensure that the special education plan of the board is reviewed annually by the board and that the review is completed prior to the 15th day of May in each year.

(4) In any year where the special education plan is amended by the board, the amendment shall be submitted to the Minister for review on or before the 15th day of May in that year.

(5) The Minister may at any time require a board to amend its special education plan in a manner that the Minister considers necessary so as to ensure that the board provides special education programs and special education services that meet the current needs of the exceptional pupils of the board.

3. (1) Commencing with the school year 1986-87 and in every second school year thereafter, every board shall, in accordance with procedures provided by the Minister, prepare and approve a report on the provision by the board of special education programs and special education services.

(2) The report referred to in subsection (1) shall be submitted to the Minister for review not later than the 15th day of May in the year 1987 and in every second year thereafter.

4. (1) Every board shall ensure that the special education plan of the board provides for the enrolment and placement of each trainable retarded child who is,
- (a) in attendance at a day nursery licensed under the *Day Nurseries Act* that has a program for developmentally handicapped children; and
- (b) qualified to be a resident pupil of the board.

(2) A copy of the provisions of the special education plan referred to in subsection (1) shall be submitted to the Minister where required by the Minister.

5. (1) Every board shall ensure that the special education plan of the board provides for the enrolment and placement of each person under the age of twenty-one years who is qualified to be a resident pupil of the board and who resides or is lodged within the area of jurisdiction of the board in a centre, facility, home, hospital or institution, other than a private school, that is approved, designated, established, licensed or registered under any Act, and in which no education program is provided by the Ministry or the Ministry of Correctional Services.

(2) Where the centre, facility, home, hospital or institution referred to in subsection (1) is situate within the area of jurisdiction of the board, the board shall make provision in its special education plan for the enrolment and placement of each person under the age of twenty-one years who,

    (a) is a resident in such centre, facility, home, hospital or institution; and

    (b) would be qualified to be a resident pupil of the board if the person's parent or guardian was also resident within the area of jurisdiction of the board.

6. Every board shall ensure that the special education plan of the board is maintained and reviewed in accordance with this Regulation and implemented by the board in accordance with the terms of the plan as to the dates by which and the extent to which special education programs and special education services shall be established or provided for its exceptional pupils.

REGULATION 307
SPECIAL GRANT
R.R.O. 1990, Reg. 307

1. Subject to the approval of the Lieutenant Governor in Council, the Minister may pay in any year, pursuant to a request from a board, in addition to the grant payable under the General Legislative Grants Regulation for such year, a special grant to such board where the General Legislative Grant otherwise payable to the board has placed or will place, in the opinion of the Minister, an undue burden upon all the ratepayers or supporters of the board or upon such of them as are assessed in a particular municipality or locality within the area of jurisdiction of the board.

2. A board to which a special grant is paid in a year under section 1 is not precluded from applying for receiving a special grant in a subsequent year.

3. The Minister, subject to the approval of the Lieutenant Governor in Council, shall prescribe the purpose to which a special grant paid under this Regulation is to be applied, and the amount of such special grant is recoverable in the year next following the year in which it is made if it is not applied as prescribed.

REGULATION 308
SUPERVISED ALTERNATIVE LEARNING FOR EXCUSED PUPILS

R.R.O. 1990, Reg. 308; Fr. version O. Reg. 665/91

1. In this Regulation,

"achievement report" means a written communication on the progress of a pupil between a parent of the pupil and the principal of the school at which the pupil is enrolled or the principal of such other school designated by a committee;

"approved work station" means the place of work approved by a committee where the pupil is employed during school hours when the pupil is excused from attendance at school either full-time or part-time under subsection 3(4);

"child" means a person of compulsory school age who has attained the age of fourteen years;

"committee" means a Supervised Alternative Learning for Excused Pupils Committee established under section 2;

"parent" includes a guardian;

"program" means a supervised alternative learning program in respect of a pupil that is approved by a committee and that may include one or more of,

    (a) full-time or part-time employment at an approved work station for such term or period of time as is fixed or determined under the program,

    (b) completion of a life-skills course, and

    (c) such continuing studies or other activity directed towards the pupil's needs and interests as may be acceptable to the committee,

pursuant to which a pupil is excused from attendance at school either full-time or part-time and by which regular contact with the pupil is maintained by a teacher or other staff member who is employed at or associated with the school where the pupil is enrolled, or such other school as may be designated by the committee, to ensure that the pupil continues to conform to the program;

"pupil" means a child for whom a program has been prescribed under subsection 3(4).

2. (1) A board shall establish a committee to be known as the Supervised Alternative Learning for Excused Pupils Committee for the purposes of this Regulation and designate the secretary of it.

(2) A committee shall be composed of such persons, not fewer than three, as may be appointed by a board in each year, and a quorum of a committee shall consist of,

    (a) a member of the board;

    (b) a supervisory officer who qualified as such as a teacher and is employed by the board, or, where the board does not employ a supervisory officer, the appropriate provincial supervisory officer for the area in which the board has jurisdiction; and

    (c) at least one person who is not an employee of the board in addition to those referred to in clauses (a) and (b).

(3) A committee shall designate a member as chair.

(4) Where a committee considers that it is in the best interests of a pupil, it may designate a school for the purposes of a program that is not the school where the pupil is enrolled.

3. (1) A parent of a child may apply in writing to the principal of the school where the child is enrolled or has a right to attend to have the child participate in a program and the parent shall state in the application why he or she considers that the child should participate in a program.

(2) Where an application is made under subsection (1), the principal shall forthwith forward the application to the secretary of the committee and a copy thereof to the school attendance counsellor, and the committee shall consider the application and any oral or written submission made by any person in support thereof or in opposition thereto and may require the principal and any other employee of the board to report to the committee upon the child in respect of whom the application is made and to make recommendations in respect of the application.

(3) The parent of a child may examine the written reports and recommendations, if any, in respect of the child made under subsection (2).

(4) The committee shall, after interviewing the child, his or her parent and, where the committee considers it appropriate, any other person,

(a) reject the application, in which case the child shall attend school as required by subsection 21(1) of the Act; or

(b) approve the application, in which case the committee shall prescribe a program directed towards the child's needs and interests,

and the secretary of the committee shall notify in writing the principal, the school attendance counsellor, the child and the parent of the decision of the committee.

4. (1) Where the parent of a child disagrees with the determination of the committee to reject the application under clause 3(4)(a) and wishes to bring further relevant information to the attention of the committee, or disagrees with the program prescribed by the committee and notifies the secretary in writing of the disagreement setting out the reasons therefor, the committee may review the decision with which the parent disagrees and, as the case requires, with or without hearing the parent,

(a) approve the application and prescribe a program;

(b) confirm or alter the program; or

(c) refuse to review its determination or the program that it has prescribed,

and the committee shall notify in writing the principal, the school attendance counsellor, the child and the parent of the decisions it has taken in respect of the notification given by the parent.

(2) A pupil shall conform to the program as prescribed for the pupil by the committee under subsection 3(4) or subsection (1) of this section or as altered under subsection 6(2), and the pupil is excused from attendance at school so long as the pupil conforms to the program.

(3) A pupil who is excused from attendance at school either full-time or part-time as determined by the committee under subsection 3(4) or subsection (1) of this section or as altered under subsection 6(2), shall be recorded as a full-time pupil on the register of the school in which the pupil is enrolled or of such other school as was designated by the committee, until the pupil is no longer of compulsory school age.

5. (1) Where the parent of a child disagrees with the determination of the committee to,
  (a) reject the application under clause 3(4)(a); or
  (b) refuse to review its determination under clause 4(1)(c),

the parent may in writing notify the provincial school attendance counsellor of his or her disagreement and the reasons therefor, and the provincial school attendance counsellor may,

  (c) inquire into the validity of the parent's request to have a program prescribed for the child and recommend that the child attend school as required by subsection 21(1) of the Act; or
  (d) recommend, where he or she is satisfied that the child should be excused from attendance at school under this Regulation, that a program be prescribed for the pupil and remit the application to the committee for reconsideration,

and a copy of the recommendation shall be delivered to the board, the principal, the school attendance counsellor, the child and the parent.

(2) Where the provincial school attendance counsellor remits an application to the committee under clause (1)(d), the committee shall reconsider the application.

6. (1) Where a parent of a pupil or a pupil wishes to alter the program prescribed for the pupil under subsection 3(4) or 4(1), the parent may apply in writing to the secretary of the committee for approval of such alteration by the committee.

(2) Where a parent applies under subsection (1) or where a report is made under subsection 7(2), the committee may, after discussion of the application or the report with the pupil and his or her parent, alter the program prescribed for the pupil and shall notify in writing the principal, the school attendance counsellor, the pupil and the parent of the decision of the committee.

7. (1) The school attendance counsellor shall have the same powers and shall perform the same duties in respect of a pupil as in the case of a child who is not excused from attendance at school.

(2) The teacher or other staff member responsible for maintaining regular contact with the pupil shall report to the committee when requested by the committee, and the principal of the school where the pupil is enrolled or of such other school as was designated by the committee shall report to the parent whenever achievement reports are issued by the principal.

(3) A school attendance counsellor of a board shall report as required by the board to the appropriate supervisory officer of the board who shall report to the provincial school attendance counsellor through the chief executive officer of the board on or before the 30th day of September in each year on the number of pupils who under this Regulation during the preceding school year,

  (a) were excused from attendance at school;
  (b) were required to attend school on a part-time basis only;
  (c) returned to full-time attendance at school; and
  (d) ceased to be excused from attendance under section 8.

(4) The parent of a pupil may examine a report in respect of the pupil under subsection (2).

8. Where a pupil and his or her parent move from the area of jurisdiction of the board under which the program is prescribed for the pupil to the area of jurisdiction of another board, the pupil shall be removed from the roll on which he or she was included under subsection 4(3), and the board of which the pupil is then qualified to be a resident pupil shall refer to its committee the question of whether the pupil should be excused from attendance at a school operated by it, and the committee shall make the determination in accordance with subsections 3(2) and (4) and may prescribe a program for the pupil in accordance with subsection 3(4), and for such purpose the committee shall, where it has obtained the consent in writing of the parent, have access to all reports, recommendations and submissions made to the committee of the board that previously prescribed a program for the pupil.

9. Where a pupil resides within the area of jurisdiction of the board under which the program for the pupil is administered but ceases to be a resident pupil of such board by reason of the parent of the pupil ceasing to reside within the area of jurisdiction of the board, the pupil shall continue in the program in accordance with this Regulation without payment of a fee.

10. Where a pupil has ceased to reside within the area of jurisdiction of the board under which the program for the pupil was prescribed and the pupil is not qualified to be a resident pupil of the board in whose area of jurisdiction he or she has taken up residence, the pupil is not excused from attendance at school unless the pupil continues to conform to the program that was prescribed for him or her and, where the pupil continues to conform to the program the pupil shall do so without the payment of a fee and shall remain enrolled as a full-time pupil of the school where the pupil was enrolled immediately before his or her change of residence and the school attendance counsellor for the board that has jurisdiction in the area in which the pupil resides shall give such assistance and cooperation to the teacher or other staff member who makes the reports to the committee under subsection 7(2) as the committee may require.

REGULATION 309
SUPERVISORY OFFICERS
R.R.O. 1990, Reg. 309, as am. O. Reg. 665/92; 162/93

PART I

QUALIFICATIONS OF SUPERVISORY OFFICERS

1. (1) In this Part,

"acceptable university degree" means a degree from an Ontario university or post-secondary institution that is an ordinary member of the Association of Universities and Colleges of Canada or a degree that is equivalent thereto from a university other than such Ontario university or post-secondary institution;

"architect" means a person who is an architect within the meaning of the *Architects Act*;

"certified general accountant" means a member of the Certified General Accountants Association of Ontario;

"certified management accountant" means a registered or certified member of The Society of Management Accountants of Ontario;

"chartered accountant" means a member of The Institute of Chartered Accountants of Ontario;

"lawyer" means a member of the Law Society of Upper Canada;

"Principal's Certificate" means a permanent principal's certificate;

"professional engineer" means a person who is a professional engineer within the meaning of the *Professional Engineers Act*;

"program in school board management" means two compulsory graduate courses approved by the Minister that are offered by a university, one of which is a course in school board finance and the other in school board administration, and four optional graduate courses approved by the Minister that are offered by a university in education, public administration or political science;

"university" means,
- (a) an Ontario university or post-secondary institution that is an ordinary member of the Association of Universities and Colleges of Canada,
- (b) a Canadian university in a province other than Ontario that is an ordinary member of the Association of Universities and Colleges of Canada,
- (c) a university in the United States that is recognized by,
    - (i) Middle States Association of Colleges and Schools,
    - (ii) New England Association of Schools and Colleges,
    - (iii) North Central Association of Colleges and Schools,
    - (iv) Northwest Association of Schools and Colleges,
    - (v) Southern Association of Colleges and Schools,
    - (vi) Western Association of Schools and Colleges, or
- (d) a university that is located in a country other than Canada or the United States and that is a member of the association of Commonwealth Universities or the International Association of Universities.

REGULATIONS UNDER THE EDUCATION ACT

son who holds or who under this Regulation is deemed to hold a Supervisory 'icate is, subject to subsection 6(1), qualified as a supervisory officer for the Act and this Regulation.

(3) A person referred to in subsection 3(4) who is employed by a board is qualified as a business supervisory officer for the purposes of the Act and this Regulation for the period during which the person is employed by the board in a position referred to in that subsection.

(4) For the purposes of this Regulation, a person who is the holder of a Master's degree that is an acceptable university degree and who successfully completes a graduate course, either as part of or in addition to the courses necessary to obtain the degree, in each of school board finance and school board administration at a university shall be deemed to have completed a program in school board management.

(5) For the purposes of this Regulation, a person who is the holder of an acceptable university degree and who is a certified general accountant, a certified management accountant or a chartered accountant shall be deemed to be a person who has completed the four optional graduate courses as part of a program in school board management.

O. Reg. 665/92, s. 1.

2. The Minister shall issue a Supervisory Officer's Certificate to a person if the person applies for it and the Ontario College of Teachers certifies that the person meets the qualifications of a Supervisory Officer. O. Reg. 665/92, s. 2, *part*; O. Reg. 182/97, s. 1.

2.1 (1) On application, the Minister shall issue a Business Supervisory Officer's Certificate to a person who meets the following qualifications:

1. The person has at least seven years of successful experience in business administration, including at least three years in a managerial role relevant to the role of business supervisory officer.
2. The person holds an acceptable university degree.
3. The person,
    i. holds a master's degree from a university, or
    ii. is qualified to practise as an architect, certified general accountant, certified management accountant, chartered accountant, lawyer or professional engineer, or is qualified to practise in another professional capacity that, in the opinion of the Minister, provides experience appropriate for the position of business supervisory officer.
4. The person has successfully completed a program in school board management.
5. The person has successfully completed the business supervisory officer's qualifications program described in section 2.2 within five years after starting the program.

(2) A person shall be deemed to meet the qualifications set out in paragraphs 1 to 4 of subsection (1) if, not later than the 31st day of December, 1997, the person obtains the qualifications that were required of a candidate for a Business Supervisory Officer's Certificate under subsection 2(3) of this Regulation as it read immediately before the 6th day of November, 1992. O. Reg. 665/92, s. 2, *part*.

2.2 The business supervisory officer's qualifications program referred to in section 2.1 shall have the following features:

1. The program shall be provided by an organization or institution that has entered into

a contract with the Minister to provide the instruction and arrange for the practical experience referred to in paragraphs 3 and 4.
2. No person shall be admitted to the program unless the person has submitted proof to the organization or institution that provides the program that the person meets the qualifications set out in paragraphs 1 to 4 of subsection 2.1(1).
3. The program shall consist of,
   i. four instructional modules, each consisting of at least fifty hours of instruction, and
   ii. one module consisting of at least fifty hours of practical experience in the workplace.
4. The instructional modules shall provide instruction that, in the opinion of the Minister, is relevant to the position of business supervisory officer, in the following subject areas:
   i. Statutes, regulations and government policies affecting education in Ontario.
   ii. Curriculum guidelines and other reference material pertaining to elementary and secondary education in Ontario.
   iii. Theories and practices of supervision, administration and business organization. O. Reg. 665/92, s. 2, *part*; O. Reg. 182/97, s. 2.

3. (1) A supervisory officer responsible for the development, implementation, operation and supervision of educational programs in schools shall,
   (a) hold a Supervisory Officer's Certificate; or
   (b) be a person who is deemed to hold a Supervisory Officer's Certificate under section 4.

(2) A senior business official who,
   (a) reports to a director of education;
   (b) reports to an assistant director of education or associate director of education; or
   (c) is employed by a board that has an enrolment of more than 600 pupils and that does not employ a director of education,

shall, subject to subsections (4) and (5), be a person who holds, or who under this Regulation is deemed to hold, a Business Supervisory Officer's Certificate.

(3) A business official who;
   (a) is assigned one or more of the duties of a supervisory officer;
   (b) reports to a senior business official referred to in subsection (2); and
   (c) has been appointed to a position designated by a board as superintendent, assistant superintendent, comptroller, assistant comptroller, business administrator or assistant business administrator or to a position that the board considers equivalent thereto and that has been approved by the Minister,

shall, subject to subsection (4), be a person who holds, or who under this Regulation is deemed to hold, a Business Supervisory Officer's Certificate.

(4) A board may appoint a person who does not hold or who under this Regulation is not deemed to hold a Business Supervisory Officer's Certificate as a senior business official referred to in subsection (2) or as a business official referred to in subsection (3) for a term of not more than two years if the person,

(a) holds an acceptable university degree or is qualified to practise as an architect, certified general accountant, certified management accountant, chartered accountant, lawyer or professional engineer, or in another professional capacity that, in the opinion of the Minister, provides experience appropriate for the position of business supervisory officer; and

(b) has entered into an agreement in writing with the Board that sets out that the person will endeavour to obtain a Business Supervisory Officer's Certificate within the term of the appointment. O. Reg. 665/92, s. 3(2).

(5) Despite subsection (4), a board may employ a person appointed under that subsection for an additional period of not more than two years if the person continues to make progress towards obtaining a Business Supervisory Officer's Certificate.

(6) A person who was appointed under subsection (4) before the 6th day of November, 1992 may, by agreement with the board, amend the agreement under clause (4)(b) to be consistent with the new requirements of that clause. O. Reg. 655/92, s. 3(3).

4. A person who, prior to the 1st day of July 1974,

(a) held an Elementary School Inspector's Certificate, a Public School Inspector's Certificate, a Secondary School Principal's Certificate, or a Secondary School Principal's Certificate, Type A; or

(b) served as a provincial inspector of secondary schools or a municipal inspector of secondary schools,

is deemed to hold a Supervisory Officer's Certificate.

5. (1) A person who was in the employ of a board on the 31st day of August, 1975, in a position referred to in subsection 3(2) or (3), is deemed to hold a Supervisor Officer's Certificate.

(2) A person employed in the Ministry on the 31st day of August, 1975, in a position that the Minister considers similar to one of those referred to in subsection 3(2) or (3) is deemed to hold a Supervisory Officer's Certificate.

6. (1) A person who,

(a) holds a Supervisory Officer's Certificate and was not required, at the time the certificate was obtained, to have seven years of successful teaching experience;

(b) is deemed to hold a Supervisory Officer's Certificate under section 5; or

(c) holds a Business Supervisory Officer's Certificate,

is qualified as a supervisory officer under this Regulation for business administration purposes only.

(2) A supervisory officer other than a supervisory officer referred to in subsection (1) who, on the 30th day of September, 1986, was performing the duties,

(a) of a senior business official referred to in clause 3(2)(c) and who reports as referred to in clauses 3(2)(a) and (b); or

(b) of a business official referred to in clause 3(3)(c) who reports to a senior business official referred to in subsection 3(2),

is deemed to hold a Business Supervisory Officer's Certificate. O. Reg. 665/92, s. 4.

PART II

TRANSFER AND DISMISSAL

7. (1) In this section, "redundant" in respect of the position of a supervisory officer means no longer required to be filled by reason of,
- (a) the implementation by a board of a long range organizational plan of operation in respect of schools or of supervisory services that eliminates the position or merges it with another position;
- (b) a reduction in the number of classes or in the business functions of the board for which supervision is required; or
- (c) a change in duties or requirements placed upon boards by or under any Act that renders a supervisory service unnecessary or reduces the need for such service.

(2) Where a board declares the position of a supervisory officer redundant, the board shall,
- (a) give the supervisory officer at least three months' notice in writing that the position has been declared redundant;
- (b) transfer the supervisory officer to a position for which he or she is qualified, with supervisory and administrative responsibilities as similar as possible to those of his or her previous position; and
- (c) pay the supervisory officer for at least one year following the date of the transfer with no reduction in his or her rate of salary.

8. (1) A board shall not suspend or dismiss a supervisory officer without first giving the supervisory officer reasonable information about the reasons for the suspension or dismissal and an opportunity to make submissions to the board.

(2) A supervisory officer who wishes to make submissions to the board may make them orally or in writing. O. Reg. 162/93, s. 1.

9. [Revoked O. Reg. 162/93, s. 1.]

10. [Revoked O. Reg. 162/93, s. 1.]

11. [Revoked O. Reg. 162/93, s. 1.]

12. [Revoked O. Reg. 162/93, s. 1.]

13. [Revoked O. Reg. 162/93, s. 1.]

14. [Revoked O. Reg. 162/93, s. 1.]

15. [Revoked O. Reg. 162/93, s. 1.]

REGULATION 310
TEACHERS' CONTRACTS
R.R.O. 1990, Reg. 310

Form of Contracts

1. (1) Every contract between a board and a permanent teacher shall be in Form 1.

(2) Every contract between a board and a probationary teacher shall be in Form 2.

(3) Except where otherwise provided under subsection 259(5) or (6) of the Act, every contract between a board and a continuing education teacher shall be in Form 3.

Payment of Salaries

2. (1) Subject to subsection (4), a board shall pay the salary of a teacher under contract in Form 1 or Form 2 in the number of payments set out in the contract.

(2) Subject to subsection (4), a board shall pay the salary of a teacher under contract in Form 3 in the number of payments or on the dates set out in the contract.

(3) In the case of a contract in Form 1 or Form 2, the contract shall provide for not fewer than ten salary payments.

(4) Where during the term of a contract between a board and a teacher the salary of the teacher is changed by mutual agreement in writing between the board and the teacher, the contract shall be deemed to be varied accordingly.

FORM 1

Education Act

PERMANENT TEACHER'S CONTRACT

This Agreement made in duplicate this .... day of .... , 19 ...., between .... hereinafter called the "Board" and .... of
(   )
(the .... of .... in the County   )
(   )
((or as the case may be) of ....   )
(   )

hereinafter called the "Teacher".

1. The Board agrees to employ the Teacher as a permanent teacher and the Teacher agrees to teach for the Board commencing the .... day of .... , 19 ....

at a yearly salary of .... Dollars, subject to any changes in salary mutually agreed upon by the Teacher and the Board, payable in ....

(not fewer than ten)

payments, less any lawful deduction, in the following manner:

    i. Where there are ten payments, one-tenth on or before the last teaching day of each teaching month.

    ii. Where there are more than ten payments, at least one-twelfth on or before the last teaching day of each teaching month, any unpaid balance being payable on or before the last teaching day of June, or at the time of leaving the employ of the Board, whichever is the earlier.

  2. This Agreement is subject to the Teacher's continuing to hold qualifications in accordance with the Acts and the regulations administered by the Minister.

  3. The Teacher agrees to be diligent and faithful in his or her duties during the period of employment, and to perform such duties and teach such subjects as the Board may assign under the Acts and the regulations administered by the Minister.

  4. Where the Teacher attends an educational conference for which the school has been legally closed and his or her attendance at it is certified by the supervisory officer concerned or by the chair of the conference, the Board agrees to make no deductions from the Teacher's salary for his or her absence during that attendance.

  5. Where an Act of Ontario or a regulation thereunder authorizes the Teacher to be absent from school without loss of pay, the Board agrees that no deduction from his or her pay will be made for the period of absence so authorized.

  6. This Agreement may be terminated,

    (a) at any time by the mutual consent in writing of the Teacher and the Board;

    (b) on the 31st day of December in any year of the Teacher's employment by either party giving written notice to the other on or before the last preceding 30th day of November; or

    (c) on the 31st day of August in any year of the Teacher's employment by either party giving written notice to the other on or before the last preceding 31st day of May.

  7. The Teacher agrees with the Board that if the Teacher enters into an agreement with another board he or she will within forty-eight hours notify the Board in writing of the termination of this Agreement unless the notice has already been given.

  8. Where the Teacher is to be transferred by the Board from a school in one municipality to a school in another municipality, the Board agrees to notify the Teacher in writing on or before the 1st day of May immediately prior to the school year for which the transfer is effective, but nothing in this paragraph prevents the transfer of a teacher at any time by mutual consent of the Board and the Teacher.

  9. This Agreement shall remain in force until terminated in accordance with any Act administered by the Minister or the regulations thereunder.

FORM 2 REGULATIONS UNDER THE EDUCATION ACT

In witness whereof the Teacher has signed and the Board has affixed hereto its corporate seal attested by its proper officers in that behalf.

....
(signature of Chair of the Board)

....
(signature of Secretary of the Board)

....
(signature of Teacher)

FORM 2

Education Act

PROBATIONARY TEACHER'S CONTRACT

This Agreement made in duplicate this .... day of .... , 19 ...., between .... hereinafter called the "Board" and .... of
( )
(the .... of .... in the County)
( )
((or as the case may be) of ....)
( )
hereinafter called the "Teacher".

1. The Board agrees to employ the Teacher as a probationary teacher for a probationary period of .... years and the Teacher agrees to teach for the Board commencing the .... day of .... , 19 .... at a yearly salary of .... Dollars, subject to any changes in salary mutually agreed upon by the Teacher and the Board, payable in ....
(not fewer than ten)
payments, less any lawful deduction, in the following manner:

   i. Where there are ten payments, one-tenth on or before the last teaching day of each teaching month.
   ii. Where there are more than ten payments, at least one-twelfth on or before the last teaching day of each teaching month, any unpaid balance being payable on or before the last teaching day of June, or at the time of leaving the employ of the Board, whichever is the earlier.

2. This Agreement is subject to the Teacher's continuing to hold qualifications in accordance with the Acts and regulations administered by the Minister.

REGULATION 310 **FORM 3**

3. The Teacher agrees to be diligent and faithful in his or her duties during the period of employment, and to perform such duties and teach such subjects as the Board may assign under the Acts and regulations administered by the Minister.

4. Where the Teacher attends an educational conference for which the school has been legally closed and his or her attendance at it is certified by the supervisory officer concerned or by the chair of the conference, the Board agrees to make no deductions from the Teacher's salary for his or her absence during that attendance.

5. Where an Act of Ontario or a regulation thereunder authorizes the Teacher to be absent from school without loss of pay, the Board agrees that no deduction from his or her pay will be made for the period of absence so authorized.

6. Despite anything in this contract this Agreement may be terminated,
    (a) at any time by the mutual consent in writing of the Teacher and the Board;
    (b) on the 31st day of December in any year of the Teacher's employment by either party giving written notice to the other on or before the last preceding 30th day of November; or
    (c) on the 31st day of August in any year of the Teacher's employment by either party giving written notice to the other on or before the last preceding 31st day of May.

7. The Teacher agrees with the Board that if the Teacher enters into an agreement with another board he or she will within forty-eight hours notify the Board in writing of the termination of this Agreement unless the notice has already been given.

8. Where this Agreement is not terminated under paragraph 6 at the conclusion of the probationary period in paragraph 1, the Teacher is deemed to be employed as a permanent teacher by the Board.

In witness whereof the Teacher has signed and the Board has affixed hereto its corporate seal attested by its proper officers in that behalf.

....
(signature of Chair of the Board)

....
(signature of Secretary of the Board)

....
(signature of Teacher)

FORM 3

Education Act

CONTINUING EDUCATION TEACHER'S CONTRACT

This Agreement made in duplicate this ....

day of .... , 19 ....
between .... hereinafter
called the "Board" and .... of

FORM 3

REGULATIONS UNDER THE EDUCATION ACT

(the .... of .... in the county)
(or as the case may be) of ....)
  hereinafter called the "Teacher".

    1. For the session commencing on the ....
day of .... , 19 .... ,
and ending on the .... day
of .... , 19 .... ,
the Board agrees to employ the Teacher as a continuing education teacher and the Teacher agrees to teach for the Board as a continuing education teacher at a salary of $ ....
  (specify amount per hour or per session)

    2. The salary specified in paragraph 1, subject to any changes in salary mutually agreed upon by the Teacher and the Board, is reduced by any lawful deductions and is payable as follows:

....
  (specify number of payments or dates of payment)

    3. This Agreement is subject to the Teacher continuing to hold qualifications in accordance with the Acts and the regulations administered by the Minister.

    4. During the session specified in paragraph 1, the Teacher agrees to perform such duties as the Board may assign under the Acts and the regulations administered by the Minister and to be diligent and faithful in the performance of the Teacher's duties.

    5. Despite anything in this contract, this Agreement may be terminated prior to the end of the session mentioned in paragraph 1,

    (a) at any time by mutual consent in writing of the Teacher and the Board;

    (b) if the Teacher has entered upon the teaching duties referred to in paragraph 4, at any time by either party giving written notice to the other not less than forty-eight hours before the date of termination specified in the notice; or

    (c) by the Board at any time without advance notice to the Teacher where, before the commencement of the course or class or teaching in the subject, the Board has resolved not to offer the course, class or subject in the session mentioned in paragraph 1.

IN WITNESS WHEREOF the Teacher has signed and the Board has affixed hereto its corporate seal attested by its proper officers.

                                                     ....

                                                     ....

                                                     ....
                                                         (signature of Teacher)

REGULATION 311
TERRITORY WITHOUT MUNICIPAL ORGANIZATION ATTACHED TO A DISTRICT MUNICIPALITY
R.R.O. 1990, Reg. 311

1. (1) Those portions of the territory without municipal organization situate in the Territorial District of Thunder Bay being,

(a) the geographic townships of Atikameg, Bomby, Brothers, Bryant, Cecil, Cecile, Davies, Flood, Foote, Grenville, Herbert, Knowles, Laberge, McCron, McGill, Mikano, Nickle, Roberta, Shabotik and Spooner; and

(b) all lands in unsurveyed territory within an area the boundary sides of which are as follows:

1. On the east side, the easterly boundary of the Territorial District of Thunder Bay.
2. On the south side, the International Boundary.
3. On the west side, the line described as commencing at the point of intersection of the 86th Meridian and the International Boundary, extending northerly along the said Meridian until it meets the 48th Parallel, then easterly along the said Parallel until it meets the high water mark on the shoreline of the geographic Township of Homer, then southerly and southeasterly along the said high water mark to the intersection of the easterly boundary of the geographic Township of Homer, then northerly along the said easterly boundary of the geographic Township of Homer to the intersection of the boundary of Pukaskwa National Park, then northeasterly and along the boundary of the said National Park to the northerly boundary of the said National Park, thence westerly along the said northerly boundary to the point of intersection thereof with the 86th Meridian, then northerly along the said Meridian until it meets the southerly boundary of the geographic Township of Lecours to the southwest angle of the geographic Township of Bomby, then northerly along the said westerly boundary of the geographic Township of Bomby to the northwest angle of the said Township, then westerly along the northerly boundary of the geographic Township of Lecours to the point of intersection with the 86th Meridian, then northerly along the said Meridian until it meets the southerly boundary of the geographic Township of Grenville, then westerly along the southerly boundary of the geographic Township of Grenville to the southwest angle thereof, then northerly along the westerly boundary of the geographic townships of Grenville and Davies to the northwest angle of the geographic Township of Davies.
4. On the north side, the lien formed by the northerly boundary of the Township of Manitouwadge and the extension westerly of the northerly boundary of the Township of Manitouwadge to the northwest angle of the geographic Township of Davies and the extension easterly of the northerly boundary of the Township of Manitouwadge along the northerly boundary of the geographic townships of Nickle, Herbert and Foote to the easterly boundary of the District of Thunder Bay,

are attached to the Township of Manitouwadge.

(2) Those portions of the territory without municipal organization situate in the Territorial District of Thunder Bay being,

S. 1 REGULATIONS UNDER THE EDUCATION ACT

    (a) the geographic Township of Pic not included in former school section No. 1. Pic; and

    (b) the geographic Township of Coldwell not included in former school section No. 1. Port Coldwell,

are attached to the Town of Marathon.

(3) Those portions of Territory without municipal organization situate in the Territorial District of Thunder Bay being,

    (a) the geographic townships of Byron, Cotte, Grain, Homer, Lecours and O'Neill; and

    (b) all lands in unsurveyed territory within an area the boundary sides of which are described as follows:

1. On the east side, the line described in paragraph 3 of clause (1)(b).
2. On the south side, the International Boundary.
3. On the west side, the Meridian 86°30'.
4. On the north side, the line former by the projection westerly of the northerly boundary of the geographic Township of Davies until it meets the Meridian 86°30',

are attached to the Town of Marathon.

(4) The portion of the territory without municipal organization comprising the geographic Township of Syine not included in the former school section No. 1. Jackfish is attached to the Township of Terrace Bay.

(5) Those portions of the territory without municipal organization situate in the Territorial District of Thunder Bay being,

    (a) the geographic townships of Strey, Tuuri and Walsh;

    (b) all lands in unsurveyed territory within an area the boundary sides of which are described as follows:

1. On the east side, the Meridian 86°30'.
2. On the south side, the International Boundary.
3. On the west side, the line described as commencing at the intersection of the southeast angle of the Township of Terrace Bay and the International Boundary, then northerly along the easterly limit of the Township of Terrace Bay to the northeast angle thereof, then westerly along the northerly boundary of the Township of Terrace Bay to the point of intersection thereon of the easterly limit of the geographic Township of Strey, then continuing along the northerly limit of the Township of Terrace Bay and the southerly limit of the geographic Township of Strey to the southwest angle of the geographic Township of Strey, then northerly along the westerly limit of the geographic Township of Strey and its projection northerly parallel to the 87th Meridian to the point of intersection with a line that is the projection westerly of the northerly limit of the geographic Township of Davies.
4. On the north side, a line that is the projection westerly of the northerly limit of the geographic Township of Davies,

are attached to the Township of Terrace Bay.

(6) The portion of territory without municipal organization comprising the geographic Township of Lahontan not included in former school section No. 1. Rossport is attached to the Township of Schreiber.

(7) Those portions of the territory without municipal organization situate in the Territorial District of Thunder Bay being,
- (a) the geographic townships of Killraine, Priske, Wiggins and Yesno; and
- (b) all lands in unsurveyed territory, exclusive of St. Ignace Island, within an area the boundary sides of which are described as follows:
  1. On the east side, the line described in paragraph 3 of clause (5)(b).
  2. On the south side, the International Boundary.
  3. On the west side, a line that is the extension southerly to the International Boundary of the westerly limit of the geographic Township of Wiggins, the said westerly limit of the said geographic Township of Wiggins and the line that is the projection northerly of the said westerly limit of the geographic Township of Wiggins to the point of intersection of a line that is the projection westerly of the northerly limit of the geographic Township of Davies.
  4. On the north side, a line that is the projection westerly of the northerly limit of the geographic Township of Davies,

are attached to the Township of Schreiber.

REGULATION 312
TRAINING ASSISTANCE
R.R.O. 1990, Reg. 312

[Editor's note: Although not revoked at the time of publication, this regulation refers to provisions in s. 135 of the Education Act that have been repealed.]

REGULATION 313
TRUSTEE DISTRIBUTION
R.R.O. 1990, Reg. 313, as am. O. Reg. 47/91; Fr. version O. Reg. 378/92; 143/94; 71/97

[Editor's note: Although not revoked at the time of publication, this regulation refers to matters that no longer apply after the Education Quality Improvement Act, 1997.]

REGULATION 7/91
CALCULATION OF ENROLMENT
IN PART XIII OF THE ACT
O. Reg. 7/91

[Editor's note: Although not revoked at the time of publication, this regulation refers to Part XIII of the Education Act, which has been repealed.]

REGULATION 731/92
TRANSITIONAL PROVISIONS RELATING TO THE KIRKLAND LAKE — TIMISKAMING SEPARATE SCHOOL ZONE BOUNDARY CHANGES
O. Reg. 731/92; Fr. version O. Reg. 776/92, as am. O. Reg. 683/94; 95/95

[Editor's note: Although not revoked at the time of publication, this regulation refers to matters that are no longer relevant after the Education Quality Improvement Act, 1997.]

REGULATION 183/97
LETTERS OF PERMISSION
O. Reg. 183/97

1. (1) The Minister may grant to a board a Letter of Permission for a period specified in the letter if the director of education or secretary of the board submits to the Ministry, in duplicate, an application in Form 1 or 1a together with evidence that,
- (a) the board has publicly advertised, on at least three occasions, a position for which a teacher is required under the regulations;
- (b) at least one advertisement was published in a daily newspaper having provincial circulation in Ontario;
- (c) at least one advertisement appeared during the 30 days preceding the start of employment;
- (d) seven days have passed since the date of the final advertisement; and
- (e) no teacher has applied for the position or no teacher who has applied for the position has accepted it.

(2) The period for which a Letter of Permission is granted,
- (a) shall not exceed one year; and
- (b) shall not extend beyond the end of a school year unless the period begins after the end of a school year and ends before the beginning of the next school year.

2. Regulation 297 of the Revised Regulations of Ontario, 1990 and Ontario Regulations 34/91, 415/91, 243/92, 687/92, 559/93 and 729/94 are revoked.

FORM 1

Education Act

APPLICATION FOR LETTER OF PERMISSION

On behalf of ....
(name of board)

A LETTER OF PERMISSION is requested to employ
....
(name in full)

Social Insurance Number ....

as a teacher of the .... division

at .... school,

from........................ 19.......... to .... 19..........

I certify and attach evidence that the Board has complied with section 1 of the Ontario Regulation 183/97, including a copy of the most recent advertisement of the position for which the Letter of Permission is required.

FORM 1A REGULATIONS UNDER THE EDUCATION ACT

Date ....
 Director of Education or Secretary of the Board

LETTER OF PERMISSION IS HEREBY GRANTED

Date ....
 (*Name*)
 Delegate of the Deputy Minister

FORMULE 1A

Loi sur l'éducation

DEMANDE DE PERMISSION INTÉRIMAIRE

Au nom du ....
 (nom du conseil)

Une PERMISSION INTÉRIMAIRE est demandée pour l'emploi de:

....
 (prénoms et nom)

dont le numéro d'assurance sociale est ....

en qualité d'enseignant au cycl ....

à l'écote ....

du 19 .... au .... 19......

Je certifie et joins la preuve que le Conseil s'est conformé à l'article 1 du Règlement de l'Ontario 183/97. Vous trouverez également ci-joint une copie de l'annonce la plus récente du poste pour lequel la permission intérimaire est demandée.

Date: ....
 Le directeur de l'éducation ou le secrétaire du Conseil,

LA PERMISSION INTÉRIMAIRE EST ACCORDÉE PAR LA PRÉSENTE

Date: ....
 Le délégué du sous-ministre,
 (*nom*)

REGULATION 185/97
ESTABLISHMENT, AREAS OF JURISDICTION AND NAMES OF DISTRICT SCHOOL BOARDS
O. Reg. 185/97, as am. O. Reg. 278/97; 80/98; 213/98

1. Thirty-one English-language public district school boards are established.

2. The name of each English-language public district school board is ''English-language Public District School Board No. ____'' (inserting a number between 1 and 29 or a combination of numbers and letters as set out in each paragraph of section 3) unless otherwise specified in the Schedules. O. Reg. 80/98, s. 2; 213/98, s. 1.

3. The following are the areas of jurisdiction of the English-language public district school boards:
  1. The area of jurisdiction of the District Ontario North East consists of,
      i. in the Territorial District of Algoma, the geographic townships of Ebbs and Templeton,
      ii. in the Territorial District of Cochrane,
         A. the City of Timmins,
         B. the Towns of Cochrane, Hearst, Iroquois Falls, Kapuskasing and Smooth Rock Falls,
         C. the Townships of Glackmeyer, Mattice-Val Cote, Moonbeam, Opasatika and Val Rita-Harty,
         D. the portion of the Township of Black River-Matheson that on December 31, 1996 was not part of the geographic townships of Barnet, Frencheville, Garrison, Harker, Holloway, Lamplugh, Marriott, McCool, Michaud, Rand or Stoughton,
         E. the portion of the Township of Fauquier-Strickland that on December 31, 1996 was not part of the geographic townships of Beardmore, Carmichael, MacVicar or Stringer,
         F. the geographic townships of Aurora, Barker, Blount, Brower, Calder, Casgrain, Clute, Colquhoun, Fournier, Fox, Hanlan, Hanna, Irish, Kendall, Kennedy, Lamarche, Landry, Leitch, Lowther, McCowan, Mortimer, Nansen, Newmarket, O'Brien, Ottaway, Pyne, St. John, Stimson, Stoddard, Studholme, Teefy and Way.
         G. the portion of the geographic township of Benoit that is not part of the Township of Black-River Matheson
         H. the portion of the geographic township of Haggart that is not part of the Township of Fauquier-Strickland, and
         I. the portion of the geographic township of Owens that is not part of the Township of Val Rita-Harty,
      iii. in the Territorial District of Nipissing,
         A. the Municipality of Temagami, except for the portion of the Municipality that was formerly part of the geographic townships of Clement and Scholes, and

S. 3 REGULATIONS UNDER THE EDUCATION ACT

      B. the geographic townships of Eldridge, Flett, Gladman, Gooderham, Hammell, Hartle, Hobbs, Kenny, McCallum, McLaren and Thistle, and
    iv. in the Territorial District of Timiskaming,
      A. the Towns of Charlton, Cobalt, Englehart, Haileybury, Kirkland Lake, Latchford and New Liskeard,
      B. the Village of Thornloe,
      C. the Townships of Armstrong, Brethour, Casey, Chamberlain, Coleman, Dack, Dymond, Evanturel, Gauthier, Harley, Harris, Hilliard, Hudson, James, Kerns, Larder Lake, Matachewan and McGarry,
      D. the geographic townships of Auld, Barber, Barr, Bayly, Beauchamp, Boston, Brigstocke, Bryce, Cane, Catharine, Chown, Corkill, Davidson, Eby, Farr, Firstbrook, Grenfell, Haultain, Henwood, Ingram, Kittson, Lawson, Lebel, Lorrain, Lundy, Maisonville, Marquis, Marter, McElroy, Mickle, Milner, Mulligan, Nicol, Otto, Pacaud, Pense, Roadhouse, Robillard, Savard, Sharpe, Smyth, South Lorrain, Truax, Tudhope, Willet and Willison, and
      E. the portion of the geographic township of Gillies Limit that is not part of the Township of Coleman.
2. The area of jurisdiction of the Algoma District School Board consists of,
    i. in the Territorial District of Algoma,
      A. the Cities of Elliot Lake and Sault Ste. Marie,
      B. the towns of Blind River, Bruce Mines and Thessalon,
      C. the Villages of Hilton Beach and Iron Bridge,
      D. the Townships of Day and Bright Additional, Dubreuilville, Hilton, Hornepayne, Jocelyn, Johnson, Laird, Michipicoten, Plummer Additional, Prince, Shedden, St. Joseph, The North Shore, Thessalon, Thompson and White River,
      E. the Township of MacDonald, Meredith and Aberdeen Additional,
      F. the Township of Tarbutt and Tarbutt Additional,
      G. the geographic townships of Aberdeen, Archibald, Aweres, Bridgland, Bright, Chenard, Cobden, Dennis, Deroche, Dunphy, Esquega, Fenwick, Fiddler, Finon, Fisher, Galbraith, Gaudette, Gladstone, Gould, Grasett, Haughton, Havilland, Herrick, Hodgins, Home, Huotari, Jarvis, Jogues, Juillette, Kamichisitit, Kars, Kincaid, Kirkwood, Ley, Mack, McMahon, Montgomery, Morin, Nouvel, Parkinson, Patton, Peever, Pennefather, Rix, Rose, Ryan, Scarfe, Shields, Slater, Tilley, Timmermans, Tupper, VanKoughnet and Wells,
      H. the portion of the geographic township of Striker not included in the Township of The North Shore,
      I. all the islands in the North Channel of Lake Huron lying south of the geographic townships of Bright, Cobden, and the portion of Striker that is not part of the Township of The North Shore, and
      J. the mining locations known as Montreal Mining Southern Location, Montreal Mining Northern Location, A. McDonnell Mining Location, Kincaid Mining Location 5, 6, 7 and 8 and Rankin Mining Location, and

ii. in the Territorial District of Sudbury,
- A. The Township of Chapleau, and
- B. the geographic townships of Caverley, Chapleau, de Gaulle, Eisenhower, Gallagher, Genier, Halsey, Kaplan and Panet.

3. The area of jurisdiction of the Rainbow District School Board consists of,
    i. in the Territorial District of Manitoulin, all of the said territorial district except the geographic townships of Carlyle, Humboldt and Killarney,
    ii. in the Territorial District of Sudbury,
    - A. The Regional Municipality of Sudbury,
    - B. the Town of Espanola,
    - C. the Townships of Baldwin and Hagar,
    - D. the Township of Casimir, Jennings and Appleby,
    - E. the Municipality of French River,
    - F. the Township of Nairn and Hyman,
    - F.1 the portion of the Municipality of West Nipissing that was formerly part of the geographic township of Janes,
    - G. the Township of Ratter and Dunnet,
    - H. the geographic townships of Allen, Awrey, Burwash, Cartier, Cascaden, Cleland, Cox, Curtin, Davis, Foster, Foy, Hart, Harty, Hawley, Hendrie, Henry, Hess, Laura, Loughrin, Moncrieff, Mongowin, Roosevelt, Scadding, Secord, Servos, Street, and Truman,
    - I. the portions of the geographic townships of Dill, Dryden, Eden, Tilton and Trill that are not part of The Regional Municipality of Sudbury,
    - J. the portion of the geographic township of Janes that is not part of the Municipality of West Nipissing, and
    - K. the portions of the geographic townships of Bigwood, Cherriman and Haddo that are not part of the Municipality of French River.
    iii. the portion of the Township of The Sables — Spanish Rivers that is in the Territorial District of Sudbury.

4. The area of jurisdiction of the Near North District School Board consists of,
    i. in the Territorial District of Nipissing,
    - A. the City of North Bay,
    - B. the Towns of Kearney and Mattawa,
    - C. the Townships of Bonfield, Calvin, Chisholm, East Ferris, Field, Mattawan and Papineau-Cameron,
    - D. the portion of the Municipality of West Nipissing that was not formerly part of the geographic townships of Bertram, Dana, Fell, Latchford or McWilliams, and
    - E. the geographic townships of Blyth, Boyd, Clarkson, Commanda, Deacon, Eddy, French, Jocko, Lauder, Lyman, Merrick, Notman, Pentland, Phelps, Poitras and Wyse,
    ii. the Territorial District of Parry Sound, and
    iii. in the District Municipality of Muskoka, the Freeman Ward of the Township of Georgian Bay.

S. 3 REGULATIONS UNDER THE EDUCATION ACT

5. The area of jurisdiction of the Keewatin-Patricia District School Board consists of, in the Territorial District of Kenora,
   i. the City of Dryden,
   ii. the Towns of Jaffray Melick, Keewatin, Kenora and Sioux Lookout,
   iii. the Townships of Ear Falls, Ignace, Machin and Sioux Narrows,
   iv. the geographic townships of Boys, Britton, Buller, Colenso, Dome, Eton, Hartman, Ilsley, Kirkup, Ladysmith, Melgund, Mutrie, Pellatt, Redditt, Redvers, Rowell, Rugby, Smellie, Southworth, Van Horne, Wabigoon, Wainwright and Zealand,
   v. the portion of the geographic township of Aubrey that is not part of the Township of Machin,
   vi. all the lands in unsurveyed territory in the vicinity of the station house of the Canadian National Railways at Minaki described as follows:

   commencing at a point distant 4 kilometres measured east astronomically from the northeast corner of the said station house,

   thence north astronomically 4 kilometres,

   thence west astronomically 8 kilometres,

   thence south astronomically 8 kilometres,

   thence east astronomically 8 kilometres,

   thence north astronomically 4 kilometres to the point of commencement,
   vii. except for those parts of the mainland which are crossed by the said line, all lands lying north of a line extending from the southernmost extremity of the geographic Township of Boys to the southwest corner of the geographic Township of Kirkup and south of the southerly boundaries of the geographic townships of Boys and Pellatt, the Towns of Jaffray Melick, Keewatin and Kenora,
   viii. all lands within an area of 6.4 kilometres in width and lying on both sides of the centre line of tertiary road Number 804 and within 3.2 kilometres of the said centre line measured at right angles thereto, and not in the Township of Ear Falls, and
   ix. all lands within an area of 6.4 kilometres in width and lying on both sides of the centre line of that part of the King's Highway known as Number 105 and within 3.2 kilometres of and measured at right angles to that portion of the centre line of the said part of the highway extending in a generally northerly and northwesterly direction from its intersection with the centre line of Pickerel Creek to its intersection with the southerly limit of the Municipality of Red Lake, and not in the Township of Ear Falls or referred to in subparagraph H.
6. The area of jurisdiction of the Rainy River District School Board, consists of,
   i. in the Territorial District of Kenora,
      A. the Township of Lake of the Woods,
      A.1 the geographic townships of Godson, Phillips and Tweedsmuir, and
      B. all lands in, other than the geographic townships of Godson, Phillips and Tweedsmuir and the Township of Lake of the Woods, within an area the boundary sides of which are as follows:
         1. on the west side, the International Boundary between the point of

intersection thereon of the 49th degree parallel of north latitude and the point of intersection of the production westerly of the north boundary of the geographic township of Tweedsmuir along the 4th base line,

2. on the south side, the line described as commencing at the point of intersection of the 49th degree parallel of north latitude with the International Boundary,

   thence due east 24 kilometres more or less along the 49th degree parallel of north latitude to the east shore of the Lake of the Woods,

   thence north easterly and northerly along the east shore of the Lake of the Woods and the south and east shores of Sabaskong Bay of the Lake of the Woods to the point of intersection of the westerly production of the south boundary of the geographic township of Godson,

   thence due east along the said south boundary of the said geographic Township and along their production due east being along O.L.S. Gillon's base line of 1919 to the 24th mile post on O.L.S. Alexander Niven's 6th meridian line,

3. on the east side, O.L.S. Alexander Niven's 6th meridian line between the 24th mile post thereon and the point of intersection on the said meridian line of the production due east along the 4th base line of the north boundary of the geographic township of Tweedsmuir,

4. on the north side, the production along the 4th base line westerly to the International Boundary and easterly to O.L.S. Alexander Niven's 6th meridian line of the north boundary of the geographic township of Tweedsmuir, and

ii. in the Territorial District of Rainy River,
   A. the Towns of Fort Frances and Rainy River,
   B. the Townships of Alberton, Atikokan, Chapple, Dawson, Emo, La Vallee, Lake of the Woods and Morley,
   C. the Township of McCrosson and Tovell,
   D. the geographic townships of Asmussen, Baker, Bennett, Claxton, Croome, Dance, Dewart, Farrington, Fleming, Griesinger, Halkirk, Hutchinson, Kingsford, Mathieu, McCaul, McLarty, Menary, Miscampbell, Nelles, Pratt, Rowe, Senn, Sifton, Spohn, Sutherland, Tanner, Trottier and Watten,
   E. all the lands in unsurveyed territory described as follows:

   commencing at the southwest corner of the geographic township of Bennett,

   thence south astronomically 9.6 kilometres,

   thence east astronomically to a point distant 9.6 kilometres measured south astronomically from the southeast corner of the geographic township of Baker, thence north astronomically 9.6 kilometres more or less to the southeast corner of the geographic township of Baker,

thence west astronomically to the point of commencement,

F. all the lands in unsurveyed territory described as follows:

commencing at the southwest corner of the geographic township of McCaul,

thence south astronomically 9.6 kilometres,

thence east astronomically to a point distant 9.6 kilometres measured south astronomically from the southeast corner of the geographic township of Trottier,

thence north astronomically 9.6 kilometres more or less to the southeast corner of the geographic township of Trottier,

thence west astronomically to the point of commencement,

G. the Wild Land Reserve, and

H. all lands in unsurveyed territory within an area the boundary sides of which are as follows:

1. on the north side, the northerly limit of the Territorial District of Rainy River commencing at the point of intersection of the 49th degree parallel of north latitude with the International Boundary,

   thence due east 24 kilometres more or less along the 49th degree parallel of north latitude to the east shore of the Lake of the Woods,

   thence north easterly and northerly along the east shore of the Lake of the Woods and the south and east shores of Sabaskong Bay of the Lake of the Woods to the point of intersection of the westerly production of the north boundaries of the geographic townships of Claxton and McLarty,

   thence due easterly along the said north boundaries of the said geographic townships and along their production due east being along O.L.S. Gillon's base line of 1919 to the 24th mile post on O.L.S. Alexander Niven's 6th meridian line,

   thence due south along the said meridian line 9.6 kilometres to the 18th mile post thereon in latitude 49° 0' 6" north,

   thence due east to the point of intersection of the production north of the east boundary of the geographic township of Farrington,

2. on the east side, the line formed by the east boundary of the geographic township of Farrington, the production of the said east boundary due north to the north boundary of the Territorial District of Rainy River and the production due south of the said east boundary to the International Boundary,

3. on the south side, the International Boundary from the mouth of the Rainy River easterly to the point of intersection on the International Boundary of the production due south of the east boundary of the geographic township of Farrington,

4. on the west side, the international Boundary from the mouth of the Rainy River northerly to the point of intersection on the International Boundary of the 49th degree parallel of north latitude.

7. The area of jurisdiction of the Lakehead District School Board consists of, in the Territorial District of Thunder Bay,
    i. the City of Thunder Bay,
    ii. the Municipalities of Neebing and Oliver Paipoonge,
    ii.1 the Townships of Conmee, Gillies, O'Connor and Shuniah,
    iii. the geographic townships of Blackwell, Conacher, Devon, Forbes, Fraleigh, Goldie, Gorham, Hagey, Laurie, Lismore, Lybster, Marks, Michener, Robson, Sibley, Strange and Ware,
    iv. the Dawson Road Lots, and
    v. the area bounded by the easterly boundary of Lot 1, concessions 1 and 2 of the Dawson Road Lots; the southerly boundary of the geographic township of Forbes; and westerly shore of the Kaministiquia River (sometimes known as the Dog River) and the northerly shore of the Shebandowan River (sometimes known as the Matawin River).

8. The area of jurisdiction of the Superior-Greenstone District School Board consists of, in the Territorial District of Thunder Bay,
    i. the Town of Geraldton, Longlac and Marathon,
    ii. the Townships of Beardmore, Dorion, Manitouwadge, Nipigon, Red Rock, Schreiber and Terrace Bay,
    iii. the geographic townships of Atikameg, Ashmore, Bomby, Boothe, Brothers, Bryant, Byron, Cecil, Cecile, Coldwell, Corrigal, Cotte, Daley, Davies, Errington, Flood, Foote, Grain, Grenville, Herbert, Homer, Houck, Killraine, Knowles, Laberge, Lahontan, Lecours, Leduc, Lyon, McCron, McGill, Mikano, Nickle, Oakes, O'Neill, Pic, Priske, Roberta, Shabotik, Spooner, Stirling, Strey, Syine, Tuuri, Walsh, Wiggins and Yesno, and
    iv. all lands in unsurveyed territory within an area described as follows:
        A. on the north side, the extension of the north side of the geographic township of Davies westerly to intersect with the boundary formed by extending the west side of the geographic township of Wiggins northerly until it meets the said extension,
        B. on the east side, the extension of the east side of the geographic township of Spooner southerly until the Canada-United States border,
        C. on the south side, the Canada-United States border, and
        D. on the south side, the extension of the west side of the geographic township of Wiggins southerly until the Canada-United States border, excluding St. Ignace Island.

9. The area of jurisdiction of the Bluewater District School Board consists of the Counties of Bruce and Grey.

10. The area of jurisdiction of the Avon Maitland District School Board consists of the Counties of Huron and Perth.

11. The area of jurisdiction of the Greater Essex County District School Board consists of the County of Essex, including the Township of Pelee.

S. 3 REGULATIONS UNDER THE EDUCATION ACT

12. The area of jurisdiction of the Lambton Kent District School Board consists of the Counties of Kent and Lambton.
13. The area of jurisdiction of the Thames Valley District School Board consists of the Counties of Elgin, Middlesex and Oxford.
14. The area of jurisdiction of the Toronto District School Board consists of the urban area of the City of Toronto incorporated by the *City of Toronto Act, 1997*.
15. The area of jurisdiction of the Durham District School Board consists of The Municipality of Durham, except for the Municipality of Clarington.
16. The area of jurisdiction of the Kawartha Pine Ridge District School Board consists of the Counties of Northumberland (including that portion of the City of West Quinte which on January 1, 1997 was part of the County of Northumberland) and Peterborough and the Municipality of Clarington in The Regional Municipality of Durham.
17. The area of jurisdiction of the Trillium Lakelands District School Board consists of the District Municipality of Muskoka, except the Freeman Ward of the Township of Georgian Bay, and the Counties of Haliburton and Victoria.
18. The area of jurisdiction of the York Region District School Board consists of The Regional Municipality of York.
19. The area of jurisdiction of the Simcoe County District School Board consists of the County of Simcoe.
20. The area of jurisdiction of the Upper Grand District School Board consists of the Counties of Dufferin and Wellington.
21. The area of jurisdiction of the Peel District School Board consists of The Regional Municipality of Peel.
22. The area of jurisdiction of the Halton District School Board consists of The Regional Municipality of Halton.
23. The area of jurisdiction of the Hamilton-Wentworth District School Board consists of The Regional Municipality of Hamilton-Wentworth.
24. The area of jurisdiction of the District School Board of Niagara consists of The Regional Municipality of Niagara.
25. The area of jurisdiction of the Grand Erie District School Board consists of The Regional Municipality of Haldimand-Norfolk and the County of Brant.
26. The area of jurisdiction of the Waterloo Region District School Board consists of The Regional Municipality of Waterloo.
27. The area of jurisdiction of the Ottawa-Carleton District School Board consists of The Regional Municipality of Ottawa-Carleton.
28. The area of jurisdiction of the Upper Canada District School Board consists of the County of Lanark, the United Counties of Leeds and Grenville, the United Counties of Prescott and Russell and the United Counties of Stormont, Dundas and Glengarry.
29. The area of jurisdiction of the Limestone District School Board consists of the Counties of Frontenac and Lennox and Addington.
30. The area of jurisdiction of the Renfrew County District School Board consists of the County of Renfrew.
31. The area of jurisdiction of the Hastings and Prince Edward District School Board consists of the County of Hastings (including that portion of the City of West Quinte

which on January 1, 1997 was part of the County of Hastings) and the County of Prince Edward. O. Reg. 278/97, s. 1; 80/98, s. 3; 213/98, ss. 2, 15, 19.

4. Twenty-nine English-language separate district school boards are established.

5. The name of each English-language separate district school board is "English-language Separate District School Board No. ____" (inserting a number between 30 and 55 or a combination of numbers and letters as set out in each paragraph of section 6) unless otherwise specified in the Schedules. O. Reg. 80/98, s. 4; 213/98, s. 3.

6. The following are the areas of jurisdiction of the English-language separate district school boards:
1. The area of jurisdiction of the Northeastern Catholic District School Board consists of,
    i. in the Territorial District of Algoma, the geographic townships of Ebbs and Templeton,
    ii. in the Territorial District of Cochrane,
        A. the City of Timmins,
        B. the Towns of Cochrane, Hearst, Iroquois Falls, Kapuskasing and Smooth Rock Falls,
        C. the Townships of Glackmeyer, Mattice-Val Cote, Moonbeam, Opasatika and Val Rita-Harty,
        D. the portion of the Township of Black River-Matheson that on December 31, 1996 was not part of the geographic townships of Barnet, Frecheville, Garrison, Harker, Holloway, Lamplugh, Marriott, McCool, Michaud, Rand or Stoughton,
        E. the portion of the Township of Fauquier-Strickland that on December 31, 1996 was not part of the geographic townships of Beardmore, Carmichael, MacVicar or Stringer,
        F. the geographic townships of Aurora, Barker, Blount, Brower, Calder, Casgrain, Clute, Colquhoun, Fournier, Fox, Hanlan, Hanna, Irish, Kendall, Kennedy, Lamarche, Landry, Leitch, Lowther, McCowan, Mortimer, Nansen, Newmarket, O'Brien, Ottaway, Pyne, St. John, Stimson, Stoddard, Studholme, Teefy and Way.
        G. the portion of the geographic township of Benoit that is not part of the Township of Black River-Matheson,
        H. the portion of the geographic township of Haggart that is not part of the Township of Fauquier-Strickland,
        I. the portion of the geographic township of Owens that is not part of the Township of Val Rita-Harty,
    iii. in the Territorial District of Nipissing,
        A. the Municipality of Temagami, except for the portion of the Municipality that was formerly part of the geographic townships of Clement and Scholes, and
        B. the geographic townships of Eldridge, Flett, Gladman, Gooderham, Hammell, Hartle, Hobbs, Kenny, McCallum, McLaren and Thistle, and

S. 6 REGULATIONS UNDER THE EDUCATION ACT

      iv. in the Territorial District of Timiskaming,
- A. the Towns of Charlton, Cobalt, Englehart, Haileybury, Kirkland Lake, Latchford and New Liskeard,
- B. the Village of Thornloe,
- C. the Townships of Armstrong, Brethour, Casey, Chamberlain, Coleman, Dack, Dymond, Evanturel, Gauthier, Harley, Harris, Hilliard, Hudson, James, Kerns, Larder Lake, Matachewan and McGarry,
- D. the geographic townships of Auld, Barber, Barr, Bayly, Beauchamp, Boston, Brigstocke, Bryce, Cane, Catharine, Chown, Corkill, Davidson, Eby, Farr, Firstbrook, Grenfell, Haultain, Henwood, Ingram, Kittson, Lawson, Lebel, Lorrain, Lundy, Maisonville, Marquis, Marter, McElroy, Mickle, Milner, Mulligan, Nicol, Otto, Pacaud, Pense, Roadhouse, Robillard, Savard, Sharpe, Smyth, South Lorrain, Truax, Tudhope, Willet and Willison, and
- E. the portion of the geographic township of Gillies Limit that is not part of the Township of Coleman.

2. The area of jurisdiction of the Nipissing-Parry Sound Catholic District School Board consists of,
   i. in the Territorial District of Nipissing,
   - A. the City of North Bay,
   - B. the Towns of Kearney and Mattawa,
   - C. the Townships of Bonfield, Calvin, Chisholm, East Ferris, Mattawan and Papineau-Cameron,
   - D. the portion of the Municipality of West Nipissing that was not formerly part of the geographic townships of Bertram, Dana, Fell, Latchford or McWilliams, and
   - E. the geographic townships of Blyth, Boyd, Clarkson, Commanda, Deacon, Eddy, French, Jocko, Lauder, Lyman, Merrick, Notman, Pentland, Phelps, Poitras and Wyse, and

   ii. in the Territorial District of Parry Sound,
   - A. the Towns of Kearney, Powassan and Trout Creek,
   - B. the Villages of Burk's Falls, South River and Sundridge,
   - C. the Townships of Armour, Joly, Machar, McMurrich/Monteith, Nipissing, North Himsworth, Perry, Ryerson, South Himsworth and Strong,
   - D. the portion of the Township of Seguin which on January 1, 1997 was part of the geographic township of Monteith,
   - E. the geographic townships of Laurier, Lount, Patterson and Pringle, and
   - F. the portion of the Township of Magnetawan that was not formerly part of the geographic township of Croft.

3. The area of jurisdiction of the Huron-Superior Catholic District School Board consists of,
   i. in the Territorial District of Algoma,
   - A. the Cities of Elliott Lake and Sault Ste. Marie,
   - B. the Town of Blind River,
   - C. the Village of Iron Bridge,

D. the Townships of Johnson, Laird, Michipicoten, The North Shore, Prince, Shedden, Thompson and White River,
E. the Township of Day and Bright Additional,
F. the Township of Macdonald, Meredith and Aberdeen Additional,
G. the Township of Tarbutt and Tarbutt Additional,
H. the geographic townships of Archibald, Aweres, Bright, Cobden, Dennis, Deroche, Esquega Fenwick, Fiddler, Fisher, Gaudette, Gladstone, Grasett, Havilland, Herrick, Hodgins, Home, Jarvis, Jogues, Juillette, Kamichisitit, Kars, Kincaid, Ley, Mack, Montgomery, Nouvel, Parkinson, Patton, Peever, Pennefather, Rix, Ryan, Scarfe, Shields, Slater, Tilley, Timmermans, Tupper and VanKoughnet,
I. the mining locations known as Montreal Mining Southern Location, Montreal Mining Northern Location, A. McDonnell Mining Location, Kincaid Mining Locations, 5,6, 7 and 8 and Rankin Mining Location,
J. the portion of the geographic Township of Striker that is not part of the Township of The North Shore, and
K. all the islands of the North Channel of Lake Huron lying south of the geographic townships of Bright, Cobden and the portion of Striker that is not part of the Township of the North Shore, and

ii. in the Territorial District of Sudbury,
A. the Town of Espanola,
B. the Townships of Baldwin and Chapleau,
B.1 the Township of Nairn and Hyman, and
C. the geographic townships of Caverley, Chapleau, Curtin, de Gaulle, Eisenhower, Foster, Gallagher, Genier, Halsey, Kaplan, Mongowin, Panet, Roosevelt and Truman.
D. [Revoked O. Reg. 213/98, s. 4(12).]

ii.1 the portion of the Township of The Sables — Spanish Rivers that is in the Territorial District of Sudbury, and

iii. in the Territorial District of Manitoulin, Ward No. 2 of the Town of Northeastern Manitoulin and the Islands,

4. The area of jurisdiction of the Sudbury Catholic District School Board consists of,
i. in the Territorial District of Sudbury,
A. The Regional Municipality of Sudbury,
B. the Township of Casimir, Jennings and Appleby,
C. the Municipality of French River,
D. the Township of Hagar,
E. the Township of Ratter and Dunnet,
E.1 the portion of the Municipality of West Nipissing that was formerly part of the geographic township of Janes,
F. the geographic townships of Allen, Awrey, Burwash, Cartier, Cascaden, Cleland, Cox, Davis, Foy, Hart, Harty, Hawley, Hendrie, Henry, Hess, Laura, Loughrin, Moncrieff, Scadding, Secord, Servos and Street,
G. the portions of the geographic townships of Dill, Eden and Tilton that are not part of The Regional Municipality of Sudbury,

S. 6 REGULATIONS UNDER THE EDUCATION ACT

      H. the portion of the geographic township of Dryden that is not part of The Regional Municipality of Sudbury,
      I. the portion of the geographic township of Trill that is not part of The Regional Municipality of Sudbury,
      J. the portion of the geographic township of Janes that is not part of the Municipality of West Nipissing, and
      K. the portions of the geographic townships of Bigwood, Cherriman and Haddo that are not part of the Municipality of French River,
  ii. in the Territorial District of Manitoulin, the Township of Rutherford and George Island, and
  iii. in the Territorial District of Parry Sound, the geographic townships of Henvey and Wallbridge.

5. The area of jurisdiction of the Northwest Catholic District School Board is
  i. in the Territorial District of Kenora,
      A. the City of Dryden,
      B. the Town of Sioux Lookout,
      C. the Townships of Lake of the Woods and Machin,
      D. the geographic townships of Britton, Buller, Colenso, Eton, Godson, Hartman, Ilsley, Ladysmith, Melgund, Mutrie, Phillips, Redvers, Rowell, Rugby, Smellie, Southworth, Tweedsmuir, Van Horne, Wabigoon, Wainwright and Zealand,
      E. the portion of the geographic township of Aubrey that is not part of the Township of Machin, and
      F. all lands, other than the geographic townships of Godson, Phillips and Tweedsmuir and the Township of Lake of the Woods, within an area the boundary sides of which are as follows:
        1. on the west side, the International Boundary between the point of intersection thereon of the 49th degree parallel of north latitude and the point of intersection of the production westerly of the north boundary of the geographic township of Tweedsmuir along the 4th base line.
        2. on the south side, the line described as commencing at the point of intersection of the 49th degree parallel of north latitude with the International Boundary; thence due east 24 kilometres more or less along the 49th degree parallel of north latitude to the east shore of the Lake of the Woods; thence north easterly and northerly along the east shores of Sabaskong Bay of the Lake of the Woods to the point of intersection of the westerly production of the south boundary of the geographic township of Godson; thence due east along the said south boundary of the said geographic township and along its production due east being along O.L.S. Gillon's base line of 1919 to the 24th mile post on O.L.S. Alexander Niven's 6th meridian line.
        3. on the east side, O.L.S. Alexander Niven's 6th meridian line between the 24th mile post thereon and the point of intersection on

the said meridian line of the production due east along the 4th base line of the north boundary of the geographic township of Tweedsmuir.
            4. on the north side, the production along the 4th base line westerly to the International Boundary and easterly to O.L.S. Alexander Niven's 6th meridian line of the north boundary of the geographic township of Tweedsmuir, an
    ii. in the Territorial District of Rainy River,
        A. the Towns of Fort Frances and Rainy River,
        B. the Townships of Alberton, Chapple, Dawson, Emo, La Vallee, Lake of the Woods and Morley,
        C. [Revoked O. Reg. 213/98, s. 4(13).]
        D. the geographic townships of Claxton, Croome, Dance, Dewart, Farrington, Fleming, Griesinger, Halkirk, Kingsford, Mathieu, McLarty, Menary, Miscampbell, Nelles, Pratt, Rowe, Senn, Sifton, Spohn, Sutherland and Watten,
        E. the Wild Land Reserve,
        F. all lands in unsurveyed territory within an area the boundary sides of which are as follows:
            1. on the north side, the northerly limit of the Territorial District of Rainy River commencing at the point of intersection of the 49th degree parallel of north latitude with the International Boundary; thence due east 24 kilometres more or less along the 49th degree parallel of north latitude to the east shore of the Lake of the Woods; thence north easterly and northerly along the east shore of the Lake of the Woods and the south and east shores of the Lake of the Woods and the south and east shores of Sabaskong Bay of the Lake of the Woods to the point of intersection of the westerly production of the north boundaries of the geographic townships of Claxton and McLarty; thence due easterly along the said north boundaries of the geographic townships of Claxton and McLarty; thence due easterly along the said north boundaries of the said geographic townships and along their production due east being along O.L.S. Gillon's base line of 1919 to the 24th mile post on O.L.S. Alexander Niven's 6th meridian line; thence due south along the said meridian line 9.6 kilometres to the 18th mile post thereon in latitude 49°0' 6" north; thence due east to the point of intersection of the production north of the east boundary of the geographic township of Farrington.
            2. on the east side, the line formed by the east boundary of the geographic township of Farrington, the production of the said east boundary due north to the north boundary of the Territorial District of Rainy River and the production due south of the said east boundary to the International Boundary.
            3. on the south side, the International Boundary from the mouth of

the Rainy River easterly to the point of intersection on the International Boundary of the production due south of the east boundary of the geographic township of Farrington.
4. on the west side, the International Boundary from the mouth of the Rainy River northerly to the point of intersection on the International Boundary of the 49th degree parallel of north latitude.

6. The area of jurisdiction of the Kenora Catholic District School Board consists of, in the Territorial District of Kenora,
    A. the Towns of Jaffray Melick, Keewatin and Kenora,
    B. the Township of Sioux Narrows,
    C. the geographic townships of Boys, Kirkup, Pellatt and Redditt,
    D. all the lands in unsurveyed territory in the vicinity of the station house of the Canadian National Railways at Minaki described as follows:

    commencing at a point distant 4 kilometres measured east astronomically from the northeast corner of the said station house;

    thence north astronomically 4 kilometres;

    thence west astronomically 8 kilometres;

    thence south astronomically 8 kilometres;

    thence east astronomically 8 kilometres;

    thence north astronomically 4 kilometres to the point of commencement; and
    E. except for those parts of the mainland which are crossed by the said line, all lands lying north of a line extending from the southernmost extremity of the geographic township of Boys to the southwest corner of the geographic township of Kirkup and south of the southerly boundaries of the geographic townships of Boys and Pellatt, the Towns of Jaffray, Melick, Keewatin and Kenora.

7. The area of jurisdiction of the Thunder Bay Catholic District School Board consists of, in the Territorial District of Thunder Bay,
    i. the City of Thunder Bay,
    ii. the Municipalities of Neebing and Oliver Paipoonge,
    ii.1 the Townships of Conmee, Gillies, O'Connor and Shuniah,
    iii. the geographic townships of Blackwell, Conacher, Devon, Forbes, Fraleigh, Goldie, Golding, Gorham, Hagey, Laurie, Lismore, Lybster, Marks, Michener, Robson, Sibley, Strange and Ware,
    iv. the Dawson Road Lots, and
    v. the area bounded by the easterly boundary of Lot 1, concessions 1 and 2 of the Dawson Road Lots; the southerly boundary of the geographic township of Forbes; the westerly shore of the Kaministiquia River (sometimes known as the Dog River) and the northerly shore of the Shebandowan River (sometimes known as the Matawin River).

8. The area of jurisdiction of the Superior North Catholic District School Board consists of, in the Territorial District of Thunder Bay,
    i. the Towns of Geraldton, Longlac and Marathon,
    ii. the Townships of Beardmore, Dorion, Manitouwadge, Nakina, Nipigon, Red Rock, Schreiber and Terrace Bay,

iii. the geographic townships of Ashmore, Atikameg, Bomby, Boothe, Brothers, Bryant, Byron, Ceci, Cecile, Coldwell, Corrigal, Cotte, Daley, Davies, Errington, Flood, Foote, Grain, Grenville, Herbert, Homer, Houck, Killraine, Knowles, Laberge, Lahontan, Lecours, Leduc, Lyon, McCron, McGill, Mikano, Nickle, Oakes, O'Neill, Pic, Priske, Roberta, Shabotik, Spooner, Stirling, Strey, Syine, Tuuri, Walsh, Wiggins and Yesno,

iv. all lands, excluding St. Ignace Island, in unsurveyed territory within an area described as follows;

    A. on the north side, the extension of the north side of the geographic township of Davies westerly to intersect with the boundary formed by extending the west side of the geographic township of Wiggins northerly until it meets the said extension,

    B. on the east side, the extension of the east side of the geographic township of Spooner southerly until the Canada-United States border,

    C. on the south side, the Canada-United States border, and

    D. on the west side, the extension of the west side of the geographic township of Wiggins southerly until the Canada-United States border.

9. The area of jurisdiction of the Bruce-Grey Catholic District School Board consists of the Counties of Bruce and Grey.

10. The area of jurisdiction of the Huron Perth Catholic District School Board consists of the Counties of Huron and Perth.

11. The area of jurisdiction of the Windsor-Essex Catholic District School Board consists of the County of Essex including the Township of Pelee.

12. The area of jurisdiction of English-language Separate District School Board No. 38 consists of the Counties of Elgin, Middlesex and Oxford.

13. The area of jurisdiction of the St. Clair Catholic District School Board consists of the Counties of Kent and Lambton.

14. The area of jurisdiction of the Toronto Catholic District School Board consists of the urban area of the City of Toronto incorporated by the *City of Toronto Act, 1997*.

15. The area of jurisdiction of the Peterborough Victoria Northumberland and Clarington Catholic District School Board consists of the Counties of Northumberland (including that portion of the City of West Quinte which on January 1, 1997 was part of the County of Northumberland), Peterborough and Victoria and the Municipality of Clarington in The Regional Municipality of Durham.

16. The area of jurisdiction of the York Catholic District School Board consists of The Regional Municipality of York.

17. The area of jurisdiction of the Dufferin-Peel Catholic District School Board consists of The Regional Municipality of Peel and the County of Dufferin.

18. The area of jurisdiction of the Simcoe Muskoka Catholic District School Board consists of the District Municipality of Muskoka, the County of Simcoe, and, in the Territorial District of Parry Sound, Wards 3, 4 and 6 of the Township of Seguin.

19. The area of jurisdiction of the Durham Catholic District School Board consists of The Regional Municipality of Durham, except for the Municipality of Clarington.

20. The area of jurisdiction of the Halton Catholic District School Board consists of The Regional Municipality of Halton.

21. The area of jurisdiction of the Hamilton-Wentworth Catholic District School Board consists of The Regional Municipality of Hamilton-Wentworth.
22. The area of jurisdiction of the Wellington Catholic District School Board consists of the County of Wellington.
23. The area of jurisdiction of the Waterloo Catholic District School Board consists of The Regional Municipality of Waterloo.
24. The area of jurisdiction of the Niagara Catholic District School Board consists of The Regional Municipality of Niagara.
25. The area of jurisdiction of the Brant/Haldimand-Norfolk Catholic District School Board consists of The Regional Municipality of Haldimand-Norfolk and the County of Brant.
26. The area of jurisdiction of the Catholic District School Board of Eastern Ontario consists of the County of Lanark, the United Counties of Leeds and Grenville, the United Counties of Prescott and Russell and the United Counties of Stormont, Dundas and Glengarry.
27. The area of jurisdiction of the Ottawa-Carleton Catholic District School Board consists of The Regional Municipality of Ottawa-Carleton.
28. The area of jurisdiction of the Renfrew County Catholic District School Board consists of the County of Renfrew.
29. The area of jurisdiction of the Algonquin and Lakeshore Catholic District School Board consists of the Counties of Frontenac, Lennox and Addington, Hastings (including that portion of the City of West Quinte which on January 1, 1997 was part of the County of Hastings) and Prince Edward, and, in the Territorial District of Nipissing,
    i. the Township of South Algonquin,
    ii. O. Reg. 278/97, s. 2; 80/98, s. 5; 213/98, ss. 4, 13, 16, 20.

7. Four French-language public district school boards are established.

8. The name of each French-language public district school board in "Conseil de district des écoles publiques de langue française n°_____" (inserting a number between 56 and 59) unless otherwise specified in the Schedules. O. Reg. 80/98, s. 6; 213/98, s. 5.

9. The following are the areas of jurisdiction of the French-language public district school boards:
1. The area of jurisdiction of the Conseil scolaire de district du Nord-Est de l'Ontario consists of the District Municipality of Muskoka, the Territorial District of Parry Sound, and
    i. In the Territorial District of Algoma, the Township of Hornepayne and the geographic townships of Ebbs and Templeton,
    ii. in the Territorial District of Cochrane,
        A. the City of Timmins,
        B. the Towns of Cochrane, Hearst, Iroquois Falls, Kapuskasing and Smooth Rock Falls,
        C. the Townships of Glackmeyer, Mattice-Val Cote, Moonbeam, Opasatika and Val Rita-Harty,
        D. the portion of the Township of Black River-Matheson that on December

31, 1996 was not part of the geographic townships of Barnet, Frecheville, Garrison, Harker, Holloway, Lamplugh, Marriott, McCool, Michaud, Rand or Stoughton,

E. the portion of the Township of Fauquier-Strickland that on December 31, 1996 was not part of the geographic townships of Beardmore, Carmichael, MacVicar or Stringer,

F. the geographic townships of Aurora, Barker, Blount, Brower, Calder, Casgrain, Clute, Colquhoun, Fournier, Fox, Hanlan, Hanna, Irish, Kendall, Kennedy, Lamarche, Landry, Leitch, Lowther, McCowan, Mortimer, Nansen, Newmarket, O'Brien, Ottaway, Pyne, St. John, Stimson, Stoddard, Studholme, Teefy and Way,

G. the portion of the geographic township of Benoit that is not part of the Township of Black River-Matheson,

H. the portion of the geographic township of Haggart that is not part of the Township of Fauquier-Strickland, and

I. the portion of the geographic township of Owens that is not part of the Township of Val Rita-Harty,

iii. in the District Municipality of Muskoka,

iv. in the Territorial District of Nipissing,

A. the City of North Bay,

B. the Towns of Kearney and Mattawa,

C. the Townships of Bonfield, Calvin, Chisholm, East Ferris, Mattawan and Papineau-Cameron,

C.1 the portion of the Municipality of West Nipissing that was not formerly part of the geographic townships of Bertram, Dala, Fell, Latchford and McWilliams,

D. the Municipality of Temagami, except for the portion of the Municipality that was formerly part of the geographic townships of Clement and Scholes,

E. the geographic townships of Blyth, Boyd, Clarkson, Commanda, Deacon, Eddy, Eldridge, Flett, French, Gladman, Gooderham, Hammell, Hartle, Hobbs, Jocko, Kenny, Lauder, Lyman, McCallum, McLaren, Merrick, Notman, Pentland, Phelps, Poitras, Thistle and Wyse,

v. the Territorial District of Parry Sound,

vi. in the Territorial District of Timiskaming,

A. the Towns of Charlton, Cobalt, Englehart, Haileybury, Kirkland Lake, Latchford and New Liskeard,

B. the Village of Thornloe,

C. the Townships of Armstrong, Brethour, Casey, Chamberlain, Coleman, Dack, Dymond, Evanturel, Gauthier, Harley, Harris, Hilliard, Hudson, James, Kerns, Larder Lake, Matachewan and McGarry,

D. the geographic townships of Auld, Barber, Barr, Bayly, Beauchamp, Boston, Brigstocke, Bryce, Cane, Catharine, Chown, Corkill, Davidson, Eby, Farr, Firstbrook, Grenfell, Haultain, Henwood, Ingram, Kittson, Lawson, Lebel, Lorrain, Lundy, Maisonville, Marquis, Marter, McElroy,

Mickle, Milner, Mulligan, Nicol, Otto, Pacaud, Pense, Roadhouse, Robillard, Savard, Sharpe, Smyth, South Lorrain, Truax, Tudhope, Willet and Willison, and

E. the portion of the geographic township of Gillies Limit that is not part of the Township of Coleman.

2. The area of jurisdiction of the Conseil scolaire de district du Grand Nord de l'Ontario consists of,
   i. in the Territorial District of Algoma,
      A. the Cities of Elliot Lake and Sault Ste. Marie,
      B. the Towns of Blind River, Bruce Mines and Thessalon,
      C. the Villages of Hilton Beach and Iron Bridge,
      D. the Townships of Day and Bright Additional, Dubreuilville, Hilton, Jocelyn, Johnson, Laird, Michipicoten, Plummer Additional, Prince, Shedden, St. Joseph, The North Shore, Thessalon, Thompson, and White River.
      E. the Township of MacDonald, Meredith and Aberdeen Additional.
      F. the Township of Tarbutt and Tarbutt Additional,
      G. the geographic townships of Aberdeen, Archibald, Aweres, Bridgland, Bright, Chenard, Cobden, Dennis, Deroche, Dunphy, Esquega, Fenwick, Fiddler, Finon, Fisher, Galbraith, Gaudette, Gladstone, Gould, Grasett, Haughton, Havilland, Herrick, Hodgins, Home, Huotari, Jarvis, Jogues, Juillette, Kamichisitit, Kars, Kincaid, Kirkwood, Ley, Mack, McMahon, Montgomery, Morin, Nouvel, Parkinson, Patton, Peever, Pennefather, Rix, Rose, Ryan, Scarfe, Shields, Slater, Tilley, Timmermans, Tupper, VanKoughnet and Wells,
      H. the portion of the geographic township of Striker not included in the Township of The North Shore,
      I. all the islands in the North Channel of Lake Huron lying south of the geographic townships of Bright, Cobden, and the portion of Striker that is not part of the Township of The North Shore, and
      J. the mining locations known as Montreal Mining Southern Location, Montreal Mining Northern Location, A. McDonnell Mining Location, Kincaid Mining Locations 5, 6, 7 and 8 and Rankin Mining Location,
   ii. in the Territorial District of Kenora,
      A. the City of Dryden,
      A.1 the Municipality of Red Lake,
      B. the Towns of Jaffray Melick, Keewatin, Kenora and Sioux Lookout,
      C. the Townships of Ear Falls, Ignace, Lake of the Woods, Machin and Sioux Narrows,
      D. the geographic townships of Boys, Britton, Buller, Colenso, Dome, Eton, Godson, Hartman, Ilsley, Kirkup, Ladysmith, Melgund, Mutrie, Pellatt, Phillips, Redditt, Redvers, Rowell, Rugby, Smellie, Southworth, Tweedsmuir, Van Horne, Wabigoon, Wainwright and Zealand,
      D.1 the portions of the geographic Townships of Baird and Heyson that are not part of the Municipality of Red Lake,

REGULATION 185/97 **S. 9**

E. the portion of the geographic township of Aubrey that is not part of the Township of Machin,

F. all the lands in unsurveyed territory in the vicinity of the station house of the Canadian National Railways at Minaki described as follows:

commencing at a point distant 4 kilometres measured east astronomically from the northeast corner of the said station house,

thence north astronomically 4 kilometres,

thence west astronomically 8 kilometres,

thence south astronomically 8 kilometres,

thence east astronomically 8 kilometres,

thence north astronomically 4 kilometres to the point of commencement,

G. except for those parts of the mainland which are crossed by the said line, all lands lying north of a line extending from the southernmost extremity of the geographic township of Boys to the southwest corner of the geographic township of Kirkup and south of the southerly boundaries of the geographic townships of Boys and Pellatt, the towns of Jaffray Melick, Keewatin and Kenora,

H. all lands within an area of 6.4 kilometres in width and lying on both sides of the centre line of tertiary road Number 804 and within 3.2 kilometres of the said centre line measured at right angles thereto, and not in the Township of Ear Falls,

I. all lands within an area of 6.4 kilometres in width and lying on both sides of the centre line of that part of the King's Highway known as Number 105 and within 3.2 kilometres of and measured at right angles to that portion of the centre line of the said part of the highway extending in a generally northerly and northwesterly direction from its intersection with the centre line of Pickerel Creek to its intersection with the southerly limit of the Municipality of Red Lake, and not in the Township of Ear Falls or referred to in subparagraph H, and

J. all lands, other than the geographic townships of Godson, Phillips and Tweedsmuir and the Township of Lake of the Woods, within an area the boundary sides of which are as follows:

1. on the west side, the International Boundary between the point of intersection thereon of the 49th degree parallel of north latitude and the point of intersection of the production westerly of the north boundary of the geographic Township of Tweedsmuir along the 4th base line,

2. on the south side, the line described as commencing at the point of intersection of the 49th degree parallel of north latitude with the International Boundary,

thence due east 24 kilometres more or less along the 49th degree parallel of north latitude to the east shore of the Lake of the Woods,

thence north easterly and northerly along the east shore of the Lake of the Woods and the south and east shores of Sabaskong Bay of the Lake of the Woods to the point of intersection of the westerly production of the south boundary of the geographic township of Godson,

thence due east along the said south boundary of the said geographic Township and along their production due east being along O.L.S. Gillon's base line of 1919 to the 24th mile post on O.L.S. Alexander Niven's 6th meridian line.

3. on the east side, O.L.S. Alexander Niven's 6th meridian line between the 24th mile post thereon and the point of intersection on the said meridian line of the production due east along the 4th base line of the north boundary of the geographic township of Tweedsmuir,

4. on the north side, the production along the 4th base line westerly to the International Boundary and easterly to O.L.S. Alexander Niven's 6th meridian line of the north boundary of the geographic township of Tweedsmuir,

iii. in the Territorial District of Manitoulin, all of the said territorial district except the geographic townships of Carlyle, Humboldt and Killarney,

iv. in the Territorial District of Rainy River,

   A. the Towns of Fort Frances and Rainy River,

   B. the Townships of Alberton, Atikokan, Chapple, Dawson, Emo, La Vallee, Lake of the Woods and Morley,

   C. [Revoked O. Reg. 213/98, s. 6(8).]

   D. the geographic townships of Asmussen, Baker, Bennett, Claxton, Croome, Dance, Dewart, Farrington, Fleming, Griesinger, Halkirk, Hutchinson, Kingsford, Mathieu, McCaul, McLarty, Menary, Miscampbell, Nelles, Pratt, Rowe, Senn, Sifton, Spohn, Sutherland, Tanner, Trottier and Watten,

   E. all the lands in unsurveyed territory described as follows:

commencing at the southwest corner of the geographic township of Bennett,

thence south astronomically 9.6 kilometres,

thence east astronomically to a point distant 9.6 kilometres measured south astronomically from the southeast corner of the geographic township of Baker,

thence north astronomically 9.6 kilometres more or less to the southeast corner of the geographic township of Baker,

thence west astronomically to the point of commencement,

   F. all the lands in unsurveyed territory described as follows:

commencing at the southwest corner of the geographic township of McCaul,

thence south astronomically 9.6 kilometres,

thence east astronomically to a point distant 9.6 kilometres measured south astronomically from the southeast corner of the geographic township of Trottier,

thence north astronomically 9.6 kilometres more or less to the southeast corner of the geographic township of Trottier,

thence west astronomically to the point of commencement,

G. the Wild Land Reserve,

H. all lands in unsurveyed territory within an area the boundary sides of which are as follows:
  1. on the north side, the northerly limit of the Territorial District of Rainy River commencing at the point of intersection of the 49th degree parallel of north latitude with the International Boundary,

    thence due east 24 kilometres more or less along the 49th degree parallel of north latitude to the east shore of the Lake of the Woods,

    thence north easterly and northerly along the east shore of the Lake of the Woods and the south and east shores of Sabaskong Bay of the lake of the Woods to the point of intersection of the westerly production of the north boundaries of the geographic townships of Claxton and McLarty,

    thence due easterly along the said north boundaries of the said geographic townships and along their production due east being along O.L.S. Gillon's base line of 1919 to the 24th mile post on O.L.S. Alexander Niven's 6th meridian line,

    thence due south along the said meridian line 9.6 kilometres to the 18th mile post thereon in latitude 49° 0' 6" north,

    thence due east to the point of intersection of the production north of the east boundary of the geographic township of Farrington,

  2. on the ease side, the line formed by the east boundary of the geographic township of Farrington, the production of the said east boundary due north to the north boundary of the Territorial District of Rainy River and the production due south of the said east boundary to the International Boundary,

  3. on the south side, the International Boundary from the mouth of the Rainy River easterly to the point of intersection on the International Boundary of the production due south of the east boundary of the geographic township of Farrington,

  4. on the west side, the International Boundary from the mouth of the Rainy River northerly to the point of intersection on the International Boundary of the 49th degree parallel of north latitude,

v. in the Territorial District of Sudbury,
  A. The Regional Municipality of Sudbury,
  B. the Town of Espanola,
  C. the Townships of Chapleau, Baldwin and Hagar,

D. the Township of Casimir, Jennings and Appleby,
E. the Municipality of French River,
F. the Township of Nairn and Hyman,
G. the Township of Ratter and Dunnet,
G.1 the portion of the Municipality of West Nipissing that was formerly part of the geographic township of Janes,
H. the geographic townships of Allen, Awrey, Burwash, Cartier, Cascaden, Caverley, Chapleau, Cleland, Cox, Curtin, Davis, de Gaulle, Eisenhower, Foster, Foy, Gallagher, Genier, Halsey, Hart, Harty, Hawley, Hendrie, Henry, Hess, Kaplan, Laura, Loughrin, Moncrieff, Mongowin, Panet, Roosevelt, Scadding, Secord, Servos, Street, and Truman,
I. the portions of the geographic townships of Dill, Dryden, Eden, Tilton and Trill that are not part of The Regional Municipality of Sudbury.
J. the portion of the geographic township of Janes that is not part of the Municipality of West Nipissing, and
K. the portions of the geographic townships of Bigwood, Cherriman and Haddo that are not part of the Municipality of French River, and

vi. in the Territorial District of Thunder Bay,
   A. the City of Thunder Bay,
   B. the Towns of Geraldton, Longlac and Marathon,
   B.1 the Municipalities of Neebing and Oliver Paipoonge,
   C. the Townships of Beardmore, Conmee, Dorion, Gillies, Manitouwadge, Nipigon, O'Connor, Red Rock, Schreiber, Shuniah and Terrace Bay,
   D. the geographic townships of Atikameg, Ashmore, Blackwell, Bomby, Boothe, Brothers, Bryant, Byron, Cecil, Cecile, Coldwell, Conacher, Corrigal, Cotte, Daley, Davies, Devon, Errington, Flood, Foote, Forbes, Fraleigh, Goldie, Golding, Gorham, Grain, Grenville, Hagey, Herbert, Homer, Houck, Killraine, Knowles, Laberge, Lahontan, Laurie, Lecours, Leduc, Lismore, Lybster, Lyon, Marks, McCron, McGill, Michener, Mikano, Nickle, Oakes, O'Neill, Pic, Priske, Roberta, Robson, Shabotik, Sibley, Spooner, Stirling, Strange, Strey, Syine, Tuuri, Walsh, Ware, Wiggins and Yesno,
   E. the Dawson Road Lots,
   F. the area bounded by the easterly boundary of Lot 1, concessions 1 and 2 of the Dawson Road Lots; the southerly boundary of the geographic township of Forbes; the westerly shore of the Kaministiquia River (sometimes known as the Dog River) and the northerly shore of the Shebandowan River (sometimes known as the Matawin River), and
   G. all lands in unsurveyed territory within an area described as follows:
      1. on the north side, the extension of the north side of the geographic township of Davies westerly to intersect with the boundary formed by extending the west side of the geographic township of Wiggins northerly until it meets the said extension,
      2. on the east side, the extension of the east side of the geographic

township of Spooner southerly until the Canada-United State border,
3. on the south side, the Canada-United States border, and
4. on the west side, the extension of the west side of the geographic township of Wiggins southerly until the Canada-United States border, excluding St. Ignace Island, and

vii. the portion of the Township of The Sables — Spanish Rivers that is the Territorial District of Sudbury.

3. The area of jurisdiction of the Conseil Scolaire de district du Centre Sud-Ouest consists of the urban area of the City of Toronto incorporated by the *City of Toronto Act, 1997*, the Regional Municipalities of Durham, Haldimand-Norfolk, Halton, Hamilton-Wentworth, Niagara, Peel, Waterloo and York and the Counties of Brant, Bruce, Dufferin, Elgin, Essex (including the Township of Pelee), Grey, Haliburton, Huron, Kent, Lambton, Middlesex, Northumberland (including that portion of the City of West Quinte which on January 1, 1997 was part of the County of Northumberland), Perth, Peterborough, Oxford, Simcoe, Victoria and Wellington.

4. The area of jurisdiction of French-language Public District School Board No. 59 consists of the Regional Municipality of Ottawa-Carleton and the Counties of Frontenac, Hastings (including that portion of the City of West Quinte which on January 1, 1997 was part of the County of Hastings), Lanark, Lennox and Addington, Prince Edward, Renfrew and The United Counties of Leeds and Grenville, The United Counties of Prescott and Russell and The United Counties of Stormont, Dundas and Glengarry. O. Reg. 278/97, s. 3; 80/98, s. 7; 213/98, ss. 6, 17, 21.

10. Eight French-language separate district school boards are established.

11. The name of each French-language separate district school board is "Conseil de district des écoles séparées de langue française n°____" (inserting a number between 60 and 66 or a combination of numbers and letters as set out in each paragraph of section 12) unless otherwise specified in the Schedules. O. Reg. 80/98, s. 8; 213/98, s. 7.

12. The following are the areas of jurisdiction of the French-language separate district school boards:

1. The area of jurisdiction of the Conseil scolaire de district catholique des Grandes Rivières consists of,
   i. in the Territorial District of Algoma, the geographic townships of Ebbs and Templeton.
   ii. in the Territorial District of Cochrane,
      A. the City of Timmins,
      B. the Towns of Cochrane, Hearst, Iroquois Falls, Kapuskasing and Smooth Rock Falls,
      C. the Townships of Glackmeyer, Mattice-Val Cote, Moonbeam, Opasatika and Val Rita-Harty,
      D. the portion of the Township of Black River-Matheson that on December 31, 1996 was not part of the geographic townships of Barnet, Frencheville, Garrison, Harker, Holloway, Lamplugh, Marriott, McCool, Michaud, Rand or Stoughton,

S. 12   REGULATIONS UNDER THE EDUCATION ACT

E. the portion of the Township of Fauquier-Strickland that on December 31, 1996 was not part of the geographic townships of Beardmore, Carmichael, MacVicar or Stringer,

F. the geographic townships of Aurora, Barker, Blount, Brower, Calder, Casgrain, Clute, Colquhoun, Fournier, Fox, Hanlan, Hanna, Irish, Kendall, Kennedy, Landry, Lamarche, Leitch, Lowther, McCowan, Mortimer, Nansen, Newmarket, O'Brien, Ottaway, Pyne, St. John, Stimson, Stoddard, Studholme, Teefy and Way,

G. the portion of the geographic township of Benoit that is not part of the Township of Black River-Matheson,

H. the portion of the geographic township of Haggart that is not part of the Township of Fauquier-Strickland, and

I. the portion of the geographic township of Owens that is not part of the Township of Val Rita-Harty,

iii. in the Territorial District of Nipissing,

A. the Municipality of Temagami, except for the portion of the Municipality that was formerly part of the geographic townships of Clement and Scholes, and

B. the geographic townships of Eldridge, Flett, Gladman, Gooderham, Hammell, Hartle, Hobbs, Kenny, McCallum, McLaren and Thistle, and

iv. in the Territorial District of Timiskaming,

A. the Towns of Cobalt, Charlton, Englehart, Haileybury, Kirkland Lake, Latchford and New Liskeard,

B. the Village of Thornloe,

C. the Townships of Armstrong, Brethour, Casey, Chamberlain, Coleman, Dack, Dymond, Evanturel, Gauthier, Harley, Harris, Hilliard, Hudson, James, Kerns, Larder Lake, Matachewan and McGarry,

D. the geographic townships of Auld, Barber, Barr, Bayly, Beauchamp, Boston, Brigstocke, Bryce, Cane, Catharine, Chown, Corkill, Davidson, Eby, Farr, Firstbrook, Grenfell, Haultain, Henwood, Ingram, Kittson, Lawson, Lebel, Lorrain, Lundy, Maisonville, Marquis, Marter, McElroy, Mickle, Milner, Mulligan, Nicol, Otto, Pacaud, Pense, Roadhouse, Robillard, Savard, Sharpe, Smyth, South Lorrain, Truax, Tudhope, Willet and Willison, and

E. the portion of the geographic township of Gillies Limit that is not part of the Township of Coleman.

2. The area of jurisdiction of the Conseil scolaire de district catholique Franco-Nord consists of,

i. in the Territorial District of Nipissing,

A. The City of North Bay,

B. the portion of the Municipality of West Nipissing that was not formerly part of the geographic townships of Bertram, Dana, Fell, Latchford and McWilliams,

C. the Towns of Kearney and Mattawa,

REGULATION 185/97 **S. 12**

      D. the Townships of Bonfield, Calvin, Chisholm, East Ferris, Mattawan and Papineau-Cameron, and

      E. the geographic townships of Blyth, Boyd, Clarkson, Commanda, Deacon, Eddy, French, Jocko, Lauder, Lyman, Merrick, Notman, Pentland, Phelps, Poitras and Wyse, and

    ii. in the Territorial District of Parry Sound,

      A. the Towns of Kearney, Powassan and Trout Creek,

      B. the Villages of Burk's Falls, South River and Sundridge,

      C. the Townships of Armour, Joly, Machar, McMurrich/Monteith, Nipissing, North Himsworth, Perry, Ryerson, South Himsworth and Strong,

      D. the portion of the Township of Seguin which on January 1, 1997 was part of the geographic township of Monteith,

      E. the geographic townships of Laurier, Lount, Patterson and Pringle, and

      F. the portion of the Township of Magnetawan that was not formerly part of the geographic township of Croft.

3. The area of jurisdiction of the Conseil scolaire de district catholique du Nouvel-Ontario consists of,

    i. in the Territorial District of Algoma,

      A. the Cities of Elliot Lake and Sault Ste. Marie,

      B. the Town of Blind River,

      C. the Village of Iron Bridge,

      D. the Township of Day and Bright Additional,

      E. the Township of Macdonald, Meredith and Aberdeen Additional,

      F. the Township of Tarbutt and Tarbutt Additional,

      G. the Townships of Johnson, Laird, Michipicoten, The North Shore, Prince, Shedden, Thompson and White River,

      H. the geographic townships of Archibald, Aweres, Bright, Cobden, Dennis, Deroche, Esquega, Fenwick, Fiddler, Fisher, Gaudette, Gladstone, Grasett, Havilland, Herrick, Hodgins, Home, Jarvis, Jogues, Juillette, Kamichisitit, Kars, Kincaid, Ley, Mack, Montgomery, Nouvel, Parkinson, Patton, Peever, Pennefather, Rix, Ryan, Scarfe, Schields, Slater, Tilley, Timmermans, Tupper and VanKoughnet,

      I. the mining locations known as Montreal Mining Southern Location, Montreal Mining Northern Location, A. McDonnell Mining Location, Kincaid Mining Locations, 5, 6, 7 and 8 and Rankin Mining Location,

      J. the portion of the geographic township of Striker that is not part of the Township of The North Shore, and

      K. all the islands of the North Channel of Lake Huron lying south of the geographic townships of Bright, Cobden and the portion of Striker that is not part of the Township of the North Shore,

    ii. in the Territorial District of Manitoulin,

      A. the Township of Rutherford and George Island, and

      B. Ward No. 2 of the Town of Northeastern Manitoulin and the Islands,

    iii. in the Territorial District of Parry Sound, the geographic townships of Henvey and Wallbridge,

iv. in the Territorial District of Sudbury,
- A. The Regional Municipality of Sudbury,
- B. the Town of Espanola,
- C. the Township of Casimir, Jennings and Appleby,
- D. the Municipality of French River,
- E. the Township of Nairn and Hyman,
- F. the Township of Ratter and Dunnet,
- G. the Townships of Baldwin, Chapleau and Hagar,
- G.1 the portion of the Municipality of West Nipissing that was formerly part of the geographic township of Janes,
- H. the geographic townships of Allen, Awrey, Burwash, Cartier, Cascaden, Caverley, Chapleau, Cleland, Cox, Curtin, Davis, de Gaulle, Eisenhower, Foster, Foy, Gallagher, Genier, Halsey, Hart, Harty, Hawley, Hendrie, Henry, Hess, Kaplan, Laura, Loughrin, Moncrieff, Mongowin, Panet, Roosevelt, Scadding, Secord, Servos, Street and Truman,
- I. the portions of the geographic townships of Dill, Eden and Tilton that are not part of The Regional Municipality of Sudbury,
- J. the portion of the geographic township of Dryden that is not part of The Regional Municipality of Sudbury, and
- K. the portion of the geographic township of Trill that is not part of The Regional Municipality of Sudbury,
- L. the portion of the geographic township of Janes that is not part of the Municipality of West Nipissing, and
- M. the portions of the geographic townships of Bigwood, Cherriman and Haddo that are not part of the Municipality of French River.

v. the portion of the Township of The Sables — Spanish Rivers that is in the Territorial District of Sudbury.

4. The area of jurisdiction of the Conseil scolaire de district catholique des Aurores boréales consists of,
    i. in the Territorial District of Kenora,
    - A. the City of Dryden,
    - B. the Towns of Jaffray Melick, Keewatin, Kenora and Sioux Lookout,
    - C. the Townships of Lake of the Woods, Machin and Sioux Narrows,
    - D. the geographic townships of Boys, Britton, Buller, Colenso, Eton, Godson, Hartman, Ilsley, Kirkup, Ladysmith, Melgund, Mutrie, Pellatt, Phillips, Redditt, Redvers, Rowell, Rugby, Smellie, Southworth, Tweedsmuir, Van Horne, Wabigoon, Wainwright and Zealand,
    - E. the portion of the geographic township of Aubrey that is not part of the Township of Machin,
    - F. all the lands in unsurveyed territory in the vicinity of the station house of the Canadian National Railways at Minaki described as follows:

        commencing at a point distant 4 kilometres measured east astronomically from the northeast corner of the said station house,

        thence north astronomically 4 kilometres,

thence west astronomically 8 kilometres,

thence south astronomically 8 kilometres,

thence east astronomically 8 kilometres,

thence north astronomically 4 kilometres to the point of commencement,

G. except for those parts of the mainland which are crossed by the said line, all lands lying north of a line extending from the southernmost extremity of the geographic township of Boys to the southwest corner of the geographic township of Kirkup and south of the southerly boundaries of the geographic townships of Boys and Pellatt, the towns of Jaffray Melick, Keewatin and Kenora, and

H. all lands, other than the geographic townships of Godson, Phillips and Tweedsmuir and the Township of Lake of the Woods, within an area the boundary sides of which are as follows:
1. on the west side, the International Boundary between the point of intersection thereon of the 49th degree parallel of north latitude and the point of intersection of the production westerly of the north boundary of the geographic Township of Tweedsmuir along the 4th base line,
2. on the south side, the line described as commencing at the point of intersection of the 49th degree parallel of north latitude with the International Boundary,

    thence due east 24 kilometres more or less along the 49th degree parallel of north latitude to the east shore of the Lake of the Woods,

    thence north easterly and northerly along the east shore of the Lake of the Woods and the south and east shores of Sabaskong Bay of the Lake of the Woods to the point of intersection of the westerly production of the south boundary of the geographic township of Godson,

    thence due east along the said south boundary of the said geographic township and along its production due east being along O.L.S. Gillon's base line of 1919 to the 24th mile post on O.L.S. Alexander Niven's 6th meridian line,
3. on the east side, O.L.S. Alexander Niven's 6th meridian line between the 24th mile post thereon and the point of intersection on the said meridian line of the production due east along the 4th base line of the north boundary of the geographic township of Tweedsmuir,
4. on the north side, the production along the 4th base line westerly to the International Boundary and easterly to O.L.S. Alexander Niven's 6th meridian line of the north boundary of the geographic township of Tweedsmuir.

ii. in the Territorial District of Rainy River,
    A. the Towns of Fort Frances and Rainy River,

B. the Townships of Alberton, Chapple, Dawson, Emo, La Vallee, Lake of the Woods and Morley,

C. [Revoked O. Reg. 213/98, s. 8(13).]

D. the geographic townships of Claxton, Croome, Dance, Dewart, Farrington, Fleming, Griesinger, Halkirk, Kingsford, Mathieu, McLarty, Menary, Miscampbell, Nelles, Pratt, Rowe, Senn, Sifton, Spohn, Sutherland and Watten,

E. the Wild Land Reserve, and

F. all lands in unsurveyed territory within an area the boundary sides of which are as follows:

  1. on the north side, the northerly limit of the Territorial District of Rainy River commencing at the point of intersection of the 49th degree parallel of north latitude with the International Boundary,

  thence due east 24 kilometres more or less along the 49th degree parallel of north latitude to the east shore of the Lake of the Woods,

  thence north easterly and northerly along the east shore of the Lake of the Woods and the south and east shores of Sabaskong Bay of the Lake of the Woods to the point of intersection of the westerly production of the north boundaries of the geographic townships of Claxton and McLarty,

  thence due easterly along the said north boundaries of the said geographic townships and along their production due east being along O.L.S. Gillon's base line of 1919 to the 24th mile post on O.L.S. Alexander Niven's 6th meridian line,

  thence due south along the said meridian line 9.6 kilometres to the 18th mile post thereon in latitude 49° 0' 6" north,

  thence due east to the point of intersection of the production north of the east boundary of the geographic township of Farrington,

  2. on the east side, the line formed by the east boundary of the geographic township of Farrington, the production of the said east boundary due north to the north boundary of the Territorial District of Rainy River and the production due south of the said east boundary to the International Boundary,

  3. on the south side, the International Boundary from the mouth of the Rainy River easterly to the point of intersection on the International Boundary of the production due south of the east boundary of the geographic township of Farrington,

  4. on the west side, the International Boundary from the mouth of the Rainy River northerly to the point of intersection on the International Boundary of the 49th degree parallel of north latitude, and

iii. in the Territorial District of Thunder Bay,

  A. the City of Thunder Bay,

  B. the Towns of Geraldton, Longlac and Marathon,

  B.1 the Municipalities of Neebing and Oliver Paipoonge,

C. the Townships of Beardmore, Conmee, Dorion, Gillies, Maintouwadge, Nakina, Nipigon, O'Connor, Red Rock, Schreiber, Shuniah and Terrace Bay,

D. the geographic townships of Ashmore, Atikameg, Blackwell, Bomby, Boothe, Brothers, Bryant, Byron, Cecil, Cecile, Coldwell, Conacher, Corrigal, Cotte, Daley, Davies, Devon, Errington, Flood, Foote, Forbes, Fraleigh, Goldie, Golding, Gorham, Grain, Grenville, Hagey, Herbert, Homer, Houck, Killraine, Knowles, Laberge, Lahontan, Laurie, Lecours, Leduc, Lismore, Lybster, Lyon, Marks, McCron, McGill, Michener, Mikano, Nickle, Oakes, O'Neill, Pic, Priske, Roberta, Robson, Shabotik, Sibley, Spooner, Stirling, Strange, Strey, Syine, Tuuri, Walsh, Ware, Wiggins and Yesno,

E. the Dawson Road Lots,

F. the area bounded by the easterly boundary of Lot 1, concessions 1 and 2 of the Dawson Road Lots, the southerly boundary of the geographic township of Forbes, the westerly shore of the Kaministiquia River (sometimes known as the Dog River) and the northerly shore of the Shebandowan River (sometimes known as the Matawin River), and

G. all lands, excluding St. Ignace Island, in unsurveyed territory within an area described as follows:
  1. on the north side, the extension of the north side of the geographic township of Davies westerly to intersect with the boundary formed by extending the west side of the geographic township of Wiggins northerly until it meets the said extension,
  2. on the east side, the extension of the east side of the geographic township of Spooner southerly until the Canada-United States border,
  3. on the south side, the Canada-United States border, and
  4. on the west side, the extension of the west side of the geographic township of Wiggins southerly until the Canada-United States border.

5. The area of jurisdiction of the Conseil scolaire de district des écoles catholiques du Sud-Ouest consists of the Counties of Bruce, Grey, Huron, Perth, Oxford, Middlesex, Elgin, Lambton, Kent and Essex (including the Township of Pelee).

6. The area of jurisdiction of the Conseil scolaire de district catholique Centre-Sud consists of the urban area of the City of Toronto incorporated by the *City of Toronto Act, 1997*, the Regional Municipalities of Durham, York, Peel, Haldimand-Norfolk, Halton, Hamilton-Wentworth, Niagara, Waterloo and the Counties of Brant, Dufferin, Northumberland (including that portion of the City of West Quinte which on January 1, 1997 was part of the County of Northumberland), Peterborough, Simcoe, Victoria and Wellington, the District Municipality of Muskoka, and in the Territorial District of Parry Sound, Wards 3, 4 and 6 of the Township of Seguin.

7. The area of jurisdiction of the Conseil scolaire de district catholique de l'Est Ontarien consists of the United Counties of Stormont, Dundas and Glengarry and the United Counties of Prescott and Russell.

8. The area of jurisdiction of the Conseil scolaire de district catholique du Centre-Est de l'Ontario consists of the Regional Municipality of Ottawa-Carleton, the Counties of Frontenac, Hastings (including that portion of the City of West Quinte which on January 1, 1997 was part of the County of Hastings), Lanark, Lennox and Addington, Prince Edward, Renfrew and the United Counties of Leeds and Grenville, and, in the Territorial District of Nipissing, the Township of South Algonquin. O. Reg. 278/97, s. 4; 213/98, ss. 8, 14, 18, 22.

13. (1) The name of each district school board listed in Column 1 of Schedule 1 is changed to the name listed opposite in Column 2 of Schedule 1.

(2) The name of each district school board listed in Column 1 of Schedule 2 is changed to the name listed opposite in Column 2 of Schedule 2.

(3) [Revoked 213/98, s. 9(2).]

(4) [Revoked 213/98, s. 9(2).]

14. (1) A reference to a district school board using the name listed in Column 1 of a Schedule to this Regulation shall be construed as if it were a reference to the district school board using the name listed opposite in Column 2 of the Schedule.

(2) Subsection (1) applies to a reference in any document of legal effect made before January 1, 1999, whether before or after the coming into force of this section.

(3) For this purposes of subsection (2), a document includes but is not limited to a regulation, directive, order or agreement. O. Reg. 213/98, s. 10.

15. (1) A description set out in a paragraph of this Regulation of the area of jurisdiction of a district school board shall be interpreted as of the day the paragraph comes into force.

(2) Subsection (1) applies regardless of changes in the boundaries, name or status of one or more municipal entities or geographical areas.

(3) Despite subsections (1) and (2), where a paragraph or portion of a paragraph that sets out a description or a part of a description of the area of jurisdiction of a district school board is amended, the paragraph or portion of a paragraph as amended shall be interpreted as of the day the amendment comes into force. O. Reg. 213/98, s. 10.

Schedule 1
O. Reg. 80/98, s. 10

COLUMN 1 Old Name	COLUMN 2 New Name
English-language Public District School Board No. 2	Algoma District School Board
English-language Public District School Board No. 4	Near North District School Board
English-language Public District School Board No. 5A	Keewatin-Patricia District School Board
English-language Public District School Board No. 5B	Rainy River District School Board

REGULATION 185/97

Schedule

Column 1 Old Name	Column 2 New Name
English-language Public District School Board No. 6A	Lakehead District School Board
English-language Public District School Board No. 6B	Superior-Greenstone District School Board
English-language Public District School Board No. 7	Bluewater District School Board
English-language Public District School Board No. 8	Avon Maitland District School Board
English-language Public District School Board No. 9	Greater Essex County District School Board
English-language Public District School Board No. 11	Thames Valley District School Board
English-language Public District School Board No. 12	Toronto District School Board
English-language Public District School Board No. 13	Durham District School Board
English-language Public District School Board No. 17	Simcoe County District School Board
English-language Public District School Board No. 19	Peel District School Board
English-language Public District School Board No. 21	Hamilton-Wentworth District School Board
English-language Public District School Board No. 23	Grand Erie District School Board
English-language Public District School Board No. 24	Waterloo Region District School Board
English-language Public District School Board No. 25	Ottawa-Carleton District School Board
English-language Public District School Board No. 28	Renfrew County District School Board
English-language Public District School Board No. 29	Hastings and Prince Edward District School Board
English-language Separate District School Board No. 30A	Northeastern Catholic District School Board

Schedule

REGULATIONS UNDER THE EDUCATION ACT

Column 1 Old Name	Column New Name
English-language Separate District School Board No. 30B	Nipissing-Parry Sound Catholic District School Board
English-language Separate District School Board No. 31	Huron-Superior Catholic District School Board
English-language Separate District School Board No. 32	Sudbury Catholic District School Board
English-language Separate District School Board No. 33A	Northwest Catholic District School Board
English-language Separate District School Board No. 33B	Kenora Catholic District School Board
English-language Separate District School Board No. 34A	Thunder Bay Catholic District School Board
English-language Separate District School Board No. 34B	Superior North Catholic District School Board
English-language Separate District School Board No. 35	Bruce-Grey Catholic District School Board
English-language Separate District School Board No. 36	Huron Perth Catholic District School Board
English-language Separate District School Board No. 42	York Catholic District School Board
English-language Separate District School Board No. 44	Simcoe Muskoka Catholic District School Board
English-language Separate District School Board No. 45	Durham Catholic District School Board
English-language Separate District School Board No. 47	Hamilton-Wentworth Catholic District School Board
English-language Separate District School Board No. 48	Wellington Catholic District School Board
English-language Separate District School Board No. 49	Waterloo Catholic District School Board
English-language Separate District School Board No. 50	Niagara Catholic District School Board
English-language Separate District School Board No. 51	Brant/Haldimand-Norfolk Catholic District School Board

Schedule

Column 1 Old Name	Column New Name
English-language Separate District School Board No. 53	Ottawa-Carleton Catholic District School Board
English-language Separate District School Board No. 54	Renfrew County Catholic District School Board
Conseil de district des écoles publiques de langue française n° 57	Conseil scolaire de district du Grand Nord de l'Ontario

Schedule

REGULATIONS UNDER THE EDUCATION ACT

Schedule 2

O. Reg. 213/98, s. 12.

COLUMN 1 Old Name	COLUMN 2 New Name
English-language Public District School Board No. 1	District School Board Ontario North East
English-language Public District School Board No. 3	Rainbow District School Board
English-language Public District School Board No. 10	Lambton Kent District School Board
English-language Public District School Board No. 14	Kawartha Pine Ridge District School Board
English-language Public District School Board No. 15	Trillium Lakelands District School Board
English-language Public District School Board No. 16	York Region District School Board
English-language Public District School Board No. 18	Upper Grand District School Board
English-language Public District School Board No. 20	Halton District School Board
English-language Public District School Board No. 22	District School Board of Niagara
English-language Public District School Board No. 26	Upper Canada District School Board
English-language Public District School Board No. 27	Limestone District School Board
English-language Separate District School Board No. 37	Windsor-Essex Catholic District School Board
English-language Separate District School Board No. 39	St. Clair Catholic District School Board
English-language Separate District School Board No. 40	Toronto Catholic District School Board
English-language Separate District School Board No. 41	Peterborough Victoria Northumberland and Clarington Catholic District School Board
English-language Separate District School Board No. 43	Dufferin-Peel Catholic District School Board

Schedule

Column 1 Old Name	Column 2 New Name
English-language Separate District School Board No. 46	Halton Catholic District School Board
English-language Separate District School Board No. 52	Catholic District School Board of Eastern Ontario
English-language Separate District School Board No. 55	Algonquin and Lakeshore Catholic District School Board
Conseil de district des écoles publiques de langue française n° 56	Conseil scolaire de district du Nord-Est de l'Ontario
Conseil de district des écoles publiques de langue française n° 58	Conseil scolaire de district du Centre Sud-Ouest
Conseil de district des écoles séparées de langue française n° 60A	Conseil scolaire de district catholique des Grandes Rivières
Conseil de district des écoles séparées de langue française n° 60B	Conseil scolaire de district catholique Franco-Nord
Conseil de district des écoles séparées de langue française n° 61	Conseil scolaire de district catholique du Nouvel-Ontario
Conseil de district des écoles séparées de langue française n° 62	Conseil scolaire de district catholique des Aurores boréales
Conseil de district des écoles séparées de langue française n° 63	Conseil scolaire de district des écoles catholiques du Sud-Ouest
Conseil de district des écoles séparées de langue française n° 64	Conseil scolaire de district catholique Centre-Sud
Conseil de district des écoles séparées de langue française n° 65	Conseil scolaire de district catholique de l'Est ontarien
Conseil de district des écoles séparées de langue française n° 66	Conseil scolaire de district catholique du Centre-Est de l'Ontario

REGULATION 250/97
REPRESENTATION ON DISTRICT SCHOOL BOARDS—1997 REGULAR ELECTION

O. Reg. 250/97, as am. O. Reg. 279/97; 396/97

INTERPRETATION

1. (1) In this Regulation,

"board" means a district school board; ("conseil")

"board area" means the area of jurisdiction, expressed in square kilometres, of a board, as set out in the Schedule; ("territoire du conseil")

"Commission" means the Education Improvement Commission established under section 334 of the Act; ("Commission")

"committee" means an education improvement committee referred to in clause 335(3)(1) of the Act; ("comité")

"density" means the quotient obtained by dividing the population of the relevant electoral group by the board area; ("densité")

"density member position" means a board position determined by the application of Tables 2 and 3, but not Table 1; ("poste de membre lié à la densité")

"election" means the regular election to be held in 1997 referred to in subsection 4(1) of the *Municipal Elections Act, 1996*; ("élection")

"electoral group" means a public school English-language electoral group, a separate school English-language electoral group, a public school French-language electoral group or a separate school French-language electoral group; ("groupe électoral")

"existing board" has the same meaning as "board" in subsection 1(1) of the Act but does not include a school authority; ("conseil existant")

"high density board" means a board that has,

    (a) eight members or less, of whom not more than one occupies a density member position, or

    (b) nine or more members, of whom not more than two occupy density member positions; ("conseil d'un territoire à forte densité")

"low density board" means a board that is not a high density board; ("conseil d'un territoire à faible densité")

"population member position" means a board position determined by the application of Table 1, but not Tables 2 and 3; ("poste de membre lié à la population")

"start date" means the later of,

    (a) the date on which this Regulation is filed,

    (b) the date on which the clerk of the municipality in the area of jurisdiction of the board that has the largest population of the relevant electoral group receives the results of a determination of population under subsection 2(4) or (5),

(c) the date on which the supervisory officer receives the last direction under subsection 2(7) or (8), and
(d) the date on which the supervisory officer receives the last estimate of results under subsection 2(9); ("date de commencement")

"supervisory officer" means the person referred to in subsection 4(5); ("agent de supervision")

"ward" does not include a ward of a regional or district municipality ("quartier")

(2) A reference in this Regulation, other than in clause 6(3)(e), to a municipality or ward shall be deemed to be a reference to the part of a municipality or ward that is within the area of jurisdiction of the board.

(3) A reference in this Regulation to the clerk shall be deemed to be a reference to,

(a) if the clerk is the clerk of a municipality in respect of which an order has been implemented under section 25.2 or 25.3 of the *Municipal Act* and the order assigns responsibility for conducting the election in the municipality to a person other than the clerk, that other person;

(b) if the clerk is the clerk of an area municipality in The Municipality of Metropolitan Toronto, the person designated under paragraph 2 of section 23 of the *City of Toronto Act, 1997*.

(4) For the purposes of this Regulation,

(a) the relevant electoral group for an English-language public district school board is the group of persons who are members of a public school English-language electoral group and who reside in the area of jurisdiction of the English-language public district school board;

(b) the relevant electoral group for an English-language separate district school board is the group of persons who are members of a separate school English-language electoral group and who reside in the area of jurisdiction of the English-language separate district school board;

(c) the relevant electoral group for a French-language public district school board is the group of persons who are members of a public school French-language electoral group and who reside in the area of jurisdiction of the French-language public district school board; and

(d) the relevant electoral group for a French-language separate district school board is the group of persons who are members of a separate school French-language electoral group and who reside in the area of jurisdiction of the French-language separate district school board.

(5) In this section,

"public school English-language electoral group", "separate school English-language electoral group", "public school French-language electoral group" and "separate school French-language electoral group" have the same meaning as in Part VIII of the *Education Act* as it read on January 1, 1997. ("groupe électoral de langue anglaise des écoles publiques"), ("groupe électoral de langue anglaise des écoles séparées"), ("groupe électoral de langue française des écoles publiques"), ("groupe électoral de langue française des écoles séparées") O. Reg. 279/97, s. 1.

POPULATION DATA

2. (1) The assessment commissioner shall provide to the Commission the results of the determination of population provided to the secretary of each existing board and the clerk of each municipality under subsections 230(6) and 329(3) of the Act.

(2) The secretary of each existing board shall provide the results to the members of the committee.

(3) If a municipality or ward that is to be used for the election is composed of a part of one or more municipalities or wards in respect of which results were provided under subsections 230(6) and 329(3) of the Act, the assessment commissioner shall determine the populations of the relevant electoral groups of the municipality or ward.

(4) As soon as possible, the assessment commissioner shall provide the results of the determination under subsection (3) to,

   (a) the Commission;
   (b) the secretary of each existing board whose members are elected by members of an electoral group that is part of the relevant electoral group; and
   (c) the clerk of each municipality in the area of jurisdiction of the board that is also in the area of jurisdiction of the assessment commissioner.

(5) On receipt of the results, the Commission shall provide them to the clerk of each municipality in the area of jurisdiction of the board who has not received them from the assessment commissioner.

(6) If the assessment commissioner does not provide the results within seven days after the date of filing of this Regulation, he or she shall notify the Commission of the municipalities and wards for which the results have not been provided.

(7) If results have been provided for two or more adjacent municipalities or wards in the area of jurisdiction of a board, the Commission may, on receipt of the notice, direct that,

   (a) the clerks referred to in subsection 5(1) include those municipalities or wards wholly within a geographic area identified under rule 2 of subsection 8(5) in the case of a high density board with no low population areas;
   (b) the committee include those municipalities or wards wholly within the low population area or wholly outside of it and the clerks include them wholly within a geographic area identified under rule 5 or rule 7 of subsection 8(6), as the case may be, in the case of a high density board with one or more low population areas; or
   (c) the committee include those municipalities or wards wholly within a geographic area identified under rule 3 of subsection 9(2) in the case of a low density board.

(8) The Commission may, if it considers it appropriate to do so, make a direction before receiving the notice from the assessment commissioner.

(9) If the Commission gives no direction under subsection (7) or (8), it shall estimate the results for the municipalities or wards referred to in subsection (3).

(10) The Commission shall give any direction or estimate within 14 days after the date of filing of this Regulation.

(11) The Commission shall provide the supervisory officer with any direction or estimate, who shall provide a copy of it to the clerks referred to in subsection 5(1) and to the committee at the beginning of the meeting convened under that subsection.

(12) The clerks and the committee shall comply with any direction or use any estimate in respect of municipalities and wards referred to in subsection (3) instead of the results provided under subsections 230(6) and 329(3) of the Act.

3. If a municipality or ward that is to be used for the election is composed of a part of one or more of the municipalities or wards in respect of which results were provided under subsection 230(6) and 329(3) of the Act and the boundaries of the municipality or ward are established for the purpose of electing members to boards more than seven days after the date of filing of this Regulation, the municipalities and wards that existed on January 1, 1997 shall be deemed to exist for purposes of the election, and this Regulation and other applicable law shall apply to such municipalities and wards as if their boundaries had not changed since January 1, 1997.

IDENTIFICATION OF MUNICIPALITIES BY SUPERVISORY OFFICER AND MEETING

4. (1) A supervisory officer shall identify the three municipalities within the area of jurisdiction of the board that have successively the largest populations of the relevant electoral group.

(2) Subject to subsections (3) and (4), the identification shall be based on the results provided under subsections 230(6) and 329(3) of the Act or on any results or estimate under section 2.

(3) The identification shall not be based on the results or estimate under section 2 if the municipality or ward to be used for the election does not exist at the time the identification is made unless an order has been implemented under section 25.2 or 25.3 of the *Municipal Act* making a person responsible for conducting the election in the municipality or unless the election in the municipality will be conducted by the person designated under paragraph 2 of section 23 of the *City of Toronto Act, 1997*.

(4) If two or more English-language public district school boards, English-language separate district school boards, French-language public district school boards or French-language separate district school boards have jurisdiction in the same municipality and the boundary between them is also a boundary between wards in the municipality, the identification shall be based on the sum of the results for the relevant electoral group in the wards of the municipality in the area of jurisdiction of the board.

(5) The supervisory officer is,

(a) for English-language public district school boards, the appropriate English-language supervisory officer of the board of education, other than a board of education that operates only French-language instructional units, that has jurisdiction in the municipality in the area of jurisdiction of the board having the largest population of the relevant electoral group;

(b) for English-language separate district school boards, the appropriate English-language supervisory officer of the county or district combined separate school board, other than a county combined separate school board that operates only French-language instructional units, that has jurisdiction in the municipality in the area of jurisdiction of the board having the largest population of the relevant electoral group;

(c) for French-language public district school boards, the appropriate French-language supervisory officer of the board of education, other than a board of education that may not operate a school or class under Part XII of the Act, that has jurisdiction in the municipality in the area of jurisdiction of the board having the largest population of the relevant electoral group;

(d) for French-language separate district school boards, the appropriate French-language supervisory officer of the county or district combined separate school board, other than a county combined separate school board that may not operate a school or class under Part XII of the Act, that has jurisdiction in the municipality in the area of jurisdiction of the board having the largest population of the relevant electoral group. O. Reg. 279/97, s. 2.

5. (1) The supervisory officer shall take all necessary steps to convene a meeting of the clerks of the three municipalities within the area of jurisdiction of the board that have successively the largest population of the relevant electoral group.

(2) The Commission shall establish one committee for each board.

(3) As soon as possible after the start date, the Commission shall provide, in writing, the names and addresses of the members of the committee to,

(a) the clerks referred to in subsection (1);

(b) the secretary of each existing board whose members are elected by members of an electoral group that is part of the relevant electoral group; and

(c) the supervisory officer.

(4) On receipt of the names and addresses of the committee members, the supervisory officer shall give at least two days notice of the time and place of the meeting to the members of the committee, who may attend the meeting.

(5) If the supervisory officer does not receive the names and addresses of all of the committee members within three days after the start date, the Commission,

(a) has the powers and duties of the committee under this Regulation until the supervisory officer receives all the names and addresses; and

(b) may appoint a representative to exercise any powers and duties of the Commission under clause (a) and to attend the meeting on its behalf.

(6) The supervisory officer shall give at least two days notice of the time and place of the meeting to any other clerk who is the clerk of a municipality that is divided into wards situated within the area of jurisdiction of the board.

(7) The supervisory officer shall convene the meeting within 10 days after the start date.

DETERMINATION AND DISTRIBUTION OF BOARD MEMBERS

6. (1) At the meeting, the clerks shall,

(a) determine the population of the relevant electoral group, the board area and its density; and
(b) determine the number of members of the board in accordance with section 7.

(2) Subject to subsection (3), a determination of the number of members of the board under section 7 and a distribution of members under section 8 or 9 shall be based on the results provided to the clerks by the assessment commissioner under subsections 230(6) and 329(3) of the Act.

(3) If the results provided to the clerks by the assessment commissioner are for municipalities or wards that are not to be used for purposes of the election,
   (a) the result for a municipality that has the same boundaries as a ward that is to be used for the election is the result for the ward;
   (b) if a municipality or ward that is to be used for the election is composed of not less than all of one or more of the municipalities or wards in respect of which results were provided under subsections 230(6) and 329(3) of the Act, the result for the municipality or ward is the sum of the results for the relevant electoral group for each of the municipalities and wards of which the municipality or ward is composed;
   (c) if a municipality or ward that is to be used for the election is composed of a part of one or more of the municipalities or wards in respect of which results were provided under subsection 230(6) and 329(3) of the Act, the result for the municipality or ward is the result or estimate provided under section 2;
   (d) the result for a group of adjacent municipalities and wards in respect of which a direction has been given is the sum of the results for the relevant electoral group for each of the municipalities and wards; and
   (e) if a municipality or ward that is to be used for the election is composed of one or more municipalities or wards in respect of which results were provided under subsection 230(6) and 329(3) of the Act and territory outside the area of jurisdiction of the board, those results are the result for the part of the municipality or ward within the area of jurisdiction of the board.

DETERMINATION OF NUMBER OF BOARD MEMBERS

7. (1) Subject to an addition of members pursuant to regulations made under subclause 327(3)(d)(vi) or (vii) of the Act, the number of members for a board shall be determined by applying the following rules in order, beginning with rule 1:

1. Subject to rules 2 and 3, a board shall have the number of members set out in Column 2 of Table 1 opposite the population of the relevant electoral group for the board set out in Column 1 of that Table.
2. Subject to rule 3, and in addition to the number of members determined under rule 1, a board shall have the number of members set out in Column 2 of Table 2 opposite the density for the board set out in Column 1 of that Table.
3. The number of additional members that a board shall have as a result of the application of rule 2 shall not exceed the number set out in Column 2 of Table 3 opposite the board area set out in Column 1 of that Table.

(2) For the purpose of rule 2 of subsection (1), the calculation of density shall be correct to two decimal places, with the number 0.005 being raised to 0.01.

DISTRIBUTION OF MEMBERS OF HIGH DENSITY BOARDS

8. (1) A distribution of the members of a board determined to be a high density board under section 7 shall be made, in accordance with the rules set out in this section, in respect of the geographic area identified under rule 2 of subsection (5) and rules 5 and 7 of subsection (6).

(2) The committee shall,

(a) identify the municipalities or wards, if any, that are low population areas, and

(b) if low population areas are identified, determine the low population factor, which shall be,

(i) in the case of a high density board with not more than one density member position, a number greater than zero but less than or equal to one, and

(ii) in the case of a high density board with not more than two density members positions, a number greater than zero but less than or equal to two.

(3) In carrying out its duties under subsection (2), the committee shall have regard to the following principles:

1. Municipalities and wards with a low population of the relevant electoral group should receive reasonable representation.
2. Evidence of historic, traditional or geographic communities within the relevant electoral group should be taken into account.
3. To the extent possible, the identification of low population municipalities and wards should permit the establishment of geographic areas that coincide with school communities.
4. Representation should not deviate unduly from the principle of representation by population.

(4) On any vote taken by the members of the committee in respect of an identification or determination under subsection (2) that results in a tie, the clerks shall break the tie by majority vote.

(5) If no low population areas are identified under clause (2)(a), the clerks shall distribute the members of the board by applying the following rules in order, beginning with rule 1:

1. Calculating the electoral quotient for each municipality and ward using the following formula:

$$\text{electoral quotient} = \frac{a \times b}{c}$$

where a = the population of the relevant electoral group that is resident in the municipality or ward,

b = the total number of members on the board,

c = the total population of the relevant electoral group.

2. Identify,

i. one or more municipalities

ii. one or more wards in a municipality, or

iii. any combination of municipalities and wads

that shall form geographic areas in which the sum of the electoral quotients of the municipalities or wards is, as nearly as practicable, an integer.

3. The number of members for a geographic area in a high density board with no low population areas shall be, as nearly as practicable, the sum of the electoral quotients of the municipalities or wards that form the geographic area.

(6) If one or more low population areas are identified under clause (2)(a), the clerks shall distribute the members of the board by applying the following rules in order, beginning with rule 1:

1. Place the municipalities and wards in two groups, one of which shall be comprised of the low population areas and one of which shall be comprised of the remaining municipalities and wards.

2. Calculate an electoral quotient for each municipality and ward using the following formula:

$$\text{electoral quotient} = \frac{a \times (b + c - d)}{e}$$

where a = the population of the relevant electoral group that is resident in the municipality or ward,

b = the total number of population member positions on the board,

c = the total number of density member positions on the board,

d = the low population factor,

e = the total population of the relevant electoral group.

3. Add the low population factor to the sum of the electoral quotients of the low population areas.

4. Calculate an electoral quotient for each municipality and ward in the low population area using the following formula:

$$\text{electorial quotient} = \frac{a \times b}{c}$$

where a = the population of the relevant electoral group that is resident in the municipality or ward,

b = the number calculated under rule 3,

c = the total population of the relevant electoral group that is resident in the low population areas.

5. Among the low population areas, identify,

i. one or more municipalities,

ii. one or more wards in a municipality, or

iii. any combination of municipalities and wards,

that shall form geographic areas in which the sum of the electoral quotients calculated under rule 4 of the municipalities or wads is, as nearly as practicable, an integer.

6. The number of members for a geographic area in a low population area in a high density board shall be, as nearly as practicable, the sum of the electoral quotients calculated under rule 4 of the municipalities or wards that form the geographic area.

7. Among the municipalities and wards that are not low population areas, identify,
    i. one or more municipalities,
    ii. one or more wards in a municipality, or
    iii. any combination of municipalities and wards,

that shall form geographic areas in which the sum of the electoral quotients calculated under rule 2 of the municipalities or wards is, as nearly as practicable, an integer.

8. The number of members for a geographic area in a high density board that is not in a low population area shall be, as nearly as practicable, the sum of the electoral quotients calculated under rule 2 of the municipalities or wards that form the geographic area.

(7) If another clerk is the clerk of a municipality that is divided into wards situated within the area of jurisdiction of the board, he or she may make recommendations to the clerks or to the committee in respect of the distribution to be made to wards in his or her municipality.

DISTRIBUTION OF MEMBERS OF LOW DENSITY BOARDS

9. (1) A distribution of the members of a board determined to be a low density board under section 7 shall be made, in accordance with the rules set out in subsection (2), in respect of the geographic area identified under rule 3 of that subsection.

(2) The members of a low density board shall be disturbed by applying the following rules in order, beginning with rule 1:

1. Adjust the number of population member positions and the number of density member positions so that the population member positions form at least a simple majority of the member positions determined under section 7.

2. Calculate the electoral quotient for the population member positions for each municipality and ward using the following formula:

$$\text{electorial quotients} = \frac{a \times b}{c}$$

where a = the population of the relevant electoral group that is resident in the municipality or ward,

b = the total number of population member positions for the board as adjusted under rule 1,

c = the total population of the relevant electoral group.

3. Identify geographic areas composed of
    i. one or more municipalities,
    ii. one or more wards in a municipality, or

iii. any combination of municipalities and wards.
4. Add a number to the sum of the electoral quotients for each geographic area such that the total of the numbers added equals the number of density member positions as adjusted under rule 1.
5. The number of members for a geographic area in a low density board shall be, as nearly as practicable, the sum determined under rule 4.

(3) The clerks shall carry out all the actions required by rules 1, 2 and 5 of subsection (2).

(4) The committee shall carry out all the actions required by rules 3 and 4 of subsection (2), having regard to the following principles:
1. Municipalities and wards with a low population of the relevant electoral group should receive reasonable representation.
2. Evidence of historic, traditional or geographic communities within the relevant electoral group should be taken into account.
3. To the extent possible, geographic areas to which member positions are distributed should coincide with school communities.
4. Representation should not deviate unduly from the principle of representation by population.

(5) Despite subsection (4), on any vote taken by the members of the committee in respect of the application of rules 3 and 4 of subsection (2) that results in a tie, the clerks shall break the tie by majority vote.

(6) Any other clerk who is the clerk of a municipality that is divided into wards situated within the area of jurisdiction of the board may make recommendations to the committee in respect of the distribution of members to be made to wards in his or her municipality.

10. A committee whose powers and duties have been exercised by the Commission or its representative under subsection 5(5) shall adopt or vary the actions taken by the Commission or its representative in the exercise of those powers and duties before taking any actions on its own behalf under this Regulation.

11. (1) On completion of the determination and distribution of members of the board, the clerks shall prepare a report consisting of,
(a) the results of the determination and distribution;
(b) a copy of any direction received under subsection 2(7) or (8); and
(c) a copy of the data and calculations by which the determination and the distribution were made, including a copy of any estimate received under subsection 2(9).

(2) The clerks shall provide a copy of the report to the committee.

(3) The committee shall review the report and submit its comments in writing to the clerks within three days after receiving the report.

(4) After considering the comments, the clerks shall confirm or vary their original determination or distribution.

(5) The clerks shall confirm their original determination and distribution if no comments are received within the allotted time.

(6) Within 28 days after the start date, the clerk of the municipality having the largest population of the relevant electoral group shall send the supervisory officer a copy of,

(a) the final results of the determination and distribution;
(b) any direction received under subsection 2(7) or (8); and
(c) the data and calculations by which the final determination and distribution were made including a copy of any estimate received under subsection 2(9).

(7) On receipt of the material referred to in subsection (6), the supervisory officer shall send a copy of the material to the Minister, the secretary of each existing board whose members are elected by members of an electoral group that is part of the relevant electoral group and the clerks of all municipalities within the area of jurisdiction of the board.

(8) The supervisory officer shall send the material referred to in subsection (7) no later than 30 days after the start date.

APPEALS

12. (1) A committee and a minority-language section, within the meaning of Part XIII of the Act, of an existing board may, in the name of their members, be a party to an appeal under this section.

(2) Subject to subsection (3), the committee, a council of a municipality in the area of jurisdiction of a board and an existing board in respect of representation of members of the relevant electoral group on a board for territory without municipal organization in its area of jurisdiction may appeal to the Commission the application of,

(a) all of the rules in subsection 8(5);
(b) all of the rules in subsection 8(6); or
(c) rules 1, 2 and 5 of subsection 9(2).

(3) An appeal on a distribution under subsection (2) may only be made if the distribution allots to a geographic area a number of members that is different from the sum of the applicable electoral quotients for the geographic area by an amount that is greater than 0.05 times the total number of members.

(4) A council of a municipality in the area of jurisdiction of a board, an existing board whose members are elected by members of an electoral group that is part of the relevant electoral group and a minority-language section, within the meaning of Part XIII of the Act, of such an existing board may appeal to the Commission the application of,

(a) subsection 8(2); or
(b) rules 3 and 4 of subsection 9(2).

(4.1) Despite subsections (2) and (4), an existing board that represents the interests of both public and separate school supporters may not appeal the distribution of member positions on an English-language separate district school board or a French-language separate district school board.

(5) An appellant under this section shall provide notice of the appeal to the supervisory officer.

(6) On receipt of the notice of appeal, the supervisory officer shall send a copy of it to the clerk of each municipality in the area of jurisdiction of the board.

(7) An appeal shall be commenced within 10 days after the receipt of the copies referred to in subsection 11(7), failing which the board shall be deemed to be properly constituted despite any defect in the distribution of members.

(8) The Commission shall dispose of the appeal within 14 days after the date on which it is commenced.

(9) The Commission may confirm or vary the distribution that is the subject of the appeal.

(10) The Commission's decision on the appeal is final.

(11) The Commission shall provide written notice of its decision to the supervisory officer who is responsible for providing a copy of the notice to the clerks of each municipality within the area of jurisdiction of the board and to the secretary of each existing board referred to in subsection 11(3) of the *Municipal Elections Act, 1996*. O. Reg. 297/97, s. 3.

NOMINATION OF CANDIDATES FOR BOARD ELECTIONS

13. (1) If a geographic area is composed of all or part of two or more municipalities, the nomination shall be submitted to the clerk of the municipality having the largest population of the relevant electoral group resident in the geographic area.

(2) The clerk who conducts the nominations shall send, by registered mail within 48 hours after the closing of nominations, to the clerk of each municipality that is included in the geographic area, the names of the candidates who have qualified.

(2.1) If the distance between the residence of a person seeking nomination and the office for submission of nominations is greater than 100 kilometres, the clerk referred to in subsection (1) shall delegate such of his or her powers as may be necessary to the clerk of the municipality in which the person resides to permit the person or the person's agent to file the nomination at the latter clerk's office.

(3) The clerk of a municipality is responsible for conducting the election in the municipality.

(4) The clerk of a municipality shall report the vote recorded to the clerk to whom nominations were submitted under subsection (1), who shall prepare the final summary and announce the result of the vote.

(4.1) The clerk referred to in subsection (1) shall forward the results of the vote and the names of the candidates who have been elected to the supervisory officer, who shall forward them to the Commission.

(5) In this section,

"municipality" includes territory without municipal organization that is deemed to be a district municipality under section 15. O. Reg. 279/97, s. 4.

14. (1) The secretary of an existing board who receives extracts of the preliminary list of electors based on school support shall, on request, provide a copy of the extracts to any candidate for office on a board for which members of an electoral group of the existing board may vote.

(2) The Commission may exercise the powers of a board for purposes of clause 57(1)(b) of the *Municipal Elections Act, 1996* if, within 20 days after the clerk's declaration of the

results of the election, the committee for the board requires that a recount under that clause be held.

TERRITORY WITHOUT MUNICIPAL ORGANIZATION

15. (1) Each part of territory without municipal organization that is within the area of jurisdiction of an English-language public district school board and, under the Act, is deemed to be a district municipality for purposes of elections to a divisional board, is deemed to be a district municipality for purposes of the election of members to the English-language public district school board.

(2) Each part of territory without municipal organization that is within the area of jurisdiction of an English-language separate district school board and, under the Act, is deemed to be a district municipality for purposes of elections to a county or district combined separate school board, is deemed to be a district municipality for purposes of the election of members to the English-language separate district school board.

(3) Each part of territory without municipal organization that is within the area of jurisdiction of a French-language public district school board and, under the Act, is deemed to be a district municipality for purposes of elections to a divisional board, is deemed to be a district municipality for purposes of the election of members to the French-language public district school board.

(4) Each part of territory without municipal organization that is within the area of jurisdiction of a French-language separate district school board and, under the Act, is deemed to be a district municipality for purposes of elections to a county or district combined separate school board, is deemed to be a district municipality for purposes of the election of members to the French-language separate district school board.

(5) Each part of territory without municipal organization that is within the area of jurisdiction of an English-language public district school board and that, by a regulation made under the Act, is attached to a district municipality for purposes of elections to a divisional board, is deemed to be attached to the same district municipality for purposes of the elections of members to the English-language public district school board.

(6) Each part of territory without municipal organization that is within the area of jurisdiction of a French-language public district school board and that, by a regulation made under the Act, is attached to a district municipality for purposes of elections to a divisional board, is deemed to be attached to the same district municipality for purposes of the elections of members to the French-language public district school board.

(7) The secretary of an existing board, who was deemed for purposes of the 1994 regular elections to be the clerk for trustee distribution purposes for a part of territory without municipal organization that is deemed to be a district municipality under subsections (1) to (4), shall be the clerk in such part for the purposes of this Regulation.

(8) Except as otherwise provided in this Regulation, the secretary of each existing board referred to in subsections (1) to (4) is responsible for conducting the election of members to district school boards from parts of territory without municipal organization deemed under the Act to be a district municipality for the purposes of the existing board and in each case, for the

purposes of the election of members to a district school board, the *Municipal Elections Act, 1996* applies as if the secretary were the clerk, the existing board were the council of a local municipality and the deemed district municipality were the geographic area of a local municipality.

(9) Except as otherwise provided in this Regulation, for the purposes of the election, officers appointed by an existing board have the same powers and duties with respect to the election of members to a district school board from parts of territory without municipal organization deemed under the Act to be a district municipality for the purposes of the existing board as those officers are given under sections 54 and 103 of the Act with respect to the election of members of the existing board from those parts.

(10) Expenses incurred by an existing board in connection with the election of members to a district school board from parts of territory without municipal organization deemed under the Act to be a district municipality for the purposes of the existing board shall, for the purposes of sections 54 and 103 of the Act, be deemed to be expenses incurred in connection with election of members of the existing board from those parts. O. Reg. 279/97, s. 5; O. Reg. 396/97, s. 1.

MISCELLANEOUS

16. (1) A by-law of a municipality made under the authority of subsection 230(25) of the Act does not apply to the election.

(2) A by-law of a municipality or a local board under section 220.1 of the *Municipal Act* does not apply to a board or an existing board in respect of any service, activity, cost or use of property relating to the election of members of boards in the election.

17. A clerk of a municipality may delegate any of his or her powers and duties under this Regulation to election officials of another municipality, including territory without municipal organization deemed to be a district municipality under section 15.

TRANSITIONAL MATTERS

18. (1) In this section and in sections 19, 20 and 21,

"new office" means the office of member of a district school board; ("nouveau poste")

"old office" means an office on an existing board. ("ancien poste")

(2) A new office and an old office correspond if the relevant electoral group for the new office includes all or part of the electoral group for the old office. O. Reg. 279/97, s. 6.

19. (1) The clerk shall send to every candidate for an old office at the election a notice,

(a) advising of the candidate's right to file a nomination for a new office;

(b) explaining the candidate's options under section 20.

(2) The notice shall be sent by registered mail or delivered personally on or before August 30, 1997. O. Reg. 279/97, s. 6.

20. (1) The rules set out in subsection (2) apply to a candidate for an old office who files a nomination for a corresponding new office on or before September 13, 1997.

(2) The rules referred to in subsection (1) are:
1. The nomination filing fee paid with respect to the nomination for the old office shall be deemed to have been paid with respect to the nomination for the new office.
2. The campaign for the old office shall be deemed to form part of the campaign for the new office.
3. The campaign for the new office shall be deemed to have begun on the day the candidate was nominated for the old office and not as provided in section 68 of the *Municipal Elections Act, 1996*.

(3) The rules set out in subsection (4) apply to a candidate for an old office who does not file a nomination for a corresponding new office as described in subsection (1).

(4) The rules referred to in subsection (3) are:
1. The candidate's election campaign period ends on the day that is 60 days after the date of publication of this Regulation in *The Ontario Gazette*.
2. The nomination for the old office shall be deemed to have been withdrawn on the day referred to in paragraph 1.

(5) Subsections (3) and (4) do not apply to a candidate who actually withdraws the nomination. O. Reg. 279/97, s. 6.

21. A candidate for a new office is entitled,

(a) to carry forward, for the purposes of clause 79(3)(b) of the *Municipal Elections Act, 1996*, any deficit accumulated in a campaign for a corresponding old office in the 1994 regular election or in an intervening by-election;

(b) receive payment, under subsection 79(8) of the *Municipal Elections Act, 1996*, of any surplus accumulated in such a campaign. O. Reg. 279/97, s. 6.

22. (1) Subsection 37(3) of the *Municipal Elections Act, 1996* shall be read without reference,

(a) to the words "among the members representing an electoral group" in the part of the subsection before paragraph 1; and

(b) to the words "for the electoral group" in the third line of paragraphs 1 and 2.

(2) Subsection 38(1) of the *Municipal Elections Act, 1996* shall be read without reference,

(a) to the words "to represent the electoral group" in the third and fourth lines; and

(b) to the words "of the members representing the electoral group" in the fifth and sixth lines.

(3) Clause 38(2)(a) of the *Municipal Elections Act, 1996* shall be read without reference to the words "representing the electoral group".

(4) An application for a compliance audit referred to in subsection 81(1) of the *Municipal Elections Act, 1996* made before January 1, 1998 shall be made to the Commission.

(5) On receiving an application referred to in subsection (4), the Commission shall, as soon as practicable, refer it to the board to which the candidate sought election, and the 30-day period provided in subsection 81(3) of the *Municipal Elections Act, 1996* for a decision on the application runs from the day the board receives the application.

REGULATION 250/97 **Schedule**

(6) Prior to January 1, 1998, for the purposes of subsection 84(5) of the *Municipal Elections Act, 1996*, a clerk who receives a disclaimer shall send it to the Commission and not to the secretary of the local board. O. Reg. 279/97, s. 6.

Schedule
am. O. Reg. 279/97, s. 7

Board Number	Area of Board in square kilometres
01	24,283
02	9,151
03	11,584
04	15,998
05A	4,682
05B	10,054
06A	4,919
06B	16,987
07	8,673
08	5,599
09	1,887
10	5,542
11	7,174
12	631
13	1,868
14	6,706
15	11,756
16	1,787
17	4,983
18	4,178
19	1,246
20	951
21	1,137
22	1,868
23	4,108
24	1,404

Schedule

REGULATIONS UNDER THE EDUCATION ACT

Board Number	Area of Board in square kilometres
25	2,894
26	12,165
27	7,199
28	8,042
29	7,221
30A	24,283
30B	11,653
31	8,739
32	7,432
33A	11,008
33B	731
34A	4,919
34B	17,261
35	8,673
36	5,599
37	1,887
38	7,174
39	5,542
40	631
41	9,804
42	1,787
43	2,736
44	8,735
45	1,868
46	951
47	1,136
48	2,691
49	1,404
50	1,868
51	4,108
52	12,165

REGULATION 250/97 **Table 1**

Board Number	Area of Board in square kilometres
53	2,894
54	8,042
55	15,357
56	44,428
57	57,206
58	67,473
59	37,514
60A	24,283
60B	10,520
61	16,189
62	34,133
63	28,819
64	37,751
65	5,421
66	33,042

TABLE 1
MEMBER DETERMINATION BY ELECTORAL POPULATION

COLUMN 1	COLUMN 2
Total Population of the Relevant Electoral Group	Total Number of Members
Less than 30,000 persons	5
30,000 up to 44,999	6
45,000 up to 59,999	7
60,000 up to 99,999	8
100,000 up to 149,999	9
150,000 up to 249,999	10
250,000 up to 399,999	11
400,000 up to 999,999	12
1,000,000 up to 1,499,999	17

Table 2 REGULATIONS UNDER THE EDUCATION ACT

Column 1	Column 2
1,500,000 and over	22

TABLE 2
MEMBER DETERMINATION BY POPULATION DENSITY

Column 1	Column 2
Density of the Board	Number of Additional Density-Based Members
Less than 1.0	7
From 1.0 up to but not including 1.25	6
From 1.25 up to but not including 1.5	5
From 1.5 up to but not including 2.0	4
From 2.0 up to but not including 3.0	3
From 3.0 up to but not including 4.0	1

TABLE 3
AREA FACTOR ADJUSTMENT
(DENSITY FACTOR ADJUSTED BY A BOARD'S AREA)
am. O. Reg. 279/97, s. 8.

Column 1	Column 2
Area of the Board	Maximum Number of Additional Density-Based Members
40,000 square kilometres or more	the lesser of 7 and the difference between 12 and the number of population member positions
Equal to or more than 25,000 square kilometres but less than 40,000 square kilometres	6
Equal to or more than 12,000 square kilometres but less than 25,000 square kilometres	3

Table 3

Column 1	Column 2
Equal to or more than 8,000 square kilometres but less than 12,000 square kilometres	1
Less than 8,000 square kilometres	0

REGULATION 460/97
TRANSITION FROM OLD BOARDS TO DISTRICT SCHOOL BOARDS
O. Reg. 460/97, as am. O. Reg. 93/98; 477/98

PART I
DEFINITIONS

1. In this Regulation,

"assets" includes real and personal property; ("éléments d'actifs")

"assets, liabilities and employees" associated with an old board means,
- (a) the assets and liabilities that the designated board associated with the old board acquired as a result of the merger under section 2 of the old board with the designated board, and
- (b) the employees who were transferred under section 2 from the old board to the designated board associated with the old board; ("éléments d'actif, éléments de passif et employés")

"Commission" means Education Improvement Commission; ("Commission")

"designated board" associated with an old board means the district school board that is listed in column 2 of Schedule 1, opposite the old board listed in column 1 of Schedule 1; ("conseil désigné")

"supported board" associated with an old board means the district school board that is listed in column 3 of Schedule 1, opposite the old board listed in Column 1 of Schedule 1. ("conseil secondé")

PART II
MERGER OF OLD BOARDS WITH DISTRICT SCHOOL BOARDS AND RELATED EMPLOYEE TRANSFERS

2. Effective January 1, 1998,
- (a) each employee of each old board listed in column 1 of Schedule 1 is transferred to the district school board and listed opposite in column 2 of Schedule 1; and
- (b) immediately after the transfer under clause (a), each old board listed in column 1 of Schedule 1 is merged with and continued as the district school board listed opposite in column 2 of Schedule 1.

PART III
INTERIM ROLE OF DESIGNATED BOARD

3. (1) Until an order under this Regulation determining the disposition of an asset, liability or employee associated with an old board takes effect, the designated board associated with the old board shall manage the asset, liability or employee.

(2) Where a designated board is required to manage assets, liabilities or employees under subsection (1), it shall do so for and on behalf of,

(a) itself; and

(b) the supported board associated with the old board.

4. (1) The designated board associated with an old board shall exercise the powers and carry out the duties of the supported board associated with the old board as necessary in order to,

(a) provide continuity in the education of pupils who have the right to attend schools governed by the supported board; and

(b) permit a smooth transition from governance by the old board to governance by the district school boards.

(2) The designated board shall not exercise any power or carry out any duty of the supported board under this section after the earlier of,

(a) December 31, 1998; and

(b) a date specified for the purposes of this subsection by the Commission in relation to the designated board and the supported board, in a written notice to the two boards.

5. (1) For the purposes of sections 3 and 4, in order to ensure that the governance role of the supported board associated with an old board is respected as required by subsection 58.2.1(7) of the Act, the designated board associated with the old board shall,

(a) be guided by the principles underlying sections 312, 318 and 325 of the Act, as it read immediately before January 1, 1998; and

(b) follow any directives issued by the Commission under subsection (2).

(2) The Commission may issue directives to district school boards respecting how the requirements of the following provisions are to be met:

1. Subsection (1) of this section.
2. Sections 3 and 4.
3. Subsection 58.2.1(7) of the Act.

(3) In issuing a directive under subsection (2), the Commission shall be guided by the principles underlying sections 312, 318 and 325 of the Act, as it read immediately before January 1, 1998.

6. (1) This section applies where,

(a) on December 31, 1997, there is an agreement in effect between two old boards; and

(b) on January 1, 1998, the old boards are merged with district school boards.

(2) Until January 1, 1999, the district school boards referred to in clause (1)(b) may not amend or revoke the agreement referred to in clause (1)(a) without the prior written approval of the Commission.

(3) The Commission shall not give the approval without giving each district school board with an interest in the agreement an opportunity to make representations to the Commission.

PART IV

ORDERS ON JOINT REQUEST

Joint Request for Order

7. (1) The supported board associated with an old board and the designated board associated with the old board may jointly request, in writing, that the Commission make an order with respect to any asset, liability or employee associated with the old board.

(2) A joint request may be made under subsection (1) at any time before the Commission makes an order under this Regulation determining the disposition of the asset, liability or employee.

(3) A joint request may be in respect of any group of assets, liabilities and employees associated with one or more old boards with which both the designated board and the supported board are associated.

(4) The joint request must identify the assets, liabilities and employees that are the subject of the request and, with respect to each, state whether the asset, liability or employee should be transferred to the supported board or remain with the designated board.

(5) The joint request may include representations respecting the proposed disposition, including but not limited to representations respecting,

(a) the timing of any transfer; and
(b) the terms and conditions to which the transfer order should be subject.

Authority of Commission to Make Order on Joint Request

8. (1) The Commission may make an order under this Part determining the disposition of assets, liabilities and employees that are the subject of a joint request.

(2) Subject to subsections (4) and (5) and section 9, the order may be in accordance with the joint request or may vary from it, as the Commission considers appropriate having regard to,

(a) the needs of the designated board,
(b) the needs of the supported board; and
(c) where applicable, the interests described in subsection 33(4).

(3) In addition to the matters mentioned in clauses (2)(a) to (c), in the case of an order respecting an employee, the Commission may take into account the preferences of the employee where the Commission considers it appropriate to do so.

(4) Subject to subsections (5) and (6) and section 9, the order,

(a) shall specify the time at which the disposition of each asset, liability or employee is to take effect; and
(b) may be made subject to the terms and conditions that the Commission considers appropriate having regard to the matters referred to in clauses (2)(a) to (c).

(5) The Commission shall not make an order respecting any asset, liability or employee under this Part unless,

(a) the Commission is satisfied that the order will not unduly impair the ability of the designated board to exercise its powers, carry out its duties and conduct its day-to-day operations;

(b) the Commission is satisfied that the supported board will be able to discharge its administrative and operational responsibilities for the assets, liabilities and employees that will be transferred to it under the order; and

(c) the designated board and the supported board state in writing that they agree with the order.

(6) In addition, the Commission shall not make an order under this Part determining whether an employee is to be transferred to a supported board or is to remain with a designated board unless,

(a) the employee agrees to the determination in writing;

(b) the employee has been notified in accordance with directives issued by the Commission of the proposal with respect to him or her in the joint request, 15 days have elapsed from the notification and no dispute resolution process is ongoing under Part V with respect to the employee; or

(c) the employee has been the subject of a dispute resolution process under Part V and that process is no longer ongoing, whether because of the issuance of a notice under section 13 or because the process as established by the Commission's directives has been completed.

Timing of Orders on Joint Request

9. (1) Subject to subsections (2) and (4), an order under this Part determining the disposition of an asset, liability or employee shall not be made after August 31, 1998 and shall not provide for the transfer of any asset, liability or employee after August 31, 1998.

(2) The Commission may make an order under this Part determining the disposition of an asset or liability at any time before January 1, 1999 if, on August 31, 1998, a dispute resolution process under Part V as to the disposition is ongoing.

(3) An order made under subsection (2) shall not provide for the transfer of any asset or liability after December 31, 1998.

(4) The Commission may make an order under this Part determining the disposition of an employee at any time before October 31, 1998 if,

(a) on August 31, 1998, the employee was employed by the Algoma District School Board or the Rainbow District School Board; and

(b) on or after August 31, 1998, a dispute resolution process under Part V as to the disposition of the employee was ongoing.

(5) An order made under subsection (4) shall not provide for the transfer of an employee after October 30, 1998. O. Reg. 477/98, s. 1.

PART V

DISPUTE RESOLUTION PROCESS

10. (1) The Commission shall establish a process for resolving disputes with respect to the holding in trust, transfer and vesting of assets, the transfer of liabilities and the transfer of employees of old boards to and among district school boards.

(2) A hearing under the dispute resolution process, whether written or oral, shall be held by the Commission or by a panel, established under section 27, of one or more members of the Commission.

(3) The Commission may issue directives for the purpose of implementing the dispute resolution process.

11. (1) Subject to subsection (1.1) the Commission shall take such steps and issue such directives as it considers necessary to ensure that, by August 31, 1998, all dispute resolution processes respecting employees,

- (a) are completed in accordance with the Commission's directives establishing the dispute resolution process; or
- (b) are discontinued because of the issuance of a notice under subsection 13.

(1.1) The Commission shall take such steps and issue such directives as it considers necessary to ensure that, by October 30, 1998, all dispute resolution processes respecting employees described in clause 9(4)(a),

- (a) are completed in accordance with the Commission's directives establishing the dispute resolution process; or
- (b) are discontinued because of the issuance of a notice under section 13.

(2) The Commission shall take such steps and issue such directives as it considers necessary to ensure that, by December 31, 1998, all dispute resolution processes respecting assets and liabilities,

- (a) are completed in accordance with the Commission's directives establishing the dispute resolution process; or
- (b) are discontinued because of the issuance of a notice under section 13. O. Reg. 477/98, s. 2.

12. (1) Subject to section 13, the dispute resolution process applies to every asset and liability associated with an old board the disposition of which has not been determined by an order under Part IV before April 1, 1998.

(2) Subject to section 13, the dispute resolution process applies to every employee associated with an old board whose disposition has not been determined by an order under Part IV before March 1, 1998.

(3) Subject to section 13, the dispute resolution process applies to every asset, liability or employee in respect of which notice is given under subsection (4).

(4) A designated board associated with an old board or a supported board associated with an old board may, in accordance with the directive issued under section 10, give written notice invoking the dispute resolution process in respect of any asset, liability or employee associated with the old board.

S. 13　REGULATIONS UNDER THE EDUCATION ACT

(5) A notice under subsection (4) may be given in respect of an asset or liability at any time before April 1, 1998 and in respect of an employee at any time before March 1, 1998.

(6) Subject to section 13, the dispute resolution process applies to every employee in respect of whom notice is given under subsection (7).

(7) An employee associated with an old board may, in accordance with the directives issued under section 10, give written notice invoking the dispute resolution process in respect of himself or herself.

(8) A notice under subsection (7) may be given at any time before March 1, 1998.

13. (1) The Commission shall monitor all dispute resolution processes in order to identify, in each case as soon as is reasonably possible,
- (a) each asset or liability with respect to which there is agreement between the supported board and the designated board; and
- (b) each employer with respect to whom there is agreement among the employee, the supported board and the designated board.

(2) The Commission shall issue such directives as it considers appropriate to assist it in carrying out its obligations under subsection (1).

(3) When the Commission identifies an asset, liability or employee under subsection (1), the Commission shall, as soon as reasonably possible, issue a written notice to that effect.

(4) The notice under subsection (3) shall be given to the supported board and the designated board.

(5) Where the notice under subsection (3) relates to an employee, the notice shall also be given to the employee.

(6) The dispute resolution process ceases to apply to an asset, liability or employee when the Commission issues,
- (a) a notice under subsection (3); or
- (b) an order under this Regulation determining the disposition of the asset, liability or employee.

PART VI

ORDERS WITHOUT JOINT REQUEST

14. (1) Subject to subsection 3 at any time before August 31, 1998, the Commission may make an order determining the disposition of any asset, liability or employee associated with an old board the disposition of which has not been determined by an order made under this Regulation if,
- (a) the asset, liability or employee has been the subject of a dispute resolution process under Part V; and
- (b) that asset, liability or employee is no longer the subject of the dispute resolution process, whether because of the issuance of a notice under section 13 or because the process as established by the Commission's directives has been completed.

(2) An order made under subsection (1) shall not provide for the transfer of any asset, liability or employee after August 31, 1998.

(3) At any time before October 31, 1998, the Commission may make an order determining the disposition of an employee, the disposition of whom has not been determined by an order made under this Regulation if,
- (a) on August 31, 1998, the employee was an employee of the Algoma District School Board or the Rainbow District School Board;
- (b) on or after August 31, 1998, a dispute resolution process under Part V as to the disposition of the employee was ongoing; and
- (c) the employee is no longer the subject of the dispute resolution process, whether because of the issuance of a notice under section 13 or because the process as established by the Commission's directives has been completed.

(4) An order made under subsection (3) shall not provide for the transfer of any employee after October 30, 1998. O. Reg. 477/98, s. 3.

15. (1) On August 31, 1998, the Commission shall make an order determining the disposition of each employee associated with an old board whose disposition has not been determined by an order made under this Regulation.

(2) An order made under subsection (1) shall not provide for the transfer of any employee after August 31, 1998.

(2.1) Subsections (1) and (2) do not apply to an employee if,
- (a) on August 31, 1998, the employee is employed by the Algoma District School Board or the Rainbow District School Board; and
- (b) on or after August 31, 1998, a dispute resolution process under Part V as to the disposition of the employee is ongoing.

(2.2) On October 30, 1998, the Commission shall make an order determining the disposition of each employee referred to in subsection (2.1) whose disposition has not been determined by an order made under this Regulation.

(2.3) An order made under subsection (2.2) shall not provide for the transfer of any employee after October 30, 1998.

(3) Subsection (4) applies if the dispute resolution process under Part V in respect of an asset or liability is no longer ongoing, whether because of the issuance of a notice under section 13 or because the process as established by the Commission's directives has been completed.

(4) On August 31, 1998, the Commission shall make an order determining the disposition of each asset or liability associated with an old board the disposition of which has not been determined by an order made under this Regulation.

(5) An order made under subsection (4) shall not provide for the transfer of any asset or liability after August 31, 1998. O. Reg. 477/98, s. 4.

16. (1) At any time after August 31, 1998 and before December 31, 1998, the Commission may make an order determining the disposition of any asset or liability associated with an old board the disposition of which has not been determined by an order made under this Regulation, if the dispute regulation process under Part V in respect of the asset or liability is no longer ongoing, whether because of an issuance of a notice under section 13 or because the process as established by the Commission's directives has been completed.

(2) An order made under subsection (1) shall not provide for the transfer of any asset or liability after December 31, 1998.

S. 17 REGULATIONS UNDER THE EDUCATION ACT

17. (1) On December 31, 1998, the Commission shall make an order determining the disposition of each asset and liability associated with each old board the disposition of which has not been determined by an order made under this Regulation.

(2) An order made under subsection (1) shall not provide for the transfer of any asset or liability after December 31, 1998.

18. (1) In making an order under this Part, the Commission shall have regard to,
   (a) the needs of the designated board;
   (b) the needs of the supported board; and
   (c) where applicable, the interests described in subsection 33(4).

(2) In making an order under this Part respecting an employee, the Commission may also take into account the preferences of the employee where the Commission considers it appropriate to do so.

(3) An order made under this Part shall specify, subject to subsections 14(2), 14(4), 15(2), 15(2.3), 15(5), 16(2) and 17(2), the time at which the disposition of each asset, liability or employee is to take effect.

(4) An order made under this Part may be made subject to the terms and conditions that the Commission considers appropriate having regard to the matters referred to in clauses (1)(a) to (c). O. Reg. 477/98, s. 5.

PART VII

PAYMENT BY SUPPORTED BOARD FOR SERVICES OF DESIGNATED BOARD

Definitions

19. In this Part,

"designated board's actual costs" means the actual costs incurred by a designated board associated with an old board in managing the assets, liabilities and employees associated with the old board; ("frais réels")

"exclusive jurisdiction costs" means costs incurred by a designated board for which payment is required under section 20; ("frais de compétence exclusive")

"1997 expenditure allocation form" means the form that,
   (a) is referred to in the B4 memorandum to directors of education dated November 18, 1997; and
   (b) was provided by the Ministry for the purpose of determining the French-English split of 1997 expenditures by old boards; ("formule de répartition des dépenses pour 1997")

"supported board's common jurisdiction expenditure costs" means the common jurisdiction expenditure costs of a supported board associated with an old board, as calculated under the legislative grant regulation applicable to the period beginning January 1, 1998 and ending August 31, 1998. ("frais qui incombent au conseil secondé au titre des dépenses de compétence commune")

Exclusive Jurisdiction Expenditures for January 1, 1998 to August 31, 1998

20. (1) This section applies where the old board that was merged under section 2 with a designated board had a minority language section within the meaning of the Act, as it read immediately before January 1, 1998.

(2) The supported board associated with an old board shall pay to the designated board associated with the old board the total of the designated board's actual costs incurred during the period beginning January 1, 1998 and ending August 31, 1998 for matters listed as exclusive jurisdiction expenditures on the 1997 expenditure allocation form for the old board.

Common Jurisdiction Expenditures for January 1, 1998 to August 31, 1998 Where No Transfer Occurs Befire August 31, 1998

21. (1) This section applies whether or not the old board that was merged under section 2 with a designated board had a minority language section within the meaning of the Act, as it read immediately before January 1, 1998.

(2) This section applies in respect of the period beginning January 1, 1998 and ending August 31, 1998 where, throughout that period, no asset, liability or employee associated with an old board is transferred from the designated board associated with the old board to the supported board associated with the old board.

(3) The supported board associated with an old board shall pay to the designated board associated with the old board the supported board's common jurisdiction expenditure costs.

Other Expenditures

22. (1) This section applies whether or not the old board that was merged under section 2 with a designated board had a minority language section within the meaning of the Act, as it read immediately before January 1, 1998.

(2) This section applies to costs incurred by a designated board associated with an old board in respect of which payment is not provided by section 20 or 21.

(3) Examples of costs to which this section applies include:

1. Costs, other than exclusive jurisdiction costs, in respect of the period beginning January 1, 1998 and ending August 31, 1998 where, during that period, one or more assets, liabilities or employees associated with the old board are transferred from the designated board associated with the old board to the supported board associated with the old board.
2. Costs in respect of the period beginning January 1, 1998 and ending August 31, 1998 where the old board had no minority language section and was, immediately before January 1, 1998, purchasing English-language or French-language educational programs or services, as the case may be, for its minority language pupils.
3. Costs in respect of the period beginning September 1, 1998 and ending December 31, 1998.

(4) The supported board associated with an old board shall pay to the designated board associated with the old board amounts determined in accordance with directives issued by the Commission under subsection (5).

(5) The Commission shall issue directives respecting the amounts payable under subsection (4), in order to provide for payments by the supported board to the designated board in respect of costs incurred by the designated board in meeting requirements under Part III of this Regulation.

23. (1) This section applies to district school boards affected by the operation of section 6 or 33.

(2) A district school board shall pay to another district school board amounts determined in accordance with directives issued by the Commission under subsection (3).

(3) The Commission shall issue directives respecting amounts payable under subsection (2), in order to provide for payments by one district school board to another district school board in respect of costs incurred by the second district school board in meeting requirements under clause 58.1(2)(q) of the Act.

(4) A directive under subsection (3) may provide for an adjustment of amounts that would otherwise be payable under section 20, 21 or 22.

23.1 An order of the Education Improvement Commission that provides for the transfer of employees of the Algoma District School Board or the Rainbow District School Board after August 31, 1998, shall also provide for an adjustment of amounts payable from September 1, 1998 to the date of the transfer by the board to which they are transferred to the Algoma District School Board or the Rainbow District School Board, as the case may be. O. Reg. 477/98, s. 6.

Dispute Resolution

24. (1) The Commission shall establish a process for resolving disputes with respect to payments to be made under this Part.

(2) The Commission may issue directives for the purpose of implementing the dispute resolution process.

General

25. (1) On application made from time to time by a supported board associated with an old board or a designated board associated with an old board, the Commission may order payments to be made or accounts to be adjusted for the purpose of ensuring that the requirements of this Part are met.

(2) An order under this section may be made subject to the terms and conditions that the Commission considers appropriate.

(3) An order under this section shall be in respect of costs incurred during the period beginning January 1, 1998 and ending December 31, 1998.

(4) An order under this section may be made at any time before September 1, 1999.

26. (1) The Commission may issue directives respecting the making of interim or periodic payments under this Part.

(2) Without limiting the generality of subsection (1), the directives may require interim or periodic payments to be made in respect of matters listed as common jurisdiction expenditures on the 1997 expenditure allocation form, before the legislative grant regulation applicable to the period beginning January 1, 1998 and ending August 31, 1998 is made.

(3) The directives may include provisions respecting the payment of interest and the allowance of discounts in circumstances specified in the directives.

(4) Where the directives include provisions respecting interest payments and discount allowances, the rate of interest payable or the rate of discount allowable, as the case may be, is the lowest prime rate reported to the Bank of Canada by any of the banks listed in Schedule 1 to the *Bank Act* (Canada) at the relevant date.

PART VIII

GENERAL POWERS AND DUTIES OF THE COMMISSION

27. The Commission may establish panels of one or more members to exercise specified powers and carry out specified duties of the Commission in the place of the Commission.

28. The Commission may issue directives respecting the procedures to be followed and deadlines to be met in connection with anything done under this Regulation.

29. Any directive issued under this Regulation may be general or particular.

30. (1) The Commission may vary any of its orders under this Regulation by varying the date on which the order, or any part of the order, is to take effect.

(2) Subsection (1) is subject to any provision of this Regulation that sets a date by which an order must be made or by which an order must take effect.

31. Where the Commission is required by this Regulation or the directives issued under it to give a notice to an employee and the employee is represented by a bargaining agent for collective bargaining purposes, the Commission shall also give the notice to the bargaining agent.

32. (1) In addition to the powers and duties of the Commission under Parts II to VII of this Regulation, the Commission has the following powers and shall exercise the following duties:

1. The power and duty to issue directives to district school boards and other classes of persons or bodies specified by the Commission respecting criteria to be applied and processes to be followed in developing recommendations to the Commission with respect to any matter referred to in clauses 58.1(2)(p) and 58.2(1)(b) and (c) of the Act.
2. The power and duty to issue directives respecting the participation of classes of persons or bodies specified by the Commission in the development of recommendations referred to in paragraph 1.
3. The power and duty to make determinations respecting the holding in trust, transfer and vesting of assets, the transfer of liabilities and the transfer of employees of old boards to and among district school boards for the purpose of making orders under this Regulation.

4. The power and duty to determine by or against which district school boards legal and other proceedings commenced by or against old boards shall be continued.
5. The power and duty to determine by or against which district school boards orders or determinations of a court or other authority affecting old boards shall be enforced.
6. The power and duty to issue orders that the Commission considers necessary or advisable to give effect to the determination made under this section and to impose terms and conditions on its orders.

(2) Without limiting the generality of paragraph 4, a determination under paragraph 4 may substitute or add persons as parties to a proceeding continued under paragraph 4.

(3) Without limiting the generality of paragraph 5, a determination under paragraph 5 may substitute or add persons against which or by which an order or determination referred to under paragraph 5 may be enforced.

PART IX

TRANSFERS BETWEEN PUBLIC BOARDS AND ROMAN CATHOLIC BOARDS

33. (1) In this section,

"Schedule 2 public old boards" means an old board listed in column 2 of Schedule 2; ("ancien conseil public mentionné à l'annexe 2")

"Schedule 2 Roman Catholic old board" means an old board listed in column 1 of Schedule 2. ("ancien conseil catholique mentionné à l'annexe 2")

(2) This section applies where the area of jurisdiction of a designated board that is a public district school board includes some or all of the area of jurisdiction of a Schedule 2 Roman Catholic old board.

(3) In making an order under this Regulation that affects a designated board referred to in subsection (2), the Commission shall take into account the interests of,

(a) the designated board associated with the relevant Schedule 2 Roman Catholic old board; and
(b) the supported board associated with the relevant Schedule 2 Roman Catholic old board.

(4) For the purposes of subsection (3), a designated board referred to in clause (3)(a) and a supported board referred to in clause (3)(b) has an interest in an asset or liability of the designated board referred to in subsection (2) only if, before January 1, 1998, the asset or liability related, in whole or in part, to the education of pupils,

(a) who attended a school of a Schedule 2 public old board listed in Schedule 2 opposite the relevant Schedule 2 Roman Catholic old board; and
(b) whose parent or guardian was a separate school supporter.

(5) Where the Commission considers it appropriate to do so having regard to the interests described in subsection (4), the Commission may transfer an asset or liability from the designated board referred to in subsection (2) to a designated board referred to in clause (3)(a) or a supported board referred to in clause (3)(b).

REGULATION 460/97 **Schedule 1/Annexe 1**

PART X

REVOCATION AND COMMENCEMENT

34. Ontario Regulation 357/97 is revoked.

35. This Regulation comes into force on the day section 32 of the *Education Quality Improvement Act, 1997* comes into force.

Schedule 1/Annexe 1

O. Reg. 93/98

Item/Point	Column 1/Colonne 1 Old Boards/ Anciens conseils	Column 2/ Colonne 2 Designated Boards/ Conseils Désignés	Column 3/ Colonne 3 Supported Boards/ Conseils secondés
1.	The Timmins Board of Education	1	56
2.	The Kapuskasing-Smooth Rock Falls and District Board of Education/Le conseil de l'éducation de Kapuskasing-Smooth Rock Falls et de son district	1	56
3.	The Hearst Board of Education	1	56
4.	The Cochrane-Iroquois Falls, Black River-Matheson Board of Education	1	56
5.	The Kirkland Lake Board of Education	1	56
6.	The Timiskaming Board of Education	1	56
7.	The Chapleau Board of Education	2	57
8.	The Michipicoten Board of Education	2	57
9.	The Sault Ste. Marie Board of Education	2	57
10.	The Central Algoma Board of Education	2	57
11.	The North Shore Board of Education	2	57
12.	The Hornepayne Board of Education	2	56
13.	The Sudbury Board of Education	3	57
14.	The Espanola Board of Education	3	57
15.	The Manitoulin Board of Education	3	57
16.	The Nipissing Board of Education	4	56
17.	The East Parry Sound Board of Education	4	56

Schedule 1/Annexe 1 REGULATIONS UNDER THE EDUCATION ACT

Item/Point	Column 1/Colonne 1 Old Boards/ Anciens conseils	Column 2/ Colonne 2 Designated Boards/ Conseils Désignés	Column 3/ Colonne 3 Supported Boards/ Conseils secondés
18.	The West Parry Sound Board of Education	4	56
19.	The Kenora Board of Education	5A	57
20.	The Red Lake Board of Education	5A	57
21.	The Dryden Board of Education	5A	57
22.	The Fort Frances-Rainy River Board of Education	5B	57
23.	The Atikokan Board of Education	5B	57
24.	The Lakehead Board of Education	6A	57
25.	The Beardmore, Geraldton, Longlac and Area Board of Education/Conseil de l'éducation de Beardmore, de Geraldton, de Longlac et des environs	6B	57
26.	The Nipigon-Red Rock Board of Education	6B	57
27.	The Lake Superior Board of Education/Le conseil scolaire du Lac Supérieur	6B	57
28.	The Bruce County Board of Education	7	58
29.	The Grey Board of Education	7	58
30.	The Huron County Board of Education	8	58
31.	The Perth County Board of Education	8	58
32.	The Board of Education for the City of Windsor	9	58
33.	The Essex County Board of Education	9	58
34.	The Kent County Board of Education	10	58
35.	The Lambton County Board of Education/ Conseil de l'éducation du comté de Lambton	10	58
36.	The Board of Education for the City of London/Le conseil de l'éducation de la ville de London	11	58
37.	The Middlesex Board of Education	11	58
38.	The Elgin County Board of Education	11	58

REGULATION 460/97　　**Schedule 1/Annexe 1**

Item/Point	Column 1/Colonne 1 Old Boards/ Anciens conseils	Column 2/ Colonne 2 Designated Boards/ Conseils Désignés	Column 3/ Colonne 3 Supported Boards/ Conseils Secondés
39.	The Oxford County Board of Education	11	58
40.	The Metropolitan Toronto School Board	12	58
41.	The Board of Education for the City of North York	12	58
42.	The Board of Education for the City of Scarborough	12	58
43.	The Board of Education for the City of Etobicoke	12	58
44.	The Board of Education for the City of Toronto	12	58
45.	The Board of Education for the City of York	12	58
46.	The Board of Education for the Borough of East York	12	58
47.	The Durham Board of Education	13	58
48.	The Northumberland & Clarington Board of Education	14	58
49.	The Peterborough County Board of Education	14	58
50.	The Victoria County Board of Education	15	58
51.	The Haliburton County Board of Education	15	58
52.	The Muskoka Board of Education	15	56
53.	The York Region Board of Education	16	58
54.	The Simcoe County Board of Education	17	58
55.	The Wellington County Board of Education	18	58
56.	The Dufferin County Board of Education	18	58
57.	The Peel Board of Education	19	58
58.	The Halton Board of Education	20	58
59.	The Board of Education for the City of Hamilton/Le conseil de l'éducation de la ville de Hamilton	21	58

Schedule 1/Annexe 1 REGULATIONS UNDER THE EDUCATION ACT

Item/Point	Column 1/Colonne 1 Old Boards/ Anciens conseils	Column 2/ Colonne 2 Designated Boards/ Conseils Désignés	Column 3/ Colonne 3 Supported Boards/ Conseils Secondés
60.	The Wentworth County Board of Education	21	58
61.	The Lincoln County Board of Education	22	58
62.	The Niagara South Board of Education/ Conseil scolaire de Niagara Sud	22	58
63.	The Haldimand Board of Education	23	58
64.	The Norfolk Board of Education	23	58
65.	The Brant County Board of Education	23	58
66.	The Waterloo County Board of Education	24	58
67.	The Ottawa Board of Education	25	
68.	The Carleton Board of Education	25	
69.	The Lanark County Board of Education	26	59
70.	The Leeds & Grenville County Board of Education	26	59
71.	The Prescott & Russell County Board of Education	26	59
72.	The Stormont, Dundas & Glengarry County Board of Education	26	59
73.	The Lennox & Addington County Board of Education	27	59
74.	The Frontenac County Board of Education	27	59
75.	The Renfrew County Board of Education	28	59
76.	The Prince Edward County Board of Education	29	59
77.	Hastings County Board of Education	29	59
78.	The Hearst District Roman Catholic Separate School Board	60A	30A
79.	The Cochrane, Iroquois Falls/Black River – Matheson District Roman Catholic Separate School Board	60A	30A

REGULATION 460/97 **Schedule 1/Annexe 1**

Item/Point	Column 1/Colonne 1 Old Boards/ Anciens conseils	Column 2/ Colonne 2 Designated Boards/ Conseils Désignés	Column 3/ Colonne 3 Supported Boards/ Conseils secondés
80.	The Timmins District Roman Catholic Separate School Board/Le conseil des écoles séparées catholiques du district de Timmins	60A	30A
81.	The Kapuskasing District Roman Catholic Separate School Board/Conseil des écoles séparées catholiques du district de Kapuskasing	60A	30A
82.	The Kirkland Lake-Timiskaming District Roman Catholic Separate School Board/ Conseil des écoles séparées catholiques du district de Kirkland Lake-Timiskaming	60A	30A
83.	The Nipissing District Roman Catholic Separate School Board	60B	30B
84.	The Sault Ste. Marie District Roman Catholic Separate School Board	31	61
85.	The Michipicoten District Roman Catholic Separate School Board	31	61
86.	The North Shore District Roman Catholic Separate School Board	31	61
87.	The Chapleau District Roman Catholic Separate School Board	61	31
88.	The Sudbury District Roman Catholic Separate School Board/Le conseil des écoles séparées catholiques romaines de Sudbury	61	32
89.	The Fort Frances-Rainy River District Roman Catholic Separate School Board	33a	62
90.	The Dryden District Roman Catholic Separate School Board	33a	62
91.	The Kenora District Roman Catholic Separate School Board	33b	62
92.	The Lakehead District Roman Catholic Separate School Board/Le conseil des écoles séparées catholiques du district de Lakehead	34a	62

Schedule 1/Annexe 1   REGULATIONS UNDER THE EDUCATION ACT

Item/Point	Column 1/Colonne 1 Old Boards/ Anciens conseils	Column 2/ Colonne 2 Designated Boards/ Conseils Désignés	Column 3/ Colonne 3 Supported Boards/ Conseils secondés
93.	The Geraldton District Roman Catholic Separate School Board/Le conseil des écoles séparées catholiques du district de Geraldton	34b	62
94.	The North of Superior District Roman Catholic Separate School Board/Le conseil des écoles séparées catholiques du district Supérieur Nord	34b	62
95.	The Bruce-Grey County Roman Catholic Separate School Board	35	63
96.	The Huron-Perth County Roman Catholic Separate School Board	36	63
97.	The Windsor Roman Catholic Separate School Board/Le conseil de l'éducation catholique de Windsor	37	63
98.	The Essex County Roman Catholic Separate School Board/Conseil des écoles séparées catholiques du comté d'Essex	37	63
99.	The London and Middlesex County Roman Catholic Separate School Board/Le conseil des écoles catholiques de London et du comté de Middlesex	38	63
100.	The Elgin County Roman Catholic Separate School Board	38	63
101.	The Oxford County Roman Catholic Separate School Board/Conseil des écoles séparées catholiques romaines du comté d'Oxford	38	63
102.	The Kent County Roman Catholic Separate School Board/Conseil des écoles séparées catholiques de Kent	39	63
103.	The Lambton County Roman Catholic Separate School Board/Conseil des écoles séparées catholiques du comté de Lambton	39	63

REGULATION 460/97 Schedule 1/Annexe 1

ITEM/POINT	COLUMN 1/COLONNE 1 OLD BOARDS/ ANCIENS CONSEILS	COLUMN 2/ COLONNE 2 DESIGNATED BOARDS/ CONSEILS DÉSIGNÉS	COLUMN 3/ COLONNE 3 SUPPORTED BOARDS/ CONSEILS SECONDÉS
104.	The Metropolitan Separate School Board/ Conseil des écoles catholiques du Grand Toronto	40	64
105.	The Peterborough, Victoria, Northumberland & Clarington Roman Catholic Separate School Board	41	64
106.	The York Region Roman Catholic Separate School Board/Conseil des écoles séparées catholiques de la région de York	42	64
107.	The Dufferin-Peel Roman Catholic Separate School Board/Conseil des écoles séparées catholiques de Dufferin & Peel	43	64
108.	The Simcoe County Roman Catholic Separate School Board	44	64
109.	The Durham Region Roman Catholic Separate School Board/Conseil des écoles séparées catholiques de la région de Durham	45	64
110.	The Halton Roman Catholic Separate School Board/Conseil des écoles séparées catholiques de Halton	46	64
111.	The Hamilton-Wentworth Roman Catholic Separate School Board/Le conseil des écoles séparées catholiques romaines de Hamilton-Wentworth	47	64
112.	The Wellington County Roman Catholic Separate School Board/Conseil des écoles séparées catholiques de Wellington	48	64
113.	The Waterloo Region Roman Catholic Separate School Board/Le conseil des écoles séparées catholiques de la région de Waterloo	49	64
114.	The Lincoln County Roman Catholic Separate School Board/Le conseil des écoles catholiques du comté de Lincoln	50	64

Schedule 1/Annexe 1   REGULATIONS UNDER THE EDUCATION ACT

Item/Point	Column 1/Colonne 1 Old Boards/ Anciens conseils	Column 2/ Colonne 2 Designated Boards/ Conseils Désignés	Column 3/ Colonne 3 Supported Boards/ Conseils secondés
115.	The Welland County Roman Catholic Separate School Board/Le conseil des écoles séparées catholiques romaines du comté de Welland	50	64
116.	The Haldimand-Norfolk Roman Catholic Separate School Board/Le conseil des écoles séparées catholiques de Haldimand-Norfolk	51	64
117.	The Brant County Roman Catholic Separate School Board/Le conseil des écoles séparées catholiques du compté de Brant	51	64
118.	The Lanark, Leeds & Grenville County Roman Catholic Separate School Board	52	66
119.	The Prescott & Russell County Roman Catholic English-Language Separate School Board	52	
120.	The Stormont, Dundas and Glengarry County Roman Catholic Separate School Board/Le conseil des écoles séparées catholiques des comtés de Stormont, Dundas et Glengarry	65	52
121.	The Ottawa Roman Catholic Separate School Board	53	
122.	The Carleton Roman Catholic Separate School Board	53	
123.	The Renfrew County Roman Catholic Separate School Board	54	66
124.	The Hastings-Prince Edward County Roman Catholic Separate School Board	55	66
125.	The Frontenac-Lennox and Addington County Roman Catholic Separate School Board	55	66

REGULATION 460/97　　**Schedule 2/Annexe 2**

Item/Point	Column 1/Colonne 1 Old Boards/ Anciens conseils	Column 2/Colonne 2 Designated Boards/ Conseils Désignés	Column 3/Colonne 3 Supported Boards/ Conseils secondés
126.	Conseil des écoles française de la communauté urbaine de Toronto/The Metropolitan Toronto French-Language School Conseil	12	58
127.	Le Conseil des écoles publiques d'Ottawa-Carleton	59	
128.	Conseil des écoles séparées catholiques de langue française de Prescott-Russell	65	
129.	Conseil des écoles catholiques de langue française de la région d'Ottawa-Carleton	66	

Schedule 2/Annexe 2

Item/Point	Column 1/Colonne 1 Old Boards/ Anciens conseils	Column 2/Colonne 2 Old Boards/ Anciens conseils
1.	The Chapleau District Roman Catholic Separate School Board	The Chapleau Board of Education
2.	The Michipicoten District Roman Catholic Separate School Board	The Michipicoten Board of Education
3.	The North Shore District Roman Catholic Separate School Board	The North Shore Board of Education The Espanola Board of Education
4.	The Dryden District Roman Catholic Separate School Board	The Dryden Board of Education
5.	The Fort Frances-Rainy River District Roman Catholic Separate School Board	The Fort Frances-Rainy River Board of Education

Schedule 2/Annexe 2 REGULATIONS UNDER THE EDUCATION ACT

Item/ Point	Column 1/Colonne 1 Old Boards/ Anciens conseils	Column 2/Colonne 2 Old Boards/ Anciens conseils
6.	The Geraldton District Roman Catholic Separate School Board/Le conseil des écoles séparées catholiques du district de Geraldton	The Beardmore, Geraldton, Longlac and Area Board of Education/Conseil de l'éducation de Beardmore, de Geraldton, de Longlac et des environs
7.	The North of Superior District Roman Catholic Separate School Board/Le conseil des écoles séparées catholiques du district Supérieur Nord	The Nipigon-Red Rock Board of Education The Lake Superior Board of Education/Le conseil scolaire du Lac Supérieur

REGULATION 461/97
PUPIL REPRESENTATION ON BOARDS
O. Reg. 461/97

1. (1) Every board shall develop and implement a policy providing for the representation of the interests of pupils on the board.

(2) The policy shall be in accordance with this regulation and with any policies and guidelines issued by the Minister under paragraph 3.5 of subsection 8(1) of the Act.

2. (1) Each board shall have one pupil representative or such greater number of pupil representatives as is specified in the policy.

(2) A pupil representative must be in the last two years of the intermediate division or in the senior division at the time that he or she is elected or appointed.

3. (1) The policy shall specify whether the pupil representatives are to be chosen by peer election or by appointment and shall specify the procedures to be followed for the purpose.

(2) The procedures specified under subsection (1) shall ensure that the elections or appointments occur not later than June 30 in each school year, to take effect with respect to the following school year.

(3) The policy shall provide for,

(a) the type and extent of participation by pupil representatives;
(b) disqualification of pupil representatives;
(c) the filling of vacancies;
(d) the term of office of pupil representatives.

(4) With respect to the type and extent of participation by pupil representatives, the policy shall provide that, subject to subsections 55(3) and (5) of the Act, pupil representatives have at least the same opportunity for participation at meetings of the board and at meetings of committees of the board as a board member has.

4. (1) The policy may provide for reimbursement of pupil representatives for all or part of their out-of-pocket expenses reasonably incurred in connection with carrying out the responsibilities of pupil representatives.

(2) Where reimbursement of expenses is provided for under subsection (1), it shall be according to the same policies as govern the reimbursement of board members for such expenses.

5. This Regulation comes into force on the day section 30 of the *Education Quality Improvement Act, 1997* comes into force.

REGULATION 462/97
NATIVE REPRESENTATION ON BOARDS
O. Reg. 462/97

1. (1) Where a board has entered into one or more agreements under section 188 of the Act, the council of the band, or the councils of the bands, to which the Indian pupils who are, under the agreement or agreements, enroled in the schools operated by the board or in the schools in which the board provides all the instruction, belong, may, subject to subsection (4), name one person to represent on the board the interests of the Indian pupils.

(2) Where a person is named under subsection (1), the board shall, subject to subsection (5), appoint the person a member of the board.

(3) The member appointed under subsection (2) shall be deemed to be an elected member of the board, except that,

    (a) where the agreement with the board under this section or, where there is more than one such agreement, all the agreements with the board under this section are in respect of secondary school pupils only, the member so appointed is a member for secondary school purposes only and shall not vote on a motion or otherwise take part in any proceedings that affect elementary schools exclusively; and

    (b) where the agreement with the board under this section or, where there is more than one such agreement, all the agreements with the board under this section are in respect of elementary school pupils only, the member so appointed is a member for elementary school purposes only and shall not vote on a motion or otherwise take part in any proceedings that affect secondary schools exclusively.

(4) Where the number of Indian pupils enrolled in the schools under the jurisdiction of a board under one or more agreements made under this section exceeds 25 per cent of the average daily enrolment in the schools of the board, two persons may be named under subsection (1), and subsection (1) to (3) apply with necessary modifications in respect of the two persons.

(5) Where the number of Indian pupils enrolled in the schools under the jurisdiction of the board under one or more agreements made under this section is fewer than the lesser of 10 per cent of the average daily enrolment in the schools of the board and 100, the appointment under subsection (2) may be made at the discretion of the board.

(6) For the purpose of determining the number of Indian pupils enrolled in the schools under the jurisdiction of a board referred to in subsection (4) or (5), the number of Indian pupils in Indian schools in which the board provides all the instruction shall be included.

(7) Where the agreement is, or the agreements are, in respect of elementary school pupils only or secondary school pupils only, the enrolment referred to in subsections (4) and (5) shall be that of elementary school pupils only or secondary school pupils only, as the case may be.

(8) The term of office of a member appointed under this section terminates on the same date as the term of office of the elected members.

(9) Where a regulation made under clause 67(2)(a) of the Act provides for the appointment of one or more members to represent on the board the interests of Indian pupils, this section does not apply.

(10) Where the office of a member of a board appointed under this section becomes vacant for any reason, it shall be filled in accordance with this section and the person so appointed shall hold office for the remainder of the term of his or her predecessor.

2. This Regulation comes into force on the day section 95 of the *Education Quality Improvement Act, 1997* comes into force.

REGULATION 463/97
ELECTRONIC MEETINGS
O. Reg. 463/97

1. Subject to any conditions or limitations provided for under the Act or under this regulation, a member of a district school board who participates in a meeting through electronic means in accordance with this regulation shall be deemed to be present at the meeting for the purposes of every Act.

2. (1) Every district school board shall develop and implement a policy providing for the use of electronic means for the holding of meetings of a district school board and meetings of a committee of a district school board, including a committee of the whole board.

(2) The policy shall be in accordance with this regulation and with any policies established and guidelines issued by the Minister under paragraph 3.6 of subsection 8(1) of the Act.

3. (1) The policy shall provide for the following:
1. At the request of any board member or pupil representative, the board shall provide the member or representative with electronic means for participating in one or more meetings of the board or of a committee of the board, including a committee of the whole board.
2. The electronic means required by paragraph 1 shall permit the member or representative to hear and be heard by all other participants in the meeting.
3. The electronic means shall be provided in such a way that the rules governing conflict of interest of members are complied with.

(2) The policy shall ensure that pupil representatives who are participating through electronic means do not participate in any proceedings that are closed to the public in accordance with the Act.

4. (1) Subsection (2) applies in respect of meetings of the board or of a committee of the board, including a committee of the whole board, that are open to the public.

(2) Every board shall determine, in accordance with any policies established and guidelines issued under paragraph 3.6 of subsection 8(1) of the Act, whether electronic means should be provided at one or more locations within the area of jurisdiction of the board, to permit participation by members of the public in meetings or classes of meetings.

(3) Where the board determines that electronic means should be provided under this section, the board's policy shall,
(a) provide for the extent and manner of participation by members of the public through electronic means; and
(b) ensure that members of the public who are participating through electronic means do not participate in any proceedings that are closed to the public in accordance with the Act.

5. (1) The policy shall require that, at every meeting of the board or of a committee of the whole board, the following persons be physically present in the meeting room of the board:
1. The chair of the board or his or her designate.
2. At least one additional member of the board.

3. The director of education of the board or his or her designate.

(2) The policy shall require that, at every meeting of a committee of the board, except a committee of the whole board, the following persons be physically present in the meeting room of the committee:

1. The chair of the committee or his or her designate.
2. The director of education of the board or his or her designate.

(3) Despite paragraph 1 of subsection 3(1), the policy shall include provisions permitting the board to refuse to provide a member with electronic means of participation in a meeting of the board, a meeting of a committee of the whole board or a meeting of any other committee of the board, where to do so is necessary to ensure compliance with this section.

6. (1) The meeting room of the board or of a committee of the board, as the case may be, shall be open to permit physical attendance by members of the public at every meeting of the board or of the committee of the board.

(2) For the purposes of subsection (1), the meeting room of a committee of the whole board is the meeting room of the board.

(3) Subsection (1) does not apply where a meeting is closed to the public in accordance with the Act.

7. This Regulation comes into force on the day section 107 of the *Education Quality Improvement Act, 1997* comes into force.

REGULATION 464/97
SPECIAL EDUCATION ADVISORY COMMITTEES
O. Reg. 464/97

1. In this Regulation,

"local association" means an association or organization of parents that operates locally within the area of jurisdiction of a board and that is affiliated with an association or organization that is not an association or organization of professional educators but that is incorporated and operates throughout Ontario to further the interests and well-being of one or more groups of exceptional children or adults.

2. (1) Every district school board shall establish a special education advisory committee that shall consist of,

(a) subject to subsections (2) and (3), one representative from each of the local associations that operates locally within the area of jurisdiction of the board, as nominated by the local association and appointed by the board;

(b) one alternate for each representative appointed under clause (a), as nominated by the local association and appointed by the board;

(c) such number of members from among the board's own members as is determined under subsection (4), as appointed by the board;

(d) where the number of members appointed under clause (c) is less than three, one alternate, as appointed by the board from among its own members, for each member appointed under clause (c);

(e) one or two persons to represent the interests of Indian pupils, as provided by section 4; and

(f) one or more additional members appointed under subsection (5).

(2) The board shall not appoint more than 12 representatives under clause (1)(a).

(3) Where there are more than 12 local associations within the area of jurisdiction of the board, the board shall select the 12 local associations that shall be represented.

(4) The number to be appointed by the board under clause (1)(c) shall be the lesser of,

(a) three; and

(b) 25 per cent of the total number of members of the board, rounded down to the nearest whole number.

(5) For the purposes of clause (1)(f), the board may appoint one or more additional members who are neither representatives of a local association nor members of the board or another committee of the board.

3. (1) Every school authority, other than a board established under section 68 of the Act, shall establish a special education advisory committee that shall consist of,

(a) two representatives from the local associations that operate locally within the area of jurisdiction of the board, as nominated by the local associations and appointed by the board;

(b) one alternate for each representative appointed under clause (a), as nominated by the local associations and appointed by the board;

(c) one member from among the board's own members, as appointed by the board;

(d) one alternate, as appointed by the board from among its own members, for the member appointed under clause (c); and

(e) one or two persons to represent the interests of Indian pupils, as provided by section 4.

(2) Where no local association or associations have been established, instead of the members and alternates required by clauses (1)(a) and (b), the board shall appoint two members and two alternates who are not members of the board.

4. (1) Where a board has one member appointed in accordance with a regulation made under section 188 of the Act, the special education advisory committee shall include one person appointed to represent the interests of Indian pupils.

(2) Where a board has more than one member appointed in accordance with a regulation made under section 188 of the Act, the special education advisory committee shall include two persons appointed to represent the interests of Indian pupils.

(3) One alternate shall be appointed for each person appointed in accordance with subsection (1) or (2).

(4) The representatives and alternates shall be nominated by the councils of the bands with which the board has entered into agreements under section 188 of the Act.

(5) The board shall appoint the persons nominated under subsection (4).

5. (1) A person is not qualified to be nominated or appointed under section 2 or 3 to a special education advisory committee of a board unless the person is qualified to vote for members of that board and is resident in its area of jurisdiction.

(2) Subsection (1) does not apply in respect of persons appointed under section 4.

(3) A person is not qualified to be nominated or appointed under section 2, 3 or 4 if the person is employed by the board.

6. Subject to section 7, each of the persons appointed to a special education advisory committee of a board shall hold office during the term of office of the members of the board and until a new board is organized.

7. (1) A member of a special education advisory committee vacates his or her seat if he or she,

(a) is convicted of an indictable offence;

(b) absents himself or herself without being authorized by resolution entered in the minutes from three consecutive regular meetings of the committee; or

(c) ceases to hold the qualifications to be appointed to the committee.

(2) An alternate for a member of a special education advisory committee vacates his or her position if he or she,

(a) is convicted of an indictable offence;

(b) absents himself or herself without being authorized by resolution entered in the minutes from three consecutive regular meetings of the committee in respect of which the alternate received a notice under subsection 9(9); or

(c) ceases to hold the qualifications to be appointed as an alternate.

(3) Where a seat or position becomes vacant under this section, section 8 applies with respect to filling the vacancy.

(4) Despite subsection (3), where a member of the committee or an alternate for a member of a committee is convicted of an indictable offence, the vacancy or position shall not be filled until the time for taking any appeal that may be taken from the conviction has elapsed, or until the final determination of any appeal so taken, and in the event of the quashing of the conviction the seat or position shall be deemed not to have been vacated.

8. (1) If a seat or position on a special education advisory committee becomes vacant, the board that appointed the person whose seat or position has become vacant shall appoint a qualified person to fill the vacancy for the remainder of the term of the person whose seat or position has become vacant.

(2) The nomination requirements of sections 2, 3 and 4 apply with respect to appointments under this section.

(3) Where a seat of a member of the committee is vacant and has not yet been filled, the alternate for the member, if there is an alternate, shall act in the member's place for all purposes of this Regulation.

9. (1) A majority of the members of a special education advisory committee is a quorum, and a vote of a majority of the members present at a meeting is necessary to bind the committee.

(2) Every member present at a meeting, or his or her alternate when attending the meeting in his or her place, is entitled to one vote.

(3) The members of the committee shall, at their first meeting, elect one of their members as chair and one of their members as vice-chair.

(4) The vice-chair shall assist the chair and shall act for the chair at meetings in his or her absence.

(5) The chair or, in the absence of the chair, the vice-chair, shall preside at meetings.

(6) If at any meeting the chair and vice-chair are not present, the members present may elect a chair for that meeting.

(7) The chair may vote with the other members of the committee and any motion on which there is an equality of votes is lost.

(8) The committee shall meet at least 10 times in each school year.

(9) Where a member for whom an alternate has been appointed cannot attend a meeting of the committee, the member shall so notify the alternate.

(10) Where an alternate receives a notice under subsection (9), he or she shall attend the meeting and act at the meeting in the member's place.

10. (1) The board shall make available to its special education advisory committee the personnel and facilities that the board considers necessary for the proper functioning of the committee, including the personnel and facilities that the board considers necessary to permit the use of electronic means for the holding of meetings of the committee in accordance with the regulations made under section 208.1 of the Act.

(2) Within a reasonable time after a special education advisory committee is appointed, the board shall provide the members of the committee and their alternates with information and orientation respecting,

(a) the role of the committee and of the board in relation to special education; and
(b) Ministry and board policies relating to special education.

11. (1) A special education advisory committee of a board may make recommendations to the board in respect of any matter affecting the establishment, development and delivery of special education programs and services for exceptional pupils of the board.

(2) Before making a decision on a recommendation of the committee, the board shall provide an opportunity for the committee to be heard before the board and before any other committee of the board to which the recommendation is referred.

12. (1) The board shall ensure that its special education advisory committee is provided with the opportunity to participate in the board's annual review, under Regulation 306 of the Revised Regulations of Ontario, 1990, of its special education plan.

(2) The board shall ensure that its special education advisory committee is provided with the opportunity to participate in the board's annual budget process under section 231 of the Act, as that process relates to special education.

(3) The board shall ensure that its special education advisory committee is provided with the opportunity to review the financial statements of the board, prepared under section 252 of the Act, as those statements relate to special education.

13. This Regulation comes into force on the day section 31 of the *Education Quality Improvement Act, 1997* comes into force.

REGULATION 465/97
REGULATION UNDER SECTION 46.1 OF THE ACT
(PRESCRIBED MUNICIPALITIES, DEFENCE PROPERTY)
O. Reg. 465/97

1. The municipalities named in Column 1 are prescribed for the purposes of subsection 46.1(2) of the *Education Act*.

2. The lands and premises with the assessment roll numbers set out in Column 2 are prescribed for the purposes of the definition of "defence property" in subsection 46.1(1) of the Act.

Column 1	Column 2
Town of Petawawa	47 79 078 015 44100
	47 79 079 010 08400
City of Kingston	10 11 090 090 27100
	10 11 090 090 27200
	10 11 090 090 27300
	10 11 090 090 27500
City of Quinte West	12 04 211 085 75100
	12 04 211 085 75200
City of Gloucester	06 06 000 030 00121
City of Ottawa	06 14 010 402 59605
Township of Essa	43 21 010 012 00100
Township of Adjala-Tosorontio	43 01 020 007 20402
City of North Bay	48 44 050 076 50000
City of Toronto	19 08 031 580 00151

3. This Regulation comes into force on the day section 22 of the *Education Quality Improvement Act, 1997* comes into force.

REGULATION 466/97
BORROWING FOR PERMANENT IMPROVEMENTS: ISSUANCE OF DEBENTURES
O. Reg. 466/97

1. A board that, under subsection 247(1) or (2) of the Act, borrows money or incurs a debt for permanent improvements or issues debentures for the money borrowed or the debt incurred shall do so only in accordance with this Regulation.

2. (1) A board may pass a money by-law for the issuing of debentures.

(2) Subsections 140(1) and (2) of the *Municipal Act* apply to the money by-law.

3. (1) A board may by by-law authorize,

(a) the borrowing of money by the issuance of instalment debentures that comply with subsection (2); and

(b) the issuance of debentures to refund at maturity outstanding debentures of the board in accordance with subsection (3).

(2) The last instalment of an instalment debenture shall mature no earlier than five years after the date upon which the debenture was issued and the debenture shall specify the sum of principal payable under the debenture in the final year that the board shall raise by issuing refunding debentures under clause (1)(b).

(3) A refunding debenture mentioned in clause (1)(b) shall be payable within the maximum period of years that the board authorized by by-law for the repayment of the debt for which it issued debentures, commencing on the date it issued the original debentures.

(4) A by-law passed under subsection (1) shall provide that the sums of principal and interest payable on the debentures issued under the by-law shall be provided for in accordance with subsections 247(5) and (6) of the Act.

4. (1) Subject to subsections (2) to (7), the following provisions of the *Municipal Act* apply to money by-laws passed and debentures issued under this Regulation:

1. Subsections 140(5) to (10), (12), (13) and (15) to (18).
2. Subsections 141(1), (2), (3), (5) to (8), (10) and (11).
3. Sections 142 and 143.
4. Subsections 144(1), (2.1), (2.2) and (3) to (9).
5. Subsections 145(1) and (3).
6. Subsection 150(1).
7. Sections 151 and 152.
8. Sections 169, 170, 171, 172, 174 and 175.
9. Subsection 176(2).
10. Section 177.
11. Sections 179, 180, 181.1 and 182.
12. Subsections 185(1) and (2).
13. Sections 186 and 188.

(2) In the provisions mentioned in subsection (1),

(a) references to a council, corporation, municipality, municipal corporation or council of a city shall be deemed to be references to the board that issued the debentures; and

(b) references to the treasurer of a municipality shall be deemed to be references to the treasurer of the board that issued the debentures.

(3) In subsection 141(5) of the *Municipal Act*, the reference to a retirement fund referred to in clause 141(4)(b) of that Act shall be deemed to be a reference to the retirement fund mentioned in clause 5(1)(b) of this Regulation.

(4) In subsection 144(3) of the *Municipal Act*, the reference to clause 144(2)(b) of that Act shall be deemed to be a reference to clause 6(1)(b) of this Regulation.

(5) In subsection 144(5) of the *Municipal Act*, the reference to section 167 of that Act shall be deemed to be a reference to section 241 of the *Education Act*.

(6) In subsections 144(7) and (8) of the *Municipal Act*, references to the 31st day of December shall be deemed to be references to August 31.

(7) In subsection 176(2) of the *Municipal Act*, the reference to subsection 176(1) of that Act shall be deemed to be a reference to section 10 of this Regulation.

(8) In section 177 of the *Municipal Act*, the reference to levying the amount required to be raised for a sinking fund shall be deemed to be a reference to setting aside the amount required to be set aside for a sinking fund.

5. (1) A by-law passed with respect to extendible or retractable term debentures shall provide for the setting aside in each year of the currency of the debentures of,

(a) an amount sufficient to pay the interest payable on the debentures in that year; and
(b) a specified amount to form a retirement fund.

(2) The specified amount for the retirement fund shall be equal to or greater than the amount that would have been required to have been set aside and paid in each year in respect of the principal amount of the debentures if,

(a) the principal had been payable in equal annual instalments; and
(b) the board had issued the debentures for the maximum period that it authorized by by-law for the repayment of the debt for which it issued the debentures, commencing on the date of the debentures.

(3) A by-law mentioned in subsection (1) shall provide that the amounts payable under that subsection shall be set aside and paid in accordance with subsections 247(5) and (6) of the Act.

6. (1) A money by-law for the issuing of sinking fund debentures shall provide for the setting aside in each year of the currency of the debentures of,

(a) an amount sufficient to pay the interest payable on the debentures in that year; and
(b) a specified amount for the sinking fund that, with interest at a rate not to exceed 8 per cent per annum compounded yearly, will be sufficient to pay the principal of the debentures at maturity.

(2) A by-law mentioned in subsection (1) shall provide that the amounts payable under that subsection shall be set aside and paid in accordance with subsections 247(5) and (6) of the Act.

(3) The principal and interest payable under refinancing debentures issued under subsection 144(2.1) of the *Municipal Act* shall be raised in accordance with subsections (1) and (2) of this section.

7. (1) A money by-law for the issuing of term debentures shall provide for,
- (a) the setting aside, in each year of the currency of the debentures, of an amount sufficient to pay the interest payable on the debentures; and
- (b) the setting aside, in each year of the currency of the debentures in which no other debentures issued under the same by-law become due and payable, of a specified amount to form a retirement fund for the debentures that, with interest at a rate not to exceed 8 per cent per annum compounded yearly, will be sufficient to pay the principal of the debentures at maturity.

(2) A by-law mentioned in subsection (1) shall provide that the amounts payable under that subsection shall be set aside and paid in accordance with subsection 247(5) and (6) of the Act.

8. The repealing by-law mentioned in subsection 150(1) of the *Municipal Act* shall recite the facts on which it is founded and shall be appointed to take effect on August 31 in the fiscal year of its passing.

9. (1) Subject to subsections (5) and (6), a board that receives money from the sale or hypothecation of debentures shall ensure that the money,
- (a) is kept in a separate account;
- (b) is used only for the purposes for which the board issued the debentures; and
- (c) is not applied towards payment of the current or other expenditures of the board,

(2) Despite subsection (1) and section 175 of the *Municipal Act*, a board that receives money from the sale of debentures that is not required immediately for the purpose or purposes for which the board issued the debentures may invest the money in the general fund of the board.

(3) The board shall ensure that,
- (a) the part of the money invested that is described in subsection (4) is returned to the debenture account no later than August 31 of the fiscal year in which the board invested the money; and
- (b) interest is credited to the debenture account on the money invested, at a rate equal to the rate currently applicable to the temporary borrowings of the board.

(4) The part of the money invested to which clause (3)(a) applies is the lesser of the whole of the money invested and the amount sufficient to pay,
- (a) the interest and principal payment on the debentures that become due and payable during the fiscal year following the fiscal year in which the board invested the money; and
- (b) the amounts required to be paid, during the fiscal year following the fiscal year in which the board invested the money, into a sinking fund or retirement fund established in respect of the debentures mentioned in clause (a).

(5) Subject to subsection (6), if the amount realized from the debentures is in excess of that required for the purpose or purposes for which the board issued the debentures, the board shall ensure that the excess amount is applied as follows:

1. If the amount is sufficient to redeem one or more debentures of the latest maturity, it shall be applied for that purpose if any of those debentures are redeemable.
2. If none of the debentures mentioned in paragraph 1 are redeemable or if the amount is not sufficient to redeem a debenture or if a balance remains after redemption as required by paragraph 1, the amount or the balance, as the case may be, shall be applied on the annual payments of principal and interest on the debentures until the amount or the balance, as the case may be, has all been so applied, and the amounts to be set aside and paid for that purpose shall be reduced accordingly.

(6) If the whole or any part of the amount realized from the sale or hypothecation of any debentures is not required for the purpose or purposes for which the debentures were issued, it may be applied to buy back the debentures or may be applied to meet the whole or a portion of any other capital expenditure of the board.

(7) If real or personal property acquired with all or part of the proceeds of the sale of debentures is sold while any part of the debentures remains outstanding, the net proceeds of the sale, to the extent of the amount of principal and interest then outstanding on the debentures, shall be applied in accordance with subsection (5) and (6).

10. The treasurer of a board in respect of which a sum is required by law to be set aside for a sinking fund shall prepare and lay before the board in every year, before the board adopts the estimates, a statement showing what amount will be required for that purpose.

11. If a deficit is sustained on the sale of all or part of an issuance of debentures of a board and all or part of the amount of the deficit is required for the purposes for which the board issued the debentures, the board shall ensure that,

(a) the amount required is added to the sum to be raised in the first year for the payment of principal and interest on the debentures and the amount to be set aside in the first year is increased accordingly; or

(b) the amount required is raised by the issuance of other debentures for the same or similar purpose.

12. (1) A board may by by-law borrow money for permanent improvements by way of a loan from a bank or trust company or a credit union within the meaning of the *Credit Unions and Caisses Populaires Act, 1994* with an initial maturity of more than one year.

(2) A board that obtains a loan mentioned in subsection (1) shall ensure that the proceeds of it are used for permanent improvements.

13. This Regulation comes into force on the latter of January 1, 1998 and the day that subsection 113(1) of the *Education Quality Improvement Act, 1997* comes into force.

REGULATION 467/97
DEEMED DISTRICT MUNICIPALITIES
(SCHOOL AUTHORITY JURISDICTION) — TAX RATES
O. Reg. 467/97

1. For the purpose of clause 257.12(3)(a) of the Act, each of the following district school areas shall be deemed to be a district municipality, unless and until it becomes or is included in a municipality:

1. The Mine Centre District School Area.
2. The Summer Beaver District School Area.
3. The Kashabowie District School Area.
4. The Caramat District School Area.
5. The Collins District School Area.
6. The Kilkenny District School Area.
7. The Slate Falls District School Area.
8. The Sturgeon Lake District School Area.
9. The Upsala District School Area.
10. The Asquith-Garvey District School Area.
11. The Missarenda District School Area.
12. The Murchison, Lyell and Sabine District School Area.
13. The Umphreville District School Area.

2. For the purpose of clause 257.12(3)(a) of the Act, each of the following former school sections shall be deemed to be a district municipality, unless and until it becomes or is included in a municipality:

1. The former school section known as The Allanwater District School Area.
2. The former school section known as The Armstrong District School Area.
3. The former school section known as The Auden District School Area.
4. The former school section known as The Ferland District School Area.
5. The former school section known as The Savant Lake District School Area.

3. For the purpose of clause 257.12(3)(a) of the Act, each of the following areas shall be deemed to be a district municipality, unless and until it becomes or is included in a municipality:

1. All land within The Foleyet District School Area or the separate school zone of The Foleyet Roman Catholic Separate School Board.
2. All land within The Gogama District School Area or the separate school zone of The Gogama Roman Catholic Separate School Board.

4. For the purpose of clause 257.13(3)(a) of the Act, the portion of The James Bay Lowlands Secondary School District that is not within the Moosonee Development Area shall be deemed to be a district municipality, unless and until it becomes or is included in a municipality.

5. For the purpose of clause 257.12(3)(a) of the Act, the portions of the geographic townships of Baird and Heyson that are not within The Township of Red Lake in the Territorial

District of Kenora shall be deemed to be a district municipality, unless and until they become or are included in a municipality.

6. This Regulation comes into force on the later of January 1, 1998 and the day section 31 of the *Education Quality Improvement Act, 1997* comes into force.

REGULATION 468/97
DEEMED DISTRICT MUNICIPALITIES (DISTRICT SCHOOL BOARD JURISDICTION) — TAX RATES
O. Reg. 468/97

1. (1) Subject to subsection (2), for the purpose of clause 257.12(3)(a) of the Act, each of the following that is not within a district municipality set out in O. Reg. 467/97 (*Deemed District Municipalities (School Authority Jurisdiction)—Tax Rates*) shall be deemed to be a district municipality, unless and until it becomes or is included in a municipality:

1. Every school section in existence on December 31, 1968 that comprised only territory without municipal organization, except a school section established under section 67 or 68.
2. Any part of territory without municipal organization that on December 31, 1968 was part of a high school district but was not in a school section.
3. Any part of territory without municipal organization that was designated by a regulation made under subsection 55(1) of the Act, as it read on December 31, 1997, or a predecessor of that subsection, as a district municipality or that was added to a school division without being so designated and that on December 31, 1968 was not in a school section or in a high school district.

(2) For the purpose of clause 257.12(3)(a) of the Act, if an area described in subsection (1) is partly within a separate school zone,

  (a) the portion of the area that is within the separate school zone shall be deemed to be a district municipality, unless and until it becomes or is included in a municipality; and

  (b) the portion of the area that is outside the separate school zone shall be deemed to be a district municipality, unless and until it becomes or is included in a municipality.

2. For the purpose of clause 257.12(3)(a) of the Act, the geographic township of Dickens in the Territorial District of Nipissing and the portion of the geographic township of Murchison, in the Territorial District of Nipissing, that is not in The Murchison, Lyell and Sabine District School Area, shall be deemed to be a district municipality, unless and until they become or are included in a municipality.

3. This Regulation comes into force on the later of January 1, 1998 and the day section 32 of the *Education Quality Improvement Act, 1997* comes into force.

REGULATION 469/97
DEBT AND FINANCIAL OBLIGATION LIMITS
O. Reg. 469/97

[Revoked O. Reg. 472/98.]

REGULATION 470/97
FINANCIAL STATEMENTS AND AUDITOR'S REPORTS FOR OLD BOARDS
O. Reg. 470/97

1. (1) A district school board shall at its first meeting in 1998 or as soon as possible after the first meeting require its treasurer to prepare the financial statements for 1997 for each old board that was merged into the district school board by a regulation made under clause 58.1(2)(h) of the Act.

(2) Instead of requiring its treasurer to prepare the financial statements mentioned in subsection (1), the district school board may require the person who was the treasurer of the old board to prepare the old board's financial statements if that person is an employee of the district school board.

(3) A person required to prepare financial statements under this section shall do so in accordance with the direction of the district school board and shall do so as soon as reasonably possible.

2. (1) A district school board shall obtain an auditor's report on the financial statements required to be prepared under section 1 as soon as reasonably possible after the financial statements have been prepared.

(2) Upon receipt of the auditor's report, the treasurer of the district school board shall promptly give the Ministry of Education and Training two copies of the auditor's report and two copies of the financial statements mentioned in subsection (1).

(3) Within one month after the district school board has received the auditor's report, the treasurer of the district school board shall,

- (a) publish the financial statements to which the auditor's report relates, and the auditor's report, in a daily or weekly newspaper that, in the opinion of the treasurer, has sufficient circulation within the area of jurisdiction of the old board in respect of which the financial statements were prepared, to provide reasonable notice to those affected by them; or
- (b) mail or deliver a copy of the financial statements and auditor's report to each of the old board's supporters.

(4) The financial statements and auditor's report published, mailed or delivered under subsection (3) shall be in the same form as financial statements and auditor's report prepared under subsection 252(2) of the Act.

(5) For purposes of obtaining the auditor's report mentioned in subsection (1), the district school board shall retain the person who was the auditor of the old board to prepare the audit report on the financial statements of the old board, unless that is not reasonably possible and, if that person is retained, the district school board is subject to the same rights and obligations as the old board would have been had the retainer of the auditor by the old board been continued.

3. The Regulation comes into force on the day that section 113 of the *Education Quality Improvement Act, 1997* comes into force.

REGULATION 471/97
ELIGIBLE INVESTMENTS
O. Reg. 471/97

1. A board does not have the power under section 241 of the Act to invest in a security other than a security prescribed under this Regulation.

2. The following are prescribed as securities that a board may invest in:

1. Bonds, debentures, promissory notes or other evidence of indebtedness issued or guaranteed by,
    i. Canada or a province or territory of Canada,
    ii. an agency of Canada or a province or territory or Canada,
    iii. a municipality in Canada,
    iv. a board of similar entity in Canada,
    v. the Municipal Finance Authority of British Columbia.
2. Bonds, debentures, promissory notes or other evidence of indebtedness of a corporation if,
    i. the bond, debenture or other evidence of indebtedness is secured by the assignment to a trustee, as defined in the *Trustee Act*, of payments that Canada or a province or territory of Canada has agreed to make or is required to make under a federal, provincial or territorial statute, and
    ii. the payments referred to in subparagraph i are sufficient to meet the amounts payable under the bond, debenture or other evidence of indebtedness, including the amounts payable at maturity.
3. Deposit receipts, deposit notes, certificates of deposit or investment, acceptances or similar instruments issued, guaranteed or endorsed by,
    i. a bank listed in Schedule I or II to the *Bank Act* (Canada),
    ii. a loan corporation or trust corporation registered under the *Loan and Trust Corporations Act*,
    iii. a credit union or league to which the *Credit Unions and Caisses Populaires Act, 1994* applies, or
    iv the Province of Ontario Savings Office.
4. Bonds, debentures or evidences of long-term indebtedness issued or guaranteed by an institution listed in paragraph 3.
5. Short term securities, the terms of which provide that the principal and interest shall be fully repaid no later than three days after the day the investment was made, that are issued by,
    i. the board of governors of a college of applied arts and technology established under section 5 of the *Ministry of Colleges and Universities Act*,
    ii. a degree granting institution as authorized under section 3 of the *Degree Granting Act*, or
    iii. a board as defined in the *Public Hospitals Act*.

3. (1) A board shall not invest in a security under paragraph 4 of section 2 unless the bond, debenture, promissory note or evidence of indebtedness is rated,

(a) by Canadian Bond Rating Service Inc. as "AA—" or higher;

(b) by Dominion Bond Rating Service Limited as "AA(low)" or higher;
(c) by Moody's Investors Services Inc. as "Aa3" or higher; or
(d) by Standard and Poor's Inc. as "AA—" or higher.

(2) If an investment made under paragraph 4 of section 2 falls below the standard required under subsection (1), the board shall sell the investment within 90 days after the day the investment falls below the standard.

4. A board shall not invest in a security issued or guaranteed by a board or similar entity unless,

(a) the money raised by issuing the security is to be used for school purposes; and
(b) the security is to be repaid entirely from the taxes or charges levied on property, with grants or appropriations made by the government of Canada or a province or territory of Canada or a municipality, or from a combination of such taxes, charges, grants and appropriations.

5. (1) A board shall not invest in a security that is expressed or payable in any currency other than Canadian dollars.

(2) Subsection (1) does not prevent a board from continuing an investment, made before this Regulation comes into force, that is expressed and payable in the currency of the United States of America or the United Kingdom.

6. Before a board invests in a security prescribed under this Regulation, the board shall, if it has not already done so, adopt a statement of the board's investment policies and goals.

7. (1) If a board has an investment in a security prescribed under this Regulation, the board shall require the treasurer of the board to prepare and provide to the board, each year or more frequently if so required by the board, an investment report.

(2) The investment report referred to in subsection (1) shall contain,

(a) a statement about the performance of the portfolio of investments of the board during the period covered by the report;
(b) a description of the estimated proportion of the total investments of a board that are invested in its own long-term and short-term securities to the total investment of the board and a description of the change, if any, in that estimated proportion since the previous year's report;
(c) a statement by the treasurer as to whether or not, in his or her opinion, all investments were made in accordance with the investment policies and goals adopted by the board;
(d) a record of the date of each transaction in or disposal of its own securities, including a statement of the purchase and sale price of each security; and
(e) such other information that the board may require on that, in the opinion of the treasurer, should be included.

8. (1) Despite this Regulation, an investment by an old board or a school authority in bonds, debentures or other indebtedness of a corporation made before the day this Regulation comes into force may be continued if the bond, debenture or other indebtedness is rated,

(a) by Canadian Bond Rating Service Inc. as "AA—" or higher;
(b) by Dominion Bond Rating Service Limited as "AA(low)" or higher;
(c) by Moody's Investors Services Inc. as "Aa3" or higher; or

(d) by Standard and Poor's Inc. as "AA—" or higher.

(2) If the rating of an investment continued under subsection (1) falls below the standard required by that subsection, the board shall sell the investment within 90 days after the day the investment falls below the standard.

9. This Regulation comes into force on the day that section 113 of the *Education Quality Improvement Act, 1997* comes into force.

REGULATION 472/97
PRINCIPALS AND VICE-PRINCIPALS OF SCHOOL AUTHORITIES
O. Reg. 472/97

1. Each of the following provisions apply, as of the day the provision comes into force, to principals and vice-principals who are employed by a school authority both on December 31, 1997 and January 1, 1998:

1. Subsection 277.11(2) to (5) of the Act.
2. Subsection 287.2(2) of the Act.
3. Subsection 287.2(3) of the Act.

2. This Regulation comes into force on January 1, 1998.

3. This Regulation is revoked on September 1, 2000.

REGULATION 494/97
LEVYING AND COLLECTING BY ALTERNATIVE BOARDS
O. Reg. 494/97

1. The Foleyet Roman Catholic Separate School Board shall perform the duties imposed on The Foleyet District School Area Board by subsection 255(1) section 256 and paragraph 3 of subsection 257.7(1) of the Act and subsection 21.1(1) of the *Provincial Land Tax Act* respecting the levying and collecting of rates, taxes or tax rates, as the case may be, in the area of jurisdiction of The Foleyet District School Area Board.

2. The Gogama Roman Catholic Separate School Board shall perform the duties imposed on The Gogama District School Area Board by subsection 255(1), section 256 and paragraph 3 of subsection 257.7(1) of the Act and subsection 21.1(1) of the *Provincial Land Tax Act* respecting the levying and collecting of rates, taxes or tax rates, as the case may be, in the area of jurisdiction of The Gogama District School Area Board.

3. English-language Separate District School Board No. 55 shall perform the duties imposed by paragraphs 2 and 3 of subsection 257.7(1) of the Act in the geographic township of Dickens in the Territorial District of Nipissing and the portion of the geographic township of Murchison, in the Territorial District of Nipissing, that is not in The Murchison, Lyell and Sabine District School Area.

4. The James Bay Lowlands Secondary School Board shall perform the duties imposed on The Moose Factory Island District School Area Board by subsection 255(1), section 256 and paragraph 3 of subsection 257.7(1) of the Act and subsection 21.1(1) of the *Provincial Land Tax Act* respecting the levying and collecting of rates, taxes or tax rates, as the case may be, in the area of jurisdiction of The Moose Factory Island District School Area Board.

5. This Regulation comes into force on the later of January 1, 1998 and day subsection 113(2) of the *Education Quality Improvement Act, 1997* comes into force.

REGULATION 495/97
CURRENT BORROWING LIMITS
O. Reg. 495/97

1. (1) For the purposes of subsection 243(4) of the Act, the maximum amount that a board may borrow at any one time during the period specified in subsection (3), together with the total of any similar borrowings that have not been repaid and any accrued interest on those borrowings, shall be determined by the board as follows:
1. Estimate the revenue fund expenditures of the board for the fiscal year January 1, 1998 to August 31, 1998.
2. Subtract, from the amount determined under paragraph 1, the amount of revenue fund revenues of the fiscal year January 1, 1998 to August 31, 1998 already received by the board.

(2) For the purposes of paragraph 1 of subsection (1), revenue fund revenues do not include revenues derivable or derived from the sale of assets, current borrowings or issues of debentures or instruments prescribed under clause 247(3)(f) of the Act or from a surplus including arrears of taxes and proceeds from the sale of assets.

(3) The period referred to in subsection (1) begins on January 1, 1998 and ends on the earlier of,
- (a) August 31, 1998; and
- (b) the day on which the estimates for the fiscal year ending on August 31, 1998 are adopted.

2. This Regulation comes into force on the day subsection 113(1) of the *Education Quality Improvement Act, 1997* comes into force.

REGULATION 496/97
RESERVE FOR WORKING FUNDS LIMIT
O. Reg. 496/97

1. The maximum amount that a district school board may provide for a reserve for working funds for the period January 1, 1998 to August 31, 1998 is 5 per cent of the amount estimated by the board as its revenue fund expenditures for the period January 1, 1998 to August 31, 1998.

2. This Regulation comes into force on the day subsection 113(1) of the *Education Quality Improvement Act, 1997* comes into force.

REGULATION 497/97
DISPOSITION OF SCHOOL SITES
O. Reg. 497/97, Fr. version O. Reg. 152/98

[Revoked O. Reg. 445/98.]

REGULATION 498/97
ALLOCATIONS TO RESERVE FUND FOR PERMANENT IMPROVEMENTS
O. Reg. 498/97

[Revoked O. Reg. 447/98.]

REGULATION 20/98
EDUCATION DEVELOPMENT CHARGES — GENERAL
O. Reg. 20/98, Fr. version O. Reg. 151/98, as am. O. Reg. 473/98

PART I

INTERPRETATIONS

Definitions

1. For the purposes of Division E of Part IX of the Act and in this Regulation,

"existing industrial building" means a building classified as land in the industrial property class according to the last returned assessment roll;

"gross floor area" means the total floor area, measured between the outside of exterior walls or between the outside of exterior walls and the centre line of party walls dividing the building from another building, of all floors above the average level of finished ground adjoining the building at its exterior walls.

Exclusion from Education Land Costs: Excess Land

2. (1) Costs that are attributable to excess land of a site are prescribed, for the purposes of paragraph 2 of subsection 257.53(3) of the Act, as costs that are not education land costs.

(2) Subsection (1) does not apply to costs described in paragraph 5 of subsection 257.53(2) of the Act.

(3) Land is not excess land if it is reasonably necessary,

(a) to meet a legal requirement relating to the site; or

(b) to allow the facilities for pupil accommodation that the board intends to provide on the site to be located there and to provide access to those facilities.

(4) This section does not apply to land,

(a) that has already been acquired by the board before February 1, 1998, or

(b) in respect of which there is an agreement, entered into before February 1, 1998, under which the board is required to, or has an option to, purchase the land.

(5) In this section,

"excess land" means the part of a school site that exceeds the maximum area determined, under the table to this section, based on the number of pupils that can be accommodated in the school to be built on the site.

ELEMENTARY SCHOOLS	
Number of pupils	Maximum area (acres)
1 to 400	5
401 to 500	5

ELEMENTARY SCHOOLS	
Number of pupils	Maximum area (acres)
501 to 600	6
601 to 700	7
701 or more	8
SECONDARY SCHOOLS	
Number of pupils	Maximum area (acres)
1 to 1000	12
1001 to 1100	13
1101 to 1200	14
1201 to 1300	15
1301 to 1400	16
1401 to 1500	17
1501 or more	18

PART II
EXEMPTIONS

Additional Dwelling Unit Exemptions

3. For the purposes of clause 257.54(3)(b) of the Act, the following table sets out the name and description of the classes of residential buildings that are prescribed, the maximum number of additional dwelling units that are prescribed for buildings in those classes and the restriction for each class.

NAME OF CLASS OF RESIDENTIAL BUILDING	DESCRIPTION OF CLASS OF RESIDENTIAL BUILDINGS	MAXIMUM NUMBER OF ADDITIONAL DWELLING UNITS	RESTRICTIONS
Single detached dwellings	Residential buildings, each of which contains a single dwelling unit, that are not attached to other buildings.	Two	The total gross floor area of the additional dwelling unit or units must be less than or equal to the gross floor area of the dwelling unit already in the building.

Name of Class of Residential Building	Description of Class of Residential Buildings	Maximum Number of Additional Dwelling Units	Restrictions
Semi-detached dwellings or row dwellings	Residential buildings, each of which contains a single dwelling unit, that have one or two vertical walls, but no other parts, attached to other buildings.	One	The gross floor area of the additional dwelling unit must be less than or equal to the gross floor area of the dwelling unit already in the building.
Other residential buildings	A residential building not in another class of residential building described in this table.	One	The gross floor area of the additional dwelling unit must be less than or equal to the gross floor area of the smallest dwelling unit already in the building.

Replacement of Dwelling Unit Exemption

4. (1) Subject to subsection (2), a board shall exempt an owner with respect to the replacement, on the same site, of a dwelling unit that was destroyed by fire, demolition or otherwise, or that was so damaged by fire, demolition or otherwise as to render it uninhabitable.

(2) A board is not required to exempt an owner if the building permit for the replacement dwelling unit is issued more than two years after,

(a) the date the former dwelling unit was destroyed or became uninhabitable; or

(b) if the former dwelling unit was demolished pursuant to a demolition permit issued before the former dwelling unit was destroyed or became uninhabitable, the date the demolition permit was issued.

Replacement of Non-Residential Building Exemption

5. (1) Subject to subsections (2) and (3), a board shall exempt an owner with respect to the replacement, on the same site, of a non-residential building that was destroyed by fire, demolition or otherwise, or that was so damaged by fire, demolition or otherwise as to render it unusable.

(2) If the gross floor area of the non-residential part of the replacement building exceeds the gross floor area of the non-residential part of the building being replaced, the board is only required to exempt the owner with respect to the portion of the education development charge calculated in accordance with the following formula:

$$Exempted\ portion = \frac{GFA\ (old)}{GFA\ (new)} \times EDC$$

where,

"Exempted portion" means the portion of the education development charge that the board is required to exempt;

"GFA (old)" means the gross floor area of the non-residential part of the building being replaced;

"GFA (new)" means the gross floor area of the non-residential part of the replacement building;

"EDC" means the education development charge that would be payable in the absence of the exemption.

(3) A board is not required to exempt an owner if the building permit for the replacement building is issued more than five years after,

  (a) the date the former building was destroyed or became unusable; or
  (b) if the former building was demolished pursuant to a demolition permit issued before the former building was destroyed or became unusable, the date the demolition permit was issued.

(4) This section does not apply with respect to education development charges on residential development.

Toronto Railway Lands Exemption

6. (1) In this section,

"agreement" means the agreement entitled "Development Levy Agreement—Railway Lands Central and West" made as of October 21, 1994 among The Corporation of the City of Toronto, Canadian National Railway Company, CN Transactions Inc., The Board of Education for the City of Toronto, Metropolitan Separate School Board and The Metropolitan Toronto School Board, and registered in the Land Registry Office for the Land Titles Division of Metropolitan Toronto (No. 66) as Instrument No. C920254;

"lands" means the lands described in Schedules A and B to the agreement.

(2) A board shall exempt an owner from education development charges on the lands to the extend provided for in the agreement.

PART III

DETERMINATION OF CHARGES AND PASSAGE OF BY-LAW

Determination of Education Development Charges

7. Before an education development charge by-law is passed, the board shall do the following for the purposes of determining the education development charges:

1. The board shall estimate the number of new dwelling units in the area in which the charges are to be imposed for each of the 15 years immediately following the day the board intends to have the by-law come into force. The board's estimate shall include only new dwelling units in respect of which education development charges may be imposed.
2. The board shall identify different types of new dwelling units and estimate, for each type, the average number of new elementary school pupils and the average number of new secondary school pupils generated by each new dwelling unit who will attend schools of the board.
3. For each of the 15 years referred to in paragraph 1, the board shall estimate the total number of new elementary school pupils and new secondary school pupils using the estimated number of new dwelling units and the estimated average number of new pupils generated by each new dwelling unit subject to the following adjustments,
    i. the board shall reduce the number of new elementary school pupils by the number of existing elementary school pupil places that, in the opinion of the board, could reasonably be used to accommodate those new pupils,
    ii. the board shall reduce the number of new secondary school pupils by the number of existing secondary school pupil places that, in the opinion of the board, could reasonably be used to accommodate those new pupils.
4. The board shall estimate the net education land cost for the elementary school sites and secondary school sites required to provide pupil places for the new elementary school pupils and new secondary school pupils.
5. The board shall estimate the balance of the education development charge reserve fund, if any, relating to the area in which the charges are to be imposed. The estimate shall be an estimate of the balance immediately before the day the board intends to have the by-law come into force.
6. The board shall adjust the net education land cost with respect to any balance estimated under paragraph 5. If the balance is positive, the balance shall be subtracted from the cost. If the balance is negative, the balance shall be converted to a positive number and added to the cost.
7. The net education land cost as adjusted, if necessary, under paragraph 6, is the growth-related net education land cost.
8. The board shall choose the percentage of the growth-related net education land cost that is to be funded by charges on residential development and the percentage, if any, that is to be funded by charges on non-residential development. The percentage that is to be funded by charges on non-residential development shall not exceed 40 percent.
9. The board shall determine the charges on residential development subject to the following,
    i. the charges shall be expressed as a rate per new dwelling unit,
    ii. the rate shall be the same throughout the area in which charges are to be imposed under the by-law,
    iii. the rate shall be an amount determined by the board so that if applied, over the 15 year period referred to in paragraph 1, to the estimated residential development in the area to which the by-law would apply and for which charges

may be imposed, the percentage of the growth-related net education land cost that is to be funded by charges on residential development would not be exceeded.
10. If charges are to be imposed on non-residential development, the board shall determine the charges subject to the following,
   i. the charges shall be expressed as one of the following types of rate, as selected by the board,
      A. a rate to be applied to the gross floor area of the development, or
      B. a rate to be applied to the declared value of the development,
   ii. the board may choose to have one type of rate for some parts of the area in which charges are to be imposed and the other type of rate to apply to the other parts of the area in which charges are to be imposed.
   iii. the board may not choose to have both types of rate apply within a city, town, village or township,
   iv. if only one type of rate applies under the by-law, the rate shall be the same throughout the area in which charges are to be imposed under the by-law,
   v. if both types of rate are to apply under the by-law, each of those rates shall be the same throughout the area in which each type of rate applies,
   vi. the rate (or rates if both types of rate are to apply under the by-law) shall be determined by the board so that if applied over the 15 year period referred to in paragraph 1, to the estimated non-residential development in the area to which the by-law would apply and for which charges may be imposed, the percentage of the growth-related net education land cost that is to be funded by charges on non-residential development would not be exceeded.

Application of Charge if Based on Declared Value of Development

8. An education development charge expressed as a rate to be applied to the declared value of a development shall be applied to the declared value used to calculate the building permit fee, if that fee is calculated using the declared value of the development.

Background Study Contents

9. (1) The following information is prescribed, for the purposes of clause 257.61(2)(d) of the Act, as information that must be included in the education development charge background study relating to an education development charge by-law:
1. The following estimates that the board intends to use in determining the education development charges,
   i. the board's estimates under paragraph 1 of section 7, for each of the years required under that paragraph, of the number of new dwelling units in the area in which the charges are to be imposed,
   ii. the board's estimates under paragraph 2 of section 7, for each type of dwelling unit identified by the board, of the average number of elementary school pupils

and the average number of secondary school pupils generated by each new dwelling unit who will attend schools of the board, and
      iii. the board's estimates under paragraph 3 of section 7, for each of the years required under that paragraph, of the total number of new elementary school pupils and the total number of new secondary school pupils, without the adjustments set out in that paragraph being made and with the adjustments set out in that paragraph being made.
2. For each elementary school and secondary school in the area in which the board intends to impose education development charges,
      i. the number of existing pupil places, and
      ii. the number of pupils who attend the school.
3. For every existing elementary school pupil place in the board's jurisdiction that the board does not intend to use in the adjustment under subparagraph i of paragraph 3 of section 7, an explanation as to why the board does not intend to do so.
4. For every existing secondary school pupil place in the board's jurisdiction that the board does not intend to use in the adjustment under subparagraph ii of paragraph 3 of section 7, an explanation as to why the board does not intend to do so.
5. For each elementary school site and secondary school site, the net education land cost of which the board intends to include in its estimation under paragraph 4 of section 7,
      i. the location of the site,
      ii. the area of the site and if the area of the site exceeds the maximum area determined, under the table to section 2, based on the number of pupils that can be accommodated in the school to be built on the site, an explanation of whether the costs of the excess land are education land costs and if so, why,
      iii. the estimated education land costs of the site including a separate statement of the board's estimation of,
            A. the costs described in paragraph 1 of subsection 257.53(2) of the Act,
            B. the costs of providing services described in paragraph 2 of subsection 257.53(2) of the Act,
            C. the costs of preparing the site described in paragraph 2 of subsection 257.53(2) of the Act, and
            D. the interest described in paragraph 4 of subsection 257.53(2) of the Act, and
      iv. the number of pupil places the board estimates will be provided by the school to be built on the site and the number of those pupil places that the board estimates will be used to accommodate the number of new pupils estimated under paragraph 3 of section 7.
6. A statement of the board's policy concerning possible arrangements with municipalities, school boards or other persons or bodies in the public or private sector, including arrangements of a long-term or co-operative nature, which would provide accommodation for the new elementary school pupils and new secondary school pupils estimated under paragraph 3 of section 7, without imposing education development charges, or with a reduction in such charges.

7. If a previous education development charge background study completed by the board included a statement under paragraph 6, a statement of how the policy referred to in the statement was implemented and, if it was not implemented, an explanation of why it was not implemented.
8. A statement from the board stating that it has reviewed its operating budget for savings that could be applied to reduce growth-related net education land costs, and the amount of any savings which it proposes to apply, if any.

(2) The information prescribed under paragraph 5 of subsection (1) shall be as specific as can reasonably be provided by the board in the circumstances.

Conditions of Passage of By-Law

10. The following conditions are prescribed, for the purpose of subsection 257.54(6) of the Act, as conditions that must be satisfied in order for a board to pass an education development charge by-law:

1. The Minister has approved,
    i. the board's estimates under paragraph 3 of section 7, for each of the years required under that paragraph, of the total number of new elementary school pupils and the total number of new secondary school pupils, without the adjustments set out in that paragraph being made, and
    ii. the board's estimates of the number of elementary school sites and the number of secondary school sites used by the board to determine the net education land cost under paragraph 4 of section 7.
2. Either,
    i. the estimated average number of elementary school pupils of the board over the five years immediately following the day the board intends to have the by-law come into force exceeds the total capacity of the board to accommodate elementary school pupils throughout its jurisdiction on the day the by-law is passed, or
    ii. the estimated average number of secondary school pupils of the board over the five years immediately following the day the board intends to have the by-law come into force exceeds the total capacity of the board to accommodate secondary school pupils throughout its jurisdiction on the day the by-law is passed.
3. The board has given a copy of the education development charge background study relating to the by-law to the Minister and each board having jurisdiction within the area to which the by-law would apply.

Notice of Public Meeting

11. (1) The notice of the public meeting the board is required to give under clause 257.63(1)(b) of the Act shall be given in one of the following ways:

1. To every owner of land in the area to which the proposed by-law would apply, by personal service, fax or mail.

2. By publication in a newspaper that is, in the secretary of the board's opinion, of sufficiently general circulation in the area to which the proposed by-law would apply to give the public reasonable notice of the meeting.

(2) For the purposes of paragraph 1 of subsection (1), the owners are the owners shown on the last revised assessment roll, subject to any written notice of a change of ownership of land the secretary of the board may have received. A notice given by mail to an owner shall be mailed to the address shown on the last revised assessment roll or, if applicable, to the address shown on the notice of a change of ownership of land received by the secretary of the board.

Notice of By-Law

12. (1) This section applies to the notices relating to the passage of an education development charge by-law that the secretary of the board is required to give under section 257.64 of the Act.

(2) Notice shall be given in one of the following ways:

1. By personal service, fax or mail to every owner of land in the area to which the by-law applies.
2. By publication in a newspaper that is, in the secretary of the board's opinion, of sufficiently general circulation in the area to which the by-law applies to give the public reasonable notice of the by-law.

(3) Subsection 11(2) applies, with necessary modifications, for the purposes of paragraph 1 of subsection (2).

(4) In addition to the notice under subsection (2), notice shall be given, by personal service, fax or mail, to the following:

1. Every person and organization that has given the secretary of the board a written request for notice of the passing of the by-law and has provided a return address.
2. The Minister.
3. Unless notice is given under paragraph 2 of subsection (2),
    i. the clerk of every municipality having jurisdiction within the area to which the by-law applies, and
    ii. the secretary of every board having jurisdiction within the area to which the by-law applies.

(5) Each notice shall set out the following:

1. A statement that the board has passed an education development charge by-law.
2. A statement setting out when the by-law was passed and what its number is.
3. A statement that any person or organization may appeal the by-law to the Ontario Municipal Board under section 257.65 of the Act by filing with the secretary of the board a notice of appeal setting out the objection to the by-law and the reasons supporting the objection.
4. A statement setting out what the last day for appealing the by-law is.
5. An explanation of the education development charges imposed by the by-law on residential development and non-residential development.

6. A description of the lands to which the by-lay applies.
7. A key map showing the lands to which the by-law applies or an explanation of why a key map is not provided.
8. An explanation of where and when persons may examine a copy of the by-law.
9. A statement that notice of a proposed by-law amending the education development charge by-law or the passage of such an amending by-law is not required to be given to any person or organization, other than to certain clerks of municipalities or secretaries of school boards, unless the person or organization gives the secretary of the board a written request for notice of any amendments to the education development charge by-law and has provided a return address.

PART IV

AMENDMENT TO BY-LAW

Re Determination of Education Development Charges

13. (1) This section applies if an amendment to an education development charge by-law would change any of the rates for determining the amount of an education development charge.

(2) Section 7 applies with the following modifications and such other modifications as are necessary:

1. References to the 15 years referred to in paragraph 1 of section 7 shall be deemed to be references to the portion of the 15 years immediately following the day the board intends to have the amending by-law come into force.
2. The estimate under paragraph 5 of section 7 shall be an estimate of the balance immediately before the day the board intends to have the amending by-law come into force.

Notice of Proposed Amendment to By-Law

14. (1) This section applies to the notices relating to a proposed by-law amending an education development charge by-law that a board is required to give under section 257.72 of the Act.

(2) Notice shall be given to the following:

1. Every person and organization that has given the secretary of the board a written request for notice of any amendments to the education development charge by-law and has provided a return address.
2. The clerk of every municipality having jurisdiction within the area to which the education development charge by-law applies.
3. The secretary of every board having jurisdiction within the area to which the education development charge by-law, as amended, applies.

(3) Notice to a person or organization described in paragraph 1 of subsection (2) shall be given by personal service, fax or mail.

(4) Notice to a person described in paragraph 2 or 3 of subsection (2) shall be given by personal service, fax or mail or by publication in a newspaper that is, in the secretary of the board's opinion, of sufficiently general circulation in the area to which the education development charge by-law applies to give the public reasonable notice.

(5) Each notice shall set out the following:
1. A statement that the board proposes to amend the education development charge by-law.
2. An explanation of the education development charges imposed by the education development charge by-law on residential development and non-residential development.
3. An explanation of the proposed amending by-law.
4. A description of the lands to which the education development charge by-law applies.
5. A key map showing the lands to which the education development charge by-law applies or an explanation of why a key map is not provided.
6. If the lands to which the education development charge by-law would apply will be different if the proposed amending by-law is passed, a description of the lands to which the education development charge by-law, as amended, would apply and a key map showing those lands or an explanation of why a key map is not provided.
7. An explanation of where and when persons may examine a copy of the proposed amending by-law.

Notice of the Passage of Amending By-Law

15. (1) This section applies to the notices relating to the passage of a by-law amending an education development charge by-law that the secretary of a board is required to give under section 257.73 of the Act.

(2) Notice shall be given to the following:
1. Every person and organization that has given the secretary of the board a written request for notice of any amendments to the education development charge by-law and has provided a return address.
2. The Minister.
3. The clerk of every municipality having jurisdiction within the area to which the education development charge by-law, as amended, applies.
4. The secretary of every board having jurisdiction within the area to which the education development charge by-law, as amended, applies.

(3) Notice to a person or organization described in paragraph 1 or 2 of subsection (2) shall be given by personal service, fax or mail.

(4) Notice to a person described in paragraph 3 or 4 of subsection (2) shall be given by personal service, fax or mail or by publication in a newspaper that is, in the secretary of the board's opinion, of sufficiently general circulation in the area to which the education development charge by-law applies to give the public reasonable notice.

(5) Each notice shall set out the following:
1. A statement that the board has passed a by-law amending the education development charge by-law.
2. A statement setting out when the amending by-law was passed and what its number is.
3. A statement that any person or organization may appeal the amending by-law to the Ontario Municipal Board under section 257.74 of the Act by filing with the secretary of the board a notice of appeal setting out the objection to the amending by-law and the reasons supporting the objection.
4. A statement setting out what the last day for appealing the amending by-law is.
5. A statement that an appeal may not raise an issue that could have been raised in an appeal of the education development charge by-law under section 257.65 of the Act.

PART V

MISCELLANEOUS

Education Development Charge Reserve Fund

16. (1) A board shall, under section 257.82 of the Act, establish an education development charge reserve fund established under subsection (1) for the area to which an education development charge by-law applies.

(2) Money from an education development charge reserve fund may be used only,

(a) for growth-related net education land costs;
(b) as provided for under clause 241(1)(a) or section 257.99 of the Act;
(c) to pay the reasonable costs of preparing, revising and distributing the pamphlet for the by-law as required under section 21;
(d) to pay the service charges of a financial institution relating to the reserve fund; or
(e) if an education development charge has been paid but the building permit for the development is revoked, to refund the education development charge plus interest at a rate not exceeding the rate prescribed under section 18.

O. Reg. 473/98, s. 1.

16.1 (1) If paragraph 4 of section 3 of Ontario Regulation 446/98 applies to the proceeds of a sale, lease or other disposition of real property by a board, the board shall establish an education development charge reserve fund.

(2) Money from an education development charge reserve fund established under subsection (1) may be used only to fund costs that meet all of the following criteria:

1. The costs are education land costs.
2. The costs are growth-related net education capital costs within the meaning of Part III of the *Development Charges Act* as it read on January 31, 1998.
3. The costs are incurred for the purpose of acquiring land or an interest in land in the region prescribed under clause 257.101(d) of the Act in which the real property referred to in subsection (1) is located. O. Reg. 473/98, s. 2.

Expiry of By-Laws—Special Rule

17. (1) This section governs the expiry of an education development charge by-law of a board (the "new by-law") if, when the new by-law is passed, an education development charge by-law of another board (an "existing overlapping by-law") applies to any part of the area to which the new by-law applies.

(2) The new by-law expires on the earliest of the expiry dates of the existing overlapping by-laws, as they read on the day the new by-law is passed.

(3) For greater certainty, a by-law continued under section 257.103 of the Act is not an existing overlapping by-law.

Interest

18. The interest rate that shall be paid under subsections 257.69(3) and 257.90(2) of the Act and the minimum interest rate that boards shall pay under section 257.99 of the Act is the lowest prime rate reported to the Bank of Canada by any of the banks listed in Schedule I to the *Bank Act* (Canada) at the beginning of the period for which interest is to be paid.

Regions

19. (1) The area of the jurisdiction of a board is divided into regions for the purposes of section 257.57 of the Act in accordance with the following:
1. The part of the jurisdiction that is in the area described in an item of the Schedule to this Regulation is a region.
2. The part of the jurisdiction that is not in any area described in an item of the Schedule to this Regulation is a region.

(2) The references in the Schedule to municipalities or areas are references to those municipalities or areas as they were on December 31, 1997, except where a contrary intention appears.

Monthly Reports

20. (1) The following information, as it relates to land in the municipality, is prescribed as information to be included in a monthly report under section 257.97 of the Act:
1. The total education development charges that are collected in respect of residential development.
2. The number of building permits, for each type of new dwelling unit the board identified under paragraph 2 of section 7, in respect of which education development charges were imposed.
3. The location of the lands to which the building permits described in paragraph 2 pertained.
4. The total education development charges collected in respect of non-residential development.

5. The number of building permits issued for non-residential development in respect of which an education development charge is imposed by the board.
6. The total gross floor area of the non-residential development in respect of which education development charges, determined using a rate applied to the gross floor area of the development, are imposed by the board. The total gross floor area shall not include the gross floor area of a development with respect to which subsection 257.55(3) of the Act or subsection 5(2) of this Regulation applies.
7. The total declared value of the non-residential development in respect of which education development charges, determined using a rate applied to the declared value of the development, are imposed by the board. The total declared value shall not include the declared value of a development with respect to which subsection 257.55(3) of the Act or subsection 5(2) of this Regulation applies.
8. For each development with respect to which subsection 257.55(3) of the Act applies and in respect of which education development charges are imposed by the board,
    i. the gross floor area of the existing building,
    ii. the gross floor area of the enlargement, and
    iii. if the education development charges are determined using a rate applied to the declared value of the development, the declared value upon which the charges for the development are determined.
9. For each development with respect to which subsection 5(2) of this Regulation applies and in respect of which education development charges are imposed by the board,
    i. the gross floor area of the non-residential part of the building being replaced,
    ii. the gross floor area of the non-residential part of the replacement building, and
    iii. if the education development charges are determined using a rate applied to the declared value of the development, the declared value upon which the charges for the development are determined.
10. The number of building permits issued for residential development in an area to which the education development charge by-law applies in respect of which no education development charge is imposed.
11. The number of building permits issued for non-residential development in an area to which the education development charge by-law applies in respect of which no education development charge is imposed.

(2) The report shall cover the period,
(a) beginning at the end of the period covering by the previous report by the municipality or, if there was no previous report, beginning on the first day that an education development charge by-law of the board applied to land in the municipality;
(b) ending at the end of the 25th day of the month before the month in which the report is due.

Pamphlets Explaining By-Law

21. (1) A board shall prepare a pamphlet for each education development charge by-law in force setting out,
(a) a description of the general purpose for which the education development charges under the by-law are being imposed; and

(b) the rules for determining if an education development charge is payable in a particular case and for determining the amount of the charge.

(2) The board shall prepare the pamphlet,

(a) if the by-law is not appealed to the Ontario Municipal Board, within 60 days after the by-law comes into force;

(b) if the by-law is appealed to the Ontario Municipal Board, within 60 days after the Ontario Municipal Board's decision or, if the Ontario Municipal Board orders the board to amend the by-law, within 60 days after the board does so.

(3) If an education development charge by-law is amended, the board shall revise the pamphlet for the by-law as necessary.

(4) If the board is required to revise the pamphlet, it shall do so,

(a) if the amending by-law is not appealed to the Ontario Municipal Board, within 60 days after the amending by-law comes into force;

(b) if the amending by-law is appealed to the Ontario Municipal Board, within 60 days after the Ontario Municipal Board's decision or, if the Ontario Municipal Board orders the board to amend the amending by-law, within 60 days after the board does so.

(5) Upon preparing or revising a pamphlet, the board shall give a copy of the pamphlet to the Minister.

(6) The board shall give a copy of the most recent pamphlet, without charge, to any person who requests one.

(7) The board may charge a fee for additional copies of a pamphlet given to the person but the fee must be no more than is needed to pay for the cost of the additional copies.

(8) A person may reproduce and distribute the pamphlet in any form.

PART VI

TRANSITION FROM OLD DEVELOPMENT CHARGES ACT

Successor Boards

22. (1) Each board set out in column 2 of the following table is prescribed as a successor board of the corresponding old board set out in column 1 for the purposes of Division E of Part IX of the Act.

(2) For the purposes of this Part, the predecessor of a board set out in Column 2 of the table referred to in subsection (1) is the corresponding old board set out in Column 1.

Item	Column 1 Old Boards	Column 2 Successor Boards
1.	The York Region Board of Education	English-language Public District School Board No. 16 Conseil de district des écoles publiques de langue française n° 58

Item	Column 1 Old Boards	Column 2 Successor Boards
2.	The York Region Roman Catholic Separate School Board/Conseil des écoles séparées catholiques de la région de York	English-language Separate District School Board No. 42 Conseil de district des écoles séparées de langue française n° 64
3.	The Carleton Board of Education	English-language Public District School Board No. 25
4.	The Carleton Roman Catholic Separate School Board	English-language Separate District School Board No. 53
5.	The Durham Board of Education	English-language Public District School Board No. 13 Conseil de district des écoles publiques de langue française n° 58
6.	The Durham Region Roman Catholic Separate School Board/Conseil des écolees séparées catholiques de la région de Durham	English-language Separate District School Board No. 45 Conseil de district des écoles séparées de langue française n° 64
7.	The Halton Board of Education	English-language Public District School Board No. 20 Conseil de district des écoles publiques de langue française n° 58
8.	The Halton Roman Catholic Separate School Board/Conseil des écoles catholiques de Halton	English-language Separate District School Board No. 46 Conseil de district des écoles séparées de langue française n° 64
9.	The Peel Board of Education	English-language Public District School Board No. 19 Conseil de district des écoles publiques de langue française n° 58
10.	The Dufferin County Board of Education	English-language Public District School Board No. 18 Conseil de district des écoles publiques de langue française n° 58
11.	The Dufferin-Peel Roman Catholic Separate School Board/Conseil des écoles séparées catholiques de Dufferin & Peel	English-language Separate District School Board No. 43 Conseil de district des écoles séparées de langue française n° 64

Item	Column 1 Old Boards	Column 2 Successor Boards
12.	The Wentworth County Board of Education	English-language Public District School Board No. 21 Conseil de district des écoles publiques de langue française n° 58
13.	The Hamilton-Wentworth Roman Catholic Separate School Board/ Le conseil des écoles séparées catholiques romaines de Hamilton-Wentworth	English-language Separate District School Board No. 47 Conseil de district des écoles séparées de langue française n° 64
14.	Le Conseil des écoles publiques d'Ottawa-Carleton	Conseil de district des écoles publiques de langue française n° 59
15.	Conseil des écoles catholiques de langue française de la région d'Ottawa-Carleton	Conseil de district des écoles séparées de langue française n° 66

O. Reg. 473/98, s. 3.

Joint Education Development Charge Accounts

23. (1) For each joint education development charge account held by old boards set out in column 1 of the table to section 22 on December 31, 1997, the successor boards to the old boards shall establish an education development charge account to be held jointly by the successor boards.

(2) If, under the old Act, the amounts collected under an education development charge by-law would have been deposited into a joint education development charge account, the amounts paid under the by-law, as continued under section 257.103 of the Act, shall be deposited into the corresponding education development charge account established under subsection (1).

(3) The *Development Charges Act* and Regulation 268 of the Revised Regulations of Ontario, 1990, as they read on January 31, 1998, continue to apply, with necessary modifications, to money collected by the treasurer of a municipality under an education development charges by-law continued under section 257.103 of the Act and to a joint education development charge account established under subsection (1), subject to the following rules:

1. In addition to the money that a successor board may withdraw under subsection 5(7), of Regulation 268 of the Revised Regulations of Ontario, 1990 as it read on January 31, 1998 from the account established under subsection (1), the successor board may withdraw from the account an amount that will be applied to costs that meet all of the following criteria:
    i. The costs are education land costs.

ii. The costs are growth-related net education capital costs within the meaning of Part III of the *Development Charges Act* as it read on January 31, 1998.

iii. The costs are incurred for the purpose of acquiring land or an interest in land in the area to which applied the successor board's predecessor by-law for the account established under subsection (1).

2. Subsection 5(6) of Regulation 268 of the Revised Regulations of Ontario, 1990 as it read on January 31, 1998 does not apply to withdrawals under paragraph 1.

3. The total amount that may be withdrawn under paragraph 1 by a successor board shall not exceed the amount determined in accordance with the following formula:

$$\frac{A \times B \times (D + E + F + G + H + I - J - K - L - M - N - P - Q)}{B + C}$$

where,

A = the factor set out in Column 3 of the Table to this section opposite the name of the successor board set out in Column 1 and the name of the successor board's predecessor set out in Column 2,

B = the revenue raised by charges imposed by the successor board's predecessor by-law for the account established under subsection (1),

C = the revenue raised by charges imposed by the other education development charge by-law under which amounts were deposited into the predecessor account of the account established under subsection (1),

D = the income earned by the predecessor account of the account established under subsection (1),

E = the income that has been earned by the account established under subsection (1),

F = the future income that will be earned by the account established under subsection (1),

G = the sum of all the amounts that were deposited into the predecessor account of the account established under subsection (1),

H = the sum of all the amounts that have been deposited by the treasurer of a municipality into the account established under subsection (1),

I = the sum of all future amounts that will be deposited by the treasurer of a municipality into the account established under subsection (1),

J = the sum of all the amounts that were withdrawn from the predecessor account of the account established under subsection (1) under subsection 5(7) of Regulation 268 of the Revised Regulations of Ontario, 1990 as it read on January 31, 1998,

K = the sum of all the amounts that have been withdrawn from the account established under subsection (1) under subsection 5(7) of Regulation 268 of the Revised Regulations of Ontario, 1990 as it read on January 31, 1998,

L = the sum of all future amounts that will be withdrawn from the account established under subsection (1) under subsection 5(7) of Regulation 268 of the Revised Regulations of Ontario, 1990 as it read on January 31, 1998,

M = the sum of all future amounts that will be withdrawn under clause (6)(a) from reserve funds established under paragraph 1 of subsection (4) to which money will be distributed under subsection (5) from the account established under subsection (1),

N = the sum of all the amounts that were refunded from the predecessor account of the account established under subsection (1), including interest,

P = the sum of all the amounts that have been refunded from the account established under subsection (1), including interest,

Q = the sum of all future amounts that will be refunded from the account established under subsection (1), including interest.

(4) The following rules apply if an education development charge by-law is repealed or expires and amounts paid under the by-law were required, before it was repealed or expired, to be deposited into an education development charge account established under subsection (1):

1. The successor board whose by-law was repealed or expired shall establish an education development charge reserve fund that is in addition to any other education development charge reserve fund that the board may have established.

2. If, after the repeal or expiry, no amounts under an education development charge by-law of any other board will be required to be deposited into the education development charge account, a surplus in the account shall be distributed in accordance with subsection (5) to the education development charge reserve funds that have been established in respect of the account under paragraph 1.

(5) If paragraph 2 of subsection (4) requires a surplus in an education development charge account established under subsection (1) to be distributed in accordance with this subsection, the surplus shall be distributed so that the education development charge reserve fund established by each successor board under paragraph 1 of subsection (4) in respect of the account receives from the account the amount determined in accordance with the following formula:

$$\frac{A \times B \times (D + E + F + G - H - I - J - K - L)}{B + C} - M$$

where,

A = the factor set out in Column 3 of the Table to this section opposite the name of the successor board set out in Column 1 and the name of the successor board's predecessor set out in Column 2,

B = the revenue raised by charges imposed by the successor board's predecessor by-law for the account established under subsection (1),

C = the revenue raised by charges imposed by the other education development charge by-law under which amounts were deposited into the predecessor account of the account established under subsection (1),

D = the income earned by the predecessor account of the account established under subsection (1),

E = the income that has been earned by the account established under subsection (1),

F = the sum of all the amounts that were deposited into the predecessor account of the account established under subsection (1),

G = the sum of all the amounts that have been deposited by the treasurer of a municipality into the account established under subsection (1),

H = the sum of all the amounts that were withdrawn from the predecessor account of the account established under subsection (1) under subsection 5(7) of Regulation 268 of the Revised Regulations of Ontario, 1990 as it read on January 31, 1998,

I = the sum of all the amounts that have been withdrawn from the account established under subsection (1) under subsection 5(7) of Regulation 268 of the Revised Regulations of Ontario, 1990 as it read on January 31, 1998,

J = the sum of all future amounts that will be withdrawn under clause (6)(a) from reserve funds established under paragraph 1 of subsection (4) to which money will be distributed under this subsection from the account established under subsection (1),

K = the sum of all the amounts that were refunded from the predecessor account of the account established under subsection (1), including interest,

L = the sum of all the amounts that have been refunded from the account established under subsection (1), including interest,

M = the total of all the amounts that have been withdrawn from the account established under subsection (1) by the successor board under paragraph 1 of subsection (3).

(6) Money from an education development charge reserve fund established under paragraph 1 of subsection (4) may be used only to,

(a) pay amounts that are required to be paid under agreements entered into on or before the date referred to in subsection 257.103(4) of the Act and that could have been withdrawn under subsection 5(7) of Regulation 268 as it read on January 31, 1998 from the account established under subsection (1) or from the predecessor account of the account established under subsection (1); or

(b) fund costs that meet all of the following criteria:
  1. The costs are education land costs.
  2. The costs are growth-related net education capital costs within the meaning of Part III of the *Development Charges Act* as it read on January 31, 1998.
  3. The costs are incurred for the purpose of acquiring land or an interest in land in the area to which applied the successor board's predecessor by-law for the account established under subsection (1).

(6.1) For the purposes of paragraph 5 of section 7, if a board proposes to pass a new education development charge by-law for all or part of an area to which, when the new by-law comes into force, an education development charge by-law of the board that was continued under subsection 257.103(2) of the Act will still apply, the board's estimate shall be an estimate of the amounts that will be distributed under subsection (5) to education development charge reserve funds established by the board on the expiry or repeal of the continued by-law, less any amount that the board has entered into an agreement to pay and that the board is authorized to withdraw but has not yet withdrawn from the education development charge accounts established under subsection (1) in respect of the continued by-law.

(6.2) For the purposes of paragraph 5 of section 7, if a board proposes to pass a new education development charge by-law for all or part of an area in respect of which, when the new by-law comes into force, money from education development charge reserve funds established under paragraph 1 of subsection (4) may be used, the board's estimate shall be an estimate of the amount that will be in the reserve funds immediately before the new by-law comes into force, less any amount that the board has entered into an agreement to pay and that the board is authorized to withdraw but has not yet withdrawn from the reserve funds.

(7) For the purposes of the application of the provisions referred to in subsection 257.103(3) of the Act, references in those provisions to an education development charge reserve fund shall be deemed to be references to an education development charge reserve amount.

(8) In this section,

"predecessor account" means, with respect to an account established under subsection (1), the joint account established under the *Development Charges Act*, as it read on January 31, 1998, into which amounts were deposited that, under subsection (2), are required to be deposited into the account established under subsection (1);

"predecessor by-law" means, with respect to a successor board and an account established under subsection (1), the education development charge by-law of the successor board's predecessor under which amounts were deposited into the predecessor account of the account established under subsection (1).

Table

Item	Column 1 Successor Board	Column 2 Predecessor	Column 3 Factor
1.	Conseil de district des écoles publiques de langue française no° 59	Le Conseil des écoles publiques d'Ottawa-Carleton	1.00000
2.	Conseil scolaire de district catholique Centre-Sud	The Dufferin-Peel Roman Catholic Separate School Board	0.01685
3.	Conseil scolaire de district catholique Centre-Sud	The Durham Region Roman Catholic Separate School Board	0.03843
4.	Conseil scolaire de district catholique Centre-Sud	The Halton Roman Catholic Separate School Board	0.03633
5.	Conseil scolaire de district catholique Centre-Sud	The Hamilton-Wentworth Roman Catholic Separate School Board	0.02826
6.	Conseil scolaire de district catholique Centre-Sud	The York Region Roman Catholic Separate School Board	0.02061
7.	Conseil scolaire de district catholique du Centre-Est de l'Ontario	Conseil des écoles catholiques de langue française de la région d'Ottawa-Carleton	1.00000
8.	Conseil scolaire de district du Centre Sud-Ouest	The Dufferin County Board of Education	0.00410

S. 24   REGULATIONS UNDER THE EDUCATION ACT

Item	Column 1 Successor Board	Column 2 Predecessor	Column 3 Factor
9.	Conseil scolaire de district du Centre Sud-Ouest	The Durham Board of Education	0.00910
10.	Conseil scolaire de district du Centre Sud-Ouest	The Halton Board of Education	0.00860
11.	Conseil scolaire de district du Centre Sud-Ouest	The Peel Board of Education	0.01050
12.	Conseil scolaire de district du Centre Sud-Ouest	The Wentworth County Board of Education	0.00680
13.	Conseil scolaire de district du Centre Sud-Ouest	The York Region Board of Education	0.00840
14.	Dufferin-Peel Catholic District School Board	The Dufferin-Peel Roman Catholic Separate School Board	0.98315
15.	Durham Catholic District School Board	The Durham Region Roman Catholic Separate School Board	0.96157
16.	Durham District School Board	The Durham Board of Education	0.99090
17.	Halton Catholic District School Board	The Halton Roman Catholic Separate School Board	0.96367
18.	Halton District School Board	The Halton Board of Education	0.99140
19.	Hamilton-Wentworth Catholic District School Board	The Hamilton-Wentworth Roman Catholic Separate School Board	0.97174
20.	Hamilton-Wentworth District School Board	The Wentworth County Board of Education	0.99320
21.	Ottawa-Carleton Catholic District School Board	The Carleton Roman Catholic Separate School Board	1.00000
22.	Ottawa-Carleton District School Board	The Carleton Board of Education	1.00000
23.	Peel District School Board	The Peel Board of Education	0.98950
24.	Upper Grand District School Board	The Dufferin County Board of Education	0.99590
25.	York Catholic District School Board	The York Region Roman Catholic Separate School Board	0.97939
26.	York Region District School Board	The York Region Board of Education	0.99160

O. Reg. 473, s. 4.

Monthly Reports for Continued By-Laws

24. The following apply with respect to a report required under section 257.97 of the Act as that section applies under subsection 257.103(3) of the Act:

REGULATION 20/98 **Schedule**

1. The period that the report must cover is the period referred to in subsection 37(5) of the old Act.
2. The information that the report shall contain is the information that was prescribed under section 14 of Regulation 268 of the Revised Regulations of Ontario, 1990, as it read on January 31, 1998.

PART VII

COMMENCEMENT

25. This Regulation comes into force on February 1, 1998.

SCHEDULE (REGIONS)

Northern Ontario

1. The area of jurisdiction of the former Atikokan Board of Education as it existed on December 31, 1997.
2. The area of jurisdiction of the former Beardmore, Geraldton, Longlac and Area Board of Education as it existed on December 31, 1997.
3. The area of jurisdiction of the former Central Algoma Board of Education as it existed on December 31, 1997.
4. The area of jurisdiction of the former Chapleau Board of Education as it existed on December 31, 1997.
5. The area of jurisdiction of the former Cochrane-Iroquois Falls, Black River-Matheson Board of Education as it existed on December 31, 1997.
6. The area of jurisdiction of the former Dryden Board of Education as it existed on December 31, 1997.
7. The area of jurisdiction of the former East Parry Sound Board of Education as it existed on December 31, 1997.
8. The area of jurisdiction of the former Espanola Board of Education as it existed on December 31, 1997.
9. The area of jurisdiction of the former Fort Frances-Rainy River Board of Education as it existed on December 31, 1997.
10. The area of jurisdiction of the former Hearst Board of Education as it existed on December 31, 1997.
11. The area of jurisdiction of the former Horneypayne Board of Education as it existed on December 31, 1997.
12. The area of jurisdiction of the former Kapuskasing-Smooth Rock Falls and District Board of Education as it existed on December 31, 1997.
13. The area of jurisdiction of the former Kenora Board of Education as it existed on December 31, 1997.
14. The area of jurisdiction of the former Kirkland Lake Board of Education as it existed on December 31, 1997.

Schedule
REGULATIONS UNDER THE EDUCATION ACT

15. The area of jurisdiction of the former Lake Superior Board of Education as it existed on December 31, 1997.
16. The area of jurisdiction of the former Lakehead Board of Education as it existed on December 31, 1997.
17. The area of jurisdiction of the former Manitoulin Board of Education as it existed on December 31, 1997.
18. The area of jurisdiction of the former Michipicoten Board of Education as it existed on December 31, 1997.
19. The area of jurisdiction of the former Muskoka Board of Education as it existed on December 31, 1997.
20. The area of jurisdiction of the former Nipigon-Red Rock Board of Education as it existed on December 31, 1997.
21. The area of jurisdiction of the former Nipissing Board of Education as it existed on December 31, 1997.
22. The area of jurisdiction of the former North Shore Board of Education as it existed on December 31, 1997.
23. The area of jurisdiction of the former Red Lake Board of Education as it existed on December 31, 1997.
24. The area of jurisdiction of the former Sault Ste. Marie Board of Education as it existed on December 31, 1997.
25. The area of jurisdiction of the former Sudbury Board of Education as it existed on December 31, 1997.
26. The area of jurisdiction of the former Timiskaming Board of Education as it existed on December 31, 1997.
27. The area of jurisdiction of the former Timmins Board of Education as it existed on December 31, 1997.
28. The area of jurisdiction of the former West Parry School Board of Education as it existed on December 31, 1997.
29. In the Territorial District of Nipissing, the Township of Airy and the geographic townships of Sabine, Murchison, Lyell and Dickens.

Counties

30. The County of Brant.
31. The County of Bruce.
32. The County of Dufferin.
33. The County of Elgin.
34. The County of Essex, excluding the City of Windsor and including the Township of Pelee.
35. The County of Frontenac.
36. The County of Grey.
37. The County of Haliburton.
38. The County of Hastings.
39. The County of Huron.
40. The County of Kent.

REGULATION 20/98 — Schedule

41. The County of Lambton.
42. The County of Lanark.
43. The United Counties of Leeds and Grenville.
44. The County of Lennox and Addington.
45. The County of Middlesex, excluding the City of London.
46. Northumberland County and the Municipality of Clarington in the Regional Municipality of Durham.
47. The County of Oxford.
48. The County of Perth.
49. The County of Peterborough.
50. The United Counties of Prescott and Russell.
51. The County of Prince Edward.
52. The County of Renfrew.
53. The County of Simcoe.
54. The United Counties of Stormont, Dundas and Glengarry.
55. The County of Victoria.
56. The County of Wellington.

Regional municipalities

57. The Regional Municipality of Durham, except for the Municipality of Clarington.
58. The portion of the Regional Municipality of Haldimand-Norfolk that on December 31, 1997 was the school division of The Haldimand County Board of Education.
59. The portion of the Regional Municipality of Haldimand-Norfolk that on December 31, 1997 was the school division of The Norfolk County Board of Education.
60. The Regional Municipality of Halton.
61. The Regional Municipality of Hamilton-Wentworth, excluding the City of Hamilton.
62. The portion of the Regional Municipality of Niagara that on December 31, 1997 was the school division of The Lincoln County Board of Education.
63. The portion of the Regional Municipality of Niagara that on December 31, 1997 was the school division of The Niagara South Board of Education.
64. The Regional Municipality of Ottawa-Carleton, excluding the City of Ottawa, the City of Vanier and the Village of Rockliffe Park.
65. The Regional Municipality of Peel.
66. The Regional Municipality of Waterloo.
67. The Regional Municipality of York.

Cities

68. The City of Hamilton.
69. The City of London.
70. The City of Ottawa, the City of Vanier and the Village of Rockliffe Park.
71. The City of Toronto as it existed on January 1, 1998.
72. The City of Windsor.

REGULATION 21/98
DEVELOPMENT CHARGES ACT
O. Reg. 21/98

Note to the Reader: This Regulation is included to indicate that certain regulatory provisions that applied to school boards have been revoked.

1. Regulation 268 of the Revised Regulation of Ontario, 1990 and Ontario Regulations 229/92, 813/94, 15/96 and 475/97 are revoked.

2. This Regulation comes into force on February 1, 1998.

REGULATION 79/98
BY-ELECTIONS
O. Reg. 79/98

1. In this Regulation,

"geographic area" means a geographic area established for the 1997 regular election under the Act.

2. This Regulation applies to by-election, within the meaning of the *Municipal Elections Act, 1996*, held on or before March 31, 2000 to fill one or more offices on a district school board.

3. (1) Territory that is without municipal organization on the first day of the period described in paragraph 2 of subsection 65(4) of the *Municipal Elections Act, 1996* and that is the same as or is a part of territory deemed to be a distinct municipality under section 15 of Ontario Regulation 250/97 is deemed to be a district municipality for the purposes of this Regulation.

(2) Territory that is without municipal organization on the first day of the period described in paragraph 2 of subsection 65(4) of the *Municipal Elections Act, 1996* and that is the same as or is a part of territory deemed to be attached to a district municipality under section 15 of Ontario Regulation 250/97 is deemed to be attached to the same district municipality for the purposes of this Regulation.

4. (1) If a geographic area in which a by-election is to be held is composed of all or part of two or more municipalities, the nominations shall be submitted to the clerk of the municipality to whom nominations were submitted for the geographic area at the 1997 regular election, or to such other clerk as may have assumed his or her responsibilities in relation to by-elections.

(2) The clerk referred to in subsection (1) is the clerk for the purposes of section 76 of the *Municipal Elections Act, 1996*.

(3) As soon as possible after the closing of nominations, the clerk referred to in subsection (1) shall provide a list of certified candidates to the clerk of each municipality that is included in the geographic area.

(4) If the distance between the residence of a person seeking nomination and the office for submission of nominations is greater than 100 kilometres, the clerk referred to in subsection (1) shall delegate such of his or her powers as may be necessary to the clerk of the municipality in which the person resides to permit the person or the person's agent to file a nomination at the latter clerk's office.

(5) The clerk of each municipality in the geographic area is responsible for conducting the election in the municipality.

(6) The clerk of each municipality in the geographic area shall report the vote recorded to the clerk referred to in subsection (1), who shall prepare the final summary and announce the result of the vote.

(7) The clerk referred to in subsection (1) shall forward the results of the vote and the names of the candidates who have been elected to the Education Improvement Commission.

5. Officers appointed by a board have all the same powers and duties with respect to by-elections of members of the board in areas deemed to be district municipalities as similar officers have in a municipality with respect to by-elections.

6. Officers of a municipality have all the same powers and duties with respect to by-elections of members of a board in areas deemed to be attached to the municipality as they have with respect to by-elections in any part of the area of jurisdiction of the board that is within the municipality.

7. A clerk of a municipality may delegate any of his or her powers and duties under this Regulation to election officials for another municipality, including officials acting under section 5 or 6 of this Regulation.

REGULATION 90/98
PRINCIPALS AND VICE-PRINCIPALS — REDUNDANCY AND REASSIGNMENT
O. Reg. 90/98

1. (1) This Regulation applies when a board declares the position of a principal or vice-principal to be redundant.

(2) This Regulation applies when any of the following positions is declared to be redundant:

1. Principal or vice-principal of continuing education courses and classes that are offered for credit during the day on instructional days.
2. Principal or vice-principal who administers the board's program of continuing education courses and classes that are offered for credit.

(3) This Regulation does not apply when the position of principal or vice-principal of continuing education courses and classes that is not described in subsection (2) is declared to be redundant.

(4) A position is redundant if the board decides that the position is no longer required because of,

(a) the implementation of a restructuring plan that eliminates the position or merges it with another position;

(b) a reduction in the number of classes or schools of the board; or

(c) a change in the board's duties under any Act.

2. (1) The board shall give the affected principal or vice-principal notice in writing that his or her position is declared to be redundant.

(2) The notice must be given at least 90 days before the date on which the position becomes redundant.

(3) The notice must specify the date on which the position becomes redundant.

(4) The board may rescind the notice at any time.

(5) A notice given under this section is not notice of the termination of the principal's or vice-principal's permanent teacher's contract or probationary teacher's contract.

(6) Subsection (5) is revoked on September 1, 1998.

3. (1) The board shall assign the principal or vice-principal to another position for which he or she is qualified.

(2) The principal or vice-principal may be assigned to a position in a teachers' bargaining unit if the position is vacant after the procedures under the applicable collective agreement for filling it have been exhausted.

(3) The assignment take effect on the date on which the principal's or vice-principal's position becomes redundant, or on such other date as the board and the principal or vice-principle may agree upon.

4. (1) The following rule applies if the principal or vice-principal is employed by a district school board and is assigned to a position in which he or she is employed, other than as a principal or vice-principal, to teach:

S. 5 REGULATIONS UNDER THE EDUCATION ACT

1. For the purpose of determining his or her seniority under the applicable collective agreement, his or her length of service when he or she begins work in the new position is the sum of,
    i. the length of his or her service before January 1, 1998 while employed by the district school board or a predecessor board to teach, and
    ii. the length of his or her service after December 31, 1997 while employed, other than as a principal or vice-principal, by the district school board or a predecessor board to teach.

(2) The following rule applies if the principal or vice-principal is employed by a school authority and is assigned to a position in which he or she is employed, other than as a principal or vice-principal, to teach:

1. For the purpose of determining his or her seniority under the applicable collective agreement, his or her length of service when he or she begins work in the new position is the sum of,
    i. the length of his or her service before January 1, 1998 while employed by the school authority to teach, and
    ii. the length of his or her service after December 31, 1997 while employed, other than as a principal or vice-principal, by the school authority to teach.

(3) The following rule applies if the principal or vice-principal is assigned to a position other than one described in subsection (1) or (2):

1. For one year after he or she begins work in the new position, he or she is entitled to be paid the salary that he or she would have been paid as principal or vice-principal.

5. On August 31, 2001, section 4 is revoked and the following substituted:

4. (1) The following rule applies if the principal or vice-principal is assigned to a position other than one described in subsecton (2):

1. For one year after he or she begins work in the new position, he or she is entitled to be paid the salary that he or she would have been paid as principal or vice-principal.

(2) Subsection (1) does not apply if the principal or vice-principal is assigned to a position in which he or she is employed, other than as a principal or vice-principal, to teach.

6. This Regulation comes into force on April 1, 1998.

REGULATION 92/98
INTERIM PAYMENTS IN RESPECT OF LEGISLATIVE GRANTS FOR THE PERIOD JANUARY 1, 1998 TO AUGUST 31, 1998
O. Reg. 92/98, as am. O. Reg. 164/98

1. (1) A district school board or school authority may, before the coming into force of a regulation prescribing the conditions governing the payment of legislative grants for educational purposes for the short year, be paid an interim payment in respect of a grant of that kind.

(2) An interim payment under subsection (1) shall not exceed the sum of,

(a) 41.6 per cent of the amount shown in the Table opposite the name of the district school board or school authority; and

(b) in the case of a district school board, the amount allocated for the short year, in respect of an allocation made under the Capital Grant Plan established and maintained by the Minister, to each old board that is the district school board's predecessor.

(3) In this Regulation,

"old board" means an old board listed in column 1 of Schedule 1 to Ontario Regulation 460/97;

"short year" means the period beginning January 1, 1998 and ending August 31, 1998. O. Reg. 164/98, s.1.

2. Secton 1 applies with respect to all of the short year, including any period before this Regulation or any amendments to it are made. O. Reg. 164/98, s. 2.

3. Regulation 299 of the Revised Regulations of Ontario, 1990 is revoked.

Table REGULATIONS UNDER THE EDUCATION ACT

TABLE

DISTRICT SCHOOL BOARDS	1998 BASE
DISTRICT SCHOOL BOARD NO. 1	53,935,080
DISTRICT SCHOOL BOARD NO. 2	73,212,554
DISTRICT SCHOOL BOARD NO. 3	73,427,340
DISTRICT SCHOOL BOARD NO. 4	66,176,949
DISTRICT SCHOOL BOARD NO. 5A	32,560,067
DISTRICT SCHOOL BOARD NO. 5B	17,039,312
DISTRICT SCHOOL BOARD NO. 6A	51,926,859
DISTRICT SCHOOL BOARD NO. 6B	17,662,984
DISTRICT SCHOOL BOARD NO. 7	93,602,665
DISTRICT SCHOOL BOARD NO. 8	73,494,941
DISTRICT SCHOOL BOARD NO. 9	125,958,926
DISTRICT SCHOOL BOARD NO. 10	103,789,101
DISTRICT SCHOOL BOARD NO. 11	278,059,738
DISTRICT SCHOOL BOARD NO. 12	530,338,599
DISTRICT SCHOOL BOARD NO. 13	205,244,832
DISTRICT SCHOOL BOARD NO. 14	144,059,023
DISTRICT SCHOOL BOARD NO. 15	76,790,937
DISTRICT SCHOOL BOARD NO. 16	173,907,200
DISTRICT SCHOOL BOARD NO. 17	157,122,519
DISTRICT SCHOOL BOARD NO. 18	107,759,707
DISTRICT SCHOOL BOARD NO. 19	238,502,098
DISTRICT SCHOOL BOARD NO. 20	106,641,309
DISTRICT SCHOOL BOARD NO. 21	175,469,197
DISTRICT SCHOOL BOARD NO. 22	149,157,051
DISTRICT SCHOOL BOARD NO. 23	114,482,261
DISTRICT SCHOOL BOARD NO. 24	172,764,217
DISTRICT SCHOOL BOARD NO. 25	242,129,284
DISTRICT SCHOOL BOARD NO. 26	144,614,474
DISTRICT SCHOOL BOARD NO. 27	90,710,912
DISTRICT SCHOOL BOARD NO. 28	44,624,479
DISTRICT SCHOOL BOARD NO. 29	76,613,476
DISTRICT SCHOOL BOARD NO. 30A	21,473,504
DISTRICT SCHOOL BOARD NO. 30B	21,782,444
DISTRICT SCHOOL BOARD NO. 31	34,312,708
DISTRICT SCHOOL BOARD NO. 32	45,171,564
DISTRICT SCHOOL BOARD NO. 33A	5,999,909
DISTRICT SCHOOL BOARD NO. 33B	5,567,120
DISTRICT SCHOOL BOARD NO. 34A	36,831,381
DISTRICT SCHOOL BOARD NO. 34B	4,939,402
DISTRICT SCHOOL BOARD NO. 35	21,771,626
DISTRICT SCHOOL BOARD NO. 36	21,527,665
DISTRICT SCHOOL BOARD NO. 37	104,524,004

TABLE

DISTRICT SCHOOL BOARDS | 1998 BASE

DISTRICT SCHOOL BOARD NO. 38	92,978,259
DISTRICT SCHOOL BOARD NO. 39	62,272,281
DISTRICT SCHOOL BOARD NO. 40	329,052,070
DISTRICT SCHOOL BOARD NO. 41	55,448,522
DISTRICT SCHOOL BOARD NO. 42	155,805,786
DISTRICT SCHOOL BOARD NO. 43	271,944,251
DISTRICT SCHOOL BOARD NO. 44	67,443,865
DISTRICT SCHOOL BOARD NO. 45	96,844,931
DISTRICT SCHOOL BOARD NO. 46	71,721,530
DISTRICT SCHOOL BOARD NO. 47	103,024,674
DISTRICT SCHOOL BOARD NO. 48	28,296,545
DISTRICT SCHOOL BOARD NO. 49	90,586,771
DISTRICT SCHOOL BOARD NO. 50	96,302,731
DISTRICT SCHOOL BOARD NO. 51	40,111,662
DISTRICT SCHOOL BOARD NO. 52	65,047,255
DISTRICT SCHOOL BOARD NO. 53	150,528,001
DISTRICT SCHOOL BOARD NO. 54	26,785,606
DISTRICT SCHOOL BOARD NO. 55	55,021,681
CONSEIL SCOLAIRE DE DISTRICT #56	5,377,628
CONSEIL SCOLAIRE DE DISTRICT #57	14,225,258
CONSEIL SCOLAIRE DE DISTRICT #58	17,999,908
CONSEIL SCOLAIRE DE DISTRICT #59	40,796,208
CONSEIL SCOLAIRE DE DISTRICT #60-A	55,960,446
CONSEIL SCOLAIRE DE DISTRICT #60-B	21,086,502
CONSEIL SCOLAIRE DE DISTRICT #61	50,135,245
CONSEIL SCOLAIRE DE DISTRICT #62	3,202,139
CONSEIL SCOLAIRE DE DISTRICT #63	30,932,965
CONSEIL SCOLAIRE DE DISTRICT #64	49,885,441
CONSEIL SCOLAIRE DE DISTRICT #65	78,815,393
CONSEIL SCOLAIRE DE DISTRICT #66	69,417,645

SCHOOL AUTHORITIES | 1998 BASE

AIRY AND SABINE DSA BOARD	183,800
ASQUITH AND GARVEY DSA BOARD	437,950
CARAMATA DSA BOARD	536,938
COLLINS DSA BOARD	269,417
CONNELL AND PONSFORD DSA BOARD	982,038
FOLEYET DSA BOARD	491,648
GOGAMA DSA BOARD	280,788
JAMES BAY LOWLANDS SECONDARY SCHOOL BD	3,477,856
KASHABOWIE DSA BOARD	62,451

TABLE

SCHOOL AUTHORITIES	1998 BASE
KILKENNY DSA BOARD	17,244
MINE CENTRE DSA BOARD	87,459
MISSARENDA DSA BOARD	243,680
MOOSE FACTORY ISLAND DSA BOARD	1,696,699
MOOSONEE DSA BOARD	2,518,481
MURCHISON AND LYELL DSA BOARD	219,488
NAKINA DSA BOARD	688,795
NORTHERN DSA BOARD	1,223,328
STURGEON LAKE DSA BOARD	78,180
SUMMER BEAVER DSA BOARD	0
UPSALA DSA BOARD	485,112
ATIKOKAN RCSS BOARD	1,546,062
DUBREUILVILLE RCSS BOARD	1,007,228
FOLEYET RCSS BOARD	603,526
GOGAMA RCSS BOARD	624,422
HORNEPAYNE RCSS BOARD	882,518
IGNACE RCSS BOARD	554,168
MOOSONEE RCSS BOARD	1,569,662
RED LAKE AREA COMBINED RCSS BOARD	1,132,151
THE PARRY SOUND RCSS BOARD	723,230
BLOORVIEW MACMILLAN SCHOOL AUTHORITY	1,841,934
CAMPBELL CHILDREN'S SCHOOL BD OF ED	323,315
CARDIFF-BICROFT RCSS BOARD	140,330
ESSEX CITY CHILDREN'S REHAB BD OF ED	655,502
NIAGARA PEN CPLD CHLD TMT CTRE B OF E	1,211,788
OTTAWA CHILDREN'S TRTMT CTRE BD OF ED	734,269
PENETANGUISHENE PROTESTANT SEP SCH BD	1,000,620
WATERLOO NORTH CHILDREN'S CTR BD OF ED	655,000

REGULATION 118/98
CLASS SIZE
O. Reg. 118/98

PART I

ELEMENTARY SCHOOL CLASSES

1. (1) In this Part,

"class" means a group of pupils who are scheduled to spend more than 50 per cent of their instructional time together during the cycle that includes October 31, but does not include a class established for exceptional pupils; ("classe")

"cycle" means the number of days for which a schedule of classes in a school continues before the schedule is repeated; ("horaire")

"part-time", in relation to a class, means a class scheduled to meet,

(a) on half-days, or

(b) on average, on three or fewer days per week. ("temps partiel")

(2) For the purposes of subsection (1), pupils include pupils enrolled in a full-time or part-time junior kindergarten or kindergarten.

(3) For the purposes of subsection (1), a class can consist of pupils enrolled in the same grade or in different grades.

(4) For the purposes of subsection (3), kindergarten and junior kindergarten are to be considered grades.

2. (1) For the purposes of subsection 170.1(1) of the Act, the average size of the elementary school classes of a board, in the aggregate, shall be determined in each year as of October 31, as follows:

1. Determine the number of pupils enrolled in classes in all elementary schools of the board.
2. Determine the number of classes in all elementary schools of the board.
3. Divide the number determined under paragraph 1 by the number determined under paragraph 2.

(2) For the purposes of paragraph 1 of subsection (1), a pupil enrolled in a part-time junior kindergarten or kindergarten class shall be counted as one-half and every other pupil shall be counted as one.

(3) For the purposes of paragraph 2 of subsection (1), a part-time junior kindergarten or kindergarten class shall be counted as one-half and every other class shall be counted as one.

PART II

SECONDARY SCHOOL CLASSES

3. (1) In this Part,

"class" means,

(a) a group of pupils,
  i. who are scheduled to be together for instructional purposes during a scheduled part of the day school program provided on instructional days, and
  (ii) who are each eligible to earn the same number of credits or credit equivalents on successfully completing the course or the part of the grade nine program that he or she is taking during that scheduled part of the day school program provided on instructional days, or
(b) a co-operative education class,

but does not include a class established for exceptional pupils; ("classe")

"co-operative education class" means a group of pupils,
  (a) who are enrolled in a co-operative education program,
  (b) who are scheduled to spend some instructional time together in school during the school year in connection with the co-operative education program, and
  (c) who are each eligible to earn the same number of credits on successfully completing the course that he or she is taking in the co-operative education program; ("class d'éducation coopérative")

"course" means a course at the secondary school level that is assigned a common course code in the list of common course codes published by the Ministry; ("cours")

"cycle" means the number of days for which a schedule of classes in a school continues before the schedule is repeated; ("horaire")

"instructional day" has the same meaning as in Regulation 304 of the Revised Regulations of Ontario, 1990. ("journée d'enseignement")

(2) For the purposes of subsection (1), a class can consist of pupils enrolled in the same grade or in different grades and in the same course or in difference courses.

(3) For the purposes of subsection (1), a pupil taking a course as an independent study course shall not be considered a class or a part of a class.

4. (1) In the case of non-semestered classes, calculations under this Part shall be based on enrolment data for the cycle that includes October 31 of the school year.

(2) In the case of semestered classes held in the first semester, calculations under this Part shall be based on enrolment data for the cycle that includes October 31 of the school year.

(3) In the case of semestered classes held in the second semester, calculations under this Part shall be based on registration data available on October 31 of the school year, for the cycle that includes March 31 of the school year.

5. For the purposes of this Part, the credit value or credit equivalent value of a class is the number of credits or credit equivalents that each pupil in the class is eligible to earn on successfully completing the course or the part of the grade nine program that he or she is taking in connection with the class.

6. For the purposes of subsections 170.1(2) of the Act, the average size of the secondary school classes of a board, in the aggregate, shall be determined in each year, as follows:

1. For each class in each secondary school of the board, multiply the number of pupils enrolled in the class by the credit value or credit equivalent value of the class.

2. Total the results obtained under paragraph 1. The result is the number of pupil credits for the board.
3. Determine the credit value or credit equivalent value of each class in each secondary school of the board.
4. Total the numbers determined under paragraph 3. The result is the number of classroom credits for the board.
5. Divide the number of pupil credits for the board, determined under paragraph 2, by the numer of classroom credits for the board, determined under paragraph 4.

PART III

REPORTING

7. (1) In time to meet the deadlines specified in sections 10 and 11, the director of education for each board shall prepare a report on the average size of classes in its elementary schools and in its secondary schools.

(2) The report shall include,

(a) the average size of the elementary school classes of the board, in the aggregate, as determined under Part I;
(b) the average size of the secondary school classes of the board, in the aggregate, as determined under Part II; and
(c) the average size of the classes in each school of the board, determined in accordance with sections 8 and 9.

8. (1) For the purposes of clause 7(2)(c), the average class size of an elementary school shall be determined as of October 31, as follows:

1. Determine the number of pupils enrolled in classes in the elementary school.
2. Determine the number of classes in elementary school.
3. Divide the number determined under paragraph 1 by the number determined under paragraph 2.

(2) Section 1 and subsections 2(2) and (3) apply with necessary modifications for the purposes of this section.

9. (1) For the purposes of clause 7(2)(c), the average class size of a secondary school shall be determined as follows:

1. For each class in the secondary school, multiply the number of pupils enrolled in the class by the credit value or credit equivalent value of the class.
2. Total the results obtained under paragraph 1. The result is the number of pupil credits for the secondary school.
3. Determine the credit value or credit equivalent value of each class in the secondary school.
4. Total the numbers determined under paragraph 3. The result is the number of classroom credits for the secondary school.
5. Divide the number of pupil credits for the secondary school, determined under

paragraph 2, by the number of classroom credits for the secondary school, determined under paragraph 4.

(2) Sections 3, 4 and 5 apply with necessary modifications for the purposes of this section.

10. (1) The director of education shall ensure that, by December 15 in each year,

(a) a copy of the report is submitted to the chair of the board;

(b) copies of the report are available to the public at the head office of the board and at the office of each school of the board; and

(c) a copy of the report is submitted to the chair of the school council for each school of the board.

(2) The director of educaton shall make the report available to the public in any additional manner that the board considers appropriate.

11. The director of education shall also ensure that, by December 15 in each year, a copy of the parts of the report that deal with the matters referred to in clauses 7(2)(a) and (b) is submitted to the Minister, in a format acceptable to the Minister.

12. Where a board does not have a director of education, the secretary of the board shall perform the duties imposed by this Part on directors of education.

REGULATION 124/98
TRANSITION ASSISTANCE GRANTS
O. Reg. 124/98

1. A board specified in column 1 of Table 1 shall be paid a grant in the amount specified in column 2 of Table 1 opposite the board's name.

TABLE 1

Item	Column 1	Column 2
1.	Conseil de district des écoles publiques de langue française n° 56	$1,250,000
2.	Conseil scolaire de district du Grand Nord de l'Ontario	1,250,000
3.	Conseil de district des écoles publiques de langue française n° 58	500,000
4.	Conseil de district des écoles publiques de langue française n° 59	350,000
5.	Conseil de district des écoles séparées de langue française n° 60A	1,250,000
6.	Conseil de district des écoles séparées de langue française n° 60B	1,000,000
7.	Conseil de district des écoles séparées de langue française n° 61	750,000
8.	Conseil de district des écoles séparées de langue française n° 62	1,000,000
9.	Conseil de district des écoles séparées de langue française n° 63	1,000,000
10.	Conseil de district des écoles séparées de langue française n° 64	1,000,000
11.	Conseil de district des écoles séparées de langue française n° 65	350,000
12.	Conseil de district des écoles séparées de langue française n° 66	350,000
13.	York Catholic District School Board	2,900,000

REGULATION 181/98
IDENTIFICATION AND PLACEMENT OF EXCEPTIONAL PUPILS

O. Reg. 181/98

PART I

GENERAL

1. (1) In this Regulation,

"committee" means a special education identification, placement and review committee established under Part II and includes a committee established under Regulation 305 of the Revised Regulations of Ontario, 1990;

"designated representative" means,

(a) in relation to a board that has a director of education, the director of education of the board, and

(b) in relation to a board that does not have a director of education, the secretary or equivalent of the board;

"parent" includes a guardian;

"special education appeal board" means a special education appeal board established under Part VI.

(2) In this Regulation, a reference to the category and definition of an exceptionality is a reference to the category and definition of the exceptionality as established under subsection 8(3) of the Act.

2. Where the time limited by this Regulation for doing anything expires or falls on a school holiday within the meaning of Regulation 304 of the Revised Regulations of Ontario, 1990, the time so limited extends to and the thing may be done on the next day following that is not a school holiday.

3. (1) Subject to subsection (2), mail shall be deemed to have been received by the person to whom it was sent on the fifth day after the day on which it was mailed.

(2) If the fifth day is a school holiday within the meaning of Regulation 304 of the Revised Regulations of Ontario, 1990, the mail shall be deemed to have been received by the person to whom it was sent on the first day after the fifth day that is not a school holiday.

4. A person or body required by this Regulation to communicate in writing to a parent or pupil shall, at the request of the parent or pupil, use a braille, large print or audio-cassette format for the communication.

5. (1) A parent of a pupil and, where the pupil is 16 years of age or older, the pupil, are entitled,

(a) to be present at and participate in all committee discussions about the pupil; and

(b) to be present when the committee's identification and placement decisions are made.

(2) A parent of a pupil and, where the pupil is 16 years of age or older, the pupil, are entitled to be present at and participate in all discussions about the pupil at the meeting held by the special education appeal board under section 28.

(3) A person who has a right under subsection (1) or (2) to participate in a discussion also has the right to have a representative present at the discussion, to speak on behalf of the person or otherwise support the person.

(4) A person who has a right under clause (1)(b) to be present also has the right to have a representative present to support the person.

(5) At least 10 days in advance of a meeting of a committee or special education appeal board, the chair of the committee or board shall give written notice of the time and place of the meeting to a parent of the pupil and, where the pupil is 16 years of age or older, the pupil.

6. (1) Subsection (2) applies when,
- (a) a board implements a placement decision under section 20;
- (b) a board implements a placement decision under section 31 following an appeal to a special education appeal board in respect of a committee decision under Part IV; or
- (c) a board implements a placement decision following an appeal to the special Education Tribunal in respect of a committee decision under Part IV.

(2) The board shall promptly notify the principal of the school at which the special education program is to be provided of the need to develop an individual education plan for the pupil in consultation with the parent and, where the pupil is 16 years of age or older, the pupil.

(3) The individual education plan must include,
- (a) specific educational expectations for the pupil;
- (b) an outline of the special education program and services to be received by the pupil; and
- (c) a statement of the methods by which the pupil's progress will be reviewed.

(4) Where the pupil is 14 years of age or older, the individual education plan must also include a plan for transition to appropriate post-secondary school activities, such as work, further education and community living.

(5) subsection (4) does not apply in respect of a pupil identified as exceptional solely on the basis of giftedness.

(6) In developing the individual education plan, the principal shall,
- (a) consult with the parent and, where the pupil is 16 years of age or older, the pupil; and
- (b) take into consideration any recommendations made by the committee or the Special Education Tribunal, as the case may be, regarding special education programs or special education services.

(7) In developing a transition plan under subsection (4), the principal shall consult with such community agencies and post-secondary educational institutions as he or she considers appropriate.

(8) Within 30 days after placement of the pupil in the program, the principal shall ensure that the plan is completed and a copy of it sent to a parent of the pupil and, where the pupil is 16 years of age or older, the pupil.

7. (1) Subsection (2) applies when,

(a) a board implements a change in placement under section 25;
(b) a board implements a change in placement under section 31 following an appeal to a special education appeal board in respect of a committee decision under Part V;
(c) a board implements a change in placement in accordance with a decision of the Special Education Tribunal following an appeal to the Special Education Tribunal in respect of a committee decision under Part V;
(d) an existing placement is confirmed in a statement of decision under Part V and a parent of the pupil consents in writing to the decision or the time period provided in section 31 for filing a notice of appeal from the decision expires without a notice of appeal being filed;
(e) an existing placement is confirmed in a decision under subsection 30(1) and a parent consents in writing to the decision or the time period provided in section 31 expires without an appeal being commenced;
(f) an existing placement is confirmed in a decision under subsection 30(1), an appeal from the decision is made under section 57 of the Act to the Special Education Tribunal and the appeal is dismissed or abandoned; or
(g) an existing placement is confirmed in an order of the Special Education Tribunal granting an appeal under section 57 of the Act.

(2) The board shall promptly notify the principal of the school at which the special education program is to be provided of the need to review the pupil's individual education plan to determine whether it needs to be updated.

(3) In reviewing the plan, the principal shall,

(a) consult with the parent and, where the pupil is 16 years of age or older, the pupil; and
(b) take into consideration any recommendations of the committee or the Special Education Tribunal, as the case may be, regarding special education programs or special education services.

(4) Where an individual education plan does not include a plan for transition to appropriate post-secondary school activities and the pupil has attained the age of 14 or will attain the age of 14 within the school year, the principal shall ensure that a transition plan is developed and included in the individual education plan.

(5) Subsection (4) does not apply in respect of a pupil identified as exceptional solely on the basis of giftedness.

(6) In reviewing an individual education plan that includes a transition plan or in developing a transition plan under subsection (4), the principal shall consult with such community agencies and post-secondary educational institutions as he or she considers appropriate.

(7) Within 30 days of an implementation of a change in placement or, where the placement is confirmed, within 30 days of receiving the notice under subsection (1), the principal shall ensure that,

(a) the plan has been reviewed and updated as appropriate;
(b) a transition plan has been added to the individual education plan where required by subsection (4); and

(c) a copy of the individual education plan has been sent to a parent of the pupil and, where the pupil is 16 years of age or older, the pupil.

8. The principal shall ensure that.the individual education plan for a pupil is included in the record kept in respect of the pupil under clause 265(d) of the Act, unless a parent of the pupil has objected in writing.

9. (1) In accordance with requirements under the *Education Act*, no pupil is to be denied an education program pending a meeting or decision under this Regulation.

(2) Where an education program is provided to a pupil pending a meeting or decision under this Regulation,

- (a) the program must be appropriate to the pupil's apparent strengths and needs;
- (b) the placement for the program must be consistent with the principles underlying section 17; and
- (c) appropriate education services must be provided to meet the pupil's apparent needs.

PART II

ESTABLISHMENT OF COMMITTEES AND COMMITTEE PROCEDURES

10. Each board shall, in accordance with section 11, establish one or more committees for the identification and placement of exceptional pupils, determine the jurisdiction of each committee and establish the manner of selecting the chair of each committee.

11. (1) A board shall appoint three or more persons to each committee that it establishes.

(2) The board shall appoint, as one of the members of each committee,

- (a) a principal employed by the board;
- (b) a supervisory officer employed by the board under Part XI of the Act; or
- (c) a supervisory officer whose services are used by the board under Part XI of the Act.

(3) A principal or supervisory officer appointed under subsection (2) may designate a person to act in his or her place as a member of the committee without the approval of the board.

(4) Only a person who is eligible to be appointed to the committee under subsection (2) may be designated to act on the committee under subsection (3).

(5) No member of the board may be appointed to a committee under subsection (2) or designated to act on the committee under subsection (3).

12. (1) A board may establish procedures for committees in addition to those set out in this Regulation.

(2) Committee decisions made under this Regulation must be consistent with the board's special education plan.

PART III

PARENTS' GUIDE

13. (1) Each board shall prepare a guide for the use and information of parents and pupils that,

(a) explains the function of a committee on a referral under Part IV and on a review under Part V;
(b) outlines the procedures set out in this Regulation or established under section 12 that a committee must follow in identifying a pupil as exceptional and in deciding the pupil's placement;
(c) explains the committee's duty to describe pupils' strengths and needs and to include, in its statements of decision, the categories and definitions of any exceptionalities it identifies;
(d) explains the function of a special education appeal board under Part VI and the right of parents to appeal committee decisions to it;
(e) lists the parent organizations that are, to the best of the board's knowledge, local associations of the board, within the meaning of Ontario Regulation 464/97;
(f) includes the names, addresses and telephone numbers of the provincial and demonstration schools in Ontario;
(g) indicates the extent to which the board provides special education programs and special education services and the extent to which it purchases those programs and services from another board;
(h) explains that no committee placement decision can be implemented unless,
  (i) a parent has consented to the decision, or
  (ii) the time limit for filing a notice of appeal in respect of the decision has expired and no such notice has been filed.

(2) The board shall. ensure that copies of the guide are available at each school in the board's jurisdiction and at the board's head office and shall provide a copy to the appropriate district office of the Ministry.

(3) The board shall, at the request of a parent or pupil, provide the parent or pupil with a guide in a braille, large print or audio-cassette format.

PART IV

REFERRAL OF PUPILS TO COMMITTEES

14. (1) The principal of the school at which a pupil is enrolled,

(a) may on written notice to a parent of the pupil; and
(b) shall at the written request of a parent of the pupil,

refer the pupil to a committee established by the board, for a decision as to whether the pupil should be identified as an exceptional pupil and, if so, what the placement of the pupil should be.

(2) Where a decision is made that a pupil is to leave a demonstration school and enter a school of a board, the superintendent of the demonstration school shall so notify the designated representative of the board.

(3) On receiving the notice under subsection (2), the designated representative of the board shall ensure that the pupil is referred to a committee established by the board, for a decision as to what the placement of the pupil should be.

(4) The superintendent of the demonstration school acting under subsection (2) and the designated representative of the board acting under subsection (3) shall use their best efforts to ensure that the committee meets as soon as possible after the decision is made to move the pupil from the demonstration school to the school of the board.

(5) Where more than one committee has been established by the board, the referral under subsection (1) or (3) shall be to the committee that the principal or the designated representative, as the case may be, considers to be the most appropriate for the pupil, having regard to the jurisdiction of the committees.

(6) Within 15 days of giving a notice under clause (1)(a) or receiving a request under clause (1)(b), the principal shall provide the parent with,
- (a) a copy of the guide prepared under section 13;
- (b) a written statement of approximately when the principal expects that a committee will meet for the first time to discuss the pupil; and
- (c) in the case of a request under clause (1)(b), a written acknowledgement of the request.

(7) Within 15 days of receiving a notification under subsection (2), the designated representative shall provide the parent with,
- (a) a copy of the notification under subsection (2);
- (b) a copy of the guide prepared under section 13; and
- (c) a written statement of approximately when the designated representative expects that a committee will meet for the first time to discuss the pupil.

15. (1) A committee that has received a referral under section 14 shall obtain and consider an educational assessment of the pupil.

(2) Subject to the *Health Care Consent Act, 1996*, the committee shall also obtain and consider a health assessment of the pupil by a qualified medical practitioner if the committee determines that the assessment is required to enable it to make a correct identification or placement decision.

(3) Subject to the *Health Care Consent Act, 1996*, the committee shall also obtain and consider a psychological assessment of the pupil if the committee determines that the assessment is required to enable it to make a correct identification or placement decision.

(4) Where the committee determines that it would be useful to do so and the pupil is less than 16 years of age, the committee shall, with the consent of a parent, interview the pupil.

(5) A parent of the pupil has a right to be present at the interview.

(6) The committee shall also consider any information about the pupil submitted to it by a parent of the pupil and, where the pupil is 16 years of age or older, the pupil.

(7) In addition to complying with this section, the committee shall consider any information submitted to it that it considers relevant.

(8) As soon as possible after the chair of the committee obtains any information relating to the pupil, the chair shall provide the information to,
- (a) a parent of the pupil; and
- (b) the pupil, where the pupil is 16 years of age or older.

(9) Subsection (8) does not apply to oral information submitted at a meeting that the committee holds in respect of the pupil in accordance with this Regulation.

16. (1) The committee may discuss any proposal for special education services or special education programs and shall do so at the request of a parent or a pupil who is 16 years of age or older.

(2) The committee may make recommendations regarding special education programs and special education services.

(3) The committee may recommend that an exceptional pupil who is 21 years of age or older remain in a secondary day school program.

(4) Despite subsections (1) to (3), the committee shall not make decisions about special education services or special education programs.

(5) Despite subsection (4), a recommendation of a committee under subsection (3) is effective for the purposes of subsection 49.2(7) of the Act.

(6) A recommendation under this section is not a decision for the purposes of subsection 26(1).

17. (1) When making a placement decision on a referral under section 14, the committee shall, before considering the option of placement in a special education class, consider whether placement in a regular class, with appropriate special education services,

(a) would meet the pupil's needs; and
(b) is consistent with parental preferences.

(2) If, after considering all of the information obtained by it or submitted to it under section 15 that it considers relevant, the committee is satisfied that placement in a regular class would meet the pupil's needs and is consistent with parental preferences, the committee shall decide in favour of placement in a regular class.

18. (1) As soon as possible after making its decisions on a referral under section 14, the chair of the committee shall send a written statement of decision to,

(a) a parent of the pupil;
(b) the pupil, where the pupil is 16 years of age or older;
(c) the principal who made the referral, where the referral was made by a principal; and
(d) the designated representative of the board that established the committee.

(2) In the case of a referral by a principal under subsection 14(1), the statement of decision shall,

(a) state whether the committee has identified the pupil as an exceptional pupil;
(b) where the committee has identified the pupil as an exceptional pupil, include,
    (i) the committee's description of the pupil's strengths and needs,
    (ii) the categories and definitions of any exceptionalities identified by the committee,
    (iii) the committee's placement decision, and
    (iv) the committee's recommendation under subsection 16(2), if any; and
(c) where the committee has decided that the pupil should be placed in a special education class, state the reasons for that decision.

(3) In the case of a referral by a designated representative under subsection 14(3), the statement of decision shall,

(a) include,

(i) the committee's description of the pupil's strengths and needs,
(ii) the categories and definitions of any exceptionalities identified by the committee,
(iii) the committee's placement decision, and
(iv) the committee's recommendation under subsection 16(2), if any; and
(b) where the committee has decided that the pupil should be placed in a special education class, state the reasons for that decision.

19. (1) A parent who receives a statement of decision under section 18 may, by written notice delivered to the person specified in subsection (2) within 15 days of receipt of the statement of decision, request a meeting with the committee.

(2) The notice under subsection (1) shall be delivered to the principal in the case of a referral under subsection 14(1) and to the designated representative in the case of a referral under subsection 14(3).

(3) On receiving the request, the principal or designated representative, as the case may be, shall arrange for the committee to meet as soon as possible with the parent and, where the pupil is 16 years of age or older and wishes to attend, the pupil, to discuss the statement of decision.

(4) As soon as possible following a meeting under this section, the chair of the committee shall send a written notice to each of the persons described in subsection 18(1), stating whether any changes in its decisions were made as a result of the meeting.

(5) If changes in the committee's decisions were made as a result of the meeting, the notice under subsection (4) shall be accompanied by a revised statement of decision, together with written reasons for the changes.

20. (1) A board shall implement a placement decision made by a committee under this Part when one of the following two events occurs:

1. A parent of the pupil consents in writing to the placement.
2. The time period provided in subsection 26(2) for filing a notice of appeal from the decision expires without a notice of appeal being filed.

(2) The board shall implement a placement decision made by a committee under this Part as soon as possible after an event described in paragraph 1 or 2 of subsection (1) occurs.

(3) A board that, without the written consent of a parent of the pupil, implements a placement decision made by a committee under this Part shall give written notice of the implementation to a parent of the pupil.

PART V

COMMITTEE REVIEWS

21. (1) The principal of the school at which a pupil's special education program is being provided,
(a) may on written notice to a parent of the pupil;
(b) shall at the written request of a parent of the pupil; and
(c) shall, at the written request of the designated representative of the board that is providing the special education program to the pupil,

refer the pupil to a committee established by the board that is providing the special education program to the pupil, for a review of the identification or placement of the pupil.

(2) A request by a parent under clause (1)(b) may be made at any time after a placement has been in effect for three months but may not be made more often than once in every three month period.

(3) Subject to subsection (4), the designated representative shall make a request under clause (1)(c) when in his or her opinion it is necessary to do so in order to ensure that a review in respect of the pupil is held under this Part at least once in each school year.

(4) Subsection (3) does not apply where,
- (a) a committee proceeding with respect to the pupil was held under Part IV during the school year; or
- (b) a parent of the pupil gives a written notice dispensing with the annual review to the principal of the school at which the special education program is being provided.

(5) Within 15 days of giving a notice under clause (1)(a) or receiving a request under clause (1)(b) or (c), the principal shall provide the parent with a written statement of the approximate time when the review meeting will take place.

22. (1) Where more than one committee has been established by a board, the principal of the school at which the special education program is provided shall determine which of the committees most appropriate for the pupil, having regard to the jurisdiction of the committees.

(2) Where one board purchases a special education program from another board, the board that is providing the special education program to the pupil shall invite the purchasing board to select a representative who may,
- (a) be present at and participate in all committee discussions about the pupil; and
- (b) be present when the committee's identification and placement decisions are made.

23. (1) Sections 15 and 16 apply with necessary modifications to a committee engaged in a review under this Part.

(2) With the written permission of a parent of the pupil, a committee conducting a review under this Part shall consider the pupil's progress with reference to the pupil's individual education plan.

(3) As soon as possible after a committee engaged in a review under this Part decides that it is satisfied with the identification and placement of a pupil, the chair of the committee shall send a written statement of decision confirming the identification and placement to,
- (a) a parent of the pupil;
- (b) the pupil, where the pupil is 16 years of age or older;
- (c) the principal of the school at which the pupil's special education program is being provided;
- (d) the designated representative of the board that is providing the special education program to the pupil; and
- (e) in the circumstances described in subsection 22(2), the designated representative of the board that is purchasing the special education program.

(4) As soon as possible after a committee engaged in a review under this Part decides that the identification or placement or both should be changed, the chair of the committee shall send a written statement of decision to the persons described in subsection (3).

(5) A statement of decision under subsection (4) shall state,
(a) the reasons for the committee's decision that the pupil's identification or placement or both should be changed;
(b) whether the committee considers that the pupil should continue to be identified as an exceptional pupil;
(c) where the committee considers that the pupil should continue to be identified as an exceptional pupil,
   (i) the committee's placement decision,
   (ii) the committee's description of the pupil's strengths and needs, and
   (iii) the categories and definitions of any exceptionalities identified by the committee; and
(d) where the committee considers that the pupil should be placed in a special education class, the reasons for that decision.

(6) Section 17 applies with necessary modifications where a committee is considering the option of placing a pupil in a special education class and the pupil is not already in such a placement.

24. (1) A parent who receives a confirmation under subsection 23(3) or a statement of decision under subsection 23(4) may request a meeting with the committee by written notice, delivered within 15 days of receiving the confirmation or statement of decision, to the principal of the school at which the pupil's special education program is being provided.

(2) On receiving the request for a meeting, the principal shall arrange for the committee to meet as soon as possible with the parent and, where the pupil is 16 years of age or older and wishes to attend, the pupil, to discuss the statement of decision.

(3) As soon as possible following a meeting under this section, the chair of the committee shall send a written notice to each of the persons described in subsection 23(3), stating whether any changes in its decisions were made as a result of the meeting.

(4) If changes in the committee's decisions were made as a result of the meeting, the notice under subsection (3) shall be accompanied by a revised statement of decision, together with written reasons for the changes.

25. (1) A board shall implement a change in placement as a result of a decision made by a committee under this Part when one of the following two events occurs:
1. A parent of the pupil consents in writing to the placement.
2. The time period provided in subsection 26(3) for filing a notice of appeal from the decision expires without a notice of appeal being filed.

(2) The board shall implement a change in placement as a result of a decision made by a committee under this Part as soon as possible after an event described in paragraph 1 or 2 of subsection (1) occurs.

(3) A board that, without the written consent of a parent of the pupil, implements a change in placement as a result of a decision made by a committee under this Part shall give written notice of the implementation to a parent of the pupil.

PART VI

APPEALS FROM COMMITTEE DECISIONS

26. (1) A parent of a pupil may, by filing a notice of appeal in accordance with subsection (2) or (3), require a hearing by a special education appeal board in respect of,
- (a) a committee decision under Part IV or V that the pupil is an exceptional pupil;
- (b) a committee decision under Part IV or V that the pupil is not an exceptional pupil; or
- (c) a committee decision under Part IV or V on placement of the pupil.

(2) A notice of appeal in respect of a committee decision under Part IV shall be filed with the secretary of the board,
- (a) if no meeting is held under section 19, within 30 days of receipt of the statement of decision under section 18 by the parent who is seeking to appeal; or
- (b) if a meeting is held under section 19, within 15 days of receipt of the notice under subsection 19(4) by the parent who is seeking to appeal.

(3) A notice of appeal in respect of a committee decision under Part V shall be filed with the secretary of the board,
- (a) if no meeting is held under section 24, within 30 days of receipt of the confirmation under subsection 23(3) or the statement of decision under subsection 23(4) by the parent who is seeking to appeal; or
- (b) if a meeting is held under section 24, within 15 days of receipt of the notice under subsection 24(3) by the parent who is seeking to appeal.

(4) A notice of appeal shall indicate which of the decisions referred to in subsection (1) the parent disagrees with and shall include a statement that sets out the nature of the disagreement.

(5) The special education appeal board shall not reject or refuse to deal with an appeal by reason of any actual or alleged deficiency in the statement referred to in subsection (4) or by reason of the failure of the parent, in the opinion of the special education appeal board, to accurately indicate in the notice of appeal the subject of the disagreement.

27. (1) The special education appeal board shall be composed of,
- (a) one member selected by the board in which the pupil is placed;
- (b) one member selected by a parent of the pupil; and
- (c) a chair, selected jointly by the members selected under clauses (a) and (b) or, where those members cannot agree, by the appropriate district manager of the Ministry.

(2) Selections under clauses (1)(a) and (b) shall be made within 15 days of receipt of the notice of appeal by the secretary of the board.

(3) The selection of a chair under clause (1)(c) shall be made within 15 days of the last selection under clause (1)(a) and (b).

(4) No member or employee of the board providing or purchasing the special education program and no employee of the Ministry may be selected under subsection (1).

(5) No person who has had any prior involvement with the matter under appeal may be selected under subsection (1).

(6) The chair of the committee the decision of which is being appealed shall provide the special education appeal board with the record of the committee proceeding, including the statement of decision and any reports, assessments or other documents considered by the committee.

(7) The board shall provide the special education appeal board with the secretarial and administrative services it requires and shall, in accordance with the rules and policies that apply to members of the board under section 191.2 of the Act, pay the travelling and other expenses incurred by the members of the special education appeal board while engaged in their duties.

28. (1) The chair of the special education appeal board shall arrange for a meeting of the members of the special education appeal board to discuss the matters under appeal and shall give notice of the meeting, in accordance with subsection 5(5), to a parent of the pupil and, where the pupil is 16 years of age or older, the pupil.

(2) The meeting shall be arranged to take place at a convenient place and at a time that is no more than 30 days after the day on which the chair is selected and shall be conducted in an informal manner.

(3) Despite subsection (2), with the written consent of the parents of the pupil and the designated representative of the board, the meeting may be scheduled for a time that is more than 30 days after the day on which the chair is selected.

(4) Any person who in the opinion of the chair of the special education appeal board may be able to contribute information with respect to the matters under appeal shall be invited to attend the meeting.

(5) Where the pupil's special education program is being purchased by one board from another board, the chair shall invite the purchasing board to select a representative who may be present at and participate in all discussions about the pupil at the meeting held by the special education appeal board under section 28.

(6) Where the special education appeal board is satisfied that the opinions, views and information that bear on the appeal have been sufficiently presented to it, the special education appeal board shall end the meeting and, within three days of ending the meeting, shall,

(a) agree with the committee and recommend that its decisions be implemented; or
(b) disagree with the committee and make a recommendation to the board about the pupil's identification, placement or both.

29. (1) The special education appeal board shall send a written statement of its recommendations under section 28 to,

(a) a parent of the pupil;
(b) where the pupil is 16 years of age or older, the pupil;
(c) the chair of the committee;
(d) the principal of the school in which the pupil is placed;
(e) the designated representative of the board in which the pupil is placed; and
(f) in the circumstances described in subsection 28(5), the designated representative of the board that is purchasing the special education program.

(2) The written statement shall be accompanied by written reasons for the recommendations.

30. (1) Within 30 days of receiving the special education appeal board's written statement, the board shall consider the special education appeal board's recommendations, shall decide what action to take with respect to the pupil and shall give notice in writing of the decision to each of the persons described in subsection 29(1).

(2) In deciding what action to take with respect to a pupil, the board is not limited to the actions that the special education appeal board recommended or could have recommended.

(3) Notice to a parent under subsection (1) shall include an explanation of the further right of appeal provided by section 57 of the Act.

31. (1) The board shall implement a decision under subsection 30(1) when one of the following events occurs:

1. A parent of the pupil consents in writing to the decision.
2. Thirty days have elapsed from receipt of the notice under subsection 30(1) by a parent of the pupil and no appeal has been commenced in respect of the decision under section 57 of the Act.
3. An appeal under section 57 of the Act from the decision is dismissed or abandoned.

(2) In accordance with an agreement between the board and a parent or the pupil, the board may change a decision made by it under section 30,

(a) while an appeal under section 57 of the Act is pending; or

(b) before the end of the period referred to in paragraph 2 of subsection (1).

(3) Where the board changes a decision under subsection (2), the board shall give notice in writing of the change in decision to each of the persons described in subsection 29(1).

(4) Subsections 30(2) and (3) apply with necessary modifications in respect of a change in decision under subsection (2).

PART VII

TRANSITIONAL PROVISIONS

Interpretation

32. In this Part,

"old regulation" means Regulation 305 of the Revised Regulation of Ontario, 1990.

Committees Established Before September 1, 1998

33. (1) Where a matter was referred to a committee under section 2 of the old Regulation, the matter shall be dealt with on and after September 1, 1998 as if it had been referred to a committee under Part IV of this Regulation and, for the purpose, the provisions of this Regulation apply to the committee proceeding and to all related proceedings, including appeals, with appropriate modifications.

(2) Where a matter was referred to a committee under section 8 of the old Regulation, the matter shall be dealt with on and after September 1, 1998 as if it had been referred to a

committee under Part V of this Regulation and, for the purpose, the provisions of this Regulation, apply to the committee proceeding and to all related proceedings, including appeals, with appropriate modifications.

(3) The modifications required by subsections (1) and (2) are such modifications as the person or body exercising a power or meeting a requirement under this Regulation considers appropriate having regard to the stage to which the matter has proceeded.

Parents' Guide

34. Until December 31, 1998, a board may meet the requirements of subsection 13(2) and clauses 14(6)(a) and 14(7)(b) using copies of a guide prepared under section 2 of the old regulation.

Individual Education Plans

35. Subsections 7(2) to (7) apply with necessary modifications if, as a result of a decision of a committee, a special education appeal board or the Special Education Tribunal,
- (a) an existing placement of an exceptional pupil who does not yet have an individual education plan is confirmed; or
- (b) a board implements a change in placement of an exceptional pupil who does not yet have an individual education plan.

Appeals Filed Before September 1, 1998

36. (1) This section applies if a notice of appeal is given under section 4 of the old regulation before September 1, 1998 but the appeal is not finally determined before that date.

(2) If three people are appointed before September 1, 1998 under section 7 of the old regulation to form an appeal board to hear the appeal, the appeal shall be held in accordance with the old regulation as it read immediately before it was revoked.

(3) If three people are not appointed before September 1, 1998 under section 7 of the old regulation to form an appeal board to hear the appeal, the appeal shall be held in accordance with this Regulation.

(4) For the purposes of subsection (3),
- (a) the notice given under section 4 of the old regulation shall be deemed to be a notice properly given under section 26 of this Regulation; and
- (b) selections under clauses 27(1)(a) and (b) shall be made on or before September 15, 1998 rather than within the times specified in subsections 27(2) and (3).

37. (1) This section applies where an appeal is held in accordance with the old regulation as a result of the application of subsection 36(2) of this Regulation.

(2) If the board receives the report of the appeal decision under subsection 7(10) of the old regulation before September 1, 1998, subsection 7(11) of the old regulation applies as it read immediately before it was revoked.

(3) If the board does not receive the report of the appeal decision under subsection 7(10) of the old regulation before September 1, 1998, sections 30 and 31 of this Regulation apply as

if the report of the appeal decision given under subsection 7(10) of the old regulation were a statement given under section 29 of this Regulation.

PART VIII

REVOCATION

38. Regulation 305 of the Revised Regulations of Ontario, 1990 and Ontario Regulation 663/91 are revoked.

PART IX

COMMENCEMENT

39. (1) This Regulation, except subsection 13(3), comes into force on September 1, 1998.

(2) Subsection 13(3) comes into force on January 1, 1999.

REGULATION 283/98
CALCULATION OF AVERAGE DAILY ENROLMENT FOR THE PERIOD JANUARY 1, 1998 TO AUGUST 31, 1998
O. Reg. 283/98

1. (1) In this Regulation,

"cycle" means the number of school days for which a schedule of classes in a school continues before the schedule is repeated; ("horaire")

"full-time pupil" means a pupil who,
   (a) is enrolled in day school other than in junior kindergarten or kindergarten, and
   (b) in respect of a cycle, is registered for classroom instruction for an average of at least 210 minutes per school day; ("élève à temps plein")

"half-time pupil" means a pupil who is enrolled in junior kindergarten or kindergarten and, in respect of a cycle, is registered for classroom instruction for an average of at least 150 minutes per school day; ("élève à mi-temps")

"independent study course" means a credit course that is provided to a pupil other than a full-time pupil and that,
   (a) meets the criteria set out in the independent study course register for inclusion in the determination of day school enrolment, or
   (b) is approved by the Minister as an independent study course to be included in the determination of day school enrolment; ("cours d'études personnelles")

"non-resident pupil" of a board means a pupil, other than a pupil from outside Ontario enrolled at a school under a student exchange program approved by the board, who is enrolled at a school operated by the board and,
   (a) in respect of whom the Minister would be required to pay the cost of education for the short year if the rules set out in sections 31 to 34 of Ontario Regulation 78/97 applied in respect of the short year,
   (b) in respect of whom the board charges a fee to another board,
   (c) in respect of whom the board may charge a fee to,
      (i) the Crown in right of Canada, or
      (ii) a party resident outside Ontario,
   (d) in respect of whom the board may charge a fee to a band, the council of a band or an education authority where the band, council of a band or education authority is authorized by the Crown in right of Canada to provide education for Indians,
   (e) in respect of whom the board is required by subsection 49(6) of the Act to charge the maximum fee calculated in accordance with the regulations,
   (f) who the board is required to admit under section 42 of the Act, excluding pupils counted as resident pupils of the board under paragraph 2 or 3 of subsection 14(4) of the short year grant regulation, or
   (g) who is a registered Indian residing on a reserve, within the meaning of the *Indian Act* (Canada); ("élève non résident")

"part-time pupil" means a pupil who, is enrolled in day school and is neither a full-time nor a half-time pupil; ("élève à temps partiel") "resident-internal pupil" of a board means a pupil, other than a non-resident pupil, who is enrolled at a school operated by the board; ("élève résident interne")

"resident-external pupil" of a board means a pupil in respect of whom a fee is payable by the board to another board; ("élève résident externe")

"short year" means the period beginning January 1, 1998 and ending August 31, 1998; ("année abrégée")

"short year fees regulation" means Ontario Regulation 284/98; ("règlement sur les droits de l'année abrégée")

"short year grant regulation" means Ontario Regulation 285/98. ("règlement sur les subventions de l'année abrégée")

(2) For the purposes of section 2, a pupil is a pupil of a board if he or she is a resident-internal pupil of the board, a resident-external pupil of the board or a non-resident pupil of the board.

(3) Sections 2 and 3 of this Regulation apply for the purposes of the short year fees regulation and the short year grant regulation.

2. Day school average daily enrolment for a board for the short year is the sum of,
  (a) the product of 0.5 and the sum of,
     (i) the number of full-time pupils of the board enrolled on March 31, 1998,
     (ii) 0.5 times the number of half-time pupils of the board enrolled on that day, and
     (iii) the quotient obtained by determining, for each part-time pupil of the board enrolled on that day, the number of minutes for which the pupil is registered for classroom instruction in the cycle that includes that day, in a course other than an independent study course, and dividing the sum of the numbers so determined by the product of 300 and the number of days in the cycle;
  (b) the product of 0.1 and the sum of,
     (i) the number of full-time pupils of the board enrolled on October 31, 1997, and
     (ii) 0.5 times the number of half-time pupils of the board enrolled on that day, and
     (iii) the quotient obtained by determining, for each part-time pupil of the board enrolled on that day, the number of minutes for which the pupil is registered for classroom instruction in the cycle that includes that day, in a course other than an independent study course, and dividing the sum of the numbers so determined by the product of 300 and the number of days in the cycle; and
  (c) an amount in respect of each pupil of the board who is enrolled in an independent study course, calculated as follows:

$$\frac{A \times B}{7.5}$$

where,

A = the number of credits and partial credits that may be earned by the pupil on successful completion of the course,

B = the fraction representing the portion of the total quantity of work required for completion of the course that is completed by the pupil during the period from January 1, 1998 to June 30, 1998.

3. Continuing education average daily enrolment for a board for the period from January 1, 1998 to August 31, 1998 is the sum of,

   (a) an amount in respect of each pupil who is enrolled in a continuing education class or course established by the board, other than a continuing education course delivered primarily through means other than classroom instruction, calculated as follows:

$$\frac{A \times B}{300 \times 185}$$

where,

   A = the number of sessions for which the pupil is enrolled in the period from January 1, 1998 to August 31, 1998,

   B = the number of minutes in each session; and

   (b) an amount in respect of each pupil who is enrolled in a continuing education course established by the board and delivered primarily through means other than classroom instruction calculated as follows:

$$A \times 0.1134 \times B$$

where,

   A = the number of credits and partial credits that may be earned by the pupil on successful completion of the course,

   B = the fraction representing the portion of the total quantity of work required for completion of the course that is completed by the pupil during the period from January 1, 1998 to August 31, 1998.

4. Despite section 4 of Ontario Regulation 79/97, that Regulation does not apply to the short year or to any school year after the short year.

REGULATION 284/98
CALCULATION OF FEES FOR PUPILS FOR THE PERIOD JANUARY 1, 1998 TO AUGUST 31, 1998
O. Reg. 284/98

Interpretation

1. (1) In this Regulation,

"continuing education A.D.E." for a board means the continuing education average daily enrolment for the board, as calculated under section 3 of the short year A.D.E. regulation; ("effectif quotidien moyen de l'éducation permanente")

"day school A.D.E." for a board means the day school average daily enrolment for the board, as calculated under section 2 of the short year A.D.E. regulation; ("effectif quotidien moyen de jour")

"high cost program" means,

(a) a special education program, other than a program provided in a school of a board in lieu of an education program provided by a provincial school for the blind and deaf or other similar program for which a legislative grant is payable, or

(b) a technological education program that qualifies for one or more credits toward the secondary school graduation diploma or the Ontario secondary school diploma; ("programme à coût élevé")

"P.A.C." for a pupil means the pupil accommodation charge for a pupil as determined under subsections (3) and (4); ("frais de pension")

"section 68 board" means a board established under section 68 of the Act; ("conseil créé en vertu de l'article 68")

"short year A.D.E. regulation" means Ontario Regulation 283/98. ("règlement sur l'effectif quotidien moyen de l'année abrégée")

(2) For the purposes of this Regulation, the day school A.D.E. of a pupil enrolled in a school operated by a board is the day school A.D.E. for the board calculated as if that pupil were the board's only pupil.

(3) Subject to subsection (4), the P.A.C. for a pupil is the product of the day school A.D.E. of the pupil and $141 in the case of an elementary school pupil or $282 in the case of a secondary school pupil.

(4) If a board has entered into an agreement under subsection 188(3) of the Act that provides for a payment by the Crown in right of Canada to provide classroom accommodation for a specified number of pupils, the P.A.C. for each pupil accommodated as a result of the agreement is zero.

Application

2. This Regulation applies in respect of the period January 1, 1998 to August 31, 1998.

Fees Paid to Boards Other Than Section 68 Boards —General

3. (1) This section applies in respect of a pupil who is enrolled in a school operated by a board, other than a section 68 board, if a fee in respect of the pupil is receivable by the board from,

(a) another board;

(b) the Crown in right of Canada;

(c) a band, the council of a band or an education authority where the band, council of a band or education authority is authorized by the Crown in right of Canada to provide education for Indians.

(2) This section also applies in respect of a pupil who is enrolled in a school operated by a board, other than a section 68 board, if subsection 49(6) of the Act applies to the pupil.

(3) The fee in respect of a pupil described in subsection (1) or (2) shall be calculated as follows:

1. Take the amount calculated for the old board that operated the school in 1997 under paragraphs 1 to 4 of subsection 3(1) of Ontario Regulation 81/97, except that the current cost of operating used in the calculation shall be increased by the excess described as B in the definition of "maximum recognized day school O.E." in Ontario Regulation 78/97, as calculated for the old board that operated the school in 1997.

2. Multiply the day school A.D.E. of the pupil by the sum of,
    i. the amount determined under paragraph 1, and
    ii. the P.A.C. for that pupil.

(4) The fee in respect of a pupil referred to in subsection (1) or (2) who is enrolled in a Native language program and whose fee is receivable from the Crown in right of Canada or from a band, the council of a band or an education authority where the band, council of a band or education authority is authorized by the Crown in right of Canada to provide education for Indians, may, at the option of the board, be increased by an amount equal to the portion of the eligible sum for Native as a second language that would be generated for the pupil if he or she were a resident pupil of the board.

(5) For the purposes of subsection (4), the eligible sum for Native as a second language is,

(a) in respect of an elementary school pupil,
   (i) $219, where the pupil is enrolled in a Native language program for an average of 20 or more minutes but less than 40 minutes per school day; or
   (ii) $389, where the pupil is enrolled in a Native language program for an average of 40 or more minutes per school day, and

(b) in respect of a secondary school pupil enrolled in a Native language program, the product obtained by multiplying the number of credits or credit equivalents that may be granted to the pupil for the program by,
   (i) $57 in the case of a program offered in the intermediate division, or
   (ii) $75 in the case of a program offered in the senior division.

(6) The fee in respect of a pupil referred to in subsection (1) or (2) who is enrolled in a high cost program may, at the option of the board, be increased by multiplying the fee by a factor agreed on by the board providing the instruction and the party from whom the fee is receivable or, in the absence of agreement, by a factor determined in accordance with subsection (7).

(7) If the board providing the instruction and the party from whom the fee is receivable cannot agree on a factor, the factor shall be determined by three arbitrators, appointed as follows:
1. One arbitrator shall be appointed by the board that provides the instruction.
2. One arbitrator shall be appointed by the party from whom the fee is receivable.
3. One arbitrator shall be appointed by the arbitrators appointed under paragraphs 1 and 2.

(8) The decision of the arbitrators or a majority of them is final and binding on the board providing the instruction and the party from whom the fee is receivable.

(9) The number of pupils in a high cost program provided by the board in respect of whom the fee receivable by the board from one party may be increased under subsection (6) or (7) shall not exceed the amount obtained by,
   (a) multiplying the day school A.D.E. of the pupils in respect of whom fees are receivable by the board from the party by the ratio of the day school A.D.E. of the pupils registered in the high cost program to the day school A.D.E. of the pupils enrolled in schools operated by the board; and
   (b) subtracting the product obtained under clause (a) from the day school A.D.E. of the pupils registered in the high cost program in respect of whom fees are receivable by the board from the party.

4. (1) Despite subsection 3(1), the fee in respect of a pupil who is 21 years of age or more on December 31, 1997 and who is enrolled in a secondary school and is referred to in subsection 3(1), shall be equal to the product of the day school A.D.E. of the pupil and the sum of $2,257 and the P.A.C. for the pupil or such other amount that is agreed on by the board providing the instruction and the party from whom the fee is receivable.

(2) This section does not apply in respect of a pupil to whom subsection 49(6) of the Act applies or in respect of a pupil enrolled in a school operated by a section 68 board.

Fees Paid to Section 68 Boards

5. The fee in respect of a pupil enrolled in a school operated by a section 68 board shall be calculated as follows:
1. Take the board's cost of operating for the short year.
2. Deduct the legislative grants payable to the board for the short year.
3. Divide by the sum of the days for which each pupil of the school is enrolled at the school.
4. Multiply by the number of days for which the pupil whose fee is being calculated is enrolled at the school.

Fees Charged To Persons Residing In Ontario

6. (1) This section does not apply in respect of a pupil whose fee is receivable from another board, from the Crown in right of Canada or from a band, the council of a band or an education authority where the band, council of a band or education authority is authorized by the Crown in right of Canada to provide education for Indians.

(2) The fee charged in respect of a pupil enrolled in a school of a board, other than a section 68 board, to a parent or guardian who is resident in Ontario shall not exceed the fee referred to in subsection (3) or (4), as the case requires.

(3) The fee in respect of a pupil enrolled in a school of a board who resides with his or her parent or guardian in a school section, separate school zone or secondary school district on land that is exempt from taxation for school purposes shall not exceed $74 for each month or part of a month the pupil is enrolled in a school operated by the board.

(4) In the case of a pupil enrolled in a school of a board who is qualified to be a resident pupil of a school section, separate school zone or secondary school district, the fee in respect of the pupil shall not exceed, for each month or part of a month the pupil is enrolled in a school operated by the board, the amount charged by the board that the school in 1997 as determined under subsection 5(4) of Ontario Regulation 81/97.

(5) If a pupil is enrolled in a high cost program, the amount calculated under subsection (4) may, at the option of the board, be increased by an amount that does not exceed the additional cost to the board of providing the high cost program to the pupil.

Fees Charged to Parents not Residing in Ontario

7. (1) The fee in respect of a pupil who is enrolled in a school of a board, other than a section 68 board, and whose parent or guardian does not reside in Ontario shall be such fee as the board may determine, but shall not exceed the maximums set by subsections (2) and (3).

(2) Except as is provided in subsection (3), the fee in respect of a pupil who is enrolled in a school of a board and whose parent or guardian does not reside in Ontario shall not exceed the amount calculated as follows:

1. Add the amount determined under paragraph 1 of subsection 3(3) and the P.A.C. for the pupil.
2. Multiply the amount obtained under paragraph 1 by 0.1.
3. Multiply the result obtained under paragraph 2 by the number of months or part months during which the pupil is enrolled in a school operated by the board.

(3) Where the pupil is enrolled in a high cost program, the maximum set by subsection (2) shall be increased by an amount that does not exceed the additional cost to the board of providing the high cost program to the pupil.

(4) This section does not apply in respect of a pupil to whom subsection 49(6) of the Act applies.

Fees For Programs In Facilities

8. (1) The fee charged by a board other than a section 68 board in respect of a pupil who is not qualified to be a resident pupil of the board and for whom an educational program is provided by the board in a hospital or treatment centre shall be such fee as may be agreed on between the board that provides the program and,

   (a)   the board of which the pupil is qualified to be a resident pupil; or
   (b)   if the pupil is not qualified to be a resident pupil of a board, the parent or guardian of the pupil.

(2) Subsection (1) does not apply to a board that provides the educational program if the board received a grant under section 27 of Ontario Regulation 78/97 with respect to the educational program.

(3) Subsection (1) applies despite subsection 3(2).

Fees for Continuing Education and Summer School

9. Despite sections 3 to 8, the fee charged by a board in respect of a pupil who is enrolled in a continuing education program or a summer school operated by the board shall be such as the board providing the instruction may determine except that the fee shall not exceed the product of,

   (a)   the continuing education A.D.E. of the pupil; and
   (b)   the quotient obtained by dividing the expenditure of the board for continuing education and summer school courses or classes for the period January 1, 1998 to August 31, 1998 by the continuing education A.D.E. of the board.

REGULATION 285/98
LEGISLATIVE GRANTS FOR THE PERIOD JANUARY 1, 1998 TO AUGUST 31, 1998

O. Reg. 285/98, as am. O. Reg. 358/98; 467/98; 210/99

PART I

GENERAL

DEFINITIONS

1. In this Regulation,

"designated board associated with an old board" means the district school board that is listed in column 2 of Schedule 1 to Ontario Regulation 460/97, opposite the old board listed in column 1 of that Schedule; ("conseil désigné rattaché à un ancien conseil")

"isolate board" is a school authority other than a section 68 board; ("conseil isolé")

"Metropolitan Toronto area board" means,
   (a) The Board of Education for the Borough of East York,
   (b) The Board of Education for the City of Etobicoke,
   (c) The Board of Education for the City of North York,
   (d) The Board of Education for the City of Scarborough,
   (e) The Board of Education for the City of Toronto, and
   (f) The Board of Education for the City of York; ("conseil de secteur de la communauté urbaine de Toronto")

"old board" does not include the Metropolitan Toronto area boards or The Metropolitan Toronto French-Language School Council; ("ancien conseil")

"section 68 board" is a board established under section 68 of the Act; ("conseil créé en vertu de l'article 68")

"short year" means the period beginning January 1, 1998 and ending August 31, 1998; ("année abrégée")

"short year fees regulation" means Ontario Regulation 284/98; ("règlement sur les droits de l'année abrégée")

"short year A.D.E. regulation" means Ontario Regulation 283/98; ("règlement sur l'effectif quotidien moyen de l'année abrégée")

"supported board associated with an old board" means the district school board that is listed in column 3 of Schedule 1 to Ontario Regulation 460/97, opposite the old board listed in column 1 of that Schedule. ("conseil secondé rattaché à un ancien conseil")

General

2. (1) The legislative grant payable for the short year to a district school board is the amount calculated under Part II.

(2) The legislative grant payable for the short year to an isolate board is the amount calculated under Part IV.

(3) The legislative grant payable for the short year to a section 68 board is the amount calculated under Part IV.

3. A legislative grant payable under this Regulation shall be paid on an estimated basis during the short year and such adjustments as may be necessary shall be made after the actual financial data and average daily enrolments are available.

4. (1) In subsection (2),

"unextended old board" means an old board to which subsection 4(1) of Ontario Regulation 78/97 applied.

(2) For the purposes of this Regulation, all calculations relating to an unextended old board shall be made separately for elementary school purposes and for secondary school purposes.

5. It is a condition of the payment of a grant to a board under this Regulation that the board comply with all Acts administered by the Minister and with all regulations, policies, guidelines, directives and similar instruments made under an Act administered by the Minister.

6. Where a board contravenes an Act administered by the Minister or a regulation, policy, guideline, directive or similar instrument made under an Act administered by the Minister, the Minister may withhold all or part of a grant otherwise payable to the board under the Act until the board takes the steps necessary to correct the situation.

7. (1) Where the amount payable to an old board under a general legislative grant regulation was overpaid, the overpayment shall be deducted from the grants payable under this Regulation to the designated board associated with the old board and to the supported board associated with the old board, in accordance with the appropriate distribution ratios as determined under the directives published in September, 1997 by the Education Improvement Commission and titled "Directives for the Distribution of Assets and Liabilities Among District School Boards".

(2) Where an amount payable to an old board under a general legislative grant regulation was underpaid, the underpayment shall be added to the grants payable under this Regulation to the designated board associated with the old board and to the supported board associated with the old board, in accordance with the appropriate distribution ratios as determined under the directives published in September, 1997 by the Education Improvement Commission and titled "Directives for the Distribution of Assets and Liabilities Among District School Boards".

8. For the purposes of this Regulation, if the Minister reasonably concludes that an amount reported at a code point in a financial statement is incorrect because of an error in calculation, because of an error in filling out the form for the financial statement or because an amendment to a previous legislative grant regulation was not taken into account in calculating the amount, the Minister shall make the appropriate correction and the corrected amount shall be deemed to be the amount reported at the code point in the financial statement.

PART II

GRANTS TO DISTRICT SCHOOL BOARDS

Interpretation

9. (1) In this Part and in Part III,

"1997 actual expenditure allocation form" means the form provided by the Ministry, as part of the 1997 financial statement package, for the purpose of determining the French-English split of 1997 actual expenditures by old boards; ("formule de répartition des dépenses réelles de 1997")

"English-language instructional unit" means a class, group of classes or school in which the English language or American sign language is the language of instruction and includes a class, group of classes or school established under paragraph 25 of subsection 8(1) of the Act; ("module scolaire de langue anglaise")

"English-language portion" of an old board means the notional portion of the old board to which the expenses related to educating pupils in English-language instructional units are allocated in the 1997 actual expenditure allocation form; ("part de langue anglaise")

"French-language portion" of an old board means the notional portion of the old board to which the expenses related to educating pupils in French-language instructional units are allocated in the 1997 actual expenditure allocation form; ("part de langue française")

"language portion" of an old board means,

(a) the English-language portion of the old board, and
(b) the French-language portion of the old board. ("part linguistique")

(2) For the purposes of this Part and Part III, an old board is a predecessor of a district school board if the district school board is listed in column 2 or 3 of Schedule 1 of Ontario Regulation 460/97, opposite the old board listed in column 1 of that Schedule.

(3) For the purposes of this Part and Part III,

(a) a reference to the relevant language portions of the old boards that are the predecessors of an English-language district school board is a reference to the English-language portions of the old boards; and
(b) a reference to the relevant language portions of the old boards that are the predecessors of a French-language district school board is a reference to the French-language portions of the old boards.

Grant Entitlement

10. A district school board shall be paid a grant in an amount determined as follows:

1. Total the revenue guarantees for the relevant language portions of the old boards that are the predecessors of the district school board, in accordance with sections 11 to 16.
2. Deduct the short year tax revenue of the district school board, as determined under section 17.

3. Add the amount determined under section 18, if applicable.
4. Add the amount determined under section 19, if applicable.
5. Deduct the amount determined under section 20, if applicable.
6. Deduct the amount that is in the district school board's reserve fund under section 233(1) of the Act on August 31, 1998, immediately before the transfer under subsection 233(2) of the Act.
7. Add the amount determined under section 21, if applicable.
8. Deduct the amount determined under section 22, if applicable.
9. Add the amount in respect of accumulated deficits of old boards attributable to the board, determined in accordance with subsection (2), if that amount is not less than zero.

(2) The amount referred to in paragraph 9 of subsection (1) shall be determined as follows:

1. Multiply the amount of any year-end under requisitions at code point 0245 as reported in the audited 1997 financial statements of each of the old boards attributable to the board by the appropriate factor for each of those old boards, as set out in the Ministry document entitled "Distribution Ratios" and dated August 4, 1998, which document is available for public inspection at the Capital and Operating Grants Administration Branch of the Ministry, located on the 21st floor, 900 Bay Street, Toronto.
2. Total the amounts determined under paragraph 1.
3. Deduct the assistance for extraordinary 1997 tax write-offs as calculated under subsection 19(1) or (2), as the case may be.
4. Add the adjustment for 1997 extraordinary supplementary taxes as calculated under subsection 20(1) or (2), as the case may be.

O. Reg. 467/98, s. 1.

Revenue Guarantee

11. The revenue guarantee for a language portion of an old board shall be determined as follows:

1. Multiply the 1997 revenue for the old board, as determined under section 12, by the allocation ratio for the language portion, as determined or specified under section 13.
2. Multiply the amount obtained under paragraph 1 by 0.62.
3. Multiply the amount obtained under paragraph 2 by the enrolment adjustment factor for the language portion as determined under section 14.
4. Add to the amount obtained under paragraph 3 the junior kindergarten adjustment for the language portion as determined under section 15, if applicable.
5. Add to the amount obtained under paragraph 4 the summer school adjustment for the language portion as determined under section 16, if applicable.

1997 Revenue for an Old Board

12. (1) The 1997 revenue for an old board is the sum of,

(a) the taxes levied under the Act for the purposes of the old board in 1997;
(b) amounts that are receivable by the old board in 1997 under subsection 159(22) of the *Municipal Act*, as it read immediately before January 1, 1998;
(c) payments in lieu of taxes, as defined in section 1 of Ontario Regulation 78/97, that are receivable by the old board in 1997;
(d) the total of 1996 taxes refunded by the old board as a result of withdrawal of employee services or lock-out of employees, as reported in the audited 1997 financial statements of the old board at code point 0246;
(e) the lesser of,
    (i) the old board's over-requisitions and reserve transfers, as determined under subsection (2), and
    (ii) the amount set out in Table 1 opposite the old board;
(f) the supplementary taxes of the old board as determined for revenue guarantee purposes under subsection (4);
(g) the grant payable to the old board under Ontario Regulation 78/97, not including amounts payable under section 50 of that Regulation;

less the sum of,

(h) the amount, if any, by which the sum of the amounts calculated as grants for the old board for 1997 under sections 8 to 45 of Ontario Regulation 78/97 is less than zero; and
(i) the tax write-off for the old board as determined for revenue guarantee purposes under subsection (6).

(2) For the purposes of subclause (1)(e)(i), the amount of an old board's over-requisitions and reserve transfers is the old board's 1996 over-requisition, as reported in the audited 1997 financial statements of the old board at code point 0244, adjusted as follows:

1. Where the estimates adopted by the old board in 1997 report a net amount transferred from its reserve for working funds, add that net amount to the 1996 over-requisition.
2. Where the estimates adopted by the old board in 1997 report a net amount transferred to its reserve for working funds, deduct that net amount from the 1996 over-requisition.

(3) For the purposes of subclause (1)(e)(i), if the amount obtained under subsection (2) is a negative amount, the amount shall be deemed to be zero.

(4) For the purposes of clause (1)(f), the supplementary taxes of an old board for revenue guarantee purposes is the lesser of,

(a) the taxes receivable in 1997 by the old board under section 35 of the *Assessment Act*; and
(b) the greater of,
    (i) the amount included in the 1997 estimates of the old board in respect of the taxes receivable in 1997 by it under section 35 of the *Assessment Act*, and
    (ii) the average of the amounts received by the old board in 1992, 1993, 1994, 1995 and 1996 under section 35 of the *Assessment Act*.

(5) Calculations under clauses (1)(g) and (h) shall be made as if there was no withdrawal of employee services and no lock-out of employees during 1997.

S. 13 REGULATIONS UNDER THE EDUCATION ACT

(6) For the purposes of clause (1)(i), the tax write-off for an old board for revenue guarantee purposes is the lesser of,
- (a) the amounts charged to the old board in 1997 by a municipal council under section 421 of the *Municipal Act*, not including taxes receivable in 1997 by the old board to the extent that such taxes were cancelled or reduced as a result of a resolution of the old board; and
- (b) the greater of,
    - (i) the amounts included in the 1997 estimates of the old board in respect of the amounts chargeable in 1997 to it by a municipal council under section 421 of the *Municipal Act*, not including taxes receivable in 1997 by the old board to the extent that such taxes were cancelled or reduced as a result of a resolution of the old board; and
    - (ii) the average of the amounts charged to the old board in 1992, 1993, 1994, 1995 and 1996 by a municipal council under section 421 of the *Municipal Act*, not including taxes receivable in those years by the old board to the extent that such taxes were cancelled or reduced as a result of a resolution of the old board.

(7) For the purposes of subclauses (4)(b)(ii) and (6)(b)(ii), if the amount received or charged, as the case may be, in any one of the five years exceeds the five-year average by 75 per cent or more, the average shall be calculated excluding that year.

Allocation Ratio

13. (1) Subject to subsection (3), the allocation ratio for the English-language portion of an old board is the ratio specified for English-language expenditures on the 1997 actual expenditure allocation form for the old board.

(2) Subject to subsection (3), the allocation ratio for the French-language portion of an old board is the ratio specified for French-language expenditures on the 1997 actual expenditure allocation form for the old board.

(3) The English-language district school board and the French-language district school board of which an old board is a predecessor may by agreement specify different allocation ratios for the English-language portion and French-language portion of the old board.

(4) If an old board has no French-language expenditures to note on the 1997 actual expenditure allocation form, the allocation ratio for the English-language portion of the old board is one and the allocation ratio for the French-language portion of the old board is zero.

(5) If an old board has no English-language expenditures to note on the 1997 actual expenditure allocation form, the allocation ratio for the French-language portion of the old board is one and the allocation ratio for the English-language portion of the old board is zero.

Enrolment Adjustment Factor

14. (1) The enrolment adjustment factor for the English-language portion of an old board is determined by dividing the 1997-1998 school year English-language average daily enrolment

REGULATION 285/98 S. 14

for the old board area, as determined under subsection (2), by the 1997 calendar year English-language average daily enrolment for the old board, as determined under subsection (3).

(2) The 1997-1998 school year English-language average daily enrolment for the old board area is the sum of the following amounts:

1. The portion of the day school A.D.E. of resident-internal pupils and of the day school A.D.E. of resident-external pupils of the old board that is in respect of the period from September 1, 1997 to December 31, 1997, excluding pupils enrolled in a French-language instructional unit. For the purposes of this paragraph, "day school A.D.E. of resident-internal pupils" and "day school A.D.E. of resident-external pupils" have the same meaning as in Ontario Regulation 78/97.

2. The average daily enrolment calculated under section 2 of the short year A.D.E. regulation in respect of pupils who reside in the area of jurisdiction of the old board and who are resident pupils of an English-language district school board, excluding pupils enrolled in a secondary school who are 21 years of age or more on December 31, 1997 and pupils enrolled in a junior kindergarten program. For the purposes of this paragraph, a pupil is a resident pupil of a district school board if he or she is a resident-internal pupil or a resident-external pupil of the board within the meaning of the short year A.D.E. regulation.

3. The portion of the day school A.D.E. of non-resident pupils of the old board that is in respect of the period from September 1, 1997 to December 31, 1997, excluding pupils in respect of whom the Minister did not pay the cost of education under sections 31 to 34 of Ontario Regulation 78/97 and pupils enrolled in a French-language instructional unit. For the purposes of this paragraph, "day school A.D.E. of non-resident pupils" has the same meaning as in Ontario Regulation 78/97.

4. The average daily enrolment calculated under section 2 of the short year A.D.E. regulation in respect of non-resident pupils of an English-language district school board who reside in the area of jurisdiction of the old board and who would qualify for assistance for the cost of education under the rules set out in sections 31 to 34 of Ontario Regulation 78/97, if those rules applied in respect of the short year. For the purposes of this paragraph, a pupil is a non-resident pupil of a district school board if he or she is a non-resident pupil of the board within the meaning of the short year A.D.E. regulation.

5. The product of,
    i. 7, and
    ii. the sum of the number of teachers and one-half of the number of teachers' assistants employed by the old board to provide English-language instruction, within the meaning of subsection 58.1(1) of the Act, in programs approved by the Minister under section 27 of Ontario Regulation 78/97 for the purposes of the 1997-1998 school year.

(3) The 1997 calendar year English-language average daily enrolment for the old board is the sum of the following amounts:

1. The 1997 day school A.D.E. of resident-external pupils and the 1997 day school A.D.E. of resident-internal pupils of the old board, excluding pupils enrolled in a

French-language instructional unit. For the purposes of this paragraph, "day school A.D.E. of resident-external pupils" and "day school A.D.E. of resident-internal pupils" have the same meaning as in Ontario Regulation 78/97.

2. The day school A.D.E. of non-resident pupils of the old board, excluding pupils in respect of whom the Minister did not pay the cost of education under sections 31 to 34 of Ontario Regulation 78/97 and pupils enrolled in a French-language instructional unit. For the purposes of this paragraph, "day school A.D.E. of non-resident pupils" has the same meaning as in Ontario Regulation 78/97.

3. The product of,
   i. 7, and
   ii. the sum of the number of teachers and one-half of the number of teachers' assistants employed to provide English-language instruction, within the meaning of subsection 58.1(1) of the Act, in programs approved by the Minister under section 27 of Ontario Regulation 78/97 for the purposes of the 1997 calendar year.

(4) The following rules apply in respect of subsections (2) and (3):

1. This rule applies for the purposes of paragraphs 1 and 3 of subsection (2) and paragraphs 1 and 2 of subsection (3). A secondary school pupil of the old board who took some but not all of his or her credits in a French-language instructional unit shall be counted partly as a pupil enrolled in a French-language instructional unit and partly as a pupil not enrolled in such a unit, in the proportion that the credits taken by the pupil in a French-language instructional unit bears to the total credits taken by the pupil.

2. This rule applies for the purposes of paragraph 2 of subsection (2) where, on October 31, 1997, a pupil was enrolled in a secondary school of a public old board and the pupil's parent or guardian was a separate school supporter whose 1997 taxes for secondary school purposes were applied to the support of the public old board. If the pupil is enrolled on March 31, 1998 in a secondary school of the district school board that, on March 31, 1998, governs the school that the pupil was enrolled in on October 31, 1997, he or she shall be counted as a resident pupil of the public district school board. For the purposes of this rule, "public old board" means an old board other than a Roman Catholic school board within the meaning of the *Education Act* as it read immediately before January 1, 1998.

3. This rule applies for the purposes of paragraph 2 of subsection (2) where, on October 31, 1997, a pupil was a resident pupil of an old board enrolled in an English-language instructional unit. If the pupil is enrolled on March 31, 1998 in a school governed by an English-language district school board of which the old board is a predecessor board, the pupil shall be counted as a resident pupil of the English-language district school board. For the purposes of this rule, a pupil was a resident pupil of an old board if the pupil was a resident-internal or resident-external pupil of the old board within the meaning of Ontario Regulation 78/97.

(5) Subsections (1) to (4) apply, with necessary modifications, in respect of the enrolment adjustment factor for the French-language portion of an old board and, for the purpose,

(a) a reference to English-language shall be deemed to be a reference to French-language; and

(b) a reference to French-language shall be deemed to be a reference to English-language.

(6) Where the enrolment adjustment factor calculated in accordance with subsections (1) to (5) is less than 1.0, the enrolment adjustment factor shall be adjusted by adding to it 50 per cent of the amount by which the factor is less than one.

Junior Kindergarten Adjustment

15. (1) In this section,

"resident-internal pupil" has the same meaning as in Ontario Regulation 78/97.

(2) Subsection (3) applies where an old board operated a junior kindergarten that was an English-language instructional unit in one or more of its schools in September, 1997 and,

- (a) did not operate a junior kindergarten that was an English-language instructional unit in any of its schools before September, 1997; or
- (b) was in September, 1997 following an implementation plan for junior kindergarten that involved phasing in junior kindergarten across the old board.

(3) Subject to subsection (2), the junior kindergarten adjustment for the English-language portion of an old board is the product of,

- (a) $2,033; and
- (b) 37.2 per cent of the number of resident-internal pupils enrolled on October 31, 1997 in a junior kindergarten that,
    - (i) was operated by the old board in a school in which junior kindergarten was not provided before September 1, 1997, and
    - (ii) was not a French-language instructional unit.

(4) Subsection (5) applies where an old board operated a junior kindergarten that was a French-language instructional unit in one or more of its schools in September, 1997 and,

- (a) did not operate a junior kindergarten that was a French-language instructional unit in any of its schools before September, 1997; or
- (b) was in September, 1997 following an implementation plan for junior kindergarten that involved phasing in junior kindergarten across the old board.

(5) Subject to subsection (4), the junior kindergarten adjustment for the French-language portion of an old board is the product of,

- (a) $2,033; and
- (b) 37.2 per cent of the number of resident-internal pupils enrolled on October 31, 1997 in a junior kindergarten that,
    - (i) was operated by the old board in a school in which junior kindergarten was not provided before September 1, 1997, and
    - (ii) was a French-language instructional unit.

Summer School Adjustment

16. (1) In this section,

"day school A.D.E. of resident-external pupils" has the same meaning as in Ontario Regulation 78/97; ("effectif quotidien moyen des élèves résidents externes de jour")

"day school A.D.E. of resident-internal pupils" has the same meaning as in Ontario Regulation 78/97; ("effectif quotidien moyen des élèves résidents internes de jour")

"summer school A.D.E. for grant purposes" has the same meaning as in Ontario Regulation 78/97. ("effectif quotidien moyen des cours d'été aux fins des subventions")

(2) The summer school adjustment for the English-language portion of an old board is the product of,
- (a) the 1997 summer school A.D.E. for grant purposes, excluding pupils enrolled in a French-language instructional unit less the product of,
    - (i) the 1997 day school A.D.E. of resident-external pupils and resident-internal pupils, excluding pupils enrolled in a French-language instructional unit, and
    - (ii) 0.004;
- (b) $2,257; and
- (c) 0.38.

(3) The summer school adjustment for the French-language portion of an old board is the product of,
- (a) the 1997 summer school A.D.E. for grant purposes, excluding pupils enrolled in an English-language instructional unit less the product of,
    - (i) the 1997 day school A.D.E. of resident-external pupils and resident-internal pupils, excluding pupils enrolled in an English-language instructional unit, and
    - (ii) 0.004;
- (b) $2,257; and
- (c) 0.38.

Short Year Tax Revenue of a District School Board

17. (1) For the purposes of paragraph 2 of section 10, the short year tax revenue of a district school board shall be determined as follows:
1. Add,
    i. the total of the amounts distributed to the board in respect of the 1998 calendar year under subsections 237(12) and 238(2), section 239, subsection 240(5), sections 250 and 251 and subsections 257.8(2) and 257.9(1) of the Act, under sections 447.20 and 447.52 of the *Municipal Act* and under section 10 of Ontario Regulation 509/98,
    ii. the amounts, if any, received by the board in respect of the 1998 calendar year from a municipality under subsection 445(4) of the *Municipal Act*,
    iii. the total of the payments in lieu of taxes distributed to the board in respect of the 1998 calendar year under subsection 371.1(1) of the *Municipal Act*,
    iv. the total of the amounts, if any, received by the board in respect of the 1998 calendar year under the *Municipal Grants Act* (Canada) or under any Act of Canada that permits a payment to be made by a government or a government agency in lieu of taxes on real property, and

v. the amounts, if any, shared with the board in respect of the 1998 calendar year under subsection 442.1(11.3) of the *Municipal Act*.
2. Multiply by 0.62.
3. Add,
    i. the total of the amounts, if any, distributed to the board in the short year under subsection 2(2) of Ontario Regulation 365/98, and
    ii. the total of the amounts, if any, paid to the board in the short year under clause 3(1)(a) of Ontario Regulation 366/98.
4. Deduct the cost incurred in the short year by the board under section 257.7 of the Act in collecting taxes for school purposes in territory without municipal organization, to a maximum of 2 per cent of 62 per cent of the total amount of taxes levied by it for 1998 for school purposes in territory without municipal organization.
5. Deduct the total of the amounts paid as rebates by the board under section 257.2.1 of the Act in the short year.
6. Deduct 62 per cent of the total amounts, if any, paid by the board in respect of the 1998 calendar year under subsections 442.1(7) and 442.2(8.1) of the *Municipal Act*.

(2) Amounts paid by the Minister to the board in respect of the 1998 calendar year under section 257.11 of the Act shall be deemed to be amounts distributed to the board in respect of the 1998 calendar year under a provision of the Act referred to in subparagraph i of paragraph 1 of subsection (1). O. Reg. 210/99, s. 1.

Assistance Related to Negative Grants

18. (1) This section applies where the sum of the amounts calculated as grants under sections 8 to 45 of Ontario Regulation 78/97 for a predecessor old board of a district school board is less than zero.

(2) In the case of an English-language district school board, the amount to be added under paragraph 3 of section 10 shall be determined as follows:
1. Determine the amount by which the sum of the amounts calculated as grants for the predecessor old board for 1997 under sections 8 to 45 of Ontario Regulation 78/97 is less than zero.
2. Multiply the amount determined under paragraph 1 by 0.62.
3. Multiply the amount determined under paragraph 2 by the allocation ratio for the English-language portion of the old board, as determined or specified under section 13.

(3) In the case of a French-language district school board, the amount to be added under paragraph 3 of section 10 shall be determined as follows:
1. Determine the amount by which the sum of the amounts calculated as grants for the predecessor old board for 1997 under sections 8 to 45 of Ontario Regulation 78/97 is less than zero.
2. Multiply the amount determined under paragraph 1 by 0.62.
3. Multiply the amount determined under paragraph 2 by the allocation ratio for the French-language portion of the old board, as determined or specified under section 13.

(4) Calculations under this section shall be made as if there was no withdrawal of employee services and no lock-out of employees during 1997.

Assistance for Extraordinary 1997 Tax Write-offs

19. (1) In the case of an English-language district school board, the amount to be added under paragraph 4 of section 10 shall be determined as follows:
1. For each predecessor old board of the English-language district school board, determine the amount, if any, by which the amount determined under clause 12(4)(a) exceeds the amount determined under clause 12(6)(b).
2. Multiply the amount determined under paragraph 1 for each predecessor old board of the English-language district school board by the appropriate distribution ratio, as determined under the directives published in September, 1997 by the Education Improvement Commission and titled "Directives for the Distribution of Assets and Liabilities Among District School Boards".
3. Total the amounts determined under paragraph 2 for each old board that is a predecessor of the English-language district school board.

(2) In the case of a French-language district school board, the amount to be added under paragraph 4 of section 10 shall be determined as follows:
1. For each predecessor old board of the French-language district school board, determine the amount, if any, by which the amount determined under clause 12(6)(a) exceeds the amount determined under clause 12(6)(b).
2. Multiply the amount determined under paragraph 1 for each predecessor old board of the French-language district school board by the appropriate distribution ratio, as determined under the directives published in September, 1997 by the Education Improvement Commission and titled "Directives for the Distribution of Assets and Liabilities Among District School Boards".
3. Total the amounts determined under paragraph 2 for each old board that is a predecessor of the French-language district school board.

Adjustment for 1997 Extraordinary Supplementary Taxes

20. (1) In the case of an English-language district school board, the amount to be deducted under paragraph 5 of section 10 shall be determined as follows:
1. For each predecessor old board of the English-language district school board, determine the amount, if any, by which the amount determined under clause 12(4)(a) exceeds the amount determined under clause 12(4)(b).
2. Multiply the amount determined under paragraph 1 for each predecessor old board of the English-language district school board by the appropriate distribution ratio, as determined under the directives published in September, 1997 by the Education Improvement Commission and titled "Directives for the Distribution of Assets and Liabilities Among District School Boards".

3. Total the amounts determined under paragraph 2 for each old board that is a predecessor of the English-language district school board.

(2) In the case of an French-language district school board, the amount to be deducted under paragraph 5 of section 10 shall be determined as follows:
1. For each predecessor old board of the French-language district school board, determine the amount, if any, by which the amount determined under clause 12(4)(a) exceeds the amount determined under clause 12(4)(b).
2. Multiply the amount determined under paragraph 1 for each predecessor old board of the French-language district school board by the appropriate distribution ratio, as determined under the directives published in September, 1997 by the Education Improvement Commission and titled "Directives for the Distribution of Assets and Liabilities Among District School Boards".
3. Total the amounts determined under paragraph 2 for each old board that is a predecessor of the French-language district school board.

Assistance for Programs in Lieu

21. (1) This section applies where,
(a) a pupil who was not a resident pupil of a predecessor old board of a district school board immediately before the short year becomes a resident pupil of the district school board during the short year;
(b) the pupil requires a special education program in lieu of an education program provided in a provincial school for blind, deaf or deaf-blind pupils; and
(c) the district school board hires additional employees in order to establish or expand a special education program of the type described in clause (b) for the pupil.

(2) The amount to be added under paragraph 7 of section 10 shall be determined as follows:
1. Determine the number of teachers and one-half the number of teacher assistants employed by the board in accordance with the Minister's approval for the purpose of educating each pupil in the circumstances described in subsection (1).
2. In the case of an elementary school pupil, multiply the number determined for the pupil under paragraph 1 by $48,200. Multiply the product by 0.1 for each month or part of a month that the program is provided by the board to the pupil during the short year.
3. In the case of a secondary school pupil, multiply the number determined for the pupil under paragraph 1 by $55,400. Multiply the product by 0.1 for each month or part of a month that the program is provided by the board to the pupil during the short year.
4. Determine the number of interpreters employed by the board in accordance with the Minister's approval for the purpose of educating each pupil in the circumstances described in subsection (1).
5. Multiply the number determined for the pupil under paragraph 4 by $34,000. Multiply the product by 0.1 for each month or part of a month that the program is provided by the board to the pupil during the short year.

6. Determine the number of transcribers employed by the board in accordance with the Minister's approval for the purpose of educating each pupil in the circumstances described in subsection (1).
7. Multiply the number determined for the pupil under paragraph 6 by $28,000. Multiply the product by 0.1 for each month or part of a month that the program is provided by the board to the pupil during the short year.
8. Total the amounts determined under paragraphs 2, 3, 5 and 7.

(3) For the purposes of subsection (2), a number can be a whole number, a fraction or a mixed number.

(4) For the purposes of paragraph 4 of subsection (2), an interpreter shall be counted only if he or she,
   (a) is qualified as an interpreter in accordance with Policy/Program Memorandum #76-C; and
   (b) is employed by the board to assist an exceptional pupil who is otherwise admissible to a program in a provincial school for deaf or hard-of-hearing pupils.

(5) For the purposes of paragraph 6 of subsection (2), a transcriber shall be counted only if he or she,
   (a) is qualified as a transcriber in accordance with Policy/Program Memorandum #76-C; and
   (b) is employed by the board to assist an exceptional pupil who is otherwise admissible to a program in a provincial school for blind pupils.

Adjustment for Teachers' Withdrawal of Services

22. (1) In the case of an English-language district school board, the amount to be deducted under paragraph 8 of section 10 shall be determined as follows:
1. For each predecessor old board of the English-language district school board, determine the amount, if any, that was transferred at the end of 1997 from the reserve of the old board established under section 237 or 238 of the *Education Act*, as it read on December 31, 1997, to the general revenue fund of the old board.
2. Multiply the amount determined under paragraph 1 for each predecessor old board of the English-language district school board by the appropriate distribution ratio, as determined under the directives published in September, 1997 by the Education Improvement Commission and titled "Directives for the Distribution of Assets and Liabilities Among District School Boards".
3. Total the amounts determined under paragraph 2 for each old board that is a predecessor of the English-language district school board.

(2) In the case of a French-language district school board, the amount to be deducted under paragraph 8 of section 10 shall be determined as follows:
1. For each predecessor old board of the French-language district school board, determine the amount, if any, that was transferred at the end of 1997 from the reserve of

the old board established under section 237 or 238 of the *Education Act*, as it read on December 31, 1997, to the general revenue fund of the old board.
2. Multiply the amount determined under paragraph 1 for each predecessor old board of the French-language district school board by the appropriate distribution ratio, as determined under the directives published in September, 1997 by the Education Improvement Commission and titled "Directives for the Distribution of Assets and Liabilities Among District School Boards".
3. Total the amounts determined under paragraph 2 for each old board that is a predecessor of the French-language district school board.

Capital Project Grant

23. (1) In this section,

"capital asset" means,
 (a) a school site that provides or is capable of providing pupil accommodation and an addition or improvement to such a school site,
 (b) a school building, including a fixture of a school building, and an addition, alteration, renovation or major repair to a school building or a fixture of a school building,
 (c) furniture and equipment to be used in school buildings,
 (d) library materials for the initial equipping of a library in a school building, and
 (e) a water supply or electrical power supply on school property or the means of conveying water or electrical power to school property from outside the property; ("immobilisation")

"capital project" means a project for the acquisition of capital assets. ("projet d'immobilisations")

(2) For the purposes of this section, a capital project is an approved short year capital project if the Minister gives a final written approval for the project during the short year.

(3) For the purposes of this section,
 (a) an approved short year capital project is an approved short year growth capital project if the project is intended to result in an increase in the pupil places of a board or the purchase of land for the purposes of increasing the pupil places of a board; and
 (b) an approved short year capital project is an approved short year non-growth capital project if it is not an approved short year growth capital project.

(4) A district school board shall be paid a grant in respect of each approved short year capital project of the board equal to the product of,
 (a) the lesser of the project cost specified in the final approval for the project referred to in subsection (2) and the actual expenditure of the district school board on the project; and
 (b) the rate determined under subsections (6) to (10).

(5) Despite section 3, the total of the instalments paid to the district school board in the short year on account of a grant payable under subsection (4) shall not exceed the total of the actual expenditures of the board on the project in the short year.

(6) The rate for an approved short year non-growth capital project of a district school board is the rate set out in Column 3 of Table 2, opposite the listing in column 1 for the district school board and the listing in column 2 for the predecessor old board that proposed the project.

(7) The rate for an approved short year growth capital project of a district school board is the rate set out in Column 4 of Table 2, opposite the listing in column 1 for the district school board and the listing in column 2 for the predecessor old board that proposed the project.

(8) Despite subsections (6) and (7), the rate for an approved short year capital project in respect of a secondary school of a French-language district school board is the rate set out in Column 5 of Table 2, opposite the listing in column 1 for the district school board and the listing in column 2 for the predecessor old board that proposed the project.

(9) Subsections (6) to (8) do not apply to,

(a) approved short year capital projects that fall under the 1998 facilities renewal program described in the Ministry memorandum dated March 12, 1998 to directors of education respecting the 1998 facilities renewal project; or

(b) approved short year capital projects in respect of which no written approval specifying an estimated project cost was given by the Minister before January 1, 1998.

(9.1) The agreement dated December 22, 1997 between the Minister and Stormont, Dundas and Glengarry County Roman Catholic Separate School Board and Stormont, Dundas and Glengarry County Board of Education is not a written approval specifying an estimated project cost for the purposes of clause (9)(b).

(10) The rate for an approved short year capital project to which subsection (9) applies shall be deemed to be 1.0.

(11) Any grant or portion of a grant that is payable to a district school board in respect of a capital project under a previous legislative grant regulation and that is not paid before January 1, 1998 shall be deemed, until the end of the short year, to be a grant payable under this Regulation.

(12) Despite section 3, the total of the instalments paid to the district school board in the short year on account of a grant or portion of a grant payable under subsection (11) shall not exceed the total of the actual expenditures of the board on the project in the short year.

(13) Any grant or portion of a grant that is payable under subsection (11) is not payable during the short year under any previous legislative grant regulation. O. Reg. 358/98, s. 1.

PART III

PAYMENTS BY SUPPORTED BOARD FOR SERVICES OF DESIGNATED BOARD

24. (1) In this section,

"common jurisdiction expenditure item revenue" means revenue associated with an item described as revenue or as recovery on the section of the 1997 actual expenditure allocation form that deals with common jurisdiction expenditures.

(2) For the purposes of the definition of "supported board's common jurisdiction expenditure costs" in section 19 of the Ontario Regulation 460/97, the common jurisdiction expen-

diture costs of a supported board associated with an old board shall be determined as follows where the supported board is an English-language district school board:
1. Take the amount shown on the old board's 1997 actual expenditure allocation form, under the column heading "English Language Portion", as the total net common jurisdiction expenditures.
2. Where, during the short year, the supported board receives some or all of the common jurisdiction expenditure item revenues directly, rather than through the designated board associated with the old board, add the amounts that are shown in relation to those items on the old board's 1997 actual expenditure allocation form under the column heading "English Language Portion".
3. Multiply by 0.62.
4. Multiply by the enrolment adjustment factor for the English-language portion of the old board, as determined under section 14.

(3) For the purposes of the definition of "supported board's common jurisdiction expenditure costs" in section 19 of Ontario Regulation 460/97, the common jurisdiction expenditure costs of a supported board associated with an old board shall be determined as follows where the supported board is a French-language district school board:
1. Take the amount shown on the old board's 1997 actual expenditure allocation form, under the column heading "French Language Portion", as the total net common jurisdiction expenditures.
2. Where, during the short year, the supported board receives some or all of the common jurisdiction expenditure item revenues directly, rather than through the designated board associated with the old board, add the amounts that are shown in relation to those items on the old board's 1997 actual expenditure allocation form under the column heading "French Language Portion".
3. Multiply by 0.62.
4. Multiply by the enrolment adjustment factor for the French-language portion of the old board, as determined under section 14.

PART IV

GRANTS TO SCHOOL AUTHORITIES

Grants to Isolate Boards

25. (1) For the purposes of this section, the approved expenditure of an isolate board is the expenditure that is acceptable to the Minister as shown on the board's actual grant calculation form for the short year.

(2) For the purposes of this section, the short year tax revenue of an isolate board shall be determined as follows:
1. Add,
    i. the total of the amounts distributed to the board in respect of the 1998 calendar year under subsections 237(12) and 238(2), section 239, subsection 240(5), sections 250 and 251 and subsections 257.8(2) and 257.9(1) of the Act, under

sections 447.20 and 447.52 of the *Municipal Act* and under section 10 of Ontario Regulation 509/98,
    ii. the amounts, if any, received by the board in respect of the 1998 calendar year from a municipality under subsection 445(4) of the *Municipal Act*,
    iii. the total of the payments in lieu of taxes distributed to the board in respect of the 1998 calendar year under subsection 371.1(1) of the *Municipal Act*,
    iv. the total of the amounts, if any, received by the board in respect of the 1998 calendar year under the *Municipal Grants Act* (Canada) or under any Act of Canada that permits a payment to be made by a government or a government agency in lieu of taxes on real property, and
    v. the amounts, if any, shared with the board in respect of the 1998 calendar year under subsection 442.1(11.3) of the *Municipal Act*.
2. Multiply by 0.62.
3. Add,
    i. the total of the amounts, if any, distributed to the board in the short year under subsection 2(3) of Ontario Regulation 365/98, and
    ii. the total of the amounts, if any, paid to the board in the short year under clause 3(1)(a) of Ontario Regulation 366/98.
4. Deduct the cost incurred in the short year by the board under section 257.7 of the Act in collecting taxes for school purposes in territory without municipal organization, to a maximum of 2 per cent of 62 per cent of the total amount of taxes levied by it for 1998 for school purposes in territory without municipal organization.
5. Deduct the total of the amounts paid as rebates by the board under section 257.2.1 of the Act in the short year.
6. Deduct 62 per cent of the total of the amounts, if any, paid by the board in respect of the 1998 calendar year under subsections 442.1(7) and 442.2(8.1) of the *Municipal Act*.

(3) Amounts paid by the Minister to the isolate board in respect of the 1998 calendar year under section 257.11 of the Act shall be deemed to be amounts distributed to the board in respect of the 1998 calendar year under a provision of the Act referred to in subparagraph i of paragraph 1 of subsection (2).

(4) Paragraph 4 of subsection (2) shall not be interpreted to preclude including in the isolate board's approved expenditure an amount on account of the costs incurred by the board in collecting taxes in territory without municipal organization, where those costs exceed the amount deducted under paragraph 4 of subsection (2).

(5) Where the approved expenditure of an isolate board exceeds its short year tax revenue, the board shall be paid a grant equal to the excess. O. Reg. 210/99, s. 2.

Grants to Section 68 Boards

26. (1) For the purposes of this section, the cost of operating of a section 68 board for the short year shall be determined as follows:
1. Take the expenditure of the board for the short year that is acceptable to the Minister for grant purposes, excluding,

i. expenditures for debt charges,
ii. expenditures for the purchase of capital assets within the meaning of section 23,
iii. expenditures for the restoration of destroyed or damaged capital assets, and
iv. provisions for reserves for working funds and provisions for reserve funds.
2. Deduct any transfers from reserves for working funds or from reserve funds made during the short year.
3. Deduct the revenue of the board for the short year, not including revenue from,
   i. legislative grants,
   ii. an organization on whose property a school of the board is located, and
   iii. refunds of expenditure of the kind described in subparagraph i, ii or iii of paragraph 1.

(2) A section 68 board shall be paid a grant equal to the sum of,

(a) 80 per cent of the salaries of teachers, temporary teachers and teacher assistants employed by the board during the short year;

(b) 80 per cent of the expenditure of the board for the short year approved by the Minister for grant purposes for daily transportation of pupils and for board, lodging and weekly transportation of pupils; and

(c) 50 per cent of the excess of,
   (i) the cost of operating for the board for the short year,

over,

   (ii) the board's expenditure for the short year for,
      a. salaries of teachers, temporary teachers and teacher assistants,
      b. daily transportation of pupils, and
      c. board, lodging and weekly transportation of pupils.

PART V

PAYMENTS TO GOVERNING AUTHORITIES

27. In this Part,

"Crown establishment" means an establishment maintained by a Department of the Government of Canada, a federal Crown company, The Royal Canadian Mounted Police or Atomic Energy of Canada Limited, on lands held by the Crown in right of Canada that are not assessable for school purposes, and includes a reserve as defined in the *Indian Act* (Canada).

28. (1) This section applies where a pupil who is not resident in a Crown establishment,

(a) resides in a territorial district on land that is not part of a school section or separate school zone and attends an elementary school supported by local taxation in Manitoba or Quebec; or

(b) resides in a territorial district on land that is not part of a secondary school district and attends a secondary school supported by local taxation in Manitoba or Quebec.

(2) The Minister shall pay the governing authority of the school attended by the pupil the amount agreed on between the governing authority and the Minister.

S. 29   REGULATIONS UNDER THE EDUCATION ACT

29. (1) This section applies where,

(a) a pupil who resides in a territorial district is resident in a school section, separate school zone or a Crown establishment and attends an elementary school supported by local taxation in Manitoba or Quebec; and

(b) the Minister is of the opinion that,

    (i) daily transportation to the elementary school in Ontario that the pupil would be required to attend is impracticable due to distance and terrain, and

    (ii) the provision of board, lodging and weekly transportation is impracticable because of the age or handicap of the pupil.

(2) The Minister shall pay the governing authority of the elementary school attended by the pupil the amount agreed on between the governing authority and the Minister.

30. (1) This section applies where a pupil who resides in a territorial district,

(a) is not resident in a school section, a separate school zone or a Crown establishment; and

(b) attends a school on a reserve that is operated by,

    (i) the Crown in right of Canada, or

    (ii) a band, the council of a band or an education authority where the band, council of a band or education authority is authorized by the Crown in right of Canada to provide education for Indians.

(2) The Minister shall pay the governing authority of the school attended by the pupil the amount agreed on between the governing authority and the Minister.

TABLE 1/TABLEAU 1

Item/Point	Name of old board/Nom de l'ancien conseil	Maximum eligible amount/Somme maximale admissible $
	Public old board/Ancien conseil public	
1.	Brant County Board of Education	501 463
2.	Bruce County Board of Education	540 458
3.	Carleton Board of Education	3 830 971
4.	Central Algoma Board of Education	106 603
5.	Cochrane-Iroquois Falls, Black River Matheson Board of Education	323 339
6.	Dufferin County Board of Education	480 678
7.	Durham Board of Education	3 451 323
8.	East Parry Sound Board of Education	249 018
9.	Elgin County Board of Education	0

Table 1

REGULATION 285/98

Item/ Point	Name of old board/Nom de l'ancien conseil	Maximum eligible amount/ Somme maximale admissible $
10.	Essex County Board of Education	1 207 639
11.	Frontenac County Board of Education	496 340
12.	Grey County Board of Education	772 829
13.	Haldimand Board of Education	476 079
14.	Halton Board of Education	543 276
15.	Hamilton Board of Education	994 958
16.	Hastings County Board of Education	0
17.	Hearst Board of Education	12 780
18.	Huron County Board of Education	0
19.	Education/Conseil de l'éducation de Kapuskasing-Smooth Rock Falls et de son district	56 400
20.	Kenora Board of Education	643 270
21.	Kent County Board of Education	33 871
22.	Kirkland Lake Board of Education	39 967
23.	Lakehead Board of Education	594 283
24.	Lambton County Board of Education	1 027 473
25.	Lanark County Board of Education	525 890
26.	Leeds and Grenville County Board of Education	908 434
27.	Lennox and Addington County Board of Education	644 380
28.	Lincoln County Board of Education	0
29.	London Board of Education	0
30.	Metro Toronto Board of Education	40 313 015
31.	Middlesex County Board of Education	0
32.	Muskoka Board of Education	2 534 676
33.	Niagara South Board of Education/Conseil scolaire de Niagara Sud	0
34.	Nipissing Board of Education	0
35.	Norfolk Board of Education	263 018
36.	Northumberland & Clarington Board of Education	0
37.	Ottawa Board of Education	4 282 775
38.	Conseil des écoles publiques d'Ottawa-Carleton	243 027
39.	Oxford County Board of Education	93 019

Table 1 REGULATIONS UNDER THE EDUCATION ACT

Item/ Point	Name of old board/Nom de l'ancien conseil	Maximum eligible amount/ Somme maximale admissible $
40.	Peel Board of Education	12 907 956
41.	Perth County Board of Education	0
42.	Peterborough County Board of Education	0
43.	Prescott and Russell County Board of Education	188 381
44.	Prince Edward County Board of Education	204 688
45.	Renfrew County Board of Education	597 595
46.	Sault Ste Marie Board of Education	595 365
47.	Stormont, Dundas & Glengarry County Board of Education	517 310
48.	Sudbury Board of Education	950 266
49.	Timiskaming Board of Education	25 427
50.	Timmins Board of Education	231 429
51.	Victoria County Board of Education	0
52.	Waterloo County Board of Education	4 151 389
53.	Wellington County Board of Education	0
54.	Wentworth County Board of Education	1 668 954
55.	Windsor Board of Education	1 701 116
56.	York Region Board of Education	0
	Separate old board/ Ancien conseil séparé	
57.	Brant County Roman Catholic Separate School Board/Conseil des écoles séparées catholiques du comté de Brant	196 373
58.	Bruce-Grey County Roman Catholic Separate School Board	172 432
59.	Carleton Roman Catholic Separate School Board	1 129 288
60.	Chapleau District Roman Catholic Separate School Board	0
61.	Cochrane, Iroquois Falls/Black River Matheson District Roman Catholic Separate School Board	67 998
62.	Dryden District Roman Catholic Separate School Board	10 295
63.	Dufferin Peel Roman Catholic Separate School Board/Conseil des écoles séparées catholiques de Dufferin & Peel	8 510 093

Table 1

REGULATION 285/98

Item/ Point	Name of old board/Nom de l'ancien conseil	Maximum eligible amount/ Somme maximale admissible $
64.	Durham Region Roman Catholic Separate School Board/Conseil des écoles séparées catholiques de la région de Durham	982 708
65.	Elgin County Roman Catholic Separate School Board	0
66.	Essex County Roman Catholic Separate School Board/Conseil des écoles séparées catholiques du comté d'Essex	793 507
67.	Fort Frances-Rainy River District Roman Catholic Separate School Board	2 979
68.	Frontenac-Lennox-Addington County Roman Catholic Separate School Board	349 349
69.	Geraldton District Roman Catholic Separate School Board/Conseil des écoles séparées catholiques du district de Geraldton	10 878
70.	Haldimand-Norfolk County Roman Catholic Separate School Board/Conseil des écoles séparées catholiques de Haldimand-Norfolk	221 553
71.	Halton Roman Catholic Separate School Board/ Conseil des écoles catholiques de Halton	1 209 133
72.	Hamilton-Wentworth Roman Catholic Separate School Board/Conseil des écoles séparées catholiques romaines de Hamilton-Wentworth	844 267
73.	Hastings-Prince Edward County Roman Catholic Separate School Board	0
74.	Hearst District Roman Catholic Separate School Board	52 881
75.	Huron-Perth County Roman Catholic Separate School Board	87 719
76.	Kapuskasing District Roman Catholic Separate School Board/Conseil des écoles séparées catholiques du district de Kapuskasing	141 935
77.	Kenora District Roman Catholic Separate School Board	0
78.	Kent County Roman Catholic Separate School Board/ Conseil des écoles séparées catholiques de Kent	313 216

Table 1   REGULATIONS UNDER THE EDUCATION ACT

Item/ Point	Name of old board/Nom de l'ancien conseil	Maximum eligible amount/ Somme maximale admissible $
79.	Kirkland Lake-Timiskaming District Roman Catholic Separate School Board/Conseil des écoles séparées catholiques du district de Kirkland Lake-Timmiskaming	94 597
80.	Lakehead District Roman Catholic Separate School Board/Conseil des écoles séparées catholiques du district de Lakehead	457 171
81.	Lambton County Roman Catholic Separate School Board/Conseil des écoles séparées catholiques du comté de Lambton	391 418
82.	Lanark-Leeds-Grenville County Roman Catholic Separate School Board	225 099
83.	Lincoln County Roman Catholic Separate School Board/Conseil des écoles catholiques du comté de Lincoln	0
84.	London-Middlesex County Roman Catholic Separate School Board/Conseil des écoles catholiques de London et du comté de Middlesex	0
85.	Metropolitan Separate School Board/Conseil des écoles catholiques du Grand Toronto	9 625 081
86.	Michipicten District Roman Catholic Separate School Board	12 571
87.	Nipissing District Roman Catholic Separate School Board	349 177
88.	North of Superior District Roman Catholic Separate School Board/Conseil des écoles séparées catholiques du district Supérieur Nord	47 821
89.	North Shore District Roman Catholic Separate School Board	206 757
90.	Conseil des écoles catholiques de langue française de la région d'Ottawa-Carleton	1 015 050
91.	Ottawa Roman Catholic Separate School Board	963 275
92.	Oxford County Roman Catholic Separate School Board/Conseil des écoles séparées catholiques romaines du comté d'Oxford	12 722
93.	Peterborough, Victoria, Northumberland & Clarington Roman Catholic Separate School Board	0

REGULATION 285/98 Table 1

ITEM/ POINT	NAME OF OLD BOARD/NOM DE L'ANCIEN CONSEIL	MAXIMUM ELIGIBLE AMOUNT/ SOMME MAXIMALE ADMISSIBLE $
94.	Prescott-Russell County Roman Catholic English Language Separate School Board	69 901
95.	Conseil des écoles catholiques de langue française de Prescott-Russell	372 836
96.	Renfrew County Roman Catholic Separate School Board	0
97.	Sault Ste. Marie District Roman Catholic Separate School Board	312 568
98.	Simcoe County Roman Catholic Separate School Board	0
99.	Stormont, Dundas and Glengarry County Roman Catholic Separate School Board/Conseil des écoles séparées catholiques des comtés de Stormont, Dundas et Glengarry	395 823
100.	Sudbury District Roman Catholic Separate School Board/Conseil des écoles séparées catholiques de Sudbury	770 947
101.	Timmins District Roman Catholic Separate School Board/Conseil des écoles séparées catholiques de Timmins	261 147
102.	Waterloo County Roman Catholic Separate School Board/Conseil des écoles séparées catholiques de la région de Waterloo	1 112 046
103.	Welland County Roman Catholic Separate School Board/Conseil scolaire des écoles catholiques romaines du comté de Welland	0
104.	Wellington County Roman Catholic Separate School Board/Conseil des écoles catholiques du comté de Wellington	377 455
105.	Windsor Roman Catholic Separate School Board/ Conseil de l'éducation catholique de Windsor	964 980
106.	York Region Roman Catholic Separate School Board/ Conseil des écoles séparées catholiques de la région de York	0
	Public old board — In unextended areas/ Ancien conseil public — dans les secteurs ayant parachevé	
107.	Atikokan Board of Education	

Table 1 REGULATIONS UNDER THE EDUCATION ACT

Item/ Point	Name of old board/Nom de l'ancien conseil	Maximum eligible amount/ Somme maximale admissible $
108.	elementary/élémentaire	0
109.	secondary/secondaire	218 001
110.	Beardmore, Geraldton, Longlac & Area Board of Education/Conseil de l'éducation de Beardmore, de Geraldton, de Longlac et des environs	
111.	elementary/élémentaire	32 996
112.	secondary/secondaire	27 915
113.	Chapleau Board of Education	
114.	elementary/élémentaire	0
115.	secondary/secondaire	31 452
116.	Dryden Board of Education	
117.	elementary/élémentaire	56 632
118.	secondary/secondaire	26 278
119.	Espanola Board of Education	
120.	elementary/élémentaire	40 917
121.	secondary/secondaire	269 428
122.	Fort Frances-Rainy River Board of Education	
123.	elementary/élémentaire	0
124.	secondary/secondaire	149 254
125.	Haliburton County Board of Education	
126.	elementary/élémentaire	2 354
127.	secondary/secondaire	76 507
128.	Hornepayne Board of Education	
129.	elementary/élémentaire	21 640
130.	secondary/secondaire	3 012
131.	Lake Superior Board of Education/Conseil scolaire du Lac Supérieur	
132.	elementary/élémentaire	57 521
133.	secondary/secondaire	62 107
134.	Manitoulin Board of Education	
135.	elementary/élémentaire	130 713
136.	secondary/secondaire	0
137.	Michipicoten Board of Education	

Table 1

REGULATION 285/98

ITEM/ POINT	NAME OF OLD BOARD/NOM DE L'ANCIEN CONSEIL	MAXIMUM ELIGIBLE AMOUNT/ SOMME MAXIMALE ADMISSIBLE $
138.	elementary/élémentaire	50 995
139.	secondary/secondaire	96 703
140.	Nipigon-Red Rock Board of Education	
141.	elementary/élémentaire	45 044
142.	secondary/secondaire	68 776
143.	North Shore Board of Education	
144.	elementary/élémentaire	78 940
145.	secondary/secondaire	0
146.	Red Lake Board of Education	
147.	elementary/élémentaire	0
148.	secondary/secondaire	228 640
149.	Simcoe County Board of Education	
150.	elementary/élémentaire	0
151.	secondary/secondaire	0
152.	West Parry Sound Board of Education	
153.	elementary/élémentaire	0
154.	secondary/secondaire	441 687

TABLE 2/TABLEAU 2 — 1998

Item/ Point	Column 1/ Colonne 1 District School Board/Conseil scolaire de district	Column 2/ Colonne 2 Old Board Name/ Nom de l'ancien conseil	Column 3/ Colonne 3 Non-Growth projects/ Projets non liés à la croissance	Column 4/ Colonne 4 Growth projects/ Projets liés à la croissance	Column 5/ Colonne 5 French language secondary school projects/ Projets visant les écoles secondaires de langue française
1.	English-language Public District School Board No. 1	Cochrane-Iroquois Falls, Black River-Matheson Board of Education	81.864%	70.950%	98.716%
2.	English-language Public District School Board No. 1	Hearst Board of Education	77.112%	63.339%	98.380%
3.	English-language Public District School Board No. 1	Kapuskasing-Smooth Rock Falls Board of Education/Conseil de l'éducation de Kapuskasing-Smooth Rock Falls et de son district	72.924%	56.630%	96.083%
4.	English-language Public District School Board No. 1	Kirkland Lake Board of Education	84.300%	74.852%	98.888%
5.	English-language Public District School Board No. 1	Timiskaming Board of Education	77.573%	64.077%	98.412%
6.	English-language Public District School Board No. 1	Timmins Board of Education	79.293%	66.832%	98.534%
7.	Algoma District School Board	Central Algoma Board of Education	83.742%	73.958%	98.849%
8.	Algoma District School Board	Chapleau Board of Education	82.893%	72.605%	97.302%

REGULATION 285/98 **Table 2**

Item/ Point	Column 1/ Colonne 1 District School Board/Conseil scolaire de district	Column 2/ Colonne 2 Old Board Name/ Nom de l'ancien conseil	Column 3/ Colonne 3 Non-Growth projects/ Projets non liés à la croissance	Column 4/ Colonne 4 Growth projects/ Projets liés à la croissance	Column 5/ Colonne 5 French language secondary school projects/ Projets visant les écoles secondaires de langue française
9.	Algoma District School Board	Hornepayne Board of Education	84.071%	74.487%	98.280%
10.	Algoma District School Board	Michipicoten Board of Education	71.584%	54.492%	96.492%
11.	Algoma District School Board	North Shore Board of Education	84.899%	75.814%	98.082%
12.	Algoma District School Board	Sault Ste Marie Board of Education	75.356%	60.526%	98.255%
13.	English-language Public District School Board No. 3	Espanola Board of Education	76.304%	62.051%	97.359%
14.	English-language Public District School Board No. 3	Manitoulin Board of Education	71.558%	54.442%	97.067%
15.	English-language Public District School Board No. 3	Sudbury Board of Education	76.302%	62.041%	98.322%
16.	Near North District School Board	East Parry Sound Board of Education	76.827%	62.883%	98.359%
17.	Near North District School Board	Nipissing Board of Education	79.558%	67.257%	98.553%
18.	Near North District School Board	West Parry Sound Board of Education	53.530%	25.567%	94.995%
19.	Keewatin-Patricia District School Board	Dryden Board of Education	74.316%	58.863%	97.199%
20.	Keewatin-Patricia District School Board	Kenora Board of Education	66.763%	46.763%	97.647%
21.	Keewatin-Patricia District School Board	Red Lake Board of Education	82.546%	72.044%	98.072%

Table 2   REGULATIONS UNDER THE EDUCATION ACT

Item/ Point	Column 1/ Colonne 1 District School Board/Conseil scolaire de district	Column 2/ Colonne 2 Old Board Name/ Nom de l'ancien conseil	Column 3/ Colonne 3 Non-Growth projects/ Projets non liés à la croissance	Column 4/ Colonne 4 Growth projects/ Projets liés à la croissance	Column 5/ Colonne 5 French language secondary school projects/ Projets visant les écoles secondaires de langue française
22.	Rainy River District School Board	Atikokan Board of Education	83.931%	74.263%	97.904%
23.	Rainy River District School Board	Fort Frances-Rainy River Board of Education	77.913%	64.624%	97.564%
24.	Lakehead District School Board	Lakehead Board of Education	71.425%	54.230%	97.977%
25.	Superior-Greenstone District School Board	Beardmore, Geraldton, Longlac & Area Board of Education/Conseil de l'éducation de Beardmore, de Geraldton, de Longlac et des environs	78.808%	66.060%	97.348%
26.	Superior-Greenstone District School Board	Lake Superior Board of Education/Conseil scolaire du Lac Supérieur	77.900%	64.605%	97.606%
27.	Superior-Greenstone District School Board	Nipigon-Red Rock Board of Education	76.856%	62.934%	97.379%
28.	Bluewater District School Board	Bruce County Board of Education	78.008%	64.774%	98.443%
29.	Bluewater District School Board	Grey County Board of Education	74.551%	59.237%	98.198%
30.	Avon Maitland District School Board	Huron County Board of Education	77.006%	63.170%	98.372%
31.	Avon Maitland District School Board	Perth County Board of Education	73.888%	58.174%	98.151%

Table 2

	Column 1/ Colonne 1	Column 2/ Colonne 2	Column 3/ Colonne 3	Column 4/ Colonne 4	Column 5/ Colonne 5
ITEM/ POINT	DISTRICT SCHOOL BOARD/CONSEIL SCOLAIRE DE DISTRICT	OLD BOARD NAME/ NOM DE L'ANCIEN CONSEIL	NON-GROWTH PROJECTS/ PROJETS NON LIÉS À LA CROISSANCE	GROWTH PROJECTS/ PROJETS LIÉS À LA CROISSANCE	FRENCH LANGUAGE SECONDARY SCHOOL PROJECTS/ PROJETS VISANT LES ÉCOLES SECONDAIRES DE LANGUE FRANÇAISE
32.	Greater Essex County District School Board	Essex County Board of Education	76.721%	62.713%	98.352%
33.	Greater Essex County District School Board	Board of Education for the City of Windsor	70.364%	52.529%	97.902%
34.	English-language Public District School Board No. 10	Kent County Board of Education	77.588%	64.101%	98.413%
35.	English-language Public District School Board No. 10	Lambton County Board of Education/ Conseil de l'éducation du comté de Lambton	73.096%	56.907%	98.095%
36.	Thames Valley District School Board	Elgin County Board of Education	79.333%	66.896%	96.537%
37.	Thames Valley District School Board	Board of Education for the City of London/Le conseil de l'éducation de la ville de London	70.748%	53.145%	97.929%
38.	Thames Valley District School Board	Middlesex County Board of Education	77.653%	64.205%	98.418%
39.	Thames Valley District School Board	Oxford County Board of Education	74.079%	58.480%	96.165%
40.	Toronto District School Board	Metropolitan Toronto School Board	43.066%	8.805%	95.969%
41.	Durham District School Board	Durham Board of Education	74.576%	59.276%	98.200%

Table 2

REGULATIONS UNDER THE EDUCATION ACT

Item/ Point	Column 1/ Colonne 1 District School Board/Conseil scolaire de district	Column 2/ Colonne 2 Old Board Name/ Nom de l'ancien conseil	Column 3/ Colonne 3 Non-Growth projects/ Projets non liés à la croissance	Column 4/ Colonne 4 Growth projects/ Projets liés à la croissance	Column 5/ Colonne 5 French language secondary school projects/ Projets visant les écoles secondaires de langue française
42.	English-language Public District School Board No. 14	Northumberland & Clarington Board of Education	77.945%	64.674%	98.439%
43.	English-language Public District School Board No. 14	Peterborough County Board of Education	68.740%	49.929%	97.787%
44.	English-language Public District School Board No. 15	Haliburton County Board of Education	49.937%	19.810%	94.808%
45.	English-language Public District School Board No. 15	Muskoka Board of Education	48.697%	17.825%	96.368%
46.	English-language Public District School Board No. 15	Victoria County Board of Education	74.148%	58.591%	98.170%
47.	English-language Public District School Board No. 16	York Region Board of Education	55.430%	28.609%	96.845%
48.	Simcoe County District School Board	Simcoe County Board of Education	71.999%	55.149%	97.032%
49.	English-language Public District School Board No. 18	Dufferin County Board of Education	78.853%	66.128%	98.503%
50.	English-language Public District School Board No. 18	Wellington County Board of Education	71.817%	54.858%	98.005%
51.	Peel District School Board	Peel Board of Education	59.615%	35.313%	97.141%

Table 2

REGULATION 285/98

	Column 1/ Colonne 1	Column 2/ Colonne 2	Column 3/ Colonne 3	Column 4/ Colonne 4	Column 5/ Colonne 5
ITEM/ POINT	DISTRICT SCHOOL BOARD/CONSEIL SCOLAIRE DE DISTRICT	OLD BOARD NAME/ NOM DE L'ANCIEN CONSEIL	NON-GROWTH PROJECTS/ PROJETS NON LIÉS À LA CROISSANCE	GROWTH PROJECTS/ PROJETS LIÉS À LA CROISSANCE	FRENCH LANGUAGE SECONDARY SCHOOL PROJECTS/ PROJETS VISANT LES ÉCOLES SECONDAIRES DE LANGUE FRANÇAISE
52.	English-language Public District School Board No. 20	Halton Board of Education	61.389%	38.154%	97.266%
53.	Hamilton-Wentworth District School Board	Board of Education for the City of Hamilton/Conseil de l'éducation de la ville de Hamilton	69.510%	51.162%	97.841%
54.	Hamilton-Wentworth District School Board	Wentworth County Board of Education	72.067%	55.258%	98.022%
55.	English-language Public District School Board No. 22	Lincoln County Board of Education	71.930%	55.038%	98.013%
56.	English-language Public District School Board No. 22	Niagara South Board of Education/Conseil scolaire de Niagara Sud	73.106%	56.922%	98.096%
57.	Grand Erie District School Board	Brant County Board of Education	76.010%	61.573%	98.302%
58.	Grand Erie District School Board	Haldimand Board of Education	76.216%	61.904%	98.316%
59.	Grand Erie District School Board	Norfolk Board of Education	79.649%	67.402%	98.559%
60.	Waterloo Region District School Board	Waterloo County Board of Education	73.006%	56.763%	98.089%
61.	Ottawa-Carleton District School Board	Carleton Board of Education	74.234%	58.729%	98.176%
62.	Ottawa-Carleton District School Board	Ottawa Board of Education	45.120%	12.095%	96.115%

Table 2 REGULATIONS UNDER THE EDUCATION ACT

	Column 1/ Colonne 1	Column 2/ Colonne 2	Column 3/ Colonne 3	Column 4/ Colonne 4	Column 5/ Colonne 5
Item/ Point	District School Board/Conseil scolaire de district	Old Board Name/ Nom de l'ancien conseil	Non-Growth projects/ Projets non liés à la croissance	Growth projects/ Projets liés à la croissance	French language secondary school projects/ Projets visant les écoles secondaires de langue française
63.	English-language Public District School Board No. 26	Lanark County Board of Education	79.078%	66.488%	98.519%
64.	English-language Public District School Board No. 26	Leeds and Grenville County Board of Education	73.157%	57.004%	98.100%
65.	English-language Public District School Board No. 26	Prescott and Russell County Board of Education	86.188%	77.876%	99.022%
66.	English-language Public District School Board No. 26	Stormont, Dundas & Glengarry County Board of Education	79.678%	67.449%	98.561%
67.	English-language Public District School Board No. 27	Frontenac County Board of Education	71.893%	54.978%	98.010%
68.	English-language Public District School Board No. 27	Lennox and Addington County Board of Education	79.818%	67.673%	98.571%
69.	Renfrew County District School Board	Renfrew County Board of Education	77.946%	64.674%	98.439%
70.	Hastings and Prince Edward District School Board	Hastings County Board of Education	75.521%	60.791%	98.267%
71.	Hastings and Prince Edward District School Board	Prince Edward County Board of Education	75.575%	60.876%	98.271%

REGULATION 285/98 **Table 2**

Item/Point	Column 1/Colonne 1 District School Board/Conseil scolaire de district	Column 2/Colonne 2 Old Board Name/Nom de l'ancien conseil	Column 3/Colonne 3 Non-Growth projects/Projets non liés à la croissance	Column 4/Colonne 4 Growth projects/Projets liés à la croissance	Column 5/Colonne 5 French language secondary school projects/Projets visant les écoles secondaires de langue française
72.	Northeastern Catholic District School Board	Cochrane, Iroquois Falls/Black River—Matheson District Roman Catholic Separate School Board	84.675%	75.452%	98.915%
73.	Northeastern Catholic District School Board	Hearst District Roman Catholic Separate School Board	84.366%	74.958%	98.893%
74.	Northeastern Catholic District School Board	Kapuskasing District Roman Catholic Separate School Board/Conseil des écoles séparées catholiques du district de Kapuskasing	82.526%	72.011%	98.763%
75.	Northeastern Catholic District School Board	Kirkland Lake-Timiskaming District Roman Catholic Separate School Board/Conseil des écoles séparées catholiques du district de Kirkland Lake-Timmiskaming	91.397%	86.219%	99.391%
76.	Northeastern Catholic District School Board	Timmins District Roman Catholic Separate School Board/Conseil des écoles séparées catholiques de Timmins	80.819%	69.277%	98.642%

Table 2

REGULATIONS UNDER THE EDUCATION ACT

Item/ Point	Column 1/ Colonne 1 — District School Board/Conseil scolaire de district	Column 2/ Colonne 2 — Old Board Name/ Nom de l'ancien conseil	Column 3/ Colonne 3 — Non-Growth projects/ Projets non liés à la croissance	Column 4/ Colonne 4 — Growth projects/ Projets liés à la croissance	Column 5/ Colonne 5 — French language secondary school projects/ Projets visant les écoles secondaires de langue française
77.	Nipissing-Parry Sound Catholic District School Board	Nipissing District Roman Catholic Separate School Board	83.724%	73.929%	98.848%
78.	Huron-Superior Catholic District School Board	Chapleau District Roman Catholic Separate School Board	91.494%	86.367%	N/A
79.	Huron-Superior Catholic District School Board	Michipicoten District Roman Catholic Separate School Board	83.504%	73.561%	N/A
80.	Huron-Superior Catholic District School Board	North Shore District Roman Catholic Separate School Board	88.220%	81.120%	N/A
81.	Huron-Superior Catholic District School Board	Sault Ste. Marie District Roman Catholic Separate School Board	79.712%	67.503%	98.564%
82.	Sudbury Catholic District School Board	Sudbury District Roman Catholic Separate School Board/Conseil des écoles séparées catholiques de Sudbury	81.894%	70.998%	98.718%
83.	Northwest Catholic District School Board	Dryden District Roman Catholic Separate School Board	84.728%	75.522%	N/A

REGULATION 285/98 **Table 2**

Item/Point	Column 1/Colonne 1 District School Board/Conseil scolaire de district	Column 2/Colonne 2 Old Board Name/Nom de l'ancien conseil	Column 3/Colonne 3 Non-Growth projects/Projets non liés à la croissance	Column 4/Colonne 4 Growth projects/Projets liés à la croissance	Column 5/Colonne 5 French language secondary school projects/Projets visant les écoles secondaires de langue française
84.	Northwest Catholic District School Board	Fort Frances-Rainy River District Roman Catholic Separate School Board	87.619%	80.156%	N/A
85.	Kenora Catholic District School Board	Kenora District Roman Catholic Separate School Board	83.998%	74.368%	98.867%
86.	Superior North Catholic District School Board	Geraldton District Roman Catholic Separate School Board/Conseil des écoles séparées catholiques du district de Geraldton	88.353%	81.332%	N/A
87.	Superior North Catholic District School Board	North of Superior District Roman Catholic Separate School Board/Conseil des écoles séparées catholiques du district Supérieur Nord	81.044%	69.619%	N/A
88.	Thunder Bay Catholic District School Board	Lakehead District Roman Catholic Separate School Board/Conseil des écoles séparées catholiques du district de Lakehead	80.133%	68.177%	98.593%

Table 2

REGULATIONS UNDER THE EDUCATION ACT

Item/ Point	Column 1/ Colonne 1 District School Board/Conseil scolaire de district	Column 2/ Colonne 2 Old Board Name/ Nom de l'ancien conseil	Column 3/ Colonne 3 Non-Growth projects/ Projets non liés à la croissance	Column 4/ Colonne 4 Growth projects/ Projets liés à la croissance	Column 5/ Colonne 5 French language secondary school projects/ Projets visant les écoles secondaires de langue française
89.	Bruce-Grey Catholic District School Board	Bruce-Grey County Roman Catholic Separate School Board	85.745%	77.167%	98.991%
90.	Huron Perth Catholic District School Board	Huron-Perth County Roman Catholic Separate School Board	84.421%	75.046%	98.897%
91.	English-language Separate District School Board No. 37	Essex County Roman Catholic Separate School Board/Conseil des écoles séparées catholiques du comté d'Essex	84.604%	75.339%	98.910%
92.	English-language Separate District School Board No. 37	Windsor Roman Catholic Separate School Board/Conseil de l'éducation catholique de Windsor	79.706%	67.494%	98.563%
93.	English-language Separate District School Board No. 38	Elgin County Roman Catholic Separate School Board	83.645%	73.803%	98.842%
94.	English-language Separate District School Board No. 38	London and Middlesex County Roman Catholic Separate School Board/Conseil des écoles catholiques de London et du comté de Middlesex	81.530%	70.416%	98.692%

REGULATION 285/98 **Table 2**

Item/ Point	Column 1/ Colonne 1 District School Board/Conseil scolaire de district	Column 2/ Colonne 2 Old Board Name/ Nom de l'ancien conseil	Column 3/ Colonne 3 Non-Growth projects/ Projets non liés à la croissance	Column 4/ Colonne 4 Growth projects/ Projets liés à la croissance	Column 5/ Colonne 5 French language secondary school projects/ Projets visant les écoles secondaires de langue française
95.	English-language Separate District School Board No. 38	Oxford County Roman Catholic Separate School Board/Conseil des écoles séparées catholiques romaines du comté d'Oxford	82.993%	72.758%	98.796%
96.	English-language Separate District School Board No. 39	Kent County Roman Catholic Separate School Board/Conseil des écoles séparées Catholiques de Kent	86.053%	77.661%	99.013%
97.	English-language Separate District School Board No. 39	Lambton County Roman Catholic Separate School Board/Conseil des écoles séparées catholiques du comté de Lambton	83.132%	72.982%	98.806%
98.	English-language Separate District School Board No. 40	Metropolitan Separate School Board/Conseil des écoles catholiques du Grand Toronto	67.664%	48.205%	97.711%
99.	English-language Separate District School Board No. 41	Peterborough, Victoria, Northumberland & Clarington Roman Catholic Separate School Board	85.431%	76.664%	98.969%

Table 2 REGULATIONS UNDER THE EDUCATION ACT

Item/ Point	Column 1/ Colonne 1 District School Board/Conseil scolaire de district	Column 2/ Colonne 2 Old Board Name/ Nom de l'ancien conseil	Column 3/ Colonne 3 Non-Growth projects/ Projets non liés à la croissance	Column 4/ Colonne 4 Growth projects/ Projets liés à la croissance	Column 5/ Colonne 5 French Language Secondary School projects/ Projets visant les écoles secondaires de langue française
100.	York Catholic District School Board	York Region Roman Catholic Separate School Board/Conseil des écoles séparées catholiques de la région de York	75.559%	60.851%	98.270%
101.	English-language Separate District School Board No. 43	Dufferin Peel Roman Catholic Separate School Board/Conseil des écoles séparées catholiques de Dufferin & Peel	80.006%	67.974%	98.584%
102.	Simcoe Muskoka Catholic District School Board	Simcoe County Roman Catholic Separate School Board	83.859%	74.147%	98.857%
103.	Durham Catholic District School Board	Durham Region Roman Catholic Separate School Board/Conseil des écoles séparées catholiques de la région de Durham	83.579%	73.698%	98.837%
104.	English-language Separate District School Board No. 46	Halton Roman Catholic Separate School Board/Conseil des écoles catholiques de Halton	78.052%	64.845%	98.446%

Table 2

Item/ Point	Column 1/ Colonne 1 District School Board/Conseil scolaire de district	Column 2/ Colonne 2 Old Board Name/ Nom de l'ancien conseil	Column 3/ Colonne 3 Non-Growth projects/ Projets non liés à la croissance	Column 4/ Colonne 4 Growth projects/ Projets liés à la croissance	Column 5/ Colonne 5 French language secondary school projects/ Projets visant les écoles secondaires de langue française
105.	Hamilton-Wentworth Catholic District School Board	Hamilton-Wentworth Roman Catholic Separate School Board/Conseil des écoles séparées catholiques romaines de Hamilton-Wentworth	77.833%	64.493%	98.431%
106.	Wellington Catholic District School Board	Wellington County Roman Catholic Separate School Board/Conseil des écoles catholiques du comté de Wellington	80.507%	68.777%	98.620%
107.	Waterloo Catholic District School Board	Waterloo County Roman Catholic Separate School Board/Conseil des écoles séparées catholiques de la région de Waterloo	83.008%	72.783%	98.797%
108.	Niagara Catholic District School Board	Lincoln County Roman Catholic Separate School Board/Conseil des écoles catholiques du comté de Lincoln	82.361%	71.746%	98.751%

Table 2 REGULATIONS UNDER THE EDUCATION ACT

Item/Point	Column 1/Colonne 1 District School Board/Conseil scolaire de district	Column 2/Colonne 2 Old Board Name/Nom de l'ancien conseil	Column 3/Colonne 3 Non-Growth projects/Projets non liés à la croissance	Column 4/Colonne 4 Growth projects/Projets liés à la croissance	Column 5/Colonne 5 French language secondary school projects/Projets visant les écoles secondaires de langue française
109.	Niagara Catholic District School Board	Welland County Roman Catholic Separate School Board/Conseil scolaire des écoles catholiques romaines du comté de Welland	81.883%	70.981%	98.717%
110.	Brant/Haldimand-Norfolk Catholic District School Board	Brant County Roman Catholic Separate School Board/Conseil des écoles séparées catholiques du comté de Brant	86.654%	78.622%	99.055%
111.	Brant/Haldimand-Norfolk Catholic District School Board	Haldimand-Norfolk County Roman Catholic Separate School Board/Conseil des écoles séparées catholiques de Haldimand-Norfolk	83.018%	72.798%	98.798%
112.	English-language Separate District School Board No. 52	Lanark-Leeds & Grenville County Roman Catholic Separate School Board	86.200%	77.896%	99.023%
113.	English-language Separate District School Board No. 52	Prescott Russell County Roman Catholic English-language Separate School Board	82.430%	71.857%	98.756%

Table 2

REGULATION 285/98

Item/ Point	Column 1/ Colonne 1 District School Board/Conseil scolaire de district	Column 2/ Colonne 2 Old Board Name/ Nom de l'ancien conseil	Column 3/ Colonne 3 Non-Growth projects/ Projets non liés à la croissance	Column 4/ Colonne 4 Growth projects/ Projets liés à la croissance	Column 5/ Colonne 5 French language secondary school projects/ Projets visant les écoles secondaires de langue française
114.	English-language Separate District School Board No. 52	Stormont, Dundas and Glengarry County Roman Catholic Separate School Board/Conseil des écoles séparées catholiques des comtés de Stormont, Dundas et Glengarry	87.213%	79.519%	99.095%
115.	Ottawa-Carleton Catholic District School Board	Carleton Roman Catholic Separate School Board	85.606%	76.944%	98.981%
116.	Ottawa-Carleton Catholic District School Board	Ottawa Roman Catholic Separate School Board	67.600%	48.103%	97.706%
117.	Renfrew County Catholic District School Board	Renfrew County Roman Catholic Separate School Board	85.159%	76.228%	98.949%
118.	English-language Separate District School Board No. 55	Frontenac-Lennox & Addington County Roman Catholic Separate School Board	82.665%	72.234%	98.773%
119.	English-language Separate District School Board No. 55	Hastings-Prince Edward County Roman Catholic Separate School Board	85.151%	76.215%	98.949%

505

Table 2

REGULATIONS UNDER THE EDUCATION ACT

Item/ Point	Column 1/ Colonne 1 — District School Board/Conseil scolaire de district	Column 2/ Colonne 2 — Old Board Name/ Nom de l'ancien conseil	Column 3/ Colonne 3 — Non-Growth projects/ Projets non liés à la croissance	Column 4/ Colonne 4 — Growth projects/ Projets liés à la croissance	Column 5/ Colonne 5 — French language secondary school projects/ Projets visant les écoles secondaires de langue française
120.	Conseil de district des écoles publiques de langue française No. 56	Cochrane-Iroquois Falls, Black River-Matheson Board of Education	81.864%	70.950%	98.716%
121.	Conseil de district des écoles publiques de langue française No. 56	East Parry Sound Board of Education	76.827%	62.883%	98.359%
122.	Conseil de district des écoles publiques de langue française No. 56	Hearst Board of Education	77.112%	63.339%	98.380%
123.	Conseil de district des écoles publiques de langue française No. 56	Hornepayne Board of Education	84.071%	74.487%	98.280%
124.	Conseil de district des écoles publiques de langue française No. 56	Kapuskasing-Smooth Rock Falls Board of Education/Conseil de l'éducation de Kapuskasing-Smooth Rock Falls et de son district	72.924%	56.630%	98.083%
125.	Conseil de district des écoles publiques de langue française No. 56	Kirkland Lake Board of Education	84.300%	74.852%	98.888%
126.	Conseil de district des écoles publiques de langue française No. 56	Muskoka Board of Education	48.697%	17.825%	96.368%

Table 2

REGULATION 285/98

	Column 1/ Colonne 1	Column 2/ Colonne 2	Column 3/ Colonne 3	Column 4/ Colonne 4	Column 5/ Colonne 5
ITEM/ POINT	DISTRICT SCHOOL BOARD/CONSEIL SCOLAIRE DE DISTRICT	OLD BOARD NAME/ NOM DE L'ANCIEN CONSEIL	NON-GROWTH PROJECTS/ PROJETS NON LIÉS À LA CROISSANCE	GROWTH PROJECTS/ PROJETS LIÉS À LA CROISSANCE	FRENCH LANGUAGE SECONDARY SCHOOL PROJECTS/ PROJETS VISANT LES ÉCOLES SECONDAIRES DE LANGUE FRANÇAISE
127.	Conseil de district des écoles publiques de langue française No. 56	Nipissing Board of Education	79.558%	67.257%	98.553%
128.	Conseil de district des écoles publiques de langue française No. 56	Timiskaming Board of Education	77.573%	64.077%	98.412%
129.	Conseil de district des écoles publiques de langue française No. 56	Timmins Board of Education	79.293%	66.832%	96.534%
130.	Conseil de district des écoles publiques de langue française No. 56	West Parry Sound Board of Education	53.530%	25.567%	94.995%
131.	Conseil scolaire de district du Grand Nord de l'Ontario	Atikokan Board of Education	83.931%	74.263%	97.904%
132.	Conseil scolaire de district du Grand Nord de l'Ontario	Central Algoma Board of Education	83.742%	73.958%	98.849%
133.	Conseil scolaire de district du Grand Nord de l'Ontario	Chapleau Board of Education	82.893%	72.605%	97.302%
134.	Conseil scolaire de district du Grand Nord de l'Ontario	Dryden Board of Education	74.316%	58.863%	97.199%
135.	Conseil scolaire de district du Grand Nord de l'Ontario	Espanola Board of Education	76.304%	62.051%	97.359%

Table 2

REGULATIONS UNDER THE EDUCATION ACT

Item/ Point	Column 1/ Colonne 1 District School Board/Conseil scolaire de district	Column 2/ Colonne 2 Old Board Name/ Nom de l'ancien conseil	Column 3/ Colonne 3 Non-Growth projects/ Projets non liés à la croissance	Column 4/ Colonne 4 Growth projects/ Projets liés à la croissance	Column 5/ Colonne 5 French language secondary school projects/ Projets visant les écoles secondaires de langue française
136.	Conseil scolaire de district du Grand Nord de l'Ontario	Fort Frances-Rainy River Board of Education	77.913%	64.624%	97.564%
137.	Conseil scolaire de district du Grand Nord de l'Ontario	Beardmore, Geraldton, Longlac & Area Board of Education/Conseil de l'éducation de Beardmore, de Geraldton, de Longlac et des environs	78.808%	66.060%	97.348%
138.	Conseil scolaire de district du Grand Nord de l'Ontario	Kenora Board of Education	66.763%	46.763%	97.647%
139.	Conseil scolaire de district du Grand Nord de l'Ontario	Lake Superior Board of Education/Conseil scolaire du Lac Supérieur	77.900%	64.605%	97.606%
140.	Conseil scolaire de district du Grand Nord de l'Ontario	Lakehead Board of Education	71.425%	54.230%	97.977%
141.	Conseil scolaire de district du Grand Nord de l'Ontario	Manitoulin Board of Education	71.558%	54.442%	97.067%
142.	Conseil scolaire de district du Grand Nord de l'Ontario	Michipicoten Board of Education	71.584%	54.492%	96.492%
143.	Conseil scolaire de district du Grand Nord de l'Ontario	Nipigon-Red Rock Board of Education	76.856%	62.934%	97.379%

Table 2

Item/Point	Column 1/Colonne 1 District School Board/Conseil scolaire de district	Column 2/Colonne 2 Old Board Name/Nom de l'ancien conseil	Column 3/Colonne 3 Non-Growth projects/Projets non liés à la croissance	Column 4/Colonne 4 Growth projects/Projets liés à la croissance	Column 5/Colonne 5 French language secondary school projects/Projets visant les écoles secondaires de langue française
144.	Conseil scolaire de district du Grand Nord de l'Ontario	North Shore Board of Education	84.899%	75.814%	98.082%
145.	Conseil scolaire de district du Grand Nord de l'Ontario	Red Lake Board of Education	82.546%	72.044%	98.072%
146.	Conseil scolaire de district du Grand Nord de l'Ontario	Sault Ste. Marie Board of Education	75.356%	60.526%	98.255%
147.	Conseil scolaire de district du Grand Nord de l'Ontario	Sudbury Board of Education	76.302%	62.041%	98.322%
148.	Conseil de district des écoles publiques de langue française No. 58	Brant County Board of Education	76.010%	61.573%	98.302%
149.	Conseil de district des écoles publiques de langue française No. 58	Bruce County Board of Education	78.008%	64.774%	98.443%
150.	Conseil de district des écoles publiques de langue française No. 58	Dufferin County Board of Education	78.853%	66.128%	98.503%
151.	Conseil de district des écoles publiques de langue française No. 58	Durham Board of Education	74.576%	59.276%	98.200%

Table 2 REGULATIONS UNDER THE EDUCATION ACT

Item/ Point	Column 1/ Colonne 1 District School Board/Conseil scolaire de district	Column 2/ Colonne 2 Old Board Name/ Nom de l'ancien conseil	Column 3/ Colonne 3 Non-Growth projects/ Projets non liés à la croissance	Column 4/ Colonne 4 Growth projects/ Projets liés à la croissance	Column 5/ Colonne 5 French language secondary school projects/ Projets visant les écoles secondaires de langue française
152.	Conseil de district des écoles publiques de langue française No. 58	Elgin County Board of Education	79.333%	66.896%	98.537%
153.	Conseil de district des écoles publiques de langue française No. 58	Essex County Board of Education	76.721%	62.713%	98.352%
154.	Conseil de district des écoles publiques de langue française No. 58	Grey County Board of Education	74.551%	59.237%	96.198%
155.	Conseil de district des écoles publiques de langue française No. 58	Haldimand Board of Education	76.216%	61.904%	98.316%
156.	Conseil de district des écoles publiques de langue française No. 58	Haliburton County Board of Education	49.937%	19.810%	94.808%
157.	Conseil de district des écoles publiques de langue française No. 58	Halton Board of Education	61.389%	38.154%	97.266%
158.	Conseil de district des écoles publiques de langue française No. 58	Board of Education for the City of Hamilton/Conseil de l'éducation de la ville de Hamilton	69.510%	51.162%	97.841%

Table 2

REGULATION 285/98

Item/ Point	Column 1/ Colonne 1 District School Board/Conseil scolaire de district	Column 2/ Colonne 2 Old Board Name/ Nom de l'ancien conseil	Column 3/ Colonne 3 Non-Growth projects/ Projets non liés à la croissance	Column 4/ Colonne 4 Growth projects/ Projets liés à la croissance	Column 5/ Colonne 5 French language secondary school projects/ Projets visant les écoles secondaires de langue française
159.	Conseil de district des écoles publiques de langue française No. 58	Huron County Board of Education	77.006%	63.170%	98.372%
160.	Conseil de district des écoles publiques de langue française No. 58	Kent County Board of Education	77.588%	64.101%	96.413%
161.	Conseil de district des écoles publiques de langue française No. 58	Lambton County Board of Education/ Conseil de l'éducation du comté de Lambton	73.096%	56.907%	98.095%
162.	Conseil de district des écoles publiques de langue française No. 58	Lincoln County Board of Education	71.930%	55.038%	98.013%
163.	Conseil de district des écoles publiques de langue française No. 58	Board of Education for the City of London/Le conseil de l'éducation de la ville de London	70.748%	53.145%	97.929%
164.	Conseil de district des écoles publiques de langue française No. 58	Metropolitan Toronto School Board	43.066%	8.805%	95.969%
165.	Conseil de district des écoles publiques de langue française No. 58	Middlesex County Board of Education	77.653%	64.205%	98.418%

Table 2 REGULATIONS UNDER THE EDUCATION ACT

Item/ Point	Column 1/ Colonne 1 District School Board/Conseil scolaire de district	Column 2/ Colonne 2 Old Board Name/ Nom de l'ancien conseil	Column 3/ Colonne 3 Non-Growth projects/ Projets non liés à la croissance	Column 4/ Colonne 4 Growth projects/ Projets liés à la croissance	Column 5/ Colonne 5 French language secondary school projects/ Projets visant les écoles secondaires de langue française
166.	Conseil de district des écoles publiques de langue française No. 58	Niagara South Board of Education/Conseil scolaire de Niagara Sud	73.108%	56.922%	98.096%
167.	Conseil de district des écoles publiques de langue française No. 58	Norfolk Board of Education	79.649%	67.402%	98.559%
168.	Conseil de district des écoles publiques de langue française No. 58	Northumberland & Clarington Board of Education	77.945%	64.674%	98.439%
169.	Conseil de district des écoles publiques de langue française No. 58	Oxford County Board of Education	74.079%	58.480%	98.165%
170.	Conseil de district des écoles publiques de langue française No. 58	Peel Board of Education	59.615%	35.313%	97.141%
171.	Conseil de district des écoles publiques de langue française No. 58	Perth County Board of Education	73.888%	58.174%	98.151%
172.	Conseil de district des écoles publiques de langue française No. 58	Peterborough County Board of Education	68.740%	49.929%	97.787%

Table 2

REGULATION 285/98

Item/ Point	Column 1/ Colonne 1 District School Board/Conseil scolaire de district	Column 2/ Colonne 2 Old Board Name/ Nom de l'ancien conseil	Column 3/ Colonne 3 Non-Growth projects/ Projets non liés à la croissance	Column 4/ Colonne 4 Growth projects/ Projets liés à la croissance	Column 5/ Colonne 5 French language secondary school projects/ Projets visant les écoles secondaires de langue française
173.	Conseil de district des écoles publiques de langue française No. 58	Simcoe County Board of Education	71.999%	55.149%	97.032%
174.	Conseil de district des écoles publiques de langue française No. 58	Victoria County Board of Education	74.148%	58.591%	98.170%
175.	Conseil de district des écoles publiques de langue française No. 58	Waterloo County Board of Education	73.006%	56.763%	98.089%
176.	Conseil de district des écoles publiques de langue française No. 58	Wellington County Board of Education	71.817%	54.858%	98.005%
177.	Conseil de district des écoles publiques de langue française No. 58	Wentworth County Board of Education	72.067%	55.258%	98.022%
178.	Conseil de district des écoles publiques de langue française No. 58	Board of Education for the City of Windsor	70.364%	52.529%	97.902%
179.	Conseil de district des écoles publiques de langue française No. 58	York Region Board of Education	55.430%	28.609%	96.845%

Table 2

REGULATIONS UNDER THE EDUCATION ACT

Item/Point	Column 1/Colonne 1 District School Board/Conseil scolaire de district	Column 2/Colonne 2 Old Board Name/Nom de l'ancien conseil	Column 3/Colonne 3 Non-Growth projects/Projets non liés à la croissance	Column 4/Colonne 4 Growth projects/Projets liés à la croissance	Column 5/Colonne 5 French language secondary school projects/Projets visant les écoles secondaires de langue française
180.	Conseil de district des écoles publiques de langue française No. 59	Frontenac County Board of Education	71.893%	54.978%	98.010%
181.	Conseil de district des écoles publiques de langue française No. 59	Hastings County Board of Education	75.521%	60.791%	96.267%
182.	Conseil de district des écoles publiques de langue française No. 59	Lanark County Board of Education	79.078%	66.488%	98.519%
183.	Conseil de district des écoles publiques de langue française No. 59	Leeds and Grenville County Board of Education	73.157%	57.004%	98.100%
184.	Conseil de district des écoles publiques de langue française No. 59	Lennox and Addington County Board of Education	79.818%	67.673%	98.571%
185.	Conseil de district des écoles publiques de langue française No. 59	Conseil des écoles publiques d'Ottawa-Carleton	82.577%	72.093%	N/A
186.	Conseil de district des écoles publiques de langue française No. 59	Prescott and Russell County Board of Education	86.188%	77.876%	99.022%

Table 2

REGULATION 285/98

Item/ Point	Column 1/ Colonne 1 District School Board/Conseil scolaire de district	Column 2/ Colonne 2 Old Board Name/ Nom de l'ancien conseil	Column 3/ Colonne 3 Non-Growth projects/ Projets non liés à la croissance	Column 4/ Colonne 4 Growth projects/ Projets liés à la croissance	Column 5/ Colonne 5 French language secondary school projects/ Projets visant les écoles secondaires de langue française
187.	Conseil de district des écoles publiques de langue française No. 59	Prince Edward County Board of Education	75.575%	60.876%	98.271%
188.	Conseil de district des écoles publiques de langue française No. 59	Renfrew County Board of Education	77.946%	64.674%	98.439%
189.	Conseil de district des écoles publiques de langue française No. 59	Stormont, Dundas & Glengarry County Board of Education	79.678%	67.449%	98.561%
190.	Conseil de district des écoles séparées de langue française No. 60A	Cochrane, Iroquois Falls/Black River-Matheson District Roman Catholic Separate School Board	84.675%	75.452%	98.915%
191.	Conseil de district des écoles séparées de langue française No. 60A	Hearst District Roman Catholic Separate School Board	84.366%	74.958%	98.893%
192.	Conseil de district des écoles séparées de langue française No. 60A	Kapuskasing District Roman Catholic Separate School Board/Conseil des écoles séparées catholiques du district de Kapuskasing	82.526%	72.011%	98.763%

Table 2

REGULATIONS UNDER THE EDUCATION ACT

Item/Point	Column 1/Colonne 1 District School Board/Conseil scolaire de district	Column 2/Colonne 2 Old Board Name/Nom de l'ancien conseil	Column 3/Colonne 3 Non-Growth projects/Projets non liés à la croissance	Column 4/Colonne 4 Growth projects/Projets liés à la croissance	Column 5/Colonne 5 French language secondary school projects/Projets visant les écoles secondaires de langue française
193.	Conseil de district des écoles séparées de langue française No. 60A	Kirkland Lake-Timiskaming District Roman Catholic Separate School Board/Conseil des écoles séparées catholiques du district de Kirkland Lake-Timiskaming	91.397%	86.219%	99.391%
194.	Conseil de district des écoles séparées de langue française No. 60A	Timmins District Roman Catholic Separate School Board/Conseil des écoles séparées catholiques de Timmins	80.819%	69.277%	98.642%
195.	Conseil de district des écoles séparées de langue française No. 60B	Nipissing District Roman Catholic Separate School Board	83.724%	73.929%	98.848%
196.	Conseil de district des écoles séparées de langue française No. 61	Chapleau District Roman Catholic Separate School Board	91.494%	86.367%	N/A
197.	Conseil de district des écoles séparées de langue française No. 61	Michipicoten District Roman Catholic Separate School Board	83.504%	73.561%	N/A
198.	Conseil de district des écoles séparées de langue française No. 61	North Shore District Roman Catholic Separate School Board	88.220%	81.120%	N/A

Table 2

Item/ Point	Column 1/ Colonne 1 District School Board/Conseil scolaire de district	Column 2/ Colonne 2 Old Board Name/ Nom de l'ancien conseil	Column 3/ Colonne 3 Non-Growth projects/ Projets non liés à la croissance	Column 4/ Colonne 4 Growth projects/ Projets liés à la croissance	Column 5/ Colonne 5 French language secondary school projects/ Projets visant les écoles secondaires de langue française
199.	Conseil de district des écoles séparées de langue française No. 61	Sault Ste. Marie District Roman Catholic Separate School Board	79.712%	67.503%	98.564%
200.	Conseil de district des écoles séparées de langue française No. 61	Sudbury District Roman Catholic Separate School Board/Conseil des écoles séparées catholiques de Sudbury	81.894%	70.998%	98.718%
201.	Conseil de district des écoles séparées de langue française No. 62	Dryden District Roman Catholic Separate School Board	84.728%	75.522%	N/A
202.	Conseil de district des écoles séparées de langue française No. 62	Fort Frances-Rainy River District Roman Catholic Separate School Board	87.619%	80.156%	N/A
203.	Conseil de district des écoles séparées de langue française No. 62	Geraldton District Roman Catholic Separate School Board/Conseil des écoles séparées catholiques du district de Geraldton	88.353%	81.332%	N/A
204.	Conseil de district des écoles séparées de langue française No. 62	Kenora District Roman Catholic Separate School Board	83.998%	74.368%	98.867%

Table 2 — REGULATIONS UNDER THE EDUCATION ACT

Item/Point	Column 1/Colonne 1 District School Board/Conseil scolaire de district	Column 2/Colonne 2 Old Board Name/Nom de l'ancien conseil	Column 3/Colonne 3 Non-Growth projects/Projets non liés à la croissance	Column 4/Colonne 4 Growth projects/Projets liés à la croissance	Column 5/Colonne 5 French Language Secondary School projects/Projets visant les écoles secondaires de langue française
205.	Conseil de district des écoles séparées de langue française No. 62	Lakehead District Roman Catholic Separate School Board/Conseil des écoles séparées catholiques du district de Lakehead	80.133%	68.177%	98.593%
206.	Conseil de district des écoles séparées de langue française No. 62	North of Superior District Roman Catholic Separate School Board/Conseil des écoles séparées catholiques du district Supérieur Nord	81.044%	69.619%	N/A
207.	Conseil de district des écoles séparées de langue française No. 63	Bruce-Grey County Roman Catholic Separate School Board	85.745%	77.167%	98.991%
208.	Conseil de district des écoles séparées de langue française No. 63	Elgin County Roman Catholic Separate School Board	83.645%	73.803%	98.842%
209.	Conseil de district des écoles séparées de langue française No. 63	Essex County Roman Catholic Separate School Board/Conseil des écoles séparées catholiques du comté d'Essex	84.604%	75.339%	98.910%
210.	Conseil de district des écoles séparées de langue française No. 63	Huron-Perth County Roman Catholic Separate School Board	84.421%	75.046%	98.897%

Table 2

REGULATION 285/98

Item/ Point	Column 1/ Colonne 1 District School Board/Conseil scolaire de district	Column 2/ Colonne 2 Old Board Name/ Nom de l'ancien conseil	Column 3/ Colonne 3 Non-Growth projects/ Projets non liés à la croissance	Column 4/ Colonne 4 Growth projects/ Projets liés à la croissance	Column 5/ Colonne 5 French language secondary school projects/ Projets visant les écoles secondaires de langue française
211.	Conseil de district des écoles séparées de langue française No. 63	Kent County Roman Catholic Separate School Board/Conseil des écoles séparées catholiques de Kent	86.053%	77.661%	99.013%
212.	Conseil de district des écoles séparées de langue française No. 63	Lambton County Roman Catholic Separate School Board/Conseil des écoles séparées catholiques du comté de Lambton	83.132%	72.982%	98.806%
213.	Conseil de district des écoles séparées de langue française No. 63	London-Middlesex County Roman Catholic Separate School Board/Conseil des écoles catholiques de London et du comté de Middlesex	81.530%	70.416%	98.692%
214.	Conseil de district des écoles séparées de langue française No. 63	Oxford County Roman Catholic Separate School Board/Conseil des écoles séparées catholiques romaines du comté d'Oxford	82.993%	72.758%	98.796%
215.	Conseil de district des écoles séparées de langue française No. 63	Windsor Roman Catholic Separate School Board/Conseil de l'éducation catholique de Windsor	79.706%	67.494%	98.563%

Table 2

REGULATIONS UNDER THE EDUCATION ACT

Item/ Point	Column 1/ Colonne 1 District School Board/Conseil scolaire de district	Column 2/ Colonne 2 Old Board Name/ Nom de l'ancien conseil	Column 3/ Colonne 3 Non-Growth projects/ Projets non liés à la croissance	Column 4/ Colonne 4 Growth projects/ Projets liés à la croissance	Column 5/ Colonne 5 French language secondary school projects/ Projets visant les écoles secondaires de langue française
216.	Conseil de district des écoles séparées de langue française No. 64	Brant County Roman Catholic Separate School Board/Conseil des écoles séparées catholiques du comté de Brant	86.654%	78.622%	99.055%
217.	Conseil de district des écoles séparées de langue française No. 64	Dufferin Peel Roman Catholic Separate School Board/Conseil des écoles séparées catholiques de Dufferin & Peel	80.006%	67.974%	98.584%
218.	Conseil de district des écoles séparées de langue française No. 64	Durham Region Roman Catholic Separate School Board/Conseil des écoles séparées catholiques de la région de Durham	83.579%	73.698%	98.837%
219.	Conseil de district des écoles séparées de langue française No. 64	Haldimand-Norfolk County Roman Catholic Separate School Board/Conseil des écoles séparées catholiques de Haldimand-Norfolk	83.018%	72.798%	98.798%
220.	Conseil de district des écoles séparées de langue française No. 64	Halton Roman Catholic Separate School Board/Conseil des écoles catholiques de Halton	78.052%	64.845%	98.446%

Table 2

REGULATION 285/98

ITEM/POINT	Column 1/Colonne 1 DISTRICT SCHOOL BOARD/CONSEIL SCOLAIRE DE DISTRICT	Column 2/Colonne 2 OLD BOARD NAME/NOM DE L'ANCIEN CONSEIL	Column 3/Colonne 3 NON-GROWTH PROJECTS/PROJETS NON LIÉS À LA CROISSANCE	Column 4/Colonne 4 GROWTH PROJECTS/PROJETS LIÉS À LA CROISSANCE	Column 5/Colonne 5 FRENCH LANGUAGE SECONDARY SCHOOL PROJECTS/PROJETS VISANT LES ÉCOLES SECONDAIRES DE LANGUE FRANÇAISE
221.	Conseil de district des écoles séparées de langue française No. 64	Hamilton-Wentworth Roman Catholic Separate School Board/Conseil des écoles séparées catholiques romaines de Hamilton-Wentworth	77.833%	64.493%	98.431%
222.	Conseil de district des écoles séparées de langue française No. 64	Lincoln County Roman Catholic Separate School Board/Conseil des écoles catholiques du comté de Lincoln	82.361%	71.746%	98.751%
223.	Conseil de district des écoles séparées de langue française No. 64	Metropolitan Separate School Board/Conseil des écoles catholiques du Grand Toronto	67.664%	48.205%	97.711%
224.	Conseil de district des écoles séparées de langue française No. 64	Muskoka Board of Education	48.697%	17.825%	96.368%
225.	Conseil de district des écoles séparées de langue française No. 64	Peterborough, Victoria, Northumberland & Clarington Roman Catholic Separate School Board	85.431%	76.664%	98.969%
226.	Conseil de district des écoles séparées de langue française No. 64	Simcoe County Roman Catholic Separate School Board	83.859%	74.147%	98.857%

Table 2

REGULATIONS UNDER THE EDUCATION ACT

Item/ Point	Column 1/ Colonne 1 — District School Board/Conseil scolaire de district	Column 2/ Colonne 2 — Old Board Name/ Nom de l'ancien conseil	Column 3/ Colonne 3 — Non-Growth projects/ Projets non liés à la croissance	Column 4/ Colonne 4 — Growth projects/ Projets liés à la croissance	Column 5/ Colonne 5 — French Language Secondary School projects/ Projets visant les écoles secondaires de langue française
227.	Conseil de district des écoles séparées de langue française No. 64	Waterloo County Roman Catholic Separate School Board/Conseil des écoles séparées catholiques de la région de Waterloo	83.008%	72.783%	98.797%
228.	Conseil de district des écoles séparées de langue française No. 64	Welland County Roman Catholic Separate School Board/Conseil scolaire des écoles catholiques romaines du comté de Welland	81.883%	70.981%	98.717%
229.	Conseil de district des écoles séparées de langue française No. 64	Wellington County Roman Catholic Separate School Board/Conseil des écoles catholiques du comté de Wellington	80.507%	68.777%	96.620%
230.	Conseil de district des écoles séparées de langue française No. 64	York Region Roman Catholic Separate School Board/Conseil des écoles séparées catholiques de la région de York	75.559%	60.851%	98.270%
231.	Conseil de district des écoles séparées de langue française No. 65	Conseil des écoles séparées catholiques de langue française de Prescott-Russell	87.154%	79.423%	N/A

REGULATION 285/98 **Table 2**

Item/ Point	Column 1/ Colonne 1 District School Board/Conseil scolaire de district	Column 2/ Colonne 2 Old Board Name/ Nom de l'ancien conseil	Column 3/ Colonne 3 Non-Growth projects/ Projets non liés à la croissance	Column 4/ Colonne 4 Growth projects/ Projets liés à la croissance	Column 5/ Colonne 5 French language secondary school projects/ Projets visant les écoles secondaires de langue française
232.	Conseil de district des écoles séparées de langue française No. 65	Stormont, Dundas and Glengarry County Roman Catholic Separate School Board/Conseil des écoles séparées catholiques des comtés de Stormont, Dundas et Glengarry	87.213%	79.519%	99.095%
233.	Conseil de district des écoles séparées de langue française No. 66	Frontenac-Lennox and Addington County Roman Catholic Separate School Board	82.665%	72.234%	98.773%
234.	Conseil de district des écoles séparées de langue française No. 66	Hastings-Prince Edward County Roman Catholic Separate School Board	85.151%	76.215%	98.949%
235.	Conseil de district des écoles séparées de langue française No. 66	Lanark, Leeds & Grenville County Roman Catholic Separate School Board	86.200%	77.896%	99.023%
236.	Conseil de district des écoles séparées de langue française No. 66	Conseil des écoles catholiques de langue française de la région d'Ottawa-Carleton	75.893%	61.386%	N/A
237.	Conseil de district des écoles séparées de langue française No. 66	Renfrew County Roman Catholic Separate School Board	85.159%	76.228%	98.949%

REGULATION 286/98
CALCULATION OF AVERAGE DAILY ENROLMENT FOR THE 1998-99 FISCAL YEAR

O. Reg. 286/98, as am. O. Reg. 468/98; 211/99

1. In this Regulation,

"1998-99 fiscal year" means the period beginning September 1, 1998 and ending August 31, 1999; ("exercice 1998-1999")

"cycle" means the number of school days for which a schedule of classes in a school continues before the schedule is repeated; ("horaire")

"full-time pupil" means a pupil who,

(a) is enrolled in day school other than in junior kindergarten, and

(b) in respect of a cycle, is registered for classroom instruction for an average of at least 210 minutes per school day; ("élève à temps plein")

"half-time pupil" means,

(a) a pupil who is enrolled in junior kindergarten and, in respect of a cycle, is registered for classroom instruction for an average of at least 150 minutes per school day, and

(b) a pupil who is enrolled in kindergarten and, in respect of a cycle, is registered for classroom instruction for an average of 150 minutes or more per school day but less than 210 minutes per school day; ("élève à mi-temps")

"independent study course" means a credit course that is provided to a pupil other than a full-time pupil and that,

(a) meets the criteria set out in the independent study course register for inclusion in the determination of day school enrolment, or

(b) is approved by the Minister as an independent study course to be included in the determination of day school enrolment; ("cours d'études personnelles")

"part-time pupil" means a pupil who is enrolled in day school and is neither a full-time nor a half-time pupil. ("élève à temps partiel")

2. Day school average daily enrolment for a board for the 1998-99 fiscal year is the sum of,

(a) the product of 0.5 and the sum of,

(i) the number of full-time pupils enrolled on October 31, 1998 in schools operated by the board,

(ii) 0.5 times the number of half-time pupils enrolled on that day in schools operated by the board, and

(iii) the quotient obtained by determining, for each part-time pupil enrolled on that day in a school operated by the board, the number of minutes for which the pupil is registered for classroom instruction in the cycle that includes that day, in a course other than an independent study course, and dividing the sum of the numbers so determined by the product of 300 and the number of days in the cycle;

(b) the product of 0.5 and the sum of,
   (i) the number of full-time pupils enrolled on March 31, 1999 in schools operated by the board,
   (ii) 0.5 times the number of half-time pupils enrolled on that day in schools operated by the board, and
   (iii) the quotient obtained by determining, for each part-time pupil enrolled on that day in a school operated by the board, the number of minutes for which the pupil is registered for classroom instruction in the cycle that includes that day, in a course other than an independent study course, and dividing the sum of the numbers so determined by the product of 300 and the number of days in the cycle; and
(c) an amount in respect of each pupil enrolled in a school of the board who is registered for an independent study course, calculated as follows:

$$\frac{A \times B}{7.5}$$

where,

A = the number of credits and partial credits that may be earned by the pupil on successful completion of the course,

B = the fraction representing the portion of the total quantity of work required for completion of the course that is completed by the pupil during the 1998-99 fiscal year.

3. (1) Continuing education average daily enrolment for a board for the 1998-99 fiscal year is the sum of,

(a) an amount in respect of each pupil who is enrolled in a continuing education class or course established by the board, other than a summer school class or course within the meaning of section 4 or a continuing education course delivered primarily through means other than classroom instruction, calculated as follows:

$$\frac{A \times B}{300 \times 190}$$

where,

A = the number of sessions for which the pupil is enrolled in the 1998-99 fiscal year,

B = the number of minutes in each session; and

(b) an amount in respect of each pupil who is enrolled in a continuing education course established by the board and delivered primarily through means other than classroom instruction calculated as follows:

$$A \times 0.1134 \times B$$

where,

A = the number of credits and partial credits that may be earned by the pupil on successful completion of the course,

B = the fraction representing the portion of the total quantity of work required for completion of the course that is completed by the pupil during the period from September 1, 1998 to August 31, 1999.

(2) A course may be considered a continuing education course for the purposes of subsection (1) only if it is approved by the Minister and it is,

    (a) a course, including a course delivered primarily through means other than classroom instruction, established for adults for which one or more credits or credit equivalents may be granted, so long as in the case of a course offered by a school authority that is only authorized to provide elementary education, the course is in the intermediate division;

    (b) a class or course in citizenship and, where necessary, in language instruction in the English or the French language for persons admitted to Canada as permanent residents under the *Immigration Act* (Canada);

    (c) a class or course in English or French for adults whose first language learned and still understood is neither English nor French and that is not a class or course in which a pupil may earn a credit in English or French as a second language; or

    (d) a course of Native language instruction for adults.

(3) In calculating the continuing education average daily enrolment for a board under subsection (1) with respect to a course established for adults and referred to in clause (2)(a), any pupils in the course who are not adults shall be included.

(4) In calculating the continuing education average daily enrolment for a board under subsection (1) with respect to a class or course referred to in subsection (5),

    (a) if the number of pupils in the class or course is 10 or more and less than 15, that number shall be increased to 15; and

    (b) if the number of pupils in the class or course is less than 10, that number shall be increased by five.

(5) Subsection (4) applies with respect to,

    (a) a class or course referred to in clause (2)(b), (c) or (d); and

    (b) a class or course referred to in clause (2)(a), other than a course delivered primarily through means other than classroom instruction, if the class or course is offered in a secondary school that has an enrolment of fewer than 120 pupils per grade and that is located in a territorial district more than 80 kilometres from all other secondary schools in the Province that have the same language of instruction.

O. Reg. 468/98, s. 1.

4. (1) In this section,

"summer school class or course" means a class or course provided by a board between the hours of 8 a.m. and 5 p.m. if,

    (a) the class or course starts after the completion of the 1998-1999 school year and ends before the start of the 1999-2000 school year, and

    (b) the class or course,

        (i) is for developmentally delayed pupils,

        (ii) is one in which a pupil may earn a credit or a credit equivalent, or

        (iii) is for pupils who have completed grade 8 in the 1998-99 school year and for whom a remedial program has been recommended by the principal of the school at which the pupil completed grade 8.

(2) Only pupils who were enrolled in a day school program offered by a board in the 1998-99 school year shall be counted for the purposes of this section.

(3) Summer school average daily enrolment for a board for the 1998-99 fiscal year is the sum of the amounts in respect of each pupil enrolled in a summer school course or class that is provided by the board, other than a course delivered primarily through means other than classroom instruction, calculated as follows:

$$\frac{A \times B}{300 \times 190}$$

where,

A = the number of sessions of the summer school course or class in which the pupil is enrolled in the 1998-99 fiscal year,

B = the number of minutes in each session.

O. Reg. 211/99, s. 1.

REGULATION 287/98
STUDENT FOCUSED FUNDING-LEGISLATIVE GRANTS FOR THE SCHOOL BOARD 1998-99 FISCAL YEAR

O. Reg. 287/98, as am. O. Reg. 469/98; 537/98; 560/98; 651/98; 212/99

PART I

GENERAL

Interpretation

1. In this Regulation,

"1998-99 A.D.E. regulation" means Ontario Regulation 286/98; (''règlement sur l'effectif quotidien moyen de 1998-1999'')

"1998-99 fees regulation" means Ontario Regulation 288/98; (''règlement sur les droits de 1998-1999'')

"1998-99 fiscal year" means the fiscal year from September 1, 1998 to August 31, 1999; (''exercice 1998-1999'')

"ALF" stands for actualisation linguistique en français; (''ALF'')

"capital asset" means,

(a) a school site that provides or is capable of providing pupil accommodation and an addition or improvement to such a school site,

(b) a school building, including a fixture of a school building, and an addition, alteration, renovation or major repair to a school building or a fixture of a school building,

(c) furniture and equipment to be used in school buildings,

(d) library materials for the initial equipping of a library in a school building, and

(e) a water supply or electrical power supply on school property or the means of conveying water or electrical power to school property from outside the property; (''immobilisation'')

"cycle" has the same meaning as in the 1998-99 A.D.E. regulation; (''horaire'')

"designated board associated with an old board" means the district school board that is listed in Column 2 of Schedule 1 to Ontario Regulation 460/97, opposite the old board listed in Column 1 of that Schedule; (''conseil désigné rattaché à un ancien conseil'')

"elementary school pupil" means a pupil who is enrolled in any of junior kindergarten, kindergarten and grades one to eight; (''élève de l'élémentaire'')

"ESD" stands for English skills development; (''ESD'')

"ESL" stands for English as a second language; (''ESL'')

"full-time pupil" has the same meaning as in the 1998-99 A.D.E. regulation; (''élève à temps plein'')

"half-time pupil" has the same meaning as in the 1998-99 A.D.E. regulation; (''élève à mi-temps'') "independent study course" has the same meaning as in the 1998-99 A.D.E. regulation; ("cours d'études personnelles")

"ISA" stands for intensive support amount; ("AAS")

"isolate board" is a school authority other than a section 68 board; ("conseil isolé")

"Metropolitan Toronto area board" means,
- (a) The Board of Education for the Borough of East York,
- (b) The Board of Education for the City of Etobicoke,
- (c) The Board of Education for the City of North York,
- (d) The Board of Education for the City of Scarborough,
- (e) The Board of Education for the City of Toronto, and
- (f) The Board of Education for the City of York; ("conseil de secteur de la communauté urbaine de Toronto")

"old board" does not include the Metropolitan Toronto area boards or The Metropolitan Toronto French-Language School Council; ("ancien conseil")

"part-time pupil" has the same meaning as in the 1998-99 A.D.E. regulation; ("élève à temps partiel")

"PDF" stands for perfectionnement du français; ("PDF")

"secondary school pupil" means a pupil who is enrolled in any of grades nine to twelve or in a course leading to an OAC credit; ("élève du secondaire")

"section 68 board" is a board established under section 68 of the Act; ("conseil créé en vertu de l'article 68")

"supported board associated with an old board" means the district school board that is listed in Column 3 of Schedule 1 to Ontario Regulation 460/97, opposite the old board listed in Column 1 of that Schedule; ("conseil secondé rattaché à un ancien conseil")

"unextended old board" means an old board to which subsection 4(1) of Ontario Regulation 78/97 applied. ("ancien conseil non parachevé")

2. (1) Subject to subsections (2) to (5), for the purposes of this Regulation, a pupil is a pupil of a board if he or she is enrolled in a school operated by the board.

(2) A pupil who receives instruction in an education program provided by a board in a facility described or mentioned in subsection 19(2) is not a pupil enrolled in a school of the board for the purposes of subsection (1).

(3) Subsection (4) applies where,
- (a) the area of jurisdiction of a separate district school board includes all or part of the area that was, immediately before January 1, 1998, the area of jurisdiction of an unextended old board;
- (b) the separate district school board does not operate a secondary school in the area that was, immediately before January 1, 1998, the area of jurisdiction of the unextended old board; and
- (c) the separate district school board has entered into a purchase of services agreement with a public board to provide instruction, in schools located in the area that was, immediately before January 1, 1998, the area of jurisdiction of the unextended old

board, to secondary school pupils who are qualified to be resident pupils of the separate board.

(4) For the purposes of this Regulation, pupils receiving instruction under an agreement referred to in clause (3)(c) are pupils of the separate district school board and are not pupils of the public board.

(5) For the purposes of this Regulation, the following are not pupils of a board even if they are enrolled in a school of the board:

1. A pupil who is a registered Indian residing on a reserve within the meaning of the *Indian Act* (Canada).
2. A pupil who is liable to pay fees as specified in subsection 49(6) of the *Education Act* because he or she is a visitor within the meaning of the *Immigration Act* (Canada) or is in possession of a student authorization issued under that Act.
3. A pupil in respect of whom the board may charge a fee under section 5 of the 1998-99 fees regulation.

3. (1) For the purposes of this Regulation, the 1998-99 day school average daily enrolment of pupils of a board is the day school average daily enrolment for the board determined under section 2 of the 1998-99 A.D.E. regulation, counting only pupils of the board, excluding secondary school pupils who are 21 years of age or more on December 31, 1998, and counting kindergarten pupils in accordance with subsection (5).

(2) For the purposes of this Regulation, the 1998-99 day school average daily enrolment of elementary pupils of a board is the day school average daily enrolment for the board determined under section 2 of the 1998-99 A.D.E. regulation, counting only the elementary school pupils of the board and counting kindergarten pupils in accordance with subsection (5).

(3) For the purposes of this Regulation, the 1998-99 day school average daily enrolment of secondary pupils of a board is the day school average daily enrolment for the board determined under section 2 of the 1998-99 A.D.E. regulation, counting only secondary school pupils of the board and excluding secondary school pupils who are 21 years of age or more on December 31, 1998.

(4) For the purposes of this Regulation, the day school full-time equivalent enrolment for a board as of October 31, 1998 is the sum of,

(a) the number of full-time pupils of the board enrolled on October 31, 1998, excluding secondary school pupils who are 21 years of age or more on December 31, 1998 and counting kindergarten pupils in accordance with subsection (5);

(b) 0.5 times the number of half-time pupils of the board enrolled on October 31, 1998, excluding secondary school pupils who are 21 years of age or more on December 31, 1998 and counting kindergarten pupils in accordance with subsection (5); and

(c) the quotient obtained by determining, for each part-time pupil of the board enrolled on October 31, 1998, other than secondary school pupils who are 21 years of age or more on December 31, 1998, the number of minutes for which the pupil is registered for classroom instruction in the cycle that includes October 31, 1998, in a course other than an independent study course, and dividing the sum of the numbers so determined by the product of 300 and the number of days in the cycle.

(5) For the purposes of subsections (1), (2) and (4), if the number of kindergarten full-time pupils of the board on October 31, 1998 exceeds the number of kindergarten full-time pupils of the board on March 31, 1998, determined in accordance with subsection (6), the kindergarten pupils of the board shall be counted in accordance with the following rules:
1. When applying the formula set out in section 2 of the 1998-99 A.D.E. regulation,
    i. the maximum number that may be counted as kindergarten full-time pupils of the board on the count date of October 31, 1998 or March 31, 1999 is the number of kindergarten full-time pupils of the board on March 31, 1998, determined in accordance with subsection (6), and
    ii. any remaining kindergarten full-time pupils of the board shall be counted as half-time pupils of the board.
2. When applying the formula set out in subsection (4).
    i. the maximum number that may be counted as kindergarten full-time pupils of the board on the count date of October 31, 1998 is the number of kindergarten full-time pupils of the board on March 31, 1998, determined in accordance with subsection (6), and
    ii. any remaining kindergarten full-time pupils of the board shall be counted as half-time pupils of the board.

(6) For the purposes of subsection (5), a pupil is a kindergarten full-time pupil of a board on March 31, 1998 if,
   (a) the pupil was enrolled in a kindergarten in a school governed by the board on March 31, 1998;
   (b) in respect of the cycle that includes March 31, 1998, the pupil was registered for classroom instruction for an average of at least 210 minutes per school day;
   (c) on March 31, 1998, the pupil was not receiving instruction in an education program provided by the board in a facility described or mentioned in subsection 19(2); and
   (d) on March 31, 1998, the pupil was not a pupil described in subsection 2(5).

(7) Where this Regulation requires that pupils be counted but does not provide that the count shall be on the basis of average daily enrolment or on the basis of full-time equivalent enrolment, each pupil, whether full-time, half-time or part-time, shall be counted as one.

4. (1) A count of pupils for the purposes of this Regulation on the basis of average daily enrolment or on the basis of full-time equivalent enrolment shall be accurate to two decimal places.

(2) A count of teachers for the purposes of this Regulation on the basis of full-time equivalence shall be accurate to one decimal place.

General

5. (1) The legislative grant payable for the 1998-99 fiscal year to a district school board is the amount calculated under Part II.

(2) The legislative grant payable for the 1998-99 fiscal year to an isolate board is the amount calculated under Part III.

(3) The legislative grant payable for the 1998-99 fiscal year to a section 68 board is the amount calculated under Part III.

6. Except as otherwise provided in sections 48 and 49, a legislative grant payable under this Regulation shall be paid on an estimated basis during the 1998-99 fiscal year and such adjustments as may be necessary shall be made after the actual financial, enrolment and other data are available.

7. (1) It is a condition of the payment of a grant to a board under this Regulation that the board comply with all Acts administered by the Minister and with all regulations, policies, guidelines, directives and similar instruments made under an Act administered by the Minister.

(2) Where a board contravenes an Act administered by the Minister or a regulation, policy, guideline, directive or similar instrument made under an Act administered by the Minister, the Minister may withhold all or part of a grant otherwise payable to the board under the Act until the board takes the steps necessary to correct the situation.

8. Where the amount payable to an old board under a general legislative grant regulation was overpaid, the overpayment shall be deducted from the grants payable under this Regulation to the designated board associated with the old board and to the supported board associated with the old board, in accordance with the appropriate distribution ratios as determined under the directives published in September, 1997 by the Education Improvement Commission and titled "Directives for the Distribution of Assets and Liabilities Among District School Boards".

9. Where the amount payable to an old board under a general legislative grant regulation was underpaid, the underpayment shall be added to the grants payable under this Regulation to the designated board associated with the old board and to the supported board associated with the old board, in accordance with the appropriate distribution ratios as determined under the directives published in September, 1997 by the Education Improvement Commission and titled "Directives for the Distribution of Assets and Liabilities Among District School Boards".

PART II

GRANTS TO DISTRICT SCHOOL BOARDS

Grant Entitlement

10. (1) For the purposes of this Part, the following are types of allocations:
1. Foundation allocation.
2. Special education allocation.
3. Language allocation.
4. Small schools allocation.
5. Remote and rural allocation.
6. Learning opportunity allocation.
6.1 Summer school remedial allocation.
7. Adult education, continuing education and summer school allocation.
8. Teacher compensation allocation.
8.1 Retirement gratuity allocation.
9. Early learning allocation.

10. Transportation allocation.
11. Administration and governance allocation.
12. Pupil accommodation allocation.
13. Debt charges allocation.

(2) For the purposes of this Regulation, an old board is a predecessor of a district school board if the district school board is listed in Column 2 or 3 of Schedule 1 to Ontario Regulation 460/97, opposite the old board listed in Column 1 of that Schedule. O. Reg. 537/98, s. 1; 212/99, s. 1.

11. A district school board shall be paid a grant in an amount determined as follows:

1. Determine the 1998-99 tax revenue of the board, in accordance with section 12.
2. Determine the amount of each type of allocation for the board, in accordance with sections 13 to 38.
3. Total the amounts determined for the board under paragraph 2.
4. Adjust the amount determined under paragraph 3 in accordance with section 40.
5. Deduct the amount determined under paragraph 1 for the board from the amount determined under paragraph 4 for the board.
6. Deduct the fees revenue received by the board under section 4 of the 1998-99 fees regulation.
7. Deduct the amount that is in the board's reserve fund under subsection 233(1) of the Act on August 31, 1999, immediately before the transfer under subsection 233(2) of the Act.
8. Add the total of the amounts determined for the board for capital projects under subsection 48(4).
9. Add the total of the amounts determined for the board for capital projects under subsection 49(1).

1998-99 Tax Revenue of a District School Board

12. (1) For the purposes of paragraph 1 of section 11, the 1998-99 tax revenue of a district school board shall be determined as follows:

1. Add,
    i. 38 per cent of the total of the amounts distributed to the board in respect of the 1998 calendar year under subsections 237(12) and 238(2), section 239, subsection 240(5), sections 250 and 251 and subsections 257.8(2) and 257.9(1) of the Act, under sections 447.20 and 447.52 of the *Municipal Act* and under section 10 of Ontario Regulation 509/98,
    ii. 62 per cent of the total of the amounts distributed to the board in respect of the 1999 calendar year under subsections 237(12) and 238(2), section 239, subsection 240(5), sections 250 and 251 and subsections 257.8(2) and 257.9(1) of the Act, under sections 447.20 and 447.52 of the *Municipal Act* and under section 10 of Ontario Regulation 509/98,
    iii. 38 per cent of the amounts, if any, received by the board in respect of the 1998 calendar year from a municipality under subsection 445(4) of the *Municipal Act*,

iv. 62 per cent of the amounts, if any, received by the board in respect of the 1999 calendar year from a municipality under subsection 445(4) of the *Municipal Act*,
v. the total of the taxes received by the board in respect of the 1998 calendar year under section 35 of the *Assessment Act*,
vi. 38 per cent of the payments in lieu of taxes distributed to the board in respect of the 1998 calendar year under subsection 371.1(1) of the *Municipal Act*,
vii. 62 per cent of the payments in lieu of taxes distributed to the board in respect of the 1999 calendar year under subsection 371.1(1) of the *Municipal Act*,
viii. 38 per cent of the amounts, if any, received by the board in respect of the 1998 calendar year under the *Municipal Grants Act* (Canada) or under any Act of Canada that permits a payment to be made by a government or a government agency in lieu of taxes on real property,
ix. 62 per cent of the amounts, if any, received by the board in respect of the 1999 calendar year under the *Municipal Grants Act* (Canada) or under any Act of Canada that permits a payment to be made by a government or a government agency in lieu of taxes on real property,
x. 38 per cent of the amounts, if any, shared with the board in respect of the 1998 calendar year under subsection 442.1(11.3) of the *Municipal Act*,
xi. the total of the amounts, if any, distributed to the board in the 1998-99 fiscal year under subsection 2(2) of Ontario Regulation 365/98, and
xii. the total of the amounts, if any, paid to the board in the 1998-99 fiscal year under clause 3(1)(a) of Ontario Regulation 366/98.
2. Deduct the cost incurred in the 1998-99 fiscal year by the board under section 257.7 of the Act in collecting taxes for school purposes in territory without municipal organization, to a maximum of 2 per cent of the sum of,
   i. 38 per cent of the total amount of taxes levied by it for 1998 for school purposes in territory without municipal organization, and
   ii. 62 per cent of the total amount of taxes levied by it for 1999 for school purposes in territory without municipal organization.
2.1 Deduct an amount approved by the Minister in respect of,
   i. costs additional to those deducted under paragraph 2 that are incurred in the 1998-99 fiscal year by the board under section 257.7 of the Act in collecting taxes for school purposes in territory without municipal organization, and
   ii. costs that are incurred in the 1998-99 fiscal year by the board under section 21.1 of the *Provincial Land Tax Act* in collecting taxes in territory without municipal organization.
2.2 Deduct an amount approved by the Minister in respect of financing costs that are incurred by the board as a result of the delayed levy of 1998 taxes for school purposes in territory without municipal organization.
3. Deduct the amounts charged to the board in the 1998 calendar year by a municipal council under section 421 of the *Municipal Act*, including amounts charged under that section as a result of private legislation.
4. Deduct the total of the amounts paid as rebates by the board under section 257.2.1 of the Act in the 1998-99 fiscal year.

5. Deduct 38 per cent of the total of the amounts, if any, paid by the board in respect of the 1998 calendar year under subsections 442.1(7) and 442.2(8.1) of the *Municipal Act*.
6. Deduct 62 per cent of the total of the amounts, if any, paid by the board in respect of the 1999 calendar year under subsections 442.1(7) and 442.2(8.1) of the *Municipal Act*.

(2) Amounts paid by the Minister to the board in respect of the 1998 calendar year under section 257.11 of the Act shall be deemed to be amounts distributed to the board in respect of the 1998 calendar year under a provision of the Act referred to in subparagraph i of paragraph 1 of subsection (1).

(3) Amounts, if any, paid by the Minister to the board in respect of the 1999 calendar year under section 257.11 of the Act shall be deemed to be amounts distributed to the board in respect of the 1999 calendar year under a provision of the Act referred to in subparagraph ii of paragraph 1 of subsection (1). O. Reg. 212/99, s. 2.

Foundation Allocation

13. For the purposes of paragraph 2 of section 11, the amount of the foundation allocation for a district school board shall be determined as follows:
1. Take the 1998-99 day school average daily enrolment of elementary pupils of the board.
2. Multiply the number determined under paragraph 1 by $3,367.
3. Take the 1998-99 day school average daily enrolment of secondary pupils of the board.
4. Multiply the number determined under paragraph 3 by $3,953.
5. Total the products obtained under paragraphs 2 and 4.

Special Education Allocation

14. For the purposes of paragraph 2 of section 11, the amount of the special education allocation for a district school board shall be determined as follows:
1. Determine the enrolment-based special education amount for the board, in accordance with section 15.
2. Determine the equipment ISA for the board, in accordance with section 16.
3. Determine the program ISA for the board, in accordance with section 17.
4. Determine the programs in facilities amount for the board, in accordance with section 19.
5. Total the amounts determined under paragraphs 1 to 4.

15. For the purposes of paragraph 1 of section 14, the enrolment-based special education amount for the board shall be determined as follows:
1. Take the 1998-99 day school average daily enrolment of elementary pupils of the board.
2. Multiply the number determined under paragraph 1 by $347.

3. Take the 1998-99 day school average daily enrolment of secondary pupils of the board.
4. Multiply the number determined under paragraph 3 by $214.
5. Total the amounts determined under paragraphs 2 and 4.

16. (1) For the purposes of subsection (2), an equipment ISA claim for a pupil of a board is an approved equipment ISA claim for the pupil if,

(a) the board has designated the pupil as an ISA level 1 pupil in accordance with the Ministry publication entitled "Resource Manual for the Special Education Grant Intensive Support Amount (ISA)", dated May 15, 1998;

(b) the board has made an ISA level 1 claim for expenditures in excess of $800 for special equipment for the pupil, in accordance with the Ministry publication entitled "Revenue Manual for the Special Education Grant Intensive Support Amount (ISA)", dated May 15, 1998; and

(c) the Minister has approved the designation referred to in clause (a) and the claim referred to in clause (b).

(2) For the purposes of paragraph 2 of section 14, the equipment ISA for a board shall be calculated by totalling the approved equipment ISA claims for pupils of the board.

17. For the purposes of paragraph 3 of section 14, the program ISA for a board is the greater of,

(a) the amount specified in Column 2 of Table 1, opposite the name of the board, multiplied by the 1998-99 day school average daily enrolment of pupils of the board; and

(b) the ISA level 2 and 3 funding total determined for the board under subsection 18(5).

18. (1) For the purposes of subsection (2), a pupil of a board is a pupil approved for ISA level 2 funding if,

(a) the board has designated the pupil as an ISA level 2 pupil in accordance with the Ministry publication entitled "Resource Manual for the Special Education Grant Intensive Support Amount (ISA)", dated May 15, 1998; and

(b) the Minister has approved the designation referred to in clause (a).

(2) The ISA level 2 funding for a board shall be calculated by multiplying the number of approved ISA level 2 pupils of the board by $12,000.

(3) For the purposes of subsection (4), a pupil of a board is a pupil approved for ISA level 3 funding if,

(a) the board has designated the pupil as an ISA level 3 pupil in accordance with the Ministry publication entitled "Resource Manual for the Special Education Grant Intensive Support Amount (ISA)", dated May 15, 1998; and

(b) the Minister has approved the designation referred to in clause (a).

(4) The ISA level 3 funding for a board shall be calculated by multiplying the number of approved ISA level 3 pupils of the board by $27,000.

(5) The ISA level 2 and 3 funding total for a board shall be calculated by adding the amount determined for the board under subsection (2) to the amount determined for the board under subsection (4).

19. (1) For the purposes of paragraph 4 of section 14, the programs in facilities amount for a board is the total of the amounts determined under this section for each education program provided by the board in a facility described or named in subsection (2) where,

(a) the facility is located within the area of jurisdiction of the board;
(b) the board employs a teacher to provide the education program;
(c) no education program is provided by any Ministry in the facility;
(d) the board has entered into a written agreement with the facility setting out,
   (i) the responsibilities of the facility for the provision of accommodation, and
   (ii) the responsibilities of the board for the provision of the education program, including the number of teachers to be employed by the board for the purposes of the program; and
(e) the Minister,
   (i) is satisfied that the agreement referred to in clause (d) adequately sets out the responsibilities of the board and the facility,
   (ii) has approved the board's staffing plan for the program, and
   (iii) is satisfied that there is a need for the provision of such a program by the board in the facility.

(2) The following are facilities for the purposes of this section:
1. A psychiatric facility.
2. An approved charitable institution as defined in the *Charitable Institutions Act*.
3. An agency approved under subsection 8(1) of the *Child and Family Services Act*.
4. An approved home as defined in the *Homes for Retarded Persons Act*.
5. A place of temporary detention, open custody or secure custody continued or established under section 89 of the *Child and Family Services Act*.
6. A home for special care licensed under the *Homes for Special Care Act*.
7. A facility classified as a Group K Hospital in Regulation 964 of the Revised Regulations of Ontario, 1990 made under the *Public Hospitals Act*.
8. The Hospital for Sick Children, in Toronto.
9. The Children's Hospital of Eastern Ontario, in Ottawa.
10. The London Health Sciences Centre, in London.
11. The Lyndhurst Hospital.
12. A hospital in which an education program was discontinued after December 31, 1980 as a result of the dissolution of a board established under section 68 of the Act.
13. A nursing home approved or licensed under the *Nursing Homes Act*.
14. A correctional institution as defined in the *Ministry of Correctional Services Act*.
15. A place of secure or open custody or a place of temporary detention designated for the purposes of the *Young Offenders Act* (Canada).

(3) Subject to subsections (5) and (7), the amount for an education program referred to in subsection (1) shall be determined as follows:
1. Determine the expenditure of the board in the 1998-99 fiscal year for salary and employee benefits of teachers employed by the board to provide the program. The amount determined under this paragraph shall not exceed the amount that could be expended by the board for salary and employee benefits of teachers under the staffing plan referred to in clause (1)(e).

2. Multiply the number of full-time equivalent teachers employed by the board to provide the program by $2,500. For the purposes of this paragraph, the counting practices usually followed by the board for staffing purposes shall be followed.
3. Determine the expenditure of the board in the 1998-99 fiscal year for salary and employee benefits of teacher assistants employed by the board to assist teachers in providing the program. The amount determined under this paragraph shall not exceed the amount that could be expended by the board for salary and employee benefits of teacher assistants under the staffing plan referred to in clause (1)(e).
4. Multiply the number of full-time equivalent teacher assistants employed by the board to assist teachers in providing the program by $1,220. For the purposes of this paragraph, the counting practices usually followed by the board for staffing purposes shall be followed.
5. Determine the expenditure of the board in the 1998-99 fiscal year for the purchase of furniture or equipment for any classroom used in the program. The amount determined for a classroom under this paragraph, added to the total of any amounts received under any predecessor of this paragraph for the classroom, shall not exceed $3,300.
6. Total the amounts determined under paragraphs 1 to 5.

(4) Subsection (5) applies where,

(a) the circumstances described in clauses (1)(a) to (e) apply; and

(b) the education program was previously provided in the facility by the Ministry.

(5) Subject to subsection (7), in the circumstances described in subsection (4), the amount referred to in subsection (1) shall be an amount equal to the cost for the program that is proposed by the board and approved by the Minister, instead of the amount determined under subsection (3).

(6) In giving approvals under clause (1)(e) and subsection (5), the Minister shall ensure that the total of the amounts calculated for all boards under subsections (1) to (5) does not exceed $67 million.

(7) The amount determined for an education program under subsection (3) or (5) shall be reduced by the amount specified by the Minister under subsection (8) if the program,

(a) operates on a smaller scale than was projected in the materials submitted by the board for consideration by the Minister for the purposes of clause (1)(e);

(b) does not operate during the 1998-99 school year; or

(c) ceases to operate during the 1998-99 school year.

(8) For the purposes of subsection (7), the Minister shall specify an amount, if any, that in his or her opinion is appropriate having regard to the reasonable costs of the board in connection with the program.

20. (1) Subsections (2) and (3) apply where an ISA level 1 claim has been approved for one board under section 16 in respect of a pupil and the pupil enrolls in a school operated by second board during the 1998-99 fiscal year.

(2) The equipment for which the ISA level 1 claim was approved shall move with the pupil from the first board to the second board, unless in the opinion of the second board moving the equipment is not practical.

(3) Any unspent part of the ISA level 1 claim amount approved in respect of the pupil shall be deducted from the amount determined under subsection 16(2) for the first board and added to the amount determined under subsection 16(2) for the second board.

(4) Subsection (5) applies where,

(a) the amount determined for a board under clause 17(b) is greater than the amount determined for the board under clause 17(a); and

(b) a pupil in respect of whom an amount has been calculated for the board under subsection 18(2) or (4) enrolls in a school operated by a second board during the 1998-99 fiscal year.

(5) The amount calculated for the first board under subsection 18(2) or (4) in respect of the pupil shall be apportioned between the two boards, in the proportions that the Minister considers appropriate having regard to the costs of the boards in connection with providing the pupil's special education program.

Language Allocation—English-language District School Boards

21. For the purposes of paragraph 2 of section 11, the amount of the language allocation for an English-language district school board shall be determined as follows:

1. Determine the French as a second language amount for the board, in accordance with section 22.
2. Determine the Native as a second language amount for the board, in accordance with section 23.
3. Determine the ESL/ESD amount for the board, in accordance with section 24.
4. Total the amounts determined under paragraphs 1, 2 and 3.

22. (1) For the purposes of paragraph 1 of section 21, the French as a second language amount for the board shall be determined as follows:

1. Determine the French as a second language amount for elementary pupils of the board, in accordance with subsection (3).
2. Determine the French as a second language amount for secondary pupils of the board, in accordance with subsection (5).
3. Total the amounts determined under paragraphs 1 and 2.

(2) In subsection (3),

"instruction in French" means instruction in the subject of French or instruction in any other subject if the language of instruction is French.

(3) For the purposes of paragraph 1 of subsection (1), the French as a second language amount for elementary pupils of the board shall be determined as follows:

1. Determine the number of pupils of the board enrolled in any of grades four to eight who, on October 31, 1998, are scheduled to take instruction in French for an average of 20 or more minutes but less than 60 minutes per school day. Multiply by $229.
2. Determine the number of pupils of the board enrolled in any of grades four to eight who, on October 31, 1998, are scheduled to take instruction in French for an average of 60 or more minutes but less than 150 minutes per school day. Multiply by $260.
3. Determine the number of pupils of the board enrolled in any of grades one to eight

who, on October 31, 1998, are scheduled to take instruction in French for an average of 150 or more minutes per school day. Multiply by $291.
4. Determine the number of pupils of the board enrolled in junior kindergarten or kindergarten who, on October 31, 1998, are scheduled to take instruction in French for an average of 75 minutes or more per school day. Multiply by $291.
5. Total the products obtained under paragraphs 1 to 4.

(4) In subsection (5),

"course" means a course at the secondary level that is assigned a common course code in the list of common course codes published by the Ministry; ("cours")

"credit equivalent value" of a part of a grade nine program in which a pupil in grade nine is enrolled means the number of credit equivalents that the pupil is eligible to earn on successfully completing that part of the program; ("valeur en équivalences en crédits")

"credit value" of a course in which a pupil is enrolled means the number of credits that the pupil is eligible to earn on successfully completing the course. ("valeur en crédits")

(5) For the purposes of paragraph 2 of subsection (1), the French as a second language amount for secondary pupils of the board shall be determined as follows:
1. Determine an amount for grade nine instruction in the subject of French, as follows:
    i. Determine the credit equivalent value of each part of the grade nine program taught on a non-semestered basis in which instruction is given to pupils of the board in the subject of French. Multiply the credit equivalent value by the number of grade nine pupils of the board enrolled in that part of the program on October 31, 1998, excluding pupils who are 21 years of age or more on December 31, 1998.
    ii. Determine the credit equivalent value of each part of the grade nine program taught on a semestered basis in which instruction is given to pupils of the board in the subject of French. Multiply the credit equivalent value by the total of the number of grade nine pupils of the board enrolled in that part of the program on October 31, 1998 and the number of grade nine pupils of the board enrolled in that part of the program on March 31, 1999, excluding pupils who are 21 years of age or more on December 31, 1998.
    iii. Add the products obtained for the board under subparagraphs i and ii.
    iv. Multiply the sum obtained under subparagraph iii by $57.
2. Determine an amount for grade nine instruction in a subject other than French where the language of instruction is French, as follows:
    i. Determine the credit equivalent value of each part of the grade nine program taught on a non-semestered basis in which instruction is given to pupils of the board in a subject other than French and for which the language of instruction is French. Multiply the credit equivalent value by the number of grade nine pupils of the board enrolled in that part of the program on October 31, 1998, excluding pupils who are 21 years of age or more on December 31, 1998.
    ii. Determine the credit equivalent value of each part of the grade nine program taught on a semestered basis in which instruction is given to pupils of the board in a subject other than French and for which the language of instruction is French. Multiply the credit equivalent value by the total of the number of grade

nine pupils of the board enrolled in that part of the program on October 31, 1998 and the number of grade nine pupils of the board enrolled in that part of the program on March 31, 1999, excluding pupils who are 21 years of age or more on December 31, 1998.
    iii. Add the products obtained for the board under subparagraphs i and ii.
    iv. Multiply the sum obtained under subparagraph iii by $94.
3. Determine an amount for grade ten instruction in the subject of French, as follows:
    i. Determine the credit value of each course in the subject of French that is taught to grade ten pupils of the board on a non-semestered basis. Multiply the credit value by the number of grade ten pupils of the board enrolled in the course on October 31, 1998, excluding pupils who are 21 years of age or more on December 31, 1998.
    ii. Determine the credit value of each course in the subject of French that is taught to grade ten pupils of the board on a semestered basis. Multiply the credit value by the total of the number of grade ten pupils of the board enrolled in the course on October 31, 1998 and the number of grade ten pupils of the board enrolled in the course on March 31, 1999, excluding pupils who are 21 years of age or more on December 31, 1998.
    iii. Add the products obtained for the board under subparagraphs i and ii.
    iv. Multiply the sum obtained under subparagraph iii by $57.
4. Determine an amount for grade ten instruction in a subject other than French where the language of instruction is French, as follows:
    i. Determine the credit value of each course in a subject other than French that is taught in French to grade ten pupils of the board on a non-semestered basis. Multiply the credit value by the number of grade ten pupils of the board enrolled in the course on October 31, 1998, excluding pupils who are 21 years of age or more on December 31, 1998.
    ii. Determine the credit value of each course in a subject other than French that is taught in French to grade ten pupils of the board on a semestered basis. Multiply the credit value by the total of the number of grade ten pupils of the board enrolled in the course on October 31, 1998 and the number of grade ten pupils of the board enrolled in the course on March 31, 1999, excluding pupils who are 21 years of age or more on December 31, 1998.
    iii. Add the products obtained for the board under subparagraphs i and ii.
    iv. Multiply the sum obtained under subparagraph iii by $94.
5. Determine an amount for grade eleven, twelve or OAC instruction in the subject of French, as follows:
    i. Determine the credit value of each course in the subject of French that is taught to grade eleven, twelve or OAC pupils of the board on a non-semestered basis. Multiply the credit value by the number of grade eleven, twelve or OAC pupils of the board enrolled in the course on October 31, 1998, excluding pupils who are 21 years of age or more on December 31, 1998.
    ii. Determine the credit value of each course in the subject of French that is taught to grade eleven, twelve or OAC pupils of the board on a semestered basis. Multiply the credit value by the total of the number of grade eleven, twelve

and OAC pupils of the board enrolled in the course on October 31, 1998 and the number of grade eleven, twelve or OAC pupils of the board enrolled in the course on March 31, 1999, excluding pupils who are 21 years of age or more on December 31, 1998.
    iii. Add the products obtained for the board under subparagraphs i and ii.
    iv. Multiply the sum obtained under subparagraph iii by $75.
6. Determine an amount for grade eleven, twelve or OAC instruction in a subject other than French where the language of instruction is French, as follows:
    i. Determine the credit value of each course in a subject other than French that is taught in French to grade eleven, twelve or OAC pupils of the board on a non-semestered basis. Multiply the credit value by the number of grade eleven, twelve and OAC pupils of the board enrolled in the course on October 31, 1998, excluding pupils who are 21 years of age or more on December 31, 1998.
    ii. Determine the credit value of each course in a subject other than French that is taught in French to grade eleven, twelve or OAC pupils of the board on a semestered basis. Multiply the credit value by the total of the number of grade eleven, twelve and OAC pupils of the board enrolled in the course on October 31, 1998 and the number of grade eleven, twelve and OAC pupils of the board enrolled in the course on March 31, 1999, excluding pupils who are 21 years of age or more on December 31, 1998.
    iii. Add the products obtained for the board under subparagraphs i and ii.
    iv. Multiply the sum obtained under subparagraph iii by $145.
7. Total the dollar amounts determined under paragraphs 1 to 6.

23. (1) For the purposes of paragraph 2 of section 21, the Native as a second language amount for the board shall be determined as follows:

1. Determine the Native as a second language amount for elementary pupils of the board, in accordance with subsection (2).
2. Determine the Native as a second language amount for secondary pupils of the board, in accordance with subsection (4).
3. Total the amounts determined under paragraphs 1 and 2.

(2) For the purposes of paragraph 1 of subsection (1), the Native as a second language amount for elementary pupils of the board shall be determined as follows:

1. Determine the number of elementary school pupils of the board who, on October 31, 1998, are scheduled to take instruction in the subject of a Native language for an average of 20 or more minutes but less than 40 minutes per school day. Multiply by $219.
2. Determine the number of elementary school pupils of the board who, on October 31, 1998, are scheduled to take instruction in the subject of a Native language for an average of 40 or more minutes per school day. Multiply by $389.
3. Total the products obtained under paragraphs 1 and 2.

(3) In subsection (4),

"course" means a course at the secondary level that is assigned a common course code in the list of common course codes published by the Ministry; ("cours") "credit equivalent value" of a part of a grade nine program in which a pupil in grade nine is enrolled means the number of credit equivalents that the pupil is eligible to earn on successfully completing that part of the program; ("valeur en équivalences en crédits")

"credit value" of a course in which a pupil is enrolled means the number of credits that the pupil is eligible to earn on successfully completing the course. ("valeur en crédits")

(4) For the purposes of paragraph 2 of subsection (1), the Native as a second language amount for secondary pupils of the board shall be determined as follows:

1. Determine the credit equivalent value of each part of the grade nine program taught on a non-semestered basis in which instruction is given to pupils of the board in the subject of a Native language. Multiply the credit equivalent value by the number of grade nine pupils of the board enrolled in that part of the program on October 31, 1998, excluding pupils who are 21 years of age or more on December 31, 1998. Multiply the product by $57.

2. Determine the credit equivalent value of each part of the grade nine program taught on a semestered basis in which instruction is given to pupils of the board in the subject of a Native language. Multiply the credit equivalent value by the total of the number of grade nine pupils of the board enrolled in that part of the program on October 31, 1998 and the number of grade nine pupils enrolled in that part of the program on March 31, 1999, excluding pupils who are 21 years of age or more on December 31, 1998. Multiply the product by $57.

3. Determine the credit value of each course in the subject of a Native language that is taught on a non-semestered basis to grade ten pupils of the board. Multiply the credit value by the number of grade ten pupils of the board enrolled in the course on October 31, 1998, excluding pupils who are 21 years of age or more on December 31, 1998. Multiply the product by $57.

4. Determine the credit value of each course in the subject of a Native language that is taught on a semestered basis to grade ten pupils of the board. Multiply the credit value by the total of the number of grade ten pupils of the board enrolled in the course on October 31, 1998 and the number of grade ten pupils of the board enrolled in the course on March 31, 1999, excluding pupils who are 21 years of age or more on December 31, 1998. Multiply the product by $57.

5. Determine the credit value of each course in the subject of a Native language that is taught on a non-semestered basis to grade eleven, twelve or OAC pupils of the board. Multiply the credit value by the number of grade eleven, twelve and OAC pupils of the board enrolled in the course on October 31, 1998, excluding pupils who are 21 years of age or more on December 31, 1998. Multiply the product by $75.

6. Determine the credit value of each course in the subject of a Native language that is taught on a semestered basis to grade eleven, twelve or OAC pupils of the board. Multiply the credit value by the total of the number of grade eleven, twelve and OAC pupils of the board enrolled in the course on October 31, 1998 and the number of grade eleven, twelve and OAC pupils of the board enrolled in the course of March 31, 1999, excluding pupils who are 21 years of age or more on December 31, 1998. Multiply the product by $75.

7. Total the dollar amounts determined under paragraphs 1 to 6.

24. (1) For the purposes of paragraph 3 of section 21, the ESL/ESD amount for the board shall be determined as follows:

1. Determine, as of October 31, 1998, the number of pupils of the board who entered Canada during the period beginning September 1, 1997 and ending August 31, 1998 from countries described in subsection (2), excluding pupils who are 21 years of age or more on December 31, 1998, and multiply that number by 1.0.
2. Determine, as of October 1, 1998, the number of pupils of the board who entered Canada during the period beginning September 1, 1996 and ending August 31, 1997 from countries described in subsection (2), excluding pupils who are 21 years of age or more on December 31, 1998, and multiply that number by 0.6.
3. Determine, as of October 31, 1998, the number of pupils of the board who entered Canada during the period beginning September 1, 1995 and ending August 31, 1996 from countries described in subsection (2), excluding pupils who are 21 years of age or more on December 31, 1998, and multiply that number by 0.3.
4. Multiply the 1998-99 day school average daily enrolment of pupils of the board by the percentage set out for the board in Table 2.
5. Total the products obtained under paragraphs 1 to 4.
6. Multiply the amount determined under paragraph 5 by $2,235.

(2) Paragraphs 1 to 3 of subsection (1) apply in respect of,

(a) countries where English is not the first language of a majority of the population; and
(b) countries where a majority of the population speaks a variety of English that is so different from the English used as the language of instruction in schools of the board that an ESL or ESD program should be offered to pupils from those countries.

Language Allocation—French-language District School Boards

25. For the purposes of paragraph 2 of section 11, the amount of the language allocation for a French-language district school board shall be determined as follows:

1. Determine the French as a first language amount for the board, in accordance with section 26.
2. Determine the Native as a second language amount for the board, in accordance with section 27.
3. Determine the ALF/PDF amount for the board, in accordance with section 28.
4. Total the amounts determined under paragraphs 1, 2 and 3.

26. (1) For the purposes of paragraph 1 of section 25, the French as a first language amount for the board shall be determined as follows:

1. Multiply by $291 the number of elementary school pupils of the board on October 31, 1998.
2. Multiply the 1998-99 day school average daily enrolment of secondary pupils of the board by $460.
3. Determine the start-up amount for new elementary schools of the board, in accordance with subsection (2).
4. Total the amounts determined under paragraphs 1, 2 and 3.

(2) For the purposes of paragraph 3 of subsection (1), the start-up amount for new elementary schools of the board shall be determined by multiplying the number of elementary schools of the board that are being governed for the first time by the board in September, 1998 by $10,800. O. Reg. 469/98, s. 1.

27. For the purposes of paragraph 2 of section 25, the Native as a second language amount for the board shall be determined in the manner provided in section 23 for English-language district school boards.

28. (1) For the purposes of this section, a board is coterminous with another board if the areas of jurisdiction of the two boards are wholly or partly the same.

(2) For the purposes of this section,

(a) the area of jurisdiction of a French-language public district school board is divided into portions matching the areas of jurisdiction of the coterminous English-language public district school boards;

(b) the area of jurisdiction of a French-language separate district school board is divided into portions matching the areas of jurisdiction of the coterminous English-language separate district school boards; and

(c) where the area of jurisdiction of a French-language separate district school board is the same as the area of jurisdiction of an English-language separate district school board, the total area of jurisdiction of the French-language separate district school board is one portion.

(3) For the purposes of paragraph 3 of section 25, the ALF/PDF amount for the board shall be determined as follows:

1. Determine the ALF funding level for the board in accordance with subsection (4).
2. Determine the PDF funding level for the board in accordance with subsection (11).
3. Total the amounts determined under paragraphs 1 and 2.

(4) For the purposes of paragraph 1 of subsection (3), the ALF funding level for the board shall be determined as follows:

1. Determine the number of elementary instructional units for ALF purposes for each portion of the board, in accordance with subsection (6). The determination under this paragraph shall be accurate to two decimal places.
2. Determine the number of secondary instructional units for ALF purposes for each portion of the board, in accordance with subsection (7). The determination under this paragraph shall be accurate to two decimal places.
3. For each portion of the board, add the numbers determined under paragraphs 1 and 2.
4. Determine the assimilation factor for each portion of the board, in accordance with subsection (8) or (9), as the case may be.
5. For each portion of the board, multiply the number determined under paragraph 3 by the factor determined under paragraph 4.
6. For each portion of the board, multiply the product determined under paragraph 5 by $60,000.
7. Total the amounts determined for each of the portions of the board under paragraph 6.

(5) For the purposes of subsections (6) and (7), the pupils of a board shall be counted on the basis of day school full-time equivalent enrolment for the board as of October 31, 1998.

(6) The number of elementary instructional units for ALF purposes for a portion of the board shall be determined as follows:

1. Allow 0.005 elementary instructional units for ALF purposes for each of the first 200 elementary school pupils of the board who are enrolled in schools located in the portion.
2. Allow 0.0025 elementary instructional units for ALF purposes for each of the next 1,600 elementary school pupils of the board who are enrolled in schools located in the portion.
3. Allow 0.0013 elementary instructional units for ALF purposes for each of the remaining elementary school pupils of the board who are enrolled in schools located in the portion.
4. Total the instructional units allowed for ALF purposes for the portion of the board under paragraphs 1, 2 and 3.

(7) The number of secondary instructional units for ALF purposes for a portion of the board shall be determined as follows:

1. Allow 0.0025 secondary instructional units for ALF purposes for each of the first 1,200 secondary school pupils of the board who are enrolled in schools located in the portion.
2. Allow 0.0013 secondary instructional units for ALF purposes for each of the remaining secondary school pupils of the board who are enrolled in schools located in the portion.
3. Total the instructional units allowed for ALF purposes for the portion of the board under paragraphs 1 and 2.

(8) The assimilation factor for a portion of a French-language public district school board shall be the factor specified in Table 3 for the English-language public district school board the area of jurisdiction of which matches the portion.

(9) The assimilation factor for a portion of a French-language separate district school board shall be the factor specified in Table 3 for the English-language separate district school board the area of jurisdiction of which matches the portion.

(10) For the purposes of subsection (11), a pupil is eligible for PDF funding if,

(a) the pupil was admitted to a school of the board under section 293 of the Act;
(b) the pupil entered Canada during the period beginning September 1, 1995 and ending August 31, 1998 from a country in which French is a standard language of schooling or public administration;
(c) the pupil has one or more of the following characteristics:
   1. The pupil speaks a variety of French that is so different from the French being used as the language of instruction in schools of the board that a PDF program should be offered to the pupil.
   2. The pupil's schooling has been interrupted or delayed.
   3. The pupil has little knowledge of English or French.

(11) For the purposes of paragraph 2 of subsection (3), the PDF funding level for the board shall be determined as follows:
1. Determine, as of October 31, 1998, the number of pupils of the board who are eligible for PDF funding and who entered Canada during the period beginning September 1, 1997 and ending August 31, 1998 from a country described in clause (10)(b), excluding pupils who are 21 years of age or more on December 31, 1998, and multiply that number by 1.0.
2. Determine, as of October 31, 1998, the number of pupils of the board who are eligible for PDF funding and who entered Canada during the period beginning September 1, 1996 and ending August 31, 1997 from a country described in clause (10)(b), excluding pupils who are 21 years of age or more on December 31, 1998, and multiply that number by 0.6.
3. Determine, as of October 31, 1998, the number of pupils of the board who are eligible for PDF funding and who entered Canada during the period beginning September 1, 1995 and ending August 31, 1996 from a country described in clause (10)(b), excluding pupils who are 21 years of age or more on December 31, 1998, and multiply that number by 0.3.
4. Total the products obtained under paragraphs 1, 2 and 3.
5. Multiply the amount determined under paragraph 4 by $2,235.

Small Schools Allocation

29. (1) In this section,

"small school", in relation to an English-language district school board, means,
    (a) an elementary school that has an average of less than 20 pupils per grade and is located eight or more kilometres by road from every other elementary school of the board,
    (b) a secondary school that has an average of less than 120 pupils per grade and is located 32 or more kilometres by road from every other secondary school of the board; ("petite école")

"small school", in relation to a French-language district school board, means,
    (a) an elementary school that has an average of less than 20 pupils per grade and is located eight or more kilometres by road from every other elementary school of the board that is located in the same portion of the board's area of jurisdiction,
    (b) a secondary school that has an average of less than 120 pupils per grade and is located 32 or more kilometres by road from every other secondary school of the board that is located in the same portion of the board's area of jurisdiction. ("petite école")

(2) For the purposes of this section, a board is coterminous with another board if the areas of jurisdiction of the two boards are wholly or partly the same.

(3) For the purposes of this section,
(a) the area of jurisdiction of a French-language public district school board is divided

into portions matching the areas of jurisdiction of the coterminous English-language public district school boards;

(b) the area of jurisdiction of a French-language separate district school board is divided into portions matching the areas of jurisdiction of the coterminous English-language separate district school boards; and

(c) where the area of jurisdiction of a French-language separate district school board is the same as the area of jurisdiction of an English-language separate district school board, the total area of jurisdiction of the French-language separate district school board is one portion.

(4) For the purposes of this section,

(a) junior kindergarten, kindergarten and grades one to eight are elementary grades;

(b) grades nine to twelve and OAC are secondary grades;

(c) subject to subsection (5), a school that offers instruction in one or more of the elementary grades shall be treated as an elementary school;

(d) subject to subsection (5), a school that offers instruction in one or more of the secondary grades shall be treated as a secondary school.

(5) For the purposes of this section, where a school offers instruction in one or more of the elementary grades and in one or more of the secondary grades, the school shall be treated as two schools, as follows:

1. One elementary school, offering instruction in the relevant elementary grades.
2. One secondary school, offering instruction in the relevant secondary grades.

(6) For the purposes of this section, the average number of pupils per grade of an elementary school shall be calculated as follows:

1. Determine the day school full-time equivalent enrolment for the board as of October 31, 1998, counting only the pupils enrolled in the school. For the purposes of this paragraph, a pupil who would be a pupil of a board were it not for subsection 2(5) shall be deemed to be a pupil of the board.
2. Determine the number of grades in the school, counting junior kindergarten and kindergarten as 0.5 grades each.
3. Divide the number determined under paragraph 1 by the number determined under paragraph 2.

(7) For the purposes of this section, the average number of pupils per grade of a secondary school shall be calculated as follows:

1. Determine the day school full-time equivalent enrolment for the board as of October 31, 1998, counting only the pupils enrolled in the school. For the purposes of this paragraph, a pupil who would be a pupil of a board were it not for subsection 2(4) or (5) shall be deemed to be a pupil of the board.
2. Divide the number determined under paragraph 1 by the number of grades in which instruction is provided in the school.

(8) Where two or more elementary schools of an English-language district school board are all located within eight kilometres of each other by road, their combined average number of pupils per grade is less than 20 pupils per grade and one or more of the schools in the group

is located eight or more kilometres by road from every elementary school of the board that is not in the group,
- (a) the group of two or more schools shall be deemed to be one small school for the purposes of this section; and
- (b) each of the two or more schools in the group shall be deemed not to be a small school for the purposes of this section.

(9) Where two or more elementary schools of a French-language district school board are all located in the same portion of the board's area of jurisdiction, are all within eight kilometres of each other by road, their combined average number of pupils per grade is less than 20 pupils per grade and one or more of the schools in the group is located eight or more kilometres by road from every elementary school of the board that is not in the group but is in the same portion of the board's area of jurisdiction,
- (a) the group of two or more schools shall be deemed to be one small school for the purposes of this section; and
- (b) each of the two or more schools in the group shall be deemed not to be a small school for the purposes of this section.

(10) For the purposes of this section, the combined average number of pupils per grade of a group of two or more elementary schools shall be calculated as follows:
1. Determine the day school full-time equivalent enrolment for the board as of October 31, 1998, counting only the pupils enrolled in the schools in the group. For the purposes of this paragraph, a pupil who would be a pupil of a board were it not for subsection 2(5) shall be deemed to be a pupil of the board.
2. Determine the number of grades in which instruction is given in one or more of the schools in the group, counting junior kindergarten and kindergarten as 0.5 grades each.
3. Divide the number determined under paragraph 1 by the number determined under paragraph 2.

(11) For the purposes of paragraph 2 of section 11, the amount of the small school allocation for a district school board shall be determined as follows:
1. For each elementary small school of the board,
    - i. determine the school size factor, in accordance with subsection (12),
    - ii. determine the remoteness factor, in accordance with subsection (14), and
    - iii. determine the day school full-time equivalent enrolment for the board as of October 31, 1998, counting only the pupils of the board enrolled in the school.
2. For each elementary small school of the board, multiply the school size factor by the remoteness factor. Multiply the product by the enrolment determined for the school under subparagraph iii of paragraph 1.
3. For each elementary small school of the board, multiply the product obtained under paragraph 2 by $6,000.
4. Total the amounts determined for each of the elementary small schools of the board under paragraph 3.
5. For each secondary small school of the board,
    - i. determine the school size factor, in accordance with subsection (16),

ii. determine the remoteness factor, in accordance with subsection (17), and
iii. determine the day school full-time equivalent enrolment for the board as of October 31, 1998, counting only pupils of the board enrolled in the school. For the purposes of this subparagraph, pupils enrolled in the school who would be pupils of the board were it not for subsection 2(4) shall be deemed to be pupils of the board.
6. For each secondary small school of the board, multiply the school size factor by the remoteness factor. Multiply the product by the enrolment number determined for the school under subparagraph iii of paragraph 5.
7. For each secondary small school of the board, multiply the product obtained under paragraph 6 by $7,200.
8. Total the amounts determined for each of the secondary small schools of the board under paragraph 7.
9. Total the totals determined under paragraphs 4 and 8.

(12) The school size factor for a small elementary school shall be determined as follows:
1. For a school with an average number of pupils per grade that is less than two, the school size factor is 1.
2. For a school with an average number of pupils per grade that is two or more but not more than 10, the school size factor shall be determined on a sliding scale as follows:
    i. Divide 10 by the average number of pupils per grade.
    ii. Multiply the result obtained under subparagraph i by 0.2.
3. For a school with an average number of pupils per grade that is more than 10 but less than 20, the school size factor shall be determined on a sliding scale as follows:
    i. Subtract 10 from the average number of pupils per grade.
    ii. Divide the result obtained under subparagraph i by 10.
    iii. Subtract the result obtained under subparagraph ii from one.
    iv. Multiply the result obtained under subparagraph iii by 0.2.

(13) For the purposes of subsection (12), the average number of pupils per grade of a group of two or more schools that is deemed under subsection (8) or (9) to be one small school is the combined average number of pupils per grade of the group, calculated in accordance with subsection (10).

(14) The remoteness factor for a small elementary school shall be determined as follows:
1. For a school of an English-language district board located 80 kilometres or more by road from all other elementary schools of the board, the remoteness factor is 1.5.
2. For a school of an English-language district board located more than 32 kilometres by road but less than 80 kilometres by road from all other elementary schools of the board, the remoteness factor is 1.25.
3. For all other schools of an English-language district school board, the remoteness factor is 1.0.
4. For a school of a French-language district board located 80 kilometres or more by road from all other elementary schools of the board that are located in the same portion of the board's area of jurisdiction, the remoteness factor is 1.5.
5. For a school of a French-language district board located more than 32 kilometres by road but less than 80 kilometres by road from all other elementary schools of the

board that are located in the same portion of the board's area of jurisdiction, the remoteness factor is 1.25.
   6. For all other schools of a French-language district school board, the remoteness factor is 1.0.

(15) The following rules apply for the purposes of subsection (14), where a group of two or more schools of a board is deemed under subsection (8) or (9) to be one small school:
   1. In the case of elementary schools of an English-language district school board, if one or more of the schools in the group is located 80 kilometres or more by road from every elementary school of the board that is not in the group, the deemed small school shall be deemed to be located 80 kilometres or more by road from all other elementary schools of the board.
   2. Except where paragraph 1 applies, in the case of elementary schools of an English-language district school board, if one or more of the schools in the group is located more than 32 kilometres by road from every elementary school of the board that is not in the group, the deemed small school shall be deemed to be located more than 32 kilometres by road but less than 80 kilometres by road from all other elementary schools of the board.
   3. In the case of elementary schools of a French-language district school board, if one or more of the schools in the group is located 80 kilometres or more by road from every elementary school of the board that is not in the group but that is located in the same portion of the board's area of jurisdiction, the deemed small school shall be deemed to be located 80 kilometres or more by road from all other elementary schools of the board.
   4. Except where paragraph 3 applies, in the case of elementary schools of a French-language district school board, if one or more of the schools in the group is located more than 32 kilometres by road from every elementary school of the board that is not in the group but that is located in the same portion of the board's area of jurisdiction, the deemed small school shall be deemed to be located more than 32 kilometres by road but less than 80 kilometres by road from all other elementary schools of the board.

(16) The school size factor for a small secondary school shall be determined as follows:
   1. For a school with an average number of pupils per grade that is less than 20, the school size factor is 0.45.
   2. For a school with an average number of pupils per grade that is 20 or more but not more than 60, the school size factor shall be determined on a sliding scale as follows:
      i. Divide 60 by the average number of pupils per grade.
      ii. Multiply the result obtained under subparagraph i by 0.15.
   3. For a school with an average number of pupils per grade that is more than 60 but less than 120, the school size factor shall be determined on a sliding scale as follows:
      i. Subtract 60 from the average number of pupils per grade.
      ii. Divide the result obtained under subparagraph i by 60.
      iii. Subtract the result obtained under subparagraph ii from one.
      iv. Multiply the result obtained under subparagraph iii by 0.15.

(17) The remoteness factor for a small secondary school shall be determined as follows:

1. For a school of an English-language district school board that has an average number of pupils per grade that is less than 20 and that is located 80 kilometres or more by road from all other secondary schools of the board, the remoteness factor is 2.0.
2. For a school of an English-language district school board that has an average number of pupils per grade that is 20 or more but less than 120, and that is located 80 kilometres or more by road from all other secondary schools of the board, the remoteness factor shall be determined as follows:
    i. Add 20 to the average number of pupils per grade.
    ii. Divide 40 by the sum obtained under subparagraph i.
    iii. Add one the result obtained under subparagraph ii.
3. For all other small secondary schools of a English-language district school board, the remoteness factor is 1.0.
4. For a school of a French-language district school board that has an average number of pupils per grade that is less than 20 and that is located 80 kilometres or more by road from all other secondary schools of the board that are located in the same portion of the board's area of jurisdiction, the remoteness factor is 2.0.
5. For a school of a French-language district school board that has an average number of pupils per grade that is 20 or more but less than 120, and that is located 80 kilometres or more by road from all other secondary schools of the board that are located in the same portion of the board's area of jurisdiction, the remoteness factor shall be determined as follows:
    i. Add 20 to the average number of pupils per grade.
    ii. Divide 40 by the sum obtained under subparagraph i.
    iii. Add one to the result obtained under subparagraph ii.
6. For all other small secondary schools of a French-language district school board, the remoteness factor is 1.0.

Remote and Rural Allocation

30. For the purposes of paragraph 2 of section 11, the amount of the remote and rural allocation for a district school board shall be determined as follows:
1. Determine the per pupil distance amount for the board, in accordance with the following:
    i. If the distance specified for the board in Column 2 of Table 4 is less than 151 kilometres, the per pupil distance amount is zero.
    ii. If the distance specified for the board in Column 2 of Table 4 is 151 kilometres or more but less than 650 kilometres, the per pupil distance amount shall be determined by subtracting 150 from that distance and multiplying the result by $0.962.
    iii. If the distance specified for the board in Column 2 of Table 4 is 650 kilometres or more but less than 1,150 kilometres, the per pupil distance amount shall be determined as follows: Subtract 650 from that distance. Multiply the result by $0.134. Add $481 to the product.
    iv. If the distance specified for the board in Column 2 of Table 4 is 1,150 kilometres or more, the per pupil distance amount is $548.

2. Multiply the per pupil distance amount determined for the board under paragraph 1 by the urban factor specified for the board in Column 3 of Table 4.
3. Determine the per pupil sparsity amount for the board in accordance with the following:
    i. Determine the pupil density by dividing the 1998-99 day school average daily enrolment for the board, as determined under section 2 of the 1998-99 A.D.E. regulation, not counting pupils who are 21 years of age or more on December 31, 1998, by the board's area in square kilometres, as specified in the Schedule to Ontario Regulation 250/97.
    ii. If the number determined under subparagraph i is less than one, the per pupil sparsity amount shall be determined by subtracting that number from one and multiplying the result by $400.
    iii. If the number determined under subparagraph i is one or greater than one, the per pupil sparsity amount is zero.
4. Add the per pupil sparsity amount determined for the board under paragraph 3 to the amount determined for the board under paragraph 2.
5. Multiply the amount obtained under paragraph 4 by the 1998-99 day school average daily enrolment of pupils of the board.

O. Reg. 469/98, s. 2.

Learning Opportunities Allocation

31. For the purposes of paragraph 2 of section 11, the amount of the learning opportunities allocation for a district school board shall be the amount set out in Column 2 of Table 5, opposite the name of the board.

Summer School Remedial Allocation

31.1 (1) For the purposes of paragraph 2 of section 11, the amount of the summer school remedial allocation for a district school board shall be determined as follows:
1. Determine the summer school average daily enrolment for the board for the 1998-99 fiscal year in accordance with section 4 of the 1998-99 A.D.E. regulation, counting only pupils of the board enrolled in classes or courses described in subclause (b)(iii) of the definition of "summer school class or course" in subsection 4(1) of that regulation.
2. Multiply the number determined under paragraph 1 by $2,257.
3. Add the amount determined for the board under subsection (2) on account of transportation costs related to summer school remedial instruction.

(2) For the purposes of paragraph 3 of subsection (2), an amount on account of transportation costs related to summer school remedial instruction shall be determined for the board as follows:
1. Take the amount of the transportation allocation determined for the board under section 35.

2. Divide the amount taken under paragraph 1 by the 1998-99 day school average daily enrolment of pupils of the board.
3. Multiply the result obtained under paragraph 2 by the enrolment amount determined under paragraph 1 of subsection (1).

O. Reg. 212/99, s. 3.

Adult Education, Continuing Education and Summer School Allocation

32. (1) For the purposes of paragraph 2 of section 11, the amount of the adult education, continuing education and summer school allocation for a district school board shall be determined as follows:

1. Determine the day school average daily enrolment for the board for the 1998-99 fiscal year, in accordance with section 2 of the 1998-99 A.D.E. regulation, counting only pupils of the board who are 21 years of age or more on December 31, 1998.
2. Determine the continuing education average daily enrolment for the board for the 1998-99 fiscal year, in accordance with section 3 of the 1998-99 A.D.E. regulation.
3. Determine the summer school average daily enrolment for the board for the 1998-99 fiscal year in accordance with section 4 of the 1998-99 A.D.E. regulation, counting only pupils enrolled in classes or courses described in subclause (b)(i) or (ii) of the definition of "summer school class or course" in subsection 4(1) of that regulation.
4. Add the numbers determined under paragraphs 1, 2 and 3.
5. Multiply the total determined under paragraph 4 by $2,257.
6. Determine the amount for international languages for the board, in accordance with subsections (2) to (4).
7. Total the amounts determined under paragraphs 5 and 6.

(2) Subsections (3) and (4) apply where a board establishes classes to provide instruction in a language other than English or French and the classes have been approved by the Minister as being part of an international languages elementary school program.

(3) Except as provided in subsection (4), the amount for international languages for the board shall be the number of hours of instruction provided by the board in classes described in subsection (2), multiplied by $41.

(4) Where the quotient obtained by dividing the number of elementary school pupils enrolled in classes described in subsection (2) that have been established by the board by the number of such classes is less than 25, the $41 per hour rate specified in subsection (3) shall be reduced by the product of $1 and the difference between the quotient and 25.

O. Reg. 212/99, s. 4.

Teacher Compensation Allocation

33. (1) In this section,

"OSSTF" stands for the Ontario Secondary School Teachers' Federation; ("FEESO")

"OSSTF certification" means the OSSTF certification of Group 1, Group 2, Group 3 or Group 4; ("certification de la FEESO") "qualification category" means OSSTF certification or QECO category; ("catégorie de qualifications")

"QECO" stands for Qualifications Evaluation Council of Ontario; ("COEQ")

"QECO category" means the QECO category D, C, B, A1, A2, A3 or A4; ("catégorie du COEQ")

"teacher" includes a temporary teacher and does not include an occasional teacher. ("enseignant")

(2) In this section, a cell of Table 6 is referred to by its qualification category co-ordinate followed by the number co-ordinate representing full years of teaching experience.

(3) For example, cell C-1 contains the number 0.6127 and cell A1/Group 1-3 contains the number 0.7416.

(4) For the purposes of this section, the number of teachers employed by a board is the full-time equivalent number of persons employed by the board as of October 31, 1998 to teach.

(5) For the purposes of subsection (4), the counting practices usually followed by the board for staffing purposes shall be followed, subject to the following rules:

1. A teacher who is not assigned to provide instruction to pupils in a regular timetable that is in effect as of October 31, 1998 shall not be counted for the purposes of this section.
2. The provision of library instruction or guidance to pupils shall be considered the provision of instruction to pupils for the purposes of paragraphs 1, 3 and 4.
3. Where a teacher is assigned in a regular timetable that is in effect as of October 31, 1998 to spend part of his or her time providing instruction to pupils and is also assigned, as of that date, under section 17 of Regulation 298 of the Revised Regulations of Ontario, 1990, to spend part of his or her time acting as a consultant, co-ordinator or supervisor, the full-time equivalency for the teacher shall be determined as follows:
    i. Determine the average number of hours per day in the cycle that includes October 31, 1998 for which the teacher is regularly scheduled, in accordance with the timetable, to provide instruction to pupils or to prepare for such instruction. For the purposes of this subparagraph, a count of hours shall be accurate to one decimal place.
    ii. Divide the total determined under subparagraph i by five.
4. Where a principal or vice-principal is assigned in a regular timetable that is in effect as of October 31, 1998 to spend part of his or her time providing instruction to pupils, the principal or vice-principal shall be counted as a teacher for the purposes of this section and his or her full-time equivalency as a teacher shall be determined as follows:
    i. Determine the average number of hours per day in the cycle that includes October 31, 1998 for which the principal or vice-principal is regularly scheduled, in accordance with the timetable, to provide instruction to pupils. For the purposes of this subsection, a count of hours shall be accurate to one decimal place.
    ii. Divide the number determined under subparagraph i by five.

S. 33 REGULATIONS UNDER THE EDUCATION ACT

(6) Subject to subsections (7) and (8), when determining the number of full years of teaching experience of a teacher employed by a board, the counting practices usually followed by the board when counting the amount of teaching experience shall be applied, as of October 31, 1998.

(7) Where the number of full years of teaching experience of a teacher exceeds 10, as determined under subsection (6), the number of full years of teaching experience of the teacher shall be deemed to be 10.

(8) The number of full years of teaching experience of a principal or vice-principal shall be deemed to be 10.

(9) The following rules shall be applied, as of October 31, 1998, to determine the qualification category of a teacher:

1. If a board uses a QECO categories system for salary purposes in relation to a teacher employed by it, that QECO categories system shall be used for that teacher for the purposes of this section.
2. If a board uses an OSSTF certification system for salary purposes in relation to a teacher employed by it, that OSSTF certification system shall be used for that teacher for the purposes of this section.
3. Subject to paragraph 5, if a board does not use a QECO categories system for salary purposes in relation to an elementary school teacher employed by it, the classification system used by the board for elementary school teachers in filling out the Education Relations Commission Data Form A for 1998 shall be used for that teacher for the purposes of this section.
4. Subject to paragraph 5, if a board does not use a QECO categories system or an OSSTF certification system for salary purposes in relation to a secondary school teacher employed by it, the classification system used by the board for secondary school teachers in filling out the Education Relations Commission Data Form A for 1998 shall be used for that teacher for the purposes of this section.
5. In the circumstances described in paragraph 3 or 4, the board may elect, by written notice to the Minister, to use the QECO categories system referred to by QECO as QECO Programme Level 4 or the 1992 OSSTF certification system, instead of the classification system determined under paragraph 3 or 4.
6. The qualification category of a principal or vice-principal shall be deemed to be A4/Group 4.
7. If the qualification category of a person is changed after October 31, 1998 and the change for salary purposes is retroactive to October 31, 1998 or earlier, the changed qualification category shall be used for the purposes of this section.

(10) For the purposes of paragraph 2 of section 11, the amount of the teacher compensation allocation for a district school board shall be determined as follows:

1. For each cell in Table 6, determine the number of teachers employed by the board who have the qualification category and the number of full years of teaching experience that correspond with the co-ordinates of the cell. For example, a teacher with a qualification category of D and six months of teaching experience shall be counted for the purposes of cell D-0 and a teacher with a qualification category of A2 or

Group 2 and three years and seven months of teaching experience shall be counted for the purposes of cell A2/Group 2-3.
2. For each cell in Table 6, multiply the number of teachers employed by the board who are counted for the purposes of the cell by the number set out in that cell in Table 6.
3. Add all the products obtained under paragraph 2 for the board.
4. Divide the sum obtained under paragraph 3 by the total number of teachers employed by the board.
5. Subtract one from the number obtained under paragraph 4.
6. Multiply the result obtained under paragraph 5 by $2,685.
7. Multiply the amount determined under paragraph 6 by the 1998-99 day school average daily enrolment of pupils of the board.
8. Determine the special assistance amount for re-organization of secondary school staff, in accordance with subsection (11).
9. Determine the special assistance amount for a high credit per pupil average, if any, in accordance with subsection (12).
10. Add the amounts determined under paragraphs 7, 8 and 9.

(11) For the purposes of paragraph 8 of subsection (10), the special assistance amount for re-organization of secondary school staff shall be determined by multiplying the 1998-99 day school average daily enrolment of secondary pupils of the board by $180.

(12) For the purposes of paragraph 9 of subsection (10), the special assistance amount for a high credit per pupil average shall be determined as follows:
1. Determine the average number of credits per secondary school pupil of the board for the 1997-98 school year.
2. If the number determined under paragraph 1 is 7.5 or less but more than 7.2, deduct 7.2 from the number determined under paragraph 1.
3. If the number determined under paragraph 1 is more than 7.5, deduct 7.2 from 7.5.
4. Divide the number obtained under paragraph 2 or 3, as the case may be, by 7.2.
5. Multiply the number obtained under paragraph 4 by $2,748.
6. Multiply the amount obtained under paragraph 5 by the 1998-99 day school average daily enrolment of secondary pupils of the board.

33.1 (1) In this section,

"eligible retirees" means the following persons who cease, voluntarily, to be employed by a district school board at the end of the 1997-98 school year and who are eligible to receive an immediate pension under the *Teachers' Pension Act*:
1. Teachers who are members of a teachers' bargaining unit, but not occasional teachers or continuing education teachers.
2. Principals, other than those in respect of whom the board is eligible to receive a transition assistance grant under the guideline described in subsection (6).
3. Vice-principals, other than those in respect of whom the board is eligible to receive a transition assistance grant under the guideline described in subsection (6); ("retraités admissibles")

"new teaching staff" means teachers who are hired by a district school board to begin employment with the board in September 1998 and who are members of a teachers' bargaining unit, but not occasional teachers or continuing education teachers; ("nouveau personnel enseignant")

"relevant language portion" in relation to an old board has the same meaning as in Ontario Regulation 285/98; ("part linguistique pertinente")

"retirement gratuity" means a sick leave gratuity or other lump sum allowance payable by a board in accordance with a collective agreement or board policy in effect on April 1, 1998 but not an amount payable under an early retirement incentive plan of the board; ("prime de retraite")

"short year" has the same meaning as in Ontario Regulation 285/98. ("année abrégée")

(2) For the purpose of paragraph 2 of section 11, the amount of the retirement gratuity allocation for a district school board is determined as follows:

1. Determine the amount payable by the board in respect of retirement gratuities to the board's eligible retirees.
2. Multiply the amount determined under paragraph 1 by the percentage calculated for the board under subsection (3).
3. Subtract the average annual salary of the board's new teaching staff from the average annual salary of the board's eligible retirees described in paragraph 1 of the definition of eligible retirees.
4. Determine the amount that is the lesser of,
    i. the number of the board's new teaching staff who are assigned to one or more elementary schools or to perform duties in respect of such schools all or most of the time, and
    ii. the number obtained by applying the percentage calculated for the board under subsection (3) to the number of the board's eligible retirees who, immediately before they ceased to be employed by the board, were assigned to one or more elementary schools or to perform duties in respect of such schools all or most of the time.
5. Determine the amount that is the lesser of,
    i. the number of the board's new teaching staff who are assigned to one or more secondary schools or to perform duties in respect of such schools all or most of the time, and
    ii. the number obtained by applying the percentage calculated for the board under subsection (3) to the number of the board's eligible retirees who, immediately before they ceased to be employed by the board, were assigned to one or more secondary schools or to perform duties in respect of such schools all or most of the time.
6. Add the amounts determined under paragraphs 4 and 5.
7. Multiply the amount determined under paragraph 3 by the amount determined under paragraph 6.
8. Subtract the average annual salary of the members of teachers' bargaining units (other than occasional teachers and continuing education teachers) employed by the board on September 30, 1998 from the average annual salary of the board's eligible retirees described in paragraph 1 of the definition of eligible retirees.
9. Determine the number, if any, by which the number of eligible retirees described in

subparagraph ii of paragraph 4 exceeds the number of new teaching staff described in subparagraph i of that paragraph.
10. Determine the number, if any, by which the number of eligible retirees described in subparagraph ii of paragraph 5 exceeds the number of new teaching staff described in subparagraph i of that paragraph.
11. Add the numbers determined under paragraphs 9 and 10.
12. Multiply the amount determined under paragraph 8 by the number determined under paragraph 11.
13. Add the amounts determined under paragraphs 7 and 12.
14. Multiply the amount determined under paragraph 13 by 1.03.
15. Multiply the amount determined under paragraph 14,
    i. by 1.0 for a board in respect of which an amount is subtracted under subsection 46(2) or added under subsection 47(2), and
    ii. by 0.2 for all other boards.
16. Subtract the amount determined under paragraph 15 from the amount determined under paragraph 2.

(3) For the purposes of paragraphs 2, 4 and 5 of subsection (2), a percentage shall be calculated for each board as follows:

1. Take the amount estimated by the board and approved by the Minister that would have been paid by the board as retirement gratuities in respect of the proportion of eligible retirees who would likely have retired at the end of the 1997-98 school year based on the provisions of the Ontario Teachers' Pension Plan as it existed on January 1, 1998. For the purposes of this paragraph, the Minister shall approve the amount estimated by the board if in the opinion of the Minister the estimate is reasonable having regard to the amount budgeted by the board for retirement gratuities in the short year and the amounts actually paid as retirement gratuities by the relevant language portions of the predecessor old boards of the board in 1996 and 1997.
2. Divide the amount taken under paragraph 1 by the amount determined under paragraph 1 of subsection (2).
3. Subtract the result obtained under paragraph 2 from 1.0.

(4) When determining the number of persons or eligible retirees for the purposes of this section, each board shall use its usual full-time equivalent counting practices with respect to persons who are, and eligible retirees who were, employed part-time.

(5) For the purposes of paragraph 8 of subsection (2),

(a) the average annual salary of the members of teachers' bargaining units (other than occasional teachers and continuing education teachers) employed by the board on September 30, 1998 is calculated by dividing the total annual salaries of the members, effective at the beginning of the 1998-99 school year, by the number of those members; and

(b) the average annual salary of the board's eligible retirees described in paragraph 1 of the definition of eligible retirees is calculated by dividing the total annual salaries of the eligible retirees, effective immediately before they ceased to be employed by the board, from the number of those eligible retirees.

(6) The guideline referred to in the definition of eligible retirees is entitled "School Board Restructuring Program, Phase 2, Application for Reimbursement of Labour Adjustment Costs—Guideline", and it is an attachment to the Memorandum to Directors of Education and Secretaries of District School Authorities from Veronica Lacey, Deputy Minister, dated April 17, 1998, whose subject is School Board Restructuring Program, Phase 2. O. Reg. 538/98, s. 2.

Early Learning Allocation

34. (1) For the purposes of paragraph 2 of section 11, the amount of the early learning allocation for a district school board shall be determined in accordance with this section.

(2) If a board does not provide instruction in junior kindergarten in any of its schools in September of 1998, the amount of the early learning allocation for the board shall be determined as follows:

1. Determine the day school full-time equivalent enrolment for the board as of October 31, 1998, counting only pupils of the board enrolled in any of kindergarten and grades one to three.
2. Multiply the number determined under paragraph 1 by $609.

(3) Subject to subsection (5), if a board provides instruction in junior kindergarten in one or more of its schools in September of 1998, the amount of the early learning allocation for the board shall be determined as follows:

1. Determine the day school full-time equivalent enrolment for the board as of October 31, 1998, counting only pupils of the board enrolled in any of kindergarten and grades one to three.
2. Multiply the number determined under paragraph 1 by $609.
3. Determine the 1998-99 allocation per elementary pupil of the board, in accordance with subsection (4).
4. Multiply the amount determined under paragraph 3 by the day school full-time equivalent enrolment for the board as of October 31, 1998, counting only pupils of the board enrolled in junior kindergarten.
5. Deduct the amount determined under paragraph 4 from the amount determined under paragraph 2.

(4) For the purposes of paragraph 3 of subsection (3), the 1998-99 allocation per elementary pupil of the board shall be determined as follows:

1. Total the following amounts:
    i. The remote and rural allocation amount for the board, as determined under section 30.
    ii. The learning opportunities allocation amount for the board, as determined under section 31.
    iii. The transportation allocation amount for the board, as determined under section 35.
    iv. The administration and governance allocation amount for the board, as determined under section 36.
2. Divide the total obtained under paragraph 1 by the 1998-99 day school average daily enrolment of pupils of the board.

3. Determine an amount on account of the special education allocation for elementary pupils, as follows:
    i. Multiply the 1998-99 day school average daily enrolment of elementary pupils of the board by $347.
    ii. Divide the amount determined for the board under paragraph 2 of section 14 by the 1998-99 day school average daily enrolment of pupils of the board.
    iii. Multiply the result obtained under subparagraph ii by the 1998-99 day school average daily enrolment of elementary pupils of the board.
    iv. Determine an amount on account of program ISA for elementary pupils, as follows:
        A. If the amount determined for the board under clause 17(a) is greater than the amount determined for the board under clause 17(b), multiply the 1998-99 day school average daily enrolment of elementary pupils of the board by the per pupil amount specified for the board in Column 2 of Table 1.
        B. If the amount determined for the board under clause 17(b) is greater than the amount determined for the board under clause 17(a), calculate the part of the ISA level 2 and 3 funding total determined for the board under subsection 18(5) that is generated by elementary pupils of the board.
    v. Total the amounts obtained under subparagraphs i, iii and iv.
4. Take the amount determined in relation to elementary small schools for the board under paragraph 4 of subsection 29(11).
5. In the case of an English-language district school board, determine an amount on account of the language allocation for elementary pupils, as follows:
    i. Take the French as a second language amount for elementary pupils of the board, as calculated under subsection 22(3).
    ii. Calculate the part of the ESL/ESD amount for the board, as calculated under section 24, that is generated by elementary school pupils of the board.
    iii. Add the amount taken under subparagraph i to the amount calculated under subparagraph ii.
6. In the case of a French-language district school board, determine an amount on account of the language allocation for elementary pupils, as follows:
    i. Total the amounts determined for the board under paragraphs 1 and 3 of subsection 26(1).
    ii. Divide the total determined for the board under paragraph 7 of subsection 28(4) by the total number of instructional units determined for the board under paragraph 3 of subsection 28(4). Multiply the result by the total number of elementary instructional units determined for the board under paragraph 1 of subsection 28(4).
    iii. Calculate the part of the PDF funding level for the board, as calculated under subsection 28(11), that is generated by elementary school pupils of the board.
    iv. Total the amount taken under subparagraph i, the product obtained under subparagraph ii and the amount calculated under subparagraph iii.
7. Determine an amount on account of the teacher compensation allocation for elementary pupils, by calculating what the amount calculated for the board under paragraph

7 of subsection 33(10) would be if the calculation under that paragraph were done counting only teachers employed by the board to provide instruction to elementary school pupils and counting only elementary pupils of the board.
8. Take the amount determined in relation to elementary school renewal for the board under paragraph 6 of subsection 37(7).
9. Total the amounts taken or determined for the board under paragraphs 3 to 8.
10. Divide the total obtained under paragraph 9 by the 1998-99 day school average daily enrolment of elementary pupils of the board.
11. Total the following amounts:
    i. $3,367, on account of the foundation allocation.
    ii. $520, on account of school operations.
    iii. The amount obtained under paragraph 2.
    iv. The amount obtained under paragraph 10.

(5) If one or more of the predecessor old boards of the district school board did not provide junior kindergarten in any of its schools in September of 1997 and one or more of the predecessor old boards of the district school board provided junior kindergarten at a take-up rate of more than 93 per cent, the amount determined under subsection (3) as the early learning allocation for the district school board shall be increased by the supplementary amount, if any, determined by the Minister under subsection (6).

(6) The Minister, on application by the district school board, may determine a supplementary amount that he or she considers appropriate to adjust for the effect of the circumstances described in subsection (5) on the amount obtained for the board under subsection (3).

(7) For the purposes of subsection (5), the take-up rate for an old board shall be determined by dividing the number of junior kindergarten pupils enrolled in schools of the old board on October 31, 1997 by the number of kindergarten pupils enrolled in schools of the old board on October 31, 1997.

Transportation Allocation

35. (1) In this section,

"1997 actual expenditure allocation form" means the form provided by the Ministry, as part of the 1997 financial statement package, for the purpose of determining the French-English split of 1997 actual expenditures by the old boards.

(2) Subject to any adjustment made under subsection (6), for the purposes of paragraph 2 of section 11, the amount of the transportation allocation for an English-language district school board shall be determined as follows:
1. For each predecessor old board of the district school board, take the amount shown on the old board's 1997 actual expenditure allocation form, at item 4.3.11, under the column heading "English Language Portion", as the net transportation cost.
2. For each predecessor old board of the district school board, multiply the amount determined under paragraph 1 by 100.7 per cent.
3. Total the amounts determined under paragraph 2 for each predecessor old board of the district school board.

4. Determine the 1998-99 day school average daily enrolment of pupils of the district school board.
5. For each predecessor old board of the district school board, calculate a 1997 day school average daily enrolment, as follows:
    i. Determine the day school A.D.E. of resident-internal pupils of the old board, excluding pupils enrolled in a French-language instructional unit. For the purposes of this subparagraph, "day school A.D.E. of resident-internal pupils" has the same meaning as in Ontario Regulation 78/97, except that,
        A. a pupil who is enrolled in kindergarten shall be counted as a full-time pupil if he or she, in respect of a cycle, is registered for classroom instruction for an average of at least 210 minutes per school day, and
        B. the exclusion of pupils enrolled in junior kindergarten from the definition of "day school A.D.E. of resident-internal pupils" in Ontario Regulation 78/97 does not apply.
    ii. Determine the day school A.D.E. of non-resident pupils of the old board, excluding pupils enrolled in a French-language instructional unit and pupils described in subsection 2(5). For the purposes of this subparagraph, "day school A.D.E. of non-resident pupils" has the same meaning as in Ontario Regulation 78/97, except that,
        A. a pupil who is enrolled in kindergarten shall be counted as a full-time pupil if he or she, in respect of a cycle, is registered for classroom instruction for an average of at least 210 minutes per school day, and
        B. the exclusion of pupils enrolled in junior kindergarten from the definition of "day school A.D.E. of non-resident pupils" in Ontario Regulation 78/97 does not apply.
    iii. Total the amounts determined under subparagraphs i and ii.
6. Total the numbers obtained under paragraph 5 for each predecessor old board of the district school board.
7. Divide the number obtained under paragraph 4 by the number obtained under paragraph 6.
8. Multiply the number obtained under paragraph 7 by the amount obtained under paragraph 3.

(3) In subsection (4),

"English-language instructional unit" means a class, group of classes or school in which the English language or American sign language is the language of instruction and includes a class, group of classes or school established under paragraph 25 of subsection 8(1) of the Act.

(4) Subject to any adjustment made under subsection (6), for the purposes of paragraph 2 of section 11, the amount of the transportation allocation for a French-language district school board shall be determined as follows:
1. For each predecessor old board of the district school board, take the amount shown on the old board's 1997 actual expenditure allocation form, at item 4.3.11, under the column heading "French Language Portion", as the net transportation cost.

2. For each predecessor old board of the district school board, multiply the amount determined under paragraph 1 by 100.7 per cent.
3. Total the amounts determined under paragraph 2 for each predecessor old board of the district school board.
4. Determine the 1998-99 day school average daily enrolment of pupils of the district school board.
5. For each predecessor old board of the district school board, calculate a 1997 day school average daily enrolment, as follows:
    i. Determine the 1997 day school A.D.E. of resident-internal pupils of the old board, excluding pupils enrolled in an English-language instructional unit. For the purposes of this subparagraph, "day school A.D.E. of resident-internal pupils" has the same meaning as in Ontario Regulation 78/97, except that,
        A. a pupil who is enrolled in kindergarten shall be counted as a full-time pupil if he or she, in respect of a cycle, is registered for classroom instruction for an average of at least 210 minutes per school day, and
        B. the exclusion of pupils enrolled in junior kindergarten from the definition of "day school A.D.E. of resident-internal pupils" in Ontario Regulation 78/97 does not apply.
    ii. Determine the 1997 day school A.D.E. of non-resident pupils of the old board, excluding pupils enrolled in an English-language instructional unit and pupils described in subsection 2(5). For the purposes of this subparagraph, "day school A.D.E. of non-resident pupils" has the same meaning as in Ontario Regulation 78/97, except that,
        A. a pupil who is enrolled in kindergarten shall be counted as a full-time pupil if he or she, in respect of a cycle, is registered for classroom instruction for an average of at least 210 minutes per school day, and
        B. the exclusion of pupils enrolled in junior kindergarten from the definition of "day school A.D.E. of non-resident pupils" in Ontario Regulation 78/97 does not apply.
    iii. Total the amounts determined under subparagraphs i and ii.
6. Total the numbers obtained under paragraph 5 for each predecessor old board of the district school board.
7. Divide the number obtained under paragraph 4 by the number obtained under paragraph 6.
8. Multiply the number obtained under paragraph 7 by the amount obtained under paragraph 3.

(5) Subsection (6) applies where, as of September 15, 1998, a board of area of jurisdiction of which is wholly or partly the same as that of another board has not entered into an agreement with that other board providing for co-operative transportation services for pupils of the boards and has applied in writing to the Minister for a transportation allocation adjustment as between the two boards.

(6) Where a board applies under subsection (5), the Minister may adjust the amount of the transportation allocation for each of the two boards as the Minister considers appropriate to take into account the costs related to the transportation of pupils who are enrolled in schools

of one or the other of the two boards as a result of a decision of either board to admit a pupil who is entitled to attend a school of the other board.

(7) Adjustments to transportation allocations for two boards made by the Minister under subsection (6) shall not affect the total of the allocations that would be determined for the two boards under subsections (2) and (4). O. Reg. 560/98, s. 1.

Administration and Governance Allocation

36. (1) For the purposes of paragraph 2 of section 11, the amount of the administration and governance allocation for a district school board shall be determined as follows:
1. Determine the amount for the board for board members' honoraria and expenses and for expenses relating to pupil representation, in accordance with subsection (2).
2. Determine the amount for the board for directors of education and supervisory officers, in accordance with subsection (4).
3. Determine the amount for the board for administration costs, in accordance with subsection (5).
4. Total the amounts determined under paragraphs 1, 2 and 3.

(2) The amount for the board for board members' honoraria and expenses and for expenses relating to pupil representation shall be determined as follows:
1. Multiply the number of members on the board by $5,000, on account of board members' honoraria. For the purposes of this paragraph, the number of members on the board is the sum of,
    i. the number of members determined for the board under subclause 58.1(2)(k)(i) of the Act, and
    ii. the number of Native representatives determined for the board under subsection 188(5) of the Act.
2. Multiply the number of members on the board by $5,000, on account of board members' expenses. For the purposes of this paragraph, the number of members on the board is the sum of,
    i. the number of members determined for the board under subclause 58.1(2)(k)(i) of the Act, and
    ii. the number of Native representatives determined for the board under subsection 188(5) of the Act.
3. Total the products obtained under paragraphs 1 and 2.
4. Add $10,000 to the amount determined under paragraph 3, on account of additional honoraria for the chair and vice-chair.
5. Add $5,000 to the amount determined under paragraph 4, on account of expenses relating to pupil representation.

(3) For the purposes of subsection (4), pupils shall be counted on the basis of 1998-99 day school average daily enrolment of pupils of the board.

(4) The amount for the board for directors of education and supervisory officers shall be determined as follows:
1. Allow $65,000 as a base amount.

2. Allow $67 per pupil for the first 2,000 pupils of the board.
3. Allow $25 per pupil for the next 23,000 pupils of the board.
4. Allow $21 per pupil for the remaining pupils of the board.
5. Total the amounts allowed under paragraphs 1 to 4.
6. Add 2 per cent of the amount of the board's remote and rural allocation, as determined under section 30.
7. Add 0.5 per cent of the amount of the board's learning opportunities allocation, as determined under section 31.
8. Add 1 per cent of the amount calculated for the board for new pupil places under subsection 37(8).

(5) The amount for the board for administration costs shall be determined as follows:

1. Allow $80,000 as a base amount.
2. Add the product of $174 and the 1998-99 day school average daily enrolment of pupils of the board.
3. Add 11 per cent of the amount of the board's remote and rural allocation, as determined under section 30.
4. Add 0.5 per cent of the amount of the board's learning opportunities allocation, as determined under section 31.
5. Add 1 per cent of the amount calculated for the board for new pupil places under subsection 37(8).

Pupil Accommodation Allocation

37. (1) For the purposes of paragraph 2 of section 11, the amount of the pupil accommodation allocation for a district school board shall be determined as follows:

1. Determine the amount for the board for school operations, in accordance with subsection (2).
2. Determine the amount for the board for school renewal, in accordance with subsection (7).
3. Determine the amount for the board for new pupil places, in accordance with subsection (8).
3.1 Determine the amount for the board for leased instructional space, in accordance with subsection (13).
4. Total the amounts determined under paragraphs 1, 2, 3 and 3.1.

(2) The amount for the board for school operations shall be determined as follows:

1. Determine the 1998-99 day school average daily enrolment of elementary pupils of the board.
2. Multiply the number determined under paragraph 1 by the benchmark area requirement per pupil of 9.29 metres squared, to obtain the elementary school area requirement for the board.
3. Determine the adjusted elementary school area requirement for the board in metres squared, by applying, to the amount determined under paragraph 2, the supplementary

elementary school area factor, if any, approved for the board by the Minister in accordance with subsections (3) and (4).

4. Determine the day school average daily enrolment for the board for the 1998-99 fiscal year, in accordance with section 2 of the 1998-99 day school A.D.E. regulation, counting only pupils who are 21 years of age or more on December 31, 1998.

5. Determine the continuing education average daily enrolment for the board for the 1998-99 fiscal year, in accordance with section 3 of the 1998-99 A.D.E. regulation, counting only pupils enrolled in a course for which the pupil may earn a credit or credit equivalent and in which instruction is given between 8 a.m. and 5 p.m. and excluding pupils enrolled in a continuing education course delivered primarily through means other than classroom instruction.

6. Determine the summer school average daily enrolment for the board for the 1998-99 fiscal year, in accordance with section 4 of the 1998-99 A.D.E. regulation.

7. Add the numbers determined under paragraphs 4, 5 and 6.

8. Multiply the total determined under paragraph 7 by the benchmark area requirement per pupil of 9.29 metres squared, to obtain the adult education, continuing education and summer school area requirement for the board.

9. Determine the adjusted adult education, continuing education and summer school area requirement for the board in metres squared, by applying, to the amount determined under paragraph 8, the supplementary adult education, continuing education and summer school area factor, if any, approved for the board by the Minister in accordance with subsection (5).

10. Determine the 1998-99 day school average daily enrolment of secondary pupils of the board.

11. Multiply the number determined under paragraph 10 by the benchmark area requirement per pupil of 12.07 metres squared, to obtain the secondary school area requirement for the board.

12. Determine the adjusted secondary school area requirement for the board in metres squared, by applying, to the amount determined under paragraph 11, the supplementary secondary school area factor, if any, approved for the board by the Minister in accordance with subsection (6).

13. Obtain the adjusted total area requirement for the board in metres squared by adding the following amounts:

    i. The elementary school area requirement for the board determined under paragraph 2 or, where the Minister approves a supplementary elementary school area factor for the board, the adjusted elementary school area requirement for the board determined under paragraph 3.

    ii. The adult education, continuing education and summer school area requirement for the board determined under paragraph 8 or, where the Minister approves a supplementary adult education, continuing education and summer school area factor for the board, the adjusted adult education, continuing education and summer school area requirement for the board determined under paragraph 9.

    iii. The secondary school area requirement for the board determined under paragraph 11 or, where the Minister approves a supplementary secondary school

area factor for the board, the adjusted secondary school area requirement for the board determined under paragraph 12.
14. Multiply the number obtained under paragraph 13 by the benchmark operating cost of $55.97 per metre squared.

(3) For the purposes of paragraph 3 of subsection (2), the Minister shall approve a supplementary elementary school area factor for a board if the Minister considers that it is appropriate to do so in order to make allowance for disproportionate space needs that are particular to the board and that are caused by,

(a) the fact that the board is reasonably operating a school that is too large for the community it serves, whether because of declining enrolment or for some other reason;

(b) the fact that the board is reasonably operating a school in a building the physical characteristics of which are neither compatible with nor easily modified to conform to the benchmark area requirements referred to in subsection (2);

(c) the fact that the board has disproportionately high space requirements because the board serves a disproportionately high number of pupils in special education programs or in other education programs with high space requirements; or

(d) other circumstances similar to those described in clauses (a), (b) and (c).

(4) In determining an amount for the purposes of subsection (3), the Minister shall have regard to the effect of the circumstances referred to in clauses 3(a) to (d) on the board's space needs.

(5) Subsections (3) and (4) apply with necessary modifications to authorize the Minister to approve a supplementary adult education, continuing education and summer school area factor for a board and, for the purpose, a reference to elementary school area shall be deemed to be a reference to adult education, continuing education and summer school area.

(6) Subsections (3) and (4) apply with necessary modifications to authorize the Minister to approve a supplementary secondary school area factor for a board and, for the purpose, a reference to elementary school area shall be deemed to be a reference to secondary school area.

(7) The amount for the board for school renewal shall be determined as follows:

1. Take the percentage, as calculated by the board and approved by the Minister, of the actual total elementary school area of the board that relates to buildings that are less than 20 years old.
2. Apply the percentage referred to in paragraph 1 to the benchmark renewal cost per metre squared of $6.89.
3. Take the percentage, as calculated by the board and approved by the Minister, of the actual total elementary school area of the board that relates to buildings that are 20 years old or older.
4. Apply the percentage referred to in paragraph 3 to the benchmark renewal cost per metre squared of $10.33.
5. Add the amounts obtained under paragraphs 2 and 4, to obtain a weighted average benchmark elementary school renewal cost per metre squared.
6. Multiply the amount obtained under paragraph 5 by the elementary school area requirement for the board determined under paragraph 2 of subsection (2) or, where the Minister approves a supplementary elementary school area factor for the board,

the adjusted elementary school area requirement for the board determined under paragraph 3 of subsection (2).
7. Take the percentage, as calculated by the board and approved by the Minister, of the actual total secondary school area of the board that relates to buildings that are less than 20 years old.
8. Apply the percentage referred to in paragraph 7 to the benchmark renewal cost per metre squared of $6.89.
9. Take the percentage, as calculated by the board and approved by the Minister, of the actual total secondary school area of the board that relates to buildings that are 20 years old or older.
10. Apply the percentage referred to in paragraph 9 to the benchmark renewal cost per metre squared of $10.33.
11. Add the amounts obtained under paragraphs 8 and 10, to obtain a weighted average benchmark secondary school renewal cost per metre squared.
12. Multiply the amount obtained under paragraph 11 by the secondary school area requirement for the board determined under paragraph 11 of subsection (2) or, where the Minister approves a supplementary secondary school area factor for the board, the adjusted secondary school area requirement for the board determined under paragraph 12 of subsection (2).
13. Multiply the amount obtained under paragraph 11 by the adult education, continuing education and summer school area requirement for the board determined under paragraph 8 of subsection (2) or, where the Minister approves a supplementary adult education, continuing education and summer school area factor for the board, the adjusted adult eduction, continuing education and summer school area requirement for the board determined under paragraph 9 of subsection (2).
14. Add the amounts obtained under paragraphs 6, 12 and 13.

(8) The amount for the board for new pupil places shall be the lesser of $20 million and an amount determined as follows:

1. Determine the 1998-99 day school average daily enrolment of elementary pupils of the board.
2. Subtract the elementary capacity for the board, in terms of pupil places, as determined by the Minister in accordance with subsection (10), from the number determined under paragraph 1.
3. If the number determined under paragraph 2 is a positive number, multiply it by the benchmark area requirement of 9.29 metres squared.
4. Multiply the product obtained under paragraph 3 by the benchmark construction cost of $118.40 per metre squared.
5. Determine the 1998-99 day school average daily enrolment of secondary pupils of the board.
6. Subtract the secondary capacity for the board, in terms of pupil places, as determined by the Minister in accordance with subsection (10), from the number determined under paragraph 5.
7. If the number determined under paragraph 6 is a positive number, multiply it by the benchmark area requirement of 12.07 metres squared.

8. Multiply the product obtained under paragraph 7 by the benchmark construction cost of $129.17 per metre squared.
9. Add the products obtained under paragraphs 4 and 8.
10. Multiply the sum obtained under paragraph 9 by the geographic adjustment factor specified for the board in Table 7.

(9) In subsections (10) and (11),

"instructional space" means a space in a school that can reasonably be used for instructional purposes; ("aire d'enseignement")

"school facilities data" means data relating to boards' school facilities and includes school floor plans and other data compiled in accordance with the Ministry's school facilities inventory system. ("données sur les installations scolaires")

(9.1) For the purposes of subsections (10) and (11), an instructional space leased by a board is an instructional space of that board.

(10) For the purposes of paragraphs 2 and 6 subsection (8), the Minister shall determine an elementary capacity and a secondary capacity for the board as follows:

1. Apply the loadings determined under subsection (11) to the elementary and secondary school instructional spaces of the board, as categorized under subsection (11).
2. Where applicable, adjust the result determined under paragraph 1 in accordance with subsection (12).

(11) The Minister shall determine loadings and categories of instructional space as follows:

1. Using school facilities data, the Minister shall identify categories of instructional space. In identifying categories of instructional space, the Minister shall have regard to but is not limited to the categories identified in Appendix 1 to the Ministry publication entitled "Capital Grant Plan 1979", as amended to May 30, 1990.
2. The Minister shall assign a loading to each category of instructional space identified under paragraph 1, based on the number of pupils that can reasonably be accommodated in each category of instructional space.

(12) The Minister shall make such adjustments under paragraph 2 of subsection (10) as the Minister considers appropriate to take account of funds received by one board from another board in connection with a determination made under Ontario Regulation 460/97 respecting the disposition of an asset of an old board.

(13) The amount for the board for leased instructional space shall be the lesser of,

(a) the total of the amounts reported at code point 0405 in the audited 1997 financial statements of the predecessor old boards of the board; and
(b) the total of the costs of leasing instructional space that are paid by the board in the 1998-99 fiscal year and approved by the Minister in that fiscal year. O. Reg. 538/98, s. 2.

Debt Charges Allocation

38. (1) Subject to subsections (2) and (3), for the purposes of paragraph 2 of section 11, the amount of the debt charges allocation for a district school board shall be the total of the payments on account of principal and interest that are due and payable by the board in the 1998-99 fiscal year in order to service debt incurred, by the board or by a predecessor old board of the board, to finance the acquisition of a capital asset where,

   (a) the acquisition is pursuant to a contractual obligation entered into by the board or predecessor old board before May 15, 1998; or
   (b) the acquisition is for the purposes of a capital project the estimated project cost of which was approved in writing by the Minister before May 15, 1998.

(2) With respect to debt incurred before May 15, 1998, subsection (1) ceases to apply in respect of a debt if the amount, terms or conditions of the obligation are re-negotiated on or after May 15, unless the re-negotiated amount, terms and conditions are approved in writing by the Minister.

(3) With respect to debt incurred on or after May 15, 1998, subsection (1) applies only if the amount, terms and conditions of the debt are approved in writing by the Minister.

Phase-in Funding

39. (1) In sections 40 to 47, a reference to the relevant language portion of an old board has the same meaning as in Ontario Regulation 285/98.

(2) For the purposes of sections 40 to 47, the allocation ratio for the relevant language portion of an old board is the allocation ratio specified or determined for the language portion under section 13 of Ontario Regulation 285/98.

(3) For the purposes of sections 40 to 47, if the Minister reasonably concludes that an amount reported at a code point in a financial statement is incorrect because of an error in calculation, because of an error in filling out the form for the financial statement or because an amendment to a previous legislation grant regulation was not taken into account in calculating the amount, the Minister shall make the appropriate correction and the corrected amount shall be deemed to be the amount reported at the code point in the financial statement.

40. For the purposes of paragraph 4 of section 11, the total determined for a district school board under paragraph 3 of section 11 shall be adjusted as follows:

1. Calculate the deemed operating revenue for 1997 for the board, in accordance with section 41.
2. Calculate the 1998-99 fiscal year operating revenue for the board, in accordance with section 42.
3. Using the calculations under paragraphs 1 and 2, calculate the change in operating revenue for the board, in accordance with section 43.
4. Calculate the deemed 1997 enrolment for the board, in accordance with section 44.
5. Calculate the adjusted change in operating revenue for the board, in accordance with section 45.
6. Where the adjusted change in operating revenue for the board is more than 1.04, subtract an amount determined in accordance with section 46 from the total determined for the board under paragraph 3 of section 11.
7. Where the adjusted change in operating revenue for the board or the change in operating revenue for the board is less than 0.96, add an amount determined in

accordance with section 47 to the total determined for the board under paragraph 3 of section 11.

41. (1) For the purposes of paragraph 1 of section 40, the deemed operating revenue for 1997 for a district school board shall be calculated as follows:

1. For each predecessor old board of the district school board, take the provincial grant amount as reported in the audited 1997 financial statements of the old board at code point 0274.
2. For each predecessor old board of the district school board, adjust the amount referred to in paragraph 1 to obtain the amount that would have been reported in the audited statements of the old board at code 0274 if there had been no withdrawal of employee services or lock-out of employees in 1997.
3. For each predecessor old board of the district school board, calculate a 1997 local taxation amount, as follows:
    i. Total the amounts reported in the audited 1997 financial statements of the old board at code points 0247 and 0249.
    ii. Subtract the amount reported in the audited 1997 financial statements of the old board at code point 0245 from the total determined under subparagraph i.
    iii. Add the lesser of,
        A. the amount reported in the audited 1997 financial statements of the old board at code 0248, and
        B. the greater of,
            1. the amount included in the 1997 estimates of the old board in respect of the taxes receivable in 1997 by it under section 35 of the *Assessment Act*, and
            2. the average of the amounts received by the old board in 1992, 1993, 1994, 1995 and 1996 under section 35 of the *Assessment Act*.
    For the purposes of sub-sub-subparagraph 2 of sub-subparagraph B, if the amount received in any one of the five years exceeds the five-year average by 75 per cent or more, the average shall be calculated excluding that year.
4. For each predecessor old board of the district school board, add the amount calculated under paragraph 3 to the amount referred to in paragraph 1, as adjusted, where applicable, under paragraph 2.
5. For each predecessor old board of the district school board, subtract from the amount determined under paragraph 4 the lesser of,
    i. the amount reported as tax write-offs in the audited 1997 financial statements of the old board at code point 7712, and
    ii. the greater of,
        A. the amounts included in the 1997 estimates of the old board in respect of the amounts chargeable in 1997 to it by a municipal council under section 421 of the *Municipal Act*, not including taxes receivable in 1997 by the old board to the extent that such taxes were cancelled or reduced as a result of a resolution of the old board, and
        B. the average of the amounts charged to the old board in 1992, 1993, 1994, 1995 and 1996 by a municipal council under section 421 of the *Municipal*

Act, not including taxes receivable in those years by the old board to the extent that such taxes were cancelled or reduced as a result of a resolution of the old board.

For the purposes of subparagraph B of subparagraph ii, if the amount charged in any one of the five years exceeds the five-year average by 75 per cent or more, the average shall be calculated excluding that year.

6. For each predecessor old board of the district school board, account for net capital expenditure, as follows:
    i. Subtract, from the amount determined under paragraph 5, the sum of,
        A. the total of the amounts reported in the audited 1997 financial statements of the old board at code points 0283, 7307, 7405, 7410, 8012 and 8112, and
        B. the amount reported in the audited 1997 financial statements of the old board at code point 7305 less any money from an education development charges account used by the board in accordance with section 5 of Regulation 268 of the Revised Regulations of Ontario, 1990, as it read on December 31, 1997 and recorded at code point 7305.
    ii. Add, to the amount determined under subparagraph i, the total of the amounts reported in the audited 1997 financial statements of the old board at code points 0225, 0226, 0229, 0237, 0238 and 0287.
    iii. Add, to the amount determined under subparagraph ii, that part of the amount reported in the audited 1997 financial statements of the old board at code point 0227 that was applied to expenditures that are included in the amounts shown in those financial statements at code points 7305 and 7405. This subparagraph applies only to an amount included at code point 0227 if its application to an expenditure included at code point 7305 to 7405 was authorized in 1997 by a resolution of the old board.
7. Multiply the amount determined under paragraph 6 by the allocation ratio for the relevant language portion of the old board.
8. For each predecessor old board of the district school board, account for net tuition fee revenue, as follows:
    i. Add, to the amount determined under paragraph 7, the total of the tuition fee revenues reported in the audited 1997 financial statements of the old board at code points 0201 and 0204 that, in the case of an English-language district school board, relate to pupils enrolled in English-language instructional units and, in the case of a French-language district school board, relate to pupils enrolled in French-language instructional units.
    ii. Subtract, from the amount determined under subparagraph i, the tuition fee expenditures reported in the audited 1997 financial statements of the old board at code point 7209 that, in the case of an English-language district school board, relate to pupils enrolled in English-language instructional units and, in the case of a French-language district school board, relate to pupils enrolled in French-language instructional units.

In this paragraph, ''English-language instructional unit'' means a class, group of classes or school in which the English language or American sign language is the language of instruction and includes a class, group of classes or school established under paragraph 25 of subsection 8(1) of the Act.

9. Total the amounts determined under paragraph 8 for each old board that is a predecessor of the district school board.

(2) Subsection (3) applies where the 1997 local taxation amount calculated under paragraph 3 of subsection (1) for a predecessor old board of a district school board does not reflect the old board's requirements for 1997 because the old board's 1997 requisition was not based on a plan of fully eliminating, in 1997, the deficit accumulated to the end of 1996.

(3) The amount calculated as the 1997 local taxation amount under paragraph 3 of subsection (1) for the old board shall be increased by an amount that is,

(a) calculated by the district school board under subsection (4); and
(b) approved by the Minister.

(4) For the purposes of subsection (3), the district school board shall calculate the amount by which the predecessor old board's requisition would have been higher had the requisition been based on a plan of fully eliminating, in 1997, the deficit accumulated to the end of 1996. O. Reg. 651/98, s. 1.

42. For the purposes of paragraph 2 of section 40, the 1998-99 fiscal year operating revenue for a district school board shall be calculated as follows:

1. Total the amounts determined for the board under this Regulation for each type of allocation.
2. Deduct the amount determined for the board for school renewal under subsection 37(7).
3. Deduct the amount determined for the board for new pupil places under subsection 37(8).
4. Deduct the amount of the debt charges allocation for the board, as determined under section 38.
5. Deduct the amount of the retirement gratuity allocation, as determined under section 33.1.
5.1 Deduct the amount of the summer school remedial allocation determined for the board under section 31.1.
6. Deduct the amount, if any, by which the amount determined for the board under subsection 18(5) exceeds the amount determined for the board under clause 17(a).

O. Reg. 538/98, s. 3; 651/98, s. 2; 212/99, s. 5.

43. For the purposes of paragraph 3 of section 40, the change in operating revenue for a board shall be calculated by dividing the 1998-99 fiscal year operating revenue for the board, as determined under section 42, by the deemed operating revenue for 1997 for the board, as determined under section 41.

44. (1) For the purposes of paragraph 4 of section 40, the deemed 1997 enrolment for an English-language district school board shall be calculated as follows:

1. For each predecessor old board of the district school board, calculate a 1997 enrolment number, as follows:

    i. Determine the day school A.D.E. of resident-internal pupils of the old board, excluding pupils enrolled in a French-language instructional unit and pupils

enrolled in junior kindergarten. For the purposes of this subparagraph, "day school A.D.E. of resident-internal pupil" has the same meaning as in Ontario Regulation 78/97, except that a pupil who is enrolled in kindergarten shall be counted as a full-time pupil if he or she, in respect of a cycle, is registered for classroom instruction for an average of at least 210 minutes per school day.
   ii. Determine the day school A.D.E. of non-resident pupils of the old board, excluding pupils enrolled in a French-language instructional unit, pupils described in subsection 2(5) and pupils enrolled in junior kindergarten. For the purposes of this subparagraph, "day school A.D.E. of non-resident pupil" has the same meaning as in Ontario Regulation 78/97, except that a pupil who is enrolled in kindergarten shall be counted as a full-time pupil if he or she, in respect of a cycle, is registered for classroom instruction for an average of at least 210 minutes per school day.
   iii. Total the amounts determined under subparagraphs i and ii.
2. Total the amounts determined under paragraph 1 for each old board that is a predecessor of the district school board.

(2) In subsection (3),

"English-language instructional unit" means a class, group of classes or school in which the English language or American sign language is the language of instruction and includes a class, group of classes or school established under paragraph 25 of subsection 8(1) of the Act.

(3) For the purposes of paragraph 4 of section 40, the deemed 1997 enrolment for a French-language district school board shall be calculated as follows:

1. For each predecessor old board of the district school board, calculate a 1997 enrolment number, as follows:
   i. Determine the day school A.D.E. of resident-internal pupils of the old board, excluding pupils enrolled in an English-language instructional unit and pupils enrolled in junior kindergarten. For the purposes of this subparagraph, "day school A.D.E. of resident-internal pupil" has the same meaning as in Ontario Regulation 78/97, except that a pupil who is enrolled in kindergarten shall be counted as a full-time pupil if he or she, in respect of a cycle, is registered for classroom instruction for an average of at least 210 minutes per school day.
   ii. Determine the day school A.D.E. of non-resident pupils of the old board, excluding pupils enrolled in an English-language instructional unit, pupils described in subsection 2(5) and pupils enrolled in junior kindergarten. For the purposes of this subparagraph, "day school A.D.E. of non-resident pupil" has the same meaning as in Ontario Regulation 78/97, except that a pupil who is enrolled in kindergarten shall be counted as a full-time pupil if he or she, in respect of a cycle, is registered for classroom instruction for an average of at least 210 minutes per school day.
   iii. Total the amounts determined under subparagraphs i and ii.
2. Total the amounts determined under paragraph 1 for each old board that is a predecessor of the district school board.

45. For the purposes of paragraph 5 of section 40, the adjusted change in operating revenue for a board shall be calculated by multiplying the change in operating revenue calculated for the board under section 43 by a factor obtained by dividing the deemed 1997 enrolment for the board, calculated under section 44, by the 1998-99 day school average daily enrolment of pupils of the board, excluding pupils of the board enrolled in junior kindergarten.

46. (1) This section applies where the adjusted change in operating revenue for the board, as calculated under section 45, is more than 1.04.

(2) Where this section applies, an amount calculated as follows shall be subtracted from the total determined for the board under paragraph 3 of section 11:

1. Determine the amount by which the adjusted change in operating revenue for the board, as calculated under section 45, exceeds 1.04.
2. Multiply the amount obtained under paragraph 1 by the deemed operating revenue for 1997 for the board, as calculated under section 41.

47. (1) This section applies where the adjusted change in operating revenue for the board, as calculated under section 45, or the change in operating revenue for the board, as calculated under section 43, is less than 0.96.

(2) Where this section applies, an amount calculated as follows shall be added to the total determined for the board under paragraph 3 of section 11:

1. Determine the amount by which the change in operating revenue for the board, as calculated under section 43, is less than 0.96.
2. Multiply the amount obtained under paragraph 1 by the deemed operating revenue for 1997 for the board, as calculated under section 41.
3. Determine the amount by which the adjusted change in operating revenue for the board, as calculated under section 45, is less than 0.96.
4. Multiply the amount obtained under paragraph 3 by the deemed operating revenue for 1997 for the board, as calculated under section 41.
5. Take the greater of the amounts determined under paragraphs 2 and 4.
6. Deduct from the amount determined under paragraph 5 the amount, if any, by which the amount determined for the board under subsection 18(5) exceeds the amount determined for the board under clause 17(a).

O. Reg. 651/98, s. 3.

Grants for Capital Projects for which an Estimated Cost was Approved before September 1, 1998

48. (1) In this section,

"capital project" means a project for the acquisition of capital assets; ("projet d'immobilisations")

"capital projects Table" means Table 2 to Ontario Regulation 285/98. ("tableau des projets d'immobilisations")

(2) For the purposes of this section, a capital project is an approved 1998-99 capital project if,

(a) the Minister gives an approval in writing of the estimated cost for the project on or before September 1, 1998; and

(b) the Minister gives a final approval in writing for the project during the period beginning September 1, 1998 and ending August 31, 1999.

(3) For the purposes of this section,

(a) an approved 1998-99 capital project is an approved 1998-99 growth capital project if the project is intended to result in an increase in the pupil places of a board or in the purchase of land for the purposes of increasing the pupil places of a board; and

(b) an approved 1998-99 capital project is an approved 1998-99 non-growth capital project if it is not an approved growth capital project.

(4) A district school board shall be paid a grant in respect of each approved 1998-99 capital project of the board in an amount equal to the product of,

(a) the lesser of,
   (i) the project cost specified in the final approval for the project referred to in clause (2)(b), and
   (ii) the total of the actual expenditures by the board for the project in respect of which claims are made in accordance with the directions of the Minister before August 31, 1999; and

(b) the rate determined under subsections (6) to (8).

(5) When exercising the authority provided by subsection 234(8) of the Act for the purposes of grants payable under this section, the Minister may provide for an instalment to be paid after August 31, 1999.

(6) The rate for an approved 1998-99 non-growth capital project of a district school board is the rate set out in Column 3 of the capital projects Table, opposite the listing in Column 1 for the district school board and the listing in Column 2 for the predecessor old board that proposed the project.

(7) The rate for an approved 1998-99 growth capital project of a district school board is the rate set out in Column 4 of the capital projects Table, opposite the listing in Column 1 for the district school board and the listing in Column 2 for the predecessor old board that proposed the project.

(8) Despite subsections (6) and (7), the rate for an approved 1998-99 capital project in respect of a secondary school of a French-language district school board is the rate set out in Column 5 of the capital projects Table, opposite the listing in Column 1 for the district school board and the listing in Column 2 for the predecessor old board that proposed the project.

49. (1) Any grant or portion of a grant is payable to a district school board in respect of a capital project under a previous legislative grant regulation and that is not paid before September 1, 1998 shall be deemed to be a grant payable under this Regulation.

(2) When exercising the authority provided by subsection 234(8) of the Act for the purposes of grants or portions of grants payable under this section, the Minister may provide for an instalment to be paid after August 31, 1999.

(3) Any grant or portion of a grant that is payable under subsection (1) is not payable under any previous legislative grant resolution.

Enveloping

50. It is a condition of the payment of a grant to a district school board under this Regulation that the board manage its estimates process and its expenditures so as to ensure compliance with the requirements of sections 51 to 53.

51. (1) For the purposes of this section,

(a) an expenditure by a board is a classroom expenditure if it is an expenditure categorized in the 1998-99 Uniform Code of Accounts as a classroom expenditure; and

(b) an expenditure by a board is a non-classroom expenditure if it is an expenditure categorized in the 1998-99 Uniform Code of Accounts as a non-classroom expenditure.

(2) The Minister shall prepare and publish the 1998-99 Uniform Code of Accounts, categorizing board expenditures as classroom and non-classroom expenditures, before the beginning of the 1998-99 fiscal year.

(3) In meeting the requirements of subsection (2), the Minister shall follow the categorizations of classroom and non-classroom expenditures set out in the following three documents:

1. The Ministry publication entitled "Instructions for Updating the Costing Framework for 1996 and 1997", dated May 30, 1997.
2. The Table entitled "Allocation of Grants to Expenditure Categories", published by the Minister and distributed to boards on March 25, 1998.
3. Appendix 1 to the Ministry publication entitled "Calculation of 1997 Net Expenditure", distributed to boards in April, 1998.

(4) Subsection (3) does not prevent the Minister from making minor adjustments in categorizations for the purpose of improving the accuracy with which classroom and non-classroom expenditures are distinguished.

(5) Subject to subsection (10), a district school board shall ensure that its 1998-99 net classroom expenditure amount, calculated in accordance with subsection (6), is at least equal to its 1998-99 classroom expenditure allocation amount, calculated in accordance with subsection (8).

(6) For the purposes of subsection (5), the 1998-99 net classroom expenditure amount for a board shall be determined as follows:

1. Determine the total amount of the board's classroom expenditures in the 1998-99 fiscal year.
2. Subtract the amount determined for the board under subsection (7), on account of classroom-related revenue from sources other than legislative grants and school taxes.

(7) For the purposes of paragraph 2 of subsection (6), the amount on account of classroom-related revenue from sources other than legislative grants and school taxes for the board shall be the total of the following amounts:

1. Take 68.49 per cent of the board's revenues under the 1998-99 fees regulation.
2. Determine the total of the amounts spent on classroom expenditures from reserves of the board in the 1998-99 fiscal year.
3. This paragraph applies to grants to the board, other than grants made under this Regulation, and to donations to the board, where the board is legally required to

spend the full amount of the grant or donation on expenditures that are classroom expenditures within the meaning of this section. Determine the amount received by the board in the 1998-99 fiscal year from grants and donations to which this paragraph applies.

4. This paragraph applies to grants to the board, other than grants made under this Regulation, and to donations to the board, where the board is not legally required to spend the full amount of the grant or donation on expenditures that are classroom expenditures within the meaning of this section. Determine the amount received by the board in the 1998-99 fiscal year from grants and donations to which this paragraph applies that are spent in the 1998-99 fiscal year on expenditures that are classroom expenditures within the meaning of this section.

(8) For the purposes of subsection (5), the 1998-99 classroom expenditure allocation amount for a board shall be determined as follows:

1. Determine the amount calculated for the board under paragraph 2 of section 13, on account of the foundation allocation for elementary school pupils.
2. Apply the percentage specified in Table 8 for the elementary school part of foundation allocations to the amount determined for the board under paragraph 1.
3. Determine the amount calculated for the board under paragraph 4 of section 13, on account of the foundation allocation for secondary school pupils.
4. Apply the percentage specified in Table 8 for the secondary school part of foundation allocations to the amount determined for the board under paragraph 3.
5. Determine an amount for the board on account of French as a first or second language and Native as a second language, as follows:
    i. In the case of an English-language district school board, total the amounts determined for the board under paragraphs 1 and 2 of section 21.
    ii. In the case of a French-language district school board, total the amounts determined for the board under paragraphs 1 and 2 of section 25.
6. Apply the percentage specified in Table 8 for French as a first or second language and Native as a second language to the amount determined for the board under paragraph 5.
7. Determine an amount for the board on account of ESL/ESD/ALF/PDF, as follows:
    i. In the case of an English-language district school board, take the amount determined for the board under paragraph 3 of section 21.
    ii. In the case of a French-language district school board, take the amount determined for the board under paragraph 3 of section 25.
8. Apply the percentage specified in Table 8 for ESL/ESD/ALF/PDF to the amount determined for the board under paragraph 7.
9. Determine an amount for the board on account of the elementary school part of teacher compensation allocations, by calculating what the amount calculated for the board under paragraph 7 of subsection 33(10) would be if the calculation were done counting only teachers employed by the board to provide instruction to elementary school pupils and counting only elementary pupils of the board.
10. Apply the percentage specified in Table 8 for elementary school teacher compensation to the amount determined for the board under paragraph 9.

11. Determine an amount for the board on account of the secondary school part of teacher compensation allocations, by subtracting, from the amount determined for the board under subsection 33(10), the total of,
    i. the amount determined for the board under paragraph 9, and
    ii. the special assistance amount for re-organization of secondary school staff determined for the board under paragraph 8 of subsection 33(10).
12. Apply the percentage specified in Table 8 for secondary school teacher compensation to the amount determined for the board under paragraph 11.
13. Determine the amount of each type of allocation determined for the board under sections 14, 29, 30, 31 and 34.
14. Apply the percentage specified in Table 8 for each type of allocation for which an amount is determined under paragraph 13 to the amount determined for the board under paragraph 13 for that type of allocation.
15. Multiply the enrolment number determined for the board under paragraph 1 of subsection 32(1) by $2,257, to determine an adult day school amount for the board.
16. Apply the percentage specified in Table 8 for adult day school to the amount determined for the board under paragraph 15.
16.1 Determine the retirement gratuity allocation for the board calculated under section 33.1.
16.2 Apply the percentage specified in Table 8 for retirement gratuities to the amount determined under paragraph 16.1.
17. Determine the amount, if any, calculated for the board under subsection 46(2) as a phase-in funding deduction amount. Apply the percentage determined for the board under subsection (9) to that amount.
18. Determine the amount, if any, calculated for the board under subsection 47(2) as a phase-in funding addition amount. Apply the percentage determined for the board under subsection (9) to that amount.
19. Total the amounts determined for the board under paragraphs 2, 4, 6, 8, 10, 12, 14, 16 and 16.2.
20. Where paragraph 17 applies to the board, deduct the amount obtained for the board under that paragraph from the amount obtained for the board under paragraph 19.
21. Where paragraph 18 applies to the board, add the amount obtained for the board under that paragraph from the amount obtained for the board under paragraph 19.

(9) For the purposes of paragraphs 17 and 18 of subsection (8), the board shall determine a percentage that reasonably corresponds to the way in which the board actually applies the phase-in funding deduction amount or phase-in funding addition amount, as the case may be, to classroom expenditures in the 1998-99 fiscal year.

(10) A board shall be deemed to be in compliance with subsection (5) where its 1998-99 classroom expenditure allocation, calculated in accordance with subsection (8), exceeds its 1998-99 net classroom expenditure amount, calculated in accordance with subsection (6), if the board demonstrates, in a written report to the Minister, that the excess is accounted for by reason of expenditures other than non-classroom expenditures.

(11) For example,
(a) an amount paid on account of a part of a deficit from a previous year where the part

of the deficit is reasonably attributable to classroom expenditures is not a non-classroom expenditure; and

(b) an amount placed in a reserve fund for classroom expenditures is not a non-classroom expenditure.

(12) In making the determination under subsection (9), the board shall not apply the phase-in funding addition amount to expenditures that are not classroom expenditures and shall not apply the phase-in funding deduction amount to expenditures that are classroom expenditures if doing so would reduce the board's 1998-99 net classroom expenditure allocation, calculated in accordance with subsection (8), to an amount lower than the amount for the board set out in the column entitled "1997 Net Expenditure" and the row entitled "9 Sub-total" in the Table entitled "Classroom—Non-classroom Summary Report", which Table was released by the Minister to school boards on March 25, 1998 and is available for public inspection at the offices of the Ministry of Education and Training, 900 Bay Street, Toronto, Ontario, M7A 1L2. O. Reg. 469/98, s. 4; 538/98, s. 4.

52. (1) Subject to subsection (2), a district school board shall ensure that an amount equal to the special education allocation determined for the board under section 14, less the programs in facilities amount determined for the board under section 19, is spent in the 1998-99 fiscal year on special education for pupils of the board.

(2) Where a board's expenditure on special education for its pupils in the 1998-99 fiscal year is less than the result obtained by subtracting the programs in facilities amount determined for the board under section 19 from the special education allocation determined for the board under section 14, the board shall place the difference in the board's special education reserve fund.

(3) This section shall not be interpreted as limiting the amount that a board may spend on special education.

53. (1) Subject to subsection (2), a district school board shall ensure that an amount equal to the total of the following three amounts is spent in the 1998-99 fiscal year on the acquisition of capital assets:

1. The amount determined for the board under subsection 37(7) for school renewal.
2. The amount determined for the board under subsection 37(8) for new pupil places.
3. The amount determined for the board under subsection 37(13) for leased instructional space.

(2) Where a board's expenditure in the 1998-99 fiscal year on the acquisition of capital assets is less than the total amount referred to in subsection (1), the board shall place the difference in the board's pupil accommodation allocation reserve fund.

(3) This section shall not be interpreted as limiting the amount that a board may spend on the acquisition of capital assets. O. Reg. 538/98, s. 3; 212/99, s. 6.

54. (1) It is a condition of the payment of a grant to a district school board under this Regulation that,

(a) the board manage its estimates process and its expenditures so that the total of its administration expenditures and governance expenditures in the 1998-99 fiscal year does not exceed the administration and governance allocation amount determined for it under section 36; or

(b) the board submit the plan referred to in subsection (6).

(2) For the purposes of this section,

(a) an expenditure by a board is an administration expenditure if it is an expenditure categorized in the 1998-99 Uniform Code of Accounts as an administration expenditure; and

(b) an expenditure by a board is a governance expenditure if it is an expenditure categorized in the 1998-99 Uniform Code of Accounts as a governance expenditure.

(3) The Minister shall ensure that the 1998-99 Uniform Code of Accounts, required by subsection 51(2), states which items of board expenditures are in the category of administration expenditure and which are in the category of governance expenditure.

(4) In meeting the requirements of subsection (3), the Minister shall follow the categorizations of administration expenditures and governance expenditures set out in the three documents referred to in subsection 51(3).

(5) Subsection (4) does not prevent the Minister from making minor adjustments in categorizations for the purpose of improving the accuracy with which,

(a) board expenditures that relate to administration are identified; and

(b) board expenditures that relate to governance are identified.

(6) Where the total of a board's administration expenditures and governance expenditures in the 1998-99 fiscal year exceeds the administration and governance allocation amount determined for the board under section 36, the board shall submit a written plan to the Minister outlining how it proposes to reduce the total of the amounts that it spends on administration expenditures and governance expenditures so that, by the fiscal year 2000-2001, that total does not exceed the administration and governance allocation amount determined for the board under section 36.

PART III

GRANTS TO SCHOOL AUTHORITIES

Grants to Isolate Boards

55. (1) For the purposes of this section, the approved expenditure of an isolate board is the expenditure that is acceptable to the Minister as shown on the forms provided by the Ministry to the isolate board for the purpose of calculating its 1998-99 legislative grant.

(2) In making determinations for the purposes of subsection (1), the Minister shall apply the funding formula on which the provisions of this Regulation relating to grants to district school boards is based, with such adaptations as the Minister considers advisable to take account of characteristics particular to school authorities.

(3) For the purposes of this section, the 1998-99 tax revenue of an isolate board shall be determined as follows:

1. Add,

   i. 38 per cent of the total of the amounts distributed to the isolate board in respect of the 1998 calendar year under subsections 237(12) and 238(2), section 239, subsection 240(5), sections 250 and 251 and subsections 257.8(2) and 257.9(1) of the Act, under sections 447.20 and 447.52 of the *Municipal Act* and under section 10 of Ontario Regulation 509/98,

   ii. 62 per cent of the total of the amounts distributed to the isolate board in respect of the 1999 calendar year under subsections 237(12) and 238(2), section 239, subsection 240(5), sections 250 and 251 and subsections 257.8(2) and 257.9(1) of the Act, under sections 447.20 and 447.52 of the *Municipal Act* and under section 10 of Ontario Regulation 509/98,

   iii. 38 per cent of the amounts, if any, received by the board in respect of the 1998 calendar year from a municipality under subsection 445(4) of the *Municipal Act*,

   iv. 62 per cent of the amounts, if any, received by the board in respect of the 1999 calendar year from a municipality under subsection 445(4) of the *Municipal Act*,

   v. the total of the taxes received by the board in respect of the 1998 calendar year under section 35 of the *Assessment Act*,

   vi. 38 per cent of the payments in lieu of taxes distributed to the board in respect of the 1998 calendar year under subsection 371.1(1) of the *Municipal Act*,

   vii. 62 per cent of the payments in lieu of taxes distributed to the board in respect of the 1999 calendar year under subsection 371.1(1) of the *Municipal Act*,

   viii. 38 per cent of the amounts, if any, received by the board in respect of the 1998 calendar year under the *Municipal Grants Act* (Canada) or under any Act of Canada that permits a payment to be made by a government or a government agency in lieu of taxes on real property,

   ix. 62 per cent of the amounts, if any, received by the board in respect of the 1999 calendar year under the *Municipal Grants Act* (Canada) or under any Act of Canada that permits a payment to be made by a government or a government agency in lieu of taxes on real property,

   x. 38 per cent of the amounts, if any, shared with the board in respect of the 1998 calendar year under subsection 442.1(11.3) of the *Municipal Act*,

   xi. the total of the amounts, if any, distributed to the board in the 1998-99 fiscal year under subsection 2(3) of Ontario Regulation 365/98, and

   xii. the total of the amounts, if any, paid to the board in the 1998-99 fiscal year under clause 3(1)(a) of Ontario Regulation 366/98.

2. Deduct the cost incurred in the 1998-99 fiscal year by the board under section 257.7 of the Act in collecting taxes for school purposes in territory without municipal organization, to a maximum of 2 per cent of the sum of,

   i. 38 per cent of the total amount of taxes levied by it for 1998 for school purposes in territory without municipal organization, and

   ii. 62 per cent of the total amount of taxes levied by it for 1999 for school purposes in territory without municipal organization.

2.1 Deduct any amount approved by the Minister in respect of financing costs that are incurred by the board as a result of the delayed levy of 1998 taxes for school purposes in territory without municipal organization.

3. Deduct the amounts charged to the board in respect of the 1998 calendar year by a

municipal council under section 421 of the *Municipal Act*, including amounts charged under that section as a result of private legislation.
4. Deduct the total of the amounts paid as rebates by the board under section 257.2.1 of the Act in the 1998-99 fiscal year.
5. Deduct 38 per cent of the total of the amounts, if any, paid by the board in respect of the 1998 calendar year under subsections 442.1(7) and 442.2(8.1) of the *Municipal Act*.
6. Deduct 62 per cent of the total of the amounts, if any, paid by the board in respect of the 1999 calendar year under subsections 442.1(7) and 442.2(8.1) of the *Municipal Act*.

(4) Amounts paid by the Minister to the isolate board in respect of the 1998 calendar year under section 257.11 of the Act shall be deemed to be amounts distributed to the board in respect of the 1998 calendar year under a provision of the Act referred to in subparagraph i of paragraph 1 of subsection (3).

(5) Amounts, if any, paid by the Minister to the isolate board in respect of the 1999 calendar year under section 257.11 of the Act shall be deemed to be amounts distributed to the board in respect of the 1999 calendar year under a provision of the Act referred to in subparagraph ii of paragraph 1 of subsection (3).

(6) Paragraph 2 of subsection (3) shall not be interpreted to preclude including in the isolate board's approved expenditure an amount on account of the costs incurred by the board in collecting taxes in territory without municipal organization, where those costs exceed the amount deducted under paragraph 2 of subsection (3).

(7) Where the approved expenditure of an isolate board exceeds its 1998-99 tax revenue, the board shall be paid a grant equal to the excess.

O. Reg. 212/99, s. 7.

Grants to Section 68 Boards

56. A section 68 board shall be paid a grant in an amount determined as follows:
1. Take the expenditure of the board for the 1998-99 fiscal year that is acceptable to the Minister for grant purposes, excluding,
    i. expenditures for debt charges,
    ii. expenditures for the purchase of capital assets,
    iii. expenditures for the restoration of destroyed or damaged capital assets, and
    iv. provisions for reserves for working funds and provisions for reserve funds.
2. Deduct any transfers from reserves for working funds or from reserve funds made during the 1998-99 fiscal year.
3. Deduct the revenue of the board for the 1998-99 fiscal year, not including revenue from,
    i. legislative grants,
    ii. an organization on whose property a school of the board is located, and
    iii. refunds of expenditure of the kind described in subparagraph i, ii or iii of paragraph 1.

PART IV

PAYMENTS TO GOVERNING AUTHORITIES

57. In this Part,

"Crown establishment" means an establishment maintained by a Department of the Government of Canada, a federal Crown company, The Royal Canadian Mounted Police or Atomic Energy of Canada Limited, on lands held by the Crown in right of Canada that are not assessable for school purposes, and includes a reserve as defined in the *Indian Act* (Canada).

58. (1) This section applies where a pupil who is not resident in a Crown establishment,

(a) resides in a territorial district on land that is not part of a school section or separate school zone and attends an elementary school supported by local taxation in Manitoba or Quebec; or

(b) resides in a territorial district on land that is not part of a secondary school district and attends a secondary school supported by local taxation in Manitoba or Quebec.

(2) The Minister shall pay the governing authority of the school attended by the pupil the amount agreed on between the governing authority and the Minister.

59. (1) This section applies where,

(a) a pupil who resides in a territorial district is resident in a school section, separate school zone or a Crown establishment and attends an elementary school supported by local taxation in Manitoba or Quebec; and

(b) the Minister is of the opinion that,

(i) daily transportation to the elementary school in Ontario that the pupil would otherwise attend is impracticable due to distance and terrain, and

(ii) the provision of board, lodging and weekly transportation is impracticable because of the age or disability of the pupil.

(2) The Minister shall pay the governing authority of the elementary school attended by the pupil the amount agreed on between the governing authority and the Minister.

60. (1) This section applies where a pupil who resides in a territorial district,

(a) is not resident in a school section, a separate school zone or a Crown establishment; and

(b) attends a school on a reserve that is operated by,

(i) the Crown in right of Canada, or

(ii) a band, the council of a band or an education authority where the band, council of a band or education authority is authorized by the Crown in right of Canada to provide education for Indians.

(2) The Minister shall pay the governing authority of the school attended by the pupil the amount agreed on between the governing authority and the Minister.

Table 1

REGULATIONS UNDER THE EDUCATION ACT

TABLE/TABLEAU 1

PROGRAM ISA/AAS (PROGRAMMES)

	Column/Colonne 1	Column/Colonne 2
Item/Point	Name of Board/Nom du conseil	Program ISA Amount per pupil/AAS (programmes) par élève $
1.	District School Board Ontario North East	198
2.	Algoma District School Board	225
3.	Rainbow District School Board	156
4.	Near North District School Board	236
5.	Keewatin-Patricia District School Board	256
6.	Rainy River District School Board	148
7.	Lakehead District School Board	157
8.	Superior-Greenstone District School Board	221
9.	Bluewater District School Board	212
10.	Avon Maitland District School Board	175
11.	Greater Essex County District School Board	203
12.	Lambton Kent District School Board	213
13.	Thames Valley District School Board	173
14.	Toronto District School Board	261
15.	Durham District School Board	197
16.	Kawartha Pine Ridge District School Board	175
17.	Trillium Lakelands District School Board	198
18.	York Region District School Board	223
19.	Simcoe County District School Board	198
20.	Upper Grand District School Board	180
21.	Peel District School Board	220
22.	Halton District School Board	229
23.	Hamilton-Wentworth District School Board	203
24.	District School Board of Niagara	189
25.	Grand Erie District School Board	182

Table 1

REGULATION 287/98

Item/Point	Column/Colonne 1 Name of Board/Nom du conseil	Column/Colonne 2 Program ISA Amount per pupil/AAS (programmes) par élève $
26.	Waterloo Region District School Board	176
27.	Ottawa-Carleton District School Board	290
28.	Upper Canada District School Board	212
29.	Limestone District School Board	189
30.	Renfrew County District School Board	155
31.	Hastings and Prince Edward District School Board	209
32.	Northeastern Catholic District School Board	185
33.	Nipissing-Parry Sound Catholic District School Board	214
34.	Huron-Superior Catholic District School Board	148
35.	Sudbury Catholic District School Board	180
36.	Northwest Catholic District School Board	147
37.	Kenora Catholic District School Board	212
38.	Thunder Bay Catholic District School Board	171
39.	Superior North Catholic District School Board	283
40.	Bruce-Grey Catholic District School Board	140
41.	Huron-Perth Catholic District School Board	148
42.	Windsor-Essex Catholic District School Board	130
43.	District School Board 38	143
44.	St. Clair Catholic District School Board	151
45.	Toronto Catholic District School Board	174
46.	Peterborough Victoria Northumberland and Clarington Catholic District School Board	164
47.	York Catholic District School Board	230
48.	Dufferin-Peel Catholic District School Board	136
49.	Simcoe Muskoka Catholic District School Board	162
50.	Durham Catholic District School Board	149

Table 1

REGULATIONS UNDER THE EDUCATION ACT

ITEM/POINT	COLUMN/COLONNE 1 NAME OF BOARD/NOM DU CONSEIL	COLUMN/COLONNE 2 PROGRAM ISA AMOUNT PER PUPIL/AAS (PROGRAMMES) PAR ÉLÈVE $
51.	Halton Catholic District School Board	154
52.	Hamilton-Wentworth Catholic District School Board	176
53.	Wellington Catholic District School Board	155
54.	Waterloo Catholic District School Board	159
55.	Niagara Catholic District School Board	134
56.	Brant Haldimand Norfolk Catholic District School Board	137
57.	Catholic District School Board of Eastern Ontario	169
58.	Ottawa-Carleton Catholic District School Board	242
59.	Renfrew County Catholic District School Board	187
60.	Algonquin and Lakeshore Catholic District School Board	143
61.	Conseil scolaire de district du Nord-Est de l'Ontario	186
62.	Conseil scolaire de district du Grand Nord de l'Ontario	149
63.	Conseil scolaire de district du Centre Sud-Ouest	162
64.	Conseil scolaire de district 59	136
65.	Conseil scolaire de district catholique des Grandes Rivières	162
66.	Conseil scolaire de district catholique Franco-Nord	160
67.	Conseil scolaire de district catholique du Nouvel-Ontario	189
68.	Conseil scolaire de district catholique des Aurores boréales	196
69.	Conseil scolaire de district des écoles catholiques du Sud-Ouest	144
70.	Conseil scolaire de district catholique Centre-Sud	158

REGULATION 287/98

Table 2

	COLUMN/COLONNE 1	COLUMN/COLONNE 2
ITEM/POINT	NAME OF BOARD/NOM DU CONSEIL	PROGRAM ISA AMOUNT PER PUPIL/AAS (PROGRAMMES) PAR ÉLÈVE $
71.	Conseil scolaire de district catholique de l'Est ontarien	210
72.	Conseil scolaire de district catholique du Centre-Est de l'Ontario	205

TABLE/TABLEAU 2

ESD PERCENTAGES/POURCENTAGES DES PROGRAMMES D'ESD

	COLUMN/COLONNE 1	COLUMN/COLONNE 2
ITEM/POINT	BOARD NAME/NOM DU CONSEIL	% OF POPULATION HAVING NO KNOWLEDGE OF ENGLISH OR FRENCH/% DE LA POPULATION QUI NE CONNAÎT NI L'ANGLAIS NI LE FRANÇAIS
1.	District School Board Ontario North East	0.00%
2.	Algoma District School Board	0.00%
3.	Rainbow District School Board	0.00%
4.	Near North District School Board	0.00%
5.	Keewatin-Patricia District School Board	0.19%
6.	Rainy River District School Board	0.00%
7.	Lakehead District School Board	0.00%
8.	Superior-Greenstone District School Board	0.00%
9.	Bluewater District School Board	0.12%
10.	Avon Maitland District School Board	0.13%
11.	Greater Essex County District School Board	0.53%
12.	Lambton Kent District School Board	0.17%
13.	Thames Valley District School Board	0.35%
14.	Toronto District School Board	0.64%
15.	Durham District School Board	0.04%

Table 2 REGULATIONS UNDER THE EDUCATION ACT

	COLUMN/COLONNE 1	COLUMN/COLONNE 2
ITEM/POINT	BOARD NAME/NOM DU CONSEIL	% OF POPULATION HAVING NO KNOWLEDGE OF ENGLISH OR FRENCH/% DE LA POPULATION QUI NE CONNAÎT NI L'ANGLAIS NI LE FRANÇAIS
16.	Kawartha Pine Ridge District School Board	0.07%
17.	Trillium Lakelands District School Board	0.00%
18.	York Region District School Board	0.11%
19.	Simcoe County District School Board	0.00%
20.	Upper Grand District School Board	0.06%
21.	Peel District School Board	0.23%
22.	Halton District School Board	0.00%
23.	Hamilton-Wentworth District School Board	0.17%
24.	District School Board of Niagara	0.00%
25.	Grand Erie District School Board	0.49%
26.	Waterloo Region District School Board	0.31%
27.	Ottawa-Carleton District School Board	0.29%
28.	Upper Canada District School Board	0.03%
29.	Limestone District School Board	0.00%
30.	Renfrew County District School Board	0.00%
31.	Hastings and Prince Edward District School Board	0.05%
32.	Northeastern Catholic District School Board	0.00%
33.	Nipissing-Parry Sound Catholic District School Board	0.00%
34.	Huron-Superior Catholic District School Board	0.00%
35.	Sudbury Catholic District School Board	0.00%
36.	Northwest Catholic District School Board	0.00%
37.	Kenora Catholic District School Board	0.00%
38.	Thunder Bay Catholic District School Board	0.00%
39.	Superior North Catholic District School Board	0.00%
40.	Bruce-Grey Catholic District School Board	0.00%

Table 2

REGULATION 287/98

Item/Point	Column/Colonne 1 Board Name/Nom du conseil	Column/Colonne 2 % of population having no knowledge of English or French/% de la population qui ne connaît ni l'anglais ni le français
41.	Huron-Perth Catholic District School Board	0.00%
42.	Windsor-Essex Catholic District School Board	0.13%
43.	District School Board 38	0.03%
44.	St. Clair Catholic District School Board	0.05%
45.	Toronto Catholic District School Board	0.55%
46.	Peterborough Victoria Northumberland and Clarington Catholic District School Board	0.00%
47.	York Catholic District School Board	0.05%
48.	Dufferin-Peel Catholic District School Board	0.07%
49.	Simcoe Muskoka Catholic District School Board	0.06%
50.	Durham Catholic District School Board	0.12%
51.	Halton Catholic District School Board	0.09%
52.	Hamilton-Wentworth Catholic District School Board	0.18%
53.	Wellington Catholic District School Board	0.16%
54.	Waterloo Catholic District School Board	0.04%
55.	Niagara Catholic District School Board	0.08%
56.	Brant Haldimand Norfolk Catholic District School Board	0.00%
57.	Catholic District School Board of Eastern Ontario	0.00%
58.	Ottawa-Carleton Catholic District School Board	0.08%
59.	Renfrew County Catholic District School Board	0.00%
60.	Algonquin and Lakeshore Catholic District School Board	0.18%
61.	Conseil scolaire de district du Nord-Est de l'Ontario	0.00%
62.	Conseil scolaire de district du Grand Nord de l'Ontario	0.00%

Table 3

REGULATIONS UNDER THE EDUCATION ACT

	COLUMN/COLONNE 1	COLUMN/COLONNE 2
ITEM/POINT	BOARD NAME/NOM DU CONSEIL	% OF POPULATION HAVING NO KNOWLEDGE OF ENGLISH OR FRENCH/% DE LA POPULATION QUI NE CONNAÎT NI L'ANGLAIS NI LE FRANÇAIS
63.	Conseil scolaire de district du Centre Sud-Ouest	0.00%
64.	Conseil scolaire de district 59	0.00%
65.	Conseil scolaire de district catholique des Grandes Rivières	0.00%
66.	Conseil scolaire de district catholique Franco-Nord	0.00%
67.	Conseil scolaire de district catholique du Nouvel-Ontario	0.00%
68.	Conseil scolaire de district catholique des Aurores boréales	0.00%
69.	Conseil scolaire de district des écoles catholiques du Sud-Ouest	0.00%
70.	Conseil scolaire de district catholique Centre-Sud	0.00%
71.	Conseil scolaire de district catholique de l'Est ontarien	0.00%
72.	Conseil scolaire de district catholique du Centre-Est de l'Ontario	0.00%

TABLE/TABLEAU 3

ASSIMILATION FACTORS FOR ALF FUNDING/FACTEURS D'ASSIMILATION POUR LE FINANCEMENT DES PROGRAMMES D'ALF

	COLUMN/COLONNE 1	COLUMN/COLONNE 2	COLUMN/COLONNE 3
ITEM/POINT	FRENCH LANGUAGE BOARD/CONSEIL DE LANGUE FRANÇAISE	ENGLISH LANGUAGE COTERMINOUS BOARD/CONSEIL DE LANGUE ANGLAISE COÏNCIDENT	ASSIMILATION FACTOR/FACTEUR D'ASSIMILATION
1.	Conseil scolaire de district du Nord-Est de l'Ontario	District School Board Ontario North East	1.0

Table 3

REGULATION 287/98

ITEM/ POINT	COLUMN/COLONNE 1 FRENCH LANGUAGE BOARD/ CONSEIL DE LANGUE FRANÇAISE	COLUMN/COLONNE 2 ENGLISH LANGUAGE COTERMINOUS BOARD/ CONSEIL DE LANGUE ANGLAISE COÏNCIDENT	COLUMN/ COLONNE 3 ASSIMILATION FACTOR/ FACTEUR D'ASSIMILATION
2.	Conseil scolaire de district du Nord-Est de l'Ontario	Near North District School Board	1.0
3.	Conseil scolaire de district du Nord-Est de l'Ontario	Trillium Lakelands District School Board	1.5
4.	Conseil scolaire de district du Grand Nord de l'Ontario	Algoma District School Board	1.5
5.	Conseil scolaire de district du Grand Nord de l'Ontario	Rainbow District School Board	1.0
6.	Conseil scolaire de district du Grand Nord de l'Ontario	Keewatin-Patricia District School Board	1.5
7.	Conseil scolaire de district du Grand Nord de l'Ontario	Rainy River District School Board	1.5
8.	Conseil scolaire de district du Grand Nord de l'Ontario	Lakehead District School Board	1.5
9.	Conseil scolaire de district du Grand Nord de l'Ontario	Superior-Greenstone District School Board	1.5
10.	Conseil scolaire de district du Centre Sud-Ouest	Bluewater District School Board	1.5
11.	Conseil scolaire de district du Centre Sud-Ouest	Avon Maitland District School Board	1.5
12.	Conseil scolaire de district du Centre Sud-Ouest	Greater Essex County District School Board	1.5
13.	Conseil scolaire de district du Centre Sud-Ouest	Lambton Kent District School Board	1.5
14.	Conseil scolaire de district du Centre Sud-Ouest	Thames Valley District School Board	1.5
15.	Conseil scolaire de district du Centre Sud-Ouest	Toronto District School Board	1.5
16.	Conseil scolaire de district du Centre Sud-Ouest	Durham District School Board	1.5

Table 3

REGULATIONS UNDER THE EDUCATION ACT

Item/ Point	Column/Colonne 1 French Language Board/ Conseil de langue française	Column/Colonne 2 English Language Coterminous Board/ Conseil de langue anglaise coïncident	Column/Colonne 3 Assimilation Factor/ Facteur d'assimilation
17.	Conseil scolaire de district du Centre Sud-Ouest	Kawartha Pine Ridge District School Board	1.5
18.	Conseil scolaire de district du Centre Sud-Ouest	Trillium Lakelands District School Board	1.5
19.	Conseil scolaire de district du Centre Sud-Ouest	York Region District School Board	1.5
20.	Conseil scolaire de district du Centre Sud-Ouest	Simcoe County District School Board	1.5
21.	Conseil scolaire de district du Centre Sud-Ouest	Upper Grant District School Board	1.5
22.	Conseil scolaire de district du Centre Sud-Ouest	Peel District School Board	1.5
23.	Conseil scolaire de district du Centre Sud-Ouest	Halton District School Board	1.5
24.	Conseil scolaire de district du Centre Sud-Ouest	Hamilton-Wentworth District School Board	1.5
25.	Conseil scolaire de district du Centre Sud-Ouest	District School Board of Niagara	1.5
26.	Conseil scolaire de district du Centre Sud-Ouest	Grand Erie District School Board	1.5
27.	Conseil scolaire de district du Centre Sud-Ouest	Waterloo Region District School Board	1.5
28.	Conseil scolaire de district 59	Ottawa-Carleton District School Board	1.0
29.	Conseil scolaire de district 59	Upper Canada District School Board	1.0
30.	Conseil scolaire de district 59	Limestone District School Board	1.5
31.	Conseil scolaire de district 59	Renfrew County District School Board	1.5

Table 3

REGULATION 287/98

ITEM/POINT	COLUMN/COLONNE 1 FRENCH LANGUAGE BOARD/ CONSEIL DE LANGUE FRANÇAISE	COLUMN/COLONNE 2 ENGLISH LANGUAGE COTERMINOUS BOARD/ CONSEIL DE LANGUE ANGLAISE COÏNCIDENT	COLUMN/COLONNE 3 ASSIMILATION FACTOR/ FACTEUR D'ASSIMILATION
32.	Conseil scolaire de district 59	Hastings and Prince Edward District School Board	1.5
33.	Conseil scolaire de district catholique des Grandes Rivières	Northeastern Catholic District School Board	1.0
34.	Conseil scolaire de district catholique Franco-Nord	Nipissing-Parry Sound Catholic District School Board	1.0
35.	Conseil scolaire de district catholique Centre-Sud	Simcoe Muskoka Catholic District School Board	1.5
36.	Conseil scolaire de district catholique du Nouvel-Ontario	Sudbury Catholic District School Board	1.0
37.	Conseil scolaire de district catholique du Nouvel-Ontario	Huron-Superior Catholic District School Board	1.5
38.	Conseil scolaire de district catholique des Aurores boréales	Northwest Catholic District School Board	1.5
39.	Conseil scolaire de district catholique des Aurores boréales	Kenora Catholic District School Board	1.5
40.	Conseil scolaire de district catholique des Aurores boréales	Thunder Bay Catholic District School Board	1.5
41.	Conseil scolaire de district catholique des Aurores boréales	Superior North Catholic District School Board	1.5
42.	Conseil scolaire de district des écoles catholiques du Sud-Ouest	Bruce-Grey Catholic District School Board	1.5
43.	Conseil scolaire de district des écoles catholiques du Sud-Ouest	Huron-Perth Catholic District School Board	1.5

Table 3

REGULATIONS UNDER THE EDUCATION ACT

	Column/Colonne 1	Column/Colonne 2	Column/Colonne 3
Item/Point	French Language Board/Conseil de langue française	English Language Coterminous Board/Conseil de langue anglaise coïncident	Assimilation Factor/Facteur d'assimilation
44.	Conseil scolaire de district des écoles catholiques du Sud-Ouest	Windsor-Essex Catholic District School Board	1.5
45.	Conseil scolaire de district des écoles catholiques du Sud-Ouest	St. Clair Catholic District School Board	1.5
46.	Conseil scolaire de district des écoles catholiques du Sud-Ouest	District School Board 38	1.5
47.	Conseil scolaire de district catholique Centre-Sud	Toronto Catholic District School Board	1.5
48.	Conseil scolaire de district catholique Centre-Sud	Durham Catholic District School Board	1.5
49.	Conseil scolaire de district catholique Centre-Sud	Peterborough Victoria Northumberland and Clarington Catholic District School Board	1.5
50.	Conseil scolaire de district catholique Centre-Sud	York Catholic District School Board	1.5
51.	Conseil scolaire de district catholique Centre-Sud	Wellington Catholic District School Board	1.5
52.	Conseil scolaire de district catholique Centre-Sud	Dufferin-Peel Catholic District School Board	1.5
53.	Conseil scolaire de district catholique Centre-Sud	Halton Catholic District School Board	1.5
54.	Conseil scolaire de district catholique Centre-Sud	Hamilton-Wentworth Catholic District School Board	1.5
55.	Conseil scolaire de district catholique Centre-Sud	Niagara Catholic District School Board	1.5

Table 3

REGULATION 287/98

	COLUMN/COLONNE 1	COLUMN/COLONNE 2	COLUMN/COLONNE 3
ITEM/ POINT	FRENCH LANGUAGE BOARD/ CONSEIL DE LANGUE FRANÇAISE	ENGLISH LANGUAGE COTERMINOUS BOARD/ CONSEIL DE LANGUE ANGLAISE COÏNCIDENT	ASSIMILATION FACTOR/ FACTEUR D'ASSIMILATION
56.	Conseil scolaire de district catholique Centre-Sud	Brant Haldimand Norfolk Catholic District School Board	1.5
57.	Conseil scolaire de district catholique Centre-Sud	Waterloo Catholic District School Board	1.5
58.	Conseil scolaire de district catholique du Centre-Est de l'Ontario	Ottawa-Carleton Catholic District School Board	1.5
59.	Conseil scolaire de district catholique du Centre-Est de l'Ontario	Catholic District School Board of Eastern Ontario	1.0
60.	Conseil scolaire de district catholique de l'Est ontarien	Catholic District School Board of Eastern Ontario	1.0
61.	Conseil scolaire de district catholique du Centre-Est de l'Ontario	Algonquin and Lakeshore Catholic District School Board	1.5
62.	Conseil scolaire de district catholique du Centre-Est de l'Ontario	Renfrew County Catholic District School Board	1.5

Table 4

TABLE/TABLEAU 4

O. Reg. 469/98, s. 5

DISTACE AND URBAN FACTORS FOR REMOTE AND RURAL ALLOCATIONS/
FACTEUR URBAIN ET FACTEUR D'ÉLOIGNEMENT POUR L'ÉLÉMENT CONSEILS RURAUX ET ÉLOIGNÉS

Item/Point	Column/Colonne 1 Board Name/Nom du conseil	Column/Colonne 2 Distance/Distance	Column/Colonne 3 Urban Factor/Facteur urbain
1.	District School Board Ontario North East	680 km	0.946
2.	Algoma District School Board	790 km	0.809
3.	Rainbow District School Board	455 km	0.821
4.	Near North District School Board	332 km	0.913
5.	Keewatin-Patricia District School Board	1801 km	1.000
6.	Rainy River District School Board	1630 km	1.000
7.	Lakehead District School Board	1375 km	0.549
8.	Superior-Greenstone District School Board	1440 km	1.000
9.	Bluewater District School Board	177 km	1.000
10.	Avon Maitland District School Board	<151 km	1.000
11.	Greater Essex County District School Board	<151 km	1.000
12.	Lambton Kent District School Board	<151 km	1.000
13.	Thames Valley District School Board	<151 km	1.000
14.	Toronto District School Board	<151 km	1.000
15.	Durham District School Board	<151 km	1.000
16.	Kawartha Pine Ridge District School Board	161 km	0.942
17.	Trillium Lakelands District School Board	253 km	1.000
18.	York Region District School Board	<151 km	1.000
19.	Simcoe County District School Board	<151 km	1.000
20.	Upper Grand District School Board	<151 km	1.000
21.	Peel District School Board	<151 km	1.000
22.	Halton District School Board	<151 km	1.000

Table 4

REGULATION 287/98

Item/ Point	Column/Colonne 1 Board Name/Nom du conseil	Column/ Colonne 2 Distance/ Distance	Column/ Colonne 3 Urban Factor/ Facteur urbain
23.	Hamilton-Wentworth District School Board	<151 km	1.000
24.	District School Board of Niagara	<151 km	1.000
25.	Grand Erie District School Board	<151 km	1.000
26.	Waterloo Region District School Board	<151 km	1.000
27.	Ottawa-Carleton District School Board	<151 km	1.000
28.	Upper Canada District School Board	<151 km	1.000
29.	Limestone District School Board	235 km	0.717
30.	Renfrew County District School Board	<151 km	1.000
31.	Hastings and Prince Edward District School Board	251 km	0.971
32.	Northeastern Catholic District School Board	680 km	0.946
33.	Nipissing-Parry Sound Catholic District School Board	332 km	0.913
34.	Huron-Superior Catholic District School Board	790 km	0.777
35.	Sudbury Catholic District School Board	390 km	0.780
36.	Northwest Catholic District School Board	1715 km	1.000
37.	Kenora Catholic District School Board	1855 km	1.000
38.	Thunder Bay Catholic District School Board	1375 km	0.501
39.	Superior North Catholic District School Board	1440 km	1.000
40.	Bruce-Grey Catholic District School Board	177 km	1.000
41.	Huron-Perth Catholic District School Board	<151 km	1.000
42.	Windsor-Essex Catholic District School Board	<151 km	1.000
43.	District School Board 38	<151 km	1.000
44.	St. Clair Catholic District School Board	<151 km	1.000
45.	Toronto Catholic District School Board	<151 km	1.000
46.	Peterborough Victoria Northumberland and Clarington Catholic District School Board	161 km	0.942
47.	York Catholic District School Board	<151 km	1.000

Table 4

Item/Point	Column/Colonne 1 Board Name/Nom du conseil	Column/Colonne 2 Distance/Distance	Column/Colonne 3 Urban Factor/Facteur urbain
48.	Dufferin-Peel Catholic District School Board	<151 km	1.000
49.	Simcoe Muskoka Catholic District School Board	<151 km	1.000
50.	Durham Catholic District School Board	<151 km	1.000
51.	Halton Catholic District School Board	<151 km	1.000
52.	Hamilton-Wentworth Catholic District School Board	<151 km	1.000
53.	Wellington Catholic District School Board	<151 km	1.000
54.	Waterloo Catholic District School Board	<151 km	1.000
55.	Niagara Catholic District School Board	<151 km	1.000
56.	Brant-Haldimand-Norfolk Catholic District School Board	<151 km	1.000
57.	Catholic District School Board of Eastern Ontario	<151 km	1.000
58.	Ottawa-Carleton Catholic District School Board	<151 km	1.000
59.	Renfrew County Catholic District School Board	<151 km	1.000
60.	Algonquin and Lakeshore Catholic District School Board	277 km	0.986
61.	Conseil scolaire de district du Nord-Est de l'Ontario	634 km	0.939
62.	Conseil scolaire de district du Grand Nord de l'Ontario	1191 km	0.8620
63.	Conseil scolaire de district du Centre Sud-Ouest	<151 km	1.000
64.	Conseil scolaire de district 59	<151 km	1.000
65.	Conseil scolaire de district catholique des Grandes Rivières	680 km	0.952
66.	Conseil scolaire de district catholique Franco-Nord	332 km	0.933
67.	Conseil scolaire de district catholique du Nouvel-Ontario	790 km	0.879
68.	Conseil scolaire de district catholique des Aurores boréales	1745 km	0.727

Table 5

REGULATION 287/98

Item/Point	Column/Colonne 1 Board Name/Nom du conseil	Column/Colonne 2 Distance/Distance	Column/Colonne 3 Urban Factor/Facteur urbain
69.	Conseil scolaire de district des écoles catholiques du Sud-Ouest	<151 km	1.000
70.	Conseil scolaire de district catholique Centre-Sud	<151 km	1.000
71.	Conseil scolaire de district catholique de l'Est ontarien	<151 km	1.000
72.	Conseil scolaire de district catholique du Centre-Est de l'Ontario	<151 km	1.000

TABLE/TABLEAU 5

LEARNING OPPORTUNITIES/PROGRAMMES D'AIDE À L'APPRENTISSAGE

Item/Point	Column/Colonne 1 Name of Board/Nom du conseil	Column/Colonne 2 Allocation for Learning Opportunities/Élément programmes d'aide à l'apprentissage $
1.	District School Board Ontario North East	1,474,673
2.	Algoma District School Board	2,240,042
3.	Rainbow District School Board	1,786,217
4.	Near North District School Board	1,838,599
5.	Keewatin-Patricia District School Board	855,519
6.	Rainy River District School Board	472,125
7.	Lakehead District School Board	1,904,168
8.	Superior-Greenstone District School Board	530,177
9.	Bluewater District School Board	743,017
10.	Avon Maitland District School Board	906,166
11.	Greater Essex County District School Board	3,688,449
12.	Lambton Kent District School Board	1,190,574

Table 5

Item/Point	Column/Colonne 1 Name of Board/Nom du conseil	Column/Colonne 2 Allocation for Learning Opportunities/Élément programmes d'aide à l'apprentissage $
13.	Thames Valley District School Board	6,118,828
14.	Toronto District School Board	53,334,398
15.	Durham District School Board	1,959,159
16.	Kawartha Pine Ridge District School Board	1,421,917
17.	Trillium Lakelands District School Board	339,581
18.	York Region District School Board	2,932,609
19.	Simcoe County District School Board	1,091,421
20.	Upper Grand District School Board	918,448
21.	Peel District School Board	5,949,939
22.	Halton District School Board	562,368
23.	Hamilton-Wentworth District School Board	6,740,451
24.	District School Board of Niagara	3,161,013
25.	Grand Erie District School Board	2,327,887
26.	Waterloo Region District School Board	3,638,569
27.	Ottawa-Carleton District School Board	6,623,778
28.	Upper Canada District School Board	1,112,594
29.	Limestone District School Board	1,599,350
30.	Renfrew County District School Board	632,032
31.	Hastings and Prince Edward District School Board	1,409,881
32.	Northeastern Catholic District School Board	509,798
33.	Nipissing-Parry Sound Catholic District School Board	454,337
34.	Huron-Superior Catholic District School Board	1,164,422
35.	Sudbury Catholic District School Board	945,337
36.	Northwest Catholic District School Board	122,343
37.	Kenora Catholic District School Board	102,056

Table 5

REGULATION 287/98

ITEM/POINT	COLUMN/COLONNE 1 NAME OF BOARD/NOM DU CONSEIL	COLUMN/COLONNE 2 ALLOCATION FOR LEARNING OPPORTUNITIES/ÉLÉMENT PROGRAMMES D'AIDE À L'APPRENTISSAGE $
38.	Thunder Bay Catholic District School Board	957,557
39.	Superior North Catholic District School Board	168,584
40.	Bruce-Grey Catholic District School Board	152,434
41.	Huron-Perth Catholic District School Board	130,780
42.	Windsor-Essex Catholic District School Board	2,679,022
43.	District School Board 38	3,211,654
44.	St. Clair Catholic District School Board	546,514
45.	Toronto Catholic District School Board	23,611,599
46.	Peterborough Victoria Northumberland and Clarington Catholic District School Board	533,053
47.	York Catholic District School Board	1,854,829
48.	Dufferin-Peel Catholic District School Board	4,738,086
49.	Simcoe Muskoka Catholic District School Board	366,487
50.	Durham Catholic District School Board	721,480
51.	Halton Catholic District School Board	270,379
52.	Hamilton-Wentworth Catholic District School Board	3,291,086
53.	Wellington Catholic District School Board	267,678
54.	Waterloo Catholic District School Board	1,701,138
55.	Niagara Catholic District School Board	1,507,994
56.	Brant Haldimand Norfolk Catholic District School Board	770,868
57.	Catholic District School Board of Eastern Ontario	691,106
58.	Ottawa-Carleton Catholic District School Board	3,230,651
59.	Renfrew County Catholic District School Board	445,592
60.	Algonquin and Lakeshore Catholic District School Board	1,026,142

Table 5

Item/ Point	Column/Colonne 1 Name of Board/Nom du conseil	Column/Colonne 2 Allocation for Learning Opportunities/Élément programmes d'aide à l'apprentissage $
61.	Conseil scolaire de district du Nord-Est de l'Ontario	194,663
62.	Conseil scolaire de district du Grand Nord de l'Ontario	206,980
63.	Conseil scolaire de district du Centre Sud-Ouest	649,021
64.	Conseil scolaire de district 59	690,903
65.	Conseil scolaire de district catholique des Grandes Rivières	1,406,429
66.	Conseil scolaire de district catholique Franco-Nord	650,200
67.	Conseil scolaire de district catholique du Nouvel-Ontario	1,362,379
68.	Conseil scolaire de district catholique des Aurores boréales	205,954
69.	Conseil scolaire de district des écoles catholiques du Sud-Ouest	376,990
70.	Conseil scolaire de district catholique Centre-Sud	926,681
71.	Conseil scolaire de district catholique de l'Est ontarien	1,194,650
72.	Conseil scolaire de district catholique du Centre-Est de l'Ontario	1,313,558

Table 7

TABLE/TABLEAU 6

TEACHER COMPENSATION/RÉNUMÉRATION DES ENSEIGNANTS

Full years of teaching experience/ Années complètes d'expérience en enseignement	\multicolumn{7}{c}{Qualification Categories/Catégories de qualification}						
	D	C	B	A1/ GROUP1 A1/ GROUPE1	A2/ GROUP2 A2/ GROUPE2	A3/ GROUP3 A3/ GROUPE3	A4/ GROUP4 A4/ GROUPE4
0	0.5788	0.5788	0.5788	0.6229	0.6487	0.7081	0.7449
1	0.6127	0.6127	0.6127	0.654	0.6864	0.7502	0.7926
2	0.6332	0.6332	0.6332	0.6989	0.7318	0.7969	0.8432
3	0.6523	0.6523	0.6523	0.7416	0.7743	0.8442	0.8925
4	0.7149	0.7149	0.7149	0.7814	0.8158	0.8953	0.9443
5	0.7698	0.7698	0.7698	0.8234	0.8606	0.9435	0.9975
6	0.8225	0.8225	0.8225	0.8655	0.9042	0.9866	1.0473
7	0.8694	0.8694	0.8694	0.9073	0.9472	1.0363	1.0997
8	0.8900	0.8900	0.8900	0.9485	0.9876	1.086	1.1512
9	0.9154	0.9154	0.9154	1.0025	1.0411	1.1534	1.2026
10	0.9667	0.9667	0.9667	1.0451	1.0989	1.2136	1.2949

TABLE/TABLEAU 7

GEOGRAPHIC ADJUSTMENT FACTORS FOR NEW PUPIL PLACES/FACTEURS DE REDRESSEMENT GÉOGRAPHIQUE POUR LES NOUVELLES PLACES

Item/ Point	Column/Colonne 1 District School Boards/Conseils scolaires de district	Column/Colonne 2 Geographic Adjustment Factor/Facteur de redressement géographique
1.	District School Board Ontario North East	1.120
2.	Algoma District School Board	1.106
3.	Rainbow District School Board	1.063
4.	Near North District School Board	1.042
5.	Keewatin-Patricia District School Board	1.144

Table 7

Item/ Point	Column/Colonne 1 District School Boards/Conseils scolaires de district	Column/Colonne 2 Geographic Adjustment Factor/Facteur de redressement géographique
6.	Rainy River District School Board	1.142
7.	Lakehead District School Board	1.080
8.	Superior-Greenstone District School Board	1.141
9.	Bluewater District School Board	1.007
10.	Avon Maitland District School Board	1.010
11.	Greater Essex County District School Board	1.000
12.	Lambton Kent District School Board	1.000
13.	Thames Valley District School Board	1.000
14.	Toronto District School Board	1.000
15.	Durham District School Board	1.000
16.	Kawartha Pine Ridge District School Board	1.003
17.	Trillium Lakelands District School Board	1.026
18.	York Region District School Board	1.000
19.	Simcoe County District School Board	1.000
20.	Upper Grand District School Board	1.000
21.	Peel District School Board	1.000
22.	Halton District School Board	1.000
23.	Hamilton-Wentworth District School Board	1.000
24.	District School Board of Niagara	1.000
25.	Grand Erie District School Board	1.000
26.	Waterloo Region District School Board	1.000
27.	Ottawa-Carleton District School Board	1.000
28.	Upper Canada District School Board	1.000
29.	Limestone District School Board	1.015
30.	Renfrew County District School Board	1.000
31.	Hastings and Prince Edward District School Board	1.025
32.	Northeastern Catholic District School Board	1.123

REGULATION 287/98 **Table 7**

Item/Point	Column/Colonne 1 District School Boards/Conseils scolaires de district	Column/Colonne 2 Geographic Adjustment Factor/Facteur de redressement géographique
33.	Nipissing-Parry Sound Catholic District School Board	1.042
34.	Huron-Superior Catholic District School Board	1.104
35.	Sudbury Catholic District School Board	1.048
36.	Northwest Catholic District School Board	1.149
37.	Kenora Catholic District School Board	1.143
38.	Thunder Bay Catholic District School Board	1.074
39.	Superior North Catholic District School Board	1.146
40.	Bruce-Grey Catholic District School Board	1.007
41.	Huron-Perth Catholic District School Board	1.011
42.	Windsor-Essex Catholic District School Board	1.000
43.	District School Board 38	1.000
44.	St. Clair Catholic District School Board	1.000
45.	Toronto Catholic District School Board	1.000
46.	Peterborough Victoria Northumberland and Clarington Catholic District School Board	1.003
47.	York Catholic District School Board	1.000
48.	Dufferin-Peel Catholic District School Board	1.000
49.	Simcoe Muskoka Catholic District School Board	1.000
50.	Durham Catholic District School Board	1.000
51.	Halton Catholic District School Board	1.000
52.	Hamilton-Wentworth Catholic District School Board	1.000
53.	Wellington Catholic District School Board	1.000
54.	Waterloo Catholic District School Board	1.000
55.	Niagara Catholic District School Board	1.000
56.	Brant Haldimand Norfolk Catholic District School Board	1.000
57.	Catholic District School Board of Eastern Ontario	1.000

Table 7

Item/Point	Column/Colonne 1 District School Boards/Conseils scolaires de district	Column/Colonne 2 Geographic Adjustment Factor/Facteur de redressement géographique
58.	Ottawa-Carleton Catholic District School Board	1.000
59.	Renfrew County Catholic District School Board	1.000
60.	Algonquin and Lakeshore Catholic District School Board	1.032
61.	Conseil scolaire de district du Nord-Est de l'Ontario	1.110
62.	Conseil scolaire de district du Grand Nord de l'Ontario	1.116
63.	Conseil scolaire de district du Centre Sud-Ouest	1.000
64.	Conseil scolaire de district 59	1.000
65.	Conseil scolaire de district catholique des Grandes Rivières	1.123
66.	Conseil scolaire de district catholique Franco-Nord	1.043
67.	Conseil scolaire de district catholique du Nouvel-Ontario	1.118
68.	Conseil scolaire de district catholique des Aurores boréales	1.100
69.	Conseil scolaire de district des écoles catholiques du Sud-Ouest	1.000
70.	Conseil scolaire de district catholique Centre-Sud	1.000
71.	Conseil scolaire de district catholique de l'Est ontarien	1.000
72.	Conseil scolaire de district catholique du Centre-Est de l'Ontario	1.000

TABLE/TABLEAU 8

O. Reg. 538/98, s. 5

CLASSROOM EXPENDITURE PERCENTAGES/POURCENTAGES DES DÉPENSES LIÉES AUX CLASSES

Item/Point	Column/Colonne 1 Amounts/Sommes	Column/Colonne 2 % allocated to the classroom/% alloué aux classes
1.	Elementary School Part of Foundation Allocations/Partie de l'élément éducation de base qui vise l'élémentaire	79.5%
2.	Secondary School Part of Foundation Allocations/Partie de l'élément éducation de base qui vise le secondaire	75.9%
3.	Elementary School Teacher Compensation/Rémunération des enseignants de l'élémentaire	91.2%
4.	Secondary School Teacher Compensation/Rémunération des enseignants du secondaire	84.6%
5.	Small Schools Allocations/Élément petites écoles	50.0%
6.	Remote & Rural Allocations/Élément conseils ruraux et éloignés	74.0%
7.	Early Learning Allocations/Élément apprentissage durant les premières années d'études	70.2%
8.	Adult Day School/Élèves adultes de jour	76.0%
9.	French as a First or Second Language and Native as a Second Language/Français langue première et langue seconde, et langue autochtone langue seconde	91.1%
10.	ESL/ESD/ALF/PDF	86.0%
11.	Learning Opportunities Allocations/Élément programmes d'aide à l'apprentissage	77.3%
12.	Special Education Allocations/Élément éducation de l'enfance en difficulté	92.0%
13.	Retirement gratuity allocation	88.0%

REGULATION 288/98
CALCULATION OF FEES FOR PUPILS FOR THE 1998-99 SCHOOL BOARD FISCAL YEAR
O. Reg. 288/98

1. (1) In this Regulation,

"1998-99 A.D.E. regulation" means Ontario Regulation 286/98; ("règlement sur l'effectif quotidien moyen de 1998-1999")

"1998-99 grant regulation" means Ontario Regulation 287/98. ("règlement sur les subventions de 1998-1999")

"day school A.D.E.", for a board, means the day school average daily enrolment for the board, as calculated under section 2 of the 1998-99 A.D.E. regulation; ("effectif quotidien moyen de jour")

"elementary school pupil" means a pupil who is enrolled in any of junior kindergarten, kindergarten and grades one to eight; ("élève de l'élémentaire")

"high cost program" means,

(a) a special education program, or

(b) any other program which both the board and the party from whom the tuition fee is receivable agree is a high cost program for the purposes of this Regulation; ("programme à coût élevé")

"isolate board" means a school authority other than a section 68 board; ("conseil isolé")

"P.A.C.", for a pupil, means the pupil accommodation charge for a pupil as determined under subsections (3) and (4); ("frais de pension")

"secondary school pupil" means a pupil who is enrolled in any of grades nine to twelve or in a course leading to an OAC credit; ("élève du secondaire")

"section 68 board" means a board established under section 68 of the Act. ("conseil créé en vertu de l'article 68")

(2) For the purposes of this Regulation, the day school A.D.E. of a pupil enrolled in a school operated by a board is the day school A.D.E. for the board calculated as if that pupil were the board's only pupil.

(3) Subject to subsection (4), the pupil accommodation charge for a pupil is $141 in the case of an elementary school pupil or $282 in the case of a secondary school pupil.

(4) If a board has entered into an agreement under subsection 188(3) of the Act that provides for a payment by the Crown in right of Canada to provide classroom accommodation for a specified number of pupils, the pupil accommodation charge for each pupil accommodated as a result of the agreement is zero.

(5) For the purposes of this Regulation, a pupil is a pupil of a board if he or she is a pupil of the board within the meaning of section 2 of the 1998-99 grant regulation.

Application

2. This Regulation applies in respect of the period September 1, 1998 to August 31, 1999.

Fees Paid to Boards by Canada or by Authority Providing Education for Indians

3. (1) This section applies in respect of a pupil who is enrolled in a school operated by a district school board or an isolate board if a fee in respect of the pupil is receivable by the board from,

(a) the Crown in right of Canada; or

(b) a band, the council of a band or an education authority where the band, council of a band or education authority is authorized by the Crown in right of Canada to provide education for Indians.

(2) The fee in respect of a pupil described in subsection (1) shall be calculated as follows:

1. Take the base amount determined for the pupil under subsection (3), (4) or (5), as the case may be.
2. Multiply the day school A.D.E. of the pupil by the sum of,
    i. the base amount determined under paragraph 1, and
    ii. the P.A.C. for that pupil.

(3) For the purposes of paragraph 1 of subsection (2), the base amount for an elementary school pupil described in subsection (1) who is enrolled in a school operated by a district school board shall be determined as follows:

1. Determine the amount calculated for the board under paragraph 2 of section 13 of the 1998-99 grant regulation, on account of the foundation allocation for elementary school pupils.
2. Determine an amount on account of the special education allocation for elementary school pupils, as follows:
    i. Multiply the day school A.D.E. for elementary school pupils of the board by $347.
    ii. Divide the amount determined for the board under paragraph 2 of section 14 of the 1998-99 grant regulation by the day school A.D.E. for pupils of the board.
    iii. Multiply the result obtained under subparagraph ii by the day school A.D.E. for elementary school pupils of the board.
    iv. Determine an amount on account of program ISA for elementary pupils, as follows:
        A. If the amount determined for the board under clause 17(a) of the 1998-99 grant regulation is greater than the amount determined for the board under clause 17(b) of that Regulation, multiply the day school A.D.E. for elementary school pupils of the board by the per pupil amount specified for the board in Column 2 of Table 1 of that Regulation.
        B. If the amount determined for the board under clause 17(b) of the 1998-99 grant regulation is greater than the amount determined for the board under clause 17(a) of that Regulation, calculate the part of the ISA level 2 and 3 funding total determined for the board under subsection 18(5) of that Regulation that is generated by elementary pupils of the board.
    v. Total the amounts obtained under subparagraphs i, iii and iv.

3. In the case of an English-language district school board, determine an amount on account of the language allocation for elementary school pupils, as follows:
   i. Take the French as a second language amount for elementary pupils of the board, as calculated under subsection 22(3) of the 1998-99 grant regulation.
   ii. Calculate the part of the ESL/ESD amount for the board, as calculated under section 24 of the 1998-99 grant regulation, that is generated by elementary school pupils of the board.
   iii. Add the amount taken under subparagraph i to the amount calculated under subparagraph ii.
4. In the case of a French-language district school board, determine an amount on account of the language allocation for elementary school pupils, as follows:
   i. Take the amount determined for the board under paragraph 1 of subsection 26(1) of the 1998-99 grant regulation.
   ii. Divide the total of the amounts determined for the board under paragraph 7 of subsection 28(4) of the 1998-99 grant regulation by the total number of instructional units determined for the board under paragraph 3 of subsection 28(4) of that Regulation. Multiply the result by the total number of elementary instructional units determined for the board under paragraph 1 of subsection 28(4) of that Regulation.
   iii. Calculate the part of the PDF funding level for the board, as calculated under subsection 28(11) of the 1998-99 grant regulation, that is generated by elementary school pupils of the board.
   iv. Total the amount taken under subparagraph i, the product obtained under subparagraph ii and the amount calculated under subparagraph iii.
5. Determine the amount calculated for the board under paragraph 4 of subsection 29(11) of the 1998-99 grant regulation, on account of the small schools allocation for elementary school pupils.
6. Determine an amount on account of the remote and rural allocation for elementary school pupils, as follows:
   i. Take the amount determined for the board under paragraph 5 of section 30 of the 1998-99 grant regulation.
   ii. Divide the amount determined for the board under subparagraph i by the day school A.D.E. for the board, counting only pupils of the board.
   iii. Multiply the amount determined under subparagraph ii by the day school A.D.E. for the board, counting only elementary school pupils of the board.
7. Determine an amount on account of the learning opportunities allocation for elementary school pupils, as follows:
   i. Take the amount determined for the board under section 31 of the 1998-99 grant regulation.
   ii. Divide the amount determined for the board under subparagraph i by the day school A.D.E. for the board, counting only pupils of the board.
   iii. Multiply the amount determined under subparagraph ii by the day school A.D.E. for the board, counting only elementary school pupils of the board.
8. Determine an amount on account of the teacher compensation allocation for elementary school pupils, by calculating what the amount calculated for the board under

paragraph 7 of subsection 33(10) of the 1998-99 grant regulation would be if that calculation were done counting only teachers employed by the board to provide instruction to elementary school pupils and counting only elementary school pupils of the board.

9. Determine the amount calculated for the board under paragraph 2 of subsection 34(2) or paragraph 5 of subsection 34(3) of the 1998-99 grant regulation, as the case may be, on account of the early learning allocation.
10. Determine an amount on account of the administration and governance allocation for elementary school pupils, as follows:
    i. Take the amount determined for the board under paragraph 4 of subsection 36(1) of the 1998-99 grant regulation.
    ii. Divide the amount determined for the board under subparagraph i by the day school A.D.E. for the board, counting only pupils of the board.
    iii. Multiply the amount determined under subparagraph ii by the day school A.D.E. for the board, counting only elementary school pupils of the board.
11. Determine an amount on account of the school operations part of the pupil accommodation allocation for elementary school pupils, by multiplying the elementary school area requirement determined for the board under paragraph 2 of subsection 37(2) of the 1998-99 grant regulation or, where a supplementary elementary school area factor is approved for the board under subsection 37(3) of that Regulation, the adjusted elementary school area requirement determined for the board under paragraph 3 of subsection 37(2) of that Regulation, by the benchmark operating cost of $55.97.
12. Total the amounts determined for the board under paragraphs 1 to 11.
13. Divide the total obtained under paragraph 12 by the day school A.D.E. for the board, counting only elementary school pupils of the board.
14. Where an amount calculated in accordance with section 46 of the 1998-99 grant regulation is subtracted from the total determined for the board under paragraph 3 of section 11 of that Regulation, subtract an amount calculated as follows from the amount obtained under paragraph 13:
    i. Take the amount calculated for the board under subsection 46(2) of the 1998-99 grant regulation.
    ii. Divide the amount referred to in subparagraph i by the day school A.D.E. for the board, counting only pupils of the board.
15. Where an amount calculated in accordance with section 47 of the 1998-99 grant regulation is added to the total determined for the board under paragraph 3 of section 11 of that Regulation, add an amount calculated as follows to the amount obtained under paragraph 13:
    i. Take the amount calculated for the board under subsection 47(2) of the 1998-99 grant regulation.
    ii. Divide the amount referred to in subparagraph i by the day school A.D.E. for the board, counting only pupils of the board.

S. 3   REGULATIONS UNDER THE EDUCATION ACT

(4) For the purposes of paragraph 1 of subsection (2), the base amount for a secondary school pupil described in subsection (1) who is enrolled in a school operated by a district school board shall be determined as follows:

1. Determine the amount calculated for the board under paragraph 4 of section 13 of the 1998-99 grant regulation, on account of the foundation allocation for secondary school pupils.
2. Determine an amount on account of the special education allocation for secondary school pupils, as follows:
    i. Multiply the day school A.D.E. for secondary school pupils of the board by $214.
    ii. Divide the amount determined for the board under paragraph 2 of section 14 of the 1998-99 grant regulation by the day school A.D.E. of pupils of the board.
    iii. Multiply the result obtained under subparagraph ii by the day school A.D.E. for secondary school pupils of the board.
    iv. Determine an amount on account of program ISA for secondary pupils, as follows:
        A. If the amount determined for the board under clause 17(a) of the 1998-99 grant regulation is greater than the amount determined for the board under clause 17(b) of that Regulation, multiply the day school A.D.E. for secondary school pupils of the board by the per pupil amount specified for the board in Column 2 of Table 1 of that Regulation.
        B. If the amount determined for the board under clause 17(b) of the 1998-99 grant regulation is greater than the amount determined for the board under clause 17(a) of that Regulation, calculate the part of the ISA level 2 and 3 funding total determined for the board under subsection 18(5) of that Regulation that is generated by secondary pupils of the board.
    v. Total the amounts obtained under subparagraphs i, iii and iv.
3. In the case of an English-language district school board, determine an amount on account of the language allocation for secondary school pupils, as follows:
    i. Take the French as a second language amount for secondary pupils of the board, as calculated under subsection 22(5) of the 1998-99 grant regulation.
    ii. Calculate the part of the ESL/ESD amount for the board, as calculated under section 24 of the 1998-99 grant regulation, that is generated by secondary school pupils of the board.
    iii. Add the amount taken under subparagraph i to the amount calculated under subparagraph ii.
4. In the case of a French-language district school board, determine an amount on account of the language allocation for secondary school pupils, as follows:
    i. Take the amount determined for the board under paragraph 2 of subsection 26(1) of the 1998-99 grant regulation.
    ii. Divide the total of the amounts determined for the board under paragraph 7 of subsection 28(4) of the 1998-99 grant regulation by the total number of instructional units determined for the board under paragraph 3 of subsection 28(4) of that Regulation. Multiply the result by the total number of secondary instruc-

tional units determined for the board under paragraph 2 of subsection 28(4) of that Regulation.
    iii. Calculate the part of the PDF funding level for the board, as calculated under subsection 28(11) of the 1998-99 grant regulation, that is generated by secondary school pupils of the board.
    iv. Total the amount taken under subparagraph i, the product obtained under subparagraph ii and the amount calculated under subparagraph iii.
5. Determine the amount calculated for the board under paragraph 8 of subsection 29(11) of the 1998-99 grant regulation, on account of the small schools allocation for secondary school pupils.
6. Determine an amount on account of the remote and rural allocation for secondary school pupils, as follows:
    i. Take the amount determined for the board under paragraph 5 of section 30 of the 1998-99 grant regulation.
    ii. Divide the amount determined for the board under subparagraph i by the day school A.D.E. for the board, counting only pupils of the board.
    iii. Multiply the amount determined under subparagraph ii by the day school A.D.E. for the board, counting only secondary school pupils of the board.
7. Determine an amount on account of the learning opportunities allocation for secondary school pupils, as follows:
    i. Take the amount determined for the board under section 31 of the 1998-99 grant regulation.
    ii. Divide the amount determined for the board under subparagraph i by the day school A.D.E. for the board, counting only pupils of the board.
    iii. Multiply the amount determined under subparagraph ii by the day school A.D.E. for the board, counting only secondary school pupils of the board.
8. Determine an amount on account of the teacher compensation allocation for secondary school pupils, by subtracting from the amount calculated under paragraph 10 of subsection 33(10) of the 1998-99 grant regulation the amount determined on account of teacher compensation allocation for elementary pupils calculated under paragraph 8 of subsection (3).
9. Determine an amount on account of the administration and governance allocation for secondary school pupils, as follows:
    i. Take the amount determined for the board under paragraph 4 of subsection 36(1) of the 1998-99 grant regulation.
    ii. Divide the amount determined for the board under subparagraph i by the day school A.D.E. for the board, counting only pupils of the board.
    iii. Multiply the amount determined under subparagraph ii by the day school A.D.E. for the board, counting only secondary school pupils of the board.
10. Determine an amount on account of the school operations part of the pupil accommodation allocation for secondary school pupils, as follows:
    i. Multiply the secondary school area requirement for the board determined under paragraph 11 of subsection 37(2) of the 1998-99 grant regulation or, where a supplementary secondary school area factor is approved for the board under subsection 37(6) of that Regulation, the adjusted secondary school area re-

quirement determined for the board under paragraph 12 of subsection 37(2) of that Regulation, by the benchmark operating cost of $55.97.
11. Total the amounts determined for the board under paragraphs 1 to 10.
12. Divide the total obtained under paragraph 11 by the day school A.D.E. for the board, counting only secondary school pupils of the board.
13. Where an amount calculated in accordance with section 46 of the 1998-99 grant regulation is subtracted from the total determined for the board under paragraph 3 of section 11 of that Regulation, subtract an amount calculated as follows from the amount obtained under paragraph 12:
    i. Take the amount calculated for the board under subsection 46(2) of the 1998-99 grant regulation.
    ii. Divide the amount referred to in subparagraph i by the day school A.D.E. for the board, counting only pupils of the board.
14. Where an amount calculated in accordance with section 47 of the 1998-99 grant regulation is added to the total determined for the board under paragraph 3 of section 11 of that Regulation, add an amount calculated as follows to the amount obtained under paragraph 12:
    i. Take the amount calculated for the board under subsection 47(2) of the 1998-99 grant regulation.
    ii. Divide the amount referred to in subparagraph i by the day school A.D.E. for the board, counting only pupils of the board.

(5) For the purposes of paragraph 1 of subsection (2), the base amount for a pupil described in subsection (1) who is enrolled in a school operated by an isolate board shall be determined as follows:

1. Take the approved expenditure of the board within the meaning of subsection 55(1) of the 1998-99 grant regulation.
2. Deduct the amount of the approved expenditure referred to in paragraph 1 that relates to transportation.
3. Deduct the amount of the approved expenditure referred to in paragraph 1 that relates to school renewal.
4. Divide the amount obtained under paragraph 3 by the day school A.D.E. for the board, counting only pupils of the board.

(6) The fee in respect of a pupil described in subsection (1) who is enrolled in a Native language program in a school operated by a district school board and whose fee is receivable from the Crown in right of Canada or from a band, the council of a band or an education authority where the band, council of a band or education authority is authorized by the Crown in right of Canada to provide education for Indians, may, at the option of the district school board, be increased by an amount equal to the allocation for Native as a second language that would be generated for the pupil if he or she were a pupil of the board, determined in accordance with section 23 or 27, as the case may be, of the 1998-99 grant regulation.

(7) The fee in respect of a pupil described in subsection (1) who is enrolled in a high cost program may, at the option of the board, be increased by multiplying the fee by a factor agreed on by the board providing the instruction and the party from whom the fee is receivable or, in the absence of agreement, by a factor determined in accordance with subsection (8).

(8) If the board providing the instruction and the party from whom the fee is receivable cannot agree on a factor, the factor shall be determined by three arbitrators, appointed as follows:

1. One arbitrator shall be appointed by the board that provides the instruction.
2. One arbitrator shall be appointed by the party from whom the fee is receivable.
3. One arbitrator shall be appointed by the arbitrators appointed under paragraphs 1 and 2.

(9) The decision of the arbitrators or a majority of them is final and binding on the board providing the instruction and the party from whom the fee is receivable.

(10) This section does not apply in respect of a pupil to whom subsection 49(6) of the Act applies.

Fees Charged to Parties Residing in Ontario

4. (1) This section applies in respect of a pupil described in subsection 46(2) of the Act who is enrolled in a school of a district school board or an isolate board and who resides with his or her parent or guardian in a school section, separate school zone or secondary school district on land that is exempt from taxation for school purposes.

(2) The fee that a board shall charge in respect of a pupil described in subsection (1) to the parent or guardian is $40 for each month or part of a month the pupil is enrolled in a school of the board.

(3) This section does not apply in respect of a pupil to whom subsection 49(6) of the Act applies.

Fees Charged to Parties Not Residing in Ontario

5. (1) The fee in respect of a pupil who is enrolled in a school of a district school board or an isolate board and whose parent or guardian does not reside in Ontario shall be such fee as the board may determine, but shall not exceed the maximums set by subsections (2) and (3).

(2) Except as is provided in subsection (3), the fee in respect of a pupil who is enrolled in a school of a district school board or an isolate board and whose parent or guardian does not reside in Ontario shall not exceed the amount calculated as follows:

1. Add the base amount determined under paragraph 1 of subsection 3(2) and the P.A.C. for the pupil.
2. Multiply the amount obtained under paragraph 1 by 0.1.
3. Multiply the result obtained under paragraph 2 by the number of months or part months during which the pupil is enrolled in a school operated by the board.

(3) Where the pupil is enrolled in a high cost program, the maximum set by subsection (2) shall be increased by an amount that does not exceed the additional cost to the board of providing the high cost program to the pupil.

(4) This section does not apply in respect of a pupil to whom subsection 49(6) of the Act applies.

Fees in Respect of Pupils to Whom Subsection 49(6) of the Act Applies

6. (1) The fee in respect of a pupil to whom subsection 49(6) of the Act applies shall be the amount determined in accordance with a fees policy developed for the purposes of this section by the board that operates the school in which the pupil is enrolled.

(2) The policy referred to in subsection (1) shall not, in the case of a district school board or isolate board, provide for a fee in respect of a pupil that is less than the amount that would be chargeable by the board in respect of the pupil under section 3.

(3) The policy referred to in subsection (1) shall not, in the case of a section 68 board, provide for a fee in respect of a pupil that is less than the amount that would be chargeable by the board in respect of the pupil under section 7.

Fees Paid to Section 68 Boards

7. Except where section 6 applies, the fee that a board shall charge in respect of a pupil who is enrolled in a school operated by a section 68 board and whose parent or guardian does not reside in Ontario shall be an amount determined as follows:

1. Take the expenditure of the board for the 1998-99 fiscal year that is acceptable to the Minister for grant purposes, excluding,
    i. expenditures for debt charges,
    ii. expenditures for the purchase of capital assets, as defined in the 1998-99 grant regulation,
    iii. expenditures for the restoration of destroyed or damaged capital assets, as defined in the 1998-99 grant regulation, and
    iv. provisions for reserves for working funds and provisions for reserve funds.
2. Deduct any transfers from reserves for working funds or from reserve funds made during the 1998-99 fiscal year.
3. Deduct the revenue of the board for the 1998-99 fiscal year from,
    i. any organization on whose property a school of the board is located, and
    ii. refunds of expenditure of the kind described in subparagraph i, ii or iii of paragraph 1.
4. Divide the amount obtained under paragraph 3 by the total number of pupil days for the board for the period September 1, 1998 to August 31, 1999. For the purposes of this paragraph, the total number of pupil days for the board for the period is the sum of the number of instructional days for which each pupil who was enrolled in the school during the period.
5. Multiply the result obtained under paragraph 4 by the number of instructional days for which the pupil is enrolled in the school.

No Fees Payable by Boards

8. No fee is payable under this Regulation by one board to another board.

REGULATION 346/98
SECOND INSTALMENT PAYMENT OF SCHOOL TAXES IN 1998

O. Reg. 346/98, as am. O. Reg. 500/98

1. The time for paying instalments referred to in paragraph 2 of subsection 257.11(1) of the Act is extended to October 30, 1998.

O. Reg. 500/98, s. 1

2. Instalments referred to in paragraph 2 of subsection 257.11(1) of the Act shall be paid to the Province rather than to boards.

REGULATION 365/98
PRE-1998 SCHOOL TAX ARREARS
O. Reg. 365/98

Collection in Territory without Municipal Organization

1. (1) The powers and duties of a school authority relating to the collection of arrears of taxes levied before January 1, 1998 on property in the school authority's area of jurisdiction shall be exercised and carried out by the board that collects school purpose taxes in respect of that property under Division B of Part IX of the Act.

(2) The powers and duties of an old board relating to the collection of arrears of taxes levied before January 1, 1998 on property in the old board's area of jurisdiction shall be exercised and carried out by the board that collects school purpose taxes in respect of that property under Division B of Part IX of the Act.

(3) For the purposes of section 14 of the *Interpretation Act*, a reference in this section to the powers of a school authority or an old board relating to the collection of arrears of tax includes the power to institute, continue or enforce any investigation, legal proceeding or remedy in respect of any obligation or liability related to those arrears of taxes.

Distribution of Taxes Levied for Purposes of an Old Board

2. (1) For the purposes of this section, a district school board is the successor of an old board if the district school board is listed in column 2 or 3 of Schedule 1 of Ontario Regulation 460/97 opposite the old board listed in column 1 of that Schedule.

(2) A board that collects arrears of taxes levied before January 1, 1998 for the purposes of an old board shall distribute the amounts collected to the old board's successor English-language district school board and successor French-language district school board, in accordance with the appropriate distribution ratio, as determined under the directives published in September, 1997 by the Education Improvement Commission and titled ''Directives for the Distribution of Assets and Liabilities Among District School Boards''.

(3) A board that collects arrears of taxes levied before January 1, 1998 for the purposes of a school authority shall distribute the amounts collected to the school authority.

REGULATION 366/98
TAX ARREARS IN ANNEXED AREAS
O. Reg. 366/98

1. In this Regulation,

"taxes for school purposes" includes rates levied under sections 255 and 256 of the Act or predecessors of those sections.

2. (1) This Regulation applies only in respect of municipalities formed by either of the following forms of municipal restructuring:

1. Territory without municipal organization is annexed to a municipality.
2. The inhabitants of territory without municipal organization incorporate as a municipality.

(2) This Regulation does not apply in respect of territory without municipal organization that is attached or is deemed to be attached to a district municipality for any purpose related to taxation.

3. (1) On, or before the day set out in subsection (2), a municipality shall pay to each board in accordance with the distribution rules set out in sections 257.8 and 257.9 of the Act and in Ontario Regulation 365/98 (Pre-1998 School Tax Arrears),

(a) the full amount of arrears of taxes for school purposes that on that day remain unpaid in respect of that portion of the municipality that was territory without municipal organization before the municipality was restructured; and

(b) the full amount of arrears of taxes imposed under section 21.1 of the *Provincial Land Tax Act* that on that day remain unpaid.

(2) The day referred to in subsection (1) is the later of,

(a) 90 days after the day the municipality was formed by restructuring; and
(b) 90 days after the day this Regulation is filed.

(3) Subsections 257.11(2), (3) and (4) of the Act apply with necessary modifications in respect of payments made under subsection (1).

(4) If a board entitled to payment under subsection (1) receives an amount on account of tax arrears described in subsection (1) other than from the municipality, the amount of the payments under subsection (1) shall be adjusted accordingly.

(5) For the purpose of permitting a municipality to collect the arrears of taxes to which this Regulation applies, those arrears shall be deemed to be taxes for municipal purposes levied by the municipality.

(6) A municipality has the power to institute, continue, or enforce any investigation, legal proceeding or remedy in respect of an obligation or liability related to the arrears of taxes to which this Regulation applies.

REGULATION 392/98
TAX MATTERS — TAXATION OF CERTAIN RAILWAY, POWER UTILITY LANDS

O. Reg. 392/98, as am. O. Reg. 494/98; 705/98

1. This Regulation applies with respect to land described in paragraphs 1 and 2 of subsection 368.3(1) of the *Municipal Act*.

2. The tax rates set out in Table 1 are prescribed, for the geographic areas described in subsection 368.3(6) of the *Municipal Act*, as the tax rates for school purposes for the purposes of section 257.7 of the Act.

3. (1) Despite section 2, for land that is owned by the owner on December 31, 1997, the tax rates set out in Tables 2 to 6 for the municipality or territory in which the land is located are prescribed as the tax rates for school purposes for 1998 for the purposes of section 257.7 of the Act.

(2) The headings of the columns of Tables 2 to 6 that set out the tax rates are referneces to the names of the assessed owners as they appear on the assessment rolls except that the headings set out in Table 7 refer to the names of the assessed owners indicated in that Table.

(3) If the land is leased to the assessed owner by a municipality, the applicable tax rate is the tax rate set out in Tables 2 to 6 for that assessed owner.

TABLE 1

O. Reg. 494/98

TAX RATES FOR LAND DESCRIBED IN PARAGRAPHS 1 AND 2 OF SUBSECTION 368.3(1) OF THE *MUNICIPAL ACT*

	Geographic areas as described in subsection 368.3(6) of the *Municipal Act*	Tax rates for land described in paragraphs 1 and 2 of subsection 368.3(1) of the *Municipal Act*—expressed as dollars per acre	
		Paragraph 1 (Railway rights of way)	Paragraph 2 (Electrical corridors)
1.	The City of Toronto and the regional municipalities of Durham, Halton, Peel and York	822.69	1,208.66
2.	The Regional Municipality of Ottawa-Carleton and the counties of Lanark, Leeds and Grenville, Prescott and Russell, Renfrew and Stormont, Dundas and Glengarry, including the separated municipalities situated in those counties	127.38	623.80

Table 1

REGULATION 392/98

	Geographic areas as described in subsection 368.3(6) of the *Municipal Act*	Tax rates for land described in paragraphs 1 and 2 of subsection 368.3(1) of the *Municipal Act*—expressed as dollars per acre	
		Paragraph 1 (Railway rights of way)	Paragraph 2 (Electrical corridors)
3.	The counties of Frontenac, Haliburton, Hastings, Lennox and Addington, Northumberland, Peterborough, Prince Edward and Victoria, including the separated municipalities situated in those counties	53.62	34.46
4.	The regional municipalities of Hamilton-Wentworth, Niagara and Waterloo	291.60	436.50
5.	The Regional Municipality of Haldimand-Norfolk, the County of Oxford, and the counties of Brant, Elgin, Essex, Kent, Lambton and Middlesex, including the separated municipalities situated in those counties	114.98	86.09
6.	The counties of Bruce, Dufferin, Grey, Huron, Perth, Simcoe and Wellington, including the separated municipalities situated in those counties	74.12	34.39
7.	The Regional Municipality of Sudbury and the districts of Algoma, Manitoulin and Sudbury	42.49	13.32
8.	The District Municipality of Muskoka, and the districts of Cochrane, Nipissing, Parry Sound and Temiskaming	24.78	75.99
9.	The districts of Kenora, Rainy River, and Thunder Bay	15.43	149.75

Table 2

REGULATIONS UNDER THE EDUCATION ACT

TABLE 2

O. Reg. 494/98, s. 2; 705/98, s. 1

1998 RATES FOR ONTARIO HYDRO, CANADIAN NATIONAL RAILWAY, CASO RAILWAY AND CANADIAN PACIFIC RAILWAY

Municipality or territory	Tax rates for 1998 for land owned by the owner on December 31, 1997—expressed as dollars per acre			
	Ontario Hydro	Canadian National Railway	CASO Railway	Canadian Pacific Railway
Toronto C	3,041.26	2,761.53		2,622.26
Durham R				
Oshawa C	62.60	646.25		364.18
Whitby T	23.94	73.12		65.02
Pickering T	831.14	371.46		19.01
Clarington T	54.06	22.37		16.91
Ajax T	80.71	513.03		46.77
Brock Tp	19.79	111.65		
Uxbridge Tp		6.62		
Haldimand-Norfolk R				
Nanticoke C	40.94	15.14	36.55	24.12
Dunnville T	68.99		16.75	34.99
Haldimand T	44.84	191.70	35.06	
Norfolk Tp		18.83		
Delhi Tp	18.40	236.41	21.54	
Halton R				
Burlington C	1,859.68	1,758.40		98.12
Oakville T	1,055.89	1,771.75		
Halton Hills T	69.12	588.15		
Milton T	158.02	837.54		227.40
Hamilton-Wentworth R				
Stoney Creek C	587.62	41.16		22.69
Hamilton C	4,951.99	1,225.09		1,478.76

REGULATION 392/98 **Table 2**

Municipality or territory	Tax rates for 1998 for land owned by the owner on December 31, 1997—expressed as dollars per acre			
	Ontario Hydro	Canadian National Railway	CASO Railway	Canadian Pacific Railway
Dundas T	694.95	14.97		9.20
Ancaster T	54.56	12.40		
Flamborough T	42.87	34.86		50.12
Glanbrook Tp	109.13			
Niagara R				
Niagara Falls C	1,210.76	214.00		313.67
Port Colborne C		29.22		13.29
St Catharines C	215.88	650.52		
Welland C	638.99	162.85		209.67
Thorold C	292.22	212.08		
Grimsby T	228.59	843.89		16.78
Fort Erie T		96.49		157.78
Niagara-on-the-Lake T	80.75			
Pelham T	35.13			46.87
Lincoln T	28.59	152.24		
Wainfleet Tp		12.75	11.58	13.74
West Lincoln Tp	18.47			25.57
Ottawa-Carleton R				
Nepean C	3,310.77	539.70		
Kanata C	385.16	104.36		
Gloucester C	1,798.49	176.23		297.43
Ottawa C	4,583.80	2,811.62		2,523.27
Cumberland Tp	159.63	26.92		
Goulbourn Tp	58.40	81.67		
Osgoode Tp	18.67			31.77
Rideau Tp	1,422.68			
West Carleton Tp	20.23	11.04		12.11
Peel R				

Table 2

REGULATIONS UNDER THE EDUCATION ACT

Municipality or territory	Tax rates for 1998 for land owned by the owner on December 31, 1997—expressed as dollars per acre			
	Ontario Hydro	Canadian National Railway	CASO Railway	Canadian Pacific Railway
Mississauga C	3,296.00	1,827.73		860.86
Brampton C	728.41	678.18		453.18
Caledon T	24.02			52.02
Sudbury R				
Sudbury C	218.97	662.11		879.80
Valley East T	7.13	3.83		
Onaping Falls T				4.40
Rayside Balfour T	4.81			11.93
Capreol T		55.44		
Walden T	2.35			12.67
Nickel Centre T	29.30	10.42		12.90
Waterloo R				
Cambridge C	314.59	804.51		522.96
Kitchener C	1,396.34	1,664.56		939.14
Waterloo C	301.22			
North Dumfries Tp	21.40			49.14
Wilmot Tp	25.36	52.19		
Woolwich Tp		45.39		
York R				
Vaughan C	87.57	186.35		205.32
East Gwillimbury T	33.99	47.19		
Markham T	251.19	319.36		85.49
Aurora T	60.09	101.34		
Whitchurch-Stouffville T	76.62	74.62		
Newmarket T	91.08	320.86		
Richmond Hill T	78.68	271.83		
Georgina T	161.60	22.14		
King Tp	59.18	86.12		

REGULATION 392/98 **Table 2**

Municipality or territory	Tax rates for 1998 for land owned by the owner on December 31, 1997—expressed as dollars per acre			
	Ontario Hydro	Canadian National Railway	CASO Railway	Canadian Pacific Railway
Brant Co				
Brantford C	2,439.49	220.95		169.85
Paris T	581.46	205.91		
Brantford Tp	92.88	26.53		22.73
Burford Tp		46.55		
South Dumfries Tp	28.74	16.73		
Oakland Tp				20.10
Onondaga Tp	18.82	16.65		
Bruce Co				
Walkerton T	4,697.88			
Greenock Tp	6.31			
Arran Tp	7.74			
Bruce Tp	8.31			
Teeswater-Culross Tp	7.34			
Saugeen Tp	8.65			
Brant Tp	35.86			
Dufferin Co				
Orangeville T				652.97
Shelburne T				230.43
East Luther Grand Valley Tp	25.04			
East Garafraxa Tp	20.73			
Amaranth Tp				17.92
Melancthon Tp				8.06
Elgin Co				
St Thomas C	117.64	294.21	303.30	178.38
Aylmer T		156.19		
West Elgin Tp	17.97		26.82	

Table 2
REGULATIONS UNDER THE EDUCATION ACT

Municipality or territory	Tax rates for 1998 for land owned by the owner on December 31, 1997—expressed as dollars per acre			
	Ontario Hydro	Canadian National Railway	CASO Railway	Canadian Pacific Railway
Bayham, Port Burwell, Vienna Tp		14.01		
Dutton-Dunwich Tp	15.59		29.26	
Malahide, South Dorchester, Springfield Tp	74.69	26.34	19.14	26.06
Southwold Tp	21.17	11.73	10.60	
Central Elgin Tp	28.02	53.56	12.91	15.78
Essex Co				
Windsor C	520.07	212.18	257.42	515.90
LaSalle T	238.07			
Essex T			433.49	
Leamington T		1,149.68	647.53	
Gosfield North Tp	37.83			
Mersea Tp		112.15	28.31	
Gosfield South Tp	32.18			
Rochester Tp	27.91		19.05	18.34
Colchester North Tp			30.27	
Tilbury North Tp	26.55		16.69	17.86
Sandwich South Tp	144.35	138.33	73.82	88.88
Lakeshore Tp	33.16		33.08	30.33
Tilbury West Tp	27.74		33.99	
Frontenac Co				
Kingston C	63.91	330.22		
North Frontenac Tp				2.03
South Frontenac Tp	36.94			7.30
Central Frontenac Tp				3.88
Grey Co				
Owen Sound C	21.88			778.14

REGULATION 392/98

Table 2

Municipality or territory	Tax rates for 1998 for land owned by the owner on December 31, 1997—expressed as dollars per acre			
	Ontario Hydro	Canadian National Railway	CASO Railway	Canadian Pacific Railway
Chatsworth V				15.75
Dundalk V				426.69
Markdale V				86.39
Artemesia Tp				16.04
Bentinck Tp	20.69			
Sydenham Tp	13.93			8.84
Sullivan Tp	7.05			
Proton Tp	21.17			7.68
Normanby Tp	32.44			
Holland Tp				15.52
Glenelg Tp				9.79
Derby Tp	6.41			
Egremont Tp	10.62			
Haliburton Co				
Anson, Hindon and Minden Tp	95.80			
Hastings Co				
Quinte West C	12.89	42.23		72.26
Belleville C	115.67	104.68		131.10
Bangor, Wicklow and McClure Tp	5.83			
Tyendinaga Tp	7.11	6.71		3.20
Madoc Tp	10.51			
Huron Co				
Colborne Tp	57.04			
Goderich Tp	36.20			
Morris Tp	11.45			
Turnberry Tp	10.11			

Table 2
REGULATIONS UNDER THE EDUCATION ACT

Municipality or territory	Tax rates for 1998 for land owned by the owner on December 31, 1997—expressed as dollars per acre			
	Ontario Hydro	Canadian National Railway	CASO Railway	Canadian Pacific Railway
Hullett Tp	16.00			
Kent Co				
Chatham-Kent C	55.65	43.84	25.04	69.90
Lambton Co				
Sarnia C	372.32	339.70		
Wyoming V		93.67		
Alvinston V	132.47			
Plympton Tp		12.26		
Enniskillen Tp	17.83			
Moore Tp	46.48	50.85		
Warwick Tp		16.62		
Sombra Tp		112.69		
Dawn-Euphemia Tp		11.36		9.77
Brooke Tp	23.65			
Lanark Co				
Smiths Falls ST	78.05			587.18
Mississippi Mills T				60.57
Carleton Place T				969.53
Perth T				827.21
Montague Tp	7.90			5.81
Bathurst, Burgess and Sherbrooke Tp	27.99			6.06
Lanark Highlands Tp	109.10			
Drummond-North Elmsey Tp				5.42
Beckwith Tp				5.22
Leeds and Grenville Co				
Prescott ST		141.95		
Brockville C	788.04	554.28		951.96

630

REGULATION 392/98 **Table 2**

Municipality or territory	Tax rates for 1998 for land owned by the owner on December 31, 1997—expressed as dollars per acre			
	Ontario Hydro	Canadian National Railway	CASO Railway	Canadian Pacific Railway
Cardinal V		10.84		
Merrickville-Woolford V	11.54			6.93
North Grenville Tp				13.28
Elizabethtown Tp	8.04	8.96		2.03
Augusta Tp		11.77		
Front of Leeds and Lansdowne Tp		5.44		
Front of Escott Tp		3.87		
Kitley Tp	168.51			2.72
Rideau Lakes Tp	109.92			23.22
Front of Yonge Tp		3.43		
Edwardsburgh Tp		6.93		4.11
Lennox and Addington Co				
Greater Napanee T	9.68	19.51		4.56
Stone Mills Tp		5.01		2.53
Loyalist Tp	11.00	16.53		
Addington Highlands Tp	299.75			
Middlesex Co				
London C	648.97	1,322.46		1,176.71
Strathroy T		126.92		
Newbury V		26.99		
Ailsa Craig V	2,825.79			
Glencoe V		124.38		
Metcalfe Tp	19.70			
Caradoc Tp	26.68	23.76		14.64
Biddulph Tp	53.56			
Middlesex Centre Tp	35.84	44.74		28.35

Table 2 REGULATIONS UNDER THE EDUCATION ACT

Municipality or territory	Tax rates for 1998 for land owned by the owner on December 31, 1997—expressed as dollars per acre			
	Ontario Hydro	Canadian National Railway	CASO Railway	Canadian Pacific Railway
West Nissouri Tp		25.63		45.62
Ekfrid Tp	19.72	11.81		11.36
Mosa Tp	13.93	19.10		11.30
North Dorchester Tp	50.58	81.48		43.40
Adelaide Tp		15.07		
Northumberland Co				
Cobourg T	116.75	310.63		352.47
Port Hope T	243.90	140.56		131.07
Brighton T		64.64		69.56
Colborne V		54.98		
Brighton Tp	8.27	12.83		18.03
Hamilton Tp	15.49	52.70		38.46
Cramahe Tp	12.32	13.38		15.53
Haldimand Tp	13.76	13.38		12.19
Hope Tp	20.22	20.34		26.32
Oxford Co				
Woodstock C	2,747.03	436.27		399.95
Tillsonburg T		108.85	215.90	
Ingersoll T		295.42		399.41
Zorra Tp		30.32		18.93
Norwich Tp	61.52	28.41	12.59	
Blandford-Blenheim Tp		14.88		14.77
South-West Oxford Tp	2,015.81	49.72	15.14	32.47
East Zorra-Tavistock Tp	50.54	8.16		19.08
Perth Co				
Stratford C	159.41	473.78		
St Marys ST		84.00		
North Perth T	440.98			

REGULATION 392/98 **Table 2**

Municipality or territory	Tax rates for 1998 for land owned by the owner on December 31, 1997—expressed as dollars per acre			
	Ontario Hydro	Canadian National Railway	CASO Railway	Canadian Pacific Railway
Perth South Tp	25.16	30.59		
Perth East Tp	44.13	51.31		
Peterborough Co				
Peterborough C	544.67			412.33
Asphodel-Norwood Tp	201.32			11.16
Havelock-Belmont-Methuen Tp	793.86			14.62
Otonabee-South Monaghan Tp	16.55			7.03
Cavan-Millbrook-North Monaghan Tp	75.87			15.37
Douro-Dummer Tp				4.69
Burleigh-Anstruther-Chanedos Tp				16.16
Smith, Ennismore Tp	36.25			
Prescott and Russell Co				
Hawkesbury T		152.05		
Casselman V		150.41		
Champlain Tp		14.07		
Russell Tp	26.33	11.30		
The Nation Tp		11.56		
Prince Edward Co				
Prince Edward County C	6.34			
Renfrew Co				
Pembroke C		149.22		964.85
Renfrew T				297.46
Petawawa T	81.32			127.77
Arnprior T				555.74
Cobden V				205.29

Table 2   REGULATIONS UNDER THE EDUCATION ACT

Municipality or territory	Tax rates for 1998 for land owned by the owner on December 31, 1997—expressed as dollars per acre			
	Ontario Hydro	Canadian National Railway	CASO Railway	Canadian Pacific Railway
Beachburg V		16.97		
Chalk River V				59.12
McNab-Braeside Tp				31.96
Alice and Fraser Tp		27.56		5.95
Ross Tp		2.58		3.69
Rolph, Buchanan, Wylie and McKay Tp				1.18
Horton Tp				7.15
Head, Clara and Maria Tp				1.90
Admaston Tp				4.96
Westmeath Tp		4.05		4.01
Stafford and Pembroke Tp		14.09		50.85
Simcoe Co				
Barrie C	962.98	697.49		
Collingwood T		655.17		
Innisfil T		111.75		
Bradford West Gwillimbury T		72.22		
New Tecumseth T	29.89			70.24
Severn Tp	29.47	20.11		34.59
Springwater Tp	35.46	43.58		41.84
Oro-Medonte Tp	28.28			25.70
Clearview Tp	47.71	88.58		
Tay Tp	25.69			
Ramara Tp		18.68		
Essa Tp	16.11	21.16		13.40
Stormont, Dundas and Glengarry Co				

REGULATION 392/98

Table 2

Municipality or territory	Tax rates for 1998 for land owned by the owner on December 31, 1997—expressed as dollars per acre			
	Ontario Hydro	Canadian National Railway	CASO Railway	Canadian Pacific Railway
Cornwall C	87.08	127.42		67.57
North Stormont Tp	23.26	5.65		7.31
North Glengarry Tp		16.64		4.40
South Stormont Tp	5.75	10.49		
South Glengarry Tp		21.97		7.62
South Dundas Tp	122.07	12.76		
North Dundas Tp	68.36			15.67
Victoria Co				
Manvers Tp				8.72
Fenelon Tp	1,004.87			
Ops Tp	26.93			
Mariposa Tp	19.51			
Laxton, Digby and Longford Tp	762.06			
Eldon Tp	24.06			
Wellington Co				
Guelph C	3,040.38	755.52		844.46
Erin T	25.48			
Guelph Tp	52.80	31.85		
West Garafraxa Tp	21.08			
Eramosa Tp		38.27		
Mapleton Tp	854.66			
Pilkington Tp	31.89			
Puslinch Tp	55.15	38.52		18.93
Algoma D				
Sault Ste Marie C				440.08
Blind River T				461.36

635

Table 2 REGULATIONS UNDER THE EDUCATION ACT

Municipality or territory	Tax rates for 1998 for land owned by the owner on December 31, 1997—expressed as dollars per acre			
	Ontario Hydro	Canadian National Railway	CASO Railway	Canadian Pacific Railway
Tarbutt and Tarbutt Additional Tp				3.31
Thessalon Tp				9.85
Thompson Tp				2.53
Shedden Tp				95.73
White River Tp				11.61
Macdonald, Meredith and Aberdeen Additional Tp				34.11
Hornepayne Tp		44.76		
Plummer Additional Tp				7.43
The North Shore Tp	19.70			45.21
Laird Tp				10.83
Day and Bright Additional Tp				4.97
Johnson Tp				17.75
Michipicoten Locality Education				0.52
North Shore Locality Education				11.15
Cochrane D				
Timmins C	73.16			
Iroquois Falls T	33.06			
Kapuskasing T	2.67			
Black River-Matheson Tp	169.46			
Kenora D				
Sioux Lookout T		9.67		
Kenora T				290.91
Keewatin T	12.16			30.49
Dryden T	635.29			97.31

REGULATION 392/98 Table 2

Municipality or territory	Tax rates for 1998 for land owned by the owner on December 31, 1997—expressed as dollars per acre			
	Ontario Hydro	Canadian National Railway	CASO Railway	Canadian Pacific Railway
Jaffray Melick T	31.22			4.90
Ignace Tp				10.63
Machin Tp				1.98
Red Lake Tp	149.83			
Kenora Locality Education		8.74		6.19
Dryden Locality Education (assessment roll numbers beginning with "6060")		1.78		2.01
Dryden Locality Education (assessment roll numbers beginning with "6093")				45.33
Dryden Locality Education (assessment roll numbers beginning with "6096")		1.00		1.00
Manitoulin D				
Northeastern Manitoulin & The Islands T				2.68
Muskoka D				
Huntsville T		36.80		
Gravenhurst T	49.63	22.61		
Bracebridge T	14.80	71.59		
Muskoka Lakes Tp		24.12		21.66
Georgian Bay Tp				46.44
Nipissing D				
North Bay C	1,245.51	387.03		465.13
Cache Bay T				13.31
Mattawa T				119.51
Sturgeon Falls T				916.67
East Ferris Tp		2.82		3.16

Table 2 REGULATIONS UNDER THE EDUCATION ACT

Municipality or territory	Tax rates for 1998 for land owned by the owner on December 31, 1997—expressed as dollars per acre			
	Ontario Hydro	Canadian National Railway	CASO Railway	Canadian Pacific Railway
Papineau-Cameron Tp				3.66
Springer Tp				12.99
Calvin Tp				6.18
Chisholm Tp		2.58		
Caldwell Tp	96.20			14.07
Bonfield Tp				8.30
Nipissing Combined School Boards		2.75		4.80
Field Tp	5.84			
Parry Sound D				
Trout Creek T		28.89		
Powassan T		225.05		
Parry Sound T		441.38		348.63
Burk's Falls V		16.55		
South River V		31.37		
Sundridge V		99.83		
Machar Tp		12.93		
Strong Tp		9.86		
Perry Tp		6.33		
McDougall Tp	12.66	5.18		11.58
The Archipelago Tp	46.46			9.25
Himsworth South Tp		2.87		
Seguin Tp	24.39	10.29		5.20
Himsworth North Tp		2.13		
Armour Tp		3.70		
Carling Tp				3.14
East Parry Sound BOE		3.52		
West Parry Sound BOE		1.68		2.43

REGULATION 392/98 **Table 2**

Municipality or territory	Tax rates for 1998 for land owned by the owner on December 31, 1997—expressed as dollars per acre			
	Ontario Hydro	Canadian National Railway	CASO Railway	Canadian Pacific Railway
Rainy River D				
Fort Frances T	22.30	29.20		
Rainy River T		25.20		
Emo Tp		6.46		
La Vallee Tp		3.55		
Morley Tp		1.82		
Dawson Tp		3.38		
Chapple Tp		9.86		
Alberton Tp		3.44		
Atikokan Tp	37.67	5.36		
Atikokan Locality Education		2.79		
Mine Centre Locality Education		0.62		
Fort Frances Rainy River Locality Education		0.39		
Sudbury D				
Webbwood T				42.83
Massey T				66.74
Espanola T				124.87
Hagar Tp				1.26
Ratter and Dunnet Tp				5.31
The Spanish River Tp	2.89			2.53
Chapleau Tp				94.37
Nairn and Hyman Tp				8.91
Baldwin Tp	1,379.93			3.66
Cosby, Mason and Martland Tp	16.32			
Asquith Garvey Locality Education		5.24		

639

Table 2

REGULATIONS UNDER THE EDUCATION ACT

Municipality or territory	Tax rates for 1998 for land owned by the owner on December 31, 1997—expressed as dollars per acre			
	Ontario Hydro	Canadian National Railway	CASO Railway	Canadian Pacific Railway
Gogama Locality Education		25.72		
Chapleau Locality Education				0.62
Foyelet Locality Education		17.98		
Sudbury Locality Education		2.40		4.35
Thunder Bay D				
Thunder Bay C	295.25	395.36		363.75
Marathon T	543.71			5.18
Longlac T		91.70		
Geraldton T		0.77		
Shuniah Tp	112.29	25.03		5.44
Red Rock Tp		1.72		5.17
Manitouwadge Tp		2.51		7.89
Terrace Bay Tp				13.79
Beardmore Tp		3.28		
Schreiber Tp				38.30
Oliver and Paipoonge Tp	228.73	17.09		6.05
Nipigon Tp		11.23		29.94
Dorion Tp		4.24		5.37
Conmee Tp	9.55	1.70		
Kilkenny Locality Education		0.29		
Kashabowie Locality Education		2.21		
Caramat Locality Education		0.40		
Armstrong Locality Education		7.85		
Auden Locality Education		0.29		
Ferland Locality Education		0.26		
Lakehead Locality Education		5.46		2.23

REGULATION 392/98 **Table 3**

Municipality or territory	Tax rates for 1998 for land owned by the owner on December 31, 1997—expressed as dollars per acre			
	Ontario Hydro	Canadian National Railway	CASO Railway	Canadian Pacific Railway
Lake Superior Locality Education				1.43
Nipigon Red Rock Locality Education		1.08		0.73
Geraldton Locality Education		0.51		
Upsala Locality Education				0.87
Timiskaming D				
Haileybury T	5.65			
Kirkland Lake T	170.49			
Evanturel Tp	378.97			

TABLE 3

O. Reg. 705/98, s. 2

1998 TAX RATES FOR GUELPH JUNCTION RAILWAY, ESSEX TERMINAL RAILWAY, WATERLOO-ST. JACOBS RAILWAY COMPANY LIMITED AND GODERICH EXETER RAILWAY

Municipality or territory	Tax rates for 1998 for land owned by the owner on December 31, 1997—expressed as dollars per acre			
	Guelph Junction Railway	Essex Terminal Railway	Waterloo-St. Jacobs Railway Company Limited	Goderich Exeter Railway
Waterloo R				
Kitchener C			2,958.14	
Waterloo C			1,818.97	
Woolwich Tp			154.84	
Essex Co				
Windsor C		662.12		

Table 3 REGULATIONS UNDER THE EDUCATION ACT

Municipality or territory	Tax rates for 1998 for land owned by the owner on December 31, 1997—expressed as dollars per acre			
	Guelph Junction Railway	Essex Terminal Railway	Waterloo-St. Jacobs Railway Company Limited	Goderich Exeter Railway
Amherstburg T		98.18		
LaSalle T		69.72		
Huron Co				
Goderich T				55.48
Seaforth T				51.18
Exeter T				55.56
Clinton T				116.67
Hensall V				24.83
Tuckersmith Tp				13.07
Stephen Tp				27.54
Stanley Tp				11.48
Hay Tp				11.39
Goderich Tp				13.93
Perth Co				
Stratford C				698.54
West Perth Tp				11.05
Perth South T				33.25

TABLE 4

O. Reg. 494/98, s. 3; 705/98, s. 3

1998 RATES FOR ONTARIO NORTHLAND RAILWAY, ALGOMA CENTRAL RAILWAY, ONTARIO L'ORIGNAL RAILWAY AND ARNPRIOR NEPEAN RAILWAY

Municipality or territory	Tax rates for 1998 for land owned by the owner on December 31, 1997—expressed as dollars per acre			
	Ontario Northland Railway	Algoma Central Railway	Ontario L'Orignal Railway	Arnprior Nepean Railway
Ottawa-Carleton R				
Kanata C				344.70
Nepean C				167.31
West Carleton Tp				19.04
Prescott and Russell Co				
Champlain Tp			4.34	
Renfrew Co				
Arnprior T				24.01
Stormont, Dundas and Glengarry Co				
North Glengarry Tp			4.39	
Algoma D				
Sault Ste Marie C		74.71		
Michipicoten Tp		7.46		
Dubreuilville Tp		2.27		
Michipicoten Locality Education		2.85		
Sault Ste. Marie Locality Education		3.99		
Cochrane D				
Smooth Rock Falls T	0.00			
Iroquois Falls T	0.00			
Kapuskasing T	0.00			
Hearst T	0.00	4.65		

Table 4 REGULATIONS UNDER THE EDUCATION ACT

Municipality or territory	Tax rates for 1998 for land owned by the owner on December 31, 1997—expressed as dollars per acre			
	Ontario Northland Railway	Algoma Central Railway	Ontario L'Orignal Railway	Arnprior Nepean Railway
Opasatika Tp	0.00			
Mattice-Val Cote Tp	0.00			
Val Rita-Harty Tp	0.00			
Fauquier-Strickland Tp	0.00			
Glackmeyer Tp	0.00			
Moonbeam Tp	0.00			
Black River-Matheson Tp	0.00			
Timmins C	0.00			
Moosonee Development Area Board	0.00			
Cochrane T	0.00			
Nipissing D				
North Bay C	0.00			
Temagami T	0.00			
Timiskaming Board of Education	0.00			
Timiskaming D				
New Liskeard T	0.00			
Latchford T	0.00			
Kirkland Lake T	0.00			
Haileybury T	0.00			
Cobalt T	0.00			
Englehart T	0.00			
Thornloe V	0.00			
Evanturel Tp	0.00			
Larder Lake Tp	0.00			
Harley Tp	0.00			
Chamberlain Tp	0.00			

REGULATION 392/98 **Table 5**

Municipality or territory	Tax rates for 1998 for land owned by the owner on December 31, 1997—expressed as dollars per acre			
	Ontario Northland Railway	Algoma Central Railway	Ontario L'Orignal Railway	Arnprior Nepean Railway
Dymond Tp	0.00			
Dack Tp	0.00			
Armstrong Tp	0.00			
Gauthier Tp	0.00			
Coleman Tp	0.00			
McGarry Tp	0.00			

TABLE 5

O. Reg. 705/98, s. 4

1998 RATES FOR TORONTO TERMINALS RAILWAY COMPANY LIMITED, CSX RAILWAY, CITY OF PORT COLBORNE RAILWAY AND PORT STANLEY RAILWAY

Municipality or territory	Tax rates for 1998 for land owned by the owner on December 31, 1997—expressed as dollars per acre			
	Toronto Terminals Railway Company Limited	CSX Railway	City of Port Colborne Railway	Port Stanley Railway
Toronto C	16,667.63			
Niagara R				
Port Colborne C			1,060.10	
Elgin Co				
St Thomas C				221.99
Central Elgin Tp				79.19
Southwold Tp				57.87
Kent Co				
Chatham-Kent C		59.05		
Lambton Co				
Sarnia C		300.23		

645

Table 6

REGULATIONS UNDER THE EDUCATION ACT

Municipality or territory	Tax rates for 1998 for land owned by the owner on December 31, 1997—expressed as dollars per acre			
	Toronto Terminals Railway Company Limited	CSX Railway	City of Port Colborne Railway	Port Stanley Railway
Moore Tp		114.11		
Sombra Tp		54.98		

TABLE 6

1998 RATES FOR SOUTH SIMCOE RAILWAY, TORONTO AREA TRANSIT OPERATING AUTHORITY AND VIA RAIL CANADA INC.

Municipality or territory	Tax rates for 1998 for land owned by the owner on December 31, 1997—expressed as dollars per acre		
	South Simcoe Railway	Toronto Area Transit Operating Authority	Via Rail Canada Inc.
Durham R			
Uxbridge Tp		48.99	
Ottawa-Carleton R			
Ottawa C			2,321.46
Goulbourn Tp			22.94
Rideau Tp			6.29
York R			
Whitchurch-Stouffville T		278.82	
Essex Co			
Tecumseh T			722.71
Lakeshore Tp			921.12
Rochester Tp			150.09
Tilbury North Tp			48.32
Kent Co			
Chatham-Kent C			53.59
Lanark Co			

REGULATION 392/98 **Table 7**

Municipality or territory	Tax rates for 1998 for land owned by the owner on December 31, 1997—expressed as dollars per acre		
	South Simcoe Railway	Toronto Area Transit Operating Authority	Via Rail Canada Inc.
Montague Tp			3.29
Simcoe Co			
New Tecumseth T	54.81		

TABLE 7

ASSESSED OWNERS CORRESPONDING TO CERTAIN HEADINGS IN TABLES 2 TO 6

Headings in Tables 2 to 6	Names of assessed owners
Algoma Central Railway	Algoma Central Algoma Central Railway, Inc.
Canadian National Railway	Canadian National Railway Co. Canadian National Railways CN Real Estate Management Montreal and Ottawa Railway Canadian Government Railways
Canadian Pacific Railway	CP Rail Canadian Pacific Limited Canadian Pacific Railway Company Canadian Pacific Railways Toronto Hamilton and Buffalo Railway Company Toronto Hamilton and Buffalo Railway Grand River Railway Lake Erie and Northern Railway St. Lawrence and Hudson Railway Ontario and Quebec Railway Toronto, Grey and Bruce Railway Montreal and Ottawa Railway
CASO	Caso C P Rail-Caso Conrail Consolidated Rail Corporation Canada Southern Canada Southern Railway Co.

Table 7

Headings in Tables 2 to 6	Names of assessed owners
CSX Railway	CSX St. Clair Tunnel Company The Chesapeake and Ohio Railway Company
Ontario Northland Railway	Ontario Northland Railway Nipissing Central Railway
South Simcoe Railway	South Simcoe Railway Tottenham and District Chamber of Commerce Ltd.

REGULATION 393/98
TAX MATTERS — ELIGIBLE THEATRE DEFINITION
O. Reg. 393/98

1. For the purposes of subsection 257.6(4) of the Act,

"eligible theatre" means, subject to subsection (2), land used as a theatre that contains 1,000 seats or more and that, when it is used in the taxation year, is used predominately to present live performances of drama, comedy, music or dance.

(2) The definition of "eligible theatre" in subsection (1) does not include,

(a) land used as a dinner theatre, nightclub, tavern, cocktail lounge, bar, striptease club or similar establishment; or

(b) a building that was converted to an eligible theatre unless the conversion involved modifications to the building.

REGULATION 394/98
TAX MATTERS — DEFINITION OF BUSINESS PROPERTY AND RESIDENTIAL PROPERTY
O. Reg. 394/98

1. The following classes of real property prescribed under the *Assessment Act* are prescribed for the purposes of clause (b) of the definition of "business property" in section 257.7 of the Act:

1. The office building property class.
2. The shopping centre property class.
3. The parking lots and vacant land property class.
4. The large industrial property class.

2. The new multi-residential property class prescribed under the *Assessment Act* is prescribed for the purposes of clause (b) of the definition of "residential property" in section 257.7 of the Act.

REGULATION 400/98
TAX MATTERS — TAX RATES FOR SCHOOL PURPOSES
O. Reg. 400/98, as am. O. Reg. 408/98; 438/98; 499/98; 707/98; 79/99

Residential Property

1. (1) Subject to subsection (2), 0.46 per cent of the assessed value is prescribed as the tax rate for school purposes for residential property for the purpose of section 257.7 of the Act.

(2) The tax rate for school purposes for property in the farmlands property class and the managed forests property class, as prescribed under the *Assessment Act*, is 0.115 per cent of the assessed value.

Pipeline Property Class

2. (1) This section applies with respect to property in the pipeline property class, as prescribed under the *Assessment Act*, that is in a municipality.

(2) The tax rates set out in Table 1 are prescribed as the tax rates for school purposes for the purposes of section 257.7 of the Act for the municipalities set out in Table 1 for the pipeline property class. O. Reg. 438/98, s. 1.

Business Property in Unattached Unorganized Territory

3. (1) This section applies with respect to business property that is in territory without municipal organization that is not deemed under section 56 of the Act or subsection 58.1(2) of the Act to be attached to a municipality.

(2) The tax rates set out in Table 2 are prescribed as the tax rates for school purposes for the purposes of section 257.7 of the Act for 1998 for the territories set out in Table 2 for the property classes, prescribed under the *Assessment Act*, set out in Table 2.

(3) The tax rates prescribed under subsection (2) are reduced as follows for the subclasses for vacant units and excess land prescribed under the *Assessment Act* for the commercial property class and the industrial property class:

1. The tax rate for the subclass for the commercial property class shall be reduced by 30 per cent.
2. The tax rate for the subclass for the industrial property class shall be reduced by 35 per cent.

O. Reg. 438/98, s. 2; 499/98, s. 1.

Table 1

REGULATIONS UNDER THE EDUCATION ACT

TABLE 1

O. Reg. 408/98, s. 1

TAX RATES FOR THE PIPELINE PROPERTY CLASS IN ORGANIZED TERRITORY

Municipality	Tax Rate—Expressed as a Fraction of Assessed Value
Alberton Tp	0.062012
Armour Tp	0.008822
Armstrong Tp	0.014611
Assiginack Tp	0.012224
Atikokan Tp	0.035281
Baldwin Tp	0.014073
Barrie C	0.014855
Beardmore Tp	0.008336
Belleville C	0.017704
Black River-Matheson Tp	0.012231
Blind River T	0.015832
Bonfield Tp	0.009096
Brant Co	0.022810
Brantford C	0.017356
Brethour Tp	0.035660
Brockville C	0.018169
Bruce Co	0.014273
Bruce Mines T	0.007734
Burk's Falls V	0.013177
Cache Bay T	0.005376
Caldwell Tp	0.016592
Calvin Tp	0.013086
Casimir Jennings and Appleby Tp	0.031706
Chamberlain Tp	0.014344
Chapple Tp	0.070450
Cobalt T	0.015204
Cochrane T	0.017641

REGULATION 400/98 **Table 1**

Municipality	Tax Rate—Expressed as a Fraction of Assessed Value
Coleman Tp	0.016247
Cornwall C	0.019951
Dack Tp	0.014012
Dawson Tp	0.041499
Day and Bright Additional Tp	0.019749
Dorion Tp	0.037073
Dryden T/Barclay Tp	0.018516
Dufferin Co	0.011832
Durham R	0.018213
Dymond Tp	0.012345
Ear Falls Tp	0.033943
East Ferris Tp	0.024713
Elgin Co	0.012966
Elliot Lake C	0.010017
Emo Tp	0.052512
Englehart T	0.022043
Espanola T/Merritt Tp	0.019851
Essex Co	0.022904
Evanturel Tp	0.015659
Fauquier-Strickland Tp	0.009785
Fort Frances T	0.023433
Gananoque ST	0.015028
Geraldton T	0.024124
Glackmeyer Tp	0.014490
Grey Co	0.010648
Guelph C	0.025196
Hagar Tp	0.048456
Haileybury T	0.011447
Haldimand-Norfolk R	0.020607
Halton R	0.015341

Table 1

REGULATIONS UNDER THE EDUCATION ACT

Municipality	Tax Rate—Expressed as a Fraction of Assessed Value
Hamilton-Wentworth R	0.016512
Hastings Co	0.015010
Hearst T	0.010469
Hilliard Tp	0.041021
Hudson Tp	0.008319
Huron Co	0.006334
Ignace Tp	0.013660
Iron Bridge V	0.017431
Iroquois Falls T	0.011561
Jaffray Melick T	0.015019
Johnson Tp	0.009034
Kapuskasing T	0.011303
Keewatin T	0.019864
Kenora T	0.014030
Kerns Tp	0.012386
Kingston C	0.020542
Kirkland Lake T	0.013824
La Vallee Tp	0.073849
Lambton Co	0.018201
Lanark Co	0.023074
Latchford T	0.014524
Leeds and Grenville Co	0.022591
Lennox and Addington Co	0.018761
London C	0.021806
Longlac T	0.021240
Macdonald Meredith et al Tp	0.012600
Machar Tp	0.010319
Machin Tp	0.011925
Mattawa T	0.013385
Mattawan Tp	0.028061

Table 1

REGULATION 400/98

Municipality	Tax Rate—Expressed as a Fraction of Assessed Value
Mattice-Val Cote Tp	0.006256
Middlesex Co	0.019118
Moonbeam Tp	0.015038
Morley Tp	0.072716
Municipality of Chatham-Kent	0.019955
Muskoka D	0.006717
Nairn & Hyman Tp	0.044722
Neebing Tp	0.069669
New City of Toronto	0.020294
New Liskeard T	0.012831
Niagara R	0.017524
Nipigon Tp	0.022290
North Bay C	0.014791
North Himsworth Tp	0.014820
Northeastern Manitoulin T	0.005032
Northumberland Co	0.019109
Oliver and Paipoonge Tp	0.023297
Opasatika Tp	0.007702
Orillia C	0.026367
Ottawa-Carleton R	0.019307
Owen Sound C	0.028703
Oxford Co	0.015380
Papineau-Cameron Tp	0.008269
Peel R	0.017666
Pembroke C	0.013597
Perry Tp	0.009892
Perth Co	0.022432
Peterborough C	0.016427
Peterborough Co	0.017431
Plummer Additional Tp	0.010389

Table 1

REGULATIONS UNDER THE EDUCATION ACT

Municipality	Tax Rate—Expressed as a Fraction of Assessed Value
Powassan T	0.014353
Prescott and Russell Co	0.016717
Prescott ST	0.014658
Prince Edward County C	0.006600
Quinte West C	0.018023
Rainy River T	0.029396
Ratter and Dunnet Tp	0.046088
Red Rock Tp	0.019556
Renfrew Co	0.016390
Sault Ste Marie C	0.019117
Shuniah Tp	0.036441
Simcoe Co	0.021469
Smiths Falls ST	0.018496
Smooth Rock Falls T	0.013966
South Himsworth Tp	0.013239
South River V	0.006256
Springer Tp	0.035085
St Marys ST	0.019550
St Thomas C	0.011792
Stormont, Dundas and Glengarry Co	0.016488
Stratford C	0.015397
Strong Tp	0.009397
Sturgeon Falls T	0.014582
Sudbury R	0.016137
Sundridge V	0.008047
Temagami Tp	0.014220
Thessalon T	0.008178
Thessalon Tp	0.010303
Thompson Tp	0.011678
Thunder Bay C	0.025522

REGULATION 400/98 **Table 2**

Municipality	Tax Rate—Expressed as a Fraction of Assessed Value
Timmins C	0.024840
Trout Creek T	0.015318
Val Rita-Harty Tp	0.010127
Victoria Co	0.025474
Waterloo R	0.014572
Wellington Co	0.024431
Windsor C	0.022794
York R	0.019469

TABLE 2

O. Reg. 438/98, s. 4; 707/98, s. 1; 79/99, s. 1

TAX RATES FOR BUSINESS PROPERTY IN UNATTACHED UNORGANIZED TERRITORY FOR 1998

Territory	Tax rate—expressed as a fraction of assessed value		
	Commercial Property Class	Industrial Property Class	Pipeline Property Class
Nipissing D			
Murchison Lyell Sabine Localities	0.003937	0.006648	0.000000
Timiskaming Board of Education	0.015620	0.000000	0.018386
Nipissing Combined School Boards	0.014395	0.026347	0.030798
Parry Sound D			
South River Township School Authority	0.012273	0.000000	0.000000
Magnetawan Township School Authority	0.011631	0.015393	0.000000
West Parry Sound Board of Education	0.008948	0.01656	0.000000
East Parry Sound Board of Education	0.015157	0.024196	0.015458

Table 2

REGULATIONS UNDER THE EDUCATION ACT

Territory	Tax rate—expressed as a fraction of assessed value		
	Commercial Property Class	Industrial Property Class	Pipeline Property Class
Manitoulin D			
Manitoulin Locality Education	0.011076	0.010451	0.000000
Sudbury D			
Sudbury Locality Education	0.019065	0.029054	0.024814
Espanola Locality Education	0.014744	0.008746	0.000000
Chapleau Locality Education	0.009968	0.014017	0.000000
Foleyet DSA Locality Education	0.011736	0.000000	0.000000
Gogama DSA Locality Education	0.008466	0.000000	0.000000
Asquith, Garvey DSA Locality Education	0.005257	0.011265	0.000000
Missarenda DSA Locality Education	0.007511	0.003471	0.000000
Timiskaming D			
Kirkland Lake Locality Education	0.025707	0.047797	0.020697
Timiskaming Locality Education	0.028122	0.036440	0.020063
Cochrane D			
Hearst Locality Education	0.011789	0.009736	0.007567
Kapuskasing SRF and Dist Locality Education	0.017465	0.003966	0.009969
Cochrane-Iroquois Locality Education	0.015712	0.020675	0.010310
Moosonee Dev Area Bd	0.005531	0.009842	0.000000
James Bay Lowlands Education Locality	0.031087	0.000000	0.000000

Table 2

Territory	Commercial Property Class	Industrial Property Class	Pipeline Property Class
Algoma D			
Sault Ste. Marie Locality Education	0.025144	0.02758	0.000000
Central Algoma Locality Education	0.017267	0.015304	0.011737
Michipicoten Locality Education	0.020247	0.026656	0.000000
North Shore Locality Education	0.032324	0.020308	0.016003
Thunder Bay D			
Collins DSA Locality Education	0.000000	0.000000	0.000000
Allanwater DSA Locality Education	0.006295	0.000000	0.000000
Geraldton DSA Locality Education	0.012571	0.015097	0.006327
Nipigon Red Rock Locality Education	0.005036	0.002692	0.021993
Lake Superior Locality Education	0.032354	0.032866	0.000000
Lakehead Locality Education	0.019668	0.040276	0.032870
Auden DSA Locality Education	0.006531	0.000000	0.000000
Ferland DSA Locality Education	0.000000	0.000000	0.000000
Armstrong DSA Locality Education	0.007366	0.000000	0.000000
Caramat DSA Locality Education	0.012659	0.000000	0.000000
Kashabowie DSA Locality Education	0.006439	0.000000	0.000000

Tax rate—expressed as a fraction of assessed value

Table 2

REGULATIONS UNDER THE EDUCATION ACT

Territory	Tax rate—expressed as a fraction of assessed value		
	Commercial Property Class	Industrial Property Class	Pipeline Property Class
Kilkenny DSA Locality Education	0.007474	0.000000	0.008572
Savant Lake DSA Locality Education	0.008467	0.000000	0.000000
Upsala DSA Locality Education	0.008257	0.00545	0.003984
Rainy River D			
Fort Frances/Rainy River Education Locality (assessment roll numbers beginning with "5902")	0.013169	0.01653	0.000000
Fort Frances/Rainy River Education Locality (assessment roll numbers beginning with "5903")	0.010762	0.009895	0.000000
Mine Centre DSA Locality Education	0.007418	0.003614	0.000000
Atikokan Locality Education	0.022309	0.033698	0.098442
Kenora D			
Slate Falls DSA	0.000000	0.000000	0.000000
Summer Beaver DSA Locality Education	0.010737	0.000000	0.000000
Kenora Locality Education	0.019073	0.016259	0.026538
Dryden Locality Education (assessment roll numbers beginning with "6060")	0.013218	0.016999	0.022020
Dryden Locality Education (assessment roll numbers beginning with "6091")	0.000000	0.000000	0.020106

Table 2

REGULATION 400/98

Territory	Tax rate—expressed as a fraction of assessed value		
	Commercial Property Class	Industrial Property Class	Pipeline Property Class
Dryden Locality Education (assessment roll numbers beginning with "6093")	0.016090	0.000000	0.019561
Red Lake Locality Education	0.012638	0.035416	0.023720
Dryden Locality Education (assessment roll numbers beginning with "6096")	0.013572	0.012853	0.023870
Sturgeon Lake Locality Education	0.06472	0.000000	0.000000

REGULATION 444/98
DISPOSITION OF SURPLUS REAL PROPERTY
O. Reg. 444/98, as am. O. Reg. 57/99

PART I

DISPOSITION FOR MUNICIPAL HARD SERVICES

1. (1) Subject to subsection (3), a board that has adopted a resolution under clause 194(3)(a) of the Act that real property is not required for the purposes of the board may sell, lease or otherwise dispose of the property to a person referred to in subsection (2) if the purpose of that person in acquiring the property is to provide one or more of the services described in paragraphs 1 to 7 of subsection 5(5) of the *Development Charges Act, 1997*.

(2) The persons referred to in subsection (1) are:
1. The municipality in which the property is located.
2. Any local board of the municipality in which the property is located.
3. If the property is located in a county, in a regional municipality or in The District Municipality of Muskoka, that county, that regional municipality or The District Municipality of Muskoka, as the case may be.
4. If the property is located in a county, in a regional municipality or in The District Municipality of Muskoka, any local board of that county, of that regional municipality or of The District Municipality of Muskoka, as the case may be.

(3) A sale, lease of other disposition under this section must be at fair market value.

PART II

OTHER DISPOSITIONS

Application

2. (1) This Part applies if,

(a) a board proposes to sell, lease or otherwise dispose of real property;
(b) the board has adopted a resolution under clause 194(3)(a) of the Act that the property is not required for the purposes of the board; and
(c) the sale, lease or other disposition is not permitted under section 1.

(2) If this Part applies, a board shall not sell, lease or otherwise dispose of property except after issuing a proposal in accordance with section 3 or 4, as the case may be, and except in accordance with this Part.

(3) For the purposes of this Part, a building is considered to be last used for providing pupil accommodation even if, since it was last so used, it was used by the board primarily for storage or maintenance purposes.

Bodies to Receive Proposals from District School Boards

3. (1) An English-language public district school board shall issue a proposal to sell, lease or otherwise dispose of the real property to each of the following bodies on the same day:

1. The French-language public district school board the area of jurisdiction of which includes the property.
2. The English-language separate district school board or Roman Catholic school authority the area of jurisdiction of which includes the property.
3. The French-language separate district school board the area of jurisdiction of which includes the property.
4. The board of a Protestant separate school the area of jurisdiction of which includes the property.
5. The English language college, within the meaning of Regulation 771 of the Revised Regulations of Ontario, 1990, for the area in which the property is located.
6. The French language college, within the meaning of Regulation 771 of the Revised Regulations of Ontario, 1990, for the area in which the property is located.
7. The university named in the Schedule the head office of which is nearest to the property.
8. The municipality in which the property is located.
9. If the property is located in a regional municipality, in The District Municipality of Muskoka or in the County of Oxford, that regional municipality, The District Municipality of Muskoka or the County of Oxford, as the case may be.
10. If the property is located in the geographical area within which a local services board may exercise its jurisdiction, the local services board.
11. The Crown in right of Ontario.
12. The Crown in right of Canada.

(2) A French-language public district school board shall issue a proposal to sell, lease or otherwise dispose of the real property to each of the following bodies on the same day:

1. The English-language public district school board the area of jurisdiction of which includes the property.
2. The French-language separate district school board or Roman Catholic school authority the area of jurisdiction of which includes the property.
3. The English-language separate district school board the area of jurisdiction of which includes the property.
4. The board of a Protestant separate school the area of jurisdiction of which includes the property.
5. The French language college, within the meaning of Regulation 771 of the Revised Regulations of Ontario, 1990, for the area in which the property is located.
6. The English language college, within the meaning of Regulation 771 of the Revised Regulations of Ontario, 1990, for the area in which the property is located.
7. The university named in the Schedule the head office of which is nearest to the property.
8. The municipality in which the property is located.

9. If the property is located in a regional municipality, in The District Municipality of Muskoka or in the County of Oxford, that regional municipality, The District Municipality of Muskoka or the County of Oxford, as the case may be.
10. If the property is located in the geographical area within which a local services board may exercise its jurisdiction, the local services board.
11. The Crown in right of Ontario.
12. The Crown in right of Canada.

(3) An English-language separate district school board shall issue a proposal to sell, lease or otherwise dispose of the real property to each of the following bodies on the same day:

1. The French-language separate district school board the area of jurisdiction of which includes the property.
2. The English-language public district school board or the board of district school area the area of jurisdiction of which includes the property.
3. The French-language public district school board the area of jurisdiction of which includes the property.
4. The board of a Protestant separate school the area of jurisdiction of which includes the property.
5. The English language college, within the meaning of Regulation 771 of the Revised Regulations of Ontario, 1990, for the area in which the property is located.
6. The French language college, within the meaning of Regulation 771 of the Revised Regulations of Ontario, 1990, for the area in which the property is located.
7. The university named in the Schedule the head office of which is nearest to the property.
8. The municipality in which the property is located.
9. If the property is located in a regional municipality, in The District Municipality of Muskoka or in the County of Oxford, that regional municipality, The District Municipality of Muskoka or the County of Oxford, as the case may be.
10. If the property is located in the geographical area within which a local services board may exercise its jurisdiction, the local services board.
11. The Crown in right of Ontario.
12. The Crown in right of Canada.

(4) A French-language separate district school board shall issue a proposal to sell, lease or otherwise dispose of the real property to each of the following bodies on the same day:

1. The English-language separate district school board the area of jurisdiction of which includes the property.
2. The French-language public district school board or the board of a district school area the area of jurisdiction of which includes the property.
3. The English-language public district school board the area of jurisdiction of which includes the property.
4. The board of a Protestant separate school the area of jurisdiction of which includes the property.
5. The French language college, within the meaning of Regulation 771 of the Revised Regulations of Ontario, 1990, for the area in which the property is located.

6. The English language college, within the meaning of Regulation 771 of the Revised Regulations of Ontario, 1990, for the area in which the property is located.
7. The university named in the Schedule the head office of which is nearest to the property.
8. The municipality in which the property is located.
9. If the property is located in a regional municipality, in The District Municipality of Muskoka or in the County of Oxford, that regional municipality, The District Municipality of Muskoka or the County of Oxford, as the case may be.
10. If the property is located in the geographical area within which a local services board may exercise its jurisdiction, the local services board.
11. The Crown in right of Ontario.
12. The Crown in right of Canada.

(5) If a district school board issues a proposal to the bodies mentioned in subsection (1), (2), (3) or (4), the board may, on the same day, issue the proposal to the Ontario Realty Corporation continued under the *Capital Investment Plan Act, 1993*.

(6) A body mentioned in paragraph 8 or 9 of subsection (1), (2), (3) or (4) to which a proposal is issued may refer the proposal to any of its local boards, not including a school board.

(7) The Crown in right of Ontario may refer the proposal to any agency, board or commission of the Crown in right of Ontario.

(8) The Crown in right of Canada may refer the proposal to any agency, board or commission of the Crown in right of Canada. O. Reg. 57/99, s. 1.

Bodies to Receive Proposals from School Authorities

4. (1) A board of a district school area shall issue a proposal to sell, lease or otherwise dispose of the real property to each of the following bodies on the same day:

1. A board of a secondary school district established under section 67 of the Act the area of jurisdiction of which includes the property.
2. The English-language separate district school board or Roman Catholic school authority the area of jurisdiction of which includes the property.
3. The French-language separate district school board the area of jurisdiction of which includes the property.
4. The English language college, within the meaning of Regulation 771 of the Revised Regulations of Ontario, 1990, for the area in which the property is located.
5. The French language college, within the meaning of Regulation 771 of the Revised Regulations of Ontario, 1990, for the area in which the property is located.
6. The university named in the Schedule the head office of which is nearest to the property.
7. The municipality in which the property is located.
8. If the property is located in a regional municipality, in The District Municipality of Muskoka, in the County of Oxford or in the Moosonee Development Area, that

regional municipality, The District Municipality of Muskoka, the County of Oxford or the Moosonee Development Area Board, as the case may be.
9. If the property is located in the geographical area within which a local services board may exercise its jurisdiction, the local services board.
10. The Crown in right of Ontario.
11. The Crown in right of Canada.

(2) A board of a secondary school district established under section 67 of the Act shall issue a proposal to sell, lease or otherwise dispose of the real property to each of the following bodies on the same day:

1. A board of a district school area the area of jurisdiction of which includes the property.
2. The Roman Catholic school authority the area of jurisdiction of which includes the property.
3. The English language college, within the meaning of Regulation 771 of the Revised Regulations of Ontario, 1990, for the area in which the property is located.
4. The French language college, within the meaning of Regulation 771 of the Revised Regulations of Ontario, 1990, for the area in which the property is located.
5. The university named in the Schedule the head office of which is nearest to the property.
6. The Moosonee Development Area Board.
7. If the property is located in the geographical area within which a local services board may exercise its jurisdiction, the local services board.
8. The Crown in right of Ontario.
9. The Crown in right of Canada.

(3) A Roman Catholic school authority shall issue a proposal to sell, lease or otherwise dispose of the real property to each of the following bodies on the same day:

1. A board of a secondary school district established under section 67 of the Act the area of jurisdiction of which includes the property.
2. The English-language public district school board or the board of a district school area the area of jurisdiction of which includes the property.
3. The French-language public district school board the area of jurisdiction of which includes the property.
4. The English language college, within the meaning of Regulation 771 of the Revised Regulations of Ontario, 1990, for the area in which the property is located.
5. The French language college, within the meaning of Regulation 771 of the Revised Regulations of Ontario, 1990, for the area in which the property is located.
6. The university named in the Schedule the head office of which is nearest to the property.
7. The municipality in which the property is located.
8. If the property is located in a regional municipality, in The District Municipality of Muskoka, in the County of Oxford or in the Moosonee Development Area, that regional municipality, The District Municipality of Muskoka, the County of Oxford or the Moosonee Development Area Board, as the case may be.
9. If the property is located in the geographical area within which a local services board may exercise its jurisdiction, the local services board.

10. The Crown in right of Ontario.
11. The Crown in right of Canada.

(4) A board of a Protestant separate school shall issue a proposal to sell, lease or otherwise dispose of the real property to each of the following bodies on the same day:
1. The English-language public district school board the area of jurisdiction of which includes the property.
2. The French-language public district school board the area of jurisdiction of which includes the property.
3. The English-language separate district school board the area of jurisdiction of which includes the property.
4. The French-language separate district school board the area of jurisdiction of which includes the property.
5. The English language college, within the meaning of Regulation 771 of the Revised Regulations of Ontario, 1990, for the area in which the property is located.
6. The French language college, within the meaning of Regulation 771 of the Revised Regulations of Ontario, 1990, for the area in which the property is located.
7. The university named in the Schedule the head office of which is nearest to the property.
8. The municipality in which the property is located.
9. The Crown in right of Ontario.
10. The Crown in right of Canada.

(5) If a school authority issues a proposal to the bodies mentioned in subsection (1), (2), (3) or (4), the school authority may, on the same day, issue the proposal to the Ontario Realty Corporation continued under the *Capital Investment Plan Act, 1993*.

(6) A body mentioned in paragraph 7 or 8 of subsection (1), paragraph 6 of subsection (2), paragraph 7 or 8 of subsection (3) or paragraph 8 of subsection (4) to which a proposal is issued may refer the proposal to any of its local boards, not including a school board.

(7) The Crown in right of Ontario may refer the proposal to any agency, board or commission of the Crown in right of Ontario.

(8) The Crown in right of Canada may refer the proposal to any agency, board or commission of the Crown in right of Canada. O. Reg. 57/99, s. 2.

Proposals for Lease

5. A proposal for lease issued under section 3 or 4 must specify the term of the lease of the property.

Offers

6. A body to which a board issued a proposal under section 3 or 4 or to which a proposal was referred under section 3 or 4 may make an offer to the board in response to the proposal.

7. Except as otherwise provided in sections 8 and 9, an offer under section 6 must be for sale, lease or other disposition of the property at fair market value.

8. (1) This section applies to an offer under section 6 for the sale or lease of property on which there is a building that is used or was last used for providing pupil accommodation, if,
  (a) the body making the offer is a board; or
  (b) the purpose of the body making the offer is to acquire the property in order to use the building to accommodate pupils in,
    (i) an elementary school program or program leading to a secondary school diploma in a school established or continued under section 13 of the Act, or
    (ii) an education program that, under the legislative grant regulations made under subsection 234(1) of the Act, would be considered in determining a board's programs in facilities amount.

(2) Subject to section 9, an offer to which this section applies must be for sale or lease at the lesser of fair market value and,
  (a) in the case of property on which there is a building that is used or was last used for providing accommodation for elementary school pupils, an amount calculated in accordance with subsection (3); or
  (b) in the case of property on which there is a building that is used or was last used for providing accommodation for secondary school pupils, an amount calculated in accordance with subsection (4).

(3) The amount referred to in clause (2)(a) shall be calculated as follows:
1. Determine the elementary capacity of the property by applying the most recent loadings determined by the Minister for the purpose of pupil accommodation allocations under the legislative grant regulations made under subsection 234(1) of the Act to those spaces in the property that are used or were last used for providing accommodation for elementary school pupils.
2. Multiply the capacity determined under paragraph 1 by 9.29 square metres.
3. Multiply the product obtained under paragraph 2 by,
    i. $1,259 per square metre, in the case of a proposal for sale, or
    ii. $118.40 per square metre, in the case of a proposal for lease.

(4) The amount referred to in clause (2)(b) shall be calculated as follows:
1. Determine the secondary capacity of the property, by applying the most recent loadings determined by the Minister for the purpose of the pupil accommodation allocations under the legislative grant regulations made under subsection 234(1) of the Act to those spaces in the property that are used or were last used for providing accommodation for secondary school pupils.
2. Multiply the capacity determined under paragraph 1 by 12.07 square metres.
3. Multiply the product obtained under paragraph 2 by,
    i. $1,356 per square metre, in the case of a proposal for sale, or
    ii. $129.17 per square metre, in the case of a proposal for lease.

9. This section applies to an offer under section 6 for the sale of property on which there is a building that is used or was last used for providing pupil accommodation, if,
  (a) the offer is made by a board and the proposal in respect of which the offer is made was issued under section 3 or 4; or

(b) the offer is made by the Ontario Realty Corporation and the proposal in respect of which the offer is made was issued under subsection 3(5) or 4(5),

(2) An offer to which this section applies may, if the proposal in respect of which the offer is made so provides, be for sale at no cost. O. Reg. 57/99, s. 3.

Acceptance of Offers

10. (1) A board shall not accept any offer to purchase, lease or otherwise acquire property in respect of which a proposal must be issued under section 3 or 4 before the expiration of 90 days after the day on which the board issued the proposal.

(2) At the expiration of the 90-day period referred to in subsection (1), the only offer that the board may accept, subject to subsections (3) and (4), is an offer that,

(a) complies with section 7, 8 or 9, as the case may be; and
(b) is made by the body that, in accordance with subsection (5), has the highest priority among the bodies that made offers.

(3) If the body that, in accordance with subsection (5), has the highest priority among the bodies that made offers and the board disagree on the fair market value of the property,

(a) they shall attempt, within 30 days of the 90-day period referred to in subsection (1), to negotiate the fair market value and the body shall amend its offer to reflect the agreed value;
(b) if they cannot agree under clause (a) on the fair market value, the body making the offer may, at or before the termination of the 30-day period referred to in clause (a),
   (i) withdraw its offer, or
   (ii) elect to have the fair market value determined through binding arbitration and shall amend its offer according to the fair market value determined by the arbitrator; and
(c) if no price is agreed to under clause (a) at the termination of the 30-day period referred to in clause (a) or the body withdraws its offer or does not elect binding arbitration under clause (b), the board may consider instead the offer made by the body that, in accordance with subsection (5), has the next highest priority and whose offer complies with clause (2)(a).

(4) Subsection (3) applies to each subsequent offer that the board considers under clause (3)(c) except that the reference to the 90-day period shall be read as the day on which the board acts under clause (3)(c).

(5) For the purposes of this section, priorities shall be determined in accordance with the following rules:

1. A body mentioned in a paragraph of subsection 3(1), (2), (3) or (4) or 4(1), (2), (3) or (4) has a higher priority than a body mentioned in a subsequent paragraph.
2. For the purpose of a proposal issued under subsection 3(5) or 4(5), the Ontario Realty Corporation has a lower priority than a board and a higher priority than a body that is not a board.
3. A body that receives a referral from another body under subsection 3(6), (7) or (8)

or 4(6), (7) or (8) shall be deemed to have the same priority as the body that made the referral.

4. If offers are made by two or more bodies that, under paragraph 3, have the same priority, priorities among those bodies shall be determined by the body that referred the proposal to them.

11. (1) An agreement for the sale or lease of real property to which section 8 applies shall include a condition that if the body making the offer does not use the property to provide accommodation for pupils eligible to be included in the calculation of legislative grants for new pupil places for any period of 12 consecutive months within the 25 years after the sale or the commencement of the lease,

(a) in the case of a sale, the body shall offer the property for sale to the board from which it purchased the site or part at the price the board from which it was purchased sold it to the body, within the time specified in the agreement; and

(b) in the case of a lease, the lease is terminated on the day specified in the agreement.

(2) An offer for the sale of property under clause (1)(a) or the resulting sale, or the termination of a lease under clause (1)(b), is not a closing of the school.

(3) This section applies only where the calculated amount referred to in subsection 8(2) is less than the fair market value of the property at the time of the issuance of the proposal.

Disposition to Others after Proposal Process

12. (1) If a board does not receive an offer from a body to which a proposal is issued or referred under section 3 or 4 before the expiration of the 90-day period referred to in subsection 10(1) that complies with section 7, 8 or 9, as the case may be, the board may, subject to subsections (2) and (3), sell, lease or otherwise dispose of the property at fair market value to any other body or to any person.

(2) If the proposal referred to in subsection (1) is only for the lease of property, the board that issued the proposal may, under subsection (1), lease but not sell or otherwise dispose of the property, and the lease shall be for the term specified in the proposal.

(3) A board shall not sell, lease or otherwise dispose of property under subsection (1) unless it provides written evidence satisfactory to the Minister that,

(a) it first issued a proposal of the sale or lease of the property to each body to which a proposal must be issued under section 3 or 4, as the case may be; and

(b) no offer was received by the board from a body to which the proposal was issued or referred under section 3 or 4 before the expiration of the 90-day period referred to in subsection 10(1) that complies with section 7, 8 or 9, as the case may be.

(4) For the purposes of subsections (1) and (3), the reference to compliance with section 7, 8 or 9 means as determined under subsections 10(3) and (4) if those provisions were applied in the case of the offer.

Miscellaneous

13. If a board does not sell, lease or otherwise dispose of real property in respect of which a proposal must be issued under section 3 or 4 within three years of the expiration of the 90-day period referred to in subsection 10(1) and the board wishes to sell, lease or otherwise dispose of the property, the board shall issue another proposal under section 3 or 4, as the case may be.

Schedule/Annexe

Brock University
Carleton University
Lakehead University
Laurentian University of Sudbury/Université Laurentienne de Sudbury
McMaster University
Nipissing University
Ontario College of Art
Queen's University at Kingston
Ryerson Polytechnic University
The University of Western Ontario
Trent University
University of Guelph
University of Ottawa/Université d'Ottawa
University of Toronto
University of Waterloo
University of Windsor
Wilfrid Laurier University
York University

REGULATION 446/98
RESERVE FUNDS
O. Reg. 446/98

Pupil Accommodation Allocation Reserve Fund

1. Every district school board shall allocate all pupil accommodation allocations received under the legislative grant regulations made under subsection 234(1) of the Act, except for allocations for school operations, to a reserve fund established only for the purposes of acquiring, by purchase, lease or otherwise,

(a) school sites that are acquired as part of transactions under which the board also acquires school buildings on the school sites;

(b) school buildings or fixtures of school buildings, and additions, alterations, renovations or major repairs to school buildings or fixtures of school buildings;

(c) furniture or equipment to be used in school buildings;

(d) library materials for the initial equipping of libraries in school buildings; and

(e) water supplies or electrical power supplies on school properties or the means of conveying water or electrical power to school properties from outside the properties.

Proceeds of Dispositions Reserve Fund

2. (1) Subject to subsection (3), every district school board shall allocate all proceeds of sales, leases and other dispositions of real property to a reserve fund established only for the purposes of,

(a) acquiring, by purchase, lease or otherwise,
   (i) school sites that provide or are capable of providing pupil accommodation, and additions or improvements to such school sites,
   (ii) school buildings or fixtures of school buildings, and additions, alterations, renovations or major repairs to school buildings or fixtures of school buildings,
   (iii) furniture and equipment to be used in school buildings,
   (iv) library materials for the initial equipping of libraries in school buildings, and
   (v) water supplies or electrical power supplies on school properties or the means of conveying water or electrical power to school properties from outside the properties; and

(b) subject to subsections (3) to (6), acquiring, by purchase, lease or otherwise, real property to be used by the board for board administration purposes, and additions, alterations, renovations or major repairs to real property used by the board for those purposes.

(2) Subject to subsection (3), every district school board shall allocate all proceeds of property insurance on property of a kind referred to in clause (1)(a), whether or not the property was acquired with money from a reserve fund referred to in subsection (1), to a reserve fund established only for the purposes referred to in subsection (1).

(3) Subsections (1) and (2) do not apply to,

(a) proceeds that are required by section 3 to be allocated to an education development charge account or education development charge reserve fund;

(b) proceeds that the board is required to pay to another board pursuant to an agreement approved by the Education Improvement Commission; or

(c) proceeds that the board is required to pay to the Crown in right of Canada pursuant to an agreement under subsection 188(3) of the Act.

(4) The amount that a district school board may use from the reserve fund referred to in subsection (1) for the purpose described in clause (1)(b) shall not exceed the total of the board's net proceeds from sales, leases and other dispositions of real property that, immediately before January 1, 1998, included buildings that were used by an old board for board administration purposes.

(5) Subject to subsection (6), for the purpose of subsection (4), the net proceeds from a sale, lease or other disposition is equal to the proceeds from the sale, lease or other disposition, less the following amounts:

1. Expenses incurred for commissions, legal fees, appraisal fees, registration fees, and adjustments to tax and utility accounts in respect of the sale, lease or other disposition.

2. Any amount applied under subsection 9(7) of Ontario Regulation 466/97 in respect of the sale, lease or other disposition.

(6) For the purpose of subsection (4), if more than two hectares of land are included in property that is sold, leased or otherwise disposed of, the net proceeds from the sale, lease or other disposition shall be determined in accordance with the following formula:

$$A \times (B \div C)$$

where,

A = the net proceeds from the sale, lease or other disposition, determined in accordance with subsection (5),

B = the fair market value, at the time of the sale, lease or other disposition, of a part of the property, not exceeding two hectares in area, that includes,

    i. the land on which the buildings used by the old board for board administration purposes were situated, and

    ii. any other part of the property that was required to permit those buildings to be used by the old board for board administration purposes,

C = the fair market value, at the time of the sale, lease or other disposition, of all the property.

(7) A district school board shall not use funds from the reserve fund referred to in subsection (1) for the purpose described in clause (1)(b) unless the following requirements have been met:

1. The board must publish the following in a newspaper that, in the opinion of the secretary of the board, is of general circulation in the board's area of jurisdiction:

    i. Notice of the board's proposal to withdraw funds from the reserve fund for the purpose described in clause (1)(b).

    ii. Sufficient information to permit the board's supporters to understand generally the board's reasons for the proposed withdrawal of funds, but excluding infor-

mation that, in the opinion of the board, would prejudice the board's position in negotiations for the proposed acquisition.
 iii. Sufficient information to permit the board's supporters to understand generally the board's plans respecting use of the funds, but excluding information that, in the opinion of the board, would prejudice the board's position in negotiations for the proposed acquisition.
 iv. Notice of the time and place of a meeting of the board's supporters at which the board's proposal will be discussed.
 v. Notice that the board's supporters will be given the opportunity to make representations at the meeting.

2. The board must hold the meeting referred to in subparagraph iv of paragraph 1 on a day that is at least 21 days after the requirements of paragraph 1 have been met and must provide the opportunity to make representations referred to in subparagraph v of paragraph 1.
3. Within the period that begins three months after the meeting referred to in subparagraph iv of paragraph 1 and ends one year after that meeting, the board must pass a resolution that,
 i. is consistent with the notices and information provided under paragraph 1, and
 ii. directs the withdrawal of funds from the reserve fund referred to in subsection (1) and the use of those funds for the purpose described in clause (1)(b).

Education Development Charge Reserve Funds

3. If a district school board sells, leases or otherwise disposes of real property that was acquired, in whole or in part, by the board or by another person, with funds withdrawn from an education development charges account or education development charge reserve fund, and the property was not used to provide accommodation for pupils, the board shall allocate the net proceeds (as described under subsection 2(5)) of the sale, lease or other disposition, up to the amount withdrawn for the property's acquisition, in accordance with the following rules:

1. If the board has an education development charge by-law that applies to the area in which the property is located, the proceeds shall be allocated to the education development charge accounts or education development charge reserve fund established in respect of that by-law.
2. If paragraph 1 does not apply but the board has an education development charge reserve fund established under subsection 23(4) of Ontario Regulation 20/98 from which money may be used to acquire land or an interest in land in the area in which the property is located, the proceeds shall be allocated to that reserve fund.
3. If paragraphs 1 and 2 do not apply but the board has one or more education development charge accounts or education development charge reserve funds from which money may be used to acquire land or an interest in land in any part of the region prescribed under clause 257.101(d) of the Act in which the property is located, the proceeds shall be allocated to those accounts or reserve funds.
4. If paragraphs 1, 2 and 3 do not apply, the proceeds shall be allocated to the education development charge reserve fund established under section 16.1 of Ontario Regulation 20/98.

Special Education Reserve Fund

4. (1) If a district school board's expenditures on special education for its pupils in a fiscal year, other than the board's expenditures on programs in facilities in that year, are less than the result obtained by subtracting the programs in facilities amount determined for the board for that year under the legislative grant regulations made under subsection 234(1) of the Act from the special education allocation determined for the board for that year under those regulations, the board shall allocate the difference to a reserve fund established only for the purpose of funding special education programs provided by the board, other than programs in facilities.

(2) In this section,

"programs in facilities" means, in respect of a board, education programs that are considered in determining the programs in facilities amount for the board under the legislative grant regulations made under subsection 234(1) of the Act.

REGULATION 470/98
SCHOOL ATTENDANCE RIGHTS—RESIDENT BUSINESS PROPERTY OWNERS AND TENANTS
O. Reg. 470/98

1. Subject to section 46 of the Act, a person described in subsection 43.2(1) of the Act who attains the age of six years in any year and whose parent or guardian referred to in that subsection is Roman Catholic is, after September 1 in that year, qualified to be a resident pupil in respect of the separate school zone of the English-language separate district school board or the Roman Catholic school authority for elementary school purposes in which the property referred to in that subsection is situate, until the last school day in June in the year in which the person attains the age of 21 years.

2. Subject to section 46 of the Act, a person described in subsection 43.2(1) of the Act who is a French-speaking person, who attains the age of six years in any year and whose parent or guardian referred to in that subsection is Roman Catholic is, after September 1 in that year, qualified to be a resident pupil in respect of the separate school zone of the French-language separate district school board for elementary school purposes in which the property referred to in that subsection is situate, until the last school day in June in the year in which the person attains the age of 21 years.

3. Section 1 applies with necessary modifications in relation to a Protestant separate school board.

4. Subject to section 46 of the Act, a person described in subsection 43.2(1) of the Act whose parent or guardian referred to in that subsection is Roman Catholic is qualified to be a resident pupil in respect of the separate school zone of the English-language separate district school board for secondary school purposes in which the property referred to in that subsection is situate.

5. Subject to section 46 of the Act, a person described in subsection 43.2(1) of the Act who is a French-speaking person and whose parent or guardian referred to in that subsection is Roman Catholic is qualified to be a resident pupil in respect of the separate school zone of the French-language separate district school board for secondary school purposes in which the property referred to in that subsection is situate.

REGULATION 471/98
SCHOOL ATTENDANCE RIGHTS—NON-RESIDENT BUSINESS PROPERTY OWNERS
O. Reg. 471/98

1. In this Regulation,

"assessment limit", in respect of a board, means the amount calculated dividing the day school average daily enrolment for the board calculated under section 2 of Ontario Regulation 286/98 into the sum of,

(a) the assessment of residential property taxable for the board's purposes, according to the last assessment roll, and

(b) the board's share of assessment of business property, according to the last assessment roll, for each municipality and for territory without municipal organization in each common jurisdictional area as determined by applying the enrolment proportions calculated by the Minister under subsection 257.8(3) of the Act.

2. This Regulation does not apply with respect to residential property that is assessed under the multi-residential property class.

3. (1) A person who attains the age of six years in any year is, after September 1 in that year, qualified to be a resident pupil in respect of a school section of an English-language public district school board or of a public school authority until the last school day in June in the year in which the person attains the age of 21 years if the person does not reside in that school section but the person or the person's parent or guardian,

(a) owns business property in the school section that is assessed for an amount that is not less than the board's assessment limit and is an English-language public board supporter in the school section where he or she resides; or

(b) owns residential property in the school section that is assessed for an amount that is not less than that board's assessment limit and is an English-language public board supporter in that school section.

(2) A person is qualified to be a resident pupil in respect of a secondary school district of an English-language public district school board or of a public school authority if the person does not reside in that secondary school district but the person or the person's parent or guardian,

(a) owns business property in the secondary school district that is assessed for an amount that is not less than that board's assessment limit and is an English-language public board supporter in the secondary school district where he or she resides; or

(b) owns residential property in the secondary school district that is assessed for an amount that is not less than that board's assessment limit and is an English-language public board supporter in that secondary school district.

4. (1) A person who attains the age of six years in any year is, after September 1 in that year, qualified to be a resident pupil in respect of a school section of a French-language public district school board until the last school day in June in the year in which the person attains the age of 21 years if the person does not reside in that school section but the person or the person's parent or guardian,

(a) owns business property in the school section that is assessed for an amount that is not less than that board's assessment limit and is a French-language public district school board supporter in the school section where he or she resides; or

(b) owns residential property in the school section that is assessed for an amount that is not less than that board's assessment limit and is a French-language public district school board supporter in that school section.

(2) A person is qualified to be a resident pupil in respect of a secondary school district of a French-language public district school board if the person does not reside in that secondary school district but the person or the person's parent or guardian,

(a) owns business property in the secondary school district that is assessed for an amount that is not less than that board's assessment limit and is a French-language public district school board supporter in the secondary school district where he or she resides; or

(b) owns residential property in the secondary school district that is assessed for an amount that is not less than that board's assessment limit and is a French-language public district school board supporter in that secondary school district.

5. (1) A person who attains the age of six years in any year is, after September 1 in that year, qualified to be a resident pupil in respect of a separate school zone of an English-language separate district school board or of a Roman Catholic school authority for elementary school purposes until the last school day in June in the year in which the person attains the age of 21 years if the person does not reside in that separate school zone but the person or the person's parent or guardian,

(a) owns business property in the separate school zone that is assessed for an amount that is not less than that board's assessment limit and is an English-language Roman Catholic board supporter in the separate school zone where he or she resides; or

(b) owns residential property in the separate school zone that is assessed for an amount that is not less than that board's assessment limit and is an English-language Roman Catholic board supporter in that separate school zone.

(2) A person is qualified to be a resident pupil in respect of a separate school zone of an English-language separate district school board for secondary school purposes if the person does not reside in that separate school zone but the person or the person's parent or guardian,

(a) owns business property in the separate school zone that is assessed for an amount that is not less than that board's assessment limit and is an English-language Roman Catholic board supporter in the separate school zone where he or she resides; or

(b) owns residential property in the separate school zone that is assessed for an amount that is not less than that board's assessment limit and is an English-language Roman Catholic board supporter in that separate school zone.

(3) Subsection (1), excluding clause (a), applies with necessary modifications to attendance rights in respect of a Protestant separate school board.

6. (1) A person who attains the age of six years in any year is, after September 1 in that year, qualified to be a resident pupil in respect of a separate school zone of a French-language separate district school board for elementary school purposes until the last school day in June in the year in which the person attains the age of 21 years if the person does not reside in that separate school zone but the person or the person's parent or guardian,

(a) owns business property in the separate school zone that is assessed for an amount that is not less than that board's assessment limit and is a French-language separate district school board supporter in the separate school zone where he or she resides; or

(b) owns residential property in the separate school zone that is assessed for an amount that is not less than that board's assessment limit and is a French-language separate district school board supporter in that separate school zone.

(2) A person is qualified to be a resident pupil in respect of a separate school zone of a French-language separate district school board for secondary school purposes if the person does not reside in that separate school zone but the person or the person's parent or guardian,

(a) owns business property in the separate school zone that is assessed for an amount that is not less than that board's assessment limit and is a French-language separate district school board supporter in the separate school zone where he or she resides; or

(b) owns residential property in the separate school zone that is assessed for an amount that is not less than that board's assessment limit and is a French-language separate district school board supporter in that separate school zone.

7. This Regulation comes into force on September 1, 1998.

REGULATION 472/98
DEBT AND FINANCIAL OBLIGATION LIMITS
O. Reg. 472/98

1. The debt and financial obligations and liability limits for a district school board for its fiscal year shall be determined under this Regulation using the formula described in section 3.

2. The limits, as updated under section 4, shall be used by a district school board to determine whether the approval of the Minister is required in respect of the following debts or financial obligations:

1. Long-term debt assumed by the board for which repayment will be required beyond the term for which the members of the board were elected.
2. Other financial commitments, liabilities and contractual obligations for which payment will be required beyond the term for which the members of the board were elected, including lease agreements.

3. The debt and financial obligation and liability limits shall be determined as follows:

1. Estimate the revenue fund expenditures of the board for its fiscal year.
2. Multiply the amount obtained in paragraph 1 by 10 per cent.
3. Subtract from the amount obtained in paragraph 2 all of the payments for its fiscal year in respect of the long-term debt and the other financial commitments, liabilities and contractual obligations of the board described in paragraphs 1 and 2 of section 2 other than the payments of principal and interest for that fiscal year on debentures and long-term debts of which the Minister has agreed to pay the board the amount of the yearly principal and interest payments.

4. (1) Before authorizing any specific work or class of work that would require the incurring of a long-term debt or financial obligation described in section 2, the district school board shall have its treasurer calculate updated limits using the most recent debt and financial obligation and liability limits as determined under section 3.

(2) The treasurer shall update the most recent debt and financial obligation and liability limits determined under section 3 as follows:

From the amount obtained in section 3, subtract the estimated annual amount payable in respect of any project approved by the board to be financed by long-term debt or financial obligation described in section 2 but not as yet assumed, unless the board has by resolution indicated that it will not proceed with that project.

(3) The treasurer shall calculate the estimated amount for the fiscal year payable by the board in respect of the work.

(4) If the amount calculated under subsection (3) exceeds the amount updated under subsection (2), the board must obtain the approval of the Minister before authorizing the work.

5. Ontario Regulation 469/97 is revoked.

6. This Regulation comes into force on September 1, 1998.

REGULATION 476/98
TRANSITION ASSISTANCE GRANTS, NO. 2
O. Reg. 476/98

1. (1) A board specified in Column 1 of the document referred to in section 2 shall be paid a grant with respect to a matter set out in Column 2 of the document opposite the board's name in an amount for which the board provides proof of payment satisfactory to the Minister with respect to that matter, so long as,

- (a) subject to subclause (c)(i), the total amount paid to the board with respect to that matter does not exceed the amount set out in Column 3 of the document, opposite the board's name and the matter;
- (b) the payment by the board was made in accordance with the terms and conditions set out in the memoranda and attachments described in the Schedule;
- (c) if the board is a board set out in Column 1 of Table 1 to Ontario Regulation 124/98 opposite items 1 to 12,
    - (i) the total amount of the grants paid under this Regulation to the board in respect of matters set out in Column 2 of the document referred to in section 2 opposite the board's name does not exceed the difference between the sub-total amount set out in Column 3 of that document for the board and the amount set out in Column 2 to Table 1 to Ontario Regulation 124/98 opposite the board's name,
    - (ii) the board satisfies the Minister that it has spent the amount set out in Column 2 of Table 1 to that Regulation on the matters set out in Column 2 to the document referred to in section 2 of this Regulation opposite the board, and
    - (iii) the proof of payment does not relate to any part of the amount referred to in subclause (ii); and
- (d) if the matter set out in Column 2 to the document is set out entirely in capital letters,
    - (i) the board has made the expenditure in respect of it in accordance with a communications technology plan agreed to by all of the board having jurisdiction in the area to which the plan applies, and
    - (ii) the Minister has approved the plan.

(2) The Minister shall approve a communications technology plan under clause (1)(d) if it provides for a co-ordinated system of communication that will enable the boards to which the plan applies to communicate efficiently with their schools, with each other and with the Province.

2. The document referred to in section 1 is entitled "School Board Restructuring Program—Board Summary" and dated August 10, 1998 and is available for public inspection at the Capital and Operating Grants Administration Branch of the Ministry, located on the 21st floor, 900 Bay Street, Toronto.

Schedule

1. Memorandum to Directors of Education and Secretaries of District School Authorities from Veronica Lacey, dated February 23, 1998, whose subject is School Board Restructuring Fund, including the following attachments:

1. Guideline entitled "School Board Restructuring Fund, Application for Reimbursement of Restructuring Costs—Guideline".
2. Form entitled "School Board Restructuring Fund, Board Application Summary Form".
3. Form entitled "School Board Restructuring Fund, Application for Reimbursement of Restructuring Costs, Employee Severance/Counselling/Training".
4. Form Entitled "School Board Restructuring Fund, Application for Reimbursement of Restructuring costs".

2. Memorandum to Directors of Education and Secretaries of District School Authorities from Marc Godbout, dated April 15, 1998, whose subject is School Board Restructuring Program—Project Criteria.

3. Memorandum to Directors of Education and Secretaries of District School Authorities from Veronica Lacey, dated April 17, 1998, whose subject is School Board Restructuring Program, Phase 2, with the following attachments:
1. Guideline entitled "School Board Restructuring Program, Phase 2, Application for Reimbursement of Labour Adjustment Costs—Guideline".
2. Form entitled "School Board Restructuring Fund, Phase 2, Labour Adjustment Costs".

4. Memorandum to Directors of Education and Secretaries of District School Authorities from Marc Godbout, dated June 5, 1998, whose subject is School Board Restructuring Program—Phase 2—Clarification, with the following enclosures:
1. Form A and Form B, both entitled "School Board Restructuring Program, Labour Adjustment Costs".

REGULATION 486/98
CALCULATION OF AMOUNT OF RESERVE RESULTING FROM STRIKE OR LOCK-OUT
O. Reg. 486/98

1. (1) The amount that a board shall place in a reserve under section 233 of the Act shall be calculated as follows:
1. Determine the total of the salaries, wages and fringe benefits,
    i. that are in effect on the day that the strike or lock-out commences,
    ii. that are included in the estimates of the board in the fiscal year, and
    iii. that are not payable, or are payable but reimbursable, to or in respect of employees of the board, or any class of them, in respect of the period of a strike by or lock-out of those employees, or any such class of them, that occurs in the fiscal year.
2. Subtract from that amount the expenditures incurred in the fiscal year by the board that are approved by the Minister.

(2) The Minister shall approve expenditures under paragraph 2 of subsection (1) if they are necessarily incurred by the board in connection with the strike or lock-out and the amount of those expenditures is reasonable in the circumstances.

(3) If actual financial data required for a calculation under this Regulation are not available when the calculation is required to be made, estimate data shall be used.

2. Regulation 283 of the Revised Regulations of Ontario, 1990 is revoked.

REGULATION 509/98
TAX MATTERS—RELIEF IN UNORGANIZED TERRITORY
(SECTION 257.2.1 OF THE ACT)
O. Reg. 509/98, as am. O. Reg. 622/98; 78/99

Application

1. This Regulation applies with respect to taxes for school purposes in territory without municipal organization that is not deemed to be attached to a municipality for the purposes of taxation.

Definitions

2. In this Regulation,

"levying board" means a board that levies and collects tax rates under paragraph 2 or 3 of subsection 257.7(1) of the Act or under clause 257.14(1)(a) or (b) of the Act.

Phase-in of 1998 Assessment-related Changes

3. (1) The amount of the 1998 assessment-related tax increase or decrease for a property equals the school amount determined under subsection 372.1(6) of the *Municipal Act* subject to the following:

1. In determining the 1997 school taxes (class) in the formula in subsection 372.1(6) of the *Municipal Act*, the reference to the municipality shall be deemed to be a reference to the territory described in section 1 that is within the jurisdiction of the levying board and that is within the same territory referred to in a row to Table 2 of Ontario Regulation 438/98.
2. If a new improvement to a property is reflected in the assessment used to determine the 1998 taxes but was not reflected in the assessment used to determine the 1997 taxes, the 1998 assessment (property) shall be adjusted, in the formula in subsection 372.1(6) of the *Municipal Act*, to what it would be if the improvement was not reflected in the assessment for 1998.
3. If an improvement to a property was reflected in the assessment used to determine the 1997 taxes and, because of a change related to the improvement, the improvement is not reflected in the assessment used to determine the 1998 taxes, the 1998 assessment (property) shall be adjusted, in the formula in subsection 372.1(6) of the *Municipal Act*, to what it would be if the improvement was reflected in the assessment for 1998.

(2) If the 1998 assessment-related tax increase or decrease is positive, it is a 1998 assessment-related tax increase and if it is negative, it is a 1998 assessment-related tax decrease.

4. (1) A 1998 assessment-related tax increase or decrease shall be phased-in if the property is,

(a) in the residential/farm property class prescribed under the *Assessment Act*; or

(b) in the multi-residential property class prescribed under the *Assessment Act* in the Chapleau Locality Education.

(2) The first year in which a 1998 assessment-related tax increase or decrease shall be phased-in is the 1998 taxation year and the last year is the 2002 taxation year unless the increase or decrease is fully phased-in before that year. O. Reg. 78/99, s. 1.

5. The following apply with respect to the phase-in of a 1998 assessment-related tax increase:

1. The following adjustments shall be made to the taxes for school purposes on the property,
    i. the increase shall be subtracted from the taxes,
    ii. the amount phased-in in each of the previous years shall be added to the taxes, and
    iii. the amount to be phased-in in the current taxation year shall be added to the taxes.
2. The amount of the increase phased-in in a year shall be 20 per cent of the increase. However, the amount shall be at least $30.
3. Despite paragraph 2, the amount of the increase phased-in in a year shall not exceed the amount necessary to fully phase-in the increase. O. Reg. 78/99, s. 2.

6. The following apply with respect to the phase-in of a 1998 assessment-related tax decrease:

1. The following adjustments shall be made to the taxes for school purposes on the property,
    i. the decrease shall be added to the taxes,
    ii. the amount phased-in in each of the previous years shall be subtracted from the taxes, and
    iii. the amount to be phased-in in the current taxation year shall be subtracted from the taxes.
2. The amount of the decrease phased-in in a year shall be the threshold determined in accordance with paragraph 4. However, the amount shall be at least 20 per cent of the decrease.
3. Despite paragraph 2, the amount of the decrease phased-in in a year shall not exceed the amount necessary to full phase-in the decrease.
4. The threshold referred to in paragraph 2 is the amount determined so that the total of the decreases phased-in in the year for all properties in the same class of real property prescribed under the *Assessment Act* in the territory described in paragraph 1 of subsection 3(1) equals the total of the increases phased-in in the year for all such properties.

Tax Deferrals for Low-income Seniors and Persons with Disabilities

7. (1) In this section,

"1998 assessment-related tax increase" [Revoked O. Reg. 78/99, s. 3(1).]

"owner" means the person assessed as the owner.

(2) The owner of a property in the residential/farm property class, prescribed under the *Assessment Act*, is entitled to a deferral of taxes if,
- (a) there is a 1998 assessment-related tax increase, within the meaning of section 3, that exceeds $30;
- (b) the owner or the owner's spouse occupies the property as their principal residence on January 1 of the taxation year;
- (c) the owner or the owner's spouse is, at any time during the taxation year,
    - (i) a person who is 65 years of age or older and who receives a supplement under Part II of the *Old Age Security Act* (Canada), or
    - (ii) a person who receives income support under the *Ontario Disability Support Program Act, 1997*;
- (d) the owner or the owner's spouse was assessed as the owner of the property on the 1998 assessment roll;
- (e) if the taxation year is after 1998, there was a deferral of taxes on the property under this section for the 1998 taxation year; and
- (f) a written application for the deferral, together with sufficient documentation to establish entitlement to the deferral, is given to the secretary of the levying board,
    - (i) for the 1998 taxation year, before March 31, 1999, or
    - (ii) for a taxation year after 1998, by July 1 of the taxation year.

(3) The amount of a tax deferral under this section shall be determined in accordance with the following:
1. Subject to paragraph 2, the amount of the tax deferral is the amount of the 1998 assessment-related tax increase, within the meaning of section 3, reduced by the amount of the tax increase that is not yet phased-in.
2. The sum of a tax deferral, the taxes already deferred and the interest on such amounts shall not exceed 75 per cent of the assessed value of the property.

(4) Taxes deferred under this section shall bear interest. The rate of interest for each year shall be equal to the average prime rate, within the meaning of section 21 of Regulation 1013 of the Revised Regulations of Ontario, 1990, determined as of January 15 of the year.

(5) Amounts deferred and the interest on such amounts become due,
- (a) upon the death of the owner, subject to subsection (6);
- (b) upon the transfer of the property; or
- (c) on July 1 of the first year for which the owner is not entitled to a deferral of taxes, subject to subsections (7) and (8).

(6) If the owner dies but the owner's spouse is still alive, amounts deferred and the interest on such amounts are not due as long as,
- (a) the spouse is alive;
- (b) the property is the spouse's principal residence; and
- (c) the property is not transferred, other than to the spouse.

(7) If the owner's spouse dies and, but for the spouse's death, the owner would be entitled to a deferral of taxes if an application was made in accordance with clause (2)(f), the amounts deferred and the interest on such amounts are not due as long as,

(a) the owner is alive;
(b) the property is the owner's principal residence; and
(c) the property is not transferred.

(8) If the owner would be entitled to a deferral of taxes in the taxation year if an application was made in accordance with clause (2)(f) but such an application is not made, the amounts already deferred and the interest on such amounts are not due if a written application to continue the deferral of the amounts already deferred and the interest on such amounts, together with sufficient documentation to establish entitlement to a deferral of taxes in the taxation year, is given to the secretary of the levying board, by July 1 of the taxation year.

(9) Section 382 of the *Municipal Act* applies, with necessary modifications, with respect to taxes deferred under this section and interest on such taxes. O. Reg. 622/98, s. 1; 78/99, s. 3.

Rebates to Charities

8. (1) An eligible charity is entitled to a rebate of taxes for 1998, 1999 and 2000 taxation years on property the charity occupies if,
(a) the property is in the commercial property class or the industrial property class, prescribed under the *Assessment Act*; and
(b) a written application for the rebate, together with sufficient documentation to establish eligibility for the rebate, is given to the secretary of the levying board,
   (i) for the 1998 taxation year, on or before March 31, 1999, or
   (ii) for the 1999 or 2000 taxation year, on or before June 1 of the year.

(2) For the purposes of this section, a charity is eligible if it is a registered charity as defined in subsection 248(1) of the *Income Tax Act* (Canada) that has a registration number issued by the Department of National Revenue.

(3) The amount of the rebate shall be determined in accordance with section 2 of Ontario Regulation 47/99.

(4) The levying board must pay the rebate in accordance with the following:
1. The estimated rebate for the 1998 taxation year must be paid on or before April 30, 1999.
2. The estimated rebate for the 1999 and 2000 taxation years must be paid on or before June 30 of the year.
3. Final adjustments must be made, after the taxes paid by the charity can be determined, in respect of the difference between the estimated rebate paid by the levying board and the rebate to which the charity is entitled.

(5) A charity is entitled to a rebate even if the charity does not begin to occupy property until after the amounts under paragraphs 1 and 2 of subsection (4) would otherwise be payable.

(6) A charity is not entitled to a rebate from a levying board unless the charity repays any other levying board or municipality amounts by which the rebates the charity received for the year from that other levying board or municipality exceed the rebates from that other levying board or municipality to which the charity is entitled for the year. O. Reg. 78/99, s. 4.

Gross Leases Taxes for School Purposes

90. (1) Section 444.1 of the *Municipal Act* applies, with necessary modifications, as though it formed part of this Regulation, with respect to property in territory described in section 1 with the following modifications:

1. A reference to a municipality in subsection 444.1(10) of the *Municipal Act* shall be deemed to be a reference to the territory described in section 1 that is within the jurisdiction of the levying board.
2. A reference to a local municipality in subsection 444.1(13) of the *Municipal Act* shall be deemed to be a reference to the levying board.
3. A reference to property taxes shall be deemed to be a reference to taxes for school purposes. [Revoked O. Reg. 78/99, s. 5.]

(2) O. Reg. 78/99, s. 5.

Capping of Taxes for Certain Property Taxes for 1998, 1999 and 2000—10/5/5 per cent cap

10. (1) Divisions A and B of Part XXII.2 of the *Municipal Act* apply as though they formed part of this Regulation with the modifications in this section and such other modifications as are necessary.

(2) Subject to subsections (3) and (4), Divisions A and B of Part XXII.2 of the *Municipal Act* apply with respect to the following classes of real property prescribed under the *Assessment Act*:

1. The commercial property class.
2. The industrial property class.

(3) This section does not apply with respect to property in the commercial property class in the following territories:

1. The South River Township School Area.
2. The Allan Water DSA Locality Education.
3. The Auden DSA Locality Education.
4. The Summer Beaver DSA Locality Education.

(4) This section does not apply with respect to property in the industrial property class in the following territories:

1. The Magnetawan Township School Area.
2. The West Parry Sound Board of Education.
3. The Timiskaming Locality Education.
4. The Central Algoma Locality Education.
5. The North Shore Locality Education.
6. The Upsala DSA Locality Education.
7. The Fort Francis/Rainy River Locality Education with assessment roll numbers beginning with "5903".
8. The Red Lake Locality Education.

REGULATION 509/98 **Table 1**

(5) Divisions A and B of Part XXII.2 of the *Municipal Act* apply with respect to the multi-residential property class prescribed under the *Assessment Act* in the Lake Superior Locality Education.

(6) The following apply with respect to the application of Divisions A and B of Part XXII.2 of the *Municipal Act*:

1. Sections 447.44 and 447.45 of the *Municipal Act* do not apply.
2. A reference to a municipality, including a reference in a provision of Part XXII.1 of the *Municipal Act* as it applies under Part XXII.2 of the *Municipal Act*, shall be deemed to be a reference to the levying board. However, in paragraph 2 of subsection 447.51(4) of the Municipal Act, the reference to the municipality shall be deemed to be a reference to the territory set out in Table 1 or the Lake Superior Locality Education, as applicable.
3. A reference to 1997 mill rates shall be deemed to include only mill rates for school purposes.
4. Sections 447.52 and 447.54 of the *Municipal Act* do not apply.
5. For the purposes of paragraph 1 of subsection 447.7(3) and paragraph 1 of subsection 447.10(2) of the *Municipal Act*, as they apply under section 447.38 of that Act,
    i. the factors in Table 1 are prescribed for the territories and property classes indicated, and
    ii. 0.093129 is prescribed as the factor for the multi-residential property class in the Lake Superior Locality Education.
6. Parts I and II of the Ontario Regulation 7/99 apply with respect to the territories set out in Table 2 as though those Parts formed part of this Regulation with the following modifications and such other modifications as are necessary,
    i. section 2 of Ontario Regulation 7/99 does not apply,
    ii. a reference to a municipality shall be deemed to be a reference to a territory set out in Table 2, and
    iii. a reference to Table 1 of Ontario Regulation 7/99 shall be deemed to be a reference to Table 2 of this Regulation. O. Reg. 78/99, s. 6.

TABLE 1

O. Reg. 78/99, s. 7

PRESCRIBED FACTORS

Territory	Commercial Property Class	Industrial Property Class
Nipissing D		
Murchison Lyell Sabine Localities	0.020453	0.029026
Upsala DSA Locality Education	0.090349	

Table 1
REGULATIONS UNDER THE EDUCATION ACT

Territory	Commercial Property Class	Industrial Property Class
Nipissing Combined School Boards	0.027459	0.044277
Timiskiming Board of Education	0.057696	
Parry Sound D		
East Parry Sound Board of Education	0.649964	0.571831
Magnetawan Township School Area	0.486550	
West Parry Sound Board of Education	0.496118	
Manitoulin D		
Manitoulin Locality Education	0.612715	0.496853
Sudbury D		
Asquith Garvey DSA Locality Education	0.149645	0.284654
Chapleau Locality Education	0.153825	0.207990
Espanola Locality Education	0.763200	0.817625
Foleyet DSA Locality Education	0.324997	
Gogama DSA Locality Education	0.280344	
Missarenda DSA Locality Education	0.032308	0.021249
Sudbury Locality Education	0.198351	0.263958
Timiskaming D		
Kirkland Lake Locality Education	0.191431	0.322490
Timiskaming Locality Education	0.103265	
Cochrane D		
Cochrane Iroquois Falls BR Math Locality	0.256425	0.273973
Hearst Locality Education	0.265488	0.181107
James Bay Lowlands Locality Education	0.524825	
Kap SRF And Dist Locality Education	0.303080	0.050073
Moosonee Dev Area Bd	0.159314	0.258166
Algoma D		
Central Algoma Locality Education	1.034332	
Michipicoten Locality Education	1.212400	0.657588
North Shore Locality Education	0.967128	0.628865

REGULATION 509/98 **Table 1**

TERRITORY	COMMERCIAL PROPERTY CLASS	INDUSTRIAL PROPERTY CLASS
Sault Ste. Marie Locality Education	0.297442	0.289531
Thunder Bay D		
Armstrong DSA Locality Education	0.065712	
Caramat DSA Locality Education	0.153776	
Geraldton Locality Education	0.067076	0.273529
Kashabowie DSA Locality Education	0.034789	
Kilkenny DSA Locality Education	0.013594	
Lake Superior Locality Education	0.170677	0.132710
Lakehead Locality Education	0.044092	0.074617
Nipigon Red Rock Locality Education	0.015396	
Savant Lake DSA Locality Education	0.094232	
Upsala DSA Locality Education	0.090349	
Rainy River D		
Atikokan Locality Education	0.032914	0.046970
Fort Frances/Rainy River Locality Education (assessment roll numbers beginning with "5902")	0.024234	0.029332
Fort Frances Rainy River Locality Education (assessment roll numbers beginning with "5903")	0.023827	
Mine Centre DSA Locality Education	0.049430	0.024915
Kenora D		
Dryden Locality Education (assessment roll numbers beginning with "6060")	0.048815	0.053853
Dryden Locality Education (assessment roll numbers beginning with "6093")	0.039607	
Dryden Locality Education (assessment roll numbers beginning with "6096")	0.049537	0.042325
Kenora Locality Education	0.046416	0.032721
Red Lake Locality Education	0.079659	
Sturgeon Lake Locality Education	0.582223	

Table 2

TABLE 2

O. Reg. 78/99, s. 7

EDUCATION TAX CUTS

TERRITORY	INDUSTRIAL PROPERTY CLASS (AMOUNTS IN DOLLARS)
Timiskaming D	
Kirkland Lake Locality Education	5,318
Thunder Bay D	
Lake Superior Locality Education	5,335
Lakehead Locality Education	12,817
Rainy River D	
Atikokan Locality Education	1,092

REGULATION 712/98
TAX MATTERS—RATES UNDER SUBSECTION 255(1) OF THE ACT
O. Reg. 712/98

1. This Regulation governs the levying of rates under subsection 255(1) of the Act by a board for the purposes of a recreation committee or joint recreation committee on property in territory without municipal organization.

2. (1) Subject to subsection (2), there shall be a single rate for each property class prescribed under the *Assessment Act* and the rates for different property classes shall be in the same proportion to each other as the tax rates for school purposes for those classes are to each other.

(2) If the tax rate for school purposes for a subclass prescribed under the *Assessment Act* is less than the tax rate for school purposes for the property class, there shall be a single rate under subsection 255(1) of the Act for the subclass and the rates for the subclass and property class shall be in the same proportion to each other as the tax rates for school purposes for the subclass and property class are to each other.

REGULATION 713/98
APPORTIONMENT OF RATES IN CERTAIN DISTRICT SCHOOL AREAS
O. Reg. 713/98

1. Amounts levied under subsection 257.7(1) of the Act on residential property taxable for English-language public board purposes in the Moosonee District School Area shall be apportioned and distributed entirely to The Moosonee District School Area Board.

REGULATION 714/98
LEVYING OF CERTAIN RATES FOR 1998 IN 1999
O. Reg. 714/98

1. (1) Despite any provision of the *Education Act*, the *Municipal Act* or the *Provincial Land Tax Act*, a municipality or board that is required to levy rates in territory without municipal organization for the 1998 taxation year for school purposes, for the purposes of subsection 255(1) of the *Education Act* or for the purposes of section 21.1 of the *Provincial Land Tax Act*, may meet the requirement by levying the rates at any time before March 1, 1999.

(2) For the purposes of a levy for the 1998 taxation year carried out in January or February of 1999, the board or municipality shall levy the rates on real property that is taxable for school purposes as shown on the assessment roll returned for taxation in 1998.

(3) A board or municipality shall not levy for the 1998 taxation year in January or February of 1999 unless the board or municipality has, by by-law passed under subsection 406(2) of the *Municipal Act*, fixed a time for the return of the collector's rolls that is on or before April 30, 1999.

(4) Subsection (5) applies where a board or municipality levies for the 1998 taxation year in January or February of 1999 and the board or municipality has passed a by-law under subsection 399(5) of the *Municipal Act*.

(5) The by-law applies to payments on account of taxes for the 1998 taxation year that are received in January or February of 1999.

REGULATION 715/98
DEEMED ATTACHMENT OF CERTAIN TERRITORY WITHOUT MUNICIPAL ORGANIZATION
O. Reg. 715/98

1. Territory without municipal organization that, on December 31, 1997, was attached to a municipality for school purposes and that, on January 1, 1998, was not so attached, and that is in the territorial jurisdiction of a school authority, is deemed to be attached to the municipality under section 56 of the Act, for the purposes of Division B of Part IX of the Act and for the purposes of section 21.1 of the *Provincial Land Tax Act*.

2. Territory without municipal organization that, on December 31, 1997, was attached to a municipality for school purposes and that, on January 1, 1998, was not so attached, and that is in the territorial jurisdiction of a district school board, is deemed to be attached to the municipality under clause 58.1(2)(m) of the Act, for the purposes of Division B of Part IX of the Act and for the purposes of section 21.1 of the *Provincial Land Tax Act*.

3. Section 1 or 2, as the case may be, ceases to apply where the territory without municipal organization becomes or is included in a municipality.

4. (1) On December 31, 1998, section 2 ceases to apply in the following areas in the Territorial District of Parry Sound:

1. Lands in the geographic township of Spence that, on January 1, 1998, had assessment roll numbers beginning with the number 49-96-190.
2. Lands in the geographic township of Lount that, on January 1, 1998, had assessment roll numbers beginning with the number 49-95-060.

(2) If a tax collection procedure, including a procedure under the *Municipal Tax Sales Act*, has been commenced by The Corporation of the Township of Magnetawan in respect of lands described in paragraph 1 or 2 of subsection (1), and the procedure is not completed by January 1, 1999, The Near North District School Board may continue the procedure.

(3) If The Near North District School Board collects arrears of taxes levied for the purposes of a board or an old board before January 1, 1999 by The Corporation of the Township of Magnetawan in the areas described in paragraphs 1 and 2 of subsection (1), The Near North District School Board shall pay the amounts collected to The Corporation of the Township of Magnetawan.

REGULATION 213/99
CALCULATION OF AVERAGE DAILY ENROLMENT FOR THE 1999-2000 FISCAL YEAR
O. Reg. 213/99

1. In this Regulation,

"1999-2000 fiscal year" means the period beginning September 1, 1999 and ending August 31, 2000; ("exercice 1999-2000")

"cycle" means the number of school days for which a schedule of classes in a school continues before the schedule is repeated; ("horaire")

"day school" and "day school program" do not include continuing education or summer school classes or courses; ("cours de jour", "programme scolaire de jour")

"full-time pupil" means a pupil who,
  (a) is enrolled in day school other than in junior kindergarten or kindergarten, and
  (b) in respect of a cycle, is registered for classroom instruction for an average of at least 210 minutes per school day; ("élève à temps plein")

"half-time pupil" means a pupil who is enrolled in junior kindergarten or kindergarten and, in respect of a cycle, is registered for classroom instruction for an average of at least 150 minutes per school day; ("élève à mi-temps")

"independent study course" means a credit course that is provided to a pupil other than a full-time pupil and that,
  (a) meets the criteria set out in the independent study course register for inclusion in the determination of day school enrolment, or
  (b) is approved by the Minister as an independent study course to be included in the determination of day school enrolment; ("cours d'études personnelles")

"part-time pupil" means a pupil who is enrolled in a day school and is neither a full-time nor a half-time pupil. ("élève à temps partiel")

2. Day school average daily enrolment for a board for the 1999-2000 fiscal year is the sum of,
  (a) the product of 0.5 and the sum of,
      (i) the number of full-time pupils enrolled on October 31, 1999 in schools operated by the board,
      (ii) 0.5 times the number of half-time pupils enrolled on that day in schools operated by the board, and
      (iii) the quotient obtained by determining, for each part-time pupil enrolled on that day in a school operated by the board, the number of minutes for which the pupil is registered for classroom instruction in the cycle that includes that day, in a course other than an independent study course, and dividing the sum of the numbers so determined by the product of 300 and the number of days in the cycle;
  (b) the product of 0.5 and the sum of,
      (i) the number of full-time pupils enrolled on March 31, 2000 in schools operated by the board,

(ii) 0.5 times the number of half-time pupils enrolled on that day in schools operated by the board, and

(iii) the quotient obtained by determining, for each part-time pupil enrolled on that day in a school operated by the board, the number of minutes for which the pupil is registered for classroom instruction in the cycle that includes that day, in a course other than an independent study course, and dividing the sum of the numbers so determined by the product of 300 and the number of days in the cycle; and

(c) an amount in respect of each pupil enrolled in a school of the board who is registered for an independent study course, calculated as follows:

$$\frac{A}{7.5} \times B$$

where,

A = the number of credits and partial credits that may be earned by the pupil on successful completion of the course,

B = the fraction representing the portion of the total quantity of work required for completion of the course that is completed by the pupil during the 1999-2000 fiscal year.

3. (1) Continuing education average daily enrolment for a board for the 1999-2000 fiscal year is the sum of,

(a) an amount in respect of each pupil who is enrolled in a continuing education class or course established by the board, other than a continuing education course delivered primarily through means other than classroom instruction, calculated as follows:

$$\frac{A \times B}{300 \times 190}$$

where,

A = the number of sessions for which the pupil is enrolled in the 1999-2000 fiscal year,

B = the number of minutes in each session; and

(b) an amount in respect of each pupil who is enrolled in a continuing education course established by the board and delivered primarily through means other than classroom instruction calculated as follows:

$$A \times 0.1134 \times B$$

where,

A = the number of credits and partial credits that may be earned by the pupil on successful completion of the course,

B = the fraction representing the portion of the total quantity of work required for completion of the course that is completed by the pupil during the period from September 1, 1999 to August 31, 2000.

(2) A class or course is a continuing education class or course for the purposes of subsection (1) only if it is not a summer school class or course as defined in subsection 4(1), it is approved by the Minister and it is,

(a) a class or course, including a course delivered primarily through means other than classroom instruction, established for adults for which one or more credits may be granted, so long as in the case of a class or course offered by a school authority that is only authorized to provide elementary education, the class or course is in the intermediate division;
  (b) a class or course in citizenship and, where necessary, in language instruction in the English or the French language for persons admitted to Canada as permanent residents under the *Immigration Act* (Canada);
  (c) a class or course in English or French for adults whose first language learned and still understood is neither English nor French and that is not a class or course in which a pupil may earn a credit in English or French as a second language; or
  (d) a class or course of Native language instruction for adults.

(3) In calculating the continuing education average daily enrolment for a board under subsection (1) with respect to a class or course established for adults and referred to in clause (2)(a), (c) or (d), any pupils in the class or course who are not adults shall be included.

(4) In calculating the continuing education average daily enrolment for a board under subsection (1) with respect to a class or course referred to in subsection (5),
  (a) if the number of pupils in the class or course is 10 or more and less than 15, that number shall be increased to 15; and
  (b) if the number of pupils in the class or course is less than 10, that number shall be increased by five.

(5) Subsection (4) applies with respect to,
  (a) a class or course referred to in clause (2)(b), (c) or (d); and
  (b) a class or course referred to in clause (2)(a), other than a course delivered primarily through means other than classroom instruction, if the class or course is offered in a secondary school that has an enrolment of fewer than 120 pupils per grade and that is located in a territorial district more than 80 kilometres from all other secondary schools in the Province that have the same language of instruction.

4. (1) In this section,

"summer school class or course" means a class or course provided by a board between the hours of 8 a.m. and 5 p.m. if,
  (a) the class or course starts after the completion of the 1999-2000 school year and ends before the start of the 2000-2001 school year, and
  (b) the class or course,
      (i) is for developmentally delayed pupils,
      (ii) is one in which a pupil may earn a credit, or
      (iii) is for pupils who have completed grade 8 in the 1999-2000 school year and for whom a remedial program has been recommended by the principal of the school at which the pupil completed grade 8.

(2) Only pupils who were enrolled in a day school program offered by a board in the 1999-2000 school year shall be counted for the purposes of this section.

(3) Summer school average daily enrolment for a board for the 1999-2000 fiscal year is the sum of the amounts in respect of each pupil enrolled in a summer school class or course

that is provided by the board, other than a course delivered primarily through means other than classroom instruction, calculated as follows:

$$\frac{A \times B}{300 \times 190}$$

where,

A = the number of sessions of the summer school class or course in which the pupil is enrolled in the 1999-2000 fiscal year,

B = the number of minutes in each session.

REGULATION 214/99
STUDENT FOCUSED FUNDING—LEGISLATIVE GRANTS FOR THE SCHOOL BOARD 1999-2000 FISCAL YEAR
O. Reg. 214/99

CONTENTS

		Sections
PART I	**GENERAL**	
	Interpretation	1-4
	General	5-9
PART II	**GRANTS TO DISTRICT SCHOOL BOARDS**	
	Grant entitlement	10, 11
	1999-2000 tax revenue of a district school board	12
	Foundation allocation	13
	Special education allocation	14-20
	Language allocation — English-language district school boards	21-24
	Language allocation — French-language district school boards	25-28
	Small schools allocation	29
	Remote and rural allocation	30
	Learning opportunities allocation	31
	Summer school remedial allocation	32
	Adult Education, Continuing Education and Summer School Allocation	33
	Teacher compensation allocation	34
	Early learning allocation	35
	Transportation allocation	36
	Administration and governance allocation	37
	Pupil accommodation allocation	38
	Debt charges allocation	39
	Phase-in funding	40-47
	Stable funding guarantee	48
	Grants for certain capital projects	49
	Enveloping	50-54
PART III	**GRANTS TO SCHOOL AUTHORITIES**	
	Grants to isolate boards	55
	Grants to section 68 boards	56
PART IV	**PAYMENTS TO GOVERNING AUTHORITIES**	57-60

TABLES

Table 1	ESL/ESD grant
Table 2	Assimilation Factors for ALF Funding
Table 3	Distance and Urban Factors for Remote and Rural Allocations

S. 1 REGULATIONS UNDER THE EDUCATION ACT

Table 4   Learning Opportunities
Table 5   Teacher Compensation
Table 6   Geographic Adjustment Factors for New Pupil Places
Table 7   Pupil Accommodation Grant
Table 8   Classroom Expenditure Percentages

PART I

GENERAL

Interpretation

1. In this Regulation,

"1999-2000 A.D.E. regulation" means Ontario Regulation 213/99; ("règlement sur l'effectif quotidien moyen de 1999-2000")

"1999-2000 fees regulation" means Ontario Regulation 215/99; ("règlement sur les droits de 1999-2000")

"1999-2000 fiscal year" means the fiscal year from September 1, 1999 to August 31, 2000; ("exercice 1999-2000")

"ALF" stands for actualisation linguistique en français; ("ALF")

"capital asset" means,

    (a) a school site that provides or is capable of providing pupil accommodation and an addition or improvement to such a school site,

    (b) a school building, including a fixture of a school building, and an addition, alteration, renovation or major repair to a school building or a fixture of a school building,

    (c) furniture and equipment to be used in school buildings,

    (d) library materials for the initial equipping of a library in a school building, and

    (e) a water supply or electrical power supply on school property or the means of conveying water or electrical power to school property from outside the property; ("immobilisation")

"cycle" has the same meaning as in the 1999-2000 A.D.E. regulation; ("horaire")

"designated board associated with an old board" means the district school board that is listed in Column 2 of Schedule 1 to Ontario Regulation 460/97, opposite the old board listed in Column 1 of that Schedule; ("conseil désigné rattaché à un ancien conseil")

"elementary school pupil" means a pupil who is enrolled in any of junior kindergarten, kindergarten and grades one to eight; ("élève de l'élémentaire")

"ESD" stands for English skills development; ("ESD")

"ESL" stands for English as a second language; ("ESL")

"full-time pupil" has the same meaning as in the 1999-2000 A.D.E. regulation; ("élève à temps plein") "half-time pupil" has the same meaning as in the 1999-2000 A.D.E. regulation; ("élève à mi-temps")

"independent study course" has the same meaning as in the 1999-2000 A.D.E. regulation; ("cours d'études personnelles")

"ISA" stands for intensive support amount; ("AAS")

"isolate board" is a school authority other than a section 68 board; ("conseil isolé")

"Metropolitan Toronto area board" means,
- (a) The Board of Education for the Borough of East York,
- (b) The Board of Education for the City of Etobicoke,
- (c) The Board of Education for the City of North York,
- (d) The Board of Education for the City of Scarborough,
- (e) The Board of Education for the City of Toronto, and
- (f) The Board of Education for the City of York; ("conseil de secteur de la communauté urbaine de Toronto")

"old board" does not include the Metropolitan Toronto area boards or The Metropolitan Toronto French-Language School Council; ("ancien conseil")

"part-time pupil" has the same meaning as in the 1999-2000 A.D.E. regulation; ("élève à temps partiel")

"PDF" stands for perfectionnement du français; ("PDF")

"secondary school pupil" means a pupil who is enrolled in any of grades nine to twelve or in a course leading to an OAC credit; ("élève du secondaire")

"section 68 board" is a board established under section 68 of the Act; ("conseil créé vertu de l'article 68")

"supported board associated with an old board" means the district school board that is listed in Column 3 of Schedule 1 to Ontario Regulation 460/97, opposite the old board listed in Column 1 of that Schedule; ("conseil secondé rattaché à un ancien conseil")

"unextended old board" means an old board to which subsection 4(1) of Ontario Regulation 78/97 applied. ("ancien conseil non parachevé")

2. (1) Subject to subsections (2) to (5), for the purposes of this Regulation, a pupil is a pupil of a board if he or she is enrolled in a school operated by the board.

(2) A pupil who receives instruction in an education program provided by a board in a facility described or mentioned in subsection 19(2) is not a pupil enrolled in a school operated by the board for the purposes of subsection (1).

(3) Subsection (4) applies where,
- (a) the area of jurisdiction of a separate district school board includes all or part of the area that was, immediately before January 1, 1998, the area of jurisdiction of an unextended old board;
- (b) the separate district school board does not operate a secondary school in the area that was, immediately before January 1, 1998, the area of jurisdiction of the unextended old board; and
- (c) the separate district school board has entered into a purchase of services agreement

with a public board to provide instruction, in schools located in the area that was, immediately before January 1, 1998, the area of jurisdiction of the unextended old board, to secondary school pupils who are qualified to be resident pupils of the separate board.

(4) For the purposes of this Regulation, pupils receiving instruction under an agreement referred to in clause (3)(c) are pupils of the separate district school board and are not pupils of the public board.

(5) For the purposes of this Regulation, the following are not pupils of a board even if they are enrolled in a school of the board:

1. A pupil who is a registered Indian residing on a reserve within the meaning of the *Indian Act* (Canada).
2. A pupil who is liable to pay fees as specified in subsection 49(6) of the *Education Act* because he or she is a visitor within the meaning of the *Immigration Act* (Canada) or is in possession of a student authorization issued under that Act.
3. A pupil in respect of whom the board may charge a fee under section 5 of the 1999-2000 fees regulation.

3. (1) For the purposes of this Regulation, the 1999-2000 day school average daily enrolment of pupils of a board is the day school average daily enrolment for the board determined under section 2 of the 1999-2000 A.D.E. regulation, counting only pupils of the board, excluding secondary school pupils who are 21 years of age or more on December 31, 1999.

(2) For the purposes of this Regulation, the 1999-2000 day school average daily enrolment of elementary school pupils of a board is the day school average daily enrolment for the board determined under section 2 of the 1999-2000 A.D.E. regulation, counting only the elementary school pupils of the board.

(3) For the purposes of this Regulation, the 1999-2000 day school average daily enrolment of secondary school pupils of a board is the day school average daily enrolment for the board determined under section 2 of the 1999-2000 A.D.E. regulation, counting only secondary school pupils of the board and excluding secondary school pupils who are 21 years of age or more on December 31, 1999.

(4) For the purposes of this Regulation, the day school full-time equivalent enrolment for a board as of October 31, 1999 is the sum of,

(a) the number of full-time pupils of the board enrolled on October 31, 1999, excluding secondary school pupils who are 21 years of age or more on December 31, 1999;

(b) 0.5 times the number of half-time pupils of the board enrolled on October 31, 1999, excluding secondary school pupils who are 21 years of age or more on December 31, 1999; and

(c) the quotient obtained by determining, for each part-time pupil of the board enrolled on October 31, 1999, other than secondary school pupils who are 21 years of age or more on December 31, 1999, the number of minutes for which the pupil is registered for classroom instruction in the cycle that includes October 31, 1999, in a course other than an independent study course, and dividing the sum of the numbers so determined by the product of 300 and the number of days in the cycle.

(5) Where this Regulation requires that pupils be counted but does not provide that the count shall be on the basis of average daily enrolment or on the basis of full-time equivalent enrolment, each pupil, whether full-time, half-time or part-time, shall be counted as one.

4. (1) A count of pupils for the purposes of this Regulation on the basis of average daily enrolment or on the basis of full-time equivalent enrolment shall be accurate to two decimal places.

(2) A count of teachers for the purposes of this Regulation on the basis of full-time equivalence shall be accurate to one decimal place.

General

5. (1) The legislative grant payable for the 1999-2000 fiscal year to a district school board is the amount calculated under Part II.

(2) The legislative grant payable for the 1999-2000 fiscal year to an isolate board is the amount calculated under Part III.

(3) The legislative grant payable for the 1999-2000 fiscal year to a section 68 board is the amount calculated under Part III.

6. Except as otherwise provided in section 49, a legislative grant payable under this Regulation shall be paid on an estimated basis during the 1999-2000 fiscal year and such adjustments as may be necessary shall be made after the actual financial, enrolment and other data are available.

7. (1) It is a condition of the payment of a grant to a board under this Regulation that the board comply with all Acts administered by the Minister and with all regulations, policies, guidelines, directives and similar instruments made under an Act administered by the Minister.

(2) Where a board contravenes an Act administered by the Minister or a regulation, policy, guideline, directive or similar instrument made under an Act administered by the Minister, the Minister may withhold all or part of a grant otherwise payable to the board under the Act until the board takes the steps necessary to correct the situation.

8. (1) Where the amount payable to an old board under a legislative grant regulation was overpaid, the overpayment shall be deducted from the grants payable under this Regulation to the designated board associated with the old board and to the supported board associated with the old board, in accordance with the appropriate distribution ratios as determined under the directives published in September, 1997 by the Education Improvement Commission and titled "Directives for the Distribution of Assets and Liabilities Among District School Boards".

(2) Where the amount payable to a board under a legislative grant regulation was overpaid, the overpayment shall be deducted from the grants payable under this Regulation to the board.

9. (1) Where the amount payable to an old board under a legislative grant regulation was underpaid, the underpayment shall be added to the grants payable under this Regulation to the designated board associated with the old board and to the supported board associated with the old board, in accordance with the appropriate distribution ratios as determined under the directives published in September, 1997 by the Education Improvement Commission and titled "Directives for the Distribution of Assets and Liabilities Among District School Boards".

(2) Where the amount payable to a board under a legislative grant regulation was underpaid, the underpayment shall be added to the grants payable under this Regulation to the board.

PART II

GRANTS TO DISTRICT SCHOOL BOARDS

Grant Entitlement

10. (1) For the purposes of this Part, the following are types of allocations:
1. Foundation allocation.
2. Special education allocation.
3. Language allocation.
4. Small schools allocation.
5. Remote and rural allocation.
6. Learning opportunity allocation.
7. Summer school remedial allocation.
8. Adult education, continuing education and summer school allocation.
9. Teacher compensation allocation.
10. Early learning allocation.
11. Transportation allocation.
12. Administration and governance allocation.
13. Pupil accommodation allocation.
14. Debt charges allocation.

(2) For the purposes of this Part, an old board is a predecessor of a district school board if the district school board is listed in Column 2 or 3 of Schedule 1 to Ontario Regulation 460/97, opposite the old board listed in Column 1 of that Schedule.

11. A district school board shall be paid a grant in an amount determined as follows:
1. Determine the 1999-2000 tax revenue of the board, in accordance with section 12.
2. Determine the amount of each type of allocation for the board, in accordance with sections 13 to 39.
3. Total the amounts determined for the board under paragraph 2.
4. Adjust the amount determined under paragraph 3 in accordance with section 40.
5. Add the stable funding guarantee amount, if any, determined for the board under section 48.
6. Deduct the amount determined under paragraph 1 for the board from the amount determined under paragraph 5 for the board.
7. Deduct the fees revenue received by the board under section 4 of the 1999-2000 fees regulation.
8. Deduct the amount that is in the board's reserve fund under subsection 233(1) of the Act on August 31, 2000, immediately before the transfer under subsection 233(2) of the Act.

9. Add the total of the amounts payable to the board for capital projects under section 49.

1999-2000 Tax Revenue of a District School Board

12. (1) For the purposes of paragraph 1 of section 11, the 1999-2000 tax revenue of a district school board shall be determined as follows:

1. Add,
    i. 38 per cent of the total of the amounts distributed to the board in respect of the 1999 calendar year under subsections 237(12) and 238(2), section 239, subsection 240(5), sections 250 and 251 and subsections 257.8(2) and 257.9(1) of the Act, under sections 447.20 and 447.52 of the *Municipal Act* and under section 10 of Ontario Regulation 509/98,
    ii. 62 per cent of the total of the amounts distributed to the board in respect of the 2000 calendar year under subsections 237(12) and 238(2), section 239, subsection 240(5), sections 250 and 251 and subsections 257.8(2) and 257.9(1) of the Act, under sections 447.20 and 447.52 of the *Municipal Act* and under section 10 of Ontario Regulation 509/98,
    iii. 38 per cent of the amounts, if any, received by the board in respect of the 1999 calendar year from a municipality under subsection 445(4) of the *Municipal Act*,
    iv. 62 per cent of the amounts, if any, received by the board in respect of the 2000 calendar year from a municipality under subsection 445(4) of the *Municipal Act*,
    v. the total of the taxes received by the board in respect of the 1999 calendar year under section 35 of the *Assessment Act*,
    vi. 38 per cent of the payments in lieu of taxes distributed to the board in respect of the 1999 calendar year under subsection 371.1(1) of the *Municipal Act*,
    vii. 62 per cent of the payments in lieu of taxes distributed to the board in respect of the 2000 calendar year under subsection 371.1(1) of the *Municipal Act*,
    viii. 38 per cent of the amounts, if any, received by the board in respect of the 1999 calendar year under the *Municipal Grants Act* (Canada) or under any Act of Canada that permits a payment to be made by a government or a government agency in lieu of taxes on real property,
    ix. 62 per cent of the amounts, if any, received by the board in respect of the 2000 calendar year under the *Municipal Grants Act* (Canada) or under any Act of Canada that permits a payment to be made by a government or a government agency in lieu of taxes on real property,
    x. the total of the amounts, if any, distributed to the board in the 1999-2000 fiscal year under subsection 2(2) of Ontario Regulation 365/98, and
    xi. the total of the amounts, if any, paid to the board in the 1999-2000 fiscal year under clause 3(1)(a) of Ontario Regulation 366/98.
2. Deduct the cost incurred in the 1999-2000 fiscal year by the board under section 257.7 of the Act in collecting taxes for school purposes in territory without municipal organization, to a maximum of 2 per cent of the sum of,

i. 38 per cent of the total amount of taxes levied by it for 1999 for school purposes in territory without municipal organization, and
  ii. 62 per cent of the total amount of taxes levied by it for 2000 for school purposes in territory without municipal organization.
3. Deduct an amount approved by the Minister in respect of,
  i. costs additional to those deducted under paragraph 2 that are incurred in the 1999-2000 fiscal year by the board under section 257.7 of the Act in collecting taxes for school purposes in territory without municipal organization, and
  ii. costs that are incurred in the 1999-2000 fiscal year by the board under section 21.1 of the *Provincial Land Tax Act* in collecting taxes in territory without municipal organization.
4. Deduct the amounts charged to the board in the 1999 calendar year by a municipal council under section 421 of the *Municipal Act*, including amounts charged under that section as a result of private legislation.
5. Deduct the total of the amounts paid as rebates by the board under section 257.2.1 of the Act in the 1999-2000 fiscal year.
6. Deduct 38 per cent of the total of the amounts, if any, paid by the board in respect of the 1999 calendar year under subsections 442.1(7) and 442.2(8.1) of the *Municipal Act*.
7. Deduct 62 per cent of the total of the amounts, if any, paid by the board in respect of the 2000 calendar year under subsections 442.1(7) and 442.2(8.1) of the *Municipal Act*.

(2) Amounts, if any, paid by the Minister to the board in respect of the 1999 calendar year under section 257.11 of the Act shall be deemed to be amounts distributed to the board in respect of the 1999 calendar year under a provision of the Act referred to in subparagraph i of paragraph 1 of subsection (1).

(3) Amounts, if any, paid by the Minister to the board in respect of the 2000 calendar year under section 257.11 of the Act shall be deemed to be amounts distributed to the board in respect of the 2000 calendar year under a provision of the Act referred to in subparagraph ii of paragraph 1 of subsection (1).

Foundation Allocation

13. For the purposes of paragraph 2 of section 11, the amount of the foundation allocation for a district school board shall be determined as follows:
1. Take the 1999-2000 day school average daily enrolment of elementary school pupils of the board.
2. Multiply the number determined under paragraph 1 by $3,367.
3. Take the 1999-2000 day school average daily enrolment of secondary school pupils of the board.
4. Multiply the number determined under paragraph 3 by $3,953.
5. Total the products obtained under paragraphs 2 and 4.

Special Education Allocation

14. For the purposes of paragraph 2 of section 11, the amount of the special education allocation for a district school board shall be determined as follows:
1. Determine the enrolment-based special education amount for the board, in accordance with section 15.
2. Determine the equipment ISA for the board, in accordance with section 16.
3. Determine the program ISA for the board, in accordance with section 18.
4. Determine the programs in facilities amount for the board, in accordance with section 19.
5. Total the amounts determined under paragraphs 1 to 4.

15. For the purposes of paragraph 1 of section 14, the enrolment-based special education amount for the board shall be determined as follows:
1. Take the 1999-2000 day school average daily enrolment of elementary school pupils of the board.
2. Multiply the number determined under paragraph 1 by $362.
3. Take the 1999-2000 day school average daily enrolment of secondary school pupils of the board.
4. Multiply the number determined under paragraph 3 by $229.
5. Total the amounts determined under paragraphs 2 and 4.

16. (1) For the purposes of subsection (2), an equipment ISA claim for a pupil of a board is an approved equipment ISA claim for the pupil if,
  (a) the board has designated the pupil as an ISA level 1 pupil in accordance with the Ministry publication entitled "Resource Manual for the Special Education Grant Intensive Support Amount (ISA)", dated March 17, 1999;
  (b) the board has made an ISA level 1 claim for expenditures in excess of $800 for special equipment for the pupil, in accordance with the Ministry publication entitled "Resource Manual for the Special Education Grant Intensive Support Amount (ISA)", dated March 17, 1999; and
  (c) the Minister has approved the designation referred to in clause (a) and the claim referred to in clause (b).

(2) For the purposes of paragraph 2 of section 14, the equipment ISA for a board shall be calculated by totalling the approved equipment ISA claims for pupils of the board.

17. For the purposes of section 18, a special incidence ISA claim for a pupil of a board is an approved special incidence ISA claim for the pupil if,
  (a) the pupil was a pupil approved for ISA level 3 funding for the purposes of section 18 of Ontario Regulation 287/98;
  (b) the board has designated the pupil as requiring special incidence funding in accordance with the Ministry publication entitled "Resource Manual for the Special Education Grant Intensive Support Amount (ISA)", dated March 17, 1999;
  (c) the board has made a special incidence ISA claim not exceeding $27,000 for the pupil, in accordance with the Ministry publication entitled "Resource Manual for

the Special Education Grant Intensive Support Amount (ISA)", dated March 17, 1999; and

(d) the Minister has approved the designation referred to in clause (b) and the claim referred to in clause (c).

18. For the purposes of paragraph 3 of section 14, the program ISA for a board is the total of,

(a) the program ISA determined for the board under section 17 of Ontario Regulation 287/98, as adjusted, where applicable, under section 20 of that Regulation; and

(b) the total of the approved special incidence ISA claims for pupils of the board.

19. (1) For the purposes of paragraph 4 of section 14, the programs in facilities amount for a board is the total of the amounts determined under this section for each education program provided by the board in a facility described or named in subsection (2) where,

(a) the facility is located within the area of jurisdiction of the board;
(b) the board employs a teacher to provide the education program;
(c) no education program is provided by any Ministry in the facility;
(d) the board has entered into a written agreement with the facility setting out,
  (i) the responsibilities of the facility for the provision of accommodation, and
  (ii) the responsibilities of the board for the provision of the education program, including the number of teachers to be employed by the board for the purposes of the program; and
(e) the Minister,
  (i) is satisfied that the agreement referred to in clause (d) adequately sets out the responsibilities of the board and the facility,
  (ii) has approved the board's staffing plan for the program, and
  (iii) is satisfied that there is a need for the provision of such a program by the board in the facility.

(2) The following are facilities for the purposes of this section:

1. A psychiatric facility.
2. An approved charitable institution as defined in the *Charitable Institutions Act*.
3. An agency approved under subsection 8(1) of the *Child and Family Services Act*.
4. An approved home as defined in the *Homes for Retarded Persons Act*.
5. A place of temporary detention, open custody or secure custody continued or established under section 89 of the *Child and Family Services Act*.
6. A home for special care licensed under the *Homes for Special Care Act*.
7. A facility classified as a Group K Hospital under the *Public Hospitals Act*.
8. The Hospital for Sick Children, in Toronto.
9. The Children's Hospital of Eastern Ontario, in Ottawa.
10. The London Health Sciences Centre, in London.
11. The Lyndhurst Hospital.
12. A hospital in which an education program was discontinued after December 31, 1980 as a result of the dissolution of a board established under section 68 of the Act.
13. A nursing home approved or licensed under the *Nursing Homes Act*.
14. A correctional institution as defined in the *Ministry of Correctional Services Act*.

15. A place of secure or open custody or a place of temporary detention designated for the purposes of the *Young Offenders Act* (Canada).

(3) Subject to subsections (5) and (7), the amount for an education program referred to in subsection (1) shall be determined as follows:

1. Determine the expenditure of the board in the 1999-2000 fiscal year for salary and employee benefits of teachers employed by the board to provide the program. The amount determined under this paragraph shall not exceed the amount that could be expended by the board for salary and employee benefits of teachers under the staffing plan referred to in clause (1)(e).
2. Multiply the number of full-time equivalent teachers employed by the board to provide the program by $2,500. For the purposes of this paragraph, the counting practices usually followed by the board for staffing purposes shall be followed.
3. Determine the expenditure of the board in the 1999-2000 fiscal year for salary and employee benefits of teacher assistants employed by the board to assist teachers in providing the program. The amount determined under this paragraph shall not exceed the amount that could be expended by the board for salary and employee benefits of teacher assistants under the staffing plan referred to in clause (1)(e).
4. Multiply the number of full-time equivalent teacher assistants employed by the board to assist teachers in providing the program by $1,220. For the purposes of this paragraph, the counting practices usually followed by the board for staffing purposes shall be followed.
5. Determine the expenditure of the board in the 1999-2000 fiscal year for the purchase of furniture or equipment for any classroom used in the program. The amount determined for a classroom under this paragraph, added to the total of any amounts received under any predecessor of this paragraph for the classroom, shall not exceed $3,300.
6. Total the amounts determined under paragraphs 1 to 5.

(4) Subsection (5) applies where,

(a) the circumstances described in clauses (1)(a) to (e) apply; and

(b) the education program was previously provided in the facility by the Ministry.

(5) Subject to subsection (7), in the circumstances described in subsection (4), the amount referred to in subsection (1) shall be an amount equal to the cost for the program that is proposed by the board and approved by the Minister, instead of the amount determined under subsection (3).

(6) In giving approvals under clause (1)(e) and subsection (5), the Minister shall ensure that the total of the amounts calculated for all boards under subsections (1) to (5) does not exceed $67 million.

(7) The amount determined for an education program under subsection (3) or (5) shall be reduced by the amount specified by the Minister under subsection (8) if the program,

(a) operates on a smaller scale than was projected in the materials submitted by the board for consideration by the Minister for the purposes of clause (1)(e);

(b) does not operate during the 1999-2000 school year; or

(c) ceases to operate during the 1999-2000 school year.

(8) For the purposes of subsection (7), the Minister shall specify an amount, if any, that in his or her opinion is appropriate having regard to the reasonable costs of the board in connection with the program.

20. (1) Subsection (2) applies where an ISA level 1 claim has been approved for one board under section 16 or under a predecessor of section 16 in respect of a pupil and the pupil enrolls in a school operated by a second board during the 1999-2000 fiscal year.

(2) The equipment for which the ISA level 1 claim was approved shall move with the pupil from the first board to the second board, unless in the opinion of the second board moving the equipment is not practical.

(3) Subsection (4) applies where an ISA level 1 claim has been approved for one board under section 16 in respect of a pupil and the pupil enrolls in a school operated by a second board during the 1999-2000 fiscal year.

(4) Any unspent part of the ISA level 1 claim amount approved in respect of the pupil shall be deducted from the amount determined under subsection 16(2) for the first board and added to the amount determined under subsection 16(2) for the second board.

(5) Subsection (6) applies where a pupil,

(a) was a pupil approved for ISA level 2 or level 3 funding for the purposes of section 18 of Ontario Regulation 287/98;

(b) was enrolled in a school operated by a board at the end of 1998-1999 school year; and

(c) becomes enrolled in a school operated by a different board after the end of the 1998-1999 school year.

(6) The amount calculated under section 18 for the board referred to in clause (5)(b) shall be reduced and the amount calculated under section 18 for the board referred to in clause (5)(c) shall be correspondingly increased to the extent, if any, that the Minister considers appropriate having regard to the costs of the boards in the 1999-2000 fiscal year in connection with providing the pupil's special education program.

(7) This section applies with necessary modifications in respect of second and subsequent moves from one board to another by a pupil.

Language Allocation — English-Language District School Boards

21. For the purposes of paragraph 2 of section 11, the amount of the language allocation for an English-language district school board shall be determined as follows:

1. Determine the French as a second language amount for the board, in accordance with section 22.
2. Determine the Native language amount for the board, in accordance with section 23.
3. Determine the ESL/ESD amount for the board, in accordance with section 24.
4. Total the amounts determined under paragraphs 1, 2 and 3.

22. (1) For the purposes of paragraph 1 of section 21, the French as a second language amount for the board shall be determined as follows:

1. Determine the French as a second language amount for elementary school pupils of the board, in accordance with subsection (3).
2. Determine the French as a second language amount for secondary school pupils of the board, in accordance with subsection (5).
3. Total the amounts determined under paragraphs 1 and 2.

(2) In subsection (3),

"instruction in French" means instruction in the subject of French or instruction in any other subject if the language of instruction is French.

(3) For the purposes of paragraph 1 of subsection (1), the French as a second language amount for elementary school pupils of the board shall be determined as follows:

1. Determine the number of pupils of the board enrolled in any of grades four to eight who, on October 31, 1999, are scheduled to take instruction in French for an average of 20 or more minutes but less than 60 minutes per school day. Multiply by $229.
2. Determine the number of pupils of the board enrolled in any of grades four to eight who, on October 31, 1999, are scheduled to take instruction in French for an average of 60 or more minutes but less than 150 minutes per school day. Multiply by $260.
3. Determine the number of pupils of the board enrolled in any of grades one to eight who, on October 31, 1999, are scheduled to take instruction in French for an average of 150 or more minutes per school day. Multiply by $291.
4. Determine the number of pupils of the board enrolled in junior kindergarten or kindergarten who, on October 31, 1999, are scheduled to take instruction in French for an average of 75 minutes or more per school day. Multiply by $291.
5. Total the products obtained under paragraphs 1 to 4.

(4) In subsection (5),

"course" means a course at the secondary level that is assigned a common course code in the list of common course codes published by the Ministry; ("cours")

"credit value" of a course in which a pupil is enrolled means the number of credits that the pupil is eligible to earn on successfully completing the course. ("valeur en crédits")

(5) For the purposes of paragraph 2 of subsection (1), the French as a second language amount for secondary school pupils of the board shall be determined as follows:

1. Determine an amount for grade nine and ten instruction in the subject of French, as follows:
    i. Determine the credit value of each grade nine course and grade ten course in the subject of French that is taught on a non-semestered basis. Multiply the credit value by the number of pupils of the board enrolled in the course on October 31, 1999, excluding pupils who are 21 years of age or more on December 31, 1999.
    ii. Determine the credit value of each grade nine course and grade ten course in the subject of French that is taught on a semestered basis. Multiply the credit value by the total of the number of pupils of the board enrolled in the course on October 31, 1999 and the number of pupils of the board enrolled in the course on March 31, 2000, excluding pupils who are 21 years of age or more on December 31, 1999.

iii. Add the products obtained under subparagraphs i and ii.
iv. Multiply the sum obtained under subparagraph iii by $57.
2. Determine an amount for grade nine and ten instruction in a subject other than French where the language of instruction is French, as follows:
  i. Determine the credit value of each grade nine course and grade ten course in a subject other than French that is taught in French on a non-semester basis. Multiply the credit value by the number of pupils of the board enrolled in the course on October 31, 1999, excluding pupils who are 21 years of age or more on December 31, 1999.
  ii. Determine the credit value of each grade nine course and grade ten course in a subject other than French that is taught in French on a semestered basis. Multiply the credit value by the total of the number of pupils of the board enrolled in the course on October 31, 1999 and the number of pupils of the board enrolled in the course on March 31, 2000, excluding pupils who are 21 years of age or more on December 31, 1999.
  iii. Add the products obtained under subparagraphs i and ii.
  iv. Multiply the sum obtained under subparagraph iii by $94.
3. Determine an amount for grade 11, 12 and OAC instruction in the subject of French, as follows:
  i. Determine the credit value of each grade 11 course, grade 12 course and OAC course in the subject of French that is taught on a non-semester basis. Multiply the credit value by the number of pupils of the board enrolled in the course on October 31, 1999, excluding pupils who are 21 years of age or more on December 31, 1999.
  ii. Determine the credit value of each grade 11 course, grade 12 course and OAC course in the subject of French that is taught on a semestered basis. Multiply the credit value by the total of the number of pupils of the board enrolled in the course on October 31, 1999 and the number of pupils of the board enrolled in the course on March 31, 2000, excluding pupils who are 21 years of age or more on December 31, 1999.
  iii. Add the products obtained under subparagraphs i and ii.
  iv. Multiply the sum obtained under subparagraph iii by $75.
4. Determine an amount for grade 11, 12 and OAC instruction in a subject other than French where the language of instruction is French, as follows:
  i. Determine the credit value of each grade 11 course, grade 12 course and OAC course in a subject other than French that is taught in French on a non-semestered basis. Multiply the credit value by the number of pupils of the board enrolled in the course on October 31, 1999, excluding pupils who are 21 years of age or more on December 31, 1999.
  ii. Determine the credit value of each grade 11 course, grade 12 course and OAC course in a subject other than French that is taught in French on a semestered basis. Multiply the credit value by the total of the number of pupils of the board enrolled in the course on October 31, 1999 and the number of pupils of the board enrolled in the course on March 31, 2000, excluding pupils who are 21 years of age or more on December 31, 1999.

iii. Add the products obtained under subparagraphs i and ii.

iv. Multiply the sum obtained under subparagraph iii by $145.

5. Total the dollar amounts determined under paragraphs 1 to 4.

23. (1) For the purposes of paragraph 2 of section 21, the Native language amount for the board shall be determined as follows:

1. Determine the Native language amount for elementary school pupils of the board, in accordance with subsection (2).
2. Determine the Native language amount for secondary school pupils of the board, in accordance with subsection (4).
3. Total the amounts determined under paragraphs 1 and 2.

(2) For the purposes of paragraph 1 of subsection (1), the Native language amount for elementary school pupils of the board shall be determined as follows:

1. Determine the number of elementary school pupils of the board who, on October 31, 1999, are scheduled to take instruction in the subject of a Native language for an average of 20 or more minutes but less than 40 minutes per school day. Multiply by $219.
2. Determine the number of elementary school pupils of the board who, on October 31, 1999, are scheduled to take instruction in the subject of a Native language for an average of 40 or more minutes per school day. Multiply by $389.
3. Total the products obtained under paragraphs 1 and 2.

(3) In subsection (4),

"course" means a course at the secondary level that is assigned a common course code in the list of common course codes published by the Ministry; ("cours")

"credit value" of a course in which a pupil is enrolled means the number of credits that the pupil is eligible to earn on successfully completing the course. ("valeur en crédits")

(4) For the purposes of paragraph 2 of subsection (1), the Native language amount for secondary school pupils of the board shall be determined as follows:

1. Determine the credit value of each level one course and level two course in the subject of a Native language that is taught on a non-semestered basis. Multiply the credit value by the number of pupils of the board enrolled in the course on October 31, 1999, excluding pupils who are 21 years of age or more on December 31, 1999. Multiply the product by $57.
2. Determine the credit value of each level one course and level two course in the subject of a Native language that is taught on a semestered basis. Multiply the credit value by the total of the number of pupils of the board enrolled in the course on October 31, 1999 and the number of pupils of the board enrolled in the course on March 31, 2000, excluding pupils who are 21 years of age or more on December 31, 1999. Multiply the product by $57.
3. Determine the credit value of each grade ten course in the subject of a Native language that is taught on a non-semestered basis. Multiply the credit value by the number of pupils of the board enrolled in the course on October 31, 1999, excluding pupils who are 21 years of age or more on December 31, 1999. Multiply the product by $57.
4. Determine the credit value of each grade ten course in the subject of a Native language

that is taught on a semestered basis. Multiply the credit value by the total of the number of pupils of the board enrolled in the course on October 31, 1999 and the number of pupils of the board enrolled in the course on March 31, 2000, excluding pupils who are 21 years of age or more on December 31, 1999. Multiply the product by $57.

5. Determine the credit value of each grade 11 course, grade 12 course and OAC course in the subject of a Native language that is taught on a non-semestered basis. Multiply the credit value by the number of pupils of the board enrolled in the course on October 31, 1999, excluding pupils who are 21 years of age or more on December 31, 1999. Multiply the product by $75.

6. Determine the credit value of each grade 11 course, grade 12 course and OAC course in the subject of a Native language that is taught on a semestered basis. Multiply the credit value by the total of the number of pupils of the board enrolled in the course on October 31, 1999 and the number of pupils of the board enrolled in the course of March 31, 2000, excluding pupils who are 21 years of age or more on December 31, 1999. Multiply the product by $75.

7. Total the dollar amounts determined under paragraphs 1 to 6.

24. (1) For the purposes of paragraph 3 of section 21, the ESL/ESD amount for the board shall be determined as follows:

1. Determine, as of October 31, 1999, the number of pupils of the board who entered Canada during the period beginning September 1, 1998 and ending October 31, 1999 from countries described in subsection (2), excluding pupils who are 21 years of age or more on December 31, 1999, and multiply that number by 1.0.

2. Determine, as of October 31, 1999, the number of pupils of the board who entered Canada during the period beginning September 1, 1997 and ending August 31, 1998 from countries described in subsection (2), excluding pupils who are 21 years of age or more on December 31, 1999, and multiply that number by 0.6.

3. Determine, as of October 31, 1999, the number of pupils of the board who entered Canada during the period beginning September 1, 1996 and ending August 31, 1997 from countries described in subsection (2), excluding pupils who are 21 years of age or more on December 31, 1999, and multiply that number by 0.3.

4. Total the products obtained under paragraphs 1 to 3.

5. Multiply the amount determined under paragraph 4 by $2,235.

6. Add the product obtained under paragraph 5 to the amount set out for the board in Table 1.

(2) Paragraphs 1 to 3 of subsection (1) apply in respect of,

(a) countries where English is not the first language of a majority of the population; and

(b) countries where a majority of the population speaks a variety of English that is so different from the English used as the language of instruction in schools of the board that an ESL or ESD program should be offered to pupils from those countries.

Language Allocation — French-language District School Boards

25. For the purposes of paragraph 2 of section 11, the amount of the language allocation for a French-language district school board shall be determined as follows:

1. Determine the French as a first language amount for the board, in accordance with section 26.
2. Determine the Native language amount for the board, in accordance with section 27.
3. Determine the ALF/PDF amount for the board, in accordance with section 28.
4. Total the amounts determined under paragraphs 1, 2 and 3.

26. (1) For the purposes of paragraph 1 of section 25, the French as a first language amount for the board shall be determined as follows:

1. Multiply by $291 the number of elementary school pupils of the board on October 31, 1999.
2. Multiply the 1999-2000 day school average daily enrolment of secondary school pupils of the board by $460.
3. Determine the start-up amount for new elementary schools of the board, in accordance with subsection (2).
4. Total the amounts determined under paragraphs 1, 2 and 3.

(2) For the purposes of paragraph 3 of subsection (1), the start-up amount for new elementary schools of the board shall be determined by multiplying the number of elementary schools of the board that are being governed for the first time by the board in September, 1999 by $10,800.

27. For the purposes of paragraph 2 of section 25, the Native language amount for the board shall be determined in the manner provided in section 23 for English-language district school boards.

28. (1) For the purposes of this section, a board is coterminous with another board if the areas of jurisdiction of the two boards are wholly or partly the same.

(2) For the purposes of this section,

(a) the area of jurisdiction of a French-language public district school board is divided into portions matching the areas of jurisdiction of the coterminous English-language public district school boards;
(b) the area of jurisdiction of a French-language separate district school board is divided into portions matching the areas of jurisdiction of the coterminous English-language separate district school boards; and
(c) where the area of jurisdiction of a French-language separate district school board is the same as the area of jurisdiction of an English-language separate district school board, the total area of jurisdiction of the French-language separate district school board is one portion.

(3) For the purposes of paragraph 3 of section 25, the ALF/PDF amount for the board shall be determined as follows:

1. Determine the ALF funding level for the board in accordance with subsection (4).
2. Determine the PDF funding level for the board in accordance with subsection (11).
3. Total the amounts determined under paragraphs 1 and 2.

(4) For the purposes of paragraph 1 of subsection (3), the ALF funding level for the board shall be determined as follows:

1. Determine the number of elementary instructional units for ALF purposes for each

portion of the board, in accordance with subsection (6). The determination under this paragraph shall be accurate to two decimal points.
2. Determine the number of secondary instructional units for ALF purposes for each portion of the board, in accordance with subsection (7). The determination under this paragraph shall be accurate to two decimal places.
3. For each portion of the board, add the numbers determined under paragraphs 1 and 2.
4. Determine the assimilation factor for each portion of the board, in accordance with subsection (8) or (9), as the case may be.
5. For each portion of the board, multiply the number determined under paragraph 3 by the factor determined under paragraph 4.
6. For each portion of the board, multiply the product determined under paragraph 5 by $60,000.
7. Total the amounts determined for each of the portions of the board under paragraph 6.

(5) For the purposes of subsections (6) and (7), the pupils of a board shall be counted on the basis of day school full-time equivalent enrollment for the board as of October 31, 1999.

(6) The number of elementary instructional units for ALF purposes for a portion of the board shall be determined as follows:
1. Allow 0.005 elementary instructional units for ALF purposes for each of the first 200 elementary school pupils of the board who are enrolled in schools located in the portion.
2. Allow 0.0025 elementary instructional units for ALF purposes for each of the next 1,600 elementary school pupils of the board who are enrolled in schools located in the portion.
3. Allow 0.0013 elementary instructional units for ALF purposes for each of the remaining elementary school pupils of the board who are enrolled in schools located in the portion.
4. Total the instructional units allowed for ALF purposes for the portion of the board under paragraphs 1, 2 and 3.

(7) The number of secondary instructional units for ALF purposes for a portion of the board shall be determined as follows:
1. Allow 0.0025 secondary instructional units for ALF purposes for each of the first 1,200 secondary school pupils of the board who are enrolled in schools located in the portion.
2. Allow 0.0013 secondary instructional units for ALF purposes for each of the remaining secondary school pupils of the board who are enrolled in schools located in the portion.
3. Total the instructional units allowed for ALF purposes for the portion of the board under paragraphs 1 and 2.

(8) The assimilation factor for a portion of a French-language public district school board shall be the factor specified in Table 2 for the English-language public district school board the area of jurisdiction of which matches the portion.

(9) The assimilation factor for a portion of a French-language separate district school board shall be the factor specified in Table 2 for the English-language separate district school board the area of jurisdiction of which matches the portion.

(10) For the purposes of subsection (11), a pupil is eligible for PDF funding if,

(a) the pupil was admitted to a school of the board under section 293 of the Act;

(b) the pupil entered Canada during the period beginning September 1, 1996 and ending October 31, 1999 from a country in which French is a standard language of schooling or public administration;

(c) the pupil has one or more of the following characteristics:
 1. The pupil speaks a variety of French that is so different from the French being used as the language of instruction in schools of the board that a PDF program should be offered to the pupil.
 2. The pupil's schooling has been interrupted or delayed.
 3. The pupil has little knowledge of English or French.

(11) For the purposes of paragraph 2 of subsection (3), the PDF funding level for the board shall be determined as follows:

1. Determine, as of October 31, 1999, the number of pupils of the board who are eligible for PDF funding and who entered Canada during the period beginning September 1, 1998 and ending October 31, 1999 from a country described in clause (10)(b), excluding pupils who are 21 years of age or more on December 31, 1999, and multiply that number by 1.0.
2. Determine, as of October 31, 1999, the number of pupils of the board who are eligible for PDF funding and who entered Canada during the period beginning September 1, 1997 and ending August 31, 1998 from a country described in clause (10)(b), excluding pupils who are 21 years of age or more on December 31, 1999, and multiply that number by 0.6.
3. Determine, as of October 31, 1999, the number of pupils of the board who are eligible for PDF funding and who entered Canada during the period beginning September 1, 1996 and ending August 31, 1997 from a country described in clause (10)(b), excluding pupils who are 21 years of age or more on December 31, 1999, and multiply that number by 0.3.
4. Total the products obtained under paragraphs 1, 2 and 3.
5. Multiply the amount determined under paragraph 4 by $2,235.

Small Schools Allocation

29. (1) In this section,

"small school", in relation to an English-language district school board, means,

(a) an elementary school that has an average of less than 20 pupils per grade and is located eight or more kilometres by road from every other elementary school of the board,

(b) a secondary school that has an average of less than 120 pupils per grade and is located

32 or more kilometres by road from every other secondary school of the board; ("petite école")

"small school", in relation to a French-language district school board, means,

(a) an elementary school that has an average of less than 20 pupils per grade and is located eight or more kilometres by road from every other elementary school of the board that is located in the same portion of the board's area of jurisdiction,

(b) a secondary school that has an average of less than 120 pupils per grade and is located 32 or more kilometres by road from every other secondary school of the board that is located in the same portion of the board's area of jurisdiction. ("petite école")

(2) For the purposes of this section, a board is coterminous with another board if the areas of jurisdiction of the two boards are wholly or partly the same.

(3) For the purposes of this section,

(a) the area of jurisdiction of a French-language public district school board is divided into portions matching the areas of jurisdiction of the coterminous English-language public district school boards;

(b) the area of jurisdiction of a French-language separate district school board is divided into portions matching the areas of jurisdiction of the coterminous English-language separate district school boards; and

(c) where the area of jurisdiction of a French-language separate district school board is the same as the area of jurisdiction of an English-language separate district school board, the total area of jurisdiction of the French-language separate district school board is one portion.

(4) For the purposes of this section,

(a) junior kindergarten, kindergarten and grades one to eight are elementary grades;

(b) grades nine to twelve and OAC are secondary grades;

(c) subject to subsection (5), a school that offers instruction in one or more of the elementary grades shall be treated as an elementary school;

(d) subject to subsection (5), a school that offers instruction in one or more of the secondary grades shall be treated as a secondary school.

(5) For the purposes of this section, where a school offers instruction in one or more of the elementary grades and in one or more of the secondary grades, the school shall be treated as two schools, as follows:

1. One elementary school, offering instruction in the relevant elementary grades.
2. One secondary school, offering instruction in the relevant secondary grades.

(6) For the purposes of this section, the average number of pupils per grade of an elementary school shall be calculated as follows:

1. Determine the day school full-time equivalent enrolment for the board as of October 31, 1999, counting only the pupils enrolled in the school. For the purposes of this paragraph, a pupil who would be a pupil of a board were it not for subsection 2(5) shall be deemed to be a pupil of the board.
2. Determine the number of grades in the school, counting junior kindergarten and kindergarten as 0.5 grades each.

3. Divide the number determined under paragraph 1 by the number determined under paragraph 2.

(7) For the purposes of this section, the average number of pupils per grade of a secondary school shall be calculated as follows:
1. Determine the day school full-time equivalent enrolment for the board as of October 31, 1999, counting only the pupils enrolled in the school. For the purposes of this paragraph, a pupil who would be a pupil of a board were it not for subsection 2(4) or (5) shall be deemed to be a pupil of the board.
2. Divide the number determined under paragraph 1 by the number of grades in which instruction is provided in the school.

(8) Where two or more elementary schools of an English-language district school board are all located within eight kilometres of each other by road, their combined average number of pupils per grade is less than 20 pupils per grade and one or more of the schools in the group is located eight or more kilometres by road from every elementary school of the board that is not in the group,
(a) the group of two or more schools shall be deemed to be one small school for the purposes of this section; and
(b) each of the two or more schools in the group shall be deemed not to be a small school for the purposes of this section.

(9) Where two or more elementary schools of a French-language district school board are all located in the same portion of the board's area of jurisdiction, are all within eight kilometres of each other by road, their combined average number of pupils per grade is less than 20 pupils per grade and one or more of the schools in the group is located eight or more kilometres by road from every elementary school of the board that is not in the group but is in the same portion of the board's area of jurisdiction,
(a) the group of two or more schools shall be deemed to be one small school for the purposes of this section; and
(b) each of the two or more schools in the group shall be deemed not to be a small school for the purposes of this section.

(10) For the purposes of this section, the combined average number of pupils per grade of a group of two or more elementary schools shall be calculated as follows:
1. Determine the day school full-time equivalent enrolment for the board as of October 31, 1999, counting only the pupils enrolled in the schools in the group. For the purposes of this paragraph, a pupil who would be a pupil of a board were it not for subsection 2(5) shall be deemed to be a pupil of the board.
2. Determine the number of grades in which instruction is given in one or more of the schools in the group, counting junior kindergarten and kindergarten as 0.5 grades each.
3. Divide the number determined under paragraph 1 by the number determined under paragraph 2.

(11) For the purposes of paragraph 2 of section 11, the amount of the small school allocation for a district school board shall be determined as follows:

S. 29   REGULATIONS UNDER THE EDUCATION ACT

1. For each elementary small school of the board,
   i. determine the school size factor, in accordance with subsection (12),
   ii. determine the remoteness factor, in accordance with subsection (14), and
   iii. determine the day school full-time equivalent enrolment for the board as of October 31, 1999, counting only the pupils of the board enrolled in the school.
2. For each elementary small school of the board, multiply the school size factor by the remoteness factor. Multiply the product by the enrolment determined for the school under subparagraph iii of paragraph 1.
3. For each elementary small school of the board, multiply the product obtained under paragraph 2 by $6,000.
4. Total the amounts determined for each of the elementary small schools of the board under paragraph 3.
5. For each secondary small school of the board,
   i. determine the school size factor, in accordance with subsection (16),
   ii. determine the remoteness factor, in accordance with subsection (17), and
   iii. determine the day school full-time equivalent enrolment for the board as of October 31, 1999, counting only pupils of the board enrolled in the school. For the purposes of this subparagraph, pupils enrolled in the school who would be pupils of the board were it not for subsection 2(4) shall be deemed to be pupils of the board.
6. For each secondary small school of the board, multiply the school size factor by the remoteness factor. Multiply the product by the enrolment number determined for the school under subparagraph iii of paragraph 5.
7. For each secondary small school of the board, multiply the product obtained under paragraph 6 by $7,200.
8. Total the amounts determined for each of the secondary small schools of the board under paragraph 7.
9. Total the totals determined under paragraphs 4 and 8.

(12) The school size factor for a small elementary school shall be determined as follows:

1. For a school with an average number of pupils per grade that is less than two, the school size factor is 1.
2. For a school with an average number of pupils per grade that is two or more but not more than 10, the school size factor shall be determined on a sliding scale as follows:
   i. Divide 10 by the average number of pupils per grade.
   ii. Multiply the result obtained under subparagraph i by 0.2.
3. For a school with an average number of pupils per grade that is more than 10 but less than 20, the school size factor shall be determined on a sliding scale as follows:
   i. Subtract 10 from the average number of pupils per grade.
   ii. Divide the result obtained under subparagraph i by 10.
   iii. Subtract the result obtained under subparagraph ii from one.
   iv. Multiply the result obtained under subparagraph iii by 0.2.

(13) For the purposes of subsection (12), the average number of pupils per grade of a group of two or more schools that is deemed under subsection (8) or (9) to be one small school

is the combined average number of pupils per grade of the group, calculated in accordance with subsection (10).

(14) The remoteness factor for a small elementary school shall be determined as follows:
1. For a school of an English-language district board located 80 kilometres or more by road from all other elementary schools of the board, the remoteness factor is 1.5.
2. For a school of an English-language district board located more than 32 kilometres by road but less than 80 kilometres by road from all other elementary schools of the board, the remoteness factor is 1.25.
3. For all other schools of an English-language district school board, the remoteness factor is 1.0.
4. For a school of a French-language district board located 80 kilometres or more by road from all other elementary schools of the board that are located in the same portion of the board's area of jurisdiction, the remoteness factor is 1.5.
5. For a school of a French-language district board located more than 32 kilometres by road but less than 80 kilometres by road from all other elementary schools of the board that are located in the same portion of the board's area of jurisdiction, the remoteness factor is 1.25.
6. For all other schools of a French-language district school board, the remoteness factor is 1.0.

(15) The following rules apply for the purposes of subsection (14), where a group of two or more schools of a board is deemed under subsection (8) or (9) to be one small school:
1. In the case of elementary schools of an English-language district school board, if one or more of the schools in the group is located 80 kilometres or more by road from every elementary school of the board that is not in the group, the deemed small school shall be deemed to be located 80 kilometres or more by road from all other elementary schools of the board.
2. Except where paragraph 1 applies, in the case of elementary schools of an English-language district school board, if one or more of the schools in the group is located more than 32 kilometres by road from every elementary school of the board that is not in the group, the deemed small school shall be deemed to be located more than 32 kilometres by road but less than 80 kilometres by road from all other elementary schools of the board.
3. In the case of elementary schools of a French-language district school board, if one or more of the schools in the group is located 80 kilometres or more by road from every elementary school of the board that is not in the group but that is located in the same portion of the board's area of jurisdiction, the deemed small school shall be deemed to be located 80 kilometres or more by road from all other elementary schools of the board.
4. Except where paragraph 3 applies, in the case of elementary schools of a French-language district school board, if one or more of the schools in the group is located more than 32 kilometres by road from every elementary school of the board that is not in the group but that is located in the same portion of the board's area of jurisdiction, the deemed small school shall be deemed to be located more than 32

kilometres by road but less than 80 kilometres by road from all other elementary schools of the board.

(16) The school size factor for a small secondary school shall be determined as follows:
1. For a school with an average number of pupils per grade that is less than 20, the school size factor is 0.45.
2. For a school with an average number of pupils per grade that is 20 or more but not more than 60, the school size factor shall be determined on a sliding scale as follows:
    i. Divide 60 by the average number of pupils per grade.
    ii. Multiply the result obtained under subparagraph i by 0.15.
3. For a school with an average number of pupils per grade that is more than 60 but less than 120, the school size factor shall be determined on a sliding scale as follows:
    i. Subtract 60 from the average number of pupils per grade.
    ii. Divide the result obtained under subparagraph i by 60.
    iii. Subtract the result obtained under subparagraph ii from one.
    iv. Multiply the result obtained under subparagraph iii by 0.15.

(17) The remoteness factor for a small secondary school shall be determined as follows:
1. For a school of an English-language district school board that has an average number of pupils per grade that is less than 20 and that is located 80 kilometres or more by road from all other secondary schools of the board, the remoteness factor is 2.0.
2. For a school of an English-language district school board that has an average number of pupils per grade that is 20 or more but less than 120, and that is located 80 kilometres or more by road from all other secondary schools of the board, the remoteness factor shall be determined as follows:
    i. Add 20 to the average number of pupils per grade.
    ii. Divide 40 by the sum obtained under subparagraph i.
    iii. Add one to the result obtained under subparagraph ii.
3. For all other small secondary schools of an English-language district school board, the remoteness factor is 1.0.
4. For a school of a French-language district school board that has an average number of pupils per grade that is less than 20 and that is located 80 kilometres or more by road from all other secondary schools of the board that are located in the same portion of the board's area of jurisdiction, the remoteness factor is 2.0.
5. For a school of a French-language district school board that has an average number of pupils per grade that is 20 or more but less than 120, and that is located 80 kilometres or more by road from all other secondary schools of the board that are located in the same portion of the board's area of jurisdiction, the remoteness factor shall be determined as follows:
    i. Add 20 to the average number of pupils per grade.
    ii. Divide 40 by the sum obtained under subparagraph i.
    iii. Add one to the result obtained under subparagraph ii.
6. For all other small secondary schools of a French-language district school board, the remoteness factor is 1.0.

Remote and Rural Allocation

30. For the purposes of paragraph 2 of section 11, the amount of the remote and rural allocation for a district school board shall be determined as follows:
1. Determine the per pupil distance amount for the board, in accordance with the following:
    i. If the distance specified for the board in Column 2 of Table 3 is less than 151 kilometres, the per pupil distance amount is zero.
    ii. If the distance specified for the board in Column 2 of Table 3 is 151 kilometres or more but less than 650 kilometres, the per pupil distance amount shall be determined by subtracting 150 from that distance and multiplying the result by $0.962.
    iii. If the distance specified for the board in Column 2 of Table 3 is 650 kilometres or more but less than 1,150 kilometres, the per pupil distance amount shall be determined as follows: Subtract 650 from that distance. Multiply the result by $0.134. Add $481 to the product.
    iv. If the distance specified for the board in Column 2 of Table 3 is 1,150 kilometres or more, the per pupil distance amount is $548.
2. Multiply the per pupil distance amount determined for the board under paragraph 1 by the urban factor specified for the board in Column 3 of Table 3.
3. Determine the per pupil sparsity amount for the board in accordance with the following:
    i. Determine the pupil density by dividing the 1999-2000 day school average daily enrolment for the board, as determined under section 2 of the 1999-2000 A.D.E. regulation, not counting pupils who are 21 years of age or more on December 31, 1999, by the board's area in square kilometres, as specified in the Schedule to Ontario Regulation 250/97.
    ii. If the number determined under subparagraph i is less than one, the per pupil sparsity amount shall be determined by subtracting that number from one and multiplying the result by $400.
    iii. If the number determined under subparagraph i is one or greater than one, the per pupil sparsity amount is zero.
4. Add the per pupil sparsity amount determined for the board under paragraph 3 to the amount determined for the board under paragraph 2.
5. Multiply the amount obtained under paragraph 4 by the 1999-2000 day school average daily enrolment of pupils of the board.

Learning Opportunities Allocation

31. For the purposes of paragraph 2 of section 11, the amount of the learning opportunities allocation for a district school board shall be the amount set out in Column 2 of Table 4, opposite the name of the board.

Summer School Remedial Allocation

32. (1) For the purposes of paragraph 2 of section 11, the amount of the summer school remedial allocation for a district school board shall be determined as follows:
1. Determine the summer school average daily enrolment for the board for the 1999-2000 fiscal year in accordance with section 4 of the 1999-2000 A.D.E. regulation, counting only pupils of the board enrolled in classes or courses described in subclause (b)(iii) of the definition of "summer school class or course" in subsection 4(1) of that regulation.
2. Multiply the number determined under paragraph 1 by $2,257.
3. Add the amount determined for the board under subsection (2) on account of transportation costs related to summer school remedial instruction.

(2) For the purposes of paragraph 3 of subsection (2), an amount on account of transportation costs related to summer school remedial instruction shall be determined for the board as follows:
1. Take the amount of the transportation allocation determined for the board under section 36.
2. Deduct the amount approved for the board under paragraph 7 of section 36.
3. Divide the result obtained under paragraph 2 by the 1999-2000 day school average daily enrolment of pupils of the board.
4. Multiply the result obtained under paragraph 3 by the enrolment amount determined under paragraph 1 of subsection (1).

Adult Education, Continuing Education and Summer School Allocation

33. (1) For the purposes of paragraph 2 of section 11, the amount of the adult education, continuing education and summer school allocation for a district school board shall be determined as follows:
1. Determine the day school average daily enrolment for the board for the 1999-2000 fiscal year, in accordance with section 2 of the 1999-2000 A.D.E. regulation, counting only pupils of the board who are 21 years of age or more on December 31, 1999.
2. Determine the continuing education average daily enrolment for the board for the 1999-2000 fiscal year, in accordance with section 3 of the 1999-2000 A.D.E. regulation, excluding pupils to whom subsection 49(6) of the Act applies and pupils in respect of whom the board charges a fee under subsection 8(2) of the 1999-2000 fees regulation.
3. Determine the summer school average daily enrolment for the board for the 1999-2000 fiscal year, in accordance with section 4 of the 1999-2000 A.D.E. regulation, counting only pupils enrolled in classes or courses described in subclause (b)(i) or (ii) of the definition of "summer school course or class" in subsection 4(1) of that regulation, excluding pupils to whom subsection 49(6) applies and pupils in respect of whom the board charges a fee under subsection 8(3) of the 1999-2000 fees regulation.
4. Add the numbers determined under paragraphs 1, 2 and 3.

5. Multiply the total determined under paragraph 4 by $2,257.
6. Determine the amount for international languages for the board, in accordance with subsections (2) to (4).
7. Total the amounts determined under paragraphs 5 and 6.

(2) Subsections (3) and (4) apply where a board establishes classes to provide instruction in a language other than English or French and the classes have been approved by the Minister as being part of an international languages elementary school program.

(3) Except as provided in subsection (4), the amount for international languages for the board shall be the number of hours of instruction provided by the board in classes described in subsection (2), multiplied by $41.

(4) Where the quotient obtained by dividing the number of elementary school pupils enrolled in classes described in subsection (2) that have been established by the board by the number of such classes is less than 25, the $41 per hour rate specified in subsection (3) shall be reduced by the product of $1 and the difference between the quotient and 25.

Teacher Compensation Allocation

34. (1) In this section,

"OSSTF" stands for the Ontario Secondary School Teachers' Federation; ("FEESO")

"OSSTF certification" means the OSSTF certification of Group 1, Group 2, Group 3 or Group 4; ("certification de la FEESO")

"qualification category" means OSSTF certification or QECO category; ("catégorie de qualifications")

"QECO" stands for Qualifications Evaluation Council of Ontario; ("COEQ")

"QECO category" means the QECO category D, C, B, A1, A2, A3 or A4; ("catégorie du COEQ")

"teacher" includes a temporary teacher and does not include an occasional teacher. ("enseignant")

(2) In this section, a cell of Table 5 is referred to by its qualification category co-ordinate followed by the number co-ordinate representing full years of teaching experience.

(3) For example, cell C-1 of Table 5 contains the number 0.6127 and cell A1/Group 1-3 contains the number 0.7416.

(4) For the purposes of this section, the number of teachers employed by a board is the full-time equivalent number of persons employed by the board as of October 31, 1999 to teach.

(5) For the purposes of subsection (4), the counting practices usually followed by the board for staffing purposes shall be followed, subject to the following rules:

1. A teacher who is not assigned to provide instruction to pupils in a regular timetable that is in effect as of October 31, 1999 shall not be counted for the purposes of this section.
2. The provision of library instruction or guidance to pupils shall be considered the provision of instruction to pupils for the purposes of paragraphs 1, 3 and 4.
3. Where a teacher is assigned in a regular timetable that is in effect as of October 31,

S. 34
REGULATIONS UNDER THE EDUCATION ACT

1999 to spend part of his or her time providing instruction to pupils and is also assigned, as of that date, under section 17 of Regulation 298 of the Revised Regulations of Ontario, 1990, to spend part of his or her time acting as a consultant, co-ordinator or supervisor, the full-time equivalency for the teacher shall be determined as follows:

    i. Determine the average number of hours per day in the cycle that includes October 31, 1999 for which the teacher is regularly scheduled, in accordance with the timetable, to provide instruction to pupils or to prepare for such instruction. For the purposes of this subparagraph, a count of hours shall be accurate to one decimal place.

    ii. Divide the total determined under subparagraph i by five.

4. Where a principal or vice-principal is assigned in a regular timetable that is in effect as of October 31, 1999 to spend part of his or her time providing instruction to pupils, the principal or vice-principal shall be counted as a teacher for the purposes of this section and his or her full-time equivalency as a teacher shall be determined as follows:

    i. Determine the average number of hours per day in the cycle that includes October 31, 1999 for which the principal or vice-principal is regularly scheduled, in accordance with the timetable, to provide instruction to pupils. For the purposes of this subsection, a count of hours shall be accurate to one decimal place.

    ii. Divide the number determined under subparagraph i by five.

(6) Subject to subsections (7) and (8), when determining the number of full years of teaching experience of a teacher employed by a board, the counting practices usually followed by the board when counting the amount of teaching experience shall be applied, as of October 31, 1999.

(7) Where the number of full years of teaching experience of a teacher exceeds 10, as determined under subsection (6), the number of full years of teaching experience of the teacher shall be deemed to be 10.

(8) The number of full years of teaching experience of a principal or vice-principal shall be deemed to be 10.

(9) The following rules shall be applied, as of October 31, 1999, to determine the qualification category of a teacher:

1. If a board uses a QECO categories system for salary purposes in relation to a teacher employed by it, that QECO categories system shall be used for that teacher for the purposes of this section.
2. If a board uses an OSSTF certification system for salary purposes in relation to a teacher employed by it, that OSSTF certification system shall be used for that teacher for the purposes of this section.
3. Subject to paragraph 5, if a board does not use a QECO categories system for salary purposes in relation to an elementary school teacher employed by it, the classification system used by the board for elementary school teachers in filling out the Education Relations Commission Data Form A for 1999 shall be used for that teacher for the purposes of this section.

4. Subject to paragraph 5, if a board does not use a QECO categories system or an OSSTF certification system for salary purposes in relation to a secondary school teacher employed by it, the classification system used by the board for secondary school teachers in filling out the Education Relations Commission Data Form A for 1999 shall be used for that teacher for the purposes of this section.

5. In the circumstances described in paragraph 3 or 4, the board may elect, by written notice to the Minister, to use the QECO categories system referred to by QECO as QECO Programme Level 4 or the 1992 OSSTF certification system, instead of the classification system determined under paragraph 3 or 4.

6. The qualification category of a principal or vice-principal shall be deemed to be A4/Group 4.

7. If the qualification category of a person is changed after October 31, 1999 and the change for salary purposes it retroactive to October 31, 1999 or earlier, the changed qualification category shall be used for the purposes of this section.

(10) For the purposes of paragraph 2 of section 11, the amount of the teacher compensation allocation for a district school board is the total of the amount calculated under subsection (11) and the amount calculated under subsection (12).

(11) The amount of the elementary school teacher compensation allocation for a district school board shall be determined as follows:

1. For each cell in Table 5, determine the number of teachers employed by the board to provide instruction to elementary school pupils who have the qualification category and the number of full years of teaching experience that correspond with the co-ordinates of the cell. For example, a teacher with a qualification category of D and six months of teaching experience shall be counted for the purposes of cell D-0 and a teacher with a qualification category of A2 or Group 2 and three years and seven months of teaching experience shall be counted for the purposes of cell A2/Group 2-3.

2. For each cell in Table 5, multiply the number of teachers employed by the board to provide instruction to elementary school pupils who are counted for the purposes of the cell by the number set out in that cell in Table 5.

3. Add all the products obtained under paragraph 2 for the board.

4. Divide the sum obtained under paragraph 3 by the total number of teachers employed by the board to provide instruction to elementary school pupils.

5. Subtract one from the number obtained under paragraph 4.

6. Multiply the result obtained under paragraph 5 by $2,548.

7. Multiply the amount determined under paragraph 6 by the 1999-2000 day school average daily enrolment of elementary school pupils of the board.

(12) The amount of the secondary school teacher compensation allocation for a district school board shall be determined as follows:

1. For each cell in Table 5, determine the number of teachers employed by the board to provide instruction to secondary school pupils who have the qualification category and the number of full years of teaching experience that correspond with the co-ordinates of the cell. For example, a teacher with a qualification category of D and six months of teaching experience shall be counted for the purposes of cell D-0 and

a teacher with a qualification category of A2 or Group 2 and three years and seven months of teaching experience shall be counted for the purposes of cell A2/Group 2-3.

2. For each cell in Table 5, multiply the number of teachers employed by the board to provide instruction to secondary school pupils who are counted for the purposes of the cell by the number set out in that cell in Table 5.
3. Add all the products obtained under paragraph 2 for the board.
4. Divide the sum obtained under paragraph 3 by the total number of teachers employed by the board to provide instruction to secondary school pupils.
5. Subtract one from the number obtained under paragraph 4.
6. Multiply the result obtained under paragraph 5 by $2,956.
7. Multiply the amount determined under paragraph 6 by the 1999-2000 day school average daily enrolment of secondary school pupils of the board.
8. Determine the special assistance amount, if any, for a high credit per pupil average, in accordance with subsection (13).
9. Add the amounts determined under paragraphs 7 and 8.

(13) For the purposes of paragraph 8 of subsection (12), the special assistance amount for a high credit per pupil average shall be determined as follows:

1. Determine the average number of credits per secondary school pupil of the board for the 1998-99 school year.
2. If the number determined under paragraph 1 is 7.5 or less but more than 7.2, deduct 7.2 from the number determined under paragraph 1.
3. If the number determined under paragraph 1 is more than 7.5, deduct 7.2 from 7.5.
4. Divide the number obtained under paragraph 2 or 3, as the case may be, by 7.2.
5. Multiply the number obtained under paragraph 4 by $2,748.
6. Multiply the amount obtained under paragraph 5 by the 1999-2000 day school average daily enrolment of secondary school pupils of the board.

Early Learning Allocation

35. (1) For the purposes of paragraph 2 of section 11, the amount of the early learning allocation for a district school board shall be determined in accordance with this section.

(2) If a board does not provide instruction in junior kindergarten in any of its schools in September of 1999, the amount of the early learning allocation for the board shall be determined as follows:

1. Determine the day school average daily enrolment for the board, counting only pupils of the board enrolled in any of kindergarten and grades one to three.
2. Multiply the number determined under paragraph 1 by $609.

(3) If a board provides instruction in junior kindergarten in one or more of its schools in September of 1999, the amount of the early learning allocation for the board shall be determined as follows:

1. Determine the day school average daily enrolment for the board, counting only pupils of the board enrolled in any of kindergarten and grades one to three.
2. Multiply the number determined under paragraph 1 by $609.

3. Determine the 1999-2000 allocation per elementary school pupil of the board, in accordance with subsection (4).
4. Multiply the amount determined under paragraph 3 by the day school average daily enrolment for the board, counting only pupils of the board enrolled in junior kindergarten.
5. Deduct the amount determined under paragraph 4 from the amount determined under paragraph 2.

(4) For the purposes of paragraph 3 of subsection (3), the 1999-2000 allocation per elementary school pupil of the board shall be determined as follows:

1. Total the following amounts:
    i. The remote and rural allocation amount for the board, as determined under section 30.
    ii. The learning opportunities allocation amount for the board, as determined under section 31.
    iii. The transportation allocation amount for the board, as determined under section 36.
    iv. The administration and governance allocation amount for the board, as determined under section 37.
2. Divide the total obtained under paragraph 1 by the 1999-2000 day school average daily enrolment of pupils of the board.
3. Determine an amount on account of the special education allocation for elementary school pupils, as follows:
    i. Multiply the 1999-2000 day school average daily enrolment of elementary school pupils of the board by $362.
    ii. Calculate the part of the equipment ISA determined for the board under paragraph 2 of section 14 that is generated by elementary school pupils of the board.
    iii. Calculate the part of the amount determined for the board under clause 18(a) that is generated by individuals who were elementary school pupils in the 1998-1999 school year. Where an adjustment has been made under section 20 to the amount calculated for the board under section 18, the amount calculated for the board under this subparagraph shall be increased or decreased by the amount that the Minister considers appropriate to take account of the adjustment made under section 20.
    iv. Calculate the part of the amount determined for the board under clause 18(b) that is generated by elementary school pupils of the board. Where an adjustment has been made under section 20 to the amount calculated for the board under section 18, the amount calculated for the board under this subparagraph shall be increased or decreased by the amount that the Minister considers appropriate to take account of the adjustment made under section 20.
    v. Total the amounts obtained under subparagraphs i, ii, iii and iv.
4. Take the amount determined in relation to elementary small schools for the board under paragraph 4 of subsection 29(11).
5. In the case of an English-language district school board, determine an amount on account of the language allocation for elementary school pupils, as follows:

i. Add the amount calculated under paragraph 3 of subsection 22(3) to the amount calculated under paragraph 4 of subsection 22(3).
ii. Calculate the part of the ESL/ESD amount for the board, as calculated under section 24, that is generated by elementary school pupils of the board.
iii. Add the amount calculated under subparagraph i to the amount calculated under subparagraph ii.
6. In the case of a French-language district school board, determine an amount on account of the language allocation for elementary school pupils, as follows:
    i. Total the amounts determined for the board under paragraphs 1 and 3 of subsection 26(1).
    ii. Divide the total determined for the board under paragraph 7 of subsection 28(4) by the total number of instructional units determined for the board under paragraph 3 of subsection 28(4). Multiply the result by the total number of elementary instructional units determined for the board under paragraph 1 of subsection 28(4).
    iii. Calculate the part of the PDF funding level for the board, as calculated under subsection 28(11), that is generated by elementary school pupils of the board.
    iv. Total the amount taken under subparagraph i, the product obtained under subparagraph ii and the amount calculated under subparagraph iii.
7. Take the amount determined under subsection 34(11) as the elementary school teacher compensation allocation for the board.
8. Determine an amount in relation to elementary school operations as follows:
    i. Multiply the area requirement in metres squared determined for the board under subparagraph i of paragraph 13 of subsection 38(3), by $55.97.
    ii. Add the sum determined under paragraph 16 of subsection 38(3).
9. Total the amounts taken or determined for the board under paragraphs 3 to 8.
10. Divide the total obtained under paragraph 9 by the 1999-2000 day school average daily enrolment of elementary school pupils of the board.
11. Total the following amounts:
    i. $3,367, on account of the foundation allocation.
    ii. The amount obtained under paragraph 2.
    iii. The amount obtained under paragraph 10.

Transportation Allocation

36. For the purposes of paragraph 2 of section 11, the amount of the transportation allocation for a district school board shall be determined as follows:
1. Take the amount of the transportation allocation determined for the board under section 35 of Ontario Regulation 287/98.
2. Deduct the total of the amounts spent by the board in the fiscal year September 1, 1998 to August 31, 1999 in respect of the transportation to and from the Ontario School for the Blind, an Ontario School for the Deaf or a demonstration school established by or operated under an agreement with the Minister for pupils with severe communicational exceptionalities.

3. Determine the 1999-2000 day school average daily enrolment of pupils of the district school board.
4. Take the 1998-99 day school average daily enrolment of pupils of the board, within the meaning of Ontario Regulation 287/98, except that all pupils enrolled in kindergarten during the period from September 1, 1998 to August 31, 1999 shall be counted as half-time pupils.
5. Divide the number obtained under paragraph 3 by the number obtained under paragraph 4.
6. Multiply the number obtained under paragraph 5 by the amount obtained under paragraph 2.
7. Add the amount of the expenditure of the board in the 1999-2000 fiscal year that is approved by the Minister in respect of the transportation to and from the Ontario School for the Blind, an Ontario School for the Deaf or a demonstration school established by or operated under an agreement with the Minister for pupils with severe communicational exceptionalities.

Administration and Governance Allocation

37. (1) For the purposes of paragraph 2 of section 11, the amount of the administration and governance allocation for a district school board shall be determined as follows:
1. Determine the amount for the board for board members' honoraria and expenses and for expenses relating to pupil representation, in accordance with subsection (2).
2. Determine the amount for the board for directors of education and supervisory officers, in accordance with subsection (4).
3. Determine the amount for the board for administration costs, in accordance with subsection (5).
4. Total the amounts determined under paragraphs 1, 2 and 3.

(2) The amount for the board for board members' honoraria and expenses and for expenses relating to pupil representation shall be determined as follows:
1. Multiply the number of members on the board by $5,000, on account of board members' honoraria. For the purposes of this paragraph, the number of members on the board is the sum of,
   i. the number of members determined for the board under subclause 58.1(2)(k)(i) of the Act, and
   ii. the number of Native representatives determined for the board under subsection 188(5) of the Act.
2. Multiply the number of members on the board by $5,000, on account of board members' expenses. For the purposes of this paragraph, the number of members on the board is the sum of,
   i. the number of members determined for the board under subclause 58.1(2)(k)(i) of the Act, and
   ii. the number of Native representatives determined for the board under subsection 188(5) of the Act.
3. Total the products obtained under paragraphs 1 and 2.

4. Add $10,000 to the amount determined under paragraph 3, on account of additional honoraria for the chair and vice-chair.
5. Add $5,000 to the amount determined under paragraph 4, on account of expenses relating to pupil representation.

(3) For the purposes of subsection (4), pupils shall be counted on the basis of 1999-2000 day school average daily enrolment of pupils of the board.

(4) The amount for the board for directors of education and supervisory officers shall be determined as follows:
1. Allow $200,000 as a base amount.
2. Allow $23 per pupil for the first 25,000 pupils of the board.
3. Allow $21 per pupil for the remaining pupils of the board.
4. Total the amounts allowed under paragraphs 1 to 3.
5. Add 2 per cent of the amount of the board's remote and rural allocation, as determined under section 30.
6. Add 0.5 per cent of the amount of the board's learning opportunities allocation, as determined under section 31.
7. Add 1 per cent of the amount calculated for the board for new pupil places under subsection 38(11).

(5) The amount for the board for administration costs shall be determined as follows:
1. Allow $80,000 as a base amount.
2. Add the product of $174 and the 1999-2000 day school average daily enrolment of pupils of the board.
3. Add 11 per cent of the amount of the board's remote and rural allocation, as determined under section 30.
4. Add 0.5 per cent of the amount of the board's learning opportunities allocation, as determined under section 31.
5. Add 1 per cent of the amount calculated for the board for new pupil places under subsection 38(11).

Pupil Accommodation Allocation

38. (1) For the purposes of this section,
(a) a school of a board is an elementary school if it has been identified as such by the board in accordance with the Ministry publication entitled "Data Collection Instruction Guide for the School Facilities Inventory Database", dated March 10, 1999; and
(b) a school of a board is a secondary school if it has been identified as such by the board in accordance with the Ministry publication entitled "Data Collection Instruction Guide for the School Facilities Inventory Database", dated March 10, 1999.

(2) For the purposes of paragraph 2 of section 11, the amount of the pupil accommodation allocation for a district school board shall be determined as follows:
1. Determine the amount for the board for school operations, in accordance with subsection (3).
2. Determine the amount for the board for school renewal, in accordance with subsection (10).

3. Determine the amount for the board for new pupil places, in accordance with subsection (11).
4. Determine the amount for the board for outstanding capital commitments, in accordance with subsection (21).
5. Total the amounts determined under paragraphs 1, 2, 3 and 4.

(3) The amount for the board for school operations shall be determined as follows:

1. Determine the 1999-2000 day school average daily enrolment of elementary school pupils of the board.
2. Multiply the number determined under paragraph 1 by the benchmark area requirement per pupil of 9.29 metres squared, to obtain the elementary school area requirement for the board.
3. Determine the adjusted elementary school area requirement for the board in metres squared, by applying, to the amount determined under paragraph 2, the supplementary elementary school area factor, if any, approved for the board by the Minister in accordance with subsections (4) and (5).
4. Determine the day school average daily enrolment for the board for the 1999-2000 fiscal year, in accordance with section 2 of the 1999-2000 day school A.D.E. regulation, counting only pupils who are 21 years of age or more on December 31, 1999.
5. Determine the continuing education average daily enrolment for the board for the 1999-2000 fiscal year, in accordance with section 3 of the 1999-2000 A.D.E. regulation, counting only pupils enrolled in a course for which the pupil may earn a credit and in which instruction is given between 8 a.m. and 5 p.m. and excluding,
    i. pupils enrolled in a continuing education course delivered primarily through means other than classroom instruction,
    ii. pupils to whom subsection 49(6) of the Act applies, and
    iii. pupils in respect of whom the board charges a fee under subsection 8(2) of the 1999-2000 fees regulation.
6. Determine the summer school average daily enrolment for the board for the 1999-2000 fiscal year, in accordance with section 4 of the 1999-2000 A.D.E. regulation, excluding,
    i. pupils to whom subsection 49(6) of the Act applies, and
    ii. pupils in respect of whom the board charges a fee under subsection 8(3) of the 1999-2000 fees regulation.
7. Add the numbers determined under paragraphs 4, 5 and 6.
8. Multiply the total determined under paragraph 7 by the benchmark area requirement per pupil of 9.29 metres squared, to obtain the adult education, continuing education and summer school area requirement for the board.
9. Determine the adjusted adult education, continuing education and summer school area requirement for the board in metres squared, by applying, to the amount determined under paragraph 8, the supplementary adult education, continuing education and summer school area factor, if any, approved for the board by the Minister in accordance with subsection (6).
10. Determine the 1999-2000 day school average daily enrolment of secondary school pupils of the board.

11. Multiply the number determined under paragraph 10 by the benchmark area requirement per pupil of 12.07 metres squared, to obtain the secondary school area requirement for the board.
12. Determine the adjusted secondary school area requirement for the board in metres squared, by applying, to the amount determined under paragraph 11, the supplementary secondary school area factor, if any, approved for the board by the Minister in accordance with subsection (9).
13. Obtain the adjusted total area requirement for the board in metres squared by adding the following amounts:
    i. The elementary school area requirement for the board determined under paragraph 2 or, where the Minister approves a supplementary elementary school area factor for the board, the adjusted elementary school area requirement for the board determined under paragraph 3.
    ii. The adult education, continuing education and summer school area requirement for the board determined under paragraph 8 or, where the Minister approves a supplementary adult education, continuing education and summer school areas factor for the board, the adjusted adult education, continuing education and summer school area requirement for the board determined under paragraph 9.
    iii. The secondary school area requirement for the board determined under paragraph 11 or, where the Minister approves a supplementary secondary school area factor for the board, the adjusted secondary school area requirement for the board determined under paragraph 12.
14. Multiply the number obtained under paragraph 13 by the benchmark operating cost of $55.97 per metre squared.
15. For each elementary school of the board, calculate a top up amount for school operations, as follows:
    i. Determine the 1999-2000 day school average daily enrolment of pupils of the board, counting only pupils of the board enrolled in the school.
    ii. Determine the capacity of the school, in terms of pupil places, in accordance with subsection (16). However, the capacity of a school for which the number determined under subparagraph i is zero shall be deemed, for the purposes of this paragraph, to be zero.
    iii. Multiply the number determined under subparagraph i by the benchmark area requirement per pupil of 9.29 metres squared.
    iv. Multiply the number determined under subparagraph iii by the benchmark operating cost of $55.97 per metre squared.
    v. Multiply the number determined under subparagraph iv by the supplementary elementary school area factor, if any, approved for the board by the Minister in accordance with subsections (4) and (5).
    vi. If the school is not a school to which subsection 29(8) or (9) applies, take the amount, if any, determined under paragraph 3 of subsection 29(11) for the school.
    vii. Multiply the amount taken under subparagraph vi by 0.25.
    viii. If the school is a school to which subsection 29(8) or (9) applies, take the

amount determined under paragraph 3 of subsection 29(11) for the group of schools of which the school is a part.
- ix. Multiply the amount taken under subparagraph viii by the day school full-time equivalent enrolment for the board as of October 31, 1999, counting only the pupils of the board enrolled in the school.
- x. Divide the product obtained under subparagraph ix by the day school full-time equivalent enrolment for the board as of October 31, 1999, counting only the pupils of the board enrolled in the group of schools of which the school is a part.
- xi. Multiply the quotient obtained under subparagraph x by 0.25.
- xii. Total the numbers determined under subparagraphs v, vii and xi.
- xiii. Multiply the capacity of the school, in terms of pupil places, as determined under subparagraph ii, by the benchmark area requirement per pupil of 9.29 metres squared.
- xiv. Multiply the number determined under subparagraph xiii by the benchmark operating cost of $55.97 per metre squared.
- xv. Multiply the number determined under subparagraph xiv by the supplementary elementary school area factor, if any, approved for the board by the Minister in accordance with subsections (4) and (5).
- xvi. Multiply the number determined under subparagraph xv by 0.2.
- xvii. Subtract the number determined under subparagraph xii from the number determined under subparagraph xv.
- xviii. If the number determined under subparagraph xvii is zero or a negative number or if the number determined under subparagraph i is zero, the top up amount for school operations for the school is zero. Otherwise, the top up amount for school operations for the school is the lesser of the number determined under subparagraph xvi and the number determined under subparagraph xvii.

16. Total the top amounts for school operations determined under paragraph 15 for each of the elementary schools of the board.
17. For each secondary school of the board, calculate a top up amount for school operations, as follows:
    - i. Determine the 1999-2000 day school average daily enrolment of pupils of the board, counting only pupils of the board enrolled in the school.
    - ii. Determine the capacity of the school, in terms of pupil places, in accordance with subsection (17). However, the capacity of a school for which the number determined under subparagraph i is zero shall be deemed, for the purposes of this paragraph, to be zero.
    - iii. Multiply the number determined under subparagraph i by the benchmark area requirement per pupil of 12.07 metres squared.
    - iv. Multiply the number determined under subparagraph iii by the benchmark operating cost of $55.97 per metre squared.
    - v. Multiply the number determined under subparagraph iv by the supplementary secondary school area factor, if any, approved for the board by the Minister in accordance with subsection (9).

S. 38 REGULATIONS UNDER THE EDUCATION ACT

    vi. Take the amount, if any, determined for the school under paragraph 7 of subsection 29(11).

    vii. Multiply the amount taken under subparagraph vi by 0.25.

    viii. Add the number determined under subparagraph vii to the number determined under subparagraph v.

    ix. Multiply the capacity of the school, in terms of pupil places, as determined under subparagraph ii, by the benchmark area requirement per pupil of 12.07 metres squared.

    x. Multiply the number determined under subparagraph ix by the benchmark operating cost of $55.97 per metre squared.

    xi. Multiply the number determined under subparagraph x by the supplementary secondary school area factor, if any, approved for the board by the Minister in accordance with subsection (9).

    xii. Multiply the number determined under subparagraph xi by 0.2.

    xiii. Subtract the number determined under subparagraph viii from the number determined under subparagraph xi.

    xiv. If the number determined under subparagraph xiii is zero or a negative number or if the number determined under subparagraph i is zero, the top up amount for school operations for the school is zero. Otherwise, the top up amount for school operations for the school is the lesser of the number determined under subparagraph xii and the number determined under subparagraph xiii.

18. Total the top up amounts for school operations determined under paragraph 17 for each of the secondary schools of the board.

19. Total the amounts determined for the board under paragraphs 14, 16 and 18 to obtain the amount for the board for school operations.

(4) For the purposes of paragraph 3 of subsection (3), the Minister shall approve a supplementary elementary school area factor for a board if the Minister considers that it is appropriate to do so in order to make allowance for disproportionate space needs that are particular to the board and that are caused by,

    (a) the fact that the board is reasonably operating a school that is too large for the community it serves, whether because of declining enrolment or for some other reason;

    (b) the fact that the board is reasonably operating a school in a building the physical characteristics of which are neither compatible with nor easily modified to conform to the benchmark area requirements referred to in subsection (3);

    (c) the fact that the board has disproportionately high space requirements because the board serves a disproportionately high number of pupils in special education programs or in other education programs with high space requirements; or

    (d) other circumstances similar to those described in clauses (a), (b) and (c).

(5) In determining an amount for the purposes of subsection (4), the Minister shall have regard to the effect of the circumstances referred to in clauses (4)(a) to (d) on the board's space needs.

(6) Subject to subsections (7) and (8), subsections (4) and (5) apply with necessary modifications to authorize the Minister to approve a supplementary adult education, continuing

education and summer school area factor for a board and, for the purpose, a reference to elementary school area shall be deemed to be a reference to adult education, continuing education and summer school area.

(7) The Minister shall not approve a factor for a board under subsection (6) unless the Minister has approved a factor for the board under subsection (9).

(8) The Minister shall not approve a factor for a board under subsection (6) that is greater than the factor approved for the board under subsection (9).

(9) Subsections (4) and (5) apply with necessary modifications to authorize the Minister to approve a supplementary secondary school area factor for a board and, for the purpose, a reference to elementary school area shall be deemed to be a reference to secondary school area.

(10) The amount for the board for school renewal shall be determined as follows:

1. Take the percentage, as calculated by the board and approved by the Minister, of the actual total elementary school area of the board that relates to buildings that are less than 20 years old.
2. Apply the percentage referred to in paragraph 1 to the benchmark renewal cost per metre squared of $6.89.
3. Take the percentage, as calculated by the board and approved by the Minister, of the actual total elementary school area of the board that relates to buildings that are 20 years old or older.
4. Apply the percentage referred to in paragraph 3 to the benchmark renewal cost per metre squared of $10.33.
5. Add the amounts obtained under paragraphs 2 and 4, to obtain a weighted average benchmark elementary school renewal cost per metre squared.
6. Multiply the amount obtained under paragraph 5 by the elementary school area requirement for the board determined under paragraph 2 of subsection (3) or, where the Minister approves a supplementary elementary school area factor for the board, the adjusted elementary school area requirement for the board determined under paragraph 3 of subsection (3).
7. Take the percentage, as calculated by the board and approved by the Minister, of the actual total secondary school area of the board that relates to buildings that are less than 20 years old.
8. Apply the percentage referred to in paragraph 7 to the benchmark renewal cost per metre squared of $6.89.
9. Take the percentage, as calculated by the board and approved by the Minister, of the actual total secondary school area of the board that relates to buildings that are 20 years old or older.
10. Apply the percentage referred to in paragraph 9 to the benchmark renewal cost per metre squared of $10.33.
11. Add the amounts obtained under paragraphs 8 and 10, to obtain a weighted average benchmark secondary school renewal cost per metre squared.
12. Multiply the amount obtained under paragraph 11 by the secondary school area requirement for the board determined under paragraph 11 of subsection (3) or, where the Minister approves a supplementary secondary school area factor for the board,

the adjusted secondary school area requirement for the board determined under paragraph 12 of subsection (3).

13. Multiply the amount obtained under paragraph 11 by the adult education, continuing education and summer school area requirement for the board determined under paragraph 8 of subsection (3) or, where the Minister approves a supplementary adult education, continuing education and summer school area factor for the board, the adjusted adult education, continuing education and summer school area requirement for the board determined under paragraph 9 of subsection (3).

14. For each elementary school of the board, calculate a top up amount for school renewal, as follows:
    i. Determine the 1999-2000 day school average daily enrolment of pupils of the board, counting only pupils of the board enrolled in the school.
    ii. Determine the capacity of the school, in terms of pupil places, in accordance with subsection (16). However, the capacity of a school for which the number determined under subparagraph i is zero shall be deemed, for the purposes of this paragraph, to be zero.
    iii. Multiply the number determined under subparagraph i by the benchmark area requirement per pupil of 9.29 metres squared.
    iv. Multiply the number determined under subparagraph iii by the weighted average benchmark elementary school renewal cost per metre squared, as determined for the board under paragraph 5.
    v. Multiply the number determined under subparagraph iv by the supplementary elementary school area factor, if any, approved for the board by the Minister in accordance with subsections (4) and (5).
    vi. Multiply the capacity of the school, in terms of pupil places, as determined under subparagraph ii, by the benchmark area requirement per pupil of 9.29 metres squared.
    vii. Multiply the number determined under subparagraph vi by the weighted average benchmark elementary school renewal cost per metre squared, as determined for the board under paragraph 5.
    viii. Multiply the number determined under subparagraph vii by the supplementary elementary school area factor, if any, approved for the board by the Minister in accordance with subsections (4) and (5).
    ix. Multiply the number determined under subparagraph viii by 0.2.
    x. Subtract the number determined under subparagraph v from the number determined under subparagraph viii.
    xi. If the number determined under subparagraph x is zero or a negative number or if the number determined under subparagraph i is zero, the top up amount for school renewal for the school is zero. Otherwise, the top up amount for school renewal for the school is the lesser of the number determined under subparagraph ix and the number determined under subparagraph x.

15. Total the top up amounts for school renewal determined under paragraph 14 for each of the elementary schools of the board.

16. For each secondary school of the board, calculate a top up amount for school renewal, as follows:

i. Determine the 1999-2000 day school average daily enrolment of pupils of the board, counting only pupils of the board enrolled in the school.
ii. Determine the capacity of the school, in terms of pupil places, in accordance with subsection (17). However, the capacity of a school for which the number determined under subparagraph i is zero shall be deemed, for the purposes of this paragraph, to be zero.
iii. Multiply the number determined under subparagraph i by the benchmark area requirement per pupil of 12.07 metres squared.
iv. Multiply the number determined under subparagraph iii by the weighted average benchmark secondary school renewal cost per metre squared, as determined for the board under paragraph 11.
v. Multiply the number determined under subparagraph iv by the supplementary secondary school area factor, if any, approved for the board by the Minister in accordance with subsection (9).
vi. Multiply the capacity of the school, in terms of pupil places, as determined under subparagraph ii, by the benchmark area requirement per pupil of 12.07 metres squared.
viii. Multiply the number determined under subparagraph vi by the weighted average benchmark secondary school renewal cost per metre squared, as determined for the board under paragraph 11.
viii. Multiply the number determined under subparagraph vii by the supplementary secondary school area factor, if any, approved for the board by the Minister in accordance with subsection (9).
ix. Multiply the number determined under subparagraph viii by 0.2.
x. Subtract the number determined under subparagraph v from the number determined under subparagraph viii.
xi. If the number determined under subparagraph x is zero or a negative number or if the number determined under subparagraph i is zero, the top up amount for school renewal for the school is zero. Otherwise, the top up amount for school renewal for the school is the lesser of the number determined under subparagraph ix and the number determined under subparagraph x.

17. Total the top up amounts for school renewal determined under paragraph 16 for each of the secondary schools of the board.
18. Add the amounts obtained under paragraphs 6, 12, 13, 15 and 17 to obtain the amount for the board for school renewal.

(11) The amount for the board for new pupil places shall be the lesser of $20 million and an amount determined as follows:

1. Determine the 1999-2000 day school average daily enrolment of elementary school pupils of the board.
2. Subtract the elementary capacity for the board, in terms of pupil places, as determined by the Minister in accordance with subsection (13), from the number determined under paragraph 1.
3. If the number determined under paragraph 2 is a positive number, multiply it by the benchmark area requirement of 9.29 metres squared.

4. Multiply the product obtained under paragraph 3 by the benchmark construction cost of $118.40 per metre squared.
5. Determine the 1999-2000 day school average daily enrolment of secondary school pupils of the board.
6. Subtract the secondary capacity for the board, in terms of pupil places, as determined by the Minister in accordance with subsection (13), from the number determined under paragraph 5.
7. If the number determined under paragraph 6 is a positive number, multiply it by the benchmark area requirement of 12.07 metres squared.
8. Multiply the product obtained under paragraph 7 by the benchmark construction cost of $129.17 per metre squared.
9. Add the products obtained under paragraphs 4 and 8.
10. Multiply the sum obtained under paragraph 9 by the geographic adjustment factor specified for the board in Table 6, to obtain the amount for the board for new pupil places.

(12) In subsections (13) to (17),

"instructional space" means a space in a school that can reasonably be used for instructional purposes; ("aire d'enseignement")

"school facilities data" means data relating to boards' school facilities and includes school floor plans and other data compiled in accordance with the Ministry's school facilities inventory system. ("données sur les installations scolaires")

(13) For the purposes of paragraphs 2 and 6 of subsection (11), the Minister shall determine an elementary capacity and a secondary capacity for the board as follows:

1. Apply the loadings determined under subsection (14) to the elementary and secondary school instructional spaces of the board, as categorized under subsection (14).
2. Where applicable, adjust the result determined under paragraph 1 in accordance with subsection (15).
3. Where applicable, adjust the result determined under paragraph 2 in accordance with subsections (19) and (20).

(14) The Minister shall determine loadings and categories of instructional space as follows:

1. Using school facilities data, the Minister shall identify categories of instructional space. In identifying categories of instructional space, the Minister shall have regard to but is not limited to the categories identified in the Report of the Pupil Accommodation Review Committee, dated August, 1998, which Report was released by the Ministry to school boards in August of 1998 and is available for public inspection at the offices of the Ministry of Education and Training, 900 Bay Street, Toronto, Ontario, M7A 1L2.
2. The Minister shall assign a loading to each category of instructional space identified under paragraph 1, based on the number of pupils that can reasonably be accommodated in each category of instructional space.

(15) The Minister shall make such adjustments under paragraph 2 of subsection (13) as the Minister considers appropriate to take account of funds received by one board from another

board in connection with a determination made under Ontario Regulation 460/97 respecting the disposition of an asset of an old board.

(16) For the purposes of paragraph 15 of subsection (3), paragraph 14 of subsection (10) and subsection (19), the Minister shall determine the capacity of an elementary school as follows:

1. Apply the loadings determined under subsection (14) to the instructional spaces of the school, as categorized under subsection (14).
2. Take the elementary capacity for the board that governs the school, as determined under subsection (13) but without applying paragraph 2 of that subsection.
3. Multiply the elementary capacity for the board that governs the school, as determined under subsection (13), by the amount determined under paragraph 1.
4. Divide the product obtained under paragraph 3 by the amount taken under paragraph 2.

(17) For the purposes of paragraph 17 of subsection (3), paragraph 16 of subsection (10) and subsection (20), the Minister shall determine the capacity of a secondary school as follows:

1. Apply the loadings determined under subsection (14) to the instructional spaces of the school, as categorized under subsection (14).
2. Take the secondary capacity for the board that governs the school, as determined under subsection (13) but without applying paragraph 2 of that subsection.
3. Multiply the secondary capacity for the board that governs the school, as determined under subsection (13), by the amount determined under paragraph 1.
4. Divide the product obtained under paragraph 3 by the amount taken under paragraph 2.

(18) Subsection (19) or (20) applies in relation to an elementary or secondary school of a board if,

(a) the board has submitted evidence satisfactory to the Minister that the board has,
 (i) by December 31, 1998, developed a pupil accommodation review policy containing the four elements specified in Appendix B of the technical paper published by the Ministry entitled "Student Focused Funding — Pupil Accommodation Grants", dated September, 1998,
 (ii) by December 31, 1998, passed a resolution to close the school at the end of the 1998-99 school year, and
 (iii) within 30 days of passing a resolution described in subclause (ii) in respect of the school, issued a proposal under Ontario Regulation 444/98 to dispose of the school at no cost to the Ontario Realty Corporation or to a board; or
(b) the board has notified the Minister in writing that the school will be disposed of in accordance with an order of the Education Improvement Commission under Ontario Regulation 460/97.

(19) The elementary capacity determined for the board under subsection (13) shall be adjusted as follows:

1. For each elementary school of the board to which subsection (18) applies, determine a capacity in accordance with subsection (16).
2. Total the amounts determined under paragraph 1 for elementary schools of the board.

3. Subtract the total determined under paragraph 2 from the elementary capacity determined for the board under subsection (13).

(20) The secondary capacity determined for the board under subsection (13) shall be adjusted as follows:

1. For each secondary school of the board to which subsection (18) applies, determine a capacity in accordance with subsection (17).
2. Total the amounts determined under paragraph 1 for secondary schools of the board.
3. Subtract the total determined under paragraph 2 from the secondary capacity determined for the board under subsection (13).

(21) The amount for the board for outstanding capital commitments shall be determined as follows:

1. Take the number of elementary school pupil places shown in Column 2 of Table 7, opposite the name of the board.
2. Multiply the number taken under paragraph 1 by the benchmark area requirement per pupil of 9.29 metres squared.
3. Multiply the product obtained under paragraph 2 by the benchmark construction cost of $118.40 per metre squared.
4. Take the number of secondary school pupil places shown in Column 3 of Table 7, opposite the name of the board.
5. Multiply the number taken under paragraph 4 by the benchmark area requirement per pupil of 12.07 metres squared.
6. Multiply the product obtained under paragraph 5 by the benchmark construction cost of $129.17 per metre squared.
7. Add the products obtained under paragraphs 3 and 6.

Debt Charges Allocation

39. (1) Subject to subsections (2) and (3), for the purposes of paragraph 2 of section 11, the amount of the debt charges allocation for a district school board shall be the total of the payments on account of principal and interest that are due and payable by the board in the 1999-2000 fiscal year in order to service debt incurred, by the board or by a predecessor old board of the board, to finance the acquisition of a capital asset where,

(a) the acquisition is pursuant to a contractual obligation entered into by the board or predecessor old board before May 15, 1998; or

(b) the acquisition is for the purposes of a capital project the estimated project cost of which was approved in writing by the Minister before May 15, 1998.

(2) With respect to debt incurred before May 15, 1998, subsection (1) ceases to apply in respect of a debt if the amount, terms or conditions of the obligation are renegotiated on or after May 15, unless the renegotiated amount, terms and conditions are approved in writing by the Minister.

(3) With respect to debt incurred on or after May 15, 1998, subsection (1) applies only if the amount, terms and conditions of the debt are approved in writing by the Minister.

Phase-in Funding

40. For the purposes of paragraph 4 of section 11, the total determined for a district school board under paragraph 3 of section 11 shall be adjusted as follows:
1. Calculate the operating revenue for the 1998-99 fiscal year for the board, in accordance with section 41.
2. Calculate the operating revenue for the 1999-2000 fiscal year for the board, in accordance with section 42.
3. Using the calculations under paragraphs 1 and 2, calculate the change in operating revenue for the board, in accordance with section 43.
4. Calculate the 1998-99 enrolment for the board, in accordance with section 44.
5. Calculate the adjusted change in operating revenue for the board, in accordance with section 45.
6. Where the adjusted change in operating revenue for the board is more than 10.4, subtract an amount determined in accordance with section 46 from the total determined for the board under paragraph 3 of section 11.
7. This paragraph does not apply where the adjusted change in operating revenue for the board is more than 1.04. Where the adjusted change in operating revenue for the board or the change in operating revenue for the board is less than 0.96, add an amount determined in accordance with section 47 to the total determined for the board under paragraph 3 of section 11.

41. (1) For the purposes of paragraph 1 of section 40, the operating revenue for the 1998-99 fiscal year for a district school board shall be calculated as follows:
1. Take the amount calculated for the board under section 42 of Ontario Regulation 287/98. Add back the amount, if any, deducted for the board under paragraph 6 of that section.
2. Where paragraph 6 of section 40 of Ontario Regulation 287/98 applies, adjust the amount taken under paragraph 1 by deducting the amount calculated under subsection 46(2) of Ontario Regulation 287/98.
3. Where paragraph 7 of section 40 of Ontario Regulation 287/98 applies, adjust the amount taken under paragraph 1 by adding the amount calculated under subsection 47(2) of the Ontario Regulation 287/98.
4. In the case of Conseil scolaire de district du Grand Nord de l'Ontario, deduct an amount determined as follows:
    i. Determine the 1998-99 day school average daily enrolment of pupils of the board, within the meaning of Ontario Regulation 287/98, counting only pupils of the board who were enrolled in the schools listed in subsection (2) during the period from September 1, 1998 to August 31, 1999.
    ii. Multiply the enrolment determined under subparagraph i by $11,500.
5. In the case of Conseil scolaire de district catholique du Nouvel-Ontario, add the amount determined under paragraph 4.

(2) The following are the schools referred to in subparagraph i of paragraph 4 of subsection (1):

1. École secondaire Chapleau in Chapleau.
2. École secondaire Jeunesse-Nord in Blind River.
3. École secondaire Espanola in Espanola.

42. For the purposes of paragraph 2 of section 40, the operating revenue for the 1999-2000 fiscal year for a district school board shall be calculated as follows:

1. Total the amounts determined for the board under this Regulation for each type of allocation, not including the amount of the debt charges allocation for the board, as determined under section 39, and the amount of the summer school remedial allocation for the board, as determined under section 32.
2. Deduct the amount determined for the board for school renewal under subsection 38(10).
3. Deduct the amount determined for the board for new pupil places under subsection 38(11).
4. Deduct the amount determined for the board for outstanding capital commitments under subsection 38(21).
5. Deduct the total of the approved special incidence ISA claims for pupils of the board, as determined for the purposes of clause 18(b).
6. Where an adjustment has been made under section 20 to the amount calculated for the board under section 18, the amount deducted for the board under paragraph 5 shall be increased or decreased by the amount that the Minister considers appropriate to take account of the adjustment made under section 20.

43. For the purposes of paragraph 3 of section 40, the change in operating revenue for a board shall be calculated by dividing the operating revenue for the 1999-2000 fiscal year for the board, as determined under section 42, by the operating revenue for the 1998-99 fiscal year for the board, as determined under section 41.

44. (1) For the purposes of paragraph 4 of section 40, the 1998-99 enrolment for a board is the 1998-99 day school average daily enrolment for the board, within the meaning of Ontario Regulation 287/98, except that,

(a) pupils who were enrolled in junior kindergarten during the period from September 1, 1998 to August 31, 1999 shall not be counted; and

(b) all pupils enrolled in kindergarten during the period from September 1, 1998 to August 31, 1999 shall be counted as half-time pupils.

(2) In the case of Conseil scolaire de district du Grand Nord de l'Ontario, the 1998-99 day school average daily enrolment determined under subsection (1) shall be adjusted by deducting the enrolment amount determined under subparagraph i of paragraph 4 of subsection 41(1).

(3) In the case of Conseil scolaire de district catholique du Nouvel-Ontario, the 1998-99 day school average daily enrolment determined under subsection (1) shall be adjusted by adding the enrolment amount determined under subparagraph i of paragraph 4 of subsection 41(1).

45. For the purposes of paragraph 5 of section 40, the adjusted change in operating revenue for a board shall be calculated by multiplying the change in operating revenue calculated for the board under section 43 by a factor obtained by dividing the 1998-99 enrolment for the board, calculated under section 44, by the 1999-2000 day school average daily enrolment of pupils of the board, excluding pupils of the board enrolled in junior kindergarten.

46. (1) This section applies where the adjusted change in operating revenue for the board, as calculated under section 45, is more than 1.04.

(2) Where this section applies, an amount calculated as follows shall be subtracted from the total determined for the board under paragraph 3 of section 11:

1. Determine the amount by which the adjusted change in operating revenue for the board, as calculated under section 45, exceeds 1.04. If this excess amount is greater than 0.04, reduce it to 0.04.
2. Multiply the excess amount obtained under paragraph 1 by the operating revenue for the 1998-99 fiscal year for the board, as calculated under section 41.

47. (1) This section applies,

(a) where the adjusted change in operating revenue for the board, as calculated under section 45, is less than 0.96; or
(b) where the change in operating revenue for the board, as calculated under section 43, is less than 0.96, if the adjusted change in operating revenue for the board, as calculated under section 45, is not more than 1.04.

(2) Where this section applies, an amount calculated as follows shall be added to the total determined for the board under paragraph 3 of section 11:

1. Determine the amount by which the change in operating revenue for the board, as calculated under section 43, is less than 0.96.
2. Multiply the amount obtained under paragraph 1 by the operating revenue for the 1998-99 fiscal year for the board, as calculated under section 41.
3. Determine the amount by which the adjusted change in operating revenue for the board, as calculated under section 45, is less than 0.96.
4. Multiply the amount obtained under paragraph 3 by the operating revenue for the 1998-99 fiscal year for the board, as calculated under section 41.
5. Take the greater of the amounts determined under paragraphs 2 and 4.
6. Deduct from the amount determined under paragraph 5 the total of the approved special incidence ISA claims for pupils of the board, as determined for the purposes of clause 18(b).
7. Where an adjustment has been made under section 20 to the amount calculated for the board under section 18, the amount deducted for the board under paragraph 6 shall be increased or decreased by the amount that the Minister considers appropriate to take account of the adjustment made under section 20.

Stable Funding Guarantee

48. (1) This section applies to a district school board if the amount determined under section 41 as the operating revenue for the 1998-99 fiscal year for a board exceeds the amount determined for the board in accordance with subsection (2).

(2) The second amount referred to in subsection (1) shall be determined as follows:

1. If neither paragraph 6 nor paragraph 7 of section 40 applies to the board, take the

amount determined under section 42 as the operating revenue for the 1999-2000 fiscal year for the board. Add the total of the approved special incidence ISA claims for pupils of the board, as determined for the purposes of clause 18(b), adjusted, where applicable, in accordance with subsection (3).

2. If paragraph 6 of section 40 applies to the board, take the amount determined under section 42 as the operating revenue for the 1999-2000 fiscal year for the board. Subtract the amount calculated for the board under subsection 46(2).

3. If paragraph 7 of section 40 applies to the board, take the amount determined under section 42 as the operating revenue for the 1999-2000 fiscal year for the board. Add the amount calculated for the board under subsection 47(2). Add the total of the approved special incidence ISA claims for pupils of the board, as determined for the purposes of clause 18(b), adjusted, where applicable, in accordance with subsection (3).

(3) Where an adjustment has been made under section 20 to the amount calculated for the board under section 18, the amount added for the board under paragraph 1 or 3, as the case may be, as the total of the approved special incidence ISA claims for its pupils shall be increased or decreased by the amount that the Minister considers appropriate to take account of the adjustment made under section 20.

(4) For the purposes of paragraph 5 of section 11, the stable funding guarantee amount for a district school board shall be the amount by which the operating revenue for the 1998-99 fiscal year for the board, as determined under section 41, exceeds the amount determined for the board under subsection (2).

Grants for Certain Capital Projects

49. (1) For the purposes of this section,

"Canada-Ontario Infrastructure Works capital project" means a project funded after the Canada-Ontario Infrastructure Program Agreement, dated January 1, 1994 and amended August 26, 1996.

(2) Any grant or portion of a grant that, but for this subsection, would be payable to a district school board under a previous legislative grant regulation in respect of any capital project, other than a Canada-Ontario Infrastructure Works capital project, and that is not paid before September 1, 1999 is not payable under this Regulation or under any previous legislative grant regulation.

(3) Any grant or portion of a grant that, but for this section, would be payable to a district school board under a previous legislative grant regulation in respect of a Canada-Ontario Infrastructure Works capital project and that is not paid before September 1, 1999,

    (a) is not payable under any previous legislative grant regulation; and

    (b) shall be deemed to be a grant payable under this Regulation.

(4) When exercising the authority provided by subsection 234(8) of the Act for the purposes of grants or portions of grants payable under subsection (3), the Minister may provide for an instalment to be paid after August 31, 2000.

Enveloping

50. It is a condition of the payment of a grant to a district school board under this Regulation that the board manage its estimates process and its expenditures so as to ensure compliance with the requirements of sections 51 to 53.

51. (1) For the purposes of this section,

(a) an expenditure by a board is a classroom expenditure if it is an expenditure categorized in the Ministry's 1998-99 Uniform Code of Accounts as a classroom expenditure; and

(b) an expenditure by a board is a non-classroom expenditure if it is an expenditure categorized in the Ministry's 1998-99 Uniform Code of Accounts as a non-classroom expenditure.

(2) Subject to subsection (8), a district school board shall ensure that its 1999-2000 net classroom expenditure amount, calculated in accordance with subsection (3), is at least equal to its 1999-2000 classroom expenditure allocation amount, calculated in accordance with subsection (5).

(3) For the purposes of subsection (2), the 1999-2000 net classroom expenditure amount for a board shall be determined as follows:

1. Determine the total amount of the board's classroom expenditures in the 1999-2000 fiscal year.
2. Subtract the amount determined for the board under subsection (4), on account of classroom-related revenue from sources other than legislative grants and school taxes.

(4) For the purposes of paragraph 2 of subsection (3), the amount on account of classroom-related revenue from sources other than legislative grants and school taxes for the board shall be the total of the following amounts:

1. Take 68.49 per cent of the total of the board's revenues under sections 3, 5 and 6 of the 1999-2000 fees regulation.
2. Determine the total of the amounts spent on classroom expenditures from reserves of the board in the 1999-2000 fiscal year.
3. This paragraph applies to grants to the board, other than grants made under this Regulation, and to donations to the board, where the board is legally required to spend the full amount of the grant or donation on expenditures that are classroom expenditures within the meaning of this section. Determine the amount received by the board in the 1999-2000 fiscal year from grants and donations to which this paragraph applies.
4. This paragraph applies to grants to the board, other than grants made under this Regulation, and to donations to the board, where the board is not legally required to spend the full amount of the grant or donation on expenditures that are classroom expenditures within the meaning of this section. Determine the amount received by the board in the 1999-2000 fiscal year from grants and donations to which this paragraph applies that are spent in the 1999-2000 fiscal year on expenditures that are classroom expenditures within the meaning of this section.

S. 51 REGULATIONS UNDER THE EDUCATION ACT

5. Determine the amount received by the board in the 1999-2000 fiscal year from revenue sources not mentioned in paragraphs 1 to 4 that are spent in the 1999-2000 fiscal year on expenditures that are classroom expenditures within the meaning of this section.

(5) For the purposes of subsection (2), the 1999-2000 classroom expenditure allocation amount for a board shall be determined as follows:

1. Determine the amount calculated for the board under paragraph 2 of section 13, on account of the foundation allocation for elementary school pupils.
2. Apply the percentage specified in Table 8 for the elementary school part of foundation allocations to the amount determined for the board under paragraph 1.
3. Determine the amount calculated for the board under paragraph 4 of section 13, on account of the foundation allocation for secondary school pupils.
4. Apply the percentage specified in Table 8 for the secondary school part of foundation allocations to the amount determined for the board under paragraph 3.
5. Determine an amount for the board on account of Native language and French as a first or second language, as follows:
    i. In the case of an English-language district school board, total the amounts determined for the board under paragraphs 1 and 2 of section 21.
    ii. In the case of a French-language district school board, total the amounts determined for the board under paragraphs 1 and 2 of section 25.
6. Apply the percentage specified in Table 8 for Native language and French as a first or second language to the amount determined for the board under paragraph 5.
7. Determine an amount for the board on account of ESL/ESD/ALF/PDF, as follows:
    i. In the case of an English-language district school board, take the amount determined for the board under paragraph 3 of section 21.
    ii. In the case of a French-language district school board, take the amount determined for the board under paragraph 3 of section 25.
8. Apply the percentage specified in Table 8 for ESL/ESD/ALF/PDF to the amount determined for the board under paragraph 7.
9. Take the amount determined under subsection 34(11) as the elementary school teacher compensation allocation for the board.
10. Apply the percentage specified in Table 8 for elementary school teacher compensation to the amount determined for the board under paragraph 9.
11. Take the amount determined under subsection 34(12) as the secondary school teacher compensation allocation for the board.
12. Apply the percentage specified in Table 8 for secondary school teacher compensation to the amount determined for the board under paragraph 11.
13. Determine the amount of each type of allocation determined for the board under sections 14, 29, 30, 31 and 35.
14. Apply the percentage specified in Table 8 for each type of allocation for which an amount is determined under paragraph 13 to the amount determined for the board under paragraph 13 for that type of allocation.
15. Multiply the enrolment number determined for the board under paragraph 1 of subsection 33(1) by $2,257, to determine an adult day school amount for the board.

16. Apply the percentage specified in Table 8 for adult day school to the amount determined for the board under paragraph 15.
17. Determine the amount, if any, calculated for the board under subsection 46(2) as a phase-in funding deduction amount. Apply the percentage determined for the board under subsection (6) to that amount.
18. Determine the amount, if any, calculated for the board under subsection 47(2) as a phase-in funding addition amount. Apply the percentage determined for the board under subsection (6) to that amount.
19. Take the stable funding guarantee amount, if any, determined for the board under section 48. Apply the percentage determined for the board under subsection (7) to that amount.
20. Total the amounts determined for the board under paragraphs 2, 4, 6, 8, 10, 12, 14 and 16.
21. Where paragraph 17 applies to the board, deduct the amount obtained for the board under that paragraph from the amount obtained for the board under paragraph 20.
22. Where paragraph 18 applies to the board, add the amount obtained for the board under that paragraph to the amount obtained for the board under paragraph 20.
23. Where paragraph 19 applies to the board, add the amount obtained for the board under that paragraph to the amount obtained for the board under paragraph 21 or 22, as the case may be.

(6) For the purposes of paragraphs 17 and 18 of subsection (5), the board shall determine a percentage that reasonably corresponds to the way in which the board actually applies the phase-in funding deduction amount or phase-in funding addition amount, as the case may be, to classroom expenditures in the 1999-2000 fiscal year.

(7) For the purposes of paragraph 19 of subsection (5), the board shall determine a percentage that reasonably corresponds to the way in which the board actually applies the stable funding guarantee amount to classroom expenditures in the 1999-2000 fiscal year.

(8) A board shall be deemed to be in compliance with subsection (2) where its 1999-2000 classroom expenditure allocation, calculated in accordance with subsection (5), exceeds its 1999-2000 net classroom expenditure amount, calculated in accordance with subsection (3), if the board demonstrates, in a written report to the Minister, that the excess is accounted for by reason of expenditures other than non-classroom expenditures.

(9) For example,
(a) an amount paid on account of a part of a deficit from a previous year where the part of the deficit is reasonably attributable to classroom expenditures is not a non-classroom expenditure; and
(b) an amount placed in a reserve fund for classroom expenditures is not a non-classroom expenditure.

(10) In making a determination under subsection (6) or (7), the board shall not apply the phase-in funding addition amount or the stable funding guarantee amount to expenditures that are not classroom expenditures and shall not apply the phase-in funding deduction amount to expenditures that are classroom expenditures if doing so would reduce the board's 1999-2000 net classroom expenditure allocation, calculated in accordance with subsection (5), to an amount lower than the amount for the board set out in the column entitled ''1997 Net Expenditure''

and the row entitled "9 Sub-total" in the Table entitled "Classroom — Non-classroom Summary Report", which Table was released by the Ministry to school boards on March 25, 1998 and is available for public inspection at the offices of the Ministry of Education and Training, 900 Bay Street, Toronto, Ontario, M7A 1L2.

52. (1) Subject to subsection (2), a district school board shall ensure that an amount equal to the total of the special education allocation determined for the board under section 14 and the amount placed in the board's special education reserve fund in the fiscal year beginning on September 1, 1998 and ending on August 31, 1999, less the programs in facilities amount determined for the board under section 19, is spent in the 1999-2000 fiscal year on special education for pupils of the board.

(2) Where a board's expenditure on special education for its pupils in the 1999-2000 fiscal year is less than the result obtained by subtracting the programs in facilities amount determined for the board under section 19 from the total of the special education allocation determined for the board under section 14 and the amount placed in the board's special education reserve fund in the fiscal year beginning on September 1, 1998 and ending on August 31, 1999, the board shall place the difference in the board's special education reserve fund.

(3) This section shall not be interpreted as limiting the amount that a board may spend on special education.

53. (1) Subject to subsection (2), a district school board shall ensure that an amount equal to the total of the following three amounts is spent in the 1999-2000 fiscal year on the acquisition of capital assets:

1. The amount determined for the board under subsection 38(10) for school renewal.
2. The amount determined for the board under subsection 38(11) for new pupil places.
3. The amount determined for the board under subsection 38(21) for outstanding capital commitments.

(2) Where a board's expenditure in the 1999-2000 fiscal year on the acquisition of capital assets is less than the total amount referred to in subsection (1), the board shall place the difference in the board's pupil accommodation allocation reserve fund.

(3) This section shall not be interpreted as limiting the amount that a board may spend on the acquisition of capital assets.

54. (1) It is a condition of the payment of a grant to a district school board under this Regulation that,

(a) the board manage its estimates process and its expenditures so that the total of its administration expenditures and governance expenditures in the 1999-2000 fiscal year does not exceed the administration and governance allocation amount determined for it under section 37; or

(b) the board submit the plan referred to in subsection (3).

(2) For the purposes of this section,

(a) an expenditure by a board is an administration expenditure if it is an expenditure categorized in the Ministry's 1998-99 Uniform Code of Accounts as an administration expenditure; and

(b) an expenditure by a board is a governance expenditure if it is an expenditure categorized in the Ministry's 1998-99 Uniform Code of Accounts as a governance expenditure.

(3) Where the total of a board's administration expenditures and governance expenditures in the 1999-2000 fiscal year exceeds the administration and governance allocation amount determined for the board under section 37, the board shall submit a written plan to the Minister outlining how it proposes to reduce the total of the amounts that it spends on administration expenditures and governance expenditures so that, by the fiscal year 2000-2001, that total does not exceed the administration and governance allocation amount determined for the board under section 37.

(4) Where a board to which subsection (3) applies submitted a plan under subsection 54(6) of Ontario Regulation 287/98, the board shall meet the requirements of subsection (3) by updating that plan and submitting the updated plan to the Minister.

PART III

GRANTS TO SCHOOL AUTHORITIES

Grants to Isolate Boards

55. (1) For the purposes of this section, the approved expenditure of an isolate board is the expenditure that is acceptable to the Minister as shown on the forms provided by the Ministry to the isolate board for the purpose of calculating its 1999-2000 legislative grant.

(2) In making determinations for the purposes of subsection (1), the Minister shall apply the funding formula on which the provisions of this Regulation relating to grants to district school boards is based, with such adaptations as the Minister considers advisable to take account of characteristics particular to school authorities.

(3) For the purposes of this section, the 1999-2000 tax revenue of an isolate board shall be determined as follows:
1. Add,
    i. 38 per cent of the total of the amounts distributed to the board in respect of the 1999 calendar year under subsections 237(12) and 238(2), section 239, subsection 240(5), sections 250 and 251 and subsections 257.8(2) and 257.9(1) of the Act, under sections 447.20 and 447.52 of the *Municipal Act* and under section 10 of Ontario Regulation 509/98,
    ii. 62 per cent of the total of the amounts distributed to the board in respect of the 2000 calendar year under subsections 237(12) and 238(2), section 239, subsection 240(5), sections 250 and 251 and subsections 257.8(2) and 257.9(1) of the Act, under sections 447.20 and 447.52 of the *Municipal Act* and under section 10 of Ontario Regulation 509/98,
    iii. 38 per cent of the amounts, if any, received by the board in respect of the 1999 calendar year from a municipality under subsection 445(4) of the *Municipal Act*,
    iv. 62 per cent of the amounts, if any, received by the board in respect of the 2000

calendar year from a municipality under subsection 445(4) of the *Municipal Act*,

v. the total of the taxes received by the board in respect of the 1999 calendar year under section 35 of the *Assessment Act*,

vi. 38 per cent of the payments in lieu of taxes distributed to the board in respect of the 1999 calendar year under subsection 371.1(1) of the *Municipal Act*,

vii. 62 per cent of the payments in lieu of taxes distributed to the board in respect of the 2000 calendar year under subsection 371.1(1) of the *Municipal Act*,

viii. 38 per cent of the amounts, if any, received by the board in respect of the 1999 calendar year under the *Municipal Grants Act* (Canada) or under any Act of Canada that permits a payment to be made by a government or a government agency in lieu of taxes on real property,

ix. 62 per cent of the amounts, if any, received by the board in respect of the 2000 calendar year under the *Municipal Grants Act* (Canada) or under any Act of Canada that permits a payment to be made by a government or a government agency in lieu of taxes on real property,

x. the total of the amounts, if any, distributed to the board in the 1999-2000 fiscal year under subsection 2(3) of Ontario Regulation 365/98, and

xi. the total of the amounts, if any, paid to the board in the 1999-2000 fiscal year under clause 3(1)(a) of Ontario Regulation 366/98.

2. Deduct the cost incurred in the 1999-2000 fiscal year by the board under section 257.7 of the Act in collecting taxes for school purposes in territory without municipal organization, to a maximum of 2 per cent of the sum of,

  i. 38 per cent of the total amount of taxes levied by it for 1999 for school purposes in territory without municipal organization, and

  ii. 62 per cent of the total amount of taxes levied by it for 2000 for school purposes in territory without municipal organization.

3. Deduct the amounts charged to the board in the 1999 calendar year by a municipal council under section 421 of the *Municipal Act*, including amounts charged under that section as a result of private legislation.

4. Deduct the total of the amounts paid as rebates by the board under section 257.2.1 of the Act in the 1999-2000 fiscal year.

5. Deduct 38 per cent of the total of the amounts, if any, paid by the board in respect of the 1999 calendar year under subsections 442.1(7) and 442.2(8.1) of the *Municipal Act*.

6. Deduct 62 per cent of the total of the amounts, if any, paid by the board in respect of the 2000 calendar year under subsections 442.1(7) and 442.2(8.1) of the *Municipal Act*.

(4) Amounts, if any, paid by the Minister to the board in respect of the 1999 calendar year under section 257.11 of the Act shall be deemed to be amounts distributed to the board in respect of the 1999 calendar year under a provision of the Act referred to in subparagraph i of paragraph 1 of subsection (3).

(5) Amounts, if any, paid by the Minister to the board in respect of the 2000 calendar year under section 257.11 of the Act shall be deemed to be amounts distributed to the board in

respect of the 2000 calendar year under a provision of the Act referred to in subparagraph ii of paragraph 1 of subsection (3).

(6) Paragraph 2 of subsection (3) shall not be interpreted to preclude including in the board's approved expenditure an amount on account of the costs incurred by the board in collecting taxes in territory without municipal organization, where those costs exceed the amount deducted under paragraph 2 of subsection (3).

(7) Where the approved expenditure of an isolate board exceeds its 1999-2000 tax revenue, the board shall be paid a grant equal to the excess.

Grants to Section 68 Boards

56. A section 68 board shall be paid a grant in an amount determined as follows:
1. Take the expenditure of the board for the 1999-2000 fiscal year that is acceptable to the Minister for grant purposes, excluding,
    i. expenditures for debt charges,
    ii. expenditures for the purchase of capital assets,
    iii. expenditures for the restoration of destroyed or damaged capital assets, and
    iv. provisions for reserves for working funds and provisions for reserve funds.
2. Deduct the revenue of the board for the 1999-2000 fiscal year, not including revenue from,
    i. legislative grants,
    ii. an organization on whose property a school of the board is located, and
    iii. refunds of expenditure of the kind described in subparagraph i, ii or iii of paragraph 1.

PART IV

PAYMENTS TO GOVERNING AUTHORITIES

57. In this Part,

"Crown establishment" means an establishment maintained by a Department of the Government of Canada, a federal Crown company, The Royal Canadian Mounted Police or Atomic Energy of Canada Limited, on lands held by the Crown in right of Canada that are not assessable for school purposes, and includes a reserve as defined in the *Indian Act* (Canada).

58. (1) This section applies where a pupil who is not resident in a Crown establishment,
(a) resides in a territorial district on land that is not part of a school section or separate school zone and attends an elementary school supported by local taxation in Manitoba or Quebec; or
(b) resides in a territorial district on land that is not part of a secondary school district and attends a secondary school supported by local taxation in Manitoba or Quebec.

(2) The Minister shall pay the governing authority of the school attended by the pupil the amount agreed on between the governing authority and the Minister.

59. (1) This section applies where,

S. 60   REGULATIONS UNDER THE EDUCATION ACT

    (a) a pupil who resides in a territorial district is resident in a school section, separate school zone or a Crown establishment and attends an elementary school supported by local taxation in Manitoba or Quebec; and

    (b) the Minister is of the opinion that,

        (i) daily transportation to the elementary school in Ontario that the pupil would otherwise attend is impracticable due to distance and terrain, and

        (ii) the provision of board, lodging and weekly transportation is impracticable because of the age or disability of the pupil.

(2) The Minister shall pay the governing authority of the elementary school attended by the pupil the amount agreed on between the governing authority and the Minister.

60. (1) This section applies where a pupil who resides in a territorial district,

    (a) is not resident in a school section, a separate school zone or a Crown establishment; and

    (b) attends a school on a reserve that is operated by,

        (i) the Crown in right of Canada, or

        (ii) a band, the council of a band or an education authority where the band, council of a band or education authority is authorized by the Crown in right of Canada to provide education for Indians.

(2) The Minister shall pay the governing authority of the school attended by the pupil the amount agreed on between the governing authority and the Minister.

Table/Tableau 1
ESL/ESD grant/subvention ESL/ESD

Item/Point	Column/Colonne 1 Board Name/Nom du conseil	Column/Colonne 2 Amount/Montant $
1.	District School Board Ontario North East	12,908
2.	Algoma District School Board	7,856
3.	Rainbow District School Board	16,897
4.	Near North District School Board	9,514
5.	Keewatin-Patricia District School Board	8,405
6.	Rainy River District School Board	3,127
7.	Lakehead District School Board	33,881
8.	Superior-Greenstone District School Board	531
9.	Bluewater District School Board	57,719
10.	Avon Maitland District School Board	83,985
11.	Greater Essex County District School Board	284,985
12.	Lambton Kent District School Board	72,464

Table/Tableau 1
ESL/ESD grant/subvention ESL/ESD

Item/Point	Column/Colonne 1 Board Name/Nom du conseil	Column/Colonne 2 Amount/Montant $
13.	Thames Valley District School Board	515,192
14.	Toronto District School Board	6,241,876
15.	Durham District School Board	185,698
16.	Kawartha Pine Ridge District School Board	27,701
17.	Trillium Lakelands District School Board	0
18.	York Region District School Board	701,651
19.	Simcoe County District School Board	56,266
20.	Upper Grand District School Board	183,294
21.	Peel District School Board	1,417,922
22.	Halton District School Board	153,833
23.	Hamilton-Wentworth District School Board	430,021
24.	District School Board of Niagara	134,140
25.	Grand Erie District School Board	91,497
26.	Waterloo Region District School Board	567,007
27.	Ottawa-Carleton District School Board	665,330
28.	Upper Canada District School Board	21,721
29.	Limestone District School Board	51,587
30.	Renfrew County District School Board	10,339
31.	Hastings and Prince Edward District School Board	25,470
32.	Northeastern Catholic District School Board	3,607
33.	Nipissing-Parry Sound Catholic District School Board	3,744
34.	Huron-Superior Catholic District School Board	6,603
35.	Sudbury Catholic District School Board	7,911
36.	Northwest Catholic District School Board	1,863
37.	Kenora Catholic District School Board	160
38.	Thunder Bay Catholic District School Board	17,252
39.	Superior North Catholic District School Board	0
40.	Bruce-Grey Catholic District School Board	4,143
41.	Huron Perth Catholic District School Board	10,223

Table/Tableau 1
ESL/ESD grant/subvention ESL/ESD

ITEM/POINT	COLUMN/COLONNE 1 Board Name/Nom du conseil	COLUMN/COLONNE 2 Amount/Montant $
42.	Windsor-Essex Catholic District School Board	194,873
43.	English-language Separate District School Board No. 38	156,985
44.	St. Clair Catholic District School Board	25,820
45.	Toronto Catholic District School Board	2,648,729
46.	Peterborough Victoria Northumberland and Clarington Catholic District School Board	11,994
47.	York Catholic District School Board	447,149
48.	Dufferin-Peel Catholic District School Board	1,118,966
49.	Simcoe Muskoka Catholic District School Board	30,307
50.	Durham Catholic District School Board	85,767
51.	Halton Catholic District School Board	107,220
52.	Hamilton-Wentworth Catholic District School Board	241,105
53.	Wellington Catholic District School Board	36,169
54.	Waterloo Catholic District School Board	228,853
55.	Niagara Catholic District School Board	65,110
56.	Brant/Haldimand-Norfolk Catholic District School Board	29,548
57.	Catholic District School Board of Eastern Ontario	11,571
58.	Ottawa-Carleton Catholic District School Board	311,992
59.	Renfrew County Catholic District School Board	4,204
60.	Algonquin and Lakeshore Catholic District School Board	25,315

Table/Tableau 2
Assimilation Factors for ALF Funding/
Facteurs d'assimilation pour le financement des programmes d'ALF

Item/Point	Column/Colonne 1 French Language Board/ Conseil de langue française	Column/Colonne 2 English Language Coterminous Board/ Conseil de langue anglaise coïncident	Column/Colonne 3 Assimilation Factor/ Facteur d'assimilation
1.	Conseil scolaire de district du Nord-Est de l'Ontario	District School Board Ontario North East	1.0
2.	Conseil scolaire de district du Nord-Est de l'Ontario	Near North District School Board	1.0
3.	Conseil scolaire de district du Nord-Est l'Ontario	Trillium Lakelands District School Board	1.5
4.	Conseil scolaire de district du Grand Nord de l'Ontario	Algoma District School Board	1.5
5.	Conseil scolaire de district du Grand Nord de l'Ontario	Rainbow District School Board	1.0
6.	Conseil scolaire de district du Grand Nord de l'Ontario	Keewatin-Patricia District School Board	1.5
7.	Conseil scolaire de district du Grand Nord de l'Ontario	Rainy River District School Board	1.5
8.	Conseil scolaire de district du Grand Nord de l'Ontario	Lakehead District School Board	1.5
9.	Conseil scolaire de district du Grand Nord de l'Ontario	Superior-Greenstone District School Board	1.5
10.	Conseil scolaire de district du Centre Sud-Ouest	Bluewater District School Board	1.5
11.	Conseil scolaire de district du Centre Sud-Ouest	Avon Maitland District School Board	1.5
12.	Conseil scolaire de district du Centre Sud-Ouest	Greater Essex County District School Board	1.5
13.	Conseil scolaire de district du Centre Sud-Ouest	Lambton Kent District School Board	1.5
14.	Conseil scolaire de district du Centre Sud-Ouest	Thames Valley District School Board	1.5
15.	Conseil scolaire de district du Centre Sud-Ouest	Toronto District School Board	1.5

Item/Point	Column/Colonne 1 French Language Board/ Conseil de langue française	Column/Colonne 2 English Language Coterminous Board/ Conseil de langue anglaise coïncident	Column/Colonne 3 Assimilation Factor/ Facteur d'assimilation
16.	Conseil scolaire de district du Centre Sud-Ouest	Durham District School Board	1.5
17.	Conseil scolaire de district du Centre Sud-Ouest	Kawartha Pine Ridge District School Board	1.5
18.	Conseil scolaire de district du Centre Sud-Ouest	Trillium Lakelands District School Board	1.5
19.	Conseil scolaire de district du Centre Sud-Ouest	York Region District School Board	1.5
20.	Conseil scolaire de district du Centre Sud-Ouest	Simcoe County District School Board	1.5
21.	Conseil scolaire de district du Centre Sud-Ouest	Upper Grand District School Board	1.5
22.	Conseil scolaire de district du Centre Sud-Ouest	Peel District School Board	1.5
23.	Conseil scolaire de district du Centre Sud-Ouest	Halton District School Board	1.5
24.	Conseil scolaire de district du Centre Sud-Ouest	Hamilton-Wentworth District School Board	1.5
25.	Conseil scolaire de district du Centre Sud-Ouest	District School Board of Niagara	1.5
26.	Conseil scolaire de district du Centre Sud-Ouest	Grand Erie District School Board	1.5
27.	Conseil scolaire de district du Centre Sud-Ouest	Waterloo Region District School Board	1.5
28.	Conseil de district des écoles publiques de langue française n° 59	Ottawa-Carleton District School Board	1.0
29.	Conseil de district des écoles publiques de langue française n° 59	Upper Canda District School Board	1.0

Table/Tableau 2
Assimilation Factors for ALF Funding/
Facteurs d'assimilation pour le financement des programmes d'ALF

Table/Tableau 2
Assimilation Factors for ALF Funding/
Facteurs d'assimilation pour le financement des programmes d'ALF

Item/Point	Column/Colonne 1 French Language Board/ Conseil de langue française	Column/Colonne 2 English Language Coterminous Board/ Conseil de langue anglaise coïncident	Column/Colonne 3 Assimilation Factor/ Facteur d'assimilation
30.	Conseil de district des écoles publiques de langue française n° 59	Limestone District School Board	1.5
31.	Conseil de district des écoles publiques de langue française n° 59	Renfrew County District School Board	1.5
32.	Conseil de district des écoles publiques de langue française n° 59	Hastings and Prince Edward District School Board	1.5
33.	Conseil de district catholique des Grandes Rivières	Northeastern Catholic District School Board	1.0
34.	Conseil scolaire de district catholique Franco-Nord	Nipissing-Parry Sound Catholic District School Board	1.0
35.	Conseil scolaire de district catholique Centre-Sud	Simcoe Muskoka Catholic District School Board	1.5
36.	Conseil scolaire de district catholique du Nouvel-Ontario	Sudbury Catholic District School Board	1.0
37.	Conseil scolaire de district catholique du Nouvel-Ontario	Huron-Superior Catholic District School Board	1.5
38.	Conseil scolaire de district catholique des Aurores boréales	Northwest Catholic District School Board	1.5
39.	Conseil scolaire de district catholique des Aurores boréales	Kenora Catholic District School Board	1.5
40.	Conseil scolaire de district catholique des Aurores boréales	Thunder Bay Catholic District School Board	1.5
41.	Conseil scolaire de district catholique des Aurores boréales	Superior North Catholic District School Board	1.5
42.	Conseil scolaire de district des écoles catholiques du Sud-Ouest	Bruce-Grey Catholic District School Board	1.5
43.	Conseil scolaire de district des écoles catholiques du Sud-Ouest	Huron Perth Catholic District School Board	1.5

Table/Tableau 2
Assimilation Factors for ALF Funding/
Facteurs d'assimilation pour le financement des programmes d'ALF

Item/ Point	Column/Colonne 1 French Language Board/ Conseil de langue française	Column/Colonne 2 English Language Coterminous Board/ Conseil de langue anglaise coïncident	Column/Colonne 3 Assimilation Factor/ Facteur d'assimilation
44.	Conseil scolaire de district des écoles catholiques du Sud-Ouest	Windsor-Essex Catholic District School Board	1.5
45.	Conseil scolaire de district des écoles catholiques du Sud-Ouest	St. Clair Catholic District School Board	1.5
46.	Conseil scolaire de district des écoles catholiques du Sud-Ouest	English-language Separate District School Board No. 38	1.5
47.	Conseil scolaire de district catholique Centre-Sud	Toronto Catholic District School Board	1.5
48.	Conseil scolaire de district catholique Centre-Sud	Durham Catholic District School Board	1.5
49.	Conseil scolaire de district catholique Centre-Sud	Peterborough Victoria Northumberland and Clarington Catholic District School Board	1.5
50.	Conseil scolaire de district catholique Centre-Sud	York Catholic District School Board	1.5
51.	Conseil scolaire de district catholique Centre-Sud	Wellington Catholic District School Board	1.5
52.	Conseil scolaire de district catholique Centre-Sud	Dufferin-Peel Catholic District School Board	1.5
53.	Conseil scolaire de district catholique Centre-Sud	Halton Catholic District School Board	1.5
54.	Conseil scolaire de district catholique Centre-Sud	Hamilton-Wentworth Catholic District School Board	1.5
55.	Conseil scolaire de district catholique Centre-Sud	Niagara Catholic District School Board	1.5
56.	Conseil scolaire de district catholique Centre-Sud	Brant/Haldimand-Norfolk Catholic District School Board	1.5
57.	Conseil scolaire de district catholique Centre-Sud	Waterloo Catholic District School Board	1.5
58.	Conseil scolaire de district catholique du Centre-Est de l'Ontario	Ottawa-Carleton Catholic District School Board	1.5

REGULATION 214/99 — S. 60

Table/Tableau 2
Assimilation Factors for ALF Funding/
Facteurs d'assimilation pour le financement des programmes d'ALF

Item/Point	Column/Colonne 1 French Language Board/ Conseil de langue française	Column/Colonne 2 English Language Coterminous Board/ Conseil de langue anglaise coïncident	Column/Colonne 3 Assimilation Factor/ Facteur d'assimilation
59.	Conseil scolaire de district catholique du Centre-Est de l'Ontario	Catholic District School Board of Eastern Ontario	1.0
60.	Conseil scolaire de district catholique de l'Est ontarien	Catholic District School Board of Eastern Ontario	1.0
61.	Conseil scolaire de district catholique du Centre-Est de l'Ontario	Algonquin and Lakeshore Catholic District School Board	1.5
62.	Conseil scolaire de district catholique du Centre-Est de l'Ontario	Renfrew County Catholic District School Board	1.5

Table/Tableau 3
Distance and Urban Factors for Remote and Rural Allocations/
Facteur urbain et facteur d'éloignement pour l'élément conseils ruraux et éloignés

Item/Point	Column/Colonne 1 Board Name/Nom du conseil	Column/Colonne 2 Distance/Distance	Column/Colonne 3 Urban Factor/ Facteur urbain
1.	District School Board Ontario North East	680 km	0.946
2.	Algoma District School Board	790 km	0.809
3.	Rainbow District School Board	455 km	0.821
4.	Near North District School Board	332 km	0.913
5.	Keewatin-Patricia District School Board	1801 km	1.000
6.	Rainy River District School Board	1630 km	1.000
7.	Lakehead District School Board	1375 km	0.549
8.	Superior-Greenstone District School Board	1440 km	1.000

S. 60 REGULATIONS UNDER THE EDUCATION ACT

Table/Tableau 3
Distance and Urban Factors for Remote and Rural Allocations/
Facteur urbain et facteur d'éloignement pour l'élément conseils ruraux et éloignés

Item/Point	Column/Colonne 1 Board Name/Nom du conseil	Column/Colonne 2 Distance/Distance	Column/Colonne 3 Urban Factor/ Facteur urbain
9.	Bluewater District School Board	177 km	1.000
10.	Avon Maitland District School Board	< 151 km	1.000
11.	Greater Essex County District School Board	< 151 km	1.000
12.	Lambton Kent District School Board	< 151 km	1.000
13.	Thames Valley District School Board	< 151 km	1.000
14.	Toronto District School Board	< 151 km	1.000
15.	Durham District School Board	< 151 km	1.000
16.	Kawartha Pine Ridge District School Board	161 km	0.942
17.	Trillium Lakelands District School Board	253 km	1.000
18.	York Region District School Board	< 151 km	1.000
19.	Simcoe County District School Board	< 151 km	1.000
20.	Upper Grand District School Board	< 151 km	1.000
21.	Peel District School Board	< 151 km	1.000
22.	Halton District School Board	< 151 km	1.000
23.	Hamilton-Wentworth District School Board	< 151 km	1.000
24.	District School Board of Niagara	< 151 km	1.000
25.	Grand Erie District School Board	< 151 km	1.000
26.	Waterloo Region District School Board	< 151 km	1.000
27.	Ottawa-Carleton District School Board	< 151 km	1.000
28.	Upper Canada District School Board	< 151 km	1.000
29.	Limestone District School Board	235 km	0.717
30.	Renfrew County District School Board	< 151 km	1.000
31.	Hastings and Prince Edward District School Board	251 km	0.971

Table/Tableau 3
Distance and Urban Factors for Remote and Rural Allocations/
Facteur urbain et facteur d'éloignement pour l'élément conseils ruraux et éloignés

ITEM/POINT	Board Name/Nom du conseil	COLUMN/COLONNE 1 Distance/Distance	COLUMN/COLONNE 2 Urban Factor/ Facteur urbain
32.	Northeastern Catholic District School Board	680 km	0.946
33.	Nipissing-Parry Sound Catholic District School Board	332 km	0.913
34.	Huron-Superior Catholic District School Board	790 km	0.777
35.	Sudbury Catholic District School Board	390 km	0.780
36.	Northwest Catholic District School Board	1715 km	1.000
37.	Kenora Catholic District School Board	1855 km	1.000
38.	Thunder Bay Catholic District School Board	1375 km	0.501
39.	Superior North Catholic District School Board	1440 kn	1.000
40.	Bruce-Grey Catholic District School Board	177 km	1.000
41.	Huron Perth Catholic District School Board	< 151 km	1.000
42.	Windsor-Essex Catholic District School Board	< 151 km	1.000
43.	English-language Separate District School Board No. 38	< 151 km	1.000
44.	St. Clair Catholic District School Board	< 151 km	1.000
45.	Toronto Catholic District School Board	< 151 km	1.000
46.	Peterborough Victoria Northumberland and Clarington Catholic District School Board	161 km	0.942
47.	York Catholic District School Board	< 151 km	1.000
48.	Dufferin-Peel Catholic District School Board	< 151 km	1.000

Table/Tableau 3
Distance and Urban Factors for Remote and Rural Allocations/
Facteur urbain et facteur d'éloignement pour l'élément conseils ruraux et éloignés

Item/Point	Column/Colonne 1 Board Name/Nom du conseil	Column/Colonne 2 Distance/Distance	Column/Colonne 3 Urban Factor/ Facteur urbain
49.	Simcoe Muskoka Catholic District School Board	< 151 km	1.000
50.	Durham Catholic District School Board	< 151 km	1.000
51.	Halton Catholic District School Board	< 151 km	1.000
52.	Hamilton-Wentworth Catholic District School Board	< 151 km	1.000
53.	Wellington Catholic District School Board	< 151 km	1.000
54.	Waterloo Catholic District School Board	< 151 km	1.000
55.	Niagara Catholic District School Board	< 151 km	1.000
56.	Brant/Haldimand-Norfolk Catholic District School Board	< 151 km	1.000
57.	Catholic District School Board of Eastern Ontario	< 151 km	1.000
58.	Ottawa-Carleton Catholic District School Board	< 151 km	1.000
59.	Renfrew County Catholic District School Board	< 151 km	1.000
60.	Algonquin and Lakeshore Catholic District School Board	277 km	0.986
61.	Conseil scolaire de district du Nord-Est de l'Ontario	634 km	0.939
62.	Conseil scolaire de district du Grand Nord de l'Ontario	1191 km	0.8620
63.	Conseil scolaire de district du Centre Sud-Ouest	< 151 km	1.000
64.	Conseil de district des écoles publiques de langue française n° 59	< 151 km	1.000
65.	Conseil scolaire de district catholique des Grandes Rivières	680 km	0.952

Table/Tableau 3
Distance and Urban Factors for Remote and Rural Allocations/
Facteur urbain et facteur d'éloignement pour l'élément conseils ruraux et éloignés

Item/Point	Column/Colonne 1 Board Name/Nom du conseil	Column/Colonne 2 Distance/Distance	Column/Colonne 3 Urban Factor/Facteur urbain
66.	Conseil scolaire de district catholique Franco-Nord	332 km	0.933
67.	Conseil scolaire de district catholique du Nouvel-Ontario	790 km	0.879
68.	Conseil scolaire de district catholique des Aurores boréales	1745 km	0.727
69.	Conseil scolaire de district des écoles catholique du Sud-Ouest	< 151 km	1.000
70.	Conseil scolaire de district catholique Centre-Sud	< 151 km	1.000
71.	Conseil scolaire de district catholique de l'Est ontarien	< 151 km	1.000
72.	Conseil scolaire de district catholique du Centre-Est de l'Ontario	< 151 km	1.000

Table/Tableau 4
Learning Opportunities/
Programmes d'aide à l'apprentissage

Item/Point	Column/Colonne 1 Name of Board/Nom du conseil	Column/Colonne 2 Allocation for Learning Opportunities/Élément programmes d'aide à l'apprentissage
1.	District School Board Ontario North East	1,474,673
2.	Algoma District School Board	2,240,042
3.	Rainbow District School Board	1,786,217
4.	Near North District School Board	1,838,599
5.	Keewatin-Patricia District School Board	855,519
6.	Rainy River District School Board	472,125
7.	Lakehead District School Board	1,904,168
8.	Superior-Greenstone District School Board	530,177

S. 60 REGULATIONS UNDER THE EDUCATION ACT

<table>
<tr><td colspan="3" align="center">Table/Tableau 4
Learning Opportunities/
Programmes d'aide à l'apprentissage</td></tr>
<tr><td rowspan="2">ITEM/POINT</td><td>COLUMN/COLONNE 1</td><td>COLUMN/COLONNE 2</td></tr>
<tr><td>Name of Board/Nom du conseil</td><td>Allocation for Learning Opportunities/Élément programmes d'aide à l'apprentissage</td></tr>
<tr><td>9.</td><td>Bluewater District School Board</td><td>743,017</td></tr>
<tr><td>10.</td><td>Avon Maitland District School Board</td><td>906,166</td></tr>
<tr><td>11.</td><td>Greater Essex County District School Board</td><td>3,688,449</td></tr>
<tr><td>12.</td><td>Lambton Kent District School Board</td><td>1,190,574</td></tr>
<tr><td>13.</td><td>Thames Valley District School Board</td><td>6,118.828</td></tr>
<tr><td>14.</td><td>Toronto District School Board</td><td>53,334,398</td></tr>
<tr><td>15.</td><td>Durham District School Board</td><td>1,959,159</td></tr>
<tr><td>16.</td><td>Kawartha Pine Ridge District School Board</td><td>1,421,917</td></tr>
<tr><td>17.</td><td>Trillium Lakelands District School Board</td><td>339,581</td></tr>
<tr><td>18.</td><td>York Region District School Board</td><td>2,932,609</td></tr>
<tr><td>19.</td><td>Simcoe County District School Board</td><td>1,091,421</td></tr>
<tr><td>20.</td><td>Upper Grand District School Board</td><td>918,448</td></tr>
<tr><td>21.</td><td>Peel District School Board</td><td>5,949,939</td></tr>
<tr><td>22.</td><td>Halton District School Board</td><td>562,368</td></tr>
<tr><td>23.</td><td>Hamilton-Wentworth District School Board</td><td>6,740,451</td></tr>
<tr><td>24.</td><td>District School Board of Niagara</td><td>3,161,013</td></tr>
<tr><td>25.</td><td>Grand Erie District School Board</td><td>2,327,887</td></tr>
<tr><td>26.</td><td>Waterloo Region District School Board</td><td>3,638,569</td></tr>
<tr><td>27.</td><td>Ottawa-Carleton District School Board</td><td>6,623,778</td></tr>
<tr><td>28.</td><td>Upper Canada District School Board</td><td>1,112,594</td></tr>
<tr><td>29.</td><td>Limestone District School Board</td><td>1,599,350</td></tr>
<tr><td>30.</td><td>Renfrew County District School Board</td><td>632,032</td></tr>
<tr><td>31.</td><td>Hastings and Prince Edward District School Board</td><td>1,409,881</td></tr>
<tr><td>32.</td><td>Northeastern Catholic District School Board</td><td>509,798</td></tr>
<tr><td>33.</td><td>Nipissing-Parry Sound Catholic District School Board</td><td>454,337</td></tr>
<tr><td>34.</td><td>Huron-Superior Catholic District School Board</td><td>1,164,422</td></tr>
</table>

Table/Tableau 4
Learning Opportunities/
Programmes d'aide à l'apprentissage

ITEM/POINT	COLUMN/COLONNE 1 Name of Board/Nom du conseil	COLUMN/COLONNE 2 Allocation for Learning Opportunities/Élément programmes d'aide à l'apprentissage
35.	Sudbury Catholic District School Board	945,337
36.	Northwest Catholic District School Board	122,343
37.	Kenora Catholic District School Board	102,056
38.	Thunder Bay Catholic District School Board	957,557
39.	Superior North Catholic District School Board	168,584
40.	Bruce-Grey Catholic District School Board	152,434
41.	Huron Perth Catholic District School Board	130,780
42.	Windsor-Essex Catholic District School Board	2,679,022
43.	English-language Separate District School Board No. 38	3,211,654
44.	St. Clair Catholic District School Board	546,514
45.	Toronto Catholic District School Board	23,611,599
46.	Peterborough Victoria Northumberland and Clarington Catholic District School Board	533,053
47.	York Catholic District School Board	1,854,829
48.	Dufferin-Peel Catholic District School Board	4,738,086
49.	Simcoe Muskoka Catholic District School Board	366,487
50.	Durham Catholic District School Board	721,480
51.	Halton Catholic District School Board	270,379
52.	Hamilton-Wentworth Catholic District School Board	3,291,086
53.	Wellington Catholic District School Board	267,678
54.	Waterloo Catholic District School Board	1,701,138
55.	Niagara Catholic District School Board	1,507,994
56.	Brant/Haldimand-Norfolk Catholic District School Board	770,868
57.	Catholic District School Board of Eastern Ontario	691,106

S. 60 REGULATIONS UNDER THE EDUCATION ACT

Table/Tableau 4
Learning Opportunities/
Programmes d'aide à l'apprentissage

Item/Point	Column/Colonne 1 Name of Board/Nom du conseil	Column/Colonne 2 Allocation for Learning Opportunities/Élément programmes d'aide à l'apprentissage
58.	Ottawa-Carleton Catholic District School Board	3,230,651
59.	Renfrew County Catholic District School Board	445,592
60.	Algonquin and Lakeshore Catholic District School Board	1,026,142
61.	Conseil scolaire de district du Nord-Est de l'Ontario	194,663
62.	Conseil scolaire de district du Grand Nord de l'Ontario	206,980
63.	Conseil scolaire de district du Centre Sud-Ouest	649,021
64.	Conseil de district des écoles publiques de langue française n° 59	690,903
65.	Conseil scolaire de district catholique des Grandes Rivières	1,406,429
66.	Conseil scolaire de district catholique Franco-Nord	650,200
67.	Conseil scolaire de district catholique du Nouvel-Ontario	1,362,379
68.	Conseil scolaire de district catholique des Aurores boréales	205,954
69.	Conseil scolaire de district des écoles catholique du Sud-Ouest	376,990
70.	Conseil scolaire de district catholique Centre-Sud	926,681
71.	Conseil scolaire de district catholique de l'Est ontarien	1,194,650
72.	Conseil scolaire de district catholique du Centre-Est de l'Ontario	1,313,558

REGULATION 214/99 **S. 60**

Table/Tableau 5
Teacher Compensation/Rémunération des enseignants

Full years of teaching experience/ Années complètes d'expérience en enseignement	\multicolumn{7}{c}{Qualification Categories/Catégories de qualification}						
	D	C	B	A1/group 1 A1/groupe 1	A2/group 2A2/ groupe 2	A3/group 3A3/ groupe 3	A4/group 4A4/ groupe 4
0	0.5788	0.5788	0.5788	0.6229	0.6487	0.7081	0.7449
1	0.6127	0.6127	0.6127	0.654	0.6864	0.7502	0.7926
2	0.6332	0.6332	0.6332	0.6989	0.7318	0.7969	0.8432
3	0.6523	0.6523	0.6523	0.7416	0.7743	0.8442	0.8925
4	0.7149	0.7149	0.7149	0.7814	0.8158	0.8953	0.9443
5	0.7698	0.7698	0.7698	0.8234	0.8606	0.9435	0.9975
6	0.8225	0.8225	0.8225	0.8655	0.9042	0.9866	1.0473
7	0.8694	0.8694	0.8694	0.9073	0.9472	1.0363	1.0997
8	0.8900	0.8900	0.8900	0.9485	0.9876	1.086	1.1512
9	0.9154	0.9154	0.9154	1.0025	1.0411	1.1534	1.2026
10	0.9667	0.9667	0.9667	1.0451	1.0989	1.2136	1.2949

Table/Tableau 6
Georgraphic Adjustment Factors for New Pupil Places/
Facteurs de redressement géographique pour les nouvelles places

ITEM/POINT	COLUMN/COLONNE 1 DISTRICT SCHOOL BOARDS/CONSEILS SCOLAIRES DE DISTRICT	COLUMN/COLONNE 2 Geographic Adjustment Factor/Facteur de redressement géographique
1.	District School Board Ontario North East	1.120
2.	Algoma District School Board	1.106
3.	Rainbow District School Board	1.063
4.	Near North District School Board	1.042
5.	Keewatin-Patricia District School Board	1.144
6.	Rainy River District School Board	1.142
7.	Lakehead District School Board	1.080

Table/Tableau 6
Georgraphic Adjustment Factors for New Pupil Places/
Facteurs de redressement géographique pour les nouvelles places

Item/Point	Column/Colonne 1 DISTRICT SCHOOL BOARDS/CONSEILS SCOLAIRES DE DISTRICT	Column/Colonne 2 Geographic Adjustment Factor/Facteur de redressement géographique
8.	Superior-Greenstone District School Board	1.141
9.	Bluewater District School Board	1.007
10.	Avon Maitland District School Board	1.010
11.	Greater Essex County District School Board	1.000
12.	Lambton Kent District School Board	1.000
13.	Thames Valley District School Board	1.000
14.	Toronto District School Board	1.000
15.	Durham District School Board	1.000
16.	Kawartha Pine Ridge District School Board	1.003
17.	Trillium Lakelands District School Board	1.026
18.	York Region District School Board	1.000
19.	Simcoe County District School Board	1.000
20.	Upper Grand District School Board	1.000
21.	Peel District School Board	1.000
22.	Halton District School Board	1.000
23.	Hamilton-Wentworth District School Board	1.000
24.	District School Board of Niagara	1.000
25.	Grand Erie District School Board	1.000
26.	Waterloo Region District School Board	1.000
27.	Ottawa-Carleton District School Board	1.000
28.	Upper Canada District School Board	1.000
29.	Limestone District School Board	1.015
30.	Renfrew County District School Board	1.000
31.	Hastings and Prince Edward District School Board	1.025
32.	Northeastern Catholic District School Board	1.123
33.	Nipissing-Parry Sound Catholic District School Board	1.042

Table/Tableau 6
Georgraphic Adjustment Factors for New Pupil Places/
Facteurs de redressement géographique pour les nouvelles places

Item/Point	Column/Colonne 1 DISTRICT SCHOOL BOARDS/CONSEILS SCOLAIRES DE DISTRICT	Column/Colonne 2 Geographic Adjustment Factor/Facteur de redressement géographique
34.	Huron-Superior Catholic District School Board	1.104
35.	Sudbury Catholic District School Board	1.048
36.	Northwest Catholic District School Board	1.149
37.	Kenora Catholic District School Board	1.143
38.	Thunder Bay Catholic District School Board	1.074
39.	Superior North Catholic District School Board	1.146
40.	Bruce-Grey Catholic District School Board	1.007
41.	Huron Perth Catholic District School Board	1.011
42.	Windsor-Essex Catholic District School Board	1.000
43.	English-language Separate District School Board No. 38	1.000
44.	St. Clair Catholic District School Board	1.000
45.	Toronto Catholic District School Board	1.000
46.	Peterborough Victoria Northumberland and Clarington Catholic District School Board	1.003
47.	York Catholic District School Board	1.000
48.	Dufferin-Peel Catholic District School Board	1.000
49.	Simcoe Muskoka Catholic District School Board	1.000
50.	Durham Catholic District School Board	1.000
51.	Halton Catholic District School Board	1.000
52.	Hamilton-Wentworth Catholic District School Board	1.000
53.	Wellington Catholic District School Board	1.000
54.	Waterloo Catholic District School Board	1.000
55.	Niagara Catholic District School Board	1.000
56.	Brant/Haldimand-Norfolk Catholic District School Board	1.000

Table/Tableau 6
Georgraphic Adjustment Factors for New Pupil Places/
Facteurs de redressement géographique pour les nouvelles places

Item/Point	Column/Colonne 1 DISTRICT SCHOOL BOARDS/CONSEILS SCOLAIRES DE DISTRICT	Column/Colonne 2 Geographic Adjustment Factor/Facteur de redressement géographique
57.	Catholic District School Board of Eastern Ontario	1.000
58.	Ottawa-Carleton Catholic District School Board	1.000
59.	Renfrew County Catholic District School Board	1.000
60.	Algonquin and Lakeshore Catholic District School Board	1.032
61.	Conseil scolaire de district du Nord-Est de l'Ontario	1.110
62.	Conseil scolaire de district du Grand Nord de l'Ontario	1.116
63.	Conseil scolaire de district du Centre Sud-Ouest	1.000
64.	Conseil de district des écoles publiques de langue française n° 59	1.000
65.	Conseil scolaire de district catholique des Grandes Rivières	1.123
66.	Conseil scolaire de district catholique Franco-Nord	1.043
67.	Conseil scolaire de district catholique du Nouvel-Ontario	1.118
68.	Conseil scolaire de district catholique des Aurores boréales	1.100
69.	Conseil scolaire de district catholique du Sud-Ouest	1.000
70.	Conseil scolaire de district catholique Centre-Sud	1.000
71.	Conseil scolaire de district catholique de l'Est ontarien	1.000
72.	Conseil scolaire de district catholique du Centre-Est de l'Ontario	1.000

Table/Tableau 7
Pupil Accommodation Grant/Subventions pour les installations destinées aux élèves
Grants for New Pupil Places — Outstanding Capital Commitments/
Subvention pour les nouvelles places — Engagements d'immobilisations non réalisés

Item/Point	Column/Colonne 1 District School Board/Conseil scolaire de district	Column/Colonne 2 Pupil Places — Elementary/Places à l'élémentaire	Column/Colonne 3 Pupil Places — Secondary/Places au secondaire
1.	Bluewater District School Board		111
2.	Conseil scolaire de district catholique de l'Est ontarien	41	
3.	Conseil scolaire de district catholique Centre-Sud		452
4.	Conseil scolaire de district du Centre Sud-Ouest	144	
5.	District School Board Ontario North East	281	
6.	Dufferin-Peel Catholic District School Board	274	
7.	Durham Catholic District School Board	79	
8.	Greater Essex County District School Board		122
9.	Hamilton-Wentworth Catholic District School Board	204	224
10.	Keewatin-Patricia District School Board	69	
11.	Near North District School Board	681	
12.	Ottawa-Carelton District School Board		107
13.	Peel District School Board		83
14.	Simcoe County District School Board	91	
15.	Simcoe Muskoka Catholic District School Board	274	
16.	Superior-Greenstone District School Board		80
17.	Thunder Bay Catholic District School Board	137	
18.	Toronto Catholic District School Board		25

Table/Tableau 7
Pupil Accommodation Grant/Subventions pour les installations destinées aux élèves
Grants for New Pupil Places — Outstanding Capital Commitments/
Subvention pour les nouvelles places — Engagements d'immobilisations non réalisés

Item/Point	Column/Colonne 1 District School Board/Conseil scolaire de district	Column/Colonne 2 Pupil Places — Elementary/Places à l'élémentaire	Column/Colonne 3 Pupil Places — Secondary/Places au secondaire
19.	Upper Grand District School Board		188

Table/Tableau 8
Classroom Expenditure Percentages/
Pourcentages des dépenses liées aux classes

Item/Point	Column/Colonne 1 Amounts/Sommes	Column/Colonne 2 % allocated to the classroom/% alloué aux classes
1.	Elementary School Part of Foundation Allocations/Partie de l'élément éducation de base qui vise l'élémentaire	79.5%
2.	Secondary School Part of Foundation Allocations/Partie de l'élément éducation de base qui vise le secondaire	75.9%
3.	Elementary School Teacher Compensation/Rémunération des enseignants de l'élémentaire	91.2%
4.	Secondary School Teacher Compensation/Rémunération des enseignants du secondaire	84.6%
5.	Small Schools Allocations/Élément petites écoles	50.0%
6.	Remote & Rural Allocations/Élément conseils ruraux et éloignés	74.0%
7.	Early Learning Allocations/Élément apprentissage durant les premières années d'études	70.2%
8.	Adult Day School/Élèves adultes de jour	76.0%
9.	Native Language and French as a First or Second Language/Langue autochtone et français langue première et langue seconde	91.1%
10.	ESL/ESD/ALF/PDF	86.0%

	Table/Tableau 8 Classroom Expenditure Percentages/ Pourcentages des d'aaepenses liées aux classes	
	COLUMN/COLONNE 1	COLUMN/COLONNE 2
ITEM/POINT	Amounts/Sommes	% allocated to the classroom/% alloué aux classes
11.	Learning Opportunities Allocations/Élément programmes d'aide à l'apprentissage	77.3%
12.	Special Education Allocations/Élément éducation de l'enfance en difficulté	92.0%

REGULATION 215/99
CALCULATION OF FEES FOR PUPILS FOR THE 1999-2000 SCHOOL BOARD FISCAL YEAR
O. Reg. 215/99

1. (1) In this Regulation,

"1999-2000 A.D.E. regulation" means Ontario Regulation 213/99; ("règlement sur l'effectif quotidien moyen de 1999-2000")

"1999-2000 grant regulation" means Ontario Regulation 214/99; (règlement sur les subventions de 1999-2000")

"continuing education A.D.E.", for a board, means the continuing education average daily enrolment for the board, as calculated under section 3 of the 1999-2000 A.D.E. regulation; ("effectif quotidien moyen des cours d'éducation permanente")

"continuing education class or course" has the same meaning as in section 3 of the 1999-2000 A.D.E. regulation; ("class ou cours d'éducation permanente")

"day school A.D.E.", for a board, means the day school average daily enrolment for the board, as calculated under section 2 of the 1999-2000 A.D.E. regulation; ("effectif quotidien moyen de jour")

"day school program" does not include continuing education or summer school classes or courses; (programme scolaire de jour")

"elementary school pupil" means a pupil who is enrolled in any of junior kindergarten, kindergarten and grades one to eight; ("élève de l'élémentaire")

"high cost program" means,

(a) a special education program, or

(b) any other program which both the board and the party from whom the tuition fee is receivable agree is a high cost program for the purposes of this Regulation; ("programme à coût élevé")

"isolate board" means a school authority other than a section 68 board; ("conseil isolé")

"P.A.C." for a pupil, means the pupil accommodation charge for a pupil as determined under subsections (3) and (4); ("frais de pension")

"secondary school pupil" means a pupil who is enrolled in any of grades nine to twelve or in a course leading to an OAC credit; (élève du secondaire")

"section 68 board" means a board established under section 68 of the Act; ("conseil créé en vertu de l'article 68")

"summer school A.D.E.", for a board, means the summer school average daily enrolment for the board, as calculated under section 4 of the 1999-2000 A.D.E. regulation; ("effectif quotidien moyen des cours d'éducation permanente")

"summer school class or course" means a summer school class or course as defined in subsection 4(1) of the 1999-2000 A.D.E. regulation. ("classe ou cours d'été")

(2) For the purposes of this Regulation, the day school A.D.E. of a pupil enrolled in a school operated by a board is the day school A.D.E. for the board calculated as if that pupil were the board's only pupil.

(3) Subject to subsection (4), the pupil accommodation charge for a pupil is $141 in the case of an elementary school pupil or $282 in the case of a secondary school pupil.

(4) If a board has entered into an agreement under subsection 188(3) of the Act that provides for a payment by the Crown in right of Canada to provide classroom accommodation for a specified number of pupils, the pupil accommodation charge for each pupil accommodated as a result of the agreement is zero.

(5) For the purposes of this Regulation, a pupil is a pupil of a board if he or she is a pupil of the board within the meaning of section 2 of the 1999-2000 grant regulation.

Application

2. This Regulation applies in respect of the period September 1, 1999 to August 31, 2000.

Fees Paid to Boards by Canada or Authority Providing Education for Indians

3. (1) This section applies in respect of a pupil who is enrolled in a day school program in a school operated by a district school board or an isolate board if a fee in respect of the pupil is receivable by the board from,
   (a) the Crown in right of Canada; or
   (b) a band, the council of a band or an education authority where the band, council of a band or education authority is authorized by the Crown in right of Canada to provide education for Indians.

(2) The fee in respect of a pupil described in subsection (1) shall be calculated as follows:
1. Take the base amount determined for the pupil under subsection (3),(4) or (5), as the case may be.
2. Multiply the day school A.D.E. of the pupil by the sum of,
    i. the base amount determined under paragraph 1, and
    ii. the P.A.C. for that pupil.

(3) For the purposes of paragraph 1 of subsection (2), the base amount for an elementary school pupil described in subsection (1) who is enrolled in a school operated by a district school board shall be determined as follows:
1. Determine the amount calculated for the board under paragraph 2 of section 13 of the 1999-2000 grant regulation, on account of the foundation allocation for elementary school pupils.
2. Determine an amount on account of the special education allocation for elementary school pupils, as follows:
    i. Multiply the day school A.D.E. for the board, counting only elementary school pupils of the board, by $362.
    ii. Calculate the part of the equipment ISA determined for the board under paragraph 2 of section 14 of the 1999-2000 grant regulation that is generated by elementary school pupils of the board.
    iii. Calculate the part of the amount determined for the board under clause 18(a) of the 1999-2000 grant regulation that is generated by individuals who were

elementary school pupils in the 1998-99 school year. Where an adjustment has been made under section 20 of that regulation to the amount calculated for the board under section 18 of that regulation, the amount calculated for the board under this subparagraph shall be increased or decreased by the amount that the Minister considers appropriate to take account of the adjustment made under section 20 of that regulation.
  iv. Calculate the part of the amount determined for the board under clause 18(b) of the 1999-2000 grant regulation that is generated by elementary school pupils of the board. Where an adjustment has been made under section 20 of that regulation to the amount calculated for the board under section 18 of that regulation, the amount calculated for the board under this subparagraph shall be increased or decreased by the amount that the Minister considers appropriate to take account of the adjustment made under section 20 of that regulation.
  v. Total the amounts obtained under subparagraphs i,ii,iii and iv.
3. In the case of an English-language district school board, determine an amount on account of the language allocation for elementary school pupils, as follows:
  i. Take the French as a second language amount for elementary school pupils of the board, as calculated under subsection 22(3) of the 1999-2000 grant regulation.
  ii. Calculate the part of the ESL/ESD amount for the board that is generated by elementary school pupils of the board, as follows:
    A. Calculate the part of the ESL/ESD amount for the board, as calculated under paragraph 5 of subsection 24(1) of the 1999-2000 grant regulation, that is generated by elementary school pupils of the board.
    B. Take the amount set out for the board in Table 1 of the 1999-2000 grant regulation.
    C. Divide the amount taken under sub-subparagraph B by the day school A.D.E. for the board, counting only pupils of the board.
    D. Multiply the result obtained under sub-subparagraph C by the day school A.D.E. for the board, counting only elementary school pupils of the board.
    E. Add the amounts calculated under sub-subparagraphs A and D.
  iii. Add the amount taken under subparagraph i and the amount calculated under sub-subparagraph E of subparagraph ii.
4. In the case of a French-language district school board, determine an amount on account of the language allocation for elementary school pupils, as follows:
  i. Take the amount determined for the board under paragraph 1 of subsection 26(1) of the 1999-2000 grant regulation.
  ii. Divide the total of the amounts determined for the board under paragraph 7 of subsection 28(4) of the 1999-2000 grant regulation by the total number of instructional units determined for the board under paragraph 3 of subsection 28(4) of that Regulation. Multiply the result by the total number of elementary instructional units determined for the board under paragraph 1 of subsection 28(4) of that Regulation.
  iii. Calculate the part of the PDF funding level for the board, as calculated under

subsection 28(11) of the 1999-2000 grant regulation, that is generated by elementary school pupils of the board.
　　iv. Total the amount taken under subparagraph i, the product obtained under subparagraph ii and the amount calculated under subparagraph iii.
5. Determine the amount calculated for the board under paragraph 4 of subsection 29(11) of the 1999-2000 grant regulation, on account of the small schools allocation for elementary school pupils.
6. Determine an amount on account of the remote and rural allocation for elementary school pupils, as follows:
　　i. Take the amount determined for the board under paragraph 5 of section 30 of the 1999-2000 grant regulation.
　　ii. Divide the amount determined for the board under subparagraph i by the day school A.D.E. for the board, counting only pupils of the board.
　　iii. Multiply the amount determined under subparagraph ii by the day school A.D.E. for the board, counting only elementary school pupils of the board.
7. Determine an amount on account of the learning opportunities allocation for elementary school pupils, as follows:
　　i. Take the amount determined for the board under section 31 of the 1999-2000 grant regulation.
　　ii. Divide the amount determined for the board under subparagraph i by the day school A.D.E. for the board, counting only pupils of the board.
　　iii. Multiply the amount determined under subparagraph ii by the day school A.D.E. for the board, counting only elementary school pupils of the board.
8. Determine the amount calculated for the board under paragraph 7 of subsection 34(11) of the 1999-2000 grant regulation, on account of the teacher compensation allocation for elementary school pupils.
9. Determine the amount calculated for the board under paragraph 2 of subsection 35(2) or paragraph 5 of subsection 35(3) of the 1999-2000 grant regulation, as the case may be, on account of the early learning allocation.
10. Determine an amount on account of the administration and governance allocation for elementary school pupils, as follows:
　　i. Take the amount determined for the board under paragraph 4 of subsection 37(1) of the 1999-2000 grant regulation.
　　ii. Divide the amount determined for the board under subparagraph i by the day school A.D.E. for the board, counting only pupils of the board.
　　iii. Multiply the amount determined under subparagraph ii by the day school A.D.E. for the board, counting only elementary school pupils of the board.
11. Determine an amount on account of the school operations part of the pupil accommodation allocation for elementary school pupils, by multiplying the elementary school area requirement determined for the board under paragraph 2 of subsection 38(3) of the 1999-2000 grant regulation or, where a supplementary elementary school area factor is approved for the board under subsection 38(4) of that Regulation, the adjusted elementary school area requirement determined for the board under paragraph 3 of subsection 38(3) of that Regulation, by the benchmark operating cost of $55.97.

S. 3   REGULATIONS UNDER THE EDUCATION ACT

12. Determine the amount calculated for the board under paragraph 16 of the subsection 38(3) of the 1999-2000 grant regulation, on account of the top-up amount for elementary school operations.
13. Determine a stable funding guarantee amount for elementary school pupils as follows:
    i. Take the amount determined for the board under section 48 of the 1999-2000 grant regulation.
    ii. Divide the amount determined for the board under subparagraph i by the day school A.D.E. for the board, counting only pupils of the board.
    iii. Multiply the amount determined under subparagraph ii by the day school A.D.E. for the board, counting only elementary school pupils of the board.
14. Total the amounts determined for the board under paragraphs 1 to 13.
15. Divide the total obtained under paragraph 14 by the day school A.D.E. for the board, counting only elementary school pupils of the board.
16. Where an amount calculated in accordance with section 46 of the 1999-2000 grant regulation is subtracted from the total determined for the board under paragraph 3 of section 11 of that Regulation, subtract an amount calculated as follows from the amount obtained under paragraph 15:
    i. Take the amount calculated for the board under subsection 46(2) of the 1999-2000 grant regulation.
    ii. Divide the amount referred to in subparagraph i by the day school A.D.E. for the board, counting only pupils of the board.
17. Where an amount calculated in accordance with section 47 of the 1999-2000 grant regulation is added to the total determined for the board under paragraph 3 of section 11 of that Regulation, add an amount calculated as follows to the amount obtained under paragraph 15:
    i. Take the amount calculated for the board under subsection 47(2) of the 1999-2000 grant regulation.
    ii. Divide the amount referred to in subparagraph i by the day school A.D.E. for the board, counting only pupils of the board.

(4) For the purposes of paragraph 1 of subsection (2), the base amount for a secondary school pupil described in subsection (1) who is enrolled in a school operated by a district school board shall be determined as follows:

1. Determine the amount calculated for the board under paragraph 4 of section 13 of the 1999-2000 grant regulation, on account of the foundation allocation for secondary school pupils.
2. Determine an amount on account of the special education allocation for secondary school pupils, as follows:
    i. Multiply the day school A.D.E. for the board, counting only secondary school pupils of the board, by $229.
    ii. Calculate the part of the equipment ISA determined for the board under paragraph 2 of section 14 of the 1999-2000 grant regulation that is generated by secondary school pupils of the board.
    iii. Calculate the part of the amount determined for the board under clause 18(a) of the 1999-2000 grant regulation that is generated by individuals who were

secondary school pupils in the 1998-1999 school year. Where an adjustment has been made under section 20 of that regulation to the amount calculated for the board under section 18 of that regulation, the amount calculated for the board under this subparagraph shall be increased or decreased by the amount that the Minister considers appropriate to take account of the adjustment made under section 20 of that regulation.
    iv. Calculate the part of the amount determined for the board under clause 18(b) of the 1999-2000 grant regulation that is generated by secondary school pupils of the board. Where an adjustment has been made under section 20 of that regulation to the amount calculated for the board under section 18 of that regulation, the amount calculated for the board under this subparagraph shall be increased or decreased by the amount that the Minister considers appropriate to take account of the adjustment made under section 20 of that regulation.
    v. Total the amounts obtained under subparagraphs i,ii,iii and iv.
3. In the case of an English-language district school board, determine an amount on account of the language allocation for secondary school pupils, as follows:
    i. Take the French as a second language amount for secondary school pupils of the board, as calculated under subsection 22(5) of the 1999-2000 grant regulation.
    ii. Calculate the part of the ESL/ESD amount for the board that is generated by secondary school pupils of the board, as follows:
        A. Calculate the part of the ESL/ESD amount for the board, as calculated under paragraph 5 of subsection 24(1) of the 1999-2000 grant regulation, that is generated by secondary school pupils of the board.
        B. Take the amount set out for the board in Table 1 of the 1999-2000 grant regulation.
        C. Divide the amount taken under sub-subparagraph B by the day school A.D.E. for the board, counting only pupils of the board.
        D. Multiply the result obtained under sub-subparagraph C by the day school A.D.E. for the board, counting only secondary school pupils of the board.
        E. Add the amounts calculated under sub-subparagraphs A and D.
    iii. Add the amount taken under subparagraph i and the amount calculated under sub-subparagraph E of subparagraph ii.
4. In the case of a French-language district school board, determine an amount on account of the language allocation for secondary school pupils, as follows:
    i. Take the amount determined for the board under paragraph 2 of subsection 26(1) of the 1999-2000 grant regulation.
    ii. Divide the total of the amounts determined for the board under paragraph 7 of subsection 28(4) of the 1999-2000 grant regulation by the total number of instructional units determined for the board under paragraph 3 of subsection 28(4) of that Regulation. Multiply the result by the total number of secondary instructional units determined for the board under paragraph 2 of subsection 28(4) of that Regulation.
    iii. Calculate the part of the PDF funding level for the board, as calculated under

subsection 28(11) of the 1999-2000 grant regulation, that is generated by secondary school pupils of the board.

 iv. Total the amount taken under subparagraph i, the product obtained under subparagraph ii and the amount calculated under subparagraph iii.

5. Determine the amount calculated for the board under paragraph 8 of subsection 29(11) of the 1999-2000 grant regulation, on account of the small schools allocation for secondary school pupils.

6. Determine an amount on account of the remote and rural allocation for secondary school pupils, as follows:

 i. Take the amount determined for the board under paragraph 5 of section 30 of the 1999-2000 grant regulation.

 ii. Divide the amount determined for the board under subparagraph i by the day school A.D.E. for the board, counting only pupils of the board.

 iii. Multiply the amount determined under subparagraph ii by the day school A.D.E. for the board, counting only secondary school pupils of the board.

7. Determine an amount on account of the learning opportunities allocation for secondary school pupils, as follows:

 i. Take the amount determined for the board under section 31 of the 1999-2000 grant regulation.

 ii. Divide the amount determined for the board under subparagraph i by the day school A.D.E. for the board, counting only pupils of the board.

 iii. Multiply the amount determined under subparagraph ii by the day school A.D.E. for the board, counting only secondary school pupils of the board.

8. Determine the amount calculated for the board under paragraph 9 of subsection 34(12) of the 1999-2000 grant regulation, on account of the teacher compensation allocation for secondary school pupils.

9. Determine an amount of account of the administration and governance allocation for secondary school pupils, as follows:

 i. Take the amount determined for the board under paragraph 4 of subsection 37(1) of the 1999-2000 grant regulation.

 ii. Divide the amount determined for the board under subparagraph i by the day school A.D.E. for the board, counting only pupils of the board.

 iii. Multiply the amount determined under subparagraph ii by the day school A.D.E. for the board, counting only secondary school pupils of the board.

10. Determine an amount on account of the school operations part of the pupil accommodation allocation for secondary school pupils, as follows:

 i. Multiply the secondary school area requirement for the board determined under paragraph 11 of subsection 38(3) of the 1999-2000 grant regulation or, where a supplementary secondary school area factor is approved for the board under subsection 38(9) of that Regulation, the adjusted secondary school area requirement determined for the board under paragraph 12 of subsection 38(3) of that Regulation, by the benchmark operating cost of $55.97.

 ii. Add to the amount determined under subparagraph i the amount calculated for the board under paragraph 18 of subsection 38(3) of the 1999-2000 grant regulation, on account of the top-up amount for secondary school operations.

REGULATION 215/99   S. 3

11. Determine a stable funding guarantee amount for secondary school pupils, as follows:
   i. Take the amount determined for the board under section 48 of the 1999-2000 grant regulation.
   ii. Divide the amount determined for the board under subparagraph i by the day school A.D.E. for the board, counting only pupils of the board.
   iii. Multiply the amount determined under subparagraph ii by the day school A.D.E. for the board, counting only secondary school pupils of the board.
12. Total the amounts determined for the board under paragraphs 1 to 11.
13. Divide the total obtained under paragraph 12 by the day school A.D.E. for the board, counting only secondary school pupils of the board.
14. Where an amount calculated in accordance with section 46 of the 1999-2000 grant regulation is subtracted from the total determined for the board under paragraph 3 of section 11 of that Regulation, subtract an amount calculated as follows from the amount obtained under paragraph 13:
   i. Take the amount calculated for the board under subsection 46(2) of the 1999-2000 grant regulation.
   ii. Divide the amount referred to in subparagraph i by the day school A.D.E. for the board, counting only pupils of the board.
15. Where an amount calculated in accordance with section 47 of the 1999-2000 grant regulation is added to the total determined for the board under paragraph 3 of section 11 of that Regulation, add an amount calculated as follows to the amount obtained under paragraph 13:
   i. Take the amount calculated for the board under subsection 47(2) of the 1999-2000 grant regulation.
   ii. Divide the amount referred to in subparagraph i by the day school A.D.E. for the board, counting only pupils of the board.

(5) For the purposes of paragraph 1 of subsection (2), the base amount for a pupil described in subsection (1) who is enrolled in a school operated by an isolate board shall be determined as follows:
1. Take the approved expenditure of the board within the meaning of subsection 55(1) of the 1999-2000 grant regulation.
2. Deduct the amount of the approved expenditure referred to in paragraph 1 that relates to transportation.
3. Deduct the amount of the approved expenditure referred to in paragraph 1 that relates to school renewal.
4. Divide the amount obtained under paragraph 3 by the day school A.D.E. for the board, counting only pupils of the board.

(6) The fee in respect of a pupil described in subsection (1) who is enrolled in a Native language program in a school operated by a district school board and whose fee is receivable from the Crown in right of Canada or from a band, the council of a band or an education authority where the band, council of a band or education authority is authorized by the Crown in right of Canada to provide education for Indians, may, at the option of the district school board, be increased by an amount equal to the allocation for Native language that would be

generated for the pupil if he or she were a pupil of the board, determined in accordance with section 23 or 27, as the case may be, of the 1999-2000 grant regulation.

(7) The fee in respect of a pupil described in subsection (1) who is enrolled in a high cost program may, at the option of the board, be increased by multiplying the fee by a factor agreed on by the board providing the instruction and the party from whom the fee is receivable or, in the absence of agreement, by a factor determined in accordance with subsection (8).

(8) If the board providing the instruction and the party from whom the fee is receivable cannot agree on a factor, the factor shall be determined by three arbitrators, appointed as follows:

1. One arbitrator shall be appointed by the board that provides the instruction.
2. One arbitrator shall be appointed by the party from whom the fee is receivable.
3. One arbitrator shall be appointed by the arbitrators appointed under paragraphs 1 and 2.

(9) The decisions of the arbitrators or a majority of them is final and binding on the board providing the instruction and the party from whom the fee is receivable.

(10) This section does not apply in respect of a pupil to whom subsection 49(6) of the Act applies.

Fees Charged to Parties Residing in Ontario

4. (1) This section applies in respect of a pupil described in subsection 46(2) of the Act who is enrolled in a day school program in a school of a district school board or an isolate board and who resides in a school section, separate school zone or secondary school district in which the pupil's parent or guardian resides, on land that is exempt from taxation for the purposes of any board.

(2) The fee that a board shall charge in respect of a pupil described in subsection (1) to the parent or guardian is $40 for each month or part of a month the pupil is enrolled in a school of the board.

(3) A board charging a parent or guardian a fee of $40 for any month or part of a month under subsection (2) in respect of a pupil described in subsection (1) who is enrolled in a school of the board shall not charge the parent or guardian any fee under subsection (2) for the same month or part of a month in respect of another pupil described in subsection (1) who is enrolled in a school of the board.

(4) This section does not apply in respect of a pupil to whom subsection 49(6) of the Act applies.

Fees Charged to Parties Not Residing in Ontario

5. (1) The fee in respect of a pupil who is enrolled in a day school program in a school of a district school board or an isolate board and whose parent or guardian does not reside in Ontario shall be such fee as the board may determine, but shall not exceed the maximums set by subsections (2) and (3).

(2) Except as is provided in subsection (3), the fee in respect of a pupil who is enrolled in a school of a district school board or an isolate board and whose parent or guardian does not reside in Ontario shall not exceed the amount calculated as follows:

1. Add the base amount determined under paragraph 1 of subsection 3(2) and the P.A.C. for the pupil.
2. Multiply the amount obtained under paragraph 1 by 0.1.
3. Multiply the result obtained under paragraph 2 by the number of months or part months during which the pupil is enrolled in a school operated by the board.

(3) Where the pupil is enrolled in a high cost program, the maximum set by subsection (2) shall be increased by an amount that does not exceed the additional cost to the board of providing the high cost program to the pupil.

(4) This section does not apply in respect of a pupil to whom subsection 49(6) of the Act applies.

Fees in Respect of Pupils to Whom Subsection 49(6) of the Act Applies

6. (1) The fee in respect of a pupil who is enrolled in a day school program and to whom subsection 49(6) of the Act applies shall be the amount determined in accordance with a fees policy developed for the purposes of this section by the board that operates the school in which the pupil is enrolled.

(2) The policy referred to in subsection (1) shall not, in the case of a district school board or isolate board, provide for a fee in respect of a pupil that is less than the amount that would be chargeable by the board in respect of the pupil under section 3.

(3) The policy referred to in subsection (1) shall not, in the case of a section 68 board, provide for a fee in respect of a pupil that is less than the amount that would be chargeable by the board in respect of the pupil under section 7.

Fees Paid to Section 68 Boards

7. Except where section 6 applies, the fee that a board shall charge in respect of a pupil who is enrolled in a day school program in a school operated by a section 68 board and whose parent or guardian does not reside in Ontario shall be an amount determined as follows:

1. Take the expenditures of the board for the 1999-2000 fiscal year that is acceptable to the Minister for grant purposes, excluding,
    i. expenditures for debt charges,
    ii. expenditures for the purchase of capital assets, as defined in the 1999-2000 grant regulation,
    iii. expenditures for the restoration of destroyed or damaged capital assets, as defined in the 1999-2000 grant regulation, and
    iv. provisions for reserves for working funds and provisions for reserve funds.
2. Deduct the revenue of the board for the 1999-2000 fiscal year from,
    i. any organization on whose property a school of the board is located, and

ii. refunds of expenditure of the kind described in subparagraph i, ii, or iii of paragraph 1.
3. Divide the amount obtained under paragraph 2 by the total number of pupil days for the board for the period September 1, 1999 to August 31, 2000. For the purposes of this paragraph, the total number of pupil days for the board for the period is the sum of the number of instructional days for which each pupil was enrolled in the school during the period.
4. Multiply the result obtained under paragraph 3 by the number of instructional days for which the pupil is enrolled in the school.

Fees in Respect of Summer School and Continuing Education

8. (1) The fee in respect of a pupil to whom subsection 49(6) of the Act applies and who is enrolled in a continuing education or summer school class or course provided by a district school board or an isolate board shall be the amount determined by the board.

(2) The fee in respect of a pupil described in subsection 3(1) or 5(1) who is enrolled in a continuing eduction class or course provided by a district school board or an isolate board shall be the amount agreed on by the board and the party from whom the fee is receivable or, in the absence of agreement, the amount determined as follows:
1. Determine the expenditure of the board in the 1999-2000 fiscal year for continuing education classes or courses.
2. Divide the amount determined under paragraph 1 by the continuing education A.D.E. for the board.
3. Multiply the result obtained under paragraph 2 by the continuing education A.D.E. for the board, counting only pupils described in this subsection.

(3) The fee in respect of a pupil described in subsection 3(1) or 5(1) who is enrolled in a summer school class or course provided by a district school board or an isolate board shall be the amount agreed on by the board and the party from whom the fee is receivable or, in the absence of agreement, the amount determined as follows:
1. Determine the expenditure of the board in the 1999-2000 fiscal year for summer school classes or courses.
2. Divide the amount determined under paragraph 1 by the summer school A.D.E. for the board.
3. Multiply the result obtained under paragraph 2 by the summer school A.D.E. for the board, counting only pupils described in this subsection.

No Fees Payable by Boards

9. No fee is payable under this Regulation by one board to another board.

EDUCATION QUALITY AND ACCOUNTABILITY OFFICE ACT, 1996
S.O. 1996, c. 11, as am. S.O. 1997, c. 31, s. 148

1. Definitions.— In this Act,

"board".—"board" has the same meaning as in section 1 of the *Education Act*; ("conseil")

"Office".—"Office" means the Education Quality and Accountability Office; ("Office")

"test".—"test" means any method of assessing the academic achievement of elementary and secondary school pupils. ("test")

1997, c. 31, s. 148(1).

2. Education Quality and Accountability Office established.— A corporation without share capital known in English as the Education Quality and Accountability Office and in French as Office de la qualité et de la responsabilité en éducation is established.

3. Objects.— The Office has the following objects:
1. To evaluate the quality and effectiveness of elementary and secondary school education.
2. To develop tests and require or undertake the administering and marking of tests of pupils in elementary and secondary schools.
3. To develop systems for evaluating the quality and effectiveness of elementary and secondary school education.
4. To research and collect information on assessing academic achievement.
5. To evaluate the public accountability of boards and to collect information on strategies for improving that accountability.
6. To report to the public and to the Minister of Education and Training on the results of tests and generally on the quality and effectiveness of elementary and secondary school education and on the public accountability of boards.
7. To make recommendations, in its reports to the public and to the Minister of Education and Training, on any matter related to the quality or effectiveness of elementary and secondary school education or to the public accountability of boards.

4. (1) Office may require co-operation of boards.— Without limiting the powers or capacities of the Office, for the purpose of carrying out its objects, the Office may,
   (a) require a board to administer tests to pupils enrolled in schools of the board, mark the tests and report on the results of the tests to the Office and to the general public within the jurisdiction of the board; and
   (b) require a board to provide information to the Office, including personal information within the meaning of section 38 of the *Freedom of Information and Protection of Privacy Act* and section 28 of the *Municipal Freedom of Information and Protection of Privacy Act*.

(2) [Repealed 1997, c. 31, s. 148(2).]

(3) **Directives: when a pupil need not take a test.**— The Office may issue directives regarding the circumstances in which a pupil need not take a test under this section.

(4) **Non-application of *Regulations Act*.**— A directive issued under subsection (3) is not a regulation within the meaning of the *Regulations Act*.

(5) **Compliance of boards.**— A board shall do anything that it is required or directed to do under this section, within the time and in the manner and form specified by the Office.

(6) **Compliance of pupils.**— A pupil shall take any test administered to him or her in accordance with this section.

1997, c. 31, s. 148(2).

5. (1) **Agreements re tests.**— The Office may enter into agreements with a person operating,
   (a) a private school, as defined in section 1 of the *Education Act*;
   (b) a school provided by a band, the council of a band or an education authority where the band, the council of the band or the education authority is authorized by the Crown in right of Canada to provide education for Indians; or
   (c) a school provided by the Crown in right of Canada,

about administering tests to pupils enrolled in the school, marking the tests and reporting the results of the tests.

(2) **Fees.**— Without limiting the generality of subsection (1), an agreement may provide for the charging of fees by the Office to a person operating a school described in subsection (1).

(3) **Capacity to enter agreements not limited.**— This section shall not be interpreted to limit the ability of the Office to enter into agreements with any person.

6. (1) **Minister of Education and Training: directives and policies.**— The Minister of Education and Training may issue written directives and establish policies on matters relating to the objects of the Office.

(2) **Same.**— The board of directors of the Office shall ensure that the Office operates in accordance with the directives and policies issued or established under subsection (1).

(3) **Non-application of *Regulations Act*.**— A directive issued under subsection (1) is not a regulation within the meaning of the *Regulations Act*.

7. Crown Agency.—The Office is a Crown agency as defined in the *Crown Agency Act*.

8. (1) **Delegation of powers of Minister of Education and Training.**— Any power or duty conferred or imposed on the Minister of Education and Training under any Act may be delegated by him or her to the board of directors of the Office, as he or she considers necessary or advisable for the carrying out of the Office's objects.

(2) **Delegation subject to conditions.**— A delegation under subsection (1) shall be in writing and is subject to any conditions or restrictions set out in it.

9. (1) **Capacity and powers.**—For the purposes of carrying out its objects, the Office has all the capacity and powers of a natural person, except as limited by this Act.

(2) **Real property.**— The Office may not acquire, hold or dispose of an interest in real property, other than a leasehold interest, without first obtaining the approval of the Lieutenant Governor in Council.

(3) **Borrowing.**— The Office may, if it first obtains the approval of the Lieutenant Governor in Council, borrow money or give security against its property, subject to any conditions imposed by the Minister of Finance.

(4) **Guarantee.**— The Lieutenant Governor in Council may be order authorize the Minister of Finance, on behalf of Ontario, to agree to guarantee the repayment of loans made to the Office, including interest.

(5) **Same.**— A guarantee given under subsection (4) is subject to any conditions that the Minister of Finance imposes.

(6) **Collection of personal information.**— The Office may collect personal information within the meaning of section 38 of the *Freedom of Information and Protection of Privacy Act* and section 28 of the *Municipal Freedom of Information and Protection of Privacy Act* for the purpose of carrying out its objects.

10. Non-application of certain Acts.— The *Corporations Act* and *Corporations Information Act* do not apply to the Office, except as specifically made applicable by this Act or the regulations made under this Act.

11. (1) **Board of directors.**— The Office shall be managed by its board of directors, which shall be composed of a minimum of seven and a maximum of nine directors appointed by the Lieutenant Governor in Council.

(2) **Term.**— The directors shall be appointed for such terms as may be determined by the Lieutenant Governor in Council and may be reappointed for further terms.

(3) **Remuneration.**— The directors shall receive such remuneration and expenses as may be determined by the Lieutenant Governor in Council.

(4) **Vacancies.**— If the position of a director becomes vacant, the Lieutenant Governor in Council may appoint a person to hold office for the unexpired portion of the term or for a new term.

(5) **Temporary vacancies.**— If the position of a director becomes temporarily vacant because of a leave of absence, the Lieutenant Governor in Council may appoint a person to hold office as acting director during the leave.

12. (1) **Chair.**—One director shall be designated by the Lieutenant Governor in Council to act as the chair of the board of directors.

(2) **Acting chair.**— If the chair is absent or unable to act, the directors shall appoint from among themselves an acting chair.

13. (1) **Meetings.**— The directors shall meet at the call of the chair and, in any event, at least four times a year.

(2) **Quorum.**—A majority of the directors shall constitute a quorum.

14. By-laws.— The board of directors may pass by-laws regulating its proceedings, specifying the powers and duties of the officers and employees of the Office and generally providing for the management of the Office.

15. Conflict of interest and indemnification.— Sections 132 and 136 of the *Business Corporations Act* apply with necessary modifications to the Office and to its directors and officers.

16. (1) **Chief Executive Officer.**— The Lieutenant Governor in Council shall appoint a chief executive officer, after consulting with the directors.

(2) **Powers and duties.**— The chief executive officer is responsible for the operation of the Office, the implementation of policies established by the board of directors and the performance of such other functions as are assigned by the board of directors.

(3) **Delegation.**— The board of directors may delegate any of its powers or duties, including any power or duty delegated to it by the Minister of Education and Training, to the chief executive officer, and may impose conditions and restrictions on the delegation.

(4) **Same.**— The chief executive officer may, in writing, delegate to another employee of the Office any of the chief executive officer's powers or duties, including any that have been delegated to him or her by the board of directors, and may impose conditions and restrictions on the delegation.

17. (1) **Employees.**— The employees who are considered necessary for the proper conduct of the affairs of the Office may be appointed or transferred under the *Public Service Act*.

(2) **Same.**— The chief executive officer of the Office has the powers and duties of a deputy minister under the *Public Service Act*, and may exercise the power described in section 8 of that Act.

(3) **Same.**— Despite subsection (2), the board of directors may assign some or all of the powers and duties described or referred to in subsection (2) to another employee of the Office where the chief executive officer is seconded to the Office and not appointed or transferred under the *Public Service Act*.

(4) **Professional and other assistance.**— The Office may engage persons other than those employed under subsection (1) to provide professional, technical or other assistance to or on behalf of the Office and may prescribe the terms of engagement and provide for payment of remuneration and expenses of such persons.

18. (1) **Fees.**— Subject to the approval of Management Board of Cabinet, the Office may set fees for any class of goods or services provided by it to any class of persons.

(2) **Same.**— Despite subsection (1), the approval of Management Board of Cabinet is not required in relation to fees referred to in subsection 5(2).

19. (1) **Revenues and investments.**— Despite the *Financial Administration Act*, the revenues and investments of the Office do not form part of the Consolidated Revenue Fund.

(2) **Payments to Consolidated Revenue Fund.**— When ordered to do so by the Minister of Finance, the Office shall pay into the Consolidated Revenue Fund any money that the Minister of Finance determines is surplus to its requirements.

(3) **Reserves.**— In determining the amount payable under subsection (2), the Minister of Finance shall allow such reserves for the future needs of the Office as he or she considers appropriate, and shall ensure that the payment ordered under subsection (2) will not impair the Office's ability to pay its liabilities, to meet its obligations as they become due or to fulfil its contractual commitments.

20. Temporary investments.— The Office may invest money that is temporarily surplus to its requirement in,
  (a) notes, bonds, debentures and other evidences of indebtedness issued or guaranteed as to principal and interest by Canada, a province of Canada, an agency of the Government of Canada, an agency of the government of a province of Canada, a

bank listed in Schedule I or II to the *Bank Act* (Canada) or another financial institution authorized to carry on business in Canada; and

(b) deposit receipts, deposit notes, certificates of deposit, acceptances and other investment instruments issued, guaranteed or endorsed by a financial institution authorized to carry on business in Canada.

21. Fiscal year.—The Office's fiscal year begins on the 1st day of April in each year and ends on the 31st day of March in the following year.

22. (1) **Annual budget.**—The board of directors shall submit to the Minister of Education and Training for his or her review and approval, annually, on or before a date specified by the Minister, the Office's proposed budget for the next fiscal year.

(2) **Same.**— The Minister of Education and Training may require the board of directors to make any changes to the proposed budget that he or she considers appropriate.

23. (1) **Annual plan of operation.**— The board of directors shall submit to the Minister of Education and Training for his or her review and approval, annually, on or before a date specified by the Minister, a plan for the Office's next year's operations.

(2) **Multi-year plan.**— The Minister of Education and Training may require the board of directors to submit to him or her for review and approval a plan for the Office's future operations projected over several years as specified by the Minister.

(3) **Changes required by Minister of Education and Training.**— The Minister of Education and Training may require the board of directors to make any changes to a plan submitted under this section that he or she considers appropriate.

24. (1) **Accounting.**—The board of directors shall establish and maintain an accounting system satisfactory to the Minister of Education and Training.

(2) **Auditors.**— The board of directors shall appoint one or more auditors licensed under the *Public Accountancy Act* to audit the Office's accounts and financial transactions annually.

(3) **Disclosure to Provincial Auditor.**— The board of directors shall make available to the Provincial Auditor, on his or her request, the auditor's report and all accounts, records and other documents relating to the audit.

(4) **Audit required by Minister of Education and Training.**— The Minister of Education and Training may require that any aspect of the Office's accounts or financial transactions be audited by an auditor appointed by the Minister for the purpose.

(5) **Same.**— The auditor shall submit the results of any audit performed under subsection (4) to the Minister of Education and Training and to the board of directors.

25. (1) **Annual report.**— After the end of the Office's fiscal year, the board of directors shall make an annual report to the Minister of Education and Training on the affairs of the Office.

(2) **Same.**— The annual report shall contain any information the Minister of Education and Training requires.

(3) **Tabling.**— The Minister of Education and Training shall submit the annual report to the Lieutenant Governor in Council and shall then table the report in the Assembly if it is in session or, if not, at the next session.

(4) **Other reports.**— The Minister of Education and Training may require the board of directors to submit other reports on the Office's affairs, objects, powers or duties.

(5) **Same.**— In addition to reports required under this section, the board of directors may report to the Minister of Education and Training at any time.

26. (1) **Regulations.**—The Lieutenant Governor in Council may make regulations,
   (a) governing the decision-making procedures followed at directors' meetings;
   (b) prescribing objects of the Office in addition to those set out in section 3;
   (c) making any provision of the *Business Corporations Act*, the *Corporations Act* and the *Corporations Information Act* applicable to the Office, with such modifications as the Lieutenant Governor in Council considers necessary or advisable;
   (d) authorizing personal information within the meaning of section 38 of the *Freedom of Information and Protection of Privacy Act* and section 28 of the *Municipal Freedom of Information and Protection of Privacy Act* to be collected by the Office, for the purpose of carrying out its objects, in a manner other than directly from the individual to whom the information relates and regulating the manner in which the information is collected;
   (e) respecting any matter that the Lieutenant Governor in Council considers necessary or advisable to carry out effectively the intent and purpose of this Act.

(2) **Consultation.**— Before a regulation is made under subsection (1), the Minister of Education and Training shall consult with the Office about it.

27. (1) **Obligation re personal information.**— Before disclosing personal information obtained under this Act, the person who obtained it shall delete from it all names and identifying numbers, symbols or other particulars assigned to individuals unless disclosure of the names or other identifying information is otherwise authorized under the *Freedom of Information and Protection of Privacy Act*.

(2) **Same.**— This section applies to personal information within the meaning of section 38 of the *Freedom of Information and Protection of Privacy Act* and section 28 of the *Municipal Freedom of Information and Protection of Privacy Act*.

28. (1) **Protection from personal liability.**— No proceedings for damages shall be instituted against a director, officer or employee of the Office for an act done in good faith in the execution or intended execution of any duty or authority under this Act or for any alleged neglect or default in the execution in good faith of any duty or authority under this Act.

(2) **Crown not relieved of liability.**— Despite subsections 5(2) and (4) of the *Proceedings Against the Crown Act*, subsection (1) does not relieve the Crown of liability in respect of a tort committed by a person mentioned in subsection (1) to which it would otherwise be subject.

29. [Consequential amendments are not reproduced here.]

30. **Commencement.**— This Act comes into force on a day to be named by proclamation of the Lieutenant Governor.

31. **Short title.**— The short title of this Act is the *Education Quality and Accountability Office Act, 1996*.

IMMUNIZATION OF SCHOOL PUPILS ACT

R.S.O. 1990, c. I.1, as am. 1997, c. 15, s. 9 [Not in force at date of publication.]; 1998, c. 18, Sched. G, s. 59 [Not in force at date of publication.]

1. Definitions.—In this Act,

"Board."—"Board" means the Health Protection Appeal Board under the *Health Protection and Promotion Act*; ("Commission")

"Board" means the Health Services Appeal and Review Board under the *Ministry of Health Appeal and Review Boards Act, 1998*. ("Commission")

1998, c. 18, Sched. G, s. 59(1) [Not in force at date of publication.]

"board".—"board" means a "board" as defined in the *Education Act*; ("conseil")

"designated diseases."—"designated diseases" means diphtheria, measles, mumps, poliomyelitis, rubella and tetanus; ("maladies désignées")

"immunization record."—"immunization record" means a record of immunization maintained by a medical officer of health under this Act; ("dossier d'immunisation")

"medical officer of health."—"medical officer of health" means "medical officer of health" as defined in the *Health Protection and Promotion Act*; ("médecin-hygiéniste")

"parent."—"parent" includes an individual or a corporation that has the responsibilities of a parent; ("père ou mère")

"person."—"person" includes a board; ("personne")

"physician."—"physician" means legally qualified medical practitioner; ("médecin")

"prescribed."—"prescribed" means prescribed by the regulations; ("prescrit")

"pupil."—"pupil" means a pupil who is a minor; ("élève")

"regulations."—"regulations" means regulations made under this Act; ("règlements")

"school."—"school" means a "private school" and a "school" as defined in the *Education Act* and includes a kindergarten, a junior kindergarten and a beginners class within the meaning of the Education Act; ("école")

"school day."—"school day" means "school day" as defined in the *Education Act*; ("jour de classe")

"statement of conscience or religious belief."—"statement of conscience or religious belief" means a statement by affidavit in the prescribed form by a parent of the person named in the statement that immunization conflicts with the sincerely held convictions of the parent based on the parent's religion or conscience; ("déclaration de conscience ou de croyance religieuse")

"statement of medical exemption."—"statement of medical exemption" means a statement in the prescribed form signed by a physician stating that the prescribed program of immunization in relation to a designated diseases,
   (a) may be detrimental to the health of the person named in the statement, or
   (b) is unnecessary in respect of the person named in the statement by reason of past infection or laboratory evidence of immunity. ("déclaration d'exemption médicale")

2. Purpose of Act.—The purpose of this Act is to increase the protection of the health of children against the diseases that are designated diseases under this Act.

3. (1) **Duty of parent.**—The parent of a pupil shall cause the pupil to complete the prescribed program of immunization in relation to each of the designated diseases.

(2) **Exception**—Subsection (1) does not apply to the parent of a pupil in respect of the prescribed program of immunization in relation to a designated disease specified by a physician in a statement of medical exemption filed with the proper medical officer of health and, where the physician has specified an effective time period, only during the effective time period.

(3) **Idem.**—Subsection (1) does not apply to a parent who has filed a statement of conscience or religious belief with the proper medical officer of health.

(4) **Idem.**—Subsection (1) does not apply to a parent who, before the coming into force of this section, has filed with the proper medical officer of health a statement of religious belief in the form prescribed before the coming into force of this section.

4. Offence.—Every person who contravenes section 3 is guilty of an offence and on conviction is liable to a fine of not more than $1,000.

5. Certificate by M.O.H. as evidence.—In proceedings under section 4, as certificate by a medical officer of health as to whether or not he or she has received a statement of medical exemption, a statement of conscience or religious belief or a statement of religious belief is admissible in evidence as proof in the absence of evidence to the contrary of the facts stated therein without proof of the appointment or signature of the medical officer of health.

6. (1) **Order for suspension re designated diseases.**—A medical officer of health, in the circumstances mentioned in subsection (2), by a written order may require a person who operates a school in the area served by the medical officer of health to suspend from attendance at the school a pupil named in the order.

(2) **Grounds for order re designated diseases.**—The circumstances mentioned in subsection (1) are,

(a) that the medical officer of health has not received,
  (i) a statement signed by a physician showing that the pupil has completed the prescribed program of immunization in relation to the designated diseases,
  (ii) a statement of medical exemption in respect of the pupil or, where the medical officer of health has received a statement of medical exemption, the effective time period specified in the statement has expired and the medical officer of health has not received a further statement of medical exemption, or
  (iii) a statement of conscience or religious belief in respect of the pupil; and
(b) that the medical officer of health is not satisfied that the pupil has completed, has commenced and will complete or will commence and complete the prescribed program of immunization in relation to the designated diseases.

7. Term of suspension.—A suspension under an order by a medical officer of health under section 6 is for a period of twenty school days.

8. (1) **Service of copy of order upon parent.**—A medical officer of health who makes an order under section 6 shall serve a copy of the order upon a parent of the pupil.

(2) **Written reasons.**—An order under section 6 is not valid unless written reasons for the order are included in or attached to the order.

(3) **Repeated orders.**—A medical officer of health may make orders under section 6 from time to time in respect of a pupil where the circumstances specified in the section for making the order continue to exist.

9. Rescission of order.—A medical officer of health who has made an order under section 6 shall rescind the order where the circumstances for making the order no longer exist.

10. Statement by physician.—Every physician who administers an immunizing agent to a child in relation to a designated disease shall furnish to a parent of the child a statement signed by the physician showing that the physician has administered the immunizing agent to the child.

11. (1) **Record of immunization.**—Every medical officer of health shall maintain a record of immunization in the form and containing the information prescribed by the regulations in respect of each pupil attending school in the area served by the medical officer of health.

(2) **Review of record.**—A medical officer of health shall keep under review the immunization record maintained by the medical officer of health in respect of a pupil who has not completed the prescribed program of immunization in relation to the designated diseases.

12. (1) **Order by M.O.H.**—A medical officer of health, in the circumstances mentioned in subsection (2), by a written order may require a person who operates a school located in the health unit served by the medical officer of health to exclude from the school a pupil named in the order.

(2) **Grounds for order.**—The circumstances mentioned in subsection (1) are,

(a) that the medical officer of health is of the opinion, upon reasonable and probable grounds, that there is an outbreak or an immediate risk of an outbreak of a designated disease in the school at which the pupil attends; and

(b) that the medical officer of health has not received,

  (i) a statement of immunization signed by a physician showing, or is not otherwise satisfied, that the pupil has completed the prescribed program of immunization in relation to the designated disease, or

  (ii) a statement of medical exemption in the prescribed form signed by a physician stating that the prescribed program of immunization in relation to the designated disease is unnecessary in respect of the pupil by reason of past infection or laboratory evidence of immunity.

(3) **Term of order.**—An order under subsection (1) remains in force until rescinded in writing by the medical officer of health.

(4) **Rescission of order.**—A medical officer of health who makes an order under subsection (1) shall rescind the order as soon as the medical officer of health is satisfied that the outbreak or the immediate risk of the outbreak of the designated disease has ended.

(5) **Service of copy of order.**—The medical officer of health shall serve a copy of the order under subsection (1) upon a parent of the pupil and, where the pupil is sixteen or seventeen years of age, upon the pupil.

(6) **Service of copy of rescinding order.**—The medical officer of health shall serve a rescinding order made under subsection (4) upon the person who operates the school and shall serve a copy of the order upon a parent of the pupil and, where the pupil is sixteen or seventeen years of age, upon the pupil.

(7) **Written reasons.**—An order under subsection (1) shall include written reasons for the making of the order.

13. Hearing and submissions.—A medical officer of health need not hold or afford to any person an opportunity for a hearing or afford to any person an opportunity to make submissions before making an order under this Act.

14. (1) **Notice of transfer of pupil.**—Where a pupil transfers from a school, the person who operates the school shall give notice of the transfer in the prescribed form to the medical officer of health serving the area in which the school is located.

(2) **Transmittal of copy of immunization record.**—Where the notice under subsection (1) states that the pupil is transferring to a school in an area under the jurisdiction of another medical officer of health, the medical officer of health shall send a copy of the immunization record of the pupil to the other medical officer of health.

15. (1) **Notice.**—Where a medical officer of health makes an order under this Act requiring the suspension of a pupil or requiring that a pupil be excluded from a school due to an outbreak or an immediate risk of an outbreak of a designated disease, the medical officer of health shall serve upon a parent of the pupil or, where the pupil is sixteen or seventeen years of age, upon the pupil a notice of entitlement to a hearing.

(2) **Idem.**—A notice under subsection (1) shall inform the parent or pupil, as the case may be, that the parent or pupil is entitled to a hearing by the Board if the parent or pupil mails or delivers to the medical officer of health, to the Board and to the person who operates the school, within fifteen days after the notice is served on the parent or pupil, notice in writing requiring a hearing and the parent or pupil may so require such a hearing.

(3) **Opportunity to show compliance and to examine documents.**—Where a hearing by the Board is required in accordance with this section, the medical officer of health shall afford to the parent or pupil requiring the hearing a reasonable opportunity before the hearing,

(a) to show or to achieve compliance with all lawful requirements concerning the subject-matter of the hearing; and

(b) to examine any written or documentary evidence that will be produced or any report the contents of which will be given in evidence at the hearing.

(4) **Powers of Board where hearing.**—Where a hearing is required in accordance with this section, the Board shall appoint a time and place for and hold the hearing and the Board by order may confirm, alter or rescind the decision or order of the medical officer of health and for such purposes the Board may substitute its finding for that of the medical officer of health.

(5) **Time for hearing.**—The Board shall hold a hearing under this section within fifteen days after receipt by the Board of the notice in writing requiring the hearing and the Board may, from time to time at the request or with the consent of the person requiring the hearing, extend the time for holding the hearing for such period or periods of time as the Board considers just.

(6) **Parties.**—The medical officer of health, the parent or pupil who has required the hearing and such other persons as the Board may specify are parties to the proceedings before the Board.

(7) **Effect of order.**—Despite the fact that a hearing is required in accordance with this section, an order under this Act by a medical officer of health takes effect when it is served on the person to whom it is directed.

(8) **Members holding hearing not to have taken part in investigation, etc.**—Members of the Board holding a hearing shall not have taken part before the hearing in any investigation or consideration of the subject-matter of the hearing and shall not communicate directly or indirectly in relation to the subject-matter of the hearing with any person or with any party or representative of the party except upon notice to and opportunity for all parties to participate, but the Board may seek legal advice from an adviser independent from the parties and in such case the nature of the advice shall be made known to the parties in order that they may make submissions as to the law.

(9) **Recording of evidence.**—The oral evidence taken before the Board at a hearing shall be recorded and, if so required, copies or a transcript thereof shall be furnished upon the same terms as in the Ontario Court (General Division).

(10) **Findings of fact.**—The findings of fact of the Board pursuant to a hearing shall be based exclusively on evidence admissible or matters that may be noticed under sections 15 and 16 of the *Statutory Powers Procedure Act*.

(11) **Only members at hearing to participate in decision.**—No member of the Board shall participate in a decision of the Board pursuant to a hearing unless he or she was present throughout the hearing and heard the evidence and argument of the parties and, except with the consent of the parties, no decision of the Board shall be given unless all members so present participate in the decision.

(11) [Repealed 1998, c. 18, Sched. G, s. 59(2). Not in force at date of publication.]

(12) **Release of documentary evidence.**—Documents and things put in evidence at a hearing shall, upon the request of the person who produced them, be released to the party by the Board within a reasonable time after the matter in issue has been finally determined.

16. (1) **Appeal to court.**—Any party to the proceedings before the Board under this Act may appeal from its decision or order to the Divisional Court in accordance with the rules of court.

(2) **Record to be filed in court.**—Where any party appeals from a decision or order of the Board under this Act, the Board shall forthwith file in the Ontario Court (General Division) the record of the proceedings before it in which the decision was made, which, together with the transcript of evidence if it is not part of the Board's record, shall constitute the record in the appeal.

(3) **Powers of court on appeal.**—An appeal under this section may be made on questions of law or fact or both and the court may affirm or may rescind the decision of the Board and may exercise all powers of the Board to confirm, alter or rescind the order that is the subject of the appeal and to substitute its findings for that of the person who made the order as the court considers proper and for such purposes the court may substitute its opinion for that of the person who made the order or of the Board, or the court may refer the matter back to the Board for rehearing, in whole or in part, in accordance with such directions as the court considers proper.

17. (1) Regulations.—The Lieutenant Governor in Council may make regulations,

(a) prescribing any matter referred to in this Act as prescribed by the regulations;

(a) prescribing the information that must be contained in a record of immunization required to be maintained by a medical officer of health under section 11.

1997, c. 15, s. 9(1) [Not in force at date of publication.]

(b) prescribing forms and providing for their use and requiring that statements of conscience or religious belief be in the form of affidavits;

(b) [Repealed 1997, c. 15, s. 9(1). Not in force at date of publication.]

(c) governing the custody, recording, inspection and destruction of records in respect of immunizations in relation to designated diseases;

(d) prescribing programs of immunization in respect of designated diseases, including specifying immunizing agents and the number and timing of dosages of immunizing agents;

(e) classifying children, pupils or persons and exempting any such class from any provision of this Act or the regulations and prescribing conditions to which such exemption shall be subject;

(f) requiring and governing reports by persons who operate schools to medical officers of health in respect of records and documentation related to the immunization of children applying for admission to the schools and pupils and former pupils in the schools;

(g) respecting any other matter that the Lieutenant Governor in Council considers necessary or advisable to carry out effectively the intent and purpose of this Act.

(2) **Regulations by Minister.**—The Minister may make regulations prescribing forms and providing for their use and requiring that statements of conscience or religious belief be made as affidavits.

1997, c. 15, s. 9(2) [Not in force at date of publication.]

18. (1) Service.—Any notice, order or other document under this Act or the regulations is sufficiently given, served or delivered if delivered personally or sent by ordinary mail addressed to the person to whom it is to be given, served or delivered at his or her last known address.

(2) **When service deemed made.**—A notice, order or other document sent by ordinary mail in accordance with subsection (1) shall be deemed to be given, served or delivered on the seventh day after the day of mailing, unless the person to whom it is sent establishes that, acting in good faith, the person did not receive the notice, order or other document until a later date through absence, accident, illness or other cause beyond the person's control.

REGULATION 645
GENERAL
R.R.O. 1990, Reg. 645, as am. O. Reg. 299/96

1. A record of immunization maintained by a medical officer of health with respect to a pupil shall contain,
- (a) the name of the pupil in full;
- (b) the date of birth of the pupil;
- (c) the sex of the pupil;
- (d) the name of the school attended by the pupil;
- (d.1) the pupil's health number, as defined in the *Health Cards and Numbers Control Act, 1991*; O. Reg. 299/96, s. 1
- (e) a record of all the pupil's immunization against designated diseases showing,
   - (i) the type of vaccine given,
   - (ii) the date of administration of the vaccine, and
   - (iii) any reactions to the vaccine;
- (f) any statement of medical exemption that pertains to the pupil showing the effective time period on the statement; and
- (g) any statement of religious belief that pertains to the pupil.

2. A statement of medical exemption shall be in Form 1.

3. A statement of conscience or religious belief shall be in Form 2.

4. A notice of transfer of pupil referred to in section 14 of the Act shall be in Form 3.

5. The following program of immunization in respect of designated diseases in prescribed:

Schedule

ITEM DISEASE	TYPE OF VACCINE TO BE USED	MINIMUM NUMBER OF DOSES ACCEPTED	RECOMMENDED SCHEDULE OF PRIMARY IMMUNIZATION	INTERVAL BETWEEN BOOSTER DOSES
1. Diphtheria	TOXOID	3	Two injections, 1 to 2 months apart with a further dose one year later. Children immunized in infancy require three doses 1 to 2 months apart, a further dose one year later and a booster dose at age 4–6.	10 years

Form 1   IMMUNIZATION OF SCHOOL PUPILS ACT REGULATION

Item Disease	Type of Vaccine to be Used	Minimum Number of Doses Accepted	Recommended Schedule of Primary Immunization	Interval Between Booster Doses
2. Tetanus	TOXOID	3	Two injections, 1 to 2 months apart with a further dose one year later. Children immunized in infancy require three doses 1 to 2 months apart, a further dose one year later and a booster dose at age 4–6.	10 years
3. Poliomyelitis	Inactivated Polio vaccine (IPV) or	3	Two injections, 1 to 2 months apart with a further dose one year later. Children immunized in infancy require three doses 1 to 2 months apart, a further dose one year later and a booster dose at age 4–6.	10 years
	Live Oral Polio vaccine (OPV)	3	Two doses 1 to 2 months apart with a further dose 2 to 12 months later. Children immunized in infancy require a booster dose at age 4–6.	NONE required
4. Measles	Live attenuated virus vaccine	2	One dose after the first birthday with a further dose more than one month later and preferably at age 4-6	NONE required
5. Mumps	Live attenuated virus vaccine	1 after one year of age	One dose after the first birthday.	NONE required
6. Rubella	Live attenuated virus vaccine	1 after one year of age	One dose after the first birthday.	NONE required

O. Reg. 299/96, s. 2.

FORM 1

Immunization of School Pupils Act

STATEMENT OF MEDICAL EXEMPTION

PUPIL'S NAME: ....

        Last Name   First Name

REGULATION 645   **Form 1**

ADDRESS: ....

DATE OF BIRTH: .... / .... / ....
                     Year   Month   Day

SCHOOL: .... Class or Grade: ....

I, ..., certify that, for medical reasons indicated below, the above named pupil should be exempted from the requirements of the Act.

The specific reasons and length of exemptions are checked in the boxes below. The time periods for temporary medical exemptions are indicated.

Disease	Immunity		Contraindication	Length of Exemption	
	Physician diagnosed prior disease	Test evidence of Immunity	Detrimental to Health	Permanent	Temporary From To
Diphtheria		☐	☐	☐	☐ ..... / .....
Tetanus		☐	☐	☐	☐ ..... / .....
Poliomyelitis		☐	☐	☐	☐ ..... / .....
Measles	☐	☐	☐	☐	☐ ..... / .....
Mumps	☐	☐	☐	☐	☐ ..... / .....
Rubella		☐	☐	☐	☐ ..... / .....

Use this space to define evidence of immunity: ....
....
....

Use this space for explanations of contraindications detrimental to health: ....
....
....
....

          Physician's Signature ....
          Address: ....
          Date: ....

Form 2   IMMUNIZATION OF SCHOOL PUPILS ACT REGULATION

FORM 2

Immunization of School Pupils Act

STATEMENT OF CONSCIENCE OR RELIGIOUS BELIEF

AFFIDAVIT

I, ..., parent of the following named pupil:

PUPIL'S NAME : ....
                    Last Name   First Name

ADDRESS: ....

DATE OF BIRTH: .... / .... / ....
                       Year   Month   Day

SCHOOL: .... Class or Grade: ....,

make oath or solemnly affirm and say as follows:

The requirements of the *Immunization of School Pupils Act*, conflict with my sincerely held convictions based on my religion or conscience.

I understand that section 12 of the Act provides that the Medical Officer of Health may order that the above named pupil be excluded from school if there is an outbreak or immediate risk of an outbreak of a designated disease in the school at which the pupil attends where the following have not been received:—

    1. A statement of immunization or other satisfactory evidence of immunization.

    2. A statement of medical exemption stating that immunization is unnecessary because of evidence of immunity.

SWORN OR SOLEMNLY AFFIRMED before me at)
the

.... of ....)

Municipality of .... this ....) ....
                                                                        Parent's Signature

day of ...., 199.....)

....)
        A commissioner, etc.

REGULATION 645   **Form 3**

FORM 3

Immunization of School Pupils Act

NOTICE OF TRANSFER FROM A SCHOOL

To the Medical Officer of Health ....
                                          Health Agency

Notice is hereby given that the following pupils have transferred from:

.... School, ...
                                                                    Address

Date	Name of Pupil	Sex	Date of Birth	Grade	Transferring to School	Transferring to School Board

Signed ....

for ....
                    Operator of School

LOCAL GOVERNMENT DISCLOSURE OF INTEREST ACT, 1994

S.O. 1994, c. 23, Schedule B*, as am. 1996, c. 32, s. 74; 1997, c. 31, s. 152
[Not in force at date of publication.]

1. Purpose.—The purpose of this Act is to preserve the integrity and accountability of local government decision-making.

2. (1) **Definitions.**—In this Act,

"board".—"board" means,
  (a) a local board as defined in the *Municipal Affairs Act*,
  (b) boards, agencies, corporations or other entities or classes of them established in relation to local, municipal or school purposes as may be prescribed in the regulations; ("commission")

"child".—"child" means a child under 18 years of age born within or outside marriage and includes an adopted child and a person whom a parent has demonstrated a settled intention to treat as a child of his or her family; ("enfant")

"commissioner".—"commissioner" means the commissioner appointed under this Act; ("commissaire")

"committee".—"committee" means any advisory or other committee or subcommittee composed of members of one or more boards or councils; ("comité")

"council".—"council" means the council of a municipality other than an improvement district and the board of trustees of an improvement district; ("conseil")

"meeting".—"meeting" includes any regular, special, committee or other meeting of a council or board; ("réunion")

"member".—"member" means a member of a council or of a board; ("membre")

"Minister".—"Minister" means the Minister of Municipal Affairs; ("ministre")

"municipality".—"municipality" means a local municipality, county, improvement district, metropolitan, regional or district municipality and the County of Oxford; ("municipalité")

"pecuniary interest".—"pecuniary interest" includes a direct or indirect pecuniary interest of a member and a pecuniary interest deemed to be that of a member; ("intérêt pécuniaire")

"prescribed".—"prescribed" means prescribed by regulations made under this Act; ("prescrit")

"senior officer".—"senior officer" means the chair or any vice-chair of the board of directors, the president, any vice-president, the secretary, the treasurer or the general manager of a corporation or any other person who performs functions for the corporation similar to those normally performed by a person occupying any such office; ("dirigeant")

---

* Editor's Note: On proclamation, this Act will replace the *Municipal Conflict of Interest Act*, R.S.O. 1990, c. M.50. See S.O. 1994, c. 23, sections 2(3)-(5) for transitional provisions.

"spouse".—"spouse" means a spouse as defined in Part III of the *Family Law Act'*. ("conjoint")

(2) **Non-application.**—This Act does not apply to a committee of management of a recreation centre appointed by a school board, to a local roads board or to a local services board.

(3) **Pecuniary interest.**—For the purposes of this Act, a member shall be deemed to have a pecuniary interest in a matter in which a council or board is concerned, if,
- (a) the member or his or her nominee,
    - (i) is a shareholder in, or a director or senior officer of, a corporation that does not offer its securities to the public,
    - (ii) has a controlling interest in, or is a director or senior officer of, a corporation that offers its securities to the public,
    - (iii) is a partner or agent of a person,
    - (iv) is a member of a body,
  that has a pecuniary interest in the matter;
- (b) the member or the member's spouse or child is an employee of a person or body and the member knows that the person or body has a pecuniary interest in the matter;
- (c) the member knows that the member's spouse or child has a direct or indirect pecuniary interest in the matter; or
- (d) the member knows that the member's spouse or child,
    - (i) is a shareholder in, or a director or senior officer of, a corporation that does not offer its securities to the public,
    - (ii) has a controlling interest in, or is a director or senior officer of, a corporation that offers its securities to the public,
    - (iii) is a partner or agent of a person,
    - (iv) is a member of a body,
  that has a pecuniary interest in the matter.

(4) **Definition.**—In subsection (3), "controlling interest" means the interest that a person has in a corporation when the person beneficially owns, directly or indirectly, or exercises control or direction over, equity shares of the corporation carrying more than 10 per cent of the voting rights attached to all equity shares of the corporation for the time being outstanding.

3. Exceptions.—Section 4 does not apply to a pecuniary interest in any matter that a member may have,
- (a) as a user of any public utility service supplied to the member by the municipality or board under similar conditions as other users;
- (b) as a recipient of any service or commodity or any subsidy, loan or other benefit offered by the municipality or board on terms common to other persons;
- (c) as a purchaser or owner of a debenture of the municipality or board;
- (d) as a depositor with the municipality or board, if the whole or part of the deposit is or may be returnable to the member in like manner as a deposit is or may be returnable to other persons under similar conditions;
- (e) in any property affected by a work under the *Drainage Act* or under the *Local Improvement Act*;

(f) in farm land that is exempt from taxation for certain expenditures under the *Assessment Act*;

(g) as a director or senior officer of a corporation incorporated by the municipality or to carry on business on behalf of the municipality or board or as a person nominated by the council as a director or officer of a corporation;

(h) as a member or office holder of a council, board or other body when it is required by law or by virtue of office or results from an appointment by a council or board;

(i) as a recipient of an allowance for attendance at meetings, or any other allowance, honorarium, remuneration, salary or benefit to which the member may be entitled as a member;

(j) in common with persons generally within the area of jurisdiction or, if the matter under consideration affects only part of the area, in common with persons within that part;

(k) as a member or volunteer for a charitable organization or a non-for-profit organization with objects substantially similar to those provided by section 118 of the *Corporations Act* if the member receives no remuneration or other financial benefit from the organization and the pecuniary interest is in common with other persons in the organization;

(l) as a recipient of remuneration, consideration or an honorarium under section 256 of the *Municipal Act* or as a volunteer firefighter;

(m) that is so remote or insignificant in its nature that it cannot reasonably be regarded as likely to influence the member.

4. (1) **Duty of member.**—If a member has a pecuniary interest in any matter and is or will be present at a meeting at any time at which the matter is the subject of consideration, the member,

(a) shall, before any consideration of the matter at the meeting, orally disclose the interest and its general nature;

(b) shall not, at any time, take part in the discussion of, or vote on, any question in respect of the matter;

(c) shall not, at any time, attempt, either on his or her own behalf or while acting for, by or through another person, to influence the voting on any such matter or influence employees of or persons interested in a contract with the council or board in respect of the matter;

(d) shall immediately leave the meeting and remain absent from it at any time during consideration of the matter; and

(e) shall, as soon as possible, complete and file with the clerk of the municipality or secretary of the board a written disclosure, in the prescribed form, setting out the interest and its general nature.

(2) **When absent from meeting.**—If a member is absent from all or part of a meeting in which he or she has a pecuniary interest in a matter being considered, other than an absence due to compliance with clause (1)(d), clause (1)(c) applies to that member and he or she shall,

(a) disclose the interest in the manner described in clause (1)(a) at the next meeting of the council or board that the member attends;

(b) in the case of a committee meeting, disclose the interest in the manner described in clause (1)(a) at the next meeting of the committee that the member attends; and

(c) file a written disclosure in the manner described in clause (1)(e) as soon as possible after the next meeting that the member attends.

(3) **Limitation.**—A disclosure under this section is not required to disclose that the member has a spouse or child or the name of the member's spouse or child.

(4) **Interest of member.**—Where a disclosure omits reference to a member's spouse or child, the interest shall be stated as being that of the member.

(5) **Filing.**—If a member of a committee is required to file a written disclosure under this section, the member shall file it in the manner described in clause (1)(e) with the clerk of the council or secretary of the board that appointed the member.

5. (1) **Gifts.**—A member shall not, either directly or through another person, accept a fee, gift or personal benefit except compensation authorized by law that is connected with the performance of his or her duties of office.

(2) **Exception.**—Subsection (1) does not apply to,

(a) a gift or personal benefit that is received as an incident of the protocol or social obligations that normally accompany the responsibilities of office; or

(b) a contribution that is permitted under the *Municipal Elections Act, 1996*.

1996, c. 32, s. 74(1).

(3) **Disclosure.**—A member shall complete and file a disclosure statement with the clerk of the municipality or secretary of the board as soon as possible after receiving a gift or personal benefit described under clause (2)(a) if,

(a) the value of the gift or benefit exceeds the lower of the amount prescribed or provided by by-law or resolution; or

(b) the total value received directly or indirectly from one source in one calendar year exceeds the lower of the amount prescribed or provided by by-law or resolution.

(4) **Contents.**—A disclosure statement filed under subsection (3) shall state the nature of the gift or benefit, its source and the circumstances under which it was given or accepted.

6. (1) **Financial disclosure requirement.**—This section applies only to members of,

(a) a council;

(b) a board as defined in subsection 1(1) of the *Education Act*;

(c) a public utility commission; and

(d) a police village.

1997, c. 31, s. 152.

(2) **Filing form.**—Every member shall, within 60 days of being elected or appointed, file with the clerk of the municipality or the secretary of the board a financial disclosure statement in the prescribed form.

(3) **Omissions.**—The member may with the consent of the commissioner omit or delete from the financial disclosure statement information if,

(a) disclosure would reveal a source of income for the member or the member's spouse or child from services that are customarily provided on a confidential basis; or

(b) the possibility of serious harm to a person or business justifies a departure from the general principle of public disclosure.

(4) **Changes.**—The member shall file a supplementary financial disclosure statement during the month of December of every calendar year except an election year.

(5) **Limitation.**—A financial disclosure statement under this section is not required to disclose that the member has a spouse or child or the name of the member's spouse or child.

(6) **Interest of member.**—Where a financial disclosure statement omits reference to a member's spouse or child, the financial information shall be stated as being that of the member.

7. (1) **Commissioner.**—The Minister may appoint a commissioner to exercise the powers and perform the duties set out in this Act.

(2) **Assistant commissioner.**—The commissioner may appoint one or more assistant commissioners who may exercise such powers and duties of the commissioner as the commissioner delegates to them.

(3) **Restriction.**—The commissioner and any assistant commissioner shall not be a member of the Legislative Assembly, a council or a board.

(4) **Guidelines.**—The commissioner may provide such guidelines for the proper administration of this Act as he or she considers necessary for the guidance of members, boards and municipalities.

8. (1) **Applications.**—Any person may apply in writing to the commissioner for an investigation to be carried out of an alleged contravention by a member of section 4, 5 or 6.

(2) **Timing.**—An application may only be made within 90 days after the person became aware of the alleged contravention.

(3) **Fees.**—The commissioner may establish fees in respect of applications under subsection (1) and may waive any fee in cases of hardship.

(4) **Contents.**—An application shall set out the reasons for believing that the member has contravened section 4, 5 or 6 and include a statutory declaration attesting to the fact that the person became aware of the contravention not more than 90 days before the date of the application.

(5) **Investigation.**—The commissioner, upon receiving an application, may conduct such investigation as he or she considers necessary.

(6) **Same.**—For the purpose of conducting an investigation, the commissioner,

(a) has the right of access, at all reasonable hours, to all relevant books, papers or documents of the member or applicant and of a municipality or board; and

(b) has the powers of a commission under Part II of the *Public Inquiries Act* which Part applies to the investigation as if it were an inquiry under that Act.

(7) **Timing.**—The commissioner shall complete the investigation within 180 days of receiving the completed application.

(8) **Completion.**—Upon completion of the investigation, the commissioner,

(a) shall, if he or she considers it appropriate, apply to the Ontario Court (General Division) for a determination as to whether the member has contravened section 4, 5 or 6; or

(b) shall advise the applicant that the commissioner will not be making an application to the court.

(9) **Court determination.**—The question of whether or not a member has contravened section 4, 5 or 6 may be tried and determined by the Ontario Court (General Division).

(10) **Application.**—Any person may apply to the court for a determination under subsection (9).

(11) **Requirement.**—No application may be made to the court unless the application includes a statutory declaration attesting to the fact that the person became aware of the contravention not more than 90 days before the date of the application to the commissioner under subsection (4).

(12) **Restriction.**—Despite subsection (10), no person other than the commissioner shall make an application to the court unless the person has submitted an application to the commissioner under subsection (1) and,

(a) the commissioner has notified the applicant that he or she will not be carrying out an investigation;

(b) the commissioner has failed to complete the investigation within 180 days of receiving the application; or

(c) the commissioner has notified the applicant that the commissioner will not be making an application to the court under clause (8)(b).

(13) **Limitation.**—No application shall be brought to the court under this section after the expiration of two years from the date on which the contravention is alleged to have occurred.

9. (1) **Power of court.**—If the court determines that a member or a former member while he or she was a member has contravened section 4, 5 or 6, the court,

(a) shall suspend the member without pay and benefits for a period of not more than 90 days;

(b) may, in the case of a member, declare the seat of the member vacant;

(c) may disqualify the member or former member from being a member for a period of not more than seven years; and

(d) may, where the contravention has resulted in personal financial gain, require the member or former member to make restitution to the party suffering the loss, or, where such party is not readily ascertainable, to the municipality or board of which he or she is a member or former member.

(2) **Restrictions.**—A member suspended from a council or board under subsection (1) shall not during the period of the suspension,

(a) participate in any meeting of the council or board as a member or otherwise;

(b) participate in any meeting of any body,

(i) to which the member has been appointed by the council or board, or

(ii) on which the member is required by law to sit by virtue of the member's office on the council or board;

(c) participate in any meeting of any other council or board that appointed or approved the appointment of the member to the council or board; or

(d) in the case of suspension from a council, participate in any meeting of any other council of which the member is also a member.

(3) **No vacancy.**—Clause 38(c) of the *Municipal Act* and section 229 of the *Education Act* do not apply to the seat of a member if the member is absent due to a suspension under clause 9(1)(a).

10. (1) **Appeal to Divisional Court.**—An appeal lies to the Divisional Court from a determination made under section 9 as to whether a contravention has occurred or not.

(2) **Judgment or new trial.**—The Divisional Court may give any judgment that ought to have been pronounced, in which case its decision is final, or the Divisional Court may grant a new trial for the purpose of taking evidence or additional evidence and may remit the case to the Ontario Court (General Division) and, subject to any directions of the Divisional Court, the case shall be proceeded with as if there had been no appeal.

(3) **Further appeal.**—If the case is remitted to the Ontario Court (General Division) under subsection (2), the appeal lies from the order of the court to the Divisional Court in accordance with this section.

11. Proceedings not invalidated.—The failure of any member to comply with section 4 does not of itself invalidate any proceedings in respect of any matter but the proceedings are voidable at the instance of the municipality or of the board, as the case may be, before the expiration of two years from the date of the passing of the by-law or resolution authorizing the matter unless to make void the proceedings would adversely affect the rights of any person acquired under or by virtue of the proceedings who acted in good faith and without actual notice of the failure to comply with section 4.

12. Other procedures prohibited.—The following proceedings in respect of disclosure of interest shall be taken only under this Act:

1. To suspend a member without pay or benefits.
2. To declare a seat vacant.
3. To disqualify a member or former member.
4. To require a member or former member to make restitution where a contravention has resulted in personal gain.

13. (1) **Quorum.**—If the number of members who, by reason of this Act, are disabled from participating in a meeting is such that there is no quorum, despite any other Act, any number that is not less than one-third of the total number of members of the council or board shall be deemed to constitute a quorum, but the number shall not be less than two unless an order is made under subsection (3) authorizing it.

(2) **Same.**—When the remaining number of members under subsection (1) is two, the concurrent votes of both are necessary to carry any resolution, by-law or other measure.

(3) **Order.**—If the remaining number of members who are not disabled from participating in the meeting is less than one-third of the total number of members or less than two, as the case may be, the council or board may apply to the commissioner without notice for an order authorizing the council or board to give consideration to, discuss and vote on the matter out of which the pecuniary interests arise.

(4) **Declaration.**—The commissioner may declare that section 4 does not apply to a matter that is the subject of consideration by a council or board if,

(a) the council or board applies to the commissioner under subsection (3); and

(b) the council or board submits a copy of the written disclosure statements of the members who are disabled from participating.

(5) **Conditions.**—As part of a declaration given under subsection(4), the commissioner may require the council or board to comply with any conditions the commissioner considers appropriate.

(6) **Effect.**—If a declaration is made, section 4 does not apply and the council or board may give consideration to the matter in the same manner as though none of the members had a pecuniary interest in it, subject to any conditions the commissioner sets out in the declaration.

14. Minutes.—Every oral declaration made under section 4 shall be recorded in the minutes of the meeting by the clerk of the municipality or secretary of the committee or board, as the case may be.

15. (1) Register.—The clerk of a municipality and the secretary of a board shall maintain a register of disclosures for the members of the council or board, respectively.

(2) **Contents.**—The register shall contain,

(a) the written disclosures of pecuniary interests under section 4;
(b) disclosure statements and supplementary disclosure statements of financial information under section 6; and
(c) disclosure statements of gifts or personal benefits under section 5.

(3) **Inspection.**—All documents in the register are public documents and may be inspected by any person under request at the office of the clerk or the secretary during normal office hours.

(4) **Copies.**—Any person may make extracts from the documents and is entitled to copies of them upon payment of such fees as may be charged by the municipality or board for the preparation of copies of other documents.

(5) **Retention of records.**—Despite section 116 of the *Municipal Act*, a municipality or local board shall not destroy the documents in the register until after the prescribed period.

16. Prohibition re information.—A member or former member shall not use or disclose information that is gained in the execution of his or her office and is not available to the general public to further or seek to further his or her pecuniary interests or the pecuniary interests of any other person.

17. Offence.—Every person who contravenes section 16 is guilty of an offence.

18. (1) Insurance.—Despite section 252 of the *Municipal Act*, the council of every municipality may pass by-laws,

(a) for contracting for insurance;
(b) despite the *Insurance Act*, to enable the municipality to act as an insurer; and
(c) for exchanging with other municipalities in Ontario reciprocal contracts of indemnity or inter-insurance in accordance with Part XIII of the *Insurance Act*,

to protect a member who has been found not to have contravened section 4, 5 or 6, against any costs or expenses incurred by the member as a result of a proceeding brought under this Act, and for paying on behalf of or reimbursing the member for the costs or expenses.

(2) ***Insurance Act* does not apply.**—The *Insurance Act* does not apply to a municipality acting as an insurer for the purposes of subsection (1).

(3) **Surplus funds.**—Despite subsections 387(1) and (2) of the *Insurance Act*, any surplus funds and the reserve fund of a municipal reciprocal exchange may be invested only in such securities as a municipality may invest in under section 167 of the *Municipal Act*.

1996, c. 32, s. 74(2).

(4) **Reserve funds.**—The money raised for a reserve fund of a municipal reciprocal exchange may be spent or pledged for, or applied to, a purpose other than that for which the fund was established if two-thirds of the municipalities that are members of the exchange together with two-thirds of the municipalities that previously were members of the exchange and that may be subject to claims arising while they were members of the exchange agree in writing and if section 386 of the *Insurance Act* is complied with.

(5) **Boards.**—A board has the same powers to provide insurance for or to make payments to or on behalf of its members as are conferred on a municipality under this section in respect of its members.

(6) **Former members.**—A by-law or resolution passed under this section may provide that it applies to a person who was a member at the time the circumstances giving rise to the proceeding occurred but who, before the judgment in the proceeding, had ceased to be a member.

19. By-laws.—A municipality or board may pass by-laws or resolutions providing for the maximum amount of a single gift or benefit and of the combined value of gifts and benefits under section 5.

20. Community economic development corporations.—If a director of a community economic development corporation is required to file a written disclosure or a disclosure statement under this Act, the director shall file it with the clerk of the municipality that nominated or appointed the person.

21. Regulations.—The Lieutenant Governor in Council may make regulations prescribing,

(a) financial information or classes of financial information that must be disclosed or that is exempt from being disclosed in a financial disclosure statement under section 6;

(b) the maximum amount of a single gift or benefit and of the combined value of gifts and benefits under section 5.

22. Regulations.—The Minister may make regulations,

(a) prescribing the duties of the commissioner;
(b) prescribing procedures for applications to the commissioner under section 13;
(c) prescribing forms or requiring that information required be on a form provided by the Ministry;
(d) prescribing boards, agencies, corporations or other entities or classes of them to which this Act applies;
(e) prescribing the period for the purposes of subsection 15(5).

23. Conflict.—In the event of conflict between a provision of this Act and a provision of any other Act, the provision of this Act prevails.

24. Short title.—The short title of this Act is *Local Government Disclosure of Interest Act, 1994*.

MUNICIPAL CONFLICT OF INTEREST ACT

R.S.O. 1990, c. M.50; repealed S.O. 1994, c. 23, s. 2 [Not in force at date of publication.],* as am. 1996, c. 32, s. 76; 1997, c. 25, Sched. E, s. 7; 1997, c. 31, s. 156

1. Definitions.—In this Act,

"child."—"child" means a child born within or outside marriage and includes an adopted child and a person whom a parent has demonstrated a settled intention to treat as a child of his or her family; ("enfant")

"controlling interest."—"controlling interest" means the interest that a person has in a corporation when the person beneficially owns, directly or indirectly, or exercises control or direction over, equity shares of the corporation carrying more than 10 per cent of the voting rights attached to all equity shares of the corporation for the time being outstanding; ("intérêts majoritaires")

"council."—"council" means the council of a municipality other than an improvement district and means the board of trustees of a municipality that is an improvement district; ("conseil")

"elector."—"elector" means,

(a) in respect of a municipality, or a local board thereof, other than a school board, a person entitled to vote at a municipal election in the municipality, and

(b) in respect of a school board, a person entitled to vote at the election of members of the school board; ("électeur")

"interest in common with electors generally."—"interest in common with electors generally" means a pecuniary interest in common with the electors within the area of jurisdiction and, where the matter under consideration affects only part of the area of jurisdiction, means a pecuniary interest in common with the electors within that part; ("intérêt commun à tous les électeurs")

"judge."—"judge" means a judge of the Ontario Court (General Division); ("juge")

"local board."—"means a school board, board of directors of a children's aid society, committee of adjustment, committee of management of a community recreation centre, conservation authority, court of revision, land division committee, public utilities commission, public library board, board of management of an improvement area, board of park management, board of health, police services board, planning board, district social services administration board, trustees of a police village, board of trustees of a police village, board or committee of management of a home for the aged, suburban roads commission or any other board, commission, committee, body or local authority estab-

---

* Editor's Note: Pursuant to section 2(2) of the Planning and Municipal Statute Law Amendment Act, 1994, S.O. 1994, c. 23, this Act is to be repealed and will essentially be replaced by the Local Government Disclosure of Interest Act, 1994, which is set out in Schedule B to the Planning and Municipal Statute Law Amendment Act, 1994 (see section 2(1)). As of the date of publication, the relevant legislation provisions were not yet proclaimed in force. In this Consolidation, the text of the new legislation follows the *Municipal Conflict of Interest Act*.

lished or exercising any power or authority under any general or special Act in respect of any of the affairs or purposes, including school purposes, of a municipality or of two or more municipalities or parts thereof, but does not include a committee of management of a community recreation centre appointed by a school board, a local roads board, a local services board or a negotiating committee appointed under the *Municipal Boundary Negotiations Act*; ("conseil local")

"**meeting.**"—"meeting" includes any regular, special, committee or other meeting of a council or local board, as the case may be; ("réunion")

"**member.**"—"member" means a member of a council or of a local board; ("membre")

"**municipality.**"—"municipality" means the corporation of a county, city, town, village, township or improvement district or of a metropolitan, regional or district municipality and a board, commission or other local authority exercising any power in respect of municipal affairs or purposes, including school purposes, in territory without municipal organization, but does not include a committee of management of a community recreation centre appointed by a school board, a local roads board or a local services board; ("municipalité")

"**parent.**"—"parent" means a person who has demonstrated a settled intention to treat a child as a member of his or her family whether or not that person is the natural parent of the child; ("père ou mère")

"**school board.**"—"school board" means a board as defined in subsection 1(1) of the *Education Act*, and, where the context requires, includes an old board within the meaning of subsection 1(1) of the *Education Act*; ("conseil scolaire")

"**senior officer.**"—"senior officer" means the chair or any vice-chair of the board of directors, the president, any vice-president, the secretary, the treasurer or the general manager of a corporation or any other person who performs functions for the corporation similar to those normally performed by a person occupying any such office; ("dirigeant")

"**spouse.**"—"spouse" means a person of the opposite sex to whom the person is married or with whom the person is living in a conjugal relationship outside marriage. ("conjoint")

1997, c. 31, s. 156(1).

2. Indirect pecuniary interest.—For the purposes of this Act, a member has an indirect pecuniary interest in any matter in which the council or local board, as the case may be, is concerned, if,

(a) the member or his or her nominee,

    (i) is a shareholder in, or a director or senior officer of, a corporation that does not offer its securities to the public,

    (ii) has a controlling interest in or is a director or senior officer of, a corporation that offers its securities to the public, or

    (iii) is a member of a body,

that has a pecuniary interest in the matter; or

(b) the member is a partner of a person or is in the employment of a person or body that has a pecuniary interest in the matter.

3. Interest of certain relatives deemed that of member.— For the purposes of this Act, the pecuniary interest, direct or indirect, of a parent or the spouse or any child of the member shall, if known to the member, be deemed to be also the pecuniary interest of the member.

Exceptions

4. Where s. 5 does not apply.—Section 5 does not apply to a pecuniary interest in any matter that a member may have,

(a) as a user of any public utility service supplied to the member by the municipality or local board in like manner and subject to the like conditions as are applicable in the case of persons who are not members;

(b) by reason of the member being entitled to receive on terms common to other persons any service or commodity or any subsidy, loan or other such benefit offered by the municipality or local board;

(c) by reason of the member purchasing or owning a debenture of the municipality or local board;

(d) by reason of the member having made a deposit with the municipality or local board, the whole or part of which is or may be returnable to the member in like manner as such a deposit is or may be returnable to all other electors;

(e) by reason of having an interest in any property affected by a work under the *Drainage Act* or under the *Local Improvement Act*;

(f) by reason of having an interest in farm lands that are exempted from taxation for certain expenditures under the *Assessment Act*;

(g) by reason of the member being eligible for election or appointment to fill a vacancy, office or position in the council or local board when the council or local board is empowered or required by any general or special Act to fill such vacancy, office or position;

(h) by reason only of the member being a director or senior officer of a corporation incorporated for the purpose of carrying on business for and on behalf of the municipality or local board or by reason only of the member being a member of a board, commission, or other body as an appointee of a council or local board;

(i) in respect of an allowance for attendance at meetings, or any other allowance, honorarium, remuneration, salary or benefit to which the member may be entitled by reason of being a member or under a by-law passed pursuant to section 256 of the *Municipal Act*, or as a member of a volunteer fire brigade, as the case may be;

(j) by reason of the member having a pecuniary interest which is an interest in common with electors generally; or

(k) by reason only of an interest of the member which is so remote or insignificant in its nature that it cannot reasonably be regarded as likely to influence the member.

Duty of Member

5. (1) When present at meeting at which matter considered.—Where a member, either on his or her own behalf or while acting for, by, with or through another, has any pecuniary interest, direct or indirect, in any matter and is present at a meeting of the council or local board at which the matter is the subject of consideration, the member,

(a) shall, prior to any consideration of the matter at the meeting, disclose the interest and the general nature thereof;
(b) shall not take part in the discussion of, or vote on any question in respect of the matter; and
(c) shall not attempt in any way whether before, during or after the meeting to influence the voting on any such question.

(2) **Where member to leave closed meeting.**—Where the meeting referred to in subsection (1) is not open to the public, in addition to complying with the requirements of that subsection, the member shall forthwith leave the meeting or the part of the meeting during which the matter is under consideration.

(3) **When absent from meeting at which matter considered.**—Where the interest of a member has not been disclosed as required by subsection (1) by reason of the member's absence from the meeting referred to therein, the member shall disclose the interest and otherwise comply with subsection (1) at the first meeting of the council or local board, as the case may be, attended by the member after the meeting referred to in subsection (1).

Record of Disclosure

6. (1) **Disclosure to be recorded in minutes.**—Every declaration of interest and the general nature thereof made under section 5 shall, where the meeting is open to the public, be recorded in the minutes of the meeting by the clerk of the municipality or secretary of the committee or local board, as the case may be.

(2) **Idem.**—Every declaration of interest made under section 5, but not the general nature of that interest, shall, where the meeting is not open to the public, be recorded in the minutes of the next meeting that is open to the public.

Remedy for Lack of Quorum

7. (1) **Quorum deemed constituted.**—Where the number of members who, by reason of the provisions of this Act, are disabled from participating in a meeting is such that at that meeting the remaining members are not of sufficient number to constitute a quorum, then, despite any other general or special Act, the remaining number of members shall be deemed to constitute a quorum, provided such number is not less than two.

(2) **Application to judge.**—Where in the circumstances mentioned in subsection (1), the remaining number of members who are not disabled from participating in the meeting is less than two, the council or local board may apply to a judge without notice for an order authorizing the council or local board, as the case may be, to give consideration to, discuss and vote on the matter out of which the interest arises.

(3) **Power of judge to declare s. 5 not to apply.**—The judge may, on an application brought under subsection (2), by order, declare that section 5 does not apply to the council or local board, as the case may be, in respect of the matter in relation to which the application is brought, and the council or local board thereupon may give consideration to, discuss and vote on the matter in the same manner as though none of the members had any interest therein,

Action Where Contravention Alleged

subject only to such conditions and directions as the judge may consider appropriate and so order.

8. Who may try alleged contravention of s. 5(1-3).—The question of whether or not a member has contravened subsection 5(1), (2) or (3) may be tried and determined by a judge.

9. (1) **Who may apply to judge.**—Subject to subsection (3), an elector may, within six weeks after the fact comes to his or her knowledge that a member may have contravened subsection 5(1), (2) or (3), apply to the judge for a determination of the question of whether the member has contravened subsection 5(1), (2) or (3).

(2) **Contents of notice of application.**—The elector in his or her notice of application shall state the grounds for finding a contravention by the member of subsection 5(1), (2) or (3).

(3) **Time for bringing application limited.**—No application shall be brought under subsection (1) after the expiration of six years from the time at which the contravention is alleged to have occurred.

10. (1) **Power of judge to declare seat vacant, disqualify member and require restitution.**—Subject to subsection (2), where the judge determines that a member or a former member while he or she was a member has contravened subsection 5(1), (2) or (3), the judge,

(a) shall, in the case of a member, declare the seat of the member vacant; and

(b) may disqualify the member or former member from being a member during a period thereafter of not more than seven years; and

(c) may, where the contravention has resulted in personal financial gain, require the member or former member to make restitution to the party suffering the loss, or, where such party is not readily ascertainable, to the municipality or local board of which he or she is a member or former member.

(2) **Saving by reason of inadvertence or error.**—Where the judge determines that a member or a former member while he or she was a member has contravened subsection 5(1), (2) or (3), if the judge finds that the contravention was committed through inadvertence or by reason of an error in judgment, the member is not subject to having his or her seat declared vacant and the member or former member is not subject to being disqualified as a member, as provided by subsection (1).

(3) **Member not to be suspended.**—The authority to disqualify a member in subsection (1) does not include the right to suspend a member.

(4) A disqualification of a member of a school board under this section that would have continued after December 31, 1997 but for the dissolution of the school board continues for its duration with respect to membership on any board whose members are elected by members of the electoral group who elected the member.

(5) In subsection (4),

"electoral group" has the same meaning as in Part VIII of the *Education Act* as the Part read on January 1, 1997.

1997, c. 31, s. 156, s. 2.

11. (1) **Appeal to Divisional Court.**—An appeal lies from any order made under section 10 to the Divisional Court in accordance with the rules of court.

(2) **Judgment or new trial.**—The Divisional Court may give any judgment that ought to have been pronounced, in which case its decision is final, or the Divisional Court may grant a new trial for the purpose of taking evidence or additional evidence and may remit the case to the trial judge or another judge and, subject to any directions of the Divisional Court, the case shall be proceeded with as if there had been no appeal.

(3) **Appeal from order or new trial.**—Where the case is remitted to a judge under subsection (2), an appeal lies from the order of the judge to the Divisional Court in accordance with the provisions of this section.

12. Proceedings not invalidated but voidable.—The failure of any person to comply with subsection 5(1), (2) or (3) does not of itself invalidate any proceedings in respect of any such matter but the proceedings in respect of such matter are voidable at the instance of the municipality or of the local board, as the case may be, before the expiration of two years from the date of the passing of the by-law or resolution authorizing such matter unless to make void the proceedings would adversely affect the rights of any person acquired under or by virtue of the proceedings who acted in good faith and without actual notice of the failure to comply with subsection 5(1), (2) or (3).

13. Other Proceedings prohibited.—Proceedings to declare a seat vacant or to disqualify a member or former member for conflict of interest, or to require a member or former member to make restitution where a contravention has resulted in personal financial gain, shall be had and taken only under this Act.

General

14. (1) **Insurance.**—Despite section 252 of the *Municipal Act*, the council of every municipality may at any time pass by-laws,

(a) for contracting for insurance;
(b) despite the *Insurance Act*, to enable the municipality to act as an insurer; and
(c) for exchanging with other municipalities in Ontario reciprocal contracts of indemnity or inter-insurance in accordance with Part XIII of the *Insurance Act*,

to protect a member of the council or of any local board thereof who has been found not to have contravened section 5, against any costs or expenses incurred by the member as a result of a proceeding brought under this Act, and for paying on behalf of or reimbursing the member for any such costs or expenses.

(2) *Insurance Act* **does not apply.**—The *Insurance Act* does not apply to a municipality acting as an insurer for the purposes of subsection (1).

(3) **Surplus funds.**—Despite subsections 387(1) and (2) of the *Insurance Act*, any surplus funds and the reserve fund of a municipal reciprocal exchange may be invested only in such securities as a municipality may invest in under section 167 of the *Municipal Act*.

1996, c. 32, s. 76.

(4) **Reserve funds.**—The money raised for a reserve fund of a municipal reciprocal exchange may be expended or pledged for, or applied to, a purpose other than that for which the fund was established if two-thirds of the municipalities that are members of the exchange together with two-thirds of the municipalities that previously were members of the exchange

and that may be subject to claims arising while they were members of the exchange agree in writing and if section 386 of the *Insurance Act* is complied with.

(5) **Local boards.**—A local board has the same powers to provide insurance for or to make payments to or on behalf of its members as are conferred upon the council of a municipality under this section in respect of its members.

(6) **Former members.**—A by-law passed under this section may provide that it applies to a person who was a member at the time the circumstances giving rise to the proceeding occurred but who, prior to the judgment in the proceeding, has ceased to be a member.

15. Conflict with other Acts.—In the event of conflict between any provision of this Act and any provision of any general or special Act, the provision of this Act prevails.

MUNICIPAL FREEDOM OF INFORMATION A PROTECTION OF PRIVACY ACT

R.S.O. 1990, c. M. 56, as am. 1992, c. 32, s. 23; 1995, c. 1, s. 83; 1996, c. 1, Sched. K, ss. 13-24; 1996, c. 2, s. 73; 1996, c. 32, s. 77; 1997, c. 25, Sched. E, s. 8

PURPOSES

1. (1) **Purposes.**—The purposes of this Act are,
(a) to provide a right of access to information under the control of institutions in accordance with the principles that,
   (i) information should be available to the public,
   (ii) necessary exemptions from the right of access should be limited and specific, and
   (iii) decisions on the disclosure of information should be reviewed independently of the institution controlling the information; and
(b) to protect the privacy of individuals with respect to personal information about themselves held by institutions and to provide individuals with a right of access to that information.

DEFINITIONS

2. (1) **Definitions.**—In this Act,

"head", in respect of an institution, means the individual or body determined to be head under section 3; ("personne responsable")

"Information and Privacy Commissioner" and "Commissioner" means the Commissioner appointed under subsection 4(1) of the *Freedom of Information and Protection of Privacy Act*; ("commissaire à l'information et à la protection de la vie privée", "commissaire")

"institution" means,
(a) a municipal corporation, including a metropolitan, district or regional municipality or the County of Oxford,
(b) a school board, public utilities commission, hydro-electric commission, transit commission, suburban roads commission, public library board, board of health, police commission, conservation authority, district social services administration board, local services board, planning board, local roads board, police village or joint committee of management or joint board of management established under the *Municipal Act*,
(c) any agency, board, commission, corporation or other body designated as an institution in the regulations; ("institution")

"law enforcement" means,
(a) policing,
(b) investigations or inspections that lead or could lead to proceedings in a court or tribunal if a penalty or sanction could be imposed in those proceedings, and

(c) the conduct of proceedings referred to in clause (b); (''exécution de la loi'')

''Minister'' means the Chairman of the Management Board of Cabinet; (''ministre'')

''personal information'' means recorded information about an identifiable individual, including,

    (a) information relating to the race, national or ethnic origin, colour, religion, age, sex, sexual orientation or marital or family status of the individual,

    (b) information relating to the education or the medical, psychiatric, psychological, criminal or employment history of the individual or information relating to financial transactions in which the individual has been involved,

    (c) any identifying number, symbol or other particular assigned to the individual,

    (d) the address, telephone number, fingerprints or blood type of the individual,

    (e) the personal opinions or views of the individual except if they relate to another individual,

    (f) correspondence sent to an institution by the individual that is implicitly or explicitly of a private or confidential nature, and replies to that correspondence that would reveal the contents of the original correspondence,

    (g) the views or opinions of another individual about the individual, and

    (h) the individual's name if it appears with other personal information relating to the individual or where the disclosure of the name would reveal other personal information about the individual; (''renseignements personnels'')

''personal information bank'' means a collection of personal information that is organized and capable of being retrieved using an individual's name or an identifying number or particular assigned to the individual; (''banque de renseignements personnels'')

''record'' means any record of information however recorded, whether in printed form, on film, by electronic means or otherwise, and includes,

    (a) correspondence, a memorandum, a book, a plan, a map, a drawing, a diagram, a pictorial or graphic work, a photograph, a film, a microfilm, a sound recording, a videotape, a machine readable record, any other documentary material, regardless of physical form or characteristics, and any copy thereof, and

    (b) subject to the regulations, any record that is capable of being produced from a machine readable record under the control of an institution by means of computer hardware and software or any other information storage equipment and technical expertise normally used by the institution; (''document'')

''regulations'' means the regulations made under this Act. (''règlements'')

(2) **Personal information.**—Personal information does not include information about an individual who has been dead for more than thirty years.

(3) **Bodies considered part of municipal corporation.**—Every agency, board, commission, corporation or other body not mentioned in clause (b) of the definition of ''institution'' in subsection (1) or designated under clause (c) of the definition of ''institution'' in subsection (1) is deemed to be a part of the municipal corporation for the purposes of this Act if all of its members or officers are appointed or chosen by or under the authority of the council of the municipal corporation.

1997, c. 25, Sched. E, s. 8.

3. (1) **Designation of head.**—The members of the council of a municipal corporation may by by-law designate from among themselves an individual or a committee of the council to act as head of the municipal corporation for the purposes of this Act.

(2) **Idem.**—The members elected or appointed to the board, commission or other body that is an institution other than a municipal corporation may designate in writing from among themselves an individual or a committee of the body to act as head of the institution for the purposes of this Act.

(3) **If no designation.**—If no person is designated as head under this section, the head shall be,

(a) the council, in the case of a municipal corporation; and
(b) the members elected or appointed to the board, commission or other body in the case of an institution other than a municipal corporation.

PART I

FREEDOM OF INFORMATION

Access to Records

4. (1) **Right of access.**—Every person has a right of access to a record or a part of a record in the custody or under the control of an institution unless,

(a) the record or the part of the record falls within one of the exemptions under sections 6 to 15; or
(b) the head is of the opinion on reasonable grounds that the request for access is frivolous or vexatious.

(2) **Severability of record.**—If an institution receives a request for access to a record that contains information that falls within one of the exemptions under sections 6 to 15 and the head of the institution is not of the opinion that the request is frivolous or vexatious, the head shall disclose as much of the record as can reasonably be severed without disclosing the information that falls under one of the exemptions.

1996, c. 1, Sched. K, s. 13.

5. (1) **Obligation to disclose.**—Despite any other provision of this Act, a head shall, as soon as practicable, disclose any record to the public or persons affected if the head has reasonable and probable grounds to believe that it is in the public interest to do so and that the record reveals a grave environmental, health or safety hazard to the public.

(2) **Notice.**—Before disclosing a record under subsection (1), the head shall cause notice to be given to any person to whom the information in the record relates, if it is practicable to do so.

(3) **Contents of notice.**—The notice shall contain,

(a) a statement that the head intends to release a record or a part of a record that may affect the interests of the person;
(b) a description of the contents of the record or part that relate to the person; and
(c) a statement that if the person makes representations forthwith to the head as to why

the record or part should not be disclosed, those representations will be considered by the head.

(4) **Representations.**—A person who is given notice under subsection (2) may make representations forthwith to the head concerning why the record or part should not be disclosed.

Exemptions

6. (1) **Draft by-laws, etc.**—A head may refuse to disclose a record,
   (a) that contains a draft of a by-law or a draft of a private bill; or
   (b) that reveals the substance of deliberations of a meeting of a council, board, commission or other body or a committee of one of them if a statute authorizes holding that meeting in the absence of the public.

(2) **Exception.**—Despite subsection (1), a head shall not refuse under subsection (1) to disclose a record if,
   (a) in the case of a record under clause (1)(a), the draft has been considered in a meeting open to the public;
   (b) in the case of a record under clause (1)(b), the subject-matter of the deliberations has been considered in a meeting open to the public; or
   (c) the record is more than twenty years old.

7. (1) **Advice or recommendations.**—A head may refuse to disclose a record if the disclosure would reveal advice or recommendations of an officer or employee of an institution or a consultant retained by an institution.

(2) **Exception.**—Despite subsection (1), a head shall not refuse under subsection (1) to disclose a record that contains,
   (a) factual material;
   (b) a statistical survey;
   (c) a report by a valuator;
   (d) an environmental impact statement or similar record;
   (e) a report or study on the performance or efficiency of an institution;
   (f) a feasibility study or other technical study, including a cost estimate, relating to a policy or project of an institution;
   (g) a report containing the results of field research undertaken before the formulation of a policy proposal;
   (h) a final plan or proposal to change a program of an institution, or for the establishment of a new program, including a budgetary estimate for the program;
   (i) a report of a committee or similar body within an institution, which has been established for the purpose of preparing a report on a particular topic;
   (j) a report of a body which is attached to an institution and which has been established for the purpose of undertaking inquiries and making reports or recommendations to the institution;
   (k) the reasons for a final decision, order or ruling of an officer or an employee of the institution made during or at the conclusion of the exercise of discretionary power conferred by or under an enactment or scheme administered by the institution.

(3) **Idem.**—Despite subsection (1), a head shall not refuse under subsection (1) to disclose a record if the record is more than twenty years old.

8. (1) **Law enforcement.**—A head may refuse to disclose a record if the disclosure could reasonably be expected to,

- (a) interfere with a law enforcement matter;
- (b) interfere with an investigation undertaken with a view to a law enforcement proceeding or from which a law enforcement proceeding is likely to result;
- (c) reveal investigative techniques and procedures currently in use or likely to be used in law enforcement;
- (d) disclose the identity of a confidential source of information in respect of a law enforcement matter, or disclose information furnished only by the confidential source;
- (e) endanger the life or physical safety of a law enforcement officer or any other person;
- (f) deprive a person of the right to a fair trial or impartial adjudication;
- (g) interfere with the gathering of or reveal law enforcement intelligence information respecting organizations or persons;
- (h) reveal a record which has been confiscated from a person by a peace officer in accordance with an Act or regulation;
- (i) endanger the security of a building or the security of a vehicle carrying items, or of a system or procedure established for the protection of items, for which protection is reasonably required;
- (j) facilitate the escape from custody of a person who is under lawful detention;
- (k) jeopardize the security of a centre for lawful detention; or
- (l) facilitate the commission of an unlawful act or hamper the control of crime.

(2) **Idem.**—A head may refuse to disclose a record,

- (a) that is a report prepared in the course of law enforcement, inspections or investigations by an agency which has the function of enforcing and regulating compliance with a law;
- (b) that is a law enforcement record if the disclosure would constitute an offence under an Act of Parliament;
- (c) that is a law enforcement record if the disclosure could reasonably be expected to expose the author of the record or any person who has been quoted or paraphrased in the record to civil liability; or
- (d) that contains information about the history, supervision or release of a person under the control or supervision of a correctional authority.

(3) **Refusal to confirm or deny existence of record.**—A head may refuse to confirm or deny the existence of a record to which subsection (1) or (2) applies.

(4) **Exception.**—Despite clause (2)(a), a head shall disclose a record that is a report prepared in the course of routine inspections by an agency that is authorized to enforce and regulate compliance with a particular statute of Ontario.

(5) **Idem.**—Subsections (1) and (2) do not apply to a record on the degree of success achieved in a law enforcement program including statistical analyses unless disclosure of such a record may prejudice, interfere with or adversely affect any of the matters referred to in those subsections.

9. (1) **Relations with governments.**—A head shall refuse to disclose a record if the disclosure could reasonably be expected to reveal information the institution has received in confidence from,

   (a) the Government of Canada;
   (b) the Government of Ontario or the government of a province or territory in Canada;
   (c) the government of a foreign country or state;
   (d) an agency of a government referred to in clause (a), (b) or (c); or
   (e) an international organization of states or a body of such an organization.

(2) **Idem.**—A head shall disclose a record to which subsection (1) applies if the government, agency or organization from which the information was received consents to the disclosure.

10. (1) **Third party information.**—A head shall refuse to disclose a record that reveals a trade secret or scientific, technical, commercial, financial or labour relations information, supplied in confidence implicitly or explicitly, if the disclosure could reasonably be expected to,

   (a) prejudice significantly the competitive position or interfere significantly with the contractual or other negotiations of a person, group of persons, or organization;
   (b) result in similar information no longer being supplied to the institution where it is in the public interest that similar information continue to be so supplied;
   (c) result in undue loss or gain to any person, group, committee or financial institution or agency; or
   (d) reveal information supplied to or the report of a conciliation officer, mediator, labour relations officer or other person appointed to resolve a labour relations dispute.

(2) **Consent to disclosure.**—A head may disclose a record described in subsection (1) if the person to whom the information relates consents to the disclosure.

11. Economic and other interests.—A head may refuse to disclose a record that contains,

   (a) trade secrets or financial, commercial, scientific or technical information that belongs to an institution and has monetary value or potential monetary value;
   (b) information obtained through research by an employee of an institution if the disclosure could reasonably be expected to deprive the employee of priority of publication;
   (c) information whose disclosure could reasonably be expected to prejudice the economic interests of an institution or the competitive position of an institution;
   (d) information whose disclosure could reasonably be expected to be injurious to the financial interests of an institution;
   (e) positions, plans, procedures, criteria or instructions to be applied to any negotiations carried on or to be carried on by or on behalf of an institution;
   (f) plans relating to the management of personnel or the administration of an institution that have not yet been put into operation or made public;
   (g) information including the proposed plans, policies or projects of an institution if the disclosure could reasonably be expected to result in premature disclosure of a pending policy decision or undue financial benefit or loss to a person;
   (h) questions that are to be used in an examination or test for an educational purpose;
   (i) submissions under the *Municipal Boundary Negotiations Act*, by a party municipality

or other body before the matter to which the submissions relate is resolved under that Act.

12. Solicitor-client privilege.—A head may refuse to disclose a record that is subject to solicitor-client privilege or that was prepared by or for counsel employed or retained by an institution for use in giving legal advice or in contemplation of or for use in litigation.

13. Danger to safety or health.—A head may refuse to disclose a record whose disclosure could reasonably be expected to seriously threaten the safety or health of an individual.

14. (1) **Personal privacy.**—A head shall refuse to disclose personal information to any person other than the individual to whom the information relates except,
- (a) upon the prior written request or consent of the individual, if the record is one to which the individual is entitled to have access;
- (b) in compelling circumstances affecting the health or safety of an individual, if upon disclosure notification thereof is mailed to the last known address of the individual to whom the information relates;
- (c) personal information collected and maintained specifically for the purpose of creating a record available to the general public;
- (d) under an Act of Ontario or Canada that expressly authorizes the disclosure;
- (e) for a research purpose if,
    - (i) the disclosure is consistent with the conditions or reasonable expectations of disclosure under which the personal information was provided, collected or obtained,
    - (ii) the research purpose for which the disclosure is to be made cannot be reasonably accomplished unless the information is provided in individually identifiable form, and
    - (iii) the person who is to receive the record has agreed to comply with the conditions relating to security and confidentiality prescribed by the regulations; or
- (f) if the disclosure does not constitute an unjustified invasion of personal privacy.

(2) **Criteria re invasion of privacy.**—A head, in determining whether a disclosure of personal information constitutes an unjustified invasion of personal privacy, shall consider all the relevant circumstances, including whether,
- (a) the disclosure is desirable for the purpose of subjecting the activities of the institution to public scrutiny;
- (b) access to the personal information may promote public health and safety;
- (c) access to the personal information will promote informed choice in the purchase of goods and services;
- (d) the personal information is relevant to a fair determination of rights affecting the person who made the request;
- (e) the individual to whom the information relates will be exposed unfairly to pecuniary or other harm;
- (f) the personal information is highly sensitive;
- (g) the personal information is unlikely to be accurate or reliable;
- (h) the personal information has been supplied by the individual to whom the information relates in confidence; and

(i) the disclosure may unfairly damage the reputation of any person referred to in the record.

(3) **Presumed invasion of privacy.**—A disclosure of personal information is presumed to constitute an unjustified invasion of personal privacy if the personal information,

(a) relates to a medical, psychiatric or psychological history, diagnosis, condition, treatment or evaluation;

(b) was compiled and is identifiable as part of an investigation into a possible violation of law, except to the extent that disclosure is necessary to prosecute the violation or to continue the investigation;

(c) relates to eligibility for social service or welfare benefits or to the determination of benefit levels;

(d) relates to employment or educational history;

(e) was obtained on a tax return or gathered for the purpose of collecting a tax;

(f) describes an individual's finances, income, assets, liabilities, net worth, bank balances, financial history or activities, or creditworthiness;

(g) consists of personal recommendations or evaluations, character references or personal evaluations; or

(h) indicates the individual's racial or ethnic origin, sexual orientation or religious or political beliefs or associations.

(4) **Limitation.**—Despite subsection (3), a disclosure does not constitute an unjustified invasion of personal privacy if it,

(a) discloses the classification, salary range and benefits, or employment responsibilities of an individual who is or was an officer or employee of an institution; or

(b) discloses financial or other details of a contract for personal services between an individual and an institution.

(5) **Refusal to confirm or deny existence of record.**—A head may refuse to confirm or deny the existence of a record if disclosure of the record would constitute an unjustified invasion of personal privacy.

15. Information soon to be published.—A head may refuse to disclose a record if,

(a) the record or the information contained in the record has been published or is currently available to the public; or

(b) the head believes on reasonable grounds that the record or the information contained in the record will be published by an institution within ninety days after the request is made or within such further period of time as may be necessary for printing or translating the material for the purpose of printing it.

16. Exemptions not to apply.—An exemption from disclosure of a record under sections 7, 9, 10, 11, 13 and 14 does not apply if a compelling public interest in the disclosure of the record clearly outweighs the purpose of the exemption.

Access Procedure

17. (1) **Request.**—A person seeking access to a record shall,

(a) make a request in writing to the institution that the person believes has custody or control of the record;
(b) provide sufficient detail to enable an experienced employee of the institution, upon a reasonable effort, to identify the record; and
(c) at the time of making the request, pay the fee prescribed by the regulations for that purpose.

(1.1) **Frivolous request.**—If the head of the institution is of the opinion on reasonable grounds that the request is frivolous or vexatious, subsection (2) does not apply to the request.

(2) **Sufficiency of detail.**—If the request does not sufficiently describe the record sought, the institution shall inform the applicant of the defect and shall offer assistance in reformulating the request so as to comply with subsection (1).

1996, c. 1, Sched. K, s. 14.

18. (1) **Definition.**—In this section, "institution" includes an institution as defined in section 2 of the *Freedom of Information and Protection of Privacy Act*.

(2) **Request to be forwarded.**—The head of an institution that receives a request for access to a record that the institution does not have in its custody or under its control shall make reasonable inquiries to determine whether another institution has custody or control of the record, and, if the head determines that another institution has custody or control of the record, the head shall within fifteen days after the request is received,

(a) forward the request to the other institution; and
(b) give written notice to the person who made the request that it has been forwarded to the other institution.

(3) **Transfer of request.**—If an institution receives a request for access to a record and the head considers that another institution has a greater interest in the record, the head may transfer the request and, if necessary, the record to the other institution, within fifteen days after the request is received, in which case the head transferring the request shall give written notice of the transfer to the person who made the request.

(4) **Greater interest.**—For the purpose of subsection (3), another institution has a greater interest in a record than the institution that receives the request for access if,

(a) the record was originally produced in or for the other institution; or
(b) in the case of a record not originally produced in or for an institution, the other institution was the first institution to receive the record or a copy of it.

(5) **When transferred request deemed made.**—Where a request is forwarded or transferred under subsection (2) or (3), the request shall be deemed to have been made to the institution to which it is forwarded or transferred on the day the institution to which the request was originally made received it.

19. Notice by head.—Where a person requests access to a record, the head of the institution to which the request is made or if a request is forwarded or transferred under section 18, the head of the institution to which it is forwarded or transferred, shall, subject to sections 20, 21 and 45, within thirty days after the request is received,

(a) give written notice to the person who made the request as to whether or not access to the record or a part of it will be given; and

(b) if access is to be given, give the person who made the request access to the record or part, and if necessary for the purpose cause the record to be produced.

1996, c. 1, Sched. K, s. 15.

20. (1) **Extension of time.**—A head may extend the time limit set out in section 19 for a period of time that is reasonable in the circumstances, if,

(a) the request is for a large number of records or necessitates a search through a large number of records and meeting the time limit would unreasonably interfere with the operations of the institution; or

(b) consultations with a person outside the institution are necessary to comply with the request and cannot reasonably be completed within the time limit.

(2) **Notice of extension.**—A head who extends the time limit under subsection (1) shall give the person who made the request written notice of the extension setting out,

(a) the length of the extension;

(b) the reason for the extension; and

(c) that the person who made the request may ask the Commissioner to review the extension.

20.1 (1) **Frivolous request.**—A head who refuses to give access to a record or a part of a record because the head is of the opinion that the request for access is frivolous or vexatious, shall state in the notice given under section 19,

(a) that the request is refused because the head is of the opinion that the request is frivolous or vexatious;

(b) the reasons for which the head is of the opinion that the request is frivolous or vexatious; and

(c) that the person who made the request may appeal to the Commissioner under subsection 39(1) for a review of the decision.

(2) **Non-application.**—Sections 21 and 22 do not apply to a head who gives a notice for the purpose of subsection (1).

1996, c. 1, Sched. K, s. 16.

21. (1) **Notice to affected person.**—A head shall give written notice in accordance with subsection (2) to the person to whom the information relates before granting a request for access to a record,

(a) that the head has reason to believe might contain information referred to in subsection 10(1) that affects the interest of a person other than the person requesting information; or

(b) that is personal information that the head has reason to believe might constitute an unjustified invasion of personal privacy for the purposes of clause 14(1)(f).

(2) **Contents of notice.**—The notice shall contain,

(a) a statement that the head intends to disclose a record or part of a record that may affect the interests of the person;

(b) a description of the contents of the record or part that relate to the person; and

(c) a statement that the person may, within twenty days after the notice is given, make representations to the head as to why the record or part should not be disclosed.

(2.1) **Description.**—If the request covers more than one record, the description mentioned in clause (2)(b) may consist of a summary of the categories of the records requested if it provides sufficient detail to identify them.

(3) **Time for notice.**—The notice referred to in subsection (1) shall be given within thirty days after the request for access is received or, if there has been an extension of a time limit under subsection 20(1), within that extended time limit.

(4) **Notice of delay.**—A head who gives notice to a person under subsection (1) shall also give the person who made the request written notice of delay, setting out,
- (a) that the disclosure of the record or part may affect the interests of another party;
- (b) that the other party is being given an opportunity to make representations concerning disclosure; and
- (c) that the head will within thirty days decide whether or not to disclose the record.

(5) **Representation re disclosure.**—Where a notice is given under subsection (1), the person to whom the information relates may, within twenty days after the notice is given, make representations to the head as to why the record or part should not be disclosed.

(6) **Representation in writing.**—Representations under subsection (5) shall be made in writing unless the head permits them to be made orally.

(7) **Decision re disclosure.**—The head shall decide whether or not to disclose the record or part and give written notice of the decision to the person to whom the information relates and the person who made the request within thirty days after the notice under subsection (1) is given, but not before the earlier of,
- (a) the day the response to the notice from the person to whom the information relates is received; or
- (b) twenty-one days after the notice is given.

(8) **Notice of head's decision to disclose.**—A head who decides to disclose a record or part under subsection (7) shall state in the notice that,
- (a) the person to whom the information relates may appeal the decision to the Commissioner within thirty days after the notice is given; and
- (b) the person who made the request will be given access to the record or part unless an appeal of the decision is commenced within thirty days after the notice is given.

(9) **Access to be given unless affected person appeals.**—A head who decides under subsection (7) to disclose the record or part shall give the person who made the request access to the record or part within thirty days after notice is given under subsection (7), unless the person to whom the information relates asks the Commissioner to review the decision.

1996, c. 1, Sched. K, s. 18.

22. (1) **Contents of notice of refusal.**—Notice of refusal to give access to a record or part under section 19 shall set out,
- (a) where there is no such record,
  - (i) that there is no such record, and
  - (ii) that the person who made the request may appeal to the Commissioner the question of whether such a record exists; or
- (b) where there is such a record,

(i) the specific provision of this Act under which access is refused,
(ii) the reason the provision applies to the record,
(iii) the name and position of the person responsible for making the decision, and
(iv) that the person who made the request may appeal to the Commissioner for a review of the decision.

(2) **Idem.**—A head who refuses to confirm or deny the existence of a record as provided in subsection 8(3) (law enforcement) or subsection 14(5) (unjustified invasion of personal privacy) shall state in the notice given under section 19,
  (a) that the head refuses to confirm or deny the existence of the record;
  (b) the provision of this Act on which the refusal is based;
  (c) the name and office of the person responsible for making the decision; and
  (d) that the person who made the request may appeal to the Commissioner for a review of the decision.

(3) **Idem.**—A head who refuses to disclose a record or part under subsection 21(7) shall state in the notice given under subsection 21(7),
  (a) the specific provision of this Act under which access is refused;
  (b) the reason the provision named in clause (a) applies to the record;
  (c) the name and office of the person responsible for making the decision to refuse access; and
  (d) that the person who made the request may appeal to the Commissioner for a review of the decision.

(3.1) **Description.**—If a request for access covers more than one record, the statement in a notice under this section of a reason mentioned in subclause (1)(b)(ii) or clause (3)(b) may refer to a summary of the categories of the records requested if it provides sufficient detail to identify them.

(4) **Deemed refusal.**—A head who fails to give the notice required under section 19 or subsection 21(7) concerning a record shall be deemed to have given notice of refusal to give access to the record on the last day of the period during which notice should have been given.

1996, c. 1, Sched. K, s. 18.

23. (1) **Copy of record.**—Subject to subsection (2), a person who is given access to a record or a part of a record under this Act shall be given a copy of the record or part unless it would not be reasonably practicable to reproduce it by reason of its length or nature, in which case the person shall be given an opportunity to examine the record or part.

(2) **Access to original record.**—If a person requests the opportunity to examine a record or part and it is reasonably practicable to give the person that opportunity, the head shall allow the person to examine the record or part.

(3) **Copy of part.**—A person who examines a record or a part and wishes to have portions of it copied shall be given a copy of those portions unless it would not be reasonably practicable to reproduce them by reason of their length or nature.

Information to be Published or Available

24. (1) **Publication of information re institutions.**—The Minister shall cause to be published a compilation listing all institutions and, in respect of each institution, setting out,

PART II — PROTECTION OF INDIVIDUAL PRIVACY   S. 29

(a) where a request for a record should be made; and
(b) the title of the head of the institution.

(2) **Idem.**—The Minister shall cause the compilation to be published before the 1st day of January, 1992 and at least once every three years thereafter.

25. (1) **Information available for inspection.**—A head shall cause to be made available for inspection and copying by the public information containing,

(a) a description of the organization and responsibilities of the institution;
(b) a list of the general classes or types of records in the custody or control of the institution;
(c) the title, business telephone and business address of the head; and
(d) the address to which a request under this Act should be made.

(2) **Idem.**—The head shall ensure that the information made available is amended as required to ensure its accuracy.

26. (1) **Annual report of head.**—A head shall make an annual report, in accordance with subsection (2), to the Commissioner.

(2) **Contents of report.**—A report made under subsection (1) shall specify,

(a) the number of requests under this Act for access to records made to the institution;
(b) the number of refusals by the head to disclose a record, the provisions of this Act under which disclosure was refused and the number of occasions on which each provision was invoked;
(c) the number of uses or purposes for which personal information is disclosed if the use or purpose is not included in the statements of uses and purposes set forth under clauses 34(1)(d) and (e);
(d) the amount of fees collected by the institution under section 45; and
(e) any other information indicating an effort by the institution to put into practice the purposes of this Act.

PART II

PROTECTION OF INDIVIDUAL PRIVACY

Collection and Retention of Personal Information

27. Application of Part.—This Part does not apply to personal information that is maintained for the purpose of creating a record that is available to the general public.

28. (1) **Definition.**—In this section and in section 29, "personal information" includes information that is not recorded and that is otherwise defined as "personal information" under this Act.

(2) **Collection of personal information.**—No person shall collect personal information on behalf of an institution unless the collection is expressly authorized by statute, used for the purposes of law enforcement or necessary to the proper administration of a lawfully authorized activity.

29. (1) **Manner of collection.**—An institution shall collect personal information only directly from the individual to whom the information relates unless,

(a) the individual authorizes another manner of collection;
(b) the personal information may be disclosed to the institution concerned under section 32 or under section 42 of the *Freedom of Information and Protection of Privacy Act*;
(c) the Commissioner has authorized the manner of collection under clause 46(c);
(d) the information is in a report from a reporting agency in accordance with the *Consumer Reporting Act*;
(e) the information is collected for the purpose of determining suitability for an honour or award to recognize outstanding achievement or distinguished service;
(f) the information is collected for the purpose of the conduct of a proceeding or a possible proceeding before a court or judicial or quasi-judicial tribunal;
(g) the information is collected for the purpose of law enforcement; or
(h) another manner of collection is authorized by or under a statute.

(2) **Notice to individual.**—If personal information is collected on behalf of an institution, the head shall inform the individual to whom the information relates of,

(a) the legal authority for the collection;
(b) the principal purpose or purposes for which the personal information is intended to be used; and
(c) the title, business address and business telephone number of an officer or employee of the institution who can answer the individual's questions about the collection.

(3) **Exception.**—Subsection (2) does not apply if,

(a) the head may refuse to disclose the personal information under subsection 8(1) or (2) (law enforcement);
(b) the Minister waives the notice; or
(c) the regulations provide that the notice is not required.

30. (1) **Retention of personal information.**—Personal information that has been used by an institution shall be retained after use by the institution for the period prescribed by regulation in order to ensure that the individual to whom it relates has a reasonable opportunity to obtain access to the personal information.

(2) **Standard of accuracy.**—The head of an institution shall take reasonable steps to ensure that personal information on the records of the institution is not used unless it is accurate and up to date.

(3) **Exception.**—Subsection (2) does not apply to personal information collected for law enforcement purposes.

(4) **Disposal of personal information.**—A head shall dispose of personal information under the control of the institution in accordance with the regulations.

Use and Disclosure of Personal Information

31. **Use of personal information.**—An institution shall not use personal information in its custody or under its control except,

(a) if the person to whom the information relates has identified that information in particular and consented to its use;
(b) for the purpose for which it was obtained or compiled or for a consistent purpose; or

PART II — PROTECTION OF INDIVIDUAL PRIVACY   S. 34

(c) for a purpose for which the information may be disclosed to the institution under section 32 or under section 42 of the *Freedom of Information and Protection of Privacy Act.*

32. Where disclosure permitted.—An institution shall not disclose personal information in its custody or under its control except,

(a) in accordance with Part I;
(b) if the person to whom the information relates has identified that information in particular and consented to its disclosure;
(c) for the purpose for which it was obtained or compiled or for a consistent purpose;
(d) if the disclosure is made to an officer or employee of the institution who needs the record in the performance of his or her duties and if the disclosure is necessary and proper in the discharge of the institution's functions;
(e) for the purpose of complying with an Act of the Legislature of an Act of Parliament, an agreement or arrangement under such an Act or a treaty;
(f) if disclosure is by a law enforcement institution,
    (i) to a law enforcement agency in a foreign country under an arrangement, a written agreement or treaty or legislative authority, or
    (ii) to another law enforcement agency in Canada;
(g) if disclosure is to an institution or a law enforcement agency in Canada to aid an investigation undertaken with a view to a law enforcement proceeding or from which a law enforcement proceeding is likely to result;
(h) in compelling circumstances affecting the health or safety of an individual if upon disclosure notification is mailed to the last known address of the individual to whom the information relates;
(i) in compassionate circumstances, to facilitate contact with the next of kin or a friend of an individual who is injured, ill or deceased;
(j) to the Minister;
(k) to the Information and Privacy Commissioner;
(l) to the Government of Canada or the Government of Ontario in order to facilitate the auditing of shared cost programs.

33. Consistent purpose.—The purpose of a use or disclosure of personal information that has been collected directly from the individual to whom the information relates is a consistent purpose under clauses 31(b) and 32(c) only if the individual might reasonably have expected such a use or disclosure.

Personal Information Banks

34. (1) Personal information bank index.—A head shall make available for inspection by the public an index of all personal information banks in the custody or under the control of the institution setting forth, in respect of each personal information bank,

(a) its name and location;
(b) the legal authority for its establishment;
(c) the types of personal information maintained in it;
(d) how the personal information is used on a regular basis;

(e) to whom the personal information is disclosed on a regular basis;
(f) the categories of individuals about whom personal information is maintained; and
(g) the policies and practices applicable to the retention and disposal of the personal information.

(2) **Ensure accuracy.**—The head shall ensure that the index is amended as required to ensure its accuracy.

1989, c. 63, s. 34.

35. (1) **Inconsistent use or disclosure.**—A head shall attach or link to personal information in a personal information bank,

(a) a record of any use of that personal information for a purpose other than a purpose described in clause 34(1)(d); and
(b) a record of any disclosure of that personal information to a person other than a person described in clause 34(1)(e).

(2) **Idem.**—A record of use or disclosure under subsection (1) forms part of the personal information to which it is attached or linked.

1989, c. 63, s. 35.

Right of Individual to Whom Personal Information Relates to Access and Correction

36. (1) **Right of access to personal information.**—Every individual has a right of access to,

(a) any personal information about the individual contained in a personal information bank in the custody or under the control of an institution; and
(b) any other personal information about the individual in the custody or under the control of an institution with respect to which the individual is able to provide sufficiently specific information to render it reasonably retrievable by the institution.

(2) **Right of correction.**—Every individual who is given access under subsection (1) to personal information is entitled to,

(a) request correction of the personal information if the individual believes there is an error or omission;
(b) require that a statement of disagreement be attached to the information reflecting any correction that was requested but not made; and
(c) require that any person or body to whom the personal information has been disclosed within the year before the time a correction is requested or a statement of disagreement is required be notified of the correction or statement of disagreement.

37. (1) **Request.**—An individual seeking access to personal information about the individual shall,

(a) make a request in writing to the institution that the individual believes has custody or control of the personal information;
(b) identify the personal information bank or otherwise identify the location of the personal information; and

(c) at the time of making the request, pay the fee prescribed by the regulations for that purpose.

(2) **Access procedures.**—Subsections 4(2), 17(1.1) and (2) and sections 18, 19, 20, 20.1, 21, 22 and 23 apply with necessary modifications to a request made under subsection (1).

(3) **Comprehensible form.**—If access to personal information is to be given, the head shall ensure that the personal information is provided to the individual in a comprehensible form and in a manner that indicates the general conditions under which the personal information is stored and used.

1996, c. 1, Sched. K, s. 19.

38. Exemptions.—A head may refuse to disclose to the individual to whom the information relates personal information,

(a) if section 6, 7, 8, 9, 10, 11, 12, 13 or 15 would apply to the disclosure of that personal information;
(b) if the disclosure would constitute an unjustified invasion of another individual's personal privacy;
(c) that is evaluative or opinion material compiled solely for the purpose of determining suitability, eligibility or qualifications for employment or for the awarding of contracts and other benefits by an institution if the disclosure would reveal the identity of a source who furnished information to the institution in circumstances where it may reasonably have been assumed that the identity of the source would be held in confidence;
(d) that is medical information if the disclosure could reasonably be expected to prejudice the mental or physical health of the individual; or
(e) that is a research or statistical record.

PART III

APPEAL

39. (1) Right to appeal.—A person may appeal any decision of a head under this Act to the Commissioner if,

(a) the person has made a request for access to a record under subsection 17(1);
(b) the person has made a request for access to personal information under subsection 37(1);
(c) the person has made a request for correction of personal information under subsection 36(2); or
(d) the person is given notice of a request under subsection 21(1).

(1.1) **Fee.**—A person who appeals under subsection (1) shall pay the fee prescribed by the regulations for that purpose.

(2) **Time for application.**—An appeal under subsection (1) shall be made within thirty days after the notice was given of the decision appealed from by filing with the Commissioner written notice of appeal.

S. 40 MUNICIPAL FREEDOM OF INFORMATION AND PROTECTION OF PRIVACY ACT

(2.1) **Immediate dismissal.**—The Commissioner may dismiss an appeal if the notice of appeal does not present a reasonable basis for concluding that the record or the personal information to which the notice relates exists.

(2.2) **Non-application.**—If the Commissioner dismisses an appeal under subsection (2.1), subsection (3) and sections 40 and 41 do not apply to the Commissioner.

(3) **Notice of application for appeal.**—Upon receiving a notice of appeal, the Commissioner shall inform the head of the institution concerned and any other affected person of the notice of appeal.

1996, c. 1, Sched. K, s. 20.

40. Mediator to try to effect settlement.—The Commissioner may authorize a mediator to investigate the circumstances of any appeal and to try to effect a settlement of the matter under appeal.

41. (1) **Inquiry.**—The Commissioner may conduct an inquiry to review the head's decision if,

(a) the Commissioner has not authorized a mediator to conduct an investigation under section 40; or

(b) the Commissioner has authorized a mediator to conduct an investigation under section 40 but no settlement has been effected.

(2) **Procedure.**—The *Statutory Powers Procedure Act* does not apply to an inquiry under subsection (1).

(3) **Inquiry in private.**—The inquiry may be conducted in private.

(4) **Powers of Commissioner.**—In an inquiry, the Commissioner may require to be produced to the Commissioner and may examine any record that is in the custody or under the control of an institution, despite Parts I and II of this Act or any other Act or privilege, and may enter and inspect any premises occupied by an institution for the purposes of the investigation.

(5) **Record not retained by Commissioner.**—The Commissioner shall not retain any information obtained from a record under subsection (4).

(6) **Examination on site.**—Despite subsection (4), a head may require that the examination of a record by the Commissioner be of the original at its site.

(7) **Notice of entry.**—Before entering any premises under subsection (4), the Commissioner shall notify the head of the institution occupying the premises of his or her purpose.

(8) **Examination under oath.**—The Commissioner may summon and examine on oath any person who, in the Commissioner's opinion, may have information relating to the inquiry and, for that purpose, the Commissioner may administer an oath.

(9) **Evidence privileged.**—Anything said or any information supplied or any document or thing produced by a person in the course of an inquiry by the Commissioner under this Act is privileged in the same manner as if the inquiry were a proceeding in a court.

(10) **Protection.**—Except on the trial of a person for perjury in respect of his or her sworn testimony, no statement made or answer given by that or any other person in the course of an inquiry by the Commissioner is admissible in evidence in any court or any inquiry or in any

PART IV — GENERAL   S. 45

other proceedings, and no evidence in respect of proceedings before the Commissioner shall be given against any person.

(11) **Idem.**—A person giving a statement or answer in the course of an inquiry before the Commissioner shall be informed by the Commissioner of his or her right to object to answer any question under section 5 of the *Canada Evidence Act*.

(12) **Prosecution.**—No person is liable to prosecution for an offence against any Act, other than this Act, by reason of his or her compliance with a requirement of the Commissioner under this section.

(13) **Representations.**—The person who requested access to the record, the head of the institution concerned and any affected party shall be given an opportunity to make representations to the Commissioner, but no person is entitled to be present during, to have access to or to comment on representations made to the Commissioner by any other person.

(14) **Right to counsel.**—The person who requested access to the record, the head of the institution concerned and any affected party may be represented by counsel or an agent.

1996, c. 1, Sched. K, s. 21.

42. Burden of proof.—If a head refuses access to a record or a part of a record, the burden of proof that the record or the part falls within one of the specified exemptions in this Act lies upon the head.

43. (1) **Order.**—After all of the evidence for an inquiry has been received, the Commissioner shall make an order disposing of the issues raised by the appeal.

(2) **Idem.**—If the Commissioner upholds a decision of a head that the head may refuse to disclose a record or a part of a record, the Commissioner shall not order the head to disclose the record or part.

(3) **Conditions.**—Subject to this Act the Commissioner's order may contain any conditions the Commissioner considers appropriate.

(4) **Notice of order.**—The Commissioner shall give the appellant and the persons who received notice of the appeal under subsection 39(3) written notice of order.

1996, c. 1, Sched. K, s. 22.

44. Delegation.—The Commissioner shall not delegate to a person other than an Assistant Commissioner his or her power to require a record referred to in section 8 to be produced and examined.

PART IV

GENERAL

45. (1) **Fees.**—A head shall require the person who makes a request for access to a record to pay fees in the amounts prescribed by the regulations for,

(a) the costs of every hour of manual search required to locate a record;
(b) the costs of preparing the record for disclosure;
(c) computer and other costs incurred in locating, retrieving, processing and copying a record;

(d) shipping costs; and

(e) any other costs incurred in responding to a request for access to a record.

(3) **Estimate of costs.**—The head of an institution shall, before giving access to a record, give the person requesting access a reasonable estimate of any amount that will be required to be paid under this Act that is over $25.

(4) **Waiver of payment.**—A head shall waive the payment of all or any part of an amount required to be paid under subsection (1) if, in the head's opinion, it is fair and equitable to do so after considering,

(a) the extent to which the actual cost of processing, collecting and copying the record varies from the amount of the payment required by subsection (1);

(b) whether the payment will cause a financial hardship for the person requesting the record;

(c) whether dissemination of the record will benefit public health or safety; and

(d) any other matter prescribed in the regulations.

(5) **Review.**—A person who is required to pay a fee under subsection (1) may ask the Commissioner to review the amount of the fee or the head's decision not to waive the fee.

(6) **Disposition of fees.**—The fees provided in this section shall be paid and distributed in the manner and at the times prescribed by the regulations.

1996, c. 1, Sched. K, s. 23.

46. Powers and duties of Commissioner.—The Commissioner may,

(a) offer comment on the privacy protection implications of proposed programs of institutions;

(b) after hearing the head, order an institution to,

(i) cease a collection practice that contravenes this Act, and

(ii) destroy collections of personal information that contravene this Act;

(c) in appropriate circumstances, authorize the collection of personal information otherwise than directly from the individual;

(d) engage in or commission research into matters affecting the carrying out of the purposes of this Act;

(e) conduct public education programs and provide information concerning this Act and the Commissioner's role and activities; and

(f) receive representations from the public concerning the operation of this Act.

47. (1) **Regulations.**—The Lieutenant Governor in Council may make regulations,

(0.a) prescribing standards for determining what constitutes reasonable grounds for a head to conclude that a request for access to a record is frivolous or vexatious.

(a) respecting the procedures for access to original records under section 23;

(b) prescribing the circumstances under which records capable of being produced from machine readable records are not included in the definition of ''record'' for the purposes of this Act;

(c) setting standards for and requiring administrative, technical and physical safeguards to ensure the security and confidentiality of records and personal information under the control of institutions;

(d) setting standards for the accuracy and completeness of personal information that is under the control of an institution;

(e) prescribing time periods for the purposes of subsection 30(1);
(f) prescribing the amount, the manner of payment and the manner of allocation of fees described in clause 17(1)(c) or 37(1)(c), subsection 39(1.1) or section 45 and the times at which they are required to be paid.
(g) prescribing matters to be considered in determining whether to waive all or part of the costs required under section 45;
(h) designating any agency, board, commission, corporation or other body as an institution;
(i) prescribing circumstances under which the notice under subsection 29(2) is not required;
(j) prescribing conditions relating to the security and confidentiality of records used for a research purpose;
(k) prescribing forms and providing for their use;
(l) respecting any matter the Lieutenant Governor in Council considers necessary to carry out effectively the purposes of this Act.

(2) **Categories of fees.**—A regulation made under clause (1)(f) may prescribe a different amount, manner of payment, manner of allocation or time of payment of fees for different categories of records or persons requesting access to a record.

1996, c. 1, Sched. K, s. 24.

48. (1) **Offences.**—No person shall,
(a) wilfully disclose personal information in contravention of this Act;
(b) wilfully maintain a personal information bank that contravenes this Act;
(c) make a request under this Act for access to or correction of personal information under false pretences;
(d) wilfully obstruct the Commissioner in the performance of his or her functions under this Act;
(e) wilfully make a false statement to mislead or attempt to mislead the Commissioner in the performance of his or her functions under this Act; or
(f) wilfully fail to comply with an order of the Commissioner.

(2) **Penalty.**—Every person who contravenes subsection (1) is guilty of an offence and on conviction is liable to a fine not exceeding $5,000.

(3) **Consent of Attorney General.**—A prosecution shall not be commenced under clause (1)(d), (e) or (f) without the consent of the Attorney General.

49. (1) **Delegation of head's powers.**—A head may in writing delegate a power or duty granted or vested in the head to an officer or officers of the institution or another institution subject to such limitations, restrictions, conditions and requirements as the head may set out in the delegation.

(2) **Protection from civil proceeding.**—No action or other proceeding lies against a head, or against a person acting on behalf or under the direction of the head, for damages resulting from the disclosure or non-disclosure in good faith of a record or any part of a record under this Act, or from the failure to give a notice required under this Act if reasonable care is taken to give the required notice.

(3) **Vicarious liability of institutions preserved.**—Subsection (2) does not relieve an institution from liability in respect of a tort committed by a head or a person mentioned in

subsection (2) to which it would otherwise be subject and the institution is liable for any such tort in a like manner as if subsection (2) had not been enacted.

50. (1) **Oral requests.**—If a head may give access to information under this Act, nothing in this Act prevents the head from giving access to that information in response to an oral request or in the absence of a request.

(2) **Pre-existing access preserved.**—This Act shall not be applied to preclude access to information that is not personal information and to which access by the public was available by statute, custom or practice immediately before the 1st day of January, 1991.

51. (1) **Information otherwise available.**—This Act does not impose any limitation on the information otherwise available by law to a party to litigation.

(2) **Powers of courts and tribunals.**—This Act does not affect the power of a court or a tribunal to compel a witness to testify or compel the production of a document.

52. (1) **Application of Act.**—This Act applies to any record in the custody or under the control of an institution regardless of whether it was recorded before or after the 1st day of January, 1991.

(2) **Non-application of Act.**—This Act does not apply to records placed in the archives of an institution by or on behalf of a person or organization other than the institution.

(3) **Same.**—Subject to subsection (4), this Act does not apply to records collected, prepared, maintained or used by or on behalf of an institution in relation to any of the following:

1. Proceedings or anticipated proceedings before a court, tribunal or other entity relating to labour relations or to the employment of a person by the institution.
2. Negotiations or anticipated negotiations relating to labour relations or to the employment of a person by the institution between the institution and a person, bargaining agent or party to a proceeding or an anticipated proceeding.
3. Meetings, consultations, discussions or communications about labour relations or employment-related matters in which the institution has an interest.

(4) **Exception.**—This Act applies to the following records:

1. An agreement between an institution and a trade union.
2. An agreement between an institution and one or more employees which ends a proceeding before a court, tribunal or other entity relating to labour relations or to employment-related matters.
3. An agreement between an institution and one or more employees resulting from negotiations about employment-related matters between the institution and the employee or employees.
4. An expense account submitted by an employee of an institution to that institution for the purpose of seeking reimbursement for expenses incurred by the employee in his or her employment.

1995, c. 1, s. 83.

53. (1) **Other Acts.**—This Act prevails over a confidentiality provision in any other Act unless the other Act or this Act specifically provides otherwise.

(2) **Idem.**—The following confidentiality provisions prevail over this Act;

1. Section 88(6) of the *Municipal Elections Act, 1996*.

2. Subsection 53(1) of the *Assessment Act*.

1996, c. 32, s. 77.

54. Exercise of rights of deceased, etc., persons.—Any right or power conferred on an individual by this Act may be exercised,

(a) if the individual is deceased, by the individual's personal representative if exercise of the right or power relates to the administration of the individual's estate;

(b) by the individual's attorney under a continuing power of attorney, the individual's attorney under a power of attorney for personal care, the individual's guardian of the person, or the individual's guardian of property; and

(c) if the individual is less than sixteen years of age, by a person who has lawful custody of the individual.

1992, c. 32, s. 23; 1996, c. 2, s. 73.

55. Review of this Act.—The Standing Committee on the Legislative Assembly shall, before the 1st day of January, 1994, undertake a comprehensive review of this Act and shall, within one year after beginning that review, make recommendations to the Legislative Assembly regarding amendments to this Act.

REGULATION 823
GENERAL
R.R.O. 1990, Reg. 823, as am. O. Reg. 395/91; 22/96; 480/97

1. A record capable of being produced from machine readable records is not included in the definition of "record" for the purposes of the Act if the process of producing it would unreasonably interfere with the operation of an institution.

2. (1) A head who provides access to an original record must ensure the security of the record.

(2) A head may require that a person who is granted access to an original record examine it at premises operated by the institution.

(3) A head shall verify the identity of a person seeking access to his or her own personal information before giving the person access to it.

3. (1) Every head shall ensure that reasonable measures to prevent unauthorized access to the records in his or her institution are defined, documented and put in place, taking into account the nature of the records to be protected.

(2) Every head shall ensure that only those individuals who need a record for the performance of their duties shall have access to it.

(3) Every head shall ensure that reasonable measures to protect the records in his or her institution from inadvertent destruction or damage are defined, documented and put in place, taking into account the nature of the records to be protected.

4. (1) An institution is not required to give notice of the collection of personal information to an individual to whom it relates if the head complies with subsection (2) and if,

(a) providing notice would frustrate the purpose of the collection;
(b) providing notice might result in an unjustifiable invasion of another individual's privacy; or
(c) the collection is for the purpose of determining suitability or eligibility for an award or honour.

(2) For the purpose of subsection (1), the head shall make available for public inspection a statement describing the purpose of the collection of personal information and the reason that notice has not been given.

5. (1) Personal information that has been used by an institution shall be retained by the institution for the shorter of one year after use or the period set out in a by-law or resolution made by the institution or made by another institution affecting the institution, unless the individual to whom the information relates consents to its earlier disposal.

5.1 A head of an institution that receives a request for access to a record or personal information shall conclude that the request is frivolous or vexatious if,

(a) the head is of the opinion on reasonable grounds that the request is part of a pattern of conduct that amounts to an abuse of the right of access or would interfere with the operations of the institution; or
(b) the head is of the opinion on reasonable grounds that the request is made in bad faith or for a purpose other than to obtain access. O. Reg. 22/96, s. 1.

5.2 The fee that shall be charged for the purposes of clause 17(1)(c) or 37(1)(c) of the Act shall be $5. O. Reg. 22/96, s. 1.

5.3 (1) For the purposes of subsection 39(1.1) of the Act, the fee payable for appealing a decision of a head to the Commissioner shall be,

(a) $25, if the person appealing has made a request for access to a record under subsection 17(1);

(b) $10, if the person appealing has made a request for access to personal information under subsection 37(1); and

(c) $10, if the person appealing has made a request for correction of personal information under subsection 36(2).

(2) For the purposes of subsection 39(1.1) of the Act, no fee is payable for appealing a decision of a head to the Commissioner if the person appealing is given notice of a request under subsection 21(1) of the Act. O. Re.g 22/96, s. 1.

6. The following are the fees that shall be charged for the purposes of subsection 45(1) of the Act for access to a record:

1. For photocopies and computer printouts, 20 cents per page.
2. For floppy disks, $10 for each disk.
3. For manually searching a record, $7.50 for each 15 minutes spent by any person.
4. For preparing a record for disclosure, including severing a part of the record, $7.50 for each 15 minutes spent by any person.
5. For developing a computer program or other method of producing a record from machine readable record, $15 for each 15 minutes spent by any person.
6. The costs, including computer costs, that the institution incurs in locating, retrieving, processing and copying the record if those costs are specified in an invoice that the institution has received. O. Reg. 22/96, s. 2.

6.1 The following are the fees that shall be charged for the purposes of subsection 45(1) of the Act for access to personal information about the individual making the request for access:

1. For photocopies and computer printouts, 20 cents per page.
2. For floppy disks, $10 for each disk.
3. For developing a computer program or other method of producing the personal information requested from machine readable record, $15 for each 15 minutes spent by any person.
4. The costs, including computer costs, that the institution incurs in locating, retrieving, processing and copying the personal information requested if those costs are specified in an invoice that the institution has received. O. Reg. 22/96, s. 2.

7. (1) If a head gives a person an estimate of an amount payable under the Act and that estimate is $100 or more, the head may require the person to pay a deposit equal to 50 per cent of the estimate before the head takes any further steps to respond to the request.

(2) A head shall refund any amount paid under subsection (1) that is subsequently waived. O. Reg. 22/96, s. 3.

8. The following are prescribed as matters for a head to consider in deciding whether to waive all or part of a payment required to be made under the Act:

1. Whether the person requesting access to the record is given access to it.

2. If the amount of a payment would be $5 or less, whether the amount of the payment is too small to justify requiring payment.

9. If a person is required to pay a fee for access to a record, the head may require the person to do so before giving the person access to the record.

10. (1) The following are the terms and conditions relating to security and confidentiality that a person is required to agree to before a head may disclose personal information to that person for a research purpose:

1. The person shall use the information only for a research purpose set out in the agreement or for which the person has written authorization from the institution.
2. The person shall name in the agreement any other persons who will be given access to personal information in a form in which the individual to whom it relates can be identified.
3. Before disclosing personal information to other persons under paragraph 2, the person shall enter into an agreement with those persons to ensure that they will not disclose it to any other person.
4. The person shall keep the information in a physically secure location to which access is given only to the person and to the persons given access under paragraph 2.
5. The person shall destroy all individual identifiers in the information by the date specified in the agreement.
6. The person shall not contact any individual to whom personal information relates directly or indirectly without the prior written authority of the institution.
7. The person shall ensure that no personal information will be used or disclosed in a form in which the individual to whom it relates can be identified without the written authority of the institution.
8. The person shall notify the institution in writing immediately if the person becomes aware that any of the conditions set out in this section have been breached.

(2) An agreement relating to the security and confidentiality of personal information to be disclosed for a research purpose shall be in Form 1.

11. A request for access to a record under Part II of the Act or for access to or correction of personal information under Part II of the Act shall be in Form 2 or in any other written form that specifies that it is a request made under the Act. O. Reg. 395/91, s. 1.

FORM 1

Municipal Freedom of Information and Protection of Privacy Act

Agreement

This agreement is made between ...., referred to
                                  name of researcher
below as the researcher, and ...., referred to
                              name of institution
below as the institution.

The researcher has requested access to the following records that contain personal information and are in the custody or under the control of the institution: (Describe the records below)

Form 1

REGULATION UNDER THE MFIPPA

....
....
....

The researcher understands and promises to abide by the following terms and conditions:

1. The researcher will not use the information in the records for any purpose other than the following research purpose unless the researcher has the institution's written authorization to do so: (Describe the research purpose below)

....
....
....

2. The researcher will give access to personal information in a form in which the individual to whom it relates can be identified only to the following persons: (Name the persons below)

....
....
....

3. Before disclosing personal information to persons mentioned above, the researcher will enter into an agreement with those persons to ensure that they will not disclose it to any other person.

4. The researcher will keep the information in a physically secure location to which access is given only to the researcher and to the persons mentioned above.

5. The researcher will destroy all individual identifiers in the information by ....

(date)

6. The researcher will not contact any individual to whom personal information relates directly or indirectly without the prior written authority of the institution.

7. The researcher will ensure that no personal information will be used or disclosed in a form in which the individual to whom it relates can be identified without the written authority of the institution.

8. The researcher will notify the institution in writing immediately upon becoming aware that any of the conditions set out in this agreement have been breached.

Signed at .... this ..... day of ...., 199 .....

....

Researcher	Representative of Institution
Name:	Name: ....
Address:	Position: ....
....	Institution: ....
Telephone:	Address: ....
	....
	Telephone: ....

REGULATION 823 Form 2

FORM 2

O. Reg. 580/97, s. 1

Municipal Freedom of Information and Protection of Privacy Act

Request for:	Name of Institution request made to:
☐ Access to General Records	
☐ Access to Own Personal Information	
☐ Correction of Own Personal Information	

If request is for access to, or correction of, own personal information records:

Last name appearing on records: ☐ same as below or ▶

Details

Last Name	First Name	Middle Name	☐ Mr. ☐ Mrs.
			☐ Ms. ☐ Miss

Address (Street/Apt. No./P.O. Box No./R.R. No.)	City or Town	Province

Postal Code	Telephone Number(s) Area Code	Area Code
	Day ▶	Evening ▶

Detailed description of requested records, personal information records or personal information to be corrected. (If you are requesting access to, or correction of, your personal information, please identify the personal information bank or record containing the personal information, if known)

Note: If you are requesting a correction of personal information, please indicate the desired correction and, if appropriate, attach any supporting documentation. You will be notified if the correction is not made and you may require that a statement of disagreement be attached to your personal information.

Preferred method of access to records	Signature	Date
☐ Examine Original		Day Month Year
☐ Receive Copy		

For Institution Use Only

Date received	Request Number	Comments
Day Month Year		

Personal information contained on this form is collected pursuant to the Municipal Freedom of Information and Protection of Privacy Act and will be used for the purpose of responding to your request. Questions about this collection should be directed to the Freedom of Information and Privacy Coordinator at the institution where the request is made.

1278

O. Reg. 517/90, Form 2.

ONTARIO COLLEGE OF TEACHERS ACT, 1996
1996, c. 12, as am. 1997, c. 31, s. 161

PART I
DEFINITIONS

1. Definitions.—In this Act,

"by-laws".—"by-laws" means the by-laws made under this Act; ("règlements administratifs")

"College".—"College" means the Ontario College of Teachers; ("Ordre")

"document".—"document" means a record of information in any form and includes any part of it; ("document")

"Minister".—"Minister" means the Minister responsible for the administration of this Act; ("ministre")

"regulations".—"regulations" means the regulations made under this Act; ("règlements")

"school board".—"school board" means a board as defined in subsection 1(1) of the *Education Act.* ("conseil scolaire")

1997, c. 31, s. 161.

PART II
COLLEGE

2. (1) **College established.**—The College is established under the name Ontario College of Teachers in English and Ordre des enseignantes et des enseignants de l'Ontario in French.

(2) **Body corporate.**—The College is a body corporate without share capital with all the powers of a natural person.

(3) **Non-application of certain Acts.**—The *Corporations Act* and *Corporations Information Act* do not apply to the College, except as specifically made applicable by this Act or the regulations.

3. (1) **Objects.**—The College has the following objects:
1. To regulate the profession of teaching and to govern its members.
2. To develop, establish and maintain qualifications for membership in the College.
3. To accredit professional teacher education programs offered by post-secondary educational institutions.
4. To accredit ongoing education programs for teachers offered by post-secondary educational institutions and other bodies.
5. To issue, renew, amend, suspend, cancel, revoke and reinstate certificates of qualification and registration.
6. To provide for the ongoing education of members of the College.
7. To establish and enforce professional standards and ethical standards applicable to members of the College.

8. To receive and investigate complaints against members of the College and to deal with discipline and fitness to practise issues.
9. To develop, provide and accredit educational programs leading to certificates of qualification additional to the certificate required for membership, including but not limited to certificates of qualification as a supervisory officer, and to issue, renew, amend, suspend, cancel, revoke and reinstate such additional certificates.
10. To communicate with the public on behalf of the members of the College.
11. To perform such additional functions as are prescribed by the regulations.

(2) **Duty.**—In carrying out its objects, the College has a duty to serve and protect the public interest.

4. (1) **Council.**—The College shall have a Council that shall be its governing body and board of directors and that shall manage and administer its affairs.

(2) **Composition of Council.**—The Council shall be composed of,
(a) 17 persons who are members of the College and who are elected by the members of the College in accordance with the regulations; and
(b) 14 persons who are appointed by the Lieutenant Governor in Council in accordance with the regulations.

(3) **Role of Registrar.**—The Registrar shall serve as secretary to the Council and has all the rights of participation at meetings of the Council that a member of the Council has, other than the right to vote.

(4) **Expenses and remuneration.**—Council members appointed by the Lieutenant Governor in Council shall be paid, by the Minister, such expenses and remuneration as the Lieutenant Governor in Council determines.

5. (1) **Term of office.**—No term of a Council member shall exceed three years, except as permitted by regulation.

(2) **Multiple terms.**—A person may be a Council member for more than one term but no person may be a Council member for more than 10 consecutive years.

6. (1) **Qualifications to vote.**—Subject to the regulations, every member of the College who is in good standing is entitled to vote at an election of members of the Council.

(2) **Good standing.**—A member is in good standing for the purposes of this section if,
(a) the member is not in default of payment of a membership fee prescribed by the by-laws; and
(b) the member's certificate of qualification and registration is not suspended.

7. Vacancies.—Where one or more vacancies occur in the membership of the Council, the members remaining in office constitute the Council so long as their number is not fewer than a quorum.

8. (1) **Council meetings.**—The Council shall meet at least four times a year.

(2) **Open to public.**—The meetings of the Council shall be open to the public and reasonable notice shall be given to the members of the College and to the public.

(3) **Exclusion of public.**—Despite subsection (2), the Council may exclude the public from a meeting or any part of a meeting if it is satisfied that,
(a) financial or personal or other matters may be disclosed of such a nature that the

desirability of avoiding public disclosure of them in the interest of any person affected or in the public interest outweighs the desirability of adhering to the principle that meetings be open to the public;
(b) a person involved in a civil or criminal proceeding may be prejudiced;
(c) the safety of a person may be jeopardized;
(d) personnel matters or property transactions will be discussed;
(e) litigation affecting the College will be discussed or instructions will be given to or opinions received from solicitors for the College; or
(f) the Council will deliberate whether to exclude the public from a meeting or a part of a meeting.

9. (1) **Officers.**—The Council may employ such persons as it considers advisable and shall have the officers provided for by the by-laws.

(2) **Registrar.**—The Council shall appoint one of its employees as the Registrar and may appoint one or more deputy registrars who shall have the powers of the Registrar for the purposes of this Act.

(3) **Chief executive officer.**—The Registrar shall be the chief executive officer of the College.

10. (1) **Meeting with Minister.**—The Council shall meet annually with the Minister.

(2) **Open to public.**—Subsections 8(2) and (3) apply to the annual meeting with the Minister.

11. (1) **Annual report.**—The Council shall report annually to the Minister on the activities and financial affairs of the College.

(2) **Tabling of report.**—The Minister shall submit the report to the Lieutenant Governor in Council and shall then table the report in the Assembly if it is in session or, if not, at the next session.

12. (1) **Powers of Minister.**—In addition to his or her other powers and duties under this Act, the Minister may,
(a) review the activities of the Council and require the Council to provide reports and information;
(b) require the Council to do anything that, in the opinion of the Minister, is necessary or advisable to carry out the intent of this Act;
(c) require the Council to make, amend or revoke a regulation.

(2) **Council to comply.**—If the Minister requires a Council to do anything under subsection (1), the Council shall, within the time and in the manner specified by the Minister, comply with the requirement and submit a report to the Minister respecting the compliance.

(3) **Regulations.**—If the Minister requires the Council to make, amend or revoke a regulation under clause (1)(c) and the Council does not do so within 60 days, the Lieutenant Governor in Council may, by regulation, make, amend or revoke the regulation.

(4) **Authority of Lieutenant Governor in Council.**—Subsections (3) does not give the Lieutenant Governor in Council authority to do anything that the Council does not have authority to do.

(5) **Copies of regulations, orders.**—The Council shall ensure that a copy of each regulation made under subsection (3) is available for public inspection in the Office of the College.

(6) **Same.**—The Registrar shall provide to any person, on payment of a reasonable charge, a copy of any regulation made under subsection (3).

(7) **Expenses of College.**—The Minister may pay the College for expenses incurred in complying with a requirement under subsection (1).

13. Annual meeting of members.—The College shall hold an annual meeting of the members not more than 15 months after the holding of the last preceding annual meeting of members.

14. (1) **Membership.**—Every person who holds a certificate of qualification and registration is a member of the College, subject to any term, condition or limitation to which the certificate is subject.

(2) **Resignation of membership.**—A member may resign his or her membership by filing a resignation in writing with the Registrar.

(3) **Same.**—The certificate of qualification and registration of a person who files a resignation is cancelled.

(4) **Expiry of membership.**—A certificate of qualification and registration that expires in accordance with the regulations is cancelled.

(5) **Continuing jurisdiction: revocation, cancellation.**—A person whose certificate of qualification and registration is revoked or cancelled continues to be subject to the jurisdiction of the College for professional misconduct, incompetence or incapacity referable to any time during which the person held,

    (a) a certificate of qualification and registration under this Act; or

    (b) an Ontario Teacher's Certificate or a letter of standing as a teacher under the *Education Act*.

15. (1) **Committees.**—The Council shall establish the following committees:
1. Executive Committee.
2. Investigation Committee.
3. Discipline Committee.
4. Registration Appeals Committee.
5. Fitness to Practise Committee.

(2) **Same.**—The Council may establish other committees as the Council from time to time considers necessary.

(3) **Vacancies.**—Where one or more vacancies occur in the membership of a committee, the members remaining in office constitute the committee so long as their number is not fewer than the quorum.

16. Executive Committee.—The Council may delegate to the Executive Committee the authority to exercise any power or perform any duty of the Council other than the power to make, amend or revoke a regulation or by-law.

17. (1) **Majority on committees.**—A majority of the persons appointed or elected to a Committee mentioned in subsection 15(1) shall be persons elected to the Council under clause 4(2)(a).

(2) **Panels.**—A panel of a committee mentioned in subsection 15(1) that consists of more than one person shall include at least one person elected to the Council under clause 4(2)(a) and at least one person appointed to the Council under clause 4(2)(b).

PART III

REGISTRATION

18. (1) **Registration.**—The Registrar shall issue a certificate of qualification and registration to a person who applies for it in accordance with the regulations and who fulfils the requirements specified in the regulations for the issuance of the certificate.

(2) **Grounds for refusal.**—The Registrar may refuse to issue a certificate of qualification and registration where the Registrar has reasonable grounds to believe that,
  (a) the past conduct or actions of the applicant afford grounds for belief that the applicant will not perform his or her duties as a teacher in accordance with the law, including but not limited to this Act, the regulations and the by-laws; or
  (c) the applicant does not fulfil the requirements specified in the regulations for the issuance of the certificate.

(3) **Same.**—Except as otherwise directed under this Act, the Registrar shall refuse to issue a certificate of qualification and registration to an applicant who previously held a certificate of qualification and registration that was revoked as a result of a decision of the Discipline Committee or the Fitness to Practise Committee and that was not reinstated under section 33 or 34.

(4) **Terms, etc., on consent.**—If the Registrar is of the opinion that a certificate of qualification and registration should be issued to an applicant with terms, conditions or limitations imposed and the applicant consents to the imposition, the Registrar may do so.

(5) **Same.**—Limitations that may be imposed on consent under subsection (4) include the fixing of a period of not longer than one year during which the applicant may not apply under section 22.

19. (1) **Disclosure of application file.**—The Registrar shall give an applicant for a certificate of qualification and registration, at the applicant's request, a copy of each document the College has that is relevant to the application.

(2) **Exception.**—The Registrar may refuse to give an applicant anything that may, in the Registrar's opinion, jeopardize the safety of any person.

20. (1) **Notice of proposal to refuse to issue, revoke, etc..**—Where the Registrar purposes,
  (a) to refuse to issue a certificate of qualification and registration; or
  (b) to impose terms, conditions or limitations on a certificate of qualification and registration to which the applicant has not consented,
the Registrar shall first serve notice of the proposal, with written reasons for it, on the applicant.

(2) **Exception.**—Subsection (1) does not apply where the Registrar refuses to issue a certificate under subsection 18(3).

(3) **Contents of notice.**—A notice under subsection (1) shall state that the applicant may request a review by the Registration Appeals Committee in accordance with subsection (4).

(4) **Request for review.**—The request for review must be,
  (a) in writing;
  (b) served on the Registrar within 60 days after the notice under subsection (1) is served on the applicant; and

(c) accompanied by the fee prescribed by the by-laws for the purpose.

(5) **Submissions.**—The request for review may be accompanied by written submissions.

(6) **Power of Registrar where no review.**—Where the applicant does not request a review by the Registration Appeals Committee in accordance with subsection (4), the Registrar may carry out the proposal stated in the notice under subsection (1).

(7) **Same.**—Where the Registrar imposes terms, conditions and limitations on the applicant's certificate of qualification and registration under subsection (6), the Registrar may fix a period of not longer than one year during which the applicant may not apply under section 22.

21. (1) **Review by Registration Appeals Committee.**—Where the applicant requests a review in accordance with subsection 20(4), the Registration Appeals Committee shall conduct the review.

(2) **Exception.**—Despite subsection (1), the Registration Appeals Committee may refuse to conduct a review if, in its opinion, the request for review is frivolous, vexatious or an abuse of process.

(3) **Extension of time for requesting review.**—The Registration Appeals Committee may extend the time for requesting a review under subsection 20(4) where it is satisfied that there are apparent grounds for granting relief and that there are reasonable grounds for applying for the extension.

(4) **Same.**—The Committee may give the directions that it considers appropriate consequent on the extension.

(5) **Same.**—Directions may be given under subsection (4) to the applicant, to the Registrar or to both, either before or after the Committee conducts the review.

(6) **Same.**—Directions that may be given to the Registrar under subsection (4) include but are not limited to directions to do one or more of the following:
1. Remove specified terms, conditions or limitations on a certificate of qualification and registration issued under section 20.
2. Impose specified terms, conditions or limitations on a certificate of qualification and registration issued under section 20.
3. Revoke a certificate of qualification and registration issued under section 20.
4. Vary or eliminate a period fixed under subsection 20(7).

(7) **Examination of documents, submissions.**—The Registration Appeals Committee shall ensure that the person requesting the review is given an opportunity to examine and make written submissions on any documents that the Committee intends to consider in making its decision on the review.

(8) **No hearing.**—Except as provided by section 20 and this section, the Registration Appeals Committee need not hold a hearing or afford to any person an opportunity for a hearing or an opportunity to make oral or written submissions before making a decision or giving a direction under this section.

(9) **Orders.**—After considering the request for review, the submissions and any document that the Committee considers relevant, the Registration Appeals Committee may make an order doing one or more of the following:
1. Directing the Registrar to issue a certificate of qualification and registration.
2. Directing the Registrar to issue a certificate of qualification and registration if the

applicant fulfils requirements specified in the regulations for the issuance of the certificate.
3. Directing the Registrar to issue a certificate of qualification and registration subject to specified terms, conditions or limitations.
4. Directing the Registrar to refuse to issue a certificate of qualification and registration.

(10) **Same.**—Where the Registration Appeals Committee makes an order under paragraph 3 of subsection (9), the Committee may fix a period of not longer than one year during which the person who requested the review may not apply under section 22.

(11) **Order to return fee.**—The Registration Appeals Committee may order that the fee paid under subsection 20(4) be returned to the person who requested the review where, in the opinion of the Committee, to do so would be appropriate in all the circumstances.

(12) **Service of decision on parties.**—The Registration Appeals Committee shall give its decision under this section in writing, with reasons, and shall serve the person who requested the review with a copy.

22. (1) **Application for variation.**—A member may apply to the Registration Appeals Committee for an order directing the Registrar to remove or modify any term, condition or limitation imposed by the Registrar or the Registration Appeals Committee on the member's certificate of qualification and registration.

(2) **Same.**—The application must be,
(a) in writing; and
(b) accompanied by the fee prescribed for the purpose by the by-laws.

(3) **Limitations.**—The right to apply under subsection (1) is subject to,
(a) any limitation imposed by the Registrar or Registration Appeals Committee under section 18, 20 or 21; and
(b) any limitation imposed under subsection (8) in the disposition of a previous application under this section.

(4) **Submissions.**—The application may be accompanied by written submissions.

(5) **Examination of documents, submissions.**—The Registration Appeals Committee shall ensure that the applicant is given an opportunity to examine and make written submissions on any documents that the Committee intends to consider in making its decision on the application.

(6) **No hearing.**—Except as provided by this section, the Registration Appeals Committee need not hold a hearing or afford to any person an opportunity for a hearing or an opportunity to make oral or written submissions before making a decision or giving a direction under this section.

(7) **Orders.**—After considering the application, the submissions and any document that the Committee considers relevant, the Registration Appeals Committee may make an order doing one or more of the following:
1. Refusing the application.
2. Directing the Registrar to remove any term, condition or limitation imposed on the certificate of qualification and registration.
3. Directing the Registrar to impose specified terms, conditions or limitations on the certificate of qualification and registration.

(8) **Limitations on application.**—The Registration Appeals Committee, in disposing of an application under this section, may fix a period of not longer than six months during which the applicant may not apply under subsection (1).

(9) **Order to return fee.**—The Registration Appeals Committee may order that the fee paid under subsection (2) be returned to the applicant where, in the opinion of the Committee, to do so would be appropriate in all the circumstances.

(10) **Service of decision on applicant.**—The Registration Appeals Committee shall give its decision under this section in writing, with reasons, and shall serve the applicant with a copy.

23. (1) **Register.**—The Registrar shall maintain a register.

(2) **Contents.**—Subject to any by-law respecting the removal of information from the register, the register shall contain,

- (a) each member's name and the class of certificate of qualification and registration and any certificates of additional qualifications that the member holds;
- (b) the terms, conditions and limitations imposed on each certificate of qualification and registration;
- (c) a notation of every revocation, cancellation and suspension of a certificate of qualification and registration;
- (d) information that a committee required by this Act directs shall be included; and
- (e) information that the by-laws prescribe as information to be kept in the register.

(3) **Inspection.**—Any person has the right, during normal business hours, to inspect the register.

(4) **Copies.**—The Registrar shall provide to any person, on payment of a reasonable charge, a copy of any part of the register.

24. (1) **Suspension: failure to pay fees, provide information.**—The Registrar may suspend a member's certificate of qualification and registration for,

- (a) failure to pay a fee or penalty prescribed by the by-laws; or
- (b) failure to provide information required by the by-laws.

(2) **Same.**—The Registrar shall not suspend a member's certificate of qualification and registration without first giving the member two-months notice of the default and intention to suspend.

(3) **Re-instatement.**—A person whose certificate of qualification and registration was suspended by the Registrar under subsection (1) is entitled to have the suspension removed on payment of the fees and penalties prescribed by the by-laws or on provision of the information required by the by-laws, as the case may be.

PART IV

INVESTIGATION COMMITTEE

25. (1) **Composition of Investigation Committee.**—The Council shall appoint at least seven of its members to the Investigation Committee.

(2) **Same.**—At least two of the members of the Investigation Committee shall be persons who were appointed to the Council by the Lieutenant Governor in Council.

(3) **Same.**—No person who is a member of the Discipline Committee or the Fitness to Practise Committee shall be a member of the Investigation Committee.

26. (1) **Duties of Investigation Committee.**—The Investigation Committee shall consider and investigate complaints regarding the conduct or actions of a member of the College made by,
- (a) a member of the public;
- (b) a member of the College;
- (c) the Registrar;
- (d) the Minister.

(2) **Same.**—Despite subsection (1), the Investigation Committee shall refuse to consider and investigate a complaint if, in its opinion,
- (a) the complaint does not relate to professional misconduct, incompetence or incapacity on the part of a member;
- (b) the complaint is frivolous, vexatious or an abuse of process.

(3) **Same.**—No action shall be taken by the Investigation Committee under subsection (5) unless,
- (a) a complaint in a format prescribed by the by-laws has been filed with the Registrar;
- (b) the member whose conduct or actions are being investigated has been notified of the complaint and given at least 30 days in which to submit in writing to the Committee any explanations or representations the member may wish to make concerning the matter; and
- (c) The Committee has examined or has made every reasonable effort to examine all the information and documents that the College has that are relevant to the complaint.

(4) **Same.**—Notice of a complaint under clause (3)(b) shall include reasonable information about any allegations contained in the complaint.

(5) **Same.**—The Investigation Committee in accordance with the information it receives may,
- (a) direct that the matter be referred, in whole or in part, to the Discipline Committee or the Fitness to Practise Committee;
- (b) direct that the matter not be referred under clause (a);
- (c) require the person complained against to appear before the Investigation Committee to be cautioned or admonished; or
- (d) take such action as it considers appropriate in the circumstances and that is not inconsistent with this Act, the regulations or the by-laws.

(6) **Decision and reasons.**—The Investigation Committee shall give its decision in writing to the Registrar for the purposes of subsection (7) and, except where the decision is made under clause (5)(a), its reasons for the decision.

(7) **Notice.**—The Registrar shall provide the complainant and the person complained against with a copy of the written decision made by the Investigation Committee and its reasons for the decision, if any.

(8) **No hearing.**—Except as provided by this section, the Investigation Committee need not hold a hearing or afford to any person an opportunity for a hearing or an opportunity to make oral or written submissions before making a decision or giving a direction under this section.

(9) **Timely disposal.**—The Investigation Committee shall use it best efforts to dispose of a complaint within 120 days of it being filed with the Registrar.

PART V

DISCIPLINE AND FITNESS TO PRACTISE

27. (1) **Composition of Discipline Committee.**—The Council shall appoint at least 11 of its members to the Discipline Committee.

(2) **Same.**—At least four of the members of the Discipline Committee shall be persons who were appointed to the Council by the Lieutenant Governor in Council.

(3) **Chair of Committee.**—The Council shall appoint one of the members of the Discipline Committee as the Chair.

28. (1) **Composition of Fitness to Practise Committee.**—The Council shall appoint at least five of its members to the Fitness to Practise Committee.

(2) **Same.**—At least one of the members of the Fitness to Practise Committee shall be a person who was appointed to the Council by the Lieutenant Governor in Council.

(3) **Chair of Committee.**—The Council shall appoint one of the members of the Fitness to Practise Committee as the Chair.

29. (1) **Reference by Council or Executive Committee.**—The Council or the Executive Committee may direct the Discipline Committee to hold a hearing and determine any allegation of professional misconduct or incompetence on the part of a member of the College.

(2) **Same.**—The Council or the Executive Committee may direct the Fitness to Practise Committee to hold a hearing and determine any allegation of incapacity on the part of a member of the College.

(3) **Interim suspension.**—The Council or the Executive Committee may make an interim order directing the Registrar to suspend a member's certificate of qualification and registration or impose terms, conditions or limitations on a member's certificate of qualification and registration if,
   (a) an allegation respecting the member has been referred to the Discipline Committee or to the Fitness to Practise Committee; and
   (b) the Council or the Executive Committee is of the opinion that the actions or conduct of the member exposes or is likely to expose students to harm or injury.

(4) **Restriction.**—No order shall be made under subsection (3) unless the member has been given,
   (a) notice of the Executive Committee's or the Council's intention to make the order; and
   (b) at least 14 days to make written submissions to the Executive Committee or the Council.

(5) **Same.**—Clause (4)(b) does not apply where the Executive Committee or the Council is of the opinion that the delay would be inappropriate in view of the risk of harm or injury to students.

(6) **No hearing.**—Except as provided by this section, the Executive Committee or the Council need not hold a hearing or afford any person an opportunity to make oral or written submissions before making a decision or giving a direction under this section.

(7) **Procedure following order.**—If an order is made under subsection (3) in relation to a matter referred to the Discipline Committee or the Fitness to Practise Committee,
- (a) the College shall prosecute the matter expeditiously; and
- (b) the Discipline Committee or the Fitness to Practise Committee shall give precedence to the matter.

(8) **Duration of order.**—An order under subsection (3) continues in force until the matter is disposed of by the Discipline Committee or the Fitness to Practise Committee.

30. (1) **Duties of Discipline Committee.**—The Discipline Committee shall,
- (a) hear and determine matters directed or referred to it under section 26, 29 or 33; and
- (b) perform such other duties as are assigned to it by the Council.

(2) **Professional misconduct.**—A member may be found guilty of professional misconduct by the Discipline Committee, after a hearing, if the member has been guilty, in the opinion of the Committee, of professional misconduct as defined in the regulations.

(3) **Incompetence.**—The Discipline Committee may, after a hearing, find a member to be incompetent if, in its opinion, the member has displayed in his or her professional responsibilities a lack of knowledge, skill or judgment or disregard for the welfare of a student of a nature or extent that demonstrates that the member is unfit to continue to carry out his or her professional responsibilities or that a certificate held by the member under this Act should be made subject to terms, conditions or limitations.

(4) **Powers of Discipline Committee.**—Where the Discipline Committee finds a member guilty of professional misconduct or to be incompetent, it may make an order doing one or more of the following:
1. Directing the Registrar to revoke any certificate held by the member under this Act.
2. Directing the Registrar to suspend any certificate held by the member under this Act for a stated period, not exceeding 24 months.
3. Directing the Registrar to impose specified terms, conditions or limitations on any certificate held by the member under this Act.
4. Directing that the imposition of a penalty be postponed for a specified period and not be imposed if specified terms are met within that period.

(5) **Same.**—Where the Discipline Committee finds a member guilty of professional misconduct, it may, in addition to exercising its powers under subsection (4), make an order doing one or more of the following:
1. Requiring that the member be reprimanded, admonished or counselled by the Committee or its delegate and, if considered warranted, directing that the fact of the reprimand, admonishment or counselling be recorded on the register for a specified or unlimited period.
2. Imposing a fine in an amount that the Committee considers appropriate, to a maxi-

mum of $5,000, to be paid by the member to the Minister of Finance for payment into the Consolidated Revenue Fund.
3. Directing that the finding and the order of the Committee be published, in detail or in summary, with or without the name of the member, in the official publication of the College and in any other manner or medium that the Committee considers appropriate in the particular case.
4. Fixing costs to be paid by the member to the College.

(6) **Same.**—In making an order under paragraph 4 of subsection (4), the Committee may specify the terms that it considers appropriate, including but not limited to terms requiring the successful completion by the member of specified courses of study.

(7) **Same.**—In making an order revoking or suspending a certificate or imposing terms, conditions or limitations on a certificate, the Committee may fix a period during which the member may not apply under section 33.

(8) **Publication on request.**—The Discipline Committee shall cause a determination by the Committee that an allegation of professional misconduct or incompetence was unfounded to be published in the official publication of the College, on the request of the member against whom the allegation was made.

(9) **Costs.**—Where the Discipline Committee is of the opinion that the commencement of the proceeding was unwarranted, the Committee may order that the College reimburse the member for his or her costs or such portion of them as the Discipline Committee fixes.

31. (1) **Duties of the Fitness to Practise Committee.**—The Fitness to Practise Committee shall,
 (a) hear and determine matters directed or referred to it under section 26, 29 or 33; and
 (b) perform such other duties as are assigned to it by the Council.

(2) **Incapacity.**—The Fitness to Practise Committee may, after a hearing, find a member to be incapacitated if, in its opinion, the member is suffering from a physical or mental condition or disorder such that the member is unfit to continue to carry out his or her professional responsibilities or that a certificate held by the member under this Act should be made subject to terms, conditions or limitations.

(3) **Powers of Fitness to Practise Committee.**—Where the Fitness to Practise Committee finds a member to be incapacitated, it may make an order doing one or more of the following:
1. Directing the Registrar to revoke any certificate held by the member under this Act.
2. Directing the Registrar to suspend any certificate held by the member under this Act for a stated period, not exceeding 24 months.
3. Directing the Registrar to impose specified terms, conditions or limitations on any certificate held by the member under this Act.
4. Directing that the imposition of a penalty be postponed for a specified period and not be imposed if specified terms are met within that period.

(4) **Same.**—In making an order under paragraph 4 of subsection (3), the Committee may specify the terms that it considers appropriate, including but not limited to terms requiring the production to the Committee of evidence satisfactory to it that any physical or mental condition or disorder in respect of which the penalty was imposed has been resolved.

PART V — DISCIPLINE AND FITNESS TO PRACTISE   S. 32

(5) **Same.**—In making an order revoking or suspending a certificate or imposing terms, conditions or limitations on a certificate, the Committee may fix a period during which the member may not apply under section 33.

(6) **Publication on request.**—The Fitness to Practise Committee shall cause a determination by the Committee that an allegation of incapacity was unfounded to be published in the official publication of the College, on the request of the member against whom the allegation was made.

(7) **Costs.**—Where the Fitness to Practise Committee is of the opinion that the commencement of the proceeding was unwarranted, the Committee may order that the College reimburse the member for his or her costs or such portion of them as the Committee fixes.

32. (1) **Procedure: s. 30 hearings.**—This section applies to hearings of the Discipline Committee under section 30 and to hearings of the Fitness to Practise Committee under section 31.

(2) **Parties.**—The College and the member whose conduct or actions are being investigated are parties to the hearing.

(3) **Examination of documentary evidence.**—A party to the hearing shall be given an opportunity to examine before the hearing any documents that will be given in evidence at the hearing.

(4) **Members holding hearing not to have taken part in investigation, etc..**—Members of the Discipline Committee or Fitness to Practise Committee holding a hearing shall not have taken part before the hearing in any investigation of the subject-matter of the hearing other than as a member of the Council or Executive Committee considering the referral of the matter to the Discipline Committee or Fitness to Practise Committee, and shall not communicate directly or indirectly about the subject-matter of the hearing with any person or with any party or representative of a party except on notice to and opportunity for all parties to participate.

(5) **Same.**—Despite subsection (4), the Discipline Committee or Fitness to Practise Committee may seek legal advice from an adviser independent from the parties and, in that case, the nature of the advice shall be made known to the parties so that they may make submissions as to the law.

(6) **Hearings of Discipline Committee to be public.**—A hearing of the Discipline Committee shall, subject to subsection (7), be open to the public.

(7) **Exclusion of public.**—The Discipline Committee may make an order that the public be excluded from a hearing or any part of a hearing if the Committee is satisfied that,
  (a) matters involving public security may be disclosed;
  (b) financial or personal or other matters may be disclosed at the hearing of such a nature that the desirability of avoiding public disclosure of them in the interest of any person affected or in the public interest outweighs the desirability of adhering to the principle that hearings be open to the public;
  (c) a person involved in a civil or criminal proceeding may be prejudiced;
  (d) the safety of a person may be jeopardized; or
  (e) the Committee will deliberate whether to exclude the public from a hearing or a part of a hearing.

(8) **Fitness to Practise Committee hearings to be closed.**—A hearing of the Fitness to Practise Committee shall, subject to subsection (9), be closed to the public.

(9) **Open on request of member in some cases.**—A hearing of the Fitness to Practise Committee shall be open to the public if the person who is alleged to be incapacitated requests it in a written notice received by the Registrar before the day the hearing commences, unless the Fitness to Practise Committee is satisfied that,
 (a) matters involving public security may be disclosed;
 (b) financial or personal or other matters may be disclosed at the hearing of such a nature that the desirability of avoiding public disclosure of them in the interest of any person affected or in the public interest outweighs the desirability of acceding to the request of the person who is alleged to be incapacitated;
 (c) a person involved in a civil or criminal proceeding may be prejudiced;
 (d) the safety of a person may be jeopardized; or
 (e) the Committee will deliberate whether to exclude the public from a hearing or a part of a hearing.

(10) **Recording of evidence.**—The oral evidence taken before the Discipline Committee or Fitness to Practise Committee shall be recorded and, if requested by a party, copies of a transcript shall be provided to the party at the party's expense.

(11) **Only members at hearing to participate in decision.**—No member of the Discipline Committee or Fitness to Practise Committee shall participate in a decision of the Committee following a hearing unless he or she was present throughout the hearing and heard the evidence and argument of the parties.

(12) **Release of documentary evidence.**—Documents and things put in evidence at a hearing shall, on the request of the party who produced them, be returned by the Discipline Committee or Fitness to Practise Committee within a reasonable time after the matter in issue has been finally determined.

(13) **Service of decision, reasons.**—Subject to subsection (14), the Discipline Committee or Fitness to Practise Committee shall serve its decision, with reasons,
 (a) on the parties; and
 (b) where the matter was referred to the Discipline Committee or Fitness to Practise Committee as a result of a complaint under subsection 26(1), on the complainant.

(14) **Same.**—Where the hearing was closed, the Discipline Committee or Fitness to Practise Committee may, in its discretion, serve its decision on the complainant without reasons.

PART VI

REINSTATEMENT AND VARIATION

33. (1) **Reinstatement after disciplinary proceedings.**—A person who has had a certificate revoked or suspended as a result of a proceeding before the Discipline Committee may apply in writing to the Registrar to have a new certificate issued or the suspension removed.

(2) **Variation after disciplinary proceedings.**—A person who has a certificate that is subject to terms, conditions or limitations as a result of a proceeding before the Discipline

Committee may apply in writing to the Registrar for the removal or modification of the terms, conditions or limitations.

(3) **Time of application.**—An application under subsection (1) or (2) shall not be made before the expiry of the period fixed for the purpose by the Discipline Committee under subsection 30(7) or under paragraph 6 of subsection (6), as the case may be.

(4) **Same.**—If the Discipline Committee did not fix a period under subsection 30(7) or under paragraph 6 of subsection (6), an application under subsection (1) or (2) shall not be made earlier than one year from the date of the order under section 30 or the date of the last order made under this section, as the case may be.

(5) **Referral of Discipline Committee.**—The Registrar shall refer an application under subsection (1) or (2) to the Discipline Committee.

(6) **Order.**—The Discipline Committee may, after a hearing, make an order doing one or more of the following:
1. Refusing the application.
2. Directing the Registrar to issue a certificate to the applicant.
3. Directing the Registrar to remove the suspension of the applicant's certificate.
4. Directing the Registrar to impose specified terms, conditions and limitations on a certificate of the applicant.
5. Directing the Registrar to remove any term, conditions or limitations on a certificate of the applicant.
6. Fixing a period during which the applicant may not apply under this section.

(7) **Parties.**—The College and the applicant are parties to the hearing.

(8) **Examination of documentary evidence.**—A party to the hearing shall be given an opportunity to examine before the hearing any documents that will be given in evidence at the hearing.

(9) **Closed hearings.**—Hearings of the Discipline Committee under this section shall be closed to the public.

(10) **Recording of evidence.**—If requested by a party, the oral evidence taken before the Discipline Committee under this section shall be recorded and, if requested by a party, copies of a transcript shall be provided to the party at the party's expense.

(11) **Only members at hearing to participate in decision.**—No member of the Discipline Committee shall participate in a decision of the Committee under this section unless he or she was present throughout the hearing and heard the evidence and the argument of the parties.

(12) **Release of documentary evidence.**—Documents and things put in evidence at a hearing under this section shall, on the request of the party who produced them, be returned by the Discipline Committee within a reasonable time after the matter in issue has been finally determined.

(13) **Service of decision on parties.**—The Discipline Committee shall give its decision under this section in writing, with reasons, and shall serve each party with a copy of the decision.

(14) **Fitness to Practise Committee.**—Subsections (1) to (13) apply with necessary modifications to the Fitness to Practise Committee and, for the purpose,

(a) a reference to the Discipline Committee shall be deemed to be a reference to the Fitness to Practise Committee;
(b) a reference to subsection 30(7) shall be deemed to be a reference to subsection 31(5);
(c) a reference to section 30 shall be deemed to be a reference to section 31.

34. Reinstatement: no hearing.—The Council or Executive Committee may, without a hearing, with respect to a member or former member who has had a certificate suspended or revoked for any reason under this Act, make an order doing one or more of the following:
1. Directing the Registrar to issue a certificate to the member or former member.
2. Directing the Registrar to remove the suspension of the member's or former member's certificate.

PART VII

APPEALS TO COURT

35. (1) Appeal to court.—A party to a proceeding before the Registration Appeals Committee, the Discipline Committee or the Fitness to Practise Committee may appeal to the Divisional Court, in accordance with the rules of court, from the decision or order of the committee.

(2) **Same.**—For the purposes of this section,
(a) a person who requests a review under section 21 is a party to the review under section 21 by the Registration Appeals Committee; and
(b) a person who applies for an order under section 22 is a party to the proceeding under section 22 by the Registration Appeals Committee.

(3) **Certified copy of record.**—On the request of a party desiring to appeal to the Divisional Court and on payment of the fee prescribed by the by-laws for the purpose, the Registrar shall give the party a certified copy of the record of the proceeding, including any documents received in evidence and the decision or order appealed from.

(4) **Powers of court on appeal.**—An appeal under this section may be made on questions of law or fact or both and the court may affirm or may rescind the decision of the committee appealed from and may exercise all powers of the committee and may direct the committee to take any action which the committee may take and that the court considers appropriate and, for the purpose, the court may substitute its opinion for that of the committee or the court may refer the matter back to the committee for rehearing, in whole or in part, in accordance with such directions as the court considers appropriate.

PART VIII

REGISTRAR'S POWERS OF INVESTIGATION

36. (1) Registrar's investigation.—Where the Registrar believes on reasonable and probable grounds,
(a) that a member has committed an act of professional misconduct or is incompetent or incapacitated;

PART VIII — REGISTRAR'S POWERS OF INVESTIGATION   **S. 38**

    (b) that there is cause to refuse to issue a certificate applied for under this Act;
    (c) that there is cause to suspend or revoke a certificate issued under this Act; or
    (d) that there is cause to impose terms, conditions or limitations on a certificate applied for or issued under this Act,

the Registrar may appoint one or more investigators to investigate whether such act has occurred, such incompetence or incapacity exists or there is such cause.

(2) **Approval of Executive Committee.**—The Registrar shall not make an appointment under subsection (1) without the approval of the Executive Committee.

(3) **Powers of investigator.**—The investigator may inquire into and examine the conduct or actions of the member to be investigated as the conduct or actions relate to the member's professional responsibilities.

(4) **Same.**—The investigator has, for the purposes of the investigation, all the powers of a commission under Part II of the *Public Inquiries Act.*

(5) **Same.**—The investigator may, on production of his or her appointment, enter at any reasonable time the place of work of the member or the premises of the member's employer and may examine anything found there that is relevant to the investigation.

(6) **Obstruction of investigator.**—No person shall obstruct an investigator in the course of his or her duties or withhold or conceal from him or her or destroy anything that is relevant to the investigation.

37. (1) **Entries and searches.**—A justice of the peace may, on the application of an investigator, issue a warrant authorizing the investigator to enter and search a place and examine anything that is relevant to the investigation if the justice of the peace is satisfied that the investigator has been properly appointed and that there are reasonable and probable grounds for believing that,
    (a) the member being investigated has committed an act of professional misconduct or is incompetent or incapacitated; and
    (b) there is something relevant to the investigation at the place.

(2) **Searches by day unless stated.**—A warrant issued under subsection (1) does not authorize an entry or search after sunset and before sunrise unless it is expressly stated in the warrant.

(3) **Assistance and entry by force.**—An investigator entering and searching a place under the authority of a warrant issued under subsection (1) may be assisted by other persons and may enter a place by force.

(4) **Investigator to show identification.**—An investigator entering and searching a place under the authority of a warrant issued under subsection (1) shall produce his or her identification, on request, to any person at the place.

38. (1) **Copying of documents and objects.**—An investigator may copy, at the College's expense, a document or object that an investigator may examine under section 36 or under the authority of a warrant issued under section 37.

(2) **Removal for documents and objects.**—An investigator may remove a document or object described in subsection (1) if,
    (a) it is not practicable to copy it in the place where it is examined; or

(b) a copy of it is not sufficient for the purposes of the investigation.

(3) **Return of documents and objects or copies.**—If it is practicable to copy a document or object removed under subsection (2), the investigator shall,

(a) if it was removed under clause (2)(a), return the document or object within a reasonable time; or

(b) if it was removed under clause (2)(b), provide the person who was in possession of the document or object with a copy of it within a reasonable time.

(4) **Copy as evidence.**—A copy of a document or object certified by an investigator to be a true copy shall be received in evidence in any proceeding to the same extent and shall have the same evidentiary value as the document or object itself.

39. Report of investigation.—The Registrar shall report the results of an investigation to one or more of the Executive Committee, the Investigation Committee the Discipline Committee or the Fitness to Practise Committee, as the Registrar considers appropriate.

PART IX

REGULATIONS AND BY-LAWS

40. (1) **Regulations subject to approval.**—Subject to the approval of the Lieutenant Governor in Council and with prior review by the Minister, the Council may make regulations,

1. making any provision of the *Business Corporations Act*, the *Corporations Act* and the *Corporations Information Act* applicable to the College, with such modifications as the Council considers necessary or advisable;
2. defining constituencies along regional, occupational and other lines for the purpose of electing persons to the Council under clause 4(2)(a);
3. prescribing the number of representatives for each constituency defined under paragraph 2;
4. respecting qualifications, nomination procedures and election procedures for the purpose of electing persons to the Council under clause 4(2)(a);
5. prescribing the conditions disqualifying elected members from sitting on the Council and governing the removal of disqualified members of the Council;
6. extending the term of office of Council members by up to six months;
7. governing the filling of vacancies created on the Council by the departure of elected members of the Council;
8. prescribing the quorum of the Council;
9. respecting the composition and election or appointment of committees required by this Act, other than the Investigation Committee, the Discipline Committee and the Fitness to Practise Committee;
10. governing the filling of vacancies on the committees required by this Act;
11. prescribing terms of office of members of committees required by this Act;
12. respecting practice and procedure of committees required by this Act;
13. prescribing the quorums of the committees required by this Act;
14. providing for the establishment of panels of any committee required by this Act and providing that a panel of a committee may exercise the powers and carry out the duties of the committee, subject to the restrictions, if any, specified in the regulation;

15. designating persons or bodies for the purposes of section 47;
16. prescribing classes of certificates of qualification and registration, including but not limited to classes of certificates that are temporary, provisional or otherwise limited;
17. respecting terms, conditions and limitations that may be imposed on certificates of qualification and registration;
18. respecting requirements, including but not limited to standards, qualifications, examinations and experience requirements, for the issuance of certificates of qualification and registration and providing for exemptions from those requirements;
19. respecting the accreditation of teacher education programs offered by post-secondary educational institutions and on-going education programs for teachers offered by post-secondary educational institutions and other bodies.
20. respecting requirements, including but not limited to standards, qualifications, examinations and experience requirements, for the issuance of certificates in respect of qualifications of members additional to those required for a certificate of qualification and registration, including but not limited to certificates of qualification as a supervisory officer;
21. providing for exemptions from requirements under paragraph 20;
22. respecting the development, provision and accreditation of educational programs leading to certificates in respect of qualifications of members additional to those required for a certificate of qualification and registration, including but not limited to certificates of qualification as a supervisory officer;
23. establishing processes and criteria for issuing to members certificates in respect of qualifications additional to those required for a certificate of qualification and registration, including but not limited to certificates of qualification as a supervisory officer;
24. prescribing ongoing education requirements for members;
25. establishing processes and criteria for suspending certificates of members who fail to meet ongoing education requirements;
26. establishing processes and criteria for removing the suspension of certificates where the suspension was as a result of failure to meet ongoing education requirements;
27. establishing processes and criteria for suspending a certificate of qualification and registration under section 275 of the *Education Act*;
28. respecting any matter ancillary to this Act with respect to the issuance, expiry, renewal, amendment, suspension, cancellation, revocation and reinstatement of certificates issued under this Act;
29. requiring employers of members to deduct members' fees from their salaries and to submit the fees directly to the College, in the manner and within the times specified in the regulations;
30. prescribing penalties to be paid by employers for the late submission of fees to the College;
31. defining professional misconduct for the purposes of this Act.

(2) **Copies of regulations.**—The Council shall ensure that a copy of each regulation is available for public inspection in the office of the College.

(3) **Same.**—The Registrar shall provide to any person, on payment of a reasonable charge, a copy of any regulation made under this section.

(4) **Filling of vacancies.**—The regulations under paragraphs 7 and 10 of subsection 40(1) must set out procedures for filling vacancies on the Council and required committees and must require that each procedure for filling a vacancy begin within 10 days of the vacancy arising.

41. (1) **By-laws.**—The Council may make by-laws relating to the administrative and domestic affairs of the College including but not limited to by-laws,

1. prescribing the seal and other insignia of the College and providing for their use;
2. providing for the execution of documents by the College;
3. respecting banking and finance;
4. fixing the financial year of the College and providing for the audit of the accounts and transactions of the College;
5. respecting conflict of interest rules for members of the Council, for members of committees and for officers and employees of the College;
6. respecting indemnification by the College of members of the Council, of members of committees and of officers and employees of the College;
7. respecting the calling, holding and conducting of meetings of the Council and the duties of members of the Council;
8. providing for the remuneration of members of the Council and committees, other than persons appointed by the Lieutenant Governor in Council, and for the payment of the expenses of the Council and committees in the conduct of their business;
9. respecting the calling, holding and conducting of meetings of the members;
10. authorizing voting, by mail or other means, by the members on any of the business of the College and prescribing procedures for such voting;
11. prescribing positions of officers of the College, providing for the election or appointment of officers and prescribing the duties of officers;
12. prescribing forms and formats and providing for their use;
13. providing procedures for making, amending and revoking by-laws;
14. respecting the management of property of the College;
15. respecting the borrowing of money by the College and the giving of security in respect of the borrowing;
16. providing for the method of service of any document or class of documents given or served under this Act;
17. providing for the composition, election or appointment, powers, duties, quorums, practices and procedures of committees other than those required by this Act;
18. prescribing terms of office of members of committees other than those required by this Act;
19. prescribing the conditions disqualifying elected members of the Council from sitting on committees and governing the removal of disqualified members of committees;
20. governing the filling of vacancies on committees other than those required by this Act;
21. respecting reports to Council to be made by committees;
22. prescribing professional standards and ethical standards applicable to members;
23. prescribing annual membership fees and other fees payable by members, applicants

for membership and other persons for anything the Registrar or any committee is required or authorized to do under this Act;
24. prescribing penalties to be paid by members for the late payment of any fee;
25. prescribing any fee referred to in this Act as prescribed by the by-laws;
26. respecting the reporting and publication of decisions of the College, the Council and the committees;
27. respecting the keeping of a register of members, including but not limited to by-laws prescribing the information that must be kept in the register and the information that may be removed from the register;
28. requiring members to provide the College with information necessary for establishing and maintaining the register and for establishing and maintaining records necessary for the proper functioning of the College;
29. requiring members to provide the College with information about their participation in ongoing education programs;
30. respecting membership of the College in other organizations the objects of which are not inconsistent with and are complementary to those of the College, the payment of fees to such organizations and representation at meetings of such organizations;
31. providing for the establishment and dissolution and governing the operation of groups of members and respecting grants by the College to such groups;
32. authorizing the making of grants to advance knowledge of education or to maintain or improve standards of teaching or support or encourage public information and interest in education;
33. respecting scholarships, bursaries and prizes to assist in the education of teachers or persons wishing to become teachers.

(2) **Meetings by telecommunications, etc.**—A by-law made under paragraph 7 or 9 of subsection (1) may provide for the meetings to be held in any manner that allows all the persons participating to communicate with each other simultaneously and instantaneously.

(3) **Unanimous by-laws, etc..**—A by-law or resolution signed by all the members of the Council is as valid and effective as if passed at a meeting of the Council called, constituted and held for the purpose.

(4) **Copies of by-laws.**—The Council shall ensure that a copy of each by-law is given to the Minister and is available for public inspection in the office of the College.

(5) **Same.**—The Registrar shall provide to any person, on payment of a reasonable charge, a copy of any by-law made under this section.

42. (1) **Regulations made by Lieutenant Governor in Council.**—The Lieutenant Governor in Council may make regulations,
   (a) prescribing additional functions of the College for the purposes of paragraph 11 of subsection 3(1);
   (b) respecting the appointment of persons to the Council under clause 4(2)(b), including but not limited to regulations specifying how different interests are to be represented on the Council;
   (c) governing the election of the first Council of the College, including but not limited to prescribing eligibility of persons to vote or to run as candidates, election procedures and representation;

(d) providing for such transitional matters as the Lieutenant Governor in Council considers necessary or advisable in connection with the establishment of the College or the assumption of powers and duties by the College;

(e) providing for such other matters as the Lieutenant Governor in Council considers necessary or advisable in connection with the College.

(2) **Regulations under clause (1)(c) or (d).**—In the event of a conflict between a regulation made under clause (1)(c) or (d) and this or any other Act, the regulation prevails.

(3) **Same.**—A regulation made under clause (1)(d) may be retroactive in its effect.

43. (1) **Regulations and by-laws: general or specific.**—A regulation or by-law made under any provision of this Act may be general or specific.

(2) **Same.**—Without limiting the generality of subsection (1), a regulation or by-law may be limited in its application to any class of members, certificates or qualifications.

(3) **Classes.**—A class under this Act may be defined with respect to any attribute and may be defined to consist of or to exclude any specified member of the class, whether or not with the same attributes.

PART X

MISCELLANEOUS

44. (1) **Right to use French.**—A person has the right to use French in all dealings with the College.

(2) **Council to ensure.**—The Council shall take all reasonable measures and make all reasonable plans to ensure that persons may use French in all dealings with the College.

(3) **Limitation.**—The right to use French given by this section is subject to the limits that are reasonable in the circumstances.

(4) **Definition.**—In this section,

"**dealings**".—"dealings" means any service or procedure available to the public or to members of the College and includes giving or receiving communications, information or notices, making applications, taking examinations or tests and participating in programs or in hearings or reviews.

45. Official publication.—The Council shall establish and maintain an official publication of the Council.

46. (1) **Leave of absence.**—A member of the Council or of a committee established under this Act who attends a meeting or other proceeding of the Council or the committee during work hours, or who has been asked by the Registrar or his or her delegate to do other work of the College during work hours, shall be granted, on request, a paid leave of absence by his or her employer for the purpose.

(2) **Employer reimbursement.**—If an employer has provided a leave of absence to a member under subsection (1), the College shall reimburse the employer for the salary expense, if any, incurred by the employer in temporarily hiring a person to replace the member in the workplace.

47. (1) **Right to obtain information.**—For the purpose of carrying out its objects, the College may require the Provincial Schools Authority, a school board or any other person or body designated by the regulations to provide the College with information, including personal information within the meaning of section 38 of the *Freedom of Information and Protection and Privacy Act* or section 28 of the *Municipal Freedom of Information and Protection of Privacy Act*, in respect of members of the College.

(2) **Disclosure by school board: offences.**—A school board shall promptly notify the College in writing when the board becomes aware that a member who is or has been employed by the board,
- (a) has been convicted of an offence under the *Criminal Code* (Canada) involving sexual conduct and minors; or
- (b) has been convicted of an offence under the *Criminal Code* (Canada) that in the opinion of the board indicates that students may be at risk of harm or injury.

(3) **Disclosure by school board: conduct or actions of member.**—A school board shall promptly notify the College in writing where in the opinion of the board the conduct or actions of a member who is or has been employed by the board should be reviewed by a committee of the College.

(4) **Disclosure by minority language section: conduct or actions of member.**—For the purposes of subsection (3), where a board has a French-language section or English-language section, the section has the responsibilities of the board with respect to members who are or have been employed for schools or classes governed by the section.

(5) **Information provided by Minister to College.**—If required by the College for the purpose of carrying out its objects, the Minister may provide to the College information, including personal information within the meaning of section 38 of the *Freedom of Information and Protection of Privacy Act*, in respect of its members, former members and applicants for membership.

(6) **Information provided by College to Minister.**—For the purpose of carrying out his or her duties under the *Education Act*, the Minister has the authority to collect from the College information, including personal information within the meaning of section 38 of the *Freedom of Information and Protection of Privacy Act*, in respect of its members, former members and applicants for membership.

48. (1) **Confidentiality.**—Every person engaged in the administration of this Act, including any person appointed under section 36, shall preserve secrecy with respect to all matters that come to his or her knowledge in the course of his or her duties and shall not communicate any of those matters to any other person except,
- (a) as may be required in connection with the administration of this Act and the regulations and by-laws or any proceeding under this Act or the regulations or by-laws;
- (b) to his or her counsel;
- (c) with the consent of the person to whom the information relates; or
- (d) to the extent that the information is available to the public under this Act.

(2) **Testimony in civil proceeding.**—No person to whom subsection (1) applies shall be compelled to give testimony in any civil proceeding, other than a proceeding under this Act or an appeal or judicial review relating to a proceeding under this Act, with regard to information obtained in the course of his or her duties.

(3) **Evidence on civil proceedings.**—No record of a proceeding under this Act and no document or thing prepared for or statement given at such a proceeding and no order or decision made in such a proceeding is admissible in any civil proceeding, other than a proceeding under this Act or an appeal or judicial review relating to a proceeding under this Act.

(4) **Offence.**—Every person who contravenes subsection (1) is guilty of an offence and on conviction is liable to a fine of not more than $25,000.

49. Order directing compliance.—Where it appears to the College that any person does not comply with this Act or the regulations or by-laws, despite the imposition of any penalty in respect of such non-compliance and in addition to any other rights it may have, the College may apply to a judge of the Ontario Court (General Division) for an order directing the person to comply with the provision, and the judge may make the order or such other order as the judge thinks fit.

50. Offence: obstruction of investigator.—Any person who contravenes subsection 36(6) is guilty of an offence and on conviction is liable to a fine of not more than $10,000.

51. (1) **Offence: false representation to obtain certificate.**—Every person who makes a representation, knowing it to be false, for the purpose of having a certificate issued under this Act is guilty of an offence and on conviction is liable to a fine of not more than $10,000.

(2) **Offence: assisting in false representation.**—Every person who knowingly assists a person in committing an offence under subsection (1) is guilty of an offence and on conviction is liable to a fine of not more than $10,000.

52. (1) **Service of notice or document.**—A notice or document to be given or served under this Act is sufficiently given or served if it is,
   (a)   delivered personally;
   (b)   sent by mail; or
   (c)   given or served in accordance with by-laws respecting service.

(2) **Same.**—Where a notice or document to be given under this Act is sent by mail addressed to a person at the last address of the person in the records of the College, there is a rebuttable presumption that the notice or document is delivered to the person on the fifth day after the day of mailing.

53. Registrar's certificate as evidence.—Any statement containing information from the records required to be kept by the Registrar under this Act, purporting to be certified by the Registrar under the seal of the College, is admissible in evidence in a court of law as proof, in the absence of evidence to the contrary, of the facts stated in it, without proof of the appointment or signature of the Registrar and without proof of the seal.

54. *Statutory Powers Procedure Act.*—In the event of a conflict between this Act, the regulations or the by-laws and the *Statutory Powers Procedure Act*, the provisions of this Act, the regulations and the by-laws prevail.

55. Immunity of College.—No proceeding for damages shall be instituted against the College, the Council, a committee of the College, a member of the Council or a committee of the College, or an officer, employee, agent or appointee of the College for any act done in good faith in the performance or intended performance of a duty or in the exercise or the intended exercise of a power under this Act, a regulation or a by-law, or for any neglect or default in the performance or exercise in good faith of such duty or power.

PART X — MISCELLANEOUS

56. (1) **Deemed loan.**—Any payment made by the Minister that is charged to an appropriation of the Minister of Education and Training made for the fiscal year beginning on April 1, 1994 or for any subsequent fiscal year, for the purpose of establishing or operating the College, shall be deemed to have been a loan from the Province of Ontario to the College.

(2) **Same.**—A payment for the purpose of the Ontario Teaching Council Implementation Committee established by Order in Council to advise the Minister in respect of the establishment and mandate of the College is a payment for the purpose of establishing the College within the meaning of subsection (1).

(3) **Same.**—The Minister shall notify the College of the amount of any payment described in subsection (1) and shall, by order, direct the repayment of the amount by the College to the Province of Ontario.

(4) **Same.**—The determination by the Minister of the amount of a payment described in subsection (1) is final and shall not be reviewed in any court.

(5) **Same.**—An order under subsection (3) may fix a schedule for repayment of an amount and may prescribe the rate of interest payable on the amount from the date of the order until the date on which the amount is repaid in full.

(6) **Same.**—A rate of interest prescribed in an order under subsection (3) shall not exceed the prime rate of the bank listed in Schedule I or II of the *Bank Act* (Canada) that has the highest prime rate on the day that the order is made.

(7) **Same.**—An order under subsection (3) is not a regulation within the meaning of the *Regulations Act*.

57. (1) **Guarantee of loans.**—The Lieutenant Governor in Council may, by order, authorize the Minister of Finance, on behalf of Ontario, to agree to guarantee the repayment of loans made to the College, including interest.

(2) **Same.**—A guarantee given under subsection (1) is subject to any conditions that the Minister of Finance imposes.

58. (1) **Regulations under *Teaching Profession Act*.**—The Minister may require the board of governors of The Ontario Teachers' Federation to amend or revoke a regulation made under the *Teaching Profession Act* if, in the Minister's opinion, the regulation conflicts with or overlaps with this Act or a regulation or by-law under this Act.

(2) **Same.**—If the Minister requires the board of governors of The Ontario Teachers' Federation to amend or revoke a regulation under subsection (1) and the board of governors does not do so within 60 days, the Lieutenant Governor in Council may, by regulation, amend or revoke the regulation.

(3) **Same.**—Subsection (2) does not give the Lieutenant Governor in Council authority to do anything that the board of governors of The Ontario Teachers' Federation does not have authority to do.

PART XI

TRANSITIONAL PROVISIONS

59. (1) **Appointment of Registrar.**—Despite any other provision of this Act, the Minister shall, on such terms as the Minister determines, appoint the Registrar of the College for all or part of,

    (a) the period beginning on the day this section is proclaimed in force and ending on the day of the first meeting of the first duly elected and appointed Council; and

    (b) the term of the first duly elected and appointed Council.

(2) **Expenses and salary of Registrar appointed by Minister.**—For greater certainty, the expenses and salary of a Registrar appointed by the Minister under subsection (1) remain the responsibility of the College.

(3) **Powers of Registrar appointed by Minister.**—During the period mentioned in clause (1)(a), the Registrar may do anything that the Council could do under this Act if the Council were duly elected and appointed and, without limiting the generality of the foregoing, the Registrar,

    (a) may do anything that is necessary or advisable to ensure that there is a first election of the Council and that the election is conducted in accordance with the regulations; and

    (b) may incur indebtedness on behalf of the College.

(4) **Same.**—During the period mentioned in clause (1)(b), the Registrar has the same powers and duties as if appointed by the Council.

(5) **Powers of the Minister.**—During the period mentioned in clause (1)(a), the Minister may,

    (a) review the Registrar's activities and require the Registrar to provide reports and information;

    (b) require the Registrar to do anything that in the opinion of the Minister is necessary or advisable to carry out the intent of this Act; and

    (c) require the Registrar to make, amend or revoke a regulation or by-law.

(6) **Registrar to comply.**—If the Minister requires the Registrar to do anything under subsection (5), the Registrar shall, within the time and in the manner specified by the Minister, comply with the requirement and submit a report to the Minister respecting the compliance.

(7) **Regulations.**—If the Minister requires the Registrar to make, amend or revoke a regulation under clause (5)(c) and the Registrar does not do so within 60 days, the Lieutenant Governor in Council may, by regulation, make, amend or revoke the regulation.

(8) **By-laws.**—If the Minister requires the Registrar to make, amend or revoke a by-law under clause (5)(c) and the Registrar does not do so within 60 days, the Lieutenant Governor in Council may, by order, make, amend or revoke the by-law.

(9) **Authority of Lieutenant Governor in Council.**—Subsections (7) and (8) do not give the Lieutenant Governor in Council authority to do anything that the Registrar does not have authority to do.

(10) **Copies of regulations, by-laws made by Registrar.**—Subsections 40(2) and (3) and subsections 41(4) and (5) apply, with necessary modifications, to regulations and by-laws

made by the Registrar under this section and, for the purpose, the Registrar has the duties of the Council.

(11) **Copies of regulations, by-laws made by Lieutenant Governor in Council.**—The Registrar shall ensure that a copy of each regulation and by-law made by the Lieutenant Governor in Council under this section is available for public inspection in the office of the College and shall provide to any person, on payment of a reasonable charge, a copy of any regulation or by-law made by the Lieutenant Governor in Council under this section.

(12) **Expenses.**—The Minister may pay the College for expenses incurred in complying with a requirement under subsection (5).

60. First meeting of members.—The College shall hold its first annual meeting of the members not more than 15 months after the first Council is duly elected and appointed.

61. Transition: elected Council members.—Persons elected to the first Council in the election referred to in clause 42(1)(c) shall be deemed, for the purposes of this Act, to have been elected to the Council by the members of the College under clause 4(2)(a).

62. (1) **Transition: initial membership.**—Every person who, on a day to be specified in a regulation made under subsection (2), holds an Ontario Teacher's Certificate or a letter of standing issued under the *Education Act* shall be deemed to hold a certificate of qualification and registration under this Act.

(2) **Same.**—Subject to the approval of the Lieutenant Governor in Council and with prior review by the Minister, the Council may make regulations specifying a day for the purposes of subsection (1) and providing a concordance between,

(a) qualifications held under the *Education Act* by persons affected by subsection (1) before the specified day; and
(b) certificates, including any terms, conditions or limitations on those certificates, held under this Act on and after the specified day.

(3) **Same.**—For the purposes of subsection (2), qualifications include,
(a) qualifications set out in Regulation 297 of the Revised Regulations of Ontario, 1990;
(b) qualifications set out on Ontario Teacher's Qualifications Record Cards;
(c) qualifications set out on any other records of qualification held by the Ministry in respect of any person affected by subsection (1).

(4) **Same.**—Regulations that may be made under subsection (2) include but are not limited to regulations,
(a) classifying certificates of qualification and registration that come into being as a result of subsection (1);
(b) deeming certificates of qualification and registration of any class prescribed under clause (a) to be subject to specified terms, conditions and limitations;
(c) deeming terms, conditions and limitations referred to in clause (b) to have been imposed by the Registrar under this Act;
(d) deeming any person who holds a certificate of qualification and registration of any class prescribed under clause (a) to also hold one or more additional certificates of qualification;
(e) deeming additional certificates referred to in clause (d) to have been issued under this Act.

(5) **Same.**—A regulation may be made under subsection (2) only by a duly elected and appointed Council and not by a Registrar acting under subsection 59(3).

(6) **Same.**—Subsections 40(2) and (3) apply to a regulation made under subsection (2).

63. (1) **Transition: persons in programs.**—Any person who,
- (a) is enrolled in a program of professional education within the meaning of Regulation 297 of the Revised Regulations of Ontario, 1990 on the date specified under subsection 62(2); and
- (b) fulfils the requirements for an Ontario Teacher's Certificate as they existed immediately before the date specified under subsection 62(2),

shall be deemed to have fulfilled the requirements for the issuance of a certificate of qualification and registration.

(2) **Same.**—Subject to the approval of the Lieutenant Governor in Council and with prior review by the Minister, the Council may make regulations providing for any matter that it considerers necessary or advisable in connection with the issuance of certificates of qualification and registration under subsection (1), including but not limited to regulations,
- (a) relating to terms, conditions and limitations to be imposed on the certificates;
- (b) relating to the classification of the certificates; and
- (c) respecting processes and criteria for the issuance of the certificates.

(3) **Same.**—Subsections 40(2) and (3) apply to a regulation made under subsection (2).

PART XII

CONSEQUENTIAL AMENDMENTS

64 to 67. [Consequential amendments are not reproduced here.]

PART XIII

COMMENCEMENT AND SHORT TITLE

68. Commencement.—This Act comes into force on a day to be named by proclamation of the Lieutenant governor.

69. Short title.—The short title of this Act is the *Ontario College of Teachers Act, 1996*.

REGULATION 344/96
FIRST ELECTION
O. Reg. 344/96

Definitions

1. (1) In this Regulation,

"elector" means a person who holds an Ontario Teacher's Certificate or a letter of standing issued under the *Education Act* and "electorate" has a corresponding meaning;

"supervisory officer" means a person who is qualified in accordance with the regulations made under the *Education Act* governing supervisory officers and who is employed,

(a) by a school board, or

(b) in the Ministry and designated by the Minister,

to perform such supervisory and administrative duties as are required of supervisory officers by the *Education Act* and the regulations made under it.

(2) In this Regulation, "intermediate division", "junior division", "primary division", "private school" and "senior division" have the same meaning as in subsection 1(1) of the *Education Act*.

(3) In this Regulation, "English-language section" and "French-language section" have the same meaning as in Part XIII of the *Education Act*.

(4) In this Regulation, "branch affiliate" has the same meaning as in section 1 of the *School Boards and Teachers Collective Negotiations Act*.

(5) For the purposes of sections 9 to 12, a person who is an occasional teacher within the meaning of subsection 1(1) of the *Education Act* is employed by a school board or the Provincial School Authority only if the person was employed, by one or more school boards or the Provincial School Authority or both, for a total of at least 20 days in 1996 before the date specified under subsection 19(2).

Positions Established

2. The following positions are established for purposes of the election of members of the first Council of the College:

1. Position 1: Northern Ontario Elementary
2. Position 2: Northern Ontario Secondary
3. Position 3: Southwestern Ontario Elementary
4. Position 4: Southwestern Ontario Secondary
5. Position 5: Southeastern Ontario Elementary
6. Position 6: Southeastern Ontario Secondary
7. Position 7: Central Ontario Elementary
8. Position 8: Central Ontario Secondary
9. Position 9: Public System
10. Position 10: Public System

11. Position 11: Separate System
12. Position 12: Separate System
13. Position 13: French-language Systems
14. Position 14: French-language Systems
15. Position 15: Supervisory Officers
16. Position 16: Private Schools
17. Position 17: Faculties of Education

Eligibility to Vote

3. Each elector who resides in one of the following areas is entitled to cast one vote for Position 1 and one vote for Position 2:
1. The territorial districts within the meaning of the *Territorial Division Act*.
2. The Regional County Municipalities of Abitibi, Abitibi-Ouest, Rouyn-Noranda, Témiscamingue and Valée de l'Or in the Province of Quebec.
3. The Province of Manitoba.

4. Each elector who resides in one of the following areas is entitled to cast one vote for Position 3 and one vote for Position 4:
1. The counties of Brant, Essex, Kent, Lambton, Elgin, Middlesex, Huron, Perth, Bruce, Grey, Wellington and Oxford.
2. The Regional Municipalities of Haldimand-Norfolk, Halton, Waterloo, Niagara and Hamilton-Wentworth.

5. Each elector who resides in one of the following areas is entitled to cast one vote for Position 5 and one vote for Position 6:
1. The Regional Municipality of Ottawa-Carleton.
2. The united counties of Prescott and Russell.
3. The united counties of Stormont, Dundas and Glengarry.
4. The united counties of Leeds and Grenville.
5. The counties of Haliburton, Prince Edward, Hastings, Northumberland, Victoria, Peterborough, Lanark, Renfrew, Frontenac, and Lennox and Addington.
6. The Municipality of Clarington in the Regional Municipality of Durham.
7. Any part of the Province of Quebec not mentioned in section 3.

6. Each elector who resides in one of the following areas is entitled to cast one vote for Position 7 and one vote for Position 8:
1. The Regional Municipalities of Peel and York.
2. The Regional Municipality of Durham except for the Municipality of Clarington.
3. The counties of Simcoe and Dufferin.
4. The Municipality of Metropolitan Toronto.
5. Any area not mentioned in section 3, 4, or 5.

7. Each elector is entitled to cast one vote for each of Positions 9 to 17.

Eligibility for Nomination

8. A person is eligible to be nominated for a position if the person,

(a) is an elector;
(b) is entitled under sections 3 to 7 to case a vote for the position;
(c) resides in Ontario;
(d) meets all the requirements of sections 9 to 15 that relate to the position; and
(e) is not employed by the College or Registrar, under a secondment agreement or otherwise.

9. (1) To be eligible to be nominated for any of positions 1 to 8, a person must be,
(a) employed by a school board or the Provincial Schools Authority;
(b) employed at a private school that has submitted a current notice of intention under section 16 of the *Education Act*;
(c) employed by a university included in the Schedule to the *University Foundations Act, 1992* or by a college of applied arts and technology established in accordance with section 5 of the *Ministry of Colleges and Universities Act*;
(d) employed by the Crown in right of Canada at a school operated by the Crown in right of Canada;
(e) employed by a band or the council of a band within the meaning of the *Indian Act* (Canada) at a school operated by the band or the council of the band.; or
(f) employed by an education authority within the meaning of subsection 1(1) of the *Education Act*;

(2) To be eligible to be nominated for position 1, 3, 5 or 7, a person,
(a) must be a member of a branch affiliate that represents only elementary school teachers;
(b) must be a member of a branch affiliate that represents both elementary school teachers and secondary school teachers and must be employed as an elementary school teacher; or
(c) must not be a member of any branch affiliate and must hold the qualifications required under the *Education Act* to teach in a course or class in the primary or junior division or in the first two years of the intermediate division.

(3) To be eligible to be nominated for position 2, 4, 6 or 8, a person,
(a) must be a member of a branch affiliate that represents only secondary school teachers;
(b) must be a member of a branch affiliate that represents both elementary school teachers and secondary school teachers and must be employed as a secondary school teacher; or
(c) must not be a member of any branch affiliate and must hold the qualifications required under the *Education Act* to teach in a course or class in the last two years of the intermediate division or in the senior division.

10. To be eligible to be nominated for position 9 or 10, a person,
(a) must be employed by the Provincial Schools Authority or a school board, other than a Roman Catholic separate school board; and
(b) must not be a person described in section 12 or 13.

11. To be eligible to be nominated for position 11 or 12, a person,
(a) must be employed by a Roman Catholic separate school board; and
(b) must not be a person described in subsection 12 or 13.

12. To be eligible to be nominated for position 13 or 14, a person must not be a person described in section 13 and must be one of the following:
1. A person who is employed by the Provincial Schools Authority at École Jules Léger.
2. A person who is employed by The Metropolitan Toronto French-Languages School Council, the Conseil des écoles publiques d'Ottawa-Carleton, the Conseil des écoles catholiques de langue français de la région d'Ottawa-Carleton or the Conseil des écoles séparées catholiques de langue française de Prescott-Russell.
3. A person who is employed by a school board that is a board within the meaning of subsection 309(1) of the *Education Act* and whose recruitment and assignment fall within the exclusive jurisdiction of the French-language section or outside the exclusive jurisdiction of the English-language section of the board.
4. A person who is employed by a school board that is not a board within the meaning of subsection 309(1) of the *Education Act*, to teach in a course or class in which the language of instruction is French or Quebec sign language, other than a course or class established under paragraph 25 of subsection 8(1) of the *Education Act*.

13. To be eligible to be nominated for position 15, a person must be a supervisory officer.

14. To be eligible to be nominated for position 16, a person must be employed at a private school that has submitted a current notice of intention under section 16 of the *Education Act*.

15. To be eligible to be nominated for position 17, a person must be employed by a university or college with which the Minister of Education and Training has an agreement under clause 14(1)(b) of the *Education Act*, at a school or faculty of education within the university or college.

16. (1) A person who is nominated for position 9 shall be deemed to be also nominated for position 10 and vice versa.

(2) Subsection (1) applies with necessary modifications to positions 11 and 12 and to positions 13 and 14.

General Duties of Registrar

17. (1) The Registrar shall administer the election of members of the first Council of the College and shall decide all matters incidental to the election, including but not limited to whether a person is eligible to vote for a position, whether a person is eligible to be nominated for a position and whether a nomination or vote should be accepted.

(2) The Registrar shall act as returning officer for the purposes of the election.

(3) The Registrar may,
(a) employ persons to assist in the conduct of the election; and
(b) enter into an agreement for the purpose of using electronic means for voting and for tabulating results.

(4) The Registrar shall permit any elector to inspect, during regular office hours, the list of electors identified by the Registrar as eligible to vote for any position.

Calling the Election

18. (1) The Registrar shall designate a period of one week during which the election of members of the first Council of the College will be held.

(2) The week must begin before March 1, 1997.

19. (1) The Registrar shall give notice of the election to the electors at least 90 days before the first day of the voting period.

(2) The notice shall include a nomination form, instruction on how to nominate candidates and the last date for service on the Registrar of completed nominations.

(3) The notice shall be given in a manner that, in the Registrar's opinion, is adequate to bring the election to the attention of the electorate.

20. (1) Nominations shall be in writing, in a form established by the Registrar, and shall state,

(a) the name, address and phone number of the nominee;
(b) the position sought by the nominee;
(c) the name of the nominee's employer; and
(d) any other information required by the Registrar.

(2) Where the nominee is an occasional teacher within the meaning of subsection 1(1) of the *Education Act*, the nomination shall specify the dates in 1996 on which the nominee was employed by a school board or by the Provincial Schools Authority.

(3) The nomination shall include the signatures of at least 20 electors other than the nominee, each of whom must, at the time that he or she signs, be eligible to be nominated for the position sought by the nominee.

(4) The nomination shall also include the signature of the nominee attesting to,

(a) his or her eligibility for the position sought;
(b) his or her willingness to be nominated and to serve on the Council; and
(c) the accuracy of any information about the nominee contained in the nomination.

(5) A nominee may submit a biographical statement in support of the nomination, in a form established by the Registrar and within the time specified by the Registrar.

(6) The biographical statement shall include the signature of the nominee attesting to the accuracy of any information about the nominee contained in the statement.

21. (1) No person shall sign as nominee for more than one person.

(2) The Registrar shall reject all nominations of a person who contravenes subsection (1).

22. (1) Subject to subsection (2), nomination may be served on the Registrar in accordance with section 52 of the Act or by facsimile.

(2) The Registrar shall reject a nomination that is served by facsimile if the nominee is unable to satisfy the Registrar that the facsimile is a true copy of the original nomination.

23. (1) The Registrar shall review the nominations and shall reject a nomination,

(a) if the Registrar has reason to believe that the nominee is not eligible to be nominated for the position; or
(b) if the nomination was not served on the Registrar by the date specified under subsection 19(2).

(2) The Registrar may reject a nomination where he or she reasonably determines that it does not meet the requirements of this Regulation.

24. (1) The Registrar shall give each nominee written notice as to whether the nomination has been accepted or rejected.

(2) A person whose nomination for a position has been accepted is a candidate for the position.

(3) A person who is a candidate for position 9 shall be deemed to be also a candidate for position 10 and vice versa.

(4) Subsection (3) applies with necessary modifications to positions 11 and 12 and to positions 13 and 14.

25. (1) The Registrar shall declare a person's candidacy for a position terminated where the Registrar reasonably determines that the person,

(a) was not eligible to be nominated for the position at the time the person's nomination was served on the Registrar;

(b) has ceased to be eligible to be nominated for the position since the time mentioned in clause (a); or

(c) signed as nominee for more than one position.

(2) The Registrar shall declare a person's candidacy for a position terminated on receiving written notification from the person that he or she wishes the candidacy terminated.

(3) Where a person's candidacy is terminated, the Registrar shall,

(a) give the person written notice of the termination; and

(b) take the steps that the Registrar considers feasible and appropriate to make the electorate aware that the candidacy has been terminated.

Acclamations, Vacant Positions

26. (1) Subject to subsections (2) to (4), where only one person is a candidate for a position, the Registrar shall declare the person elected to the position by acclamation.

(2) Where only one person is a candidate for positions 9 and 10, the Registrar shall declare the person elected to one of the positions by acclamation.

(3) Where the total number of candidates for positions 9 and 10 is two, the Registrar shall acclaim one as elected to position 9 and one as elected to position 10.

(4) Subsections (2) and (3) apply with necessary modifications to positions 11 and 12 and to positions 13 and 14.

27. (1) Where there is no candidate for a position, a majority of the elected members of Council shall at its first meeting elect a person to the position.

(2) A vote under subsection (1) may only be cast for a person who is at the time of the vote eligible to be nominated for the position.

Election Procedures

28. (1) The Registrar shall establish the voting procedures for the election.

(2) The procedures shall permit each elector to vote on any day during the voting period.

(3) The procedures may provide for the use of electronic means for voting and for tabulating results.

(4) The Registrar shall make reasonable efforts to ensure that any records that connect the name of an elector to the votes cast by him or her are used only to the extent necessary for the purposes of voting and tabulating results.

29. (1) At least 20 days before the first day of the voting period, the Registrar shall mail the following information to each elector identified by the Registrar as eligible to vote:
1. A list of the positions for which the elector is entitled to vote.
2. A list of the candidates, in alphabetical order, for each of positions 1 to 8 and 15 to 17 for which the elector is entitled to vote.
3. A list of the candidates, in alphabetical order, for positions 9 and 10.
4. A list of the candidates, in alphabetical order, for positions 11 and 12.
5. A list of the candidates, in alphabetical order, for positions 13 and 14.
6. The biographical statement, where submitted and prepared in accordance with the requirements of this Regulation, for each of the candidates for whom the elector is entitled to vote.
7. Instructions on how to vote, including clarifying that an elector cannot cast two votes for the same person for positions 9 and 10, for positions 11 and 12 or for positions 13 and 14.
8. A general description of the role and functions of the College and of the Council.

(2) The mailing should be by ordinary mail to the elector's current address, as ascertained by the Registrar.

(3) The Registrar shall make reasonable efforts to identify the electors, to determine the positions each elector is entitled to vote for and to ascertain the current address of each elector.

Election Results

30. (1) The Registrar shall, within two days after the last day of the voting period,
(a) ensure that the votes for each candidate are counted;
(b) declare elected the candidate who received the greatest number of votes for each of positions 1 to 8 and 15 to 17;
(c) declare elected to positions 9 and 10 the candidates for those positions who received the two highest numbers of votes for the positions;
(d) declare elected to positions 11 and 12 the candidates for those positions who received the two highest numbers of votes for the positions; and
(e) declare elected to positions 13 and 14 the candidates for those positions who received the two highest numbers of votes for the positions.

(2) The Registrar shall make the election results available to the public, including the candidate elected to each position, the total number of votes cast for each position, the number of votes cast for each candidate and the number of votes rejected, with an indication of the reasons.

(3) If fewer than 50 votes separate an elected candidate from another candidate for the same position, the Registrar shall, on the request of the other candidate, promptly re-tabulate the results of the election for the position and provide the re-tabulated results to all candidates for the position.

(4) A request by a candidate under subsection (3) may only be made within 12 days after the last day of the voting period.

(5) Where from the re-tabulation it appears to the Registrar that a wrong candidate was declared elected, the Registrar shall correct the results, declare the correct candidate as elected and make the corrected election results available to the public.

(6) The Registrar shall retain all returns from the election until the Election Review Committee authorizes their destruction or until September 1, 1997, whichever comes first.

(7) Where necessary, the Registrar shall break a tie by lot.

Right to Use French

31. (1) An elector has the right to use French or English in all dealings with the Registrar relating to the election of members of the first Council of the College.

(2) An elector has the right to vote in French or English.

Term of Office

32. The persons elected to the Council of the College under this Regulation shall hold office for a term of three years beginning on the day of the first meeting of the Council at which there is a quorum.

Election Review Committee

33. (1) After the election of the members of the first Council of the College, the Council shall appoint an Election Review Committee.

(2) Only persons who were elected to the Council under this Regulation may be appointed to the Election Review Committee.

(3) The Election Review Committee shall review the conduct of the election and make recommendations to the Council on regulations and by-laws to govern subsequent elections of members of the Council;

(4) The recommendations shall be made with a view to preserving and enhancing the efficiency and integrity of the election process.

(5) The Registrar shall cooperate with and assist the Election Review Committee in the performance of its duties.

REGULATION 345/96
APPOINTMENTS TO COUNCIL
O. Reg. 345/96

1. The Lieutenant Governor in Council shall appoint persons under clause 4(2)(b) of the Act who are, in the opinion of the Lieutenant Governor in Council, able to represent the public interest and the interests of the education community.

2. The persons appointed under clause 4(2)(b) of the Act shall hold office for the term specified in the appointment.

REGULATION 72/97
GENERAL
O. Reg. 72/97

Employers' Obligation to Submit Fees

1. In sections 2 to 4,

"due date" means the date on which the annual membership fee is due in any year, as specified in the by-laws; ("date d'échéance")

"private school" has the same meaning as in subsection 1(1) of the *Education Act*. ("école privée)

2. (1) Where, on the due date in any year, a school board employs a member, the school board shall,

(a) deduct the amount of the annual membership fee payable in respect of the year by the member from the member's salary; and

(b) submit the amount of the fee to the College.

(2) Where, on the due date in any year, the Provincial Schools Authority employs a member and the Ministry of Education and Training is responsible for paying the member's salary, the Ministry of Education and Training shall,

(a) deduct the amount of the annual membership fee payable in respect of the year by the member from the member's salary; and

(b) submit the amount of the fee to the College.

(3) Where, on the due date in any year, a private school employs a member who contributes to the Ontario Teachers' Pension Plan, the private school shall,

(a) deduct the amount of the annual membership fee payable in respect of the year by the member from the member's salary; and

(b) submit the amount of the fee to the College.

(4) Subsection (3) applies only if the private school has received notice that the member contributes to the Ontario Teachers' Pension Plan.

(5) The amounts referred to in subsections (1) to (3) shall be submitted no later than 35 days after the due date.

(6) The amount may be submitted by cheque or by any other means approved by the Registrar.

(7) When submitting an amount under this section, the school board, the Ministry of Education and Training or the private school, as the case may be, shall provide the Registrar with sufficient information to identify the member on whose behalf the amount is submitted.

(8) The Registrar may issue directions respecting the content and form of the information to be provided under subsection (7).

3. At the written request, made before the due date, of a school board, the Ministry of Education and Training or a private school, as the case may be, the Registrar may extend the period specified in subsection 2(5), if the Registrar is of the opinion that the extension is warranted because of exceptional circumstances.

4. (1) A school board, the Ministry of Education and Training or a private school, as the case may be, shall pay interest on any amount in arrears, from the day the amount was required to be submitted under section 2 or, where applicable, section 3, to the day before the day on which the payment is made.

(2) The interest shall be calculated at the bank prime rate plus 4 per cent per year.

(3) In subsection (2),

"bank prime rate" means the prime rate quoted by the College's bank of record on the day the payment was due.

Quorum at Council Meetings

5. Sixteen members of the Council, at least four of whom shall be persons appointed to the Council under clause 4(2)(b) of the Act, constitute a quorum of the Council.

Disqualification of Council Members

6. (1) The Council shall disqualify an elected member of the Council from sitting on the Council if the member,

   (a) is found by the Discipline Committee to be guilty of professional misconduct or to be incompetent;
   (b) is found by the Fitness to Practise Committee to be incapacitated;
   (c) fails, without cause, to attend three consecutive meetings of the Council;
   (d) fails, without cause, to attend half the meetings of the Council in any 12-month period;
   (e) fails, without cause, to attend three consecutive meetings of a committee of which he or she is a member;
   (f) fails, without cause, to attend a hearing of a panel of a committee for which he or she has been selected; or
   (g) fails or ceases to meet the criteria set out in the regulations for eligibility to be nominated for the position for which the member was elected, as those regulations read on the day the member was declared elected.

(2) An elected member of the Council who is disqualified from sitting on the Council ceases to be a member of the Council.

(3) An elected member of the Council who is the subject of a proceeding before the Discipline Committee or the Fitness to Practise Committee as a result of a referral under section 26 or 29 of the Act is suspended from his or her office as member of the Council pending the outcome of the proceeding.

(4) A person who is suspended under subsection (3) from his or her office as member of the Council shall not participate in any meeting or other proceeding of the Council.

Vacancies on Council

7. (1) For the purposes of this Regulation, the seat of an elected member of the Council becomes vacant if the member dies, resigns or is disqualified from sitting on the Council.

(2) For the purposes of this Regulation, the resignation of an elected member of the Council is effective when received by the Registrar, the chair or the vice-chair.

8. (1) If the seat of the elected member of the Council becomes vacant not more than six months before the expiry of the member's term of office, the Council may leave the seat vacant or may fill the vacated position by appointment.

(2) If the Council chooses to fill the vacated position by appointment, it shall appoint the person who had the most votes of all the unsuccessful candidates for the position in the last Council election, not including those persons who, as of the date of the appointment,

(a) are not willing to fill the vacancy; or
(b) do not meet the criteria set out in the regulations for eligibility to be nominated for the position, as those regulations read on the day the member was declared elected.

(3) If no person can be appointed in accordance with subsection (2), the Council may fill the vacated position by appointing any person who, as of the date of the appointment, is willing to fill the vacancy and meets the criteria set out in the regulations for eligibility to be nominated for the position, as those regulations read on the day the member was declared elected.

(4) The Council shall make its determination under subsection (1) as soon as reasonably possible and, if the Council decides to fill the vacated position, the Council shall do so as soon as reasonably possible.

9. (1) If the seat of an elected member of the Council becomes vacant more than six months before the expiry of the member's term of office, the Council shall fill the vacated position by appointing the person who had the most votes of all the unsuccessful candidates for the position in the last Council election, not including the persons who, as of the date of the appointment,

(a) are not willing to fill the vacancy; or
(b) do not meet the criteria set out in the regulations for eligibility to be nominated for the position, as those regulations read on the day the member was declared elected.

(2) If no person can be appointed in accordance with subsection (1), the Council shall fill the vacated position by appointing any person who, as of the date of the appointment, is willing to fill the vacancy and meets the criteria set out in the regulations for eligibility to be nominated for the position, as those regulations read on the day the member was declared elected.

(3) The Council shall fill the vacated position as soon as reasonably possible.

10. Within 10 days of a vacancy to which section 8 or 9 applies arising, the Registrar shall,

(a) notify the members of the Council that the vacancy has arisen;

(b) provide the members of the Council with the information that they need in order to be able to fill the vacancy; and

(c) draw the attention of the Council to its obligation under section 8 or 9, as the case may be, to act expeditiously.

11. (1) If the seat of one or more elected Council members becomes vacant and no quorum of the Council remains in office, the Registrar shall hold an election for the vacant positions and, for the purpose, shall adapt the provisions of the regulation that governed the last election to the Council, as those provisions read on the last voting day in that election, as he or she considers appropriate.

(2) Where an election is required under this section, the Registrar shall,

(a) within 10 days of the requirement to hold an election arising under subsection (1), set a date or time period during which the voting will occur; and

(b) ensure that the election is held as soon as reasonably possible.

12. A person appointed under section 8 or 9 or elected under section 11 shall hold office until the former Council member's term would have expired.

Statutory Committees

13. In sections 14 to 18,

"statutory committee" means,

(a) the Executive Committee,

(b) the Investigation Committee,

(c) the Discipline Committee,

(d) the Registration Appeals Committee, and

(e) the Fitness to Practise Committee.

14. (1) Subject to subsections 25(1), 27(1) and 28(1) of the Act, the Council shall determine the number of members to be appointed by it to the Investigation Committee, the Discipline Committee and the Fitness to Practise Committee.

(2) The members of a statutory committee to be appointed by the Council shall be appointed as soon as reasonably possible.

(3) A person appointed to a statutory committee shall continue to be a member of the committee until the first meeting of the next Council.

(4) Subject to subsection 20(1), the Council shall appoint a chair for each statutory committee, from among the members appointed to the committee.

(5) Subject to subsection 20(2), a statutory committee shall elect a vice-chair from among its members.

(6) In the absence of the chair of a statutory committee, the vice-chair shall temporarily act as and have all the powers of the chair.

(7) In the absence of the chair of a statutory committee, the vice-chair shall temporarily act as and have all the powers of the chair.

(8) The chair of a statutory committee may vote at meetings of the committee.

15. (1) Subject to subsection (4), a quorum of the Investigation Committee, the Discipline Committee or the Fitness to Practise Committee is a majority of the number of positions on the committee, as determined under subsection 14(1), whether or not one or more of the positions is vacant.

(2) Subject to subsection (4), a quorum of the Registration Appeals Committee is three.

(3) Subject to subsection (4), a quorum of the Executive Committee if four.

(4) A quorum of a statutory committee is not constituted unless at least one of the members of the committee participating in the meeting is a person appointed to the Council under clause 4(2)(b) of the Act.

16. (1) The seat of a member of a statutory committee becomes vacant if the member dies, resigns from the committee, resigns from the Council or is disqualified from sitting on the Council.

(2) For the purposes of this Regulation, the resignation of a member of a statutory committee from the committee is effective when received by the Registrar or the chair of the committee.

(3) If the seat of a member of a statutory committee becomes vacant, the Executive Committee shall, as soon as reasonably possible, appoint a member of the Council to fill the vacancy.

(4) Subsection (3) does not apply to vacancies on the Executive Committee.

(5) If the seat of a member of the Executive Committee becomes vacant, the Council shall, as soon as reasonably possible, appoint one of its members to fill the vacancy.

(6) In filling a vacancy under this section, the Executive Committee or Council, as the case may be, shall ensure that the requirements of subsections 25(2), 27(2) and 28(2) of the Act and of section 19 and subsections 23(2) and (3) of this Regulation are complied with.

(7) Within 10 days of a vacancy to which subsection (3) or (5) applies arising, the Registrar shall,

(a) notify the members of the Executive Committee or Council, as the case may be, that the vacancy has arisen;

(b) provide the members of the Executive Committee or the Council, as the case may be, with the information that they need in order to be able to fill the vacancy; and

(c) draw the attention of the Executive Committee or the Council, as the case may be, to its obligation under this section to act expeditiously.

(8) A person appointed under this section shall hold office until the former committee member's term would have expired.

(9) A person who is suspended under subsection 6(3) from his or her office as member of the Council is also suspended from his or her office as member of a statutory condition.

(10) A person who is suspended under subsection (9) from his or her office as member of a committee shall not participate in any meeting or other proceeding of the committee or of a panel of the committee.

17. (1) Each statutory committee shall meet at least once a year.

(2) Each statutory committee shall meet,

(a) when requested by its chair;

(b) when requested in writing signed by a sufficient number of members to constitute a quorum under section 15;
(c) when requested by the Council; or
(d) when requested by the Executive Committee.

18. (1) A meeting of a statutory committee may be held by any means that permit every person participating in the meeting to communicate with each other simultaneously.

(2) The chair of a statutory committee shall ensure that minutes are,
(a) taken at each meeting;
(b) reviewed and approved at the meeting following the one at which they are taken; and
(c) signed by the chair after approval.

(3) Subsections (1) and (2) apply with necessary modifications to a meeting of a panel of a statutory committee.

(4) This section does not apply to a hearing of a statutory committee or of a panel of a statutory committee.

Executive Committee

19. (1) The Council shall appoint the chairs of the following committees as members of the Executive Committee:
1. The Fitness to Practise Committee.
2. The Discipline Committee.
3. The Registration Appeals Committee.
4. The Investigation Committee.
5. The Standards of Practice and Education Committee.
6. The Finance Committee.
7. The Accreditation Committee.

(2) The Council shall also appoint the chair and vice-chair of the Council as members of the Executive Committee, where they are not appointed under subsection (1).

(3) The Council shall appoint additional members to the Executive Committee in accordance with the following rules, where applicable:
1. If all persons appointed under subsections (1) and (2) are members of the Council elected under clause 4(2)(a) of the Act, the Council shall appoint two additional persons to the Executive Committee, both of whom shall be members of the Council appointed under clause 4(2)(b) of the Act.
2. If only one of the persons appointed under subsections (1) and (2) is a member of the Council appointed under clause 4(2)(b) of the Act, the Council shall appoint one additional person to the Executive Committee, who shall be a member of the Council appointed under clause 4(2)(b) of the Act.
3. If all the persons appointed under subsections (1) and (2) are members of the Council appointed under clause 4(2)(b) of the Act, the Council shall appoint two additional persons to the Executive Committee, both of whom shall be members of the Council elected under clause 4(2)(a) of the Act.
4. If only one of the persons appointed under subsections (1) and (2) is a member of

the Council elected under clause 4(2)(a) of the Act, the Council shall appoint one additional person to the Executive Committee, who shall be a member of the Council elected under clause 4(2)(a) of the Act.

20. (1) The chair of the Council shall be the chair of the Executive Committee.

(2) The vice-chair of the Council shall be the vice-chair of the Executive Committee.

Investigation Committee

21. (1) A complaint to be considered and investigated by the Investigation Committee under section 26 of the Act shall be considered and investigated by a panel of the Committee selected for the purpose by the chair of the Committee from among its members.

(2) A panel shall be composed of at least three persons.

(3) The chair of the Committee shall appoint one of the members of the panel as its chair.

(4) A panel may exercise all the powers and carry out all the duties of the Committee, with respect to the complaint before the panel.

Discipline Committee

22. (1) A hearing on matters directed or referred to the Discipline Committee under section 26, 29 or 33 of the Act shall be conducted by a panel of the Committee selected for the purpose by the chair of the Committee from among its members.

(2) A panel shall be composed of at least three persons.

(3) The chair of the Committee shall appoint one of the members of the panel as its chair.

(4) A panel may exercise all the powers and carry out all the duties of the Committee, with respect to the matter before the panel.

(5) If the term of office of a member of a panel who has participated in a hearing expires at any time before the hearing has been completed or before a decision is given, the term shall be deemed to continue for the purpose of participating in the decision.

Registration Appeals Committee

23. (1) The Council shall appoint five of its members to the Registration Appeals Committee.

(2) At least two of the members of the Registration Appeals Committee shall be persons appointed to the Council under clause 4(2)(b) of the Act.

(3) At least two of the members of the Registration Appeals Committee shall be persons elected to the Council under clause 4(2)(a) of the Act.

24. (1) A request for review under section 21 of the Act or an application for variation under section 22 of the Act shall be decided by a panel of the Registration Appeals Committee selected for the purpose by the chair of the Committee from among its members.

(2) A panel shall be composed of at least three persons.

(3) The chair of the Committee shall appoint one of the members of the panel as its chair.

(4) A panel may exercise all the powers and carry out all the duties of the Committee, with respect to the matter before the panel.

(5) If the term of office of a member of a panel who has participated in a proceeding expires at any time before the proceeding has been completed or before a decision is given, the term shall be deemed to continue for the purpose of participating in the decision.

Fitness to Practise Committee

25. (1) A hearing on matters directed or referred to the Fitness to Practise Committee under section 26, 29 or 33 of the Act shall be conducted by a panel of the Committee selected for the purpose by the chair of the Committee from among its members.

(2) A panel shall be composed of at least three persons.

(3) The chair of the Committee shall appoint one of the members of the panel as its chair.

(4) A panel may exercise all the powers and carry out all the duties of the Committee, with respect to the matter before the panel.

(5) If the term of office of a member of a panel who has participated in a hearing expires at any time before the hearing has been completed or before a decision is given, the term shall be deemed to continue for the purpose of participating in the decision.

Designation for Purposes of Section 47 of the Act

26. The following persons or bodies are designated for the purposes of subsection 47(1) of the Act:

1. A private school, as defined in subsection 1(1) of the *Education Act*, in respect of which a current notice of intention has been filed under section 16 of that Act.
2. A college of applied arts and technology established under section 5 of the *Ministry of Colleges and Universities Act*.
3. An institution specified in the Schedule to the *University Foundations Act, 1992*.
4. The Ontario Teachers' Pension Plan Board.
5. The Ontario Teachers' Federation.
6. L'Association des enseignantes et des enseignants franco-ontariens.
7. The Federation of Women Teachers' Associations of Ontario.
8. The Ontario English Catholic Teachers' Association.
9. The Ontario Public School Teachers' Federation.
10. The Ontario Secondary School Teachers' Federation.

REGULATION 184/97
TEACHERS QUALIFICATIONS
O. Reg. 184/97

DEFINITIONS

1. (1) In this Regulation,

"acceptable university degree" means a degree that is,
- (a) granted by an Ontario university that is an ordinary member of the Association of Universities and Colleges of Canada,
- (b) granted by a Canadian university in a province other than Ontario that is an ordinary member of the Association of Universities and Colleges of Canada, and is a degree that is considered by the College to be equivalent to a degree referred to in clause (a),
- (c) granted by a university in the United States that is recognized by,
    - (i) Middle States Association of Colleges and Schools,
    - (ii) New England Association of Schools and Colleges,
    - (iii) North Central Association of Colleges and Schools,
    - (iv) Northwest Association of Schools and Colleges,
    - (v) Southern Associatin of Colleges and Schools, or
    - (vi) Western Association of Schools and Colleges

    and is considered by the College to be equivalent to a degree referred to in clause (a), and
- (d) granted by a university that is located in a country other than Canada and the United States and that is considered by the College to be equivalent to a degree referred to in clause (a);

"appropriate supervisory officer" means, in respect of a teacher, the supervisory officer assigned by a board in accordance with the *Education Act* and the regulations under it or by the Minister to provide supervisory services in respect of the performance by the teacher of his or her duties under the *Education Act* and the regulations under it;

"approved program" means a program approved by the College;

"band" and "council of the band" have the same meaning as in the *Indian Act* (Canada);

"candidate" means a candidate for any qualifications granted in a Certificate of Qualification under this Regulation;

"certificate of qualification" means a certificate of qualification referred to in subsection (2);

"division" means the primary division, junior division, intermediate division or senior division, as defined in the *Education Act*;

"general studies" means the courses developed from curriculum guidelines that are issued by the Minister for the intermediate division and senior division and listed under a heading other than "Technological Studies" in Appendix B to OSIS;

"holds a degree" means, in respect of a candidate, that he or she has completed all the requirements for and has been approved for, the granting of a degree, regardless of whether or not the degree has been conferred;

REGULATION 184/97 **S. 1**

"OSIS" means the circular entitled "Ontario Schools Intermediate and Senior Divisions Program and Diploma Requirements" issued by the Minister including any document issued by the Minister in accordance with paragraphs 1, 2, 3, 4 and 25 of subsection 8(1) of the *Education Act*;

"program of professional education" means a program approved by the College and conducted at a college, faculty or school of education in Ontario that includes,

 (a) a concentrated study of,
  (i) the primary and junior divisions, with or without a focus on the teaching of French as a second language,
  (ii) the junior division and one optional course from Schedule A that is in the intermediate division and a course related to grades 7 and 8 of the intermediate division,
  (iii) the intermediate and senior divisions including two optional courses from Schedule A, or
  (iv) technological studies, including a minimum of two optional courses from Schedule B at the basic level, or one optional course from Schedule B at the basic level and the other such course at the advanced level,
 (b) studies in education including learning and development throughout the primary, junior, intermediate and senior division,
 (c) teaching methods designed to meet the individual needs of pupils,
 (d) the acts and regulations respecting education,
 (e) a review of the curriculum guidelines issued by the Minister related to all of the divisions and a study of curriculum development, and
 (f) a minimum of 40 days of practical experience in schools or in other situations approved by the College for observation and practice teaching;

"technological qualifications" means, in respect of a candidate for a certificate of qualification, an interim certificate of qualification or a certificate of qualification (limited, restricted),

 (a) the holding of the secondary school graduation diploma or the successful completion of courses that are considered by the College to be the equivalent of such diploma,
 (b) proof of his or her competence in the area or areas of technological studies selected as options in the program of professional education, and
 (c) one of,
  (i) five years of wage-earning, business or industrial experience in the area or areas of technological studies selected as options in the program of professional education,
  (ii) a combination of education related to the area or areas of technological studies selected as options in the program of professional education beyond that referred to in clause (a) and business or industrial experience in the area or areas of technological studies selected as options in the program of technological studies that totals five years, including at least two years of wage-earning experience, no less than 16 months of which is continuous employment, or
  (iii) at least 3,700 hours of wage-earning experience and successful completion of a post-secondary education program acceptable to the College that includes at least 24 months of academic studies, if the wage-earning experience and the

education program are related to the area or areas of technological studies selected as options in the program of professional education;

"technological studies" means the courses developed from curriculum guidelines issued by the Minister and entitled "Broad-Based Technological Education, Grades 10, 11 and 12, 1995" and "Technological Studies, Intermediate and Senior Divisions, Part C: Ontario Academic Courses, 1987";

"university course" means a one-year university course beyond the Ontario Academic Credit level, or the equivalent of such one-year university course, where the course is part of a program leading to an acceptable university degree;

"university credit" means a unit of recognition in respect of the successful completion of a university course, such that 60 such university credits are required to complete a four-year university program leading to an acceptable university degree.

(2) The following shall be two classes of certificates of qualification and registration:

1. A certificate of registration, which shall set out the holder's membership relationship with the College.
2. A certificate of qualification, which shall set out the holder's qualifications for teaching.

PART I

BASIC QUALIFICATIONS

2. A candidate for the certificate of qualification shall submit to the dean of a college or faculty of education or the director of a school of education in Ontario,

(a) a certificate of birth or baptism, or other acceptable proof of the date and place of birth;

(b) in the case of a candidate who is a married woman who wishes to have her certificate issued in her married name, a certificate of marriage or other acceptable proof that she is the person referred to in the certificate or other document submitted under clause (a);

(c) a certificate of change of name where applicable;

(d) evidence satisfactory to such dean or director of his or her academic or technological qualifications;

(e) in the case of a person who was not born in Canada, the basis upon which the candidate is present in Canada;

(f) proof of freedom from active tuberculosis.

3. Where the dean of a college or faculty of education or the director of a school of education in Ontario reports to the Registrar that a candidate,

(a) has complied with section 2;

(b) holds an acceptable university degree or qualifications the College considers equivalent thereto, or technological qualifications; and

(c) has successfully completed a program of professional education, the Registrar may grant to the candidate a certificate of qualification in the form provided for in the by-laws of the College, indicating the areas of concentration successfully completed.

4. (1) An entry on a certificate of qualification in respect of a program successfully completed in Canada shall indicate by the language in which the entry is recorded whether the program was taken in English or in French.

(2) An entry on a certificate of qualification in respect of a program successfully completed out of Canada shall indicate by the language in which the entry is recorded whether the qualification referred to is for teaching in schools and classes where English is the language of instruction or in French-language schools and classes established under Part XII of the *Education Act*.

(3) Despite section 14, qualifications valid in French-language schools and classes established under Part XII of the *Education Act* are valid in French-language classes where the teacher may otherwise be assigned or appointed to teach according to subsection 19(14) of Regulation 298 of the Revised Regulations of Ontario, 1990.

5. An entry on a certificate of qualification in respect of a program in International Languages shall specify which language was studied in the program.

6. (1) Where the dean of a college or faculty of education or the director of a school of education in Ontario reports to the Registrar that a candidate,

   (a) has complied with section 2;
   (b) is of native ancestry;
   (c) holds the requirements for a Secondary School Graduation Diploma or standing the College considers equivalent thereto; and
   (d) has successfully completed a program of professional education with concentration in the primary division and the junior division,

the Registrar may grant to the candidate a certificate of qualification in the form provided for in the by-laws of the College.

(2) The Registrar may grant to a candidate a certificate of qualification (limited) valid for one year for teaching in the primary division and junior division if the dean of a college or faculty of education or the director of a school of education in Ontario reports to the Registrar that the candidate meets the qualifications of clauses (1)(a) to (c) and has successfully completed the first session of a program of professional education with concentration in the primary division and the junior division.

(3) The certificate of qualification (limited) granted under subsection (2) shall be in the form provided for in the by-laws of the College.

(4) The Registrar may renew a candidate's certificate of qualification (limited) for one year for teaching in the primary division and junior division if the candidate submits to the Registrar evidence that the candidate,

   (a) holds a certificate of qualification (limited) granted under subsection (2) that has expired or is about to expire; and
   (b) has an offer of a position as a teacher in the primary division or junior division from
      (i) a board,
      (ii) a private school,

(iii) the Provincial Schools Authority established under section 2 of the *Provincial Schools Negotiations Act*,

(iv) the Department of Indian Affairs and Northern Development of the Government of Canada, or

(v) a council of a band or an education authority, if the council of the band or the education authority is authorized by the Crown in right of Canada to provide education for Indians.

7. (1) Where the dean of a college or faculty of education or the director of a school of education in Ontario at the time of making a report under section 3, 6, 8 or 11 is of the opinion from the information provided under section 2 by the candidate in respect of whom the report is to be made, that the candidate is not entitled under the laws of Canada to obtain employment as a teacher in Canada, the dean or director at the time of making the report shall so inform the Registrar.

(2) Where the Registrar is informed as set out in subsection (1), the Registrar may refuse to grant the certificate referred to in section 3 or 6 or in the subsection 11(2), as the case may be, or may withhold the certificate of qualification (limited) referred to in section 8 or it extension under subsection 11(1), until the candidate provides proof to the Registrar that the candidate is entitled under the laws of Canada to obtain employment as a teacher in Canada.

8. Where the dean of a college or faculty of education or the director of a school of education in Ontario reports to the Registrar that a candidate,

(a) has complied with section 2;

(b) holds an acceptable university degree or qualifications the College considers equivalent thereto or technological qualifications; and

(c) has successfully completed the first session of a program of professional education,

the Registrar may grant to the candidate a certificate of qualification (limited) in the form provided for in the by-laws of the College.

9. Where a person who is the holder of a certificate of qualification (limited) granted under section 8 that has expired, or is about to expire, submits to the Registrar evidence that he or she has an offer of a position as a teacher from,

(a) a board;

(b) a private school;

(c) the Provincial Schools Authority established under section 2 of the *Provincial Schools Negotiations Act*;

(d) the Department of Indian Affairs and Northern Development of the Government of Canada; or

(e) a council of a band or an education authority where such council of the band or education authority is authorized by the Crown in right of Canada to provide education for Indians,

the Registrar may renew the certificate of qualification (limited) for a period of one year.

10. For the purposes of section 11, a person who holds a Temporary Elementary School Certificate or a Temporary Secondary School Certificate is deemed to hold a certificate of qualification (limited) granted on the date of his or her Temporary Elementary School Certificate or his or her Temporary Secondary School Certificate.

11. (1) Where the dean of a college or faculty of education or the director of a school of education in Ontario reports to the Registrar that a person who holds a certificate of qualification (limited),

(a) has taught successfully for one school year in Ontario as certified by the appropriate supervisory officer; and

(b) has successfully completed the second session of a program of professional education where such second session is not the final session of the program.,

the Registrar may extend the person's certificate of qualification (limited) for one year.

(2) Where the dean of a college or a faculty of education or the director of a school of education in Ontario reports to the Registrar that a candidate who holds a certificate of qualification (limited),

(a) has taught successfully in Ontario, as certified by the appropriate supervisory officer, for one school year after the granting of a certificate of qualification (limited) and after its extension where it was extended; and

(b) has successfully completed the final session of a program of professional education,

the Registrar may grant to the candidate a certificate of qualification in the form provided for in the by-laws of the College, indicating the areas of concentration successfully completed.

12. An applicant for an interim certificate of qualification who completed a teacher education program outside Ontario shall submit to the Registrar with the application,

(a) the items required to be submitted under section 2;

(b) evidence of his or her academic or technological qualifications;

(c) his or her teaching certificate and a transcript of his or her teacher education program;

(d) a statement from the issuing authority that his or her teaching certificate has not been suspended or cancelled;

(e) where the candidate is not a Canadian citizen or a permanent resident of Canada, evidence that the candidate is entitled under the laws of Canada to obtain employment in Canada as a teacher; and

(f) such evidence as the Registrar may require of successful teaching experience in schools and programs similar to those for which the interim certificate of qualification applied for is valid.

13. (1) Where an applicant for an interim certificate of qualification,

(a) has complied with section 12;

(b) has successfully completed in a Canadian province other than Ontario a teacher education program acceptable to the College; and

(c) holds the academic or technological qualifications required for a certificate of qualification,

the Registrar may issue to the applicant a Letter of Eligibility in the form provided for in the by-laws of the College.

(2) The Letter of Eligibility is valid for three years from its date of issue.

(3) Where an applicant who holds a Letter of Eligibility granted under this section submits to the Registrar evidence that the applicant has an offer of a position as a teacher in Ontario from,

(a) a board;

(b) a private school;
(c) the Provincial Schools Authority established under section 2 of the *Provincial Schools Negotiations Act*;
(d) the Department of Indian Affairs and Northern Development of the Government of Canada; or
(e) a council of a band or an incorporated education authority established by two or more bands where such council of the band or education authority is authorized by the Crown in right of Canada to provide education for Indians,

and that the offer is subject to the applicant obtaining an interim certificate of qualification, the Registrar may grant to the applicant an interim certificate of qualification in the form provided for in the by-laws, valid for six years from the date of issue.

14. (1) Where an applicant for an interim certificate of qualification,
(a) has complied with the requirements of section 12;
(b) has successfully completed outside Canada a teacher education program acceptable to the College; and
(c) holds the academic or technological qualifications required for a certificate of qualification,

the Registrar may issue to the applicant a Letter of Eligibility in the form provided for in the by-laws.

(2) The Letter of Eligibility is valid for three years from its date of issue.

15. Where an applicant who holds a Letter of Eligibility issued under section 14 submits to the Registrar evidence that the applicant,
(a) has an offer of a position as a teacher in Ontario from,
  (i) a board,
  (ii) a private school,
  (iii) the Provincial Schools Authority established under section 2 of the *Provincial Schools Negotiations Act*,
  (iv) the Department of Indian Affairs and Northern Development of the Government of Canada, or
  (v) a council of a band or an incorporated education authority established by two or more bands where such council of the band or education authority is authorized by the Crown in right of Canada to provide education for Indians,
and such offer is subject to his or her obtaining an interim certificate of qualification; and
(b) has successfully completed, subsequent to the date of such offer, an approved orientation program in English or French, as the case may be, for holders of Letters of Eligibility,

the Registrar may grant to the applicant an interim certificate of qualification in the form provided for in the by-laws, valid for six years from the date of issue.

16. The Registrar may grant an interim certificate of qualification, in the form provided for in the by-laws that is valid for a period of one year from the date of issue to a person who,
(a) was the holder of a letter of standing that was issued under Parts I, II, and IV of

Ontario Regulation 295/73 and that had the force of an Interim Certificate referred to in subsection 28(1); and

(b) is not the holder of a certificate of qualification or an interim certificate of qualification and who is offered a position as a teacher by,
   (i) a board,
   (ii) a private school,
   (iii) the Provincial Schools Authority established under section 2 of the *Provincial Schools Negotiations Act*,
   (iv) the Department of Indian Affairs and Northern Development of the Government of Canada, or
   (v) a council of a band or an education authority, where such council of the band or education authority is authorized by the Crown in right of Canada to provide education for Indians.

17. (1) Where a person who holds an interim certificate of qualification granted under section 13, 15 or 16, that is still valid or that has expired, submits to the Registrar evidence that the person had, while the person was the holder of the interim certificate of qualification, at least ten months of successful teaching experience in Ontario as certified by the appropriate supervisory officer, the Registrar may grant to the person a certificate of qualification in the form provided for in the by-laws, indicating the areas of concentration successfully completed.

(2) Where an interim certificate of qualification issued under section 13, 15 or 16 expires, the person who is the holder of the interim certificate of qualification is not eligible for another interim certificate of qualification.

18. (1) Where a person who holds an interim certificate of qualification granted under section 13, 15 or 16 that has expired or is about to expire, submits to the Registrar,

(a) evidence that the person had while the person was the holder of the interim certificate of qualification fewer than 10 months of successful teaching experience in Ontario, as certified by the appropriate supervisory officer; and

(b) evidence that the person has an offer of a position as a teacher from,
   (i) a board,
   (ii) a private school,
   (iii) the Provincial Schools Authority established under section 2 of the *Provincial Schools Negotiations Act*,
   (iv) the Department of Indian Affairs and Northern Development of the Government of Canada, or
   (v) a council of a band or an education authority established by two or more bands where such council of the band or education authority is authorized by the Crown in right of Canada to provide education for Indians.

the Registrar may, despite subsection 17(2), extend the period of validity of the interim certificate of qualification that has expired or is about to expire, as the case may be, for one year periods.

(2) Where the Registrar extends the period of validity of an interim certificate of qualification under subsection (1), the interim certificate of qualification issued to the person shall be altered to indicate the extended period of validity.

19. (1) Where the dean of a college or faculty of education or the director of a school of education in Ontario reports to the Registrar that a candidate,

(a) has complied with section 2;

(b) is entitled under the laws of Canada to obtain employment in Canada as a teacher, if the candidate is not a Canadian citizen or a permanent resident of Canada;

(c) is unable to undertake a program leading to the certificate of qualification by reason of impaired hearing;

(d) holds an acceptable university degree or qualifications the College considers equivalent thereto; and

(e) has successfully completed an approved program of teacher education for teaching the deaf,

the Registrar may grant to the candidate a certificate of qualification (restricted) that is in the form provided for in the by-laws and valid in Ontario for teaching the deaf.

(2) The Registrar may grant a certificate of qualification (limited, restricted) valid for one year for teaching the deaf to a candidate who has successfully completed an approved program of teacher education outside Ontario for teaching the deaf, if the candidate submits to the Registrar,

(a) evidence that the candidate has complied with section 2;

(b) evidence that the candidate is deaf or hard of hearing;

(c) evidence that the candidate is a Canadian citizen or a permanent resident of Canada or is entitled under the laws of Canada to obtain employment in Canada as a teacher;

(d) evidence that the candidate holds an acceptable university degree or qualifications that the College considers equivalent to an acceptable university degree; and

(e) if the candidate is qualified to teach outside Ontario,

(i) the candidate's teaching certificate and a transcript of the candidate's teacher education program, and

(ii) a statement from the authority that issued the candidate's teaching certificate that the certificate has not been suspended or cancelled.

(3) The certificate of qualification (limited, restricted) granted under subsection (2) shall be in the form provided for in the by-laws.

(4) The Registrar may extend a certificate of qualification (limited, restricted) granted under subsection (2) for one-year periods.

(5) The Registrar may grant a certificate of qualification (restricted) for teaching the deaf to a person who holds a certificate of qualification (limited, restricted) granted under subsection (2) if the person submits to the Registrar evidence of at least one year of experience successfully teaching the deaf in Ontario since the granting of the certificate of qualification (limited, restricted), as certified by the appropriate supervisory officer.

(6) The certificate of qualification (restricted) granted under subsection (5) shall be in the form provided for in the by-laws.

20. Where the principal of a course leading to the additional qualification of Part I Special Education, or the dean of a college or faculty of education or the director of a school of education in Ontario, repots to the Registrar that a candidate,

(a) holds one of,

(i) a Diploma in Pre-School Education obtained at Ryerson Polytechnic University,
(ii) a Diploma in Child Study obtained at the Institute of Child Study of the University of Toronto, or
(iii) a Diploma in Early Childhood Education obtained at an Ontario college of applied arts and technology;
(b) has complied with section 2;
(c) has successfully completed the program for Part I Special Education including Part I of the Teaching Trainable Retarded option; and
(d) is entitled under the laws of Canada to obtain employment in Canada as a teacher, if the candidate is not a Canadian citizen or a permanent resident of Canada,

the Registrar may grant to the candidate a certificate of qualification (limited, restricted), in the form provided for in the by-laws, that is valid for one year for teaching in schools or classes for the trainable retarded.

21. Where a person who is the holder of a certificate of qualification (limited, restricted) granted under section 20 that has expired, or is about to expire, submits to the Registrar evidence that he or she has an offer of a position as a teacher in schools or classes for the trainable retarded, the Registrar may renew the certificate of qualification (limited, restricted) for a period of one year.

22. Where the principal of a course leading to the additional qualification of Part II Special Education, or the dean of a college or faculty of education or the director of a school of education in Ontario reports to the Registrar that a candidate,

(a) holds a certificate of qualification (limited, restricted) granted under section 20;
(b) has taught successfully for one year in Ontario in a school or class for the trainable retarded as certified by the appropriate supervisory officer;
(c) is entitled under the laws of Canada to obtain employment in Canada as a teacher, if the candidate is not a Canadian citizen or a permanent resident of Canada; and
(d) has successfully completed the program for Part II Special Education including Part II of the Teaching Trainable Retarded option,

the Registrar may grant to the candidate a certificate of qualification (restricted), in the form provided for in the by-laws, that is valid for teaching in schools or classes for the trainable retarded.

23. (1) The Registrar may grant to a candidate a certificate of qualification (limited, restricted) valid for one year for the teaching of a Native language as a second language if the dean of a college or faculty of education or the director of a school of education in Ontario reports to the Registrar that the candidate,

(a) has demonstrated an acceptable degree of fluency in the Algonquin or Iroquoian language;
(b) has complied with section 2;
(c) has successfully completed the first session of an approved program for Teacher of a Native Language as a Second Language; and
(d) is entitled under the laws of Canada to obtain employment in Canada as a teacher, if the candidate is not a Canadian citizen or a permanent resident of Canada.

(2) A certificate of qualification (limited, restricted) granted under subsection (1) shall be in the form provided for in the by-laws.

24. The Registrar may extend a candidate's certificate of qualification (limited, restricted) for one year for the teaching of a Native language as a second language if the dean of a college or faculty of education or the director of a school of education in Ontario reports to the Registrar that the candidate,

(a) holds a certificate of qualification (limited, restricted) granted under section 23;

(b) has submitted evidence of at least one year of successful teaching experience in a Native language as a second language, as certified by,

(i) the appropriate supervisory officer, where the successful teaching experience was in Ontario and was not in a school operated on an Indian reserve, or

(ii) the appropriate supervisory official, where the successful teaching experience was outside Ontario or in a school operated on an Indian reserve in Ontario; and

(c) has successfully completed the second session of an approved program for Teacher of a Native Language as a Second Language after completing the experience referred to in clause (b).

25. (1) The Registrar may grant to a candidate a certificate of qualification (restricted) for the teaching of a Native language as a second language if the dean of a college or faculty of education or the director of a school of education in Ontario reports to the Registrar that the candidate,

(a) holds a certificate of qualification (limited, restricted) extended under section 24;

(b) has submitted evidence of at least one year of successful teaching experience in a Native language as a second language, following the completion of the teaching experience referred to in section 24, as certified by,

(i) the appropriate supervisory officer, where the successful teaching experience was in Ontario and was not in a school operated on an Indian Reserve, or

(ii) the appropriate supervisory official, where the successful teaching experience was outside Ontario or in a school operated on an Indian Reserve in Ontario; and

(c) has successfully completed the third session of an approved program for Teacher of a Native Language as a Second Language after completing the successful teaching experience referred to in clause (b).

(2) The certificate of qualification (restricted) granted under subsection (1) shall be in the form provided for in the by-laws.

26. (1) The Registrar may grant to a candidate a certificate of qualification (limited, restricted) valid for one year for teaching dance if the dean of a college or faculty of education or the director of a school of education in Ontario reports to the Registrar that the candidate,

(a) has complied with section 2;

(b) holds a Secondary School Graduation Diploma or has qualifications that the College considers to be equivalent to a Secondary School Graduation Diploma;

(c) has successfully completed, before August 31, 1995, the first session of the program in Dance referred to in Schedule D;

(d) is competent to perform in the areas of dance taught in elementary and secondary schools; and

(e) is entitled under the laws of Canada to obtain employment in Canada as a teacher, if the candidate is not a Canadian citizen or a permanent resident of Canada.

(2) A certificate of qualification (limited, restricted) granted under subsection (1) shall be in the form provided for in the by-laws.

(3) The Registrar may extend a candidate's certificate of qualification (limited, restricted) for one year for teaching dance if the dean of a college or faculty of education or the director of a school of education in Ontario reports to the Registrar that the candidate,

(a) holds a certificate of qualification (limited, restricted) granted under subsection (1);

(b) has submitted evidence of at least one year of experience successfully teaching dance in Ontario since the granting of the certificate of qualification (limited, restricted), as certified by the appropriate supervisory officer; and

(c) has successfully completed, before August 31, 1996, the second session of the program in Dance referred to in Schedule D.

(4) The Registrar may grant a candidate a certificate of qualification (restricted) for teaching dance if the dean of a college or faculty of education or the director of a school of education in Ontario reports to the Registrar that the candidate,

(a) holds a certificate of qualification (limited, restricted) granted under subsection (1);

(b) has submitted evidence of at least one year of experience successfully teaching dance in Ontario following the experience referred to in clause (3)(b), as certified by the appropriate supervisory officer; and

(c) has successfully completed, before August 31, 1997, the third session of the program in Dance referred to in Schedule D.

(5) The certificate of qualification (restricted) granted under subsection (4) shall be in the form provided for in the by-laws.

27. The Registrar may grant to a candidate a certificate of qualification in the form provided for in the by-laws if the candidate submits to the Registrar evidence that the candidate,

(a) holds a valid certificate of qualification (restricted);

(b) holds an acceptable university degree or qualifications that the College considers equivalent to an acceptable university degree; and

(c) has successfully completed an approved program of teacher education leading to qualifications in two areas of concentration in the primary division, junior division, intermediate division or senior division.

28. (1) A person who holds one of the following certificates and who is,

(a) a Canadian citizen; or

(b) a British subject who was granted the certificate prior to September 1, 1973,

is deemed to hold the certificate of qualification:

1. First Class Certificate valid in Secondary Schools.
2. High School Specialist's Certificate.
3. Interim Elementary School Teacher's Certificate.
4. Interim Elementary School Teacher's Certificate, Standard 1, 2, 3 or 4.
5. Interim Elementary School Teacher's Certificate, Standard 1, 2, 3 or 4 (French only).

6. Interim First Class Certificate.
7. Interim High School Assistant's Certificate.
8. Interim High School Assistant's Certificate, Type A.
9. Interim High School Assistant's Certificate, Type B.
10. Interim Occupational Certificate, Type A (Practical Subjects).
11. Interim Occupational Certificate, Type B (Practical Subjects).
12. Interim Primary School Specialist's Certificate.
13. Interim Second Class Certificate.
14. Interim Vocational Certificate, Type A.
15. Interim Vocational Certificate, Type B.
16. Occupational Specialist's Certificate (Practical Subjects).
17. Permanent Commercial—Vocational Certificate.
18. Permanent Elementary School Teacher's Certificate.
19. Permanent Elementary School Teacher's Certificate, Standard 1, 2, 3 or 4.
20. Permanent Elementary School Teacher's Certificate, Standard 1, 2, 3 or 4 (French only).
21. Permanent First Class Certificate.
22. Permanent High School Assistant's Certificate.
23. Permanent Occupational Certificate (Practical Subjects).
24. Permanent Primary School Specialist's Certificate.
25. Permanent Second Class Certificate.
26. Permanent Vocational Certificate.
27. Vocational Specialist's Certificate.

(2) The Registrar shall grant to a person referred to in subsection (1) a certificate of qualification in the form provided for in the by-laws.

(3) A person who holds an interim certificate referred to in subsection (1) continues to be qualified to teach in accordance with the certificate until the date to which the certificate is valid as shown thereon and the person may upon application be granted by the Registrar a certificate of qualification in the form provided for in the by-laws.

(4) Where a person who held a Letter of Standing granted before July 1, 1978 submits to the Registrar evidence of at least 10 months of successful teaching experience in Ontario, as certified by the appropriate supervisory officer, in a division or subject for which the Letter of Standing is valid, the Registrar may grant to the person a certificate of qualification in the form provided for in the by-laws.

29. (1) A person who holds one of the following certificates or Letters of Standing that was valid on July 1, 1978 but who was not qualified for an Ontario Teacher's Certificate under Regulation 297 of the Revised Regulations of Ontario, 1990, as it read on the day before this regulation comes into force holds a certificate of qualification (restricted) indicating qualifications to teach in the classes schools and subjects that were indicated on the person's certificate or letter of standing:

1. Elementary Certificate in Teaching Trainable Retarded Children.
2. Elementary Instrumental Music Certificate, Type A.
3. Elementary Instrumental Music Certificate, Type B.
4. Elementary Vocal Music Certificate, Type A.

5. Elementary Vocal Music Certificate, Type B.
6. Interim School Class Certificate (French only).
7. Interim Specialist Certificate in Instrumental Music.
8. Interim Specialist Certificate in Vocal Music.
9. Intermediate Certificate in Teaching Trainable Retarded Children.
10. Intermediate Industrial Arts Only Certificate.
11. Intermediate Instrumental Music Certificate, Type A.
12. Intermediate Instrumental Music Certificate, Type B.
13. Intermediate Vocal Music Certificate, Type A.
14. Intermediate Vocal Music Certificate, Type B.
15. Letter of Standing (renewable).
16. Permanent Letter of Standing (Renewable).
17. Permanent Second Class Certificate (French only).
18. Permanent Specialist Certificate in Instrumental Music.
19. Permanent Specialist Certificate in Vocal Music.
20. Specialist Certificate as Teacher of the Blind.
21. Specialist Certificates as Teacher of the Deaf.
22. Supervisor's Certificate in Instrumental Music.
23. Supervisor's Certificate in Vocal Music.
24. Teacher of the Trainable Retarded.
25. Temporary Certificate as Teacher of French to English-speaking Pupils in Elementary Schools.

(2) Where the dean of a college or faculty of education or the director of a school of education in Ontario reports to the Registrar that the candidate,

(a) has complied with section 2;

(b) is entitled under the laws of Canada to obtain employment in Canada as a teacher, if the candidate is not a Canadian citizen or a permanent resident of Canada;

(c) holds or is deemed to hold a certificate of qualification (restricted) referred to in subsection (1);

(d) holds an acceptable university degree or qualifications the College considers equivalent thereto, or technological qualifications or, in the case of a candidate for a certificate of qualification valid for teaching in French-language schools and classes established under Part XII of the *Education Act*, a Secondary School Honour Graduation Diploma; and

(e) has successfully completed approved programs with concentration in two divisions,

the Registrar may grant to the candidate a certificate of qualification in the form provided for in the by-laws, indicating the areas of concentration successfully completed.

(3) A person who holds a Deferred Elementary School Teacher's Certificate or a Deferred First Class Certificate that was valid on July 1, 1978 remains qualified to teach in the schools and classes for which he or she is qualified by the certificate and, upon submission to the College of evidence of completion of the academic requirements for an Interim Elementary School Teacher's Certificate or an Interim First Class Certificate, as the case may be, in force at the time the deferred certificate was issued, the Registrar may grant to the person a certificate of qualification in the form provided for in the by-laws.

PART II

ADDITIONAL QUALIFICATIONS FOR TEACHERS

30. A session of a course leading to an additional qualification shall consist of a minimum of 125 hours of work that is approved by the Registrar.

31. Where the dean of a college or faculty of education or the director of a school of education in Ontario reports to the Registrar that a candidate,

(a) holds or has been recommended by the dean or the director for a certificate of qualification, an interim certificate of qualification or certificate or qualification (restricted);

(b) holds an acceptable university degree or qualifications the College considers equivalent thereto; and

(c) has successfully completed an approved program leading to qualifications in an additional area of concentration in the primary division, the junior division, the intermediate division in general studies or the senior division in general studies, or has qualifications that the College considers equivalent to the successful completion of such a program,

the Registrar may have entered on the candidate's certificate of qualification such additional area of concentration.

32. (1) Subject to subsection (2), where the dean of a college or faculty of education in Ontario reports to the Registrar that a candidate,

(a) holds or has been recommended by the dean or the director for a certificate of qualification or an interim certificate of qualification;

(b) has successfully completed an approved program leading to additional qualifications in a subject listed in Schedule B, or has qualifications that the College considers equivalent to the successful completion of such a program.

(c) in the case of a candidate for a qualification listed in Schedule B at the advanced level, has produced evidence of,

 (i) twelve months of business or individual experience in the area of qualification,

 (ii) academic experience that the College considers equivalent to 12 months of business or industrial experience in the area of the qualification, or

 (iii) a combination of academic, business and industrial experience that the College considers equivalent to 12 months of business or industrial experience in the area of the qualification; and

(d) has demonstrated competence in the area referred to in clause (c),

the Registrar may have entered on the candidate's certificate of qualification the additional qualification in such subject.

(2) An additional qualification may not be entered under subsection (1) on the certificate of qualification in respect of such teacher, of a candidate whose areas of concentration in the program of professional education that qualified him or her for the certificate of qualification were not in technological studies unless the candidate meets the requirements of clause (c) of the definition of "technological qualifications" in subsection 1(1).

ONE-SESSION COURSES

33. Where the principal of a single-session course leading to a qualification listed in Schedule C or the dean of a college or faculty of education or the director of a school of education in Ontario reports to the Registrar that a candidate,

(a) holds or has been recommended by the dean or the director for a certificate of qualification or an interim certificate of qualification; and

(b) has successfully completed an approved program leading to additional qualifications in a subject listed in Schedule C, or has qualifications that the College considers equivalent to the successful completion of such a program,

the Registrar may have entered upon the candidate's certificate of qualification the additional qualification in such subject.

THREE-SESSION SPECIALIST COURSES

34. The Registrar may have entered on a candidate's certificate of qualification the Part I qualification in a subject listed in Schedule D if the principal of the first session of a three-session course leading to a specialist qualification in the subject, the dean of a college or faculty of education or the director of a school of education in Ontario reports to the Registrar that the candidate,

(a) holds a certificate of qualification or an interim certificate of qualification;

(b) has successfully completed an approved program leading to the Part I qualification; and

(c) has an entry on the candidate's certificate of qualification that shows,

(i) qualification in the primary division, the junior division, the intermediate division in general studies or the senior division in general studies, in the case of Part I qualification other than Primary Education, Junior Education or Intermediate Education,

(ii) an area of concentration for the corresponding division, in the case of a Part I qualification in Primary Education, Junior Education or Intermediate Education, or

(iii) qualification in technological studies, in the case of a Part I qualification in one of the following:

1. Actualisation linguistique en français/Perfectionnement du français (ALF/PDF).
2. Computers in the Classroom.
3. Co-operative Education.
4. Design and Technology.
5. English as a Second Language.
6. Guidance.
7. Media.
8. Multiculturalism in Education.
9. Music—Instrumental.
10. Music—Vocal (Primary, Junior).

11. Music—Vocal (Intermediate, Senior).
12. Religious Education.
13. Special Education.
14. The Blind.
15. The Deaf.
16. The Deaf/Blind.
17. Visual Arts.

35. Where the principal of the second session of a three-session course or the dean of a college or faculty of education or the director of a school of education in Ontario reports to the Registrar that a candidate,

(a) holds or is deemed to hold a certificate of qualification or an interim certificate of qualification;

(b) has successfully completed the first session, or the equivalent thereof, of a course leading to an additional qualification in a subject listed in Schedule D;

(c) has submitted evidence of at least one year of successful teaching experience in Ontario certified by the appropriate supervisory officer or of at least one year of successful teaching experience outside Ontario certified by the appropriate supervisory official; and

(d) has successfully completed the approved program for the second session of the course after completing the experience referred to in clause (c),

the Registrar may have entered upon the candidate's certificate of qualification the Part II qualification in such subject.

36. Where the principal of the third session of a three-session course or the dean of a college or faculty of education or the director of a school of education in Ontario reports to the Registrar that the candidate,

(a) holds or is deemed to hold a certificate of qualification or an interim certificate of qualification;

(b) has successfully completed the second session, or the equivalent thereof, of a course leading to an additional qualification in a subject listed in Schedule D;

(c) submits evidence of at least two years of successful teaching experience, including at least one year of experience in Ontario in the subject referred to in clause (b), certified by the appropriate supervisory officer and, if some of the experience was outside Ontario, by the appropriate supervisory official; and

(d) has successfully completed subsequent to the experience referred to in clause (c) the approved program for the third session of such course,

the Registrar may have entered upon the candidate's certificate of qualification the specialist qualification in such subject.

37. Where the dean of a college or faculty of education or the director of a school of education in Ontario reports to the Registrar that the candidate who does not hold a certificate of qualification,

(a) holds a certificate of qualification (restricted) valid in Ontario for teaching the deaf only; and

(b) has otherwise met the requirements of section 33, 34, 35, 36, 40, 46 or 47, the Registrar may grant to the candidate the appropriate additional qualification.

38. (1) A teacher who holds or is deemed to hold a certificate of qualification and who, prior to October 1, 1978, began a Master of Education program that was approved by the Minister as leading to the Specialist Certificate in Guidance, may obtain the specialist qualification in Guidance by completing the requirements for such Certificate as they existed on June 30, 1978, and the Registrar shall, upon submission to the Registrar of evidence satisfactory to the Registrar of the completion of such requirements, have entered on such teacher's certificate of qualification the specialist qualifications in Guidance.

(2) A teacher who holds or is deemed to hold a certificate of qualification and who, prior to October 1, 1978, began a Master of Library Science program that was approved by the Minister as leading to the Specialist Certificate in Librarianship, may obtain the specialist qualification in Librarianship by completing the requirements for such Certificate as they existed on June 30, 1978, and the Registrar shall, upon submission to the Registrar of evidence satisfactory to the Registrar of the completion of such requirements, have entered on such teacher's certificate of qualification the specialist qualification in Librarianship.

39. A teacher who holds a special certificate in a subject listed in Schedule C, D or E, or a special certificate no longer issued, continues to be qualified in accordance with such certificate, and the Registrar shall have the additional qualification corresponding to such special certificate recorded on the teacher's certificate of qualification where the teacher holds or is granted a certificate of qualification.

ONE-SESSION HONOUR SPECIALIST COURSE

40. (1) Where the dean of a college or faculty of education in Ontario reports to the Registrar that a candidate for an Honour Specialist qualification in a subject or subjects listed in Schedule E,

(a) holds or is deemed to hold a certificate of qualification or an interim certificate of qualification and the candidate's certificate of qualification has an entry showing qualifications in the primary division, the junior division, the intermediate division in general studies or the senior division in general studies; and

(b) holds,

(i) a degree of Bachelor of Arts or Bachelor of Science from an Ontario university in a program,

(A) that requires four years of university study, or the equivalent thereof, to a total of at least 60 university credits, and

(B) in which the candidate has obtained at least second class or equivalent standing in the subject or subjects in which the candidate seeks an Honour Specialist qualification, including, in the case of two subjects, at least 42 university credits therein and not fewer than 18 university credits in each subject or, in the case of one subject, at least 27 university credits therein, or

(ii) qualifications the College considers equivalent to the qualifications referred to in subclause (i);

(c) submits evidence of at least two years of successful teaching experience, including at least one year of experience in Ontario in the subject or one or both of the subjects in which the Honours Specialist qualification is sought, certified by the appropriate supervisory officer and, if some of the experience was outside Ontario, by the appropriate supervisory official; and

(d) has successfully completed subsequent to the experience referred to in clause (c) the approved program for the Honour Specialist qualification in the subject or subjects referred to in sub-subclause (b)(i)(B),

the Registrar may have entered upon the candidate's certificate of qualification the Honour Specialist qualification in such subject or subjects referred to in sub-subclause (b)(i)(B).

(2) A university credit that has been used to meet the requirements for an Honour Specialist qualification established by clause (1)(b) shall not be used to meet the requirements for another Honour Specialist qualifications.

(3) For the purpose of clause (1)(b), a university credit in Anthropology, Psychology or Sociology shall be deemed to be a university credit in Individual and Society.

(4) Where the dean of a college or faculty of education in Ontario reports to the Registrar that a candidate for the Honour Technological Studies Specialist Qualification,

(a) holds or is deemed to hold a certificate of qualification or an interim certificate of qualification;

(b) has entries on his or her certificate of qualification indicating qualifications in at least,

(i) three of the subjects listed in Schedule B including at least one at both the basic and the advanced level, or

(ii) four of the subjects listed in Schedule B at the basic level and an entry indicating the Specialist qualification in one of the subjects in Schedule D listed in subclause 34(c)(iii);

(c) submits evidence of at least two years of successful teaching experience, including at least one year of experience in Ontario in technological studies, certified by the appropriate supervisory officer and, if some of the experience was outside Ontario, by the appropriate supervisory official;

(d) holds a Secondary School Honour Graduation Diploma or has successfully completed the equivalent of one year's full-time study in a program in respect of which a Secondary School Graduation Diploma or its equivalent is required for admission; and

(e) has successfully completed subsequent to the experience referred to in clause (c) the approved program for the Honour Technological Studies Specialist qualification,

the Registrar may have entered upon the candidate's certificate of qualification the Honour Technological Studies Specialist qualification.

(5) The entry on a candidate's certificate of qualification indicating that he or she has completed successfully the first session of a three-session course leading to the Specialist qualification in Design and Technology or Computer Studies — Computer Technology is deemed to be equivalent to one basic level entry for the purposes of clause (4)(b).

41. (1) Where a teacher who completed prior to September 1, 1979 the first session of a two-session course leading to an Interim Vocational Certificate, Type A or an Interim Occupational Certificate, Type A completes the requirements for such certificate as they existed on June 30, 1978, the Registrar may have entered on the teacher's certificate of qualification the appropriate qualification.

(2) Where a teacher who,

(a) held an Interim High School Assistant's Certificate, Type A on July 1, 1978; or
(b) completed at a college or faculty of education in Ontario prior to July 1, 1979 the requirements for such certificate as they existed immediately before July 1, 1978,

completes the requirements for the High School Specialist Certificate as they existed immediately before July 1, 1978, the Registrar may have entered on the teacher's certificate of qualification the appropriate Honours Specialist qualification.

42. A teacher who before May 20, 1997 held an Honour Specialist qualification in Latin or Greek shall be deemed to hold an Honour Specialist qualification in Classical Studies (Latin, Greek).

PRINCIPAL'S QUALIFICATIONS

43. (1) The Principal's Qualification Program shall consist of two one-session courses.

(2) A teacher holds principal's qualifications if the teacher's certificate of qualification has an entry for Part II of the Principal's Qualification Program.

44. An applicant for admission to the Principal's Qualification Program must,

(a) hold an acceptable university degree;
(b) hold a certificate of qualification or interim certificate of qualification;
(c) hold concentrations in three divisions including the intermediate division, as indicated on the applicant's certificate of qualification;
(d) provide evidence of at least five years of successful teaching experience in a school providing elementary or secondary education, as certified by the appropriate supervisory officer or, in the case of experience outside Ontario, by the appropriate supervisory official; and
(e) hold or provide evidence of one of the following:
    1. A Specialist or Honour Specialist qualification as indicated on the applicant's certificate of qualification and,
        (i) successful completion of at least half the number of courses required to qualify for a master's degree that is an acceptable university degree, or
        (ii) an additional Specialist or Honour Specialist qualification as indicated on the applicant's certificate of qualification.
    2. A master's degree or doctorate that is an acceptable university degree.
    3. Successful completion of such number of graduate university courses as is equivalent to the number of graduate university courses that are required to qualify for a master's degree that is an acceptable university degree.

45. If the principal of a course leading to qualifications in Part I of the Principal's Qualification Program reports to the Registrar that a candidate has met the admission requirements of section 44 and has successfully completed the course, the Registrar may have the Part I qualification entered on the candidate's certificate of qualification.

46. An applicant for admission to a course leading to qualifications in Part II of the Principal's Qualification Program must have an entry on his or her certificate of qualification showing qualifications in Part I of the program.

47. If the principal of a course leading to qualifications in Part II of the Principal's Qualification Program reports to the Registrar that a candidate has met the admission requirements of section 46 or 51 and has successfully completed the course, the Registrar may have the Part II qualifications entered on the candidate's certificate of qualification.

48. Where the principal of a Principal's Development Centre reports to the Registrar that a candidate,

(a) holds principal's qualifications;

(b) has two years of successful experience as a principal or vice-principal as certified by the appropriate supervisory officer; and

(c) has successfully completed the Course.

the Registrar may have entered on the candidate's certificate of qualification the Principal's Development Course qualification.

49. A teacher who holds a High School Principal's Certificate, an Elementary School Principal's Certificate, a Secondary School Principal's Certificate, Type B, a Secondary School Principal's Certificate, Type A, a Secondary School Principal's Certificate or a Vocation School Principal's Certificate, whether such certificate is an interim certificate or a permanent certificate, remains qualified within the limitations of the certificate except that the interim qualification will not lapse after the five-year period of validity and such qualification shall be shown on his or her certificate of qualification.

50. A teacher who holds an Elementary School Inspector's Certificate shall be deemed to hold an Elementary School Principal's Certificate.

51. Despite section 46, a teacher who holds or who is deemed to hold an interim or permanent Elementary School Principal's Certificate, or who holds an interim or permanent Secondary School Principal's Certificate, Type B, an interim or permanent Vocational School Principal's Certificate, an interim Secondary School Principal's Certificate, or an interim Secondary School Principal's Certificate Type A, may be admitted to the course leading to qualifications in Part II of the Principal's Qualification Program.

52. (1) Where a teacher held an interim Elementary School Principal's Certificate, an interim Secondary School Principal's Certificate, Type B, or an interim Secondary School Principal's Certificate, Type A, on July 1, 1978 and completes the requirements for the permanent certificate that corresponds thereto as they existed immediately before July 1, 1978, the Registrar shall have entered on the teacher's certificate of qualification the appropriate qualification.

(2) A teacher who holds a permanent Secondary School Principal's Certificate, Type A or a permanent Secondary School Principal's Certificate is deemed to hold principal's qualifications.

PART IV

TEMPORARY LETTERS OF APPROVAL

53. (1) The Registrar may grant to a board a Temporary Letter of Approval for a period specified in the letter if the director of education or secretary of the board submits to the Registrar, in duplicate, an application in the form provided for in the by-laws certifying that,
- (a) the board finds it necessary to assign or appoint a teacher to teach a subject or hold a position who does not hold the qualifications required by the regulations made under the *Education Act* for teaching the subject or holding the position; and
- (b) the teacher in respect of whom the application is made,
    - (i) holds a certificate of qualification, an interim certificate of qualification, a certificate of qualification (restricted), a certificate of qualification (limited), or a certificate of qualification (limited, restricted), and
    - (ii) is considered competent to teach the subject or hold the position.

(2) The period for which a Temporary Letter of Approval is granted,
- (a) shall not exceed one year; and
- (b) shall not extend beyond the end of a school year unless the period begins after the end of a school year and ends before the beginning of the next school year.

PART V

QUALIFICATIONS OF SUPERVISORY OFFICERS

54. In this Part,

"acceptable university degree" means a degree from an Ontario university or post-secondary institution that is an ordinary member of the Association of Universities and Colleges of Canada or a degree that is equivalent thereto from a university other than such Ontario university or post-secondary institution;

"Principal's Certificate" means a permanent principal's certificate;

"university" means,
- (a) an Ontario university or post-secondary institution that is an ordinary member of the Association of Universities and Colleges of Canada,
- (b) a Canadian university in a province other than Ontario that is an ordinary member of the Association of Universities and Colleges of Canada,
- (c) a university in the United States that is recognized by,
    - (i) Middle States Association of Colleges and Schools,
    - (ii) New England Association of Schools and Colleges,
    - (iii) North Central Association of Colleges and Schools,
    - (iv) Northwest Association of Schools and Colleges,
    - (v) Southern Association of Colleges and Schools,
    - (vi) Western Association of Schools and Colleges, or
- (d) a university that is located in a country other than Canada or the United States and that is a member of the association of Commonwealth Universities or the International Association of Universities.

S. 55 REGULATIONS UNDER THE ONTARIO COLLEGE OF TEACHERS ACT

55. A person who meets the following qualifications shall have an entry recorded on his or her certificate of qualification or interim certificate of qualification indicating an additional qualification as a supervisory officer:

1. The person has at least seven years of successful teaching experience in a school providing elementary or secondary education.
2. The person holds a certificate of qualification or an interim certificate of qualification.
3. The person holds qualifications to teach in the intermediate division and at least two other divisions that are indicated on the person's certificate of qualification.
4. The person holds an acceptable university degree.
5. The person holds a master's degree from a university.
6. The person meets one or more of the following criteria:
    i. The person holds,
        A. an Elementary School Principal's Certificate,
        B. a Secondary School Principal's Certificate, Type A.
        C. a Secondary School Principal's Certificate, Type B, or
        D. a Secondary School Principal's Certificate.
    ii. The person holds a certificate of qualification indicating Part I and Part II Principal's Qualifications.
    iii. The person holds specialist or honours specialist qualifications in one or more subjects and has, in addition to the experience required by paragraph 1, at least two years of successful experience as a teacher appointed by a board under section 17 of Regulation 298 of the Revised Regulations of Ontario, 1990 to supervise or co-ordinate a subject or program or to act as a consultant for the teachers of a subject or program, as certified by the appropriate supervisory officer.
    iv. The person has, in addition to the experience required by paragraph 1, at least two years of experience,
        A. as an education officer employed by the Ministry of Education and Training, as certified by a district manager or branch director of the Ministry of Education and Training,
        B. as an employee outside Ontario in a position that is equivalent in the Registrar's opinion to the position of supervisory officer of a school board, as certified by a person acceptable to the Registrar, or
        C. as a program consultant seconded to the Ministry for French language, English language or Native language programs, as certified by a district manager or branch director of the Ministry of Education and Training.
7. The person has successfully completed the supervisory officer's qualifications program described in section 56 within five years after starting the program.

56. The supervisory officer's qualifications programs referred to in section 55 shall have the following features:

1. The program shall be provided by an organization or institution that has entered into a contract with the College to provide the instruction and arrange for the practical experience referred to in paragraphs 3 and 4.
2. No person shall be admitted to the program unless the person has submitted proof to

the organization or institution that provides the program that the person meets the qualifications set out in paragraphs 1 to 6 of section 55.
3. The program shall consist of,
    i. four instructional modules, each consisting of at least 50 hours of instruction, and
    ii. one module consisting of at least 50 hours of practical experience in the workplace.
4. The instructional modules shall provide instruction that, in the opinion of the Registrar, is relevant to the position of supervisory officer in the following subject areas:
    i. Statutes, regulations and government policies affecting education in Ontario.
    ii. Curriculum guidelines and other reference material pertaining to elementary and secondary education in Ontario.
    iii. Theories and practices of supervision, administration and business organization.

PART VI
REGISTRATION

57. A person may apply for a certificate of qualification and registration by submitting to the Registrar a completed application in the form prescribed by the by-laws together with the fee prescribed by the by-laws.

PART VII
TRANSITIONAL

58. The day prescribed for the purposes of subsection 62(1) of the Act is May 20, 1997.

59. For the purposes of subsection 62(2) of the Act, on and after May 20, 1997 any person holding a qualification referred to in one of the following paragraphs shall be deemed to have been granted by the Registrar and to hold the corresponding certificate of qualification under this Regulation containing the same terms, conditions or limitations:
1. Regulation 297 of the Revised Regulations of Ontario, 1990.
2. Ontario Teacher's Qualifications Record Cards.
3. Any other records of qualification held by the Ministry of Education and Training.

60. Any person who is deemed under subsection 63(1) of the Act to have fulfilled the requirements for the issuance of a particular certificate of qualification shall be issued that certificate containing the same terms, conditions and limitations that would have applied to their qualifications referred to in paragraphs 1, 2 and 3 of section 59 before May 20, 1997.

Schedule A

INTERMEDIATE AND SENIOR DIVISION OPTIONS TAKEN IN ENGLISH OR FRENCH

Business Studies—Accounting
Business Studies—Data Processing

Schedule B REGULATIONS UNDER THE ONTARIO COLLEGE OF TEACHERS ACT

Business Studies—Marketing and Merchandising
Business Studies—Information Management
Classical Studies—Greek
Classical Studies—Latin
Computer Science
Dance
Design and Technology
Dramatic Art
Economics
English (First language)
English (Second language)—anglais
Environmental Science
Family Studies
French (Second language)
French (First language)—français
Geography
History
Individual and Society
International Languages
Law
Mathematics
Music—Instrumental
Music—Vocal
Native Language (Second language)
Native Studies
Politics
Physical and Health Education
Religious Education
Science—General
Science—Biology
Science—Chemistry
Science—Geology
Science—Physics
Visual Arts

Schedule B

TECHNOLOGICAL STUDIES OPTIONS TAKEN IN ENGLISH OR FRENCH

BASIC LEVEL	ADVANCED LEVEL
Communications Technology	Communications Technology
Construction Technology	Construction Technology
Hospitality Services	Hospitality Services
Manufacturing Technology	Manufacturing Technology

REGULATION 184/97 **Schedule D**

Personal Services
Technological Design
Transportation Technology

Personal Services
Technological Design
Transportation Technology

Schedule C

ONE-SESSION QUALIFICATIONS TAKEN IN ENGLISH OR FRENCH

Adult Education
Associate Teacher
Childhood Education
Childhood Education in Great Britain
Community School Development
Computer Studies—Computer Technology
Driver Education Instructor
Integrated Arts
Law
Preschool Deaf Education
Teaching Children with Language Difficulties – Aphasia
Teacher of Cree
Teacher of Mohawk
Teacher of Native Children
Teacher of Ojibway
Teaching Writing

Schedule D

THREE SESSION QUALIFICATIONS TAKEN IN ENGLISH OR FRENCH

Actualisation linguistic en français/Perfectionnement du français (ACF/PDF)
Business Studies—Accounting
Business Studies—Data Processing
Business Studies—Entrepreneurship Studies
Business Studies—Marketing and Merchandising
Business Studies—Information Management
Computer Studies—Computer Science
Computers in the Classroom
Co-operative Education
Dance
Design and Technology
Dramatic Arts
English as a Second Language
Environmental Science

Schedule E REGULATIONS UNDER THE ONTARIO COLLEGE OF TEACHERS ACT

Family Studies
French as a Second Language
Guidance
Intermediate Education
International Languages
Junior Education
Librarianship
Mathematics in Primary and Junior Education
Media
Multiculturalism in Education
Music—Instrumental
Music—Vocal (Primary, Junior)
Music—Vocal (Intermediate, Senior)
Native Language as a Second Language
Physical and Health Education (Primary, Junior)
Physical and Health Education (Intermediate, Senior)
Primary Education
Reading
Religious Education
Science in Primary and Junior Education
Special Education
The Blind
The Deaf
The Deaf/Blind
Visual Arts

Schedule E

HONOUR SPECIALIST QUALIFICATIONS TAKEN IN ENGLISH OR FRENCH

Biology
Business Studies
Chemistry
Classical Studies (Latin, Greek)
Computer Science
Contemporary Studies
Dance
Dramatic Arts
English (First language)
English (Second language) – anglais
Environmental Science
Family Studies
French (Second language)
French (First language) – français

REGULATION 184/97 **Schedule E**

Geography
Geology
History
International Languages
Mathematics
Music
Physical and Health Education
Physics
Religious Education
Science
Visual Arts

REGULATION 276/97
TRANSITIONAL MATTERS—DISCIPLINE
O. Reg. 276/97

1. In this Regulation,

"transitional discipline matter" means a matter that was referred by the Minister to the Ontario Teachers' Federation before May 20, 1997 for a recommendation on whether or not a certificate of qualification or letter of standing should be suspended, cancelled or reinstated under paragraph 13 of subsection 8(1) of the *Education Act*, if the matter was not disposed of by the Minister before that date.

2. (1) If the Minister referred a transitional discipline matter to the Ontario Teachers' Federation on or after January 1, 1997, the following rules apply:

1. The Federation and its Relations and Discipline Committee shall not take any further action on the transitional discipline matter, despite the regulations made under the *Teaching Profession Act*.
2. The Minister shall refer the transitional discipline matter to the College.
3. The transitional discipline matter shall be disposed of in accordance with the *Ontario College of Teachers Act, 1996*.

(2) If the Minister referred a transitional discipline matter to the Ontario Teachers' Federation before January 1, 1997, the following rules apply:

1. The Federation and its Relations and Discipline Committee shall deal with the transitional discipline matter in accordance with the regulations made under the *Teaching Profession Act*, as they read immediately before May 20, 1997.
2. After considering any recommendation made by the Federation's Relations and Discipline Committee, the Minister may decide whether to suspend, cancel or reinstate a certificate of qualification or letter of standing under paragraph 13 of subsection 8(1) of the *Education Act*.
3. The Minister shall promptly advise the Registrar in writing of any decision under paragraph 2.
4. A decision of the Minister to suspend a person's certificate of qualification or letter of standing for a period of time under paragraph 2 shall be deemed to be a decision of the Discipline Committee of the College under section 30 of the *Ontario College of Teachers Act, 1996*,
    i. directing the Registrar to suspend the person's certificate of qualification and registration for that period of time, and
    ii. fixing a one-year period during which the person may not apply under section 33 of the Act to have the suspension removed.
5. A decision of the Minister to cancel a person's certificate of qualification or letter of standing under paragraph 2 shall be deemed to be a decision of the Discipline Committee of the College under section 30 of the *Ontario College of Teachers Act, 1996*,
    i. directing the Registrar to revoke the person's certificate of qualification and registration, and

ii. fixing a one-year period during which the person may not apply under section 33 of the Act to have a new certificate issued.
6. A decision of the Minister to reinstate a person's certificate of qualification or letter of standing under paragraph 2 shall be deemed to be a decision of the Discipline Committee of the College under section 33 of the *Ontario College of Teachers Act, 1996* directing the Registrar to issue a certificate of qualification and registration to the person.
7. A decision of the Minister not to reinstate a person's certificate of qualification or letter of standing under paragraph 2 shall be deemed to be a decision of the Discipline Committee of the College under section 33 of the *Ontario College of Teachers Act, 1996*,
    i. refusing an application under that section to have a new certificate issued, and
    ii. fixing a one-year period during which the person may not make an application under that section to have a new certificate issued.
8. Section 33 of the *Ontario College of Teachers Act, 1996* applies, with necessary modifications, to a person whose certificate of qualification and registration is suspended or revoked as a result of a decision of the Minister that is deemed under paragraph 4 or 5 to be a decision of the Discipline Committee of the College.
9. Section 35 of the *Ontario College of Teachers Act, 1996* does not apply to a decision of the Minister under paragraph 2 that is deemed under paragraph 4, 5, 6 or 7 to be a decision of the Discipline Committee of the College.

3. (1) Subject to subsection (2), section 33 of the *Ontario College of Teachers Act, 1996* applies, with necessary modifications, to a person whose certificate of qualification or letter of standing was suspended or cancelled by the Minister before May 20, 1997 under paragraph 13 of subsection 8(1) of the *Education Act*.

(2) An application may not be made under section 33 of the *Ontario College of Teachers Act, 1996* pursuant to subsection (1) unless,

(a) in the case of an application to remove a suspension, at least one year has passed since the Minister imposed the suspension; and

(b) in the case of an application to issue a new certificate,
   (i) at least one year has passed since the Minister cancelled the certificate of qualification or letter of standing, and
   (ii) if the Minister refused before May 20, 1997 to reinstate the certificate of qualification or letter of standing, at least one year has passed since the last refusal.

REGULATION 437/97
PROFESSIONAL MISCONDUCT
O. Reg. 437/97

1. The following acts are defined as professional misconduct for the purposes of subsection 30(2) of the Act:

1. Providing false information or documents to the College or any other person with respect to the member's professional qualifications.
2. Inappropriately using a term, title or designation indicating a specialization in the profession which is not specified on the member's certificate of qualification and registration.
3. Permitting, counselling or assisting any person who is not a member to represent himself or herself as a member of the College.
4. Using a name other than the member's name, as set out in the register, in the course of his or her professional duties.
5. Failing to maintain the standards of the profession.
6. Releasing or disclosing information about a student to a person other than the student or, if the student is a minor, the student's parent or guardian. The release or disclosure of information is not an act of professional misconduct if,
    i. the student (or if the student is a minor, the student's parent or guardian) consents to the release or disclosure, or
    ii. if the release or disclosure is required or allowed by law.
7. Abusing a student physically, sexually, verbally, psychologically or emotionally.
8. Practising or purporting to practise the profession while under the influence of any substance or while adversely affected by any dysfunction,
    i. which the member knows or ought to know impairs the member's ability to practise, and
    ii. in respect of which treatment has previously been recommended, ordered or prescribed but the member has failed to follow the treatment.
9. Contravening a term, condition or limitation imposed on the member's certificate of qualification and registration.
10. Failing to keep records as required by his or her professional duties.
11. Failing to supervise adequately a person who is under the professional supervision of the member.
12. Signing or issuing, in the member's professional capacity, a document that the member knows or ought to know contains a false, improper or misleading statement.
13. Falsifying a record relating to the member's professional responsibilities.
14. Failing to comply with the Act or the regulations or the by-laws.
15. Failing to comply with the *Education Act* or the regulations made under that Act, if the member is subject to that Act.
16. Contravening a law if the contravention is relevant to the member's suitability to hold a certificate of qualification and registration.
17. Contravening a law if the contravention has caused or may cause a student who is under the member's professional supervision to be put at or to remain at risk.

18. An act or omission that, having regard to all the circumstances, would reasonably be regarded by members as disgraceful, dishonourable or unprofessional.
19. Conduct unbecoming a member.
20. Failing to appear before a panel of the Investigation Committee to be cautioned or admonished, if the Investigation Committee has required the member to appear under clause 26(5)(c) of the Act.
21. Failing to comply with an order of a panel of the Discipline Committee or an order of a panel of the Fitness to Practise Committee.
22. Failing to co-operate in a College investigation.
23. Failing to take reasonable steps to ensure that the requested information is provided in a complete and accurate manner if the member is required to provide information to the College under the Act and the regulations.
24. Failing to abide by a written undertaking given by the member to the College or by an agreement entered into by the member with the College.
25. Failing to respond adequately or within a reasonable time to a written inquiry from the College.
26. Practising the profession while the member is in a conflict of interest.
27. Failing to comply with the member's duties under the *Child and Family Services Act*.

2. A finding of incompetence, professional misconduct or a similar finding against a member by a governing authority of the teaching profession in a jurisdiction other than Ontario that is based on facts that would, in the opinion of the Discipline Committee, constitute professional misconduct as defined in section 1, is defined as professional misconduct for the purposes of subsection 30(2) of the Act.

ONTARIO STUDENT RECORD (OSR) GUIDELINE

INTRODUCTION

The Ontario Student (OSR) is the record of a student's educational progress through schools in Ontario. The Education Act states that the OSR is "privileged for the information and use of supervisory officers and the principal and teachers of the school for the improvement of instruction" of the student. The authority for the collection and use of information contained in the OSR is also specified in the Education Act. Each student and the parent(s) or guardian(s) of a student who is not an adult must be made aware of the purpose and content of, and have access to, all of the information contained in the OSR.

This guideline sets out the policies of the Ministry of Education in regard to the establishment, maintenance, use, retention, transfer, and disposal of the OSR. It replaces Ontario Regulation 2.71, Pupil Records; the *Manual for the Ontario Student Record (OSR) System, 1985*, revised edition; and the following Records/Data Memoranda: No. 2, "Transfer of Ontario Student Records", revised 1982; No. 9, "OSR Requirements", November 20, 1981; and No. 12, "The Revised Ontario Student Record (OSR) System", April 30, 1985.

This guideline will be revised as needed. Each page of the guideline is dated, and replacement pages will be provided with a revision date. Selected terms used in this guideline are defined in Appendix A.

The content of this guideline has been reviewed for compliance with the provincial Freedom of Information and Protection of Privacy Act, 1987. This legislation deals with the public's right of access to provincial government information. It also deals with an individual's right of access to his or her personal information held by provincial government bodies, as well as the protection of the confidentiality of this information. Effective January 1, 1991, school boards will be required to comply with similar legislation that will apply to municipalities and local school boards.

1. ESTABLISHMENT OF THE OSR

An OSR shall be established for each student who enrols in a school operated by a board. The student and the parent(s) or guardian(s) of a student who is not an adult must be informed of the purpose and content of the OSR at the time of enrolment.

The OSR is an ongoing record and will be transferred, under the conditions outlined in section 6 of this guideline, if the student transfers to another school.

Any part or parts of the OSR may be microrecorded or stored on a computer file in a manner that permits the printing of a clear and legible reproduction. Provision should be made to retain original documents when it is important to keep an original signature or initial on a document. Any microrecording or computer file or reproduction of an OSR is subject to the security and access requirements applicable to a hard copy.

If an OSR folder is lost or inadvertently destroyed, a new OSR folder shall be created. Previous information can be obtained from the current office index card and, if applicable,

---

* Ministry of Education, Ontario Student Record (OSR) Guideline, issued December 1989. © Queen's Printer for Ontario, 1989. Reproduced with permission. **Note: The Guideline is being revised in 1999.**

from the card(s) at the previous school(s). A notation shall be made in the margin on the front of the new OSR folder that gives the date on which the new folder was created and the reason.

2. RESPONSIBILITY FOR THE OSR

School boards are responsible for ensuring compliance with the policies set out in this guideline. Boards shall specify those persons responsible for performing clerical functions with respect to the establishment and maintenance of the OSR. Boards will also develop criteria for determining the following:

— the types of information beyond those specified in this guideline that could be considered to be conducive to the improvement of the instruction of the student
— the uses of the documentation file beyond those specified in this guideline (see subsection 3.4)
— the pertinence of the materials in the OSR, with a view to removing those no longer considered to be conducive to the improvement of the instruction of the student (see section 9)
— the times other than those specified in this guideline at which it could be considered appropriate to issue report cards (see subsection 3.2.1)
— the types of information beyond those required by this guideline that could be added to the office index card (see section 3.5)

In addition, boards will develop procedures to be followed to ensure:

— the security of the information contained in the OSR during both the period of use and the period of retention and storage;
— the regular review of the OSR for the removal of any material that is no longer considered to be conducive to the improvement of the instruction of the student;
— the storage of the OSR for the period specified in the retention schedule (see section 8);
— the complete and confidential disposal of the OSR.

It is the duty of the principal of a school to:

— establish, maintain, retain, transfer, and dispose of a record for each student enrolled in the school in compliance with the criteria established by the board;
— ensure that the materials in the OSR comply with the policies of this guideline and the criteria established by the school board;
— ensure the security of the OSR;
— ensure that all persons specified by a board to perform clerical functions with respect to the establishment and maintenance of the OSR are aware of the confidentiality provisions of the Education Act and the relevant freedom of information and protection of privacy legislation.

3. COMPONENTS OF THE OSR

An OSR shall consist of the following components:

— an OSR folder in Form 1 or Form 1A
— lireport cards
— an Ontario Student Transcript, where applicable
— a documentation file, where applicable
— an office index card
— a Student Record of Accumulated Instruction in (a) French As a Second Language and/or (b) Native As a Second Language
— additional information identified as being conducive to the improvement of the instruction of the student

3.1 The OSR Folder

All schools have established a new OSR folder, Form 1A (see Appendix B), for students enrolling in school for the first time after September 1, 1985. For students who enrolled in school before that date, the OSR folder, Form 1, must be adjusted to correspond to Form 1A (see Appendix C). The folder shall contain the parts set out below in subsections 3.1.1 to 3.1.7.

3.1.1 Biographical data: Part A

The following information shall be provided:

— the student's full name and date of birth (The principal or his or her delegate shall indicate the method of verification on the folder — e.g., birth certificate, baptismal certificate, passport — and shall initial and date the folder.)
— a student number assigned by the school or the school board, where applicable
— a ministry identification number (MIN), where applicable

3.1.2 Schools attended: Part B

The following information shall be completed only when the student retires or transfers from the school:

— the name of each school that the student has attended
— the name of the board, the name of the person who operated the private school, or the name of the school operated by the Department of National Defence (see definition of DND school in Appendix A)
— the date of entry to each school
— the highest grade completed, the date of completion of this grade, and the name of a teacher contact

Where the student is transferring to a school from an educational institution that was not required to maintain an OSR, Part B may include any information that will complete the record of schools attended.

S. 3.1.3   ONTARIO STUDENT RECORD (OSR) GUIDELINE

3.1.3 Retirement from an Ontario school: Part C (Form 1A) or Parts J and K (Form 1)

The following information shall be provided on retirement (see section 7):

— the date of retirement
— the student's address at retirement
— the student's destination at retirement in respect of employment or further education

3.1.4 Names of parents or guardians: Part D

The following information shall be provided:

— the first name of the student's parent(s) or guardian(s) or the first name and surname of the student's parent(s) or guardian(s) when the surname of the latter differs from that of the student
— the date of death of a parent or guardian of a student opposite the name of the deceased (the date should be recorded promptly)

3.1.5 Special health information: Part E

A summary of a student's special health conditions shall be provided when such conditions are identified and the principal determines that such health conditions are likely to interfere with the achievement of the student. Entries in Part E shall be dated and kept current.

An adult student or the parent(s) or guardian(s) of a student who is not an adult shall be consulted and shall give written consent to any entry in, or deletion to, Part E.

3.1.6 Photographs and information on school activities: Parts F, G, and J (Form 1A) or Parts F, G, and I (Form 1)

Other information may be inserted only if it satisfies the criteria for inclusion set out by the board (see section 2).

3.1.7 Additional information: Part H

The following information shall be provided, if applicable:

— the date the student enters a Supervised Alternative Learning for Excused Pupils (SALEP) program (Ontario Regulation 532/83), as well as the SALEP committee report, which is to be inserted in the OSR documentation file (see subsection 3.4)
— the date the student enters a Linkage program and the name of the trade chosen

3.2 Report Cards

3.2.1 Completion and use

A report card shall be completed and filed in the OSR folder for each student who has been enrolled in the school for more than six weeks from the commencement of the reporting period:

ONTARIO STUDENT RECORD (OSR) GUIDELINE **S. 3.2.2**

— at the time of his or her transfer to another school or to a private or DND school; or
— liat the time of his or her retirement from school; or
— at the end of the school year; or
— at the end of each semester, if the school is organized on a semester plan; or
— at such other times that the board may stipulate.

A completed report card or an exact copy of it shall be placed in the student's OSR folder, and the report card or an exact copy of it shall be forwarded to the adult student or to the parent(s) or guardian(s) of a student who is not an adult.

3.2.2 Content

A school board shall approve, for use in its schools, report cards that include the following:

— the full name of the student as recorded on the OSR folder
— the name and address of the school and any other particulars that may be required to identify the school
— the name of the principal
— the signature of the principal or his or her delegate (A facsimile of the principal's signature or a stamped signature is not acceptable. The principal's delegate shall indicate that he or she is signing on behalf of the principal.)
— where applicable, the grade in which the student is placed
— where applicable, the grade to which the student is promoted
— the record of attendance of the student at school
— the date the report card is issued
— a concise statement of the program of study undertaken by the student, sufficient to enable a person to understand the objectives, content, and degree of difficulty of the courses included in the program of study
— the student's level of achievement (indicated by an anecdotal description, a percentage mark, or a letter grade) or a statement that there has been insufficient time to assess the achievement of the student
— for secondary school courses, the common course code and title of the course
— for secondary school courses, the value of the credits assigned to the course (expressed as an integer or a decimal) or, for courses for which credits are not awarded, the words "non-credit course"
— space for comment by the adult student or the parent(s) or guardian(s) of a student who is not an adult
— the following statement to students and parents or guardians:

To Parents or Guardians and Students

This copy of the report card should be retained for future reference. The original or an exact copy has been placed in the OSR folder in respect of the student and will be retained for five years after the student retires from school. Every effort has been made to ensure that all entries are a clear indication of the achievement of the student. If you wish to review the information contained in the OSR folder, please contact the principal. Each student and the parent(s) or guardian(s) of a student who is not an adult are entitled to have access to the student's OSR.

3.2.3 Quality of paper

The exact copy of the report card in the OSR folder shall be printed on paper that is:

— white and capable of retaining its whiteness for the retention period of the report card;
— sufficiently opaque to ensure that the information on the card is legible even when ink is applied to both sides of the paper;
— suitable for long-term storage.

3.3 The Ontario Student Transcript (OST)

The requirements for the OST are outlined in the *Manual for the Ontario Student Transcript, 1986*. The OST is a cumulative and continuous record of a student's successful completion of secondary school courses. The OST is kept in the OSR folder. A sample of the OST is contained in Appendix D.

3.4 The Documentation File

When a documentation file is required, it shall be kept in the OSR folder. A documentation file shall be established when the following information is required:

— verification of a custody order (see subsection 10.2.1)
— verification of a change-of-surname order (see subsection 10.1)
— a written requires to be named by repute (see subsection 10.1.1)
— identification and/or placement determinations; the results of a review of a placement; and the decision of an appeal board, a school board, or a tribunal with respect to an identification and/or placement made by a committee
— an individual psychological, health, or educational assessment report
— the report of a Supervised Alternative Learning for Excused Pupils (SALEP) committee
— letters of request for a correction to, or a deletion from, the record where the request has not been granted (see section 9)

A documentation file shall also be established to contain information identified in the criteria set out by the school board (see section 2).

A sample documentation file is contained in Appendix E.

3.5 The Office Index Card

The office index card provides the school with immediate access to information about a student. It shall remain at the school during the period in which the student is enrolled at the school. The card is not filed in the OSR folder and is not transferred with the OSR when the student transfers from the school.

ONTARIO STUDENT RECORD (OSR) GUIDELINE   S. 3.6

The office index card shall record the following information:

— the full name of the student as recorded on the OSR folder
— the student's number assigned by the school or school board
— a ministry identification number (MIN), where applicable
— the sex of the student
— the student's date of birth (year, month, day) and the source used to verify the date
— the name(s) of the student's parent(s) or guardian(s)
— the name(s) of the individual(s) who has (have) custody of the student and for whom verification of the custody order is included in the documentation file
— the student's current address and home telephone number as well as an emergency number, if one has been provided
— the dates (year, month, day) on which the student enrols in the school, transfers from the school, or retires from the school
— the name and address of the school to which the student transfers and the date on which the OSR is transferred
— the student's address on the date of transfer or retirement from the school
— the name and address or some other means of identification of the school from which the student is transferring or retiring
— (This information must be sufficient to identify the source of the index card.)
— other information that is identified within the criteria set out by the school board (see section 2)

When a student transfers to another school or retires from school, the office index card shall be stored at the school or at a central record office provided by the board.

3.6 Student Record of Accumulated Instruction in French As a Second Language

An individual record of accumulated instruction in French as a second language shall be established and maintained for each student enrolled in a French-as-a-second language program. The record shall be kept on a card that is in the form prescribed by the regulation (see sample in Appendix F) and shall include all of the information required for each entry. An entry shall be made on the record:

— at the end of a school year, semester, or summer course; and
— when a student transfers to another school or to a private or DND school; and
— when a student retires from school.

If the principal of a secondary school is satisfied that al of the information on a student's studies in French as a second language can be ascertained from report cards and the OST contained in the OSR folder, then information on secondary school credit courses need not be entered on the card that records the student's instruction in French as a second language. However, the card itself must be retained in the student's OSR.

If a student has had previous instruction in French but no record is available, the entries on the card must be started at least from the date of enrolment in an Ontario school. A note shall be made on the first lines of the instruction card indicating what is known about a student's previous instruction in French as a second language and in other subjects taught in French. If the number of accumulated hours must be estimated, an annotation must indicate that the figure is approximate.

The French-as-a-second-language card shall be kept in the OSR folder, but may be removed, for a temporary period, subject to the approval of the principal.

3.7 Student Record of Accumulated Instruction in Native As a Second Language

An individual record of accumulated instruction in Native as a second language as a subject shall be established and maintained for each student enrolled in a Native-as-a-second-language program. The record shall be kept on a card that is in the form prescribed by the regulation (see sample in Appendix G), and shall include all of the information required for each entry. An entry shall be made on the record:

— at the end of a school year, semester, or summer course; and
— when a student transfers to another school or to a private or DND school; and
— when a student retires from school.

If the principal of a secondary school is satisfied that all of the information on a student's studies in Native as a second language can be ascertained from report cards and the OST contained in the OSR folder, then information on secondary school credit courses need not be entered on the card that records the student's instruction in Native as a second language. However, the card itself must be retained in the student's OSR.

The entries on the card must be started from the date of enrolment in the Native-as-a-second-language program. A note shall be made on the first line of the instruction card indicating what is known about a student's previous instruction in a Native language. If the number of accumulated hours must be estimated, an annotation must indicate that the figure is approximate.

The Native-as-a-second-language card shall be kept in the OSR folder, but may be removed, for a temporary period, subject to the approval of the principal.

4. ACCESS TO THE OSR

Access to an OSR means the right of those authorized by the Education Act to examine the contents of the OSR. Under the Freedom of Information and Protection of Privacy Act, 1987, students and parents or guardians who are authorized to have access to the contents of the OSR also have the right to receive a copy of the contents of the OSR. The provisions of this section apply during both the period of use and the period of retention and storage.

4.1 Students

Every student has a right of access to his or her OSR.

4.2 Parents and Guardians

ONTARIO STUDENT RECORD (OSR) GUIDELINE   S. 5

A parent or guardian of a student who is not an adult has a right of access to the student's OSR. Under both the Children's Law Reform Act and the Divorce Act, 1985, the legal right of a non-custodial parent to have access to a child includes the right to make inquiries and to be given information concerning the child's health, education, and welfare.

4.3 Educational Personnel

Only supervisory officers and the principal and teachers of the school shall have access to the OSR, for the purpose of improving the instruction of the student, without the written consent of the adult student or of the parent(s) or guardian(s) of a student who is not an adult.

4.4 Other

No individual (including board officials) other than those identified previously in subsection 4.3 shall have access to the OSR without the written consent of the adult student or of the parent(s) or guardian(s) of a student who is not an adult. The OSR shall not be produced in the course of any legal proceedings, except as provided for below.

4.4.1 Civil suit

A principal may receive a court order, pertaining to a civil suit, that requires that certain records be produced. In such a situation, the principal shall produce the OSR in accordance with the court order. The judge should be informed that the order may contravene the Education Act. In special circumstances it may be appropriate for the school board to appeal the court order.

4.4.2 Child and Family Services Act, 1984

Under the Child and Family Services Act, 1984, it is possible for a court to order a principal of a school to produce a student's OSR for inspection and copying. A court may make such an order if it is satisfied that (a) a record contains information that may be relevant to a consideration of whether a child is suffering abuse or is likely to suffer abuse, and (b) the person in control of the record has refused to permit a Children's Aid Society director to inspect it.

4.4.3 Criminal Code

If a school principal is served with a search warrant requiring the surrender of an OSR to the police, the principal is obliged to comply with the warrant. Likewise, if a principal is served with a subpoena requiring his or her testimony in a criminal case, he or she is obliged to comply with the subpoena and produce the OSR if required.

5. USE AND MAINTENANCE OF THE OSR

Information from an OSR may be used to assist in the preparation of a report required under the Education Act or the regulations made under it.

Information from an OSR may also be used, when a written request is made by a former student, an adult student, or the parent(s) or guardian(s) of a student who is not an adult, in the preparation of a report:

— for an educational institution, or for the student or former student, with respect to an application for further education; or
— for the student or former student with respect to an application for employment.

The contents of the OSR must be reviewed according to criteria established by the school board to ensure that they remain conducive to the improvement of the instruction of the student (see section 2). Any such review must comply with the provisions of section 8 of this guideline.

6. TRANSFER OF THE OSR

The transfer of the OSR means the transfer of all parts of the OSR other than the office index card (See section 3.5 for information on the index card). Subject to the conditions outlined below, the original OSR is transferable only to schools in Ontario, to private schools in Ontario, or to DND schools.

If the original OSR is being transferred between schools operated by the same school board, it may be transferred by a delivery service provided by the board.

If the original OSR is being transferred outside the jurisdiction of the board or to a private school, it shall be transferred by Priority Post or an equivalent delivery method, approved by the board, that maintains confidentiality and guarantees prompt delivery.

If some or all of the information in the OSR has been microrecorded or stored in computer files and if the receiving school has equipment that is capable of receiving this information so that the OSR can be reproduced or viewed in the same manner as in the sending school, the information may be transmitted to the receiving school either as a microrecording or by electronic transmission rather than in printed form.

6.1 Transfer to Another School Board in Ontario

Before a principal shall transfer an original OSR to a school operated by another school board in Ontario, the principal shall have received:

— a written request for the information from the principal of the receiving school.

To expedite the transfer of such information, principals may find it useful to send with the student a brief statement to the principal of the receiving school indicating that an official request for information is required. A sample form for this purpose is provided in Appendix H.

6.2 Transfer to a Private School in Ontario

Before a principal transfers an original OSR to an inspected private school or to a non-inspected private school in Ontario, the principal shall have received:

— a written request for the information from the receiving private school, in which the private school agrees to accept responsibility for the OSR and to maintain, retain, transfer, and dispose of the OSR in accordance with this guideline (see Appendix I); and
— a written statement, signed by the adult student or the parent(s) or guardian(s) of a student who is not an adult, indicating consent to the transfer.

6.3 Transfer to a DND School

The conditions for the transfer of an OSR to a DND school are the same as those for a private school in Ontario outlined in 6.2 above.

6.4 Transfer to an Educational Institution Outside Ontario

An original OSR may not be transferred outside Ontario. Only an exact copy of the OSR shall be sent to the principal of an educational institution outside Ontario after the principal who is responsible for the OSR has received:

— a written request for the information from the principal of the educational institution outside Ontario; and
— a written statement, signed by the adult student or the parent(s) or guardian(s) of a student who is not an adult, indicating consent to the transfer.

7. RETIREMENT OF A STUDENT

A student retires from a school, a private school, or a DND school when he or she ceases to be enrolled in school. A student is not considered to have retired if he or she (a) withdraws for a temporary period with the written consent of the principal, or (b) transfers to another school, a private school, or a DND school to which the OSR (except for the office index card) is transferred.

When a student retires from a school, a private school, or a DND school that maintained an OSR for the student, the principal, on request, shall give the adult student or the parent(s) or guardian(s) of a student who is not an adult the following:

— an exact copy of the student's OST
— the information and materials stored in the OSR folder that are not required to be retained under the retention schedule provided in section 8. If this information is not requested by the adult student or the parent(s) or guardian(s) of a student who is not an adult, it shall be retained in the OSR until July 31 of the fifth year following the year in which the student retired from school, after which it shall be destroyed.

8. RETENTION, STORAGE, AND DESTRUCTION OF THE OSR

The Freedom of Information and Protection of Privacy Act, 1987, requires that personal information that has been used by an institution shall be retained by the institution for at least one year after use, unless the individual to whom the information relates consents in writing to its earlier disposal. Therefore, any personal information placed in an OSR shall be retained by the school for at least one year after use, unless the principal receives written consent to its earlier disposal from the adult student or the parent(s) or guardian(s) of a student who is not an adult.

The following components of the OSR shall be retained for five years after a student retires from school:

— report cards
— the documentation file, where applicable
— the record of instruction in French as a second language and/or Native as a second language, where applicable
— the record relating to a Linkage program, where applicable
— additional information that is identified by the school board as being conducive to the improvement of the instruction of the student

The following components of the OSR shall be retained for fifty-five years after a student retires from school:

— the OSR folder
— the OST
— the office index card

The destruction of all or any part of the OSR when its retention is no longer required under this guideline shall be effected under conditions that ensure the complete and confidential disposal of the record.

9. CORRECTION OR REMOVAL OF OSR INFORMATION

If certain information or material in an OSR folder is determined, according to the board's criteria, to be no longer conducive to the improvement of the instruction of the student, the principal shall cause the information or material to be removed from the OSR folder. Such information shall be given to the adult student or to the parent(s) or guardian(s) of a student who is not an adult, or it shall be destroyed (subject to the requirements of the relevant freedom of information and protection of privacy legislation).

An adult student or the parent(s) or guardian(s) of a student who is not an adult may be of the opinion that the information contained in the student's OSR is inaccurately recorded or that it is not conducive to the improvement of the instruction of the student. In such a case, the adult student or the parent(s) or guardian(s) of a student who is not an adult may request in writing that the principal correct the alleged inaccuracy or remove the information from the record. If the principal agrees to the request, the material shall be corrected or shall be removed from the file and destroyed or returned to the adult student or to the parent(s) or guardian(s) of a student who is not an adult. If the request is complied with, no record of the request shall be retained in the OSR. If the principal refuses to comply with such a request, the adult student or the parent(s) or guardian(s) of a student who is not an adult may require in writing that the principal refer the request to the appropriate supervisory officer. The supervisory officer shall:

— require the principal to comply with the request, in which case no record of the request shall be retained in the OSR; or
— submit the OSR and the request to a person designated by the Minister of Education.

The person designated by the minister shall hold a hearing at which the principal and the person(s) who made the request are parties to the proceedings, and the person designated shall, after the hearing, reach a decision on the matter. This decision shall be final and binding on all parties to the proceedings. If the person designated by the minister orders compliance with the request, no record of the request shall be retained in the OSR. If the person designated by the minister does not order compliance with the request, the original request, including the date on which it was made, and the statement of this final decision shall be retained in the documentation file.

Every principal shall ensure that no OSR discloses (a) the contravention or alleged contravention by the student of any statute or regulation to which the Young Offenders Act or Part V-A of the Provincial Offences Act applies, or (b) the disposition of any proceedings brought under those statutes or regulations. If an entry in an OSR does disclose such information, the principal of the school in which the student is enrolled shall ensure that the entry is deleted from the OSR.

10. SPECIAL CIRCUMSTANCES

10.1 Change of Surname

10.1.1 Change by repute

When a principal receives a written request from an adult student or the parent(s) or guardian(s) of a student who is not an adult that the student be identified by a surname other than the legal surname of the student and when (a) the student is known by a surname other than his or her legal surname, (b) the surname is a name obtained by repute, and (c) the use of the surname is in the student's best interests, the principal shall record the requested surname in Part A of the OSR folder in addition to the legal surname of the student, and the requested surname shall be used henceforth. In this case, the legal surname shall be enclosed in brackets. The written request will be stored in the documentation file (see subsection 3.4).

10.1.2 Change by marriage or by law

When a principal receives a document that establishes that a student for whom the principal maintains an OSR has had his or her surname changed, either by marriage or in accordance with the law of the province, state, or country in which the document was made, the principal shall file the document, a notarial copy of the document, or a verification of his or her knowledge of the document in the documentation file and shall change the surname of the student on all components of the OSR so that the record shall appear as if originally established in the new surname.

10.2 Adoption

10.2.1 Placement for adoption

When a principal receives a written notice, signed by a Children's Aid Society director or by a director appointed under the Child and Family Services Act, 1984, that a student for whom the principal maintains an OSR has been legally placed for adoption, the principal shall:

— prepare a new index card and OSR folder for the student in the surname of either or both of the adoptive parents and in the given name or names of the student that are desired by the adoptive parents (the names of the adoptive parents shall be used throughout);
— change the name of the student on all report cards previously prepared for the student (the new name as set out on the new index card and OSR folder shall be used);
— ensure that no contents of the OSR folder disclose the previous name of the student or the placement of the student for adoption; and
— destroy the index card and OSR folder that have been replaced.

These provisions do not apply if both the adoptive parents and the Children's Aid Society (or the licensee, if the child has been placed by a licensee referred to in Part VII of the Child and Family Services Act, 1984) agree that it is in the best interests of the student to disclose the placement for adoption, in which case the provisions outlined in subsection 10.1.2 with respect to the OSR folder, the report cards, and the index card shall apply.

10.2.2 Termination of adoption

When a principal receives a written notice, signed by a Children's Aid Society director, that a student's placement for adoption has been terminated, the principal shall:

— prepare a new index card and OSR folder for the student in the name of the student;
— change the name of the student on all report cards previously prepared for the student (the new name as set out on the new index card and OSR folder shall be used);
— ensure that no contents of the OSR folder disclose the previous name of the student or the placement of the student for adoption; and
— destroy the index card and OSR folder that have been replaced.

10.3 Reports From Third Parties

When requesting a report from a third party concerning a student, it is appropriate to advise the third party that the report will be filed in the OSR and be subject to the access provisions governing an OSR. Reports from third parties shall be added to the OSR only if:

— the principal is of the opinion that the report is conducive to the improvement of the instruction of the student; and
— the principal receives written consent from the adult student or the parent(s) or guardian(s) of a student who is not an adult to the inclusion of the report.

If consent to the inclusion of the report in the OSR is not given by either the adult student or the parent(s) or guardian(s) of a student who is not an adult, the principal shall make a notation on Part H of the OSR that the report was received. The report shall be returned to the third party or destroyed.

If a report from a third party is included in the OSR and if the principal receives a request from the student or the parent(s) or guardian(s) of a student who is not an adult to examine the OSR, the principal shall advise the student or the parent(s) or guardian(s) of a student who is not an adult that only the originator of the report can provide a full interpretation. However, the principal shall not withhold the report from the examination of the student or of the parent(s) or guardian(s) of a student who is not an adult. Copies of this report shall be made available to the student or the parent(s) or guardian(s) of a student who is not an adult according to the access provision of the relevant freedom of information and protection of privacy legislation. Reports from third parties shall not be released to any party other than those designated as having a right of access to the OSR.

December 1989

11. CONTINUING EDUCATION RECORDS

For each student enrolled in a school board continuing education course or program for the purpose of achieving an Ontario secondary school credit or credits, the principal of the continuing education course or program shall establish an office index card, which shall contain the following information:
— the full name of the student as recorded on the OSR folder
— the student's number assigned by the school or school board
— a ministry identification number (MIN), where applicable
— the sex of the student
— the student's date of birth (year, month, day) and the source used to verify the date
— the name(s) of the student's parent(s) or guardian(s)
— the name(s) of the individual(s) who has (have) custody of the student and for whom verification of the custody order is included in the documentation file
— the student's current address and home telephone number as well as an emergency number, if one has been provided
— the dates (year, month, day) on which the student enrols in the school, transfers from the school, or retires from the school
— the name and address of the school to which the student transfers and the date on which the OSR is transferred
— the student's address on the date of transfer or retirement from the school
— the name and address or some other means of identification of the school from which the student is transferring or retiring (This information must be sufficient to identify the source of the index card.)
— other information that is identified within the criteria set out by the school board (see section 2)

The OST shall be maintained by the principal of the continuing education program. However, if a student is enrolled in another school in Ontario, a copy of the OST should be forwarded to that institution after authorization by the student.

The requirements for the maintenance, retention, storage, and release of information in these two parts of the OSR are the same for a student in a continuing education program as for a student in a regular program.

APPENDIX A: DEFINITIONS

The following definitions are provided for the purposes of this guideline only. Most are based on definitions of terms in the Education Act.

adult A person who is eighteen years of age or older.

board A board of education, public school board, secondary school board, Roman Catholic separate school board, or Protestant separate school board, including a French-language board or the public sector or Roman Catholic sector of a French-language board or the minority-language section of a board.

DND school An educational institution operated either in or outside Ontario to provide education for students whose parents or guardians are members of the Canadian Forces or employees of the Department of National Defence of the Government of Canada. A DND school is deemed to be a private school in Ontario that is operated by the Government of Canada.

guardian A person who has lawful custody of a child, other than the parent of the child.

Linkage program A program authorized by the Minister of Education, the Minister of Colleges and Universities, and the Minister of Skills Development that enables a student who has obtained credits in specific technological studies courses and has successfully achieved competencies identified in approved training profiles to qualify for advanced placement when entering apprenticeship programs.

Ontario Student Transcript That component of an OSR that is used to record particulars of the secondary school courses successfully completed by a student and the credits granted in recognition thereof.

principal A teacher appointed by a board to perform in respect of a school the duties of a principal under the Education Act and the regulations made under it.

private school An institution at which instruction in any of the subjects of the elementary or secondary school courses of study is provided at any time between the hours of 9:00 a.m. and 4:00 p.m. on any school day for five or more students who are of or over compulsory school age and that is not a school as defined in the *Education Act*.

school The body of public school students, separate school students, or secondary school students that is organized as a unit for educational purposes under the jurisdiction of the appropriate board or the body of students enrolled in any of the elementary or secondary school courses of study in an educational institution operated by the Government of Ontario, as well as the teachers and other staff members associated with such unit or institution and the lands and premises used in connection therewith.

ONTARIO STUDENT RECORD (OSR) GUIDELINE   S. 11

supervisory officer A person qualified in accordance with the regulations governing supervisory officers and who is employed

(a) by a board or
(b) in the Ministry of Education and designated by the Minister of Education

to perform such supervisory and administrative duties that are required of supervisory officers by the Education Act and the regulations made under it.

teacher A person who holds a valid certificate of qualification or a letter of standing as a teacher in an elementary or secondary school in Ontario.

APPENDIX B: OSR FORMS

The following forms can be downloaded from the Ministry of Education's website address:

www.edu.gov.on.ca/eng/document/curricul/osr/osr.html.

- **Form 1A: The Ontario Student Record Folder**
  Note: Adjusting OSR Folder Form 1 to Form 1A

An OSR established on or after September 1, 1985, shall use the OSR folder referred to as Form 1A OSRs established up to and including August 31, 1985, used the OSR folder referred to as Form 1, which is now out-of-date and must be adjusted to match Form 1A. The following procedure is prescribed for adjusting the OSR folder Form 1 to Form 1A:

— *Part A on Form 1.* Use the student number assigned by the board, where applicable, and discontinue the use of the Social Insurance Number.
— *Part B on Form 1.* Use the grade designation instead of the achievement form number. If a student does not have a grade designation, use "U" for "ungraded".
— *Part C on Form 1.* Insert a current Ontario Student Transcript into each secondary school OSR folder.
— *Part H on Form 1.* Where applicable, include information related to a Linkage program and a Supervised Alternative Learning for Excused Pupils (SALEP) program.
— Insert a documentation file, where applicable.

- **Student Transcript**

- **OSR Documentation File**

- **Student Record of Accumulated Instruction in French as a Second Language**

- **Student Record of Accumulated Instruction in Native as a Second Language**

- **Student Transfer Form**

- **Request for an OSR Form From a Private School**

- **Office Index Card**

PROVINCIAL SCHOOLS NEGOTIATIONS ACT
R.S.O. 1990, c. P.35, as am. 1996, c. 12, s. 65, 1997, c. 31, s. 167

1. Definitions.—In this Act,

"agreement" means a written collective agreement made pursuant to this Act between the Authority and the employee organization in respect of matters that are negotiable under this Act; ("convention")

"Authority" means the Provincial Schools Authority; ("Administration")

"Commission" [Repealed 1997, c. 31, s. 167(1)]

"employee organization" means the organization that is formed pursuant to this Act by teachers; ("association d'employés")

"principal" means a person employed in a school,
  (a) who is appointed to be in charge of the school, and
  (b) who is a member of the Ontario College of Teachers or whose appointment is authorized by the Minister of Education and Training. ("directeur d'école")

"school" means a school operated by,
  (a) the Ministry of Correctional Services,
  (b) the Ministry of Education, or
  (c) the Ministry of Health,

but does not include a summer course or a correspondence course; ("école")

"teacher" means a person employed in a school as a teacher, but not as a supervisory officer, a principal, a vice-principal or an occasional teacher, and,
  (a) who is a member of the Ontario College of Teachers, or
  (b) whose appointment as a teacher is authorized by the Minister of Education and Training. ("enseignant")

"vice-principal" means a teacher who is appointed to be in charge of a school in the absence of the principal; ("directeur adjoint")

"written collective understanding" [Repealed 1997, c. 31, s. 167(4).]

2. (1) **Provincial Schools Authority.**—The authority known as the Provincial Schools Authority, consisting of five members appointed by the Lieutenant Governor in Council, is continued under the name of Provincial Schools Authority in English and under the name Administration des écoles provinciales in French.

(2) **Chair and vice-chair.**—The Lieutenant Governor in Council shall designate one of the members of the Authority as chair and one as vice-chair.

(3) **Secretary.**—The Authority shall appoint a secretary.

(4) **Remuneration.**—The members and the secretary of the Authority shall be paid such remuneration and expenses as are determined by the Lieutenant Governor in Council.

(5) **Money.**—The money required for the purposes of the Authority is payable out of money appropriated therefor by the Legislature.

3. (1) **Authority as employer.**—The Authority employs the teachers and principals and vice-principals and none of them is a Crown employee.

(2) **Transition.**—The following credits and benefits stand to the credit of a teacher under the Authority's retirement gratuity that is based upon sick leave credit:
1. The teacher's sick leave credits under a contract of employment that vested in the Authority on July 18, 1975.
2. The teacher's benefits under a contract of employment that vested in the Authority on July 18, 1975 respecting termination of employment.

(3) **Principals, vice-principals.**—A principal or a vice-principal may perform the duties of a teacher despite any provision of a collective agreement.

(4) **Transition.**—Sections 277.11 (election by principal, vice-principal) and 287.2 (employment terms) of the *Education Act* apply with necessary modifications with respect to principals and vice-principals who are employed as such by the Authority on both December 31, 1997 and January 1, 1998.

(5) **Repeal.**—Subsection (4) is repealed on September 1, 1998.

1997, c. 31, s. 167(5).

4. (1) **Employment of teachers.**—Subject to subsection (2), the Authority is responsible for all matters relating to the employment of teachers, and for such purpose has all the powers and is subject to the duties and liabilities of a public board under the *Education Act*.

(2) **Administration.**—All matters relating to administration in respect of teachers who teach in a school operated by a Ministry referred to in the definition of "school" in section 1 are the responsibility of the deputy minister of the Ministry, and each such Ministry that operates a school shall provide the salaries and benefits of the teachers of such school in accordance with the collective agreements that apply with respect to the teachers.

(3) [Repealed 1997, c. 31, s. 167(8).]

(4) **Pensions.**—For the purposes of the *Teachers' Pension Act*, a teacher employed by the Authority shall be deemed to be employed as a teacher by the minister of a ministry of the Government of Ontario.

(5) [Repealed 1997, c. 31, s. 167(9).]

(6) **Application of Part X of *Education Act*.**—Part X of the *Education Act* applies with necessary modifications to the teachers and to the Authority.

5. (1) **Application of the *Labour Relations Act, 1995*.**—On and after January 1, 1998, the *Labour Relations Act, 1995* applies with respect to collective bargaining between the Authority and the teachers that it employs.

(2) **Teachers' bargaining unit.**—A bargaining unit is established and is composed of the teachers employed by the Authority.

(3) **Same.**—The teachers' bargaining unit shall be deemed to be an appropriate bargaining unit.

(4) **Bargaining agent.**—The bargaining agent for the teachers' bargaining unit is the employee organization that, on December 31, 1997, represents the teachers for the purposes of this Act.

(5) **Same.**—The bargaining agent shall be deemed to be certified as the bargaining agent for the teachers' bargaining unit and shall be deemed to be a trade union for the purposes of the *Labour Relations Act, 1995*.

(6) **Same.**—No trade union is entitled to apply for certificate as the bargaining agent for the teachers' bargaining unit.

(7) **Same.**—No person is entitled to apply for a declaration that the bargaining agent no longer represents the members of the teachers' bargaining unit.

(8) **Closing of schools.**—In case of a strike against the Authority or a lockout by the Authority and subject to subsection (9), the Authority may close one or more schools if it is of the opinion that,

    (a) the safety of pupils may be endangered during the strike or lockout;
    (b) the school building or the equipment or supplies in the building may not be adequately protected during the strike or lockout; or
    (c) the strike or lockout will substantially interfere with the operation of the school.

(9) **Approval for lock-out, closure.**—Before closing a school or locking out members of a bargaining unit at a school, the Authority shall obtain the written approval of the minister responsible for the ministry that operates the school.

1997, c. 31, s. 167(10).

6. (1) **Status of collective bargaining on January 1, 1998.**—During the period beginning on January 1, 1998 and ending when the Authority and the bargaining agent enter into their first collective agreement after that date, neither party may make an application under subsection 43(1) of the *Labour Relations Act, 1995* (first agreement arbitration).

(2) **Collective agreement.**—An agreement between the Authority and the employee organization representing the teachers that is in force on January 1, 1998 constitutes a collective agreement for the purposes of the *Labour Relations Act, 1995*.

(3) **No collective agreement.**—If, on January 1, 1998, there is no collective agreement in force with respect to the teachers' bargaining unit, the terms and conditions of employment of the teachers in the bargaining unit are those established under the most recent applicable agreement.

(4) **Same.**—If, on January 1, 1998, there is no collective agreement in force with respect to the teachers' bargaining unit,

    (a) the most recent collective agreement between the Authority and the employee organization that represented the teachers in the bargaining unit shall be deemed to be an expired collective agreement; and
    (b) the Authority and the bargaining agent shall be deemed to have received a notice under clause 21(b) of the *Labour Relations Act, 1995* on December 17, 1997 that the Minister of Labour does not consider it advisable to appoint a conciliation board.

1997, c. 31, s. 167(10).

7. (1) **Regulations.**—The Lieutenant Governor in Council may make regulations governing terms and conditions of employment for principals and for vice-principals.

(2) **Same.**—A regulation may establish different requirements for different classes of principal or vice-principal.

1997, c. 31, s. 167(10).

SCHOOL BOARDS AND TEACHERS COLLECTIVE NEGOTIATIONS ACT

R.S.O. 1990, c. S. 2, as am. S.O. 1996, c. 1, Schedule Q, s. 5, 1996, c. 12, s. 66

[Repealed 1997, c. 31, s. 178.]

Note to the reader:

The *School Boards and Teachers Collective Negotiations Act* was repealed on December 31, 1997 by the *Education Quality Improvement Act, 1997*. However, it is included in this edition to enable readers to compare it to the provisions in Part X.1 of the *Education Act* that now govern teacher/school board collective bargaining. Furthermore, section 35(1.1) of the *School Boards and Teachers Collective Negotiations Act* is cross-referenced in section 277.10 of the *Education Act*. Section 277.12 of the *Education Act* "continues" certain functions of the Education Relations Commission.

PART I

GENERAL

1. Definitions.—In this Act,

"affiliate."—"affiliate" means one of the following bodies:
  1. L'Association des Enseignants Franco-Ontariens.
  2. The Federation of Women Teachers' Associations of Ontario.
  3. The Ontario English Catholic Teachers' Association.
  4. The Ontario Public School Teachers' Federation.
  5. The Ontario Secondary School Teachers' Federation; ("organisation d'enseignants")

"agreement."—"agreement" means a written collective agreement made after the 18th day of July, 1975 and pursuant to this Act between a board and a branch affiliate or branch affiliates or between two or more boards and two or more branch affiliates covering matters negotiable under this Act; ("convention")

"board."—"board" means a board of education, public school board, secondary school board, Roman Catholic separate school board or Protestant separate school board and includes a divisional board of education; ("conseil")

"branch affiliate."—"branch affiliate" means an organization composed of all the teachers employed by a board who are members of the same affiliate; ("section locale")

"Commission."—"Commission" means the Education Relations Commission; ("Commission")

"Council."—"Council" means the Ontario School Trustees' Council; ("Conseil")

"Federation."—"Federation" means the Ontario Teachers' Federation; ("Fédération")

"lock-out."—"lock-out" means the suspension of employment of, or the refusal to assign work to, teachers other than principals and vice-principals in a school or schools by a board with the view to compelling the cessation of a strike or preventing the resumption of a strike or with the view to inducing or persuading the branch affiliate that represents the teachers to enter into or renew an agreement; ("lock-out")

"**member association.**"—"member association" means one of the following bodies:
1. L'Association française des conseils scolaires de l'Ontario.
2. Northern Ontario Public and Secondary School Trustees' Association.
3. Ontario Public School Trustees' Association.
4. Ontario Separate School Trustees' Association; ("association de conseillers scolaires")

"**party.**"—"party" means a board or a branch affiliate; ("partie")

"**principal.**"—"principal" means a principal as defined in the *Education Act*; ("directeur d'école")

"**strike.**"—"strike" includes any action or activity by teachers in combination or in concert or in accordance with a common understanding that is designed to curtail, restrict, limit or interfere with the operation or functioning of a school program or school programs or of a school or schools including, without limiting the foregoing,
 (a) withdrawal of services,
 (b) work to rule,
 (c) the giving of notice to terminate contracts of employment; ("grève")

"**teacher.**"—"teacher" means,
 (a) a person who is a member of the Ontario College of Teachers, or
 (b) a person in respect of whom a letter of permission has been granted under the *Education Act*,

and who is employed by a board under a contract prescribed by the regulations under the *Education Act*, but does not include a supervisory officer as defined in the *Education Act*, an instructor in a teacher-training institution or a person employed to teach in a school for a period not exceeding one month. ("enseignant")

"**vice-principal.**"—"vice-principal" means a vice-principal within the meaning of the regulations under the *Education Act*; ("directeur adjoint")

"**vote by secret ballot.**"—"vote by secret ballot" means a vote by ballots cast in such a manner that a person expressing his or her choice cannot be identified with the choice expressed. ("scrutin secret")

1996, c. 12, s. 66.

2. Purpose of Act.—The purpose of this Act is the furthering of harmonious relations between boards and teachers by providing for the making and renewing of agreements and by providing for the relations between boards and teachers in respect of agreements.

3. (1) Application of Act.—This Act applies to all collective negotiations between boards and teachers in respect of any term or condition of employment put forward by either party for the purpose of making or renewing an agreement.

(2) **Negotiations to be in accordance with Act.**—No such collective negotiations shall be carried on between a board and the teachers employed by the board except in accordance with this Act.

4. (1) Joint negotiations.—In negotiations and procedures under this Act to make or renew an agreement or agreements, two or more boards may act jointly as a party and two or more branch affiliates may act jointly as a party, where both the boards and branch affiliates involved so agree, to make or renew an agreement between the boards and the branch affiliates or to make or renew a separate agreement between each of the boards and a branch affiliate that represents teachers employed by the board.

(2) **Idem.**—A separate agreement between a board and a branch affiliate made pursuant to subsection (1) may include terms and conditions of employment in addition to and consistent with those terms and conditions which are part of the agreement between all the boards acting as a party and all the branch affiliates acting as a party.

(3) **Branch affiliates may negotiate as one party.**—Despite subsection (1), two or more branch affiliates may act as one party in negotiations and procedures under this Act to make or renew an agreement or agreements with the same board.

(4) **Agreements between individual boards and branch affiliates.**—Where two or more boards act jointly as a party and two or more branch affiliates act jointly as a party pursuant to subsection (1), any negotiations and proceedings and resulting agreement pursuant to subsection (2) between one of the boards and a branch affiliate shall be deemed to be part of the joint negotiations and agreement in accordance with subsection (1).

(5) **Continuation of agreement to act jointly.**—A board or branch affiliate that agrees to act jointly with another board or branch affiliate pursuant to subsection (1), shall continue to act jointly with such other board or branch affiliate until an agreement is made or renewed between the parties.

5. Representation of teachers by branch affiliate.—A branch affiliate shall, in negotiations and procedures under this Act, represent all the teachers composing its membership.

6. Negotiating group.—In negotiations to make or renew an agreement, a party shall be represented by only one group of persons but may at any time increase, decrease or change the composition of the group.

7. Parties may obtain assistance.—At any time during negotiations or procedures under this Act,

(a) a board that is a party may obtain assistance from the Council, a member association or another board;

(b) a branch affiliate that is a party may obtain assistance from the Federation, an affiliate or another branch affiliate; and

(c) a party may obtain assistance from one or more advisors, agents, counsel or solicitors.

PART II

NEGOTIATIONS

8. Subject-matter of negotiations.—Negotiations shall be carried out in respect of any term or condition of employment put forward by either party.

9. Notice of desire to negotiate.—Where there is no agreement in force between a board and a branch affiliate, the branch affiliate may give to the board or the board may give to the branch affiliate written notice of its desire to negotiate with the view to making an agreement.

10. (1) **Notice of desire to negotiate for renewal of agreement.**—Either party to an agreement may give written notice to the other party within the month of January in the year in which the agreement expires of its desire to negotiate with the view to the renewal, with or without modification, of the agreement then in operation.

(2) **Where notice not given of desire to negotiate renewal of agreement.**—Where an agreement exists between a board or boards and a branch affiliate or branch affiliates and no party to the agreement gives notice in accordance with this Act of its desire to negotiate with the view to the renewal of the agreement, the agreement continues in operation and is renewed from year to year, with each yearly period expiring on the 31st day of August, until the year, if any, in which notice is given in accordance with this Act of desire to negotiate with the view to the renewal, with or without modification, of the agreement.

(3) **Working conditions may not be altered.**—Where notice has been given of desire to negotiate to make or renew an agreement, the terms and conditions of the agreement, other than a term or condition that prevents a strike, that was in force at the time of giving the notice shall not be altered until either,
- (a) an agreement or a new agreement comes into force or the agreement is renewed, as the case may be; or
- (b) subject to subsection 27(2) and subsection 68(5), sixty days have elapsed after the Commission has made public the report of the fact finder as provided in section 26,

whichever first occurs.

11. Obligation to negotiate.—The parties shall meet within thirty days from the giving of the notice and they shall negotiate in good faith and make every reasonable effort to make an agreement or to renew the agreement, as the case requires.

12. (1) **Parties may choose procedures to reach agreement.**—The parties, at any time during negotiations to make or renew an agreement, may agree to,
- (a) request the Commission to assign a person to assist the parties to make or renew the agreement;
- (b) request the Commission to appoint a fact finder as provided in Part III; or
- (c) refer all matters remaining in dispute between them that may be provided for in an agreement to,
    - (i) an arbitrator or a board of arbitration for determination as provided in Part IV, or
    - (ii) a selector for determination as provided in Part V.

(2) **Effect of choice of procedure.**—Where the parties refer all matters remaining in dispute between them to an arbitrator or a board of arbitration or to a selector pursuant to clause (1)(c), no teacher who is a member of a branch affiliate that is a party shall engage in a strike against the board that is a party and the board shall not lock out or declare a state of lock-out to exist against members of the branch affiliate that is a party.

13. Where Commission may assign person to assist parties.—The Commission may, in the exercise of its own discretion, at any time assign a person to assist the parties to make or renew an agreement.

PART III

FACT FINDING

14. Appointment of fact finder.—The Commission shall appoint forthwith a person as a fact finder during negotiations to make or renew an agreement if the parties have not referred all matters remaining in dispute between them to an arbitrator or board of arbitration as provided in Part IV or a selector as provided in Part V and,

    (a) one or both of the parties gives notice to the Commission that an impasse has been reached in the negotiations and requests the appointment of a fact finder, and the Commission approves the request;

    (b) the Commission is of the opinion that an impasse has been reached in the negotiations; or

    (c) the agreement that was in operation in respect of the parties expires during negotiations between the parties to make or renew an agreement, and fact finding has not taken place as provided in this Part.

15. Parties may proceed to make agreement or to arbitration or selection procedure.—The parties to negotiations to make or renew an agreement may, despite the appointment of a fact finder,

    (a) make or renew the agreement; or

    (b) agree to refer all matters remaining in dispute between them to,

        (i) an arbitrator or a board of arbitration for determination as provided in Part IV, or

        (ii) a selector for determination as provided in Part V,

and upon the giving of notice to the Commission by the parties that they have so acted, the appointment of the fact finder is terminated.

16. Persons prohibited as fact finder.—No person shall be appointed a fact finder who has a direct pecuniary interest in the matters coming before him or her or who is acting or has, within the period of six months immediately before the date of his or her appointment, acted as solicitor, counsel, negotiator, advisor or agent of either of the parties, but no person shall be deemed to have a direct pecuniary interest by reason only of being a ratepayer within the area of jurisdiction of the board that is a party.

17. Vacancy.—Where a fact finder ceases to act by reason of withdrawal, death or otherwise before submitting his or her report to the Commission, the Commission shall appoint another person in the fact finder's stead and such person shall commence the work of the fact finder anew.

18. Notice of appointment of fact finder.—Where the Commission appoints a fact finder, the Commission shall give written notice to each of the parties of the appointment of and the name and address of the fact finder.

19. (1) **Notice of matters agreed upon and matters in dispute.**—Within seven days after the receipt of notice from the Commission of the appointment of the fact finder, each party shall give written notice to the fact finder and to the other party setting out all the matters that the parties have agreed upon for inclusion in an agreement and all the matters remaining in dispute between the parties.

(2) **Where notice not given.**—Where a party fails to comply with subsection (1), the fact finder may make a determination of the matters mentioned in subsection (1) and may then proceed pursuant to this Part.

20. (1) **Duty of fact finder.**—It is the duty of a fact finder to confer with the parties and to inquire into, ascertain and make a report setting out the matters agreed upon by the parties for inclusion in an agreement and the matters remaining in dispute between the parties.

(2) **What report may contain.**—A fact finder may, in his or her report, include findings in respect of any matter that he or she considers relevant to the making of an agreement between the parties and recommend terms of settlement of the matters remaining in dispute between the parties.

21. **Matters that may be considered by fact finder.**—In inquiring into and ascertaining the matters remaining in dispute between the parties, the fact finder amy inquire into and consider any matter that the fact finder considers relevant to the making of an agreement between the parties including, without limiting the foregoing,
    (a) the conditions of employment in occupations outside the public teaching sector;
    (b) the effect of geographic or other local factors on the terms and conditions of employment;
    (c) the cost to the board of the proposal of either party;
    (d) the interests and welfare of the public.

22. **Procedure of fact finder.**—The fact finder shall determine his or her own procedure under guidelines established by the Commission and, where the fact finder requests information from a party, the party shall provide the fact finder with full and complete information.

23. **Submission of report of fact finder.**—The fact finder shall submit his or her report to the Commission within thirty days after the date of his or her appointment or within such longer period of time as the Commission, with the agreement of the parties, may direct and the Commission shall forthwith give a copy of the report to each of the parties.

24. **Report not binding.**—The report of the fact finder is not binding on the parties but is made for the advice and guidance of the parties and upon receipt of the report the parties shall endeavour, in good faith, to make an agreement or to renew the agreement, as the case may be.

25. (1) **Assignment of assistance.**—Where the Commission has given a copy of the report of the fact finder to each of the parties and the Commission is of the opinion that the parties will or are likely to benefit from assistance, the Commission may assign a person to assist the parties to make or renew, as the case may be, the agreement.

(2) **Idem.**—Where the Commission has given a copy of the report of the fact finder to each of the parties and both of the parties request assistance from the Commission, the Commission shall assign a person to assist the parties to make or renew, as the case may be, the agreement.

26. (1) **Where report confidential.**—If the parties make or renew, as the case may be, an agreement within fifteen days after the Commission has given a copy of the report to each of the parties, the report shall not be made public by the Commission, either of the parties or by any person.

(2) **Release of report.**—If the parties do not make an agreement, or renew the agreement, as the case may be, within the period of time specified in subsection (1), the Commission shall make public the report of the fact finder.

(3) **Deferral of release.**—Despite subsections (1) and (2), where both parties agree and the Commission approves, the Commission may defer making public the report of the fact finder for an additional period of not more than five days.

27. (1) **Parties may agree to refer matters in dispute.**—If the parties do not make or renew, as the case may be, an agreement within fifteen days after the Commission has given a copy of the report of the fact finder to each of the parties, the parties may agree to refer all matters in dispute between them that may be provided for in an agreement to,

   (a) an arbitrator or a board of arbitration for determination as provided in Part IV; or
   (b) a selector for determination as provided in Part V.

(2) **Effect of choice of procedure.**—Where, pursuant to subsection (1), the parties refer all matters remaining in dispute between them that may be provided for in an agreement to an arbitrator or a board of arbitration or refer all such matters to a selector and either of the parties submits its final offer to the selector,

   (a) the terms of the agreement, if any, in force between the parties at the time of the giving of notice of desire to negotiate pursuant to subsection 10(1) or (2), shall not be altered until an agreement is made or renewed between the parties; and
   (b) no teacher who is a member of a branch affiliate that is a party shall engage in a strike against the board that is a party and the board shall not lock out or declare a state of lock-out to exist against members of the branch affiliate that is a party.

PART IV

VOLUNTARY BINDING ARBITRATION

28. (1) **Parties to give notice to Commission where arbitration agreed upon.**—Where the parties agree to refer all matters remaining in dispute between them that may be provided for in an agreement to an arbitrator or a board of arbitration, the parties shall jointly give written notice to the Commission that they have so agreed and the notice shall state,

   (a) that the parties agree to refer the matters to an arbitrator and,
      (i) the date of appointment and the name and address of the arbitrator, or
      (ii) that the parties have not appointed the arbitrator and that the parties request the Commission to appoint the arbitrator; or
   (b) that the parties agree to refer the matters to a board of arbitration and,
      (i) that the parties have each appointed a person as a member of the board of arbitration and shall set out the names and addresses of the two members so appointed, or
      (ii) that both of the parties or one of them, as the case may be, has not appointed a person as a member of the board of arbitration and that the parties request the Commission to appoint the members or member, as the case may be, of the board,

and the notice shall state that the decision of the arbitrator or board of arbitration will be accepted by the parties as binding upon them.

(2) **Parties not to withdraw.**—Except as provided in section 56, a party shall not withdraw from arbitration proceedings under this Part after notice is given to the Commission in accordance with subsection (1).

(3) **Where appointments made by Commission.**—Where the parties, in the notice mentioned in subsection (1), request the Commission to appoint the arbitrator or the members or one of the members of the board of arbitration, the Commission shall make the appointment or appointments and shall forthwith thereafter give notice thereof to the parties setting out the name and address of the appointee or the names and addresses of the appointees, as the case may be, together with the date of the appointment or appointments.

(4) **Appointment of chair by members.**—Where the parties agree to refer all matters remaining in dispute between them to a board of arbitration, the two members of the board of arbitration shall, within ten days after the giving of notice of their appointment by the parties or by the Commission, as the case may be, appoint a third person to be chair of the board of arbitration and the chair shall forthwith give written notice to the Commission of his or her appointment.

(5) **Where Commission to appoint chair.**—Where the two members of the board of arbitration are unable to appoint or to agree on the appointment of the chair of the board of arbitration within the period of time set out in subsection (4), the Commission shall appoint the chair and shall give notice of the appointment to the two members and to the parties and the notice shall set out the name and address of the person appointed and the date of the appointment.

29. Persons prohibited as arbitrator or members or chair of board of arbitration.—No person shall be appointed an arbitrator or member or chair of a board of arbitration who has a direct pecuniary interest in the matters coming before him or her or who is acting or has, within the period of six months immediately before the date of his or her appointment, acted as solicitor, counsel, negotiator, advisor or agent of either of the parties, but no person shall be deemed to have a direct pecuniary interest by reason only of being a ratepayer within the area of jurisdiction of the board that is a party.

30. (1) **Vacancy.**—Where a member of a board of arbitration is unable to enter on or to carry on his or her duties so as to enable a decision to be rendered within the period of time required by subsection (2) or ceases to act by reason of withdrawal or death before the board of arbitration has completed its work, a replacement shall be appointed by the body that appointed the member, and the board of arbitration shall continue to function as if such member were a member of the board of arbitration from the beginning.

(2) **Where chair unable to act.**—Where the chair of a board of arbitration is unable to enter on or to carry on his or her duties so as to enable a decision to be rendered within sixty days after his or her appointment or within such longer period of time as may be provided in writing by the board of arbitration and consented to by the Commission or ceases to act by reason of withdrawal or death, the Commission shall give notice thereof to the members of the board of arbitration who shall within seven days of the giving of the notice appoint a person to

be the chair and if the appointment is not so made by the members it shall be made by the Commission, and after the chair is appointed the arbitration shall begin anew.

(3) **Where arbitrator unable to act.**—Where an arbitrator is unable to enter on or to carry on his or her duties so as to enable a decision to be rendered within sixty days after his or her appointment or within such longer period of time as may be provided in writing by the arbitrator and consented to by the Commission or ceases to act by reason of withdrawal or death, the Commission shall give notice thereof to the parties who shall within seven days of the giving of the notice appoint a person to be the arbitrator and if the appointment is not so made it shall be made by the Commission and after the arbitrator is appointed the arbitration shall begin anew.

31. Notice of matters agreed upon and matters in dispute.—Within seven days after the giving of notice that the arbitrator or the chair of the board of arbitration, as the case may be, has been appointed, each party shall give written notice to the arbitrator or chair and to the other party setting out all the matters that the parties have agreed upon for inclusion in an agreement and all the matters remaining in dispute between the parties.

32. (1) **Procedure.**—The arbitrator or board of arbitration shall determine his, her or its own procedure but shall give full opportunity to the parties to present their evidence and make their submissions.

(2) **Idem.**—If the members of a board of arbitration are unable to agree among themselves on matters of procedure or as to the admissibility of evidence, the decision of the chair governs.

(3) **Decision.**—The decision of a majority of a board of arbitration is the decision of the board, but if there is no majority, the decision of the chair is the decision of the board.

33. (1) **Powers of arbitrator or board of arbitration.**—The arbitrator or board of arbitration has power,

- (a) to summon any person,
    - (i) to give oral or written evidence on oath or affirmation to the arbitrator or board of arbitration, or
    - (ii) to produce in evidence for the arbitrator or board of arbitration such documents and other things as the arbitrator or board of arbitration may specify;
- (b) to administer oaths and affirmations;
- (c) to accept for or exclude from consideration any oral testimony, document or other thing, whether admissible in a court of law or not.

(2) **Stated case for contempt for failure to attend, etc.**—Where any person without lawful excuse,

- (a) on being duly summoned under subsection (1) as a witness before the arbitrator or board of arbitration, as the case may be, makes default in so attending;
- (b) being in attendance as a witness before the arbitrator or board of arbitration, as the case may be, refuses to take an oath or to make an affirmation legally required by the arbitrator or board of arbitration to be taken or made, or to produce any document or thing in his or her power or control legally required by the arbitrator or board of arbitration to be produced, or to answer any question to which the arbitrator or board of arbitration may legally require an answer; or

(c) does any other thing that would, if the arbitrator or board of arbitration had been a court of law having power to commit for contempt, have been contempt of that court,

the arbitrator or board of arbitration may state a case to the Divisional Court setting out the facts and that court may, on the application of the arbitrator or board of arbitration, inquire into the matter and, after hearing any witnesses who may be produced against or on behalf of that person and after hearing any statement that may be offered in defence, punish or take steps for the punishment of that person in like manner as if the person had been guilty of contempt of the court.

34. (1) **Duty of arbitrator or board of arbitration.**—The arbitrator or board of arbitration shall inquire into, consider and decide on all matters remaining in dispute between the parties.

(2) **Matters that may be considered by arbitrator or board of arbitration.**—In the conduct of proceedings and in reaching a decision in respect of a matter in dispute, the arbitrator or board of arbitration may inquire into and consider any matter that the arbitrator or board of arbitration considers relevant to the making of an agreement between the parties.

35. (1) **Time for report of arbitrator or board of arbitration.**—The arbitrator or board of arbitration shall complete the consideration of all matters in dispute between the parties and shall report in writing the decision of the arbitrator or board of arbitration on the matters to the parties and to the Commission within sixty days after the giving of notice of the appointment of the arbitrator or of the appointment of the chair of the board of arbitration, as the case may be, or within such longer period of time as may be provided in writing by the arbitrator or board of arbitration and consented to by the Commission.

(1.1) **Criteria.**—In making a decision or award, the arbitrator or board of arbitration shall take into consideration all factors it considers relevant, including the following criteria:
1. The employer's ability to pay in light of its fiscal situation.
2. The extent to which services may have to be reduced, in light of the decision or award, if current funding and taxation levels are not increased.
3. The economic situation in Ontario and in the municipality or municipalities served by the board.
4. A comparison, as between the employees and other comparable employees in the public and private sectors, of the terms and conditions of employment and the nature of the work performed.
5. The employer's ability to attract and retain qualified employees.

(1.2) **Transition.**—Subsection (1.1) does not apply if, on or before the day the *Savings and Restructuring Act, 1996* receives Royal Assent,
(a) an oral or electronic hearing has begun; or
(b) the arbitrator or board of arbitration has received all the submissions, if no oral or electronic hearing is held.

(1.3) **Restriction.**—Nothing in subsection (1.1) affects the powers of the arbitrator or board of arbitration.

(2) **Effect of decision.**—The decision of the arbitrator or board of arbitration is binding upon the parties and they shall comply in good faith with the decision.

1996, c. 1, Sch. Q., s. 5.

36. (1) Preparation and execution of document by parties.—Within thirty days after receipt by the parties of the report of the arbitrator or board of arbitration, as the case may be, the parties shall prepare a document giving effect to all matters agreed upon by the parties and the decision of the arbitrator or board of arbitration and shall execute the document and thereupon it constitutes an agreement.

(2) **Where arbitrator or board of arbitration to prepare document.**—If the parties fail to execute the document within the period of time mentioned in subsection (1), the arbitrator or board of arbitration, as the case may be, shall prepare the document and submit it to the parties and shall fix the time within which and the place where the parties shall execute the document.

(3) **Failure to execute document.**—If the parties or either of them fail to execute the document within the time fixed by the arbitrator or the board of arbitration, the document shall be deemed to be in effect as though it had been executed by the parties and the document thereupon constitutes an agreement.

PART V

FINAL OFFER SELECTION

37. (1) Parties to give notice to Commission where selection agreed upon.—Where the parties agree to refer all matters remaining in dispute between them that may be provided for in an agreement to a selector, the parties shall jointly give written notice to the Commission that they have so agreed and the notice shall state that the parties agree to refer the matters to a selector and,

(a) the date of appointment and the name and address of the selector; or

(b) that the parties have not appointed the selector and that the parties request the Commission to appoint the selector.

(2) **Statement by parties.**—The parties shall, together with the notice mentioned in subsection (1), give to the Commission a written statement signed by the parties setting out that neither party will withdraw from the proceedings after the final offers of the parties have been submitted to the selector and that the decision of the selector will be accepted by the parties as binding upon them.

(3) **Parties not to withdraw.**—Except as provided in section 56, where the parties give to the Commission a written statement in accordance with subsection (2), a party shall not withdraw from the proceedings after the final offer of either of the parties has been submitted to the selector.

(4) **Where Commission appoints selector.**—Where the parties request the Commission to appoint the selector, the Commission shall make the appointment and give notice of the appointment of the selector to the parties and the notice shall set out the name and address of the person appointed and the date of the appointment.

38. Persons prohibited as selector.—No person shall be appointed a selector who has a direct pecuniary interest in the matters coming before him or her or who is acting or has, within the period of six months immediately before the date of his or her appointment, acted as solicitor, counsel, negotiator, advisor or agent of either of the parties, but no person shall be deemed to have a direct pecuniary interest by reason only of being a ratepayer within the area of jurisdiction of the board that is a party.

39. Selector unable to act.—Where a selector is unable to enter on or to carry on his or her duties so as to enable a decision to be rendered within the time specified by this Act or such longer period of time as may be provided in writing by the selector and consented to by the Commission or ceases to act by reason of withdrawal or death, the Commission shall give notice thereof to the parties who shall within seven days of the giving of the notice appoint a person to be the selector, and if the appointment is not so made by the parties it shall be made by the Commission, and after the selector is appointed, the selection procedure shall begin anew.

40. Notice of matters agreed upon and matters in dispute.—Within seven days after the giving of notice that the selector has been appointed, the parties shall jointly give written notice to the selector setting out all matters that the parties have agreed upon for inclusion in an agreement and all the matters remaining in dispute between the parties.

41. Notice of final offer.—Within fifteen days after the giving of notice that the selector has been appointed, each party shall give written notice to the selector setting out the final offer of the party on all the matters remaining in dispute between the parties and may submit with the notice a written statement in support of the final offer set out in the notice.

42. Final offer of opposite party.—Upon receiving the notices of the parties setting out the final offer of each party, the selector shall forthwith give to each party a copy of the notice setting out the final offer of the opposite party on all the matters remaining in dispute between the parties together with a copy of the statement, if any, of the opposite party submitted in support of the final offer of the opposite party.

43. Written response.—Each party may, within ten days after being given a copy of the final offer and supporting statement, if any, of the opposite party, give to the selector a written reply and the selector shall forthwith give a copy of the reply of each party to the opposite party.

44. Hearing.—Within fifteen days after each party has been given a copy of the final offer and supporting statement, if any, of the opposite party, or within such longer period of time as may be provided in writing by the selector and consented to by the Commission, the selector shall hold a hearing in respect of the matters remaining in dispute between the parties and may, before making a selection, hold a further hearing or hearings.

45. Parties may dispense with hearing.—The parties may agree to dispense with a hearing by the selector and in such case may jointly give written notice to the selector that they have so agreed, and the selector, upon receipt of the notice, shall not hold a hearing but shall proceed to his or her decision.

46. (1) **Procedure.**—The selector shall determine his or her own procedure but, in holding a hearing, shall give full opportunity to the parties to present their evidence and make their submissions.

(2) **Powers of selector.**—The selector has power,

(a) to summon any person,

   (i) to give oral or written evidence on oath or affirmation to the selector, or

(ii) to produce in evidence for the selector such documents and other things as the selector may specify;
(b) to administer oaths and affirmations;
(c) to accept for or exclude from consideration any oral testimony, document or other thing, whether admissible in a court of law or not.

(3) **Stated case for contempt for failure to attend, etc.**—Where any person without lawful excuse,
(a) on being duly summoned under subsection (2) as a witness before the selector makes default in so attending;
(b) being in attendance as a witness before the selector, refuses to take an oath or to make an affirmation legally required by the selector to be taken or made, or to produce any document or thing in his or her power or control legally required by the selector to be produced, or to answer any question to which the selector may legally require an answer; or
(c) does any other thing that would, if the selector had been a court of law having power to commit for contempt, have been contempt of that court,

the selector may state a case to the Divisional Court setting out the facts and that court may, on the application of the selector, inquire into the matter and, after hearing any witnesses who may be produced against or on behalf of that person and after hearing any statement that may be offered in defence, punish or take steps for the punishment of that person in like manner as if the person had been guilty of contempt of the court.

47. (1) **Selection of final offer.**—The selector shall, within fifteen days after the conclusion of the hearing or hearings or within fifteen days after the giving of the notice by the parties that they have agreed to dispense with a hearing, as the case may be, or within such longer period of time as may be provided in writing by the selector and consented to by the Commission, make a decision selecting all of one of the final offers on all matters remaining in dispute between the parties given to the selector by one or the other of the parties.

(2) **Criteria.**—In making a decision, the selector shall take into consideration all factors he or she considers relevant, including the following criteria:
1. The employer's ability to pay in light of its fiscal situation.
2. The extent to which services may have to be reduced, in light of the decision, if current funding and taxation levels are not increased.
3. The economic situation in Ontario and in the municipality or municipalities served by the board.
4. A comparison, as between the employees and other comparable employees in the public and private sectors, of the terms and conditions of employment and the nature of the work performed.
5. The employer's ability to attract and retain qualified employees.

(3) **Transition.**—Subsection (2) does not apply if, on or before the day the *Savings and Restructuring Act, 1996* receives Royal Assent.
(a) an oral or electronic hearing has begun; or
(b) the selector has received all the submissions, if no oral or electronic hearing is held.

(4) **Restriction.**—Nothing in subsection (2) affects the powers of the selector.

1996, c. 1, Sch. Q., s. 5.

48. Effect of decision.—The decision of the selector is binding upon the parties and they shall comply in good faith with the decision.

49. (1) **Preparation and execution of document by parties.**—Within thirty days after receipt of notice of the decision of the selector, the parties shall prepare a document giving effect to all matters agreed upon by the parties and the decision of the selector and shall execute the document and thereupon it constitutes an agreement.

(2) **Where selector to prepare document.**—If the parties fail to execute the document within the period of time mentioned in subsection (1), the selector shall prepare the document and submit it to the parties and shall fix the time within which and the place where the parties shall execute the document.

(3) **Failure to execute document.**—If the parties or either of them fail to execute the document within the time fixed by the selector, the document shall be deemed to be in effect as though it had been executed by the parties and the document thereupon constitutes an agreement.

PART VI

AGREEMENTS

50. Term of agreement.—Every agreement shall,
  (a) provide for a term of operation of not less than one year;
  (b) state that it is effective on and after the 1st day of September in the year in which it is to come into operation; and
  (c) state that it expires on the 31st day of August in the year in which it ceases to operate.

51. (1) **Conflict.**—Where a conflict appears between a provision of an agreement and a provision of an Act or regulation, the provision of the Act or regulation prevails.

(2) **Application of *Constitution Act, 1867*—**The provisions of this Act shall not be construed as to prejudicially affect the rights and privileges with respect to the employment of teachers enjoyed by Roman Catholic and Protestant separate school boards under the *Constitution Act, 1867*.

52. (1) **Resolution of matters arising out of agreement.**—Unless an agreement otherwise provides for the final and binding settlement of all differences between the parties arising from the interpretation, application, administration or alleged contravention of the agreement, the agreement is deemed to include a provision to the following effect:

> Where a difference arises between the parties relating to the interpretation, application or administration of this agreement, or where an allegation is made that this agreement has been contravened, either of the parties may, after exhausting any grievance procedure established by this agreement, notify the other party in writing of its desire to submit the difference or allegation to arbitration and the notice shall contain the name of the first party's appointee to an arbitration board. The recipient of the notice shall within five days inform the other party either that it accepts the other party's appointee as a single arbitrator or inform the other party of the name of its appointee to the arbitration board. Where two appointees are so selected they shall, within five

days of the appointment of the second of them, appoint a third person who shall be the chair. If the recipient of the notice fails to appoint an arbitrator or if the two appointees fail to agree upon a chair within the time limited, the appointment shall be made by the Commission upon the request of either party. The single arbitrator or the arbitration board, as the case may be, shall hear and determine the difference or allegation and shall issue a decision and the decision is final and binding upon the parties and upon any employee or employer affected by it. The decision of a majority is the decision of the arbitration board, but, if there is no majority, the decision of the chair governs. The arbitrator or arbitration board, as the case may be, shall not by his, her or its decision add to, delete from, modify or otherwise amend the provisions of this agreement.

(2) **Enforcement of arbitration decision.**—Where a party or a teacher fails to comply with any of the terms of a decision of an arbitrator or arbitration board, any party or any teacher affected by the decision may file with the Ontario Court (General Division) a copy of the decision of the arbitrator or arbitration board, exclusive of the reasons therefor and certified by the arbitrator or the chair of the arbitration board to be a true copy of the decision, whereupon the decision shall be entered in the same way as an order of that court and is enforceable as such.

53. Provision against strikes and lock-outs.—Every agreement shall be deemed to provide that there will be no strike or lock-out during the term of the agreement or of any renewal of the agreement.

54. (1) **Agreement to form part of contract of employment.**—An agreement between a board and a branch affiliate shall be deemed to form part of the contract of employment between the board and each teacher who is a member of the branch affiliate.

(2) **Conflict.**—Where a conflict appears between a provision of any other part of a contract of employment and a provision of the agreement referred to in subsection (1), the provision of the agreement prevails, but no agreement shall conflict with the form of contract prescribed by the regulations under the *Education Act*.

55. Notice of agreement.—Where the parties agree on all the matters to be included in an agreement, whether during or at the conclusion of negotiations or other proceedings under this Act, the chief executive officer of the board or of each of the boards, as the case may be, that is a party shall forthwith give notice thereof to the Commission.

56. Where agreement reached.—Where the parties agree on all the matters to be included in an agreement, whether during or at the conclusion of negotiations or other proceedings under this Act, they shall prepare a document incorporating all the matters agreed upon and shall execute the document and the document thereupon constitutes an agreement.

57. Notice to Commission of execution of agreement.—Upon the execution of an agreement, each party to the agreement shall forthwith give notice thereof, together with a copy of the agreement, to the Commission.

58. Binding effect of agreement.—An agreement is binding upon the board and upon the branch affiliate that is a party to it and upon the teachers employed by the board who are members of the branch affiliate.

PART VII

EDUCATION RELATIONS COMMISSION

59. (1) Commission continued.—The Education Relations Commission is continued under the name Education Relations Commission in English and Commission des relations de travail en éducation in French.

(2) **Composition.**—The Commission shall be composed of five persons who shall be appointed by the Lieutenant Governor in Council.

(3) **Chair and vice-chair.**—The Lieutenant Governor in Council shall designate a chair and a vice-chair from among the members of the Commission.

(4) **Acting chair.**—In the case of the absence or inability to act of the chair or of there being a vacancy in the office of the chair, the vice-chair shall act as and have all the powers of the chair and in the absence of the chair and vice-chair from any meeting of the Commission, the members of the Commission present at the meeting shall appoint an acting chair who shall act as and have all the powers of the chair during the meeting.

(5) **Term of office.**—The members of the Commission shall be appointed for a term of one, two or three years so that as nearly as possible one-third of the members shall retire each year.

(6) **Vacancy.**—Every vacancy on the Commission caused by the death, resignation or incapacity of a member may be filled by the appointment by the Lieutenant Governor in Council of a person to hold office for the remainder of the term of such member.

(7) **Reappointment.**—Each of the members of the Commission is eligible for reappointment upon the expiration of his or her term of office.

(8) **Quorum.**—Three members of the Commission constitute a quorum and are sufficient for the exercise of all the authority of the Commission.

(9) **Exercising powers.**—The powers of the Commission shall be exercised by resolution and the Commission may pass resolutions governing the calling of and the proceedings at meetings and specifying the powers and duties of employees of the Commission and generally dealing with the carrying out of its duties.

(10) **Remuneration.**—The members of the Commission shall be paid such remuneration and expenses as are determined by the Lieutenant Governor in Council.

(11) **Employees.**—Subject to the approval of the Lieutenant Governor in Council, the Commission may,
 (a) establish job classifications, salary ranges and terms and conditions of employment for its employees; and
 (b) appoint and pay such employees as are considered proper.

(12) **Pension plan.**—The Commission shall be deemed to have been designated by the Lieutenant Governor in Council under the *Public Service Pension Act* as a commission whose permanent employees are required to be members of the Public Service Pension Plan.

(13) **Professional and other assistance.**—The Commission may engage persons other than those employed pursuant to subsection (11) to provide professional, technical or other

assistance to or on behalf of the Commission, and may prescribe the terms of engagement and provide for payment of the remuneration and expenses of such persons.

60. (1) **Duties of Commission.**—It is the duty of the Commission,

(a) to carry out the duties imposed on it by this Act and such other functions as may, in the opinion of the Commission, be necessary to carry out the intent and purpose of this Act;
(b) to maintain an awareness of negotiations between teachers and boards;
(c) to compile statistical information on the supply, distribution, professional activities and salaries of teachers;
(d) to provide such assistance to parties as may facilitate the making or renewing of agreements;
(e) to select and, where necessary, to train persons who may act as mediators, fact finders, arbitrators or selectors;
(f) to determine, at the request of either party or in the exercise of its discretion, whether or not either of the parties is or was negotiating in good faith and making every reasonable effort to make or renew an agreement;
(g) to determine the manner of conducting and to supervise votes by secret ballot pursuant to this Act; and
(h) to advise the Lieutenant Governor in Council when, in the opinion of the Commission, the continuance of a strike, lock-out or closing of a school or schools will place in jeopardy the successful completion of courses of study by the students affected by the strike, lock-out or closing of the school or schools.

(2) **Provision of information.**—The Commission may request a board to provide information necessary to compile the statistical information referred to in subsection (1) and a board shall comply with such a request within a reasonable period of time.

(3) **Annual report.**—The Commission shall annually prepare a report on the affairs of the Commission for the preceding year and the report shall be tabled in the Legislature.

61. **Testimony by member of Commission.**—No member of the Commission shall be required to give testimony in any proceeding under this Act with regard to information obtained in the discharge of his or her duties as a member of the Commission.

62. **Money.**—The money required for the purposes of the Commission shall be paid out of the money appropriated therefor by the Legislature.

PART VIII

STRIKES AND LOCK-OUTS

63. **Notice of strike.**—No teacher shall take part in a strike against the board that employs the teacher unless,

(a) there is no agreement in operation that is deemed under this Act to form part of the contract of employment between the board and the teacher;
(b) notice of desire to negotiate to make or renew an agreement has been given by either party;

(c) all the matters remaining in dispute between the board and the branch affiliate that represents the teacher have been referred to a fact finder and fifteen days have elapsed after the Commission has made public the report of the fact finder;

(d) the offer of the board in respect of all matters agreed upon by the parties and in respect of all matters remaining in dispute between the parties last received by the branch affiliate that represents the teacher is submitted to and rejected by the teachers composing the branch affiliate by a vote by secret ballot conducted under the supervision of and in the manner determined by the Commission;

(e) the teachers composing the branch affiliate that represents the teacher have voted, not earlier than the vote referred to in clause (d) and not before the end of the fifteen-day period referred to in clause (c), in favour of a strike by a vote by secret ballot conducted under the supervision of and in the manner determined by the Commission; and

(f) after a vote in favour of a strike in accordance with clause (e), the branch affiliate that represents the teacher gives to the board written notice of the strike and of the date on which the strike will commence at least five days before the commencement of the strike.

64. (1) **Principals and vice-principals.**—A principal and a vice-principal shall be members of a branch affiliate.

(2) **Idem, membership in branch affiliate.**—Despite subsection (1), in the event of a strike by the members of a branch affiliate each principal and vice-principal who is a member of the branch affiliate shall remain on duty during the strike or any related lock-out or state of lock-out or closing of a school or schools.

65. (1) **Unlawful strike.**—The Federation shall not and no affiliate or branch affiliate shall call or authorize or threaten to call or authorize an unlawful strike.

(2) **Idem.**—No officer, official or agent of the Federation, an affiliate or a branch affiliate or member of a branch affiliate shall counsel, procure, support or encourage an unlawful strike or threaten an unlawful strike.

66. (1) **Unlawful lock-out.**—The Council shall not and no member association or board shall call or authorize or threaten to call or authorize an unlawful lock-out.

(2) **Idem.**—No officer, official or agent of the Council, a member association or a board or member of a board shall counsel, procure, support or encourage an unlawful lock-out or threaten an unlawful lock-out.

67. (1) **Declaration of unlawful strike.**—Where the Federation, an affiliate or a branch affiliate calls or authorizes a strike or teachers take part in a strike against a board that the board, a member association, the Council or any person normally resident within the jurisdiction of the board alleges is unlawful, the board, member association, Council or person may apply to the Ontario Labour Relations Board for a declaration that the strike is unlawful, and the Board may make the declaration.

(2) **Declaration of unlawful lock-out.**—Where the Council, a member association or a board calls or authorizes a lock-out of members of a branch affiliate that the branch affiliate, an affiliate, the Federation or any person normally resident within the jurisdiction of the board alleges is unlawful, the branch affiliate, affiliate, Federation or person may apply to the Ontario

Labour Relations Board for a declaration that the lock-out is unlawful, and the Board may make the declaration.

(3) **Direction by O.L.R.B.**—Where the Ontario Labour Relations Board makes a declaration under subsection (1) or (2), the Board in its discretion may, in addition, direct what action, if any, a person, teacher, branch affiliate, affiliate, the Federation, a board, member association or the Council and their officers, officials or agents shall do or refrain from doing with respect to the unlawful strike or unlawful lock-out.

(4) **Enforcement of direction by court.**—The Ontario Labour Relations Board shall file with the Ontario Court (General Division) a copy of a direction made under subsection (3), exclusive of the reasons therefor, whereupon the direction shall be entered in the same way as an order of the court and is enforceable as such.

68. (1) **Lock-out.**—Where a lawful strike takes place against a board, the board may lock out or declare a state of lock-out to exist against all members, other than principals or vice-principals, of the branch affiliate that represents teachers engaged in the strike.

(2) **Idem.**—No board shall lock out or declare a state of lock-out to exist or close a school or schools unless and until the proposal of the branch affiliate in respect of all matters agreed upon by the parties and in respect of all matters remaining in dispute between the parties last received by the board has been presented to a meeting of the board in public session.

(3) **Idem.**—Except as provided in subsection (1), a board shall not lock out a teacher.

(4) **Closing of school.**—Where a lawful strike takes place against a board, the board may close a school or schools where the board is of the opinion that,
- (a) the safety of students may be endangered;
- (b) the school building or the equipment or supplies therein may not be adequately protected during the strike; or
- (c) the strike will substantially interfere with the operation of the school.

(5) **Payment of teachers.**—A teacher shall not be paid his or her salary in respect of the days on which,
- (a) the teacher takes part in a strike, other than a strike as defined in clause (b) of the definition of "strike" in section 1;
- (b) the teacher is locked out; or
- (c) the school in which the teacher is employed is closed pursuant to subsection (4).

(6) **Resumption of strike or new strike.**—Where a lawful strike is terminated without an agreement coming into effect, no teacher shall take part in a resumption of the strike or take part in a new strike except after the provisions of clauses 63(d), (e) and (f) have again been complied with in respect of such resumption or new strike.

(7) **Application of section.**—This section applies despite any provision of the *Education Act*.

69. Participation in lawful strike.—The contract of employment or position of a teacher shall not be terminated by reason of his or her participation in a lawful strike.

70. Resignation etc. by teacher.—Nothing in this Act precludes a teacher,
- (a) from terminating his or her employment with a board in good faith in accordance with the provisions of his or her contract of employment;

(b) from withdrawing a voluntary service in good faith on an individual basis.

PART IX

MISCELLANEOUS

71. Copies of notice to be given to Commission.—Where, under this Act, a party is required to give notice to another party, the party giving the notice shall also within the same time limit, if any, give a copy of the notice to the Commission.

72. Decisions, etc., of Commission and others not subject to review.—Except in respect of section 51, no decision, order, determination, direction, declaration or ruling of the Commission, a fact finder, an arbitrator or board of arbitration, a selector or the Ontario Labour Relations Board shall be questioned or reviewed in any court, and no order shall be made or process entered, or proceedings taken in any court, whether by way of injunction, declaratory judgment, certiorari, mandamus, prohibition, quo warranto, application for judicial review or otherwise, to question, review, prohibit or restrain the Commission, fact finder, arbitrator or board of arbitration, selector or the Ontario Labour Relations Board or the proceedings of any of them.

73. Service of notice.—Any notice or document required or authorized by this Act tó be given shall,
  (a) where it is to be given to the Commission, be delivered to the office of the Commission;
  (b) where it is to be given to a board, be delivered to the office of the board;
  (c) where it is to be given to a branch affiliate, be delivered to an officer of the branch affiliate;
  (d) where it is to be given to an affiliate, the Council, the Federation or a member association, be delivered to the office of the affiliate, the Council, the Federation or the member association, as the case requires;
  (e) where it is to be given to an arbitrator or selector, be delivered to the arbitrator or selector; and
  (f) where it is to be given to a board of arbitration, be delivered to the chair or either of the other two members of the board of arbitration.

74. (1) **Costs.**—The expenditures incurred by a party in respect of a person appointed or retained by the party for the purpose of making or renewing an agreement shall be borne by the party and all other expenses, including fees for a single arbitrator, a selector or a chair of a board of arbitration shall be shared equally by the parties and such expenditures and fees shall be paid within sixty days after the agreement or renewal of agreement is executed or is deemed in effect as though it had been executed by the parties.

(2) **Idem.**—The fees and expenses, if any, of persons assigned by the Commission to assist parties to make or renew an agreement and of fact finders appointed by the Commission shall be paid by the Commission.

75. Statement as to officers of branch affiliate.—Where the Commission so directs, a branch affiliate shall file with the Commission, within the time prescribed in the direction, a statement signed by its president or secretary setting out the names and addresses of its officers.

76. (1) **Where vote by secret ballot required.**—Subject to subsection (2), a vote conducted by a branch affiliate to give approval to the terms of an agreement shall be a vote by secret ballot.

(2) **Idem.**—A vote conducted by a branch affiliate for the purpose of section 63 or for the purpose of giving approval to the terms of an agreement after the commencement of a strike shall be a vote by secret ballot conducted under the supervision of and in the manner determined by the Commission.

77. (1) **Contravention by teacher or trustee.**—Every person who contravenes any provision of this Act is guilty of an offence and on conviction is liable to a fine of not more than $1,000 for each day upon which the contravention occurs or continues.

(2) **Contravention by Council or Federation.**—The Council and every member association and every board and the Federation and every affiliate and every branch affiliate that contravenes any provision of this Act is guilty of an offence and on conviction is liable to a fine of not more than $25,000 for each day upon which such contravention occurs or continues.

(3) **Contravention of decision, etc.**—The contravention of a decision, order, determination, direction, declaration or ruling made under this Act is deemed, for the purposes of this section, to be a contravention of this Act.

(4) **Where officers also guilty of offence.**—Where the Council or a member association or the Federation or an affiliate or a branch affiliate is guilty of an offence under this Act, every officer or representative thereof, and where a board is guilty of an offence under this Act every member of the board, who assents to the commission of the offence shall be deemed to be a party to and guilty of the offence and is liable to a fine under subsection (1) as if he or she had been convicted of an offence under subsection (1).

(5) **Information.**—An information in respect of a contravention of any provision of this Act may be for one or more offences and no information, warrant, conviction or other proceedings in any such prosecution is objectionable or insufficient by reason of the fact that it relates to two or more offences.

(6) **Consent to prosecution.**—No prosecution for an offence under this Act shall be instituted except with the consent of the Ontario Labour Relations Board which may only be granted after affording an opportunity to the person or body seeking the consent and the person or body sought to be prosecuted to be heard.

(7) **Practice and procedure of O.L.R.B.**—The Ontario Labour Relations Board shall determine its own practice and procedure but shall give full opportunity to the parties to any proceedings to present their evidence and to make their submissions, and the Ontario Labour Relations Board may, subject to the approval of the Lieutenant Governor in Council, make rules governing its practice and procedure and the exercise of its powers and prescribing such forms as are considered advisable.

(8) **Decision of O.L.R.B.**—The decision of the majority of the members of the Ontario Labour Relations Board present and constituting a quorum is the decision of the Ontario Labour Relations Board, but, if there is no majority, the decision of the chair or vice-chair governs.

78. Style of prosecution.—A prosecution for an offence under this Act may be instituted against any body, association or organization in the name of the body, association or organization whether or not the body, association or organization is a body corporate and, for the purposes of any such prosecution, any unincorporated body, association or organization shall be deemed to be a body corporate.

79. Vicarious responsibilities.—Any act or thing done or omitted by an officer, official or agent of the Federation, an affiliate, a branch affiliate, the Council, a member association or a board or by a member of a board within the apparent scope of his or her authority to act on behalf of the Federation, affiliate, branch affiliate, Council, member association or board shall be deemed to be an act or thing done or omitted by the Federation, affiliate, branch affiliate, Council, member association or board, as the case may be.

80. (1) **Application.**—The *Arbitrations Act* does not apply to proceedings under this Act.

(2) **Idem.**—The *Statutory Powers Procedure Act* does not apply to proceedings under this Act other than in respect of a determination referred to in clause 60(1)(f).

(3) **Idem.**—Despite subjection (2), but subject to section 72, the *Statutory Powers Procedure Act* applies to proceedings before the Ontario Labour Relations Board under this Act.

81. Compellability of witnesses.—Despite any other provision of this Act,
 (a) the Minister of Education;
 (b) the Deputy Minister of Education;
 (c) the chair, a vice-chair or a member of the Ontario Labour Relations Board;
 (d) an arbitrator or member or chair of a board of arbitration; or
 (e) a selector,

is not a compellable witness in any proceeding under this Act.

TEACHERS' PENSION ACT

R.S.O. 1990, c. T. 1, as am. S.O. 1991, c. 52, ss. 1-8; 1993, c. 39

DEFINITIONS

1. Definitions. In this Act,

"active plan member", of the pension plan, means a person who is making the contributions required of an active member of the plan or a person on whose behalf contributions required of an active member of the plan are being made. ("participant actif")

"Board" means the Ontario Teacher's Pension Plan Board; ("Conseil")

"Minister" [Repealed 1993, c. 39, s. 1.]

"pension fund" means the pension fund maintained to provide benefits in respect of the Ontario Teachers' Pension Plan; ("caisse de retraite")

"pension plan" means the Ontario Teachers' Pension Plan; ("régime de retraite")

"Schedule 1" or "Schedule 2" means Schedule 1 or 2, as the case may be, to the *Teachers' Pension Act, 1989*, being chapter 92, as amended from time to time. ("annexe 1", "annexe 2")

1991, c. 52, s. 1; 1993, c. 39, s. 1.

2. (1) Pension plan continued.—A pension plan known as the Ontario Teachers' Pension Plan is continued under the name Ontario Teachers' Pension Plan in English and Régime de retraite des enseignantes et des enseignants de l'Ontario in French.

(2) **Defined benefits plan.**—The pension plan is a defined benefit plan within the meaning of the *Pension Benefits Act*.

(3) **Plan documents.**—The terms of the pension plan are as set out in Schedule 1 and in such other governing documents as may be created or adopted under this Act or that Schedule.

(4) **Sufficiency of assets.**—The assets of the pension fund, including the present value of any special payments under Schedule 2 or additional contributions to be made by the Minister of Education and Training, shall be maintained at a level that, at the time of a valuation of the pension plan prepared by the plan actuary for filing with the Pension Commission of Ontario, is reasonably sufficient in the opinion of the actuary to meet the liabilities of the pension plan on a continuing basis.

1991, c. 52, s. 2; 1993, c. 39, s. 2.

3. Administrator.—The Board shall administer the pension plan and manage the pension fund in accordance with this Act, the *Pension Benefits Act* and the *Income Tax Act* (Canada).

4. Pension fund.—The pension fund is continued.

5. (1) Contributions by the Crown.—The Minister of Finance shall pay from the Consolidated Revenue Fund an amount equal to contributions under the pension plan payable by the Minister of Education and Training.

(1.1) **Matching contributions.**—The total amount of the contributions payable by the Minister of Education and Training and the employers who contribute under the pension plan in respect of any year shall not exceed the amount of contributions payable by or on behalf of active plan members in respect of credited service for that year.

(1.2) **Idem.**—For the purpose of subsection (1.1), payments made under subsections (2) to (7) shall not be included in determining the total amount of contributions payable by the Minister of Education and Training and the employers who contribute under the plan.

(2) **Payments re transitional valuation.**—The Minister of Finance shall make the payments required under Schedule 2.

(3) **Deficiency.**—If in a year the amount of cash and assets capable of sale in the pension fund is insufficient to meet the payments out of the fund in the year after the sale of the assets capable of sale, the Minister of Finance shall pay from the Consolidated Revenue Fund an amount sufficient to make up the deficiency.

(4) **Limitation.**—Subsection (3) ceases to apply if an agreement mentioned in subsection 11(1) is in force.

(5) [Repealed 1993, c. 39, s. 3(2).]

(6) [Repealed 1993, c. 39, s. 3(2).]

(7) **Solvency deficiency.**—If a solvency deficiency is disclosed by a solvency valuation under the *Pension Benefits Act*, the Minister of Education and Training may, during the five years following the date of the valuation, make additional contributions to the pension plan.

1991, c. 52, s. 3; 1993, c. 39, s. 3.

5.1 (1) **Recovery of payments.**—If a going concern valuation of the pension plan as at January 1, 1993 discloses a gain, the Crown's portion of which is greater than the special payments made by the Minister of Finance under this Act during the period beginning on January 1, 1993 and ending on March 31, 1994, the Board shall repay to the Minister an amount equal to the special payments, with appropriate adjustments for interest.

(2) **Non-application of *Pension Benefits Act*, s. 78.**—Section 78 of the *Pension Benefits Act* does not apply to a repayment under subsection (1).

1993, c. 39, s. 4.

6. (1) **Board continued.**—The Ontario Teachers' Pension Plan Board is continued as a corporation without share capital under the name Ontario Teachers' Pension Plan Board in English and Conseil de régime de retraite des enseignantes et des enseignants de l'Ontario in French.

(2) **Application of *Corporations Act*.**—The *Corporations Act* does not apply with respect to the Board.

7. Composition of the Board.—The composition of the Board shall be as is set out in the pension plan.

8. (1) **Powers, etc., of the Board.**—The powers and duties of the Board shall be those set out in the pension plan.

(2) **Protection from liability.**—No action or other proceeding for damages shall be commenced or continued against a member of the Board or against a member of a committee of the Board for an act done in good faith in the execution or intended execution of a power or duty under this Act, the pension plan or an agreement between the Minister and the executive of The Ontario Teachers' Federation in respect of the plan.

1991, c. 52, s. 4.

9. [Repealed 1991, c. 52, s. 5.]

10. (1) **Joint management.**—The Minister of Education and Training and the executive of The Ontario Teachers' Federation may enter into an agreement that provides for the following matters:

1. The joint management of the pension plan by the Minister and the executive of the Federation.
2. The composition of the Board, the appointment of the members of the Board and the delineation of the powers and duties of the Board.
3. The sharing of entitlement to gains or surplus under the plan and of liability for deficiencies in the pension fund by the Minister, the employers who contribute under the plan and the active plan members.
4. The amendment of the plan, including the amendment of Schedule 1, by agreement between the Minister and the executive of the Federation.
5. The resolution of disputes between the Minister and the executive of the Federation with respect to amendments to the plan.
6. Any other matter to which the Minister and the executive of the Federation agree.

(2) **Filing of amendment.**—An agreement amending the pension plan under paragraph 4 of subsection (1) shall be filed with the Pension Commission of Ontario and the amendment to the plan comes into force on the date of filing or on such later date as may be set out in the agreement.

(3) **Conflict with *Pension Benefits Act*.**—To the extent that an amendment to the pension plan conflicts with the *Pension Benefits Act* in a matter in which the conflict is not authorized by this Act or Schedule 1, the amendment is void.

1991, c. 52, s. 6; 1993, c. 39, s. 5.

11. (1) **Agreement for member responsibility.**—The Minister of Education and Training and the executive of the Ontario Teachers' Federation may enter into an agreement that provides,

(a) that the pension plan will continue;
(b) that the entitlement to gains or surplus and the liability for deficiencies in the pension fund are permanently assumed by the active plan members;
(c) that the liability of the Crown to contribute under the plan is limited to a specified amount or to a specified percentage of member contributions under the plan;
(d) that the members may amend the plan, subject to the restrictions described in clauses (b) and (c).

(2) **Filing of agreement.**—An agreement under subsection (1) shall be filed with the Pension Commission of Ontario and comes into force on the date of filing or on such later date as may be set out in the agreement.

(3) **Repeal of Schedule 1.**—Schedule 1 is repealed on the day the agreement under subsection (1) comes into force.

1991, c. 52, s. 7; 1993, c. 39, s. 6.

12. (1) **Investments authorized.**—Despite the *Pension Benefits Act* and the regulations thereunder, the receipt and holding by the Board of debentures issued or transferred under section 12 of the *Teachers' Pension Act, 1989*, being chapter 92, shall not be considered imprudent or unreasonable or contrary to the *Pension Benefits Act* and the regulations thereunder, and the nature, amount and terms of the debentures may be taken into account by the Board and any committee of the Board in determining future investments of the assets of the pension plan.

(2) **Transfer Teachers' Pensions.**—Section 81 of the *Pension Benefits Act* does not apply to the transfers described in section 12 of the *Teachers' Pension Act, 1989*, being chapter 92.

12.1 (1) **Special payments required by *Pension Benefits Act*.**—If the *Pension Benefits Act* or the regulations made under that Act require the Minister of Education and Training, as a result of a valuation of the pension plan, to make special payments in respect of the plan, the Minister shall not make the payments but the plan shall be amended so that the actuarial value of the changes made by the amendment is not less than the amount of the special payments.

(2) **Time for amendment.**—The amendment required by subsection (1) shall take effect not later than the 1st day of January immediately following the date of the valuation.

(3) **Actuarial gain.**—Despite the *Pension Benefits Act* and the regulations made under that Act, an implicit actuarial gain disclosed by a valuation of the pension plan made on or after the 1st day of January, 1992 need not be applied to reduce the outstanding balance of a going concern unfunded actuarial liability disclosed by the valuation required by section 3 of Schedule 2.

(4) **Interpretation.**—For the purpose of subsection (3), "implicit actuarial gain" means an amount that would be an actuarial gain but for an adjustment to the required contribution rate determined by the plan actuary in the preparation of the valuation.

1991, c. 52, s. 8; 1993, c. 39, s. 7.

13. (1) **Continued application.**—The *Teachers' Superannuation Act, 1983*, being chapter 84, as it read on the 31st day of December, 1989, continues to apply to the computation or payment of every allowance, annuity, pension or deferred pension or payment to the payment of which a person became entitled under that Act before that date, and continues to apply in respect of every person who, within the meaning of that Act, ceased to be a contributor on or before that date and is entitled to a deferred allowance under that Act.

(2) **Idem.**—The *Teachers' Superannuation Act, 1983*, being chapter 84, as it read on the 31st day of December, 1989, continues to apply in respect of every person who is entitled to a survivor benefit, death benefit, right or allowance with respect to contributions made by a person referred to in subsection (1).

14. Payment of pensions, predecessor Acts.—Every allowance, pension or deferred pension or other payment under the *Teachers' Superannuation Act, 1983*, being chapter 84, or a predecessor Act or under the *Superannuation Adjustment Benefits Act*, being chapter 490 of the Revised Statutes of Ontario, 1980, or a predecessor Act, including any payment authorized to be made from the Consolidated Revenue Fund, that, before the 1st day of January, 1990, a person was receiving, was entitled to receive, or was entitled to receive with the payment thereof deferred until the year 1990 or later, shall be paid out of the pension fund in accordance with the Act under which entitlement to the payment arose.

TEACHING PROFESSION ACT
R.S.O. 1990, c. T.2, as am. S.O. 1991, Vol. 2, c. 52, 1996, c. 12, s. 67; 1997, c. 31, s. 180

1. Definitions.—In this Act,
"Board of Governors."—"Board of Governors" means the Board of Governors of the Federation; ("conseil d'administration")
"board of trustees."—[Repealed 1997, c. 31, s. 180(1).]
"executive."—"executive" means the executive of the Federation; ("bureau")
"Federation."—"Federation" means The Ontario Teachers' Federation; ("Fédération")
"member."—"member" means a member of the Federation; ("membre")
"Minister."—"Minister" means the Minister of Education; ("ministre")
"Ministry."—"Ministry" means the Ministry of Education; ("ministère")
"regulations."—"regulations" means the regulations made under this Act; ("règlements")
"teacher."—"teacher" means a person who is a member of the Ontario College of Teachers and is employed by a board as a teacher but does not include a supervisory officer, a principal, a vice-principal or an instructor in a teacher-training institution. ("enseignant")
1996, c. 12, s. 67; 1997, c. 31, s. 180(2).

2. Body corporate.—The federation of teachers known as The Ontario Teachers' Federation is continued as a body corporate, under the name The Ontario Teachers' Federation in English and Fédération des enseignantes et enseignants de l'Ontario in French.

3. Objects.—The objects of the Federation are,

(a) to promote and advance the cause of education;
(b) to raise the status of the teaching profession;
(c) to promote and advance the interests of teachers and to secure conditions that will make possible the best professional service;
(d) to arouse and increase public interest in educational affairs;
(e) to co-operate with other teachers' organizations throughout the world having the same or like objects; and
(f) to represent all members of the pension plan established under the *Teachers' Pension Act* in the administration of the plan and the management of the pension fund.

4. (1) Membership in Federation.—Every teacher is a member of the Federation except,

(a) a teacher who has withdrawn from membership under subsection 4(1) or (2) of *The Teaching Profession Act*, being chapter 64 of the Statutes of Ontario, 1944;
(b) a teacher who,
 (i) at any time during World War II was a member of Her Majesty's forces or engaged on special war service designated by the regulations, and
 (ii) at the time of entering the forces or becoming engaged on such service was a teacher or was training to be a teacher at a provincial normal school or the Ontario College of Education, and
 (iii) notifies the Minister and the secretary of the Board of Governors of his or her

withdrawal from membership by registered letter posted not later than six months after he or she ceases to be in the forces or on special war service.

(2) **Associate members.**—Every student in a teachers' college or in a college of education in Ontario is an associate member of the Federation.

(3) **Persons receiving pension.**—Every person who was a member of the Federation upon retirement and who is receiving a pension or an allowance under the *Teachers' Pension Act* may, on request, be an associate member of the Federation.

5. (1) **Board of Governors.**—There shall be a Board of Governors of the Federation, which shall be composed of fifty members consisting of the immediate past president, the president, the first vice-president, the second vice-president and the secretary-treasurer of each of, The Ontario Secondary School Teachers' Federation, The Federation of Women Teachers' Associations of Ontario, The Ontario Public School Teachers' Federation, the Association des enseignantes et des enseignants franco-ontariens and The Ontario English Catholic Teachers' Association, and five representatives of each of such federations or associations, who shall be elected annually at the annual meeting of the federation or association from among its members.

(2) **Term of office.**—The members of the Board of Governors shall take office at the conclusion of the annual meeting of the Federation and shall hold office until their successors take office.

(3) **Vacancies.**—If a vacancy occurs on the Board of Governors, it shall be filled by the executive of the affiliated body that the person who vacated the office represented and the person so named to fill the vacancy shall hold office for the remainder of the term of the person who vacated the office.

6. (1) **Executive.**—There shall be an executive of the Federation, which shall be composed of eleven members as follows,

(a) the immediate past president, the president, the first vice-president, the second vice-president and the third vice-president of the Federation;

(b) one representative of The Ontario Secondary School Teachers' Federation, one representative of The Federation of Women Teachers' Associations of Ontario, one representative of The Ontario Public School Teachers' Federation, one representative of the Association des enseignantes et des enseignants franco-ontariens and one representative of The Ontario English Catholic Teachers' Association, who shall be elected annually at the annual meeting of the Board of Governors from among its members; and

(c) the secretary-treasurer of the Federation.

(2) **Term of office.**—The members of the executive shall take office at the conclusion of the annual meeting of the Federation and shall hold office until their successors take office.

(3) **Vacancies.**—If a vacancy occurs on the executive, it may be filled by the Board of Governors from among its members who represent the affiliated body that the person who vacated the office represented, and the person so named shall hold office for the remainder of the term of the person who vacated the office.

7. President and vice-presidents.—There shall be a president, a first vice-president, a second vice-president and a third vice-president of the Federation who shall be elected annually at the annual meeting of the Board of Governors from among its members in such a manner that the officers of the immediate past president, president, first vice-president, second vice-president and third vice-president shall represent each of the affiliated bodies.

8. Secretary-treasurer.—There shall be a secretary-treasurer of the Federation appointed by the Board of Governors who may be a member of the Board of Governors and who shall receive such remuneration as may be fixed by the Board of Governors.

9. Functions of executive.—The executive is responsible for carrying on the business of the Federation and may,

(a) subject to the approval of the Minister, acquire and hold in the name of the Federation such real and personal property as may be necessary for the purposes of the Federation and may alienate, mortgage, lease or otherwise dispose of such property as occasion may require;

(b) invest the funds of the Federation in any securities in which a trustee is authorized to invest money under the *Trustee Act*;

(c) make such grants as it considers advisable to organizations having the same or like objects as the Federation;

(d) act as the representative of the members of the pension plan established under the *Teachers' Pension Act* including carrying out the following functions:

 1. Appointing persons to be members of the Ontario Teachers' Pension Plan Board created under that Act.
 2. Entering into agreements as described in that Act.
 3. Negotiating, agreeing to or directing amendments to the plan as permitted under that Act or an agreement entered into under that Act.
 4. Entering into an agreement on behalf of the Federation to indemnify a member of the Ontario Teachers' Pension Plan Board or a member of a committee of the Board against any costs sustained with respect to legal proceedings arising out of an act or omission done in the execution of his or her duties as a member of the Board or committee.

1991, Vol. 2, c. 52, s. 9.

10. Conferences.—In the interests of the advancement of education and the improvement of teaching conditions in Ontario, the Board of Governors shall meet annually and confer with the Minister and the senior officials of the Ministry on matters touching and concerning the objects of the Federation, and the Board of Governors shall at such meeting and may at any other time make such representations and recommendations either of a general nature or which relate to any particular school, teacher or matter as it considers advisable and as are in keeping with the objects of the Federation.

11. Collection of fees.—[Repealed 1997, c. 31, s. 180(3).]

12. Regulations.—Subject to the approval of the Lieutenant Governor in Council, the Board of Governors may make regulations,

(a) prescribing a code of ethics for teachers;

(b) [Repealed 1997, c. 31, s. 180(4).]

(c) providing for voluntary membership in the Federation of persons who are not members thereof and prescribing the duties, responsibilities and privileges of voluntary members;

(d) prescribing the duties, responsibilities and privileges of associate members;

(e) providing for the suspension and expulsion of members from the Federation and other disciplinary measures;

(f) designating the services and organizations that shall be deemed to be special war services for the purposes of clause 4(1)(b);

(g) providing for the holding of meetings of the Board of Governors and of the executive and prescribing the manner of calling and the notice to be given in respect of such meetings;

(h) prescribing the procedure to be followed at meetings of the Board of Governors and of the executive;

(i) providing for the payment of necessary expenses to the members of the Board of Governors and the executive;

(j) conferring powers upon or extending or restricting the powers of and prescribing the duties of the Board of Governors and of the executive;

(k) providing for the appointment of standing and special committees;

(l) providing for the establishment of branches of the Federation or of the recognition by the Federation of local bodies, groups or associations of teachers which shall be affiliated with the Federation.

13. (1) **Restriction re by-laws.**—A by-law governing the membership of teachers in an affiliated body of the Federation shall not authorize a teacher to be a member of an affiliated body that is not his or her designated bargaining agent, if any, under Part X.1 of the *Education Act.*

(2) **Changes to regulations, by-laws.**—The Minister may request the Board of Governors to make, amend or revoke a regulation or by-law if the Minister considers it appropriate to do so.

(3) **Same.**—If the Board of Governors fails to comply with the Minister's request within 60 days after receiving it, the Lieutenant Governor in Council may, by regulation, make, amend or revoke the regulation or by-law.

1997, c. 31, s. 180(5).

REGULATION MADE UNDER THE TEACHING PROFESSION ACT*

[Updated to June 1, 1997]

Affiliated Bodies

1. The Ontario Secondary School Teachers' Federation, the Federation of Women Teachers' Association of Ontario, the Ontario Public School Teachers' Federation, l'Association des enseignantes et des enseignants franco-ontariens and the Ontario English Catholic Teachers' Association shall be affiliated with the Federation and known as "affiliated bodies."

Voluntary Membership

2. (1) The Board of Governors shall grant voluntary membership in the Federation to a person who,

(a) is not a member thereof;
(b) holds a teacher's certificate;
(c) is engaged in an educational capacity;
(d) is a member of an affiliated body; and
(e) makes application to the Board of Governors for voluntary membership in the Federation.

(2) The Board of Governors shall grant voluntary membership in the Federation to a person who is not a member thereof and who is from outside Ontario and is on an assignment of two years or less as a teacher in Ontario under a teacher exchange program.

(3) The duties of a voluntary member shall be the same as those of a member under Sections 13 to 18.

(4) A voluntary member shall have such privileges as are common to all members of the Federation.

Application for Membership by a Former Member

3. (1) A teacher who has withdrawn from membership under subsection (1) or (2) of Section 4 of the *Teaching Profession Act, 1944*, may make application to the Board of Governors for reinstatement as a member.

---

* Editor's Note: Section 1 of the Regulations Act, R.S.O. 1990, c. R.21 expressly excludes regulations made pursuant to the Teaching Profession Act from the application of the Regulations Act, R.S.O. 1990, c. R.21, and as such, they are not required to be published in the Ontario Gazette. Accordingly, the Regulation Made Under the Teaching Profession Act does not have a conventional "R.S.O. 1990, Reg. ***" or an "O. Reg. ***/9*" citation.

The text noted below was updated by verifying its accuracy with the Ontario Teachers' Federation. Section 12 of the Teaching Profession Act gives the Board of Governors of that organization the authority to pass regulations pursuant to that Act.

(2) The Board of Governors shall refer the application to the proper affiliated body for its opinion of the application.

(3) Where the Board of Governors, after considering the opinion of the affiliated body, accepts the application, the secretary-treasurer of the Federation shall notify the Minister and the applicant forthwith.

Fees

4. (1) Subject to subsections 2 and 4, a member shall pay the Federation an annual membership fee as follows:
1. A secondary school teacher, 1.18 per cent of total annual salary.
2. A statutory member of the Ontario Public School Teachers' Federation $100.00 plus 1.2 per cent of the total annual salary of the member.
3. A female public school teacher,
    (i) working more than half-time, $650.00,
    (ii) working half-time or less, $325.00.
4. A separate school teacher,
    (i) working more than half-time, $675.00,
    (ii) working half-time or less, an amount which bears the same relation to $660.00 as does the teacher's total annual salary the teacher would earn if full-time.
5. A teacher in a French-language school or class who is a member of L'Association des enseignantes et des enseignants franco-ontariens, 1.5% of the teacher's total annual salary;

where "total annual salary" means salary in accordance with the terms and conditions under which the member is employed, and includes a cost of living or other similar bonus.

(2) A member who is employed by a board exclusively in respect of the continuing education classes provided by the board shall pay the Federation an annual membership fee as follows:
1. A secondary school teacher, 1.18 per cent of the salary attributable to such teaching.
2. A statutory member of the Ontario Public School Teachers' Federation, 1.15 per cent of the salary attributable to such teaching.
3. A female public school teacher $0.20 in respect of each day on which the teacher performs teaching duties to a maximum amount of $4.00 for each month in which the teacher performs such teaching duties.
4. A separate school teacher, 1.25 per cent of the salary attributable to such teaching duties.
5. A teacher of a French-language school or class who is a member of L'Association des enseignantes et des enseignants franco-ontariens, 1.5 per cent of the salary attributable to such teaching duties.

(3) A member to whom subsection (1) applies who is also employed for the purpose of a class referred to in subsection (2) shall pay an annual membership fee that is the sum of the annual membership fee applicable to the member under subsection (1) and the annual membership fee that would be applicable to the member under subsection (2), if the member were a person employed exclusively for the purpose of a class referred to in subsection (2).

(4) Where a fee, or a portion thereof, that is payable under subsection (1) is not based upon salary, such fee or portion thereof shall be reduced, in the case of a teacher who is not employed for the full school year, by multiplying such fee or portion thereof by the ratio of the number of full and part months that the teacher was employed in the school year to ten.

(5) A board of trustees, in respect of a teacher employed by the board, shall,
- (a) where a single deduction is made, remit to the secretary-treasurer of the Federation the full annual fee,
    - (i) by the 30th day of November, or
    - (ii) in the case of a teacher whose employment commences after the first school day in November, by the last day of the first full month that the teacher is employed by the board; and
- (b) where deductions are made in instalments, place the instalment fee on deposit with the Federation on or before the 15th day of the month immediately following the month of deduction.

Meetings of the Board of Governors

5. (1) The annual meeting of the Board of Governors shall be held in each year on the days during the three weeks next preceding Labour Day that are, and at a time and place that is, determined by the president.

(2) Subject to subsection (5), there shall be a special meeting of the Board of Governors on the days during or within two weeks following each of the Christmas vacation and the Easter vacation that are, and at a time and place that is, determined by the president.

(3) The Board of Governors shall meet at such other dates and times as the executive may by resolution determine.

(4) A member of the Board of Governors shall be allowed a leave of absence not exceeding four days a year to attend meetings of the Board of Governors referred to in subsections (2) and (3).

(5) Upon the recommendation of the executive and with the approval of at least thirty-two members of the Board of Governors, the Board of Governors may, by resolution, waive the holding of one of the meetings under subsection (2).

(6) The secretary-treasurer of the Federation shall send to members of the Board of Governors a written notice of the date, time and place of a meeting of the Board of Governors,
- (a) at least fourteen days before the date of a meeting under subsection (1) or (2); and
- (b) at least three days before the date of a meeting under subsection (3).

(7) A quorum at a meeting of the Board of Governors shall be thirty-two members thereof.

Meetings of Executive

6. (1) The executive shall meet immediately before and immediately after a meeting of the Board of Governors.

(2) The secretary-treasurer of the Federation shall send to members of the executive at least seven days in advance of a meeting of the executive written notice of date, time and place of the meeting under subsection (1).

(3) The president of the Federation may at any time call a special meeting of the executive.

(4) A quorum at any meeting of the executive shall be six members thereof.

Nominating Committee

7. (1) At the meeting of the executive immediately before the annual meeting of the Board of Governors, the executive shall appoint a nominating committee and include thereon a representative of each of the affiliated bodies.

(2) The nominating committee shall meet on the first day of the annual meeting of the Board of Governors to prepare nominations for the executive for the year next following.

(3) The nominating committee shall present the report of its nominations to the Board of Governors and, upon these and other nominations which may be submitted from the floor by any member of the Board of Governors, a secret ballot shall be taken.

Relations and Discipline Committee

8. There shall be a Relations and Discipline Committee appointed by the Board of Governors.

Standing Committees

9. (1) There shall be standing committees as follows:
1. Educational finance
2. Educational Studies
3. Legislation
4. Pension
5. Teacher Education

(2) A committee under subsection (1) shall,
(a) be composed of the chairman or a member of the corresponding committee of each affiliated body, together with the president and secretary-treasurer of the Federation; and
(b) be convened by a member designated by the executive, following the annual meeting of the Board of Governors.

(3) The Board of Governors may, by by-law, establish such standing committees, in addition to those set out in subsection (1), as it considers expedient, and terminate any standing committee so established.

(4) A by-law passed under subsection (3) establishing a standing committee shall make provision for the composition of the committee.

(5) Clause (b) of subsection (2) applies to a standing committee established under subsection (3).

Special Committees

10. The Board of Governors or the executive may, by resolution, appoint such special committees as it considers necessary from time to time.

Procedure at Annual Meeting of Board of Governors

11. (1) The order of procedure at the annual meeting of the Board of Governors shall be as follows:
1. Call to order.
2. Appointment of committees.
3. Reading and confirming the minutes of the next preceding meeting.
4. Business arising from the minutes.
5. Reading of correspondence and action thereon.
6. Reports of officers.
7. Reception of delegations.
8. Reports from affiliated bodies.
9. Reports of standing and special committees.
10. General business.
11. Elections.
12. Installation of officers.
13. Adjournment.

(2) The Board of Governors may omit one or more items of the order of procedure from the agenda of the annual meeting.

Expenses

12. The Federation shall pay such necessary expenses as members of the Board of Governors and of the executive incur in carrying out their duties under the Act and this Regulation.

General Duties of Members

13. A member shall strive at all times to achieve and maintain the highest degree of professional competence and to uphold the honour, dignity, and ethical standards of the teaching profession.

Duties of a Member to his Pupils

14. A member shall,
(a) regard as his first duty the effective education of his pupils and the maintenance of a high degree of professional competence in his teaching;
(b) endeavour to develop in his pupils an appreciation of standards of excellence;
(c) endeavour to inculcate in his pupils an appreciation of the principles of democracy;
(d) show consistent justice and consideration in all his relations with pupils;
(e) refuse to divulge beyond his proper duty confidential information about a pupil; and
(f) concern himself with the welfare of his pupils while they are under his care.

Duties of a Member to Educational Authorities

15. (1) A member shall,

(a) comply with the Acts and regulations administered by the Minister;
(b) co-operate with his educational authorities to improve public education;
(c) respect the legal authority of the board of trustees in the management of the school and in the employment of teachers;
(d) make in the proper manner such reports concerning teachers under his authority as may be required by the board of trustees; and
(e) present in the proper manner to the proper authorities the consequences to be expected from policies or practices which in his professional opinion are seriously detrimental to the interests of pupils.

(2) A member shall not,
(a) break a contract of employment with a board of trustees;
(b) violate a written or oral agreement to enter into a contract of employment with a board of trustees; or
(c) while holding a contract of employment with a board of trustees, make application for another position the acceptance of which would necessitate his seeking the termination of his contract by mutual consent of the teacher and the board of trustees, unless and until he has arranged with his board of trustees for such termination of contract if he obtains the other position.

Duties of a Member to the Public

16. A member shall,
(a) endeavour at all times to extend the public knowledge of his profession and discourage untrue, unfair or exaggerated statements with respect to teaching; and
(b) recognize a responsibility to promote respect for human rights.

Duties of a Member to the Federation

17. A member shall co-operate with the Federation to promote the welfare of the profession.

Duties of a Member to Fellow Members

18. (1) A member shall,
(a) avoid interfering in an unwarranted manner between other teachers and pupils;
(b) on making an adverse report on another member, furnish him with a written statement of the report at the earliest possible time and not later than three days after making the report;
(c) refuse to accept employment with a board of trustees whose relations with the Federation are unsatisfactory; and
(d) where he is in an administrative or supervisory position, make an honest and determined effort to help and counsel a teacher before subscribing to the dismissal of that teacher.

(2) Under clause (c) of subsection (1), the onus shall be on the member to ascertain personally from the Federation whether an unsatisfactory relationship exists.

(3) A member shall not attempt to gain an advantage over other members by knowingly underbidding another member, or knowingly applying for a position not properly declared vacant, or by negotiating for salary independently of his local group of fellow-members.

Relations and Discipline Procedure

19. (1) In this section and Sections 20 to 28

(a) "Committee" means the Relations and Discipline Committee of the Ontario Teachers' Federation;

(b) "teaching certificate" means an Ontario Teacher's Certificate or other qualification to teach prescribed under Regulation 269 as amended and revised from time to time.

(2) The Committee shall be composed of ten members who are teachers, appointed by the Board of Governors, two of whom shall be from each affiliated body.

(3) A person is not eligible for appointment to the Committee who,

(a) holds office on a disciplinary body of an affiliated body;

(b) holds office on the executive of an affiliated body; or

(c) is employed by either an affiliated body or the Federation.

(4) The Committee shall appoint one of the members of the Committee to be chairman.

(5) The chairman of the Committee may assign a panel of five members of the Committee to hold a hearing.

(6) Three members of the panel assigned under subsection (5) constitute a quorum for a hearing and all disciplinary decisions require the vote of a majority of members of the Committee present at the hearing.

(7) The secretary-treasurer of the Federation shall act as secretary to the Committee but shall not participate in any decision of the Committee.

20. (1) The Committee shall,

(a) consider complaints regarding professional misconduct or unethical conduct of a member;

(b) consider applications for reinstatement of the teaching certificate of a former member or the lifting of a suspension thereof.

(2) A hearing of the Committee shall be held in camera unless the member requests otherwise by notice delivered to the Committee not later than the day before the day fixed for the hearing, in which case the Committee shall conduct the hearing in public except when,

(i) matters involving public security may be disclosed; or

(ii) the possible disclosure of intimate financial or personal matters outweighs the desirability of holding the hearing in public.

(3) No hearing in respect of alleged professional misconduct or unethical conduct shall be conducted by the Committee unless,

(a) a written signed complaint has been filed in the office of the secretary-treasurer of the Federation;

(b) a copy thereof has been served on the member whose conduct is being investigated; and

(c) the member whose conduct is being investigated has been served with notice of the time, place and purpose of the hearing.

(4) The secretary-treasurer of the Federation shall,

(a) prepare and complete or cause to be completed a written complaint and file it in the office of the secretary-treasurer of the Federation;

(b) serve upon the member whose conduct is being investigated,
- (i) a copy of the complaint; and
- (ii) a notice of the hearing which shall include,
    - A. a statement of the time, place and purpose of the hearing;
    - B. a reference to the statutory authority under which the hearing will be held;
    - C. a statement that if the party notified does not attend at the hearing the Committee may proceed in his absence and he will not be entitled to any further notice of the proceedings; and
    - D. a statement that the member may,
        1. be represented by counsel or an agent;
        2. call and examine witnesses;
        3. present arguments and submissions; and
        4. conduct cross-examination of witnesses as reasonably required for full and fair disclosure of the facts in relation to which they have given evidence; and

(c) make all necessary arrangements for the conduct of the hearing including,
- (i) the appointment of counsel for the Federation;
- (ii) the arrangement for oral evidence to be recorded; and
- (iii) the notification to all members of the Committee of the time and place of the hearing.

21. In proceedings before the Committee, the Federation and the member whose professional misconduct or unethical conduct, or reinstatement is being investigated shall be parties to the proceedings.

22. (1) A member whose professional misconduct or unethical conduct or reinstatement is being investigated shall be afforded an opportunity to examine, before the hearing, any written or documentary evidence that will be produced or any report, the contents of which will be given in evidence at the hearing.

(2) Members of the Committee conducting the hearing shall not,

(a) have taken part before the hearing in the investigation of the subject matter of the complaint;

(b) have taken part in any previous hearing involving the member whose professional misconduct, unethical conduct or reinstatement is being investigated; or

(c) communicate directly or indirectly in relation to the subject matter of the hearing with any person or with any party or representative of a party, except upon notice to and opportunity for all parties to participate.

23. (1) The evidence before the Committee shall be recorded by a person appointed by the chairman of the Committee.

(2) Nothing is admissible in evidence before the Committee that would be inadmissible in a civil case and the findings of the Committee shall be based exclusively on evidence before it.

(3) No member of the Committee shall participate in the decision of the Committee unless he has been present throughout the hearing.

24. At a hearing before the Committee, a party to the proceedings may,
- (a) be represented by counsel or an agent;
- (b) call and examine witnesses;
- (c) present arguments and submissions; and
- (d) conduct cross-examination of witnesses as reasonably required for full and fair disclosure of the facts in relation to which they have given evidence.

25. (1) A member may be found guilty by the Committee of a professional misconduct or unethical conduct if in the opinion of the Committee he has contravened any of the provisions of Sections 13 to 18.

(2) In the case of hearings into complaints of professional misconduct and unethical conduct, the Committee shall,
- (a) consider the allegations, hear the evidence and ascertain the facts of the case;
- (b) determine whether upon the evidence and the facts so ascertained the allegations have been proved;
- (c) determine whether in respect of the allegations so proved, the member is guilty of professional misconduct or unethical conduct; and
- (d) determine the penalty to be imposed, as hereinafter provided, in cases in which it finds a member guilty of professional misconduct or unethical conduct.

(3) Where the Committee finds a member guilty of professional misconduct or unethical conduct, it shall,
- (a) recommend to the Minister the cancellation of the teaching certificate of the member;
- (b) recommend to the Minister the suspension for a stated fixed period of the teaching certificate of the member; or
- (c) reprimand the member,

or proceed with any combination of the foregoing.

26. (1) Where the Federation receives a request for a recommendation in respect of the reinstatement of a teaching certificate of a former member or the lifting of the suspension thereof, the secretary-treasurer shall refer the matter to the Committee for a hearing.

(2) Following a hearing under subsection (1), the Committee shall recommend to the Minister that the teaching certificate be reinstated or the suspension lifted, or that the teaching certificate remain cancelled or the suspension not be lifted, as the case may be.

27. (1) The Committee shall give its decision and recommendation, if any, under sub-sections 25.(3) or 26.(2) in writing and shall give reasons in writing, therefor, if requested by a party.

(2) The decision of the Committee shall be served upon the parties.

28. Any notice or other document required to be served by this regulation may be served by prepaid first class mail addressed to the person to whom notice is to be given at his last known address and where notice is served by mail, the service shall be deemed to have been made on the fifth day after the day of mailing unless the person to whom the notice is given establishes that he, acting in good faith, due to absence, accident, illness or other cause beyond his control, did not receive the notice or did not receive the notice until a later date.

Evidencing Regulations and Resolutions

29. Regulations made by and resolutions passed by the Board of Governors may be evidenced by the signatures of the president and the secretary-treasurer of the Federation.

Effective Date and Transitional Provisions

30. (1) This Regulation comes into force on the 1st day of January 1986, and applies in respect of any complaint of professional misconduct or unethical conduct filed in the office of the secretary-treasurer of the Federation on or after that date, and in respect of a request referred to in Section 26 received by the Federation on or after that date.

(2) The provisions of the Regulation made under the Teaching Profession Act that are revoked by this Regulation shall continue to apply to any matter or proceeding brought thereunder and not disposed of prior to the 1st day of January 1986 notwithstanding the coming into force of this Regulation.

Index

References are to sections of the *Education Act* unless otherwise indicated: Reg.—*Education Act* regulation; EQAOA—*Education Quality and Accountability Office Act, 1996*; ISPA—*Immunization of School Pupils Act*; ISPA Reg.—Regulation under the *Immunization of School Pupils Act*; LGDIA—*Local Government Disclosure of Interest Act*; MCIA—*Municipal Conflict of Interest Act*; MFIPPA—*Municipal Freedom of Information and Protection of Privacy Act*; MFIPPA Reg.—Regulation under the *Municipal Freedom of Information and Protection of Privacy Act*; OCTA—*Ontario College of Teachers Act*; OCTA Reg.—Regulations under the *Ontario College of Teachers Act*; OSRG—Ontario Student Record Guidelines; PSNA—*Provincial Schools Negotiation Act*; SBTCNA—*School Boards and Teachers Collective Negotiations Act*; TPenAct—*Teachers' Pension Act*; TPA—*Teaching Profession Act*; TPA Reg.—Regulation under the *Teaching Profession Act*.

Aboriginal schools
admission of non-aboriginal pupils to, 12(2)-(3)
agreements by school boards, 185, 188
native representation on boards, Reg. 462/97

Admission of pupils See also **Resident pupil qualification; Continuing education.**
adult non-resident, 37
fee
    attending from other district or zone, 49(1)-(5)
    limitation of waiver, 38
    visitors to Canada, 49(6)-(7)
    waiver of, 32(2)
right to attend
    child as ward, 47
    child in custody of corporation or society, 48
    generally, 32(1)
    repeal of *London-Middlesex Act, 1992*, 48.1
    other district or zone, 39, 40
    persons unlawfully in Canada, 49.1
    residence on defence property, 46.1, Reg. 465/97
to secondary school, 41

Adult education See **Continuing education**

Advertising and announcements, Reg. 298, s. 24

Agreements with Canada
admission to aboriginal schools, 12(2)
physical fitness, 12(1)

Alternative boards
levying and collecting duties, Reg. 494/97

Anti-racism policy, 8(1) para. 29.1

Appeal against suspension, 23(2)-(2.2)

Arbitrators, 210

Assessment of academic achievement
policies and guidelines establishment, 8(1) para. 3.3
tests prescribed by Minister, 8(1) para. 3.2

Attendance of pupils
compulsory attendance
    excused, 21(2)-(3)
    duty of parent, 21(5)
    exception to, 8(8)
    generally, 21(1)
    Provincial School Attendance Counsellor, 24
    school attendance counsellors, 25. See also **School attendance counsellors**
    underaged pupil, 21(4)

INDEX

daily register, 8(1) para. 8
effect of closing, 5(2)
liability
    corporations, 30(4)
    employer, 30(3)
    habitual truants, 30(5)-(6)
    parent or guardian, 30(1)
prosecutions, 31
right to attend
    generally, 32; Reg. 470/98
    non-resident business owner, 43.2; Reg. 471/98
    non-resident property owner, 43.1

Auditors
appointment, 253
duties prescribed, 8(1) para. 30
report of old board financial statements, Reg. 470/97

Awards
approval by Minister, 8(1) para. 28

Band
defined, 1(1)

Beginners class, 34(3)

Blind, schools for
additional schools, 13(4)
admissions, Reg. 296, ss. 3-8
administration, 13(3)
continuation of, 13(2)
designations, Reg. 296, s.2
duties of pupils, Reg. 296, s.14
duties of residence counsellors, Reg. 296, s.16
duties of Superintendent, Reg. 296, ss.18-20
fees, Reg. 296, ss.9-12
parents, Reg. 296, s.17
powers of Minister, 8(1) para.20
regulations, 13(7); Reg. 296
Superintendent's Advisory Council, Reg. 296, s.22
teachers
    duties, Reg. 296, s.15
    qualifications, Reg. 296, s.23

transportation, Reg. 296, s.13

Board. See also **Alternative boards; Board members; Finance; Protestant separate school board; Roman Catholic school authority** and **School board advisory committee.**
agreements
    accommodation or services for other board, 18(1)
    admission of pupils to aboriginal schools, 185
    approved, 8(1) para.33
    co-operative, 171.1
    education at other school, 184
    education of aboriginal pupils, 188
    financial services, 249
    joint use of facilities, 183
    multi-use building, 196
    natural science programs, 197(5)
    pupils in federal establishments, 187
    right to close school, 186
    transfer of French-language secondary school, 182
appointment of school attendance counsellors, 25
appointment to teach in emergency, Reg. 298, s.21
benefits. See also **Teachers' pensions**
    group coverage for employees, 177
    liability insurance, 176
    pensions, 178
    retirement allowances, 179
    sick leave credits, 180
borrowing, 242-247
closing of school, 19
consent to advertising and announcements, Reg. 298, s.24
defined, 1(1); ISPA 1
designation of professional activity days, Reg. 304
designation of teachers, 135
development charges, see **Education development charges**
duties, 170-170.2

investment
  eligible, Reg. 471/97
  powers, 241
meetings
  electronic meetings, 8(1) para.3.6; 208; Reg. 463/97
  generally, 208
  public access to, 207
movement of pupil between boards, 42, 43
out-of-class programs, 197
native representation, Reg. 462/97
powers, 171
property. See **Property**
pupil representatives
  authority for regulations, 55
  guidelines for, 8(1) para. 3.5
  regulation, Reg. 461/97
reports, 8(1) paras. 27.1, 27.2
resident pupil qualification, 33, 34
scholarships, bursaries and prizes, 173
setting taxes, 257.15-257.29, 257.106
supervision of financial affairs by Minister, 257.30-257.52
suspensions and expulsions, 23(2)-(6)
transition to district school boards, Reg. 460/97
transportation of pupils, 190
vacancies
  appointment or election, 218, 221(1), 224, 226
  cause, 228
  elections, 222, 225
  tie vote, 227

Board members. See also **Conflict of interest.**
attendance required, 229
declaration and oath of allegiance, 209
expenses, 191.2
guidelines for, 8(1) para. 3.4
lack of members, 220(3)
qualifications, 219, 351.1
offences and penalties, 211-217
remain in office, 220(1)
remuneration, 191

resignation, 220(3)-(4)

Board officers
business administrator, 198(6)
responsibility, 199
secretary, 198(1)
security, 198(2)-(4)
treasurer, 198(5)

Boards of reference
application for, 268
costs, 276
direction and report, 273, 275
duties and powers, 272
interim appointment of teacher, 269
appointment of, 270(2)
eligibility of applicant, 270(7)
new Board required, 270(10), (11), 274
notice of, 270(1)
practice and procedure, Reg. 300
regulations, 277
representatives, 270(3)-(6), (8)

Books and other learning materials
agreements for development and production, 8(1) para. 23
duty to provide, 170(1) para. 13
procedures for selection and approval, 8(1), para. 4
publication of lists, 8(1) para. 7
purchase and distribution, 8(1) para. 5
selection and approval by Minister, 8(1) para. 6
selection by schools, Reg. 298, s. 7

Borrowing. See **Finance.**

Building. See **Property.**

Bursaries. See **Scholarships and bursaries**

Business property
defined, 1(1)
taxation of, 257.7; Reg. 394/98

By-elections, Reg. 79/98

Calculation of enrolment
average daily
  1997, Reg. 79/97

1998, Reg. 283/98
1998 - 1999 fiscal year, Reg. 286/98
1999-2000 fiscal year, Reg. 213/99

Calculation of fees for pupils, Reg. 284/98, Reg. 288/98, Reg. 215/99

Census, 27

Certificate
granted by Minister, 8(1) para. 1

Classroom teacher
defined, 170.2(1)

Class size
elementary school, Reg. 118/98, ss. 1-2
maximum and average, 170.1
regulations, 170.1(5)
reporting, Reg. 118/98, ss. 7-12
secondary school, Reg. 118/98, ss. 3-6

Closing. See **Minister; School closing**

Closing exercises, Reg. 298. s. 4

Collective bargaining. See also **Collective bargaining under the former Act.**
advice to Lieutenant-Governor in Council re jeopardy, 277.12
arbitration, 277.10
application of *Labour Relations Act*, 277.2
bargaining agents
    district school boards, 277.3(2)
    replacement, 277.6
    school authorities, 277.4(3)-(4)
bargaining units
    appropriateness, 277.8(1)
    certification, 277.8(2)-(4)
    combined, 277.7
    district school boards, 277.3(1)
    school authorities, 277.4(1)-(2)
definitions, 277.1
Education Relations Commission, 277.12
enforcement of Part X.1, 277.13.1-2
election by principal and vice-principal, 277.11

first collective agreement after transition, 277.18-21
joint negotiations, 277.9
occasional teachers, 277.5
priority of Act and regulations, 277.13
transition
    generally, 277.14
    outstanding grievances, 277.16
    right to strike, 277.17(3)
    termination of arbitrations, strikes, lockouts, 277.17(1)-(2)
    terms of employment, school authorities, 277.15

Collective bargaining under the former Act
agreements, SBTCNA, ss. 50-58
assistance to parties, SBTCNA, s. 7
application of Act, SBTCNA, s. 3(1)
contravention of Act, SBTCNA, s. 77
costs, SBTCNA, s. 74
decisions not subject to review, SBTCNA, s. 72
definitions, SBTCNA, s. 1
Education Relations Commission, SBTCNA, ss. 59-62
fact finding, SBTCNA, ss. 14-27
final offer selection, SBTCNA, ss. 37-49
joint negotiations, SBTCNA, s. 4
liability, SBTCNA, s. 79
negotiations, SBTCNA, ss. 8-13
negotiating group, SBTCNA, s. 6
non-application of *Arbitrations Act, Statutory Powers Procedure Act*, SBTCNA, s. 80
notice, SBTCNA, s. 73
officers of branch affiliate, SBTCNA, ss. 75-76
OLRB hearing and decision, SBTCNA, ss. 77(7)-(8)
purpose of Act, SBTCNA, s. 2
representation of teachers by branch affiliate, SBTCNA, s. 5
strikes and lockouts, SBTCNA, ss. 63-70

style of prosecution, SBTCNA, s. 78
witnesses not compellable, SBTCNA, s. 81
voluntary binding arbitration, SBTCNA, ss. 28-36
vote by secret ballot, SBTCNA, s. 76

Combined separate school zone
defined, 1(1)

Compulsory attendance. See **Attendance of pupils.**

Conflict of interest
appeals, MCIA, s.11
alleged contravention, MCIA, ss. 8-13
application to judge, MCIA, ss. 9-10
controlling interest defined, MCIA, s 1
definitions, MCIA, s. 1
duty to disclose interest, MCIA, s. 5
exceptions to disclosure, MCIA, s. 4
indirect pecuniary interest
    child, MCIA, s. 3
    defined, MCIA, s. 2
    director, MCIA, s. 2(a)
    employee, MCIA, s. 2(b)
    officer, MCIA. S. 2(a)
    parent, MCIA, s. 3
    partner, MCIA, s. 2(b)
    shareholder, MCIA, s. 2(a)
    spouse, MCIA, s. 3
insurance, MCIA, s. 14
interest in common with electors generally, MCIA, s. 1
Local Government Disclosure of Interest Act, LGDIA
powers of judge, MCIA, s. 10
quorum, lack of, MCIA, s. 7
record of disclosure, MCIA, s. 6
statutory conflict, MCIA, s. 15

Continuation of per-August 1, 1981 school arrangements, 1(5)

Continuing Education
admission of adults, 49.1
continuing education instructor defined, 1(1)
continuing education teacher defined, 1(1)
contracts, Reg. 310, ss. 1-2, Form 3
discontinuance of course, Reg. 285, s.10
establishment
    by board, 171(1) para. 31
    requested by parents, Reg. 285, s. 5
location, Reg. 285, ss. 2(5)-(6), 8-9
qualification of instructor, Reg. 285, s.3
regulation, Reg. 285
scheduling, Reg. 285, 1(1.1), 2(1)
types of courses, Reg. 285, ss. 1(1)-(2)

Co-operative education program
defined, 170.2(12)

Copyright licence agreements 8(1) para. 23.1

Corporation or partnership school support, 237, 257.2

Correspondence courses
development of, 8(1) para. 17
fees for, 8(1) para. 17.1

Costs of education outside Ontario, 8(1) para. 35

Council of the band
defined, 1(1)

Courses of study
prescribed by Minister, 8(1) paras. 2, 3

Credit
defined, 1(1)

Current expenditure
defined, 1(1)

Current revenue
defined, 1(1)

Deaf, schools for
additional schools, 13(4)
admissions, Reg. 296, ss. 3-8
administration, 13(3)
continuation of, 13(1)
designations, Reg. 296, s. 2

duties of pupils, Reg. 296, s. 14
duties of residence counsellors, Reg. 296, s. 16
duties of Superintendent, Reg. 296, ss. 18-21
fees, Reg. 296, ss. 9-12
parents, Reg. 296, s. 17
powers of Minister, 8(1) para. 20
regulations, 13(7), Reg. 296
teachers
    duties, Reg. 296, s. 15
    qualifications, Reg. 296, s. 23
Superintendent's Advisory Council, Reg. 296, s. 22
transportation, Reg. 296, s. 13

Debentures. See **Finance.**

Debt charge
defined, 1(1)

Development charges. See also **Education development charges.**
regulations revoked, Reg. 21/98

Diplomas
granted by Minister, 8(1) para. 1

Discipline of pupils
board committee, 23(6)
expulsion by board, 23(3)
parties to hearing, 23(4)
readmission, 23(5)
suspension, 23(1)-(2.2)

District municipality
defined, 1(1)
varying tax rates
    authorized by regulations, 257.12(3)(a)
deemed to be, Reg. 467/97

District school area
defined, 1(1)
deemed to be district municipality, Reg. 467/97
formation and alteration
    designation, Reg. 291

disposition of assets and liabilities, 60(2)
generally, 59(2)-(5)
new areas, 60(1)
school sections, 59(1)

District school board. See also **Elections, School board.**
conduct of elections, 58.7
corporate status, 58.5
debt and financial obligation limits, Reg. 472/98
deemed to be local boards, 58.6
defined, 1(1)
elections by general vote, 58.9
electronic meetings, Reg. 463/97
establishment, areas of jurisdiction and names of, Reg. 185/97
financial statements of old board, Reg. 470/97
regulations, 58.1-58.4
transitional authority, 351
transition assistance grants, Reg. 476/98
transition from old boards
    dispute resolution process, Reg. 460/97, ss. 10-13
    Education Improvement Commission powers and duties, Reg. 460/97, ss. 27-32
    employees, Reg. 460/97, s. 2, Sched. 1
    interim role of designated board, Reg. 460/97, ss. 3-6
    merger, Reg. 460/97, s.2, Sched. 1
    orders on joint request, Reg. 460/97, ss. 7-8
    orders without joint request, Reg. 460/97, ss. 14-18
    payment for services, Reg. 460/97, ss. 19-26
    transfers between public and RC boards, Reg. 460/97, s. 33

Drug education, 8(1) para. 29.2

Educational advancement programs, 8(1) para. 22(b)

Education authority
defined, 1(1)

Education development charges
amendment, 257.70-257.79, Reg. 20/98, ss. 13-15
appeal, 257.64-257.69
authority to make regulations, 257.101
background study, 257.61-257.62
by-laws
    authority, 257.54-257.59
    conditions of passage, Reg. 20/98, s. 10
    expiry, Reg. 20/98, s.17
    explanation of, Reg. 20/98, s. 21
    notice of, Reg. 20/98, s. 12
collection, 257.80-257.84
complaints, 257.85-257.91
definitions, 257.53(1), Reg. 20/98, s. 1
determination of charges, Reg. 20/98, s. 7
Development Charges Act, application of, Reg. 20/98, s. 23(3)
education land costs,
    general, 257.53(2)
    excess land, Reg. 20/98, s. 2
    exclusions, 257.53(3)
    leases, 257.53(4)
exemptions, Reg. 20/98, ss. 3-6
interest rate, Reg. 20/98, s. 18
no right of petition, 257.100
public meeting
    notice, Reg. 20/98, s. 11
    required, 257.63
regions, Reg. 20/98, s. 19
registration, 257.95
reports by municipalities, 257.97, Reg. 20/98, s. 20
reserve fund
    borrowing from, 257.99
    establishment, Reg. 20/98, ss. 16-16.1
review of policies, 257.60
special cases, 257.92-257.93
statement of treasurer, 257.98
transition from old Act, Reg. 20/98, ss. 22-24
types of boards, 257.94

Education Improvement Commission
creation of, 334
exercise of power, 350
function, 335
powers and limitations, 58.3
protection from liability, 346
regulations, 58.2(3)-(7),(15)
transition from old boards to district school boards, Reg. 460/97
use of personal information, 347

Education Quality and Accountability Office
accounting, EQAOA, s. 24
agreements re tests, EQAOA, s. 5
annual report, EQAOA, s. 25
board of directors, EQAOA, ss. 11-14
borrowing, EQAOA, ss. 9(3)-(5)
budget, EQAOA, s. 22
by-laws, EQAOA, s. 14
capacity and powers, EQAOA, ss. 8-9
chief executive officer, EQAOA, s. 16
co-operation of boards required, EQAOA, s. 4
Corporations Act, Corporations Information Act, non-applicability, EQAOA, s.10
Crown agency, EQAOA, s. 7
definitions, EQAOA, s. 1
delegation of powers by Minister, EQAOA, s. 8
directives and policies of Minister, EQAOA, s. 6
employees, EQAOA, s. 17
establishment, EQAOA, s. 2
fees, EQAOA, s. 18
fiscal year, EQAOA, s. 21
liability, EQAOA, s. 28
objects, EQAOA, s. 3
personal information. See also **Personal information; Protection of privacy.**
    collection, EQAOA, s. 9(6), 26(d)

INDEX

disclosure, EQAOA, s. 27
plan of operation, EQAOA, s. 23
regulations, EQAOA, s. 26
revenues and investments, EQAOA, ss. 19-20

Education Taxes
generally 257.5 - 257.14
interim financing 257.11(15) - (20)
tax rates
    defined for school purposes 257.12(1.1)
    setting 257.12.1 - 257.12.2

Elections
conduct of elections, 58.7
representation on district school boards - 1997
    appeals, Reg. 250/97, s. 12
    area of Board, Reg. 250/97 Sched., table 1
    clerk, Reg. 250/97, s.17
    definitions, Reg. 250/97, s. 1
    determination and distribution of members, Reg. 250/97 s. 6
    determination of number of members, Reg. 250/97, s. 7, Sched., tables 1 and 2
    distribution of members
        high density boards, Reg. 250/97, s. 8
        low density boards, Reg. 250/97, ss. 9-11
    identification of municipalities, Reg. 250/97, s. 4
    meeting, Reg. 250/97, s. 5
    municipal by-laws, Reg. 250/97, s. 16
    nomination of candidates, Reg. 250/97, ss. 13-14
    population data, Reg. 250/97, ss. 2-3
    transitional, Reg. 250/97, ss. 18-22

Elementary school
defined, 1(1)
organizational units, Reg. 298, s. 14

Elementary school boards, Reg. 298, s. 8

Emergency procedures, Reg. 298, s. 6

English-language district school board
defined, 1(1)
language of instructional units, 289

English-language public board supporter
defined, 1(1)
notice re status, 236(1)

English-language Roman Catholic board
defined, 1(1)

English-language Roman Catholic board supporter
defined, 1(1)
notice re status, 236(2)

Enrolment, calculation of
average daily, Reg. 79/97

Ethnocultural equity policy, 8(1) para. 29.1

Exceptional pupil
appeals, Reg. 181/98, ss. 26-31
continuous education, 49(7)
defined, 1(1)
demonstration schools for, 13(5)-(7)
generally, Reg. 181/98, ss. 1-9
identification, placement and review committee
    establishment and procedures, Reg. 181/98, ss. 10-12
    reviews, Reg. 181/98, ss. 21-25
parents' guide, Reg. 181/98, s. 13
referral of pupils to committees, Reg. 181/98, ss. 14-20
transitional provision, Reg. 181/98, ss. 32-37

Exchange programs, 8(1) para. 22(a)

Expropriation. See Property.

Expulsion of pupil, 23(3)

Federal grants, 8(1) para. 21

Fees
for transcripts, statements of standing and duplicate certificates or diplomas, Reg. 293

Fees for Admission. See Admission of pupils.

Finance. See also Auditor, Boards, School taxes.
appointment of auditor, 253
borrowing by boards
    authority, 241(1)(d)
    current, 243, Reg. 495/97
    debt, financial obligation and liability limits, 242
    for permanent improvements, 247, Reg. 466/97
    payments on old debentures, 245
    provincial guarantee of debentures, 244
    no obligation to raise money by rates, 246
    report, 241(5)
court proceedings, 257
custody of books, 254
education taxes, See also **Education taxes.** 257.5-257.14
estimates, 231-233
financial statements
    for old board, Reg. 470/97
    preparation by treasurer, 252
investment powers, 241
legislative committee review, 257.107
legislative grants. See **Legislative grants**
municipal grants, 235
provincial financial services corporation, 248-249
recreation committees, 255
reserve for working funds, Reg. 496/97
school rate, 240
school supporters, 236
special grant, Reg. 307
supervision of board's financial affairs, 257.30-257.52
taxes set by boards, 257.15-257.29, 257.106
when fees payable, 257.1

Financial assistance under Act
accounting statement, 9

Flags, Reg. 298, s. 5

Freedom of information
information available for inspection, MFIPPA 25
invasion of personal privacy
    criteria for, MFIPPA 14
publication of information, MFIPPA 24
records
    access to
        procedure, MFIPPA 17 - 26
        right of, MFIPPA 4
    defined, MFIPPA 2(1); MFIPPA Reg. 823, s. 1
    exemptions from disclosure, MFIPPA 6 - 16
    obligation to disclose, MFIPPA 5
    records not subject to exemption, MFIPPA 7(2)
    security, MFIPPA Reg. 823, ss. 2 - 3
    to whom disclosure may be made, MFIPPA 14

French immersion programs, 8(1) para. 25

French-language district school board
admission of non-French-speaking pupils, 293
defined, 1(1)
language of instructional units, 288

French-language district school board supporter
defined, 1(1)
qualification as elector, 58.8

French-language instructional unit
defined, 1(1)
duty to provide
    elementary school authority, 290
    secondary school district, 291
English taught, 292

INDEX

operation in district school boards, 288, 289

French-language public district school board supporter
defined, 1(1)
notice re status, 236(3)

French-language rights holder
defined, 1(1), 294(1)
entitlement to vote, 50.1(2), 54(2)
groups, 294
Languages of Instruction Commission of Ontario, 295-299

French-language separate district school board supporter
defined, 1(1)
notice re status, 236(4)

French-speaking person
defined, 1(1)

Grants. See also **Finance, Legislative grants.**
transition assistance grants, Reg. 124/98

Guardian
defined, 1(1), 18
liability of, 30(1)

Head office
defined, 1(1)

Holidays, Reg. 304, s.2(4)

Honoraria
school authorities members, 191.1
school board members, 191

Immigration Act, 49(6)-(7)

Immunization
appeal to court, ISPA, s. 16
"designated diseases" defined, ISPA, s. 1
duty of parent, ISPA, s. 3
certificate of M.O.H. as evidence, ISPA, s. 5
hearing and submissions not required, ISPA, s. 13
hearing, ISPA, s. 15
notice of transfer of pupil, ISPA, s. 14

offence, ISPA, s.4
order by M.O.H., ISPA, s. 12
order for suspension, ISPA, s. 6
purpose of legislation, ISPA, s. 2
record of immunization
    defined, ISPA, s. 1
    maintenance and review, ISPA, s. 11
    prescribed contents, ISPA Reg., s. 1
    transfer, ISPA, s. 14, ISPA Reg., s. 4, Form 3
regulations, ISPA, s. 17
rescission of order, ISPA, s. 9
service of copy of order, ISPA, ss. 8(1), 18
statement by physician, ISPA, s. 10
statement of conscience or religious belief
    defined, ISPA, s. 1
    filing by parent, ISPA, ss. 3(3)-(4)
    form, ISPA Reg. s. 3, Form 2
statement of medical exemption
    defined, ISPA, s. 1
    filing by physician, ISPA, s. 3(2)
    form, ISPA Reg. s. 2, Form 1
term of suspension, ISPA, s. 7

Indian. See also **Aboriginal schools.**
defined, 1(1)

Information and Privacy Commissioner
defined, MFIPPA 2(1)
duties, MFIPPA 46
powers, MFIPPA 46

Institution
defined, MFIPPA 2(1)
"head" of institution, defined, MFIPPA 2(1)
determination of, MFIPPA 3

Intermediate division
defined, 1(1)

James Bay Lowland Secondary School Board, Reg. 294

Judge
defined, 1(1)

Junior division
defined, 1(1)

Kindergarten
duty to operate, 170(1) para. 6.1
resident pupil qualification, 34

Labour relations. See **Collective bargaining.**

Languages of Instruction Commission of Ontario, 295-299

Law enforcement
defined, MFIPPA 2(1)

Leadership training camps, 15

Legislative committee review, 257.107

Legislative Grants
authority to make regulations,
basic per pupil grant,
board specific grants,
capital project grants,
conditions,
definitions,
interim payments,
1997 selected grants,
1998 grants, Reg. 285/98
program specific grants,
regulations governing, 234
special assistance for en bloc transfer,
special compensation for pooling,
student-focused funding, Reg. 287/98, Reg. 214/99
transportation grants - 1997,

Letter of Permission, Reg. 183/97

Lockout. See **Strike or lockout.**

Medical examinations, 8(1), para. 15

Milk
purchase for free distribution, Reg. 302

Minister
act not regulation, 8(4)
additions to enrolment, 4
administrative responsibility, 2(3)
authority, 2(2)
defined, 1(1); MFIPPA, s. 2(1)
delegation by
    application of *Executive Council Act,* 1(6)
    authorization, 2(4)
    limitations, 2(5)
closing of school or class
    issuance of guidelines, 8(1) para. 16
    order, 5(1)
powers, 8(1), 10
responsibility for special education programs, 8(3)

Ministry
defined, 1(1)

Ministry of Education and Training
Annual Report, 3
continued, 2(1)

Municipal charges, 58

Municipal corporation
bodies considered part of, MFIPPA 2(3)
head
    delegation of powers, MFIPPA 49(1)
    determination of, MFIPPA 3
    protection from civil proceeding, MFIPPA 49(2)

Municipality
defined, 1(1)

Native representation on boards, Reg. 462/97. See also **Aboriginal schools.**

Northern District School Area Board, The, Reg. 295

Occasional teacher
defined, 1(1.1)

Offences and penalties, 211-217

Officers. See **Board officers.**

Old board
defined, 1(1)

INDEX

Ontario College of Teachers. See also **Qualification of teachers, Teacher education.**
annual meeting of members, OCTA, s. 13
by-laws, OCTA, s. 41
committees, OCTA, ss. 15-17
confidentiality, OCTA, s. 48(1)
Council
    annual report, OCTA, s. 11
    appointments to, OCTA Reg., 345/96
    composition, OCTA, s. 4(2)
    disqualification of members, OCTA Reg. 72/97, s. 6
    first election of members, OCTA Reg. 344/96
    election review committee, OCTA Reg. 344/96, s. 33
    leave of absence, OCTA, s. 46
    meetings, OCTA, s. 8
    meeting with Minister, OCTA, s. 10
    officers, OCTA, s. 9(1)
    official publication, OCTA, s. 45
    positions established for first Council, OCTA Reg. 344/96, s. 2
    powers of Minister, OCTA, s. 12
    quorum, OCTA Reg. 72/97, s. 5
    Registrar, OCTA, ss. 4(3), 9(2), 36-39
    remuneration, OCTA, s. 4(4)
    statutory committees
        defined, OCTA, s. 15(1), OCTA Reg. 72/97, s 13
        Discipline Committee, OCTA, s. 27
        Executive Committee, OCTA, s. 16, OCTA Reg. 72/97, ss. 19-20
        Fitness to Practice Committee, OCTA Reg. 72/97, s. 25
        general procedures, OCTA Reg. 72/97, ss. 14-18
        Investigation Committee, OCTA, ss. 25-26
        Registration Appeals Committee, OCTA Reg. 72/97, ss. 23-24
    term of office, OCTA, s. 5, OCTA Reg. 345/96, s. 2
    vacancies, OCTA, s. 7, OCTA Reg. 72/97, ss. 7-12
    voting, OCTA, s. 6
deemed loan, OCTA, s. 56
definitions, OCTA, s. 1
discipline
    appeals to court, OCTA, s. 35
    direction to hold hearing, OCTA, s. 29(1)
    Discipline Committee, OCTA, ss. 27, 30
    Fitness to Practice Committee, OCTA, ss. 28(1), 31
    hearings, OCTA, ss. 29(6), 32
    incompetence, OCTA, s. 30(3)
    interim suspension, OCTA, ss. 29(3)-(5)
    order, OCTA, s. 33(6)
    professional misconduct, OCTA, s. 30(2), OCTA Reg. 437/97
    publication that allegation unfounded, OCTA, ss. 30(8), 31(6)
    reinstatement, OCTA, ss. 33-34
    variation, OCTA, ss. 33-34
discipline — transitional, OCTA Reg. 276/97
disclosure of prior actions and offences, OCTA, s. 47
duty to protect public interest, OCTA, s. 3(2)
establishment, OCTA, s. 2(1)
evidence in civil proceedings, OCTA, s. 48(3)
fees, OCTA Reg. 72/97, ss. 1-4
French, right to use, OCTA, s. 44, OCTA Reg. 344/96, s. 31
guarantee of loan, OCTA, s. 57
immunity, OCTA, s. 55
investigation committee
    composition, OCTA, s. 25
    decision and reasons, OCTA, s. 26(6)
    duties, OCTA, s. 26(1)-(5)
jurisdiction where certificate revoked, OCTA, s. 14(5)
membership, OCTA, s. 14
non-compliance, OCTA, s. 49

objects, OCTA, s. 3
offences
    confidentiality, OCTA, s. 48
    false representation re certificate, OCTA, s. 51
    obstruction of investigator, OCTA, s. 50
Registrar
    appointment by Council, OCTA, s. 4(3)
    calling election, OCTA Reg. 344/96, ss. 18-30
    duties generally, OCTA Reg. 344/96, s. 17
    powers of investigation, OCTA, ss. 36-39
    role, OCTA, s. 4(3)
Registrar's certificate as evidence, OCTA, s. 53
registration, OCTA, ss. 18-24
    appeals to court, OCTA, s. 35
    disclosure of file, OCTA, s. 19
    grounds for refusal, OCTA, s. 18(2)-(3)
    notice of proposal to refuse, OCTA, s. 20
    register, OCTA, s. 23
    Registration Appeals Committee review, OCTA, s. 21
    variation, OCTA, s. 22
regulations, OCTA, ss. 40, 42, 43
regulations under the *Teaching Profession Act,* OCTA, s. 58
right to obtain information. See also **Freedom of information, Protection of privacy.**
    OCTA, s. 47
service of notice or document, OCTA, s. 52
statutory conflict, OCTA, s. 54
suspension of membership, OCTA, s. 24
transitional provisions, OCTA, ss. 59-63

Ontario education numbers, 266.1-266.5

Ontario Parent Council, 17

Ontario Property Assessment Corporation
references to, 1(1.2.1)

Ontario Student Record
access to, OSRG 4
adoption, OSRG 10.2
change of surname, OSRG 10.1
components, OSRG 3
    documentation file, OSRG 3.4
    folder, OSRG 3.1
    French instruction, record of, OSRG 3.6
    Native instruction, record of, OSRG 3.7
    office index card, 3.5
    Ontario Student Transcript, OSRG 3.3
    report cards, OSRG 3.2
    reports from third parties, OSRG 10.3
continuing education students, OSRG 11
correction/removal of information, OSRG 9
definitions, OSRG App. A
destruction, OSRG 8
establishment, OSRG 1
forms, OSRG App. B
responsibility for, OSRG 2
retention, OSRG 8
storage, OSRG 8
student ceasing to be enrolled, OSRG 7
transfer, OSRG 6
use/maintenance, OSRG 5

Ontario Teacher's Certificate
fee for duplicate, Reg. 293

Ontario Teachers' Federation
affiliated bodies, TPA Reg. s. 1
annual conferences with Minister, TPA, s. 10
associate members, TPA, s. 4(2),(3)
Board of Governors
    conferences, TPA, s. 10
    expenses, TPA Reg., s. 12
    generally, TPA, s. 5
    meetings, TPA Reg., ss. 5, 6, 11
body corporate, TPA, s. 2
committees

nominating, TPA Reg. S. 7
Relations and Discipline, TPA Reg. ss. 8, 19-28
special, TPA Reg. s. 10
standing, TPA Reg. s. 9
duties of members,
    educational authorities, TPA Reg., s. 15
    fellow members, to, TPA Reg., s. 18
    general, TPA Reg., s. 13
    OTF, to, TPA Reg., s. 17
    public, to, TPA Reg., s. 16
    pupils, to, TPA Reg., s. 14
executive
    expenses, TPA Reg. s. 12
    functions, TPA, s. 9
    generally, TPA, s. 6
    meetings, TPA Reg., s. 6
name, TPA, s. 2
objects, TPA, s. 3
membership
    application by former member, TPA Reg., s. 3
    fees, TPA Reg. S. 4
    mandatory, TPA, s. 4(1)
    voluntary, TPA Reg., s. 2
president, TPA, s. 7
regulations, TPA, s. 12
Relations and Discipline Committee
    procedure, TPA Reg., s. 19-28
secretary-treasurer, TPA, s. 8
students, TPA, s. 4(2)
vice-presidents, TPA, s. 7

Opening and closing exercises, Reg. 298, s.4

Operation of schools generally, Reg. 298

Parent. See also **Ontario Parent Council.**
authority or obligation vested in pupil, 1(2)
compulsory attendance, 21(5)
dealing with principal, Reg. 298, s. 11
guide re exceptional pupils, Reg. 181/98, s. 13
immunization
    duty, ISPA, s. 3

statement of conscience or religious belief, ISPA, ss. 1, 3(3), 6(2)
indirect pecuniary interest, MCIA, ss. 2-3
information to medical officer, 266(2.1)
liability of, 30(1)
pupil records and, 266(2),(3)
religious instruction of child, 51(1)
request for continuing education program, Reg. 285, s. 5
request to school attendance counsellor, 26(1)
schools for deaf and blind, and, Reg. 296, s. 17
visit to school, 50(1)

Part-time teacher
defined, 1(1)

Permanent improvement
borrowing for, 247, Reg. 466/97
defined, 1(1)
regulations, 1(6)

Personal information
defined, MFIPPA 2(1),(2)

Personal information bank
defined, MFIPPA 2(1)

Physical fitness
agreements with Canada, 12(1)

Population
defined, 1(1)

Primary division
defined, 1(1)

Principal. See also **Vice-principal.**
as teacher, 287.1
defined, 1(1)
duties, 265; Reg. 298, s. 11
election to resign, 277.11
employed by school authority, Reg. 472/97
employment terms, 287.2
in French-language schools, Reg. 298, s. 13
qualifications, Reg. 298, ss. 9-10; Reg. 184/97, ss. 43-52

redundancy and reassignment, Reg. 90/98

Private school
agreements regarding, 16(8.1)-(8.2)
defined, 1(1)
inspection of, 16(6)-(8)
offence, 16(9)
operation, 16(1)-(5)

Professional activity days, Reg. 304

Professional development courses, 8(1) para. 16, See also **Teaching profession.**

Property
acquisition of school site, 195
agreement for multi-use building, 196
building
    approval by Minister, Reg. 298, s. 2
    powers of board, 195(5)-(7)
natural science and conservation programs, 197
disposal of realty, 194, Reg. 444/98
possession of, 193
school lands granted before 1850, 192

Protection of Privacy
appeals of decisions relating to
    fees, MFIPPA Reg. 823 s. 5.3
    general, MFIPPA 39 - 44
forms relating to, MFIPPA Reg. 823
offences, MFIPPA 48
personal information
    access
        fees for request, MFIPPA 17(1), 37(1), 45; MFIPPA Reg. 823, ss. 5.2, 6 - 9
        right to generally, MFIPPA 36 - 38
    collection
        generally, MFIPPA 29
        where notice not required, MFIPPA Reg. 823, s. 4
    correction, right to, MFIPPA 36(2)
    defined, MFIPPA 2(1),(2)
    disclosure
        oral requests, MFIPPA 50(1)
        refusal to disclose, MFIPPA 38
        vexatious requests, MFIPPA 5.1
        when permitted, MFIPPA 32
    disposal, MFIPPA 30(4)
    information otherwise available, 51(1)
    retention, MFIPPA 30; MFIPPA Reg. 823, s. 5
    use, MFIPPA 31
personal information banks, MFIPPA 34-35
regulations, MFIPPA 47

Protestant separate school
application to establish, 158
attendance rights, 167.1
corporate name of board, 166
discontinuing board, 168
distribution of tenant school support, 169
election of board members, 165, 169
notice to supporters re status, 236(5)
powers and procedures, 167, 169
qualification of voter, 164
share of legislative grants, 159

Provincial school attendance counsellor
as trustee, 29
generally, 24
reference to, 30(7)

Provincial Schools Authority
collective bargaining
    generally, PSNA, ss. 5(1)-(7)
    status on January 1, 1998, PSNA, s.6
composition, PSNA, s. 2(1)
definitions, PSNA, s.1
employment of teachers, PSNA, s. 4
status of employer, PSNA, s. 3(1)

Provincial supervisory officer
defined, 1(1)

Psychiatrists, psychologists and social workers, Reg. 298, s. 26(2)

Public district school board. See also **School board.**
area of jurisdiction
    English-language, Reg. 185/97, ss. 1-6
    French-language, Reg. 185/97, ss. 7-12

defined, 1(1)
elections and meetings, 62-64
establishment
    English-language, Reg. 185/97, s. 1
    French-language, Reg. 185/97, s. 7
inactive, 66
membership, 61(2)-(6)
name
    English-language, Reg. 185/97, s. 2
    French-language, Reg. 185/97, s. 8
public school elector defined, 61(1)
school sections, 59(1)

Public school
defined, 1(1)

Public school authority
defined, 1(1)
establishment of tax exempt land, 68
membership, 61(2)-(6)
public school elector defined, 61(1)
school sections, 59(1)

Pupil. See also **Immunization.**
assignment of Ontario education numbers, 266.1-266.5
deemed attendance during closing, 5(2)
18 or over, 1(2)
fee for transcript of standing, Reg. 293
records, 8(1) para. 27, 11(1) para. 3-4, 266.
    See Also **Ontario student record.**
requirements, Reg. 298, s. 23
representation on boards, Reg. 461/97

Qualification of teachers
additional qualifications, Reg. 184/97, ss. 30-32, Sched. B
basic qualifications, Reg. 184/97, ss. 2-29, 58-60
certificate or letter of standing
    cancelled or under suspension, Reg. 298, s. 22
    equivalent qualification, 8(1) para. 14
    fees for, Reg. 293
    suspension, cancellation and reinstatement, 8(1) para. 13
for appointment to school, 170(1) para. 12

courses
    one-session courses, Reg. 184/97, s. 33, Sched. C
    one-session honour specialist course, Reg. 184/97, ss. 40-42, Sched. E
    three-session specialist courses, Reg. 184/97, ss. 34-39, Sched. D
definitions, Reg. 184/97, s. 1
emergency appointment, Reg. 298, s. 21
generally, Reg. 298, s. 19
membership in Ontario College of Teachers, 262
Ministerial exemption
    letter of permission, 8(1) para. 10
    temporary letter of approval, 8(1) para. 11
    withdrawal of, 8(1) para. 12
registration, Reg. 184/97, s. 57
Temporary Letter of Approval, Reg. 184/97, s. 53
to supervise subject or program, Reg. 298, ss. 17-18
transitional, Reg. 184/97, ss. 58-60

Racism, policy against, 8(1) para. 29.1

Real Property. See **Property.**

Records. See **Pupil; Freedom of Information; Ontario Student Record**

Regulations
contrasted to acts of Minister, 8(4)
defined, 1(1)
fees, 11(3)-(4), (9); Reg. 293
immunization of school pupils, ISPA, s. 17
land reserved for school site, 195(7)
responsibility of Minister, 2(3)
school year prescribed, 11(7)-(7.1)
subject-matter generally, 11(1)

Religious instruction, 51; Reg. 298, ss. 27-29

Remembrance Day service, Reg. 304, s. 9

Reserve fund

defined, 1(1)
education development charge reserve funds, Reg. 446/98, s. 3
proceeds of dispositions, Reg. 446/98, s. 2
pupil accommodation allocation, Reg. 446/98, s. 1
special education, Reg. 446/98, s. 4
strike or lockout
    calculation of amount resulting from, Reg. 486/98

Resident pupil qualification
admission of adult non-resident elementary level
    choice of accessible schools, 35
    general, 33
kindergarten, 34
move into differently assessed residence, 45
movement between boards, 42, 43
one parent is sole support, 45
residence on tax-exempt lands, 46
secondary level
    generally, 36
    other district or zone, 39, 40

Residential property
defined, 1(1)
taxation of, 257.7; Reg. 394/98

Review of classroom effectiveness
conducted by Minister, 8(1) para. 3.1

Research grants, 8(1) para. 24

Revenues and expenditures. See Finance.

Roman Catholic
defined, 1(1)

Roman Catholic board
defined, 1(1)
entitlement of residents to vote, 54
religious education, 52

Roman Catholic school authority
defined, 1(1)
school extension
    adoption of plan for secondary education, 96

pre-1998, 135-135.1
teacher conduct, 136

Roman Catholic school board
deeming provision, 135.1

Rural separate school
board
    duties and powers, 90
    meetings and elections, 92
    municipality may conduct election, 93
    procedures, 89(1)-(5)
    vacancy, 223
defined, 1(1)
entitlement to vote, 89(6)-(7)

Rural separate school zone
defined, 1(1)

Safety
application of *Workplace Safety and Insurance Act, 1997,* 8(1) para. 9

Scholarships and bursaries
agreements with federal Crown, 12(4)
approval of board, 173
powers of Minister, 8(1) para. 18
variation of grant, 17

School
defined, 1(1)

School attendance counsellors. See also Attendance by pupils.
appointment, 25
inquiries, 26(4)
powers, 26(1)
prosecutions by, 31
reports of, 26(2)
reports to, 28(1)
supervision, 26(3)
where none, 28(2)

School authority
defined, 1(1)
duty to provide French-language instructional unit, 290
principals and vice-principals, Reg. 472/97

1011

remuneration of members, 191.1

School board advisory committee, 200-205

School boards. See **Board.**

School closing
by board, 19, 186
civic holiday, 20
deemed attendance, 5(2)
guidelines, 8(1) para. 26
ordered by Minister, 5(1)

School councils
establishment by Board, 170(1) para. 17.1
Ministry materials to members, Reg. 298, s. 11(12)
names made known to parents, Reg. 298, s. 11(13) - (15)
regulations, 170(3)

School day
defined, 1(1)
establishment, Reg. 298, s. 3

School operation generally, Reg. 298

School rate, 240

School section
defined, 1(1)
resolution of questions by judge, 1(3)

School site. See also **Property.**
defined, 1(1)
acquisition, 195

School support
corporation or partnership, 237
designated ratepayer, 238
individuals, 236
tenants, 239
type of board for *Assessment Act* purposes, 257.4

School taxes
apportionment in certain areas, Reg. 713/98
arrears
    annexed areas, Reg. 366/98
    pre-1998, Reg. 365/98
business property, 257.7, Reg. 394/98
deemed attachment of certain territory, Reg. 715/98
deemed to be district municipalities, Regs. 467/97; 468/97
education taxes, 257.5 - 257.14
eligible theatre
    defined, Reg. 393/98
    exemption from taxation, 257.6(4)
levying of certain 1998 rates in 1999, Reg. 714/98
railway, power utility lands, Reg. 392/98
rates for school purposes, Reg. 400/98
recreation committee rates, Reg. 712/98
regulations to limit changes in, 257.2.1
residential property, 257.7, Reg. 394/98
second instalment 1998, Reg. 346/98
set by boards, 257.15 - 257.29, 257.106
unorganized territories, in, 257.2.1, Reg. 509/98

School year
after 1997-1998, Reg. 304, s. 2(3.1)
defined, 1(1)
calendar, Reg. 304
prescribed, 11(7)-(7.1)
varied, 22

Secondary school
defined, 1(1)
organizational units, Reg. 298, s. 14

Secondary school district
defined, 1(1)
designation by Cabinet, 67
duty to provide French-language instructional unit, 291

Secretary
defined, 1(1)

Senior division
defined, 1(1)

Separate district school board
area of jurisdiction
    English-language, Reg. 185/97, s.6

INDEX

French-language, Reg. 185/97, s. 12
defined, 1(1)
establishment
    English-language, Reg. 185/97, s. 4
    French-language, Reg. 185/97. s. 10
name
    English-language, Reg. 185/97, s. 5, Sched. 1
    French-language, Reg. 185/97, s. 11, Sched. 1

Separate school. See also **Protestant separate school.**
constitutional right recognized, 1(4), (4.1),
defined, 1(1)

Separate school supporter
compulsory attendance, 21(6)
defined, 1(1)
entitlement of non-resident to vote, 88
in 1997, 1(7)

Separate school zone. See also **Roman Catholic school authority.**
boundaries, 78, 86.1
combined zones
    board membership and election, 95
    detachment from, 85
    formation of, 84
    secretary as returning officer, 94
defined, 1(1)
discontinuing board, 86
meeting to establish
    legislative grants, 83
    powers of board, 81
    procedures, 80
    right to vote, 82

Separated town
defined, 1(1)

Special education
advisory committees, 57.1, Reg. 464/97
duty of Board, 170(1) para. 7
hearing-handicapped children, Reg. 298, s. 30
maximum enrolment, Reg. 298, s. 31
Ministerial responsibility, 8(3)
programs and services, Reg. 306
regulations, 11(1) para. 5
special education plan, Reg. 306
"special education program" defined, 1(1)
"special education service" defined, 1(1)

Special education tribunals, 57

Strike or lockout
"lockout" defined, 19(4)
money placed in reserve, 233
school closing, 19(2)
"strike" defined, 19(4)
teacher salary, 19(3)

Student-focused funding
administration and governance, Reg. 214/99, s. 37
capital projects, Reg. 214/99, s. 49
debt charges, Reg. 214/99, s. 39
early learning, reg. 214/99, s. 35
foundation allocation, Reg. 214/99, ss. 13 - 20
general, Reg. 214/99
grant entitlement, Reg. 214/99, ss. 10 - 11
grants to school authorities, Reg. 214/99, ss. 55 - 56
language, Reg. 214/99, ss. 21 - 28
learning opportunities, Reg. 214/98, ss. 31 - 33
small schools, Reg. 214/99, ss. 29 - 30
payments to governing authorities, Reg. 214/99, ss. 57 - 60
pupil accommodation, Reg. 214/99, s. 38
teacher compensation, Reg. 214/99, s. 34
transportation, Reg. 214, s. 36

Supervised alternative learning for excused pupils, Reg. 308

Supervisory officer
defined, 1(1)
duties, 286; Reg. 298, s. 26
employment
    as chief executive officer, 283
    by district school boards, 279

by school authorities, 280
language, 284
qualifications, 278, Reg. 309, ss. 1-6; OCTA Reg. 184/97, ss. 54-56
responsibility, 285
suspension or dismissal, 287, Reg. 309, ss. 7-8
transfer, Reg. 309, s. 7

Support staff
"designated person" defined, 135(1)
termination, 135(24)

Suspension of pupil, 23(1)-23(2.2)

Taxes. See **School taxes.**

Teacher. See also **Collective bargaining, Ontario College of Teachers, Qualification of teachers.**
boards of reference, 267-277
conferences, 264(3)
contracts
    form of contract, Reg. 310
    regulations, 11(1)
    termination, 263
convicted of criminal offence, 170(1) para. 12.1
definitions
    "continuing education teacher" 1(1)
    "occasional teacher", 1(1.1)
    "part-time teacher", 1(1)
    "permanent teacher", 1(1)
    "probationary teacher" 1(1)
    "teacher", 1(1)
    "temporary teacher", 1(1)
discipline. See **Ontario College of Teachers.**
duties, 264(1), Reg. 298, s. 20
emergency appointment, Reg. 298, s. 21
in charge of organizational units, Reg. 298, s. 14
in French-language schools, Reg. 298, s. 13
pensions. See **Teachers' pensions.**
probationary period, 261
professional activity days, Reg. 304
refusal to give up school property, 264(2)
salary, payment of, Reg. 310, s. 2
supervision of subjects or programs, Reg. 298, ss. 17-18
transfer between boards, 135(1)

Teacher education. See also **Ontario College of Teachers, Qualification of teachers.**
fee for certificate or statement of standing, Reg. 293
professional education, 14
teachers' colleges, 8(1) para. 19

Teachers' assistants, 170.3

Teachers' pensions
"active plan member" defined, TPenAct 1
agreement for member responsibility, TPenAct 11
Ontario Teachers' Pension Plan Board, TPenAct 6 - 8
pension fund
    administration, TPenAct 3
    Crown contribution, TPenAct 5(1)
    defined, TPenAct 1
    investments, TPenAct 12(1)
Pension Benefits Act
    conflicts with *Teachers' Pension Act*, TPenAct 10(3)
    effect upon, TPenAct 12.1
pension plan
    defined, TPenAct 1
    joint management of, TPenAct 10(1)
Teachers' Superannuation Act, 1983,
    continued application of, TPenAct 13

Teaching time, 170.2

Temporary teacher
defined, 1(1)

Territory without municipal organization
authority to make regulation, 56
attached to a district municipality, Reg. 311

Tests

INDEX

prescribed by Minister, 8(1), para. 3.2

Textbooks. See **Books and other learning materials.**

Trailers, fees for, 250

Transportation
power of school board, 190

Travel expenses. See **Expenses.**

Trustee
use of term, 1(12)

Urban municipality
defined, 1(1)

Vice-principal
appointment and duties, Reg. 298, s. 12
election to resign, 277.11

employed by school authority, Reg. 472/97
in French-language school, Reg. 298, s. 13(3)
qualifications, Reg. 298, ss. 9-10
redundancy and reassignment, Reg. 90/98

Visitors
to public schools, 50
to Roman Catholic schools, 53

Voting
changing residence, 1(11)(b)
entitlement, 1(10), 50.1
owners and tenants of property, 1(9)
"qualification period" defined, 1(11)(a)
residence requirement, 1(8)
"resides" defined, 1(11)(a)

Zones. See **Separate school zone.**